NEWTON'S TELECOM DICTIONARY

The Official Glossary of Telecommunications and Voice Processing Terms

by Harry Newton

SIXTH EDITION

THE LOGIC OF MY DICTIONARY

by Harry Newton

Most technical dictionaries define terms tersely, often in other technical terms. As a result they leave you more confused. This dictionary is different, deliberately so. My definitions tell you what the term is, how it works, how you use it, what its benefits are, what its negatives are, how it fits into the greater scheme of things, and occasionally some warnings or checklists if you're buying.

This is a working dictionary. Salespeople tell me they include the definitions in proposals to customers. Novices tell me they love it because it cuts through the clutter. Users explain telecom things to their boss with my definitions. Management uses it to understand telecom technicalities. You can give it to your users, to your customers, to your boss. You can even give it to your kids to let them understand what you do.

I don't claim my dictionary is comprehensive. But each edition gets bigger and better. I add, re-work and update words. I'm always looking for new ones. That's an invitation. Send me your product names, your service descriptions, your in-house glossaries.

HOW TO USE MY DICTIONARY

My definitions are in ASCII code order — NOT alphabetical order. ASCII is almost alphabetical order. Here is the order of the more common characters you'll find in this dictionary:

Blank Space	=	ASCII 32	5	=	ASCII 53
& (Ampersand)	=	ASCII 38	6	=	ASCII 54
Hyphen -	=	ASCII 45	7	=	ASCII 55
Period .	=	ASCII 46	8	=	ASCII 56
/ (Forward slash)	=	ASCII 47	9	=	ASCII 57
0 (zero)	=	ASCII 48	: (colon)	=	ASCII 58
1	=	ASCII 49	; (semi colon)	=	ASCII 59
2	=	ASCII 50	A (capital A)	=	ASCII 65
3	=	ASCII 51	Capital letters to		ASCII 90
4	=	ASCII 52	Lower case letters		

I choose ASCII order over alphabetical order because ASCII is established. All computer sorting programs do sorts in ASCII order — unless you tell them otherwise. In contrast, when you do "alphabetical" sorts, no one seems to know which comes first: back slash or backslash etc.

ON STYLE

All high-tech industries make up new words by joining words together. They typically start by putting two words together, then, later, they join them with a hyphen. Then, with age and familiarity, the hyphen tends to disappear.

Sometimes it's just a matter of personal choice. Some people spell database as one word. Some as two, i.e. data base. I prefer it as one, since it has acquired its own logic by now.

Sometimes it's a matter of how it looks. I prefer T1 (T-one) as T-1, simply because T-1 is easier to recognize on paper.

Plurals give people trouble. In my opinion, the plural of PBX is PBXs, not PBX's. The possessive of PBX is PBX's. The New York Times disagrees with me. The Wall Street Journal agrees with me.

In this book, the numbers one through nine are spelled out. Above nine, the numbers are written as arabic numerals, i.e. 10, 11, 12, etc.

I follow the style Andy Moore established in TELECONNECT Magazine, and the one he has so rigorously held us to for over a decade. Yes, it's been that long.

THANK YOUs

A big thank you to the dozens of people and dozens of companies who helped. I bet I leave some of you out. If so, I apologize.

Among the manufacturers, special thanks to Amdahl, Anixter, Aspect, AT&T, Bellcore, Dialogic, Ecos Electronics, General Cable, Micom, MCI, NEC, Newbridge Networks, New York Telephone, Northern Telecom, Racal Data, Ricoh, Sharp and Teknekron. They'll recognize some of their words in this dictionary. Among the magazines I borrowed (or stole), the best were PC Magazine and our own TELECONNECT, Call Center and IMAGING Magazine. Special thank yous also to internetworking expert, Tad Witkowicz at CrossComm, Marlboro MA. Ken Guy of Micom, Simi Valley (near LA); local area network expert, Michael Marcus, president of Able Communications, an excellent interconnect company based in Scardsale NY, Frank Derfler of PC Magazine; Chris Gahan of 3Com; Stephen Doster of Telco Research in Nashville; bugging expert Jim Ross of Ross Engineering, Adamstown, MD; wiring experts John and Carl Siemon of The

Siemon Company, Watertown CT; Kelly Christiansen and the fine folk at Novell, the local area network company in Provo, UT; to Judy Marterie and the electricity wiring, grounding and test experts at Ecos Electronics Corporation in Oak Park, Il; to John Perri and Karen Miller of SoftCom, NYC; to John Taylor of GammaLink, a Sunnyvale, CA company which produces beautiful fax products and extremely helpful documentation on fax technology; to Bill Flanagan who's written fine books on T-1 and voice and data networking, to Jane Laino of Corporate Communications Consultants, NYC, to Henry Baird of Seattle consultants Baird & Associates; to Sharon O'Brien formerly of Hayes Microcomputer Products in Norcross (Atlanta), to Howard Bubb, Ed Margulies, Terry Henry, Jim Shinn, Nick Zwick and Sal Manetti, Manager of Technical Publications of leading voice processing company, Dialogic Corporation of Parsippany, NJ; to Al Wokas of voice processing company Rheterox in San Jose, CA. Ian Angus at the Angus TeleManagement Group in Ajax, Ontario, embarrassed me into expanding my Canadian coverage. At Ziff Davis, which publishes this dictionary on CD-ROM disks, I'm grateful to Jonathan Pollard and Paul Gudelis. In my own office, I'm very grateful to Muriel Fullam, Rose Bodin, Andy Moore and Jennifer Cooper-Farrow. Without all these wonderful people, this dictionary wouldn't be as good as it's actually turned out. If I sound surprised, you're right.

If I've left any definitions out, or if some of my definitions are unclear, contact me. This is the fifth edition of my dictionary. It's one-quarter bigger than the fourth edition which was fewer than 12 months ago. There'll be many more editions. Our industry is exploding.

I wrote this dictionary on a Toshiba T3300SL laptop using ZEdit, a very beautiful text editor, which Sammy Mitchell of Marietta, GA wrote. Andy and Jennifer typeset it on a Macintosh Quadra using QuarkXpress and Adobe Illustrator. Bookcrafters in Chelsa, Michigan printed it.

Harry Newton
12 West 21 Street
New York, NY 10010
212-691-8215 Fax 212-691-1191
MCI Mail HarryNewton /101-5032
CompuServe 70600,2451

August, 1993

NUMBERS

" Double quotation marks. Typically used to signify something your computer should print (to screen, disk or paper), as in

PRINT "Thanks for being a good guy."

Some programs allow you to use single quotation marks interchangeable with double ones. Some programs don't. Try one or the other if in doubt.

The character typically above the 3 on your keyboard. It's commonly called the pound sign, but it's also called the number sign, the crosshatch sign, the octothorpe sign and the tic-tack-toe sign. On some phones it represents "NO." And on others it represents "YES." MCI and some other long distance companies use it as the key for making another long distance credit card call without having to redial.

& The "and" sign. Its real name is an "ampersand."

* The star sign. It's often used to represent a wild card or a joker. For example, the command

ERASE JOHN.*

will erase all the files on your disk beginning with JOHN, e.g. JOHN.TXT, JOHN.NEW, JOHN.OLD, JOHN.BAK, etc.

- The dash. The minus sign. Often we take two words and join them with a dash into a new word. As the word becomes more and more common, we remove the dash and the double-word now becomes a fully-fledged single word.

/ The forward slash. Lotus made it famous.

@ The character typically above the 2 on your keyboard. It's called the "at sign." Its biggest use these days is in spreadsheets and in computer publishing.

**** The backslash. Used for designating directories on your MS-DOS machine. This dictionary is located in

C:\WORK\DICTIONA>

That means it's in the "dictiona" subdirectory of the "work" directory.

^ The character typically above the 6 on your keyboard. It was originally a circumflex. In computer language it became the symbol that was written to represent the Control (Ctrl) key. It's also called the "hat."

~ This character is a tilde. It tells you how to pronounce the n in se§or. According to William Safire, it's a Spanish word from the Latin term for a tiny diacritical mark used to change the phonetic value of a letter.

1.544 MBPS The speed of a T-1 circuit.

100BASE-VG A joint HP-AT&T proposal for fast-ethernet running at 100 million bits per second. It would use all four pairs in the 10BaseT twisted pair

1

wiring scheme to transmit or receive, rather than today's present system of using one pair to transmit and one pair to receive. 10BaseT also use Manchester coding, a less efficient coding method compared with the 5B6B coding used in 100Base-VG, which splits the signal across the four wire pairs at 25 Mhz each.

10Base-T See 802.3

10XXX CALLING An access code that is dialed, in addition to the telephone number, to connect with a long distance carrier. Each carrier has a unique three digit code represented here by XXX. 1-0-XXX calling allows customers to use long distance carriers other than one they subscribe to. AT&T's code is 1-0-288 (as in 1-0-ATT). MCI's is 1-0-222. Sprint's is 1-0-333.

110-TYPE CONNECTING BLOCK The part of a 110-type cross connect that terminates twisted-pair wiring and can be used with either jumper wires or patch cords to establish circuit connections.

110-TYPE CROSS CONNECT A compact cross connect, developed by AT&T, that can be arranged for use with either jumper wires or patch cords. Jumper wires, used for more permanent circuits, must be cut down to make circuit connections. Patch cords allow ease of circuit administration for frequently rearranged circuits. The 110-type cross connect also provides straightforward labeling methods to identify circuits.

119 Japan's equivalent of the United States' emergency 911 number.

144-LINE WEIGHTING In telephone systems, a noise weighting used in a noise measuring set to measure noise on a line that would be terminated by an instrument with a No 144-receiver, or a similar instrument.

16 BIT An adjective that describes systems and software that handle information in words that are 2 bytes (16 bits) wide.

16450/8250A Found in most current PCs, these older UART chips use a 1-byte buffer that must be serviced immediately by the CPU. If not, interrupt overruns will result. See 16550 and UART.

16550 An enhanced version of the original National Semiconductor 16xxx series UART, which sits in and controls the flow of information into and out of virtually every PC serial port in the world. The older version contains only a one-byte buffer. This can slow down the transmission of high-speed data especially when you're using a multi-tasking program, like Windows. The "solution" is to get a serial card or port containing the 16550. This chip contains two 16-byte FIFO buffers, one each for incoming and outgoing data. Also new is the 16550's level-sensitive interrupt-triggering mechanism, which controls the amount of incoming data the buffer can store before generating on interrupt request. Together, these features help reduce your CPU's interrupt overhead and thus speed up your communications. See 16450/8250A and UART.

1791 April 27, Samuel Morse born.

1793 Semaphore invented.

1840 Samuel Morse patents the telegraph.

1843 First successful fax machine patented by Sottish inventor, Alexander Bain. His "Recording Telegraph" worked over a telegraph line, using electromagnetically controlled pendulums for both a driving mechanism and timing. At the sending end, a style swept across a block of metal type, providing a voltage to be applied to a similar stylus at the receiving end, reproducing an arc of the image on a block holding a paper saturated with electrolytic solution which discolored when an electric current was applied through it. The blocks at both ends were lowered a fraction of an inch after each pendulum sweep until the image was completed. Bain's device transmitted strictly black and white images.

1844 Samuel Morse send sends first public telegraph message.

1865 First commercial fax service started by Giovanni Casselli, using his "Pantelegraph" machine, with a circuit between Paris and Lyon, which was later extended to other cities.

1876 Braving a hostile ocean, the men of the Faraday, a steam-driven ship with three masts, laid the first transatlantic cable between Ireland and America. The was made by Siemens. It could carry 22 messages at one time. And it carried the world into a new era of communications.

1876 Telephone patent issued to Alexander Graham Bell; first long distance call.

1877 First telephone in a private home. First telephone in New York City.

1880 Alexander Graham Bell develops the photophone which uses sunlight to carry messages. It was never commercially produced.

1881 First long distance line, Boston to Providence.

1887 AT&T (American Telephone & Telegraph Co.) starts business.

1889 A. B. Strowger invents the telephone switch, dial telephone.

1891 Undersea telephone cable, England to France.

1895 Guglielmo Marconi of Italy invents wireless telegraph.

1915 First transcontinental phone call in USA.

1922 First dial exchange in New York City — PE-6 from PEnnsylvania 6.

1925 IBM begins selling punch-card machinery in Japan.

1927 April 7, 1929. First public demonstration of video phone technology. Moving black and white pictures were sent over telephone wires between Secretary of Commerce Herbert Hoover in Washington DC and AT&T executives in New York. They went at 18 frames per second. Further development of this technology led to the creation of TV.

1929 Coaxial cable invented; Herbert Hoover first president to have phone installed on his desk.

1936 First TV broadcast by the BBC in Great Britain.

193RD BIT The frame bit for a T-1 frame.

1947 Transistor invented at AT&T's Bell Labs in New Jersey.

1948 May 11: Birth of the International Communications Association.

1951 Direct distance calling. Sony unveils the first transistor radio.

1954 The year William Shockley left Bell Labs to pursue the commercial opportunities offered by his invention of the transister.

1956 First transatlantic repeatered telephone cable.

1960 1. First test an of electronic switch. 2. MITI creates the Japan Electronic Computer Corporation to promote its domestic computer industry. 3. Laser invented by Theodore Maiman of the U.S. Laser stands for Light Amplification by the Stimulated Emission of Radiation.

1962 August 31, 1962 President Kennedy signed Communications Satellite Act.

1963 Touch Tone service introduced.

1964 Prototype of the first video phone made by the Bell System shown at The World's Fair in Queens, New York City. Pictures were black and white and the technology was very expensive.

1965 First trial offers for reversing telephone charges.

1966 October, 1966 the Electronic Industries Association issues its first fax standard: the EIA Standard RS-328, Message Facsimile Equipment for Operation on Switched Voice Facilities Using Data Communications Equipment. The Group 1 standard, as it later became known, made possible the more generalized business use of fax. Transmission was analog and it took four to six minutes to send a page.

1967 First 800 call made in the United States.

1969 The laser is invented.

1970 Optical fiber for long-range communications developed.

1971 Ted Hoff at Intel invents the microprocessor — a single chip that contained most of the logic elements used to make a computer. Here, for the first time, according to Robert X. Cringely's book "Accidental Empires," was a programmable device to which a clever engineer could add a few memory chips and a suppport chip or two and turn it into a real computer you could hold in your hands. See also MICROPROCESSOR.

1975 Bell System begins testmarketing Picturephone, a two-way color videoconferencing service at 12 locations around the country. Businesses rented meeting rooms equipped with the technology.

1976 First digital electronic switch installed.

1977 First lightwave system installed.

1978 CCITT comes out with Group 2 recommendation on fax.

1979 Chapter 11 Federal bankruptcy provision introduced. Chapter 11 is reorganization. Chapter 7 is liquidation.

1980 CCITT comes out with Group 3 recommendaion on fax. Group 3 machines are much faster than Group 2 or 1. With Group 3 machines, after an initial 15-second handshake that is not repeated, they can send an average page of text in 30 seconds or less.

1981 IBM PC debuts.

1982 January 8, 1982 the consent decree to break up AT&T into seven regional holding companies and what was left (long distance and manufacturing) is announced. The divestiture takes place two years later on January 1, 1984.

1983 1. Novell's first network file service software. 2. Nintendo introduces Famicom, a computer turned video game.

1984 January 1984 was the breakup of the Bell System. At the beginning of January, 1984 AT&T gave up its local operating phone companies, which got formed into seven, roughly-equal holding companies. In turn, AT&T got the Justice Department off its back for an anti-trust suit and got the right to get into industries other than telecommunications. Its chosen industry was the computer industry for which it felt it had unique skills.

1986 Novell's SFT NetWare, first fault tolerant local area network operating system.

1988 First transatlantic optical fiber cable.

1989 1. Fiber to the home field trial, Cerritos, CA. 2. Novell releases NetWare 3.0, the first 32-bit network operating system for Intel 80386/486-based servers. 3. 1989: Panasonic's household-size video phone with moving color images debuts in Tokyo.

1990 Demonstration of 2,000 kilometer link using optical amplifiers without repeaters.

1991 AT&T takes over NCR. Apple and IBM announce they're working on some deals. IBM starts to split up, selling off some divisions, setting some up as independent organizations within IBM.

1992 1. AT&T introduces VideoPhone 2500 marketed as the first home-model color video phone which works on normal dial up analog phone lines. It meets cool reception because of poor image quality and its high price, namely $1,500. 2. Microsoft Windows 3.1 and IBM's OS/2 2.0 operating systems introduced. Windows NT (32-bit operating system) debuts in beta form. 3. Wang files for Chapter 11. 4. MCI introduces VideoPhone for normal dial-up analog phone lines. It retails for $750. It is not compatible with the AT&T phone.

10 BASE 2 IEE standard for baseband Ethernet at 10 Mbps over coaxial cable to a maximum distance of 185 meters. Also knowns at THIN ETHERNET.

10 BASE-T An Ethernet local area network which works on twisted pair wiring that looks and feels remarkably like telephone cabling. Sometimes old phone cabling will work. Mostly, it won't. Be safe. Put in new cabling.

10-NET The LAN from Fox Research, Dayton, OH, now a subsidiary of DCA of Atlanta. 10-Net is a baseband, Ethernet CSMA/CD peer-to-peer LAN running on one twisted pair. It is easy to install and has many advantages. See ETHERNET.

1A AT&T's first generation of standardized KEY TELEPHONE SYSTEM equipment based on a variety of interconnected phone-line-powered relays. Prior to 1A1, key systems were often patched together from a variety of non-standard parts, with varying wiring schemes, making repairs and upgrades very difficult.

1A1 AT&T's second generation of standardized KEY TELEPHONE SYSTEM equipment. Unlike the phone-line- powered 1A1, it used commercial AC power for added features such as illuminated buttons to indicate line status.

1A2 AT&T's third generation of standardized KEY TELEPHONE SYSTEMS. It was distinctive for its use of plug-in circuit cards, making it much easier to add features or diagnose and cure problems.

1A3 A cute term for an historic TIE electronic key system that provided advanced features, but was priced competitively with 1A2 electromechanical key systems.

1FB One Flat rate Business phone line. A phone line you pay a single monthly charge for and you may make as many local phone calls as you wish for free during that month. See also 1MB.

1MB One Message rate Business phone line. A phone line you pay a single monthly charge for. That charge typically allows you to make a small number of local calls for free. But that each additional local call will cost you. That cost may be by the minute, by the distance, or just by the call. See 1FB.

1PSS Packet Switching System. The AT&T Western Electric 1PSS is a high-capacity, X.25 packet switch.

2B+D A shortened way of saying ISDN's BRI interface, namely two bearer channels and one data channel. See ISDN.

23B +D A circuit with a wide range of frequencies that is divided in 23 64 Kbps paths for carrying voice, data, video or other information simultaneously. In ISDN, it is also known as the Primary Rate Interface. It bears a remarkable similarity to today's T-1 link, except that T-1 can carry 24 voice channels. In ISDN, 23B +D gives 23 channels and one D channel for out of band signaling. In T-1, signaling is handled in-band using robbed bit signaling. So there is considerable difference between today's T-1 and tomorrow's ISDN 23B +D. See ISDN PRI and ROBBED BIT SIGNALING.

24-BIT MODE The standard addressing mode of Apple Macintosh's System 6 operating system, where only 24 bits are used to designate addresses. Limits address space to 16MB (2 to the 24th power), of which only 8MB is normally available for application memory. This mode is also used under System 7 (the Mac's more moden operating system) if 32-bit addressing is turned off. See 32-BIT.

2500 SET The "normal" single-line touchtone desk telephone. It has replaced the rotary dial 500 set in most — but definitely not all — areas of the United States and Canada.

2B+D The Basic Rate Interface (BRI) in ISDN. A single ISDN circuit divided into two 64 Kbps digital channels for voice or data and one 16Kbps channel for low speed data (up to 9,600 baud) and signaling. Either or both of the 64 Kbps channels may be used for voice or data. In ISDN 2B+D is known as the Basic Rate Interface. In ISDN, 2B+D is carried on one or two pairs of wires (depending on the interface) — the same wire pairs that today bring a single voice circuit into your home or office. See ISDN.

2B1Q Two Binary, One Quarternary. An ISDN line encoding technique which uses two bits to represent four variations in amplitude and polarity.

2W Two-Wire.

32 BIT An adjective that describes hardware or software that manages data, program code, and program address information in 32-bit-wide words.

32-BIT ADDRESSING An optional addressing mode available in Apple Macintosh System 7 operating system (or System 6 if OPTIMA is installed). Because 32 bits are used to designate address information, up to 256MB of physical RAM or up to 1024MB (one gigabyte) of virtual memory on the Quadra 900 can be addressed. Also called 32-bit mode.

32-MEGABYTE BARRIER Versions of MS-DOS prior to 4.0 had a built-in limit on the size of a disk partition. Using the original design parameters of DOS, we can show how we got to the maximum size disk partition. One word, 16 bits, is defined for DOS to access sectors within its hard disk partition. A single 16-bit binary word can represent values from zero through 65,535. This limits the partition's total sector count to 65,536. Hard disk sectors are 512 bytes long. 512 bytes times 65,536 sectors = 33,554,432. Since there are 1,048,576 bytes in each megabyte, the maximum size partition calculates to 32 megabytes. MS-DOS 4.0 and 5.X can now create partitions of and read in one go a disk of up to 512 megabytes.

3274 IBM series of Control Units or Cluster Controllers provide a control interface between host computers and clusters of 3270 compatible terminals.

327X Belonging to IBM's 3270 collection of data communications terminals.

386 See 80386.

386SLC The IBM 386SLC is IBM's improved version of Intel's 80386SX microprocessor chip. IBM designed it with Intel's help, so it's compatible with the Intel family of 8088, 80286, 80386, 80486 chips.

4004 The world's first general-purpose microprocessor (computer on a chip). The 4004 was made by Intel, was 4-bit, was released on November 15, 1971 and contained 2,300 transistors. It executed 60,000 instructions per second. The tiny 4004 had as much computing power as the the first electronic computer, ENIAC, which filled 3,000 cubic feet with 18,000 vacuum tubes when it was built in 1946. Intel introduced the 4004 in 1971. The 4004 found a home in desktop calculators, traffic lights and electronic scales. It was followed by the 8-bit 8008.

42A An early terminal block. The Model 42A is a plastic mounting base about two inches square with four screws and a cover. Before modular connections became widespread, the 42A was used to connect a phone's line cord to the wire inside a wall or running around the baseboard. Adapters, such as the No. 725A made by AT&T and Suttle Apparatus, can be used to convert a 42A into a 4-conductor modular jack. See also TERMINAL BLOCK.

486 A shortened name for Intel's family of 80486 chips, the successor to and continuation of the line of chips that started with the 8088 and grew into the 8086, the 80286 and the 80386. The 80486 is a major step forward in speed, complexity and capability. In simple terms, the 486 is a combination microprocessor, floating point math coprocessor, memory cache controller and 8K of RAM cache, all in one chip. The 486 chip contains 1.2 million transistors and is capable of 41 MIPS operating at 50 MHz. See 80486.

486DX The full-powered 80486 from Intel. See 80486.

486SL A power-saving version of Intel's '486 chip, which it introduced in the fall of 1992 and targeted at manufacturers of laptops and notebooks. The chip runs at 3.3 volts, compared with 5.0 volts for its previous power-saving chip, the '386SL.

486SLC A name given to clones of 80486 chips. These clones are made by companies other than Intel, the manufacturer of the original chip. These clones are often not identical in power with the Intel chip. The Cyrix 486SLC, for example, is really a hybrid of the 386 and 486 chips. The Cyrix chip is intended to offer notebook manufacturers an easy way to upgrade machines originally designed to run on Intel 386SX processors. Cybrix built its 486SLC chip to fit the Intel 386SX sockets already in place in many popular notebook designs, thus requiring only minimal changes to the BIOS and motherboard. As with the Intel 386SX, the Cyrix processor has a 32-bit internal data path but communicates with the rest of the computer over a 16-bit data path. However, it uses the 486SX instruction set and boasts an on-board cache, althought only 1K. The 486SLC's hardware multiplier, although not as fast as a true math coprocessor, can significantly speed some graphics calculations. Like Intel's 386SL chip, the Cyrix 486SLC operates at a low 3.3 volt. This is designed to extend battery life in portables. Despite its 486 name, though, it's probably more appropriate to compare the performance of 486SLC notebooks to machines powered by 386SX and 386SL chips, not those with Intel 486-class processors. Given their different design goals, it's not fair to expect the 486SLC to match the speed of the 486SX.

486SX The Intel 486SX processor is essentially a full-powered 486DX with its math coprocessor disconnected. Unlike the 386 line, in which the SX version used a 16-bit external path, Intel created the 486SX by simply disconnecting the 486DX's math coprocessor. The 486SX shares the DX's full 32-bit data path and 8K cache.

4A The last generation of "telco-quality" add-on speakerphones, with separately-housed microphone and speaker; made by both Western Electric (AT&T) and Precision Components, Inc.

4GL Fourth Generation Language.

500 SET The old rotary dial telephone deskset. The touchtone version was called a 2500 set.

5ESS A digital central office switching system made by AT&T. It is typically used as an "end-office," serving local subscribers.

64 BIT ARCHITECTURE The wide data path over which instructions (words composed of bits) are moved to and from Intel's i860's internal registers and memory. Most conventional mainframes use a word length of 32 bits. Intel's i860 RISC-based microprocessor line, introduced in 1989, incorporates many firsts, including more than 1 million transistors on a single chip. The line currently comprises the i860 XR, with 1.2 million transistors, and the i860 XP, with 2.5 million transistors.

64 KBPS The standard speed for V.35 interface, DDS service, and also the effective top speed of a robbed-bit 64 Kbps channel.

66-TYPE CONNECTING BLOCK A type of connecting block used to terminate twisted-pair cables. All wires are manually cut down with a special tool to terminate or connect them.

66-TYPE CROSS CONNECT A cross connect made up of the 66-type connecting blocks and jumper wires for administering circuits. All wires, including jumper wires, must be cut down (or punched down) and seated with a special tool.

6800 A Motorola microprocessor used in early Macintoshes, Mac Plus and SE, plus recent low cost units such as the Classic, Portable and PowerBook 100. The 6800 does not support virtual memory or 32-bit addressing.

68020 A Motorola microprocessor used in the Macintosh II and LC. On the Mac II there is a socket to hold a coprocessor called a PMMU which enables the Mac II to use virtual memory. There is no socket on the LC motherboard, so the processor must be upgraded in order to use virtual memory.

68030 A Motorola microprocessor used in the SE/30, PowerBook 140/145 and 170, and Modular Macs, except the LC, Mac II, and Quadras. It supports virtual memory without any additional hardware.

68040 A Motorola microprocessor used in Quadras. It supports virtual memory without any additional hardware. Has built-in floating point math capabilities (an optional coprocessor on the 68030).

7-bit ASCII The standard code for text in which a byte (eight bits) holds the seven ASCII digits that define the character plus one bit for parity.

700 SERVICE An "area code" you dial, as in 1-700-XXX-XXXX. This "area code" has been reserved for the long distance companies to do so as they will. So dial 1-700- and then certain "office codes" (the next three digits), you'll get AT&T and a service it calls Easyrech. It will give a service allowing your calls to follow you. Dial other 700 office codes, get MCI and you'll be able to make intralata "long distance" phone calls, such as those from Manhattan to Westchester County — for presumably cheaper than with the local phone company. 700 service is still evolving. Each carrier has the right to create whatever service it wants with its 700 numbers.

800 PORTABILITY The terms that refers to the fact that you can take your 800 number to any long distance carrier. 800 Portability is provided by a series of complex databases the local phone companies, under FCC mandate, have built. 800 Portability started on May 1, 1993.

800 SERVICE Eight-hundred service. A generic and common (and not trademarked) term for AT&T's, MCI's, US Sprint's and the Bell operating companies' IN-WATS service. All these IN-WATS services have "800" as their "area code." Dialing an 800-number is free to the person making the call. The call is billed to the person or company being called. The telephone company suppliers of 800 services use various ways to configure and bill their 800-services. One way: you can buy an 800 line which will ring on your normal phone line. You'll only pay per call, but you won't receive any incoming call if you're making an outgoing one. (You can even terminate an 800 number on your cellular phone.) For other 800 services you might pay a flat monthly rate plus "so-much" (i.e. timed usage) per call. That timed usage may include some calculation for the distance the incoming call traveled. 800-Service is now available for calls from Canada and some countries in

Europe. More and more long distance companies are introducing 800-service.

800 Service works like this: You're somewhere in North America. You dial 1-800 and seven digits. Your local central office sees the "1" and recognizes the call as long distance. It ships that call to a bigger central office (or perhaps processes the call itself). At that central office it's processed, a machine will recognize the 800 "area code" and examine the next three digits. Those three digits will tell which long distance carrier to ship the call to. Each long distance company has been assigned specific 800 three digit "exchanges." For example, MCI has the exchange 999. AT&T has the exchange 542. If you want a phone number beginning with 800-999, then you must subscribe to MCI 800 service. If you want a phone number beginning with 800-542, you must subscribe to AT&T 800 service. Once the 800-call is "passed off" to whichever carrier it belongs to, that carrier sends the call to a switch attached to a huge "translation" database. The call arrives at the switch. The database says the call 800-NNN-XXXX is really 212-555-1234, and sends the 800 line to that number.

As a real-life example, Telecom Library, publishers of this book, has an 800 number, namely 800-LIBRARY (or 800-542-7279). When you call that number, the following number — 212-206-6870 — in New York City rings. Dialing 800-542-7279 is effectively the same as dialing 212-206-6870, except that if you dial 212-206-6870 you'll pay. If you dial 800-542-7279, I'll pay. Because 800 long distance service is essentially a database lookup and translation telephone service, there are endless "800 services" you can create, like changing the routing instructions based on time of day, day of week, number calling etc. See EIGHT HUNDRED SERVICE for more, especially all the features you can now get on 800 service.

In May of 1993 the FCC has mandated that all 800 numbers will become "portable." That means that customers can take their 800 telephone number from one long distance company to another, and still keep the same number.

800 PORTABILITY As I write this in the winter of 1992/1993, 800 numbers were not portable. This means you could not move your 800 number from one long distance company to another in North America and keep your phone number. The FCC (Federal Communications Commission) has now mandated that, effective May 1993, you will be able to switch 800 vendors but keep your number. The idea clearly is to encourage competition among vendors of 800 lines. For this to happen, the local phone companies have to develop huge databases of which numbers should be sent where. This is a big job and may not happen by May 1993. We'll see. The big "plus" of portability will probably be lower 800 prices, though there is some hope that the carriers will create features to make 800 lines more useful.

800 VALUFLEX SERVICE A New York and New England Telephone service which lets you make and receive regular phone calls and 800-number calls from local areas on your normal business phone lines. There are big advantages here. You don't have to rent additional phone lines. You don't have to expand your existing phone system — or buy a new one (if getting extra lines means you'd grow out). And you can combine your incoming 800 lines with features you can get on business lines — like call forwarding, conferencing, etc. Have your 800 calls come into your office during the day. Have them call forwarded at night to your home. 800 Valuflex is aimed at smaller business.

8008 Intel's 8-bit 8008 microprocessor was introduced in April 1972. It contained 2300 transistors. Its typical used was in dumb terminals, general calculators and bottling machines.

802 IEEE committee on Local Area Networks (LANs) standards. See 802 STANDARDS.

802 STANDARDS The 802 Standards are a set of standards for LAN communications developed through the IEEE's Project 802. The 802 Standards segment the data link layer into two sublayers:

1. A Medium Access Control (MAC) layer that includes specific methods for gaining access to the LAN (Local Area Network). These methods — such as Ethernet's random access method and Token Ring's token procedure — are in the 802.3, 802.5 and 802.6 standards.

2. A Logical Link Control (LLC) Layer, described in 802.2 standard, that provides for connection establishment, data transfer, and connection termination services. LLC specifies three types of communications links:

● An Unacknowledged connectionless Link, where the sending and receiving devices do not set up a connection before transmitting. Instead, messages are sent on a "best try" basis and there is no provision for error detection, error recovery, and message sequencing. This type of link is best suited for applications where the higher layer protocols can provide the error correction and functions, or where the loss of broadcast messages is not critical.

● A Connection-mode Link, where a connection between message source and destination is established prior to transmission. This type of link works best in applications, such as file transfer, where large amounts of data are being transmitted at one time.

● An Acknowledged-connectionless Link that, as its name indicates, provides for acknowledgement of messages without burdening the receiving devices with maintaining a connection. For this reason, it is most often used for applications where a central processor communicates with a large number of devices with limited processing capabilities. 802.1 IEEE standard for overall architecture of LANs and internetworking.

802.1B IEEE standard for network management.

802.1D IEEE standard for inter-LAN bridges (specifically between 802.3, 802.4, and 802.5 networks). Works at the MAC level.

802.2 IEEE data link layer standard used with the IEEE 802.3, 802.4 and 802.5 standards.

802.3 IEEE standard for carrier-sense multiple access with collision detection (CSMA/CD). A physical layer standard specifying a LAN with a CSMA/CD access method on a bus topology. Ethernet and Starlan both follow the 802.3 standard. Typically they transmit at 10 megabits per second (Mbps). The theoretical limit of Ethernet, measured in 64 byte packets, is 14,800 packets per second (PPS). By comparison, Token Ring is 30,000 and FDDI is 170,000.

802.3 1Base5 IEEE standard for baseband Ethernet at 1 Mbps over twisted pair wire to a maximum distance of 500 meters. Also called Starlan.

802.3 10Base2 IEEE standard for baseband Ethernet at 10 Mbps over coaxial cable to a maximum distance of 185 meters. Also called "Cheapernet" or "Thin Ethernet."

802.3 10Base5 IEEE standard for baseband Ethernet at 10 Mbps over fax coaxial cable to a maximum distance of 500 meters.

802.3 10Broad36 IEEE standard for broadband Ethernet at 10 Mbps over broadband cable to a maximum distance of 3600 meters.

802.3 10Base-T 10Base-T is an IEEE standard for operating Ethernet local area networks (LANs) on twisted-pair cabling using the home run method of wiring (exactly the same as a phone system uses) and a wiring hub that will contain electronics performing similar functions to a central telephone switch. The full name for the standard is IEEE 802.3 10Base-T. The 10Base-T standard, issued in the fall of 1990, defined the requirements for sending information at 10 million bits per second on ordinary unshielded twisted-pair cabling. The 10Base-T standard defines various aspects of running Ethernet on twisted-pair cabling such as:

Connector types (typically eight-pin RJ-45),

Pin connections (1 and 2 for transmit, 3 and 6 for receive),

Voltage levels (2.2 volts to 2.8 volts peak), and

Noise immunity requirements to filter outside interference from telephone lines or other electronic equipment.

802.4 IEEE physical layer standard specifying a LAN with a token-passing access method on a bus topology. It is typically used with Manufacturing Automation Protocol (MAP) LANs. MAP was developed by General Motors. Typical transmission speed is 10 megabits per second.

802.5 IEEE physical layer standard specifying a LAN with a token-passing access method on a ring topology using unshielded twisted pair. Used by IBM's Token Ring hardware. Typical transmission speed is 4 or 16 megabits per second.

802.6 IEEE standard for MANs (Metropolitan Area Networks). Formerly known as QPSX (Queued Packet and Synchronous Exchange), now known as DQDB (Distributed Queue DOUBLE Bus.

802.7 IEEE technical advisory group on broadband LANs.

802.8 IEEE technical advisory group for fiber-optic LANs.

802.X The Institute of Electrical and Electronics Engineers (IEEE) committee that developed a set of standards describing the cabling, electrical topology, physical topology, and access scheme of network products; in other words, the 802.X standards define the physical and data-link layers of LAN architectures. IEEE 802.3 is the work of an 802 subcommittee that describes the cabling and signaling for a system nearly identical to classic Ethernet. IEEE 802.5 comes from another subcommittee and similarly describes IBM's Token-Ring architecture.

80286 In February, 1982 Intel unveiled its second generation (thus the 2) 8086 microprocessor chip — the 16-bit 80286. The 80286 featured 134,000 transistors. The 80286 (computer on a chip) drives the IBM AT. It is a true 16-bit processor. This chip will run at 6 MHz to 16 MHz. At 10 MHz it runs 1.5 mips. The 80286 has a 24-bit address bus and can address 16 MB of memory directly (which is two (2) raised to the 24th power). In late 1991 the chip cost $8.

80386DX Introduced in October, 1985, the 80386 is the third generation of the 8086 family (hence the 3). The Intel microprocessor (computer on a chip) which drives the IBM Model 80 and many others. It contains 275,000 transistors and is a 32-bit processor. It is typically clocked at 16 MHz, but there are now versions of it that will run at 33 MHz. Its 32-bit processor means is it can process data in 32-bit chunks, rather than the 16-bit chunks of the 80286 family. The 80386 DX comes in 20 MHz (4 MIPS), 25 MHz (6 MIPS) and 33 MHz (8 MIPS). The principal architectural advantage over its predecessors is the 386 CPU's superior memory management ability, which improves performance by enabling the CPU to work with memory segments larger than 64K and to have access to more than one megabyte of memory (both limitations of the 286). The 386 can address up to four gigabytes (billion bytes) of physical memory and 64 terabytes of virtual memory at a time. It can address the four million byte of memory because it has a 32-bit address bus which can address 2 to the 32 bytes or over 4 billion bytes! Virtual memory is an area of hard disk that is treated by the processor as part of main memory. The Intel 386 DX has a 32-bit external data bus. This 80386's 32-bit bus requires a larger bus — e.g. IBM's Micro-Channel or EISA, the Extended Industry Standard Architecture. EISA is the independent computer industry's alternate to IBM's Micro-Channel data bus architecture which IBM uses in its high end PS/2 line of desktop computers. EISA, like Micro-Channel, is a 32-bit channel. But, unlike IBM's Micro-Channel, plug-in boards which work inside the XT and AT-series of IBM and IBM clone desktop computers will work inside EISA machines. They won't work in the

Micro-Channel machines. There are now several versions of the 80386. The most important one is the 80386DX which is the "genuine" 386 and features 25 times the performance of the original IBM PC. Another important 386 is the 80386SX, also called the 80386sx. Intel calls its 386SX microprocessor "the entry level member of the Intel 386 family." It is a genuine 80386 chip, except that its external data bus is only 16 bits (i.e. the size of the normal AT bus), not 32 bits. It is capable of substained execution of 2.5 to 3.5 million instructions per second. A third 386 chip is the 80386SL introduced in October 1990 designed specially for laptop and notebook portable personal computers. The 386SL contains a 386 CPU that has been re-engineered for low-power operation. Surrounding the CPU are a memory controller and a complete set of input/output (I/O) controllors like those used in most PCs. By combining these two components with a few external devices, OEMs (Original Equipment Manufacturers) can build a complete, portable 386 PC with the same functionality as a 386 desktop with just five chips — nine, including memory. As a result, systems based on the 80386SL will consume one-third less board space and all components should fit easily on a 3" x 5" motherboard. PCs based on the 386SL SuperSet (Intel's name for its chip set) will also feature 50% longer battery life. The 386 SL will also let notebook users use "auto resume" which lets you shut your laptop off in the middle of a program, turn it on later and find yourself at exactly the place you were when you shut off, i.e. no rebooting is necessary. The 386SL contains 85,000 transistors — more than three times as many as the 386SX.

For history's sake: In 1984 the typical motherboard of a PC required about 170 components plus memory chips. By 1987 the number of components had dropped to 70 excluding memory. With Intel's 386SL, a design engineer can now implement a complete PC AT compatible in 10 components plus memory. By 1993, all of the basic legic necessary for the creation of a basic PC AT-compatible should reside on one piece of silicon.

80386SL Intel introduced the 80386SL chip in October 1990. Intel designed the chip specially for laptop and notebook portable personal computers. The 386SL contains a 386 microprocessor-compatible CPU that has been re-engineered for low-power operation. Surrounding the CPU are a memory controller and a complete set of input/output (I/O) controllors like those used in most PCs. By combining these two components with a few external devices, OEMs (Original Equipment Manufacturers) can build a complete, portable 386 PC with the same functionality as a 386 desktop with just five chips — nine, including memory. As a result, systems based on the 80386SL will consume one-third less board space and all components should fit easily on a 3" x 5" motherboard. PCs based on the 386SL SuperSet (Intel's name for its chip set) will also feature 50% longer battery life. The 386SL will also let notebook users use "auto resume" which lets you shut your laptop off in the middle of a program, turn it on later and find yourself at exactly the place you were when you shut off, i.e. no rebooting is necessary. The 80386SL contains 855,000 transistors. In September 1991,

Intel introduced a 25 MHz version of the 80386SL, which will run at 5.3 mips (million intructions per second). The 386SL contains 85,000 transistors — more than three times as many as the 386SX.

80386SX Intel calls its 80386SX microprocessor "the entry level member of the Intel 386 family." It is a genuine 80386 chip, except that its external data bus is only 16 bits (i.e. the size of the normal AT bus), not 32 bits. It is capable of substained execution of 2.5 to 3.5 million instructions per second. The 80386SX contains 275,000 transistors. See also 80386DX.

80387 The Intel 80387 SX is a high performance floating point coprocessor designed to be used in 80385 SX microprocessor-based computers. It's basically a special purpose microprocessor designed to help the main "computer on a chip," the 80387 with mathematical calculations — like recalculating spreadsheets. You can install this chip in virtually all 80386SX based computers. But having the chip is only useful if you run software that can take advantage of it. Not all can.

80486DX Introduced on June 5, 1991, The Intel 80486DX microprocessor (computer on a chip) sports 1,185,000 transistors. It has a clock speed of 20 MHz to 50 MHz. It sports 50 times the performance of the original IBM PC. The Intel 486DX running at 50 MHz will process 41 million instructions per second (MIPS). As of early November, 1991, an 80486DX running at 50 MHz costs $644 in lots of a thousand. See also 486.

80486SX The Intel 80486 microprocessor without a math coprocessor. The 80486SX is a cheaper version of the 80486 chip.

80586 An Intel microprocessor containing more than three million transistors, introduced in April, 1993 and called the Pentium. It is 80% faster than the fastest 486. It is capable of executing 112 million instructions per second.

80686 An upcoming Intel microprocessor containing more than seven million transistors. It will be capable of executing 175 million instructions per second. It is due out in 1993/1994.

80786 An upcoming Intel microprocessor containing more than 20 million transistors. It will be capable of executing 250 million instructions per second. It is due out in 1995/1996.

8080 Intel brought out the 8-bit 8080 microprocessor in April, 1974. It contained 5,000 transistors and was 10-times more powerful than the 8008. The 8080 was, probably the "first" microprocessor. When it was invented, memory for computers was very expensive. The 8080 could directly address 64 thousand bytes of information. This limit of 64K was the direct result of the fact that the CPU chip had only 16 address lines. The address lines are a set of wires coming out of the CPU which allow the CPU to indicate what item of memory it wants to read or write. In most computers, the size of the "pieces" are bytes, or 8-bit characters. These 16 wires are called the Address Bus. The voltages on the 16 address lines are interpreted as a binary number (with the first pin representing the 1's place, the second pin representing the 2's place, the third pin representing the 4's place, etc. The resultant number is the Address addressable by the CPU (Central Processing Unit). The number of distinct patterns of 16 things, each of which can have two values, is 2 raised to the 16th power, or 65,536. This number is 64 times the quantity "1K" which is 1,024. See also 8086 which was the Intel chip which following the 8080.

8086 On June 8, 1978, Intel introduced the 8086, a 16-bit microprocessor with 29,000 transistors and ten times the performance of the 8080. The 8086, or more precisely its 16-bit counterpart, the 8088, became the brain of IBM's first personal computer. The 8086 chip is an upgraded version of the basic 8080 architecture. It is basically a doubling of a small portion of the internal workings of the 8086's address circuitry. Intel basically duplicated the address register (the transistors that hold the pattern of bits to place on the address bus), slid it left four bits, and added some simple circuitry to add it arithmetically to the "old" address register. This is called the Intel Segment Register. By making this simple kluge to the 8080, Intel created the 8086 and 8088 microprocessors which now effectively had twenty address lines and could therefore address two to the 20th locations, or a little over one million bytes. See also 8088 and 80286.

8088 Introduced in June 1979 by Intel, this is the 16-bit chip which drove the original IBM PC and the subsequent IBM XT. It is identical to the 8080 except that external bus width is 8-bit (the 8080 is 16). The 8088 has a clock speed of 4.77 MHz at 0.33 mips and 8 MHz at 0.75 mips. It had 29,000 transistors. It cost between $3 and $4 in late 1991. See also V20, which is a Japanese NEC version of the 8088. It's about 10% to 20% faster than the 8088. You can pull an 8088 out of your old PC (e.g. the AT&T 6300) and replace it with this chip. You'll get about a 20% (and noticeable) increase in speed. We have. It works fine. Some key systems use this chip.

8088-2 A speeded-up version of the 8088 microprocessor. It has a clock speed of 8 mhz. See also the V20-2 which is the Japanese version of the 8088-2. It's 10% to 20% faster than the 8088-2.

82596 The 82596 is an intelligent, 16-/32-bit local area network coprocessor from Intel. The 82596 implements the CSMA/CD access method and can be configured to support all existing 802.3 standards. Coupled with the 82503 Dual Serial Transceiver, the 82596 provides the optimal Ethernet connection to Intel1386 and Intel486 client PCs and servers. The board space required for an 82596/82503 motherboard implementation is less than six square inches. provides full Ethernet bandwidth performance while allowing the CPU to work independently. An on-board four-channel DMA controller along with an intelligent micromachine automatically manages memory structures and provide command chaining and autonomous block transfers while two large independent FIFOs accomodate long bus latencies and provide programmable thresholds.

9-TRACK A standard for 1/2" magnetic tape designed for data storage. Its nine tracks hold a byte (eight bits) plus one parity bit in a row across the tape width-wise.

900 SERVICE A generic and common (and not trademarked) term for AT&T's, MCI's, Sprint's and other long distance companies' 900 services. All these services have "900" as their "area code." Dialing a 900-number is free to the company or person receiving the call, but costs money to the person making the call. Here's the story: 900 service was introduced as the industry's "information service" area code. You'd dial 1-900-WEATHER, for example, and punch in some touchtones in response to prompts and you could hear the weather in Sydney, Australia or Bagdad, Iraq, wherever you might be planning your next vacation. For this service, you'd be charged perhaps 75 to 95 cents a minute. And you'd get the bill as part of your normal monthly phone bill. That was the original idea. Then some people got the idea that 900 would make a wonderful porn number and they started advertising "Call 900-666-3333 and speak with Diana. She really wants you." And they started charging $5 a minute. When huge 900-call bills started appearing on people's bills, there was an outcry from many subscribers who wouldn't pay the bills. Some children called on their parents' phones. Employees made calls from work and the company's accountants went nuts. So the industry retreated from 900 porn. Then someone thought — "Why not sell things through an 900 number?" We could sell a set of ginzu knives for just calling this 900 number. No messing with credit cards or checks. The bill goes straight on your phone bill. At about the same time someone thought that 900 numbers would be great for running sweepstakes. "Call up, register your name for a free trip with a racing car team to the Australian Indianapolis 500. Three lucky people will be chosen. The call will cost you only $2.75." So 900 services became a new type of gambling.

The long distance companies providing 900 services reacted predictably to some of the newer services. They clamped down on who they would sign up, which service and/or product you could, or could not sell. And, rather than charging "a piece of the action" as they did in the beginning, the long distance companies began to charge for them as if they were normal long distance calls: charge a set-up fee, a fee for carrying the call, a fee for collecting the money and a fee for the possibility of bad debts. There are variations on these themes.

The 900-service business is rife with stories of people who are alleged to have made millions overnight with innovative 900 numbers. Clearly enormous monies have been made — especially in the beginning when there was novelty to 900 calls. The prognosis is that the 900 number business will grow, that it will mature and that the North American public will wake up to its various scams and discover real value in many of its services. For example, one of the author's "genuine value" and favorite 900 services is fax-back. Dial a 900 number, punch in some touchtone digits, hang up and within seconds your fax machine begins to churn out useful information.

In the summer of 1991, AT&T issued guideliness for its EXPRESS900 service. Those guidelines included:

• The predominant purpose of the calls does not include Entertainment, Children's Programming, Credit/Loan Information, Fulfillment, Political Fundraising, Games of Chance, Postcard Sweepstakes, Job Lines and Personal Lines;

• Every program must have a Preamble and Caller Grace Period, with notification to callers of the opportunity to hang up before charging begins.

• Sponsors may not route calls to any telecommunications equipment or arrangements which allow charging to begin before the caller realizes any value on the call, e.g., Automatic Call Distribution (ACD) with call queuing, or Caller Hold.

905-928 MHz A relatively new frequency range for use by, amongst other things, cordless phones. Most present cordless phones operate within the band 46-49 MHz. The 900 contains 50 channels for cordless telephone transmission. The 46-49 MHz band contains only 10.

911 SERVICE 911 is an emergency reporting system whereby a caller call dial a common number — 911 — for all emergency services. The caller will be answered at a common answering location which will figure the nature of the emergency and dispatch the proper response teams. The first 911 service came on line in 1968. Here are the reasons why 911 benefits a community: Only one number for all emergency services. It's an easy number to remember. It's an easy number to dial. It's great for travelers and new residents. Calls are received by trained personnel. See also E-911, which stands for Enhanced 911 service and typically includes ANI (Automatic Number Identification) and ALI (Automatic Location Information). 911 service is sometimes called B-911 which stands for basic 911 service. See also B-911 and E-911.

999 Great Britain's equivalent of the United States emergency number 911.

A

A 1. Abbreviation for AMP or AMPERE, a unit of electric current. See AMPERE. 2. The local wireline cellular carrier. In one of its less intelligent decisions, the FCC decided to issue two cellular franchises in each city of the United States. They gave one to the local phone company and one to a competitor. This duopoloy has naturally meant little real competition. And perhaps one day, the FCC will issue other licenses and the price of cellular phone calls will drop dramatically. Meantime, the "A" carrier on your cellular phone is the local wireline carrier, i.e. the local phone company (or that was the company who had the license originally). And "B" is the other one.

A & A1 Control leads that come from 1A2 key telephone sets to operate features like flashing of lights to indicate on hold, line ringing, etc.

A & B BITS Bits used in digital environments to convey signaling information. A bit value of one generally corresponds to loop current flowing in an analog environment. A bit zero corresponds to no loop urrent, i.e. to no connection. Other signals are made by changing bit values; for example a flash-hook is set by briefly setting the A bit to zero.

A & B LEADS Additional leads used typically with a channel bank two-wire E&M interface to certain types of PBXs (also used to return talk battery to the PBX).

A & B SIGNALING Procedure used in most T-1 transmission links where one bit, robbed from each of the 24 subchannels in every sixth frame, is used for carrying dialing and controlling information. A type of in-band signaling used in T-1 transmission. A and B signaling reduces the available user bandwidth from 1.544 to 1.536 Mbps.

A BATTERY Another term for TALK BATTERY.

A LAW The PCM coding and companding standard used in Europe. See A LAW ENCODING.

A LAW ENCODING The method of encoding sampled audio waveforms used in the 2048K bit(s) 30 channel PCM primary system, widely used outside North America.

A-B TEST Direct comparison of the sound/picture quality of two pieces of audio/TV equipment by playing one, then the other.

A/B SWITCH A feature found on all new cellular telephones permitting the user to select either the "A" (non-wireline) carrier or the "B" (wireline) carrier when roaming away from home.

A/B SWITCH BOX An external mechanical device used to switch between two devices, such as printers, modems, plotters, mice, phone lines, etc. An example of how you use such a box: You plug one phone line into the "C" or common RJ-11 jack. You plug a fax machine into the "A" jack. You plug a modem into the "B" jack. By turning the switch, you can use one phone line for either a modem or a fax. An A/B switch box comes in serial, parallel port versions and RJ-11 telephone line versions. There are also A/B/C switches that switch between three devices, e.g. a fax, a modem and a phone.

A/D Analog to Digital conversion.

A/D CONVERTER Analog to Digital converter, or digitizer. It is a device which converts analog signals (such as sound or voice from microphone), to digital data so that the signal can be processed by digital circuit such as a digital signal processor.

A/UX An alternate operating system for the Macintosh based on UNIX. A/UX has its own 32-bit addressing mode.

A20 LINE A control line on the Intel 80386 microprocessor that allows MS-DOS and an extended memory manager to create the High Memory Area, or HMA. Only one program can claim control over the A20 at a time.

AA Automated Attendant. A device which answers callers with a recording, and allows caller to route themselves to an extension.

AABS A new software feature being introduced in the telephone industry. It allows collect and third-number billed calls to be placed by the caller without using an operator in much the same way as calling card services have been automated.

AAL ATM Adaption Layer.

AAP Administrative and Accounting Package. The name of a feature on an InteCom PBX which provides call accounting reports relating to usage and cost.

AAR Automatic Alternate Routing.

ABAM A designation for 22 gauge, 110 ohm, plastic insulated, twisted pair Western Electric cable normally used in central offices.

ABANDONED CALL The nontechnical explanation is: A call that is answered, but disconnected before any conversation happens. The technical explanation is: A call which has been offered into a communications network or telephone system, but which is terminated by the person originating the call before it is answered by the person being called. Follow this sequence for an explanation: You call an airline. You hear ringing. Their phone rings. A machine, called an automatic call distributor, answers the call, plays you some dumb message, "Please don't hang up. A real human will answer eventually." You, the caller, are put on Eternity Hold. You get bored waiting and hang up before a live operator answers. You have just abandoned your phone call. Thus the term, Abandoned Call. Information about abandoned calls is useful for planning how many people (also called operators, agents or telephone attendants) an airline should employ on what days and during what times of the day. Thus you can organize to get the right percentage of incoming calls answered within the "right" amount of time and give your callers (i.e. your customers) the service they deserve (or the service you think they deserve, or, the service they think they deserve).

ABBREVIATED DIALING A feature of phone systems which allows users to place calls by dialing typically one or two digits. The system translates the abbreviated number into the destination number. See also SPEED DIALING and PREDICTIVE DIALING.

ABC Automatic Bill Calling — a method of billing for payphone calls. Changed in 1982 to Calling Card service.

ABCD SIGNALING BITS These are bits robbed from bytes in each DS-0 or T-1 channel in particular subframes and used to carry in band all status information such as E&M signaling states.

ABEND ABnormal END. When Novell's NetWare local area operating system detects a serious problem, such as a hardware or software failure, the system issues an abend (abnormal end) message. The abend stops the file server. And you're dead in the water.

ABM Asynchronous Balanced Mode.

ABN ABNormal alarm status

ABORT To stop doing something. Often to get out of a software program. Also, to discontinue sending or receiving a message.

ABOVE 890 DECISION The 1959 FCC decision which allowed companies to build their own private microwave communications systems. The decision resulted from AT&T Long Lines' reluctance to provide companies with long distance service to remote places, such as oil wells, gas pipelines, power stations and paper plants. The decision got its name because the FCC allowed privately-owned microwave systems using radio frequencies "above 890" megahertz — which are naturally called "microwave." See also MICROWAVE and ENTELEC.

ABOVE THE LINE Expenses incurred by telephone company that are charged to the ratepayer by being allowed in the company's rate-base.

ABR AutoBaud Rate detect. A process by which a receiving data device determines the speed, code level, and stop bits of incoming data by examining the first character — usually a preselected sign-on character (often a carriage return). ABR allows the receiving device to accept data from a variety of transmitting devices operating at different speeds without needing to establish data rates in advance. TELECONNECT and INBOUND/OUTBOUND Magazine's electronic mail system (212-989-4675) has ABR. It will detect automatically if you are coming in at 300, 1200 or 2400 baud. Try it.

ABRASION RESISTANCE Ability of material or cable to resist surface wear.

ABRUPT CLOSE Close of a connection on a network without any attempt to prevent any loss of data.

ABS Alternate Billing Services. These are IN (Intelligent Network) services that allow subscribers to charge a call to a number or telephone other than the one they are using. For example, by using a charge card, credit card or personal identification number.

ABSENT-SUBSCRIBER SERVICE A service offered by local telephone companies to subscribers who will be away. A live operator or a machine intercepts the calls and delivers a message. When you come back, you get your old number. But in the meantime, while you're away, you pay less money per month than you would for normal phone service.

ABSOLUTE DELAY The time interval or phase difference between transmission and reception of a signal.

ABSOLUTE GAIN 1. The ratio, usually expressed in decibels, between the signal level at the output of a device and its input under specified operating conditions; e.g., no-load gain, full-load gain, small signal gain. 2. Of an antenna, for a given direction: the ratio, usually expressed in decibels, of the power that would be required at the input of an ideal isotropic radiator to the power actually supplied to the given atenna so that the radiation intensity in the far-field region in the given direction would be the same. If no direction is quoted, that corresponding to maximum radiation is assumed.

ABSOLUTE ZERO A temperature about 460 degrees below zero in Fahrenheit.

ABSORPTION Attenuation caused by dissipation of energy.

AC Alternating Current. Typically refers to the 120 volt electricity delivered by your local power utility to the three-pin power outlet in your wall. Called "alternating current" because the polarity of the current alternates between plus and minus, 60 times a second. The other form of electricity is DC, or direct current, in which the polarity of the current stays constant. Direct current, for example, is what comes from batteries. Overseas, electricity typically alternates at 50 times a second — which is neither better nor worse than the U.S., just different.

In North America, standard 120 volt AC may be also be referred to as 110 volts, 115 volts, 117 volts or 125 volts. Con Edison told me that they are only obliged to deliver voltage to 120 volts plus or minus 10%. This means your outlet may deliver anywhere from 118 volts to 132 volts before your power company will get concerned. Your AC electrical circuit consists of two supply conductors (hot and neutral) and a load (the thing you're running). The hot, energized or live conductor is ungrounded and delivers energy to the load. The hot conductor is connected to the fuse or circuit breaker at the main service entrance. The neutral or common conductor is grounded and completes the circuit from the load back to the utility transformer. The load is any electric or electronic appliance or gadget plugged into the AC electrical outlet. It completes the circuit from the transformer through the hot conductor, to the load, through the neutral conductor and back to the utility transformer. Standard 120 volt circuits also include an equipment ground conductor. This equipment grounding conductor provides an intended path for fault current and is never intended to be a part of the load circuit. The equipment ground serves three very important purposes.

1. It maintains metal appliance cases at zero volts, thus protecting people who touch the cases from receiving an electrical shock.

2. It provides an intentional fault path of low impedance path for current flow when the hot conductor contacts equipment cases (ground fault). This current causes the fuse or circuit breaker to open the circuit to protect people from electric shock.

3. Any electronic equipment (not electrical) uses the equipment ground as a zero volt reference for logic circuits to provide proper equipment performance.

See AC POWER, GROUNDING and BATTERY.

ACO Alarm Cut Off

AC POWER The phone system runs on Alternating Current. Except for very small ones, phone systems need their own dedicated AC power line. This line should be "cleaned" with a power conditioner and voltage regulator. If possible, the phone system should also be backed by a battery-based power pack, called UPS for Uninterruptible Power Supply. The most reliable battery backup is lead acid, the same technology as used in your car. Phone systems consume more power as they process more phone calls. For example, a PBX brochure says that at minimum capacity, it needs less power than eight 100-watt light bulbs. But that at its maximum duplex capacity, it needs the same power as 26 100-watt light bulbs — or 2600 watts. See AC, GROUND and GROUNDING.

AC TO DC CONVERTER An electronic device which converts alternating current (AC) to direct current (DC). Most phone systems, computers and consumer electronic devices (from answering machines to TVs) run on DC. Most phone systems have an AC to DC converter in them. Hint: it's probably buried in the power supply.

AC-DC RINGING A type of telephone signaling that uses both AC and DC components - alternating current to operate a ringer and direct current to aid the relay action that stops the ringing when the called telephone is answered.

ACA Automatic Circuit Assurance.

ACAT Additional Cooperative Acceptance Testing. A method of testing switched access service that provides a telephone company technician at the central office and a carrier's technician at its location, with suitable test equipment to perform the required tests. ACAT may, for example, consist of the following tests: Impulse Noise, Phase Jitter, Signal-to-C-Notched Noise Ratio, Intermodulation (Nonlinear) Distortion, Frequency Shift (Offset),

Envelope Delay Distortion, Dial Pulse Percent Break.

ACB A Northern Telecom term for Architecture Control Board.

ACC Automatic Callback Calling.

ACCELERATED AGING A test performed on material or cable meant to duplicate long term environmental conditions in a short period of time.

ACCELERATED DEPRECIATION A method which allows greater depreciation charges in the early years of an asset's life and progressively smaller ones later on. The total amount of depreciation charged is still equal to 100% of the asset's value. By taking the charges early on in the asset's life, you get the time value of money, i.e. depreciation charged today (and tax saved today) is worth more than the same amount of depreciation charged (or tax saved) tomorrow.

ACCELERATOR 1. A chemical additive which hastens a chemical reaction under specific conditions. A term used in the telecommunications cable industry. 2. In a Windows program, this is a keystroke that dispatches a message to a program, invoking one of its functions. For example, Alt-F4 tells the current Windows application of Windows itself to quit.

ACCELERATOR BOARD A board added onto a personal computer's main board and designed to increase the PC's performance in writing to screen or disk, etc. See also ACCELERATOR CARD.

ACCELERATOR CARD An Apple term. An accelerator card is an add-on product that upgrades the CPU of a Macintosh to a higher speed or more powerful generation of processor. An accelerator card is usually a "daughter board" that clips onto the original CPU or is inserted into the socket that held the original CPU. You need an accelerator card to use virtual memory or enhanced 24-bit addressing on LC, Mac Plus, SE and Classic. See ACCELERATOR BOARD.

ACCEPTANCE ANGLE The angle over which the core of an optical fiber accepts incoming light. It's usually measured from the fiber axis.

ACCEPTANCE TEST The final test of a new telephone system. If the system passes the test — i.e. it meets all specifications laid down in the sales contract — and is working well, then, and only then, will the customer finish paying for it.

ACCESS As a verb, to dial into a feature, a circuit or a piece of equipment. As a noun, the point at which you enter a circuit or other communications facility. In data processing, access means to retrieve information from, or store data in memory or mass storage.

ACCESS CHARGE Under deregulation, all users having access to United States public switched long distance networks will pay an Access Charge. The charge will differ for residential and business users and may also differ between Centrex and PBX users. It varies from $1 to $6 per month. The charge is theoretically, to make up for the "subsidies" once paid by AT&T Long Lines (now called AT&T) to the local operating telephone companies — Bell and independent. A more formal definition is — A surcharge levied per the Code of Federal Regulations. Title 47, part 69, on each line or circuit that has the ability to access or be accessed by a public exchange network. The fee is paid by landline and cellular subscribers, as is a federal telephone excise tax (3% at the time of writing this dictionary).

ACCESS CODE A series of digits or characters which must be dialed, typed or entered in some way to get use of something. That "something" might be the programming of a telephone system, a long distance company, an electronic mail service, a private corporate network, a mainframe computer, a local area network. Once the user dials the main number for the service he must then enter his assigned Access Code to get permission use the system. An Access Code becomes an Account Code when it is used for identifying the caller and doing the billing. Access Code may also mean the digit, or digits, a user must dial to be connected to an outgoing trunk. For example, the user picks up his phone and dials "9" for a local line, dials "8" for long distance, dials "76" for a WATS, etc. In programming a phone system called the Norstar, there are Access Codes to begin Startup, Configuration programming, and Administration programming.

ACCESS CONTROL 1. A technique used to define or restrict the rights of individuals or application programs to obtain data from, or place data into, a storage device. 2. A service feature or technique used to permit or deny use of the components of a communication system.

ACCESS COORDINATION An MCI definition. The proces of ordering, installing, and maintaining the local access channel for MCI customers.

ACCESS COUPLER A device placed between two fiber optic ends to allow signals to be withdrawn from or entered into one of the fibers.

ACCESS CUSTOMER NAME ABBREVIATION ACNA. A three-character abbreviation assigned to each IntereXchange Carrier (IXC) and listed in the Local Exchange Routing Guide (LERG).

ACCESS EVENT Information with a logical content that the functional user and the Network Access FE (Functional Entity) exchange. Definition from Bellcore.

ACCESS GROUP All terminals or phones have identical rights to make use of the computer, the network or the data PBX.

ACCESS LEVEL Used interchangeably with ACCESS CODE. "Level" in dialing tends to mean a number.

ACCESS LINE A telephone line reaching from the telephone company central office to a point usually on your premises. Beyond this point the wire is considered inside wiring.

ACCESS METHOD The technique or the program code in a computer operating system that provides input/output services. By concentrating the control instruction sequences in a common sub-routine, the programmer's task of producing a program is simplified. The access method typically carries with it an implied data and/or file structure with logically similar devices sharing access methods. The term was coined, along with data set, by IBM in the 1964 introduction of the System/360 family. It provides a logical, rather than physical, set of references. Early communications access methods were primitive; recently they have gained enough sophistication to be very useful to programmers. Communications access methods have always required large amounts of main memory. In a medium size system supporting a few dozen terminals of dissimilar types, 80K to 100K bytes of storage is not an unusual requirement. See ACCESS METHODS.

ACCESS METHODS Techniques and rules for figuring which of several communications devices — e.g. computers — will be the next to use a shared transmission medium. This term relates especially to Local Area Networks (LANs). Access method is one of the main methods used to distinguish between LAN hardware. How a LAN governs users' physical (electrical) access to the cable significantly affects its features and performance. Examples of access methods are token passing (Arcnet and Token Ring) and Carrier Sense Multiple Access with Collision Detection (CSMA/CD) (Ethernet). See ACCESS METHOD.

ACCESS SERVICE REQUEST ASR. The ASR is used by the Carrier to request the ICSC to provide Special Accesss or Switched Access as specified in the various Access Services Tariffs.

ACCESS SIGNALING A term which Northern Telecom's Norstar telephones use to indicate their ability to access a remote system (such as a Centrex or a PBX), or dial a number on an alternate carrier by means of Access Signaling (also referred to as "End-to-End" Signaling).

ACCESS TANDEM Denotes a Local Exchange Carrier switching system that provides a concentration and distribution function for originating or terminating traffic between end offices and a Carrier's location. A type of local phone company central office specifically designed to provide equal access for all long distance carriers in that area.

ACCESS TIME 1. In a telecommunications system, the elapsed time between the start of an access attempt and successful access. Note: Access time values are measured only on access attempts that result in successful access. 2. In a computer, the time interval between the instant at which an instruction control unit initiates a call for data and the instant at which delivery of the data is completed. 3. The time interval between the instant at which storage of data is requested and the instant at which storage is started. 4. In magnetic disk devices, the time for the access arm to reach the desired track and for the rotation of the disk to bring the required sector under the read-write mechanism.

ACCESS TOOLKIT Northern Telecom makes a telephone system for up to 100 users called Norstar. The phone system is "open," meaning you can program it. To be able to program it, you need the Norstar Access Toolkit, which you may or may not have to pay for. The Norstar Access Toolkit is a basically set of C Language routines which allows programmers to build applications on an industry standard MS-DOS Personal Computer which is joined to the Norstar with a Norstar interface card. The Toolkit provides access to the D channel messages broadcast to each device on the Norstar. The PC interfaces with the D channel via a PC Interface Card which is inserted into a standard PC-AT slot (the standard ISA bus).

Through the use of the interface card and a set of TSR (Terminate and Stay Resident) drivers, PC applications can insert messages in the D channel and read messages from it which can be received by any other device on the system. Applications on the PC can also be accessed by other devices on the system. In other words, a telephone set can use a feature code which addresses an application on the PC and have access to special information on the PC. Conversely, the application on the PC can monitor a telephone on the system and control how it functions under certain sets of predefined situations.

The basic relationship established between the Norstar telephone sets and the PC is one of server and terminals. Each telephone (terminal) has access to information on the PC (server) and vice versa. No longer are users limited to the set of features and functions which have been defined by Northern Telecom, they can have a phone system which meets their needs. This means you can program a Norstar to act like an automatic call distributor or a predictive dialer or a contact management phone system, or whatever your heart desires. So long as you can program it, or buy the program from someone else who's already done it. As I wrote this in the winter of 1992, shrink-wrapped software packages for Norstar were beginning to appear, as they have appeared for over 10-years for PCs.

ACCOUNT CODE (VOLUNTARY OR ENFORCED) A code assigned to a customer, a project, a department, a division — whatever. Typically, a person dialing a long distance phone call must enter that code so the computer can bill the cost of that call at the end of the month or designated time period. Many service companies, such as law offices, engineering firms, advertising agencies, etc. use account codes to bill their clients. Some account codes are very complicated. They include the client's number and the number of the particular project. The Account Code then includes Client and Matter number. These long codes can tax many call accounting systems, even some very sophisticated ones.

ACCOUNT-A-CALL Pioneers in providing call accounting services since 1972. Account-A-Call works with telecommunications management to assist in cost allocation and analysis of telephone expenses by offering a series of reports and consulting services. One of the country's biggest service bureaus. Based in Pasadena, CA.

ACCOUNTING RATE A price used between long distance companies to "balance up" what they owe each other. For example, if AT&T sends France Telecom one million minutes of calls, but France sends only 500,000 minutes back to AT&T, then AT&T will have to pay France Telecom for the imbalance. If the accounting rate between France and the United States is $1 per minute, then AT&T will pay France Telecom $250,000 for its work in completing the 500,000 extra calls. AT&T pays France Telecom only half the cost because AT&T does half the work itself.

ACCOUNTING SERVERS A local area network costs money to set up and run. Thus it makes sense to charge for usage on it. In Novell's NetWare LANs, the network supervisor sets up accounting through a program called SYSCON. When this happens, the current file server automatically begins to charge for services. The supervisor can authorize other network services (print servers, database servers, or gateways) to charge for services, or can revoke a server's right to charge.

ACCS Automatic Calling Card Service.

ACCUCALL A PBX integration utility for voice processing from Rhetorex, Campbell, CA.

ACCUNET A family of digital long distance transmission services from AT&T. Services are leased, switched or high speed. One, called Accunet Packet Service, is a packet switching digital network. Another one is called Accunet Reserved 1.5 Service, which AT&T describes as a general purpose, common user, modal-based digital service using dual 1.544 Mbps terrestrial and satellite facilities. Accunet Spectrum of Digital Services (ASDS) is AT&T's leased line (also called private line) digital service at 56 Kbps. MCI and Sprint have similar services. It is available in N x 56/64 Kbps, for N = 1, 2, 4, 6, 8, 12.

ACCURACY Absence of error. The extent to which a transmission or mathematical computation is error-free. There are obvious ways of measuring accuracy, such as the percentage of accurate information received compared to the total transmitted.

AC/DC RINGING A common way of signaling a telephone. An alternating current (AC) rings the phone bell and a direct current (DC) is used to work a relay to stop ringing when the called person answers.

ACD See the next seven definitions, AUTOMATIC CALL DISTRIBUTOR and ACIS.

ACD APPLICATION BRIDGE Refers to the link between an ACD and a database of information resident on a user's data system. It allows the ACD to communicate with a data system and gain access to a database of call processing information such as Data Directed Call Routing.

ACD APPLICATION-BASED CALL ROUTING In addition to the traditional methods of routing and tracking calls by trunk and agent group,

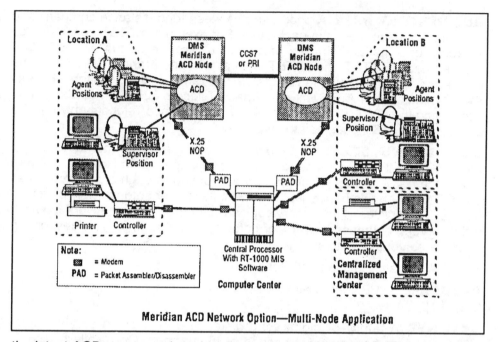

Meridian ACD Network Option—Multi-Node Application

the latest ACDs route and track calls by application. An application is a type of call, e.g. sales vs. service. Tracking calls in this manner allows accurately reported calls especially when they are overflowed to different agent groups.

ACD CALL BACK MESSAGING This ACD capability allows callers to leave messages for agents rather than wait for a live agent. It helps to balance agent workloads between peak and off-peak hours. In specific applications, it offers callers the option of waiting on hold. A good example is someone who only wishes to receive a catalog. Rather than wait while people place extensive orders, they leave their name and address as a message for later followup by an agent. This makes things simpler for them and speeds up service to those wanting to place orders.

ACD CALLER DIRECTED CALL ROUTING Sometimes referred to as an autoattendant capability within the industry, this ACD capability allows callers to direct themselves to the appropriate agent group without the an operator. The caller responds to prompts (Press 1 for sales, Press 2 for service) and is automatically routed to the designated agent group.

ACD CONDITIONAL ROUTING The ability of an ACD to monitor various parameters within the system and call center and to intelligently route calls based on that information. Parameters include volume levels of calls in queue, the number of agents available in designated overflow agent groups, or the length of the longest call. Calls are routed on a conditional basis. "If the number of calls in queue for agent group #1 exceeds 25 and there are at least 4 agents available in agent group #2, then route the call to agent group #2."

ACD DATA DIRECTED CALL ROUTING A capability whereby an ACD can automatically process calls based on data provided by a database of information resident in a separate data system. For example, a caller inputs an account number via touch tone phone. The number is sent to a data system holding a database of information on customers. The number is identified, validated and the call is distributed automatically based on the specific account type (VIP vs. regular business subscriber, as an example).

ACD INTELLIGENT CALL PROCESSING The ability of the latest ACDs to intelligently route calls based on information provided by the caller, a database on callers and system parameters within the ACD such as call volumes within agent groups and number of agents available.

ACF Advanced Communications Function. A family of software products used by IBM allowing its computers to communicate.

ACIS Automatic Customer/Caller Identification. This is a subset of many sophisticated ACD systems. ACIS allows the capture of incoming network identification digits such as DID or DNIS and interprets them to identify the call type or caller. With greater information, such as ANI, this data can identify a calling subscriber number. This is also possible by employing a voice response device to request an inbound caller to identify themselves with a unique code. This could be a phone number, a subscriber number or some other identifying factor. This data can be used to route the call, inform the agent of the call type and even pre-stage the first data screen associated with this call type automatically.

ACK In data communications, ACK is a character transmitted by the receiver of data to ACKnowledge a signal, information or packet received from the sender. See also ACKNOWLEDGMENT.

ACK1 Bisync acknowledgment for odd-numbered message.

ACKNOWLEDGMENT In data communications, the transmission of acknowledgment (ACK) characters from the receiving device to the sending device indicates the data sent has been received correctly.

ACL Applications Connectivity Link. Siemens' protocol for linking its PBX to an external computer and having that computer control the movement of calls within a Siemens PBX. See also OPEN APPLICATION INTERFACE.

ACM 1. Address Complete Message. One of the ISUP call set-up messages. A message sent in the backward direction indicating that all the address signals required for routing the call to the called party have been received. See ISUP.

2. Association for Computing Machinery. 3. Automatic Call Manager. The integration of both inbound call distribution and automated outbound call placement from a list of phone contacts to be made from a database. Telemarketing and collections applications are targets for this type of system.

ACO Alarm Cut Off

ACOUSTIC COUPLER An acoustic modem. A device used to link data terminals and computers with the telephone network. An acoustic coupler looks like the reverse of a telephone handset and is typically made of rubber. The data communications link is achieved through acoustic (sound) signals rather than through direct electrical connection. It is attached to the computer or data terminal through an RS-232-C connector. To work the acoustic coupler, start the computer's communications program, dial the distant computer on a single line telephone with a normal (e.g. old-fashioned) handset. When the distant computer answers with a higher-pitched "carrier tone," you place the telephone handset in the acoustic coupler and transmit data. Since the data is transmitted by sound between the handset and the acoustic coupler (and vice versa), the quality isn't always reliable. You can usually transmit up to 300 baud. People use acoustic couplers when they're short of time or cannot physically connect their modem electrically, e.g. they're using a coin phone.

ACOUSTIC MODEL In automatic speeech recognition, an acoustic model models acoustic behavior of words by gluing together models of smaller units, such as phonemes. (Sorry for the definition of the word model with the word model. But it's actually the best way of defining this term. HN)

ACOUSTIC (OR AIR) SUSPENSION A loudspeaker system that uses an air-tight sealed enclosure.

ACOUSTICS That branch of science pertaining to the transmission of sound. The qualities of an enclosed space describing how sound is transmitted, e.g. its clarity.

ACOUSTO-OPTIC The interactions between acoustic waves and light in a solid medium. Acoustic waves can be made to modulate, deflect, and focus light waves by causing a variation in the refractive index of the medium. See also FIBER OPTICS.

ACQUISITION 1. In satellite communications, the process of locking tracking equipment on a signal from a communications satellite. 2. The process of achieving synchronization. 3. In servo systems, the process of entering the boundary conditions that will allow the loop to capture the signal and achieve lock-on. See also phase-locked loop.

ACQUISITION TIME 1. In a communication system, the amount of time required to attain synchronism. 2. In satellite control communications, the time required for locking tracking equipment on a signal from a communications satellite. See also satellite.

ACP Activity Concentration Point.

ACRONYM A word formed from the first (or first few) letters of each word or group of words. For example, BASIC, the Beginner's All-purpose Symbolic Instruction Code, or COBOL, the computer language, which comes from COmmon Business Oriented Language.

ACS 1. Automatic Call Sequencer. A rudimentary automatic call distributor. See AUTOMATIC CALL SEQUENCER. 2. Advanced Communication System. An old name for AT&T's data communications/data processing service, later called Net 1000. In late 1986, after 10 years in birth, AT&T finally buried ACS because it offered too little in the face of what — by then — had become cheap, powerful desktop microcomputers and under $200 1200 baud modems.

ACSE Association Contol Service Element. An application-level protocol.

ACT Applied Computer Telephony is Hewlett Packard's program that is a strategy and set of open architecture commands and interfaces for integrating voice and database technologies. The idea is that with ACT a call will arrive at the telephone simultaneously with the database record of the caller. And such call and database record can be transferred simultaneously to an expert, a supervisor, etc. ACT works on both HP 3000 and HP 9000 computers. ACT essentially controls the telephone call movement within PBXs it connects to. See also OPEN APPLICATION INTERFACE.

ACTAS Alliance of Computer-Based Telephony Application Suppliers — a part of the North American Telecommunications Association (NATA). ACTAS's mission, according to ACTAS, is to deliver the benefits of computer-based telephone applications to the broadest possible range of customers. The high costs of customization and marketing currently relegate computer-based telephony applications to Fortune 100-level companies. ACTAS will work to lower the threshold for delivering the benefits of these applications, which include integrated voice and database processing systems automation and customer service, to the general business market.

ACTGA Attendant Control of Trunk Group Access. A complicated term for a simple concept, namely that your operator completes long distance calls. A primitive form of toll control.

ACTS Association of Competitive Telecommunications Suppliers. Trade association of telephone equipment dealers in Canada.

ACTIONMEDIA An imaging term. DVI Technology's product family, introduced in 1990 and consisting of single-board delivery and single board capture capability for AT or Micro Channel architecture buses (introduced with IBM), e.g. ActionMedia 750 ADP, etc.

ACTIVATION FEE Fee for the initial connection to the cellular system.

ACTIVE/PASSIVE DEVICE On a local area network, a device that supplies current for the loop is considered active. Such a device is s Token Ring MAU (Multistation Access Unit). A device which does not supply current is considered passive.

ACTIVE CALL An term which Hayes defines in its Hayes ISDN System adapter manual. An active call is a voice call to which you are connected that is not on hold.

ACTIVE CIRCUITS An MCI definition. MCI circuits for which are there is a completed "install order" and a "completed date."

ACTIVE COUPLER A fibre optic coupler that includes a receiver and one or more transmitters. It regenerates (thus "active") input signals and sends them through output fibers, instead of passively dividing input light.

ACTIVE HUB A device used to amplify transmission signals in certain local area network topologies. You can use an active hub to add workstations to a network or to lengthen the cable distance between workstations and the file saver.

ACTIVE LINE A voice or data communications channel currently in use.

ACTIVE MATRIX LIQUID CRYSTAL DISPLAY A technique of making liquid crystal displays for computers in which each of the screen's pixels — the tiny elements that make up a picture — is controlled by its own transistor.

ACTIVE MEDIUM The material in fiber optic transmission, such as crystal, gas, glass, liquid or semiconductor, which actually "lases." It's also called laser medium, lasing medium, or active material.

ACTIVE OPEN Used in TCP to request connection with another node.

ACTIVE (RECURRING) CUSTOMER An MCI definition. An MCI customer who was installed and not canceled as of the first day of the month. The system determines the customer to be recurring if the install date does not equal the current billing month.

ACTIVE SPLICING Aligning the ends of two optical fibers with the aim of minimizing the splice loss.

ACTIVE VOCABULARY A phrase used in voice recognition to mean a group of words which a recognizer has been trained to understand and is attempting to understand at a given time. It is a subset of the total vocabulary of the recognizer.

ACTIVITY CONCENTRATION POINT ACP. A location on a telecommunications network where there is high communications traffic, including voice, data, document distribution and teleconferencing. Generally, there will be some switching equipment present at the ACP.

ACTIVITY FACTOR A decimal fraction which represents the percentage of speech on a voice channel versus those periods of (non-talking) silence on that channel. Most voice channels carry actual speech 30% to 40% of the total available time. This represents an activity factor of 0.3 to 0.4.

ACTIVITY REPORT A report printed by a facsimile machine which lists all transmissions and receptions — their time, date, and number of documents; the remote unit type, diagnostic codes; and machine identification.

ACTS Automatic Coin Telephone Service includes a telephone company central office that can complete all types of payphone calls automatically without an operator. Recorded announcements are used to convey instructions to the customer.

ACU Automatic Calling Unit. Also an 801 ACU. A telephone company-provided device instructed by a computer to place a call on behalf of the computer. The call is then connected to a telephone company-provided Data Set. Anyone other than an IBM shop would simply buy a Hayes or Hayes-compatible modem, and not bother with the trouble and expense of an ACU.

ADA 1. Average Delay to Abandon. Average time a caller is held in queue before they get frustrated and decide to hang up. 2. A high level computer language which the Department of Defense has been trying to foist on its suppliers and thus, make a standard. ADA is named for British mathematician Ada Lovelace, known at the time as Lady Lovelace. She was the girlfriend of Charles Babbage, the inventor of the computer.

ADAD Automatic Dialing and Announcing Device. Device which automatically places calls and connects them to a recording or agent. A Canadian term for an automatic dialer.

ADAPTER A device used to connect a terminal to some circuit or channel so it will be compatible with the system to which it is attached.

ADAPTER SEGMENT A name sometimes used for the upper memory area of a PC, at hexadecimal addresses A000 through EFFF (640K to 1024K).

ADAPTIVE CHANNEL ALLOCATION A method of multiplexing wherein the information-handling capacities of channels are not predetermined but are assigned on demand.

ADAPTIVE COMMUNICATION Any communication system, or portion thereof, that automatically uses feedback information obtained from the system itself or from the signals carried by the system to modify dynamically one or more of the system operational parameters to improve system performance or to resist degradation.

ADAPTIVE EQUALIZATION An electronic technique that allows a modem to continuously analyze and compensate for variations in the quality of a telephone line.

ADAPTIVE INTERFRAME TRANSFORM CODING A class of compression algorithms commonly used in video codecs to reduce the data transmission rate.

ADAPTIVE LOGICALLY PROVIDED SERVICES An AT&T term for services that adapt to an end customer's needs, on demand, in any combination of voice, data or image by the dynamic allocation of network resources (bandwidth, switching, bridging, feature processing, etc.) under sophisticated software logic control.

ADAPTIVE DIFFERENTIAL PULSE CODE MODULATION See ADPCM.

ADAPTIVE PULSE CODE MODULATION A way of encoding analog voice signals into digital signals by adaptively predicting future encodings by looking at the immediate past. The adaptive part reduces the number of bits per second that another rival and more common method called PCM (Pulse Code Modulation) requires to encode voice. Adaptive PCM is not common because, even though it reduces the number of bits required to encode voice, the electronics to do it are expensive. See PULSE CODE MODULATION.

ADAPTIVE ROUTING A method of routing packets of data or data messages in which the system's intelligence selects the best path. This path might change with altered traffic patterns or link failures.

ADAS Automated Directory Assistance Service. A service from Northern Telecom which automates the greeting and inquiry portion of the directory assistance call. With ADAS, directory assistance callers are greeted by the automated system and asked to state the name of the city and the listing they are seeking. They are then connected with an operator. The ADAS service knocks a few seconds off each directory assistance call.

ADC Analog-to-Digital Converter.

ADCCP Advanced Data Communications Control Procedures, A bit-oriented ANSI-standard communications protocol. It is a link-layer protocol. ADCCP is ANSI's version of SDLC/HDLC.

ADCU Association of Data Communications Users.

ADD-IN CARD An expansion board that fits into the computer's slots and is used to expand the system's memory or extend the operation of another device.

ADD-ON 1. A telephone system feature which allows connecting a third telephone to an existing conversation. This "add-on" feature is initiated by the originator of the call. The feature is also known as "Three-Way Calling." 2. Hardware, often referred to as peripheral equipment, that is added to a system to improve its performance, add memory or increase its capabilities. Voice mail, Automated Attendant and Call Detail Recording Equipment are examples of PBX add-on devices. AT&T and some other manufacturers call them APPLICATIONS PROCESSORS.

ADD-ON CONFERENCE A PBX feature. Almost always used in conjunction with another feature called consultation hold, this feature allows an extension user to add a third person to an existing two-person conversation. The user places an existing central office call or internal call on Hold, and obtains system dial tone. The user can then call another internal extension or an outside party. After speaking with the "consulted" party, the originating phone reactivates the initiating command (typically a button push) and creates a three-party conference with the call previously placed on Hold.

ADD-ON CONFERENCE — INTERCOM ONLY Allows a telephone user to add someone else to an existing intercom (within-the-same office) conversation.

ADD-ON DATA MODULE Plug-in circuit cards which allow a PBX to send and receive analog (voice) and digital (data) signals.

ADDED BIT A bit delivered to the intended destination user in addition to intended user information bits and delivered overhead bit. An added bit might be used to round out the number of bits to some error checking scheme, for example.

ADDITIONAL COOPERATIVE ACCEPTANCE TESTING ACAT. A method of testing switched access service that provides a telephone company technician at the central office and a carrier's technician at its location, with suitable test equipment to perform the required tests. ACAT may, for example, consist of the following tests: Impulse Noise, Phase Jitter, Signal-to-C-Notched Noise Ratio, Intermodulation (Nonlinear) Distortion, Frequency Shift (Offset), Envelope Delay Distortion, Dial Pulse Percent Break

ADDITIONAL PERIOD Billing periods charged after initial, first or minimum period on a call. Usually, long distance toll/DDD has a one-minute initial period at premium rate; subsequent "additional" minutes (period) are billed at a lower rate. Additional period billing increments vary by long distance company.

ADDRESS The destination of a message sent through a communications system. A telephone number is considered the Address of the called party on a voice telephone network. In computer terms, it is a set of numbers that uniquely identifies something — a workstation on a LAN, a location in computer memory, a packet of data traveling through a network. Its meaning is similar to that used in reference to postal service.

ADDRESS FIELD In data transmission, the sequence of bits immediately following the opening flag of a frame identifying the secondary station sending, or designated to receive, the frame.

ADDRESS FILTERING A way of deciding which data packets are allowed through a device. The decision is based on the source and destination MAC (Media Access Control, the lower part of ISO layer two) addresses of the data packet.

ADDRESS SIGNALING Signals either the end user's telephone or the central office switching equipment that a call is coming in.

ADDRESS SPACE The amount of memory a PC can use directly is called its address space. MS-DOS can directly access 1024K of memory (one megabyte). A protected mode control program like Microsoft Windows 3.x or OS/2 can directly address up to 16 megabytes of memory. Here is a definition of address space, as suplied by the Personal Computer Memory Card International Association (PCMCIA) as address space applies to PCMCIA cards: "An address space is a collection of registers and storage locations contained on a PC Card which are distinguished from each other by the value of the Address Lines applied to the Card. There are three, separate, address spaces possible for a card. These are the Common Memory space, the Attribute Memory space and the I/O space."

ADDRESSABLE PROGRAMMING A cable TV (CATV) industry term. A subscriber orders a movie or sports event. He does that calling a phone number (generally an 800 number). A computer answers, grabs the calling number, confirms the request, then hangs up. The computer passes the request onto the cable company's computer, which checks the calling phone number against its accounting records. If the subscriber has good credit, the cable company sends a coded message down its cable network to the caller's set-top cable box/converter. The message temporarily enables that particular converter to descramble the channel offering the desired program.

ADDRESSABILITY 1. In computer graphics, the number of addressable points on a display surface or in storage. 2. In micrographics, the number of addressable points, within a specified film frame, written as follows: the number of addressable horizontal points by the number of addressable vertical points, for example, 3000 by 4000.

ADDRESSABLE POINT In computer graphics, any point of a device that can be addressed. See ADDRESSABILITY.

ADDRESSEE The intended recipient of a message.

ADDRESSING Refers to the way that the operating system knows where to find a specific piece of information or software in the application memory. Every memory location has an address.

ADH Average Delay to Handle. Average time a caller to an automatic call distributor waits before being connected to an agent.

ADJACENT CHANNEL INTERFERENCE When two or more carrier channels are placed too close together, they interfere with each other and mess up each other's conversations.

ADJUNCT 1. Network system in the Advanced Intelligent Network Release 1 architecture that contains SLEE (Service Logic Execution Environment) functionality, and that communicates with an Advanced Intelligent Network Release 1 Switching System in processing AIN Release 1 calls. Definition from Bellcore. See also ADJUNCT PROCESSOR.

2. An auxiliary device connected to the ISDN set, such as a speakerphone, headset adapter, or an analog interface.

ADJUNCT KEY SYSTEM A system installed behind a PBX or a Centrex. Such key system provides the users with several more features than the PBX or Centrex. Not a common term today.

ADJUNCT PROCESSOR A computer outside a telephone switching system that "talks" to the switch and gives it switching commands. An adjunct processor might include a database of customers and their recent buying activities. If the database shows that a customer lives in Indiana, the call from the customer might be switched to the group of agents handling Indiana customers. Adjunct processors might be concerned with energy management, building security etc.

ADK Application Definable Keys

ADM An AT&T term for an Add/Drop Multiplexer. A network element that can add and drop standard DSn or SONET signals from a line signal.

ADMINISTRATION A term used by the telephone industry to program features into a phone system. On a Northern Telecom Norstar system, administration includes making settings on 1. System speed dial; 2. Names on phones; 3. Time and date; 4. Restrictions; 5. Overrides; 6. Permissions; 7. Night Service and 8. Passwords.

ADMINISTRATION BY TELEPHONE The capability for the system administrator to perform most routine system administrative functions remotely from any Touch Tone pad. Such functions include mailbox maintenance (e.g. create, delete, set password, set class of service, etc.) and disk maintenance.

ADMINISTRATIVE MANAGEMENT DOMAIN An X.400 electronic mail term: A network domain maintained by a telecommunications carrier.

ADMINISTRATION SUB-SYSTEM Part of AT&T's premises distribution system that distributes hardware components for the addition or rearrangement of circuits.

ADMINISTRATIVE POINT A location at which communication circuits are administered, i.e. rearranged or rerouted, by means of cross connections, interconnections, or information outlets.

ADMINISTRATIVE SERVICE LOGIC PROGRAM ASLP. The SLP responsible for managing the feature interactions between Advanced Intelligent Network AIN Release 1 features resident on a single SLEE (Service Logic Execution Environment).

ADMINISTRATIVE SUBSYSTEM That part of a premises distribution system where circuits can be rearranged or rerouted. It includes cross connect hardware, and jacks used as information outlets.

ADN Advanced Digital Network. ADN is Pacific Bell of California's low-cost leased 56-Kbps digital service. ADN is available for intraLATA calls.

ADOBE SYSTEMS The name of the company which produces PostScript. See POSTSCRIPT and OUTLINE FONT. Adobe Systems got its name from the creek than ran past its founder's home in Los Altos, California.

ADP 1. Apple Desktop Bus. A synchronous serial bus allowing connection of the Mac keyboard, mouse and other items to the CPU. 2. Automatic Data Processing. The same as DP, data processing. 3. The name of a company which processes my payroll.

ADPCM Adaptive Differential Pulse Code Modulation. A speech coding method which calculates the difference between two consecutive speech samples in standard PCM coded telecom voice signals. This calculation is encoded using as adaptive filter and therefore, is transmitted at a lower rate than the standard 64 Kbps technique. Typically, ADPCM allows an analog voice conversation to be carried within a 32k-kbit/s digital channel; 3 or 4 bits are used to describe each sample, which represents the difference between two adjacent samples. Sampling is done 8,000 times a second.

ADRMP (pron. add-rump) AutoDialing Recorded Message Player. A device that calls a bunch of telephone numbers and upon connection will play a message to the answering person. ADRMPs are used for lead solicitation and message delivery. They are often unpopular due to their indiscriminate dialing pattern and random message playing.

ADSI Analog Display Services Interface. ADSI is a Bellcore standard defining a protocol on the flow of information between something (a switch, a server, a voice mail system, a service bureau) and a subscriber's telephone, PC, data terminal or other communicating device with a screen. The simple idea of ADSI is to add words to, and therefore a modicum of simplicity of use to a system that usually uses only touchtones. Imagine a normal voice mail system. You call it. It answers with a voice menu. Push 1 to listen to your messages, 2 to erase them, 3 to store them, 4 to forward them, etc. It's confusing. You have to remember which is which. ADSI is designed to solve that. It's designed to send to your phone's screen the choices in words that you're hearing. You then have the choice of reponding to what you hear or

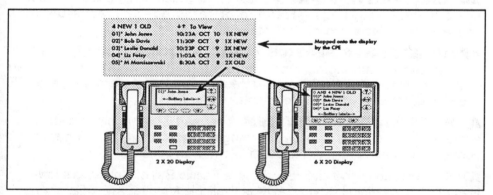

Information Page Mapping. The distant ADSI-generating device (voice-processing system, central office, by by phone, etc.) sends an Information Page to your phone. The page is 33 lines x 40 characters. The phone you own can have a display from 1 line to 20 characters all the way to 33 lines by 40 characters (in which case it would probably be a PC). This chart, courtesy Dave Werling of Northern, shows how ADSI-compatible phones "map" the incoming Information Page to the display of the phone.

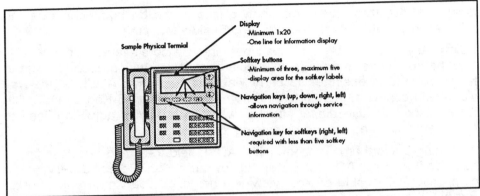

This shows the essentials of an ADSI phone, sadly called a terminal. The minimum display is 1 line by 20 characters. You need a minimum of three softkeys and four navigation keys. Don't you just love the new ADSI words like navigations?

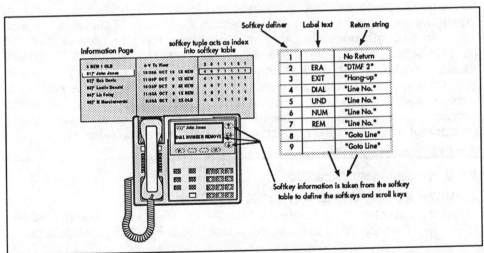

Softkey Mapping. Typically the bottom line of an ADSI-compatible phone shows words in reverse type which relate to the function of the key at that particular moment. Here we see three keys mapped to "Dial," "Number," and "Remove." Hit one and you'd dial a number, etc.

what you see. Your response is the same — a touchtone button. ADSI's signaling is DTMF and standard Bell 202 modem signals from the service to your 202-modem equipped phone. From the phone to the service it's only touchtone. With ADSI, you don't hear the modem signaling because every time the service gets ready to send you information, it first sends a "mute" tone. ADSI works on every phone line in the world.

For ADSI to work visually, you'll need a special ADSI-equipped phone or a piece of ADSI software in your PC. The nice feature of ADSI is that the standard is so flexible, it can work on cheap phones with a small display and more expensive phones with a bigger display and on a PC with a real big display. These three diagrams show a little of the basic concepts behind ADSI — Information Page Mapping and Softkey Mapping.

ADSL Asymmetrical Digital Subscriber Line. Bellcore's term for one-way T-1 to the home over the plain old, single twisted pair wiring already going to homes. ADSL is designed to carry video to the home. ADSL is one-way video with control signals returning from the home at 16 Kbps. ADSL, like ISDN, uses adaptive digital filtering, which is a way of adjusting itself to overcome noise and other problems on the line.

According to Northern Telecom, initial ADSL field trails and business cases have focused on ADSL's potential for Video on Demand service, in competition with cable pay-per-view and neighborhood video rental stores. But ADSL offers a wide range of other applications, including education and healthcare. Once telephone companies are able to deliver megabits to the home, Northern Telecom expects an explosion in potential applications including work-at-home access to corporate LANs, interactive services such as home shopping and home banking and even multi-party video gaming, interactive travelogues, and remote medical diagnosis. Multimedia retrieval will also become possible, enabling the home user to browse through libraries of text, audio, and image data — or simply subscribe to CD-quality music services. In the field of education, ADSL could make it possible to provide a low-cost "scholar's workstation" — little more than a keyboard, mouse, and screen — to every student, providing access to unlimited computer processing resources from their home. For a more modern versionn of ADSL, see DMT, which stands for Discrete Multi-Tone.

ADSTAR Automated Document STorage And Retrieval.

ADU Asynchronous Data Unit.

ADVANCED COMMUNICATION SYSTEM ACS. The old name for a proposed packet switched network from AT&T. The service was called Net 1000. AT&T finally killed the service in late 1986. For a bigger explanation, see ACS.

ADVANCED DIGITAL NETWORK ADN is Pacific Bell of California's low-cost leased 56-Kbps digital service. ADN is available for intraLATA calls.

ADVANCED INTELLIGENT NETWORK AIN. The Bell telephone companies' service-independent architecture for the 1990's and beyond.

ADVANCED 800 SERVICES AT&T's name for a family of 800 In-WATS services that include time of day and area code routing, single number 800 service (for both interstate and intrastate), automatic number identification, etc. See also 800 SERVICE and ENHANCED 800 SERVICES.

ADVANCED PRIVATE LINE TERMINATION An AT&T term which means the PBX user gets access to all the services of an Enhanced Private Switched Communications Services (EPCS) network. It also works when it is associated with AT&T's Common Control Switching Arrangement (CCSA) network.

ADVANCENET An Ethernet-based local area network from Hewlett Packard, Palo Alto, CA. See ETHERNET.

ADVANTIS A partnership between IBM and Sears Roebuck to provide advanced voice and data network services to users worldwide. As of writing, it's not exactly clear what this new company will do.

ADVISORY TONES Signals such as dial tone, busy, ringing, fast-busy, call-waiting, camp-on and all the other tones your telephone system uses to tell you that something is happening or about to happen.

AEB Analog Expansion Bus. The analog voice processing bus designed by Dialogic for interfacing DTI/124 and D/4x voice response component boards which fit in an AT-expansion slot of a PC. See also PEB, which is the more modern digital PCM expansion bus.

AECS PLAN Aeronautical Emergency Communications System Plan. The AECS Plan provides for the operation of aeronautical communications stations on a voluntary, organized basis to provide the President and the Federal Government, as well as heads of state and local governments, or their designated representatives, and the aeronautical industry, with a means of communicating during an emergency.

AEMIS Automatic Electronic Management Information System. This was the first computerized UCD/ACD reporting system introduced by AT&T for CO UCD (Uniform Call Distribution). This package was updated to become the PRO 150/500 system for UCD management on the Dimension PBX/UCD. AEMIS was the successor to the FADS or Force Administration Data System. It was an electro-mechanical system of peg counters and different colored busy lamp fields used to note trunk and position status.

AERIAL CABLE Cables strung outside and overhead. They're called aerial even though they only hang from poles or buildings. Some aerial cable hangs by its own strength. Some is supported by additional steel wire above it. Stringing aerial cable is cheaper than burying it, though buried cable lasts longer.

AERIAL DISTRIBUTION METHOD A method of running cables through the air, typically pole-to-pole. The old fashioned way. Some phone companies say aerial cable is more reliable than underground. Certainly, it's cheaper to fix or add to. It just looks less appetizing.

AERONAUTICAL RADIO INC. ARINC. The organization that coordinates the design and management of telecommunications systems for the airline industry. It's one of the largest buyers of telecommunications services and equipment in the world.

AEROSPACE Air force publicists coined the term "aerospace" to convince everyone that space was the business of those who fly in the air. According to the Economist Magazine, the "aerospace industry" was quickly accepted into the language, perhaps because President Eisenhower's alternative, the "military industrial complex," sounded rather more sinister. After the Apollo programme, which ended in 1972, the "space" in aerospace often seemed like a syllable tacked on to make building aeroplanes sound grander. But the growth in satellite use in the 1980s made space a respectable business in its own right. In America as of writing in the fall of 1991, the annual sales of space hardware are now bigger than those of civilian aircraft.

AFACTS Automatic FACilities Test System. AFACTS is a Rolm CBX feature. An automatic testing system for identifying faulty tie and central office trunks. AFACTS can pinpoint faulty trunks and generate exception and summary reports.

AFCEA Armed Forces Communications and Electronics Association. An organization of military communications personnel and suppliers who fulfill the specialized needs of government and military communications. They run an big convention each year in Washington in May-June. 703-631-4693.

AFE See ANALOG FRONT END.

AFIPS American Federation of Information Processing Societies. A national, highly-respected organization formed by data processing societies to keep abreast of advances in the field. AFIPS organizes one of the biggest trade shows in the data processing industry — the NCC (National Computer Conference).

AFNOR Acronym for Association Francais Normal. France's national standards-setting organization.

AFP AppleTalk File Protocol. Apple's network protocol, used to provide access between file servers and clients in an AppleShare network. AFP is also used by Novell's products for the Macintosh.

AFT Automatic Fine Tuning; SEE AFC.

AGC Automatic Gain Control. There are two electronic ways you can control the recording of something — Manual or Automatic Gain Control (AGC). AGC is an electronic circuit in tape recorders, speakerphones, and other voice devices which is used to maintain volume. AGC is not always a brilliant idea since it will attempt to produce a constant volume level, that is, it will try to equalize all sounds — the volume of your voice, and, when you stop talking, the circuit static and/or general room noise which you do not want amplified. Never record a seminar or speech using AGC. The recording will be decidedly amateurish. Manual Gain Control means there is record volume control and is thus, preferred in professional applications.

AGENT 1. This term comes from the huge telephone call-in reservation centers which the airlines, hotels and car rental services run. An agent is the person who answers your call, takes your order or answers your question. Agents are also called Telephone Sales Representatives or Communicators. The term "agent" was first used in the airline business. It came from gate or counter ticket agent. 2. An "Agent" is the person or persons you have legally authorized to order your telephone service and equipment from telephone companies. 3. In the computer programming sense of the word, an agent acts on behalf of another person or thing, with delegated authority. The agent's goals are those of the entity that created it. An agent is an active object with a mission, but agents are abstractions that can be implemented in any way, whereas an object has a formal definition.

AGENT SIGN ON/SIGN OFF A feature which allows any ACD agent to occupy any position in the ACD without losing his or her personal identity. Statistics are collected and consolidated about this agent and calls are routed to this agent no matter where he sits or how many positions he may occupy at one time.

AGGREGATE RATE The sum of the channel data rates for a given application.

AGGREGATOR A new breed of long distance reseller. An aggregator is essentially a sales agent for a long distance company. Here's how it works: The aggregator goes to a long distance company and says "May I sell your long distance service at a discount?" The long distance company says Yes! The aggregator hits the street and sells cut-rate long distance service to any and everyone. The long distance provider installs the service and bills it. The aggregator makes his profit by charging a fixed monthly service fee, a percentage of savings or some other arrangement. The key to it: The end user saves some money because his calls are "aggregated" with those of ALL the customers of the aggregator and the long distance company extends a bulk savings to the aggregator. Here's what TELECONNECT Magazine wrote about aggregators under the headline, "Aggregator Warning."

"Aggregators are companies which buy long distance wholesale and sell it retail. Aggregators exist because AT&T decided it wanted to win back long distance business it had lost. AT&T sliced its rates, liberalized its bulk billing rules and encouraged those consultants who had recommended their clients switch to MCI and US Sprint to become aggregators. These consultant-turned aggregators simply solicit anyone's long distance business and add it to their collection. AT&T sends their end-user a bill and the consultant-turned-aggregator a commission check.

"Should you — as an end-user — consider buying your long distance from an aggregator? The simple answer is YES? AT&T's discounts are so deep it's not uncommon for a company using AT&T today directly to switch to billing through an aggregator and save 20% to 25% — with nothing of substance happening. They still get their bills from AT&T and they still place and receive calls on AT&T as they had been doing. No wires are touched. No routing is changed.

"What about the pitfalls? There are some: First, don't buy long distance that isn't billed directly by the long distance carrier providing the service. If the aggregator does the billing, there's too much opportunity for "mischief," says

Dick Kuehn, Cleveland consultant. "There's opportunity for doing things like increasing each of your calls by 30 seconds. And because a user has no answer supervision on his call detail records, it's very hard for the user to figure his exact timing." The problem, says Dick, is there's no way for a user to verify his own bill. Dick says "Carriers are honest. Resellers (aggregators that bill) are open to question."

"TELECONNECT also believes you probably shouldn't deal with an aggregator who bills you a percentage of "savings." This is also open to abuse. There are so many rates, so many changes monthly, so many options that it's virtually impossible for the user to figure out what he would have paid had he not gone with the aggregator. The calculation is too open to abuse. TELECONNECT's feeling: pay a flat service fee.

"P.S. Imagine buying an automobile tire. The local garage carries two options: a Bridgestone for $30 and a Pirelli for $100. You opt for the Bridgestone at $30. You've thus saved $70. The garage proprietor splits your "savings" with you and charges you $35.

By late 1992, the panapoly of companies in the long distance business — not only aggregators — had expanded dramatically. And confusion between companies and what they did became rife. All, of course, purport to save you money on your long distance bills. And many do. Here's a simple explanation of the major categories:

CARRIER. Owns most of its circuits. Has own sales force and possibly independent sales agents. Best examples: AT&T, MCI, Allnet and Sprint.

TRADITIONAL RESELLER. Rents/leases most circuits or buys bulk time from carrier. Resells under own brand name, has published prices, sends own bills. Appears to be (and for all practical purposes is) same as the carriers.

AGGREGATOR. "Sponsor" who buys carrier's (typically AT&T) multi-location 800 or outbound service; enrolls other businesses as sites; volume discounts for all based on total calling at all sites. End user is still the carrier's, not the aggregator's. The carrier typically does the billing.

REBILLER: (Also called "Switchless Reseller"). Buys service as multi-location customer from carrier. Signs up individual sites (just like aggregator). Generates own end-user bills. No switch or network, but does sales, customer service, billing for long distance calls. Sometimes the rebiller's bills are more detailed than the bills you get directly from the carrier.

SALES AGENTS: Businesses or groups who are not direct employees of carrier, but who receive sales commissions from carrier. Customers belong to carrier and carrier does billing.

OTHER THIRD-PARTY MARKETERS. Buying co-ops, user groups, long distance brokers, pyramid (legal) marketing systems, shared tenant providers, Centrex aggregators, affinity groups (like college alumni and church congregation groups).

AGGREGATION An AMA (Automatic Message Accounting) function that accumulates AMA data, resulting in a less than detailed AMA record. Definition from Bellcore.

AGING The change in properties of a material with time under specific conditions.

AHD Audio High Density. System of digital audio recording on grooveless discs, employing an electronically-guided capacitance pickup.

AHOY See HELLO.

AHR Abbreviation for ampere hour, measurement of battery power: how much current may be drawn for an hour. Important specification for portable computers, cellular phones, etc.

AI Artificial Intelligence. Perhaps the next phase of computing. The present forms of AI in computer software are called Expert or Knowledge Based systems.

AIDS A Trojan Horse software program (a virus) which caused extensive damage in December 1989.

AIM Amplitude intensity modulation.

AIMS An Acronym for Auto Indexing Mass Storage. Indicates the AIMS Specification which is a standard card interface for storing large data such as image and multimedia files.

AIN Advanced Intelligent Network. An architecture being developed by Bell Communications Research Inc. for its clients, the U.S. Bell local operating telephone companies. Also, often used as shorthand for the next-generation INs. See also AIN Release 0, 1, etc.

AIN Release O Advanced Intelligent Network Release defined by individual Bell Operating Companies for initial deployment in 1991, or so.

AIN Release 1 Advanced Intelligent Network Release for initial deployment by Bell Operating Companies in 1993 that has a single functional architecture.

AIN Release 1 Logical Resources For Bell Operating Companies, the logical network resources configured and updated to provide Advanced Intelligent Network Release 1 subscriber services (e.g., SLP and trigger data). Definition from Bellcore.

AIN Release 1 Switching System An access tandem, local tandem or end office that contains an ASC (Advanced Intelligent Network Release 1 Switch Capabilities) functional group. Definition from Bellcore.

AIN Release 2 An Advanced Intelligent Network Release for initial deployment in 1995, involving from AIN Release 1 and supporting an expanded range of information networking services from the Bell operating telephone companies. Definition from Bellcore.

AIN Switch Capabilities ASC. A functional group residing in an Advanced Intelligent Network Release 1 Switching System that contains the Network Access, Service Switching, Information Management, Service Assistance and Operations FEs (Functional Entities). Definition from Bellcore.

AINTCC Automated INTtercept Call Completion. A new feature of Northern Telecom's central offices. The AINTCC feature provides options for — connecting a caller automatically to an intercepted number after hearing an announcement, or — connecting a caller to an intercepted number without an announcement.

Not using an announcement makes the number change transparent to the caller. The called (intercepted) party then has the option of informing the caller of the number change.

AIOD Automatic Identification of Outward Dialing is the ability of the telephone system to know the specific extension placing a call. It's used as part of the process of recording the detail of each telephone call for billback and cost control purposes. See AIOD LEADS and CALL ACCOUNTING SYSTEM.

AIOD LEADS Terminal equipment leads used solely to transmit automatic identified outward dialing (AIOD) data from a PBX to the public switched telephone network or to switched service networks (e.g., EPSDS), so that a vendor can provide a detailed monthly bill identifying long-distance usage by individual PBX extensions, tie-trunks, or the attendant.

AIR CONDITIONING In the Department of Defense, air conditioning is a synonym for the term "environmental control," which is the process of simultaneously controlling the temperature, relative humidity, air cleanliness, and air motion in a space to meet the requirements of the occupants, a process, or equipment.

AIR SPACE COAXIAL CABLE One in which air is the essential dielectric material. A spirally wound synthetitc filament of spacer may be used to center the conductor.

AIRBRUSH A computer imaging term. A fine-mist paint tool used to create halos, fog, clouds, and similar effects. Most paint programs let you control the size and shape of the application area. Some packages provide a transparency adjustment that determines the density of the applied color.

AIRCRAFT EARTH STATION A mobile Earth station in the aeronautical mobile-satellite service located on board an aircraft.

AIRLINE MILEAGE The monthly charge for many leased circuits is billed on the basis of "airline mileage" between the two points. Though it sounds as if it's the distance a crow would fly directly between the two points, when in reality, it is the distance in mileage between two Rate Centers whose position is laid down according to industry standards, originally created by AT&T. The entire U.S. is divided by a vertical and horizontal grid. The coordinates — vertical and horizontal — of each rate center are defined and applied to a square root formula which yields the distance between the two points. Think back to school. There's a right-angled triangle. At the top is one Rate Center. At the side is the other Rate Center. The horizontal is the horizontal coordinate. The vertical is the vertical coordinate. The formula is simple: Square the vertical distance. Square the horizontal distance. Add the two together. Then take their square root. That will give you the distance across the hypotenuse — the side opposite the right angle in the triangle. Villa, your "airline" mileage. For sample V and H city coordinates and the formula on how to calculate airline mileage, see V & H under the letter V.

AIRTIME Actual time spent talking on a cellular telephone. Most cellular carriers bill their customers based on how many minutes of airtime they use each month. Whether the calls are incoming or outgoing makes no difference, the customer is still billed. Whether the calls are going to a toll-number or a toll-free 800 number also makes no difference. The customer racks up airtime and he pays. The more minutes of time spent talking on the phone, the higher the bill. Airtime charges during peak periods of the day in North America vary from 25 to 80 cents per minute. Most carriers offer a discount on these rates for off-peak usage. Some carriers offer a discount on these rates if the customer pays a higher minimum usage charge each month.

AIS Alarm Indication Signal. Formerly called a "Blue Alarm" or "Blue Signal." A signal that replaces the normal traffic signal when a maintenance alarm indication has been activated. An AIS is a signal transmitted downstream informing that an upstream failure has been detected.

AIX Advanced Interactive eXecutive: IBM's implementation of UNIX. The Open Software Foundation (OSF) based its first operating system (OSF-1) on AIX. The next revision of the OSF operation system (OSF-2) will also be based on AIX with a Mach kernel (Mach was developed by Carnegie Melton University).

AKO Bisync acknowledgment for even-numbered message.

ALAP AppleTalk Link Access Protocol. In an AppleTalk network, this link access-layer (or data link-layer) protocol governs packet transmission on LocalTalk.

ALARM DISPLAY Attendant console indicators show the status (i.e. what's happening) in the telephone system. There are usually two types of displays — minor and major. Minor displays may be something as "minor" as a "hung" trunk, i.e. one that didn't hang up when the person speaking on it hung up. They can often be remedied by turning the PBX off, counting to ten, and then turning it on. (Before you do, check it will load itself.) Major problems — such as a blown line card in the PBX, one console out or half the trunks out — often require a service call and are often covered under the Emergency Conditions section of telephone service contracts.

ALBO Automatic Line BuildOut. ALBO is a means of automatic cable equalization used in T-1 span-line interface equipment.

ALC 1. Automatic Level Control. 2. See AUTOMATIC LIGHT CONTROL.

ALE See AUTOMATIC LINK ESTABLISHMENT

ALTERNATE ROUTE A second or subsequent choice path between two exchanges, usually consisting of two or more circuit groups in tandem. Sometimes called "alternative route" or "second-choice route."

ALTERNATE USE The ability to switch communications facilities from one type of service to another, i.e., voice to data, etc.

ALTERNATE VOICE DATA AVD. An older service which is a single transmission facility which can be used for either voice or data (up to 9600 bps). Arrangement includes a manually operated switch (on each end) to allow customers to alternately connect the line to their modem or PBX.

ALERTER In an AT&T ISDN phone, the alerter takes the place of a mechanical telephone ringer. The alerter has eight ringing signals, eight personalized ringing patterns, and the ability to play music.

ALERTING A signal sent to a customer, PBX or switching system to indicate an incoming call. A common form is the signal that rings a bell in the telephone set. Others signals can trigger such devices as whistles, gongs and chimes.

ALERTING SIGNAL A ringing signal put on subscriber access lines to indicate an incoming call.

ALGORITHM A prescribed finite set of well defined rules or processes for the solution of a problem in a finite number of steps. In normal English, it is the mathematical formula for an operation, such as computing the check digits on packets of data that travel via packet switched networks.

ALI Automatic Location Information. ALI is a feature of E-911 (Enhanced 911) systems. ALI is provided to agents answering E-911 calls. It may include information such as name, phone number, address, nearest cross street and special pre-existing conditions (i.e. hazardous materials). On some systems it may also provide the appropriate emergency service address for the particular address. ALI is retrieved from a computer database. The database may be held on site or at a remote location and may be maintained by the local phone company (or its parent) or another agency.

ALIAS 1. A feature of the Apple Macintosh System 7 allowing the user to create a file that points to the original file. When you click on an alias, the original application is launched. Aliases can work across a network; so you can access a program residing on a file server or a Mac that runs System 7 file sharing. 2. An assumed name under which users of an electronic bulletin board may post messages. For example, Jane Smith may post as "Marketing Group." The system usually provides a list of aliases and the names of the users to which they belong. Some BBS packages allow anonymous message posting.

ALIGNED BUNDLE A bundle of optical fibers in which the relative spatial coordinates of each fiber are the same at the two ends of the bundle. Also called "Coherent Bundle."

ALIT Automatic Line Insulation Testing.

ALJ An administrative law judge appointed by a State Commission to review a Commission docket, such as a rate case or incentive regulation proposal, and to make recommendations to the Commissioners.

ALL CALL PAGING With this feature, a user can broadcast an announcement — a page — to someone through the speakers of all the telephones on the system and, possibly, any external loudspeakers. If you want instant fame, ask your secretary to call all the airports in the country and page you. Mike Todd, the movie mogul, used to have this secretary perform this wonderful task. Mr. Todd gave gigantic egos a whole new meaning.

ALL CHANNEL TUNING Ability of a television set to receive all assigned channels. VHF and UHF, channels 2 through 83.

ALL DIELECTRIC CABLE Cable made entirely of dielectric (insulating) materials without any metal conductors.

ALL NUMBER CALLING Once upon a time, the first two digits of telephone exchanges sort of corresponded to their location. For example, MU-8 meant Murray Hill 8 in Murray Hill, Manhattan, New York City. Then the phone company started running out of letters, so it went to All Number Calling. The All Number Calling provides a theoretical maximum of 792 central office exchange (NNX) codes per area code (NPA). This is derived on the basis of 800 NXX code combinations (8x10x10) leaving out eight special service combinations, including 411, 611, 911.

ALL TRUNKS BUSY When a user tries to make an outside call through a telephone system and receives a "fast" busy signal (twice as many signals as a normal busy in the same amount of time), he is usually experiencing the joy of All Trunks Busy. No trunks are available to handle that call. The trunks are all being used at that time for other calls or are out of service. These days, many long distance companies are replacing a "fast" busy signal with a recording that might say something like, "I'm sorry. All circuits are busy. Please try your call later."

ALLEN, ROBERT Chairman of the board of AT&T since 1988. In 1980, he headed a task force to look into AT&T's future. The recommendation of the task force: keep equipment manufacturing at all costs.

ALLIANCE TELECONFERENCING SERVICE A direct-dial AT&T service which allows you to teleconference as few as three and as many as 59 telephones around the world. You can dial the numbers to call or you can schedule a meeting, called "Meet-Me Service." If you want to set the conference up, you dial 0-700-456-1000, then punch in the number of locations, then put in the numbers, ending each with a #. End your dialing with another # — to add yourself to the teleconference.

ALLOY A combination of two or more metals that forms a new or different metal with specific or desirable qualities.

ALOHA A method of data transmission in which the device transmits whenever it wants to. If it gets an acknowledgement from the device it's trying to reach, it continues to transmit. If not (as in the case of a collision with someone else trying to transmit simultaneously), it starts all over again. The ALOHA method get its name from a dying satellite that was donated to university researchers in the Pacific. It was used to transmit data by satellites among South Sea islands, especially Hawaii. The ALOHA "method" — called "transmit at will" — was invented because the users were short of funds to develop more sophisticated data transmission protocols, and they had a free satellite, which typically had more bandwidth than they had stuff to send.

ALPETH Aluminum-polyethlene primary covering known as the sheath for aerial cable.

ALPHA 1. Only alphabetic characters. 2. A family of microprocessors from Digital Equipment Corporation first introduced in February 1992. The first chip introduced was the 21064, described by DEC as a .75 micron CMOS-based super-scalar, super-pipelined processor using dual instruction issue and a 150 MHz cycle time. By reling on its 64-bit RISC architecture, the Alpha can deliver 400 million instructions per second.

ALPHA CHANNEL The upper 8 bits of the 32-bit data path in some 24-bit graphics adapters. The alpha channel is used by some software for controlling the color information in the lower 24 bits.

ALPHABETIC Only alphabetic characters. See also ALPHANUMERIC.

ALPHANUMERIC A set of characters that contains both letters and numbers — either individually or in combination. Numeric is 12345. Alphabetic is ABCDEF: Alphanumeric is 1A4F6HH8. American and Australian zip codes are numeric. Canadian and English postal codes are alphanumeric. No one knows why.

ALPHANUMERIC DISPLAY A display on a phone or console showing calling phone number, called number, trunk number, type of call, class of service and perhaps, some other characteristics of the call. It may also contain instructions as to how to move the call around, set up a conference call, etc. The display may be liquid crystal or light emitting diode. Typically, it's liquid crystal.

ALTAIR ETHERNET Motorola's name for its wireless local area network, which transmits at the very high frequency of 18 to 18 megahertz. Altair users need to fill out a small, one-page FCC application in order to use the system.

ALTEL Association of Long distance TELephone companies. A trade association composed of alternative (to AT&T) long distance carriers and resellers of long distance services.

ALTERNATE ANSWERING POSITION Usually refers to a second receptionist's desk which has a telephone switchboard or console identical to the main one. Also refers to when the main receptionist is away from his/her desk, or is very busy taking calls, the telephone system automatically sends the calls to another console or to a phone that will be answered.

ALTERNATE BUFFER In a data communications device, the section of memory set aside for the transmission or receipt of data after the primary buffer is full. This helps the device control the flow of data so transmission is not interrupted due to lack of space for the incoming or outgoing data.

ALTERNATE ROUTING A feature used with long distance calls that permits the telephone system (typically a PBX) to throw calls over different (alternate) phone lines, depending on the congestion of the primary phone lines the calls are to be sent over. Alternate routing is often confused with LEAST COST ROUTING, in which the telephone system chooses the least expensive way (available at that time) to route that call. Least Cost Routing typically works with so-called "look-up" tables in the memory of the PBX. These tables are put into the PBX by the user. The PBX does not automatically know how to route each call. It must be told by the user. That "telling" might be as simple as saying "all 312 area codes will go via the AT&T FX line." Or it might be as complex as actually listing which exchanges in the 312 area code go by which method. LEAST COST ROUTING tells the calls to go over the lines which are perceived by the user to be the least cost way of getting the call from point A to point B. Alternate routing happens when the least cost routes get congested and alternate routes (typically more expensive) are found from the look-up tables in the PBX's memory.

ALTERNATING CURRENT See AC.

ALTERNATIVE NON-TRAFFIC SENSITIVE COST-RECOVERY PLANS New charges proposed by the regional Bell holding companies to supplement subscriber line charges. In short, another charge on the subscriber with an interesting, though dubious, justification. They have not been fully implemented.

ALTERNATIVE REGULATORY FRAMEWORK ARF.

ALTERNATOR A machine which generates electricity which is alternating current. See AC.

ALTS Alternative Access Providers to the local telephone network i.e., Teleport.

ALU Arithmetic Logic Unit. The part of the CPU (Central Processing Unit) that performs the arithmetic and logical operations. See MICROPROCESSOR.

ALVYN Aluminum-polyethylene, the sheath used for riser cable where a flame retardant sheath is required.

AM See Amplitude Modulation.

AMA Automatic Message Accounting. AMA is the phone company's name for Call Detail Recording or Station Message Detail Recording (SMDR). See AMA TAPE.

AMA TAPE A telephone company machine-readable magnetic tape which contains the customer's long distance calling and billing data for a given month.

AMA TELEPROCESSING SYSTEM AMATPS. The primary method for delivery of AMA data from the network to billing systems. The current AMATPS architecture consists of an AMA Transmitter (AMAT) and a collector. Definition from Bellcore.

AMATPS AMA TeleProcessing System.

AMBIENT NOISE The level of noise present all the time. There is always noise, unless you're in an anechoic chamber. When measured with a sound level meter, it is usually measured in decibels above a reference pressure level of 0.00002 pascal in SI units, or 0.00002 dyne per square centimeter in cgs units.

AMERICAN BELL, INC. The old name for the unregulated telephone equipment supply subsidiary of American Telephone & Telegraph. American Bell Inc. had its name changed to AT&T Information Systems. At that point it was no longer separately incorporated. It became a division of AT&T. It has been reorganized many times. When it was American Bell, it was only selling telecommunications products and services to end users. When it become AT&T Information Systems, it sold AT&T phone systems and AT&T computer systems. It then merged with AT&T Long Lines, which was then called AT&T Communications and is now called simply AT&T. By the time you read this, it will probably be called something else. Sadly, old gadgetry, knick-knacks and momentos bearing the name American Bell, Inc. have no marketable value as antiques or examples of American folk art.

AMERICAN STANDARD CODE FOR INFORMATION INTERCHANGE ASCII. The standard 7-bit code for transferring information asynchronously on local and long distance telecommunications lines. The ASCII code enables you to represent 128 separate numbers, letters, and control characters. By using an eighth bit — as in extended ASCII or IBM's EBCDIC — you can represent 256 different characters.

ASCII often uses an eighth bit as a parity check or a way of encoding word processing symbols, not as a way of broadening the number of characters and symbols which it can represent. See also ASCII.

AMERICAN WIRE GAUGE AWG. Standard measuring gauge for non-ferrous conductors (i.e. non-iron and non-steel). AWG covers copper, aluminum, and other conductors. Gauge is a measure of the diameter of the conductor. See AWG for a bigger explanation.

AMERITECH Ameritech Corp is one of the Regional Bell operating companies formed as a result of the AT&T Divestiture. Ameritech covers five states and includes the operating telephone companies: Illinois Bell, Indiana Bell, Michigan Bell, Ohio Bell, and Wisconsin Bell. It also includes some other subsidiaries, which fit into two classifications — administrative (centralized buying, real estate, etc.) or entrepreneurial (cellular mobile radio, interconnect equipment, voice mail service bureau, venture capital, etc.). Ameritech's 1991 revenues were $10.8 billion. It has 76,000 employees and total corporate assets exceeding $20 billion.

AMI Alternate Mark Inversion. The line-coding format in T-1 transmission systems whereby successive ones (marks) are alternately inverted (sent with polarity opposite that of the preceding mark). Here's AT&T definition: A line code that employs a ternary signal to convey binary digits, in which successive binary ones are represented by signal elements that are normally of alternating, positive and negative polarity but equal in amplitude, and in which binary zeros are represented by signal elements that have zero amplitude. This is an AT&T definition.

AMIS See AUDIO MESSAGING INTERCHANGE SPECIFICATION. A standard for networking voice mail systems.

AML Anolog Microwave Link

AMPACITY The maximum current an insulated wire or cable can safely carry without excluding either the insulation or jacket materials limitations.

AMPERAGE RATING The amperage which may be safely applied to a circuit, service or equipment. See also AMPERE.

AMPERE The unit of measurement of electric current or the flow of electrons. One volt of potential across a one ohm impedance causes a current flow of one ampere. AMP is the abbreviation for ampere. It is mathematically equal to watts divided by volts. Note that in the electrical context, WATTS is spelled with two "Ts." In telecommunications, WATS, meaning Wide Area Telecommunications Service, is spelled with only one "T."

AMPERE-HOUR UNIT Measurement of battery capacity, determined by multiplying the current delivered by the time it is delivered for. See AMPERE.

AMPHENOL CONNECTOR Amphenol is a manufacturer of connectors. They make many connectors, many of which are made by other companies.

Their most famous connector was the 25-pair connector used on 1A2 key telephones and for connecting cables to many electronic key systems and PBXs. The telephone companies call the 25-pair Amphenol connector the RJ21X. The RJ21X connector is made by other companies including 3M and TRW.

AMPLIFIED HANDSET An amplified handset is the best phone gadget you can buy. You use it to crank up the volume of incoming calls and save yourself enormous amounts of money on callbacks. "We have a bad line. I'll call you back." There are three types of amplified handsets: 1. The handset with a built-in amplifier. These devices suck their power from the phone line and since the phone line doesn't have much power, you won't have much amplification. I'm not overly impressed with amplified handsets. 2. The handset with amplifying circuits built into the phone. Ditto for our comments about power. 3. The handset with the little external box amplifier which is powered by either AC or by several nicad batteries. Such an external amplifier will produce much greater amplification. This is the type we prefer at TELECONNECT Magazine.

AMPLIFIER When telephone conversations travel through a medium, such as a copper wire, they encounter resistance and thus become weaker and more difficult to hear. An amplifier is an electrical device which strengthens the signal. Unfortunately, amplifiers in analog circuits also strengthen noise and other extraneous garbage on the line. Amplifiers are used in all telephone systems, analog and digital. But in digital systems, signals are regenerated and then amplified. As a result, noise is much less prevalent and less likely to be amplified in digital systems.

AMPLITUDE The distance between high or low points of a waveform or signal. Also referred to as the wave "height." See AMPLITUDE MODULATION.

AMPLITUDE DISTORTION The difference between the output wave shape and the input wave shape.

AMPLITUDE EQUALIZER A corrective network that is designed to modify the amplitude characteristics of a circuit or system over a desired frequency range. Such devices may be fixed, manually adjustable, or automatic.

AMPLITUDE MODULATION Also called AM, it's a method of adding information to an electronic signal in which the signal is varied by its height to impose information on it. "Modulation" is the term given to imposing information on an electrical signal. The information being carried causes the amplitude (height of the sine wave) to vary. In the case of LANs, the change in the signal is registered by the receiving device as a 1 or a 0. A combination of these conveys different information, such as words, numbers or punctuation marks.

AMPS Advanced Mobile Phone Service. It's another word for analog cellular radio. Advanced Mobile Phone Service is the term used by AT&T's

Bell Laboratories (prior to the break-up in 1984) to refer to its cellular technology. The AMPS standard has been the foundation for the industry in the United States, although it has been slightly modified in recent years. "AMPS-compatible" means equipment designed to work with most analog cellular telephones.

AMS Account Management System.

ANA Assigned Night Answer.

ANALOG Comes from the word "analogous," which means "similar to." In telephone transmission, the signal being transmitted — voice, video, or image — is "analogous" to the original signal. In other words, if you speak into a microphone and see your voice on an oscilloscope and you take the same voice as it is transmitted on the phone line and ran that signal into the oscilloscope, the two signals would look essentially the same. The only difference is that the electrically transmitted signal (the one over the phone line) is at a higher frequency. In correct English usage, "analog" is meaningless as a word by itself. But in telecommunications, analog means telephone transmission and/or switching which is not digital. See ANALOG TRANSMISSION.

ANALOG BRIDGE A circuit which allows a normal two-person voice conversation to be extended to include a third person without degrading the quality of the call.

ANALOG CELLULAR The current standard for cellular communications.

ANALOG CHANNEL A channel which transmits in analog waveforms. See ANALOG.

ANALOG COMPUTER A computer that performs its tasks by measuring continuous physical variables — pressure, voltage, flow — and manipulating these variables to produce a solution, which is then converted into a numerical equivalent. Analog computers are largely used as special purpose machines in scientific or technical applications. The earliest analog computers were purely mechanical devices with levers, cogs, cams, etc., representing the data or operator values. Modern analog computers typcially employ electrical parameters such as voltage, resistance, or current to represent the quantities being manipulated.

ANALOG/DIGITAL CONVERTER An A/D Converter. Pronounced: "A to D Converter." A device which converts an analog signal to a digital signal.

ANALOG FACSIMILE Facsimile which can transmit and receive grey shadings — not just black and white. It is called analog because of its ability to transmit what appear to be continuous shades of grey. "Analog" facsimile is usually transmitted digitally.

ANALOG FRONT END The part of the fax machine that converts between the digitally modulated signal and the analog signal used on the telephone line.

ANALOG LOOP-BACK A method of testing modems and data terminals by disconnecting the device from the telephone line and looping a signal out through the device's transmit side and in through its receive side. The test tells if the trouble is with the telephone line or with the modem.

ANALOG MONITOR A computer screen that uses an analog signal, a smoothly varying value of current or voltage that varies continuously. VGA, SVGA and Macintosh models are examples of analog monitors. Most computer screens are analog. See also ANALOG.

ANALOG RECORDING System of recording in which music is converted into electrical impulses that form "patterns" in the grooves of phonograph record masters or in the oxide particles of master tapes representing (or analogous to) musical waveforms.

ANALOG SWITCH Telephone switching equipment that switches signals without changing the analog form. The major form of analog switching is circuit switching.

ANALOG SYNCHRONIZATION A synchronization control system in which the relationship between the actual phase error between clocks and the error signal device is a continuous function over a given range.

ANALOG TERMINAL ADAPTER ATA. A Northern Telecom telephone device permits analog devices (for example, faxs, answering machines, and single line telephones) to connect to the Northern Telecom Norstar telephone system.

ANALOG TRANSMISSION A way of sending signals — voice, video, data — in which the transmitted signal is analogous to the original signal. In other words, if you spoke into a microphone and saw your voice on an oscilloscope and you took the same voice as it was transmitted on the phone line and threw that signal onto the oscilloscope, the two signals would look essentially the same. The only difference would be that the electrically transmitted signal would be at a higher frequency.

ANALOGUE An English/European way of spelling ANALOG, which is the correct North American spelling. See ANALOG.

ANC All Number Calling.

AND Automatic Network Dialing.

ANECHOIC CHAMBER A perfectly quiet room. A room in which sound or radio waves do not reflect off the walls. An anechoic chamber is the only place in which a speakerphone will work perfectly. The more a room resembles an anechoic chamber — i.e. lots of drapes, plush carpet, etc. — the better a speakerphone will work.

ANGLE MODULATION Modulation in which phase angle or frequency of a sine wave carrier is varied.

ANGLE OF DEVIATION In fiber optics, the net angular deflection experienced by a light ray after one or more refractions or reflections. The term is generally used in reference to prisms, assuming air interfaces. The angle of deviation is then the angle between the incident ray and the emergent ray.

ANGLE OF INCIDENCE The angle between an incident ray and the normal to a reflecting or refracting surface.

ANGLED END An optical fiber whose end is deliberately polished at an angle to reduce reflections.

ANGSTROM A unit of length in optical measurement.

ANGULAR MISALIGNMENT LOSS The optical power loss caused by angular deviation from the optimum alignment of source to optical fiber — fiber-to-fiber, or fiber-to-detector.

ANI Automatic Number Identification. A phone call arrives at your home or office. At the front of the phone call is a series of digits which tell you, the phone number of the phone calling you. These digits may arrive in analog or digital form. They may arrive as touchtone digits inside the phone call or in a digital form on the same circuit or on a separate circuit. You will need some equipment to decipher the digits AND do "something" with them. That "something" might be throwing them into a database and bringing your customer's record up on a screen in front of your telephone agent as he answers the call. "Good morning, Mr. Smith." Some large users say they could save as much as 20 seconds on the average IN-WATS call if they knew the phone number of the person calling them. They would avoid asking regular customers for routine identification information since it would all be there in the database. ANI is touted as one of ISDN's most compelling advantages — but it is really an advantage of Signaling System 7 (and therefore distinct from ISDN). In the US, there are various types of "ANI." There's the ANI you get from a long distance phone company, which may arrive over the D channel of an ISDN PRI circuit or on a dedicated single line before the first ring. In contrast, the signaling for Caller ID, as delivered by a local phone company, is delivered between the first and second rings. In some countries — like Canada — caller ID for both local and long distance is delivered in the same technical way — between the first and second rings. In the US, there are no accepted standards, as yet. It's hard to configure a phone system to pick up calling phone numbers — both local and long distance. And of course, ANI is not available in many states or is provided with restrictions. So be careful. See CALLER ID, CLASS, COMMON CHANNEL SIGNALING, DNIS, ISDN and ISUP.

ANISOCHRONOUS Pertaining to transmission in which the time interval separating any two significant instants in sequential signals is not necessarily related to the time interval separating any other two significant instants. Isochronous and anisochronous are characteristics, while synchronous and asynchronous are relationships.

ANISOTROPIC Pertaining to a material whose electrical or optical properties vary with the direction of propagation or with different polarizations of a traveling wave.

ANM ANswer Message. The fourth of the ISUP call set-up messages. A message sent in the backward direction indicating that the call has been answered. See ISUP and COMMON CHANNEL SIGNALING.

ANNEAL The act of using heat to soften a metal such as copper, making it less brittle.

ANNOUNCEMENT SERVICE Allows a phone user to hear a recording when he dials a certain extension. These days, announcement services are provided increasingly by totally solid-state digital announcers. These gadgets are more reliable, deliver a clearer message and last much longer than analog tape-based machines (like answering machines), which use recording tape.

ANNOUNCEMENT SYSTEM A arrangement for providing information by means of recorded announcements.

ANNUAL PERCENTAGE RATE APR. A percentage calculation of the finance charge portion of financing contact.

ANNULAR RING An indicator (or ring) around the circumference of the coaxial cable every so many feet — often 2.5 meters (8.2 feet) — to indicate a point where transceivers are to be connected. Same as transceiver attachment mark.

ANNUNCIATOR Original name for the indicator on magnetic switchboards which indicates the particular line that is calling the exchange. Now it is simply a light or bell that tells you something, e.g. the ringing of a phone.

ANONYMOUS FTP A method of obtaining freeware from the Internet. With an implementation of the FTP protocol, users can get public domain software from Internet sites, using the word anonymous for a login ID, and their userid@hostname.domain as the password. A database called Archie contains a list of what is available from anonymous FTP sites, and can be reached at "archie.mcgill.ca" and at "archie.sura.net."

ANS Answer. (What else?)

ANSI American National Standards Institute. A standards-setting, non-government organization, which develops and publishes standards for "voluntary" use in the United States. The British have their own equivalent of ANSI. It's called the BSI, British Standards Institute. Standards set by national organizations are accepted by vendors in that country. ANSI is located at 1430 Broadway, New York NY 10018 212-642-4900. They put out a biweekly newsletter called "ANSI Standards in Action." See also CCITT, ECMA, IEEE, and ISO. See ANSI CHARACTER SET.

NEWTON'S TELECOM DICTIONARY

ANSI TIX9.4 ANSI's Sonet standard.

ANSI T1.110-1987 Signaling system number 7 (SS7) - General Information.

ANSI T1.111-1988 Signaling system number 7 (SS7) - Message Transfer Part (MTP)

ANSI T1.112-1988 Signaling System number 7 (SS7) - Signaling Connection Control Part (SCCP)

ANSI T1.113-1988 Signaling System 7 (SS7) - Integrated Services Digital Network (ISDN) user part.

ANSI T1.114-1988 Signaling System 7 (SS7) - Transaction Capability Application Part (TCAP)

ANSI T1.206 Digital Exchanges and PBXs - Digital circuit loopback test lines.

ANSI T1.301 ANSI ADPCM standard.

ANSI T1.401-1988 Interface between carriers and customer installations - Analog voice grade switched access lines using loop-start and ground-start signaling.

ANSI T1.501-1988 Network performance - Tandem encoding limits for 32 Kbit/s Adaptive Differential Pulse-Code Modulation (ADPCM).

ANSI T1.601-1988 Integrated Services Digital Network (ISDN) - Basic access interface for use on metallic loops for application on the network side of the NT (Layer 1 specification).

ANSI T1.605-1989 Integrated Services Digital Network (ISDN) - Basic access interface for S and T reference points (Layer 1 specification).

ANSI T1.Q1 ANSI's standard for telecommunications network performance standards, switched exchange access network transmission performance standard exchange carrier-to-interexchange carrier standards.

ANSI X3T9.5 TPDDI Twisted-Pair Distributed Data Interface (TPDDI) is a new technology that allows users to run the FDDI standard 100 Mbps transmission speed over twisted-pair wiring. Unshielded twisted-pair has been tested for distances over 50 meters (164 ft.). TPDDI is designed to help users make an earlier transition to 100 Mbps at the workstation.

ANSI CHARACTER SET The American National Standards Institute 8-bit character set. It contains 256 characters.

ANSI.SYS A device driver is used by MS-DOS to control output to the screen. Some (very few) programs require you to have the statement DEVICE=ANSI.SYS in your CONFIG.SYS file. It provides the "buttons" that these programs then push to make certain things happen on the screen. The "buttons" are pushed by ANSI.SYS commands. The commands begin with Escape (character 27 in ASCII) followed by a left bracket. You can

66
61

simply type these commands to make the screen change color, blink, etc., if you have the DEVICE=ANSI.SYS statement in your CONFIG.SYS file when you boot your PC. If you put the following line in your AUTOEXEC.BAT you will enjoy an attractive C: prompt. I use this line when I'm working on a color screen:

Prompt $e[37;44;1m $_ DATE $d TIME $t $_$P$g

But note, loading ANSI.SYS will take an extra 7,000 bytes of so of RAM. and most programs — even those that use color, including Windows — don't use ANSI.SYS. They have color commands built in. My advice is simple: Don't load ANSI.SYS unless your program specifically demands it via an error message. Save yourself the RAM memory.

ANSWER BACK A signal or tone sent by a receiving equipment or data set to the sending station to indicate that it is ready to accept transmission. Or a signal or tone sent to acknowledge receipt of a transmission. See ANSWER SUPERVISION.

ANSWER BACK SUPERVISION Another word for answer supervision. See ANSWER SUPERVISION.

ANSWER DETECT The use of a digital signal processing technique to determine the presence of voice energy on a telephone line. It is used with call (answer) supervision, to identify an answered line. It's beginning to be used with computerized dialing equipment as it eliminates the need for a telephone representative to constantly monitor call set-up progress on each telephone line in the event a call is answered. See ANSWER SUPERVISION and ANSWER SIGNAL.

ANSWER MODE When a modem is set by the user to receive data, it is in Answer Mode. In any conversation involving two computers, two terminals or one computer and one terminal, one side of the conversation must always be in Answer Mode. Putting a modem/computer in answer mode is sometimes done through software and sometimes through hardware, i.e. a switch on the side of the machine. You cannot run a data communications "conversation" if both sending and receiving equipment are in "Answer Mode." Computers — mainframe and mini — which receive a lot of phone calls are typically put in "Answer Mode." The terminals or computers calling them are typically in transmit mode.

ANSWER SIGNAL A supervisory signal, usually in the form of a closed loop, returned from the called telephone to the originating switch when the called party answers. This signal stops the ringback signal from being returned to the caller.

ANSWER SUPERVISION Follow this scenario: I call you long distance. My central office must know when you answer your phone, so my central office can start billing me for the call. It works like this: when you, the called party, answer your phone, your central office sends a signal back to my central office (the originating CO). This tells my central office to start billing me for the call. This signal is called Answer Supervision. Before the Divestiture of the Bell System in early 1984, most of the nation's long distance companies — with the exception of AT&T Communications — did not receive Answer Supervision. They did not know precisely when the called party answered. So they started their billing cycle after some time — 20 or 30 seconds after the caller completed dialing. These long distance companies presumed that after this time, some one will have answered and the call will be in progress and can then be timed and billed. Without Answer Supervision, their billing of calls is inaccurate. They may bill for calls which didn't occur. And you may pay more for calls which did occur.

With the Divestiture of the Bell System, and the introduction of Equal Access, most long distance companies will eventually be able to recognize Answer Supervision. If you choose to be equal accessed to a long distance carrier other than AT&T, most likely your long distance company will receive answer supervision from the local phone company. And therefore the pricing of your calls will be accurate. But check. If you are "accessing" your preferred long distance carrier by dialing a seven digit local number, then dialing your number and your account code, your carrier is probably not receiving Answer Supervision and the timing and billing of your long distance calls may be inaccurate. Check this out. Remember: just because your town has equal access doesn't mean your preferred long distance phone company has opted for it because it is expensive or for some other reason.

Virtually no hotels have answer supervision. So they start billing you arbitrarily. Some start billing you after three rings. Some after four. When you check out, carefully check your phone bill. You will, in most instances, find you have been billed for many uncompleted calls. Tell your family to pick up the phone quickly when you're out of town and may be calling them. Don't let the phone ring too many times as you're likely to be billed for the dubious pleasure of listening to ringing signals.

"Answer supervision" is getting better, however, as the electronics of "listening" to sounds on phone lines get better. Electronics are now available to do — to a 95% accuracy — what we as humans do — to a 100% accuracy — namely distinguish between a normal ringing sound, a fast busy sound and a person or fax machine answering the phone and saying "Hello." These electronics are getting better and less expensive, by the month.

ANSWERBACK In data communications, answerback is a response programmed into a data terminal to identify itself when polled by a remote computer or terminal. This response is usually in reply to a Control-E (ASCII Character 5, Inquiry), which is known on the Telex and TWX networks as a "Who Are You?" character, or "WRU." The Answerback allows a remote computer to verify it has dialed correctly (usually on the Telex or TWX networks) by matching the Answerback received with the Answerback expected.

ANSWERING TONE The tone an asynchronous modem will transmit when it answers the phone. The tone indicates that it is willing to accept data.

ANTENNA A device for transmitting, receiving or transmitting and receiving signals. Antennas come in all shapes and sizes. Their shape depends on the frequency signal they're receiving. Electrical signals with frequencies higher on the spectrum, for example, are shorter and more directional. As they get higher on the spectrum, they look more like light. These must be focused and thus, require antennas which are shaped like the mirror reflector of a focusing flashlight. This parabolic shape focuses the broad beam (of the bulb or the electrical signal) into a narrow, focused beam. The weaker the received signal, the bigger the antenna must be. Antennas come in many varieties and have cute names, like parabola, caresgrain, helix, lens and horn.

ANTENNA GAIN The ratio, usually expressed in decibels, of the power required at the input of a loss-free reference antenna to the power supplied to the input of the given antenna to produce, in a given direction, the same field strength, or the same irradiance, at the same distance. When not specified otherwise, the gain refers to the direction of maximum radiation. The gain may be considered for a specified polarization.

ANTENNA LOBE A picture showing an antenna's radiation pattern. A more technical explanation: A three-dimensional radiation pattern of a directional antenna bounded by one or more cones of nulls (regions of diminished intensity).

ANTENNA MATCHING The process of adjusting impedance so that the input impedance of an antenna equals or approximates the characteristic impedance of its transmission line over a specified range of frequencies. The impedance of either the transmission line, or the antenna, or both, may be adjusted to effect the match.

ANTI ALIASING A computer imaging term. A blending effect that smooths sharp contrasts between two regions of different colors. Properly done, this eliminates the jagged edges of text or colored objects. Used in voice processing, anti-aliasing usually refers to the process of removing spurious frequencies from waveforms produced by converting digital signals back to analog.

ANTI REFLECTION COATING A thin, dielectric or metallic film (or several such films) applied to an optical surface to reduce its reflectance and thereby increase the transmittance of the optical fiber. The ideal value of the refractive index of a single layer film is the square root of the product of the refractive indices on either side of the film, the ideal optical thickness being one quarter of a wavelength.

ANTI STUFFING A mechanical flap in a coin phone which prevents the blocking by paper or other material of coin chutes. An anti-stuffing flap is meant to assure that you, the user, get your money back after you've tried to make a call but didn't get through.

ANTI VIRAL PROGRAMS Programs which scan disks looking for the tell-tale signatures of computer viruses.

ANTICIPOINTMENT Raising people's levels of anticipation and then disappointing them. A definition contributed by Gerald Taylor, president, consumer division, of MCI.

ANTISTATIC A material, such as packing material, that is treated to prevent the build-up of static electricity. The static charges gradually dissipate instead of building up a sudden discharge.

ANYWHERE FIX The ability of a Global Positioning System (GPS) receiver to start position calculations without being given an approximate location and approximate time. See GPS.

AOS Alternate Operator Services. Today there are many Operator Services Providers not owned by the Bell Telephone Companies or AT&T. The AOS industry is dropping the descriptive term "alternate" and communicating that they be known as OSPs. AOS was coined by AT&T. See AOSP and OPERATOR SERVICE PROVIDERS.

AOSP Alternate Operator Service Provider. A new breed of long distance phone company. It handles operator-assisted calls, in particular Credit Card, Collect, Third Party Billed and Person to Person. Phone calls provided by OSP companies are typically fare more expensive than phone calls provided by "normal" long distance companies, i.e. those which have their own long distance networks and which you see advertised on TV. You normally encounter an OSP only when you're making a phone call from a hotel or hospital phone, or a privately-owned payphone. It's a good idea to ask the operator the cost of your call before you make it.

AOSSVR Auxiliary Operator Services System Voice Response.

AP See ADD-ON or APPLICATIONS PROCESSOR. AP is an AT&T word for a piece of equipment which hangs off the side of their PBX and makes it do more things, like voice mail.

APA All Points Addressable (APA) method of host graphics implementation which uses vertical and horizontal pixel coordinates to create a more graphic image. An SNA definition.

APAD Asynchronous Packet Assembler/Disassembler.

APC Adaptive predictive coding. A narrowband analog-to-digital conversion technique employing a one-level or multilevel sampling system in which the value of the signal at each sample time is adaptively predicted to be a linear function of the past values of the quantized signals. APC is related to linear predictive coding (LPC) in that both use adaptive predictors. However, APC uses fewer prediction coefficients, thus requiring a higher bit rate than LPC.

APCC The American Public Communications Council, which is part of the North American Telecommunications Association (NATA).

APD Avalanche PhotoDiode. A diode that, when hit by light, increases its electrical conductivity by a multiplication effect. APDs are used in lightwave receivers because the APDs have great sensitivity to weakened light signals (i.e. those which have travelled long distances over fiber). APDs are designed to take advantage of avalanche multiplication of photocurrent.

APERIODIC ANTENNA An antenna designed to have an approximately constant input impedance over a wide range of frequencies; e.g., terminated rhombic antennas and wave antennas.

APERTURE The portion of a plane surface near a directional antenna, normal to the direction of maximum radiation intensity, through which the major part of the radiation passes.

APERTURE DISTORTION In facsimile, the distortions in resolution, density, and shape of the recorded image caused by the shape and finite size of the scanning and recording apertures or spots.

API An Application Programming Interface is software that an application program uses to request and carry out lower-level services performed by the computer's or a telephone system's operating system. For Windows, the API also helps applications manage windows, menus, icons, and other GUI elements. In short, an API is a "hook" into software. An API is a set of standard software interrupts, calls, and data formats that application programs use to initiate contact with network services, mainframe communications programs, telephone equipment or program-to-program communications. For example, applications use APIs to call services that transport data across a network. Standardization of APIs at various layers of a communications protocol stack provides a uniform way to write applications. NetBIOS is an early example of a network API. Applications use APIs to call services that transport data across a network.

APL Automatic Program Load in telecom. In data processing, it's a popular programming language.

APLT See Advanced Private Line Termination.

APM 1. Average Positions Manned, the average number of ACD positions manned during the reporting period for a particular group. 2. Advanced Power Management. A technique developed by Intel and Microsoft to extend the life of batteries in smaller portable computers.

APOCALYPSE, FOUR HORSEMEN OF The four horsemen of the Apocalypse were War, Plague, Famine and Death.

APOGEE The point on a satellite orbit that is most distant from the center of the gravitational field of the Earth.

APOLOGIZE To lay the foundation for a future offense.

APPC 1. Advanced Peer-to-Peer Communications, also called Logical Unit 6.2, an IBM-specified network node definition featuring high-level program interaction capabilities on a peer-to-peer basis. Also, IBM's Advanced Peer-to-Peer Communication software. 2. Advanced Program-to-Program Communications. An IBM protocol analogous to the OSI model's session layer: it sets up the necessary conditions that enable application programs to send data to each other through the network.

APPC/PC An IBM product that implements APPC on a PC.

APPEARANCE Usually refers to a private branch exchange line or extension which is on (i.e. "appears") on a multi-button key telephone. For example, extension 445 appears on three key systems.

APPEARANCE TEST POINT The point at which a circuit may be measured by test equipment.

APPGEN A shortened form of the words APPlications GENerator.

APPLE MENU The Apple icon in the upper left hand corner of the Apple Macintosh screen. The Apple menu contains aliases, control panels, the chooser and other desk accessories.

APPLESHARE Apple Computer's local area network. It uses AppleTalk protocols. See APPLETALK.

APPLETALK Apple Computer's proprietary local area network for linking Macintosh computers and peripherals, especially LaserWriter printers. Appletalk is a CSMA/CD network that runs at 230.4 kilo bits per second and is therefore, incompatible with any other local area network. It is also a lot slower than the present top speeds of Ethernet (10 Mbps) and Token Ring (16 Mbps). Outside manufacturers, however, make gateways which will connect an Appletalk LAN to other local area and telecommunications networks — LANs, WANs and MANs.

APPLICATION A software program that carries out some useful task. Database managers, spreadsheets, communications packages, graphics programs and word processors are all applications.

APPLICATION BINARY INTERFACE ABI. The rules by which software code is written to operate specific computer hardware. Application software, written to conform to an ABI, is able to be run on a wide variety of system platforms that use the computer hardware for which the ABI is designed.

APPLICATION BRIDGE Aspect Telecommunications's ACD to host computer link. See also OPEN APPLICATION INTERFACE.

APPLICATION FOR SERVICE A standard telephone company order form that includes pertinent billing, technical and other descriptive information which enables the company to provide communications network service to the customer and its authorized users.

APPLICATION FRAMEWORK This usually means a class library with a fundamental base class for defining a complete program. The framework provides at least some of the facilities through which a program interfaces with the user, such as meus and windows, in a style that is internally consistent and abstracted from the specific environment for which it has been developed.

This is an explanation I received from Borland. I don't quite understand it, yet. An application framework is an object-oriented class library that integrates user-interface building blocks, fundamental data structures, and support for object-oriented input and output. It defines an application's standard user interface and behavior so that the programmer can concentrate on implementing the specifics of the application. An application framework allows developers to reuse the abstract design of an entire application by modeling each major component of an applications as an abstract class.

APPLICATION GENERATOR A program to generate actual programming code. An applications generator will let you produce software quickly, but it will not allow you the flexibility had you programmed it from scratch. Voice processing "applications generators," despite the name, often do no generate programming code. Instead they are self-contained environments which allow a user to define and execute applications. See APPLICATIONS GENERATOR.

APPLICATION PROGRAM A computer software program designed for a specific job, such as word processing, accounting, spreadsheet, etc.

APPLICATION PROGRAM INTERFACE API. A set of formalized software calls and routines that can be referenced by an application program to access underlying network services.

APPLICATION PROGRAMMING INTERFACE API. A set of functions and values used by one program to communicate with another program or with an operating system. See API for a better explanation.

APPLICATION SOFTWARE INTERFACE ASI. The Application Software Interface is a product of the Application Software Interface Expert Working Group of the ISDN Implementor's Workshop. The Interface focuses on the definition of a common application interface for accessing and administering ISDN services provided by hardware commonly referred to in the vendor community as Network Adapters (NAs) and responds to the applications requirements generated by the ISDN Users Workshop (IUW). The characteristics of this Application Interface shall be

● Portable across the broadest range of system architectures;

● Extensible (their words, not mine)

● Abstracted beyond ISDN to facilitate interworking;

● Defined in terms of services and facilities consistent with OSI layer interface standards.

According to Application Software Interface Group, the primary goal of the

ASI is to provide a consistent set of application software interface services and application software interface implementation agreement(s) in order that an ISDN application may operate across a broad range of ISDN vendor products and platforms. The application software interface implementation agreements will be referenced by (and tested against) the IUW (ISDN Users Workshop) generated applications. It is anticipated that the vendor companies involved in the development of these implementation agreements will build products for the ISDN user marketplace which conform to them. ASI Implementation Agreements are likely to become a US Government Federal Information Processing Standard (FIPS).

APPLICATIONS ENGINEERING Applications engineering is the process of analyzing your telephone network to find products and services that will reduce your monthly bill without sacrificing network quality. It can be as simple as calling the telephone company to convert a particular service to a Rate Stabilization Plan (RSP). In many instances, the use of applications engineering concepts will increase the quality of your network. For example, putting DIDs onto a T1 will save you money and provide your network with a digital backbone. Unfortunately, most applications engineering is done by the telephone company or by their sales agents. Their main goal is not to save you money, but rather to sell telephone company products. Therfore, they are unlikely to advise you of all the hidden costs of converting to a particular service. A true application engineer will provie you with a complete cost analysis that includes all the conversion costs, and provides you with the "break-even date." The break-even date is the date that your monthly saving offsets the initial conversion cost of the service. It is often used synonymously with the term break-even point.

APPLICATIONS GENERATOR Also called APPSGEN. Software that writes software. Applications generators are software tools that, in response to your input, write software code a computer can understand. Applications generators have three major benefits: 1. They save time. You can write software faster. 2. They are perfect for quickly demonstrating an application. 3. They can often be used by non-programmers. Applications generators have two disadvantages. 1. The code they produce is often not as efficient as the code produced by a good programmer. 2. They are often limited in what they can produce. Applications generators tend to be general purpose tools. Alternatively, they may be very specific, providing support for specific applications, such as connecting voice response units to mainframe databases, voice messaging system development, audiotex system development, etc. Applications generators are often used in programming voice processors.

One of applications generators' bigger advantages is their ability to translate user specified screens and menus into programming code. In essence, you produce the screen or menu using an interface as simple as a word processor. Then the applications generator translates that screen into programming code in a language, such as "C." Once translated into "C", a proficient programmer could go through the code and "improve" on it. See also SCRIPT LANGUAGE.

APPLICATIONS LAYER The seventh and highest layer of the Open Systems Interconnection (OSI) data communications model of the International Standards Organization (ISO). It supplies functions to applications or nodes allowing them to communicate with other applications or nodes. File transfer and electronic mail work at this layer. See OSI MODEL.

APPLICATIONS PARTNER An Applcations Partner is AT&T's new name for an outside company which will write software to work on AT&T phone systems, such as the Merlin, Legend and the Definity. AT&T is setting up an Applications Partner Program to work with companies to help them develop programs and distribute their products. See also DESKTOP CONNECTION.

APPLICATIONS PROCESSOR A special purpose computer which attaches to a telephone system and allows it (and the people using it) to perform different "applications," such as voice mail, electronic mail or packet switching. We think AT&T invented the term. See also ADD-ON.

APPLIQUE Circuit components added to an existing system to provide additional or alternate functions. Some carrier telephone equipment designed for ringdown manual operation can be modified with applique to allow for use between points having dial equipment.

APPN Advanced Peer-to-Peer Networking (APPN) is, according to its creator IBM, a leading-edge distributed networking feature IBM has added to its Systems Network Architecture (SNA). It provides optimized routing of communications between devices. In addition to simplifying the addition of workstations and systems to a network and enabling users to send data and messages to each other faster, APPN is designed to support efficient and transparent sharing of applications in a distributed computing environment. Because APPN permits direct communication between users anywhere on a network, it facilitates the development of client/server computing, in which workstation users anywhere on a network can share processing power, applications and data without regard to where the information is located. Workstations on an APPN network are dynamically defined so they can be relocated easily on the network without extensive re-programming. APPN also allows remote workstations to communicate with each other, without intervention by a central computer. Also, IBM's Advanced Peer-to-Peer Networking software.

APPN END NODE An APPN end node is the final destination of user data and cannot function as an intermediate node in an APPN network and cannot perform routing functions. See APPN.

APPROVED GROUND Grounds that meet the requirements of the NEC (National Electrical Code), such as building steel, concrete-encased electrodes, ground rings, and other devices. See AC and GROUNDING.

APPSERVER A SCSA term. AppServer defines the software environment that enables voice processing applications to run on any computing platform. AppServer sits ona PC platform equipped with call processing hardware and allows a remotely hosted application to control the call processing hardware.

APR Annual Percentage Rate. A percentage calculation of the finance charge portion of financing contact.

APS Automatic Protection Switching. An AT&T term. Protection switching is automatically initiated when the error rate on the service line exceeds a set threshold.

ARA Appletalk Remote Access. Provides an asynchronous AppleTalk connection to another Macintosh and its network services through a modem. A remote user using ARA can log on to a remote server and mount the volume on his desktop as if he were connected locally.

ARCHIE An Internet term. Located on several computers around the country, Archie is a kind of superdirectory to the files on the internet. If you're looking for a file or even a particular topic, Archie provides its specific location.

ARCHITECT One who drafts a plan of your office and then plans a draft of your money.

ARCHITECTURAL FREEDOM An AT&T term for flexibility in locating functions, such as control, storage or processing of information, at any site in or around a network, such as customer premises, central offices or regional service bureaus. Architectural freedom also means the ability to distribute functions among combinations of locations and have them interrelate through a high-throughput, low-delay, transparent network. See also ARCHITECTURE.

ARCHITECTURE The architecture of a system refers to how it is designed and how the components of the system are connected to, and operate with, each other. It covers voice, video, data and text. Architecture also includes the ability of the system to carry narrow, medium and broadband signals. It also includes the ability of the system to grow "seamlessly" (i.e. without too many large jumps in price).

ARCHIVE A backup of a file. An archived file may contain backup copies of programs and files in use or data and materials no longer in use, but perhaps needed for historical or tax purposes. Archive files are kept on paper, on microfilm, on disk, on floppies, etc. They may be kept in compressed or uncompressed form. See ARCHIVER.

ARCHIVER A software program for compressing files. If you compress files, you will save on communications charges, since you will be able to transmit those files faster as they're now smaller. My favorite MS-DOS archiver, also called file compression utility is Phil Katz's PKZIP.EXE and

PKUNZIP.EXE. You can cut a database by as much as 90% and a word processed file by maybe 30% by using PKZIP. How much you can cut is determined by how much fluff is in the file. PKZIP is the most widely-used archive and compession utility today. You can recognized "zipped" files because their extension is always ZIP. There are other compression programs out there which you will recognize by these extensions, ARC, AR7, ARJ, LZH, PAK and ZOO.

ARCHIVING FILES This is a process where the information contained in an active computer file is made ready for storing in a non-active file, perhaps in off-line or near-line storage. Typically when files are achived, they are compressed to reduce their size. To restore the file to its original size requires a process known as unarchiving. See also ARCHIVER.

ARCNET Attached Resource Computer NETwork. One of the earliest and most popular local area networks. A 2.5M-bits-per-second LAN that uses a modified token-passing protocol. Developed by Datapoint, San Antonio, TX, Arcnet interface cards are now manufactured by many vendors, including Standard Microsystems and Pure Data, Ltd. Arcnet has lost popularity in recent years to Ethernet (IEEE 802.3) and Token Ring (IEEE 802.5).

ARDIS A public data communications wireless network that allows people carrying handheld devices to send and receive short data messages. Such messages might be from sheriff standing in the street searching his department's data base for unpaid parking tickets. ARDIS is jointly owned by Motorola and IBM. It is an outgrowth of a network orginally created for IBM service technicians. A competitor to Ardis is RAM Mobile Data.

AREA CODE A three-digit code designating a "toll" center in the United States, Canada and Mexico. The first digit is any number from 2 through 9. The second digit is always a "1" or "0." These days, many cities have local exchanges with the same numbering scheme as area codes. In these cities, to dial long distance you must dial "1" first. An Area Code is also called an NPA, Numbering Plan Area. For a full listing of area codes, see NORTH AMERICAN AREA CODES.

AREA CODE RESTRICTION The ability of the telephone equipment (or its ancillary devices) to selectively deny calls to specific (but not all) area codes. Area code restriction is often confused with "0/1" (zero/one) restriction which denies calls to all area codes by sampling the first and second dialed digits (is it a 0 or 1?) and thus, identifying and blocking an attempt at making a toll call. For a full listing of area codes, see NORTH AMERICAN AREA CODES.

ARF Alternative Regulatory Framework.

ARINC Aeronautical Radio INC. The collective organization that coordinates the design and management of telecommunications systems for the airline industry. It's one of the largest buyers of telecommunications services and equipment in the world.

ARITHMETIC LOGIC UNIT ALU. The part of the CPU (Central Processing Unit) that performs the arithmetic and logical operations. See MICROPROCESSOR.

ARITHMETIC OPERATION The process that results in a mathematically correct solution during the execution of an arithmetic statement or the evaluation of an arithmetic expression.

ARITHMETIC REGISTER A register (i.e. short-term storage location) that holds the operands or the results of operations such as arithmetic operations, logic operations, and shifts.

ARITHMETIC UNIT The part of a computing system which contains the circuits that perform the arithmetic operations. See also ALU.

ARL Attendant Release Loop. A feature of the PBX console. See RELEASE.

ARMAGEDDON The fabled battlefield where God's heavenly forces are to defeat the demon-led forces of evil. The final battle.

ARMOR Mechanical protection usually accomplished by a metallic layer of tape, braid or served wires or by a combination of jute, steel tapes or wires applied over a cable sheath for additional protection. It is normally found only over the outer sheath. Armor is used mostly on cables lying on lake or river bottoms or on the shore ends of oceans. See ARMORED CABLE.

ARMORED CABLE A stainless steel handset cord which is meant to resist vandalism. Typically used on a coin phone, most stainless steel handset cords are too short. This is said to be because they were first ordered for use in prisons, where guards wanted to be certain they would not be used by the prisoners as hanging devices. Thus, they requested Western Electric to make them too short for such a use. Whether there is any validity to this story is dubious, however, it is part of telephone industry folk history and therefore, worth preserving.

ARP Address Resolution Protocol. A protocol within the Transmission Control Protocol/Internet Protocol (TCP/IP) suite that "maps" IP addresses to Ethernet addresses. TCP/IP requires ARP for use with Ethernet.

ARPA Advanced Research Projects Agency of the U.S. Department of Defense. (The whole DOD annual telecommunications bill exceeds $1 billion.) Much of the country's early work on packet switching was done at ARPA.

ARPANET Advanced Research Projects Agency NETwork. A Department of Defense data network, developed by ARPA, which ties together many users and computers in universities, government and businesses. ARPANET has been the forerunner of many developments in commercial data communications, including packet switching, which was first tested on a large scale on this network.

73

ARQ Automatic Retransmission reQuest. The standard method of checking transmitted data, used on virtually all high-speed data communications systems. The sender encodes an error-detection field based on the contents of the message. The receiver recalculates the check field and compares it with that received. If they match, an "ACK" (acknowledgment) is transmitted to the sender. If they don't match, a "NAK" (negative acknowledgment) is returned, and the sender retransmits the message. Note: this method of error correction assumes the sender temporarily or permanently stores the data it has sent. Otherwise, it couldn't possibly retransmit the data. No error detection scheme in data transmission is foolproof. This one is no exception.

ARRAY ANTENNA Take a bunch of directional antennas. Aim them at the same transmitting source. Join them together. Presto, you now have a very powerful giant antenna. Array antennas are used for picking up weak signals. They are often used in astronomical and defense communications systems.

ARRAY CONNECTOR A connector for use with ribbon fiber cable that joins 12 fibers simultaneously. A fan-out array design can be used to connect ribbon fiber cables to non-ribbon cables.

ARRAY PROCESSOR A processor capable of executing instructions in which the operands may be arrays rather than data elements.

ARRESTOR A device used to protect telephone equipment from lightning, electrical storms, etc. An arrestor is typically gas filled so when lightning strikes, the gas ionizes and, bingo, a low resistance to the ground that drains the damaging high voltage elements of the lightning away.

ARS Automatic Route Selection, also called Least Cost Routing. A way that your phone system automatically chooses the least expensive way of making the call that it is presented with. That least expensive way may be a tie line or a WATS line, etc. It may even be dial-up. See LEAST COST ROUTING and ALTERNATE ROUTING.

ARTIFICIAL INTELLIGENCE In 1950, Alan Turning, a British mathematician, challenged scientists to create a machine that could trick people into thinking it was one of them. And this for long was THE classic definition of artificial intelligence. One way to trick people is to have the computer make typing mistakes, like real humans do. The real challenge these days with artificial intelligence, now more commonly called "expert systems," is not to recreate people but to recognize the uniqueness of machine intelligence and learn to work with it in intelligent, useful ways.

ARTIFICIAL LINE INTERFACE In T-1 transmission, refers to the ability of a piece of transmission equipment to attenuate its output level to meet the required loop loss of 15-22.5 dB normally switch selectable between 0,7.5, and dB.

ARU Automatic Response Unit.

AS&C Alarm Surveillance and Control

AS/400 IBM's mid-range mini-computer. AS/400 stands for Application System/400. IBM has a product called CallPath/400 which allows AS/400 computers to link to PBXs from the leading manufacturers.

ASA Average Speed of Answer. How long the average caller has to wait before they speak to an agent. The time can vary, even over the course of one day, due to call volumes and staff levels. An important measure of service quality.

ASAI AT&T's Adjunct Switch Application Interface. A long detailed set of technical specifications for having an outside computer control an AT&T PBX. See also APPLICATIONS PARTNER, OPEN APPLICATION INTERFACE, PSAI and SCAI.

ASCII Pronounced: as'-kee. American Standard Code for Information Interchange. It's the most popular coding method used by small computers for converting letters, numbers, punctuation and control codes into digital form. Once defined, ASCII characters can be recognized and understood by other computers and by communications devices. ASCII represents characters, numbers, punctuation marks or signals in seven on-off bits. A capital "C", for example, is 1000011, while a "3" is 0110011. As a seven-bit code, and since each bit can only be a "one" or a "zero,"

ASCII can represent 128 "things," i.e. 2 x 2 x 2 x 2 x 2 x 2 x 2 which equals 128. ASCII is the code virtually every personal computer in the world encodes "things," including IBM, Apple and Radio Shack/Tandy. This compatible encoding (it was developed by ANSI — the American National Standards Institute) allows virtually all personal computers to talk to each other, if they use a compatible modem, or null modem cable and transmit and receive at the same speed. There are variations of ASCII. (Nothing is totally standard anymore.) The most important variation — one originally from IBM — is called Extended ASCII. It codes characters into eight bits (or one byte) and uses those ASCII characters above 127 to represent foreign language letters, and other useful symbols, such as those to draw boxes. But at 127 and below, extended 8-bit ASCII is identical to standard 7-bit ASCII. The CCITT calls ASCII International Telegraph Alphabet 5.

The other major method of encoding is IBM's EBCDIC (pronounced ebb'-si-dick). It's largely used on IBM and IBM-compatible mainframe computers (but not their PCs, which use ASCII and extended ASCII.) EBCDIC is an eight-bit encoding scheme, thus allowing up to 256 "things" to be encoded, i.e. 2 x 2 x 2 x 2 x 2 x 2 x 2 x 2 = 256. EBCDIC codes letters, characters and punctuation marks in a totally different way than ASCII. For ASCII files to be read by an IBM mainframe (one that reads EBCDIC), those ASCII files must be translated into EBCDIC by one of the many translation programs available. See also ASCII EDITOR and EXTENDED GRAPHICS CHARACTER SET.

ASCII EDITOR An ASCII editor (also called a "text," "DOS" or "non-document mode" editor) does NOT use extended ASCII and printer [ESCAPE] codes, which are used by word processor to create advanced features such as bold, italic, underlining, and super/subscript printing effects; and fancy formatting such as automatic paragraph reformat, pagination, hyphenation, footers, headers, and margins. I wrote this dictionary using an ASCII editor called ZEdit, which is a customized version of QEdit, undoubtedly the best editor ever written. Since an ASCII editor can't do so much, why would anyone use one? Well, its strength is in the lack of those very things a word processor has! Here are my benefits:

1. It's lightning fast. No word processor can match an ASCII editor's speed at loading itself, loading files, finding things in files, etc.

2. A file produced by an ASCII editor can be read and edited by any word processor (absolutely any). Thus it's the universal word processing file. A WordPerfect file typically can't be read by WordStar and vice versa. The reason is that every word processor uses different high-level codes for the same features (underlining, bolding, etc.) There is no consistency among word processors as to how they encode their text so they can tell printers to do bolding, etc.

3. An ASCII editor is better to type programming languages, such as EDLIN (for batch files), BASIC, FORTRAN, PASCAL, etc. If QEDIT used extended ASCII and printer codes, it could not be used by these programs...for each program interprets these "high level" codes differently from another program. An ASCII editor types straight, "vanilla" text...nothing fancy about it.

ASCII-TO-FAX CONVERSION Allows the transfer of a word-processed file directly to your fax board so it can be faxed without being scanned from a hard copy print-out. Documents faxed with ASCII-TO-FAX conversion come out much cleaner at the other end, since the scanning process always degrades the image.

ASDS Accunet Spectrum of Digital Services. AT&T's leased line (also called private line) digital service at 56 Kbps. MCI and Sprint have similar services. It is available in N x 56/64 Kbps, for N = 1, 2, 4, 6, 8, 12. The 56/64 Kbps POP-POP service (between long distance carrier central offices) costs the same as an analog line.

ASE Amplified Spontaneous Emission

ASH Ardire-Stratigakis-Hayduk, a synchronous compression algorithm that is said to offer four times throughput on a typical synchronous channel. It can be used in bridges, routers, ISDN and modems. Transcend of Cleveland, OH said at one point that it was the exclusive licensor of ASH.

ASI 1. Advanced Services Implementation. 2. Application Software Interace. An important ISDN term. See APPLICATION SOFTWARE INTERFACE. 3. Adapter Support Interface. The driver specification developed by IBM for networking over IEEE 802.5 Token-Rings.

ASIC Application Specific Integrated Circuit. Also known as a gate array. This is a chip that has been built for a specific application. Manufacturers use it to consolidate many chips into a single package, reducing system board board size and power consumption.

ASIC CHIP Application Specific Integrated Circuit Chip. A fancy name for microprocessor chips which do specific tasks. For example, an ASIC chip might be responsible for a graphics display.

ASN.1 Abstract Syntax Notation One. LAN "grammar," with rules and symbols, that is used to describe and define protocols and programming languages. ASN.1 is the OSI standard language to describe data types.

ASP 1. A Northern Telecom term for Attached Support Processor. 2. Adjunct service point. An intelligent-network feature that resides at the intelligent peripheral equipment and responds to service logic interpreter requests for service processing. See also AIN..

ASPECT RATIO The ratio of the width of a rectangular image to its height. The aspect ratio of TV is four units of width to every three units of height. This is expressed as 4 x 3 aspect ratio. A 35mm frame measures 24 x 36 mm, which means it has three units of width to two units of height. It is different in size from a TV screen. This is why the side parts of movies are chopped off on TV.

ASR 1. Automatic Speech Recognition. See INTERACTIVE VOICE RESPONSE. 2. Automatic Send-Receive teletype or telex machine. Such a machine, if left on and loaded with paper, will receive incoming messages and print them, even when nobody is present. See also AUTOMATIC SEND RECEIVE.

ASSEMBLER A program which translates an assembly programming language into the code of ones and zeros used by computers. See also ASSEMBLY LANGUAGE.

ASSEMBLY Pertaining to the translation of a program from symbolic language into machine code. See ASSEMBLY LANGUAGE.

ASSEMBLY LANGUAGE A computer language for writing software. It is a language which is converted by programs called compilers or interpreters into machine language programs which consist of only 1s and 0s and which a computer can understand. Even though an assembly language consists of recognizable nemonics and meaningful words, it's not easy to program in. It is referred to as a "low-level language". Assembly language programs run faster than high-level language programs, such as BASIC, COBOL or FORTRAN, which are much easier to learn and program in. Choosing a programming language is typically a tradeoff of ease for speed.

ASSERTED A signal is asserted when it is in the state which is indicated by the name of the signal. Opposite of Negated.

ASSIGNATION A secret romantic rendezvous. The invitation to an

NEWTON'S TELECOM DICTIONARY

assignation doesn't work if she doesn't know the meaning of the word. Are you listening Jane Laino?

ASSIGNED FREQUENCY The center of the assigned frequency band assigned to a station.

ASSIGNED FREQUENCY BAND The frequency band within which the emission of a station is authorized; the width of the band equals the necessary bandwidth plus twice the absolute value of the frequency tolerance. Where space stations are concerned, the assigned frequency band includes twice the maximum Doppler shift that may occur in relation to any point of the Earth's surface.

ASSIGNED NIGHT ANSWER ANA. After business hours or when you place your phone system on "Night Answer," this feature sends calls from specified trunks to designated extensions or departments. You may use this feature to send calls directly to modems, or to emergency numbers, or even to outside home numbers.

ASSIGNED PLANT CONCEPT A pair is dedicated from the central office to the subscriber home and maintained at that address, even when idle. See REASSIGNMENT.

ASSOCIATED COMMON-CHANNEL SIGNALING A form of common-channel signaling in which the signaling channel is associated with a specific trunk group and terminates at the same pair of switches as the trunk group. The signal channel is usually transmitted by the same facilities as the trunk group.

ASSOCIATED VOICE PORT AVP. A Northern Telecom term. A voice port is used to pass signaling and supervision information to establish a connection for the data port. The term is also used in reference to the configuration of modems and voice grade switched circuits connected to the voice-port-data-port pair.

ASSOCIATION A relationship between two connection segments that share a common Leg O (i.e., a common subscriber is in control of connection segments). Definition from Bellcore.

AST Automatic Scheduled Testing. A method of testing switched access service (Feature Groups B, C, and D) where the customer provides remote office test lines and 105 test lines with associated responders or their functions' equivalent; consists of monthly loss and C-message noise tests and annual balance test.

ASTM American Society for Testing and Materials, a non-profit industry-wide organization which publishes standards, methods of test, recommended practices, definitions and other related material.

ASYMMETRIC MULTIPROCESSING A relatively simple implementation of multiprocessing in which the operating system kernel runs

78

on one dedicated CPU and assigns tasks as they come in to other "slave processors." It is also known as "master/slave" processing.

ASYN Greek prefix meaning "not."

ASYNCHRONOUS BALANCED MODE ABM. Used in the IBM Token Ring's Logical Link Control (LLC), ABM operates at the SNA data link control and allows devices on a Token Ring to send data link commands at any time and to initiate responses independently.

ASYNCHRONOUS TRANSFER MODE ATM is the technology selected by the Consultative Committee on International Telephone & Telegraph (CCITT) International standards organization in 1988 to realize a Broadband Integrated Services Digital Network (B-ISDN). It is a fast, cell-switched technology based on a fixed-length 53-byte cell. All broadband transmissions (whether audio, data, imaging or video) are divided into a series of cells and routed across an ATM network consisting of links connected by ATM switches. Each ATM link comprises a constant stream of ATM cell slots into which transmissions are placed or left idle, if unused. The most significant benefit of ATM is its uniform handling of services allowing one network to meet the needs of many broadband services. ATM accomplishes this because its cell-switching technology combines the best advantages of both circuit-switching (for constant bit rate services such as voice and image) and packet-switching (for variable bit rate services such as data and full motion video) technologies. The result is the bandwidth guarantee of circuit switching combined with the high efficiency of packet switching.

ASYNCHRONOUS TRANSMISSION Literally, not synchronous. A method of data transmission which allows characters to be sent at irregular intervals by preceding each character with a start bit, and following it with a stop bit. It is the method most small computers (especially PCs) use to communicate with each other and with mainframes today. In every form of data transmission, every letter, number or punctuation mark is transmitted digitally as "ons" or "offs." These characters are also represented as "zeros" and "ones" (See ASCII). The problem in data transmission is to define when the letter, the number or the punctuation mark begins. Without knowing when it begins, the receiving computer or terminal won't be able to figure out what the transmission means.

One way to do this is by using some form of clocking signal. At a precise time, the transmission starts, etc. This is called SYNCHRONOUS TRANSMISSION. In ASYNCHRONOUS transmission there's no clocking signal. The receiving terminal or computer knows what's what because each letter, number or punctuation mark begins with a start bit and ends with a stop bit. Transmission of data is called SYNCHRONOUS if the exact sending or receiving of each bit is determined before it is transmitted or received. It is called ASYNCHRONOUS if the timing of the transmission is not determined by the timing of a previous character.

ASYNCHRONOUS is used in lower speed transmission and by less expensive computer transmission systems. Large systems and computer networks typically use more sophisticated methods of transmission, such as SYNCHRONOUS or BISYNCHRONOUS, because of the large overhead penalty of 20% in ASYNCHRONOUS transmission. This is caused by adding one start bit and one stop bit to an eight bit word — thus 2 bits out of ten.

The second problem with large transfers is error checking. The user sitting in front of his own screen checks his ASYNCHRONOUS transmission by looking at the screen and re-typing his mistakes. This is impractical for transferring long files at high speed if there is not a person in attendance.

In SYNCHRONOUS transmission start and stop bits are not used. According to the book Understanding Data Communications, characters are sent in groups called blocks with special synchronization characters placed at the beginning of the block and within it to ensure that enough 0 to 1 or 1 to 0 transitions occur for the receiver clock to remain accurate. Error checking is done automatically on the entire block. If any errors occur, then the entire block is retransmitted. This technique also carries an overhead penalty (nothing is free), but the overhead is far less than 20% for blocks or more than a few dozen characters.

AT 1. Access Tandem. 2. Advanced Technology. Refers to a 16 bit Personal Computer architecture using the 80 x 86 processor family which formed the basis for the ISA Bus as found in the first IBM PC.

AT COMMAND SET Also known as the Hayes Standard AT Command Set. A language that enables PC communications software to get an asynchronous and "Hayes-compatible modem" to do what you want it to do. So called "AT" because all the commands begin with "AT," which is short for ATtention. The most common commands include ATDT (touchtone a number), ATA (manually answer the phone), ATZ (reset modem — it will answer OK), ATSO=O (disable auto-answer), and ATH (hang up the phone).

To avoid having yourself knocked off your data call by the beep that comes in on the phone company's call waiting, put the following line in your modem setup: ATS10=20. That will increase your S10 register to two seconds. This register sets the time between loss of carrier (caused by the 1.5 second call waiting signal) and internal modem disconnect. Factory default on most modems is 1.4 seconds — just perfect to be cut off by the wall waiting tone! (Dumb.)

If you have to dial through several phone systems, waiting for dial tone on the way and/or going through fax/modem switches, you may consider a dial stream that looks like ATDT 1-800-433-9800 [W]212-989-4675 [W]22, where [W] means (in some software programs) "Wait for any key. When you get it, touchtone out the next digits." Iin other software programs — pure Hayes command — W means wait for second dialtone.

If [W] doesn't work for you, then change X3 in your setup line to X1; change your computer's dialed number to 9; and dial your distant computer with your phone. When you hear the modem at the other end answer, tell your computer's software to dial 9. It will dial 9, hear the modem tone at the other end and connect as though it had dialed it all by itself. X1 tells your modem to dial (or touchtone) immediately — without waiting for dial tone.

You can use several AT commands on one line. You only need AT before the first one. Some modems require commands typed in capital letters. When your dialing fails and you can't figure why, get out of your communications software program and start again. Or in total desperation, turn your computer and modem completely off and start again. The word "Hayes" comes from the manufacturer of modems called Hayes Microcomputer, Norcross, GA, the creator of the command set. Not all Hayes compatibile modems are. See also HAYES COMMAND SET.

AT LOCAL MODE One of the command modes available on the ISDN set. It is used for compatibility with existing communications packages for analog modems or for data-only application programs. See AT COMMAND SET.

AT WORK Pronounced "At Work." Microsoft's office equipment architecture announced on June 9, 1993. The simple idea is to put a set of software building blocks into both office machines and PC products, including:

- Desktop and network-connected printers.
- Digital monochrome and color copiers.
- Telephones and voice messaging systems.
- Fax machines and PC fax products.
- Handheld systems.
- Hybrid combinations of the above.

According to Microsoft, the Microsoft At Work architecture focuses on creating digital connections between machines (i.e. the ones above) to allow information to flow freely throughout the workplace. The Microsoft At Work software architecture consists of several technology components that serve as building blocks to enable these connections. Only one of the components, desktop software, will reside on PCs. The rest will be incorporated into other types of office devices (the ones above), making these products easier to use, compatible with one another and compatible with Microsoft Windows-based PCs. The components, according to Microsoft, are:

- Microsoft At Work operating system. A real-time, pre-emptive, multitasking operating system that is designed to specifically address the requirements of the office automation and communication industries. The new operating system supports Windows-compatible application programming interfaces (APIs) where appropriate for the device.

● Microsoft At Work communications. Will provide the connectivity between Microsoft At Work-based devices and PCs. It will support the secure transmission of original digital documents, and it is compatible with the Windows Messaging API and the Windows Telephony API of the Windows Open Services Architecture (WOSA).

● Microsoft At Work rendering. Will make the transmission of digital documents, with formatting and fonts intact, very fast and, consequently, cost-effective; will ensure that a document sent to any of these devices will produce high-quality output, referred to as "What You Print Is What You Fax Is What You Copy Is What You See."

● Microsoft At Work graphical user interface. Will make all devices very easy to use and will make sophisticated features accessible; will provide useful feedback to users. Leveraging Microsoft's experience in the Windows user interface, Microsoft At Work-based products will use very simple graphical user interfaces designed for people who are not computer users.

● Microsoft At Work desktop software for Windows-based PCs. Will provide Windows-based PC applications the ability to control, access and exchange information with any product based on Microsoft At Work. Desktop software is the one piece of the Microsoft At Work architecture that will reside on PCs.

See also WINDOWS, WINDOWS TELEPHONY and WOSA.

AT&T American Telephone and Telegraph Company. Not much telegraph any more and proportionately less telephone too as it moves increasingly into the computer industry. AT&T, once the largest company in the world, is now 75% smaller as a result of the Divestiture of its operating telephone companies on December 31, 1983. At one stage, it had two main divisions, AT&T Communications (the long distance phone company) and AT&T Technologies (equipment) These were merged to form one AT&T with several divisions.

Then we re-wrote this definition. Then they re-organized. Then we re-wrote. We re-wrote this definition so many times during the course of producing this dictionary that we finally gave up. Suffice, AT&T is American Telephone and Telegraph Company. At one stage it provided really good long distance service, made and sold computers (and in 1991 it bought NCR), made and sold telephone switches — from small key systems to big central offices. At one stage it was getting into wireless messaging and cable TV. It may still do all this by the time you get this dictionary. And then it may not. See also AT&T BELL LABS.

AT&T ALLIANCE A direct-dial AT&T service which allows you to teleconference as few as three and as many as 59 telephones around the world. You can dial the numbers to call or you can schedule a meeting, called "Meet-Me Service." If you want to set the conference up, you dial 0-700-456-1000, then punch in the number of locations, then put in the numbers, ending each with a #. End your dialing with another # — to add yourself to the teleconference.

AT&T APPLICATIONS PARTNER A software developer who develops applications for AT&T hardware and software. See also DESKTOP CONNECTION.

AT&T BELL LABS The research and development arm of AT&T. It used to be known simply as Bell Laboratories. It is one of the most important research laboratory in the United States. Bell Labs is credited with inventing many electronics things including the transistor.

AT&T COMMUNICATIONS AT&T-Comm or AT&T-C. The part of AT&T that was at one stage responsible for long distance services. It used to be called AT&T Long Lines, which we liked better. AT&T Communications is now the largest part of AT&T.

AT&T CREDIT CORPORATION AT&T's financing arm, which provides customized leases for telephone equipment including the MERLIN II, MERLIN Plus, Legend, SPIRIT and Definity Systems, as well as for other equipment, such as AT&T FAX Machines and computers.

AT&T FAX ATTENDANT SYSTEM A voice mail-like product providing fax store-and-forward broadcast, personal fax mailboxes for confidential reception, remote retrieval and plain paper fax. The FAX Attendant also adds Fax-on-Demand through a automated attendant/fax response. The AT&T FAX Attendant System can be integrated with AT&T's AUDIX Voice Power Voice Mail system to provide a single interface for retrieving messages and combined notification.

AT&T GBCS AT&T Global Business Communications Systems. The new name for the merger of two divisions into one division now responsible for all the business telephone system sales of AT&T worldwide. The two divisions that were merged into GBCS were called General Business Systems (office systems 80 lines and smaller) and Business Communications Systems (systems bigger than 80 lines). The merger happened during the summer of 1992.

AT&T INFORMATION SYSTEMS AT&T-IS used to be one of AT&T's sales arms. It used to be responsible for (or used to be responsible for) sales of certain equipment, including telephone systems and computers, to both end-users and some selected distributors. AT&T-IS used to be responsible for selling a service called Net 1000, which was an end-to-end data communications/data processing service, whose exact service is hard to define and has now been killed.

AT&T INTEREXCHANGE COMPANY ATTIX, a suggested name for the long distance part of AT&T, which, at the time was called AT&T Long Lines. It was then called AT&T Communications. The reason the name

ATTIX was rejected is that it reminded someone at AT&T of the word "drug addicts." No one has explained logically why AT&T ever needed to change the name "Long Lines," which most people in the industry related to very warmly. Including us.

AT&T LONG LINES The long distance part of AT&T. It was called that for over 100 years. Then they changed the name to just AT&T. Long Lines remains a favorite for all of us old timers.

AT&T NETWORK SERVICES This is an AT&T Technologies division which sells equipment primarily to Bell Operating companies, independent phone companies, overseas phone companies and large, Fortune 500-type users. It's doing very well.

AT&T TECHNOLOGIES Formerly called Western Electric, it is the equipment manufacturing arm of AT&T. No one knows why this company changed its name, since Western Electric had a wonderful reputation and is remembered with great fondness. It has an excellent reputation for high quality products and is still used as a brand name on some AT&T Technologies' products.

ATA 1. American Telemarketing Association. 2. Analog Terminal Adapter. A device for a Northern Telecom Norstar phone system that lets it use analog devices, for example FAX, answering machines, modems and single line phones, behind the Norstar's central telephone unit (its KSU). 3. AT Attachment. Refers to the interface and protocol used to access a hard disk on AT compatible computers. Disk drives adhering to the ATA protocol are commonly referred to as IDE interfaced drives for PC compatible computers.

ATA DOCUMENT The latest draft of the ANSI X3.T9 subcommittee AT Attachment document.

ATA REGISTERS These registers are accessed by a host to implement the ATA protocol for transferring data, control and status information to and from the PC Card. They are defined in the ATA Document. These registers include the Cylinder High, Cylinder Low, Sector Number, Sector Count, DriveHead, Drive Address, Device Control, Error, Feature, Status and Data registers. The I/O and memory address decoding options for these registers are defined within this specification.

ATB ALL TRUNKS BUSY. One measure which your phone company or phone systems might give you of telephone traffic in and out of your office. See ALL TRUNKS BUSY.

ATD 1. Asynchronous Time Division. 2. ATtention Dial the phone. The first three letters in the most frequently-used command in the Hayes command set for asynchronous modems — typically those used with microcomputers.

ATM 1. Automated Teller Machine. The street corner banking machine which is usually hooked up to a central computer through leased local lines and a multiplexed data network. 2. Asynchronous Transfer Mode. Very high speed telecom transmission technology. ATM is a high bandwidth, low-delay, packet-like switching and multiplexing technique. Usable capacity is segmented into fixed-size cells, consisting of header and information fields, allocated to services on demand. The CCITT has selected ATM as the basis for the future broadband network in view of its flexibility and suitability for both transmission and switching. See ASYNCHRONOUS TRANSFER MODE for a larger explanation. 3. Advanced Testing Methods.

ATT Automatic Toll Ticketing. A system which telephone companies use to automatically keep call detail records including calling number, number called, time of day and length of call. The phone company uses this information, together with the cost of phone calls, to generate an invoice to its customers.

ATTACH A command that assigns a connection number to a workstation and attaches the workstation to the LOGIN directory on the default (or specified) file server. As many as 100 workstations can be attached to a file server running NetWare v2.2. When loaded the NetWare shell (workstation file NETx.COM) automatically attaches your workstation to the nearest file server. You can also specify in SHELL.CFG which server you prefer to attach to.

ATTACH TERMINAL To assign a terminal for exclusive use by the application program. Contrast with Detach Terminal.

ATTACK TIME The time interval between the instant that a signal at the input of a device or circuit exceeds the activation threshold of the device or circuit, and the instant that the device or circuit reacts in a specified manner, or to a specified degree, to the input. The term often implies a protective action such as the provided by a clipper (peak limiter) or compressor, but may be used to describe the action of a device such as a vox (Voice Operated circuited), where the action is not protective.

ATTEMPT Trying to make a telephone call. Also defined as a call offered to a telecommunications system, regardless of whether it is completed.

ATTENDANT The "operator" of a phone system console. Typically, the first person to answer an incoming call. That person usually directs incoming calls to the proper person or department. That person may also assign outgoing lines or trunks to people requesting them. Few companies spend any time training their attendants. They should. There are two types of things attendants should be trained for: 1. Manners, including the correct way to keep people waiting and to screen incoming calls, and 2. The structure of the company. If a caller asks for some help, the attendant should know which department or person might be responsible for providing that help.

ATTENDANT BUSY LAMP FIELD Lamps, lights or LEDs that show whether a PBX or key system extension is busy or not. These days, many attendant busy lamp fields are being incorporated into CRT displays. We hope more will do this as many lamp-based attendant busy lamp fields are difficult to read.

ATTENDANT CALL WAITING INDICATION An unusual feature on a PBX console. The call waiting button on the attendant console lights to indicate a predetermined number of calls in queue. The light flashes when a second (programmable) threshold is reached.

ATTENDANT CAMP-ON If the extension is busy, the attendant or operator can place the call in a queue behind the call already in progress. When the call is over, the "camped-on" call will automatically ring the extension.

ATTENDANT CONFERENCE PBX feature that allows the attendant (or operator) to establish a conference connection between central office trunks and internal phones.

ATTENDANT CONSOLE An attendant console is the larger, specialized telephone set used by the operator or attendant to answer incoming calls and send those calls to the proper extension. Consoles are becoming more sophisticated these days in several ways. Operators need to punch fewer buttons to move calls around, while the information they present to the attendant is more useful for keeping tabs on calls and letting people know what's happening. Many consoles are acquiring TV screens that report the status of each extension, who's speaking, where the call is going, and whether there are problems, such as broken lines or trunks, etc. anywhere on the system. Some of the more modern screens will allow the operator to send messages around the company that can alert someone as to who's calling before he/she picks up the phone. You can also easily program switches through consoles with CRT (also called TV) screens. In the old days you needed to punch in complex codes. Now you can respond to "Yes/No" decisions on a screen with lots of explanatory words and help menus.

ATTENDANT CONTROL OF TRUNK GROUP ACCESS The telephone operator or attendant controls the users' access to trunks for making local and/or long distance calls. This may reduce long distance call abuse.

ATTENDANT DIRECT STATION SELECT This feature gives an operator the ability to reach an extension by simply pushing one button. In direct station select, every extension has its own button. Direct Station Select usually comes with some form of Attendant Busy Lamp Field which shows whether the extensions are busy. Some attendants like direct station select. Others don't, preferring to simply punch in 345, instead of hunting for the button which corresponds to extension 345. The best consoles these days are using some form of easy-to-read screen prompts.

ATTENDANT EXCLUSION A PBX feature which stops the attendant from listening in on a phone call once she or he has passed the call to the correct extension.

ATTENDANT FORCED RELEASE An attendant-activated (pushbutton) facility that will automatically "disconnect" all parties on a given circuit when that circuit is "entered" by the attendant.

ATTENDANT INCOMING CALL CONTROL A PBX feature which diverts incoming trunk calls automatically to a predetermined phone after a predesignated period of time or number of rings.

ATTENDANT KEY PAD Allows the attendant to perform all functions using a standard touch tone key pad on the console or adjacent to it.

ATTENDANT LOCKED LOOP OPERATION PBX feature which allows the attendant at a console to retain supervision or recall capability of any particular call which has been processed.

ATTENDANT LOCKOUT This feature denies an attendant the ability to re-enter a phone call unless specifically recalled by that PBX extension.

ATTENDANT LOOP TRANSFER Allows the attendant to transfer any call to another attendant.

ATTENDANT MONITOR A special attendant circuit which allows "listening in" on all circuits with the console handset/headset transmitter deactivated.

ATTENDANT OVERRIDE A feature that allows an attendant to enter a busy trunk connection and key the trunk number within the PBX. A warning tone will be heard by the connected parties, after which they connected parties and the attendant will be in a three-way connection.

ATTENDANT POSITION Where a telephone operator sits to answer calls and send them on to the people in the company. This is usually in front of a telephone system with buttons, toggle switches, etc. that facilitate this process.

ATTENDANT RECALL When a phone call has been transferred to a telephone extension and not answered, this telephone system feature sends the call back to the attendant. Sometimes the call will return to a special part of the attendant console which will indicate to the attendant that it is a "returned" call. It's a good idea to pay attention to the speed of recall back to the operator. People hate to be extended into endless ringing. Think of calling a hotel and how aggravating it is to wait until the call comes back to an operator after she/he extended it to the room...and it rings and rings.

ATTENDANT RECALL ON TRUNK HOLD The system will recall the attendant if a trunk placed on hold is not re-entered within a predetermined time.

ATTENDANT TRANSFER OF INCOMING CALLS A PBX and Centrex feature. A telephone extension is talking on a line but that person wants to transfer the call to someone else. The person hits their hookswitch a couple of times. (The hookswitch is the toggle switch the handset depresses when you replace it.) This flashing of the hookswitch signals the attendant to join the call. The person asks the attendant "to please transfer this call." The attendant then transfers the call to the new extension. This feature is totally inefficient as it's hard to reach the attendant, who's always busy, etc. etc. All newer phones can transfer both incoming and outgoing calls automatically by just flashing the hookswitch, dialing the extension number and hanging up.

ATTENDED A telephone system having an attendant or receptionist whose primary job is to answer all incoming calls. Many smaller systems, such as key systems, are not centrally "attended." The phone is simply answered by whoever is near. A non-attended phone system should be set up so anyone can answer an incoming call. Some systems, such as most key systems, come this way from the factory. Others, such as PBXs, have to be specially set up. Some systems can be set up so an attendant will get first shot at answering the incoming call, but then, after a couple of rings, anyone else can answer the call (perhaps a loud "night" bell will ring). This is the system we use at TELECONNECT Magazine.

ATTENDED MODE Imagine a commnications situation where your computer is connected over a phone line to another user on another computer and you are uploading and downloading files. Attended mode refers to a situation where both users manually enter the commands required to send or recieve a file concurrently, usually while conversing over the phone. Compare this to UNATTENDED MODE.

ATTENTION KEY A key or combination of keys on a computer or terminal which signals the main computer to stop its present task and wait for a new command. The ESCape key is often the Attention Key. In Crosstalk, it's Control A.

ATTENUATE To reduce the amplitude of a signal. To reduce its volume. See ATTENUATION.

ATTENUATION The decrease in power of a signal, light beam, or lightwave, either absolutely or as a fraction of a reference value. The decrease usually occurs as a result of absorption, reflection, diffusion, scattering, deflection or dispersion from an original level and usually not as a result of geometric spreading, i.e., the inverse square of the distance effect. Optical fibers have been classified as high-loss (over 100 dB/km), medium-loss (20 to 100 dB/km), and low-loss (less than 20 dB/km). In other words, attenuation is the loss of volume during transmission. The received signal is lower in volume than the transmitted signal due to losses in the transmission medium (such as that caused by resistance in the cable). Attenuation is measured in decibels. It is the opposite of Gain. Some electrical components are listed as "with attenuation" which means they will compensate for irregular electrical supply (e.g. surges). See GAIN.

ATTENUATION COFFEICIENT The rate at which average power decreases with distance.

ATTENUATION EQUALIZER Any device inserted in a transmission line or amplifier circuit to improve the shape of its frequency response.

ATTENUATOR A device to reduce signal amplitude by a known amount without introducing distortion.

ATTIX See AT&T INTEREXCHANGE COMPANY.

ATTND Attendant. (What else?)

ATTO Atto means one quintillion, which is 10 to the minus 18. See also FEMTO, which is 10 to the minus 15.

ATTRIBUTES Under MS-DOS, attributes are characteristics you can assign to a file using the ATTRIB command. You can identify a file as read-only (meaning others can't change it, but can read it) and/or as a file you want to archive when using the BACKUP, RESTORE, and XCOPY commands. The command to make a file read only is typically

ATTRIB +R filename

By using the ATTRIB command to make a file "read only," you also make it impossible to erase the file from your disk. If you want to remove the "read only" protection, i.e. make the file "read and write, the command is

ATTRIB -R filename

AUDIBLE INDICATION CONTROL Three fancy words for the ability to turn up or down the bell or beeper on your PBX attendant console.

AUDIBLE RING A sound sent from the called party's switch to inform the calling party that the called line is being rung. A long explanation for a bell or buzzer that tells you it's for you.

AUDIBLE RINGING TONE The information tone sent back to the calling telephone subscriber as an indication that the called line is being rung.

AUDIO Sound you hear which may be converted to electrical signals for transmission. A human being who hasn't had his ears blown by listening to a Sony Walkman or a ghetto blaster can hear sounds from about 15 to 20,000 hertz.

AUDIO FREQUENCY The band of frequencies (approximately 20 hertz to 15 kilohertz) that can be heard by the normal human ear.

AUDIO FREQUENCIES Those frequencies which the human ear can detect (usually in the range of 20 to 20,000 hertz). Only those from 300 to 3,000 hertz are transmitted through the phone, which is why the phone doesn't sound "Hi-Fi."

AUDIO MENU Options spoken by a voice processing system. The user can choose what he wants done by simply choosing a menu option by hitting a touchtone on his phone or speaking a word or two. Computer or voice processing software can be organized in two basic ways — menu-driven and non-menu driven. Menu-driven programs are easier for users to use, but they can only present as many options as can be reasonably spoken in a few seconds. Audio menus are typically played to callers in automated attendant/voice messaging, voice response and transaction processing applications. See also MENU and PROMPTS.

AUDIO MESSAGING INTERCHANGE SPECIFICATION AMIS. Issued in February 1990, AMIS is a series of standards aimed at addressing the problem of how voice messaging systems produced by different vendors can network or inter-network. Before AMIS, systems from different vendors could not exchange voice messages. AMIS deals only with the interaction between two systems for the purpose of exchange voice messages. It does not describe the user interface to a voice messaging system, specify how to implement AMIS in a particular systems or limit the features a vendor may implement.

AMIS is really two specifications. One, called AMIS-Digital, is based on completely digital interaction between two voice messaging systems. All the control information and the voice message itself, is conveyed between systems in digital form. By contrast, the AMIS-Analog specification calls for the use of DTMF tones to convey control information and transmission of the message itself is in analog form. AMIS was discussed in detail in the October 1990 issue of Business Communications Review. AMIS specifications are available from Hartfield Associates, Boulder CO. 303-442-5395.

AUDIO RESPONSE UNIT A device which translates computer output into spoken voice. Let's say you dial a computer and it said "If you want the weather in Chicago, push 123, then it would give you the weather. But that weather would be "spoken" by an audio response unit. Here's a slightly more technical explanation: An audio response unit is a device that provides synthesized voice responses to dual-tone multi-frequency signaling input. These devices process calls based on the caller's input, information received from a host data base, and information carried with the incoming call (e.g., time of day). ARUs are used to increase the number of information calls handled and to provide consistent quality in information retrieval. See also AUDIOTEX and INTERACTIVE VOICE RESPONSE.

AUDIOGRAPHICS The technology which allows sound and visual images to be transmitted simultaneously. According to AT&T, audiographics generally refers to single frame or slow frame visual images as opposed to continuous frame image transmission (e.g. television). Audiographic transmission is often used to teach or train people in remote locations from an educational institution or business training center, saving travel and housing expense.

AUDIOTEX A generic term for interactive voice response equipment and services. Audiotex is to voice what on-line data processing is to data terminals. The idea is you call a phone number. A machine answers, presenting you with several options, "Push 1 for information on Plays, Push 2 for information on movies, Push 3 for information on Museums." If you push 2, the machine may come back, "Push 1 for movies on the south side of town, Push 2 for movies on the north side of town, etc." See also INFORMATION CENTER MAILBOX.

AUDIOTEXT A different, and less preferred, spelling of AUDIOTEX. See AUDIOTEX.

AUDITORY PATTERN RECOGNITION Auditory pattern recognition is the ability to recognize spoken words.

AUDIT To conduct an independent review and examination of system records and activities in order to test the adequacy and effectiveness of data security and data integrity procedures, to ensure compliance with established policy and operational procedures, and to recommend any necessary changes.

AUDIT TRAIL A record of all the events that occur when users request and use specific resources. An audit trail gives you the ability to trace who did what and who was responsible for what. An audit trail is a chronological record of system activities that is sufficient to enable the reconstruction, review, and examination of the sequence of environments and activities surrounding or leading to an operation, a procedure or an event in a transaction from its inception to final results. Audit trail may apply to information in an automated information system, to the routing of messages in a communications system, or to material exchange transactions, such as in financial audit trails.

AUDITING An AT&T ISDN term for the monitoring of the status of either the network or the ISDN set.

AUGER A type of drill bit typically used to make large, deep holes for passing wire or cable through wood.

AUI Autonomous Unit Interface or Attachment Unit Interface. Most commonly used in reference to the 15 pin D type connector and cables used to connect single and multiple channel equipment in an Ethernet transceiver.

AURAL Relating to the sense of hearing.

AUTHENTICATE To establish, usually by challenge and response, that a transmission attempt is authorized and valid. To verify the identity of a user, device, or other entity in a computer system, or to verify the integrity of data that have been stored, transmitted, or otherwise exposed to possible unauthorized modification. A challenge given by voice or electrical means to attest to the authenticity of a message or transmission.

AUTHENTICATION The process whereby a user or information source proves they are who they claim to be.

AUTHORING Authoring is the process of using multimedia applications to create multimedia materials for others to view. Multimedia authoring uses many tools, from the more familiar text editor or desktop publishing application, to tools for capturing and manipulating video images or editing audio files. Authors might include specialized creators of training, sales, or corporate appplications such as insurance claims processing. Or, they might be creators of everyday business communications like voice-annotated email. Over time, everyone involved in business communications will probably have some level of multimedia authoring capability.

AUTHORIZED AGENT Also called Authorized Sales Agent. A term chosen by some of the Bell operating companies to refer to companies which sell their network services on commission. Some of these companies have specific industry knowledge and have written specialized software. The idea is to work with businesses to arm them with the absolute best package of telecommunications hardware, software and services.

AUTHORIZED BANDWIDTH The necessary bandwidth required for transmission and reception of intelligence. This defintion does not include allowance for transmitter drift or Dopler shift.

AUTHORIZED FREQUENCY A frequency that is allocated and assigned by an authority to a specific user for a specific purpose.

AUTHORIZATION Think of charging things on your MasterCard, Visa, or American Express card. If the store cannot authorize the amount of your purchase, your Visa card will not allow you to make the purchase. Authorization is needed for many long distance calls, especially those made using credit cards, telephone company calling card, etc. Authorization is done by the operator's computer checking with the remote validation database service. See BVA, BVS and VALIDATION.

AUTHORIZATION CODE A code in numbers and/or letters employed by a user to gain access to a system or service. If you are making a call out on a restricted line, the PBX will ask you for an authorization code. If you have one, your call will go through. If not, your call will be denied (i.e. not go through). Authorization codes come in various flavors. Some can be used for making long distance calls. Some can be used also for international calls, etc. See AUTHORIZED USER.

AUTHORIZED USER A person, firm, corporation or any other legal entity authorized by the provider of the service to use the service being provided.

AUTO ADJUST An AT&T ISDN term. The automatic setting of the baud rate. The baud rate is automatically set through the use of the AT portion of the command line. The speed of the computer is determined from the A and the parity is determined from the combination of the A and T. For this reason, it is not necessary to set speed and parity parameters for the ISDN set.

AUTO ANSWER The capability of a terminal, a modem or a computer to answer an incoming call and to set up a data connection without anyone being there.

AUTO BAUD Automatic speed recognition. The ability of a device to adapt to the data rate of a companion device at the other end of the link.

AUTO BAUD DETECT See AUTO BAUD.

AUTO BUSY REDIAL A feature of a phone or phone system where the phone has the ability to keep trying a busy number until answered. The circuit actually recognizes the busy tone, hangs up, and dials again. One of the greatest time-savers ever invented.

AUTO DIAL A feature of phone systems and modems which allows them to dial a long phone number (usually long distance) by punching fewer buttons than there are numbers to dial. One button auto dial on electronic phones is very common these days. Most communications software programs will allow you to auto dial a string of 35 to 40 digits, which you may need if you're dialing into a long distance company.

AUTO DIAL AUTO ANSWER A modem feature. Auto Dial lets you dial a phone number through your modem, using your personal computer or data terminal keyboard. Auto Answer permits the modem to automatically answer the incoming call without anybody having to be there.

AUTO DIALER See AUTOMATIC DIALER.

AUTO FAX TONE Also called CNG, or Calling Tone. This tone is the sound produced by virtually all Group 3 fax machines when they dial another fax machine. CNG is a medium pitch tone (1100 Hz) that lasts 1/2 second and repeats every 3 1/2 seconds. A FAX machine will produce CNG for about 45 seconds after its dials. See also CNG.

AUTO LINE FEED An instruction in a communications program which causes the program to perform a Line Fee (LF) when you hit a carriage return or the "Enter" key.

AUTO RECOGNITION A term used in file conversion in which your conversion software figures out by itself in what form the original file was — WordPerfect 5.0, Word 6.0, Wordstar 5.5 etc. See also AUTO STYLING.

AUTO SELECTION TOOL An imaging term. A tool that selects an entire area within a specified range of color values around a selected pixel.

AUTO SENSING See AUTO STYLING.

AUTO START A standby electrical power system that starts up when the normal supply of commercial power fails.

AUTO STREAM An AT&T ISDN term. The method of data flow in which both channels between the ISDN set and the application are in use simultaneously.

AUTO STYLING Auto styling is a term we found in a database conversion software program. What it means is that the program looks at the data in a field and determines from that data if the field is a numeric, character or memo, etc. The problem with auto styling is that it's frequently wrong. For example, it might check one field, find all numbers and decide it's a numeric field. Such a field might be a zip code, which actually is normally a character field. One reason why you might want you zip code to be a character field is that character fields are set left. Numeric fields are set right. (They line up at the decimal point.) Another name for auto styling is auto sensing.

AUTOBAUDING The process by which the terminal software determines the line speed on a dial-up line.

AUTODIAL BUTTON An Autodial button on a phone provides one-touch dialing of outside numbers, intercom numbers, or feature codes.

AUTODIN The worldwide data communications network of the U.S. Department of Defense. Acronym for "AUTOmatic DIgital Network."

AUTOEXEC.BAT The first file executed after a PC is started (i.e. cold or warm booted). AUTOmatic EXECute BATch file contains a list of MS-DOS commands which are executed by your PC once your machine is turned on. Essentially, once you've started your MS-DOS computer, your asks "OK, you're got me started now. What would you like me to do?" Your AUTOEXEC.BAT contains these answers. Your AUTOEXEC.BAT file allows you to tailor the MS-DOS operating system to your needs, for example, setting the PATH command. The AUTOEXEC.BAT file must be installed in the root directory of your boot disk — either hard or floppy disk (the place your computer looks for the initial MS-DOS commands).

AUTOMATED ATTENDANT A device which is connected to a PBX. When a call comes in, this device answers it and says something like, "Thanks for calling the ABC Company. If you know the extension number you'd like, pushbutton that extension now and you'll be transferred. If you don't know it, pushbutton "0" (zero) and the live operator will come on. Or, wait a few seconds and the operator will come on anyway." Sometimes the automated attendant might give you other options, such as, "dial 3" for a directory. Automated attendants are very new. They are connected also to voice mail systems ("I'm not here. Leave a message for me."). Some people react well to automated attendants. Others don't. A good rule to remember is before you spring an automated attendant on your people/customers/subscribers, etc., let them know. Train them a little. Ease them into it. They'll probably react more favorably than if it comes as a complete surprise. The first impression is rarely forgotten, so try to make it a good experience for the caller. See also DIAL BY NAME.

AUTOMATED COIN TOLL SERVICE ACTS. In the old days, operators handled routine toll calls by counting the sound of coins hitting the box, checking prices, putting calls through, figuring and collecting overtime charges, etc. ACTS does all this automatically. It figures charges, tells those charges by digitized computerized voice to the customer, counts the coins as they are deposited and then sets up the call.

AUTOMATED INTERCEPT CALL COMPLETION AINTCC. A new feature of Northern Telecom's central offices. The AINTCC feature provides options for — connecting a caller automatically to an intercepted number after hearing an announcement, or — connecting a caller to an intercepted number without an announcement.

Not using an announcement makes the number change transparent to the

---

caller. The called (intercepted) party then has the option of informing the caller of the number change.

AUTOMATED MARITIME TELECOMMUNICATIONS SYSTEM An automatic, integrated and interconnected maritime communications system serving ship stations on specified inland and coastal waters of the United States.

AUTOMATED RADIO A radio with the capability for automatically controlled operation by electronic devices that requires little or no operator intervention.

AUTOMATED TACTICAL COMMAND AND CONTROL SYSTEM A command and control system or part thereof which manipulates the movement of information from source to user without intervention. Automated execution of a decision without human intervention is not mandatory.

AUTOMATIC BUTTON RESTORATION When the telephone handset of a multi-line instrument (typically a 1A2 multi-line key set) is placed back in its cradle, the line button being used automatically "pops" back up. Conversely, when a user picks up the handset, he must always push down a line button to make a call. Most phones with this feature can be disabled, so the buttons stay down when the handset sits on the cradle. A twist of a single screw inside the instrument will usually solve the aggravation of the automatic button restoration. Some people like automatic button restoration because it saves a user from accidentally barging into someone else's call. This was a much greater problem with 1A2 key systems. It no longer is a problem with most electronic key systems since they usually extend the user automatic privacy once they get on a call so no one else can barge in, even if they want to.

AUTOMATIC CALL DISTRIBUTOR ACD. A specialized phone system used for handling many incoming calls. Once used only by airlines, rent-a-car companies, mail order companies, hotels, etc., it is now used by any company that has many incoming calls (e.g. order taking, dispatching of service technicians, taxis, railroads, help desks answering technical questions, etc.). There are very few large companies today that don't have at least one ACD. One ACD belongs to General Electric and is used specifically for answering calls regarding the home appliances and equipment they sell.

An ACD performs four functions. 1. It will recognize and answer an incoming call. 2. It will look in its database for instructions on what to do with that call. 3. Based on these instructions, it will send the call to a recording that "somebody will be with you soon, please don't hang up!" or to a voice response unit (VRU). 4. It will send the call to an agent as soon as that operator has completed his/her previous call, and/or the caller has heard the canned message.

The term Automatic Call Distributor comes from distributing the incoming calls in some logical pattern to a group of operators. That pattern might be Uniform (to distribute the work uniformly) or it may be Top-down (the same agents in the same order get the calls and are kept busy. The ones on the top are kept busier than the ones on the bottom). Or it may be Speciality Routing, where the calls are routed to answerers who are most likely to be able to help the caller the most. Distributing calls logically is the function most people associate with an ACD, though it's not the most important.

The management information which the ACD produces is much more valuable. This information is of three sorts: 1. The arrival of incoming calls (when, how many, which lines, from where, etc.) 2. How many callers were put on hold, asked to wait and didn't. This is called information on ABANDONED CALLS. This information is very important for staffing, buying lines from the phone company, figuring what level of service to provide to the customer and what different levels of service (how long for people to answer the phone) might cost. And 3. Information on the origination of the call. That information will typically include ANI (Automatic Number Identification — picking up the calling number and DNIS (Direct Number Identification Service) picking up the called number. Knowing the ANI allows the ACD and its associated computer to look up the caller's record and thus offer the caller much faster service. Knowing the DNIS may allow the ACD to route the caller to particular agent or keep track of the success of various advertising campaigns. Ad agencies will routinely run the same ad in different towns using different 800 phone numbers. Picking up which number was called identifies which TV station the ad ran on.

The seven definitions that follow the definition "ACD" show some of the features which newer ACDs have. See also 800 SERVICE, ACD and AUTOMATIC CALL SEQUENCER.

AUTOMATIC CALLING UNIT ACU. A device that places a telephone call on behalf of a computer.

AUTOMATIC CALL INTERCEPT A feature of a Rolm ACD. This feature automatically forwards calls to an attendant if the dialed number is not installed or out of order. It can also intercept an attempted trunk call that is in violation of a Class of Service restriction. Automatic Call Intercept will also recall the attendant after a predetermined period of offhook inactivity (e.g. flash or hold).

AUTOMATIC CALL SEQUENCER A device for handling incoming calls. Typically it performs three functions. 1. It answers an incoming call, gives the caller a message, and puts them on "Hold." 2. It signals the agent (the person who will answer the call) which call on which line to answer. Typically, the call which it signals to be answered is the call which has been on "hold" the longest. 3. It provides management information, such as how many abandoned calls there were, how long the longest person was kept on hold, how long the average "on hold" was, etc.

There are three types of devices which handle incoming calls. The least expensive is the Automatic Call Sequencer which is traditionally used with key systems. It differs from Uniform Call Distributors (UCDs) and Automatic Call Distributors (ACDs) in that it has no internal switching mechanism and does not affect the call in any way. It simply recommends which call should be picked up and keeps statistical information on the progress of calls. A more expensive type of device is the UCD.

The most full-featured and expensive is the ACD. Distinctions between ACDs and UCDs and/or PBXs with features called UCDs and ACDs are blurring as UCDs get more sophisticated. The main difference, as we understand it, is that a UCD offers fewer options for routing an incoming call and answering calls in any particular order. ACDs typically produce the most detailed management information reports. One company also makes something called an Electronic Call Distributor. It is essentially an automatic call distributor.

AUTOMATIC CALLBACK When a caller dials another internal extension and finds it busy, the caller dials some digits on his phone or presses a special "automatic callback" button. When the person he's calling hangs up, the phone system rings his number and the number of the original caller and the phone system automatically connects the two together. This feature saves a lot of time by automatically retrying the call until the extension is free. See also CAMP ON. Wouldn't it be nice if they had this feature on long distance calls?

AUTOMATIC CIRCUIT ASSURANCE ACA is a PBX feature that helps you find bad trunks. The PBX keeps records of calls of very short and very long duration. If these calls exceed a certain parameter, the attendant is notified. The logic is that a lot of very short calls or one very long call may suggest that a trunk is hung, broken or out of order. The attendant can then physically dial into that trunk and check it.

AUTOMATIC COVER LETTER In a fax transmission, an automatic cover letter allows the user to automatically attach a cover letter to the document being sent. This is especially convenient when sending material directly from your PC.

AUTOMATIC DIALER or AUTODIALER A device which allows the user to dial pre-programmed telephone numbers by pushing one or two buttons. Sometimes referred to as a "repertory" dialer. Dialers can be bought as a separate device and added to a phone, however, today most telephone sets are outfitted with autodialers. There are four basic measures of an automatic dialer's efficiency.

1. What's the longest number it will dial automatically? This is important because using some of AT&T's long distance competitors requires dialing lots of numbers, with lots of pauses. 2. How many numbers will it dial? Some people like to have a dialer which dials hundreds of numbers. Others like a small one, just for their most frequently called numbers. 3. Will the dialer recognize dial tone? This is important because using a long distance

company or dialing through a PBX requires one to recognize consecutive dial tones. 4. Can you "chain" dial? In other words, can you hit one speed dial button after another and have the machine dial through a complex network and throw in authorization codes, etc.?

AUTOMATIC DIALING See SPEED DIALING.

AUTOMATIC DIRECTORY PROPAGATION In electronic mail, automatic directory propagation is the ability to update addresses automatically in one domain after manually entering address changes in another domain, whether on the same LAN or another LAN connected by a gateway. In general, automatic directory propagation can be peer-to-peer, where changes in any post office are sent to all other post offices, or master-to-slave, where changes in the master post office are sent to the slaves, but changes in the slave post office do not go to the master.

AUTOMATIC EQUALIZATION The process of compensating for distortion of data communications signals over an analog circuit.

AUTOMATIC EXCHANGE A term for a central office which automatically and electronically switches calls between subscribers without using an operator. Not a common term.

AUTOMATIC FACILITIES TEST SYSTEM AFACTS is a Rolm CBX feature. It is an automatic testing system for identifying faulty tie and central office trunks. AFACTS can pinpoint faulty trunks and generate exception and summary reports.

AUTOMATIC FALLBACK A modem's ability to negotiate an appropriate data rate with the modem on the other end of the link, depending on line quality. For example, if two 2400 baud modems can not pass data at 2400 baud, they would "fall back" to 1200 baud automatically in order to transmit data without excessive errors.

AUTOMATIC FREQUENCY CONTROL A circuit in a radio receiver which automatically brings the tuning units of the set into resonance with a wave which is partially tuned in.

AUTOMATIC GAIN This is an electronic circuit which automatically increases the volume when someone is speaking quietly and drops it when someone is speaking loudly. The idea is to keep the transmitted signal even. Most tape recorders, for example, have automatic gain circuits. This allows them to pick up voices of people in a room, even though the volume of each person's conversation arriving at the tape recorder is different. The problem with automatic gain circuits is they're always looking for something to amplify. Such that when it's quiet (and meant to be) the automatic gain circuit will also try and amplify the ambient noise in the room — to keep the sound level constant. All professionally recorded tapes are done on tape reorders with manual volume controls.

AUTOMATIC HOLD — STATION or INTERCOM When a user is

having a conversation and receives another call, he may press the button to answer that new call. The call he was on originally is automatically put on hold.

AUTOMATIC IDENTIFIED OUTWARD DIALING AIOD. The toll calls placed by all extensions on the telephone systems are automatically recorded. This information allows bills to be sent, long distance lines to be chosen, etc. See CALL ACCOUNTING, CALL DETAIL RECORDING, SMDR and AIOD.

AUTOMATIC LEVEL CONTROL ALC. A control system that adjusts the incoming signal to a predetermined level. Somewhat similar to automatic gain control. See AUTOMATIC GAIN CONTROL.

AUTOMATIC LIGHT CONTROL ALC. Vidicon camera control which automatically adjusts the target voltage to compensate for variations in light levels. See also AUTOMATIC GAIN.

AUTOMATIC LINE HOLD A PBX feature. As long as a phone does not go "on-hook," activation of various line pushbuttons will automatically place the first line on hold without the use of special "hold" button.

AUTOMATIC LINK ESTABLISHMENT ALE. The capability of an HF radio station to contact, or initiate a circuit, between itself and another specified radio station, without operator assistance and usually under computer control. ALE techniques include automatic signaling, selective calling, and automatic handshaking. Other automatic techniques that are related to ALE are channel scanning and selection, Link Quality Analysis (LQA), polling, sounding, message store and forward, address protection, and anti-spoofing.

AUTOMATIC MESSAGE ACCOUNTING AMA. 1. Service mark of AT&T. A system which records and documents billing information for long distance calls made by a corporate subscriber. The calls must be made to billable destinations to be documented. The information recorded is generally either 20% of all information (CCSA networks) or 100% of the information (all others). 2. The network functionality that measures, collects, formats, and outputs subscriber network-usage data to upstream billing OSs and other OSs (Operations Systems). Definition from Bellcore.

AUTOMATIC MESSAGE SWITCHING A technique of sending messages to their appropriate destination through information contained in the message itself — typically in its "address."

AUTOMATIC NETWORK DIALING A Rolm feature which is said to simplify on-network calling among multiple business locations by providing single-step dialing for private networks and a single numbering/dialing plan.

AUTOMATIC NUMBER IDENTIFICATION ANI. Being able to recognize the phone number of the person calling you. You must have equipment at your office. And the network must have the ability to send the calling number to you. For a much longer explanation, see ANI, CALLER ID, CLASS, ISDN and System Signaling 7.

AUTOMATIC OVERFLOW TO DDD Toll calls jump to expensive direct distance dialed calls, when all lower cost FX, WATS lines, etc. are busy.

AUTOMATIC PHONE RELOCATION The Automatic Phone Relocation feature now available on some phone systems allows a telephone to retain its personal and system programming when it is reconnected to another physical location.

AUTOMATIC PRIVACY When someone is speaking on a phone line or on an intercom, this feature ensures no one else can accidentally or deliberately butt into that conversation. If you did, however, want somebody else to come into the conversation (for example, someone to provide some additional information), there's usually another feature called Privacy Release. By pushing this button on the phone, other people who have the same extension button or intercom button on their phones can then push their buttons and join the conversation. Or you can bring them into your conversation by dialing them in. Most modern key systems come with Automatic Privacy. Many people don't like it, especially those who live in small offices. Some newer phone systems are coming standard without it. And you have to program it in, if you want it.

AUTOMATIC PROGRAM LOAD APL is a PBX feature that allows it to load its own software into RAM from a local device such as a hard disk or a floppy disk. All this takes place automatically without human intervention. APL is an important feature since it often determines how fast a PBX can get back into service after some sort of failure — usually a failure in commercial power.

AUTOMATIC PROTECTION SWITCHING Switching architecture designed for SONET to perform error protection and network managment from any point on the signal path.

AUTOMATIC QUEUING Queuing is exactly as it sounds. Something you want is being used. So you get placed in line for that device. There are two types of queuing — automatic and manual. Manual is when you're put in queue by a person, for example an operator. Automatic is when you're put in queue by a machine, for example a PBX aided by its software.

AUTOMATIC RECALL A PBX feature which returns a call to the PBX attendant (or alerts the attendant) if a call extended to a telephone is not answered within a pre-set period of time. The most logical time is three rings, or 18 seconds. This feature allows the attendant to give the caller some information, take a message or connect the caller to someone else. Most hotel switches have this feature. And when the call doesn't get answered, the switch sends it back to the operator. The sad thing is that the hotel operator is usually so busy, he/she keeps you waiting another 20 or 30 seconds, irritating you.

100

AUTOMATIC RECOVERY Your telephone system dies — typically because its power is cut off. Once the power comes on, instructions in the machine direct it to reload its software so that within minutes the system can be back and running normally. Those "instructions" are normally not affected by power drops.

AUTOMATIC RINGDOWN TIE TRUNK A direct path signaling facility to a distant phone. Signaling happens automatically when you lift the receiver on either phone. See also MANUAL RINGDOWN TIE TRUNK.

AUTOMATIC ROLLBACK A feature of the Transaction Tracking System (TTS) that returns a database on a Novell NetWare local area network to its original state. When a network running under TTS fails during a transaction, the database is "rolled back" to its most recent complete state. This prevents the database from being corrupted by the incomplete transaction.

AUTOMATIC ROUTE SELECTION Your phone system automatically chooses the least cost way of sending a long distance call. See LEAST COST ROUTING and ALTERNATE ROUTING.

AUTOMATIC SCHEDULED TESTING AST. A method of testing switched access service (Feature Groups B, C, and D) where the customer provides remote office test lines and 105 test lines with associated responders or their functions' equivalent; consists of monthly loss and C-message noise tests and annual balance test.

AUTOMATIC SECURE VOICE COMMUNICATIONS NETWORK AUTOSEVOCOM. A worldwide, switched, secure voice network developed to fulfill DoD long-haul, secure voice needs.

AUTOMATIC SEND/RECEIVE ASR. A data device in which the transmitting thing is different from the receiving part, thus enabling the device to receive calls and transmit them simultaneously. See ASR for a different definition. We're not sure precisely which one is right. Both could be.

AUTOMATIC SEQUENTIAL CONNECTION A service feature provided by a data service to connect automatically, in a predetermined sequence, the terminals at each of a set of specified addresses to a single terminal at a specified address.

AUTOMATIC SPEED MATCHING The ability of an asynchronous modem to automatically determine whether it is expected to communicate at 300, 1200 or 2400 bps.

AUTOMATIC TIME-OUT ON UNCOMPLETED CALL A PBX feature. If a phone stays "off-hook" without dialing for a predetermined time interval, or stays connected to a busy signal longer than the predetermined time interval, the intercom switching equipment will automatically connect this phone to intercept.

AUTOMATIC TOLL TICKETING A system which makes a record of the

NEWTON'S TELECOM DICTIONARY

calling phone number, the called number, the time of day, the length of the call, etc. and then generates an instant phone bill for that call. Often used in hotel/motels.

AUTOMATIC TRAFFIC OVERLOAD PROTECTION ATOP. A Rolm feature defined as a dynamic form of line-load control, which automatically denies a dial tone during those periods when the Rolm CBX may become overloaded. One wonders why someone would create this feature.

AUTOMATIC VOICE NETWORK AUTOVON. The principal long-haul, unsecure voice communications network within the Defense Communications System.

AUTOMATIC VOLUME CONTROL A circuit in a radio receiver; automatically maintains various received transmissions at approximately the same volume.

AUTOMATIC WAKEUP The capability for the user to schedule a wake-up call to a predetermined telephone number, either one time or or daily.

AUTOMATIC WAKEUP SERVICE The guest or the operator dials into a machine which records a request for a guest wakeup call the following morning. The auto wakeup machine is a glorified, programmable auto-dial answering machine. The machine is said to save hotels money and make wakeup calls more reliable, and certainly more anonymous.

AUTOSCALING A drawing feature that automatically adjusts the axis units of a graph to the minimum and maximum numerical values of a set of data.

AUTOSEARCH See RECORDER.

AUTOSEVOCOM The AUTOmatic SEcure VOce COMmunications system of the U.S. Department of Defense. A worldwide, switched, secure voice network developed to fulfill DoD long-haul, secure voice needs.

AUTOTIMED RECALL When a user places a call on hold and forgets about it, Autotimed Recall will ring that user or the receptionist after a predetermined time. That time is usually programmable. It shouldn't be longer than 30 seconds, otherwise your customers, sitting endlessly on your eternity hold, will go nuts and go elsewhere.

AUTOTIMED TRANSFER This telephone system feature switches unanswered incoming calls to a backup answering position after a predetermined (usually adjustable) interval of time.

AUTOVON AUTOmatic VOice Network. The principal long-haul, unsecure voice communications network within the Defense Communications System.

AUXILIARY EQUIPMENT See also PERIPHERAL DEVICE or APPLICATIONS PROCESSOR.

AUXILIARY EQUIPMENT ACCESS The ability of a telephone system

NEWTON'S TELECOM DICTIONARY

to interface with (i.e. talk to) auxiliary equipment such as a paging system or dial dictation system.

AUXILIARY LINE A telephone trunk in addition to the main number you rent from the phone company. Phone systems are often equipped for calls to hunt from a busy main number to one or more auxiliary lines (Incoming Service Group, or ISG). For example, The Telecom Library's main number is 212-691-8215. But The Telecom Library also has 8216, 8217, 8218 and several unmarked or coded trunks. These are auxiliary lines and they don't receive their own billing or listing from the phone company. Sometimes, people have single line private lines which "appear" on their phone and no one else's. Sometimes they call these auxiliary lines. Sometimes these are called private lines.

AUXILIARY NETWORK ADDRESS In IBM parlance, in ACF/VTM, any network address except the main network address, assigned to a logical unit which is capable of having parallel sessions.

AUXILIARY POWER An alternate source of electric power, serving as backup for the primary power at the station main bus or prescribed sub-bus. An off-line unit provides electrical isolation between the primary power and the critical technical load; an on-line unit does not. These are government defintions: A Class A power source is primary power source; i.e., a source that assures an essentially continuous supply of power. Types of auxiliary power service include: Class B: a standby power plant to cover extended outages (days); Class C: a quick-start (10 to 60 seconds) unit to cover short-term outages (hours); Class D: an uninterruptible (no-break) unit using stored energy to provide continuous power within specified voltage and frequency tolerances.

AUXILIARY RINGER This is a separate external telephone ringer or bell. It can be programmed to ring when a line or a telephone, or both ring; or, when Night Service is turned on.

AUXILIARY STORAGE A mass storage device capable of holding a larger amount of information than the main memory (i.e. RAM) of the computer or telephone system, but with slower access time. For example — magnetic tape, floppy disks, etc.

AUTOVON The AUTOmatic VOice Network used worldwide by the US Department of Defense. The system includes conferencing and secure voice communications (scrambling), among other features.

AVAILABLE In automatic call distribution language, an agent state, between calls, when an agent, having finished the previous transaction, returns to accept the next inbound caller. See also AVAILABILITY.

AVAILABILITY The amount of time a computer or a telephone system is available for processing transactions or telephone calls. Here's a more technical definition: The ratio of the total time a functional unit is capable of being used during a given interval to the length of the interval; e.g., if the unit

103

is capable of being used for 100 hours in a week, the availability is 100/168. Contrast this with the term Reliability, which is different. See RELIABILITY.

AVALANCHE PHOTO DIODE APD. A fiber optic transmission device. A light detector that generates an output current many times the light energy striking its face. A photodiode that shows gain in its output power compared to the optical power that it receives through avalanche multiplication (signal gain) of the current that flows through a photosensitive device. This type of diode is used in receivers requiring high light sensitivity. See APD.

AVALANCHING The process by which an electrical signal is multiplied within a device by electron impact ionization.

AVERAGE CUSTOMER ARRIVAL RATE Represents the number of entities (humans, packets, calls, etc.) reaching a queuing system in a unit of time. This average is denoted by the Greek letter lambda. One would prefer to know, if possible, the full distribution of the calls arriving.

AVERAGE LATENCY The time required for a disk to rotate one-half revolution.

AVERAGE PULSE DENSITY In T-1 bipolar transmissions, refers to the number of "1" pulses per "0" conditions and is usually tied to a maximum number of "0"s in a row (i.e., FCC Part 68 requires 12.5% pulse density and no more than 80 consecutive "0"s where as AT&T Pub 62411 uses a formula and no more than 15 consecutive "0"s).

AVC Automatic Volume Control. In radio it maintains constant sound level despite undesired differences in strength of incoming signal.

AVD Alternative Voice Data. See AVD CIRCUITS.

AVD CIRCUITS Alternate Voice Data Circuits. Telephone lines which have been electrically treated to handle both voice and data signals. Typically used on leased overseas circuits to save money.

AVERAGE CALL DURATION Divide the total number of minutes of conversation by the number of conversations. Bingo, that's your average call duration.

AVERAGE HOLDING TIME The sum of the lengths (in minutes or seconds) of all phone calls during the busiest hour of the day divided by the number of calls. There are two definitions. The one above refers to average speaking time (it's the more common one). There's a second definition for "average holding time." This refers to how long each call was on hold, and thus not speaking. This second definition is typically found in the automatic call distribution business (ACD). Check before you do your calculations.

AVERAGE TRANSFER DELAY Average time between the arrival of a packet to a station interface and its complete delivery to the destination station.

AVOIDABLE COSTS A wonderful concept used by the regulated telephone industry. It refers to those costs which would be avoided (i.e. not incurred) if the service were not offered. Examples of costs to avoid are maintenance, taxes, labor, and other direct costs. The concept of Avoidable Costs is to allow the phone industry the justification to price a competitive service very low.

AVOX A code name for Northern Telecom's "dumb" (i.e. programmable) switch which it intends to release in the North America some time in mid 1992.

AVP A Northern Telecom word for Associated Voice Port.

AVP-L A Northern Telecom word for Associated Voice Port and Line.

AWC Area-Wide Centrex.

AWG American Wire Gauge. Standard measuring gauge for non-ferrous conductors (i.e. non-iron and non-steel). AWG covers copper, aluminum, and other conductors. Gauge is a measure of the diameter of the conductor. Also known as the Brown and Sharpe (B&S) Wire Gauge. A method of measuring the thickness of cable. The AWG numbering system is backwards: The higher the AWG number the thinner the wire. For example, heavy industrial wiring may be No. 2. Homes are typically wired with No. 12 or No. 14. Telephone systems typically use No. 22, No. 24 or No. 26. The thicker the wire, the more current it can carry further. The thicker the wire, the less resistance the current will encounter and therefore the longer it will travel. You need thicker phone cabling when your phones are further away. Some vendors save money by installing systems with thin wire. Make sure you specify.

AXIAL RATIO Of a wave having elliptical polarization, the ratio of the major axis to the minor axis of the ellipse described by the tip of the electric field vector.

AXIAL RAY A ray that travels along the axis of an optical fiber.

AXIAL SLAB INTERFEROMETRY Synonym for Slab Interferometry.

AXIS The center of an optical fiber.

AZIMUTH The horizontal angle which the radiating lobe of an antenna makes in angular degrees, in a clockwise direction, from a north-south line in the northern hemisphere. In the southern hemisphere, the reference is the south-north line. Azimuth actually involves a lot more than antennas. For example, it covers the alignment of a recording head in a tape recorder.

B

B The local wireline cellular carrier. In one of its less intelligent decisions, the Federal Communications Commission decided to issue two cellular franchises in each city of the United States. They gave one to the local phone company and one to a competitor. This duopoly has naturally meant little real price competition. And perhaps one day, the FCC will issue other licenses and the price of cellular phone calls will drop dramatically. Meantime, the "A" carrier on your cellular phone is the local wireline carrier. And the "B" is the other one.

B BATTERY A section of a phone system POWER SUPPLY that provides unfiltered Direct Current, for operating relays and various other components. Typically 20 volts. See A BATTERY.

B CHANNEL A "bearer" channel is a fundamental component of ISDN interfaces. It carries 64,000 bits per seconds in either direction, is circuit switched and should be able to carry either voice or data. Whether it does or not depends on how your local telephone company has tariffed its ISDN service. See BASIC RATE INTERFACE (BRI) and ISDN.

B CONNECTOR A commonly-used wire-splicing device consisting of a flexible plastic sleeve over a toothed metal cylinder that bites through insulation when crimped with a plier or special tool. It is about one inch long and can hold three or four wires. A gel-filled version is available for installation in damp or humid areas.

B-911 Basic 911. B-911 is a centralized emergency reporting system which may have many features but which does NOT provide ALI (Automatic Location Information) to the 911 operator. In most cases, it does not provide ANI (Automatic Number Identification) either. B-911 provides a common emergency response number and relies on Emergency Hold and Forced Disconnect to maintain effective service.

B-CDMA Broadband Code Division Multiple Access.

B-CRYPT A symmetric cryptographic algorithm designed by British Telecom.

B-DCS Broadband Digital Cross-connect System. B-DCS is a generic term for an electronic digital cross-connect system capable of cross-connecting signals at or above the DS3 rate.

B-ISDN Broadband ISDN. Normal ISDN tends to assume all "conversations" are in chunks of 64 Kbps. CCITT recommendation I.113 [45] defines Broadband as "a service or system requiring transmission channels capable of supporting (transmission) rates greater than the primary rate." Thus, broadband ISDN is a new concept in information transfer, although exactly what it is isn't clear yet. It could assume information comes in chunks as large as 150-million bits per second. In another CCITT recommendation (I.121 [47]), the CCITT presents an overview of what it sees as B-ISDN capabilities:

"B-ISDN supports switched, semi-permanent and permanent point-to-point and point-to-multipoint connections and provides on demand, reserved and permanent services. Connections in B-ISDN support both circuit mode and packet mode services of a mono- and/or multi-media type and of connectionless or connection-oriented nature and in a bidirectional or unidirectional configuration. A B-ISDN will contain intelligent capabilities for the purpose of providing advanced service characteristics, supporting powerful operation and maintenance tools, network control and management." According to the latest news, CCITT is to decide on an international standard for B-ISDN by 1996.

Bellcore says that "National and international standards bodies have made the Asynchronous Transfer Mode (ATM) the target solution for providing the flexibility required by B-ISDN. ATM provides a common platorm capable of suporting both broadband and narrow-band services ... The physical layer-transmission standard for B-ISDN is the Synchronous Optical Network (SONET), also known as the Synchronous Digital Hierarchy (SDH). See N-ISDN and SONET."

B3ZS Bipolar 3-Zero Substitution.

B8ZS Binary 8 Zero Substitution. A technique used to accommodate the ones density requirement for digital T-carrier facilities in the public network, while allowing 64 Kbps clear data per channel. Rather than inserting a one for every seven consecutive zeroes, B8ZS inserts two violations of the bipolar line encoding technique for digital transmission links.

BABBLE Just what it sounds like — crosstalk from several interfering communications circuits or channels.

BABBLING TRIBUTARY "A station that continuously transmits meaningless messages," as defined by John McNamara, of DEC and author of "Local Area Networks, an introduction to the technology." Some people might argue this was another word for Harry Newton, the author who didn't know when to stop and wanted to make this dictionary the most comprehensive telecom dictionary ever.

BABT British Approvals Board for Telecommunications.

BACK BOARD A piece of plywood mounted on a wall. Phone equipment is mounted on the plywood. It is more efficient to first mount phone equipment on plywood in the service bay, test it out while it's convenient and diagnostic tools are handy. Then take the phone equipment and the back board (which typically consists of the KSU, power supply and 66-blocks) and install them on the customer's premises. This "pre-installation" makes enormous sense — economically and reliably. Sadly, few installation companies do it.

BACK HAUL When a communications channel takes traffic beyond its destination and hauls it back — all because it is cheaper to go that route instead of going directly.

BACK TO BACK CHANNEL BANK The connection of voice frequency and signaling leads between channel banks to allow dropping (i.e. removing) and inserting (i.e. adding) of channels.

BACK TO BACK CONNECTION A connection between the output of a transmitting device and the input of an associated receiving device. When used for equipment measurements or testing purposes, this eliminates the effects of the transmission channel or medium.

BACK UP SERVER A program or device that copies files so at least two up-to-date copies always exist.

BACK-END Database server functions and procedures for manipulating data on a network.

BACKBONE The backbone is the part of the communications network which carries the heaviest traffic. The backbone is also that part of a network which joins LANs together — either inside a building or across a city or the country. LANs are connected to the backbone via bridges and/or routers and the backbone serves as a communications highway for LAN-to-LAN traffic. The backbone is one basis for design of the overall network service. The backbone may be the more permanent part of the network. A backbone in a LAN, a WAN, or a combination of both dedicated to providing connectivity between subnetworks in an enterprise-wide network.

BACKBONE CLOSET The closet in a building where the backbone cable is terminated and cross connected to either horizontal distribution cable or other backbone cable.

BACKBONE NETWORK Transmission facility, or arrangement of such facilities, designed to connect lower speed channels or clusters of dispersed users or devices.

BACKBONE SUBSYSTEM See RISER SUBSYSTEM.

BACKBONE TO HORIZONTAL CROSS-CONNECT BHC. Point of interconnection between backbone wiring and horizontal wiring.

BACKBONE WIRING The physical/electrical interconnections between telecommunications closets and equipment rooms. Cross-Connect hardware and cabling in the Main and Intermediate Cross-Connects are considered part of the backbone wiring.

BACKFEED PULL A method used to pull cable into a conduit or a duct liner when the cable is long or when placing cable into controlled environmental vaults, central offices, or under streets. With this method, the cable pays off its reel at an intermediate manhole and is first pulled in one direction. The remaining cable is then removed from the reel, laid on the ground, and then pulled in the opposite direction.

BACKFILLING To designate memory on an expanded memory card and make it available for use as conventional memory.

BACKGROUND See BACKGROUND PROCESSING.

BACKGROUND MUSIC This feature allows music to be played through speakers in the ceiling and/or through speakers in each telephone, throughout the office, or office-by-office, or selectively. Background music is typically played through paging speakers. In fact, the two — paging and background music — often go hand-in-hand. When you want to page someone, the music turns off automatically and comes back on when the paging is over. The same thing happens on airplanes. Background music is said to motivate workers, often into shutting it off.

BACKGROUND NOISE The noise you hear when nothing else is being transmitted.

BACKGROUND PROCESSING The automatic execution of lower priority computer programs when higher priority programs are not using the computer's resources. A higher priority task would be completing calls. A lower priority task would be running diagnostics. Some PBXs have this feature. Some insist on running their diagnostics even though they are choked with calls. The smarter ones tone down their diagnostics when they get busier, which makes sense.

BACKGROUND PROGRAM A low priority program operating automatically when a higher priority (foreground) program is not using the computer system's resources.

BACKGROUND TASK A secondary job performed while the user is performing a primary task. For example, many network servers will carry out the duties of the network (like controlling who is talking to whom) in the background, while at the same time the user is running his own foreground application (like word processing). See also BACKGROUND PROCESSING.

BACKOFF When a device attempts to transmit data and it finds trouble, the sending device must try again. It may not try again immediately. It may "back off" for a little time so the trouble on the line can be cleared. This happens with LANs. For example, an earlier attempt to transmit may have resulted in a collision in a CSMA/CD (Carrier Sense Multiple Access/Collision Detection) Local Area Network (LAN). So the device "backs off," waits a little and then tries again. How long it waits is determined by preset protocols.

BACKOFF ALGORITHM The formula built into a contention local area network used after collision by the media access controller to determine when to try again to get back onto the LAN. See also BACKOFF.

BACKPLANE The high-speed communications line to which individual components of a modern electronic system are connected. For example, all the extensions of a PBX are connected to line cards (circuit boards) which slide into the PBX's cage. At the rear of the PBX cage, there are several connectors. Each of these connectors is plugged into the PBX's Backplane. Also called a Backplane Bus. This backplane bus is typically very high speed, since it carries many conversations, address information and considerable signaling. These days, the backplane bus is typically a time division multiplexed line — somewhat like a train with many cars, each representing a time slice of another conversation. The backplane's capacity determines the overall capacity of the switch.

BACKPRESSURE Propagation effects in a communications network of hop-by-hop flow control to upstream nodes.

BACKSCATTERING 1. In fiber optics, the scattering of light into a direction opposite to the original one. 2. Radio wave propagation in which the direction of the incident and scattered waves resolved along a reference direction (usually horizontal) are oppositely directed. A signal received by backscattering is often referred to as "backscatter."

BACKSLASH Also called a virgule, the backslash key achieved fame because Microsoft used it to bring distinguish between subdirectories in MS-DOS.

BACKUP A copy of computer data on an external storage medium, such as a floppy disk or tape. Computers and telephone systems (which are computers) are notoriously unreliable. They glitch and lose data for all sorts of unusual and impossible-to-predict reasons. Thus the necessity for backups. The theory is when (not "if") a glitch will occur and the PBX's data base will disappear off the face of the earth. If this happens, you have a backup and you simply retrieve the back-up file, load it up and, presto, you're back live.

Only information changed in the original (since the backup was made) is thus lost. Backups save time in restoring the system after a loss. Most modern PBXs work with a data base and other extensive customized instructions the user loads in. Most PBX users forget to make and keep backups of their PBX data. They expect their vendor to make backups, but he rarely does. This carelessness costs weeks of aggravation, as the PBX's data base and instruction set is manually (and painfully) put back together.

The method by which backups are maintained is also important. The medium should clearly be reliable, i.e. the best quality magnetic medium. The method of backing up is also important. For example, a streaming tape backup is less reliable than a file-by-file backup. In a streaming backup, the backup medium simply captures the original data one bit after another in one long stream. In a file-by-file backup, the data moves over in logical segments — command files, data files, etc. Streaming backups will work if their data is placed back on the same precise device from which they were originally taken. But, if they are placed on a different device (even though the same model number, etc.), they may barf because the tape assumes bad sectors are in the same place. This will probably not be true. Streaming tape backup devices are less expensive to buy and much faster to use. Avoid them.

BACKUP LINK A resilient (fault tolerant) link which is not used until the primary link fails.

BACKWARD CHANNEL In data transmission, a secondary channel whose direction of transmission is constrained to be opposite to that of the primary (or forward) channel. The direction of transmission in the backward channel is restricted by the control interchange circuit that controls the direction of transmission in the primary channel. The channel of a data circuit that passes data in a direction opposite to that of its associated forward channel. The backward channel is usually used for transmission of supervisory, acknowledgement, or error-control signals. The direction of flow of these signals is opposite to that in which information is being transferred. The band-width of this channel is usually less than that of the forward channel; i.e., the information channel.

BACKWARD LEARNING Routing algorithm based on assumed symmetric network conditions. Source node assumes best route to given destination is via neighbor node that was on best route from destination to source.

BACKWARD RECOVERY The reconstruction of an earlier version of a file by using a newer version of data recorded in a journal.

BACKWARD SIGNAL A signal sent in the direction from the called to the calling station, or from the original communications sink to the original communications source. The backward signal is usually sent in the backward channel and usually consists of supervisory, acknowledgement, or error control signals.

BACKWARD SUPERVISION The use of supervisory sequences from a secondary to a primary station.

BAD BLOCK A defective unit on a storage medium that software cannot read or write.

BAD LINE KEY When the PX attendant encounters a bad trunk, he/she pushes this button on the console, automatically flagging the trunk for later checking and repair.

BAD LINE REPORTING Automatically reports a poor connection without interrupting the current call.

BAD SECTORS Defective areas on a hard or soft disk. The MS-DOS FORMAT command locks out bad sectors so they are never used. Other operating systems have similar commands.

BAFFLE A partition used with a loud speaker to prevent air vibrations from the back of the diaphragm from cancelling out the vibrations from the front of the diaphragm. Particularly valuable in the reproduction of bass notes.

BAG PHONE A slang expression for a transportable cellular phone whose characteristics are 3 WATT output, heavy weight (for a portable), and a bag with a handle. Bag phones are not designed for carrying around. They are designed to carry from one place to another and use at that place for serious conversations. Their big "plus" is that they give off five times as much power as your typical pocket handheld cellular phone. This makes them useful for semi-permanent "installation" in places like construction sites, etc. They are as powerful as a car phone.

BAKELITE An obsolete insulating material of the phenolic (synthetic resin) group. Jewelry made of bakelite is now particularly prized.

BALANCE To equalize load or current between parts or elements of a telephone line or circuit. Balancing helps get the best out of a phone line. In more technical terms, balancing a lne is to adjust the impedance of circuits and balance networks to achieve specified return loss objectives at junctions of two-wire and four-wire circuits.

BALANCED CIRCUIT Telephone circuit in which the two conductors are electrically balanced to each other and to the ground. A balanced electrical interface generally allows data to be transmitted over longer distances than does an unbalanced circuit. See BALANCE.

BALANCED CONFIGURATION Point-to-point network configuration in HDLC with two combined stations.

BALANCED ELECTRICAL INTERFACE An electrical interface on which each circuit consists of a separate pair of wires. A balanced electrical interface generally allows data to be transmitted over longer distances than does an unbalanced electrical interface.

BALANCED LINE A transmission line which has two conductors and a ground. When the voltages of the two conductors are equal in strength but opposite in direction, then you have a balanced line.

BALANCED MODE TRANSMISSION Data transmission with information conveyed by differences in voltages on two circuits to minimize effects of induced voltages.

BALANCED MODULATOR An amplitude modulating circuit that suppresses the carrier signal, producing an output consisting only of upper and lower sidebands.

BALANCED RETURN LOSS A measure of the effectiveness with which a balancing network simulates the impedance of the two-wire circuit at a hybrid coil. More generally, a measure of the degree of balance between two impedances connected to two conjugate sides of a hybrid set, network, or junction.

BALANCED-TO-GROUND In a two-conductor circuit, a balanced-to-ground ground condition exists where the impedance-to-ground on one wire equals the impedance-to-ground on the other. This is the preferred condition for decent data communications.

BALANCING NETWORK A network used in a set ending a four-wire circuit to match the impedance of the two-wire circuit. 2. Sometimes employed as a synonym for balun.

BALCONY A little platform up a telephone pole where people can work or sleep safely.

BALUN BALanced/UNbalanced. An impedance matching transformer. Baluns are small, passive devices that convert the impedance of coaxial cable so that its signal can run on twisted-pair wiring. They are used often so that IBM 3270-type terminals, which traditionally require coaxial cable connection to their host computer, can run off twisted-pair. Works for some types of protocols and not for others. There is often some performance degradation with baluns. And the signal cannot run as far on twisted wire as it can on coaxial cable.

BAND 1. Usually refers to AT&T's WATS Bands. AT&T WATS service is organized into circles of increasing distance from the caller. Each circle or BAND (also called SERVICE AREA), costs more per minute. But within each service area, each call costs the same per minute, even though the distances the calls travel might be different. There are typically six interstate bands covering the US and several intrastate bands (depending on how large the state is) which a customer can buy. The word "band" was invented by AT&T Communications (originally known as AT&T Long Lines) when it introduced WATS service. Recently it changed the word "band" to "Service Area." Nobody knows why. See WATS. 2. BAND can also refer to the range of frequencies between two defined limits. For example, the band of frequencies able to be heard by the human ear ranges between 30 to 25,000 hertz. The ear can hear a band (or more typically bandwidth) of about 25,000 hertz. See also POSTALIZED.

BAND SPLITTER Time-division multiplexer (TDM) or frequency division multiplexer (FDM) that divides the composite bandwidth into independent and narrower channels.

BAND-STOP FILTER A device that bars passage of frequencies within its designed range(s), and allows passage of higher or lower frequencies, or both.

BAND, CITIZENS One of two bands used for low power radio transmissions in the United States — either 26.965 to 27.225 megahertz or 462.55 to 469.95 megahertz. Citizens band radio is not allowed in many countries, even some civilized countries. In some countries they use different frequencies. CB radios, in the United States, are limited by FCC rule to four WATTS of power, which gives each CB radio a range of several miles. Some naughty people boost their CBs with external power. The author of this dictionary has actually spoken to Australia while driving on the Santa Monica Freeway in Los Angeles. See also CB.

BAND, FREQUENCY The frequencies between the upper and lower bands. See also BAND. Here is the accepted explanation of "bands:"

Below 300 Hertz	ELF	Extremely low frequency
300 — 3,000 Hertz	ILF	Infra Low Frequency
3 — 30 kHz	VLF	Very Low Frequency
30 — 300 kHz	LF	Low Frequency
300 — 3,000 kHz	MF	Medium Frequency
3 — 30 MHz	HF	High Frequency
30 — 300 MHz	VHF	Very High Frequency
300 — 3,000 MHz	UHF	Ultra High Frequency
3 — 30GHz	SHF	Super High Frequency
30 — 300GHz	EHF	Extremely High Frequency
300 — 3,000 GHz	THF	Tremendously High Frequency

BANDED RATE A price range for regulated telephone service that has a minimum floor and maximum ceiling. The minimum covers the cost of service; the maximum is the rate filed in the price list.

BANDMARKING A continuous circumferential band applied to an insulated conductor at regular intervals for identification.

BANDPASS The range of frequencies that a channel will transmit (i.e. pass through) without excessive attenuation.

BANDPASS FILTER A device which transmits a band of frequencies and blocks or absorbs all other frequencies not in the specified band. Often used in frequency division multiplexing to separate one conversation from many.

BANDPASS LIMITER A device that imposes hard limiting on a signal and contains a filter that suppresses the unwanted products of the limiting process.

BANDWIDTH The range of electrical frequencies a device can handle. The amount of bandwidth a channel is capable of carrying tells you what kinds of communications can be carried on it. A wide band circuit, for example, can carry a TV channel. A wide band circuit capable of providing one video channel can also provide 1,200 voice telephone channels.

BANDWIDTH COMPRESSION A technique to reduce the bandwidth needed to transmit a given amount of information. Bandwidth compression is used typically in "picture type" transmissions — such as facsimile or video-conferencing. For example, early facsimile machines scanned each bit of the document to be sent and sent a YES or NO (if there was material in that spot or not). More modern machines simply skip over all the blank spaces and transmit a message to the receiving facsimile machine when to start printing dots again. (A facsimile "picture" is made up of tiny dots, similar to printing photos in a magazine.) Today, bandwidth compression is used to transmit voice, video and data. There are many techniques, few of which are standard. The key, of course, is that if you're going to compress a "conversation" at one end, you must "de-compress" it at the other end. Thus, in every bandwidth compressed conversation there must be two sets of equipment, one at each end.

BANDWIDTH LIMITED OPERATION The condition prevailing when the system bandwidth, rather than the amplitude (or power) of the received signal, limits performance. The condition is reached when the system distorts the shape of the signal waveform beyond specified limits. For linear systems, bandwith-limited operation is equivalent to distortion-limited operation.

BANDWIDTH ON DEMAND Just what it sounds like. You want two 56 Kbps circuits this moment for a videoconference. No problem. Use one of the newer pieces of telecommunications equipment and "dial up" the bandwidth you need. An example of such a piece of equipment is an inverse multiplexer. Uses for bandwidth on demand include videoconferencing, LAN interconnection and disaster recovery. Bandwidth on demand is typically only for digital circuits and it's typically carved out via a T-1 permanently connected from a customer's premises to a long distance carrier's central office, also called a POP — Point of Presence.

BANK SWITCHING A technique for sequentially reading page frames in a PC's expanded memory. The 64K page frames are brought into the upper memory block from an expanded memory card, then read and swapped back to the card so that the next 64K page frame can be brought in.

BAR CODE A bunch of lines of varying width printed on something. The bar code is designed to be read optically by some data capturing device. Bar codes are turning up on letters. They are read by image scanning devices in the post office and allegedly help the mails move faster. Bar codes are on most things you buy now in supermarkets. By scanning those bar codes at the checkout counter, the supermarket knows what's being sold and not being sold. And presumably the supermarket, or its computer, can order supplies to keep the supermarket stocked with goods that are selling and not re-order those which aren't.

BARBIE, JANE The electronic "Voice With A Smile" on most telephone company intercept recordings. Ms. Barbie does her work for the Audichron Company of Atlanta, GA.

BARE WIRE An electrical conductor having no covering or insulation.

BARGE-IN Interrupting a call in progress.

BARGE-OUT Leaving a call in progress without notice.

BARIUM FERRITE A type of magnetic particle used in some recording media including Floptical diskettes.

BARREL An imaging term. Distortion that swells an image in the middle, narrows it at the top and the bottom.

BARREL CONNECTOR This connector is a cylindrical (barrel-shaped) connector used to splice together two lengths of thick Ethernet coaxial cable.

BARREL CONTACT A term in cabling. A barrel contact is an insulation displacement type contact consisting of a slotted tube that cuts the insulation when the wire is inserted.

BARREL DISTORTION When a screen is distorted — with the top, bottom and sides pushing outwards (like a beer barrel) — the screen is said to be suffering barrel distortion.

BARTON Enos Barton once said he was "disgusted" when told that it would be possible to send conversation along a wire. He later co-founded (with Elisha GRAY) the Western Electric Company, which became AT&T's manufacturing subsidiary and was once the largest electrical equipment manufacturer in the US. In addition to phones, the company made sewing machines, typewriters, movie sound equipment, radio station gear, radar systems and guided missle parts. See also GRAYBAR.

BASE ADDRESS The first address in a series of addresses in memory, often used to describe the beginning of a network interface card's I/O space.

BASE LOAD In trunk forecasting, an amount of telephone traffic measuring during a certain defined time. See BASE PERIOD.

BASE PERIOD In trunk forecasting, a time span of consecutive study during which a base load is determined.

BASE-1 SERVICE An MCI definition. MCI Service providing customers network management capabilities by allowing them to operate and administer their own telecommunications usage.

BASEBAND A form of modulation in which signals are pulsed directly on the transmission medium without frequency division. Local area networks as a rule, fall into two categories — broadband and baseband. The simpler, cheaper and less sophisticated of the two is baseband. In baseband LANs, the entire bandwidth (capacity) of the LAN cable is used to transmit a single digital signal. In broadband networks, the capacity of the cable is divided into many channels, which can transmit many simultaneous signals. While a baseband channel can only transmit one signal and that signal is usually digital, a broadband LAN can transmit video, voice and data simultaneously by splitting the signals on that cable using frequency division multiplexing. The electronics of a baseband LAN are simpler than a broadband LAN. The digital signals from the sending devices are put directly onto the cable without modulation of any kind. Only one signal is transmitted at a time. Multiple "simultaneous" transmissions can be achieved by a technique called time division multiplexing (see multiplexing). In contrast, broadband networks (which typically run on coaxial cable) need more complex electronics to decipher and pick off the various signals they transmit. Attached devices on a broadband network require modems to transmit. Attached devices to baseband networks do not.

Baseband LANs typically work with one high speed channel, which all the attached devices — printers, computers, databases — share. They share it by using it in turns — for example, passing a "token" to the next device. That token entitles the device with the token to transmit. IBM's LAN is a token ring passing local area network. Another way of sharing the baseband LAN is that each device, when it is ready to transmit, simply transmits into the channel and waits for a reply. If it doesn't receive a reply, it retransmits. Thus there are two main network or baseband access control schemes — Token Ring Passing and CSMA/CD. See also CSMA/CD, BROADBAND and LOCAL AREA NETWORKS.

BASEBAND MODEM A modem which does not apply a complex modulation scheme to the data before transmission, but which applies the digital input (or a simple transformation of it) to the transmission channel. This technique can only be used when a very wide bandwidth is available. It and only operates over short distances where signal amplification is not necessary. Sometimes called a limited distance or short-haul modem.

BASEBAND SIGNALING Transmission of a digital or analog signal at its original frequencies, i.e., a signal in its original form, not changed by modulation.

BASEBOARD A term used in voice processing to mean a printed circuit board without any daughterboards attached.

BASEBOARD RACEWAY A floor distribution method in which metal or wood channels, containing cables, run along the baseboards of the building. The front panel of the baseboard channel is removable, and outlets may be placed at any point along the channel.

BASELINE 1. The line from which a graph is drawn. The base line is the X axis on vertically oriented graphs, the Y axis on horizontal bar graphs, or the line representing zero if the data contains both positive and negative numbers.

2. The imaginary line extending through a font and representing the line on which characters are aligned for printing. In conventional, alphanumeric fonts, the baseline is usually defined as the imaginary line touching the bottom of uppercase characters.

BASIC Beginners All-purpose Symbolic Instruction Code. A programming language. BASIC is an easy easy language to learn. It's worth learning. Not all "Basics" are the same. A sort of de facto standard is Microsoft Basic. If you're wish to learn some programming, we recommend you begin with the latest version of Microsoft's QuickBasic. We've tried it. We're very impressed with it.

BASIC BUDGET SERVICE An inexpensive local phone service often restricted to people with limited incomes; may not include any outgoing calls.

BASIC CALL A call between two users that does not require Advanced

NEWTON'S TELECOM DICTIONARY

Intelligent Network Release 1 features (e.g. a POTS call). Definition from Bellcore.

BASIC CALL STATE MODEL BCSM. An abstraction of the ASC call processing activities for a basic two-party call. The BCSM is split into Originating and Terminating BCSMs.

BASIC EXCHANGE TELECOMMUNICATIONS RADIO SERVICE BETRS. A service that can extend telephone service to rural areas by replacing the local loop with radio communications, sharing the UHF and VHF common carrier and private radio frequencies.

BASIC MODE LINK CONTROL Control of data links by use of the control characters of the 7-bit character set for information processing interchange as given in ISO Standard 646-1983 and CCITT Recommedation V.3-1972.

BASIC RATE INTERFACE BRI. There are two "interfaces" in ISDN: BRI and PRI. In BRI, you get two bearer B-channels at 64 kilobits per second and a data D-channel at 16 kilobits per second. The bearer B-channels are designed for PCM voice, videoconferencing, group 4 facsimile machines, or whatever you can squeeze into 64,000 bits per second full duplex. The data D-channel is for bringing in information about incoming calls and taking out information about outgoing calls. It is also for access to slow-speed data networks, like videotex, packet switched networks, etc. One BRI standard is the "U" interface, which uses two wires. Another BRI standard is the "T" interface which uses four wires. See ISDN.

BASIC SERVICE A telephone company service limited to providing local switching and transmission. Basic Service does not include equipment. The term Basic Service is unclear and varies between telephone companies and data communications service providers. Check.

BASIC SERVICE ELEMENTS BSEs. An Open Network Architecture term. BSE's are services which value-added companies could get from their phone company. BSEs are optional basic network functions that are not required for an ESP to have a BSA, but when combined with BSEs can offer additional features and services. Most BSEs allow an ESP to offer enhanced services to their customers. BSEs fall into four general categories: Switching, where call routing, call management and processing are required; Signaling, for applications like remote alarm monitoring and meter reading; Transmission, where dedicated bandwidth or bit rate is allocated to a customer application; and Network Management, where a customer is given the ability to monitor network performance and reallocate certain capabilities. The selection of available BSEs is an ongoing process, with new arrangements being developed. ANI, Audiotext "Dial-It" Services, and Message Waiting Notification are all examples of BSEs. See OPEN NETWORK ARCHITECTURE.

BASIC SERVING ARRANGEMENT BSA. Under ONA, a BSA is the

basic interconnection access arrangement which offers a customer access to the public network and provides for the selection of available Basic Service Elements. It includes an ESP access link, the features and functions associated with that access link at the central office serving the ESP and/or other offices, and the transport (dedicated or switched) within the network that completes the connection from the ESP to the central office serving its customers or to capabilities associated with the customer's complementary network services. Each component may have a number of categories of network characteristics. Within these categories of network characteristics are alternatives from among which the customer must choose. Examples of BSA components are ESP access link, transport and/or usage. See OPEN NETWORK ARCHITECTURE.

BATCH FILE A text file for personal computers with the extension .BAT that contains MS-DOS commands. When you type the name of the file, DOS carries out the commands in the file. Many computer programs are installed on you hard disk or loaded using batch files, as are many LAN operating systems. Batch files simplify life. If used wisely, you can save yourself typing things over and over again. It also means you don't have to remember all the commands to do something, just the first one. Batch files can be used to load other programs or to change the parameters of your computer. Anything that can be done from DOS (and some things that can't) can be done from a batch file. Norton Utilities has an enhanced version of DOS's Batch file.

BATCH PROCESSING There are two basic types of data processing. One is batch processing. Also called deferred time processing and off-line processing. Batch processing occurs where everything relating to one complete job — such as preparing this week's payroll — is bunched together and transmitted for processing (locally, in the same building or long distance, across the country), usually by the same computer and under the same application program. Batch processing does not permit interaction between the program and the user once the program has been read (i.e. fed into) the computer. In batch processing with telecommunications (i.e. sending the task to be done over the phone line), network response time is not critical, since no one is sitting in front of a screen waiting for a response. On the other hand, accuracy of communications is very critical, since no one is sitting in front of a screen checking entries and responses.

The second type of processing is called INTERACTIVE or REAL TIME processing. Under this method of processing, a user sends in transactions and awaits a response from the distant computer before continuing. In this case, response time on the data communications facility is critical. Seconds count, especially if a customer is sitting at the other end of a voice call awaiting information on whether there's space on that airline flight, for example. See BATCH FILE.

BATCH FILE A batch file on a computer contains sequential instructions to

NEWTON'S TELECOM DICTIONARY

perform one task after another. Batch files on a MS-DOS machine are identified by the extension .BAT. When the MS-DOS operating system sees them, it recognizes the file and executes the instructions inside the file. DOS has a special (though limited) language for writing programs in. There are also programs for converting DOS batch files into .EXE or .COM files. This makes them run faster.

BATCH JOB FILE See BATCH FILE.

BATTERY All telephone systems work on DC (direct current). DC power is what you use to talk on. Often the DC power is called "talking battery." Most key systems and many PBXs plug directly into an AC on the wall, but that AC power is converted by a built-in power supply to the DC power the phone system needs. All central offices (public exchanges) used rechargeable lead acid batteries to drive them. These batteries perform several functions: 1. They provide the necessary power. 2. They serve as a filter to smooth out fluctuations in the commercial power and remove the "noise" that power often carries. 3. They provide necessary backup power should commercial power stop, as in a "blackout" or should it get very weak, as in a "brownout."

In short, "battery" is the term used to reference the DC power source of a telephone system. Often called "Talking Battery." 2. Storage battery used with central office switching systems and PBXs serving locations which cannot tolerate outages. Batteries serve the following purposes: Act as a filter across the generator or power rectifier output to smooth out the current and reduce noise; provide a cushion against periodic overloads exceeding the generator/rectifier capacity; supply emergency power for a limited time in event of commercial power failure. See also AC, AC POWER, BATTERY RESERVE and CENTRAL OFFICE BATTERY.

BATTERY BACKUP A battery which provides power to your phone system when the main AC power fails especially during blackouts and brownouts. Hospitals, brokerage companies, airlines and hotel reservation services must have battery backup because of the integral importance of their phone systems to their business.

BATTERY ELIMINATOR A device which has a rectifier and (hopefully) a filter. This device will convert AC power into the correct DC voltages necessary to drive a telephone system. Such a battery eliminator, or power supply, should deliver "clean" power, i.e. with little "noise" and of low impedance.

BATTERY RESERVE The capability of the fully charged battery cells to carry the central office power load imposed when commercial power fails and the primary power source (generators/rectifiers) is out of service. Properly described in terms of the number of hours the batteries can furnish operating power for dependent CO apparatus for a demand equal to that on the CO during its busy hour. A busy-hour reserve of eight hours is typical for a telephone office battery plant.

BAUD RATE A measure of transmission speed over an analog phone line — i.e. a common POTS line. (POTS stands for Plain Old Telephone Service).

120

Imagine that you want to send digital information (say from your computer) over a POTS phone line. You buy a modem. A modem is a device for converting digital on-off signals which your computer speaks to the analog, sine-wave signals your phone line speaks. For your modem to put data on your phone line means it must send out an analog sine wave (called the carrier signal) and change that carrier signal in line with the data it's sending. Baud rate measures the number of number of changes per second in that analog sine wave signal. According to Bell Labs, the most changes you can get out of a 3 KHz (3000 cycles per second) voice channel (which is what all voice channels are) is theoretically twice the bandwidth, or 6,000 baud.

Baud rate is often confused with bits per second, which is a transfer rate measuring exactly how many bits of computer data per second can be sent over a telephone line. You can get more data per second — i.e. more bits per second — on a voice channel than you can change the signal. You do this through the magic of coding techniques, such as phase-shift keying. Advanced coding techniques mean that more than one bit can be placed on a baud, so to speak. To take a common example, a 9600 bit per second modem is in reality a 2,400 baud modem with advanced coding such that four bits are impressed on each baud. The continuing development of newer and newer modems point to increasingly advanced coding techniques, bringing higher and higher bit per second speeds. My latest modem, for example, is 14,400 bits per second.

BAUDOT CODE The code set used in Telex Transmission, named for French telegrapher Emile Baudot (1845-1903) who invented it. Also known by the CCITT approved name, International Telegraph Alphabet 2. The Baudot code has only five bits, meaning that only 32 separate and distinct characters are possible from this code, i.e. 2 x 2 x 2 x 2 x 2 equals 32. By having one character called Letters (usually marked LTRS on the keyboard) which means "all the characters that follow are alphabetic characters," and having one other key called Figures (marked FIGS), meaning "all characters that follow are numerals or punctuation characters," the Baudot character set can represent 52 (26 x 2) printing characters. The characters "space," "carriage return," "line feed" and "blank" mean the same in either FIGS or LTRS. See also MORSE CODE and ASCII.

BAY A telephone industry term for the space between the vertical panels or mounting strips ("rails") of the rack. One rack may contain several bays. A bay is another place you put equipment.

BBS Bulletin Board System. Another term for an electronic bulletin board. Typically a PC, modem/s and communications bulletin board software attached to the end of one or more phone lines. Callers can call the BBS, read messages and download public domain software. TELECONNECT Magazine has a BBS. We call it our InfoBoard. It's open to our readers and friends. Its number is 212-989-4675. Settings to call this number are 8 bit, no parity, one stop bit, 2400 baud. The person who operates a BBS is called a SYSOP (pronounced "sis-op"). See also ELECTRONIC BULLETIN BOARD.

BCC 1. Bellcore Client Company. 2. Block Check Character. A control character appended to blocks in character-oriented protocols and used for figuring if the block was received in error. BCC is especially used in longitudinal and cyclic redundancy checking. As a packet (or in IBM jargon, a frame) is assembled for transmission, the bits are passed through an algorithm to come up with a BCC. When the packet is received at the other end, the receiving computer also runs the same algorithm. Both machines should come up with the same BCC. If they do, the transmission is correct and the receiving computer sends an ACK — a positive acknowledgement. If they don't, an error has occurred during transmission, and they don't have the same bits in the packet. The receiver transmits a signal (a NAK, for negative acknowledgement) that an error has occurred, and the sender retransmits the packet. This process goes on until the BCC checks.

BCD Binary Coded Decimal. A system of binary numbers where each digit of a number is represented by four bits. See BINARY.

BCM Bit Compression Multiplexer.

BDLC Buroughs Data Link Control, a bit oriented protocol.

BEACON A token ring frame sent by an adapter indicating that it has detected a serious ring problem, such as a broken cable or a MAU. An adapter sending such frames is said to be beaconing.

BEAM DIAMETER The distance between the diametrically opposed points on a plane perpendicular to the beam axis at which the irradiance is a specified fraction of the beam's peak irradiance. The term is most commonly applied to beams that are circular or nearly circular in cross-section.

BEAM DIVERGENCE 1. The increase in diameter with increase in distance along the beam axis from the appropriate aperture. 2. For beams that are circular or nearly circular in cross-section, the angle subtended by the far-field beam diameter. 3. For beams that are not circular or nearly circular in cross-section, for far-field angle subtended by two diametrically opposed points in a plane perpendicular to the beam axis, at which points the power density is a specified fraction of the beam's peak power density. Generally, for noncircular beams, only the maximum and minimum divergences (corresponding to the major and minor diameters of the far-field irradiance) need be specified.

BEAMSPLITTER A device for dividing an optical beam into two or more separate beams, often a partially reflecting mirror.

BEANS Telco-slang for B-connectors, which are about the size and shape of common beans.

BEAT FREQUENCY An old radio term: The frequency resulting when an oscillation of one frequency is "beat" or heterodyned against an oscillation of different frequency. The figure given is normally in cycles per second.

BEAT RECEPTION An old radio term. The resultant audible frequency when two sources of unequal undamped electrical oscillations of constant amplitude act simultaneously in the same circuit. See BEAT FREQUENCY.

BEATING The phenomenon in which two or more periodic quantities having slightly different frequencies produce a resultant having periodic variations in amplitude.

BECN Backward Explicit Congestion Notification. This bit notifies the user that congestion-avoidance procedures should be initiated for traffic in the opposite direction of the received frame. It indicates that the frames that the user transmits on this logical connection may encounter congested resources.

BED OF NAILS CORD A description of a type of alligator clip that attaches to the end of a craft test set, also called a butte set.

BEL A relative measurement, denoting a factor of ten change. Rarely used in practice; most measurements are in decibels (0.1 bel).

BELDEN A major manufacturer of communications cable. Belden is such a high quality manufacturer and has set many cabling standards that some many other manufacturers follow their specs.

BELL A bell in a telephone instrument rings when a 20 Hz signal of about 90 volts AC is applied to the subscriber loop. In contrast, the normal voltage applied to a subscriber loop and used for speaking and listening is 48 volts DC.

BELL 103 AT&T specification for a modem providing asynchronous originate/answer transmission at speeds up to 300 bits per second (300 baud). This is the most common standard for modems running with personal computers. Every dial service in the U.S. adheres to this standard. The second most common standard is Bell 212. See below.

BELL 201 AT&T specification for a modem providing synchronous data transmission at 2,400 bits per second.

BELL 202 AT&T specification for a modem providing asynchronous data transmission at speeds up to 1,800 bits per second. Requires four-wire line for full duplex transmission.

BELL 208 AT&T specification for a modem providing synchronous data transmission at speeds up to 4,800 bits per second.

BELL 209 AT&T specification for a modem providing synchronous data transmission at speeds up to 9,600 bits per second.

BELL 212 AT&T specification for a modem providing full duplex asynchronous or synchronous data transmission at speeds up to 1,200 bits per second on the voice dial-up phone network. This is the second most common standard for modems running with personal computers. The first is Bell 103.

BELL 43401 Bell Publication defining requirements for transmission over telco-supplied circuits that have dc continuity (that are metallic).

BELL ATLANTIC Formed as a holding company after the AT&T Divestiture. Includes Bell of Pennsylvania, C&P Telephone Companies of D.C., Maryland, Virginia, and West Virginia, Diamond State Telephone (Md.), New Jersey Bell and several Bell Atlantic business activities. Check out Bell Atlantic's logo. It has a wonderful, small wave in the "A" in Atlantic. Very charming. Very subtle.

BELL COMMUNICATIONS RESEARCH Bellcore. Formed at Divestiture to provide certain centralized services to the seven Regional Bell Holding Companies (RHCs) and their operating company subsidiaries. Also serves as a coordinating point for national security and emergency preparedness communications matters of the federal government. Bellcore does not work on customer premise equipment or other areas of potential competition among its owners — the seven Regional Bell Operating companies. Bellcore also works on standardizing methods by which customers of long distance companies will reach their favorite long distance companies. At time of writing, around 8,000 people worked at Bellcore, mostly in northern New Jersey. Bellcore has the unenviable task of trying to service the needs of the seven competitors, which own it. Its annual budget is around $1 billion, paid for by the seven Bell regional operating companies. It has been doing work on ISDN and common channel signaling standards. See also BELLCORE.

BELL COMPATIBLE A term sometimes applied to modems. A modem is said to be "Bell compatible" if it conforms to the technical specifications set forth by AT&T for the various devices, such as Bell 212.

BELL OPERATING COMPANY BOC. The 22 regulated telephone companies of the former Bell System, which was broken apart (the Divestiture of the Bell System) at midnight on December 31, 1983. At Divestiture, the Bell operating companies were grouped into seven Regional Holding Companies (RHCs). According to the terms of the Divestiture Agreement between the Federal Courts, the Federal Government and AT&T, the divested companies must limit their activities to local telephone services, directory service, customer premise equipment, cellular radio and any other ventures as the Federal Court may approve from time to time. See also REGIONAL BELL OPERATING COMPANY.

BELL SPEAK A term coined by Michael Marcus for insider jargon spoken by "real" telephone people — those who practiced pre-divestiture. Such old jargon is usually incomprehensible to anyone in today's telephone industry who is younger than 46.

BELL SYSTEM The entire AT&T organization prior to when it was broken up — at the end of 1984. The Bell System included Bell Labs, Long Lines, Western Electric and the 23 Bell operating companies.

BELLBOY A public paging system run by local Bell phone companies. The name survived for many years and only drew criticism in the middle to late seventies with the rise of the Women's Liberation movement. It's now not used. Shucks.

BELLCORE Bell Communications Research. Formed at Divestiture to provide certain centralized services to the seven Regional Bell Holding Companies (RBOCs) and their operating company subsidiaries. Also serves as a coordinating point for national security and emergency preparedness, and communications matters of the federal government. Bellcore does not work on customer premise equipment (e.g. the telephone set) or other areas of potential competition between its owners — the seven Regional Bell Operating Companies. It is a key player in the design of AIN — the Advanced Intelligent Network. You'll find many AIN definitions in this dictionary. You can acquire Bellcore documents from Bellcore — Document Registrar, 445 South Street, Room 2J-125, P.O. Box 1910, Morristown, NJ 07962-1910. Fax 201-829-5982. See also BELL COMMUNICATIONS RESEARCH.

BELLCORE AMA FORMAT BAF. The standard data format for AMA (Automatic Message Accounting) data to be delivered to the Revenue Accounting Office (RAO) in Advanced Intelligent Network Release 1.

BELLCORE MULTI-VENDOR INTERACTIONS MVI. The process for coordinating the efforts of Bellcore, the Bell Operating telephone companies and vendors to address technical issues associated with Advanced Intelligent Network.

BELLMAN-FORD-ALGORITHM Shortest-path routing algorithm that figures on number of hops in a route to find shortest-path spanning tree.

BELLSOUTH CORPORATION The largest regional Bell holding company formed at the Divestiture of AT&T. Includes Southern Bell and South Central Bell and several other BellSouth businesses. Revenues of Bellsouth were over $14.4 billion in 1992. It had 18 million access lines in service. It employs more than 96,000 people worldwide.

BELOW-THE-LINE Expenses incurred that are charged to shareholders of regulated operating telephone companies, not ratepayers.

BENCHMARK A standardized task to test the capabilities of various devices against each other for such measures as speed.

BEND LOSS A form of increased attenuation caused by allowing high-order signals to radiate from the side of the fiber. The two common types of bend losses are those occuring when the fiber is curved and microbends caused by small distortions of the fiber imposed by poor cabling techniques.

BENDING RADIUS The smallest bend which may be put into a cable under a stated pulling force. Bending radius affects size of bends in conduit, trays or ducts. It affects pulley size. It affects the size of openings at pull boxes where loops may form. Very critical in all aspects of cable laying, especially with under-carpet cabling and fiber optic cable.

BEP Back End Processor.

BER Bit Error Rate. The ratio of error bits to the total number of bits transmitted. If the BER gets too high, it might be worth while to go to a slower baud rate. Otherwise, you would spend more time retransmitting bad packets than getting good ones through. The theory is that the faster the speed of data transmission the more likelihood of error. This is not always so. But if you are getting lots of errors, the first — and easiest — step is to drop the transmission speed. See also BIT ERROR RATE.

BERNOULLI Daniel Bernoulli was the 18th century Swiss mathematician who first expressed the principle of fluid dynamics — the basis of Bernoulli "boxes" also called disk cartridges. A Bernoulli box uses both floppy and hard disk technologies. Bernoulli disks can hold up to 90 megabytes of data.

BERT Bit Error Rate Test, or Tester. A known pattern of bits is transmitted, and errors received are counted to figure the BER. The idea is to measure the quality of data transmission. The bit error rate is the ratio of received bits that are in error, relative to the number of bits received. Usually expressed in a power of 10. Sometimes called Block Error Rate Tester.

BETA 1. Refers to the final stages of development and testing before a product is released to market. "Alpha" is the term used when a product is in preliminary development). "Her baby is in beta," according to Peter Lewis of the New York Times, means she is expecting soon. In the software industry, beta has been known to last a year or more. Microsoft's Bill Gates has given the word "beta" a whole new meaning by having as many as 50,000 "beta testers" for his new Windows NT operating system. At this level, beta testing is no longer testing, it's marketing. And it's positively brilliant. See BETA TEST.

2. Business Equipment Trade Association (UK).

BETA TEST Typically the last step in the testing of a product before it is officially released. A beta test is often conducted with customers in their offices. Some customers pay for the equipment or software they get under a beta test; some don't. Some beta tests stay in (if they work). Some don't. Most products don't work when they're first introduced. So beta tests are a good idea. Unfortunately, most manufacturers don't do sufficient beta testing. They want to get their product to market before the competition does. This often means we now have two or three new products on the market, none of which work reliably or do exactly what they're meant to do. Our rule: always wait several months after a product is introduced before buying it. By then the major bugs will have been fixed. The test before the beta test is obviously called the Alpha. It isn't that common. See BETA.

BETRS Basic Exchange Telecommunications Radio Service. A service that can extend telephone service to rural areas by replacing the local loop with radio communications, sharing the UHF and VHF common carrier and private radio frequencies.

BEZEL The metal or plastic part — in short, the frame — that surrounds a cathode ray tube — a "boob" tube.

BHC Backbone to Horizontal Cross-connect. Point of interconnection between backbone wiring and horizontal wiring.

BI A Latin prefix meaning twice.

BIAS 1. A systemic deviation of a value from a reference value. 2. The amount by which the average of a set of values departs from a reference value.

3. An electrical, mechanical, magnetic, or other force field applied to a device to establish a reference level to operate the device. 4. Effect on telegraph signals produced by the electrical characteristics of the terminal equipment.

BIAS DISTORTION Distortion affecting a two-condition (binary) coding in which all the significant intervals corresponding to one of the two siginficant conditions have uniformly longer or shorter durations than the corresponding theoretical durations. The magnitude of the distortion is expressed in percent of a perfect unit pulse length.

BIAS GENERATOR A CBX printed circuit card that generates a signal that reduces idle channel noise for all coders installed in the CBX.

BIAS POTENTIAL The potential impressed on the grid of a vacuum tube to cause it to operate at the desired part of its characteristic curve.

BICONIC Fiber Optic Connector developed by AT&T.

BICONICAL ANTENNA An antenna consisting of two conical conductors having a common axis and vertex. Excitation occurs at the common vertex. If one of the cones is flattened into a plane, the antenna is called a discone.

BIDIRECTIONAL COUPLERS Fiber optic couplers that operate in the same way regardless of the direction light passes through them.

BIDIRECTIONAL PRINTING A typewriter always prints from left to right. So did the early computer printers. The newer computer printers will print from left to right, drop down a line, then print from right to left. This increases the printer's speed.

BIGAMY The only crime in which two rites make a wrong.

BIFURCATED ROUTING Routing that may split one traffic flow among multiple routes.

BILATERAL SYNCHRONIZATION A synchronization control system between exchanges A and B in which the clock at exchange A controls the received data at exchange B and the clock at exchange B controls the received data at exchange A. Normally implemented by deriving the receive timing from the incoming bit stream.

BILDSCHIRMTEXT German word for interactive videotex. The German Bundespost likes this service. But the German version isn't as successful as the French because the French gave away the videotex terminals. And the Germans didn't. Also, the French really encourage videotex entrepreneurs by giving a real piece of the action — 60% of the collected revenues.

BILL OF MATERIALS A list of specific types and amounts of direct materials expected to be used to produce a given job or quantity of output.

BILLBOARD ANTENNA A broadside antenna array with flat reflectors.

BILLED NUMBER SCREENING You (at home or your business) establish who can and cannot charge a call to your phone by making an agreement with your local telephone company to screen your calls. (e.g. Refusal of all collect call requests.)

BILLED TELEPHONE NUMBER BTN. The primary telephone number used for billing regardless of the number of telephone lines associated with that number.

BILLIBIT Someone's absolutely awful term for one billion bits. Also (and better) called a gigabit.

BILLING INCREMENT The increments of time in which the phone company (long distance or local) bills. Some services are measured and billed in one minute increments. Others are measured and billed in six or ten second increments. The billing increment is a major competitive weapon between long distance companies. Short billing increments become important to you, as a user, when your average calls are very short — for example, if you're making a lot of very short data calls (say for credit card authorizations).

BILLING MEDIA CONVERTER A Billing Media Converter, as made by the Cook division of Northern Telecom, provides a means of transporting Automatic Message Accounting (AMA) data from DMS-10 central offices to regional accounting offices with the physical transfer of magnetic tapes. The BMC is polled.

BILLING TELEPHONE NUMBER A Billing Telephone Number is the number to which calls to given location are billed. It is the seven-digit number with the area code followed by an alphanumeric code assigned by the local telephone company (e.g. NPA-NXX-XXXX).

BILLING VALIDATION SERVICE See BVA and BVS

BINARY Where only two values or states are possible for a particular condition, such as "ON" or "OFF" or "One" or "Zero." Binary is the way digital computers function because they can only represent things as "ON" or "OFF." This binary system contrasts with the "normal" way we write numbers — i.e. decimal. In decimal, every time you push the number one position to the left, it means you increase it by ten. For example, 100 is ten times the number 10. Computers don't work this way. They work with binary notation.

Every time you push the number one position to the right it means you double it. In binary, only two digits are used — the "0" (zero) and the "1" (the one). If you write the number 10101 in binary, and you want to figure it in decimal as we know it, here's how you do it. 1 is one thing; Zero x 2 = zero; 1 times 2 x 2 = 4; 0 x 2 x 2 x 2 = 0; 1 x 2 x 2 x 2 x 2 = 16. Therefore the total 10101 in binary = 1 + 0 + 4 + 0 + 16 = 21 in decimal.

Binary notation differs slightly from notation used in ASCII or EBCDIC. In ASCII and EBCDIC, the binary values are used for coding of individual characters or keys or symbols on keyboards or in computers. So each string of seven (as in ASCII) or eight (as in EBCDIC) ones and zeros is a unique value — but not a mathematical one.

ASCII uses a seven bit coding scheme. Thus, the maximum number of different things you can code using seven bits is 128, i.e. 2 x 2 x 2 x 2 x 2 x 2 x 2 = 128. The maximum number represented by a byte (8 bits) or the IBM EBCDIC coding system is 256. i.e. 2 x 2 x 2 x 2 x 2 x 2 x 2 x 2 = 256.

BINARY CODED DECIMAL BCD. A system of binary numbering that uses a 4-bit code to represent each decimal digit from 0 to 9 and multiple 4-bit patterns for higher numbers.

BINARY NOTATION Any notation that uses two different characters, usually the binary digits O and 1.

BINARY SYNCHRONOUS COMMUNICATIONS BISYNC or BSC. 1. In data transmission the synchronization of the transmitted characters by timing signals. The timing elements at the sending and receiving terminal define where one character ends and another begins. There are no start or stop elements in this form of transmission. 2. Also a uniform discipline or protocol for synchronized transmission of binary coded data using a set of control characters and control character sequences.

BINARY TO DECIMAL CONVERSION Conversion from base 2 to base 10. See BINARY.

BINARY TRANSFER A transfer between two computers from files that may not be text based information, and therefore, if sent as ASCII characters, would not be received properly. A Binary Transfer keeps the integrity of the data by sending it in some manner of Error Correcting Protocol such as SNA, or XMODEM.

BIND To set up a condition in a receiving device where it is unreceptive to receiving data it doesn't want.

BINDER A helically applied colored thread, yarn, or plastic ribbon used to confine and sometimes separate and identify groups of fibers or wires in a cable. Binders are usually used for holding assembled cable components in place.

BINDER GROUP A group of wires within a large cable that can be distinguished from other groups because it is wrapped with colored threads.

Normal telephone color-coding provides for only 25 pairs of wire, so binder groups allow multiple pairs of the same color wire to be in one cable. A 50-pair cable has blue and orange binder groups; a 75-pair cable has blue, orange, and green groups. Since several wire pairs have the same color markings, installers must be careful when stripping cable insulation so they do not destroy the binder threads.

BINDERY A Novell NetWare database containing definitions for entities such as users, groups, and workgroups. The bindery contains three components: objects, properties, and property data sets. Objects represent any physical or logical entity, including users, user groups, file servers, print servers, or any other entity given a name. Properties are the characteristics of each bindery object, including passwords, account restrictions, account balances, internetwork addresses, list of authorized clients, workgroups, and group members. Property data sets are values assigned to entities bindery properties.

BINDING POST A screw with a small nut. You take your wires and join them together on a binding post by wrapping them together around the screw and then tightening the nut on them. These days, 66-blocks have effectively replaced binding posts. 66-blocks are easier and faster to use.

BIOS Basic Input/Output System of desktop computers. The BIOS contains the buffers for sending information from a program to the actual hardware device the information should go to.

BIOSENORS Devices such as fingerprint readers and signature recognition systems.

BIP-N Bit Interleaved Parity N. A method of error monitoring. With even parity, an N bit code is generated by the transmitting equipment over a specified portion of the signal in such a manner that the first bit of the code provides even parity over the first bit of all N-bit sequences within the specified portion, etc. Even parity is generated by setting the BIP-N bits so that there are an even number of 1s in each of all N-bit sequences including the BIP-N.

BIPOLAR The predominant signaling method used for digital transmission services, such as DDS and T-1. The signal carrying the binary value alternates between positive and negative. Zero and one values are represented by the signal amplitude at either polarity, while no-value "spaces" are at zero amplitude.

BIPOLAR CODING The T carrier line coding system that inverts the polarity of alternate "one" bits.

BIPOLAR SIGNAL A signal having two polarities, both of which are not zero. It must have two-state or three-state binary coding scheme. It is usually symmetrical with respect to zero amplitude.

BIPOLAR VIOLATION The presence of two consecutive "one" bits of the same polarity on the T carrier line. See also BIPOLAR CODING.

BIRD A satellite.

BIRTHDAYS January 4, 1847 Thomas Edison born February 16, 1982 Michael Allen Newton born February 20, 1980 Claire Elizabeth Newton born February 22, 1956 Andy Moore born in Zanesville, OH March 3, 1847 Alexander Graham Bell born March 15, 1949 Gerry Friesen born April 27, 1791 Samuel Morse born May 11, 1948 International Communications Association born June 10, 1942 Harry Newton born in Sydney Australia June 13, 1961 TeleCommunications Association born June 25, 1952 Paula Friesen born June 27, 1968 Caterfone decision handed down by FCC July 4, 1943 Susan Newton born August 31, 1962 President Kennedy signed Communications Satellite Act September 12, 1948 Communications Managers Association December 10, William G. McGowan, founder of MCI

BIS The French term for "second" or "encore." It is used by the CCITT to designate the second in a family of related standards. "ter" designates the third in a family. See V SERIES.

BISDN Broadband ISDN. See ISDN.

BISTABLE TRIGGER CIRCUIT A trigger circuit that has two stable states.

BISYNC (pron. Bye-sink). BISYNChronous Transmission. A half-duplex, character-oriented, synchronous data communications transmission method originated by IBM in 1964. See SYNCHRONOUS.

BISYNCHRONOUS TRANSMISSION Also called BISYNC. A data character-oriented communications protocol developed by IBM for synchronous transmission of binary-coded data between two devices. BISYNC uses a specific set of control characters to synchronize the transmission of that binary coded data. See also BINARY SYNCHRONOUS COMMUNICATION.

BIT Bit is a contraction of the term BInary digiT. It is the smallest unit of information (data) a computer can process, representing either high or low, yes or no, or 1 or O. It is the basic unit in data communications. A bit can have a value of zero (a mark) or one (a space).

BIT BUCKET Slang for throwing out bits — into a wastepaper bucket.

BIT BUFFER A section of memory capable of temporarily storing a single BInary uniT (bit) of information. Used to make data transmission accurate or consistent.

BIT CHECK A bit added to a digital signal and used for error checking, i.e. a parity bit. See also PARITY.

BIT DURATION The time it takes one bit to pass a point on the transmission medium. Used to measure delay times, especially in high speed communications.

BIT ERROR The value of an encoded bit can be changed due to a transmission problem (e.g. noise on the line) and then interpreted incorrectly by the receiver.

BIT ERROR RATE BER. The percentage of received bits in error compared to the total number of bits received. Usually expressed as a number to the power of 10. For example, 10 to the fifth power means that one in every 100,000 bits transmitted will be wrong. In transmitting data a high error rate on the transmission medium (i.e. some noise), doesn't mean there'll be lots of problems with the final transmission. It just means there'll have to be lots of re-transmissions — "until one gets it right." These re-transmissions reduce the amount of data transmitted in a unit of time and therefore, increase the time needed to send that information. If the BER gets too high, it might be worth while to go to a slower transmission rate. Otherwise, you would spend more time retransmitting bad packets than getting good ones through. The theory is that the faster the speed of data transmission the more likelihood of error. This is not always so. But if you are getting lots of errors, the first — and easiest — step is to drop the transmission speed.

BIT INTERLEAVING/MULTIPLEXING In multiplexing, individual bits from different lower speed channel sources are combined one bit at a time/one channel at a time into one continuous higher speed bit stream compare with byte interleaving/ multiplexing.

BIT ORIENTED Used to describe communications protocols in which control information may be coded in fields as small as a single bit.

BIT ORIENTED PROTOCOL BOP. See BIT ORIENTED TRANSMISSION.

BIT ORIENTED TRANSMISSION An efficient transmission protocol that encodes communications control information in fields of bits rather than characters or bytes.

BIT PATTERN A group of bits arranged in specified ways to represent numbers, letters or symbols, forming a unique binary number for each character. For example, the 7-bit ASCII code produces 128 different characters, i.e. $2 \times 2 \times 2 \times 2 \times 2 \times 2 \times 2 = 128$.

BIT RATE The number of bits of data transmitted over a phone line per second. You can usually figure how many characters per second you will be transmitting — in asynchronous communications — if you divide the bit rate by ten. For example, if you are transmitting at 1200 bits per second, you will be transmitting 120 characters per second. In real life, it's never this simple, however. The total bits transmitted will depend on re-transmissions, which depends on the noise of the line, etc.

BIT ROBBING The use of the least significant bit per channel in every sixth frame for signaling. See BIT STUFFING and ROBBED BIT SIGNALING.

BIT STREAM A continuous stream of data bits transmitted over a communications line with no break or separators between the characters.

BIT STUFFING Process in some data communications protocols where a string of "one" bits is broken by an inserted "zero." This inserted zero is added by the sender and stripped by the receiver. The idea of inserting the zero is to avoid confusing the receiver into thinking the series of one bits mean something else, like a flag control character. See ZERO STUFFING.

BIT TRANSFER RATE The number of bits transferred per unit time. Usually expressed in Bits Per Second (BPS).

BIT PARITY A binary bit appended to an array of bits to make the sum of all the bits always odd or always even. See PARITY.

BITMP A sequential collection of bits that represents, in memory, an image to be displayed on the screen or printer. Each bit in a bitmap corresponds to one pixel or dot on the output device. A Microsoft Windows TrueType definition.

BITRONIX Hewlett Packard's term for its bidirectional parallel port communications "standard." It introduced this standard with its 600 dps Lasetjet 4 plain paper printer in the fall of 1992. It is hoping other manufacturers will adopt the standard. The big plus of the standard is that it allows a printer to tell a connected computer that it (the printer) has run out of paper, or the paper has jammed, etc. Having that communications back and forth will allow the user to clear the problem and get the printer and up ang running faster. It will also stop the computer locking up.

BITS PER SECOND The number of bits passing a specific point per second. A KILObit is one thousand bits per second. A MEGAbit is one million bits per second (thousands of kilos). A GIGAbit is one billion bits per second (thousands of millions). A TERAbit is one trillion bits per second (thousands of billions). A PETAbit is equal to 10 to the 15th or 1,000 terabits.

BL Business Line

BLACK BODY A totally absorbing body that does not reflect radiation (i.e. light). In thermal equilibrium, a black body absorbs and radiates at the same rate; the radiation will just equal absorption when thermal equilibrium is maintained.

BLACK BOX An electronic device that you don't want to take the time to understand. As in, "We'll put the data through a black box that will put it into X.25 format." The term has recently come also to mean PBX switches. While "Black Box" is a generic term, The Black Box Corporation of Pittsburgh, PA, has had the audacity (and brilliance) to register the term as a trademark.

The Phone Phreak community has used the term black box to describe a device that's put on phone lines in electromechanical central office areas (they don't work under ESS offices). To the phone phreak community, a black box made up of a resistor, a capacitor and a toggle switch that would "fool" the central office into thinking the phone had not been picked up when receiving a long distance call. Since the call was not "answered," the call could not be billed. Clever, eh? (Illegal, too.) See BLUE BOX and RED BOX.

BLACK FACSIMILE TRANSMISSION 1. In facsimile systems using amplitude modulation, that form of transmission in which the maximum transmitted power corresponds to the maximum density of the subject copy. 2. In facsimile systems using frequency modulation, that form of transmission in which the lowest transmitted frequency corresponds to the maximum density of the subject copy.

BLACK MATRIX Picture tube in which the color phosphors are surrounded by black for increased contrast.

BLACK RECORDING 1. In facsimile systems using amplitude modulation, that form of recording in which the maximum received power corresponds to the maximum received power corresponds to the maximum density of the record medium.

2. In a facsimile system using frequency modulation, that form of recording in which the lowest received frequency corresponds to the maximum density of the record medium.

BLACK SIGNAL 1. In facsimile, the signal resulting from the scanning of a maximum-density area of the subject copy. 2. In cryptographic systems, a signal containing only unclassified or encrypted information.

BLANK A character on teletype terminals that does not punch holes in paper tape (except for feed holes to push the paper through). Also the character between words, usually called a "Space" is referred to in IBM jargon as a Blank.

BLANKING The suppression of the display of one or more display elements or display segments.

BLAST BLocked ASynchronous Transmission.

BLEND A computer imaging term. The smooth transition from one color to another. Blending tools give a realistic look to a drawing, especially if you want to create a smooth shadow.

BLERT BLock Error Rate Test.

BLINKING An intentional periodic change in the intensity of one or more display elements or display segments.

BLF The Busy Lamp Field is a visual display of the status of all or some of your phones. Your BLF tells you if a phone is busy or on hold. Your Busy Lamp Field is typically attached to or part of your operator's phone. See BUSY LAMP FIELD.

BLIND TRANSFER Someone transfers a call to someone else without telling the person who's calling.

BLISTER PACK A pocketed polyvinyl chloride shipping container with a snap-on cover.

BLOB Binary Large OBjects. When a database includes not only the traditional character, numeric, and memo fields but also pictures or other stuff consuming of large space, a database is said to include BLOBs — binary large objects.

BLOCK In data communications, a group of bits transmitted as a unit and treated as a unit of information. Usually consists of its own starting and ending control deliminators, a header, the text to be transmitted and check characters at the end used for error correction. Sometimes called a Packet.

BLOCK CHARACTER CHECK BCC. The result of transmission verification algorithm accumulated over a transmission block, and normally appended at the end, e.g. CRC, LRC.

BLOCK DIAGRAM A graphic way to show different elements of a program or process by the use of squares, rectangles, diamonds and various shapes connected by lines to show what must be done, when it must be done and what happens if it's done this way or that. In short, it shows how all the small decision points add up to the whole process.

BLOCK MISDELIVERY PROBABILITY The ratio of the number of misdelivered blocks to the total number of block transfer attempts during a specified period.

BLOCK MULTIPLEXER CHANNEL An IBM mainframe input/output channel that allows interleaving of data blocks.

BLOCK PARITY The designation of one or more bits in a block as parity bits whose purpose is to ensure a designated parity, either odd or even. Used to assist in error detection or correction, or both.

BLOCK TRANSFER The process of sending and receiving one or more blocks of data.

BLOCK TRANSFER ATTEMPT A coordinated sequence of user and telecommunication system activities undertaken to effect transfer of an individual block from a source user to a destination user. A block transfer attempt begins when the first bit of the block crosses the functional interface between the source user and the telecommunication system. A block transfer attempt ends either in successful block transfer or in block transfer failure.

BLOCK TRANSFER EFFICIENCY The average ratio of user information bits to total bits in successfully transferred blocks.

BLOCK TRANSFER FAILURE Failure to deliver a block successfully. Normally the principal block transfer failure outcomes are: lost block, misdelivered block, and added block.

BLOCK TRANSFER RATE The number of successful block transfers made during a period of time.

BLOCK TRANSFER TIME The average value of the duration of a successful block transfer attempt. A block transfer attempt is successful if 1. The transmitted block is delivered to the intended destination user within the maximum allowable performance period and 2. The contents of the delivered block are correct.

BLOCKED CALLS DELAYED A variable in queuing theory to describe what happens when the user is held in queue because his call is blocked and he can't complete it instantly.

BLOCKED CALLS HELD A variable in queuing theory to describe what happens when the user redials the moment he encounters blockage.

BLOCKED CALLS RELEASED A variable in queuing theory to describe what happens when the user, after being blocked, waits a little while before redialing.

BLOCKING When a telephone call cannot be completed it is said that the call is "blocked." Blocking is a fancy way to say that the caller is "receiving a busy." There are many places a call can be blocked: at the user's own telephone switch — PBX or key system, at the user's local central office or in the long distance network. Blocking happens because switching or transmission capacity is not available at that precise time.

The number of calls you try compared to the number of times you get blocked measures "the grade of service" on that network. Blocked calls are different from calls that are not completed because the called number is busy. This is because numbers that are busy are not the fault of the telephone switching and transmission network. One might think the fewer blocked calls, the better.

From the user's point of view, the answer is obviously YES, it is better. Less blockage, fewer busies and less frustration. But as one designs a switching and transmission network for less and less blocking, the network becomes more and more expensive. Logarithmically so. We keep adding extra circuits and extra equipment. Thus, in any telecommunications network design there is always a trade-off: What are you prepared to pay, compared to what can you tolerate?

Everyone designs their network with different tradeoffs depending on what they and their users or customers, can tolerate and/or are willing to pay. Most companies are willing to pay more for better service if someone explains the logic of telephone design to them. Many network salesmen, however, don't believe this. They practice the sales "theory" of selling better service for less money. This doesn't work in business, and especially not in telephony.

The "Grade of Service" is a measurement of blocking. It varies from almost zero (best, but most expensive case, no calls blocked) to one (worst case, all calls blocked). Grade of Service is written as P.05 (five percent blocking). "Blocking" used to be a technical term but has now become a sales tool especially among PBX manufacturers, who increasingly claim their switch to be "non-blocking." This means it will not, they claim, block a call in the switch.

There are several flaws in this logic: First, it's not logical or useful to buy a non-blocking PBX if the chances of being blocked elsewhere — the local lines, the local exchange or the long distance network — are very high. Second, a true non-blocking PBX can be very expensive, perhaps too much power and too much money for most peoples' needs. Third, most manufacturers define "non-blocking" differently. One defines it strictly in terms of switching capability and ignores the fact that his PBX might not have sufficient other "things," like devices which ring bells on phones (to indicate an incoming call) or devices which deliver dial tone to a phone (to indicate the PBX is ready to receive instructions).

BLOCKING FACTOR The number of records in a block; the number is computed by dividing the size of the block by the size of each record contained therein. Each record in the block must be the same size.

BLOCKING FORMULAS Specific probability distribution functions that closely approximate the call pattern of telephone users probable behavior in failing to find idle lines.

BLOWER A microphone.

BLOWN FIBER A method for installing optical fibers in which fibers are blown through glass.

BLOWN FUSE A broken fuse.

BLU Northern Telecom word for Basic Link Unit.

BLUE ALARM Used in T-1 transmission. Also known as the AIS (Alarm Indication Signal). The blue alarm is turned on when two consecutive frames have fewer than three zeros in the data bit stream. A blue alarms sends 1's (ones) in all bits of all time slots on the span. See T-1 and AIS.

BLUE BOX A device used to steal long distance phone calls. The classic blue box was slightly larger than a cigarette container. It had a touchtone pad on the front and a single button on top. Typically, you went to a coin phone and dialed an 800 number. While the distant number was ringing, you punched the single button on the top of the blue box. That button caused the blue box's speaker to emit a 2600 Hz tone. This disconnected the ringing at the other end but left the user inside the long distance network. The user then punched in a series of digits on the touchtone pad. The phone network heard those tones and sent the call according to the instructions in the tones. The tones duplicated the tones which the touchtone pads of long distance operators emitted. They are different from those emitted by normal telephones. The first blue box was "discovered" at MIT in a small utility box that was painted blue, thus the term blue box. When they were young, Steve Jobs and Steve Wozniak, founders of Apple Computer, sold blue boxes, which Wozniak built. People who used blue boxes in their salad days included characters with adopted pseudonyms like Dr. No, The Snark and Captain Crunch, who got his name from the free 2600 Hz whistle included as a promotion in boxes of Captain Crunch breakfast cereal. With the advent of CCIS, Common Channel Interoffice Signaling (i.e. out-of-band signaling), blue boxes no longer work.

BLUE COLLAR COMPUTER A colloquial term for a handheld computer which is used by "blue collar" workers for tasks such taking inventory, tracking goods, etc. Such computer may have a pen, a large pen-sensitive or touch-sensitive screens, a bar code scanner and a modem. It may be able to capture signatures — useful for confirmation of the delivery of goods.

BLUE GROMMET The rubber collar over the joint between the handset and the armored cable on a pay phone. Blue identifies a "hearing aid compatible" handset.

BLUE PAGES Section of phone directory commonly used for government phone numbers, as distinct from white and yellow pages.

BM Burst Modem.

BNA Burroughs Network Architecture. Communications architecture of Burroughs, now Unisys.

BNC A bayonet-locking connector for slim coaxial cables, like those used with Ethernet. BNC is an acronym for Bayonet-Neill-Concelman. Don't ask who Neill and Concelman are. Someone also says it also stands for British National Connector.

BNC BARREL CONNECTORS These connectors join two lengths of thin Ethernet coaxial cable together. See also BNC.

BNC CONNECTORS The connectors for thin Ethernet coaxial cable are BNC connectors. BNC connectors are used on thin Ethernet cable. The BNC connectors on each end of thin Ethernet cable connect to T-connectors, barrel connectors, and other network hardware. See BNC.

BNC FEMALE TO N-SERIES FEMALE ADAPTER The BNC female to N-Series female adapter is a connector which enables you to connect thin coaxial cable to thick coaxial cable. The BNC female connector attaches to the thin cable and the N-Series male connector attaches to the thick Ethernet cable.

BNC T-CONNECTORS The top of the T in a BNC T-connector functions as a barrel connector and links two lengths of thin Ethernet coaxial cable; the third end connects to the SpeedLink/PC 16.

BNC TERMINATORS 50-ohm terminators are used to block electrical interference on a Ethernet coaxial cable network and to terminate the network at certain spots. You attach a BNC terminator to one plug on a T-connector if you will not be attaching a length of cable to that plug. You may also need to use a BNC terminator with a grounding wire to ground the network. See BNC.

BNR Bell Northern Research. Northern Telecom's research arm.

BNS 1000/2000 AT&T's Broadband Networking Systems using fast-packet, cell relay switching providing dynamic bandwidth allocation on demand with interfaces to a variety of LAN routers, including AT&T's LCS200, Wellfleet, Cisco Systems and NCR StarWAN products.

BOARD 1. Short for printed circuit board. In display/monitor terminology it refers to the adapter (or controller) that serves as an interface between computer and monitor. Portables generally have built-in interfaces (typically VGA) so that you can plug in an external monitor without an additional board or "card." 2. An SCSA term. Any hardware module that controls its own physical interface to the S Cbus or SCxbus. From a programming point of view, a board is an addressable system component that contains resources.

BOC Bell Operating Company. The local Bell operating telephone company. These days there are 22 Bell Operating Companies. They are organized into (i.e. owned by) seven Regional Bell holding companies, also called RBOCs, pronounced "R-bocks," or RHCs. See BELL OPERATING COMPANY.

BOND The electrical connection between two metallic surfaces established to provide a low resistance path between them.

BONDING 1. In electrical engineering, the process of connecting together metal parts so that they make low resistance electrical contact for direct current and lower frequency alternating currents. 2. The process of establishing the required degree of electrical continuity between two or more conductive surfaces that are to be joined. 3. The process by which all building and equipment electrical grounds are joined together to eliminate differences in electrical ground potentials. 4. A new group know as the Bandwidth ON Demand INteroperability Group (BONDING). The group's charter is to develop common control and synchronization standard needed to manage high speed data as it travels through the public network. This will allow equipment from vendors to interoperate over existing Switched 65 and ISDN services.

BONG A tone that long distance carriers and value added carriers make in order to signal you that they now require additional action on your part — usually dialing more digits.

BONTs Broadband Optical Network Terminations.

BOOLEAN EXPRESSION An expression composed of one or more relational expressions; a string of symbols that specifies a condition that is either true or false.

BOOLEAN LOGIC Boolean Logic is named after the 19th century mathematician, George Boole. Boolean logic is algebra reduced to either TRUE or FALSE, YES or NO, ON or OFF. Boolean logic is important for computer logic because computers work in binary — TRUE or FALSE, YES or NO, ON or OFF.

BOOLEAN OPERATORS See BOOLEAN LOGIC. Boolean operators are AND, OR, XOR, NOR, NOT. The result of an equation with one or more of the boolean operators is that the result will either be true or false.

BOOLEAN VALUED EXPRESSION An expression that will return a "true" or "fale" evaluation.

BOOT Abbreviation for the verb to bootstrap. A technique or device designed to bring itself into a desired state where it can operate on its own. For example, one type of boot is a routine whose first few instructions are sufficient to bring the rest of itself into memory from an input device. See BOOTSTRAP.

BOOT ROM A read-only memory chip allowing a workstation to communicate with the file server and to read a DOS boot program from the server. Workstations can thus operate on the network without having a disk drive. These are commonly called diskless PCs or diskless workstations.

BOOTSTRAP The process of starting up a computer. Think about the following explanation in regard to your desktop MS-DOS machine. Usually, when the computer is turned on, it goes to a location of permanent Read Only Memory (See ROM) for instructions. These instructions, in turn, load the first instructions from the disk telling the computer what tasks to start performing. The name of this process comes from the expression "pulling oneself up by one's own bootstraps." The typical personal computer BOOT (startup) throws a message on the screen instructing the user to "insert a disk."

To confuse matters, there are WARM boots and COLD boots. Cold boots occur when the ac power switch on the computer is turned on. Warm boots occur when you hit the reset button (or CTL/ALT/DELETE) while the ac power switch stays on. A warm boot — reset — is done when you're changing disks or programs, or have done something dumb, like tried to access a drive that didn't access, or tried to print without connecting up to a printer.

You do a cold boot when the machine locks up rock hard and a warm boot doesn't work. To do a cold boot with your computer, turn the ac power off, count to ten and then turn it on. Remember: never leave disks in your computer when you're turning it on and off. The surge of electricity might destroy the disks. When modems give trouble, do a cold boot on them. In fact, when phone systems give trouble, do a cold boot on them also. See also BOOT RAM, DEVICE DRIVER and MS-DOS.

BOP Bit Oriented Protocol. See BIT ORIENTED TRANSMISSION.

BORSCHT A group of functions provided in Line Circuits (LC). It stands for

B: Battery supply to subscriber line.

O: Overvoltage protection.

R: Ringing current supply.

S: Supervision of subscriber terminal.

C: Coder and decoder.

H: Hybrid (2 wire to 4 wire conversion).

T: Test.

BOTTOM LINE A phrase that can mean net profit, the lowest possible price that someone will take or the basic meaning with all the frills and nonsense cut away.

BOUND MODE In an optical fiber, a mode whose field decays monotonically in the transverse direction everywhere external to the core and which does not lose power to radiation. Except in a single-mode fiber, the power in bound modes is predominantly contained in the core of the fiber.

BOUNDARY FUNCTION Capability in SNA sub-area node to handle some functions that nearby peripheral nodes are not capable of handling.

BOUNDRY NODE In IBM's SNA, a subarea node that can provide certain protocol support for adjacent subarea nodes, including transforming network addresses to local addresses, and vice versa, and performing session level sequencing and flow control and less intelligent peripheral nodes.

BPAD Bisynchronous Packet Assembler/Disassembler.

BPI Bytes Per Inch. How many bytes are recorded per inch of recording surface. Typically used in conjunction with magnetic tape.

BPON Broadband Passive Optical Network.

BPS Bits Per Second. A measure of the speed of data communications. There are many ways to measure bits per second. So don't assume that just because one LAN or other data communications system has a faster bits per seconds, it will transmit your information faster. You have to factor in speed of writing and reading from the disk and the accuracy of transmission. All datacom schemes have error-checking systems, some better than others. Typically such systems force a re-transmission of data if a mistake is detected. You might have a fast, but "dirty" (i.e. lots of errors) transmission medium, which may need lots of re-transmissions. Thus, the "effective" bps of data communications network may actually be quite low. See also BAUD.

BPSK Binary Phase-Shift Key.

BRA Basic Rate Access. A Canadian term for the ISDN 2B+D standard, which is called BRI in the U.S. — Basic Rate Interace.

BRAGG REFLECTOR A device designed to finely focus a semiconductor laser beam. Dennis Hall, a professor at the University of Rochester's Institute of Optics in New York, told the Economist Magazine in the Spring of

1993 that he and his colleague Gary Wicks have etched into the surface of his gallium-arsenide laser a grating of 600 concentric grooves, each a quarter of a millionith of a meter apart. The grating acts as what is known as a Bragg reflector. As the waves of laser light pass throgh each of its ridges, they are reflected by each of its ridges, a process which causes them to come together into an even, circular beam.

BRAID A fibrous or metallic group of filaments interwoven cylindrically to form a covering over one or more insulated conductors.

BRAINERD, PAUL S. Founder of Aldus Corporation of 1984, Mr. Brainerd is reputed to be "the father of desktop publishing." His program Aldus PageMaker allowed the average PC user to produce professional-looking documents.

BRANCH A path in the program which is selected from two or more paths by a program instruction. "To branch" means to choose one of the available paths.

BRANCH FEEDER A cable between the distribution cable and the main feeder cable to connect phone users to the central office. An outside plant term.

BRANCHING FILTER A device placed in a waveguide to separate or combine different microwave frequency bands.

BRCS Business and Residence Customer Services. An approach that the AT&T 5ESS switch employs to provision revenue-generating services.

BREADBOARD A circuit board made by hand, usually in building a prototype. No one knows where the word breadboard came from. Maybe because it looks a little like a breadboard?

BREAK An interruption. As in "Make and Break." Make means contacts which are usually open, but which close during an operation. "Make and Break" accurately describes rotary dialing.

BREAK IN The attendant can interrupt conversations and announce an emergency or an important call.

BREAK KEY A Break Key is found on some PCs. It is usually used to interrupt the current task running on a remote host. Break is not an ASCII character, it is simply a period of start (space) polarity.

BREAK OUT BOX A testing device that permits a user to cross-connect and tie individual leads of an interface cable using jumper wires to monitor, switch, or patch the electrical output of the cable. The most common break out box in our industry is probably the RS-232 box. Some of these boxes have LEDs (Light Emitting Diodes), which allow you to see which lead is "live." See also BREAKOUT BOX.

BREAK TEST ACCESS Method of disconnecting a circuit, which has been electrically bridged, to allow testing on either side of the circuit. Devices that provide break test access include: bridge clips, plug-on protection modules, and plug-on patching devices. Break test access also provides a demarcation point.

BREAKDOWN VOLTAGE The voltage at which the insulation between two conductors breaks down.

BREAKING STRENGTH The amount of force needed to break a wire or fiber.

BREAKOUT A wire or group of wires in a multi-conductor configuration which terminates somewhere other than at the end of the configuration.

BREAKOUT BOX A device that is plugged in between a computer terminal and its connecting cable to re-configure the way the cable is wired. When hooking up a terminal that is wired as if it were a computer itself (such as a VT-100), a break out box is used to break out, or fan out the 25 connections in the RS-232 cable. Each wire in the break out box goes through a switch that can be turned off, and a wire jumper is provided to connect each pin on one side to one or the other pin on the other side. This allows you, for example, to switch pins 2 & 3, thus fooling two computer devices into thinking one is talking to a terminal. (Now you have the essence of a null modem cable.) Break out boxes are necessary because there is no such thing as "standard" pinning on an RS-232 cable. To connect one computer to a printer one minute and to another computer the next minute, usually requires totally different wiring in the RS-232 cable, i.e. two sets of cables. This lack of standardization is why you'll always see dozens of RS-232 cables lying around where computers are used.

BRI Basic Rate Interface. There are two subscriber "interfaces" in ISDN. This one and PRI (Primary Rate Interface). In BRI, you get two bearer B-channels at 64 kilobits per second and a data D-channel at 16 kilobits per second. The bearer B-channels are designed for PCM voice, slow-scan videoconferencing, group 4 facsimile machines, or whatever you can squeeze into 64,000 bits per second full duplex. The data (or D) channel is for bringing in information about incoming calls and taking out information about outgoing calls. It is also for access to slow-speed data networks, like videotex, packet switched networks, etc. See BASIC RATE INTERFACE and ISDN.

BRICK A colloquial expression for a handheld two-way radio. In more technical language, a "brick" is a station in the mobile service consisting of a hand-held ratiotelephone unit licensed under a site authorization. Each unit can work while being hand-carried.

BRIDGE Verb: 1. To connect one circuit or component to another in parallel. When two single line phones share the same number — line or trunk — they are bridged. Sometimes a bridge has associated components — e.g. amplifiers — to compensate for losses. Most of today's phone systems insist that the cabling from the central switching cabinet to the phone not be bridged — but be a direct run from the phone to the cabinet.

Noun: 2. A device that connects LANs using similar or dissimilar media and signaling systems such as Ethernet, Token-Ring, and X.25. It operates at the data-link layer of the OSI model. Bridges sometimes work within a PC and sometimes within a special purpose computer. Bridges read and filter data packets and frames. A bridge is also called a data link relay or level 2 relay."

When used for connecting LANs, a bridge connects LANs at the Medium Access Control (MAC) sub-layer of the OSI model's Data Link Layer. Bridges forward packets destined for another LAN. Bridges can be classified as source routing bridges, which are used in IBM environments, or transparent bridges, which operate primarily in non-IBM environments. A third bridging method, Source Routing Transparent (SRT), enables a bridge to act as both a transparent and a source routing bridge. See INTERNETWORKING, ROUTERS, SOURCE ROUTING, and TRANSPARENT ROUTING.

BRIDGE AMPLIFIER An amplifier installed on a CATV trunk cable to feed branching cables.

BRIDGE EQUIPMENT Equipment which connects different LANs, allowing communication between devices. As in "to bridge" several LANs. Bridges are protocol-independent but hardware-specific. They will connect LANs with different hardware and different protocols. An example would be a device that connects an Ethernet network to a Starlan network. With this bridge it is possible to send signals between the two networks, and only these two networks.

These signals will be understood only if the protocols used on each LAN are the same, e.g. XNS or TCP/IP, but they don't have to be the same for the bridge to do its job for the signals to move on either LAN. They just won't be understood. This differs from gateways and routers. Routers connect LANs with the same protocols but different hardware. The best examples are the file servers that accommodate different hardware LANs. Gateways connect two LANs with different protocols by translating between them, enabling them to talk to each other. The bridge does no translation. Bridges are best used to keep networks small by connecting many of them rather than making a large one. This reduces the traffic faced by individual computers and improves network performance.

BRIDGE LIFTER A device that removes, either electrically or physically, bridged telephone pairs. Relays, saturable inductors, and semiconductors are used as bridge lifters.

BRIDGE TAP An undetermined length of wire attached between the normal endpoints of a circuit that introduces unwanted impedance imbalances for data transmission. Also called bridging trap or bridged tap. See BRIDGED TAP.

BRIDGED RINGING A system where ringers on a phone line are connected across that line.

BRIDGED TAP 1. Any section of a cable pair not on the direct electrical path between the central office and the user's premises. 2. The multiple appearances of the same cable pair at several distribution points.

BRIDGING Bridging across a circuit is done by placing one test lead from a test set or a conductor from another circuit and placing it on one conductor of another circuit. And then doing the same thing to the second conductor. You bridge across a circuit to test the circuit by listening in on it, by dialing on it, by running tests on the line, ec. You can bridge across a circuit by going across the pair in wire, by stripping it, etc. You can bridge across a pair (also called a circuit path) by installing external devices across quick clips on a connecting block.

BRIDGING ADAPTER A box containing several male and female electrical connectors that allows various phones and accessories to be connected to one cable. Bridging adapters work well with 1A2 key systems and single line phones behind PBXs, not so well with electronic key systems and electronic telephones behind PBXs.

BRIDGING CLIP A small piece of metal with a U-shape cross-section which is used to connect adjacent terminals on 66-type connecting blocks.

BRIDGING CONNECTION A parallel connection by means of which some of the signal energy in a circuit may be extracted, usually with negligible effect on the normal operation of the circuit. Most modern phone systems don't encourage bridging connections, since the negigible is rarely negligible.

BRIDGING LOSS The loss at a given frequency resulting from connecting an impedance across a transmission line. Expressed as the ratio (in decibels) of the signal power delivered to that part of the system following the bridging point before bridging, to the signal power delivered to that same part after the bridging.

BRIGHTNESS An attribute of visual reception in which a source appears to emit more or less light. Since the eye is not equally sensitive to all colors, brightness cannot be a quantitative term.

BRITTLE Easily broken without much stretching.

BROADBAND A transmission facility that has a bandwidth (capacity) greater than a voice grade line of 4 kHz. (Some say that to be "broadband" it should be 20 kHz.) Such a broadband facility — typically coaxial cable — may carry numerous voice, video and data channels simultaneously. Each "channel" will take up a different frequency on the cable. There'll be "guardbands" (empty spaces) between the channels to make sure each channel doesn't interfere with its neighbor.

A coaxial CATV cable is the "classic" broadband channel. Simultaneously it carries many TV channels. Broadband cables are used in some office LANs.

But more common are the BASEBAND variety which have the capacity for one channel only. Everything on that cable to be transmitted or received must use that one channel. That one channel is very fast, so each device needs only to use that high speed channel for only a little of the time. The problem is getting onto the channel. See BASEBAND.

BROADCAST To send information to two or more receiving devices simultaneously — over a data communications network, a voice mail, electronic mail system, a local TV or radio station or a satellite system.

BROADCAST STORM A pathological condition that may occur in a TCP/IP network that can cause large number of broadcast packets to be propagated unnecessarily across an enterprise-wide network, thereby causing network overload. Broadcast storms happen when users mix old TCP/IP routers with routers supporting the new releases of TCP/IP protocol. Routers use broadcast packets to resolve IP addressing requests from stations on LANs. If a station running an old version of TCP/IP sends such a request, TCP/IP routers in an enterprise-wide network misunderstand it and send multiple broadcasts to their brother and sister routers. In turn, these broadcasts cause each router to send more broadcasts, and so on. This chain reaction can produce so many broadcast messages that the network can shut down. It should be noted that this is extremely rare and it happens only in TCP/IP networks that use two specific TCP/IP protocol releases.

BROADCAST LIST A list of two or more system users to whom messages are sent simultaneously. Master Broadcast Lists are shared by all system users and are set up by the System Administrator. Personal Lists are set up by individual subscribers.

BROADCAST MESSAGE A message from one user sent to all users. Just like a TV station signal. On LANs, all workstations and devices receive the message. Broadcast messages are used for many reasons, including acknowledging receipt of information and locating certain devices. On voice mail systems, broadcast messages are important announcement messages from the system administrator that provide information and instructions regarding the voice processing system. Broadcast messages play before standard Voice Mail or Automated Attendant messages.

BROADCAST NET A British Telecom turret feature that allows each trader single key access to a group of outgoing lines. This is designed primarily for sending short messages to multiple destinations. The "net" function allows the user to set up and amend his broadcast group.

BROADCAST TRANSMISSION A fax machine feature that allows automatic transmission of a document to several locations.

BROKERNET A virtual private dedicated network offering from New York Telephone and provided within Manhattan aimed at brokerage, banking and message industries. It uses digital switching to provide virtual private lines, specifically "hot line" service.

BRONZE A mixture of copper and tin and small amounts of other metals.

BROUTER In local area networking, a brouter is a device that combines the dynamic routing capability of an internetwork router with the ability of a bridge to interconnect dissimilar local area networks (LANs). It has the ability to route one or more protocols, such as TCP/IP and XNS, and bridge all other traffic.

BROWSER A developed tool used to inspect a class hierarchy in an object-oriented software system.

BROWSING The act of searching through automated information system storage to locate or acquire information without necessarily knowing of the existence or the format of the information being sought.

BRUSH A computer imaging term. A paint package's most basic image-creation tool. Most packages let you select a variety of sizes and shapes. Many let you customize shapes.

BSA See both BASIC SWITCHING ARRANGEMENT and OPEN NETWORK ARCHITECTURE.

BSC Binary Synchronous Communication. A set of IBM operating procedures for synchronous transmission used in teleprocessing networks.

BSE Basic Switching Element. See OPEN NETWORK ARCHITECTURE.

BSP Bell System Practice. A very defined way of writing and presenting instruction and installation manuals. BSPs also establish standards for splicing cable, for installing phones, answering phones, collecting debts, finding phonetaps, climbing poles. They are (or once were) the instruction manuals that dictated how to do everything. Divestiture has changed the rules. BSPs are not as important as they were when AT&T handed down all the BSPs.

BSS GSM Base Station System. See also GSM.

BT British Telecom.

BTAM Basic Telecommunications Access Method. One of IBM's early host-based software programs for controlling remote data communications interface to host applications, supporting pre-SNA protocols. See IBM.

BTI British Telecom International.

BTL Bell Telephone Laboratories.

BTN Billed Telephone Number. The primary telephone number used for billing, regardless of the number of phone lines associated with that number.

BTRIEVE Btrieve is a key-indexed database record management system. You can retrieve, insert, update, or delete records by key value, using sequential or random access methods. First introduced in 1983, Btrieve was one of the first databases designed for LANs. Novell bought the company in the late 1980s. Now called NetWare Betrieve, it is included with most versions of NetWare 2.x and NetWare 3.x. There are Btrieve developer products for DOS, OS/2 and Windows.

BTRL British Telecom Research Laboratories.

BTU Basic Transmission Unit.

BUFFER 1. In data transmission, a buffer is a temporary storage location for information being sent or received. Usually located between two different devices that have different abilities or speeds for handling the data. The buffer acts like a dam, capturing the data and then trickling it out at speeds the lower river can handle without, hopefully, flooding or overflowing the banks. 2. A coating material used to cover and protect the fiber. The buffer can be constructed using either a tight jacket or loose tube technique.

BUFFER COATING Protective material applied to fibers. Increases apparent fiber size. May be more than one layer. Stated in microns. Usually thicker or multi-coated on tight-buffer cables. BUFFER STORAGE Electronic circuitry where data is kept during buffering.

BUFFERED REPEATER A device that amplifies and regenerates signals so they can travel farther along a local area cable. This type of repeater also controls the flow of messages to prevent collisions.

BUG 1. A concealed microphone or listening device or other audiosurveillance device. 2. To install the means for audio surveillance. 3. A semiautomatic telegraph key. 5 A problem in software or hardware. The original computer bug, a moth, is enshrined at the Washington Navy Yard. It was the cause of a hardware failure in an early computer in 1945. The story goes like this: a team of top Navy scientists was developing one of the world's first electronic computers. Suddenly, in the middle of a calculation, the computer ground to a halt, dead. Engineers poured over every wire and every inch of the massive machine. Finally, one of the technicians discovered the cause of the problem. Buried deep insides its electronic innards, crushed between two electric relays, lay the body of a moth. These days, "bugs" in telecom or computer systems are not insects. They're indescribable glitches that adversely affect smooth operations. Bugs usually originate in software. Some programmers call bugs "undocumented features." And they are, indeed.

BUILDING ENTRANCE AREA The area inside a building where cables enter the building and are connected to riser cables within the building and where electrical protection is provided. The network interface as well as the protectors and other distribution components for the campus subsystem may be located here. Typically this area is the end of the local telephone company's responsibility. From here on it's your responsibility. You should protect your equipment inside the building from spikes and surges and other electrical nonsenses which the phone company's cables might bring in. For the best disaster protection, it's wise to have two building entrances by which your telecommunications cables can enter. And they should enter from separate telephone central offices. Some telephone companies, e.g. New York Telephone, are now tariffing such services.

BUILDING FOOTING The concrete base under the foundation of a building in which copper wire may be laid to form an electrical ground.

BUILDING OUT The process of adding a combination of inductance, capacitance,and resistance to a cable pair so that its electrical length may be increased by a desired amount to control impedance characteristics.

BUILDING STEEL The structural steel beams that make up the frame of a building. If the steel frame is buried in the earth, it can be used as an electrical ground.

BULK BILLING A method of billing for long distance telephone services where no detail of calls made is provided. WATS is a bulk billed service. Therein lies the problem for the cost conscious user. There's no verification of calls made. See CALL DETAIL RECORDING.

BULK STORAGE Lots of storage. Usually reels of magnetic tape or hard disks.

BULLETIN BOARD SYSTEM A fancy name for an electronic message system running on a microcomputer. Call up, leave messages, read messages. The system is like a physical bulletin board. That's where the name comes from. Some people call bulletin board systems electronic mail systems. TELECONNECT and Inbound/Outbound Magazines and Telecom Library Inc. have them, too. We call our our InfoBoard. Call us on 212-989-4675. You can use any computer, any communications software and virtually any 300, 1,200 or 2,400 baud modem. You have 15 minutes before our system cuts you off. You can pick up free software and leave us messages and order books and subscriptions. See also BBS.

BULK ENCRYPTION Simultaneous encryption of all channels of a multichannel telecommunications trunk.

BUMPER BEEPER Radio beacon transmitter, hidden in or on a vehicle for use with radio tailing equipment.

BUNCHED FRAME-ALIGNMENT SIGNAL A frame-alignment signal in which the signal elements occupy consecutive digit positions.

BUNDLE 1. A group of fibers or wires within a cable sharing a common color-code. 2. In T-1, specifically M44 Multiplexing, a bundle consists of 12 nibbles (4 bits) and may represent 11 channels of 32 Kbps compressed information plus a delta channel. A bundle is typically a subset of a DSI and treated as an entity with its own signaling delta channel.

BUNDLED Combining several services under one telephone tariff item at a single charge.

BUNDLED RATES Several service combined into one offering for one charge.

BURDEN TEST A semi-legitimate test used in regulation to determine if the offering of a new or continued service will cause consumers of other services to pay prices no higher than if the service were not offered. In other words, the question is "Who carries the Burden?" It's sometimes called the "avoidable cost test."

BURFORD COURIER An MCI definition. A communications software package developed for use with Wang VS mainframes enabling users to communicate directly with MCI International's Telex messaging services.

BURN-IN To run new devices and printed circuits cards, often at high temperatures, in order to pinpoint early failures. The theory is all semiconductor devices show their defects — if any — in the first few weeks of operation. If they pass this "burn-in" period, they will work for a long time, so the theory goes. "Burn-in" should probably be 30-days under full power and working load. Burn-in should also take place in a room with lots of heat and at least 50% humidity, since this will simulate the poorly-ventilated places most people install telephone systems.

BURNING A POLE Slang expression to describe when an installer accidentally slides down a telephone pole.

BURRUS DIODE A surface-emitting LED with a hole etched to accommodate a light-collecting fiber. Named after its inventor, Charles Burrus.

BURST 1. In data communication, a sequence of signals, noise, or interface counted as a unit in accordance with some specific criterion or measure. 2. To separate continuous-form or multipart paper into discrete sheets.

BURST ISOCHRONOUS Isochronous burst transmission.

BURST MODE A way of doing data transmission in which a continuous block of data is transferred between main memory and an input/output device without interruption until the transfer has been completed.

BURST SWITCHING In a packet-switched network, a switching capability in which each network switch extracts routing instructions from an incoming packet header to establish and maintain the appropriate switch connection for the duration of the packet, following which the connection is automatically released. In concept, burst switching is similar to connectionless mode transmission, but it differs from the latter in that burst switching implies an intent to establish the switch connection in near real time so that only minimum buffering is required at the node switch.

BURST TRANSMISSION 1. A method of transmission that combines a very high data signaling rate with very short transmission times. 2. A method of operating a data network by interrupting, at intervals, the data being transmitted. The method enables communication between data terminal equipment and a data network operating at dissimilar data signaling rates.

BURSTY INFORMATION Information that flows in short bursts with relatively long, silent intervals between.

BUS An electrical connection which allows two or more wires or lines to be connected together. Typically, all circuit cards receive the same information that is put on the BUS. Only the card the information is "addressed" to will use that data. This is convenient so that a circuit card may be plugged in "anywhere on the Bus." See also BACKPLANE and BUS NETWORK.

BUS HOG A device which gets control of and hogs a backplane bus.

BUS NETWORK All communications devices share a common path. Typically in a bus network, a "conversation" from each device is sampled quickly and interleaved using time division multiplexing. Bus networks are very high-speed — millions of bits per second — forms of transmission (e.g. on a local area network) and switching. They often form the major switching and transmission backbone of a modern PBX. The printed circuit cards which connect to each trunk and each line are plugged into the PBX's high-speed "backbone" — i.e. the bus network. See also BUS.

BUS TOPOLOGY A network topology in which nodes are connected to a single cable with terminators at each end.

BUSINESS ID An MCI definition. A five-digit numeric code identifying the business to which a customer is assigned. The first two digits indicate division number, the third indicate service type, and the fourth and fifth indicate billing cycle. These are assigned during order entry and passed to MCI A/R with the customer install/ transaction.

BUSY In use. "Off-hook". There are slow busies and fast busies. Slow busies are when the phone at the other end is busy or off-hook. They happen 60 times a minute. Fast busies (120 times a minute) occur when the network is congested with too many calls. Your distant party may or may not be busy, but you'll never know because you never got that far.

BUSY BACK A busy signal.

BUSY CALL FORWARDING When you call a busy phone extension, your call is automatically sent to another predetermined telephone extension.

BUSY HOUR The hour of the day (or the week, or the month, or the year, — check) during which a telephone system carries the most traffic. For many offices, it is 10:30 A.M. to 11:30 A.M. The "busy hour" is perhaps the most important concept in traffic engineering — the science of figuring what telephone switching and transmission capacities one needs. Since the "busy hour" represents the most traffic carried in a hour, the idea is if you create enough capacity to carry that "busy hour" traffic, you will be able to carry all other traffic. In actuality, one never designs capacity sufficient to carry 100% of the busy hour traffic. That would be too expensive. So, the argument then comes down to, "What percentage of my peak busy or busy hour traffic am I prepared to block?" This percentage might be as low as half of one percent or as high as 10%. Typically, it's between 2% and 5%, depending on what business you're in and the cost to you — in lost sales, etc. — of blocking calls.

BUSY LAMP A light on a telephone showing a certain line or phone is busy. See BUSY LAMP FIELD.

BUSY LAMP FIELD A device with rows of tiny lights that shows which phones in a telephone system are speaking and which aren't. Each light corresponds to a telephone extension on the system. The busy lamp field usually sits attached to the attendant's console, telling the attendant if an extension is busy, free, on hold, etc. The benefit of having a busy lamp field is that the operator doesn't have to dial the number to find out what's happening with the extension. This saves the attendant time in handling incoming calls and gives the caller better service. A busy lamp field is often combined with DSS (DIRECT STATION SELECT). Next to each light on the busy lamp field there is a button which the operator can push which will dial the corresponding extension (i.e. directly select it) and will typically transfer the call automatically. This button is like an autodial button. This saves the time of dialing the two, three or more numbers of the extension. These days, busy lamp fields are often built into phones on a key system, and everyone, not just the operator, can have one. This gives everyone information on what's happening in the system. It makes transferring calls, etc. easier.

BUSY OUT To cause a line to return a busy signal to a caller. Busying out lines going into a computer is useful when the computer is not available, i.e. during maintenance periods. This way callers do not get connected to modems with no computers to talk to. This is also known as "taking the phone off the hook." In a voice phone system with trunks that rotary (or hunt) on, sometimes busying one or more broken trunks out helps calls rotary on to trunks that are still working. This way, someone doesn't end up on your third trunk with endless ringing, while your 4th, 5th, 6th etc. trunks are free, leaving them wondering where you are and wondering why you're not getting any calls.

BUSY OVERRIDE A feature of some PBXs which allows the attendant or other high priority user to barge in on a telephone conversation. A warning tone is usually thrown into the conversation to alert the parties of an override. The feature is also called "Barge-In." Sometimes when conversations are overridden, only the person within the organization can hear the barge-in.

BUSY SEASON An annual recurring and reasonably predictable period of maximum busy hour requirements — normally three months of the year, and typically the three months preceding Christmas.

BUSY SIGNAL A signal indicating the line called is busy. The busy signal is generated by the central office. There are two types of busy signals. See BUSY.

BUSY TEST A method of figuring whether something which can carry traffic is actually doing so or whether it's broken or free and available for use.

BUSY VERIFICATION OF STATION LINES 1. An attendant can confirm that a line is actually in use by establishing a connection (dialing in and listening) to that apparently busy line. 2. In the public switched telephone network, a switching system service feature that permits an attendant to verify the busy or idle state of station lines and to break into the conversation. An alternating tone of 440 Hz is applied to the line for 2 seconds, followed by a 0.5-second burst every 10 seconds to alert both parties that the attendant is connect to the circuit.

BUTTINSKY Or Butt Set. The one-piece telephone carried on the hips of telephone technicians. It's called buttinsky or butt set because it allows technicians to "butt in" on phone calls, not because the device is worn on their butts. Butt sets used to be essentially telephones without ringers. But now they are much more sophisticated. They will pulse out in rotary or dial out in touchtone and allow you to talk or to monitor a call. They will run computerized tests on the line. Some even have the equivalent of an asynchronous computer terminal built in, which can be used to talk to a distant computer over a phone line. This distant computer could assign them their next jobs, allow them to check and assign features (touchtone, rotary, hunt), report the time spent on this job, etc. In short, the terminal and the computer could replace a raft of clerks and a deluge of paperwork.

BUTTON CAPS Interchangeable plastic squares fit over the buttons of electronic telephones, and are used to label the features programmed onto each programmable button location. Button caps can be either pre-printed or have clear windows which allow features, lines, and Autodial numbers to be labelled on the button.

BUTT SET See BUTTINSKY.

BUZZ 1. To check the continuity of a cable pair by putting an audible buzzer on one end and then checking with a "buttinsky" to see if you can hear the buzz and thus identify the correct cable pair. 2. A feature of a Rolm CBX which lets the user signal one Rolm desktop product without picking up the handset. Only one buzz per extension is permitted.

BUZZER An electromechanical device that makes a buzzing noise when power is applied, often used to signal someone to answer an intercom call. Battery-powered buzzers were once used to help trace phone circuits. TONE GENERATORS are more common today, but old terminology is still used, as in "buzzing out a line."

BUZZER LEADS The wires inside a telephone intended for the connection of a buzzer, usually as part of an intercom system.

BVA AT&T's exclusively-owned Billing Validation Application database. Today, BVA contains all the Regional Bell Operating Companies (RBOCs) calling cards, and other billing information such as billed number screening and payphone numbers. The RBOCs and AT&T access that database today. Prior to Divestiture three market players, the RBOCs, AT&T and most Independent Companies, dominated the "O" Operator Services business which provided alternate billing arrangements such as collect calls, bill to third number and charging calls to calling cards. The three market players still exclusively employ BVA which allows them to validate or authorize alternate billing arrangements. No other long distance carrier or a company needing access to the data for billing validation can use the system. The database is owned by AT&T and is updated daily by the RBOCs and Independent Companies with local exchange information, billing number screening and calling card information. The scenario is further complicated by the 1984 AT&T Plan of Reorganization's exclusive BVA access restrictions. In other words, the three original market players (AT&T, the RBOCs and Independent Companies) have exclusive access to BVA for a predetermined contract length. In most cases these arrangements run into the 1990's. See BVS.

BVS Business Validation Service. US West Service Link was the first in the nation to develop and make available a nationwide Billing Validation Service open to any company that needs to verify the legitimacy of their callers' requests to place charge calls to their local telephone calling cards. US West Service Link developed BVS in 1987 and turned up the system for "on-line" customers in early 1988. Today, the US West BVS system is a national validation source containing calling card data of customers served by the RBOCs GTE, Southern New England Telephone, United Telecommunications, Cincinnati Bell, Rochester Telephone and Telecomm Canada, a consortium representing all of Canada's local telephone operating companies. In all, more than 60 million records are stored. US Sprint, MCI and ITI are among the carriers using BVS. BVS uses X.25 and SS7 protocol. See BVA.

BX.25 AT&T's rules for establishing the sequences of events and the specific types and forms of signals required to transfer data between computers. BX.25 includes the international rules known as X.25 and more.

BYPASS A term coming from the idea of using a method of local communications other than the local telephone company. The theory is you bypass the local phone company for typically two reasons: 1. Because the phone company is too expensive. 2. Because the phone company can't get you the bandwidth, the quality, the fast delivery or the service you want.

Bypass means you might be transmitting between two of your offices in the same city, perhaps between your office and your factory, etc. You might also be transmitting directly to your friendly long distance telephone company, which then carries your calls to distant cities. Bypass means you might be using one, several or many technologies, including your own private microwave, your own cable (metal or fiber), using the local CATV company, using the local bypass company, of which there are now dozens.

Bypass is a word created by the local telephone industry to sound very threatening. The theory is major users will bypass their local phone company, depriving their phone company of needed revenues. This will drive the phone company close to imminent bankruptcy, or at the very least, to the state regulators for huge rate increases, hurting everyone. The reality of this threat has not been proven. Nevertheless, the rhetoric frightens sufficient regulators to look at the evils of bypass and to outlaw it, or at least severely restrict it — as several states have done. This will strengthen the phone company's local monopoly, the objective of the exercise in the beginning. The reality is that bypass in all its forms is expanding, under encouragement from large users and from the FCC. See also 700 SERVICE.

BYPASS CABLING Bypass cabling or relays are wired connections in a local area ring network that permit traffic between two nodes that are not normally wired next to each other. Such bypass cabling might be used in an emergency or while other parts of the system are being serviced. Usually such bypass relays are arranged so that any node can be removed from the ring and the two nodes on either side of the removed node can then talk.

BYPASS TRUNK GROUP A trunk group circumvents one or more tandems in its routing ladder.

BYTE A popular microcomputer magazine, which derives its name from the true meaning of BYTE, which is eight bits of information composed of zeros or ones, one of which may include a parity bit. Most character sets, e.g. ASCII or EBCDIC, use one byte per character of information such as a letter, a number or digit, a punctuation mark or a symbol, such as $. A byte is to a bit what a word is to a character. In some circles a byte is called an octet. See BYTE COUNT.

BYTE COUNT The number of 8-bit bytes in a message. Since ASCII characters typically have 8-bits, the byte count is also called the character count.

BYTE COUNT PROTOCOL A class of data link protocols in which each frame has a header containing a count of the total number of data characters in the body of the frame.

BYTE MULTIPLEXER CHANNEL An IBM mainframe input/output channel that allows for the interleaving, or multiplexing, of data in bytes. Compare with block multiplexer channel.

BYTE MULTIPLEXING A byte (or character) from one channel is sent as a unit and bytes from different channels follow in successive time slots.

BYTE TIMING CIRCUIT Optional X.21 circuit used to maintain byte or character synchronization.

BZT Bundesamt fuer Zulassungen in der Telekommunikation. The name of the German telecom approval authority.

C

C The programming language AT&T uses for several of its central office switches. It is also used as the programming language of choice for interactive voice response (voice processing) systems. C operates under UNIX, MS-DOS and other operating systems. It is very powerful and is becoming somewhat of a standard for programming telecom switches. AT&T writes its C programs under the operating system UNIX, because UNIX is a true multi-tasking system.

C BAND Portion of the electromagnetic spectrum used heavily for satellite transmission. The uplink frequency is at 6 GHz and the downlink is at 4 GHz. Contrast with KU BAND.

C BATTERY A source of low potential used in the grid circuit of a vacuum tube to cause operation to take place at the desired point on the characteristic curve.

C LEAD The third of three wires which make up trunk lines between central office switches. There are three wires — positive, negative, and the "c lead." The purpose of the "c lead" is to control the grounding, holding and releasing of trunks.

C MESSAGE WEIGHTING This definition from James Harry Green, author of the excellent Dow Jones Handbook of Telecommunications. C Message Weighting is a factor in noise measurements to approximate the lesser annoying effect on the human ear of high and low-frequency noise compared to mid-range noise.

C2 Command and Control. The exercise of authority and direction by a properly designated commander over assigned forces in the accomplishment of the mission. Command and control functions are performed through an arrangement of personnel equipment, communications, facilities, and procedures employed by a commander in planning, directing, coordinating, and controlling forces and operations in the accomplishment of the mission. See C3.

C3 Command, Control and Communications. The capabilities required by military commanders to exercise command and control of their forces. See C2.

C7 European equivalent of the North American System Signaling 7. C7 is not 100% compatible with North American System Signaling 7 and that's where gateway switches come in. These switches convert the signaling between one and the other and do it in real time.

C&C NEC Corp.'s idea of combining Computers and Communications into something truly wondrous.

C-DTE Character mode Data Terminal Equipment. A term to describe most PCs (personal computers) and printer-terminals that use asynchronous signals for data communications.

C-LINK A signaling link used to connect mated pairs of Signal Transfer Points (STPs). An Ericsson term.

C-MESSAGE WEIGHTING A type of telephone weighting network that allows for equal attenuation of all frequencies within the voice band in the same manner as it appears to be attenuated by the media.

C/A CODE The standard Clear/Acquisition GPS (Global Positioning Code) — a sequence of 1023 pseudo-random, binary biphase modulations on the GPS carrier at the chip rate of 1,023 MHz. Also known as the "civilian code." See GPS.

CA Call Appearance

CABLE May refer to a number of different types of wires or groups of wires capable of carrying voice or data transmissions. The most common interior telephone cable has been two pair. It's typically called quad wiring. It consists of four separate wires each covered with plastic insulation and with all four wires wrapped in an outer plastic covering. The wire and cable business is immense. The assortment of stuff it produces each year is mind-boggling. In telecommunications, there is one rule: The quality of a circuit is only as good as its weakest link. Often that "weak link" is the quality of the wiring or cabling (we used the words interchangeably) that the user himself puts in. Please put in decent quality wiring. Don't skimp.

CABLE ASSEMBLY A completed cable and its associated hardware ready to install.

CABLE BAYS Lots of cable arranged like bays in a harbor.

CABLE BUSINESS A magazine on cabling run by Steve Paulov and family in Mesquite (Dallas), TX. A great magazine. 214-270-0860.

CABLE CUTOFF WAVELENGTH For a cabled single-mode optical fiber, Cable Cutoff Wavelength specifies a complex inter-relation of specified length, bend, and deployment conditions. It is the wavelength at which the fiber's second order mode is attenuated a measurable amount when compared to a multimode reference fiber or to a tightly bent single-mode fiber.

CABLE DIAMETER Expressed in millimeters or inches. Affects space occupied, allowable bend radius, reel size, length on a reel and reel weight. Also affects selection of pulling grips.

CABLE DOG Slang expression. In the West, lifelong cable installer who seeks no upward mobility. In the East, worker who deals with underground cable.

CABLE LOSS The amount of radio frequency (RF) signal attenuated (lost) while it travels on a cable. There are many reasons for cable loss, including the cable's shape, its type, its size, its length and what it's made of. For coaxial cable, higher frequencies have greater loss than lower frequencies and follow a logarithmic function. Cable losses are usually calculated for the highest frequency carried on the cable. See ATTENUATION.

CABLE PROTECTION There are three basic types of protection in addition to standard plastic cladding:

ElectroMagnetic (EM) Shielding: Prevents passive coupling. EM shielding can be a metallic conduit or metal wrapping-with appropriate grounding-on the wires.

Pentration-Resistant Conduit: Used to secure the cable from cutting or tapping. Note, however, not all penetration-resistant conduits provide EM shielding.

Pressurized Conduit: Detects intrusion by monitoring for pressure loss. Fiber optic cable is extremely difficult to tap and if tapped, the intrusion can be detected through signal attenuation. But since fiber optic cable can be cut, penetration-resistant conduit is recommended to protect the cable.

CABLE RACKING Framework fastened to bays to support cabling between them.

CABLE RISER Cable running vertically in a multi-story building to serve the upper floors.

CABLE RUN Conduit used to run cables through a building. Also, path taken by a cable or group of cables.

CABLE SHIELD A metallic component of the cable sheath which prevents outside electrical interference and drains off current induced by lightning.

CABLE TELEVISION RELAY STATION CARS. A fixed or mobile station used for the transmission of television and related audio signals, signals of standard and FM broadcast stations, signals of instructional television fixed stations, and cablecasting from the point of reception to a terminal point from which the signals are distributed to the public.

CABLE TYPE The type of cable used. Also called the media. Examples are coaxial, UTP (Unshielded Twisted Pair), STP (Shielded Twisted Pair) and fiber. Factors including cost, connectivity and bandwidth are important in determining cable type. Choosing cable is getting more and more complex. Our tip: Choose and buy well in advance of when you'll need it. The cable you want will not always be in stock.

CABLE VAULT Room under the main distribution frame in a central office building. Cables from the subscribers lines come into the building through the cable vault. From here they snake their way up to the main distribution frame. The cable vault looks like a bad B-movie portrayal of Hell, replete with thousands of dangerous black snakes. Cable vaults are prime targets for the spontaneous starting of fires. They should be protected with Halon gas, but usually aren't because some parts of the phone industry think Halon is too expensive.

CABLE WEIGHT Expressed in lbs. per 1000 (without reel weight included). Affects sag, span and size of messenger in aerial applications.

CABLEGRAM SERVICE An MCI definition. An MCI International service which provides cablegram communication to International destinations through the use of a computerized messagd switching center in New York City.

CAC Customer Administration Center. A type of terminal used by a PBX user to maintain and troubleshoot his PBX.

CACHE A cache is high-speed memory designed to hold upcoming to-be-accessed and/or recently-accessed data. A cache speeds up a computer's operation because high-speed memory sends information to and from the computer's central microprocessor much faster than a hard disk could. Cache memory gives the computer user the impression that the computer and its programs are actually running a lot faster than they are theoretically capable of. Cache memory comes in RAM on a computer's motherboard and on hard disk controller cards. The value of a cache is directly related to how good the software is that runs it. There are wide variations in the quality of caching software. A cache is especially important in a LAN file server. It can be used to "speed up" access to a database stored on the file server, thereby saving workstation users time and aggravation. Caches work because of a phenomenon known as the locality principle which states that a von Neumann CPU (i.e. one that performs instructions one after another) tends to access the same memory locations over and over again. A cache works like this: when the CPU needs data from memory, the cache hardware and software checks to see if the information is already in the cache. If it is, it grabs that information. This is called a cache hit. If it isn't, it's called a cache miss and the computer has to access the disk, which is slower. Data retrieved during a cache miss is often written into the cache. See also CACHE MEMORY.

CACHE HIT When the data you want is actually in cache. Thus you don't have to access your hard disk and your computing is fast. See CACHE and CACHE MEMORY.

CACHE MEMORY Available Random Access Memory that you set up to allow your computer to "remember" stuff — so the next time your computer wants that information, it can find it fast from RAM, instead of searching through a hard disk which is slow. This high speed cache memory eliminates the CPU wait state. When the CPU reads data from main memory, a copy of this data is stored in the cache memory. The next time the CPU reads the same address, the data is transferred from the cache memory instead of from main memory. Novell's NetWare, for example, uses cache memory to improve file server access time. In NetWare, cache memory contains the directory and file caches, along with the FAT (File Allocation Table), the turbo FAT, the Hash table, and an open space for other functions. See also CACHE.

CACHE MISS When the caching software guesses wrongly and you have to read your data off your hard disk rather than reading it from the cache. See also CACHE and CACHE MEMORY.

CAD 1. Computer Aid Disptach. 2. Computer Aided Design. A computer and its related software and terminals used to design things. A CAD system might be as simple as computerized drafting tools or as complex as detailed layouts of integrated circuits. CAD systems often have terminals on peoples' desks and a central maxi-computer in the company's main computer room. CAD terminals are often run over LANs (local area networks) or through telephone systems. The terminals are often moved, thus having universal wiring and a universal switching system — a LAN or a phone system — is extremely useful.

CAD/CAM Computer Aided Design/Computer Aided Manufacturing. See CAD.

CADB Calling Area Data Base. An MCI definition. An MCI System that stores reference data for various MCI Systems and reconciles MCI Calling Areas with those of Bell.

CADENCE In voice processing, cadence is used to refer to the pattern of tones and silence intervals generated by a given audio signal. Examples are busy and ringing tones. A typical cadence pattern is the US ringing tone, which is one second of tone followed by three seconds of silence. Some other countries, such as the UK, use a double ring, which is two short tones within about a second, followed by a little over two seconds of silence.

CADS Code Abuse Detection System.

CAE Computer Aided Engineering.

CAGE ANTENNA An antenna having conductors arranged cylindrically.

CAGR Compounded Annual Growth Rate.

CAI 1. Computer Assisted Instruction. See also CAD for a discussion on telecom needs. 2. Common Air Interface, the standard interface that allows a wireless handset to communicate with a base station.

CALIBRATE To test and reset a measuring or timing device against a standard to make sure it is functioning correctly.

CALL My definition: Two people on the phone. One calls the other. People who speak on phones are called "parties." No one knows why. Bellcore's definition: An arrangement providing for a relation between two or more simultaneously present users for the purpose of exchanging information.

CALL ACCOUNTING SYSTEM A computer, a magnetic storage device (floppy or hard disk), software and some mechanical method of attaching itself to a telephone system. A call accounting system is used to record information about telephone calls, organize that information and upon being asked, prepare reports — printed or to disk. The information which it records (or "captures") about telephone calls typically includes from which extension the call is coming, which number it is calling (local or long distance), which circuit is used for the call (WATS, MCI, etc.), when the call started, how long it lasted, for what purpose the call was made (which client? which project?). A call accounting system might also include information on incoming calls — which trunk was used, where the call came from (if ANI or interactive voice response was used), which extension took the call, if it was transferred and to where and how long it took.

There are eleven basic uses for call accounting systems:

1. Controlling Telephone Abuse. It's the 90-10 rule. 10% of your people sit on long distance calls all day to their friends and family. The others work. Some people still think WATS calls are free. Knowing who's calling where and how much they're spending is useful. Often they appreciate being told they're spending money. Big money...and they stop.

2. Controlling Telephone Misuse. I figured once you could call between two major cities for five cents a minute and $1 a minute. That's a 20-fold difference! Often you need different lines. Often a company has different lines. Sometimes the phone system makes the dialing decision. Sometimes the person makes the dialing decision. Whoever's doing it can be wrong. A call accounting system is a good check to see if you're spending money needlessly.

3. Allocating telephone calling costs among departments and divisions. Telephones — voice, data, video and imaging — are some of your biggest expenses. They're a cost that should be allocated to the products you're making, or the departments or divisions in your company. Telephone costs can determine which product is profitable. Which isn't. Item: A software company recently dropped one of its three "big" software packages because phone calls for support got too expensive.

4. Billing Clients and Projects back for telephone charges incurred on their behalf. Every lawyer, government contractor, etc. does it. Makes sense.

5. Sharing and Resale of long distance and local phone calls, as in a hotel/motel, hospital, shared condominium, etc. Someone's got to send out the bills. And it's not the phone company. In fact, with a call accounting system you can be your own phone company!

6. Motivation of Salespeople. The more phone calls they make the more they sell. This rule is as obvious as the nose on your face. You WANT salespeople to make more calls? Hang a list of all their calls on the wall. Give prizes to those make the most! Or those who make more than last week. Or those who set a new record.

7. Personnel Evaluation. Which employees are doing better at being productive on the phone (however you define "productive"). You want them to get on and off the phone fast? Or you want them to stay on and coddle your customers? You can now correlate phone calls with income — from service or just straightout sales.

8. Network Optimization. Two fancy words for figuring which is the best combination of MCI, AT&T, MCI, Sprint, Wiltel, etc. lines. And which is the best combination of all the various services each offer. A rule of thumb: There's a 20-fold difference in per minute telephone calling costs between any two major cities in the US. And — amazing — you won't hear any difference in quality, despite the huge difference in price. I think it's the biggest price difference in any product anywhere. It's amazing.

9. Phone System Diagnostics. Is the phone system working as well as it should? Are all the lines working? Are all the circuit packs (circuit cards) working? Call accounting systems can tell you which lines you're getting no traffic on. Or which line carried the 48 hour call to Germany (it's happened). Either way, you can figure quickly which lines are working and which aren't.

10. Long Distance Bill Verification. Was the bill accurate we received from our chosen long distance phone company? Mostly it isn't. In fact, there's no such thing as an accurate phone bill. That's an oxymoron. Using your call accounting systems to check your long distance gives you some peace of mind. It's cheap peace of mind. Everyone should have one.

11. Tracing Calls. True story: Every third or fourth Friday afternoon a large factory in the south received bomb threats. They'd clear the factory, search the factory and not find anything. By the time they'd checked, it was too late to start up production. One day they checked their call accounting records. The calls were coming from a phone on the factory floor. The whole thing was a ruse to get an afternoon off...And now that many phones give you the number of who's calling, call accounting systems are turning out to be great for checking the effectiveness of regonal ad campaigns, figuring the profitability of direct mailings and even figuring the profitability of individual customers.

CALL ANNOUNCEMENT A PBX operator can announce a call to the called party before putting the call through. All modern PBXs have this feature.

CALL ATTEMPT A try at making a telephone call to someone. Tally up call attempts and compare them to completions and you'll have some idea of corporate frustration and thus, the need for more lines or more phone equipment. The measures in this in call attempts, calls answered, calls overflowed, and calls abandoned.

CALL BARRING The ability to prevent all or certain calls from reaching to or from a phone.

CALL BEFORE DIG A preventive maintenance measure in which signs are posted near buried cables advising people to phone before digging in the area.

CALL BLOCK A name for a Pacific Bell (and possibly other local telephone companies') service which helps you avoid unwanted calls by rejecting calls from numbers you specify. BellSouth describes its service called "Call Block" as "prevents the number received from getting through again. It also lets the subscriber pre-select up to six phone numbers to be blocked.

CALL BLOCKING Check into a hotel. Dial a 0+ call. You're connected to an Alternate Operator Service company. But you know their rates may be high. You ask to be connected to AT&T or MCI, or whoever is the carrier of your choice. Sadly, the AOS cannot connect and neither can (nor will) your hotel's operator. This is called "Call Blocking." The FCC has disbarred the practice. But it continues. See also CALL SPLASHING.

CALL CENTER A place where calls are answered and calls are made. A call center will typically have lots of people (also called agents), an automatic call distributor, a computer for order-entry and lookup on customers' orders. A Call Center could also have a predictive dialer for making lots of calls quickly. The term "call center" is broadening. It now includes help desks and service lines. For more information on Call Centers, please read CALL CENTER Magazine. 212-691-8215.

CALL CLEAR PACKET An information packet that ends an X.25 communications session, performing the equivalent of hanging up the phone.

CALL CLEARING The process by which a call connection is released from use.

CALL COLLISION 1. Contention that occurs when a terminal and a DCE simultaneously transfer a call request and an incoming call specifying the same logical channel. The DCE will proceed with the call request and cancel the incoming call. 2. That condition arising when a trunk or channel is seized at both ends simultaneously, thereby blocking a call.

CALL COMPLETION RATE The ratio of successfully completed calls to the total number of attempted calls. This ratio is typically expressed as either a percentage or a decimal fraction.

CALL CONTROL Used generally by the telephone industry to describe setup, monitoring, and tearing down of telephone calls.

CALL CONTROL SIGNAL Any one of the entire set of interactive signals necessary to establish, maintain, and release a call.

CALL DELAY The delay encountered when a call reaches busy switching equipment. In normal POTS telephone service, the delay is considered OK if no more than one and a half percent of the calls are delayed by three seconds during the busy hour.

CALL DETAIL RECORDING A feature of a telephone system which allows the system to collect and record information on outgoing phone calls — who made them, where they went, what time of day they were placed, how long they took, etc. It is usually needed if you are to install a Call Accounting System. See also CALL ACCOUNTING SYSTEM.

NEWTON'S TELECOM DICTIONARY

CALL DIVERTER 1. A device which when connected to a called telephone number intercepts calls to that number and connects them to a telephone operator or prerecorded message. 2. An ancillary device which is connected to a telephone line. The device will, when the called telephone rings, initiate a telephone call on another line to a different telephone number. The calling party may or may not be aware that his call has been diverted to another telephone.

CALL DURATION The time from when the call is actually begun (i.e. answered) to the instant either party hangs up. Call Duration is an important concept for traffic engineering.

CALL ESTABLISHMENT The process by which a call connection is created.

CALL FORWARDING A service available in many central offices, and a feature of many PBXs and some hybrid PBX/key systems, which allows an incoming call to be sent elsewhere. There are many variations on call forwarding: Call forwarding busy. Call forwarding don't answer. Call forwarding all calls, etc.

A useful feature. For example, you're going to a meeting but you're expecting an important call. Pick up your phone, punch in some digits and all your calls will go to the new number — perhaps the phone outside the meeting room.

The big disadvantage is that many people return to their offices but forget they forwarded their calls elsewhere. As a result, they usually miss a whole bunch of important calls. Some electronic phones now have a reminder light or message on them saying "all calls are being forwarded." Some people program their PBXs to cancel all call forwards at noon and at midnight every day. This makes sense.

To begin call forwarding, the code is 72# and the number you want to be forwarded to. To cancel it, you punch in 73#.

CALL FRAME Harris' PBX to computer link. Harris' protocol for linking its PBX to an external computer and having that computer control the movement of calls within a Harris PBX. See also OPEN APPLICATION INTERFACE.

CALL HOLD If you hang the phone up, you lose the caller. Call hold — a feature of most phone systems — allows you to "hold" the call, so the other person can't hear you. You can then return to the conversation by pushing a button on your phone, typically the button flashing which shows which line the person is sitting on hold. Call hold is useful when you have someone on another line calling you.

CALL IDENTIFIER A network utility that is an identifying name assigned by the originating network for each established or partially established virtual call and, when used in conjunction with the calling DTE address, uniquely identifies the virtual call over a period of time.

CALL IN ABSENCE HORN ALERT A cellular car phone feature that sounds your car's horn when you are receiving a call.

CALL IN ABSENCE INDICATOR A cellular car phone feature that ensures that power to the cellular phone is not lost if the car's ignition is turned off.

CALL LETTERS Certain combinations of letters assigned to radio stations by the FCC. The group of letters assigned the U.S. by the International Radiotelegraph Convention are all three and four letter combinations beginning with N and/ or W and all combinations of KDA to KZZ inclusive.

CALL ME CARD A special AT&T Card number which permits others to call you, and only you, and have the call charged to your telephone. Give an AT&T CALL ME Card to your very best customers to encourage them to call you. A Call Me Card is like having a private unlisted 800 toll-free number.

CALL ME MESSAGE A Rolm/IBM feature on their CBX that allows internal users to leave other users a message showing the time, date and the caller's extension number.

CALL MODEL An abstraction of the call processing functionality of the architecture and the relationship that exists between the functionality of the Service Switching FE in an ASC and the Service Logic and Control FE in a SLEE (Service Logic Execution Environment). The call model consists of two components: Connection View and Basic Call State Model. Definition from Bellcore in reference to Advanced Intelligent Network.

CALL NOT ACCEPTED SIGNAL A call control signal sent by the called terminal to indicate that it does not accept the incoming call.

CALL PACKET A block of data carrying addressing and other information that is needed to establish an X.25 switched virtual circuit (SVC).

CALL PARK The phone call is not for you. Or maybe it is, but you don't want to answer it on your phone. Put it into CALL PARK, then you or anyone else can answer it from any other phone. Call Park is similar to placing a call on hold. The attendant may have a call for you, but you're not there. So he places the call in Call Park, pages you and tells you the call is in Call Park. You pick up the nearest phone, dial one or two digits (the code for grabbing the call out of Call Park) and you have the call. It's faster than looking for you, then telling you to hang up while she transfers the call.

CALL PICKUP A phone is ringing but not yours. With call pickup, you can punch in a button or two on your phone and answer that person's ringing phone. Saves time. See CALL PICKUP GROUP.

CALL PICKUP GROUP All the phones in an area that can be answered by each other by simply punching in a couple of digits. See CALL PICKUP.

CALL PROCESSING The system and process that sets up the intended connection in a switching system. The system scans the trunk and/or station ports for any "requests" for service. Upon detecting a request, the system checks the stored instructions and look-up tables and sets the connection up accordingly.

CALL PROGRESS TONE A tone sent from the telephone switch to tell the caller of the progress of the call. Examples of the common ones are dial tone, busy tone, ringback tone, error tone, re-order, etc. Some phone systems provide additional tones, such as confirmation, splash tone, or a reminder tone to indicate that a feature is in use, such as confirmation, hold reminder, hold, intercept tones.

CALL QUEUING Incoming or outgoing calls may be queued pending an answer. The idea of call queuing is to save money. See also CALLBACK QUEUING.

CALL RECORD The data record of a call transaction. The record is made up of event details that typically include date, time, trunk(s) used, station(s) used and duration. In an ACD, these events may also include time in queue, call route used, system disposition flag, inbound or outdialled digits and wrap-up data entered.

CALL REFERENCE Information element that identifies to which call a Layer 3 message pertains.

CALL RELEASE TIME The time it takes from sending equipment a signal to close down the call to the time a "free condition" appears and the system is ready for another call.

CALL RESTRICTOR Equipment inserted in a telephone line or trunk which restricts outgoing calls in some way. Usually from making a toll call.

CALL REQUEST PACKET In packet data switching, a call request packet carries information, such as sender and recipient identification, that is needed to establish an X.25 circuit. In more technical terms, a call request packet is sent by the originating data terminal equipment (DTE) showing requested network terminal number (NTN), network facilities and either X.29 control information or call user data.

CALL RETURN A name for a Pacific Bell (and possibly other local telephone companies') service which allows you to dial the last caller, even if you did not answer the telephone.

CALL SCREENING There are several definitions. Here are two. 1. A PBX feature that looks at the digits dialed by the caller to figure whether the call should be completed. 2. A receptionist or secretary answers the "executive's" phone and checks out that the person calling is important enough be put through to the almighty executive whose calls are being screened.

CALL SECOND A unit for measuring communications traffic. Defined as one user making one second of a phone call. One hundred call seconds are called "ccs," as in Centum call seconds. "ccs" is the U.S. standard of telephone traffic. 3600 call-seconds = 1 call hour. 3600 call-seconds per hour = 36 CCS per hour = 1 call-hour = 1 erlang = 1 traffic unit. See also ERLANG and TRAFFIC ENGINEERING.

CALL SELECTOR A local phone company service which alerts the subscriber with a distinctive ring that one of the six numbers your pre-selected is calling.

CALL SEQUENCER A call sequencer, also called an Automatic Call Sequencer, is a piece of equipment which attaches to a key system or a PBX. The Call Sequencer's main function is to direct incoming calls to the next available person to answer that phone. It typically does this by causing lights on telephones to flash at different rates. The light with the fastest flashing is the one whose call has been waiting longest. This call is answered first. Call Sequencers also might answer the phone, deliver a message and put the person on hold. They might keep statistical tabs of incoming calls, how fast they were answered, how long the people waited, how many people abandoned (hung up while they were on hold waiting for their call to be answered by a human being), etc. Call Sequencers are usually simple and inexpensive. Better, but much more expensive devices for answering incoming phone calls are Automatic Call Distributors. These are the devices which typically answer when you call an airline. See AUTOMATIC CALL DISTRIBUTOR.

CALL SETUP The first six PICs (Point In Call) of the Originating BCSM (Basic Call State Model), or the first four PICs of the Terminating BCSM. Definition from Bellcore in reference to Advanced Intelligent Network.

CALL SETUP TIME The amount of time it takes for a circuit-switched call to be established between two people or two data devices. Call set-up includes dialing, wait time and time to move through central offices and long distance services. You don't pay for call set-up, but you will need extra lines to take care of it. See also ANSWER SUPERVISION and TRAFFIC ENGINEERING.

CALL SPILL-OVER In common-channel signaling, the effect on a traffic circuit of the arrival at a switching center of an abnormally delayed call control signal relating to a previous call, while a subsequent call is being set up on the circuit.

CALL SPLASHING A "splash" happens when an Alternate Operator Service (AOS) company, located in a city different to the one you're calling from, connects your call to the long distance carrier of your choice in the city the AOS operator is in. Let's say you're calling from a Hotel in Chicago. You ask AT&T handle your call. The AOS, located in Atlanta, "splashes" your call over to AT&T in Atlanta. But you're calling Los Angeles. Bingo. Your AT&T call to LA is now more expensive than it would be — if you had been connected to AT&T in Chicago.

CALL SPLITTING A feature allowing a phone user to speak privately with either party of a conference call by alternating between the two. Call splitting by an attendant allows the attendant to speak to the called person privately while effectively putting the calling person on hold, or vice versa.

CALL STALKER An AT&T PC-based product which gives the 911 attendant the phone number and address of the person calling.

CALL STORE The temporary memory used in a stored program control switch (SPC) to hold records of calls in progress. These records are then transferred to permanent memory.

CALL TRACE A name for local telephone company service which permits the tracing of the last call received and holds the results for later use by an authorized law enforcement agency. (Results of the trace are not available to the customer.)

CALL TRANSFER Allows you to transfer a call from your phone to someone else's. On some phones you do this by punching in a bunch of numbers. Some you do it by hitting the "transfer" button and then the number you want to send the call to. The fewer buttons and numbers you have to punch, the easier it will be for your people.

If you're choosing a telephone system, check how easy it is to transfer a call. It is the most commonly used (and misused) feature on a phone system. How many times have you been told, "I'll transfer you to Mr. Smith, but if we get disconnected, please call back on extension 234." If your people are saying this to your customers or prospects, you are giving the outside world the wrong impression of your business. And since 97% of your prospects' contact with your company is first through your phone system, you could be losing precious business.

CALL USER DATA In packet data networking technology, user information transmitted in a call request packet to the destination data terminal equipment (DTE).

CALL WAITING There are three types of call waiting: 1. From an attendant.

2. From an originating user. 3. To a terminating user. The general concept is as follows: You're speaking on the phone. A call comes in for you. You might hear a beep in your ear or see a light on your phone turn on. Or you might hear a beep and see a message come across the screen of your phone. When you hear the beep, you can, if you wish, put the present call on hold and answer the new one. Or you can ignore the new one, hoping it will go away, and perhaps return to your attendant/operator. The above scenario relates to call waiting put on you by an attendant, another internal user or which you buy as a monthly service from the phone company.

Call Waiting is provided by most modern telephone systems — private ones and central offices. They have slightly different ways of working. These days, even some hotel phones have call waiting. So listen for beep tones. It may be the call you're expecting. Better yet, ask your hotel to put you in a room with two lines.

A major problem with call waiting is if you're on a data call from your PC, the call waiting "beep" will often cause your modem to hang up, thus destroying your data call. There are two solutions to this, the obvious one being turn off call waiting. Some phone systems will allow you to turn it off. The less obvious one is modify your modem. Here's how. In all Hayes and Hayes-compatible modems, there's a S10 register. It tells the modem how long before it hangs up after losing carrier. In Hayes modems, the S10 register is set for 1.4 seconds. The typical call waiting tone is 1.5 seconds. Solution, increase the S10 register to six seconds (to be sure). Use your communications software. Go into terminal mode, then type: ATS10=60. You must put this command in every time you power up, because the Hayes 1200 modem (and others) have volatile memory. But the Hayes 2400 and the 9600 (and other 2400 baud and higher asynchronous modems) have non-volatile memory. They remember the six seconds after they've been switched off. The command to write this to memory is ATS10=60&W. The "&W" means write it to memory.

CALLBACK A feature of some voice and data telephone systems. You dial someone. Their phone or computer is busy. You hit a button or code for "call-back." When their phone becomes free, the phone system will call you and them simultaneously. You can only use this call-back feature on things internally in your phone system — calling other people, calling long distance lines (which might be busy), calling the dictation pool, etc. See CALLBACK QUEUING and CALL WAITING.

CALLBACK MODEM A modem that calls you back. Here's how it works. You dial into a network. A modem answers. You put your password in. It accepts the password. It says "Please hang up. I will now call you back." You hang up. It calls you back. There are two reasons for doing this instead of allowing you to just go straight into the network. 1. It's better security. You have to be at a pre-determined place — an authorized phone number. 2. It may save on phone calls. The modem uses the company's communications network, which is probably cheaper than what the person calling in can use.

CALLBACK QUEUING An option on a PBX which allows outgoing calls to be put in line for one or several trunks. When a trunk becomes available, the PBX calls the user, his phone rings and then the PBX dials the distant party on the trunk it grabbed before calling the user. PBXs typically have two types of queuing. The first is called Hold-On Queuing. With this, the user dials his long distance number, the PBX searches for the correct trunk, finds it's not available and tells the user with a beep or message. The user then elects to stay on the line and wait. The instant the trunk becomes free, the PBX connects the user to it. The second type of queuing is called Callback Queuing. The user hangs up and the phone system calls you back, as we explained above.

There are tradeoffs between the two types of queuing. Callback queuing obviously can tolerate longer queues. The longer you wait, the more chance you have of reaching a very low-cost trunk. But users don't like waiting so long for a trunk. And when the call does come, it may likely reach a phone, newly-deserted by a user who's gone to the bathroom.

In contrast, hold-on queuing is more efficient of the user's time, but less efficient of the user's trunks. The less time you wait, the less chance you have of reaching a low-cost trunk. Life is a trade-off. Queuing is no exception. See also QUEUING.

CALLBRIDGE Rolm to non-IBM computers open architecture interface. A method of connecting a Rolm CBX (telephone system) to a non-IBM computer, so that the computer may "talk" to the PBX and make certain things happen, e.g. moving a screen of client information around simultaneously with the phone call from the client. This feature is especially useful in customer service and customer order-entry environments — for example with direct mail order catalog companies, etc. See OPEN APPLICATION INTERFACE.

CALLED DTE A DTE which receives a call from another DTE.

CALLED LINE IDENTIFICATION FACILITY A service feature provided by a network (private or public), which enables a calling terminal to be notified by the network of the address to which the call has been connected. See CALLER ID.

CALLER ID Your phone rings. A name pops upon on your phone's screen. It's the name of the person calling you. Or it may be just the caller's phone number. It's called Caller ID and the information about name and/or calling phone number is passed to your phone by your telephone company's central switch. There are basically two forms of "caller ID" — one provided by your local phone company and one provided by your long distance company (chiefly on 800 calls). Caller ID, generic term, is a term most commonly applied to the service your local phone company provides, usually called CLASS. In CLASS, the information about who's calling and/or their phone number is passed to your phone between the first and second ring signaling an incoming call. There is considerable controversy about local calling ID, since some people say it invades peoples' privacies (the caller's privacy). And there are states in which Caller ID hasn't been allowed, or where it's been allowed with restrictions, or where they're still arguing about it. There are standards for local caller ID. There are standards for long distance Caller ID. And they're not the same. However, there are tests underway and one day you may actually have a phone in your home or your office which will tell you who's calling on all your calls — local and long distance. Don't hold your breath! See also CLASS and ANI.

CALLER INDEPENDENT VOICE RECOGNITION Having a voice response unit recognize the voice of a caller without having been trained on the caller's voice.

CALLED LINE IDENTIFICATION SIGNAL A sequence of characters transmitted to the calling terminal to permit identification of the called line.

CALLED PARTY SUBADRESS Information element that is passed transparently by the SPCS (if certain conditions are met) and can be used to further identify the destination party.

CALLED PARTY CAMP-ON A communication system service feature that enables the system to complete an access attempt in spite of issuance of a user blocking signal. Systems that provide this feature monitor the busy user until the user blocking signal ends, and then proceed to complete the requested access. This feature permits holding an incoming call until the called party is free.

CALLING CARD A sort of credit card issued by Bell operating companies, AT&T, MCI and others used for charging long distance calls. Typically, the number on your calling card is the phone number at which you receive bills (home or business phone) plus a four digit Personal Identification Number (PIN number). Some phone companies — local and long distance — charge more for a call made with a Calling Card. Some don't.

CALLING DTE A DTE (Data Terminal Equipment) which places a call to another DTE.

CALLING LINE ID You are called. As the call comes in, you receive the phone number of the person calling you. Calling Line ID is another term for AUTOMATIC NUMBER IDENTIFICATION. Calling Line ID is used increasingly for the phone numbers of local calls, while ANI tends to be used for the phone numbers of distant phone numbers. Essentially they're the same. See also ANI, CALLING NUMBER DISPLAY, ISDN and SIGNALING SYSTEM 7.

CALLING LINE IDENTIFICATION FACILITY A service feature, provided by a network, that enables a called terminal to be notified by the network of the address from which the call has originated. See CALLING LINE ID.

CALLING NUMBER DISPLAY Your phone has a LCD (Liquid Crystal Display) or LED (Light Emitting Diode) display. When your phone rings, it will show which telephone number (internal or external) is calling you. Some phone systems allow you to add the person's name to the calling number display. See also ANI and CALLER ID.

CALLING PARTY The person who makes (originates) the phone call.

CALLING PARTY CAMP-ON A feature that enables the system to complete an access attempt in spite of temporary unavailablitity of transmission or switching facilities. Systems that provide this feature monitor the system facilities until the necessary facilities become available, and then proceed to complete the requested access. Such systems may or may not issue a system blocking signal to let the caller know of the access delay.

CALLING PARTY IDENTIFICATION A new service being tested in some areas which tells the person being called the number calling them. They can then decide to answer or not answer it. See ANI, which stands for Automatic Number Identification.

CALLING PARTY NUMBER Information element that identifies the number of the originating party. An AIN term.

CALLING PARTY SUBADDRESS Information element that is passed transparently by the SPCS (if certain conditions are met) and can be used to further identify the originating party. An AIN term.

CALLING SEQUENCE A sequence of instructions together with any associated data necessary to perform a call.

CALLPATH IBM's announced telephone system link to IBM's computers. See CALLPATH SERVICES ARCHITECTURE, CALLPATH CICS, and CALLPATH HOST.

CALLPATH CICS Enabling software that connects your telephone systems with your IBM 370 or 390 (i.e. the mainframe version of CallPath/400, which works on the AS/400 platform).

CALLPATH HOST IBM and ROLM's CICS-based integrated voice and data applications platform which links to ROLM's 9751 PBX. See CALLPATH SERVICES ARCHITECTURE.

CALLPATH SERVICES ARCHITECTURE CSA. IBM's program for intergrating voice and data technologies. It is both a strategy and set of open architecture commands and interfaces for integrating voice and database technologies. The idea is that with CallPath a call will arrive at a computer terminal simultaneously with the database record of the caller. And such call and database record can be transferred simultaneously to an expert, a supervisor, etc. The first implementation is CallPath/400 which works with the IBM AS/400 minicomputer. CallPath CICS works with IBM mainframes. See OPEN APPLICATION INTERFACE and DIRECTTALK.

CAM 1. Call Applications Manager. The name of the Tandem software interface which provides the link between a call center switch telepone switch (either a PBX or an ACD) and all Tandem NonStop (fault tolerant) computers. CAM supports most major PBXs and automatic call distributors. 2. Computer-Aided Manufacture. The actual production of goods implemented and controlled by computers and robots. Often used in conjunction with CAD. Only a few factories are completely automated. Usually, there is some human intervention in the actual construction of the product, often to make sure a part is placed in the robot correctly.

CAMA Centralized Automatic Message Accounting. See CAMA/LAMA.

CAMA/LAMA Centralized Automatic Message Accounting/Local Automatic Message Accounting. Specific versions of AMA in which the

NEWTON'S TELECOM DICTIONARY

ticketing of toll calls is done automatically at a central location for several COs (CAMA) or only at the local office for that office's subscribers.

CAMP-ON You want to transfer a call to a phone but it's busy. This telephone system feature will allow you to lock the call you're trying to transfer onto the line that's busy. When it becomes free, the phone will ring and the "camped-on" call will be connected automatically.

CAMPUS BACKBONE Wiring between buildings.

CAMPUS ENVIRONMENT An environment in which users — voice, video and data — are spread out over a broad geographic area, as in a university, hospital, medical center, prison. There may be several telephone systems. There may be several LANs on a campus. They will be connected with bridges and/or routers communicating over telephone, microwave or fiber optic cable.

CAMPUS SUBSYSTEM The part of a premises distribution system which connects buildings together. The cable, interbuilding distribution facilities, protectors, and connectors that enable communication among multiple buildings on a premises.

CANCEL By touching the "cancel" button on a phone system you're telling the phone system to ignore the last command you gave it. That command might have been transfer, hold, park, etc. The "cancel" button is often mistakenly confused with the "release" button. The "release" button acts the same as hitting "Enter" on a computer system, i.e. it tells the system to go ahead and do what you just told it to do, no matter how stupid your command. In short, "Cancel" means kill the last command. You use when you make a mistake. "Release" means "Enter" — Do it and do it now.

CANNIBALIZE To devour a phone system by stripping parts from it to repair another system. A common technique for maintaining equipment whose original manufacturer no longer supplies parts. Before you cannibalize, check out the monthly publication Telecom Gear. That publication lists sources of secondary telecom equipment. Good stuff, too.

CAP 1. Customer Administration Panel. A simplified alternative to CAC, which is a Customer Administration Center. These are AT&T words. 2. Computer Aided Professional Publishing. The computerization of professional publishing (as opposed to desktop operations), including true color representation of the layout on the workstation screen.

CAP'N CRUNCH see CAPTAIN CRUNCH.

CAPACITANCE The capacity of a medium (wire, cable, resistor, bus) to store an electrical charge. Capacitance is measured in farads.

CAPACITIVE COUPLING The transfer of energy from one circuit to another by virtue of the mutual capacitance between the circuits.The coupling may be deliberate or inadvertent. Capacitive coupling favors

173

transfer of higher frequency components, whereas inductive coupling favors transfer of lower frequency components.

CAPACITY 1. The information carrying ability of a telecommunications facility. What the "facility" is determines the measurement. You might measure a date line's capacity in bits per second. You might measure a switch's capacity in the maximum number of calls it can switch in one hour, or the maximum number of calls it can keep in conversation simultaneously. You might measure a coaxial cable's capacity in bandwidth. 2. The measure of the amount of electrical energy a condenser can store up. The unit of capacity is the farad.

CAPACITY TRANSFER CONTROL A Northern Telecom term for a feature which permits single allocation of capacity to be shared among members in a digital switched broadcast connection. For teleconferencing, for instance, a conference leader can transfer transmission capacity among the digital ports in the circuits. 95% of such transfers will take place within 10 seconds.

CAPS 1. Code Abuse Prevention System. 2. Competitive Access Providers to the local telephone network i.e., Teleport or Metropolitan Fiber System.

CAPSIZING When downsizing, rightsizing and upsizing fail. Contributed by Fred Schindler of IBM.

CAPSTAN 1. A flangeless pulley used to control speed and motion of magnetic tape through a recorder or playback unit. 2. A rotating drum or cylinder used for pulling cables by exerting traction upon a rope or pull line passing around the drum.

CAPTAIN Character And Pattern Telephone Access Information Network System. A form of videotext developed in Japan and operated through the public switched telephone network. Displays are on a TV set. It's interactive.

CAPTAIN CRUNCH At one point in the 1960s, a breakfast cereal had a promotion. It was a toy whistle. When you blew the whistle, it let out a precise 2,600 Hz tone. If you blew that whistle into the mouthpiece of a telephone after dialing any long distance number, it terminated the call as far as the AT&T long distance phone system knew, while still allowing the connection to remain open. If you dialed an 800 number, blew the whistle and then touchtoned in a series of tones (called MF tones) you could make long distance and international calls for free. The man who discovered the whistle was called John Draper and he picked up the handle of Cap'n Crunch in the nether world of the late 1960s phone phreaks. A marvellous account of the exploits of phone phreaks was published in the October 1971 issue of Esquire Magazine. That article described how the Cap'n would call himself (he needed two lines) — choosing to route the connection through Tokyo, India, Greece, South Africa, South America, London, New York and California — to make his second phone next to him ring. He'd have a wonderful time talking to himself, albeit with a round-the-world delay (despite the speed of light) of as long as 20 seconds. Later, AT&T closed the loophole Cap'n Crunch had discovered. AT&T turned from in-band signaling to out-of-band signaling. Cap'n Crunch's legacy (he got put in jail four times during the 1970s) is System Signaling 7, a system of immense benefit to us all. See MULTI-FREQUENCY SIGNALING and SIGNALING SYSTEM 7.

CAPTIVE EFFECT An effect associated with the reception of frequency-modulated signals in which, if two signals are received on or near the same frequency, only the stronger of the two will appear in the output. The complete suppression of the weaker carrier occurs at the receiver limiter, where it is treated as noise and rejected. Under conditions where both signals are fading randomly, the receiver may switch from one to the other.

CAPTURE EFFECT An effect associated with the reception of frequency-modulated signals in which, if two signals are received on or near the same frequency, only the stronger of the two will appear in the output. The complete suppression of the weaker carrier occurs at the receiver limiter, where it is treated as noise and rejected. Under conditions where both signals are fading randomly, the receiver may switch from one to the other.

CAPTURE RATIO The ability of a tuner or receiver to select the stronger of two signals at or near the same frequency. Expressed in decibels, the lower the figure, the better.

CAR PHONE The type of cellular phone that's installed in a vehicle. There are four types of cellular phones being sold today— mobile, transportable, portable and personal. A car phone (also called a mobile unit) is attached to the vehicle, its power comes from the vehicle's battery and the car phone has an external antenna, which works best if it's mounted in the middle of the highest point of the car and wired directly with no breaks in the wire. Many window-mounted antennas have a break in their wiring. The wiring snacks to the inside window whence it stops. There is no electrical connection between the inside of the window and the antenna glued onto the outside of the window. The "connection" is done through signal radiation. In North America, the car phone transmits with a standard three watts of power.

CARBON BLOCK A device for protecting cable from lightning strikes. The carbon block consists of two electrodes spaced so that any voltage above the design level is arced from line to ground. Carbon block protectors are used commonly in both local customer offices and central offices. They are effective, but can be destroyed if high voltage is directly applied — as in a direct strike by lightning. A more expensive, but more effective method of protection is the gas tube. These are glass capsules that are connected between the circuit and the ground. When a voltage higher than the design voltage strikes the line, the gas ionizes and conducts the excess voltage to ground. When the voltage is gone, the protector restores itself to normal. Gas tubes, however, take a tiny time to ionize. This may not be fast enough for very sensitive things, like PBX circuit cards. So gas tube protectors are often equipped with diodes, which clamp the interfering voltage to a safe level until the gas tube ionizes.

CARBON FIBER A strong synthetic material that is low in mass with excellent damping characteristics, used in the manufacture of tonearms.

CARBON RHEOSTAT A rheostat using carbon as the resistance material. See RHEOSTAT.

CARBON TRANSMITTER The microphone of a telephone set which uses carbon granules and a diaphragm. The diaphragm responds to our voice and varies the pressure on the granules and hence, their resistance. If your carbon mike isn't working well, tap it lightly on your desk. The carbon granules will line up and it will work much better. Carbon microphones are very reliable but are being increasingly replaced with more sensitive electronic mikes. Some say electronic mikes are too sensitive, so recently, some manufacturers have gone back to carbon mikes.

CARD AUTHORIZATION CENTER CAC. A computer directly linked to MCI switches for authorization and determination of billing center ID for MCI card calls.

CARD DIALER A device attached to a telephone which accepts a special plastic card and then automatically dials the number on the card as indicated by the holes punched in it. A card dialer is now obsolete except for unusual applications, like systems whereby you carry your card with you and use it as a security device.

CARD SERVICES The software layer above Socket Services that coordinates access to PCMCIA cards, sockets and system resources. Card Services is a software management interface that allows the allocation of system resources (such as memory and interrupts) automatically once the Socket Services detects that a PC Card has been inserted. Socket Services is a BIOS level software interface that provides a method for accessing the PCMCIA slots of a computer. Card Services is a software management interface that allows the allocation of system resources (such as memory and interrupts) automatically once the Socket Services detects that a PC Card has been inserted. Both of these specifications are contained in the PCMCIA Standards document. See PCMCIA.

CARET The symbol ^ which is found above 6 on most keyboards. Also used to indicate the "Ctrl" key in some instruction manuals.

CAROT Centralized Automatic Reporting On Trunks. A test and maintenance facility associated primarily with electronic toll switching systems like the AT&T Communication's #4-ESS. CAROT is a computerized system that automatically accesses and tests trunks for a maximum of fourteen offices simultaneously. It enables rapid routine testing of all trunks to ensure quick identification of faults and potential failures.

CARPEL TUNNEL SYNDROME Carpel tunnel syndrome is a serious disorder of the arm caused by fast, repetitive work, such as typing without support for your wrists or with insufficient time for rest. In carpel tunnel syndrome, the tendons passing through the wrist bones swell and press on the median nerve. Surgery to take pressure off the nerve can relieve numbness and pain, but it's not always effective and many victims remain permanently disabled.

CARRIAGE RETURN By hitting this key, the printing head or the cursor on your screen will return to the left hand margin. Usually hitting a Carriage Return or the "Enter" key includes a line feed, i.e. the paper will move up one line or the cursor will drop down one line. "Usually" does not mean always. So check. You can usually correct the problem of not having a line feed with a carriage return by moving a dip switch on the printer, changing one of the parameters of the telecommunications software program (the part where it says something about auto linefeed) or changing the computer's operating system (by doing a "Config" or the like). In most microcomputers, a Carriage Return is equivalent to a "Control M," or ASCII 13. A line feed is a "Control J".

CARRIER 1. A company which provides communications circuits. Carriers are split into "private" and "common." A private carrier can refuse you service. A "common" carrier can't. Most of the carriers in our industry — your local phone company, AT&T, MCI, US Sprint, etc. — are common carriers. Common carriers are regulated. Private carriers are not. 2. An electrical signal at a continuous frequency capable of being modified to carry information. It is the modifications or the changes from the carrier's basic frequency that become the information carried. Modifications are made via amplitude, frequency or phase. The process of modifying a carrier signal is called modulation. A carrier is modulated and demodulated (the signal extracted at the other end) according to fixed protocols. Some of the wideband (i.e. multi-frequency) circuits are also called "carriers." T1, which typically has 24-channel PCM voice circuits, is known as a carrier system.

CARRIER BAND A band of continuous frequencies that can be modulated with a signal.

CARRIER BYPASS A long distance phone company provides a direct link between its own switching office and a customer's office, thus bypassing the local phone company. Bypass is done to save the customer or the long distance company money. Bypass is also done to get service faster. Sometimes the local phone company simply can't deliver fast enough.

CARRIER COMMON LINE CHARGE Also called Access Charge. The charge which long distance phone companies pay to local phone companies to complete their long distance calls. These charges typically are much more than the local phone company gets from its normal business and residential users for completing local phone calls of the same distance. High access charges are designed to help the local phone company financially. That they do. They also encourage bypass and may, in the long term, be self-defeating.

(There are advantages to either way. There is no "right" way. Our own preference, however, is to use "carrier detect.") All asynchronous modems have the ability to adjust to either way of handling "carrier detect." In a Hayes or Hayes compatible modem with dip switches, Switch 6 determines whether the carrier detect is "forced true," i.e. the program and the modem will ignore the presence or absence of carrier, or whether it responds to carrier detect. In a Hayes or Hayes compatible modem without dip switches but with "switches" in memory, the command is AT&C1. If your modem has non-volatile memory, the command is AT&C1&W.

CARRIER DETECT CIRCUITRY Electronic components which detect the presence of a carrier signal and thus determine if a transmission is about to happen. Used in modems. See CARRIER DETECT.

CARRIER FREQUENCY 1. The frequency of a carrier wave. 2. The frequency of an unmodulated wave capable of being modulated or impressed with a second (information-carrying) signal. In frequency modulation, the carrier frequency is also referred to as the "center frequency."

CARRIER IDENTIFICATION CODES CIC. Three digit numbers used by end-user customers to reach the services of interexchange carriers through equal access arrangements. The primary carrier of choice is reached by dialing "1" plus the area code and called party number. Secondary IX carriers can still be reached by dialing 10 plus the CIC assigned to the carrier desired. CIC numbers are used to dial around the carrier presubscribed to the calling telephone (e.g. 10-XXX or 950-0XXX where XXX is the CIC).

CARRIER LEAK The unwanted carrier remaining after carrier suppression in a suppressed carrier transmission system.

CARRIER LIAISON COMMITTEE CLC. A committee formed to help industry participants work together to resolve the issues of implementing 800 Portability. CLC is sponsored by the Exchange Carriers Standards Association (ECSA) and is comprised of the LECs (local exchange carriers), long distance carriers and users of 800 service.

CARRIER LOSS In T-1, carrier loss means too many zeros. A carrier loss in T-1 is said to occur when 32 consecutive zeros appear on the network. Carrier is said to return when the next 1 is detected.

CARRIER NOISE LEVEL The noise level resulting from undesired variations of a carrier in the absence of any intended modulation.

CARRIER POWER (OF A RADIO TRANSMITTER) The average power supplied to the antenna transmission line by a transmitter during one radio frequency cycle taken under the condition of no modulation. Does not apply to pulse modulation or frequency-shift keying.

CARRIER PROVIDED LOOP MCI is responsible for ordering coordinating, maintaining, and billing the local loop.

NEWTON'S TELECOM DICTIONARY

CARRIER SELECT KEYS Buttons at the bottom of a payphone used to choose a long distance carrier.

CARRIER SELECTION As a result of Judge Greene's Modified Final Judgment which lead to the breakup of the Bell System, most local phone companies must offer their customers (business and home) the opportunity to select which long distance company they would like to be use on a "primary" basis. That means when you dial 1+ (one plus) you get that carrier. To use any other long distance company you have to dial more digits, e.g. 1-0288 (for AT&T).

CARRIER SENSE In a local area network, a PC or workstation uses its network card to detect if another station is transmitting. See CSMA.

CARRIER SENSE MULTIPLE ACCESS CSMA. In local area networking, CSMA is a way of getting onto the LAN. Before starting to transmit, personal computers on the LAN "listen" to make sure no other PC is transmitting. Once the PC figures out that no other PC is transmitting, it sends a packet and then frees the line for other PCs to transmit. With CSMA, though stations do not transmit until the medium is clear, collisions still occur. Two alternative versions (CSMA/CA and CSMA/CD) attempt to reduce both the number of collisions and the severity of their impact. See CSMA/CA and CSMA/CD.

CARRIER SENSE MULTIPLE ACCESS WITH COLLISION AVOIDANCE CSMA/CA. A protocol that requires the PC to sense if another PC is transmitting. If not, it begins transmitting. Under CSMA/CA, a data station that intends to transmit sends a jam signal; after waiting a sufficient time for all stations to pick up the jam signal, it sends a transmission frame; if while transmitting, it detects another station's jam signal, it stops transmitting for a designated time and then tries again.

CARRIER SENSE MULTIPLE ACCESS/COLLISION DETECTION A network control scheme. It is a contention access control scheme. It "listens" for conflicting traffic to avoid data collisions. The Ethernet LAN uses CSMA/CD, then waits a small amount of time and then tries again. See CSMA/CD and ETHERNET.

CARRIER SHIFT 1. A method of keying a radio carrier for transmitting binary data or teletypewriter signals, which consists of shifting the carrier frequency in one direction for a marking signal and in the opposite direction for a spacing signal. 2. In amplitude modulation, a condition resulting from imperfect modulation whereby the positive and negative excursions of the envelope pattern are unequal, thus effecting a change in the power associated with the carrier. There can be positive or negative carrier shift.

CARRIER SIGNAL A continuous waveform (usually electrical) whose properties are capable of being modulated or impressed with a second information-carrying signal. The carrier itself conveys no information until altered in some fashion, such as having its amplitude changed (amplitude modulation), its frequency changed (frequency modulation) or its phase changed (phase modulation). These changes convey the information.

CARRIER SYNCHRONIZATION In a radio receiver, the generation of a reference carrier with a phase closely matching that of a received signal.

CARRIER SYSTEM A system where several different signals can be combined onto one carrier by changing some feature of the signals transmitting them (modulation) and then converting the signals back to their original form (demodulation).

CARRIER TERMINAL The modulation, demodulation and multiplex equipment used to combine and separate individual channels at the ends of a transmission system.

CARRIER TO NOISE RATIO CNR. In radio receivers, the ratio, expressed in decibels, of the level of the carrier to that of the noise in the receiver bandwidth before any nonlinear process such as amplitude limiting and detection takes place.

CARRIER WAVE The radio frequency wave generated at a transmitting station for the purpose of carrying the modulated or audio frequency wave.

CARRIED LOAD The traffic that occupies a group of servers on a LAN.

CARRIED TRAFFIC The part of the traffic offered to a group of servers that successfully seizes a server on a LAN.

CARS Cable Television Relay Service Station. A fixed or mobile station used for the transmission of television and related audio signals, signals of standard and FM broadcast stations, signals of instructional television fixed stations, and cablecasting from the point of reception to a terminal point from which the signals are distributed to the public.

CARTERFONE A device for connecting a two-way mobile radio system to the telephone network invented by Thomas Carter. The device was made out of bakelite. It was electrically connected to the base station of the mobile radio system. When someone on the radio wanted to speak on a "landline" (the phone system), the base station operator would dial the number on a separate phone then place the telephone handset in the Carterfone device. The handset was acoustically, not electrically, connected to the phone system. No more than 4,000 Carterfones were ever installed, yet the Bell System thought they were the most dangerous device ever invented. Tom Carter died in Gun Barrel, TX where he lived, in the early part of 1991. He died not a rich man. See CARTERFONE DECISION.

CARTERFONE DECISION In the summer of 1968 the FCC said that the Carterfone and other customer phone devices could be connected to the nation's phone network — if they were "privately beneficial, but not publicly harmful." The Carterfone decision was a landmark. It allowed the connection of non-telephone company equipment to the public telephone network. This decision marked the beginning of the telephone interconnect business as we know it today. The Carterfone decision made a lot of lawyers rich before all the rules on connection to the network got cleared up, and finally codified in something called Part 68 of the FCC's Rules. See CARTERFONE and NETWORK HARM.

CARTRIDGE 1. A device which holds magnetic tape of some kind. 2. A device to translate (transduce) stylus motion to electrical energy in a phonograph. It comes in three basic types — moving magnetic coil, induced magnet and ceramic. A phono cartridge is also call a pickup. Most record players use ceramic cartirdges because they have higher output than the three magnetic types and can work with a less powerful (i.e. cheaper) amplifier.

CAS 1. Centralized Attendant Service. One group of switchboard operators answers all the incoming calls for several telephone systems located throughout one city. CAS is used by customers with several locations in the same geographic area, i.e. retail stores, banks. 2. Communicating Applications Specification. A high-level API (Application Programming Interface) developed by Intel and DCA that was introduced in 1988 to define a standard software API for fax modems. CAS enables software developers to integrate fax capability and other communication functions into their applications.

CASCADE To connect the output of a device into the input of another device, often the same type as the first.

CASCADE AMPLIFICATION The method of successively using two or more vacuum tubes for amplification at radio, intermediate or audio frequencies.

CASCADED STARS Local area network topology in which a centralized multiport repeater serves as the focal point for many other multiport repeaters.

CASCADING NOTIFICATION A feature of some sophisticated voice mail systems. Let's say someone leaves a message for you in your voice mail box. Your voice mail system then automatically goes out to find you, i.e. to notify you. It may start by lighting your message light, calling your home phone number, calling your cellular phone, calling your beeper, etc. I like this feature because when I want you, I want you. And a little mechanized help is much appreciated. I first saw the feature in Macrotel's MVX voice mail series.

CASE Computer Aided Software Engineering. CASE is a new, faster, more efficient way of writing software for some applications. The idea with CASE is to sketch out relations between databases, events, and options and then have the computer write the code.

CASSEGRAIN ANTENNA An antenna in which the feed radiator is mounted at or near the surface of a concave main reflector and is aimed at a convex secondary reflector slightly inside the focus of the main reflector. Energy from the feed unit illuminates the secondary, reflects it back to the main reflector, which then forms the desired forward beam. This technique is adapted from optical telescope technology and allows the feed monitor radiator to be more easily supported.

CASSETTE TAPE A slow, inefficient method of storing and retrieving data which uses the same technology as audio cassettes — like the Sony Walkman. Some PBXs use cassette tape to backup their user programming and database.

CASTELLATION A series of ribs and metallized indentations that defines edge contact regions.

CAT Computerized Axial Tomography. CAT allows X-rays of the brain.

CATEGORY OF PERFORMANCE The EIA/TIA Technical Sysems Bulletin (TSB) 36 for unshielded twisted pair (UTP) wire and the impending release of EIA/TIA TSB 40 for cross-connect hardware provide the performance benchmarks that the cabling industry must meet in order to claim a particular category of performance. The table below highlights the different categories and their supported data rates:

Category	Data Rate Supported
1,2	Voice
3	10 Mbps
4	20 Mbps
5	100 Mbps

CATHODE The heated element which emits electrons in a vacuum tube. It may be a filament, or may be a separate element, heated by proximity to a filament. It is maintained at a negative potential in respect to the anode or plate. Cathodes have other applications, also.

CATHODE RAY The beam of electrons emitted by a cathode. See CATHODE RAY TUBE.

CATHODE RAY TUBE CRT. A TV screen. A CRT is a tube of glass, used in television, oscilloscope and computer terminals, from which air has been removed (i.e. vacuum tube). At the back of the CRT is an electron gun which directs an electron beam to the front of the tube. The inside front of the tube has been coated with fluorescent material which reacts to and lights up once the electron beams hit. CRTs are very reliable if they are vented, since the electron gun gets hot. CRTs have a "memory." They will memorize what's been left on their screen for a while, i.e. the image is burned into the screen. And you'll see it even though the screen is turned off. In short, turn your screen off when you're not using it. Or run a "CRT-saving" program which varies the image on the screen.

CATLAS AT&T software standing for Centralized Automatic Trouble

Locating and Analysis System. CATLAS is used as a maintenance tool for locating and diagnosing problems in AT&T electronic central offices.

CATV Community Antenna TeleVision or CAble TeleVision. CATV is a broadband transmission facility. It generally uses a 75-ohm coaxial cable which simultaneously carries many frequency-divided TV channels. Each channel is separated by guard channels. See ADDRESSABLE PROGRAMMING and BROADBAND.

CAU Northern Telecom term for Connection Arrangement Unit.

CAVITY A volume defined by conductor-dielectric or dielectric-dielectric reflective boundaries, or a combination of both, and having dimensions designed to produce specific interference effects (constructive or destructive) when excited by an electromagnetic wave.

CB Why 10-4, good buddy, that stands for Citizens Band. Also known as Children's Band, not because of Radio Shack's toy walkie talkies, but for the inane chatter that sometimes goes on in these channels. In short, CB is low-power (up to four WATTS permitted) public radio. You do not need permission from the FCC to transmit or receive at these frequencies. Thus CB's great popularity. CB went through a boom (perhaps a craze?), then it ran out of radio frequencies and public enthusiasm. Its original frequencies were 26.965 to 27.225 Mhz. Now the FCC's given it new frequencies — 462.55 to 469.95 MHz. These new frequencies are much better, clearer and less congested. If you buy a CB set, make sure you get one that operates in these higher frequencies. In some countries they use different frequencies. CB radio is not allowed in many countries, even some civilized countries, though it will obviously work there.

CBEMA Computer Business Equipment Manufacturers Association. A lobbying group created to protect the interests of its members.

CBF Computer Based Fax.

CBK Change BacK.

CBR Constant Bit Rate. It refers to processes such as voice that require a constant, repetitive or uniform transfer of information.

CBTA Canadian Business telecommunications Alliance. The largest organizationn of business telecom users in Canada.

CBX Computerized Branch eXchange. CBX is a registered trademark of the ROLM Corporation, Santa Clara, CA. Rolm is now owned by Siemens and IBM, but largely by Siemens. What CBX is to Rolm, PBX or PABX is to other companies. The term CBX has not received wide acceptance, except at Rolm.

CBX II A Rolm communications controller for larger systems. Two versions exist: the CBX II 8000 (16-bit CPU) and the CBX II 9000 (32-bit CPU).

CCC 1. Clear Coded Channel. A 64 kbps channel in which all 64 kbps is available for data. 2. Clear Channel Capability. The bandwidth of a data transmission path available to end users after control and signaling bits are accounted for. 3. Communications Competition Coalition. Lobbying organization establised to encourage competition in telecommunications in Canada.

CCD 1. Charge-Coupled Devices. An imaging technology used in cameras in which the image is focused by a lens on one or several charged devices which regiser the colors. 2. Change Coupled Device.

CCDN Corporate Consolidated Data Network. An IBM word.

CCFL Cold Cathode Fluorescent Lamp. A technology several laptop computer manufacturers use to light their LCD screens.

CCIA Computer and Communications Industry Association. A trade organization of computer, data communications and specialized common carrier services companies headquartered in Arlington VA. It runs seminars, does lobbying and generally tries to take care of the common interests of its members. See CBEMA.

CCIR Comite' Consultatif International des Radiocommunications (Consultative Committee on International Radiocommunications France). Also used to describe 625-line television system used primarily in Western Europe. The US system of TV is 525. The high definition TV is scheduled to be 1,125.

CCIS Common Channel Interoffice Signaling. A way of carrying telephone signaling information along a path different from the path used to carry voice. CCIS occurs over a separate packet switched digital network. CCIS is separate from the talk path. A special version of CCIS is called Signaling System #7. SS#7 is integral to ISDN. CCIS offers basically two benefits: first, it dramatically speeds up the setting up and tearing down of phone calls. Second, it allows much more information to be carried about the phone call than what is carried on in-band (old-fashioned) signaling. That information can include the calling number, a message, etc.

Signaling for a group of voice telephone circuits is done on CCIS by encoding the information digitally on one of the voice circuits. In the previous method of signaling — the one replaced by CCIS — multi-frequency tones were sent down the same talkpath and the conversation would eventually travel. By taking the signaling information out of the talk path, the "phone phreak" community could no longer get free calls by using so-called "blue boxes" which duplicated the multi-frequency tones used by switching machines. CCIS is a much more efficient method of signaling, since it doesn't require a full voice grade channel just to check if the called party in LA is free and whether the call coming in from New York should be put through. See also COMMON CHANNEL SIGNALING, SYSTEM SIGNALING 7, ISDN and COMMON CHANNEL INTEROFFICE SIGNALING.

CCITT Comite Consultatif Internationale de Telegraphique et Telephonique, which, in English, means the Consultative Committee on International Telegraphy and Telephony. The CCITT is one of the four permanent parts of the International Telecommunications Union, the ITU, based in Geneva Switzerland. The scope of its work is now much broader than just telegraphy and telephony. It now also includes telematics, data, new services, systems and networks (like ISDN). The ITU is a United Nations Agency and all UN members may also belong to the ITU (at present 164), represented by their governments.

In most cases the governments give their rights on their national telecom standards to their telecommunications administrations (PITs). But other national bodies ((in the US, for exmaple, the State Department) may additionally authorize Recognised Private Operating Agencies (RPOAs) to participate in the work of the CCITT. After approval from their relevant national governmental body, manufacturers and scientific organisations may also be admitted, as well as other international organisations. This means, says the ITU, that participants are drawn from the broad arena. The activities of the CCITT divide into three areas:

Study Groups (at present 15) to set up standard ("recommendations") for telecommunications equipment, systems, networks and services.

Plan Committees (World Plan Committee and Regional Plan Committee) for developing general plans for a harmonised evolution of networks and services.

Specialized Autonomous Groups (GAS, at present three) to produce handbooks, strategies and case studies for support mainly of developing countries.

Each of the 15 Study Groups draws up standards for a certain area - for example, Study Group XVIII specializes in digital networks, including ISDN. Members of Study Groups are experts from administrations, RPOAs, manufacturing companies, scientific or other international organisations - at times there are as many as 500 to 600 delegates per Study Group. They develop standards which have to be agreed upon by consensus. This, says the ITU, can sometimes be rather time-consuming, yet it is a democratic process, permitting active participation from all CCITT member organisations.

The long-standing term for such standards is "CCITT recommendations." As the name implies, recommendations have a non-binding status and they are not treaty obligations. Therefore, everyone is free to use CCITT recommendations without being forced to do so. However, there is increasing awareness of the fact that using such recommendations facilitates interconnection and interoperability in the interest of network providers, manufacturers and customers. This is the reason why CCITT recommendations are now being increasingly applied — not by force, but because the advantages of standardized equipment are obvious. ISDN is a good example of this.

CCITT has no power of enforcement, except moral persuasion. Sometimes, manufacturers adopt the CCITT specs. Sometimes they don't. Mostly they do.

CCITT V.24 In data communications, a set of standards specifying the characteristics for interfaces. Those standards include descriptions of the various functions provided by each of the pins. This standard is similar (but not identical) the RS-232-C as established by the American TIA/EIA — Telecommunications Industry Association/Electronics Industries Association.

CCIU Northern Telecom word for Conference Control Interface Unit.

CCO SYSTEM DEC VAX and IBM mini/mainframe telecommunications management software from the folks at Telco Research Nashville, TN. Includes cost allocation, directory, inventory management, problem recovery, traffic statistics, trouble tickets, work orders, student resale, tenant resale, bill verification, cable and wire, and network optimization applications. Also has a PC-based graphical interface to Telco Research's mini/mainframe telemanagement system.

CCR Customer Controlled Reconfiguration. An AT&T service that lets users make changes in their digital access and cross connect (DACS) network configurations at a DSO Level in either real time or according to a preplanned schedule.

CCS One hundred call seconds or one hundred seconds of telephone conversation. One hour of telephone traffic is equal to 36 CCS (60 x 60 = 3600 divided by 100 = 36) which is equal to one erlang. CCS are used in network optimization. Lee Goeller calls CCS an obsolete traffic unit. He says "When given traffic in CCS, always divide by 36 immediately. It is not obvious that 5 trunks cannot carry 185 CCS, but you don't have to be a rocket scientist to know that you can't average 5.14 calls on a five trunk group." See also TRAFFIC ENGINEERING.

CCSA Common Control Switching Arrangement. A private network set up by AT&T for very large users and using parts of the public switched network. One important feature of a CCSA is that any user anywhere in a CCSA network can reach any other user by dialing only seven digits. Only very large customers subscribe to this service. It's expensive. AT&T has fewer than 100 customers.

CCSA ACCESS A PBX feature which allows a PBX user to get into a CCSA network. See CCSA.

CCS7 COMMON CHANNEL SIGNALING 7. See ISDN.

CCT CONTINUITY CHECK TONE.

CCTV Closed Circuit TV.

CCU Communication Control Unit - Processor, often a minicomputer, associated with a host mainframe computer that performs a number of communications-related functions. Compare with cluster control unit.

CD 1. Carrier Detect. CD is a signal generated by dial-up modem. CD indicates its connection status. If your CD light is on, then your modem is speaking to another modem. 2. Compact Disc. A 4.5 inch diameter disk containing digital audio or digital computer information, which can be played back and (now recorded) on a laser-equipped player. It was introduced by Sony and Philips in 1982. A compact disc originally came in only one flavor — read only. And most music tapes can only be listened to, not recorded to. For music it was a major breakthrough. It recorded music digitally (that is, coded as the zeros and ones of computer-speak) instead of trying to make an electrical copy of the sound waves themselves as devices like audio cassettes and LP records had. The Economist described the CD well. It said, "Instead of using a needle, the sound was plucked from the CD's surface by a tiny beam of laser light and then processed by a microcomputer. To the ear, the leap in performance between a compact disc and a long-playing record was even greater than the difference between color and black and white TV was to eye."

Each month, a division of Ford Motor Co. publishes a CD-ROM inventory of 300,000 parts for its 2,400 dealers. A CD can typically hold 660 megabytes of information. That is the equivalent of 1,500 floppies or 250,000 pages of print. Most computer CD-ROM drives can play audio CD disks — if they have the software and the speakers. Audio CD players, though, cannot play computer CD-ROM disks. But most computer CD-ROM players can play CD audio disks. See CD-R, CD-ROM, CD-I, CD-V and WORM.

CD I See CD-I below.

CD-I Compact Disc Interactive. Geared toward home entertainment, the drive connects to a television.

CD-R Recordable CD disk. A standard and technology allowing you to write to and read from a Compact Disk. This new technology will be compatible with existing CDs, i.e. you should be able to read these disks in existing CD-players. See CD-ROM.

CD-ROM Compact Disc Read Only Memory. Also called CD or CD-ROM. The familiar Compact Disc which you see in the audio stores, but now made for computers. These disks hold huge amounts of data — as much as 660 megabytes. Put into a computer drive, the retrieval time is about 10 times slower than on a hard disk. At the time I wrote this dictionary, response time on typical CD-ROM drives was 300 milliseconds, versus 11 milliseconds for some of the faster hard disks. As I wrote this, I saw an ad for an NEC drive advertising 150 milliseconds, which is very fast for a CD-ROM drive. CD-ROMs will be the basis of the new imaging computers, which will combine voice, data, video and imaging into one system and put it on the desktop. See CD, CD-ROM XA, CD-V and CD-WO.

CD-ROM XA Stands for Compact Disc - Read Only Memory eXtended Architecture. Microsoft's extensions to CD-ROM that let you interleave audio with data. Though it is not a video specification, limited video can be included on disc. Demand for multimedia applications is increasing use of CD-ROM XA. To use it, you must have a drive that reads the audio portions of the disc and audio card in your computer that translates the digital into sound. Not all drives can recognize the extensions. See CD-WO.

CD-V Compact Disc Video. A format for putting 5 minutes of video on a 3-inch disc. This format has come and gone. Video is shifting towards CD-ROM XA.

CD-WO Compact Disc Write Once. A CD-ROM version of the WORM (Write Once Read Many) technology. For companies performing all CD-ROM publishing in-house, this format is useful for creating test discs before sending the master for duplication. CD-WO discs conform to ISO 9669 standards and can be played in CD-ROM drives.

CDAR Customer Dialed Account Recording.

CDDI Copper Distributed Data Interface is a version of FDDI (Fiber Distributed Data Interface— a 100 million bit per second local area network) that runs on unshielded twisted-pair cabling rather than optical fiber.

CDEV Control panel DEVice. An Apple Macintosh term.

CDFP Centrex Data Facility Pooling.

CDH INTERFACE An interface once required by the Bell System to protect their phone lines from "foreign" (i.e. non-AT&T) phone equipment. CDH devices were eventually ruled a total waste of money and the phone companies refunded the money — at least to the subscribers who asked. If you still have the stuff installed, you may be due a huge refund. Watch out for the statute of limitations.

CDLC Cellular Data Link Control. A public domain data communications protocol used in cellular telephone systems. In other words, you can attach a data terminal to a cellular telephone and send and receive information. There are more 5,000 modems using CDLC on the Vodaphone Cellular System in the UK, where it is the de facto standard for cellular data communications. Features like improved synchronization field, forward error correction, bit interleaving, and selective retransmission make CDLC ideal for cellular transmissions, according to Millidyne who makes the CDLC modems in the US.

CDMA 1. Call Division Multiple Access. 2. Code Division Multiple Access, also called Spread Spectrum, is a name for a new form of digital cellular phone service. Motorola, a leading cellular manufacturer, says CDMA is a spread spectrum technology that assigns a code to all speech bits, sends a scrambled transmission of the encoded speech over the air and reassembles the speech to its original format. The major benefits of CDMA is increased capacity (up to 10 times analog) and more efficient use of spectrum. More importantly, CDMA technology provides three features that improve system quality: 1) The "soft hands-off" feature ensures that a call is connected before handoff is completed, reducing the probability of a dropped call. 2) Variable rate vocoding allows speech bits to be transmitted at only the rates necessary for high quality which conserves the battery power of the subscriber unit. 3) Multipath signal processing techniques combines power for increased signal integrity. Additional benefits to the subscriber include increased talk times for handportable units, more secure transmissions and special service options such as data, intergrated voice and data, fax and tiered services.

CDMA works by combinging each phone call with a code which only one cellular phone plucks from the air. Business Week said CDMA works "by spreading all signals across the same broad frequency spectrum and assigning a unique code to each. The dispersed signals are pulled out of the background noise by a receiver which knows the code. This method, developed by a San Diego company called Qualcomm Inc. is very new. According to the Wall Street Joournal, CDMA systems are said to offer up to 20 times more call handling capacity than the conventional cellular systems by assigning a special electronic code to each call signal, allowing more calls to occupy the same space and be spread over an entire frequency band. Much of the equipment to support CMDA, like cellular switches, however, have not yet been developed."

CDMA is about to be used in inside-building wireless PBX conversations by companies including SpectraLink of Boulder, CO. SpectraLink's explanation: "One of several technologies used to separate multiple transmissions over a finite frequency allocation. CDMA operates in conjunction with spread spectrum transmission. Spread spectrum takes the original information signal and combines it with a correlating code, resulting in a signal which occupies a much greater bandwidth than the original. By assigning a unique correlating code to each transmitter, several simultaneous conversations can share the same frequency allocation. The process of using spread spectrum in conjunction with individual correlating codes is known as Code Division Multiple Access." See also CODE DIVISION MULTIPLE ACCESS.

CDO Community Dial Office. A small automatic central office switching system that is completely unattended. Routine maintenance is provided by a traveling technician once or twice each year, or as troubles develop. Such an office usually serves a small community with a few hundred lines in a rural area.

CDPD Cellular Digital Packet Data. CDPD is a new, open standard for the use cellular as a means of wireless data transmission. The technology allows data files to be broken into packets and sent along idle channels of existing cellular voice networks.

CDR Call Detail Recording. See CALL ACCOUNTING.

CDR EXCLUDE TABLE A table listing local central office codes which are not monitored (i.e. ignored) by a call accounting system.

CEBIT CeBIT is the world's largest computer and office automation show. It attracts 600,000 or so people to Hannover, Germany in March or so of each year. It is also called the Hannover Fair. It is about five times the size of Comdex, which is North America's largest computer show. Many of the "booths" at Hannover are really small buildings, which are used year-round. Space at the show is sometimes rented for four years.

CED 1. CallEd station iDentification. A 2100 Hz tone with which a fax machine answers a call. See CNG. 2. Capacitance Electronic Disc. System of video recording a grooved disc, employing a groove-guided capacitance pickup.

CED COMPRESSION A method of compression used in faxing.

CEDAR A Rolm desktop computer phone that is part IBM PC, part Rolm phone.

CEI Comparable Efficient Interface. The idea is that the telephone industry will let all its information providers have this interface — defined by technical specs and pricing — and, if it does, then the phone companies can themselves use this information to become information providers themselves. The concept has merit. Implementation has been agonizingly slow.

CEILING DISTRIBUTION SYSTEMS Cable distribution system that use the space between a suspended or false ceiling and the structural floor for running cable. Methods used in ceiling distribution systems include zone, home-run, raceway, and poke-through.

CEKS Centrex Electronic Key Set.

CELL 1. The basic geographic unit of a cellular system. Also, the basis for the generic industry term "cellular." A city or county is divided into smaller "cells," each of which is equipped with a low-powered radio transmitter/receiver. The calls can vary in size depending upon terrain, capcacity demands, etc. By controlling the transmission power, the radio frequencies assigned to one cell can be limited to the boundaries of that cell. When a cellular phone moves from one cell toward another, a computer at the Mobile Telephone Switching Office (MTSO) monitors the movement and at the proper time, transfers or hands off the phone call to the new cell and another radio frequency. The handoff is performed so quickly that it's not noticeable to the callers. 2. The basic unit of a battery, consisting of plates, electrolyte and a container. A chemical device that produces electricity through electrolysis.

CELL REVERSAL The reversal of the polarity of the terminals of a battery cell as the result of discharging.

CELL SITE CONTROLLER The cellular radio unit which manages the radio channels within a cell.

CELL SPLITTING A means of increasing the capacity of a cellular system by subdividing or splitting cells into two or more smaller cells.

CELLULAR DATA LINK CONTROL CDLC is a public domain data communications protocol used in cellular telephone systems. In other words, you can attach a data terminal to a cellular telephone and send and receive information. There are more 5,000 modems using CDLC on the Vodaphone Cellular System in the UK, where it is the de facto standard for cellular data communications. Features like improved synchronization field, forward error correction, bit interleaving, and selective retransmission make CDLC ideal for cellular transmissions, according to Millidyne who makes the CDLC modems in the US.

CELLULAR FLOOR METHOD A floor distribution method in which cables pass through floor cells, constructed of steel or concrete, that provide a ready-made raceway for distributing power and communication cables.

CELLULAR PROTOCOLS Conventions and procedures which relate to the format and timing of device communications. In data transmission communications, there are currently three major protocols, which are converging into a de facto standard: MNP, SPCL, and PEP.

CELLULAR RADIO A mobile radio system. In the old days, there was one central antenna and everything homed in on that and emanated from it. With cellular radio, a city is broken up into "cells," each maybe no more than several city blocks. Every cell is handled by one transceiver (receiver/transmitter). As a cellular mobile radio moves from one cell to another, it is "handed" off to the next cell by a master computer, which determines from which cell the strength is strongest. Cellular mobile radio has several advantages:

1. You can handle many simultaneous conversations on the same frequencies. One frequency is used in one cell and then re-used in another cell. You can't do this on a normal mobile radio system.

2. Because one cellular system can accommodate many more subscribers than a normal mobile radio system, and therefore because it can achieve certain economies of scale, it has the potential of achieving much lower transmission costs.

3. Because the transceiver is always closer to the user than in a normal mobile system, and the user's radio device thus needs less power, the device can be cheaper and smaller. Cellular radios started at over $5,000 and are now well under $500. From the first portable units, weight has already dropped to under one pound. There are several units that will fit in your breast pocket and not overly stretch your suit.

The following are specific cellular radio terms, or general telecom terms that mean something special in cellular radio:

● A/B Switch Permits user to select either the wireline (B system) or the nonwireline (A system) carrier when roaming.

● Alphanumeric memory. Capability to store names with phone numbers.

● Call-in-absence horn alert. User-activated feature that sounds car horn upon receiving a call.

● Call-in-absence indicator. Feature that displays what calls came in while user was absent.

● Call-in-progress override. Insures that power to the phone is not lost if the car's ignition is turned off.

● Call restriction. Security feature that limits phone's use without completely locking it. Variations might include dial from memory only, dial last number only, seven-digit dial only, no memory access, etc.

● Call timer. Displays information on call duration and quantity. Variations might include present call, last call, total number of calls, or total accumulated time since last reset. Call-timer beep serves as a reminder to help keep calls brief. It might be set to go off once a minute, ten seconds before the minute, for example.

● Continuous DTMF (touch-tones). Sends DTMF (dual-tone, multi-frequency) tones — also called touchtones — allowing access to voice mail and answering machines that require long-duration tones. "Continuous" means you get the tone so long as your finger is on the button. This may seem obvious to you and me, except that some "modern" phones just give a short tone no matter how long you keep your finger on the touchtone button.

● Dual NAM. Allows user to have two phone numbers with separate carriers (see multi-NAM).

● Electronic lock. Provides security by completely locking phone so it can't be used by unauthorized persons.

● Expanded spectrum. Full 832-channel analog cellular spectrum currently available to users.

● Hands-free operation. Allows user to receive calls and converse while leaving handset in cradle (similar to office speakerphone).

● Hands-free answering. Phone automatically answers incoming call after a fixed number of rings and goes to hands-free operation.

● Memory linkage. Allows programming specific memory locations to dial a sequence of other memory locations.

● Multi-NAM. A cellular telephone term to allow a phone to have more than two phone numbers, each of which can be on a different cellular system if desired. This lets the user register with both carriers in home city, expanding available geographic coverage.

● Mute. Silences the telephone's microphone to allow private conversations without discontinuing the phone call. Audio mute turns off the car stereo automatically when the phone is in use, and turns it back on when the call is completed.

● NAM. Numerical Assignment Module. Basically, your cellular phone number, although it refers specifically to the component or module in the phone where the number is stored.

● On-hook dialing. Allows dialing with the handset in the cradle.

● Roaming. Using any cellular system outside your home system. Roaming usually incurs extra charges.

● Scratch pad. Allows storage of phone numbers in temporary memory during a call. Silent scratch pads allows number entry into scratch pad without making beep tones.

● Signal strength indicator. Displays strength of cellular signal to let user know if a call is likely to be dropped.

● Speed dialing. Dialing phone number from memory by pressing a single button.

● Standby time. Maximum time cellular phone operating on battery power can be left on to receive incoming calls.

● Talk time. Maximum time cellular phone operating on battery power can transmit.

● Voice-activated dialing. Your cellular phone recognizes your words and dial accordingly. You say "Dial Mom" and it dials mom.

CELLULAR RADIO SWITCHING OFFICE The electronic switching office which switches calls between cellular (mobile) phones and wireline (i.e. normal wired) phones. The switch controls the "handoff" between cells and monitors usage. Different manufacturers call their equipment different things, as usual.

CELLUPLAN II A proposed national standard to place packets of data between idle spaces on a cellular voice network.

CELP Code Excited Linear Prediction. An analog-to-digital voice coding scheme. Sun is proposing the use of CELP so that a user could send realtime voice communications over local area or wide are network — bypassing the phone system!

CEMH Controlled Environment ManHole. Environmental control of the CEMH is maintained by a heat pump (a fancy name for an airconditioner — cooler and heater).

CENLEC European Electrical Standards Institute (Comite European de Normalization Electrique).

CENTEL CORPORATION A telephone company serving over one million customer lines. It's based near the Chicago O'Hare Airport. During 1992 it was absorbed by Sprint.

CENTRAL OFFICE Telephone company facility where subscribers' lines are joined to switching equipment for connecting other subscribers to each other, locally and long distance. Also called CO, as in See-Oh. Sometimes the term central office is the same as the overseas term "public exchange." Sometimes, it means a wire center in which there might be several switching exchanges.

CENTRAL OFFICE BATTERY A group of wet cells joined in series to provide 48 volts DC. Central office batteries are typically charged off the main 120 volts AC. The batteries have two basic functions. 1. To provide a constant source of DC power for eight hours or so after AC powers drops, and 2. To isolate the central office from glitches on the AC line.

CENTRAL OFFICE CODE Part of the national numbering plan, the central office code is the second three digits of a subscriber's telephone number, which identifies the local switching office.

CENTRAL OFFICE CONNECTION COC. An MCI charge (monthly and installation) for each local access channel. If no access channels are provided, one COC is charged for each serving MCI terminal.

CENTRAL OFFICE OVERRIDE A third party may interrupt or join in your conversation.

CENTRAL OFFICE TRUNK 1. A trunk between central offices. It may be between major switches or between a major and a minor switch. 2. A trunk between public and private switches.

CENTRAL PROCESSING UNIT CPU. The part of a computer which performs the logic, computational and decision-making functions. It interprets and executes instructions as it receives them. Personal computers have one CPU, typically a single chip. It is the so-called "computer on a chip." That chip identifies them as an 8-bit, 16-bit or 32-bit machine.

Telephone systems, especially smaller ones, are not that different. Typically they have one main CPU — a chip — which controls the various functions in the telephone. Today's telephone systems are in reality nothing more than special purpose computers. As phone systems get bigger, the question of CPUs - - central processing units — becomes harder to figure. The design of phone systems has, of late, tended away from single processor-controlled telephone systems (as in single processor controlled PCs). There are several reasons for this move. First, it's more economical for growth. Make modules of "little" switches and join little ones together to make big ones. Second, it's more reliable. It's obviously better not to rely on one big CPU, but to have several. In short, the issue of Central Processing Units — CPUs — is blurring. But the concept is still important because by understanding how your telephone switch works (its architecture), you will understand its strengths and weaknesses.

CENTRALIZED ATTENDANT SERVICE Calls to remote (typically branch) locations are automatically directed to operators at a central location. Imagine four retail stores in a town. There are three branch stores and one main, downtown store, each having their own local phone numbers, which customers call. It's clearly inefficient to put operators at each of the stores — when one group is busy, the other will be free, etc. What this feature does is to direct all the calls coming into each of the stores into one bank of operators, who then send those calls back to the outlying stores.

Despite the extra schlepping of calls around town, having one large group of operators is cheaper than maintaining many small groups. Each store has its own local Listed Directory Number (LDN) Service. Special Release Link Trunk circuits connect each unattended location (each store) to the main attendant location. These trunks are only temporarily used during call processing. An incoming call to an unattended store seizes such a trunk circuit for completion of the call to the centralized attendant, who then uses the same trunk circuit to process the call to the remote location's internal extension. (After all if the caller was calling that store, they obviously want to talk to someone in that store.) The circuit is then released and is available for other calls. Since such special trunk circuits are only used during that part of a call that requires connection between locations, such trunks are more efficient than normal tie trunk circuits.

CENTRALIZED AUTOMATIC MESSAGE ACCOUNTING CAMA. The recording of toll calls at a centralized point.

CENTRALIZED ORDERING GROUP COG. An organization provided by some communications service providers (like a local phone company) to coordinate services between the companies and vendors.

CENTREX Centrex is a business telephone service offered by a local telephone company from a local central office. Centrex is basically single line telephone service delivered to individual desks (the same as you get at your house) with features, i.e. "bells and whistles," added. Those "bells and whistles" include intercom, call forwarding, call transfer, toll restrict, least cost routing and call hold (on single line phones).

Think about your home phone. You can often get "Custom Calling" features. These features are typically fourfold: Call forwarding, Call Waiting, Call Conferencing and Speed Calling. Centrex is basically Custom Calling, but instead of four features, it has 19 features. Like Custom Calling, Centrex features are provided by the local phone company's central office.

Phone companies peddle centrex is leased to businesses as a substitute for that business buying or leasing its own on-premises telephone system — its own PBX, key system or ACD. Before Divestiture in 1984, Centrex was presumed dead. AT&T was, at that time, intent on becoming a major PBX and key system supplier. Then Divestiture came, and the operating phone companies recognized they were no longer part of AT&T, no longer had factories to support, but did have a huge number of Centrex installations providing large monthly revenues. As a result, the local operating companies have injected new life into Centrex, making the service more attractive in features, price, service and attitude. Here are the main reasons businesses go with Centrex as opposed to going with a stand-alone telephone system:

1. Money. Centrex is typically cheaper to get into (the central office already exists). Installation charges can be low. Commitment can also be low, since most Centrex service is leased on a month-to-month basis. So it's perfect for companies planning an early move. There may be some economies of scale, also. Some phone companies are now offering low cost, large size packages.

2. Multiple locations. Companies with multiple locations in the same city are often cheaper with Centrex than with multiple private phone systems and tie lines, or with one private phone system and OPX lines. (An OPX line is an Off Premise eXtension, a line going from a telephone system in one place to a phone in another. It might be used for an extension to the boss's home.)

3. Growth. It's theoretically easier to grow Centrex than a standalone PBX or key system, which usually has a finite limit. With Centrex, because it's provided by a huge central office switch, it's hard, theoretically, to run out of paths, memory, intercom lines, phones, tie lines, CO lines, etc. The limit on the growth of a Centrex is your central office, which may be many thousands of lines.

4. Footprint Space Savings. You don't have to put any switching equipment in your office. All Centrex switching equipment is at the central office. All you need at your office are phones.

5. Fewer Operators because of Centrex's DID features. Fewer operator positions saves money on people and space.

6. Give better service to your customers. With Centrex, each person has their own direct inward dial number. Many people prefer to dial whomever they want directly rather than going through a central operator. Saves time.

7. Better Reliability. When was the last time a central office crashed? Here are some of the features built into modern central offices: redundancy, load-sharing circuitry, power back-up, on-line diagnostics, 24-hour on-site personnel, mirror image architecture, 100% power failure phones, complete DC battery backup and battery power. Engineered to suffer fewer than three hours down time in every 40 years.

8. Non-blocking. Trunking constraints are largely eliminated with Centrex, since a central office is so large.

9. Minimal Service Costs. Repair is cheap. Service time is immediate. People are right next to the machine 24-hours a day. Phones and wires are the only things that require repair on the customers' premises. You can easily plug new phones in, plug them out yourself. All other equipment is in the central office. You need not hold inventory or test equipment.

10. No technological obsolescence. Renting Centrex means a user has the ultimate flexibility — ability to jump quickly into new technology. Central offices are moving quickly into new technologies, such as ISDN.

11. Ability to manage it yourself. You can now get two important features previously available only on privately-owned self-contained phone systems (like PBXs): 1. The ability for you, the user, to make changes to the programming of your own Centrex installation without having to personally call a phone company representative. 2. The ability to get call detail accounting by extension and then have reports printed by a computer in your office. The phone company does this call accounting by installing a separate data line which carries Centrex call records back to the customer as those calls are made.

The above arguments are pro-Centrex. There are also anti-Centrex arguments. And there's plenty of evidence to argue exactly the opposite. For example, central offices often run out of capacity. The "big" key to Centrex traditionally comes down to price. And, in fact, in some cities the price of Centrex lines is lower than "normal" PBX lines. Of course, you can buy Centrex lines and attach your own PBX or key system to those Centrex lines. The big disadvantage of Centrex is that there are no specialized Centrex phones able to take better advantage of Centrex central office features than normal electronic phones can.

Centrex is known by many names among operating phone companies, including Centron and Cenpac. Centrex comes in two variations — CO and CU. CO means the Centrex service is provided by the Central Office. CU means the central office is on the customer's premises. See the following CENTREX definitions.

CENTREX CO Indicates that all equipment except the attendant's position and station equipment is located in the central office. See CENTREX.

CENTREX CU Indicates that all equipment including the dial switching equipment, is located on the customer's premises. See CENTREX.

CENTREX CCRS Centrex Customer Rearrangement System. Computer software from New York Telephone that allows their Centrex customers to make certain changes in their own line and features arrangements. Other phone companies have similar services under different names.

CENTREX LAN SERVICE Put a modem on a dedicated central office line. Connect that line to a switch. Bingo you have a switched, relatively high-speed service that can connect synchronous and asynchronous terminals and other equipment at speeds up to 19.2 Kbps. Centrex LAN service works with existing wiring Centrex central office to customer premise wiring. Centrex LAN is a name given this service by New York Telephone. Other phone companies have similar services under different names. It's not a very successful service, since it's very slow. Compare 19,200 bits per second to Ethernet, which is 10 million bits per second!

CENTRONICS The name of the printer manufacturer whose method of data transmission between a computer and a parallel printer has become an industry standard. See CENTRONICS PRINTER STANDARD.

CENTRONICS PRINTER STANDARD The Centronics standard was developed by the Centronics company which makes computer printers. The Centronics standard is a 36-pin single plug/connector with eight of the 36-pins carrying their respective bits in parallel (eight bits to one character), which means it's much faster than serial transmission which sends only one bit a time. There are several types of Centronics male and female plugs and receptacles. So know which you want before you buy. The pinning — the location of and function of each of the 36-individual wires, is standard from one Centronics cable to another.

The Centronics printer standard has been adopted by many printer and PC companies, including IBM. It is a narrower standard than the RS-232-C standard. The Centronics works only between a computer and a printer. It won't work over phone lines, unless conversion is done at either end. However, it is standard and has none of the dumb interface problems the RS-232-C standard does.

CENTUM CALL SECOND 1/36th of an erlang. The formula for a centum call second is the number of calls per hour multiplied by their average duration in seconds, all divided by 100.

CEPT Conference des administrations Europeenes des Postes et Telecommunications (European Conference of Postal and Telecommunications Administrations). Standards-setting body whose membership includes European Post, Telephone, and Telegraphy Authorities (PTTs).

CEPT FORMAT Defines how the bits of a PCM carrier system of the 32 channel European type T-1/E-1 will be used and in what sequence. To correctly receive the transmitted intelligence, the receiving end equipment must know exactly what each bit is used for. CEPT format uses 30 VF channels plus one channel for supervision/control (signaling) and one channel for framing (synchronizing). All 8 bits per channel are used to code the waveshape sample. For a much better explanation, see T-1.

CERB Centralized Emergency Reporting Bureau. A Canadian term similar to PSAP — Public Safety Answering Position. See PSAP.

CERN European Laboratory for Particle Physics in Geneva.

CERTIFIED Several companies in the "secondary" industry test used equipment, parts and/or systems. They have various ways of testing them. Typically they test with working phones operating for extended periods at different temperatures. The idea is to check that this used equipment works the way it's meant to work — to the original manufacturer's design specification. Once these tests have been completed a secondary dealer will "certify" such equipment, usually in writing. Such certification carries the assurance that the used equipment works as it's meant to. Sometimes certified equipment is upgraded to the most current revision level of hardware and software. Sometimes it's not. You, the buyer, must check. Certified equipment typically carries a guarantee — that guarantee being as good, obviously, as the company that backs it.

CESIUM CLOCK A clock containing a cesium standard as a frequency-determining element. It's a very accurate clock. See CESIUM STANDARD.

CESIUM STANDARD A primary frequency standard in which a specified hyperfine transition of cesium-133 atoms is used to control the output frequency. Its accuracy is intrinsic and achieved without calibration.

CEV Controlled Environmental Vault. A below ground room that houses electronic and/or optical equipment under controlled temperature and humidity.

CFA Carrier Failure Alarm. The alarm which results from an out-of-frame or loss of carrier condition and which is combined with trunk conditioning to create a CGA.

CFAC Call Forward All Calls.

CFAMN Call Forwarding Address Modified Notification.

CFB Call Forward Busy.

CFDA Call Forward Don't Answer.

CFGDA Call Forward Group Don't Answer.

CFP Channel Frame Processor.

CFRP Carbon Fiber Reinforced Plastic. A light and durable material, which has been used (for the wings of advanced fighter jets) in the defense business and which Toshiba introduced in 1991 as casing for a line of notebook sized computer laptops.

CFW Call Forward.

CGA 1. Carrier Group Alarm. A service alarm generated by a channel bank when an out-of-frame (OOF) condition exists for some predetermined length of time (generally 300 milliseconds to 2.5 seconds). The alarm causes the calls using a trunk to be dropped and trunk conditioning to be applied.

2. Color Graphics Adapter. An IBM standard for displaying material on personal computer screens. The simplest (and conventional) CGA displays 320 horizontal picture elements, known as pels or pixels, by 200 pels vertically. There is also an Enhanced CGA, which is 640 x 400, or 128,000 pixels per screen. Older portables may use CGA monochrome mode. See MONITOR.

CGSA Cellular Geographic Service Area. The actual area in which a cellular company provides cellular service. This area may be somewhat smaller than the MSA (Metropolitan Statistical Area) surrounding it.

CHAD 1. The little solid round dots of paper made when paper tape is punched with information. 2. CHAnge Display.

CHAD TAPE Punched tape used in telegraphy/teletypewriter operation. The perforations, called "chad," are severed from the tape, making holes representing the characters.

CHADLESS TAPE 1. Punched tape that has been punched in such a way that chad is not formed. 2. A punched tape wherein only partial perforation is completed and the chad remains attached to the tape. This is a deliberate process and should not be confused with imperfect chadding. See CHAD.

CHAINING A programming technique linking one activity to another, as in a chain. Each link in the chain may contain a pointer to the next link, or there may be a master control or program instructing the programs to link together.

CHAIN MAILBOXES Mailboxes that are connected together to provide a service or a number of messages (e.g. Directory, Product Information, etc.).

CHANNEL 1. Typically what you rent from the telephone company. A voice-grade transmission facility with defined frequency response, gain and bandwidth. Also, a path of communication, either electrical or electromagnetic, between two or more points. Also called a circuit, facility, line, link or path. 2. An SCSA term. A transmission path on the SCbus or SCxbus Data Bus that transmits data between two end points. 3. A channel of a GPS (Global Positioning System) receiver consists of the circuitry necessary to tune the signal from a single GPS satellite.

CHANNEL ATTACHED Describing the attachment of devices directly to the input/output channels of a (mainframe) computer. Devices attached to a controlling unit by cables rather than by telecommunications circuits. Same as locally attached (IBM).

CHANNEL BANK A multiplexer. A device which puts many slow speed voice or data conversations onto one high-speed link and controls the flow of those "conversations." Typically the device that sits between a digital circuit — say a T-1 — and a couple of dozen voice grade lines coming out of a PBX. One side of the channel bank will be connections for terminating two pairs of wires or a coaxial cable — those bringing the T-1 carrier in. On the other side are connections for terminating multiple tip and ring single line analog phone lines or several digital data streams. Sometimes you need channel banks. Sometimes, you don't. For example, if you're shipping a bundle of voice conversations from one digital PBX to another across town in a T-1 format — and both PBXs recognize the signal — then you will probably not need a channel bank. You'll need a Channel Service Unit (CSU). If one, or both, of the PBXs is analog, then you will need a channel bank at the end of the transmission path whose PBX won't take a digital signal. See CHANNEL SERVICE UNIT and T-1.

CHANNEL CAPACITY A measure of the maximum possible bit rate through a channel, subject to specified constraints.

CHANNEL IDENTIFICATION Information element that requests or identifies the channel to be used for a call. An AIN term.

CHANNEL GATE A device for connecting a channel to a highway, or a highway to a channel, at specified times.

CHANNEL LOOPBACK In network management systems, diagnostic test that forms a loop at the multiplexor's channel interface that returns transmitted signals to their source. See also LOOPBACK.

CHANNEL MODE An AT&T term for a method of communications whereby a fixed bandwidth is established between two or more points on a network as a semi-permanent connection and is rearranged only occasionally.

CHANNEL MODEM That portion of multiplexing equipment required to derive a desired subscriber channel from the local facility.

CHANNEL PACKING A technique for maximizing the use of voice frequency channels used for data transmission by multiplexing a number of lower data rate signals into a single higher speed data stream for transmission on a single voice frequency channel.

CHANNEL QUEUE LIMIT Limit on number of transmit buffers used by a station to guarantee that some receive buffers are always available.

CHANNEL SERVICE UNIT CSU. A device used to connect a digital phone line (T-1 or Switched 56 line) coming in from the phone company to either a multiplexer, channel bank or directly to another device producing a digital signal, e.g. a digital PBX, a PC, or data communications device. A CSU performs certain line-conditioning, and equalization functions, and responds to loopback commands sent from the central office. A CSU regenerates digital signals. It monitors them for problems. And it provides a way of testing your digital circuit. You can buy your own CSU or rent one from your local or long distance phone company. See also CSU and DSU.

CHANNEL TIER An AT&T term for the tier within the Universal Information Services network that partitions transmission capacity into channels and offers the channels to the nodes' higher tiers.

CHANNEL TIME SLOT A time slot starting at a particular instant in a frame and allocated to a channel for transmitting a character, in-slot signal, or other data. Where appropriate a modifier may be added.

CHANNEL TRANSLATOR Device used in broadband LANS to increase carrier frequency, converting upstream (toward the head-end) signals into downstream signals (away from the head-end).

CHANNELIZATION Subdividing a wideband channel into many smaller channels so it may carry many different streams of information.

CHAPTER 11 The Chapter 11 process is started when a company files a reorganization petition with the federal Bankruptcy Court. From that moment on, creditors are prevented from suing the company, and any creditor lawsuits in process are halted, pending the outcome of the Chapter 11 reorganization. Creditors of the company file claims with the Bankruptcy Court. A creditors committee, usually made up of the seven creditors who have filed the largest claims against the company, represents the interest of all creditors. Under Chapter 11 protection, the company's management usually continues to manage the company's business, subject to judical review. In rare circumstances, such as fraud, a party may ask the court to appoint a trustee to manage the company during reorganization. The ultimate objective of a Chapter 11 reorganization is to restructure creditors' claims so that the company can move ahead with its business. Company mangement includes a negotiated partial payment to creditors. The plan also can include exchanges of debt for equity, a moratorium on repayment or a combination of these actions. In some cases, more than one plan may be proposed. For example, a creditor, or group of creditors, may develop its own plan. The complex process of reaching a consensual plan entails extensive negotiations among the company, its creditors and its shareholders.

Once developed, the company's reorganization plan — or one of the competing plans — must be accepted by specified margins of creditors and shareholders. Creditors representing two-thirds of the total dollar amount of bankruptcy claims against the company and 51 percent of the total number of those voting must accept the plan, and two-thirds of the amount of shares represented by shareholders voting on the plan must approve it for a plan to be accepted. Once accepted, the Bankruptcy Court reviews the plan to ensure that it conforms to certain additional statutory requirments before confirming it. With a restructed balance sheet, the company then emerges from Chapter 11 protection to implement the plan. Some companies emerge from Chapter 11 and become normal operating companies again. Some don't and move into Chapter 7 bankruptcy, which is complete and relatively immediate liquidation of the company (i.e. sale of all the company's assets).

CHAPTER 7 See Chapter 11.

CHARACTER A letter, a number or a symbol. A character is sometimes described by the digit represented by the bit pattern that makes up the Character. i.e., the letter A is ASCII code 65, a carriage return is ASCII code 13.

CHARACTER CELL In text mode on a PC, each pel is called a character cell. Character cells are arranged in rows and columns. A typical PC will support two text modes — 80 columns by 25 rows and 40 columns by 25 rows. The default text mode on virtually all PCs is 80 x 25.

CHARACTER CODE One of several standard sets of binary representations for the alphabet, numerals and common symbols, such as ASCII, EBCDIC, BCD.

CHARACTER DISTORTION In telegraphy, the distortion caused by transients that, as a result of previous modulation, are present in the transmission channel. It effects are not consistent. Its influence upon a given transition is to some degree dependent upon the remnants of transients affecting previous signal elements.

CHARACTER GENERATOR A functional unit that converts the coded representation of a character into the graphic representation of the character for display.

CHARACTER IMPEDANCE The impedance termination of an electrically uniform (approximately) transmission line that minimizes reflections from the end of the line.

CHARACTER INTERVAL The total number of unit intervals (including synchronizing, information, error checking, or control bits) required to transmit any given character in any given communication system. Extra signals that are not associated with individual characters are not included. An example of an extra signal that is excluded in the above definition is any additional time added between the end of the stop element and the beginning of the next start element as a result of a speed change, buffering, etc. This additional time is defined as a part of the intercharacter interval.

CHARACTER ORIENTED PROTOCOL A communications protocol in which the beginning of the message and the end of a block of data are flagged with special characters.

CHARACTER ORIENTED WINDOWS (COW) INTERFACE An SAA-compatible user interface for OS/2 applications.

CHARACTER PRINTER A device which prints a single character at a time. Contrast with a line printer, which prints blocks of characters and is much faster.

CHARACTER SET All the letters, numbers and characters which a computer can use. The symbols used to represent data. The ASCII standard has 256 characters, each represented by a binary number from 1 to 256. This set includes all the letters in the alphabet, numbers, most punctuation marks, some mathematical symbols and some other characters typically used by computers.

CHARACTERISTIC FREQUENCY A frequency that can be easily identified and measured in a given emission. A carrier frequency may, for example, be designated as the characteristic frequency.

CHARACTERISTIC IMPEDANCE The impendance of a circuit that, when connnected to the output terminals of a uniform transmission line of arbitrary length, causes the line to appear infinitely long. A line terminated in its characteristic impedance will have no standing waves, no reflections from the end, and a constant ratio of voltage to current at a given frequency at every point on the line.

CHARACTERS PER SECOND The number of characters that can be printed on paper or displayed on a CRT screen per horizontal (linear) inch.

You can usually figure the number of characters per second by dividing by eight the number of bits transmitted each second. The end result won't be that accurate unless you allow for re-transmissions because of errors on the line.

CHAT A common name for a type of messaging done over a network, involving short, usually one or two line messages sent from one node to another. Usually, a chatting facility is RAM-resident, meaning it can be "popped up" inside an application program. Users are usually notified of an incoming chat by a beep and a message at the bottom of their screens.

CHEAPERNET A slang name for the thin wire coaxial cable (0.2-inch, RG58A/U 50-ohm) that uses a smaller diameter coaxial cable than standard thick Ethernet. Thin Ethernet is also called "Cheapernet" due to the lower cabling cost. Thin Ethernet systems tend to have transceivers on the network interface card, rather than in external boxes. PCs connect to the Thin Ethernet bus via a coaxial "T" connector. Thin Ethernet is now the most common Ethernet coaxial cable, though twisted pair is gaining. Thin Ethernet is also referred to as ThinNet or ThinWire. See also 10BASE-T.

CHECK BIT A bit added to a unit of data, say a byte or a word, and used for performing an accuracy check. See also PARITY.

CHECK CHARACTERS Characters added to the end of a block of data which is determined by an algorithm using the data bits which are sent. The receiving device computes its own check characters. It compares them with those sent by the transmitter. If they do not match, the receiver requests the sender to send the block again. If the check characters match, then all the bits used to compute the check characters have been received properly.

CHECK-IN MAILBOX The Centigram VoiceMemo II mailbox used to assign names and passcodes for guests checking into a hotel.

CHECK-OUT MAILBOX The Centigram VoiceMemo II mailbox used to clear out guest mailboxes when the guest checks out of the hotel.

CHECKPOINT CYCLE HDLC error recovery cycle formed by pairing an F bit with a previous P bit or vice versa.

CHECKPOINTING HDLC error recovery based on pairing of P and F bits and giving the equivalent of a negative acknowledgment without using either REJ or SREJ.

CHECKSUM The sum of a group of data items used for error checking. Checksum is computed by the sending computer based upon an algorithm that counts the bits going out in a packet. The check digit is then sent to the other end as the tail, or trailer of the packet. As the packet is being received, the receiving computer goes through the same algorithm, and if the check digit it comes up with is the same as the one received, all is well. Otherwise, it requests the packet be sent again.

CHEMICAL RECTIFIER A chemical device for changing alternating current to pulsating direct, usually used to storage battery charging.

CHEMICAL STRIPPING Soaking an optical fiber in a chemical to remove its coating.

CHEMICAL VAPOR DEPOSITION TECHNIQUE CVD. In optical fiber manufacturing, a process in which deposits are produced by heterogeneous gas-solid and gas-liquid chemical reactions at the surface of a substrate. The CVD method is often used in fabricating optical fiber preforms by causing gaseous materials to react and deposit glass oxides. The preform may be processed further in preparation for pulling into an optical fiber.

CHIEF INFORMATION OFFICER The person responsible for planning, choosing, buying, installing — and ultimately taking the blame for — a company's computer and information processing operation. Originally, CIOs were called data processing managers. Then they became Management Information System (MIS) managers. Then, CIOs. The idea of calling them CIOs was to reflect a new idea that the information they controlled was a critical corporate advantage and one that could give the company a competitive edge over its competitors — if played correctly.

CHILL Ccitt HIgh Level Language. A computer language developed by the CCITT for the standardization of software in telecommunications switches. Not widely adopted. C is more widely adopted.

CHIME An electromechanical or electronic substitute for the conventional telephone bell, that sounds like a musical chime being struck, typically in a "bing-bong" sequence.

CHIMNEY EFFECT Picture a phone system. We have an upright, rectangular cabinet full of printed circuit cards and all getting hot. How to cool them? Simple, raise the machine a little off the ground, put holes in the bottom of the cabinet and holes in the top of the cabinet. Hot air rises. Bingo, air will rise through the top of the cabinet and cool air will get sucked in the bottom of the cabinet. And bingo, you don't need a fan. This natural cooling technique is called the Chimney Effect and many modern phone systems now use it.

CHIP 1. An integrated circuit. The physical structure upon which integrated circuits are fabricated as components of telephone systems, computers, memory systems, etc. 2. The transition time for individual bits in the pseudo-random sequence transmitted by the GPS satellite.

CHIRPING 1. A rapid change (as opposed to a long-term drift) of the wavelength of an electromagnetic wave. Chirping is most often observed in pulsed operation of a source. 2. A pulse compression technique that uses (usually linear) freqeuency modulation during the pulse.

CHOKE An obsolete term: An inductance with either and air or iron core, designed to retard certain frequencies; as a radio frequency choke or an audio frequency choke.

CHOKE COIL A coil so wound as to offer a retarding or self inductance effect to an alternating current.

CHOKE PACKET Packet used for flow control. Node detecting congestion generates choke packet and sends it toward source of congestion, which is required to reduce input rate.

CHOOSER A desk accessory onn the Apple Macintosh that allows a user to choose items such as a printer or file server by clicking on an icon of the device.

CHOPPER A device for rapidly opening and closing a circuit. An ancient radio term.

CHROMA Name sometimes applied to color intensity control in a receiver.

CHROMATIC DISPERSION One of the mechanisms that limits the bandwidth of optical fibers by producting pulse spreading because of the various colors of light traveling in the fiber. Different wavelengths of light travel at different speeds. Since most optical sources emit light containing a range of wavelengths, each of these wavelengths arrive at different times and thereby cause the transmitted pulse to spread as it travels down the fiber.

CHROMINANCE Portion of color TV signal representing colors.

CHROMIUM DIOXIDE Tape whose coating is of chromium dioxide particles. Noted for its superior frequency output.

CHURN Cellular phone and beeper users drop their monthly subcriptions often. The industry calls This phenomenon "churn." Sometimes it's as high as 2% or 3% a month. It drives the cellular and beeper business mad. It's very expensive to sign up a new customer.

CHUTZPAH A New York Jewish word which means unmitigated gall (audacity). The word is best exemplified by the story of the 15-year old who goes into court having killed his father and mother and falls on the mercy of the court. Now that's Chutzpah! Telecom companies without competition show they understand the meaning of chutzpah very well.

CI Customer Interface.

CIC Carrier Identification Code. See CARRIER IDENTIFICATION CODE.

CICS Customer Information Control System. An IBM program environment designed to allow transactions entered at remote computers to be processed concurrently by a mainframe host. Also, IBM's Customer Information Control System software.

CIF A videophone ISDN standard which is part of the CCITT's H.261. It produces a color image of 352 by 288 pixels. The format uses two B channels, with voice taking 32 kbps and the rest for video.

CIGOS Canadian Interest Group on Open Systems. Canadian organization which promotes OSI.

CIIG Canadian ISDN Interest Group. Canadian organization which promotes ISDN.

CIM 1. Computer-Integrated Manufacturing. 2. An MCI definition. Customer Information Manager.

CIPHERTEXT The result of processing plaintext (unencrypted information) through an encryption algorithm.

CIRCUIT The physical connection (or path) of channels, conductors and equipment between two given points through which an electric current may be established. Includes both sending and receiving capabilities.

CIRCUIT BOARD Same as a Printed Circuit Board, namely a board with microprocessors, transistors and other small electronics components. Such a board slides into a the slot in a telephone system or personal computer.

CIRCUIT BREAKER A special type of switch arranged to open a circuit when overloaded, without injury to itself.

CIRCUIT MODE 1. An AT&T term for the method of communications in which a fixed bandwidth circuit is established from point to point through a network and held for the duration of a telephone call. 2. An AIN term for a type of switching that causes a one-to-one correspondence between a call and a circuit. That is, a circuit or path is assigned for a call between each switching node, and the circuit or path is not shared with other calls.

CIRCUIT NOISE LEVEL At any point in a transmission system, the ratio of the circuit noise at that point to some arbitrary amount of circuit noise chosen as a reference.

CIRCUIT ORDER MANAGEMENT SYSTEM COMS. An automated processing system of MCI circuit- and service-related information. Processes hardwire service circuit orders from order entry through scheduling and completion. COMS also provides circuit order data, hardwire customer data, and circuit inventory data to other MCI systems in Finance, Engineering, and Operations.

CIRCUIT ORDER RECORD COR. Report generated by the COR Tracking System within NOBIS, indicating circuit installations, changes, and disconnects.

CIRCUIT PROVISIONING The telephone operating company process that somehow organizes to get you a trunk or other special service circuit.

CIRCUIT SEGREGATION Differentiating between services that are maintained by separate technicians or departments. Can be accomplished through visual and/or mechanical means.

CIRCUIT SWITCHING The process of setting up and keeping a circuit open between two or more users, such that the users have exclusive and full use of the circuit until the connection is released. There are basically three types of switching — CIRCUIT, PACKET and MESSAGE.

• PACKET SWITCHING is like circuit switching in that you can also switch information between people or devices, but in packet switching (as in circuit switching), no circuit is left open on a dedicated basis. Circuit switching is like having your own railroad track for your conversation to travel on that's yours as long as you keep the connection open. Once you hang up, the next caller gets to use that track.

• PACKET SWITCHING is a data switching technique only. In packet switching, the addresses on your packets are read by the switches as they approach, and are switched down the tracks. The next packet is read to throw the switches to send THAT packet where it needs to go. The data conversation is sent in packets. Each packet can be sent along different tracks as they are open. The packets are assembled at the other end — typically in the last switching office before the packets reach the distant computer or distant user.

• MESSAGE SWITCHING sends a message from one end to the other. But it's not interactive, as in packet or circuit switching. In message switching, the message is typically received in one block, stored in one central place, then retrieved or sent in one clump to the other end.

CIRCUIT TIER An AT&T term for the tier within the Universal Information Services network that provides real-time circuit switching of channels.

CIRCUIT, FOUR WIRE A path in which four wires are presented to the terminal equipment (phone or data), thus allowing for simultaneous transmission and reception. Two wires are used for transmission in one direction and two in the other direction.

CIRCULAR EXTENSION NETWORK Permits two or more single-line phones connected to a PBX, each with its own extension, to operate like a "square" key telephone system. An incoming call directed to any non-busy phone in the group will ring at all of the non-busy phones. The first extension to answer will be connected to the incoming call. At any time, a non-busy extension can make or receive calls.

CIRCULAR HUNTING When calling a station, the switching system makes a complete search of all numbers within the hunting group, regardless of the location within that group of the called number. For example, the hunt group is 231, 232, 233 and 234, the call is directed to 233. If it is busy, the equipment will search 234, 231, and 232 to find a non-busy station.

CIRCULAR MIL The measure of sectional area of a wire.

CIRCULAR POLARIZATION In electromagnetic wave propagation, polarization such that the tip of the electric field vector describes a circle in any fixed plane intersecting, and normal to, the direction of propagation. The magnitude of the electric field vector is constant. A circularly polarized wave may be resolved into two linearly polarized waves in phase quadrature with their planes of polarization at right angles to each other.

CIRCULATOR 1. In networking, a passive junction of three or more ports in which the ports can be accessed in such an order that when power is fed into any port it is transferred to the next port, the port counted as following the last in order. 2. In radar, a device that switches the antenna alternately between the transmitter and reciever.

CIRCUMNAURAL A type of headphone that almost totally isolates the listener from room sounds.

CIS Contact Image Sensor. A type of scanner technology in which the photodetectors come in contact with the original document.

CISC Complex Instruction Set Computing. The "old" way (i.e. the present way) of doing computing as against RISC — Reduced Instruction Set Computing. See RISC.

CIT Computer Integrated Telephone is Digital Equipment Company's program, announced in October 1987, that provides a framework for functionally integrating voice and data in an applications environment so that the telephone and terminal on the desktop can be synchronized, the call arriving as the terminal's screen on the caller arrives. CIT uses the DEC VAX line of computers. According to DEC, CIT supports both inbound and outbound telecommunications applications. In an inbound scenario, the application may recognize the caller's originating phone number through Automatic Number Identification (ANI) and/or the dialed number through Dialed Number Identification Service (DNIS), match the information to corresponding data base records and automatically deliver the call and the data to the call center agent. In an outbound application, dialing can be automated, increasing the number of connected calls. In either scenario, the telephone calls and associated data can be simultaneously transferred to alternate locations within an organization, adding a new level of customer service to call center applications. Digital made its first CIT announcements at Telecom '87 in Geneva, Switzerland. The CIT product set, consisting of client and server software implementing a variety of switch-to-computer link protocols, and providing a robust applications interface, was first shipped in 1989. The company announced its latest release, CIT Version 2.1, in January 1991. See also OPEN APPLICATION INTERFACE.

CITIZENS BAND One of two bands used for low power radio transmissions in the United States — either 26.965 to 27.225 megahertz or 462.55 to 469.95 megahertz. Citizens band radio is not allowed in many countries, even some civilized countries. In some countries they use different frequencies. CB radios, in the United States, are limited by FCC rule to four WATTS of power, which gives each CB radio a range of several miles. Some naughty people boost their CBs with external power. The author of this dictionary has actually spoken to Australia while driving on the Santa Monica Freeway in Los Angeles. See also CB.

CLADDING 1. When referring to an optical fiber, a layer of material of lower refractive index, in intimate contact with a core material of higher refractive index. 2. When referring to a metallic cable, a process of covering with a metal (usually acheived by pressure rolling, extruding, drawing, or swaging) until a bond is achieved.

CLADDING DIAMETER The diameter of the circle that includes the cladding layer in an optical fiber.

CLADDING MODE In an optical fiber, a transmission mode supported by the cladding; i.e., a mode in addition to the modes supported by the core material.

CLADDING MODE STRIPPER A device for converting optical fiber cladding modes to radiation modes; as a result, the cladding modes are removed from the fiber. Often a material such as the fiber coating or jacket having a refractive index equal to or greater than that of the fiber cladding will perform this function.

CLADDING RAY In an optical fiber, a ray that is confined to the core and cladding by virtue of reflection from the outer surface of the cladding. Cladding rays correspond to cladding modes in the terminology of mode descriptors.

CLAIRE Harry Newton's favorite daughter. Why "favorite?" Simple. She's his only daughter. When he wrote this, she was 12 1/2 going on 35. Her full name is Claire Elizabeth Newton.

CLAMN 1. Called Line Address Modification Notification

CLAMPER An electronic circuit which sets the level of a signal before the scanning of each line begins to insure that no spurious electronic noise is introduced into the picture signal from the electronics of the video equipment.

CLAS Centrex Line Assignment Service. A service from New York Telephone and other Bell operating companies, which allows Centrex subscribers to change their class of service by dialing in on a personal computer, reaching the phone company's computer and then changing things themselves — without phone company personnel assisting or hindering.

Load your PC with communications software. Dial your local central office. Change your Centrex phone numbers. Turn on, turn off features. Change pickup groups. Add numbers to speed dialing, etc. Your on-line changes are checked by the phone company's computers. If they make sense (i.e. one change doesn't conflict with another), they take effect by early the following day — at which time you can call up and get a report on which took, which didn't and who's got what. Saves calling in person. Is more accurate. And, best of all, saves money. Typically just one flat monthly charge. No charge for any of your changes.

CLASS 1. Custom Local Area Signaling Services. It is based on the availability of channel interoffice signaling. Class consists of number-translation services, such as call-forwarding and caller identification, available within a local exchange of Local Access and Transport Area (LATA). CLASS is a service mark of Bellcore. Some of the phone services which Bellcore promotes for CLASS are Automatic Callback, Automatic Recall, Calling Number Delivery, Customer Originated Trace, Distinctive Ringing/Call Waiting, Selective Call Forwarding and Selective Call Rejection. See also CALLING LINE IDENTIFICATION. 2. In an object-oriented programming environment, a class defines the data content of a specific type of object, the code that manipulates it, and the public and private programming interfaces to that code. See ANI and ISDN.

CLASS 1 The Class 1 interface is an extension of the EIA/TIA's (Electronics Industry Association and the Telecommunications Industry Association) specification for fax communication, known as Group III. Class I is a series of Hayes AT commands that can be used by software to control fax boards. In Class 1, both the T.30 (the data packet creation and decision making necessary for call setup) and ECM/BFT (error-correction mode/binary file transfer) are done by the computer. A specification being developed (fall of 1991) Class 2, will allow the modem to handle these functions in hardware. Industry analysts believe Class 2 will be the standard for the long haul, but approval is slow. Even so, some modem makers will shortly deliver data/fax modems. See also CLASS 1 OFFICE.

CLASS 1 OFFICE A regional toll telephone switching center. The highest level toll office in AT&T's long distance switching hierarchy. There are essentially five levels in the hierarchy, with the lowest level — Class 5 — being those central offices owned by the local telephone companies. Each of the classes can complete calls between themselves. But, if the routes are busy, then calls automatically climb the hierarchy. A Class 1 office is the office of "last resort."

CLASS 2 A proposed standard similar to Class 1 that would place more of the task of establishing the fax connection onto the faxmodem, while continuing to rely on the host's processor to send and receive the image data. The Class 2 standard (known as PN-2388) is still under study by the EIA's (Electronic Industries Association) TR.29 committee, with further revisions expected. See CLASS 1.

CLASS 2 OFFICE The second level in AT&T's long distance toll switching hierarchy.

CLASS 3 OFFICE The third level in AT&T's long distance toll switching hierarchy.

CLASS 4 OFFICE The fourth level in AT&T's long distance toll switching hierarchy — the major switching center to which toll calls from Class 5 offices are sent. In U.S. common carrier telephony service, a toll center designated "Class 4C" is an office where assistance in completing incoming calls is provided in addition to other traffic. A toll center designated "Class 4P" is an office where operators handle only outbound calls, or where switching is performed without operator assistance.

CLASS 5 OFFICE An end office. Your local central office. The lowest level in the hierarchy of local and long distance switching which AT&T set up when it was "The Bell System." A class 5 office is a local Central Office that serves as a network entry point for station loops and certain special-service lines. Also called an End Office. Classes 1, 2, 3, and 4 are toll offices in the telephone network.

CLASS OF EMISSION The set of characteristics of an emission, designated by standard symbols, e.g., type of modulation of the main carrier, modulating signal, type of information to be transmitted, and also if appropriate, any additional signal characteristics.

CLASS OF OFFICE A ranking assigned to switching points in the telephone network, determined by function, interfaces and transmission needs.

CLASS OF SERVICE 1. Each phone in a system may have a different collection of privileges and features assigned to it, such as access to WATS lines. Class of Service assignments if properly organized, can become an important tool in controlling telephone abuse. 2. A subgrouping of telephone users for the sake of rate distinction. This may distinguish between individual and party lines, between Government lines and others, between those permitted to make unrestricted international dialed calls and others, between business or residence and coin, between flat rate and message rate, and between restricted and extended area service. 3. A category of data transmission provided in a public data network in which the data signaling rate, the terminal operating mode, and the code structure (if any) are standardized. This is defined within CCITT Recommendations X.1.

CLASSMARK A designator used to describe the service feature privileges, restrictions, and circuit characteristics for lines or trunks accessing a switch; e.g., precedence level, conference privilege, security level, zone restriction. See CLASS OF SERVICE.

CLC Carrier Liaison Committee. A committee formed to help industry participants work together to resolve the issues of implementing 800 Portability. CLC is sponsored by the Exchange Carriers Standards Association (ECSA) and is comprised of the LECs (local exchange carriers), long distance carriers and users of 800 service.

CLEAR To cause one or more storage locations to be in a prescribed state, usually that corresponding to a zero or to the space character.

CLEAR CHANNEL 1. Characteristic of a transmission path where the full bandwidth is available to the user. Primarily of digital circuits that do not require some part of the channel to be reserved for carrier framing or control bits. 2. An SCSA term. A channel which is used exclusively for data transmission, with no bandwidth required for administrative messages such as signaling or synchronization. All SCbus data channels are clear.

CLEAR CONFIRMATION SIGNAL A call control signal to acknowledge reception of the DTE clear request by the DCE or the reception of the DCE clear indication by the DTE.

CLEAR COLLISION Contention that occurs when a DTE and a DCE simultaneously transfer a clear request packet and a clear indication packet specifying the same logical channel. The DCE will consider that the clearing is completed and will not transfer a DCE clear confirmation packet.

CLEAR TO SEND CTS. One of the standard attributes of a modem in which the receiving modem indicates to the calling modem that it is now ready to accept data. One of the standard pins used by the RS-232-C standard. In CCITT V.24, the corresponding pin is called Ready For Sending.

CLEARLINE 1.5 A Sprint name for T-1 service. It is an all digital 1.544 Mbps private line service that connects two customer sites via dedicated T-1 access lines.

CLEARLINE 45 A Sprint name for DS-3 service. This high-capacity point-to-point private line service transmits voice, data, and video at 44.736 Mbps.

CLEARLINE FRACTIONAL 1.5 A Sprint name for all all digital private line service which transmits voice, data, and video at speeds from 112/123 Kbps up to 672/768 Kbps - a fraction of a T-1, also called a DS-1. The service may be ordered in 56/64 Kbps increments from two channels (112/128 Kbps) to 12 channels (672/768 Kbps). Point-to-point service connects customer sites via dedicated T-1 access lines.

CLEAVING The controlled breaking of a fiber so that its end surface is smooth.

CLEOS Conference of the Lasers and Electro-Optics Society.

CLID Calling Number IDentification. Same as ANI (Automatic Number Identification), except CLID tends to refer to identification of local calling numbers. CLID tends to be referred to as a service of CLASS. See also CLASS and ANI.

CLIENT A computer that is configured to request services from a network. Client can also refer to the code at one end of the network connection. The client end of the connection is also referred to as the user end. See also CLIENT/SERVER COMPUTING and CLIENT SERVER.

CLIENT SERVER A computer on a local area network that you can request information or applications from. The idea is that you — the user — are the client and it — the slave — is the server. That was the original meaning of the term. Over time, client server began to refer to a computing system that splits the workload between PCs and one or more larger computers on a network. A good analogy, according to Peter Lewis of the New York Times is to think of client-server as a restaurant where the waiter takes your order for a hamburger, goes to the kitchen and comes back with some raw meat and a bun. You get to cook the burger at your table and add your favorite condiments. In computerese, this is distributed computing, where some processing work is done by the customer at his or her table, instead of entirely in the kitchen (centralized computing in the old mainframe days). It sounds like more work, but it has many advantages. The service is faster. The food is cooked exactly to your liking, and the giant, expensive stove in the kitchen can be replaced by lots of cheap little grills. See DOWNSIZING, REENGINEERING and SERVER.

CLIENT SERVER MODEL In most cases, the "client" is a desktop computing device or program "served" by another networked computing device. Computers are integrated over the network by an application, which provides a single system image. The server can be a minicomputer, workstation, or microcomputer with attached storage devices. A client can be served by multiple servers.

CLIP ON TOLL FRAUD Clip on toll fraud occurs when someone connects a phone between someone else's phone (typically a coin phone) and the central office and makes unlawful toll calls. The term "clip on" comes because the telephone service thief "clips on" to the line. Clip on toll fraud is often done on COCOT (Customer Owned Coin Operated Telephone) phone lines because these lines do not enjoy the same protection from toll fraud which is afforded to coin phone lines which local telcos provide to their own coin phones.

CLIPPER A circuit or device that limits the instantaneous output signal amplitude to a predetermined maximum value, regardless of the amplitude of the input signal.

CLIPPING Clipping has two basic meanings. The first refers to the effect caused by a simplex (one way at a time) speakerphone. Here the conversation goes one way. When the other person wants to talk, the voice path has to reverse (to "flip"). While the flipping takes place, a few sounds are "clipped" from that person's conversation. This phenomenon happens on some long distance and many overseas channels. These channels are so expensive, they are simultaneously shared by many conversations. Gaps in your conversation are filled by other people's conversation. But when you start talking, the equipment has to recognize you're now talking, find some capacity for your conversation, and send it. In the process of doing this, your first word or part of your first word might be "clipped" and the conversation will sound "broken."

The second way your voice is clipped is what happens every day on the telephone. You're squeezing your own voice which typically spans 10,000 Hertz into a voice channel which is only 3,000 Hertz. This clips the extremes of your conversation — the higher sounds. As a result, your voice sounds

NEWTON'S TELECOM DICTIONARY

flatter over the phone. As you become more economical and try to squeeze your voice into smaller capacity channels, so it becomes increasingly clipped.

CLOCK Exactly as it sounds. An oscillator-generated signal that provides a timing reference for a transmission link. A clock provides providing signals used in a transmission system to control the timing of certain functions such as the duration of signal elements or the sampling rate. It also generates periodic, accurately spaced signals used for such purposes as timing, regulation of the operations of a processor, or generation of interrupts. In short, a clock has two functions: 1. To generate periodic signals for synchronization on a transmission facility. 2. To provide a time base for the sampling of signal elements. Used in computers, a clock synchronizes certain procedures, such as communication with other devices. It simply keeps track of time, which allows computers to do the same things at the same time so they don't "bump into each other."

CLOCK BIAS The difference between the GPS clock's indicated time and true universal time. GPS is Global Positioning System. See GPS.

CLOCK CYCLE The time that elapses from one read or write operation to another in the main memory of a computer's central processing unit (CPU). The more tasks that can be accomplished per cycle, the more efficient the chip. Some chips like the i860 chip can execute two instructions and three operations per clock cycle.

CLOCK DIFFERENCE A measure of the separation between the respective time marks of two clocks. Clock differences must be reported as algebriac quantities measured on the same time scale. The date of the measurement should be given.

CLOCK SPEED Each CPU contains a special clock circuitry which is connected to a quartz crystal (same as the one in your watch). The quartz crystal's vibrations, which are very fast, coordinate the CPU's operation, keeping everything in step. CPU clock speeds are measured in megahertz, or MHz, which stands for "million cycles per second." The clock speeds of today's computer range from a slow of 4.77 MHz (the original IBM PC) to 25 MHz with some Intel 80386 based machines. Clock speed is a misleading term. It is only one way of measuring the speed of a computer. One other critical way is how fast you can read and write information to the hard disk. How important that is depends on whether you're running a program with lots of access to your hard disk (like a database program) or running a program which uses a lot of calculations in RAM, i.e. a spreadsheet.

CLOCK TOLERANCE The maximum permissible departure of a clock indication from a designated time reference such as Coordinated Universal Time.

CLOCKWISE POLARIZED WAVE An elliptically or circularly polarized electromagnetic wave in which the direction of rotation of the electric vector is clockwise as seen by an observer looking in the direction of propagation of the wave.

CLOSE COUPLING The condition in which two coils are placed in close magnetic relation to each other, thus establishing a high degree of mutual induction.

CLOSE TALK A voice recognition term. An arrangement where a microphone is fewer than four inches from the speaker's mouth.

CLOSED ARCHITECTURE Proprietary design that is compatible only with hardware and software from a single vendor of single product family. Contrast with OPEN ARCHITECTURE.

CLOSED END The end of a Foreign Exchange — FX — line which ends on a PBX, a key system or a telephone. The closed end is the end of the circuit beyond which a call cannot progress further. The other end of the FX circuit is called the "open end," because calls can progress further.

CLOSED LOOP SYSTEM A closed electrical circuit into which a standard signal is feed and received instantly. A measure of the difference between the input signal and the output signal is a measure of the error, and potentially what's causing it.

CLOSED USER GROUP A group of specified users of a data network that is assigned a facility that permits them to communicate with each other but precludes communications with other users of the service or services.

CLOSURE A cabinet, pedestal, or case used to enclose cable sheath openings necessary for splicing or terminating fibers.

CLOUD Some of the newer high-speed data, phone company-offered services resemble a local area netowrk. You connect to them directly. To make a call, you don't actually dial a number as you do on a circuit-switched service, you just transmit, putting an address at the front of your transmission. The service reads the address and sends it where you want. Like a LAN, everything is connected and on line. The concept is get stuff sent from one place to another much faster than would be possible if you had to wait to dial, for the circuit to be set up, for the machine at the other end to answer, etc. In these high-speed services, the circuit is "always set up." The provider (the phone company) refers to its network as a "cloud." And when you see diagrams of these newer high-speed services, like SMDS and frame relay, you see the carrier portion drawn as a cloud (like the one you see in the sky). Services with "clouds" are also called "connectionless." See the various definitions below beginning with CONNECTIONLESS.

CLTS ConnectionLess Transport Service.

CLUSTER 1. Collection of terminals or other devices in a single location. A cluster control unit and a cluster controller in IBM 3270 systems are devices that control the input/output operations of a group (cluster) of display stations. 2. Unit of storage allocation used by MS-DOS usually consisting of four or more 512-byte sectors.

CLUSTER CONTROLLER A device that can control input/output operations of more than one device connected to it (e.g. a terminal). An interface between several bisynchronous devices and a PAD, NC or communication facility. The cluster controller handles remote communications processing for its attached devices. Most common types are IBM 327X.

CLUT An imaging term. Color Look-Up Table. The palette used in an indexed color system. Usually consists of 256 colors.

CMIP Common Management Information Protocol. A protocol formally adopted by the International Standards Organization in Paris (ISO), used for exchanging network management information. Typically, this information is exchanged between two management stations. CMIP can, however, be used to exchange information between an application and a management station. CMIP has been designed for OSI networks, but it is transport independent. Theoretically, it could run across a variety of transports, including, for example, IBM's Systems Network Architecture.

CMOL Short for "CMIP Over Logical Link Control". An implementation of the CMIP protocol over the second layer of the OSI protocol stack, to be proposed as a standard by 3 Com Corp. and IBM. The goal of CMOL is to create agents that require significantly less memory than CMIP implemented over OSI, or SNMP implemented over UDP.

CMOS Complementary Metal Oxide Semiconductor. A technology for making integrated circuits known for requiring less electricity. See also COMPLEMENTARY METAL OXIDE SEMICONDUCTOR.

CMOS RAM Complementary Metal Oxide Semiconductor Random Access Memory. Memory which contains a personal computer's configuration information. CMOS RAM must have continuous power to preserve its memory. This power is typically supplied by a lithium battery.

CMOS SETUP A program which prepares the system to work. CMOS setup records your PC's hardware configuration information into CMOS RAM. It must be modified when you add, change or remove hardware.

CMOT CMIP Over TCP/IP. An internet standard defining the use of CMIP for managing TCP/IP local area networks.

CMP Communications Plenum Cable.

CMS 1. Call Management System. This is the AT&T label for their inbound call distribution management reporting package. CMS is found on the Horizon, the Merlin, S/75 and S/85 PBX/ACDs. CMS is the successor product to AEMIS/PRO 150/500. 2. Call Management Services. Canadian term for local calling features based on CLID (Calling Line Identification).

CMS 8800 Cellular Mobile Telephone Service (North American version).

CMY A computer imaging term. A color model used by the printing industry that is based on mixing cyan, magenta, and yellow. It's also referred to as CMYK, with the K denoting black. The K was added after printers discovered they could obtain a darker black using special black colorants rather than by combining cyan, magenta, and yellow alone. See also CMYK.

CMYK A computer imaging term. A color model used by the printing industry that is based on mixing cyan, magenta, yellow and black (called "K.") It used to be called CMY. The K was added after printers discovered they could obtain a darker black using special black colorants rather than by combining cyan, magenta, and yellow. CMYK is the basis of what's known now as "four-color" printing. But there is also five, six, sevem and eight color printing, etc. Each of these "extra" colors are basically "colors" which are better printed as their own color rather than by printing a combination the basic three. Silver, copper, gold, aluminum, etc. are all printed traditionally as extra colors, and extra passes through the printer.

CNA Cooperative Network Architecture.

CNC Complementary Network Service. See OPEN NETWORK ARCHITECTURE.

CND Calling Number Delivery.

CNE Certified (local area) Network Engineer. When you graduate from Novell's third level class, you become a certified network engineer. It costs a small fortune to go to all the required Novell classes. As a result, there are few CNE around. They're a rare breed.

CNET Centre National d'etudes de Telecommunication. The French organization that approves telecommunications products for sale in France.

CNG Also called Auto Fax Tone, or Calling Tone. This tone is the sound produced by virtually all fax machines when they dial another fax machine. CNG is a medium pitch tone (1100 Hz) that lasts 1/2 second and repeats every 3 1/2 seconds. A fax machine will produce CNG for about 45 seconds after it dials. The CNG tone is useful for owners of fax/phone/modem switches. Such switches answer an incoming call. If they hear a CNG tone, they will transfer the call to a fax machine. If they don't, they'll transfer the call to a phone, answering machine or perhaps a modem. Depends on how they're set up. See CED and FACSIMILE.

CNM An SMDS (Switched Megabit Data Service) term. Customer Network Management. All activities that customers perform to manage their communications networks. SMDS CNM service enables customers to directly manage many aspects of the SMDS service provided by telecommunications carriers.

CNR Telephone company term for re-scheduling a telephone installation appointment because the "Customer is Not Ready."

CNRI Corporation for National Research Initiatives.

CNS Complementary Network Service. CNSs are basic services associated with end user's lines that make it easier for Enhanced Service Providers (ESPs) to offer them enhanced services. Some examples of CNSs include Call Forwarding Busy/Don't Answer, Three Way Calling, and Virtual Dial Tone. See OPEN NETWORK ARCHITECTURE.

CO Central Office. In North America, a CO is that location which houses a switch to serve local telephone subscribers. Sometimes the words "central office" are confused with the switch itself. In Europe and abroad, the words "central office" are not known. The more common words are "public exchange." But those words tend to refer more to the switch itself, rather than the site, as in North America. CO was the name of a magazine published by Telecom Library Inc, the publisher of this dictionary. See also CENTRAL OFFICE or PUBLIC EXCHANGE.

CO LINES These are the lines connecting your office to your local telephone company"s Central Office which in turn connects you to the nationwide telephone system.

CO LOCATION The ability of a someone who is not the local phone company to put their equipment in the phone company's offices and join their equipment to the phone company's equipment. That "someone" who might co-locate their equipment on the phone company's premises might be an end-user or it might be another local or long distance telecommunications company. It might even be a competitor of the local phone company. The idea of co-location is to save money, give better service, ensure better interconnection, get technical problems solved faster, etc. Not all local phone companies offer their customers co-location. New York Telephone and New England Telephone are two that now do.

CO SIMULATOR A desktop device which pretends to act like a mini-central office. The smallest version will consist of two lines and two RJ-11 jacks. Plug a phone into both jacks. Pick up one phone. You hear dial tone. Dial or touchtone two or three digits. Bingo, the second phone rings. You pick up the second phone. You can have a conversation with yourself or with a machine — like a voice processing system. Most central office simulators can simulate normal on-hook, off-hook, dialing, answering, speaking, etc. Some now can simulate caller ID features — inlcuding number of person calling.

COAM Customer Owned And Maintained equipment.

COASTING MODE In timing-dependent systems, a free-running operational timing mode in which continuous or periodic measurement of timing error is not available. In some systems, operation in this mode can be enhanced for a period of time by using clock or timing error (or correction) information obtained during a prior tracking mode to estimate clock or timing corrections to be made in the free-running mode.

COATED FILAMENT A vacuum tube filament coated with a metallic oxide to provide greater electron emission and longer life.

COATING A protective material (usually plastic) applied to the optical fiber immediately after drawing to preserve its mechanical strength and cushion it from external forces that can induce microbending losses.

COAXIAL CABLE A cable composed of an insulated central conducting wire wrapped in another cylindrical conducting wire. The whole thing is usually wrapped in another insulating layer and an outer protective layer. A coaxial cable has great capacity to carry great quantities of information. It is typically used to carry high-speed data (as in connections of 327X terminals to computer hosts) and in CATV (multiplexed TV stations).

COB Close Of Business.

COBOL Common Business Oriented Language. A very popular computer programming language for business applications.

COBRA An MCI defintion. Surveillance and test equipment for LADNER monitoring: not yet functioning.

COC Central Office Connection. Separately tariffed part of T-1 circuit.

COCOT Customer Owned Coin Operated Telephone. See also CLIP ON TOLL FRAUD.

CODE The system of dots and dashes used to represent the letters of the alphabet, numerals, punctuation and other symbols.

CODE BIT The smallest signaling element used by the Physical Layer for transmission on the fiber cable.

CODE BLOCKING A switch's ability to block calls to a specified area code, central office code or phone number.

CODE CALL ACCESS A very useful PBX feature. It allows attendants and extension users to activate, by dialing an access code followed by a two or three digit called code, customer-provided signaling devices throughout the premises. The signaling devices then issue a series of tones or visual coded signals corresponding to the called code. The called or paged party responds by dialing a meet-me answering code from any phone and is then connected to the paging party.

CODE CONVERSION A process which converts the codes coming in from one network into codes that can be recognized on another network, such as converting from the Baudot code in a telex network to the ASCII code on the TWX network. Usually, the hardware will convert differences in transmission speed.

CODE DIVISION MULTIPLE ACCESS CDMA, also called Spread Spectrum, is a name for a new form of digital cellular phone service. The idea is that each phone call is combined with a code which only one cellular phone plucks from the air. Business Week said CDMA works "by spreading all signals across the same broad frequency spectrum and assigning a unique code — the company says one of 42 billion — to each. The dispersed signals are pulled out of the background noise by a receiver which knows the code. This method, developed by a San Diego company called Qualcomm Inc. is very new. Much of the equipment to support it — like the cellular switches have not yet been developed." CDMA is also being used by wireless PBXs. See CDMA for a longer and better explanation.

CODE-EXCITED LINEAR PREDICTION CELP. An analog-to-digital voice coding scheme.

CODE LEVEL Number of bits used to represent a character.

CODEC CODer-DECoder. This equipment converts voice signals from their analog form to digital signals acceptable to more modern digital PBXs and digital transmission systems. It then converts those digital signals back to analog so that you may hear and understand what the other party is saying. In some phone systems, the CODEC is in the PBX and shared by many analog phone extensions. In other phone systems, the CODEC is actually in the phone. Thus the phone itself sends out a digital signal and can, as a result, be more easily designed to accept a digital RS-232-C signal.

CODED CHARACTER SET A set of unambiguous rules that establish a character set and the one-to-one relationships between the characters of the set and their coded representations.

CODED IMAGE A representation of an image in a form suitable for storage and processing.

CODED TRUNKS You buy several trunks. They hunt on. The main number is 555-3000. If the main number is busy, the call goes to the next line. There are two types of "next lines." One type can have an actual number, like 555-3001, which you can call directly. The other can be a coded trunk with no actual number and which you can't call directly. It's better to have no coded trunks because it's hard to test coded trunks. You can't dial them directly. Actual dial-able numbers are better.

CODER An analog-to-digital converter that changes analog voice signals to their digital equivalents. See CODEC.

CODIAL OFFICE CDO. A small central office designed for unattended operation in a distant community. Usually a community dial office is fairly small, rarely more than 10,000 lines.

CODING THEORY Mathematical theory describing how to encode data into streams of digital symbols at transmitter and decode it at receiver to maximize accuracy of data presented to user.

COHERENCE AREA In optical communications, the area in a plane perpendicular to the direction of propagation over which light may be considerd highly coherent.

COHERENCE LENGTH The propagation distance over which a light beam may be considered coherent. See COHERENT LIGHT.

COHERENT LIGHT Light emitted from laser and some light-emitting-diodes. It is made up of light of a single frequency in which all the light waves are in phase (i.e., their wave peaks and troughs are all in alignment so the waves reinforce or amplify each other.)

COIL A number of turns of wire, so wound as to afford inductance.

COIL ANTENNA One consisting of one or more complete turns of wire. See LOOP ANTENNA.

COIN ACCEPTOR/REJECTOR A mechanical or electro-mechanical device that checks and validates the coins deposited in a coin pay phone. They measure the coin's size and weight and steel content. These coin acceptor/rejector units transmit the value of the coin deposits to the processing part of a smart payphone or they signal the information to the telephone company central office via coded tones.

COIN SUPERVISORY TRUNK GROUP A trunk group that lets a switchboard operator collect overtime monies due on coin phones and check for stuck coins.

COIN TELEPHONE A pay telephone that takes coins. The coin telephone was invented by William Gray, an American whose previous inventions included the inflatable chest protector for baseball players. Mr. Gray's first phone lacked a dial. Its instructions read: "Call Central in the usual manner. When told by the operator, drop coin in proper channel and push plunger down." In today's nomenclature, Mr. Gray's original phone is known as a post-pay coin phone. See also PAYPHONE and several entries following it.

COLD START Everything starts from scratch. The power to the computer or telephone system is turned off. Everything in the system's volatile memory is erased. A cold start may be needed on a microcomputer when something has happened to "lock up" the keyboard and the Reset button (if there is one) doesn't clear the problem completely. A Cold Start is also needed when you want to load a new operating system. When your phone system gives troubles you find hard to diagnose, turn it off, count to ten and turn it on. This cold boot to your phone system will often fix the problem, as it will typically do on a computer system.

COLLABORATION A multimedia term. Collaboration involves two or more people working together in real-time, or in a "store-and-forward" mode. Applications will enable a group of people to collaborate in real-time over the network using shared screens, shared whiteboards, and video conferencing. Collaboration can range from two people reviewing a slide set on line to a conference of doctors at different locations sharing patient files and discussing treatment options.

COLLECT CALL A telephone call generally requiring operator-assistance. The called party is verbally asked by an operator if they will pay for the call. The called party is ultimately billed for the call.

COLLECTOR RING Metallic ring generally on the armature of a generator in contact with brushes for completing the circuit to a rotating member.

COLLIMATE The condition of parallel light rays.

COLLIMATION The process by which a divergent or convergent beam of electromagnetic radiation is converted into a beam with the minimum divergence or convergence possible for that system (ideally, a parallel bundle of rays).

COLLINEAR ANTENNA A cellular car antenna which looks like a pigtail, because it has a little curlicue in the middle. The curlicue is not a spring, but a clever bit of electro-mechanical magic known as a phasing network, which allows the antenna to boost the effective power of the transmitter's signal. Typically a collinear cellular car antenna is 13 inches high.

COLLISION The result of two workstations trying to use a shared transmission medium (cable) simultaneously. The electrical signals, which carry the information they are sending bump into each other. This ruins both signals and both will have to re-transmit their information. In most systems, a built in delay will make sure the collision does not occur again. The whole process takes fractions of a second. Collisions in LANs make no sound. Collisions do, however, slow a LAN down. See ALOHA, COLLISION DETECTION and CONTENTION.

COLLISION DETECTION The process of detecting that simultaneous (and therefore damaging) transmission has taken place. Typically, each transmitting workstation that detects the collision will wait some period of time and try again. Collision detection is an essential part of the CSMA/CD access method. Workstations can tell that a collision has taken place if they do not receive an acknowledgement from the receiving station within a certain amount of time (fractions of a second). See ALOHA, CONTENTION and ETHERNET.

COLLISION WINDOW The time it takes for a data pulse to travel the length of the network. During this interval, the network is vulnerable to collision.

COLOCATION A competing local phone company can locate its switches within a local exchange company's (LEC) central office. See also CO LOCATION.

COLOPHON Did you ever notice a paragraph at the end of a book describing the typefaces used, the production methods, and so forth? That little paragraph is called a colophon.

COLOR CODE A color system for circuit identification by use of solid colors, tracers, braids, surface marking, etc.

COLOR MODEL A technique for describing a color (see CMY, HSL, HSV, and RGB).

COLUMN A database definition: The logical equivalent of a field, a column contains an individual data item within a row or record.

COMBAT NET RADIO CNR. A radio operating in a network, providing a half-duplex circuit employing a single radio frequency or a discrete set of radio frequencies (frequency hopping). Combat net radios are primarily used for command and control of combat, combat support, and combat service support operations between and among ground, naval, and airborne forces.

COMCODE AT&T's numbering system for telecom equipment, replacing older KS-prefix numbers, and supplements standard industry part designations. Comcode No. 102092848 is touch-tone Princess phone with a transparent plastic housing. How many would you like to order? See also KS NUMBER.

COMBINATION TRUNK A central office trunk circuit which is available as either an incoming or outgoing circuit to the attendant and also available through dial access to internal phone users for outgoing calls.

COMBINED DISTRIBUTION FRAMEE CDF. A distribution frame that combines the functions of main and intermediate distribution frames. The frame contains both vertical and horizontal terminating blocks. The vertical blocks are used to terminate the permanent outside lines entering the station. Horizontal blocks are used to terminate inside plant equipment. This arrangement permits the association of any outside line with any desired terminal equipment. These connections are made with equipment. These connections are made with twisted pair wire, normally referred to as jumper wire, or with optical fiber cables, normally referred to as jumper cables. In technical control facilities, the vertical side may be used to terminate equipment as well as outside lines. The horizontal side is then used for jackfields and battery terminations.

COMBINED STATION MDLC station containing both a primary and a secondary and used in asynchronous balanced mode.

COMINT COMunications INTelligence.

COMMA-FREE CODE A code constructed such that any partial code word, beginning at the start of a code word but terminating prior to the end of that code word, is not a valid code word. The comma-free property permits the proper framing of transmitted code words, provided that: (a) external synchronization is provided to identify the start of the first code word in a sequence of code words, and (b) no uncorrected errors occur in the symbol stream. Huffman codes (variable length) are examples of comma-free codes.

COMMAND AND CONTROL C2. The exercise of authority and direction by a properly designated commander over assigned forces in the accomplishment of the mission. Command and control functions are performed through an arrangement of personnel equipment, communications, facilities, and procedures employed by a commander in planning, directing, coordinating, and controlling forces and operations in the accomplishment of the mission.

COMMAND AND CONTROL SYSTEM The facilities, equipment, communications, procedures, and personnel essential to a commander for planning, directing and controlling operations of assigned forces pursuant to the missions assigned. See COMMAND, CONTROL and COMMUNICATIONS.

COMMAND BUFFER A segment of memory used to temporarily store commands. The command buffer only holds a copy of the last command issued.

COMMAND CONFERENCE SYSTEM A conference calling arrangement in a Northern Telecom PBX which allows a designated phone to originate a conference to and between a group of PBX extensions. Any phone that is busy when the conference begins is automatically connected to the conference as soon as that phone becomes free.

COMMAND, CONTROL AND COMMUNICATIONS C3. The capabilities required by military commanders to exercise command and control of their forces.

COMMAND LINE INTERPRETER CLI. A Rolm user interface to the CBX software and used for things like testing.

COMMAND NET A communications network which connects an echelon of command with some or all of its subordinate echelons for the purpose of command control. See C2 and C3.

COMMAND PATH The list of path names that tells MS-DOS where to look for files that aren't in the current directory.

COMMAND PORT In network management systems an interface used to monitor and control the system.

COMMAND PROCESSOR The MS-DOS program, COMMAND.COM, that contains all DOS's internal commands, like DIR, ERASE and REName. Once you have your hard disk set up, it's a good idea to made your COMMAND.COM "read only." This way it will be difficult for anyone to erase the file. If you don't have COMMAND.COM on your disk, or don't have it in a place where MS-DOS can find it, your disk will not boot (i.e. start) your computer. The command to make COMMAND.COM read only is ATTRIB +R COMMAND.COM.

A mistake many novices make is to "open" COMMAND.COM using their word processor, find that it's full of "junk," then save the file. Saving COMMAND.COM with a word processor destroys COMMAND.COM. The next time you start your computer it will "hang." The solution: Boot from a floppy. Erase COMMAND.COM and REName COMMAND.BAK to COMMAND.COM. Reboot your machine again. This time it should work. If it doesn't, copy COMMAND.COM from your original MS-DOS disk.

COMMAND PROMPT The MS-DOS command prompt appears on the screen as the default drive letter followed by a greater-than > sign. The command prompt lets you know MS-DOS is ready to receive a command. You can use the PROMPT command to change the command prompt. The PROMPT I prefer is prompt. $_DATE $d TIME $t $_$P$g And it looks like this DATE Sat 7-13-1991 TIME 14:49:00.00 C:\BIN\HARRY> Don't forget to type the period after the word "prompt."

COMMDESK BANKER A communications software package offered by MCI International that provides all the capabilities of COMMDesk, plus a security feature essential for financial transactions.

COMMDesk MANAGER An MCI defintion. A communications software package designed to run on an IBM PC/XT/AT or compatible that gives the user full access to all MCI International and MCI communications services.

COMMON AUDIBLE The same as Common Bell. Ringer wiring is such that ringing occurs on more than one CO or PBX line.

COMMON BATTERY A battery (or several batteries) that acts as a central source of energy for many pieces of equipment. In many telecommunications applications, a common battery provides 48 volts of power to a central office switch and to all its phones.

COMMON BATTERY SIGNALING A system in which the signaling power of a telephone is supplied by the battery at the servicing switchboard. Switchboards may be manual or automatic, and "talking power" may be supplied by common or local battery.

COMMON BELL A bell or ringer which sounds when any of the lines terminating on that phone rings. A term harking back to 1A2 key system days.

COMMON BUSINESS LINE CBL. An option with 800 Service that has been replaced by 800 Business Line.

COMMON CARRIER A company that furnishes communications services to the general public. It is typically licensed by a state or federal government agency. A common carrier cannot refuse to carry you, your information or your freight as long as you conform to the rules and regulations as filed with the state or federal authorities. See OTHER COMMON CARRIER.

COMMON CARRIER BUREAU A department of the Federal Communications Commission responsible for recommending and implementing regulatory policies on interstate and international common carrier (voice, video, data) activities.

COMMON CHANNEL INTEROFFICE SIGNALING CCIS. A way of

transmitting all signaling information for a group of trunks by encoding that information and transmitting it over a separate channel using time-division digital methods. By transmitting that signaling information over a separate channel, CCIS saves huge long distance bandwidth, which in the past was used to switch calls across the country only to find a busy signal and then come all the way back again to signal the calling party a busy. For the biggest explanation of common channel signaling, see SIGNALING SYSTEM 7. See also MTP, SCCP, ISUP, ISDN and TCAP.

COMMON CHANNEL SIGNALING This is a Bellcore definition: A network architecture which uses Signaling System 7 (SS7) protocol for the exchange of information between telecommunications nodes and networks on an out-of-band basis. It performs three major functions: 1. It allows the exchange of signaling information for interoffice circuit connections. 2. It allows the exchange of additional information services and features, e.g. CLASS, database query/response, etc. 3. It provides improved operations procedures for network management and administration of the telecommunications network. For the biggest explanation of common channel signaling, see SIGNALING SYSTEM 7. See also ISDN, ISUP, MTP, SCCP, STP and TCAP.

COMMON CHANNEL TRANSIT EXCHANGE An intermediate exchange where networking of common channel signaling systems occurs.

COMMON CONTROL A switching arrangement where the control of all activities is located centrally. This is in contrast to the control being distributed around the system with multiple control devices.

COMMON CONTROL SWITCHING ARRANGEMENT CCSA. An AT&T offering for very big companies. Those big companies can create their own private networks and dial anywhere on them by dialing a standard seven digit number, similar to a local phone number. The corporate subscriber rents private, dedicated lines and then shares central office switches. CCSA uses special CCSA software at the central office.

COMMON COSTS Costs of the provision of some group of services that cannot be directly attributed to any one of those services.

COMMON EQUIPMENT In telephone systems Common Equipment are items that are used by several or all phones for processing calls. On a key system, the device that permits a light on any instrument to flash on and off may be Common Equipment when used to control all lights on all instruments.

COMMON INTERMEDIATE FORMAT A videophone ISDN standard which is part of the CCITT's H.261. It produces a color image of 352 by 288 pixels. The format uses two B channels, with voice taking 32 kbps and the rest for video.

COMMON MODE INTERFERENCE 1. Interference that appears between signal leads, or the terminals of a measuring circuit and ground. 2.

A form of coherent interference that affects two or more elements of a network in a similar manner (i.e., highly coupled) as distinct from locally generated noise or interference that is statistically independent between pairs of network elements.

COMMON MODE REJECTION RATIO CMRR. The ratio of the common mode interference voltage at the input of a circuit to the corresponding interference voltage at the output.

COMMON MODE VOLTAGE 1. The voltage common to both input terminals of a device. 2. In a differential amplifier, the unwanted part of the voltage between each input connection point and ground that is added to the voltage of each original signal.

COMMON RETURN A return path that is common to two or more circuits and that serves to return currents to their source or to ground.

COMMON RETURN OFFSET The dc common return potential difference of a line.

COMMON TRUNK In telephone systems having a grading arrangement, a trunk accessible to all groups of the grading.

COMMON USER CIRCUIT A circuit designated to furnish a communication service to a number of users.

COMMON USER NETWORK A system of circuits or channels allocated to furnish communication paths between switching centers to provide communication service on a common basis to all connected stations or subscribers.

COMMONALITY 1. A quality that applies to material or systems: (a) possessing like and interchangeable characteristics enabling each to be utilized, or operated and maintained by personnel trained on the others without additional specialized training; (b) having interchangeable repair parts and/or components; (c) applying to consumable items interchangeably equivalent without adjustment. 2. A term applied to equipment or systems that have the quality of one entity possessing like and interchangeable parts with another equipment or system entity.

COMMUNICATING OBJECTS A term created in the fall of 1992 by Mitel's VP Tony Bawcutt for a new Mitel division which specializes in making PC printed cards for and software drivers and developer tools for those cards. Those cards are designed to be the building blocks of what Mitel calls multimedia applications — but what are more properly called PC-based voice and call processing telecom developer building blocks. One of the first cards Mitel introduced was an ISDN S-access card which converts PCs into ISDN telephones, also called voice and data workstations.

COMMUNICATING WORD PROCESSOR A dedicated word processor that includes software for sending word processed files over phone lines. Communicating word processors have now largely been replaced by PCs (Personal Computers) running word processing programs and asynchronous communications software programs.

COMMUNICATION CHANNEL A two-way path for transmitting voice and/or data signals. See also CIRCUIT.

COMMUNICATION WORKERS OF AMERICA CWA. A national union of telephone industry employees, currently very worried about its future membership growth given the phone industry's propensity to let its surplus workers go.

COMMUNICATIONS ACT OF 1934 Federal legislation which established national telecommunications goals and created the Federal Communications Commission to regulate all interstate and international communications.

COMMUNICATIONS ACT RE-WRITE A plan to re-write the Communications Act of 1934 to bring telecommunications regulation into the twentieth century. The Act will undoubtedly never been re-written, since Congress typically has more important things to do. However, it is not the function of a dictionary to make predictions. Suffice, a lot of people have spent and are continuing to spend a lot of money to get the Act re-written. They are making a lot of lawyers and a lot of lobbyists rich, but not dictionary writers.

COMMUNICATIONS ADAPTER Device attached to an IBM System 3X computer or an IBM PC that allows communications over RS-232 lines.

COMMUNICATIONS CONTROL CHARACTER A character intended to control or help transmission over data networks. There are ten control characters specified in ASCII which form the basis for character-oriented communications control procedures.

COMMUNICATIONS PROTOCOL 1. Specifications which define hardware and software requirements for that type of communications. 2. The format governing the communication and the transfer of data between two or more devices.

COMMUNICATIONS SATELLITE A satellite circling the earth, usually at a distance of about 22,000 miles, with electronic equipment for relaying signals received from the earth back to other points on the earth. See GEOSTATIONARY SATELLITE.

COMMUNICATIONS SERVER Also called an asynchronous server or asynchronous gateway. A communications server is a type of gateway that translates the packetized signals of a LAN to asynchronous signals, usually used on telephone lines or on direct connections to DEC and other minicomputers and mainframes. It handles different asynchronous protocols and allows nodes on a LAN to share modems or host connections. Usually one machine on a LAN will act as a gateway, sharing its serial ports or an RS-232 connection to a minicomputer. All devices on the LAN can use this machine to get to the modems and the minicomputer.

COMMUNICATIONS SYSTEM ENGINEERING The translation of user requirements for the exchange of information into cost-effective technical solutions of equipment and subsystems.

COMMUNICATIONS ZONE A military term: Rear part of theater of operations (behind but contiguous to the combat zone), which contains the lines of communications, establishments for supply and evacuation, and other agencies required for the immediate support and maintanance of the field forces.

COMMUNICATOR Crosstalk's new PC telecommunications program. It's essentially a reduced and slightly easier-to-use version of Crosstalk M.K.4, the top of the line. Crosstalk is owned by DCA, based in Atlanta.

COMMUNITY ANTENNA TELEVISION CATV. Signals from distant TV stations are picked up by a large antenna, typically located on a hill, then amplified and piped all over the community below on coaxial cable.

COMMUNITY CHECK A check to determine whether electrical current flows continuously throughout the length of a single wire on individual wires in a cable.

COMMUNITY OF INTEREST A grouping of telephone users that call each other with a high degree of frequency. Often several Communities of Interest exist within an organization. This phenomenon can influence design for service when new switches are planned.

COMMUTATOR A device used on a dynamo to reverse the connection periodically in order to cause the current flow in one direction, i.e., to produce direct current.

COMPACT DISC See CD-ROM.

COMPANDER See COMPANDING.

COMPANDING The word is a contraction of the words "compressing" and "expanding." Companding is the process of compressing signals for economical transmission and then expanding them back to their original form at the receiving end.

COMPARTMENTATION A military/government term: A method employed to segregate information of different desired accessibilities from each other. It may be used for communications security purposes.

COMPATIBLE A widely misused word. In the computer world, two computers are said to be compatible when they will produce the identical result if they run identical programs. Another meaning is whether equipment — peripherals and components — can be used interchangeably with each other, from one computer to another. Compatibility used to be regarded as a useful trait in 1A2 key telephones. But then the electronics revolution came along and now there are almost no compatible electronic key telephones from different manufacturers — although TIE and Vodavi are making an effort with their 612/616 and 1A3 electronic key systems, respectively. And TIE and Toshiba have some compatibility among their own different phone systems.

COMPATIBLE SIDEBAND TRANSMISSION That method of independent sideband transmission wherein the carrier is deliberately reinserted at a lower level after its normal suppression to permit reception by conventional AM receivers. The normal method of transmitting compatible SSB (AME) is the emission of the carrier plus the upper sideband.

COMPELLED SIGNALING A signaling method in which the transmission of each signal in the forward direction is inhibited until an acknowledgement of the satisfactory receipt of the previous signal has been sent back from the receiver terminal.

COMPILATION The translation of programs written in a language understandable to programmers into instructions understandable to the computer. Think of programmers writing in every language but Greek and computers understanding only Greek. In this case, Greek is called machine language. The other languages (the programmer languages) are called things like COBOL, FORTRAN, Pascal, dBASE. A compiler is a special program that translates from all these other languages into machine language.

COMPILER A program that takes the source code a programmer has written and translates it into object code the computer can understand. A computer program used to convert symbols meaningful to a human into codes meaningful to a computer. For example, a compiler takes instructions written in a "higher" level language such as BASIC, COBOL or ALGOL and converts them into machine code which can be read and acted upon by a computer. Compilers converts large sections of code at one time, compared to an interpreter which translates commands one at a time.

COMPLEMENTARY METAL OXIDE SEMICONDUCTOR CMOS. A method of building chips which produces a logic circuit family which uses very little power.

COMPLEMENTARY NETWORK SERVICE CNS. CNSs are basic services associated with end user's lines that make it easier for ESPs to offer them enhanced services. Some examples of CNSs include Call Forwarding Busy/Don't Answer, Three Way Calling, and Virtual Dial Tone. See OPEN NETWORK ARCHITECTURE.

COMPLETE DOCUMENT RECOGNITION The ability to perform recognition on documents, retaining as much information as possible about the features and formatting of the original, and including the ability to capture images as well as text.

COMPLETED CALL Careful with this one. In telephone dialect, a Completed Call is one that has been switched to its destination and conversation has begun but has not yet ended.

COMPLETION RATIO The proportion of the number of attempted calls to the number of completed calls.

COMPLIMENTARY NETWORK SERVICES CNS. The means for an enhanced-service provider's customer to connect to the network and to the enhanced service provider. Complimentary network services usually consist of the customer's local service (e.g.,business or residence line) and several associated service options, e.g., call-forwarding service.

COMPOSITE Output of a multiplexor that includes all data from the multiplexed channels. Contrast with AGGREGATE.

COMPOSITE LINK The datastream composed of all the input channels and control and signaling information in a multiplexed circuit. The Composite Link Speed is the transmission speed of the circuit.

COMPOSITE MATERIALS Composite materials consist of two or more components. They make it possible to combine the best properties of different materials; for example, the compression strength and low price of concrete with the tensile strength of reinforcing rods. Composite materials include: Reinforced concrete, fiber-reinforced plastic, fiber-reinforced metals, plywood, chipboard and ceramics. The composites mainly considered for antennas are fiber-reinforced plastics. They combine the low weight and protective properties of plastics with the stiffness and strength of fiber.

COMPOSITE SIGNALING A direct current signaling system that separates the signals from the voice band by filters. Also called CX Signaling.

COMPOSITED CIRCUIT A circuit that can be used simultaneously for telephony and dc telegraphy, or signaling; separation between the two being accomplished by frequency discrimination.

COMPOUND A term used to designate an insulating or jacketing material made by mixing two or more ingredients.

COMPOUND DOCUMENT A document composed of a variety of data types and formats. Each data type is linked to the application that created it. A compound document might include audio, video, images, text, and graphics. Compound documents first became possible to the world of PCs with the introduction of Windows 3.1, which included OLE (Object Linking and Embedding). OLE allows you to write a letter in your favorite Windows word processor, embed a small voice icon in your document, send your letter to someone else, have them open your letter, place their mouse on the voice icon and hear whatever comments you recorded. To make this possible, both you (the creator) and your recipient would need access to programs that could read both the text and the voice. Ideally, you would both be on a LAN (Local Area Network) and would both get access to the identical applications software, resident, presumably, on the LAN's file server. See COMPOUND MAILBOX.

COMPOUND DOCUMENT MAIL See COMPOUND DOCUMENT.

COMPOUND MAILBOX A mailbox for mail from all sources — fax, voice mail, e-mail, pager, etc. See COMPOUND DOCUMENT.

COMPRESSED VIDEO Television signals transmitted with much less than the usual bit rate. Full standard coding of broadcast quality television typically requires 45 to 90 megabits per second. Compressed video includes signals from 3 mb/s down to 56 kb/s. The lower bit rates typically involve some compromise in picture quality, particularly when there's rapid motion on the screen.

COMPRESSION Reducing the representation of the information, but not the information itself. Reducing the bandwidth or number of bits needed to encode information or encode a signal, typically by eliminating long strings of identical bits or bits that do not change in successive sampling intervals (e.g., video frames). Compression saves transmission time or capacity. It also saves storage space on storage devices such as hard disks, tape drives and floppy disks.

COMPRESSION ALGORITHM The arithmetic formulae which convert a signal into smaller bandwidth or few bits.

COMPRESSOR See COMPANDING.

COMPROMISE EQUALIZER Equalizer set for best overall operation for a given range of line conditions. This is often fixed but may be manually adjustable.

COMPSURF COMPprehensive SURFace Analysis. A Novell program that checks the surface of a hard disk, marks off sections that are lousy and therefore shouldn't be written to, and then low level formats the disk. The program is slow, but thorough and rigorous. No hard disk should ever be used on a file server on a Novell local area network without being subjected to this wonderful program. Don't believe Novell when it says that you don't need to subject new disks to COMPSURF. You should submit ALL disks.

COMPUCALL Northern Telecom DMS central office link to computer interface. An open architecture specification. Northern Telecom spells it as CompuCALL. According to Northern Telecom's own words, CompuCALL employs the Switch Computer Application Interface (SCAI) open architecture standard to connect the central office with customers' general-purpose business computers.

CompuCALL consists of:

● The CompuCALL base software (NTXJ59AA) in the Northern Telecom DMS-100 switch, or the Meridian Automatic Call Distribution (ACD) Server, that sends and receives SCAI messages; and

● The CompuCALL transport mechanism that physically links the switch to the computer or other external processor and carries the SCAI message.

Northern Telecom also supplies the Meridian ACD CompuCALL Options (NTXJ39AA) and other applications software which rely on the CompuCALL base. Computers and software vendors provide application programming interface (API) software as well as business application software. The API, which resides in the business computer, converts SCAI messages into information that can be used by computer-based business application software.

The first applications of CompuCALL integrate computer databases with voice telephony:

● CompuCALL Coordinated Voice and Data provides an agent a screen of information about a caller concurrently with receipt of a call.

● CompuCALL Voice Processing Integration uses Interactive Voice Response (IVR) systems and Voice Response Units (VRU) to obtain additional information about callers and direct them to the appropriate agent.

● CompuCALL Third-Party Call Control lets the customer's computer place outgoing calls.

Successful implementation of CompuCALL requires interaction with application software on a business computer. CompuCALL consists of:

● The CompuCALL base software residing in the Northern Telecom DMS-100 central office switch that sends and receives SCAI messages; and

● The CompuCALL transport mechanism that physically links the switch to the computer or other external processor and carries the SCAI message.

Computer and software vendors provide application programming interface (API) software as well as business application software. The API, which resides in the business computer, converts SCAI messages into information that can be used by computer-based business application software.

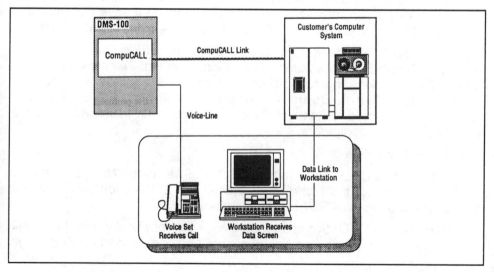

CompuCALL is based on the seven-layer protocol defined by the International Telegraph and Telephone Consultative Committee's (CCITT) Open System Interconnection (OSI) reference model. The product is transport independent. With BCS33, CompuCALL is scheduled to be available for Verifications Office (VO) on X.25. In 1993, it will be available on Integrated Services Digital Network Basic Rate Interface (ISDN BRI).

See also OPEN APPLICATION INTERFACE.

COMPUNICATIONS A recent creation meaning the combination of telephones, computers, television and data systems.

COMPUTER This is a definition straight from AT&T Bell Laboratories. "An electronic device that accepts and processes information mathematically according to previous instructions. It provides the result of this processing via visual displays, printed summaries or in an audible form."

COMPUTER AIDED DIALING A newer (and allegedly less offensive) term for predictive dialing. See also PREDICTIVE DIALING.

COMPUTER AIDED PROFESSIONAL PUBLISHING CAP. The computerization of professional publishing (as opposed to desktop operations), including true color representation of the layout on the workstation screen.

COMPUTER AND BUSINESS EQUIPMENT MANUFACTURERS ASSOCIATION CBEMA. Association active before Congress and the FCC promoting the interests of the competitive terminal, computer and peripheral equipment industries.

COMPUTER AND COMMUNICATIONS INDUSTRY ASSOCIATION CCIA. Organization of data processing and communications companies which promotes their interests before Congress and the FCC.

COMPUTER INQUIRY A series of ongoing FCC proceedings examining the distinctions between communications and information processing to determine which services are subject to common carrier regulation. The FCC decision in 1980 resulting from the second inquiry was to limit common carrier regulation to basic services. Enhanced services and customer premises equipment are not to be regulated. This meant the Bell operating companies had to set up separate subsidiaries if they were to offer non-regulated services.

Computer Inquiry III, adopted by the FCC in May, 1986, removed the structural separation requirement between basic and enhanced services for the BOCs and for AT&T. CI III replaced that requirement with "nonstructural safeguards." This action resulted in the imposition of such concepts as "comparably efficient interconnection" (CEI) and Open Network Architecture (ONA). The FCC's jurisdiction regarding Computer Inquiry I, II and III has now been usurped by Judge Greene, who insists on fairly tight control over the non-basic telephone company activities of the Bell operating companies.

Sometimes he gives dispensations (waivers). Sometimes he doesn't. His word these days is final law on what the Bell operating companies can and can't do.

COMPUTER SUPPORT TELEPHONY See CST.

COMPUTER-LIKE TRANSPORT An AT&T term for the carrying of digital information with the potential for acting on that information at any network node as appropriate.

COMSAT The COMmunications SATellite corporation was created by Congress as the exclusive provider to the U.S. of satellite channels for international communications. COMSAT is also the U.S. representative to Intelsat and Inmarsat, two international groups responsible for satellite and maritime communications. Comsat is now being merged with Continental Telephone, also known as Contel.

COMSPEC COMmand SPECification. A configuration command that tells MS-DOS where to find the program that interprets what is typed at the prompt. Except in unusual circumstances, that program is COMMAND.COM. COMSPEC is typically used when you have the program COMMAND.COM somewhere other than in the root directory of your C: drive (if you have a hard disk machine) or your A: drive if you have a floppy system. Let's say you want to tell your computer to find COMMAND.COM on your D: drive, the command in your AUTOEXEC.BAT program would be:

SET COMSPEC=D:\COMMAND.COM

COMSTAR A domestic communications satellite system from Comsat.

CONCATENATION Joining several fibers together end-to-end.

CONCENTRATION A fundamental concept to telephony. Communications from a number of phones are sent out on a smaller number of outgoing lines. The theory is that, since not all the phones are being used at any one time, fewer trunks than phones are needed. Some phone system designs assume that only 5% of the phones will be in use at any one time. Some phone systems design assume 10%. In some phone-intensive industries, you can't make any assumptions about concentration. You have to assume one line per phone. No concentration. TELECONNECT Magazine is around one phone per line. We are very phone intensive. See CONCENTRATION RATIO.

CONCENTRATION RATIO The ratio between lines and trunks in a concentrated carrier system or line concentrator.

CONCENTRATOR 1. This telecommunications device allows a number of circuits (typically slow speed ones) to be connected to a smaller number of lines for transmission under the assumption that not all of the larger group of lines will be used at the same time. The concentrator allows a shared transmission medium to accommodate more data sources than there are channels currently available within the transmission medium. A concentrator's job is to save money on transmission. 2. Some LANs use concentrators, or access units, that allow network devices to be interconnected through a central point. The wiring is star, also called home run. Attaching devices through a central concentrator typically simplifies the maintenance of the LAN. A concentrator is used when connecting a LAN over the "normal" twisted wires in a building which were put there originally to carry voice and which now have to be used because — for one reason or another — it's not possible to connect the LAN using its normal bus coaxial cable connection.

CONCENTRICITY In a wire or cable, the measurement of the location of the center of the conductor with respect to the geometric center of the circular insulation.

CONCENTRICITY ERROR The amount by which a fiber's core is not centered in its cladding. The distance between the center of the two concentric circles specifying the cladding diameter and the center of the two concentric circles specifying the core diameter.

CONCERT NETWORK MANAGEMENT SYSTEM British Telecom operating environment.

CONCURRENCY 1. The shared use of resources by multiple interactive users or applications at the same time. 2. When more than one user accesses a particular use of records of files at the same time.

CONCURRENCY CONTROL A feature that allows multiple users to execute database transactions simultaneously without interfering with each other.

CONCURRENT SITE LICENSE Companies that buy software for multiple computers typically buy one copy of the program and a license to reproduce it up to a certain number of times. This is called a site license, though it may apply to its use throughout an organization. Site licenses vary. Some require that a copy be bought for each potential user — the only purpose being to indicate the volume discount and keep tabs. Others allow for a copy to be placed on a network server but limit the number of users who can gain simultaneous access. This is called a Concurrent Site License. And many network administrators prefer this concurrent license, since it gives them greater control. For example, if the software is customized, it need be customized only once, namely on the server.

CONDENSER A device for storing up electrical energy and consisting of two or more conducting surfaces or electrodes separated by an insulating medium called a dialectic.

CONDENSER ANTENNA An antenna consisting of two capacity areas.

CONDENSER MICROPHONE Microphone which operates through changes in capacitance caused by vibrations of its conductive diaphragm.

CONDITIONED CIRCUIT A circuit that has conditioning equipment to obtain the desired characteristics for voice or data transmission. See CONDITIONING.

CONDITIONED LOOP A loop that has conditioning equipment to obtain the desired line characteristics for voice or data transmission. See CONDITIONING.

CONDITIONING Electrical treatment of transmission lines to improve their performance for specific uses such as data transmission. The "tuning" or addition of equipment to improve the transmission characteristics of a leased voice-grade line so that it meets the specifications for higher-speed data transmission. Voice-grade lines often have too much "noise" on them. By altering the equipment at both ends of the line, this noise on the line can be overcome. This allows transmission of data, which is much more sensitive to noise than voice.

Here is another definition of conditioning: A procedure used to make circuit transmission impairments lie within certain acceptable limits which are specified in a tariff (typically used on telephone lines leased for data transmission to improve transmission speed and quality). Usually done with special equipment or routing.

CONDOFIBER A shared tenancy cable or shared ownership facility such as a transatlantic fiber cable. Multiple vendors such as Sprint, MCI and AT&T may all own a group of fibers with responsibility for maintaining their own operation while at the same time paying an overall "association" fee for the common maintenance of the overall cable.

CONDUCTANCE The opposite of resistance; a measure of the ability of a conductor to carry an electrical charge. Conductance is a ratio of the current flow to the potential difference causing the current flow. The unit of conductance is Mho (a reversed spelling of Ohm).

CONDUCTING MATERIALS Substances which offer relatively little resistance to the passage of an electric current.

CONDUCTIVITY A term used to describe the ability of a material to carry an electrical charge. The opposite of specific resistance. Usually expressed as a percentage of copper conductivity - copper being one hundred percent. Conductivity is expressed for a standard configuration of conductor.

CONDUCTOR Any substance, usually a wire or cable, that can carry (i.e. offer a relatively small opposition to the passage of) an electrical current.

CONDUIT A pipe, usually metal, that runs either from floor to floor or along a floor or ceiling to protect cables. A conduit protects the cable and prevents burning cable from spreading flames or smoke. Many fire codes in large cities thus require that cable be placed in metal conduit. In the riser subsystem when riser closets are not aligned, conduit is used to protect cable as well as to provide the means for pulling cable from floor to floor. In the horizontal wiring subsystem, conduit may be used between a riser or satellite closet and an information outlet in an office or other room. Conduit is also used for in-conduit campus distribution, where it is run underground between buildings and intermediate manholes and encased in concrete. Multiduct, clay tile conduit may also be used.

CONDUIT RUN The path taken by a conduit or group of conduits.

CONFEREE Participant in a conference call who is not the call controller. This definition courtesy Hayes. According to Hayes, a "controller" is the person who sets up the conference call.

CONFERENCE BRIDGE A telecommunications facility or service which permits callers from several diverse locations to be connected together for a conference call. The conference bridge contains electronics for amplifying and balancing the conference call so everyone can hear each other and speak to each other. The conference call's progress is monitored through the bridge in order to produce a high quality voice conference and to maintain decent quality as people enter or leave the conference.

CONFERENCE CALL Connecting three or more people into one phone conversation. You used to have to place conference calls through an AT&T operator (you still can). But now you can also organize conference calls with most modern phone systems or a conference bridge. If conferencing is important to you, make sure your conferencing device has amplification and balancing. If not, it will simply electrically join the various conversations together and people at either end won't be able to hear each other. There are different types of conference devices you can buy, including special teleconferencing devices that sit on conference tables and perform the function of a speakerphone, albeit a lot better. There are also dial-in devices called conference bridges. But, however, you use these devices, they will requires lines (and/or trunks). If you install one inside your phone system, be careful have the extra spare extensions. For a conference of 10 people, you'll typically need 10 extensions connected to your conference bridge. See CONFERENCE BRIDGE.

CONFERENCE, MEET-ME A conference call in which each of the people wishing to join the conference simply dials a special "Meet-Me" Conference phone number, which automatically connects them into the conference. It is a feature of some PBXs and also some special Conferencing Equipment. See CONFERENCE BRIDGE.

CONFERENCING Several parties can be added to a phone conversation through Conferencing.

CONFIDENCER A noise-cancelling microphone for use on a telephone in noisy places. A confidencer is not an easy device to use.

CONFIDENTIAL RECEPTION The ability to receive a facsimile transmission directly into memory which can be printed out or viewed at a later time.

CONFIDENTIAL TRANSMISSION A facsimile message that is sent confidentially into memory or a private mailbox, to be retrieved by the receiver at a later time. It's usually retrieved by using a confidential passcode or password.

CONFIG.SYS A file of commands used to set up the computer. MS-DOS reads it each time it starts. This is where you put commands for device drivers for a mouse, a RAM drive, instructions on where to put DOS, how much memory to set for your cache, etc. Other configuration parameters like how many open files are allowed, how many buffers, how many drives, etc. are also put in this file. Here is my CONFIG.SYS. I'm using MS-DOS 5.0 and have 6 megabytes of RAM. My CONFIG.SYS puts DOS high, sets up 1 meg for expanded memory and two megs for a cache:

```
device=C:\dos\HIMEM.SYS
device=C:\dos\EMM386.EXE 1024
DOS=HIGH,umb
device=c:\dos\smartdrv.sys 2048
FILES=40
STACKS=0,0
lastdrive=d
```

CONFIGURATION The hardware and software arrangements that define a computer or telecommunications system and thus determine what the system will do and how well it will do it. This information can be entered in the CMOS and EEPROM setup programs.

CONFIGURATION DATABASES Rolm/IBM words for those databases which represent unique user specifications relating to system and phone features. These databases can be entered on-site and are not part of the generic software which runs the phone system.

CONFIGURATION FILE An unformatted ASCII file that stores initialization information for an application.

CONFORMANCE TEST A test performed by an independent body to determine if a particular piece of equipment or system satisfies the criteria of a particular standard, sometimes a contract to buy the equipment.

CONFIRMING DESIGN LAYOUT REPORT DATE CDLRD. The date a common carrier accepts the facility designed proposed by the Telco.

CONFORMING END OFFICE Central office with the ability to provide originating and terminating feature group D local access and transport area access service.

CONNECT TIME 1. Measure of computer and telecommunications system usage. The interval during which the user was on-line for a session. 2. Interval during which a request for a connection is being completed.

CONNECTED A voice recognition term for words spoken clearly in succession without pasues. For recognition to occur, words or utterances must be separated by at least 50 milliseconds (1/20th of a second). Generally refers to digit recognition and sometimes used to describe fast discrete recognition.

CONNECTING ARRANGEMENT The manner in which the facilities of a common carrier (phone company) and the customer are interconnected.

CONNECTING BLOCK A plastic block containing metal wiring terminals to establish connections. from one group of wires to another. Usually each wire can be connected to several other wires in a bus or common arrangement. A 66-type block is the most common type of connecting block. It was invented by Western Electric. Northern Telecom has one called a Bix block. There are others. These two are probably the most common. A connecting block is also called a terminal block, a punch-down block, a quick-connect block, a cross-connect block. A connecting block will include insulation displacement connections (IDC). In other words, with a connecting block, you don't have to remove the plastic shielding from around your wire conductor before you "punch it down."

CONNECTION 1. A path between telephones that allows the transmission of speech and other signals. 2. An electrical continuity of circuit between two wires or two units, in a piece of apparatus.

CONNECTION ORIENTED OPERATION A communications protocol in which a logical connection is established between communicating devices. Connection-oriented service is also referred to as virtual-circuit service.

CONNECTION ORIENTED TRANSMISSION Data transmission technique involving setting up connection before transmission and disconnecting it afterward. A type of service in which information always traverses the same pre-established path or link between two points. See CONNECTIONLESS SERVICE.

CONNECTIONLESS MODE TRANSMISSION In packet data transmission, a mode of operation in which each packet is encoded with a header containing destination address sufficient to permit the indepedent delivery of the packet without the aid of additional instruments. See also CLOUD, CONNECTIONLESS NETWORK and CONNECTIONLESS SERVICE.

CONNECTIONLESS NETWORK A type of communications network in which no logical connection (i.e. no leased line or dialed-up channel) is required between sending and receiving stations. Each data unit (datagram) is sent and addressed independently. IEEE 802 LAN standards specify connectionless networks. Connectionless networks are becoming more common in broadband city networks now increasingly offered by phone companies.

CONNECTIONLESS SERVICE A networking mode in which individual data packets in a network (local or long distance) traveling from one point to another are directed from one intermediate node to the next until they reach their ultimate destination. Because packets may take different routes, they must be reassembled at their destination. The receipt of a transmission is typically acknowledged from the ultimate destination to the point of origin. A connectionless packet is frequently called a datagram. A connectionless service is inherently unreliable in the sense that the service provider usually cannot provide assurance against the loss, error insertion, misdelivery, duplication, or out-of-sequence delivery of a connectionless packet. Connectionless networks may be better than connection-oriented ones for obtaining management information over a failing network because a device doesn't have the additional burden of maintaining a network connection.

CONNECTIONLESS TRANSMISSION Data transmission without prior establishment of a connection.

CONNECTIONS PER CIRCUIT HOUR CCH. A unit of traffic measurement; the number of connections established at a switching point per hour.

CONNECTIVITY Property of a network that allows dissimilar devices to communicate with each other.

CONNECTOR A device that electrically connects wires or fibers in cable to equipment, or other wires or fibers. Wire and optical connectors most often join transmission media to equipment (host computers and terminal devices) or cross connects. A Connector at the end of a telephone cable or wire is used to join that cable to another cable with a matching Connector or to some other telecommunications device. Residential telephones use the RJ-11C connector. Computer terminals with an RS-232-C interface, use the DB-25 connector. The RS-232-C standard is actually the electrical method of using the pins on a DB-25. See RS-232-C.

CONSENT DECREE 1982 The agreement which divested the Bell Operating Companies from AT&T. It took effect at midnight on December 31, 1983.

CONSERVATION OF RADIANCE A basic principle stating that no passive optical system can increase the quantity L/n2, where L is the radiance of a beam and n is the local refractive index. Formerly called conservation of brightness, or the brightness theorem.

CONSOLE 1. A large telephone which a PBX attendant uses to answer incoming calls and transfer them around the organization. Before you buy a PBX for your company, make sure your operator has checked out its console. Some are very difficult to use. Some are easy. Some operators hate some consoles. Some consoles hate some operators. You can measure the efficiency of consoles by comparing keystrokes to do simple jobs and comparing them — e.g. answer an incoming line, dial an extension and transfer the call. How many keystrokes does your PBX take? 2. The device which allows communications between a computer operator and a computer. 3. The console is the Novell NetWare name for the monitor and keyboard of the file server. Here you can view and control the file server or router activity. At the console, you can enter commands to control disk drives, send messages, set the file server or router clock, shut down the file server, and view file server information. NetWare commands you can enter only from the console (for example, MONITOR) are called console commands. Keep your file server locked up and away from prying eyes. It's clearly not just a case of changing passwords and getting in and mucking around. There have been examples of thieves simply removing the file server's hard disk, putting it in their briefcase and walking off with it.

CONSOLELESS OPERATION Some PBXs can work without a console. Some must have a console. It's good to check. Consoles are expensive. If you don't want one — because your company is small — you don't want to be forced to buy one, only to have it sit idly by.

CONSTANT CARRIER Physical line specification selection indicating full duplex line in bisync network.

CONSULT To seek another's endorsement of a decision you've already made.

CONSULTANT See CONSULT and CONSULTANT LIAISON PROGRAMS.

CONSULTANT LIAISON PROGRAMS Large users often use communications consultants to help them choose systems and long distance phone lines. In recognition of the important role consultants play, many suppliers have consultant liaison programs. Such programs typically consist of a toll-free number and somebody on the other end to answer technical and pricing questions, a three-ring containing information on all the company's products and services, occasional seminars and, for those extra-privileged consultants, trips to all expense paid trips to exotic places and "something" else. With MCI that "something else" is a dial-up, toll-free, bulletin board. Dial it up with your PC, you can download MCI's latest prices and services. It's truly splendid as most of the paperwork others issue is obsolete the moment it's issued.

CONSULTATION See CONSULTATION HOLD.

CONSULTATION HOLD PBX feature which allows an extension to place a call on hold while speaking with another call. The idea is "consulting with" someone while you have someone else on the phone.

CONTACT A strip or piece of metal which makes an electrical contact when some electromechanical device like a relay or a magnet operates. Contacts are often plated with precious metal to prevent them from oxidizing (i.e. rusting) and thus messing up the switch.

CONTACT IMAGE SENSOR Uses a flat bar of light-emitting diode that directly touches the original. It eliminates the step of having the diodes move through the lens, which causes poorer resolution. This method is a more sophisticated than the charged-coupled device scanning method.

CONTACT REGION The section of the jack wire inside the plug opening as shown in Subpart F of FCC rule 6B, figures 6B.500 (a) (3) and 6B.500 (b) (3).

CONTENDED ACCESS In local area networking technology it's the shared access method that allows stations to use the medium on a first-come, first-served basis.

CONTENDING PORT A programmable port type which can initiate a connection only to a preprogrammed port or group of ports.

CONTENTION Contention occurs when several phones are vying for access to a line and only one of them can get it at one time. Some method is usually established for selecting the winner (first in, first out, campon, etc.) and accommodating the loser(s) (.e.g. giving them a busy tone). When you cannot get an outside line from your extension you have been in contention and lost.

CONTEXT DEPENDENT SOFT KEYS Many telephones now have an LCD screen. Sometimes such screens have unmarked keys underneath them and/or at their side. What these keys do depends on the "labels" appearing on the screen. They are called "context dependent" because what those keys do depends on where the call is at that time. The first context dependent soft keys were on the Mitel SuperSet 4 phones. When the handset was resting on the phone, only three of the six context sensitive keys had meaning. One said "Program," one said "Msg" and one said "Redial." When you picked the phone up, three buttons would now be alive. One would say "Page," one would say "Redial" and one would say "Hangup." If the phone rang and you picked it up, one button would now say "transf/conf" (meaning transfer/conference. When another phone was ringing. one button would say "Pickup," letting you push that button and answer someone else's phone. And so on. The neatest implementation of context sensitive keys was probably on the Telenova (now no longer manufactured). At one point when you were in voice mail, this phone's six buttons looked exactly like a cassette recorder — record, play, fast forward, fast reverse, etc. It was brilliant. No one has ever made using voice mail so easy.

CONTEXT SENSITIVE A term from the computer industry which means that "Help" is only a keystroke away. Hit F1 and Help information will flash on the screen. That information will be relevant to what you're doing now, i.e. that help is within the context of what's going on right this moment. See also CONTEXT DEPENDENT SOFT KEYS.

CONTEXT SWITCH The technique with which an Intel 80x86 microprocessor handles multitasking is called a context switch. The CPU performs a context switch when it transfers control from one task to another. In the process, it saves the processor state (including registers) of one task, then loads the values for the task that is taking control. Context switching is the kind of multitasking that is done in standard mode Windows, where the CPU switches from one task to another, rather than allocating time to each task in turn, as in timeslicing.

CONTIGUOUS PORT Ports occurring in unbroken numeric sequence.

CONTIGUOUS UNITED STATES The area within the boundaries of the District of Columbia and the 48 contiguous states as well as the offshore areas outside the boundaries of the coastal states of the 48 contiguous states, (including artificial islands, anchored vessels and fixed structures erected in such offshore areas for the purpose of exploring for, developing, removing and transporting resources therefrom) to the extent that such areas appertain to and are subject to the jurisdiction and control of the United States within the meaning of the Outer Continental Shelf Land Act, 43 U.S.C. Section 1331, et seq.

CONTINENTAL TELECOM INC. CONTEL. A telephone company made up of more than 600 small phone companies. In 1990 it merged with GTE in a tax-free swap of shares. Contel was formed and grown by Charles Wohlstetter, an ex-stockbroker, who became comfortable in the process of growing Contel. In late 1990, Contel merged with GTE, which is a euphemism for GTE buying Contel.

CONTINUITY An uninterrupted electrical path.

CONTINUITY CHECK TONE CCT. A single frequency of 2000 Hz which is transmitted by the sending exchange and looped back by the receiving exchange. Reception of the returned indicates availability of the channel. See CCITT Recommendation.271.

CONTINUOUS A word used in voice recognition to mean a type of recognition that requires no pause between utterances.

CONTINOUS DTMF This is a feature of some phones (especially cellular phones) that sends touch-tone sounds for as long as the key is held down, allowing access to services such as voice mail and answering machines that need long-duration tones. Some phones automatically have continuous DTMF; some don't. It's worth checking. Continuous DTMF makes a lot more sense.

CONTINUOUS WAVES A series of wave or cycle of current all of which have a constant or unvarying amplitude.

CONTINUOUSLY VARIABLE Capable of having one of an infinite number of values, differing from each other by an arbitrarily small amount. Usually used to describe analog signals or analog transmission.

CONTROL CABLE A multiconductor cable made for operation in control or signal circuits.

CONTROL CHARACTER A non-printing ASCII character which controls the flow of communications or a device. Control characters are entered from computer terminal keyboards by holding down the Control key (marked CTRL on most keyboards) while the letter is pressed. To ring a bell at remote telex terminal, an operator could hold down the CTRL key, and tap the "G" key, since Control-G is the BELL character. Most computers display Control as the "^" character in front of the designated letter. For example, ^M is the Carriage Return character.

CONTROL CIRCUIT X.21 interface circuit used to send control information from DTE to DCE.

CONTROL EQUIPMENT 1. The central "brains" of a telephone system. That part which controls the signaling and switching to the attached telephones. Known as the KSU (or key service unit) in a key system. 2. Equipment used to transmit orders from an alarm center to remote site to enable you to do things by remote control.

CONTROL FIELD Field in frame containing control information.

CONTROL OF ELECTROMAGNETIC RADIATION 1. Measures taken to minimize electromagnetic radiation emanating from a system or component, or to minimize electromagnetic interference. Such measures are taken for purposes of security and/or the reduction of interference, especially on ships and aircraft. 2. A national operational plan to minimize the use of electromagnetic radiation in the United States and its possessions and the Panama Canal Zone in the event of attack of imminent threat thereof, as an aid to the navigation of hostile aircraft, guided missiles, or other devices.

CONTROL OF FLOW LANGUAGE Programming-like constructs (IF, ELSE, WHILE, GOTO, and so on) provided by Transact-SQL so that the user can control the flow of execution of SQL Server queries, stored procedures, and triggers. This definition from Microsoft SQL server.

CONTROL PANEL The control panel on the Apple Macintosh is for general hardware and software settings. Icons allow a user to customize the system or application, or select a particular service, such as a specific printer, set the sound level, the date and time and choose an Ethernet connection through the network control panel.

CONTROL SEGMENT A world-wide network of Global Positioning System monitoring and control installations that ensure the accuracy of satellite positions and their clocks.

CONTROL SIGNAL Modem interface signal used to announce, start, stop or modify a function. Here's a table showing common RS-232-C and CCITT V.24 control signals

Pin	Control Signal	From	To
4	Request-To-Send (RTS)	DTE	DCE

5	Clear-To-Send (CTS)	DCE	DTE
6	Data Set Ready (DSR)	DCE	DTE
8	Carrier Detect (CD)	DCE	DTE
20	Data Terminal Ready (DTR)	DTE	DCE
22	Ring Indicator (RI)	DCE	DTE

CONTROL STATION On multiaccess link, station that is in charge of such functions as selection and polling.

CONTROL TIER An AT&T term for the tier within the Universal Information Services network node that provides the transport network's connection control function.

CONTROL UNIT An architectural component of a processor chip which orchestrates processor activity and handles timing to make sure the processor doesn't overlap functions.

CONTROL PACKAGE NETWORK A Rolm/IBM term for a multinode network used by the processors in one CBX node to communicate with the processors in other nodes. CPN-1 is used with RolmBus 74. CPN-2 is used with Rolmbus 295. Formerly called HUB.

CONTROLLED ENVIRONMENT VAULT CEV. It is a low maintenance, water-tight concrete or fiberglass container typically buried in the ground which provides permanent housing for remote switches, remote line concentrators, pair gain and fiber transmission systems. Because it is buried, it can often be installed in utility easements or other places where local building laws may be a problem. This below ground room that houses electronic and/or optical equipment is under controlled temperature and humidity conditions.

CONTROLLER 1. In the truest sense, a device which controls the operation of another piece of equipment. In its more common data communications sense, a device between a host and terminals that relays information between them. It administers their communication. Controllers may be housed in the host, can be stand-alone, or can be located in a file server. Typically one controller will be connected to several terminals. The most common controller is the IBM Cluster Controller for their 370 family of mainframes. In an automated radio, a controller is a device that commands the radio transmitter and receiver, and that performs processes, such as automatic link establishment, channel scanning and selection, link quality analysis, polling, sounding, message store and forward, address protection, and anti-spoofing. 2. Participant in a conference call who sets up the conference call.

CONTROLLER CARD Also called a hard disk/diskette drive controller. It's an add-in card which controls how data is written to and retrieved from your PC's various floppy and hard drives. Controller cards come in various flavors, including MFN and SCSI. Controller cards are the devices used to format hard drives. Controller cards are not hard drive specific (except within categories). Controller cards will format many drives. But once you have a hard drive that has been formatted by that one controller card, it tends to prefer talking to that controller card forever. If you switch your hard disk to another machine, switch the controller card along with it. If you switch your hard disk to another machine, but not the controller card, then format the hard disk. That's not a "100% Do It Or Else You'll Be Disappointed" rule. But just a "Play It Safe and Switch Them" rule.

CONTURING In digital facsimile, density step lines in received copy resulting from analog-to-digital conversion when the original image has observable gray shadings between the smallest density steps of the digital system.

CONUS A military term for CONtiguous United States (lower 48 states). See CONTIGUOUS UNITED STATES.

CONVECTION COOLING Design techniques used in switching system construction to permit safe heat dissipation from the equipment without the need for cooling fans.

CONVECTOR The device which covers the steam heating radiator in buildings and typically sits underneath a window. Also called a weathermaster.

CONVECTOR AREA An area allocated for heat circulation and distribution. Convector areas, typically built into a wall, can be used as a satellite location only if a more suitable area is unavailable.

CONVERGENCE 1. A measure of the clarity of a color monitor. A measure of how closely the red, green and blue guns in a color monitor track each other when drawing a color image. The other measures are focus and dot pitch. 2. A LAN term. The point at which all the internetworking devices share a common understanding of the routing topology. The slower the covergence time, the slower the recovery from link failure.

CONVERSATION PATH The route from originating port to terminating port for a two-way call. A conversation thus typically requires two ports on most PBXs.

CONVERSATION TIME The time spent on a conversation from the time the person at the other end picks up to the time you or him hang up. Conversation time plus dialing, searching and ringing time equal the time your circuit will be used during a call.

CONVERSATIONAL MODE TELEX An MCI International product providing realtime exchange between Telex terminals or other compatible devices that allows instantaneous, two-way conversations in writing.

CONVERTER 1. A vacuum tube which combines the functions of oscillator and mixed tube. 2. A device for changing A.C to D.C and vice versa. An ancient radio term. 3. An adapter, such as one that allows a modular phone to be plugged into a 4-hole jack.

CONVOLUTIONAL CODE Error protection code encoding data bits in a continuous stream. An error-correction code in which each m-bit information symbol to be encoded is transformed into an n-bit symbol (n>m) where the transformation is a function of the last k information symbols, and k is referred to as the constraint length of the code. Convolutional codes are often used to improve the performance of radio and satellite links.

COOPERATIVE PROCESSING Mainframe and intelligent workstations dividing application code between them.

COPOLYMER Compound resulting from the polymerization of two different monomers.

COPROCESSOR 1. An additional processor which takes care of specific tasks, the objective being to reduce the load on the main CPU. Many IBM PCs and IBM clones have the capacity to install a coprocessor chip which does only arithmetic functions. This significantly speeds up your computer if you do a lot of calculations. See MATH COPROCESSOR.

COPW Customer Owned Premises Wire. You own the telephone wiring in your office.

COPY A nice new programming feature. We found it on Northern Telecom's Norstar phone. With this button, certain programmed settings can be copied from one line to another, or from one telephone to another. Line programmable settings that can be copied on the Norstar are Line Data, Restrictions, Overrides, and Night Service. Telephone settings that can be copied are Line Access, Restrictions, Overrides, and Permissions.

CORD A small, flexible insulated cable.

CORD BOARD The earliest manual PBX. Usually an elegant wooden device consisting of lots of cords with plugs on them. These cords sat horizontally sticking up, like missiles in a silo. Each cord corresponded to an extension. Whenever the phone rang, the cord board attendant would answer it. Each incoming line was a vertical hole. When the operator had figured for whom the call was, he/she would simply plug the cord corresponding to the desired extension into the hole corresponding to the incoming trunk. The operator would reverse the process if the internal user wanted to make an external call. Either the operator would dial the call first, or simply plug in the user's extension and thus allow the user to dial the call directly. The tip of the plug and the circular ring of the plug gave the term "tip and ring" to telephony. In electronics, it's known as positive and negative. See CORD CIRCUIT.

CORD CIRCUIT A switchboard circuit, terminated in two plug-ended cords, used to establish connections manually between user lines or between trunks and user lines. A number of cord circuits are furnished as part of the manual switchboard position equipment. The cords may be referred to as front cord and rear cord or trunk cord and station cord. In modern cordless switchboards, the cord circuit is switch operated. See CORD BOARD.

CORD LAMP The lamp associated with a cord circuit that indicates supervisory conditions for the respective part of the connection. See CORD BOARD.

CORDBOARD See CORD BOARD.

CORDLESS TELEPHONE A telephone with no cord between handset and base. Each piece contains a radio transmitter, receiver, and antenna. The handset contains a rechargable battery; the base must be plugged into an AC outlet. Depending on product design, radio frequency, environmental conditions, and national law, range between handset and base can be 10 feet to several miles. Cordless phones were once all analog. Now a breed of digital ones is coming out. They work much better in electrically noisy environments — like the typical office.

CORDLESS SWITCHBOARD A telephone switchboard in which manually operated keys are used to make connections. See CORD BOARD.

CORE The central glass element of a fiber optic cable through which the light is transmitted (typically 8-12 microns in diameter for single mode fiber and 50-100 microns in diameter for multimode fiber). This light conducting portion of the fiber is defined by the high refraction index region. The core is normally in the center of the fiber, bounded by the cladding material.

CORE NON-CIRCULARITY The percent that the shape of the core's cross section deviates from a circle. Sometimes referred to as core ovality.

CORE SIZE Primary description of a fiber. Stated in microns. Does not include cladding. Determines end surface area which accepts and transmits light.

CORNER REFLECTOR 1. A device, normally consisting of three metallic surfaces or screens perpendicular to one another, designed to act as a radar target or marker. 2. In radar interpretation, an object that, by means of multiple reflections from smooth surfaces, produces a radar return of greater magnitude than might be expected from the physical size of the object. 3. A reflected electromagnetic wave to its point of origin. Such reflectors are often used as radar targets. 4. Passive optical mirror, that consists of three mutually perpendicular flat, intersecting reflecting surfaces, which returns an incident light beam in the opposite direction. 5. A reflector consisting of two mutually intersecting conducting flat surfaces.

CORPORATE ACCOUNT SERVICE An MCI specific service involving a single, unified reporting system for multiple business that the customer owns, franchises, manages, or directs.

CORPORATE ID NUMBER The MCI term for the number which identifies a customer on a corporate level. (Not all MCI customers have a corporate ID number.)

CORPORATE NETWORK Also called an internetwork or a wide-area network. A network of networks (the mother of all networks) that connects most or all of a corporation's voice, data, and video resources using various methods, including the phone system, LANs, private data networks, leased telecommunications lines, and public data networks. Connections between networks are made with bridges and routers.

Corporate networks come in many shapes and sizes. Often, they will consist of networks within the same building or facility. Here, networks are combined using bridges and routers. Corporate networks may also span great distances. Such internetworks require different types of connections than single-facility internetworks, though the fundamentals are similar. Internetworks that connect remote facilities usually rely on some type of public or leased data communications network provided by the phone company or a data network service company. Bridges and routers are still required to connect networks to the long-distance data service, whether it's an X.25 packet switched network, a T-1 line, or even a regular phone line. See also BRIDGE and ROUTER.

CORRELATION The AMA (Automatic Message Accounting) function that permits the association of AMA data generated at the same network system or at physically separate network systems. There are three levels of correlation that affect Advanced Intelligent Network Release 1: record level, service level, and customer level. Definition from Bellcore in reference to Advanced Intelligent Network.

CORRIDOR OPTIONAL CALLING PLAN New York Telephone offers a discounted way for subscribers in the 212 and 718 area codes to call five northern New Jersey counties — Bergen, Essex, Hudson, Passaic and Union.

CORROSION The destruction of the surface of a metal by chemical reaction.

COS 1. See CLASS OF SERVICE. 2. Compatible for Open Systems. 3. Corporation for Open Systems international. A Federal Government blessed organization which aims towards standardizing OSI and ISDN. COS members includes everyone from end-users to manufacturers. COS deals with private and public networking issues.

COSNAME Identifies class of service SNA.

COST OF SERVICE PRICING A procedure, rationale or methodology for pricing services strictly on the basis of the cost to provide those services.

COT 1. Continuity Check Message. The second of the ISUP call set-up messages. Indicates success or failure of continuity check if one is needed. See ISUP and COMMON CHANNEL SIGNALING. 2. Central Office Terminal

COTS COnnection Transport Service.

COULOMB The quantity of electricity transferred by a current of one ampere in one second. One unit of quantity in measuring electricity.

COUNTER-ROTATING RING An arrangement whereby two signal paths, whose direction opposite to each other, exists in a ring topology.

COUNTERPOISE A system of electrical conductors used to complete the antenna system in place of the usual ground connection.

COUNTRY CODE 1. The one, two or three digit number that, in the world numbering plan, identifies each country or integrated numbering plan in the world. 2. In international record carrier transmissions, the country code is a two or three alpha or numeric abbreviation of the country name following the geographical place name.

COUPLED MODES 1. In fiber optics, a condition wherein energy is transferred among modes. The energy share of each mode does not differ after the equilibrium length has been reached 2. In microwave transmission, a condition where energy is transferred from the fundamental mode to higher order modes. Energy transferred to coupled modes is undesirable in usual microwave transmission in a waveguide. The frequency is kept low enough so that propagation in the waveguide is only in the fundamental mode.

COUPLING Any means by which energy is transferred from one conductive or dielectric medium (e.g., optical waveguide) to another, including fortuitous occurrences. Types of electrical coupling include capacitive (electrostatic) coupling, inductive coupling, and conductive (hard wire) coupling. Coupling may occur between optical fibers unless specific action is taken to prevent it. Coupling between fibers is very effectively prevented by the polymer overcoat, which also prevents the propagation of cladding modes, and provides some degree of physical protection.

COUPLING LOSS The power loss suffered when coupling light from one optical device to another.

COURIER DISPATCH The Courier Dispatch service offered by MCI International allows customers to generate and send high-priority messages from their own Telex terminals to any destination in the Continental U.S. and Hawaii.

COVERAGE The percent of completeness with which a metal braid covers the underlying surface.

COVERAGE AREA The geographic area served by a cellular system; that is, the area in which service is available to users of the system.

COW INTERFACE Character-Oriented Windows Interface. An SAA-compatible user interface for OS/2 applications.

CP Connection Point in Northern Telecom parlance.

CP/M Control Program for Microcomputers. An erstwhile popular operating system for primarily 8-bit microcomputer systems based on the family of Intel 8080 family of microprocessor chips. The system was originally by Gary Kidall a programmer and consultant who later formed a company called Intergalatic Digital Research (later just Digital Research). Sadly, that company never upgraded CP/M to 16-bit machines. Thus it left the way open for Bill Gates and the company he formed, Microsoft, to create MS-DOS, which, in its initial form, bore a remarkable resemblance to CP/M.

CPC Calling Party Connected.

CPE Customer Provided Equipment, or Customer Premise Equipment. Originally it referred to equipment on the customer's premises which had been bought from a vendor who was not the local phone company. Now it simply refers to telephone equipment — key systems, PBXs, answering machines, etc. — which reside on the customer's premises. "Premises" might be anything from an office to a factory to a home.

CPI Computer to PBX Interface. This proprietary hardware/software interface provides direct connectivity between a PBX's switching network and a host computer to allow switched access between the host computer and data terminal equipment connected with the PBX. The interface is based on the North American Standard T-Carrier specification (24 multiplexed 64 kbps channels operating at a combined speed of 1,544 Mbps). Developed by Northern Telecom, Inc. this interface uses in-band signaling and provides bidirectional data transmission at speeds up to 56 Kbps synchronous per channel. See OPEN APPLICATION INTERFACE.

CPI-C IBM SAA Common Programming Interface-Communication between SNA and OSI environments.

CPM Critical Path Method. See also CP/M.

CPN Computer PBX Network.

CPODA Compression Priority Demand Assignment. Another protocol for converting voice into data bits. See also PCM.

CPS Characters per second, or cycles per second.

CPU The Central Processing Unit. The computing part of a computer. The "brain" of the computer. It manipulates data and processes instructions coming from software or a human operator. See CENTRAL PROCESSING UNIT.

CR 1. Carriage Return. The key on a computer called Carriage Return or sometimes "ENTER." Touching this key usually signals the computer that the entry has been completed and is now ready for processing by the computer. See CARRIAGE RETURN. 2. Critical (alarm status). Indicates a failure affecting more than 96 customers. An AT&T defintion. 3. Call Reference.

CRACKER A person who "cracks" computer and telephone systems by gaining access to passwords, or by "cracking" the copy protection of computer software. A cracker usually does illegal acts. A Cracker is a "Hacker" whose hacks are beyond the bounds of propriety, and usually beyond the law. See HACKER.

CRAFT Cooperative Research Action For Technology.

CRASH The complete failure of a hardware device or a software operation. Usually used to mean a "fatal" crash in which the device or software must be started from a "power up" condition. See BOOT.

CRC Cyclic Redundancy Check. A process used to check the integrity of a block of data. A CRC character is generated at the transmission end. Its value depends on the hexadecimal value of the number of ones in the data block. The transmitting device calculates the value and appends it to the data block. The receiving end makes a similar calculation and compares its results with the added character. If there is a difference, the recipient requests retransmission. CRC is a common method of establishing that data was correctly received in data communications. See CRC CHARACTER and CYCLIC REDUNDANCY CHECK.

CRC CHARACTER A character used to check the integrity of a block of data. The character is generated at the transmission end. Its value depends on the hexadecimal value of the number of ones in the data block. And it is added to the data block. The receiving end makes a similar calculation and compares its results with the added character. If there's a difference, there's been a mistake in transmission. So, please, re-send the data.

CRD Contention Resolution Device.

CREAM SKIMMING Selecting only the most profitable markets or services to sell into. Choosing the cream of the market. An erstwhile popular economic theory to deny new entrants into the telephone industry.

CREDENTIALS A way of establishing, via a trusted third party, that you are who you claim to be.

CREDIT CARD PHONE A pay telephone that accepts credit cards with magnetic strips on them instead of coins.

CRITICAL ANGLE The smallest angle at which a ray will be totally reflected within a fiber.

CRITICAL TECHNICAL LOAD That part of the total technical power load required for synchronous communcations and automatic switching equipment.

CROSS ASSEMBLER An assembler that can run symbolic-language on one type of computer and produce machine-language output for another type of computer.

CROSS BORDER DIGITAL DATA SERVICE CDDS. An MCI International digital, private-line service that provides customers with service that provides customers with 56 kbps dedicated terrestrial channels between the U.S. and Canada.

CROSS BORDER TERRESTRIAL DIGITAL DATA SERVICE CTDDS. An MCI International point-to-point dedicated, leased channel service enabling customers to transmit traffic between the U.S. and Canada over digital terrestrial facilities at a transmission speed of 1.544 Mbps.

CROSS CONNECT Distribution system equipment used to terminate and administer communication circuits. In a wire cross connect, jumper wires or patch cords are used to make circuit connections. In an optical cross connect, fiber patch cords are used. The cross connect is located in an equipment room, riser closet, or satellite closet.

CROSS CONNECT FIELD Wire terminations grouped to provide cross connect capability. The groups are identified by color-coded sections of backboards mounted on the wall in equipment rooms, riser closets, or satellite closets, or by designation strips placed on the wiring block or unit. The color coding identifies the type of circuit that terminates at the field.

CROSS CONNECTION Cross-connection is the connection of one wire to another usually by anchoring each wire to a connecting block and then placing a third wire between them so that an electrical connection is made.

CROSS COUPLING The coupling of a signal from one channel, circuit, or conductor to another, where it becomes an undesired signal. See COUPLING.

CROSS EXTENSION CABLE When you make an RJ-11 cable and use it as a phone extension cord, the wiring becomes like this diagram.

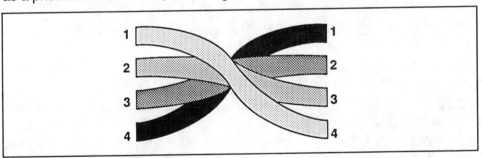

CROSS PLAN TERMINATION The conversion of ten-digit telephone numbers to seven digits, or vice versa.

CROSS POLARIZATION The relationship between two radio waves where one is polarized vertically and the other horizontally.

CROSS SUBSIDIZATION Supporting one area of a business from revenues generated by another area.

CROSS WYE A cable used at the host system, or network interface equipment that changes pin/signal assignment in order to conform to a given wiring standard (USOC, AT&T PDS, DEC MMJ, etc).

NEWTON'S TELECOM DICTIONARY

CROSSBAR A switching system that uses a centrally-controlled matrix switching network of electro-mechanical switches which worked with magnets and which connected horizontal and vertical paths to establish a path through the network. Crossbar is known for its reliability but is now largely obsolete because it takes up a lot of space and isn't programmable.

CROSSCOMM A networking company specializing in token ring internetworking and enterprise-wide networks. Located in Marlboro, MA.

CROSSLINK An X.25 link connecting two XTX NCs on the same level.

CROSSOVER CABLE Another word for NULL MODEM CABLE. A cable used to joined two computers together. Usually conductors 2 & 3 are reversed in an RS-232 connection.

CROSSPOINT A single element in an array of elements that comprise a switch. It is a set of physical or logical contacts that operate together to extend the speech and signal channels in a switching network.

CROSSPOLARIZED OPERATION The use of two transmitters operating on the same frequency, with one transmitter-receiver pair being vertically polarized and the other pair horizontally polarized (orthogonal polarization).

CROSSTALK Crosstalk occurs when you can hear someone you did not call talking on your telephone line to another party you did not call. There are several technical causes for this phenomenon. They relate to wire placement, shielding and transmission techniques. CROSSTALK is also the name of a very popular telecommunications software program for 8- and 16-bit microcomputers. The program is produced by Microstuf, which is now called Crosstalk Communications, Norcross, GA and is now a subsidiary of DCA.

CROSSTALK ATTENUATION The extent to which a communications system resists crosstalk.

CRT Cathode Ray Tube. The glass display device found in television sets and video computer terminals. See CATHODE RAY TUBE.

CRTC Canadian Radio Television and Telecommunications Commission. Canada's federal telecom regulator.

CRYPTANALYSIS 1. The steps and operations performed in converting encrypted messages into plain text without initial knowledge of the key employed in the encryption. 2. The study of encrypted texts. The steps or processes involved in converting encrypted text into plain text without initial knowledge of the key employed in the encryption.

CRYPTO A term used to describe encrypted information. The use of encryption on data communications circuits lessens the chance that the information will be successfully copied by eavesdroppers.

CRYPTOCHANNEL A complete system of crypto-communications between two or more holders. The basic unit for naval cryptographic communication. It includes: (a) the cryptographic aids prescribed; (b) the holders thereof; (c) the indicators or other means of identification; (d) the area or areas in which effective; (e) the special purpose, if any, for which provided; and (f) pertinent notes as to distribution, usage, etc. A cryptochannel is analogous to a radio circuit.

CRYPTOGRAPHY The process of concealing the contents of a message from all except those who know the key.

CRYSTAL MICROPHONE A microphone, the diaphragm of which is attached to a piezo-electric crystal, which generates electrical currents when torque is applied, due to the vibration of the diaphragm. The earliest form of microphone, now obsolete. See also CONDENSER and ELECTRET MICROPHONE.

CS Convergence Sublayer. The upper portion of BISDN Layer 3.

CSA 1. Callpath Services Architecture — IBM's computer host to PBX interface. It links computer and telephone systems. See also CALLBRIDGE and OPEN APPLICATION INTERFACE. 2. Canadian Standards Association — a non-profit, independent organization which operates a listing service for electrical and electronic materials and equipment. It is the body that establishes telephone equipment (and other) standards for use in Canada. The Canadian counterpart of the Underwriters Laboratories.

CSC 1. Customer Service Center 2. Customer Service Consultant 3. Customer Service Coordinator 4. Customer Support Center 5. Customer Support Consultant.

CSDC Circuit Switched Digital Capability. AT&T defines it as a technique for making end-to-end digital connections. Customers can place telephone calls normally, then use the same private connection to transmit high-speed data. CSDC is a circuit-switched, 56-kbps, full-duplex data service that provides high-speed data communications over regular telephone lines.

CSFI IBM Communications Subsystem For Interconnection: networking software.

CSI 1. Called Subscriber Identification. This is an identifier whose coding format contains a number, usually a phone number from the remote terminal used in fax. 2. Capability Set I. A set of service-independent building blocks for the creation of IN services developed by the European Telecommunications Standards Institute and the CCITT.

CSMA Carrier Sense Multiple Access. In local area networking, CSMA is a way of getting onto the LAN. Before starting to transmit, personal computers on the LAN "listen" to make sure no other PC is transmitting. Once the PC figures out that no other PC is transmitting, it sends a packet and then frees the line for other PCs to transmit. With CSMA, though stations do not transmit until the medium is clear, collisions still occur. Two alternative versions (CSMA/CA and CSMA/CD) attempt to reduce both the number of collisions and the severity of their impact. See CSMA/CA and CSMA/CD.

CSMA/CA Carrier Sense Multiple Access (CSMA) with Collision Avoidance. In local area networking, CSMA technique that combines slotted time-division multiplexing (TDM) with carrier sense multiple access/collision detection (CSMA/C) to avoid having collisions occur a second time. CSMA/CA works best if the time allocated is short compared to packet length and if the number of stations (these days PCs) is small. See CARRIER SENSE MULTIPLE ACCESS/COLLISION AVOIDANCE and CSMA.

CSMA/CD Carrier Sense Multiple Access with Collision Detection. In local area networking technology, CSMA technique that also listens while transmitting to detect collisions. CSMA/CD is a leading control technique for getting onto and off a local area network. All devices attached to the network listen for transmissions in progress (i.e. carrier sense) before starting to transmit (multiple access). If two or more begin transmitting at the same time and their transmissions crash into each other, each backs off (collision detection) for a different amount of time (determined by an algorithm) before again attempting to transmit.

If you didn't understand the above definition, try this one: CSMA/CD: Abbreviation for Carrier Sense Multiple Access with Collision Detection, a method of having multiple workstations access a transmission medium (multiple access) by listening until no signals are detected (carrier sense), then transmitting and checking to see if more than one signal is present (collision detection). Each workstation attempts to transmit when they "believe" the network to be free. If there is a collision, each workstation attempts to retransmit after a preset delay, which is different for each workstation. It is one of the most popular access methods for PC-based LANs. Think of it as entering a highway from an access road, except that you can crash and still try again. Or think of it as two polite people who start to talk at the same time. Each politely backs off and waits a random amount of time before starting to speak again. Ethernet-based LANs use CSMA/CD. See Ethernet and IEEE 802.3.

CSMDR Centralized Station Message Detail Recording.

CSR 1. Customer Station Rearrangement (as in Centrex). 2. Customer Service Record. Computer printout that details the fixed monthly charges billed by your local telephone company. The CSR is composed of computer codes called USOCs, which in turn correspond to a particular tariffed service. USOCs tell the telephone company's billing system what tariff rate should be billed for a particular service. In order to ensure your telephone bill is correct you must request and review this document. No telcom manager should be without this important document.

CST Computer Supported Telephony, a term coined by Siemens. Here is an an explanation from Dr. Peter Pawlita of Siemens. "More people communicate by telephone than by any other means. The reason is simple: The telephone bridges any distance, saves travel time and can be used spontaneously and is universally available. Unfortunately telephone usage is often associated with annoying delays and frayed nerves resulting from such things as time wasted in finding a number, dialing errors, and the absence of the dialed party. Added to this the person to whom you are speaking does not have the knowledge you require, or has to spend a long time looking or documents. What could be more obvious, therefore, than to turn these problems over to the computer — to implement Computer Supported Telephony (CST). CST denotes the functional connection of a computer system to a PBX at the application level. CST applications can automatically initiate calls, receive incoming calls, and provide "just-in-time" business data, documents and notes on the screen. All this makes telephony more convenient, time-saving, efficient and largely error-free."

CSTA Computer Supported Telephony Application. A standard from the European Computer Manufacturers Association for linking computers to telephone systems. See also CST and OPEN APPLICATION INTERFACE.

CSTP Customer Specific Term Plan. See CUSTOMER SPECIFIC TERM PLAN.

CSU 1. Channel Service Unit. Also called a Data Service Unit. A device to terminate a digital channel on a customer's premises. It performs certain line-conditioning and equalization functions, and responds to loopback commands sent from the central office. A CSU sits between the digital line coming in from the central office and devices such as channel banks or data communications devices. See CHANNEL SERVICE UNIT.

2. Channel Sharing Unit. Line bridging devices that allow several inputs to share one output. CSUs exist to handle any input/output combination of sync or async terminals, computer ports, or modems and thus these units are variously called modem sharing units, digital bridges, port sharing units, digital sharing devices, modem contention units, multiple access units, control signal activated electronic switches or data-activated electronic switches.

CSUA Canadian Satellite Users Association. Trade assocation of satellite users.

CT Cordless Telephone.

CT-2 Interim Standard for the Telepoint service favored by UK Memorandum of Understanding with other network operators.

CT1 Cordless Telephony Generation 1. A new type of low-cost public cordless telephone system getting popular in Europe. You carry a cheap handset. You go to within several hundred yards of a local antenna and you make your phone call. You can't receive calls as you can on a cellular radio. You can't make calls unless you're close to the antenna. The service helps overcome the serious lack of street-side coin and public phones in Europe. CT1 is the the analog version of the interface specification. See CT2 and CT2+.

CT2 Cordless Telephony Generation 2, interface specification for digital technology, currently in use in the U.K. for Telepoint (payphone) applications. See CT1.

CT2+ An expansion of the CT2 interface specification that would extend network capabilities and allow backwards compatibility with CT2 handsets. See CT1 and CT2.

CTA Competitive Telecommunications Association. Trade association of alternate long distance carriers (resellers) in Canada.

CTCA Canadian Telecommunications Consultants Association. Professional organization of telecommunications consultants.

CTD Continuity Tone Detector.

CTE 1. Channel Translation Equipment. 2. Coefficient of thermal expansion.

CTI Computer Telephone Integration. Basically a polite term for connecting a computer to a telephone switch and having the computer issue the switch commands to move calls around. The most classic application for CTI is in call centers. Picture this: A call comes in. That call carries some form of caller ID — either ANI or Class Caller ID. The switch "hears" the calling number, strips it off, sends it to the computer. The computer does a lookup, sends back the switch instructions on what to do with the call. The switch follows orders. It might send the call to a specialized agent or maybe just to the agent the caller dealt with last time. There are emerging standards for CTI. But they've been complex. See also WINDOWS TELEPHONY.

CTIA Cellular Telecommunications Industry Association. Washington, D.C.-based industry association.

CTS 1. Clear To Send. Pin 5 on the 25-conductor RS-232-C interface or an RS-232-C signal used in the exchange of data between the computer and a serial device. 2. Communication Transport System. CTS is The Siemon Company's proprietary structured wiring system. It consists of the methodology and the connecting hardware products to plan, design, and implement the communications wiring infrastructure for commercial buildings (for more information see the company's CTS Design Workbook and CTS Training Videotape). The Siemon Company is based in Watertown, CT. 3. Conformance Testing Services.

CTTU Centralized Trunk Test Unit. An operational support system providing centralized trunk maintenance through a data link on a switch.

CTX Centrex.

CUA Common User Access.

CUCKOO-CLOCK Telecom slang for some 6- and 10-button models of AT&T 1A2 wall phones shaped vaguely like traditional cuckoo-clocks. These were probably the first multi-line phones to come with handsets that plugged into the base with Trimline-style 5-pin plugs, before the current modular connectors were adopted. Often seen in in hospitals on TV shows.

CUG Closed User Group. Selected collection of terminal users that do not accept calls from sources not in their group and also often restricted from sending messages outside the group.

CURIE POINT The temperature at which certain elements (usually so-called "rare earth" elements) relax their resistance to magnetic changes. In a magneto-optic disk drive the surface to be marked is heated briefly by a laser light to its Curie point. Magnetism is then applied in the proper polarity to make the spot a "1" or a "0." It cools, and is locked in that position, until it re-heated and changed again. This is how magneto-optic drives can be erasable.

CURRENT A measure of how much electricity passes a point on a wire in a given time frame. Current is measured in amperes, or amps. The abbreviation for current is I. See OHM'S LAW.

CURRENT CARRYING CAPACITY The maximum current an insulated conductor can safely carry without exceeding its insulation and jacket temperature limitations.

CURRENT LOOP Transmission technique that recognizes current flows, rather than voltage levels. It has traditionally been used in teletypewriter networks incorporating batteries as the transmission power source. In this serial transmission system, a pair of wires connecting the receiving and sending devices transmit binary 0 (zero) when no current flows and a binary 1 (one) when current is flowing.

CURSOR A symbol on a screen indicating where the next character may be typed. Cursors may be solid, blinking, underlines, etc. Many programs, computers and phone systems allow you to reprogram the cursor to what you like. One author of this dictionary, Harry Newton, likes a non-blinking solid block, which came standard with his original CP/M version of WordStar, but doesn't any longer.

CURSOR SUBMARINING A liquid crystal display on a computer laptop screen doesn't write to screen very fast. When you move a cursor across your screen or move your mouse quickly across the screen, the cursor disappears. This phenomenon is known as cursor submarining. Cute.

CURVES AND ARCS A computer imaging term. Paint packages handle curves and acrs in a variety of ways. Examples include spline curves, where-in you specify a series of points and the package draws a curve that smoothly approaches those points, and "three point" curves, in which the first two points anchor the ends of the curve and third selects the apex.

CUSTOM CALLING A group of special services available from the central office switching system which the telco can offer its subscribers without the need for any special terminal equipment on their premises. Basic custom calling features now available include call waiting, 3-way calling, abbreviated dialing (speed calling), call forwarding, series completing (busy or no answer) and wake up or reminder service.

CUSTOM LOCAL AREA SIGNALING SERVICES CLASS. A generic term (like WATS) describing several enhanced local service offerings such as incoming-call identification, call trace, call blocking, automatic return of the most recent incoming call, call redial, and selective forwarding and programming to permit distinctive ringing for incoming calls. See CLASS.

CUSTOMER CONTROL An AT&T term for the ability for an end user to monitor, choose, modify, redesign and/or program the type of service received from a network.

CUSTOMER INFORMATION MANGER CIM. An MCI definition. A component of the NCS which supports the creation and maintenance of customer databases fror Vnet customers. Customers have remote access to and control over their portion of the NCS database via a terminal at the customer's location.

CUSTOMER PREMISES EQUIPMENT CPE. Terminal equipment supplied by either the telephone common carrier or by a competitive supplier, which is connected to the nationwide telephone network and resides on the customer's premises.

CUSTOMER-PROVIDED LOOP The customer assumes responsibility for ordering, coordinating, maintaining, and billing for the local loop.

CUSTOMER PROVIDED TERMINAL EQUIPMENT Or just Customer Provided Equipment (CPE). Terminal equipment connected to the telephone network which is owned by the user or leased from a supplier other than the local telephone operating company.

CUSTOMER SERVICE CENTER CSC. MCI organization responsible for installing, verifying, and maintaining MCI customers and customer service.

CUSTOMER SERVICE RECORD CSR. Computer printout that details the fixed monthly charges billed by your local telephone company. The CSR is composed of computer codes called USOCs, which in turn correspond to a particular tariffed service. USOCs tell the telephone company's billing system what tariff rate should be billed for a particular service. In order to ensure your telephone bill is correct you must request and review this document. No telcom manager should be without this important document.

CUSTOMER SERVICE UNIT CSU. A device that provides an accessing arrangement at a user location to either switched or point-to-point, digital circuits. A CSU provides local loop equalization, transient protection, isolation, and central office loop-back testing capability. See also CSU/DSU.

CUSTOMER SPECIFIC TERM PLAN A Customer Specific Term Plan is an option offered by AT&T on the purchase of its 800 services whereby customers can earn additional discounts by committing to a multiyear contract. This also is one of two plans used by aggregators to resell 800 services. The other is the Revenue Volume Pricing Plan.

CUT To transfer a service from one facility to another.

CUT BACK TECHNIQUE A technique for measuring optical fiber attenuation or distortion by performing two transmission measurements. One is at the output end of the full length of the fiber. The other is within 1 to 3 meters of the input end. Without disturbing the source-to-fiber coupling, access to the short length output is accomplished by "cutting back" the test fiber.

CUT DOWN A method of securing a wire to a wiring terminal. The insulated wire is placed in the terminal groove and pushed down with a special tool. As the wire is seated, the terminal cuts through the insulation to make an electrical connection, and the tool's spring-loaded blade trims the wire flush with the terminal. Also called punch down.

CUT THROUGH The act of connecting one circuit to another, or a phone to a circuit. This is when a user dials the access code for the circuit and is immediately "cut through" to the tie line. The user controls the call. It is a tie line operation.

CUT THROUGH RESISTANCE A measure of an insulation's ability to withstand penetration by sharp edges.

CUTOFF ATTENUATOR A waveguide of adjustable length that varies the attenuation of signals passing through the waveguide.

CUTOFF FREQUENCY 1. The frequency above which, or below which, the output current in a circuit, such as a line or a filter, is reduced to a specified level. 2. The frequency below which a radio wave fails to penetrate a layer of the ionosphere at the angle of incidence required for transmission between two specified points by reflection from the layer.

CUTOFF MODE The highest order mode that will propagate in a given waveguide at a given frequency.

CUTOVER The physical changing of lines from one phone system to another, or the installation of a new system. It's usually done over the weekend, accompanied by heavy praying that everything will go right. There are two types of cutovers — flash cuts and parallel cuts. Parallel cuts occur when the old phone system is left functioning and the new one, central switching equipment and phones, is installed around it. This means that for some weeks there are two sets of phones, two sets of wires, two switches, two sets of phone lines, etc. The parallel cut is a far more reliable method of cutting over a new switch. But it's also more expensive.

A "flash cut" occurs in a flash. On Friday, everyone is using the old switch. When everyone comes to work on Monday, the old switch and its phones have disappeared. In its place, there's a brand new system. Sometimes it works. More often than not, there are remaining nagging problems. With any

Cutover, it's a good idea to set up a Complaint or Cutover Number. Thus, if anyone's having trouble with their phone, they can call this number and get their problems taken care of. How well these problems are taken care of will determine how well the cutover went and how well the employees perceive the new switch is working. Perception, not reality, is what's at stake here.

CV Old Bell-Speak for single-line phone. Origin is obscure. If you know it, we'll send you a free copy of the next edition of this book.

CVD Chemical Vapor Deposition.

CVSD Continuously Variable Slope Delta modulation. A method for coding analog voice signals into digital signals that uses 16,000 to 64,000 bps bandwidth, depending on the sampling rate.

CW 1. Call Waiting (as in Custom Calling Service). 2. Continuous Wave.

CWA Communications Workers of America. A national union of telephone industry employees, currently very worried about its future membership growth given the phone industry's propensity to let its surplus workers go.

CXR Carrier.

CX SIGNALING A direct current (DC) signaling system that separates the signal from the voice band by filters. Also called Composite Signaling.

CYCLIC DISTORTION In telegraphy, distortion that is neither characateristic, bias, nor fortuitous, and which in general has a periodic character. Its causes are, for example, irregularities in the duration of contact time of the brushes of a transmitter distributor or interference by distributing alternating currents.

CYBERPUNK A work coined by a book called "Cyberpunk: Outlaws and Hackers on the Computer Frontier" by Katie HaFner and John Markoff. The book defines Cyberpunk as what you and I know as a computer hacker — a person who manages to get into other people's computer systems. He does this usually through telephone lines. In most cases, hackers see themselves as harmless electronic joyriders. But they occasionally pinch data, inject viruses and misleading information and disrupt legitimate business and research. Sometimes they get caught.

CYBERSPACE Difficult to describe, but roughly the largely incomprehensible world of computer networks that can be explored with the proper addresses and codes. People who use the system for hours on end are said to be lost in cyberspace.

CYCLE One complete sequence of an event or activity. Often refers to electrical phenomena. One electrical cycle is a complete sine wave. (A complete set of one positive and one negative alternation of current.)

CYCLE MANAGER EXTRACTION An MCI system which selects processable calls from Distribution and forwards them to the appropriate MCI Reference System for billing.

CYCLE POOLS Where dial-up call records are stored in MCI's Revenue System until extracted for billing.

CYCLE SLIP A discontinuity in the measured carrier beat phase resulting from a temporary loss-of-lock in the carrier tracking loop of a Global Positioning System receiver.

CYCLE TIME The time to complete a cycle. In microcomputers, it's the time between successive RAM read or write operations.

CYCLIC REDUNDANCY CHECK CRC. A check performed on data to see if an error has occurred in the transmitting, reading or writing of the data. A CRC is performed by reading the data, calculating the CRC character and comparing its value to the CRC character already present in the data. If they are equal, the new data is presumed to be the same as the old data. Otherwise, it's wrong. Re-send the data. A CRC character is figured by treating a block of data as a string of bits that are equal to a binary number. Then we divide that number by another predetermined binary number and append the remainder from the division to the data. We call that appended number the CRC character.

CYLINDER A hard disk drive contains a number of platters, which are divided into tracks. A cylinder is a collection of all corresponding tracks on all sides of the platters in a disk drive. Think of a hard disk consisting of dozens of concentric cylinders, each of slightly different diameters. These distinct concentric storage areas on the hard disk roughly correspond to the tracks on a floppy diskette. Generally, the more cylinders a hard disk has, the greater its storage capacity.

CYPRESS A Rolm/IBM desktop device which combines a data terminal, a igital phone and several time management software features.

D

D CHANNEL In an ISDN interface, the "D" channel (the Data channel) is used to carry control signals and customer call data in a packet switched mode. In the BRI (Basic Rate Interface, i.e. the lowest ISDN service) the "D" channel operates at 16,000 bits per second, part of which will carry setup, teardown, ANI and other characteristics of the call. 9,600 bps will be free for a separate conversation by the user. In the PRI (Primary Rate Interface, i.e. ISDN equivalent of T-1), the "D" channel runs at 64,000 bits per second. The D channel provides the signaling information for each of the 23 voice channels (refered to as "B channels"). The actual data which travels on the D channel is much like that of a common serial port. Bytes are loaded from the network and shifted out to the customer site in a serial bit stream. The customer site of course responds with its serial bit stream, too. An example of a data packet sent from the network to indicate a new call has the following components:

- CUSTOMER SITE ID
- TYPE OF CHANNEL REQUIRED (Usually a B channel)
- CALL HANDLE (Not unlike a file handle)
- ANI AND DNIS INFORMATION
- CHANNEL NUMBER REQUESTED -
- A REQUEST FOR A RESPONSE

This packet is responded to by the customer site with a format similar to:

- NETWORK ID
- CHANNEL TYPE IS OK
- CALL HANDLE

The packets change as the state of the call changes, and finally ends with one side or the other sending a disconnect notice. The important concept here is the fact the information on the D channel could actually be anything — any kind of serial data. It could just as well be sports scores! So with that in mind, consider the CHANNEL NUMBER REQUESTED packet above. This is the networks' selected channel for the customer site to use. Normally, this number is between 1 and 23, but could be a higher number if needed. This is what NFAS is all about. NFAS (Non Facility Associated signaling, pronounced N-FAST without the T) allows a D channel to carry call information regarding channels which may not even exist in the same PBX or PC system. See also ISDN and DS-0.

D CONDITIONING A type of conditioning which controls harmonic distortion and signal-to-noise ratio so that they lie within specified limits.

D REGION That portion of the ionosphere existing approximately 50 to 90 km above the surface of the Earth. Attenuation of radio waves, caused by ionospheric free-electron density generated by cosmic rays from the sun, is pronounced during daylight hours.

D TYPE The standard connector used for RS-232-C, RS-423 and RS-422 communications. D-type connectors are typically seen in nine, 15 and 25 pin configurations.

D-BANK Another name for channel bank. A device that multiplexes groups of 24 channels of digitized voice input at 64 Kbps into T-1 aggregate outputs of 1,544 Mbps.

D-BIT Also called DBIT. The delivery confirmation bit in an X.25 packet used to indicate whether or not the DTE wishes to receive an end-to-end acknowledgment of delivery. In short, a bit in the X.25 packet header that assures data integrity between the TPAD and the HPAD.

D-INSIDE WIRE Direct-Inside Wire. Made of 24-gauge, annealed-copper conductors with color-added PVC, which allows it to be pulled in conduit without the aid of lubricants. Generally used in the horizontal subsystem.

D/A Digital to Analog conversion.

D/A CONVERTER Digital to Analog converter. A device which converts digital pulses, i.e. data, into analog signals so that the signal can be used by analog device such as amplifier, speaker, phone, or meter.

D/I Drop and Insert. See BIT STUFFING and BIT ROBBING.

D1, D1D, D2, D3, D4 and D5 T-1 framing formats developed for channel banks. All formats contain a framing bit in every 193rd bit position. The Superframe (introduced in D2 channel banks) is made up of 12 193-bit frames, with the 193rd bit sequence being repeated every 12 frames. D2 framing also introduced robbed bit signaling, where the eighth bit in frames 6 and 12 were "robbed" for signaling information (like dial pulses). D1D was introduced after D2 to allow backwards compatibility of Superframe concepts to D1 banks.

D3 FORMAT 24 data channels on one standard (North American standard) T1/D3 span line. Each data channel is 8-bits wide and has a bandwidth of 8KHz. See also DS-1.

D3/D4 Refers to compliance with AT&T TR (Technical Reference) 62411 definitions for coding, supervision and alarm support. D3/D4 compatibility ensures support of digital PBXs, M24 services, Megacom services and Mode 3 D3/D4 channel banks at a DS-1 level.

D4 CHANNELIZATION Refers to compliance with AT&T TR (Technical Reference) 62411 in regards to the DSI frame layout (the sequential assignment of channels and time slot numbers within the DSI).

D4 FRAMING First read T-1 FRAMING. The most popular framing format in the T1 environment is D-4 framing. The name stems from the way framing is performed in the D-series of channel banks from AT&T. There are 12 separate 193-bit frames in a super-frame. The D-4 framing bit is used to identify both the channel and the signaling frame. In voice communications, signaling is an important function that is simulated and carried by all the equipment in the transmission path. In D-4 framing, signaling for voice channels is carried "in-band" by every channel, along with the encoded voice. "Robbed-bit-signaling" is a technique used in D-4 channel banks to convey signaling information. With this technique, the eighth bit (least significant bit) of each of the 24 8-bit time slots is "robbed" every sixth frame to convey voice-related signaling information (on-hook, off-hook, etc.) for each voice channel. See also EXTENDED SUPER-FRAME FORMAT.

DA 1. Doesn't answer, as in "The phone rang DA." 2. Directory Assistance. 3. Demand Assignment. 4. Discontinued Availability. Meaning a circuit that was once available is now no longer. 4. Destination Address, a field in FDDI, Ethernet and Token Ring packets which identifies the unique MAC (Media Access Control, the lower part of ISO layer two) address of the recipient. 5. Desk Accessory. Standard desk accessories on the Apple Macintosh include a calculator, alarm clock and the chooser. Desk accessories are available to the user regardless of the application currently in use, networked or non-networked. Desk accessories are installed in the Apple menu and accessed from there.

DAA Data Access Arrangement. A device required before the FCC registration program if a customer was going to hook up CPE (Customer Provided Equipment), usually modems and other data equipment, to the telephone network. Today, equipment is FCC registered (under Part 68) meaning that the device itself is approved for connection to the phone network. DAAs can still be found in old DP (data processing) installations.

DAB Dynamically Allocable Bandwidth.

DAC Digital to Analog Converter. A device which converts digital pulses, i.e. data, into analog signals so that the signal can be used by analog device such as amplifier, speaker, phone, or meter.

DACC Digital Access Cross-Connect.

DACD Digital Automatic Call Distributor. New York Telephone's name for its central office provided ACD.

DAC Digital-to-analog converter. A chip that converts the binary numbers that represent particular colors to analog red, green and blue signals that a color monitor displays.

DACS Digital Access and Cross-connect System. A digital switching device for routing and switching T-1 lines, and DS-0 portions of lines, among multiple T-1 ports. It performs all the functions of a normal "switch," except connections are typically set up in advance of the call, not together with the call, as in most, normal low-bandwidth communications systems (e.g. voice-band voice and data). A DACS is in essence a manual T-1 switch.

DACS/CCR Digital Access Crosscontrol System/Customer Controlled Reconfiguration is a feature of AT&T Accunet T1.5 service. DACS/CCR allows Accunet subscribers to redirect T-1 trunk or DS-0 data traffic over the public network from a terminal on their own premises.

DAF Destination Address Field.

DAISY CHAIN A method of connecting devices in a series. The computer's signals are passed through the chain from one device to the next. A SCSI adapter can support a daisy chain of up to seven devices.

DAISY WHEEL PRINTER A printer that prints its characters on paper using a rotating wheel with "fingers." Mounted on the fingers are the various characters. The wheel rotates, bringing the character in line with the paper, then a hammer strikes the character against the ribbon, forming an image on the paper. Daisy wheel printers are typically used for "letter quality" correspondence and are popular for word processing. Their letters are crisp and attractive. But the speed of printing is slow because of the time it takes to rotate the wheel into place. These days, more and more of what used to be printed by daisy wheel printers is now printed by laser and inkjet printers which print faster, more quietly and do a nicer job.

DAL Dedicated Access Line. A private tie line from you to your long distance or local phone company. The line may be analog or digital, e.g. a T-1 circuit.

DAMA Demand Assigned Multiple Access. A way of sharing a channel's capacity by assigning capacity on demand to an idle channel or an unused time slot.

DAMPED WAVE A wave consisting of a series of oscillations or cycles of current gradually decreasing amplitude.

DAMPING 1. The decreasing of the amplitude of oscillations caused by resistance in the circuit. 2 The progressive diminution with time of certain quantities characteristic of a phenomenon. 3. The progressive decay with time in the amplitude of the free oscillations in a circuit. 4. More generally, decreasing some dimension of a phenomenon, such as its power.

DAP INFORMATION DISTRIBUTOR DID. An MCI definition. Software which directs the distribution of network information from the Operational Data Integrator to the Data Access Points.

DARK CURRENT The external current that, under specified biasing conditions, flows in a photosensitive detector when there is no incident radiation.

DARK FIBER Unused fiber through which no light is transmitted or installed fiber optic cable not carrying a signal. Sometimes dark fiber is sold by a carrier without the (usually) accompanying transmission service. It's "dark" because it's sold without light communications transmission. The customer is expected to put his own electronics and signals on the fiber and make it light.

DARPA INTERNET World's largest internetwork, linking together thousands of networks around world. Sponsored by U.S. Defense Advanced Research Projects Agency.

DASD Direct Access Storage Device (pronounced "dazz-dee").

DAT Digital Audio Tape used to identify a type of digital tape recorder and player as well as the tape cassette. DAT tape machines record music that is much crisper, and free of the hisses and pops that mar traditional analog recordings. The drawback with DAT tape machines is they require a lot more tape to store music digitally. In a DAT machine, the music is recorded by sampling the music 48,000 each second. Each of those samples is represented by a number that is written as a 16-digit string of zeros and ones. There are two such signals, once for each stereo channel, meaning that storing a single second of music requires about 1.5 million bits. On top of that, extra bits are added to allow the system to mathematically correct errors and help the machine automatically find a particular song on the tape. All together, according to Andrew Pollack writing in the New York Times, a single second of music on a digital audio tape requires 2.8 million bits. The most powerful floppy disks now used in personal computers would be able to handle only four seconds of such digitized music.

DATA This is AT&T Bell Labs' definition: "A representation of facts, concepts or instructions in a formalized manner, suitable for communication, interpretation or processing." Typically anything other than voice.

DATA ABSTRACTION A term in object-oriented programming. An object is sometimes referred to as an instance of an abstract data type or class. Abstract data types are constructed using the built-in data types supported by the underlying programming language, such as integer and date. The common characteristics (both attributes and methods) of a group of similar objects are collected to create a new data type or class. Not only is this a natural way to think about the problem domain, it is a very efficient way to write programs. Instead of individually describing several dozen instances, the programmer describes the class once. Once identified, each instance is complete with the exception of its instance variables. The instance variables are associated with each instance, i.e., each object; methods exist only with the classes. See OBJECT ORIENTED PROGRAMMING.

DATA ACCESS ARRANGEMENT DAA. Equipment that allows you to attach your data equipment to the nation's phone system. At one stage, DAAs were required by FCC "law." Now, their limited functions are built into directly attached devices, such as terminals, computers, etc.

DATA ACCESS POINT DAP. MCI computer that holds the number translation and call-routing information for 800 and Vnet services. These computers respond to inquiries from MCI switches on how to handle these calls.

DATA BASE ADMINSTRATOR DBA. A computer at MCI that maintains the master file of Vnet translation information. The master file is created when a customer begins service and can be changed at anytime through CIM. The updated copies of the database are downloaded each night to the DAPs.

DATA ARRANGEMENT In the public switched telephone networks, a single item or group of items present at the customer side of the purposes, including all equipment that may affect the characteristics of the interface.

DATA ATTRIBUTE A characteristic of a data element such as length, value, or method of representation.

DATA BANK A collection of data in one place. The data is not necessarily logically related, nor is it necessarily consistently maintained. See DATABASE.

DATA BASE See DATABASE, which is our preferred spelling.

DATA BUBBLE A new organization within BellSouth to provide high-speed digital services. No one seems to know why it's called "Data Bubble," except that someone inside BellSouth clearly thinks the term is cute.

DATA BURST Burst transmission.

DATA BUS A bus transmits and receives data signals throughout the computer or telephone system. See BUS.

DATA CIRCUIT TERMINATING EQUIPMENT See DATA COMMUNICATIONS EQUIPMENT and DCE.

DATA COMMUNICATIONS The transfer of data between points. This includes all manual and machine operations necessary for this transfer. In short, the movement of encoded information by means of electrical transmission systems. See DATA COMMUNICATIONS EQUIPMENT.

DATA COMMUNICATIONS CHANNEL A three-byte, 192 kbps portion of the SONET signal that contains alarm, survillance and performance information. It can be used for internally or externally generated messages, or for manufacturer specific messages.

DATA COMMUNICATIONS EQUIPMENT DCE. A definition of an interface standard between computers and printers. A device typically comes configured as a DCE or DTE. See DCE and DTE. Which way it comes determines how you connect it to another device.

DATA COMPRESSION Reducing the size of a file of data by eliminating unnecessary information, such as blanks and redundant data. The idea of reducing the size is to save money on transmission or to save money on storing the data. The file or program which has been compressed is useless in its compressed form and must be "decompressed," i.e. brought back to normal before use. One method of data compression replaces a string of repeated characters by a character count. Another method uses fewer bits to represent the characters that occur more frequently. See also COMPRESSION.

Here's another definition, courtesy the US Department of Commerce: 1. The process of reducing (a) bandwidth, (b) cost, and (c) time for the generation, transmission, and storage of data by employing techniques designed to remove data redundancy. 2. The use of techniques such as null suppression, bit mapping, and pattern substitution for purposes of reducing the amount of space required for storage of textual files and data records. Some data compaction methods employ fixed tolerance bands, variable tolerance bands, slope-keypoints, sample changes, curve patterns, curve fitting, floating- point coding, variable precision coding, frequency analysis, and probability analysis. Simply squeezing noncompacted data into a smaller space, e.g., by transferring data on punched cards onto magnetic tape, is not considered data compression.

DATA COMPRESSION PROTOCOLS All current high-speed dial-up modems also support data compression protocols. This means the sending modem will compress the data on-the-fly (as it transmits) and the receiving modem will decompress the data (as it receives it) to its original form. There are two standards for data compression protocols, MNP-5 and CCITT V.42 bis. Some modems also use proprietary data compression protocols. A modem cannot support data compression without using an error control protocol, although it is possible to have a modem that only supports an error control protocol but not any data compression protocol. A MNP-5 modem requires MNP-4 error control protocol and a V.42 bis modem requires V.42 error control protocol. Note that although V.42 include MNP-4, V.42 bis does not include MNP-5. However, virtually all high-speed modems that support CCITT V.42 bis also incorporate MNP-5. The maximum compression ratio that a MNP-5 modem can achieve is 2:1. That is to say, a 9,600 bps MNP-5 modem can transfer data up to 19,200 bps. The maximum compression ratio for a V.42 bis modem is 4:1. That is why all those V.32 (9,600 bps) modem manufacturers claim that their modems provide throughput up to 38,400 bps.

Are MNP-5 and V.42 bis useful? Don't be fooled by the claim. It is extremely rare, if ever, that you will be able to transfer files at 38,400 or 57,600 bps. In fact, V.42 bis and MNP-5 are not very useful when you are downloading files from online services. Why? How well the modem compression works depends on what kind of files are being transferred. In general, you will be able to achieve twice the speed for transferring a standard text file (like the one you are reading right now). V.42 bis and MNP-5 modem cannot compress a file which is already compressed by software. In the case of MNP-5, it will even try to compress a precompressed file and actually expand it, thus slow down the file transfer! The above information courtesy modem expert, Patrick Chen.

DATA COMPRESSORS Also called compactors. These devices take over where high speed modems and statistical multiplexers leave off. They save phone lines by a doubling of data throughput by further compressing async or sync data streams.

DATA CONTAMINATION Data corruption.

DATA CONTROL BLOCK A data block usually at the beginning of a file containing descriptive information about the file.

DATA CONVERSION Converting data from one format to another. Conversion typically falls into three basic categories. 1. To convert to a form usable by the equipment you have, e.g. you convert some data from tape to disk (because you don't have a tape drive). Or you may convert from one method of encoding data to another, say from EBCDIC to ASCII, because you don't have software which can understand IBM's EBCDIC method of coding. 3. Or you may convert from one format to another, e.g. from the dBASE method of encoding databases to the Paradox method, or from WordStar to WordPerfect. There are many service bureaus whose job is to convert computer data from one form to another and there are now many programs out to do the conversion. Our favorite programs are Word-for-Word for converting word processing formats and Data Junction for converting database formats. See also DATA COMPRESSION.

DATA COUNTRY CODE A 3-digit numerical country identifier that is part of the 14-digit network terminal number plan. This prescribed numerical designation further constitutes a segment of the overall 14-digit X.121 numbering plan for a CCITT X.25 network.

DATA DICTIONARY 1. A part of a database management system that provides a centralized meaning, relationship to other data, origin, usage, and format. 2. An inventory that describes, defines, and lists all of the data elements that are stored in a database.

DATA DIRECTORY An inventory that specifies the source, location, ownership, usage, and destination of all of the data elements that are stored in a database.

DATA ELEMENT 1. A named unit of data that, in some contexts, is considered indivisible and in other contexts may consists of data items. 2. A named identifier of each of the entities and their attributes that are represented entities and their attributes that are represented in a database. 3. A basic unit of information having a unique meaning and subcategories (data items) of distinct units or values. Examples of data elements are military personnel grade, sex, race, geographic location, and military unit.

DATA ENCRYPTION STANDARD DES. A crytographic algorithm for the protection of unclassifed computer data issued as Federal Information Processing Standard Publication. The DES, which was promulgated by the National Institute of Standards and Technology (NIST)—formerly the National Bureau of Standards (NBS)—is intended for public and Government use.

DATA ENTRY Using an I/O device (input/output device), such as a keyboard on a terminal, to enter data into a computer.

DATA FILE A database typically contains multiple files of information. Each file contains multiple records. Each record is made up of one or more fields. Each field contains one or more bytes of data. The terms file, record and field find their roots in manual office filing systems.

DATA FILL One name for the specifications your ISDN phone lines. Ask for your ISDN Data Fill. It will give you useful information, such as how your lines are set up — voice, data, data/voice, etc.

DATA GRADE CIRCUIT A circuit which is suitable for transmitting data. High speed data needs better quality phone lines than normal dial-up phone circuits. You can acquire such circuits from many telephone companies. To upgrade voice phone lines to high-speed data circuits, you must sometimes "condition" the phone line. See CONDITIONING.

DATA GROUP A number of data lines providing access to the same resource.

DATA INTEGRITY A performance measure based on the rate of undetected errors. A measure of how consistent and accurate computer data is. Data integrity can be threatened by hardware problems, power failures and disk crashes, but most often by application software. In a database system, data integrity can be threatened if two users are allowed to update the same item or record of data at the same time. Record locking, where only a single user at a time is allowed access to a given data record, is a method of insuring data integrity.

DATA LINE INTERFACE The point at which a data line is connected to a telephone system.

DATA LINE MONITOR A measuring device that bridges a data line and looks at how clean the data is, whether the addressing is accurate, the protocol, etc. Being only a monitor, it does not in any way affect the information traveling on the line. See DATA MONITOR.

DATA LINE PRIVACY Prohibits activities which would insert tones on a data station line used by a facsimile machine, a computer terminal or some other device sensitive to extraneous noise.

DATA LINK A term used to describe the communications link used for data transmission from a source to a destination. In short, a phone line for data transmission. Or, A fiber optic transmitter, cable, and receiver that transmits digital data between two points.

DATA LINK CONTROL DLC. Characters used in data communications that control transmission by performing various error checking and housekeeping functions — connect, initiate, terminate, etc.

DATA LINK LAYER The second layer of the Open Systems

Interconnection data communications model of the International Standards Organization. It puts messages together and coordinates their flow. Also used to refer to a connection between two computers over a phone line. See OSI MODEL.

DATA MESSAGE A message included in the GPS (Global Positioning System) signal which reports the satellite's location, clock corrections and health. Included is rough information on the other satellites in the constellation.

DATA MONITOR A device used to look at a bit stream as it travels on a circuit. It will show the user what is going down both sides of a data channel. It will show what the user at his terminal is typing, and what the computer is responding with. Extremely useful for troubleshooting data communications problems. Also called a Data Scope.

DATA NETWORK IDENTIFICATION CODE DNIC. In the CCITT International X.121 format, the first four digits of the 14-digit international data number; the set of digits that may comprise the three digits of the data country code (DCC) and the 1-digit network code (which is called the "network digit"). See DNIC.

DATA NUMBERING PLAN AREA DNPA. In the U.S. implementation of the CCITT X.25 network, the first three digits of a network terminal number (NTN). The 10-digit NTN is the specified addressing information for an endpoint terminal in an X.25 network.

DATA OBJECT An individually addressable unit of information, specified by a data template and its content, that can persist independently of the invocation of a service.

DATA OVER VOICE A device that takes a voice grade line and multiplexes it so it can carry a voice and a data signal. Typically the data is carried in analog form. Thus, to put data on this type of circuit, you need a modem. It is called Data Over Voice, because the data streams (transmission and reception) travel at a higher frequency than the voice conversations using a technique called frequency division multiplexing (FDM).

DATA PACKET SWITCH System-common equipment that electronically distributes information among data terminal equipment connected to a data transmission network. The switch distributes information by means of information packets addressed to specific terminal devices.

DATA PBX A PBX for switching lots of low-speed asynchronous data. A switch that allows a user on an attached circuit to select from among other circuits, usually one at a time and on a contention basis, for the purpose of establishing a through connection. Distinguished from a PBX in that only digital transmissions, and not analog voice, is supported. Like a telecommunications PBX that makes and breaks phone connections, a data PBX makes and breaks connections between computers and peripherals. In response to dynamic demand, it establishes communications paths between devices attached to its input/output ports by receiving, transmitting and processing electrical signals. Usually, data PBXs work off PCs' serial ports rather than through cable attached to a network interface card. For that reason, they are restricted to serial speeds, topping out at about 19.2K bits per second. For switching lots of low-speed asynchronous data, a data PBX (also called a line selector) can be better than a LAN. Total throughput can actually be higher. See also LINE SELECTOR.

DATA PHASE A phase of a data call during which data signals may be transferred between DTEs that are interconnected via the network.

DATA PORT Point of access to a computer that uses trunks or lines for transmitting or receiving data.

DATA RATE The measurement of how quickly data is transmitted. Expressed in bps (bits-per-second).

DATA RECORD See DATA FILE and DATABASE MANAGEMENT SYSTEM.

DATA SCRAMBLER A device used in digital transmission systems to convert an input digital signal into a pseudorandom sequence free from long runs of marks, spaces, or other simple repetitive patterns.

DATA SCOPE See DATA MONITOR.

DATA SECURE LINE A single tip and ring line off the PBX which is protected against any tones (like call waiting) or break-ins that would otherwise mess up any ongoing data transmission call.

DATA SECURITY The protection of data from unauthorized (accidental or intentional) modificiation, destruction, disclosure, or delay.

DATA SERVICE UNIT DSU. Device designed to connect a DTE (Data Terminal Equipment like a PC or a LAN) to a digital phone line to allow fully-digital communications. A DSU is sort of the digital equivalent of a modem. In more technical terms, a DSU is a type of short-haul, synchronous-data line driver, normally installed at a user location that connects a user's synchronous equipment over a 4-wire circuit to a serving dial-central-office. This service can be for a point-to-point or multipoint operation in a digital data network. DSUs are typically used for leased lines. For switched digital services, you need a CSU/DSU also called a DSU/CSU. See CSU/DSU and DSU/CSU.

DATA SET In AT&T jargon, a data set is a modem, i.e. a device which performs the modulation/demodulation and control functions necessary to provide compatibility between business machines which work in digital (on-off) signals and voice telephone lines. In IBM jargon however, a data set is a collection of data, usually in a file on a disk. See also MODEM.

DATA SET READY One of the control signals on a standard RS-232-C connector. It indicates whether the data communications equipment is connected and ready to start handshaking control signals so that transmission can start. See RS-232-C and the Appendix.

DATA SHEETS What Business Communications Review calls its statistical and descriptive material comparing PBXs. BCR includes these data sheets in its excellent BCR Manual of PBXs. This manual is the most extensive write-up of larger (more than 200 line) PBXs in the world. It is available from Telecom Library on 1-800-LIBRARY.

DATA SIGNALING RATE The total of the number of bits per second in the transmission path of a data transmission system. A measurement of how quickly data is transmitted, expressed in bps, bits-per-second.

DATA SOURCE The originating device in a data communications link.

DATA STREAM Collection of characters and data bits transmitted through a channel.

DATA SWITCHING EXCHANGE DSE. The equipment installed at a single location to perform switching functions such as circuit switching, message switching, and packet switching.

DATA TERMINAL EQUIPMENT DTE. A definition of hardware specifications that provides for data communications. There are two basic specs your hardware can conform to, DTE (Data Terminal Equipment) or DCE (Data Communications Equipment). See DCE and DTE.

DATA TERMINAL READY One of the control signals on a standard RS-232-C connector. It indicates if the data terminal equipment is present, connected and ready and has had handshaking signals verified. See RS-232-C and the Appendix.

DATA TRANSFER RATE The average number of bits, characaters, or blocks per unit time passing in a data transmission system.

DATA TRANSFER REQUEST SIGNAL A call control signal transmitted by a DCE to a DTE to indicate that a distant DTE wants to exchange data.

DATA TRANSFER TIME The time that elapses between the initial offering of a unit of user data to a network by transmitting data terminal equipment and the complete delivery of that unit to receiving data terminal equipment.

DATA TYPING When converting a database from one format to another, several conversion programs will convert the data to a common format before converting it to the final version. During the conversion process a program may check through the data in the database to determine what it is and arbitrarily make one field numeric, one field character, one field memo, etc.

DATABASE A collection of data structured and organized in a disciplined fashion so that access is possible quickly to information of interest. There are many ways of organizing databases. Most corporate databases are not one single, huge file. They are multiple databases related to each other by some common thread, e.g. an employee identification number. Databases are made up of two elements, a record and a field. A record is one complete entry in a database, e.g. Gerry Friesen, 12 West 21 Street, New York, NY

10010, 212-691-8215. A field would be the street address field, namely 12 West 21 Street.

Databases are stored on computers in different ways. Some are comma delineated. They differentiate between their fields with commas — like Gerry's record above. A more common way of storing databases is with fixed length records. Here, all the fields and all the records are of the same length. The computer finds fields by index and by counting. For example, Gerry's first name might occupy the first 15 characters. Gerry's last name might be the next 20 characters, etc. Where Gerry's names are too short to fill the full 15 or 20 characters, their fields are "padded" with specially-chosen characters which the computer recognizes as padded characters to be ignored. The most important thing to remember about databases is that all the common database programs, like dBASE, Paradox, Rbase, etc. don't automatically make backups of their files like word processing programs do. Therefore, before you muck with a database file — sort it, index it, restructure it, etc. Please make sure you make a backup of the main database file.

DATABASE MANAGEMENT SYSTEM DBMS. Computer software used to create, store, retrieve, change, manipulate, sort, format and print the information in a database. Database management systems are probably the fastest growing part of the computer industry. Increasingly, databases are being organized so they can be accessible from places remote to the computer they're kept on. The "classic" database management system is probably an airline reservation system.

DATABASE OBJECT One of the components of a database: a table, view, index, procedure, trigger, column, default, or rule.

DATABASE SERVER A specialized computer that doles out database data to PCs on a LAN the way a file server doles out files. Where a traditional DBMS runs both a database application and the DBMS program on each PC on the LAN, a database server splits up the two processes. The application you wrote with your DBMS runs on your local PC, while the DBMS program runs on the database server computer. With a regular file server setup, all the database data has to be downloaded over the LAN to your PC, so that the DBMS can pick out what information your application wants. With a database server, the server itself does the picking, sending only the data you need over the network to your PC. So a database server means vastly less network traffic in a multi-user database system. It also provides for better data integrity since one computer handles all the record and file locking. See SERVER.

DATAGRAM A transmission method in which sections of a message are transmitted in scattered order and the correct order is re-established by the receiving workstation. Used on packet-switching networks. The Dow Jones Handbook of Telecommunications defines it as, "A single unacknowledged packet of information that is sent over a network as an individual packet without regard to previous or subsequent packets." Here's another definition I found. A finite-length packet with sufficient information to be independently routed from source to destination. In packet switching, a self-contained packet, independent of other packets, that carriers information sufficient for routing from the originating data terminal equipment to the destination data terminal equipment, without relying on earlier exchanges between the equipment and the network. Unlike virtual call service, there are no call establishment or clearing procedures, and the network does not generally provide protection against loss, duplication, or misdelivery. Datagram transmission typically does not involve end-to-end session establishment and may or may not entail delivery confirmation acknowledgment. See CONNECTIONLESS MODE TRANSMISSION.

DATAKIT VCS The Datakit VCS is an AT&T packet switch that can switch over 44,000 packets per second and support up to 3,500 simultaneous virtual circuits. According to AT&T, the Datakit VCS is a digital virtual circuit switch with an architecture that combines the advantages of LANs, PBXs, data circuits and X.25 packet switches.

DATAP The programmer and system house in Atlanta which provides several long distance carriers with value-added services — what Sprint calls its SCADA system manufacturer.

DATAPATH A name that's becoming generic for a data service that provides digital, full-duplex data transmission at speeds of 300 bps through 19.2 Bps asynchronous and 1,200 through 64 Kbps synchronous. Datapath has built in autobaud and hand-shaking protocols.

DATAPHONE A service mark of AT&T for various data hardware products such as modems and printers and services. See also DDS.

DATASPAN DataSPAN is generally characterized as a "fast packet" service and is based on frame relay standards recommended by the International Consultative Committee for Telephone & Telegraph (CCITT) and the American National Standards Institute (ANSI). Northern Telecom has introduced DataSPAN as a new DMS SuperNode value-added, data-communications service that is targeted toward connecting high-speed Local Area Networks. Northern Telecom asserts that DataSPAN's rapid and efficient data transport assures reliable delivery and substantial performance improvement over current LAN interconnect solutions. DataSpan switching and transmission delay is less than 3 ms per node; X.25 switching and transmission delay can be up to 50 ms per node. Using Frame Relay, wide-area packet switching can be accomplished with the same level of performance that is traditionally limited to complex, dedicated private-line networks. DataSPAN is accessed through standard DS-0 or DS-1 links.

DATE AND TIME STAMP Many voice mail systems will append the date and time of receipt of voice messages for their users/subscribers.

DATEL SERVICES An MCI International service that carries data for medium-volume users. This service provides two-way data and voice transmission for simplex, half-duplex, and full duplex operations.

DATING FORMAT The format employed to express the time of an event. The time of an event on the UTC time scale is given in the following sequence; hour, day, month, year; e.g., 0917 UT, 30 August 1997. The hour is designated by the 24-hour system. UTC stands for Coordinated Universal Time, believe it or not.

DAUGHTERBOARD First there is the motherboard. That's the main circuit board of a computer system. The motherboard contains edge connectors or sockets so other PC (printed circuit) boards can be plugged into it. Those PC boards are called Fatherboards. Some fatherboards have pins on them into which you can plug smaller boards. Those boards are called Daughterboards. In a voice processing system, you might have a Fatherboard to do faxing. And you might have a range of Daughterboards, which allow you to connect different types of phone connections. Different boards exist for standard analog tip and ring, digital switched 56, etc. See also MOTHERBOARD.

DB Should really be written as dB. Decibel. A unit of measure of signal strength, usually the relation between a transmitted signal and a standard signal source. Therefore, 6 dB of loss would mean that there is 6 dB difference between what arrives down a communications circuit and what was transmitted by a standard signal generator. See DECIBEL for a better explanation.

DB LOSS BUDGET Should be written as dB. dB Loss Budget is the amount of light available to overcome the attenuation in the optical link and still maintain specifications.

DB-9 This is the standard nine-pin RS-232-C serial port on the IBM AT and most laptop computers. The term DB-9 is used to describe both the male and female plug. So be careful when you order. See also the Appendix in this Dictionary for more information on the pinning of RS-232-C plugs.

DB-15 A standardized connector with 15 pins. It can be used Ethernet transceivers. It can also be used for connecting VGA monitors.

DB-25 The standard 25-pin connector used for RS-232-C serial data communications. In a DB-25 there are 25-pins, with 13 pins in one row and 12 in the other row. DB-25 is used to describe both the male and female plug. So be careful when you order. See also the Appendix in this Dictionary for more information on the pinning of RS-232-C plugs.

DB2 IBM's relational database system that runs on System 370-compatible mainframes under the MVS operating system.

DBA 1. Dynamic Bandwidth Allocation. 2. Database administrator. The individual in the organization with the responsibility for the design and control of databases.

DBIT Also called D-BIT. The delivery confirmation bit in an X.25 packet that is used to indicate whether or not the DTE wishes to receive an end-to-end acknowledgment of delivery. In short, a bit in the X.25 packet header that assures data integrity between the TPAD and the HPAD.

DBM Decibels below 1mW. This should be written as dBm. Output power of a signal referenced to an input signal of 1mW (Milliwatt). Similarly, dBm0 refers to output power, expressed in dBm, with no input signal. (O dBM = 1 milliwatt and -30 dBm = 0.001 milliwatt). See DECIBEL.

DBMS Database management system. A computer program that manages data by providing the services of centralized control, data independence, and complex physical structures. Advantages include efficient access, integrity, recovery, concurrency control, privacy, and security. A DBMS enables users to perform a variety of operations on data, including retrieving, appending, editing, updating, and generating reports.

DBRN A ratio expressed in DeciBels above Reference Noise.

DBT Deutsche Bundespost Telecom.

DBU Decibels below 1uW.

DC Direct Current. The flow of free electrons in one direction within an electrical conductor, such as a wire. DC also stands for Delayed Call.

DC SIGNALING A collection of ways of transmitting communications signals using direct current — the type of current produced by a dry cell household "D" cell battery. DC signaling is only used on cable. It's an out-of-band signal.

DCC 1. Data Communications Channel. Channels contained within section and line overhead used as embedded operations channels to communicate to each network element. An AT&T SONET term. 2. Digital Compact Cassette. A digital version of the familiar analog audio cassette. A DCC recorder can play and record both analog and digital cassettes. But the digital ones will sound a lot better.

DCE Data Communications Equipment. In the RS-232-C "standard" developed by the Electronic Industries Association, there are DCE devices (typically modems or printers) and DTE (Data Terminal Equipment) devices, which are typically personal computers or data terminals. The main difference between a DCE and DTE is the wiring of pins two and three. But there is, of course, no standardization. When wiring one RS-232-C device to another, it's good to know which device is wired as a DCE and which as a DTE. But it's actually best to go straight to the wiring diagram in the appendix of the device's instruction manual. Then you compare the wiring diagram of the device you want to connect and build yourself a cable that takes into account the peculiar (i.e. strange) vagaries of the engineers who designed each product. In short, with an RS-232-C connection, the modem is usually regarded as DCE, while the user device (terminal or computer) is DTE. In a X.25 connection, the network access and packet switching node is viewed as the DCE. DCE devices typically transmit on pin 3 and receive on pin 2. DTE (Data Terminal Equipment) devices typically transmit on pin 2 and receive on pin 3. See also the Appendix.

DCH D-Channel Handler.

DCM Digital Circuit Multiplication. A means of increasing the effective capacity of primary rate and higher level PCM hierarchics, based upon speech coding at 64 kbit/s. Also a Digital Carrier Module.

DCP Digital Communications Protocol.

DCP TELEPHONE A digital voice telephone of the AT&T model 7400 series, operated with the Digital Communications Protocol (DCP) used in System 75/85 digital PBXs.

DCS 1. Distributed Communications system. See DISTRIBUTED SWITCHING. 2. Desktop Color Separation. 3. Digital Crossconnect System. A device for switching and rearranging private line voice, private line analog data and T-1 lines. A DCS performs all the functions of a normal "switch," except that connections are typically set up in advance of when the circuits are to be switched — not together with the call. You make those "connections" by calling an attendant who makes them manually, or dialing in on a computer terminal — one similar to an airline agent's. See also NETWORK RECONFIGURATION SERVICE. 3. Digital Cellular System.

DCT Digital Carrier Termination.

DCTI Desktop Computer Telephone Integration. Basically, providing a way for your computer to control your telephone set.

DDA Domain Defined Attribute. A way of adding additional information to the address of your electronic mail in order to avoid confusion between people of the same or similar name.

DDB Digital Data Bank.

DDC Direct Department Calling.

DDCMP Digital Data Communications Message Protocol. A byte-oriented, link-layer protocol from Digital Equipment Corp., used to transmit messages between stations over a communications line. DDCMP supports half- or full-duplex modes, and either point-to-point or mulitpoint lines in a DNA (Digital Network Architecture) network.

DDD Direct Distance Dialing. The "brand name" the Bell System used to call its Message Toll Telephone Network. It used the words "Direct Distance Dialing" to convince the public to dial their own long distance calls directly without the help of an operator.

DDE See DYNAMIC DATA EXCHANGE

DDEML Dynamic Data Exchange Management Library. A feature of Microsoft Windows.

DDI Direct Dialing In.

DDN Defense Data Network. A network that provides long haul and area data communications and interconnectivity for DoD systems, and supports the DoD suite of protocols (especially TCP and IP). All equipment attached to the DDN by military subscribers must incorporate, or be compatible with, the DoD Internet and transport protocols. DDN was split off from ARPANET to handle U.S. military needs. It is also called MILNET.

DDP Distributed Data Processing. See DISTRIBUTED SWITCHING.

DDS Dataphone Digital Service, also called Digital Data System. DDS is private line digital service, typically with data rates at 2,400; 4,800; 9,600 and 56,000 bits per second. DDS is offered on an inter-LATA basis by AT&T and on an intra-LATA basis by the Bell operating companies. AT&T has now incorporated it into their Accunet family of offerings. But, by the time your read this, they may have a new name for the service.

DDSD Delay Dial Start Dial. A start-stop protocol for dialing into a switch.

DE FACTO Used to describe standards. Reflecting current or actual practice, but not having approval or sanction by any official standards-setting organization. usually created by an individual manufacturer or developer - hence, often used as a synonym for proprietary. The Hayes At auto-dial modem command language is an example of a de facto standard. Very often, de facto standards form the basis for de jure standards (Ethernet was the basis of Institute of Electrical and Electronic Engineers or IEEE standard 802.3). Contrast with DE JURE.

DE FOREST, LEE Lee de Forest invented the vacuum tube in 1907. Until the invention of the transistor after World War II, all radio, long distance telephony and complicated electronics, including electronic computers, were derived from de Forest's invention.

DE JURE Used to describe standards approved or sanctioned by an official standards setting organization. CCITT Recommendation X.25 for packet data networks is an example of a de jure standard. Contrast with DE FACTO.

DEAD SECTOR In facsimile, the elapsed time between the end of scanning of one line and the start of scanning of the following line.

DEADLINE During the Civil War, captured troops were placed in a field. They were told they could move wherever they wanted in the field except beyond a line that was drawn around the field. If they did, they would be shot. Thus the origin of the word deadline.

DEADLOCK See DEADLY EMBRACE.

DEADLY EMBRACE Stalemate that occurs when two elements in a process are each waiting for the other to respond. For example, in a network, if one user is working on file A and needs file B to continue, but another user is working on file B and needs file A to continue, each one waits for the other. Both are temporarily locked out. The software must be able to deal with this.

DEALER BOARD British term meaning "trading turret."

DEALING ROOM British term meaning "trading room."

DEBIT CARD A new form of bank card that handles transactions in the same way as your personal checking account. In a debit card, you get no credit. The instant you make a purchase with your debit card, the money is extracted from your bank account and placed in the bank account of your supplier. Such a card hasn't caught on in a big way, but may if we finally start to trust banks.

DEBUG A MS-DOS program to examine or alter memory, load and look at sectors of data from disk and create simple assembly-language programs. MS-DOS DEBUG.COM lets you write some small programs. You can use DEBUG to correct problems in some programs.

DEC Digital Equipment Corporation. A leading manufacturer of minicomputers. The Unix operating system, developed at Bell Labs, runs on DEC computers. DEC, with its headquarters in Massachusetts and having sold so many computers to Western Electric for inclusion in central office switches and toll switches, is sometimes referred to as "Eastern Electric." Kenneth H. Olsen founded DEC in 1957 with three employees in 8,500 square feet of leased space in a corner of an old woolen mill.

DECags DEC ASAI Gateway Services. Two-directional link to AT&T's Definity. See also OPEN APPLICATION INTERFACE.

DECIBEL dB. A unit for measuring the power of a sound or the strength of a signal. It is expressed as the ratio of two values. Here is an explanation from James Harry Green's excellent book The Dow Jones-Irwin Handbook of Telecommunications. (Get a copy from Telecom Library 1-800-LIBRARY.) Mr. Green writes, "The power in telecommunications circuits is so low that it is normally measured in milliwatts. However, the milliwatt is not a convenient way to express differences in power level between circuits. Voice frequency circuits are designed around the human ear, which has a logarithmic response to changes in power. (Likewise, the human eye has a logarithmic response to changes in light.) Therefore in telephony, the decibel, which is a logarithmic rather than a linear measurement, is used as a measure of relative power between circuits or transmission level points. A change in level of 1 dB is barely perceptible under ideal conditions...Increases or reductions of 3 dB result in doubling or halving the power in a circuit. This ratio is handy to remember when evaluating power differences. The corresponding figure for doubling or halving voltage is 6 dB. See DB.

DECIMAL Our normal numbering system. It is to the base 10.

DECISION CIRCUIT A circuit that measures the probable value of a signal element and makes an output signal decision based on the value of the input signal and a predetermined criterion or criteria.

DECISION INSTANT In the reception of a digital signal, the instant at which a decision is made by a receiving device as to the probable value of a signal condition.

DECISION SUPPORT SYSTEMS DSS. Computerized systems for transforming data into useful information, such as statistical models or predictions of trends, which is used by management in the decision-making process. There are several aspects of the best decision support systems: First, they are connected to mainframe databases. Second, they are accessible by executives from their desktops. Third, there are usually lots of programs for producing graphs, charts and writing simple reports, i.e. for the executives to extract and portray information in forms that are most useful to them.

DECNET DEC's proprietary Ethernet LAN that works across all of the company's machines, endowed with a peer-to-peer methodology. See DEC.

DECODER A device that converts information from one form to another — typically from analog to digital and vice versa. See DECODING.

DECODING Changing a digital signal into analog form or into another type of digital signal. The opposite of Encoding. See also MODEM. Decoding and coding should not be confused with deciphering and ciphering. See DES.

DECOLLIMATION In optics, that effect wherein a beam of parallel light rays is caused to diverge or converge from parallelism. Any of a large number of factors may cause this effect, e.g., refractive index inhomogeneities, occlusions, scattering, deflection, diffraction, reflection, refraction.

DECOLUMNIZATION The process of reformatting multi-column documents into a signal column. Generally, when you are processing a document for use in a word processing program, a single column of text is preferable to multiple columns.

DECOMPRESSION Decompression is the process of expanding a compressed image or file so it can be viewed, printed, faxed or otherwise processed.

DECRYPT To convert encrypted text into its equivalent plain text by means of a cryptosystem. This does not include solution by cryptanalysis. The term decrypt covers the meanings of decipher and decode.

DECT Digital European Cordless Telecommunictions, an interface specification under development and consideration throughout Europe.

DEDICATED ACCESS A connection between a phone or phone system (like a PBX) and an InpereXchange Carrier (IXC) through a dedicated line. All calls over the line are automatically routed to a particular IXC.

DEDICATED ATTENDANT LINK Assures that there will always be an intercom link available for your attendant or receptionist or operator to announce incoming calls.

DEDICATED CHANNEL OR CIRCUIT A channel leased from a common carrier by an end user used exclusively by that end user. The channel is available for use 24 hours a day, seven days a week, 52 weeks of the year, assuming it works that efficiently.

DEDICATED CIRCUIT A circuit designated for exclusive use by specified users. See also DEDICATED CHANNEL.

DEDICATED LINE Another name for a private leased line or dedicated channel. A dedicated line provides the ability to have constant transmission path from point A to point B. A dedicated line may be leased or owned. It may be assigned a single purpose, such as monitoring a distant building. It may be part of a network, with the ability for many to dial into it. It may be a tie-line between your offices or it may be a line to a long distance carrier. In this case, you do not have to dial a local connection number or put in an authorization code. A WATS line is in effect a Dedicated Line to AT&T or whomever you purchased WATS from.

DEDICATED MACHINE A computer designed to run only one program or do one thing. This machine cannot easily be re-programmed to do another task, as, for example, a general-purpose machine can. A general-purpose machine, however, can be dedicated to running only one task if programmed to do so.

DEDICATED MODE When a file server or router on a local area network is set up to work only as a file server or router, it runs in dedicated mode.

DEDICATED SERVER A computer on a network that performs specialized network tasts, such as storing files. The word "dedicated" means that the computer is used exclusively as a server. It is not used as a workstation, which means no one is sitting in front of it, using it. A dedicated server sits all alone, attached to its network, working happily all by itself.

DEDICATED SERVICE A communication network devoted to a single purpose or group of users, e.g., AUTOVON, FTS. It may also be a subset of a larger network; e.g., AUTOVON, FTS.

DEDICATED TRUNK A trunk which bypasses the Attendant Console and rings through to a particular phone, hunt group or distribution group.

DEEP SPACE Space at distances from the Earth approximately equal to or greater than the distance between the Earth and the Moon.

DEFACTO STANDARD Standards, widely accepted and used, but lacking formal approval by a recognized standards organization. For example TCP/IP.

DEFAULT The default is a factory-set hardware of software setting or configuration. It is the preset value that the program or equipment comes with. It will work with default values in the absence of any other command from the user. For example, communications software programs, such as Crosstalk, Blast, etc., have as their default settings 300 baud, 8 bit, one stop bit, no parity. If you want to run at 1,200 baud, you have to change that "default" setting.

DEFAULT CARRIER Generic name given to the long distance carrier which will carry the traffic of customers who haven't presubscribed to a long distance carrier.

DEFENSE DATA NETWORK DDN. The Department of Defense integrated packet switching network capable of worldwide multilevel secure and non-secure data transmission.

DEFERRED PROCESSING Performing operations as a group or batch, all at once. Using batch mode, you can quickly prescan your documents, capturing just the image of each page, then perform recognition on these images later, freeing your computer for interactive work.

DEFINITION A figure of merit for image quality. For video-type displays, it is normally expressed in terms of the smallest resolvable element of the reproduced received image.

DEGAUSSER Device to demagnetize color picture tube for color purity.

DEGRADATION In communications, that condition in which one or more of the established performance parameters fall outside predetermined limits, resulting in a lower quality of service.

DEGRADED SERVICE STATE The condition wherein degradation prevails in a communication link. For some applications e.g., automatic switching to a nondegraded standby link, degradation must persist for a specified period of time before a degraded service state is considered to exist.

DEGREE OF COHERENCE A measure of the coherence of a light source.

DEGREE OF ISOCHRONOUS DISTORTION In data transmission, the ratio of (a) the absolute value of the maximum measured difference between the actual and the theoretical intervals separating any two significant instants of modulation (or demodulation) to (b) the unit interval. These instants are not necessarily consecutive. The degree of isochronous distortion is usually expressed as a percentage. The result of the measurement should be completed by an indication of the period, usually limited, of the observation.

DEGREE OF START-STOP DISTORTION 1. In asynchronous data transmission, the ratio of (a) the absolute value of the maximum measured difference between the actual and theoretical intervals separating any significant instant of modulation (or demodulation) from the significant instant of the start element immediately preceding it to (b) the unit interval. 2. The highest absolute value of individual distortion affecting the significant instants of a start-stop modulation. The degree of distortion of a start-stop modulation (or demodulation) is usually expressed as a percentage.

DEJITTERIZER A device for reducing jitter in a digital signal, consisting essentially of an elastic buffer into which the signal is written and from which it is read at a rate determined by the average rate of the incoming signal. Such a device is largely ineffective in dealing with low-frequency impairments such as waiting-time jitter.

DELAY The wait time between two events, such as the time from when a signal is sent to the time it is received. There are all sorts of reasons for delays, such as propagation delays, satellite delays, etc.

DELAY ANNOUNCEMENTS These are pre-recorded announcements to incoming callers that they are being delayed and being placed in an ACD queue. Sample: "Please wait. All our agents are permanently busy. You are being placed on Eternity Hold. Don't go away or you'll never be allowed back." Some announcements are giving callers sales pitches and some idea of how long they'll have to stay on line until someone helps them.

DELAYED DELIVERY FACILITY A facility that employs storage within the data network whereby data destination for delivery to one or more addresses may be held for subsequent delivery at a later time.

DELAY DISTORTION The difference, expressed in time, for signals of different frequencies to pass through a phone line.

DELAY ENCODING A method of encoding binary data to form a two-level signal. A binary zero caused no change of signal level unless it is followed by another zero, in which case a transition takes place at the end of the first bit period. A binary "1" causes a transition from one level to the other in the middle of the bit period. Used primarily for encoding of radio signals since the spectrum of the encoding of signal contains less low frequency energy than an NRZ signal and less high frequency energy than a biphase signal.

DELAY EQUALIZER A corrective piece of electronic circuitry designed to make communications circuit delays constant over a desired frequency range.

DELAY LINE A transmission line, or equivalent device, designed to introduce delay.

DELAY MODULATION A modulation scheme that uses different forms of delay in a signal element. Frequently used in radio, microwave and fiberoptic systems.

DELAYED RING TRANSFER An optional KTU facility that provides for automatic transfer to the ringing signal from a principal telephone set to the attendant telephone station after an adjustable number of rings.

DELAYED TRANSMISSION A fax machine feature that allows a document to be transmitted automatically at a specific time.

DELAYED SENDING A feature of fax machines which allows the machine to be programmed to send its transmissions at a later time — to take advantage of lower phone rates, for example.

DELIMITER A special word or character that allows a computer to recognize the beginning or end of a portion of a program or segment of data.

DELIVERED BLOCK A successfully transferred block.

DELIVERED OVERHEAD BIT A bit transferred to a destination user, but having its primary functional effect within the telecommunication system.

DELIVERED OVERHEAD BLOCK A successfully transferred block that contains no user information bits.

DELIVERY CONFIRMATION Information returned to the originator indicating that a given unit of information has been delivered to the intended addresses.

DELPHI FORECASTING One of the silliest methods of forecasting the future. Namely, to ask a bunch of alleged experts (often academic eggheads) what they think might happen and then averaging out their opinions, sort of.

DELTA CHANNEL In T-carrier/ISDN communications, a delta channel/"D channel" contains signaling and status information.

DELTA MODULATION A method for converting analog voice to digital form for transmission. It is the second most common method of digitizing voice after Pulse Code Modulation, PCM. Sampling is done in all conversion of analog voice to digital signals. The method of sampling is what distinguishes the various methods of digitization (Delta vs.' PCM, etc.). In delta modulation, the voice signal is scanned 32,000 times a second, and a reading is taken to see if the latest value is greater or less than it was at the previous scan. If it's greater, a "1" is sent. If it's smaller, a "0" is sent.

Delta modulation's sampling rate of 32,000 times a second is four times faster than PCM. But Delta records its samples as a zero (0) or a one (1), while PCM takes an 8-bit sample. Thus PCM encodes voice into 64,000 bits per second, while Delta codes it into 32,000. Because delta has fewer bits, it could theoretically produce a poorer representation of the voice. In actual fact, the human ear can't hear the difference between a PCM and a Delta encoded voice conversation.

Delta modulation has much to recommend it, especially its use of fewer bits. Unfortunately no two delta modulation schemes are compatible with each other. So to get one delta-mod digital PBX to speak to another, you have to convert the voice signals back to analog. With AT&T making T-1 a de facto digital encoding scheme, PCM has become the de facto standard for digitally encoding voice. And although there are three types of PCM in general use, they can be made compatible on direct digital basis (i.e. without having to go back to analog voice). One problem with PCM is that

American manufacturers typically put twenty four 64,000 bit per second voice conversations on a channel and call it T-1. The Europeans put 30 conversations on their equivalent transmission path. Thus, you can't directly interface the American and the European systems. But there are "black boxes" available...(In this business, there are always black boxes available.)

DELTA SIGMA MODULATION A variant of delta modulation in which the integral of the input signal is encoded rather than the signal itself. A normal delta modulation encoder by an integrating network. See DELTA MODULATION.

DELUXE QUEUING A feature that allows incoming calls from phone users, tie trunks and attendants to be placed in a queue when all routes for completing a particular call are busy. The queue can be either a Ringback Queue (RBQ) — the user hangs up and is called back when a trunk becomes available — or an Off-Hook Queue (OHQ) — the user waits off-hook and is connected to the next available trunk. Deluxe Queuing is a term used mainly by AT&T. Most modern PBXs have this feature. Most have simpler names, however.

DEMAND ASSIGNED MULTIPLE ACCESS See DAMA.

DEMAND ASSIGNMENT A technique where users share a communications channel. Aga user needing to communicate with another user on the network activates the required circuit. Upon completion of the call, the circuit is deactivated and the capacity is available for other users.

DEMAND FACTOR The ratio of the maximum demand on a power system to the total connected load of the system.

DEMAND LOAD In general, the total power required by a facility. The demand load is the sum of the operational load (including any tactical load) and nonoperational demand loads. It is determined by applying the proper demand factor to each of the connected loads and a diversity factor to the sum total.

DEMAND PAGING The common implementation in a PC of virtual memory, where pages of data are read into memory from storage in response to page faults.

DEMAND SERVICE In ISDN applications, a telecommunications service that establishes an immediate communication path in response to a user request made through user-network signaling.

DEMARC or DEMARK (Pronounced D-Mark.) The demarcation point between the wiring that comes in from your local telephone company and the wiring you install to hook up your own telephone system — your CPE (Customer Provided Equipment) wiring. A De-Marc might be anything as simple as an RJ-11C jack (one trunk) or an RJ-14C (two trunks) or an RJ-21X (up to 25 trunks) or a 66-block — a punchdown block on one side of which the telephone company punches down its trunks and on the other, you punch down your connections into your phone system. On a 66 block, there are little metal clips called "bridging clips" between you and the phone company. Lifting these clips off cuts your equipment from the phone company's trunks. This way you can quickly see whose fault it is. Often it's yours. But, if you think it's theirs and they come and find it's yours, they'll bill you megabucks. See DEMARCATION POINT or DEMARCATION STRIP.

DEMARCATION POINT The point or interconnection between telephone company facilities and your terminal equipment. The demarcation point shall be located on the subscriber's side of the telephone company's protector or the equivalent thereof in cases where a protector is not required.

DEMARCATION STRIP The terminal strip or block (typically a 66 block) which is the physical interface between the phone company's lines and the lines going directly to your own phone system. See also DEMARC.

DEMKO Denmark Elektriske MaterielKOntrol (Denmark Testing Laboratory).

DEMOCRATICALLY SYNCHRONIZED NETWORK A mutually synchronized network in which all clocks in the network are of equal status and exert equal amounts of control on the others.

DEMODULATION The process of retrieving an electrical signal from a carrier signal or wave. The reverse of modulation. See MODEM.

DEMULTIPLEX DEMUX. To separate two or more signals previously combined by compatible multiplexing equipment.

DEMULTIPLEXER A device that pulls several streams of data out of a bigger, fatter or faster stream of data.

DEMULTIPLEXING A process applied to a multiplex signal for recovering signals combined within it and for restoring the distinct individual channels of the signals.

DENIAL OF SERVICE The removal of a LAN service from a user, usually for malicious purposes.

DENIS THE LITTLE The 6th century monk who decided that history should be split between B.C. and A.D.

DENSITY 1. The number of bits (or bytes) in a defined length on a magnetic medium. Density describes the amount of data that can be stored. 2. The number of circuits that can be packed into an integrated circuit. 3. In a facsimile system, a measure of the light transmission or reflection properties of an area, expressed by the logarithm of the ratio of incident to transmitted or reflected light flux.

DEPARTURE ANGLE The angle between the axis of the main lobe of an antenna pattern and the horizontal plane at the transmitting antenna.

DEPERSONALIZATION In 1879 a flu epidemic in Lowell, MA make it likely that all four of the telephone operators would get sick simultaneously. To help substitute operators, management numbered each of the exchange's two hundred plus customers. No problem. The customers accepted the change easily.

DEPLANING Getting off a plane. See DETRAINING.

DEPOLARIZATION 1. In electromagnetic wave propagation, that condition wherein a polarized transmission being transmitted through a nonhomogeneous medium has its polarization reduced or randomized by the effects of the medium being traversed. 2. Prevention of polarization in an electric cell or battery.

DEPOPULATE A technique to reduce the traffic load on a switch by removing devices from the shelf or cabinet. Depopulating reduces the effective device capacity of a switch but can increase switching capacity. This is a ploy used to give older PBX systems traffic capacity nearer true ACD systems.

DEPRESSED CLADDING FIBER An optical fiber construction, usually single mode, that has double cladding, the outer cladding having an index of refraction intermediate between the core and the inner cladding.

DEREGULATION The removal of regulatory authority to control certain activities of telephone companies. An attempt by federal authorities to make the telephone industry more competitive. Deregulation is meant to benefit the consumer. Sometimes it does. Sometimes it doesn't. Often, it's a scapegoat for whatever subsequently goes wrong.

DERIVATION EQUIPMENT Produces narrow band facilities from a wider band facility. Such equipment can, for instance, derive telegraph grade lines from the unused portion of a voice circuit.

DES Data Encryption Standard. An algorithm for encrypting (coding) data designed by the National Bureau of Standards so it is impossible for anyone without the decryption key to get the data back in unscrambled form. The DES standard enciphers and deciphers data using a 64-bit key specified in the Federal Information Processing Standard Publication 46, dated January 15, 1977. DES is not the most advanced system in computer security and there are possible problems with its use. Proprietary encryption schemes are also available. Some of these are more modern and more secure. The quality of your data security is typically a function of how much money you spend.

DESCENDERS Those parts (or tails) of the letters p, y, j and g which descend below the base line. This typestyle is much easier to read than one in which the tails rest on the base line. Watch out for true (i.e. real) descenders when you're buying a system. Most have them these days, but many telephone screens don't. Careful.

DESCRAMBLER A device which corrects a signal (often video) that has been intentionally distorted to prevent unauthorized viewing. Used with satellite TV systems. See DES.

DESI STRIP A slang term for Designation Strip, the small printed piece of paper that slides into or attaches onto a telephone and tells you which button answers which line or which button does what in the way of features or intercom.

DESIGN LAYOUT REPORT DLR. A record containing the technical information that describes the facilities and terminations provided by a local telephone company to a long distance telephone company. The technical information is needed by the long distance carrier to design the overall service and includes such items as cable makeup (gauge, loading, length, etc), carrier channel bank type and system mileage, signaling termination compatibility, etc. The DLR is sent to the designated Carrier representative via the local Telephone Company's Engineering Department.

DESIGNATION STRIP Also called Desi Strip. A designation Strip is the the small printed piece of paper that slides into or attaches onto a telephone and tells you which button answers which line or which button does what in the way of features or intercom.

DESKEW An imaging term. An imaging board that can deskew can correct for a page that is scanned in crookedly.

DESKTOP The computer's working environment. The screen layout, the menu bar, and the program icons associated with the machine's operating environment. Apple's Macintosh really started the word "desktop." But, with the introduction of Windows 3.0, IBM PCs and clones now also have desktops.

DESKTOP CONNECTION AT&T's code name for hardware which includes an AT&T serial port adaptor, DSS cable and a 9 to 25 pin connector and some software to make it work. The new name for desktop connection is PassageWay. It attaches to the back of the AT&T phone. The cable connects the adaptor to your PC's serial port. In AT&T's words, the AT&T PassageWay integrates telephone functions with a Microsoft Windows 3.1 or greater application, facilitiating outdialing using the Hayes Command Set used by modems, linking caller identification to PC business applications, and paving the way to an open interface between the PC software and the telephone. As a development platform, AT&T PassageWay offers an application layer access to features of the telephone including receiving information on visual/audible alerts and telephone displays, activating button presses, turning the speakerphone on or off, adjusting the volume of the telephone and dialing, including some call state progress. In addition, operating with Windows provides a unique way of accessing and sharing information between applications that co-reside on a PC. Windows provides a Graphic User Interface (GUI) that allows software packages to be easily developed. Windows also offers the Dynamic Data Exchange (DDE) interface between coresident applications that is a standard for sharing information on DOS PCs. AT&T PassageWay also passes information using Microsoft's DDE standard. See also AT&T APPLICATIONS PARTNER.

DESKTOP METAPHOR A desktop metaphor is the conceptual way a workstation screen area is used to emulate a user's physical desktop through graphic icon images. The icon maps directly to its real life function. For example, a trash can icon will allow a user to "throw out" a document. Gives an application a "user friendly" feel. Desktop metaphors are consistent throughout all Windows and windows-like applications, like Sparc's OPEN LOOK.

DESPUN ANTENNA Of a rotating communications satellite, an antenna, the direction of whose main beam with respect to the satellite is continually adjusted so that it illuminates a given area on the surface of the Earth, i.e., the footprint does not move.

DESTINATION ADDRESS That part of a message which indicates for whom the message is intended. Usually a collection of characters or bits. Just like putting a destination address on an envelope. On a token ring network this is a 48-bit sequence that uniquely defines the physical name of the computer to which a LAN data packet is being sent. The IEEE assures that in the world of LANs no two devices have the same physical address. It does so by assigning certain numbers to vendors of token ring adapters, the devices that connect computers to a token ring network.

DESTINATION CODE See DESTINATION FIELD.

DESTINATION FIELD The field in a message header that contains the network address of the individual for whom the message is meant and who will (with luck and good management) receive the message.

DESTINATION NODE Those system nodes which receive messages over the control packet network from the source or transmitting node.

DESTUFFING The controlled deletion of stuffing bits from a stuffed digital signal, to recover the original signal.

DETECTOR 1. In a radio receiver, a circuit or device that recovers the signal of interest from the modulated wave. 2. In an optical communications receiver, a device that converts the received optical signal to another form. Currently, this conversion is from optical to electrical power; however, optical-to-optical techniques are under development.

DETEM An opto-electronic transducer that combines the function of an optical detector and emitter in a single device or module.

DETRAINING Getting off a train. An absolutely ghastly word invented by the railroad industry to keep them on a par with new, awful language invented by the airline industry. See also DEPLANING.

DETECTOR A device which converts or rectifies high frequency oscillations into a pulsating direct current or which translates radio frequency power into a form suitable for the operation of an indicator. This is most frequently a vacuum tube, less commonly a crystal. Coherers and delicate chemical rectifiers were used in former years.

DETENT TUNER "Click" type of TV tuner.

DEVICE CONTROL A multimedia definition. Device control enables you to control different media devices over the network through software. The media devices include VCRs, laser disc players, video cameras, CD players, and so on. Control capabilities are available on the workstation through a graphical user interface. They are similar to the controls on the device itself, such as play, record, reverse, eject, and fast forward. Device control is important because it enables you to control video and audio remotely — without requiring physical access.

DEVICE DRIVER A special type of program that controls devices attached to the computer, such as a printer, a scanner, a diskette drive, hard disk, monitor or mouse. Device drivers are typically loaded low into the memory of IBM machines/clones by the CONFIG.SYS Device command, or they're loaded high using the Devicehigh command. A device driver is software that expands an operating system's ability to work with peripherals. A device driver controls the software routines that make peripherals (an audio response unit, a RAM disk, a print spooler) work. They may be part of another program (many applications include device drivers for printers) or they may be separate programs. DOS comes with two device drivers: ANSI.SYS and VDISK.SYS. The first is to expand the capabilities of the keyboard. The second is used to carve a RAM (Random Access Memory) disk out of the 640K of RAM that MS-DOS can address. These two device drivers are loaded from your CONFIG.SYS file when you boot up the computer. See COMMAND PROCESSOR.

DFA Doped Fiber Amplifier.

DFI Digital Facility Interface. An 5ESS switch circuitry in a DTLU responsible for terminating a single digital facility and generating one PIDB.

DG Directorate General (CEC).

DGPS Differential Global Positioning Service — a new venture of the US Coast Guard, which it hopes to have ready by 1996. It will use an existing network of radio beacons throughout the US to create a fixed grid of known reference points in order to improve the accuracy of the Defense Department's GPS signal. The Coast Guard hopes to achieve an accuracy of about 10 meters.

DGT Direccion General de Telecommunicaciones (Spanish General Directorate of Telecommunications).

DHRYSTONES Benchmark program for testing the speed of a computer. It tests a general mix of instructions. The results in Dhrystones per second are the number of times the program can be executed in one second. The Dhrystone benchmark program is used as a standard indicating aspects of a computer system's performance in areas other than its floating-point performance, for instance, integer processes per second, enumeration, record and pointer manipulation. Since the program does not use any floating-point operations, performs no I/O, and makes no operating system calls, it is most applicable to measuring the performance of systems programming applications. The program was developed in 1984 and was originally written in Ada, although the C and PASCAL versions became more popular by 1989. See WHETSTONES.

DIA/DCA Document Interchange Architecture/Document Content Architecture. IBM promulgated architectures, part of SNA, for transmission and storage of documents over networks, whether text, data, voice or video. Becoming industry standards by default.

DIAGNOSTIC PROGRAMS Programs run by the computer portion of a PBX to detect faults in the system. Such programs may run automatically at regular intervals or continuously. The goal of diagnostic programs is to detect faults before they become serious and to alert someone — typically the attendant — to do fix it. Some diagnostic programs stop running when the switch gets too busy. Some don't. You can dial into some diagnostic programs from afar. And you can't in some. Remote diagnostic programs are probably the greatest boons to improved reliability of telephone systems.

DIAL A PRAYER A sarcastic name for the local 611 number run by the local telephone companies as their centralized number for repair.

DIAL BACKUP A network scheme using dial-up phone lines as a replacement for failed leased data lines. In one typical case, two dial-up lines can be used. One dial-up link is used to transmit data and the other to receive data, thus giving us full-duplex data transmission.

DIAL BY NAME You can dial someone by spelling their name out on the touchtone pad. Typically, the system plays a recorded announcement giving directions for using the Dial by Name feature: the caller then inputs the appropriate digits/letters. When the system recognizes a match, a recorded announcement states the name of the dialed party for confirmation by the caller before automatically completing the call. If the input digits are not uniquely associated with a particular station the system may ask the caller to pick a name from a menu of choices. Dial by name is getting cheaper. Automated attendants are being programmed to have the feature. And you shouldn't buy an auto attendant unless it has this feature.

DIAL CALL PICKUP A phone user on a PBX or hybrid can dial a special code and answer calls ringing on any other phone within his own predefined pickup group.

DIAL DICTATION ACCESS A service feature available with some switching systems that permits dialing a special number to access centralized dictation equipment.

DIAL IT 900 SERVICE A special one-way mass calling service that allows prospects, customers and others to reach you from anywhere across the country. In contrast to 800-service, the caller pays the 900 charge, generally one charge for the first minute, with a lesser charge for each additional minute. DIAL-IT 900 Service is a great way to involve your customers and prospects in a promotion! Premium Billing lets you select a rate above standard DIAL-IT 900 rates. The long distance carriers (through their deals with local phone companies) handle the billing. You, the information provider, split the revenues with the long distance provider. International DIAL-IT 900 service is currently available from a growing number of countries.

DIAL LEVEL The selection of stations or services associated with a PBX, based on the first digit(s) dialed.

DIAL PICK-UP PBX feature. A phone on a PBX can answer another ringing phone by dialing a few digits. Also called an access code.

DIAL PULSING A means of signaling consisting of regular momentary interruptions of a direct or alternating current at the sending end in which the number of interruptions corresponds to the value of the digit or character. In short, the old style of rotary dialing. Dial the number "five" and you'll hear five "clicks." See DIAL SPEED, DIAL TRAIN and DTMF.

DIAL PULSE SIGNALING A type of address signaling in which dial pulse is implemented to signal the distant equipment. See DIAL PULSING.

DIAL REPEATING TRUNKS PBX tie trunks used with terminating PBX equipment capable of handling telephone signaling without attendant involvement.

DIAL SERVICE ASSISTANCE DSA. A service feature associated with the switching center equipment to provide operator services, such as information, intercepting, random conferencing, and precedence calling assistance.

DIAL SPEED The number of pulses a rotary dial can send in a given period of time, typically 10 per second. A Hayes modem with a communications package, like Crosstalk, can send 20 pulses per second.

DIAL STRING In ISDN lingo, a dial string is a phone number.

DIAL THROUGH A technique, applicable to access circuits, that permits an outgoing routine call to be dialed by the PBX user after the PBX attendant has established the initial connection.

DIAL TONE The sound you hear when you pick up a telephone. Dial tone is a signal (350 + 440 Hz) from your local telephone company that it is alive and ready to receive the number you dial. If you have a PBX, dial tone will typically be provided by the PBX. Dial tone does not come from God or the telephone instrument on your desk. It comes from the switch to which your phone is connected to.

DIAL TONE DELAY The specific time that transpires between a subscriber's going off-hook and the receipt of dial tone from a servicing telephone central office. It's a measure of the time needed to provide dial tone to customers. Many of the local public service commissions in the United States say that 90% of customers should receive dial tone in fewer than three seconds.

DIAL TONE FIRST COIN SERVICE A type of pay phone service in which dial tone is received when the caller goes off-hook and coins must be inserted only after the call is connected.

DIAL TRAIN The series of pulses or tones sent from the phone that's calling and the switching system it's attached to in order to signify the call's destination.

DIAL UP The use of a dial or pushbutton telephone to create a telephone or data call. Dial-up calls are usually billed by time of day, duration of call and distance traveled. See DIAL UP LINE.

DIAL UP LINE A telephone line which is part of the switched nationwide telephone system.

DIAL ZERO PHONE A telephone on a Northern Telecom Norstar phone system which is assigned to ring when someone dials 0 (zero) from another Norstar telephone.

DIALAN DMS Integrated Access Local Area Network

DIALED NUMBER IDENTIFICATION SERVICE See DNIS and 800 SERVICE.

DIALED NUMBER RECORDER Also called a Pen Register. An instrument that records telephone dial pulses as inked dashes on paper tape. A touch-tone decoder performs the same thing for a touch-tone telephone.

DIALING PLAN A description of the dialing arrangements for customer use on a network.

DIALOG BOX A dialog box is a temporary window which prompts you to input information or make selections necessary for a task to continue.

DIALOGIC Dialogic Corporation, Parsippany, NJ, is one of the leading manufacturers of interactive voice processing equipment and software. They sell equipment through value added resellers, dealers and distributors. Many of their dealers "add value" to the Dialogic components by doing their own specialized software programming, tailoring Dialogic products to particular specialized (and useful) applications.

DIAPHRAGM The thin flexible sheet which vibrates in response to sound waves (as in a microphone) or in response to electrical signals (as in a speaker or the receiver of telephone handset).

DIBIT A group of two bits which can be represented by a single change of modulation of the carrier signal. On phase modulation, one of four phases in four-phase modulation is used to represent 00, 01, 10 or 11.

DICHROIC FILTER An optical filter designed to transmit light selectively according to wavelength (most often, a high-pass or low-pass filter).

DICHROIC MIRROR A mirror designed to reflect light selectively according to wavelength.

DICTATION ACCESS AND CONTROL A telephone system feature which allows a user to dial a dictation machine and use that machine (giving it instructions by pushbutton) as if it were in his office. Typically, the material on that dictation machine is taken off by one or several typists of a centralized pool and word processed into letters, reports, legal briefs, etc. Telephone suppliers usually don't supply the dictation equipment. Newer telephone dictation machinery is, in reality, a specialized application of voice processing equipment. See VOICE PROCESSING.

DICTATION TANK A recording gadget which receives messages dictated through the telephone system. This tank contains tape which can then be transcribed into letters or documents. See DICTATION ACCESS AND CONTROL.

DID Direct Inward Dialing. You can dial inside a company directly without going through the attendant. This feature used to be an exclusive feature of Centrex but it can now be provided by virtually all modern PBXs and some modern hybrids.

DIEL Advisory committee on telecommunications for DIsabled and Elderly People (UK).

DIELECTRIC A nonconducting or insulating substance which resists passage of electric current, allowing electrostatic induction to act across it, as in the insulating medium between the plates of a condenser. Also an insulating material otherwise used (e.g. a Bakelite panel, or the cambric covering of a wire is a dielectric material). See also SEMICONDUCTOR.

DIELECTRIC ABSORPTION The penetration of a dielectric by the electric strain during a period of time.

DIELECTRIC CONSTANT The ratio of the capacity of a condenser with a given dielectric to the capacity of the same condenser with air as the dielectric.

DIELETRIC LENS A lens made of dieletric material that refracts radio waves in the same material that an optical lens refracts light waves.

DIELECTRIC PROCESS A printing process that uses a specially treated, charge-sensitive paper. Paper is roller-fed past an electrode array where an electrical charge is applied on line-by-line to form a latent image, then passed through a toner. The toner adheres to the charged image and heat fuses the toner to the paper to create the printed document.

DIELECTRIC SHEATH OR CABLE A sheath or cable that contains no electrically conducting materials such as metals. Dielectric cables are sometimes used in areas subject to high lightning or electro-magnetic interference. Synonym for nonmetallic cable.

DIELECTRIC STRENGTH The property of material which resists the passage of an electric current. It is measured in terms of voltage required to break down this resistance (such as volts per mil.).

DIELECTRIC TEST A test in which a voltage higher than the rated voltage is applied for a specified time to determine the adequacy of the insulation under normal conditions.

DIFFERENTIAL MODULATION Modulation in which information is encoded into differences of successive signals. Delta modulation is an example.

DIFFERENTIAL PHASE-SHIFT KEYING DPSK. A modulation technique in which the relative changes of the carrier signal's phase are coded according to the data to be transmitted. See PHASE SHIFT KEYING.

DIFFERENTIAL POSITIONING Precise measurements of the relative positions of two receivers tracking the same GPS (Global Positioning System) signals.

DIFFIE-HELLMAN KEY A technique of changing encryption techniques on the fly. In a landmark 1976 paper, called New Directions in Cryptograph, IEEE Transactions on Information Theory, W. Diffie and M. Hellman describe a method by which a secret key can be exchanged using messages that do not need to be kept secret. This type of "public" key management provides a significant cost advantage by eliminating the need for a courier service. In addition, security can be considerably enhanced by permitting more frequent key changes and eliminating the need for any individual to have access to the key's actual value.

DIFFRACTION The deviation of a wavefront from the path predicted by geometric optcis when a wavefront is restricted by an opening or an edge. Diffraction is usually most noticeable for openings of the order of a wavelength.

DIFFRACTION GRATING An array of fine, parallel, equally spaced reflecting or transmitting lines that mutually enhance the effects of diffraction at the edges of each so as to concentrate the diffracted light very close to a few directions depending on the spacing of the lines and the wavelength of the diffracted light.

DIGIPATH A New York and New England Telephone service, Digipath

Digital Service provides point-to-point and multi-point full duplex, two-way, private digital data communications at synchronous data rates of 2.4, 4.8, 9.6, 19.2 and 56 Kbps within a New York State Regional Calling Area (RCA).

DIGIPATH OPTION: SECONDARY CHANNEL CAPABILITY An optional feature for New York Telephone's 56 Kbps Digipath service. It allows customers a second channel at 2.6 Kbps, independent of the primary channel. Customers usually use this "extra" channel for diagnosing the line; for running network management over the same line; or to transmit a second, lower speed data stream through the same line.

DIGIT Any whole number from 0 to 9.

DIGIT DELETION It's nice to make it easy for people to dial their desired numbers. Part of making it "nice" is to keep their pattern of dialing consistent. The charm of our ten-digit numbering system in North America — the three digit area code and seven digit local number — is its consistency, making for easy use and easy remembering. Some corporate networks, however, don't use a common numbering scheme. They might use tie trunks to get to Chicago, and insist on the user dialing 69, instead of the more common 312 area code. They might insist on the user dialing 73 when he wants to go to Los Angeles. But if he wants to reach the LA office, he might dial 235. This can be awfully confusing. So some switches — central office and PBXs — have the ability to insert or delete digits. That is, they will recognize the number dialed and change it as it progresses through the network. The user, however, knows nothing of this. He simply dials a normal phone number and listens as his call progresses normally. Digit insertion and digit deletion are components of a PBX feature called common number dialing.

DIGIT INSERTION See DIGIT DELETION.

DIGITAL 1. In displays, the use of digits for direct readout. 2. In telecommunications, in recording or in computing, digital is the use of a binary code to represent information. See PCM (as in Pulse Code Modulation.) Analog signals — like voice or music — are encoded digitally by sampling the voice or music analog signal many times a second and assigning a number to each sample. Recording or transmitting information digitally has two major benefits. First, the signal can be reproduced precisely. In a long telecommunications transmission circuit, the signal will progressively lose its strength and progressively pick up distortions, static and other electrical interference "noises."

In analog transmission, the signal, along with all the garbage it picked up, is simply amplified. In digital transmission, the signal is first regenerated. It's put through a little "Yes-No" question. Is this signal a "one" or a "zero?" The signal is reconstructed (i.e. squared off) to what it was identically. Then it is amplified and sent along its way. So digital transmission is much "cleaner" than analog transmission. The second major benefit of digital is that the electronic circuitry to handle digital is getting cheaper and more powerful. It's the stuff of computers. Analog transmission equipment doesn't lend itself to the technical breakthroughs of recent years in digital. See also PCM, as in Pulse Code Modulation.

DIGITAL ACCESS AND CROSS-CONNECT SYSTEM See DACS and DIGITAL CROSS-CONNECT SYSTEM.

DIGITAL AUDIO The storage and processing of audio signals digitally. It usually requires at least 16 bits of linear coding to represent each digital sample.

DIGITAL AUDIO TAPE See DAT.

DIGITAL CELLULAR The state of the art in cellular communications technology. Implementation will result in substantial increases in capacity (up to 15 times that of analog technology). In addition, digital will virtually eliminate three major problems encountered by users of analog cellular: static, loss/interruption of signal when passing between cells (during handoff), and failure to get a connection because of congested relays.

DIGITAL CIRCUIT MULTIPLICATION DCM is a variation of analog TASI — Time Assigned Speech Interpolation. In DCM, speech is encoded digitally and advanced voiceband coding algorithms are applied to TASI's old speech interpolation techniques. DCM delivers a four to fivefold increase in the effective capacity of normal pulse code modulation (PCM) T-1 links operating at 1.544 megabits per second. DCM equipment is used on the TAT-8 transatlantic optical fiber submarine cable. Most DCM equipment has three operating elements: a speech activity detector. An assignment mapping and message unit, and a speech reconstitution unit. See February, 1987 issue of Data Communications for more.

DIGITAL COMMAND SIGNAL Signal sent by a fax machine or card when the caller is transmitting, which tells the answerer how to receive the fax. Modem speed, image width, image encoding and page length are all included in this frame.

DIGITAL COMMUNICATIONS MANAGER DCM. An MCI monitoring system that maintains communications through the network with the Site Controllers, the Extended Super-frame Monitoring Units, and the 1/O DXCs. The DCM issues requests for data and collects alarm and performance information, which is processed and stored in real-time for further computation and display.

DIGITAL COMPACT CASSETTE DCC. A digital version of the familiar analog audio cassette. A DCC recorder can play and record both analog and digital cassettes. But the digital ones will sound a lot better.

DIGITAL CROSS-CONNECT SYSTEM DACS or DCS. A specialized type of high-speed data channel switch. It differs from a normal voice switch, which switches transmission paths in response to dialing instructions. In a digital cross-connect system, you give it separate and specific instructions to connect this line to that. These instructions are given independently of any calls that might flow over the system. This contrasts with a normal voice switching in which switching instructions and conversations go together. Commands to a digital cross-connect system can be given by an operator at a console or can be programmed to switch at certain times. For example, you might want to change the T-1 24-voice conversation circuit to Chicago at 11 A.M. each day to allow for the president's 30 minute video-conference call.

DIGITAL ECHO CANCELLER A Digital Echo Canceller is an echo canceller as opposed to an echo suppresser. An echo canceller filtersout unwanted echoes among incoming signals, while the echo suppresser shut-offs the entire signal, by using an analog voice switch. The Digital Echo Canceller is one application of a digital transversal filter.

DIGITAL ENVELOPING Digital enveloping is an application in which someone "seals" a message m in such a way that no one other than the intended recipient, say "Bob," can "open" the sealed message. The typical implementation of digital enveloping involves a secret-key algorithm for encrypting the message (i.e., a content-encryption algorithm) and a public-key algorithm for encrypting the secret key (i.e., a key-encryption algorithm)

DIGITAL FACILITIES MANAGEMENT SYSTEM A Northern Telecom software which integrates the maintenance of all types of digital facilities from T-1 to the high-bit fiber. Largely used by telephone companies.

DIGITAL FACSIMILE EQUIPMENT Facsimile equipment that employs digital techniques to encode the image detected by the scanner. The output signal may be either digital or analog. Examples of digital facsimile equipment are CCITT Group 3, CCITT Group 4, STANAG 5000 Type I and STANAG 5000 Type II.

DIGITAL FREQUENCY MODULATION The transmission of digital data by frequency modulation of a carrier, as in binary frequency-shift keying.

DIGITAL LAT PROTOCOL The LAT protocol, announced by Digital in the mid '80s, is today one of the industry's most widely used protocols for supporting character terminals over Ethernet networks. See LAT.

DIGITAL LOOPBACK A diagnostic feature on a modem, a short-haul microwave or some other digital transmission equipment which allows the user to loop a signal back from one part of the system to another to test the circuit or the equipment. Digital loopbacks can be as long or as short as are necessary to isolate the problem. By looping a signal back and measuring it at both ends of the loop (at the beginning and at the end), you can see if the device carried the message cleanly and is thus, operating correctly.

DIGITAL MICROWAVE A microwave system in which the modulation of the radio frequency carrier is digital. The carrier is still a standard microwave radio wave. The digital modulation may be frequency or phase shift, but the control of that modulation is the digital bit stream.

DIGITAL MONITOR Opposite of analog. Receives discrete binary signals at two levels; one level corresponds to Logic 1 (true) while the other corresponds to Logic O (false). Monitors generally were of this type before VGA models appeared. Digital monitors do not have as wide a range of color choices as analog types; digital EGA monitors, for example, can display just 16 colors out of a palette of 64.

DIGITAL MULTIPLEXER A device for combining digital signals. Usually implemented by interleaving bits, in rotation, from several digital bit streams either with or without the addition of extra framing, control, or error detection bits. In short, equipment that combines by time-division multiplexing several signals into a single composite digital signal.

DIGITAL MULTIPLEX HIERARCHY An ordered scheme for the combining of digital signals by the repeated application of digital multiplexing. Digital multiplexing schemes may be implemented in many different configurations depending upon the number of channels desired, the signaling system to be used, and the bit rate allowed by the communication medium. Some currently available multiplexers have been designated as D1-, DS-, or M-series, all of which operate at T-carrier rates. Extreme care must be exercised when selecting equipment for a specific system to ensure interoperability, because there are incompatibilities among manufacturers' designs (and various nations' standards).

DIGITAL NETWORK A network in which the information is encoded as a series of ones and zeros rather than as a continuously varying wave — as in traditional analog networks. Digital networks have several major pluses over analog ones. First, they're "cleaner." They have far less noise, static, etc. Second, they're easier to monitor because you can measure them more easily. Third, you can typically pump more digital information down a communications line than you can analog information.

DIGITAL PHASE-LOCKED LOOP A phase-locked loop in which the reference signal, the controlled signal, or the controlling signal, or any combination of these, is in digital form.

DIGITAL PHASE MODULATION The process whereby the instantaneous phase of the modulated wave is shifted between a set of predetermined discrete values in accordance with the significant conditions of the modulating digital signal.

DIGITAL PORT ADAPTER DPA. A device which provides conversion from the RS449/422 interface to the more common interfaces of RS-232-C, v.35, WE-306 and others.

DIGITAL RECORDING A system of recording by conversion of musical information into a series of pulses that are translated into a binary code intelligible to computer circuits and stored on magnetic tape or magnetic discs. Also called PCM - Pulse Code Modulation.

DIGITAL SELECTIVE CALLING DSC. A synchronous system developed by the International Radio Consultative Committee (CCIR), used to establish contact with a station or group of stations automatically by radio. The operational and technical characteristics of this system are contained in CCIR Recommendation 493.

DIGITAL SIGNAL A discontinuous signal. One whose state consists of discrete elements, representing very specific information. When viewed on an oscilloscope, a digital signal is "squared." This compares with an analog signal which typically looks more like a sine wave, i.e. curvy. Usually amplitude is represented at discrete time intervals with a digital value.

DIGITAL SIGNAL PROCESSOR A specialized digital microprocessor that performs calculations on digitized signals that were originally analog (e.g. voice) and then sends the results on. The big advantage of a DSP lies in the programmability of digital microprocessors. DSPs are beginning to be used extensively in telecommunications for tasks such as echo cancellation, call progress monitoring, voice processing and for the compression of voice signals to as few as 4,800 bps. They are also used for everything from fetal monitors, to anti-skid brakes, seismic and vibration sensing devices, super-sensitive hearing aids, multimedia presentations and low-cost desktop fax machines. DSPs will do (and are already doing) for the telecom industry what the general purpose microprocessor (e.g. Intel's 80286 or 80386) did for the personal computer industry. DSPs are made by Analog Devices, AT&T, Motorola, NEC and Texas Instruments, among others.

DIGITAL SIGNATURE The network equivalent of signing a message so that you cannot deny that you sent it and that the recipient knows it must have come from you.

DIGITAL SPEECH INTERPOLATION DSI. A type of multiplexing. A way of sharing bandwidth among a larger number of users than we really have circuits for. DSI allocates the silent periods in human speech to active users. At least 50% of a voice conversation is always quiet. The technique was originally called TASI (Time Assigned Speech Interpolation). TASI and DSI are lousy for data because they "clip" the first little bit of every new snippet of conversation — unless you hog the channel the whole time by talking incessantly or transmitting continuously. If you pause, you'll get clipping as the system drops you and then reconnects you. Clipping can ruin the meaning of the beginning of data conversations, unless the header knows that TASI or DSI is coming up or the data transmission is following some reasonable protocol and can resend the data. Unfortunately, this slows transmission. DSI and TASI are somewhat similar techniques to STATISTICAL MULTIPLEXING.

DIGITAL SUBSCRIBER LINE A fancy name for an ISDN BRI channel.

Here's AT&T's definition: "A three-channel digital line that links the ISDN customer's terminal to the telephone company switch with four ordinary copper telephone wires. Operated at the Basic Rate Interface (with two 64-kilobit per second circuit-switched channels and one 16-kilobit packet switched channel), the DSL can carry both voice and data signals at the same time, in both directions, as well as the signaling date used for call information and customer data. With the introduction of the AT&T 5E5 generic, up to eight different users can be served by a single DSL." See also ISDN.

DIGITAL SWITCHING A connection in which binary encoded information is routed between an input and an output port by means of time-division multiplexing rather than by a dedicated circuit.

DIGITAL TO ANALOG CONVERSION A circuit that accepts digital signals and converts them into analog signals. A modem typically has such a circuit. It also has other circuits, such as those doing with signaling. See MODEM.

DIGITAL VIDEO INTERACTIVE DVI. A compression and playback technology originally developed by RCA's Sarnoff Research Institute and eventually acquired by Intel Corp. DVI is not a compression technique per se but a brand name for a set of processor chips that Intel is developing to compress video onto disk and to de-compress it for playback in real time at the U.S. standard motion video rate of 30 frames per second. The chip set includes both a pixel processor, which performs most of the decompression and also handles special video effects, and a display processor, which performs the rest of the decompression and produces the video output. DVI's greatest long-term advantage, according to Nick Arnett writing in PC Magazine, is that its microprocessors are programmable, so DVI can be adapted to a variety of compression and decompression schemes.

DIGITIZE Converting an analog or continuous signal into a series of ones and zeros, i.e. into a digital format. See DELTA MODULATION and PULSE CODE MODULATION. See also the Appendix.

DIGITIZED VOICE Analog voice signals represented in digital form. There are many ways of digitizing voice. See PULSE CODE MODULATION for the most common.

DIGITIZER 1. A device that converts an analog signal into a digital representation of that signal. Usually implemented by sampling the analog signal at a regular rate and encoding each sample into a numeric representation of the amplitude value of the sample. 2. A device that converts the position of a point on a surface into digital coordinate data.

DIGROUP Two groups of 12 digital channels combined to form one single 24-channel T-1 system.

DIKES A wire-cutter.

DILUTION OF PRECISION The multiplicative factor that modifies the ranging error. It is caused solely by the geometry between the user and his set of GPS (Global Positioning System) satellites. Known as DOP or GDOP.

DIM Document Image Management. The electronic access to and manipulation of documents stored in image format, accomplished through the use of automated methods such as high-powered graphical workstations, sophisticated database manangement techniques and networking.

DIMENSION An analog PBX that used PAM techniques, first introduced in the late 1970s by Western Electric (now AT&T Technologies) for AT&T. Now effectively discontinued except for the hotel/motel version. Some claim Archie McGill was responsible for Dimension. Others claim it was Bob Hawke.

DIMS Document Image Management System.

DIN Deutsche Institut fur Normung (German Institute for Standardization).

DINA Distributed Intelligence Network Architecture.

DIOCES Distributed Interoperable and Operable Computing Environments and Systems.

DIODE This wonderful explanation comes from George Gilder's book Microcosm: "Named from the Greek words meaning two roads, an ordinary diode is one of the simplest and most useful of tools. It is a tiny block of silicon made positive on one side and negative on the other. At each end it has a terminal or electrode (route for electrons). In the middle of the silicon block, the positive side meets the negative side in an electrically complex zone called a positive-negative, or p-n, junction. Because a diode is positive on one side and negative on the other, it normally conducts current only in one direction. Thus diodes play an indispensable role as rectifiers. That is, they can take alternating current (AC) from your wall and convert it into direct current (DC) to run your computer.

"In this role, diodes demonstrate a prime law of electrons. Negatively charged, electrons flow only toward a positive voltage. They cannot flow back against the grain. Like water pressure, which impels current only in the direction of the pressure, voltage impels electrical current only in the direction of the voltage. To attempt to run current against a voltage is a little like attaching a gushing hose to a running faucet.

"It had long been known, however, that if you apply a strong enough voltage against the grain of a diode, the p-n wall or junction will burst. Under this contrary pressure, or reverse bias, the diode will eventually suffer what is called avalanche breakdown. Negative electrons will overcome the p-n barrier by brute force of numbers and flood "uphill" from the positive side to the negative side. In erasable programmable read-only memories (EPROMs), this effect is used in programming computer chips used to store permanent software, such as the Microsoft operating system in your personal computer (MS-DOS). Avalanche breakdown is also used in Zener diodes to provide a stable source of voltage unaffected by changes in current."

DIODE MATRIX RINGING A method of connecting a common audible line to a system so that all stations do not ring on all lines. See also MATRIX RINGING.

DIODEA A semiconductor device which allows electricity to pass through it in only one direction, restricting flow the other way.

DIP 1. See DIP SWITCH. 2. Document Image Processing. A term for converting paperwork into electronic images manipulable by a computer. Components of include input via scanner, storage on optical media and output via video display terminal, printer, fax, micrographics, etc.

DIP SWITCH Dual In-Line Package. A teeny tiny switch usually attached to a printed circuit board. It may peek through an opening in a piece of equipment. It may not. It usually requires a ball point pen or small screwdriver to change. There are only two settings — on or off. Or 1 or 0. But printed circuit boards often have many DIP switches. They're used to configure the board in a semipermanent way. The DIP switches are similar to integrated circuit chips which have two rows (dual) of pins in a row (in-line) that fit into holes on a printed circuit board. If something doesn't work when you first install it, check the dip switches first. Then check the cable connecting it to something else.

DIPLEXER A device that permits parallel feeding of one antenna from two transmitters at the same or different frequencies without the transmitters interfering with each other. Diplexers couple transmitter and receiver to the same antenna for use in mobile communications.

DIPOLE Antenna fed from the center. Name often applied to "rabbit ear" antenna.

DIRECT BOND An electrical connection using continuous metal-to-metal contact between the things being joined.

DIRECT BROADCAST SATELLITE DBS. A satellite transmitting TV programs which can be received by small and somewhat inexpensive dish antennas often installed in backyards or on the roofs of houses. Direct broadcast satellites have generated more interest in Europe, which suffers from a lack of TV programs (good and bad), than in the U.S. which has plenty. The backyard satellite antennas you see in America are not receiving signals from Direct Broadcast Satellites. They are receiving them from satellites designed to transmit and receive from large, commercial dishes.

DIRECT CONNECT A term describing a customer hooking directly into a long-distance telephone company's switching office, bypassing the local phone company. Such "direct connect" could be via a leased copper pair, a specially-run copper pair, a fiber optic or a private microwave system. See DIRECT ELECTRICAL CONNECTION, which is different. See DIRECT CONNNECT MODEM.

DIRECT CONNECT MODEM A modem connected to telephone lines using a modular plug or wired directly to the outside phone line. It thus transfers electrical signals directly to the phone network without any intermediary protective device. Direct connect modems must be certified by the FCC. Direct connect modems are more much reliable and more accurate than acoustically coupled modems. Virtually all modems these days are directly connected. One day payphones will even come with RJ-11 jacks into which you can plug the modem of your portable laptop computer.

DIRECT CONTROL SWITCHING The switching path is set up directly through the network by dial pulses without the use of central control. The telex network is an example of direct control switching. A step by step central office also uses direct control switching.

DIRECT CURRENT DC. A flow of electricity always in the same direction. Contrast with alternate current (AC).

DIRECT CURRENT SIGNALING DX. A method whereby the signaling circuit E & M leads use the same cable pair as the voice circuit and no filter is required to separate the control signals from the voice transmission.

DIRECT DEPARTMENT CALLING DDC. A telephone service that routes incoming calls on a specific trunk or group of trunks to specific phones or groups of phones.

DIRECT DISTANCE DIALING DDD. A telephone service which lets a user dial long distance calls directly to telephones outside the user's local service area without operator assistance.

DIRECT ELECTRICAL CONNECTION A metallic connection between two things. The normal electrical way of connecting two things. This dumb definition is included in this dictionary because there was a time back in the early 1970s and before, when you couldn't (i.e. weren't allowed to) directly electrically connect your own phone or phone system to the nation's phone network. Those were the "good old days" when they (the Bell System) were trying to convince the world that electrically connecting anyone else's phones could harm the network. They never did prove this, and so today we have direct electrical connection of FCC-certified phone equipment. It's certified so it won't cause any harm to the network. See PART 68.

DIRECT IN TERMINATION Incoming calls on a PBX may be programmed to route directly to preselected telephones without the attendant intervening. DIT features may be assigned to trunk circuits on a day, night or full time basis. Direct In Termination is slightly different from DIRECT INWARD DIALING, though how different depends on whose PBX you're using.

DIRECT INTERLATA CONNECTING TRUNK GROUPS Those trunk groups used for switched LATA access that interconnect Interexchange Carriers (IXCs) used to connect that Point of Presence (POPs) directly with the Bell Operating Company (BOC) end office switching system.

DIRECT INWARD DIALING DID. The ability for a caller outside a company to call an internal extension without having to pass through an operator or attendant. In large PBX systems, the dialed digits are passed down the line from the CO (central office). The PBX then completes the call. Direct Inward Dialing is often proposed as Centrex's major feature. See also DIRECT INWARD SYSTEM ACCESS (DISA) for another approach to DID.

DIRECT INWARD SYSTEM ACCESS DISA. This feature of a telephone system allows an outside caller to dial directly into the telephone system and to access all the system's features and facilities. DISA is typically used for making long distance calls from home using the company's less expensive long distance lines, like WATS or tie lines. It's also used for leaving dictation for the typing pool. With DISA, you can dial individual extensions without the aid (or hindrance) of an operator. To use DISA, one must punch in from your touchtone phone a short string of numbers as a password code.

The problem with DISA is that "phone phreakers" (i.e. unauthorized people) often acquire that number or figure it out and run up expensive long distance phone calls. It's best to restrict DISA to trusted people and check the numbers called and bills generated. Changing the password code from time to time can help prevent this. DISA is acquiring a whole new life. It's becoming something called AUTOMATED ATTENDANT. An additional piece of equipment, called an automated attendant, is placed next to the phone system. You dial a special phone number (as you do with DISA). You're answered by a recording that says "Dial the extension you want." In DISA, the response is typically just a tone. An automated attendant is designed to save on operators and speed up outside people getting to talk to your inside people. Automated attendant is being suggested as a lower-cost alternative to Centrex.

The following is excerpted from a document Northern Telecom sent to its PBX users. Read it. It's well-done:

PBX features that are vulnerable to unauthorized access include call forwarding, call prompting and call processing features. But the most common ways hackers enter a company's PBX is through Direct Inward System Access (DISA) and voice mail systems. They often search a company's trash for directories or call detail reports that contain 800 numbers and codes. They have also posed as systems administrators and conned employees into telling them PBX authorization codes. More "sophisticated" hackers use personal computers and modems to break into databases containing customer records showing phone numbers and voice mail access codes, or simply dial 800 numbers with the help of sequential number generators and computers until they find one code that gives access to a phone system. Once these thieves have the numbers and codes, they can call into the PBX and place calls out to other locations. In many cases, the PBX is only the first point of entry for such criminals. They can also use the PBX to access the company's data system. Call-sell operators can even hide their activities from law enforcement officials by using "PBX-looping" - using one PBX to place calls out through another switch in another state.

To minimize the vulnerability of the Meridian 1 system to unauthorized access through DISA, the following safeguards are suggested:

1) Assign restricted Class of Service, TGAR and NCOS to the DISA DN.

2) Require users to enter a security code upon reaching the DISA DN.

3) In addition to a security code, require users to enter an authorization code. The calling privileges provided will be associated with the specific authorization code.

4) Use Call Detail Recording (CDR) to identify calling activity associated with individual authorization codes. As a further precaution, you may choose to limit printed copies of these records.

5) Change security codes frequently.

6) Limit access to administration of authorization codes to a few, carefully selected employees.

DIRECT LINE TERMINATIONS The term refers to central office/PBX lines which terminate directly on telephones, and are generally common to all instruments within the system. In a square configuration on a Key Telephone System, these lines must appear at the same button location on each phone.

DIRECT MEMORY ACCESS DMA is a technique in which on adapter bypasses a computer's CPU, and handles the transfer of data between itself and the system's memory directly.

DIRECT OUTWARD DIALING DOD. The ability to dial directly from an extension without having to go through an operator or attendant. In PBX and hybrid phone systems, you dial 9, listen for a dial tone, and then dial the number you want to reach. In some phone systems, you don't have to listen for the second dial tone. You can dial straight through. All phone systems now have DOD. The older ones didn't, especially cordboard PBXs. Some Club Meds and lots of cheap hotels (especially the ones Harry — the editor — stays in) do not have DOD.

DIRECT STATION SELECT DSS. A piece of key system equipment usually attached to an operator's phone set. When the operator needs to call a particular extension he/she simply touches the corresponding button on the Direct Station Select equipment. Typically DSS equipment/feature is part of a Busy Lamp Field (BLF), which shows with lights what's happening at each extension. Is it busy? Is it on hold, etc.?

DIRECT STATION SELECT INTERCOM DSS. An interoffice caller can punch one button on his or her phone and dial his desired person, instead of dialing the full intercom number. Direct station select is like having an auto dial or speed dial button for everyone in the office. DSS saves time, but adds more buttons to the phone — one button for each extension the user wants to dial.

DIRECT TERMINATION OVERFLOW DTO. An optional MCI Vnet and 800 Service feature, which allows a call to "overflow" to shared lines for completion by the local telephone company if the dedicated line is busy.

DIRECT TRUNK A trunk between two class 5 central offices.

DIRECT TRUNK ACCESS A PBX feature. By dialing some digits, the attendant can directly access any specific trunk. You'd do this if you want to check the trunk for problems, etc.

DIRECT TRUNK SELECT Permits you, the user, or the attendant to access an individual outgoing trunk instead of one chosen by the PBX from a group of trunks. You may want to grab a special trunk to get access to a specially conditioned data line, for example.

DIRECTED CALL PICKUP An extension user on a phone system user can answer calls — ringing or holding — on any other phone by dialing a unique answer code. If the call has already been answered by the called phone, the user who dials the answer code will join the connection in conference. Some tones will alert the conversing parties to the intrusion.

DIRECTIONAL ANTENNA An antenna which impels electrical waves with more energy in one direction than in another, or which receives electrical waves more readily from one direction than from another.

DIRECTIONAL COUPLER 1. A device put in a microwave system's waveguide to couple a transmitter and receiver to the same antenna. 2. A transmission coupling device for separately sampling (through a known coupling loss) either the forward (incident) or the backward (reflected) wave in a transmission line. A directional coupler may be used to sample either a forward or backward wave in a transmission line. A unidirectional coupler has available terminals or connections for sampling only one direction of transmission; a bidirectional coupler has available terminals for sampling both directions. For optical fiber applications.

DIRECTORIES Are places within a hard disk volume where you can store files or subdirectories. The term subdirectory is relative. A directory is a subdirectory only in relation to the directory above it. To a directory below it, the same directory is a parent directory.

DIRECTORY A list of all the files on a floppy diskette or hard disk. A directory may also contain other information such as the size of the files and the amount of free space remaining. 2. Also a telephone directory.

DIRECTORY ASSISTANCE DA. Formerly known as "Information", but changed because they were getting too many stupid questions. DA is provided by the local telephone company. It allows the subscriber to call for phone numbers. In most states, the local phone company charges for this service, or will begin to very shortly. AT&T and MCI charge for long distance directory assistance. Most local phone companies will give you the person's address as well as his phone number if you ask for it.

DIRECTORY CACHING A method of decreasing the time it takes to find a file's location on a PC's disk. The FAT (File Allocation Table) and directory entry table are written into the file server's memory. The area holding all directory entries is called the directory cache. The file server can find a file's address (from directory cache) and the file data (from the file cache) much faster than retrieving the information from disk.

DIRECTORY NUMBER 1. The full complement of digits associated with the name of a subscriber in a telephone directory. This is a very long way of saying the obvious, namely your phone number. 2. A unique phone number which is automatically assigned to each telephone or Data Terminal during System Startup. The DN, also referred to as an intercom number, is often used to identify a telephone when settings are assigned during programming.

DIRECTORY PACKAGE The process of adding, deleting and moving people attached to PBX or Centrex phones is more than simply programming in new extensions. Or should be. First, there are the changes necessary for the call accounting system. Second, there are changes necessary for "The Corporate Phone Directory". In the past, the directory bore little relation to the telephone system and it was often months, and sometimes years behind the actual phone system. Now some phone systems are incorporating various Directory Software Packages into the PBXs.

Some features included in these systems are the ability to dial someone by name — both for the attendant and for the individual phone user, i.e. dial HARRY, or HAR, instead of 3245. Some also include the ability to interface to the call accounting system. So that who's in what corporate department corresponds to which department's bill. There's also that important thing called a Telephone Directory. It would be useful if you could hook a laser printer to the telephone system and tell it to print, in neat, photo-ready columns, an alphabetical (by last name), departmental or any other sorted telephone directory. Some of the newer PBXs have "directory package" features which include some or all of the above. Most users find today's necessity of at least three different systems to be a pain in the behind. Rightly so. The three different systems are CDR, phone directory and extension dialing in the PBX. The three are often out of synch.

DIRECTORY SERVICE 1. A simple term for the information service which the telephone company runs on 411 or 555-1212. Also, 2. A computer networking term. The facility within networking software that provides information on resource available on the network, including files, users, printers, data sources, applications, and so on. The directory service provides users with access to resources and information on extended networks.

DIRECTORY TREE A list of directories. A directory tree looks like an organizational chart and shows how your directories and subdirectories are related. Our favorite program that shows the directory tree in your hard disk is called CTREE. You can pick it up from many electronic bulletin boards for free, including from TELECONNECT Magazine's on 212-989-4675.

DIRECTTALK A family of IBM voice processing products introduced in the summer of 1991. According to IBM, its "new IBM CallPath DirectTalk product line lets businesses automate routine operations and also provide callers with easy access to many kinds of information over the telephone — at any hour of the day and with greater accuracy. Businesses can raise the level of service they provide and do it with fewer people and with greater efficiency." According to IBM's press release, the North Carolina Employment Security Commission is using the DirectTalk product to automate the filing of unemployment benefit claims. For several years, the state has allowed claimants to verify their unemployment status by answering a series of questions on a postcard. Based on initial results, Claimants who use the telephone to answer the questions can receive checks up to four days sooner than if they answer by mail. For a Directtalk demo, call 1-800-IBM-4211.

DIRTBAGS Digitally Initiated Reorigination of Telecommunications Bypass Access Generated by Scum. A term created by Karen Corcoran of MCI's Atlanta office to describe as a group the various hackers, phreakers, and others who invade our networks and/or steal long distance service.

DIRTY POWER Dirty power typically refers to alternating current that is not a perfect sine wave and not perfectly 120 volt. There are all sorts of ways electricity can be made "dirty." It can be affected by spikes. Spikes are transient impulses (sometimes called glitches) of relatively high amplitude but very short duration. Spikes so short that a very high-speed oscilloscope is needed to observe them can often cause problems. Many spikes can occur in a fraction of a cycle.

Power can also be affected by sags and surges. Sags and surges are rapid changes in the amplitude of an AC voltage. These are generally caused by abrupt changes in the load on a power source or circuit (such as when an airconditioner starts up), and can range from a fraction of a cycle to several complete cycles. Power can also be delivered consistantly beyond its rating. In New York Con Edison guarantees 120 volts plus or minus 10%. Any level below 108 volts or above 132 volts Con Edison would consider dirty power. These are called low or high average variations. And they occur when the average voltage is above or below a desired level for significant periods of time, usually measured in seconds, minutes or longer.

Other kinds of dirty power include: Blackouts or brownouts. They occur when the power is switched off or lost completely (blackout), or when the voltage feeding a load is deliberately or inadvertently reduced significantly for a sustained period (brownout). Common-mode noise is a small (+1V-2V) signal that appears between a neutral line and ground (earth) where there should be no signal. High/low frequency variations occur when the instantaneous frequency of an AC power source differs from its normal frequency, e.g., 60 Hz, by 0.5 Hz or more. Phase-angle variations can be observed in three-phase systems whenever the phase relationships vary from their normal 120-degrees.

DIS Draft International Standard. As specified by ISO, a development step representing near final status on a specification. Once a specification has reached DIS status, companies are encouraged to develop actual products based on it.

DISA 1. Direct Inward System Access. DISA is a way of dialing into a phone system. It's been the major way crooks have dialed into PBXs and stolen toll calls. See DIRECT INWARD SYSTEM ACCESS. 2. Data Interchange Standards Association, Inc. DISA is the Secretariat and administrative arm of the Accredited Standards Committee (ASC) X12 which has responsibility for developing Electronic Data Interchange (EDI) standards. DISA OnLine is an electronic messaging and information system designed for use by DISA's member constituency.

DISABLE You figured this one. It means to prevent a hardware device from working. Unplugging it is the easiest way. It also refers to a tone or other signal which you send over a phone line to disable the equipment at the other end.

DISC An older method of spelling DISK, as in Floppy DISK. Disc (spelled with a C) is now more commonly used to refer to optical storage devices, like CD (Compact Discs) and MO (Magneto Optical) discs. See also MS-DOS.

DISCHARGE BLOCK A protective device through which unwanted voltages discharge to ground.

DISCO TECH Slang expression for a technician who only handles disconnections.

DISCONNECT The breaking or release of a circuit connecting two telephones or data devices. 2. The occasional April Fools issue of TELECONNECT Magazine. Sometimes funny. Sometimes not. Always offensive.

DISCONNECT FRAME Indicates in a fax call that the call is done. The sending fax machine sends the disconnect frame before hanging it. It does not wait for a response.

DISCONNECT SIGNAL The signal sent from one end to indicate to the other to shut down the connection.

DISCONNECT SUPERVISION The change in electrical state from off-hook to on-hook. This indicates that the transmission connection is no longer needed.

DISCONNECT SWITCH In a power system, a switch used for closing, opening, or changing the connections in a circuit or system or for purposes of isolation. It has no interrupting rating and is intended to be operated only after the circuit hs been opened by some other means, such as by a circuit breaker or variable transformer.

DISCONTINUITY An interruption or drop out of the optical signal.

DISCO TECH Slang expression for a technician who only handles disconnections.

DISCOUNTED PAYBACK PERIOD The number of years in which a stream of cash flows, discounted at an organization's cost of money, repays an initial investment.

DISCOUNTING The process of computing the present worth of a future cash flow by reducing it by a factor equivalent to the organization's cost of money (or some other measure of the value of money as measured by an interest rate) and the time until the cash flow occurs.

DISCRETE In voice recognition, refers to an isolated word. A discete word is preceded and followed by silence, hence isolated in speech. Discrete words need to be separated by about half a second of silence when spoken to a discrete recognizer.

DISCRETE MULTI-TONE See DMT.

DISCRETIONARY PREVIEW DIALING A single button dialing technique where the agent initiates a call with a single key stroke. Often used in association with a CRT tied to a database. Upon hitting a single button the system selects the phone number field from the screen and dials the number. Contrast this with Forced Preview Dialing. When the call ends, the computer brings up the next screen and starts dialing the call without the agent helping or hindering.

DISCRIMINATING RINGING See DISTINCTIVE RINGING.

DISCUSSION A method of confirming others in their errors.

DISENGAGEMENT DENIAL Disengagment failure due to excessive delay by the telecommunication system.

DISENGAGEMENT FAILURE Failure of a disengagement attempt to return a communication system to the idle state, for a given user, within a specified maximum disengagement time.

DISH Typically a parabolic microwave antenna — used for receiving line-of-sight terrestrial signals or signals from satellites.

DISK A piece of plastic or metal upon which a coating has been applied and which can thus, record computer information magnetically. The present convention is that a "disk" with a K refers to magnetic storage, while "disc" with a C refers to optical storage. See also MS-DOS.

DISK CACHE On a PC, a disk cache is the part of RAM that is set aside to temporarily hold data read from disk. A disk cache doesn't have to hold an entire file, as a RAM disk does, but can hold parts of running application software or parts of a data file. Disk-caching software manages the process of swapping data to and from the disk cache. See DISK CACHING.

DISK CACHING A technique used to speed up processing. Each time your application retrieves data from the disk, a special program, called a disk caching program, stores data read from the disk in an area of RAM. When the application next requests more data, some of it may already be in RAM, thereby dramatically speeding the retrieval of data. See DISK CACHE and CACHING.

DISK CONTROLLER A hardware device that controls how data is written to and retrieved from the disk drive. The disk controller sends signals to the disk drive's logic board to regulate the movement of the head as it reads data from or writes data from or writes data to the disk.

DISK DRIVE A device containing motors, electronics and other gadgetry for storing (writing) and retrieving (reading) data on a disk. See also MS-DOS.

DISK DUPLEXING A method of failsafe protection, occasionally used on file servers on local area networks. Disk duplexing involves copying data onto two hard disks, each on a separate disk channel. Disk duplexing protects data against the failure of a hard disk or of the hard disk channel between the disk and the file server. The hard disk "channel" includes the disk controller and interface cable. If any component on one channel fails, the other channel continues to operate normally. (You hope.) The operating system sends a warning message to the workstations to indicate the failure. It's a good idea then to fix the problem fast. See also DISK MIRRORING.

DISK MIRRORING A technique for protecting the information on your hard disk. Disk mirroring writes data simultaneously to two identical hard disks using the same hard disk controller. Here's how it works: You have a special hard disk controller card. That's the card which organizes getting information into and off your hard disk. When you come to write information to your hard disk, your hard disk controller writes first to the first hard disk, called the primary hard disk. The controller retains that information in its memory and then writes it to the second hard disk. This causes a 50% degradation in performance since it now takes twice as long to write to the disk. When the controller comes to read, it reads only from the primary disk. Thus there is no performance degradation in reading. Mirroring is designed to protect against mechanical problems with one of your hard disks. If one of the hard disks break, the other one will take over instantly. You will get a

NEWTON'S TELECOM DICTIONARY

warning message. You will be told to repair the broken disk and you will be told to designate the other disk now as your primary disk (it may already be). That primary disk will now become your bootable disk, the one you boot your computer from. Mirroring does not protect against viruses, or corrupt data or losing data. Any idiocy you can perform on one hard disk you can now happily perform on two. Mirroring does not protect you against a lightning strike which could knock out both your hard disks. Mirroring does not protect against the loss of a controller card since you're only using one. Another protection technique called disk duplexing uses two separate controllers to drive two separate hard disks.

DISK OPERATING SYSTEM See DOS.

DISK PACK A series of disks mounted horizontally and arranged as a single unit. A disk pack contains more space for storing and retrieving information than one single disk.

DISK SECTOR Magnetic diskettes are typically divided into tracks, each of which contains a number of sectors. A sector typically contains a predetermined amount of data, such as 256 bytes.

DISK SERVER A device equipped with disks and a program that permits users to create and store files on the disks. Each user has access to their own section of the disk. It gives users disk space which they would not normally have at their own personal computers. Some sort of connection between the disk server and PC is needed, like a LAN. Compare with file server, which allows users to share files.

DISK/FILE SERVER A mass storage device that can be accessed by several computers, usually through a local area network (LAN).

DISKLESS PC Just what it says: a PC without a disk drive. Used on a LAN, a diskless PC runs by booting DOS from the file server. It does this via a read-only memory chip on its network interface card called a remote boot ROM. Diskless PCs are cheaper than PCs with disks, they're more compact and they offer better security since users can't make off with floppy disks of important and sensitive data or add their own virus-ridden programs to file servers. Diskless PCs appeal primarily to users interested in security. One system of diskless PCs allow the system operator to disable and physically lock the machine's various ports and the computer case itself. Should something go wrong with the machine, the ports can be restored to operating condition by letting the system allow a technician to attach a laptop computer and run diagnostic programs.

DISKLESS WORKSTATION See DISKLESS PC.

DISOSS IBM's Distributed Office Support System.

DISPERSION A term used to describe how an electromagnetic signal is distorted because the various frequency components of that signal have different propagation characteristics. Dispersion is the degree of scattering

NEWTON'S TELECOM DICTIONARY

taking place in the light beam as it travels along the fiber optic. Or the overlapping of a light signal on one wavelength to different wavelengths because of reflected rays and the different refractive index of the core fiber material.

DISPLAY The visual presentation of information, usually on a TV-like screen or an array of illuminated digits.

DISTANCE SENSITIVE PRICING Product pricing based on the distance (airline mileage) between the originating and terminating locations of a call/data transmission.

DISTANT LEARNING A Pacific Bell term for students sitting in front of TVs and phones and participating in classes that are being held and delivered elsewhere. In one of PacBell's trials, they used a T-1 signal, so the distant lecturer could see and hear his distant students using full-color video.

DISTINCTIVE DIAL TONES In some phone systems, dial tones sound different. An internal dial tone sounds different to an external dial tone. The logical reason for this is simply to alert the user as to whether he or she is making an intercom or an outside local or long distance call.

DISTINCTIVE RINGING Enables telephone users to distinguish types of incoming calls such as outside calls and inside (intercom) calls by the tone of the ringing.

DISTORT To change some characteristic of a signal during its transmission. See DISTORTION.

DISTORTION 1. The difference in values between two measurements of a signal — for example, between the transmitted and received signal. "Distortion" typically refers to analog signals. 2. Ini images, distortion is any deformation of the on-screen image. Two common types of distortion are pincushion and barrel.

DISTRIBUTED CAPACITY The capacity in a coil due to the proximity of the turns.

DISTRIBUTED COMMON CONTROL There are two elements of telephone switching: The switching itself and the control of that switching. The earliest step-by-step telephone switches had their "Control" built into them. The dialing information at the beginning of the call physically moved switches. You could say, as a result, that control was distributed throughout the switching system. Then came the 1940s and crossbar exchanges, and the economics pointed to centralizing control. Then came computerized or stored program control (SPC) switches in which large computers were used centrally to perform virtually all the functions of the erstwhile electromechanical senders, registers, markers, etc. — those things which affect the setting up and tearing down of the call. As computers got smaller and as microprocessors appeared (the so-called computer on a chip), it became economical and efficient to place inexpensive microprocessors in the telephone circuits themselves, in essence getting much of the processing done before it hits the central processing unit. Increasingly, as special microprocessors (so-called "computers on a chip") for telecommunications evolve, we will see more and more of the processing being distributed to further and further away from the central point and closer and closer to the originating telephone instrument. It will be rare in coming years for telephones to come without microprocessors. One day, each phone will have its own switch and the rest of the system will just be one gigantic loop of cable — not unlike today's local area networks.

DISTRIBUTED COMPUTING ENVIRONMENT DCE. A new idea from Digital Equipment Corporation. Distributed Computing Environment (DCE) is a comprehensive integrated set of services that supports the development, use, and maintenance of distributed applications. Digital's DCE is an implementation of the Open Software Foundation's DCE (OSF DCE). In response to OSF's request for distributed computing technology, Digital submitted for consideration four of Digital's established distributed computing technologies:

Remote Procedure Call (RPC), a joint effort with HP/Apollo; Threads Service, based on Digital DECthreads; Cell Directory Service (CDS), based on the Digital Distributed Name Service (DECdns); Distributed Time Service (DTS), based on the Digital Distributed Time Service (DECdts).

DISTRIBUTED DATA PROCESSING DDP. A data processing arrangement in which the computers are decentralized — i.e. scattered in various places. Hence, processing occurs in a number of distributed locations and only semi-processed information is communicated on data communications lines from remote points to the central computers. The object of DDP is to save telecommunications charges and to improve network response time.

DISTRIBUTED FILE SYSTEM A type of file system in which the file system itself manages and transparently locates pieces of information from remote files and distributes files across a network. It can recognize multiple servers and be accessed independently of where it physically resides on the network.

DISTRIBUTED MANAGEMENT ENVIRONMENT A compilation of technologies now being selected by the Open Software Foundation to create a unified network and systems management framework, as well as applications. Those technologies will complement OSF's own Unix implementation, OSF/1, as well as other operating systems.

DISTRIBUTED MICROPROCESSOR COMMON CONTROL This means that the system employs many individual microprocessors to control system and telephone phone functions. The microprocessors may be located in central processing equipment or in the telephones themselves.

DISTRIBUTED NETWORK SERVICE Introduced in March 1991, AT&T's

Distributed Network Service was designed expressly for the switchless resale community unlike SDN. It allows resellers to purchase large volumes of services and receive progressive discounts on all direct dial domestic and international calls. Resellers may designate any number of locations to participate in the plan with the flexibility of adding locations.

DISTRIBUTED NODES PBX and its "slave" switches which are physically in separate buildings, in separate areas of the campus, in separate parts of the town.

DISTRIBUTED PROCESSING A network of computers such that the processing of information is initiated in local computers, and the resultant data is sent to a central computer for further processing with the data from other local systems. The term also covers computing jobs "farmed out" from a central site to remote processors where faster processing or specialized databases are available. Distributed Processing is often a more efficient use of computer processing power since each CPU can be devoted to a certain task. A LAN is the perfect example of distributed processing. See also DISTRIBUTED DATA PROCESSING.

DISTRIBUTED QUEUE DUAL BUS DQDB. A connectionless packet-switched protocol, normally residing in the Medium-Access Control sublayer of the data link layer. Definition from Bellcore in reference to Advanced Intelligent Network.

DISTRIBUTED SWITCHING When electronics and computers were expensive it made sense to centralize them and run individual lines out for miles to subscribers. Then the economies changed. Electronics and computers became cheaper and running phone lines for miles became very expensive. So switching companies started building small switches which they could put closer to subscribers. Thus, individual local loops would be shorter and the long lines going back to the larger central office would be more efficiently used — namely by more people. The remote, or distributed switches, are called everything from remote switches to slave switches (because they slave off the main one which is distant). Usually these remote switches are unattended.

DISTRIBUTION Refers to the arrangement of premises wiring runs and their associated hardware required to implement the planned customer premises wiring system extending from the Network Interface Jack to each Communications Outlet.

DISTRIBUTION CABLE Part of the outside cable plant connecting feeder or subfeeder cables to drop wires or buried service wires that connect to the customer's premises. In simpler language, it's the cable from the serving area interface — a box on a pole, in the ground, etc. — to the lightning protection at the entrance to the customer's premises. See also FEEDER PLANT and DROP WIRE.

DISTRIBUTION CABLE, INSIDE PLANT Cables usually running

horizontally from a closet on a given floor within a building. Distribution cables may be under carpet, simplex, duplex, quad, or higher fiber count cables.

DISTRIBUTION CABLE, OUTSIDE PLANT The cable running from a central office or remote terminal to the side of a subscriber's lot.

DISTRIBUTION FRAME Cables coming in from thousands of subscribers need to connect to the correct ports on a central office. Similarly, cables coming in from many PBX extensions need to connect to the PBX. The cables could be directly wired to the CO or to the PBX. This would be inflexible. It would make future moves and changes a nightmare. So the solution is something called a Distribution Frame. Basically it's a giant wire connecting devices made of metal. There are no electronics in it whatsoever. On one side we punch down the wires coming in from the outside world. On the other side, we punch down the wires coming in from the CO or PBX. Both sides are connected with wire that's called "jumper" wire. By pulling off one end of the jumper wire and moving it to another location we can quickly change phone numbers, add or subtract cabling (one, two or three pairs for normal or electronic phones, etc.). In big central offices, distribution frames can span whole city blocks and the "jumper" wires can be several hundred yards long. Designing distribution frames and their layout in advance is critical, otherwise it becomes a mess and tracing where jumper wires go becomes an enormously time-consuming job.

DISTRIBUTION GROUP A group of telephone extensions on an automatic call distributor (ACD). The ACD answers the incoming calls then checks to see if any agents' phones are free. If none are free, it delivers the caller a message and then puts the caller on hold. Which line the call has come in on may determine which group of agents should handle that call. They would be called a Distribution Group. Once the call is released from hold, it may be sent to a member of that Distribution Group following some pre-determined mathematical formula — for example, so that everyone's workload is kept constant, or a group of people are kept busy.

DISTRIBUTION SERVICE In ISDN applications, a telecommunications service that allows one-way of information from one point in the network to other points in the network with or without user individual presentation control.

DISTRIBUTION VOLTAGE DROP The voltage drop between any two defined points of interest in a power distribution system.

DITHERING Dithering is patterning black and white dots to approximate shades of grey on a scanned image.

DIURNAL PHASE SHIFT The phase shift of electromagentic signals associated with daily changes in the ionosphere. The major changes usually occur during the period of time when sunrise or sunset is present at critical points along the path. Significant phase shifts may occur on paths wherein a relfection area of the path is subject to a large tidal range. In cable systems, significant phase shifts can be occasioned by diurnal temperature variance.

DIVERSITY In microwave communications, the strength of a microwave signal can decrease for many reasons — heat, rain, fog, etc. This is not good if the objective is to get reliable communications. One solution is to simultaneously send and receive two microwave signals at slightly different frequencies. Since different frequencies respond differently to weather problems, the likelihood is that at least one will get through well. This is called diversity.

DIVERSITY COMBINER A circuit or device for combining two or more signals carrying the same information received via separate paths or channels with the objective or providing a single resultant signal that is superior in quality to any of the contributing signals.

DIVESTITURE On January 8, 1982 AT&T signed a Consent Decree with the U.S. Department of Justice, stipulating that on midnight December 30, 1983, AT&T would divest itself of its 22 telephone operating companies. According to the terms of the Divestiture, those 22 operating Bell telephone companies would be formed into seven regional holding companies of roughly equal size. Terms of the Divestiture placed business restrictions on AT&T and the BOCs. Those restrictions were threefold: The BOCs weren't allowed into long distance, equipment manufacturing, or information services. AT&T wasn't allowed into local telecommunications (i.e. to compete with the BOCs). But it was allowed into computers. The federal Judge overseeing Divestiture, Judge Harold Greene, is slowing the lifting the restrictions against the BOCs being allowed into information services. He has stayed firm on the other two — equipment manufacturing and long distance.

DIW Type D Inside Wire. Originated as a specific AT&T cable. Now commonly used to describe any 22, 24, or 26 gauge PVC jacketed twisted-pair cable used primarily for inside telephony wiring.

DIX CONNECTORS A local area network connector. DIX connectors on the transceiver local area network cable link it to the network; the male DIX connector plugs into the SpeedLink/PC16 and the female DIX connector attaches to an external transceiver.

DIX ETHERNET The DEC, Intel, Xerox Ethernet standard, also known as Version 1 or Bluebook Ethernet. There are subtle differences between IEEE 802.3 and the DIX Ethernet.

DLC 1. Digital Loop Carrier. 2. See DATA LINK CONTROL.

DLE Data Link Escape. A control character used exclusively to provide supplementary line control signals, control character sequences or DLE sequences. In packet switching, Data Link Escape is a name applied to the Control P non-print character which is used to swap the PAD from the data mode to the command mode in packet switched networks.

DLL 1. Data Link Layer driver. A driver specification developed by DEC primarily to work with DECnet PCSA for DOS. DLL is a shared driver specification, allowing multiple protocol stacks to share a single network interface card. 2. Dynamic Link Library. A feature of OS/2 and Windows that allow executable code modules to be loaded on demand and linked at run time. This lets library code be field-updated — transparent to applications — and then unloaded when they are no longer needed.

DLSE Dial Line Service Evaluation.

DLTU Digital Link Trunk Unit. An AT&T term for a device which provides the interface to digital trunks and lines such as T1, EDSL, and remote line units.

DM Delta Modulation.

DMA Direct Memory Access. A fast method of moving data from a storage device or LAN interface card directly to RAM which speeds processing. In essence, DMA is direct access to memory by a peripheral device that bypasses the CPU.

DMB Digital Multipoint Bridge.

DMI Digital Multiplexed Interface. AT&T's Digital Multiplexed Interface. A PBX to computer interface that divides the T-1 trunk into 23 user channels and one signaling channel. Also used as a T-1 PBX to computer interface. See OPEN APPLICATION INTERFACE.

DMI-BOS Digital Multiplexed Interface-Bit Oriented Signaling. A form of signaling, which uses the 24th channel of each DSI to carry signaling information, allowing clear channel 64 Kbps functionality.

DMO Digital Modification Order.

DMS Digital Multiplex System. Also the name of a line of digital central office switches from Northern Telecom. There are DMS-10s, DMS-100s, DMS-100Fs and DMS-200s and, by the time you read this, probably more. See also DMS SUPERNODE.

DMS INTEGRATED ACCESS LOCAL AREA NETWORK Shortened to DIALAN. A central office provided local area network offering completely digital, full duplex data transmission at speeds of 300 bps through 19.2 asynchronous and 1,200 bps through 64 kbps synchronous. DIALAN users use existing telephone sets and an Integrated Voice and Data Multiplexer (IVDM) that plugs into a telephone jack.

DMS SUPERNODE The SuperNode is a very flexible central office switch from Northern Telecom which can be configured as a high-capacity local or tandem switch with Common Channel Signaling 7 (CCS7) Service Switching Point (SSP) function, a Signaling Transfer Point (STP), a Service Control Point (SCP), a Digital Network CrossConnect (DNX) system or a network service node with custom programming applications. In 1988, the DMS SuperNode offered twice the capacity of the DMS-100 switch (the older Northern Telecom central office) based on the NT40 processor.

NEWTON'S TELECOM DICTIONARY

DMS-INODE DMS Integrated STP/SSP Node.

DMT Discrete Multi-Tone. A new technology using digital signal processors to pump more than 6 megabits per second of video, data, image and voice signals over today's existing one pair copper wiring. DMT technology, according to Northern Telecom, provides the following:

● Four "A" channels at 1.5 Mbps. Each "A" channel may carry a "VCR"-quality video signal, or two channels may be merged to carry a "sports"-quality real-time video signal. In the future, all four channels operating together will be able to transport an Extended Definition TV signal with significantly improved quality over anything available today. ("A" channels are asymmetric — carrying information only from the telephone company to the subscriber's residence. All other channels within ADSL are symmetric or bi-directional.)

● One ISDN "H zero" channel at 384 kbps (kilobits per second). This channel is compatible with Northern Telecom's multirate ISDN Dialable Wideband Service or equivalent services. This channel could also be used for fast, efficient access to corporate LANs for work-at-home applications, using Northern Telecom's DataSPAN or other frame-relay services.

● One ISDN Basic Rate channel, containing two "B" channels (64 kbps) and one "D" channel (16 kbps). Basic Rate access allows the home user to access the wide range of emerging ISDN services without requiring a dedicated copper pair or the expense of a dedicated NT1 unit at the home. It also permits the extension of Northern Telecom's VISIT personal videoconferencing to the home at fractional-T1 rates (Px64).

● One signalling/control channel, operating at 16 kbps giving the home user VCR-type controls over movies and other services provided on the "A" channel including fast-forward, reverse, search, and pause.

● Embedded operations channels for internal system maintenance, audits, and telephone company administration.

● Finally, the home user can place or recieve telephone calls over the same copper pair without affecting the digital transmission channels listed above. And since ADSL is passively coupled to the POTS line, the subscriber's POTS capability is unimpaired in the event of a system failure.

DN Directory number or subscriber number or telephone number entries. See DIRECTORY NUMBER.

DNA 1. Digital Network Architecture. The framework within which Digital Equipment Corporation (DEC) designs and develops all of its communications products. DNA includes many standards of the OSI Model. Some of these standards will be adopted into ISDN. Acronym also by Network Development Corporation for their network offering. 2. Dynamic Node Access. A high-speed bus invented by Dialogic to join together multiple voice processing PEB-based systems. PEB stands for PCM Expansion Bus. See PEB.

DNAR Directory Number Analysis Reporting.

DNC Dynamic Network Controller.

DNIC Data Network Identification Code. An address to reach a host computer system residing on a different packet switched network than the one you're on. The data equivalent of a telephone number with country code and area code. Typically the DNIC is a four digit number. The first three digits of a DNIC specify a country. The fourth digit specifies a public data network within that country. See also DATA NETWORK IDENTIFICATION CODE.

DNIS Dialed Number Identification Service. DNIS is a feature of 800 and 900 lines. Let's say you subscribe to several 800 numbers. You use one line for testing your advertisements on TV stations in Phoenix; another line for testing your ads on TV stations in Chicago; and yet another for Milwaukee. Now you get an automatic call distributor and you terminate all the lines in one group on your ACD. You do that because it's cheaper to man and run one group of incoming lines. One queue is more efficient than several small ones, etc. You have all your people answering all the calls. You now need to know which calls are coming from where. So your long distance carrier sends you the call's DNIS — the numbers the person dialed to reach you. Those DNIS digits might come to you in many ways, depending on the technical arrangement you have with your long distance company. In-band or out-of-band. ISDN or data channel, etc. Make sure you understand the difference between DNIS and ANI. DNIS tells you the number your caller called. ANI is the number your caller called from. See 800 SERVICE and 900 SERVICE.

DNPA Data Numbering Plan Area. In the U.S. implementation of the CCITT X.25 network, the first three digits of a network terminal number (NTN). See also DATA NUMBERING PLAN AREA.

DNPIC Directory Number Primary InterLATA Carrier.

DNR 1. Dialed Number Recorder. Also called a Pin Register. An instrument that records telephone dial pulses as inked dashes on paper tape. A touch-tone decoder performs the same thing for a touch-tone telephone. 2. Dynamic Network Reconfiguration. Allows IBM networks to change addresses without reloading and bringing the network down.

DNS 1. Domain Name Service. A TCP/IP protocol for discovering and maintaining local area network network resource information distributed among different servers. 2. See DISTRIBUTED NETWORK SERVICE.

DO A word in a high-level language program which comes before a collection of things to be done, i.e. statements to be executed.

DO-NOT-DISTURB Makes a telephone appear busy to any incoming calls. May be used on intercom-only, by extension line-only or both.

DO-WHILE A programming statement used to perform instructions in a loop while a certain condition exists — i.e. do something while the variable Y is less than 20.

DOC 1. Department of Communications. Canadian government department. 2. See DYNAMIC OVERLOAD CONTROL.

DOC-IT Okidata's name for a combination scanner, printer, copier, fax machine. A truly wonderful machine.

DOCUMENT IMAGE MANAGEMENT DIM. The electronic access to and manipulation of documents stored in image format, accomplished through the use of automated methods such as high-powered graphical workstations, sophisticated database manangement techniques and networking.

DOCUMENT RECOGNITION The ability to capture all the information on a page (text and images) and perform not only character recognition, but page structure analysis as well.

DOCUMENTATION Written text describing the system, how it works and how to work it. In most cases of high technology products, documentation is awful. Better documentation helps sell equipment and software. Please write your instruction manuals better. Please.

DOCKET Formal FCC/State regulatory commission proceeding, also referred to as a case.

DOCKING STATION Base station for a laptop that includes a power supply and expansion slots as well as monitor and keyboard connectors.

DOD Department of Defense.

DOD MASTER CLOCK The U.S. Naval Observatory master clock, which has been designated as the DOD Master Clock to which DoD time and frequency measurements are referenced. This clock is one of two standard time references for the U.S. Government in accordance with Federal Standard 1002; the other standard time reference is the National Institute for Standards and Technology (NIST) master clock.

DOLBY A system of noise/hiss reduction invented by Ray Dolby, widely used in consumer, professional and broadcast audio applications.

DOMAIN A term defined differently by various electronic mail vendors. PC Magazine's Frank Derfler defines a domain as referring to a set of hosts on a single LAN that needs only one intermediary post office to move mail from one host to another. A domain may also consist of only one host, depending on its design and implementation. In IBM's SNA, domain is a host-based systems services control point (SSCP), the physical units (PUs), logical units (LUs), links, link stations and all the affiliated resources that the host (SSCP) can control. See DOMAIN NAMING SYSTEM.

DOMAIN NAMING SYSTEM A hierarchical system of host naming that groups hosts into categories. For instance, in the Internet naming scheme, names with extensions of "COM" identify hosts in commerical businesses, and names with extensions of "EDU" identify hosts in educational institutions.

DOMESTIC ARC The portion of the geostationary orbit allowing a satellite to return a footprint that almost covers the continental United States.

DOMINANT CARRIER The long distance service provider which dominates a particular market and is subject to tougher regulation than its competitors. An FCC term. Essentially it means AT&T.

DON'T ANSWER RECALL Allows an extension user on a PBX to automatically retry a call by dialing a special digit code.

DONGLE A device to prevent copies made of software programs. A dongle is a small device supplied with software that plugs into a computer port. The software interrogates the device's serial number during execution to verify its presence. If it's not there, the software won't work. A dongle is also called a hardware key. See HARDWARE KEY.

DOOR A software program that allows access to files and programs not built into an electronic bulletin board system, thus letting users run them on-line.

DOPPLER AIDING A signal processing strategy that uses a measured doppler shift to help the GPS Global Positioning System) receiver smoothly track the GPS signal. It allows more precise velocity and position measurement.

DOPPLER SHIFT The apparent shift in the frequency of a signal caused by the relative motion of the transmitter and the receiver.

DOS Disk Operating System, as in MS-DOS, which stands for MicroSoft Disk Operating System. DOS is the software that organizes how a computer reads, writes and reacts with its disks — floppy or hard — and talks to its various input/output devices, including keyboards, screens, serial and parallel ports, printers, modems, etc. The most popular operating system for PCs is MS-DOS from Microsoft, Bellevue, WA.

DOS 3.1 was the first version of MS- and PC-DOS that offered functions supporting LANs. It has hooks so that programs can lock data records and files, crucial in multi-user LAN applications.

DOS 5.0 came out in the summer of 1991. It has major advantages, including

● The ability to load most of itself and various TSR (terminate and stay resident) program into higher memory, thus freeing up considerably more of below 640K memory for operating programs, like Lotus, WordPerfect, etc.

● The ability to work seamlessly with hard disk drives of much larger than 32 megs.

● Much better, broader, easier-to-use commands, like an improved DIR.

● Newer commands like DOSKEY, SMARTDRIVE (disk caching) and UNDELETE and UNFORMAT.

The real key to the excitement of DOS 5.0 is LOADHIGH — a feature that enables DOS 5.0 to load some TSRs above 640K on '386 and '486 PCs. DEVICEHIGH does the same for device drivers. These two features can save enormous below-640K memory, perhaps even allowing you to run programs or combinations of programs you couldn't run with earlier versions of DOS.

If you want to free up as much memory below 640K as you can, use the CONFIG.SYS:

```
device=c:\dos\himem.sys
device=c:\dos\emm386.exe 2304
dos=high,umb
file=20
buffers=4
stacks=0,0
lastdrive=d
```

If you are using Windows 3.1 (as I am), let Windows do your memory management and use the following Config.sys

```
device=C:\dos\HIMEM.SYS
DOS=HIGH,umb
FILES=60
buffers=30
lastdrive=d
```

DOS 6.0 is out. Its major feature is disk compression. It has a number of features which have long been available from third party vendors (i.e. not Microsoft), including disk compression. I haven't yet upgraded so I can't give you a report. As yet I haven't found a compelling reason to upgrade.

DOS EXTENDER A MS-DOS extender is a programming technique. The extender allows an application to run in protected mode under MS-DOS. It shifts the CPU up from real mode to protected mode when the program starts. When the program accesses DOS, everything downshifts into real mode, then upshifts back to protected mode when DOS access is complete. The problem with the DOS extender, as with expanded memory, is that it is a work-around and not a full solution. Heavy-duty programs that need the 32-bit power can get it via the DOS extender, allowing users to retain their DOS programs. But the DOS extender leaves untouched many areas that only a new, protected mode operating system can handle: data integration, addressing new hardware, a new file system, etc.

DOT ADDRESSABLE GRAPHICS Refers to the mode of operation on a dot matrix printer which allows you to control each element in the dot matrix printhead. With this feature, you may produce complex graphics drawings.

DOT PITCH A measure of the clarity of a color monitor. Dot pitch measures the vertical distance between the centers of like-colored phosphors on your screen. The smaller the distance, the sharper the monitor. Dot pitch is the major determinant in the clarity of an image on screen. And you can't do anything about it. When you buy a monitor, you buy it with a certain dot pitch and you're stuck with that dot pitch. You may be able, however, to do something about improving convergence and focus — the other measures of the clarity of a color monitor.

DOT ZERO When new software is issued, it often bears the number .0 (i.e. dot zero) as in MS-DOS 5.0. The theory among software gurus is that you should always avoid a "Dot Zero" revision, since it will likely contain bugs and that one should wait for 4.01 or 5.01 etc. This theory has some validity, although MS-DOS 5.0 came out very clean and was not revised until 6.0.

DOUBLE BUFFERING The use of two buffers rather than one to temporarily hold data being moved to and from an I/O device. Double buffering increases data transfer speed because one buffer can be filled while the other is being emptied.

DOUBLE CAMP-ON INDICATION A PBX feature. A phone attempting to camp on to another phone which is already being "camped on" shall receive a distinctive audible signal and may be denied the ability to camp-on.

DOUBLE CLICK With a Mac and an IBM-compatible PC running Windows, double-clicking carries out an action, such as beginning a new program. Press and release the mouse button twice in rapid succession to double-click. If you don't double click fast enough, it won't work.

DOUBLE CRUCIBLE METHOD A method of fabricating optical fiber by melting core and clad glasses into two suitably joined concentric crucibles and then drawing a fiber from the combined melted glass.

DOUBLE DENSITY Refers to a diskette which can contain twice the amount of data in the same amount of space as a single-density diskette. For example, a double-density 360k diskette has a 720k storage capacity. These days double density is an obsolete term, since there are now disks that are "double double" density. Most 3 1/2 inch disks will now hold twice 720K — or 1,440,000 bytes. These are called high density disks. Toshiba has introduced a "double double double" floppy, which will hold 2,880,000 bytes. But it hasn't caught on, yet.

DOUBLE ENDED SYNCHRONIZATION A synchronization control system between two exchanges, in which the phase error signals used to control the clock at one exchange are derived from comparison with the phase of the internal clock at both exchanges.

DOUBLE INTERRUPTED RING Two quick rings followed by a period of silence indicating the arrival of an outside call in some systems.

DOUBLE MODULATION Modulation of a carrier wave of one frequency by a signal wave, this carrier then being used to modulate another carrier wave of different frequency.

DOUBLE POLE A double pole switch is one which opens and closes both sides of the same circuit simultaneously. Most electrical circuits open and close with only one side being broken.

DOUBLE PULL A method for pulling cable into conduit or duct liner that is similar to backfeed pulling except that it eliminates the need to lay the backfeed cable on the ground.

DOUBLE SIDEBAND CARRIER TRANSMISSION That method of transmission in which frequencies produced by the process of amplitude modulation are symmetrically spaced above and below the carrier. The carrier level is reduced for transmission at a fixed level below that which is provided to the modulator. Carrier is usually transmitted at a level suitable for use as a reference by the receiver except in those cases where it is reduced to the minimum practical level (suppressed carrier).

DOUBLEWIDE Two trailer homes stapled together with a modest gabled roof.

DOUBLY CLAD FIBER An optical fiber, usually single mode, that has a core surrounded by an inner cladding of lower refractive index, which is in turn surrounded by an outer cladding, which has a higher refractive index than the inner cladding. This type of construction is often employed in singel-mode fibers to reduce bending losses.

DOV Data Over Voice. A technology used primarily with local Centrex services or special customer premises PBXs for transmitting data and voice simultaneously over twisted-pair copper wiring. Typical data rates for Centrex operation are 9.6 Kbps and 19.2 Kbps.

DOVPATH TRANSPORT SERVICE A New York and New England Telephone service which lets you transmit both voice and data simultaneously on one phone line. The data is carried on a higher frequency, i.e. "Over the Voice." Hence the name Data Over Voice, or DOV. DOVPATH lets you transmit up to 19.2 Kbps asynchronous data, which could be fast enough for talking to a distant mainframe computer.

DOWN-CONVERTER A device for performing frequency translation in such a manner that the output frequencies are lower in the spectrum than the input frequencies.

DOWNLINE LOADING A system in which programs are loaded into the memory of a computer system, such as a LAN bridge, router or server, via the same communication line(s) the system normally uses to communicate with the rest of a network. As opposed to systems in which all programs are loaded into the computer from a disk or tape associated with the computer. A PC connected to a LAN may use this type of loading when it is first turned on in the morning to get the information it needs from a file server. Diskless PCs always work this way.

DOWNLINK 1. The part of a transmission link reaching from a satellite to the ground. Some satellite transmission circuits, especially international ones, are priced and billed separately for the uplink and the downlink. This is because their transmissions are provided by different carriers. 2. In packet data communications, a downlink is a link from an NC or PAD to another NC or PAD on a different level. The defining of downlinks and uplinks depends on the network configuration of PADs, their relationships to each other and the direction of data transmission.

DOWNLOADING The act of receiving data from another computer into your computer. It's also called to RECEIVE. The opposite is UPLOAD or TRANSMIT. You have to be very careful distinguishing between the two. Choosing the "Download" option in some communications programs automatically erases a file of the same name that was meant for transmission.

DOWNSIZING Downsizing is what happens when companies move from large computer systems to smaller systems. There are four major reasons companies downsize from mainframe-based computer to local area network-based computing:

1. They save money. There are several reasons: a. Mainframe computers cost lots each month in maintenance. They require costly maintenance agreements with the supplier, e.g. IBM. Servers are usually bought without maintenancce agreements. When they break, the managers or the workers simply replace the broken parts themselves. b. Mainframe computers cost lots to program. There are comparatively few programs available for mainframes, compared to the plethora of off-the-shelf programs available for workstations. c. Servers require a far less costly home to live. You don't need airconditioning, special buildings with raised floors, etc. 2. Servers today have the power of mainframes 10 years ago. In fact, servers are now beginning to acquire more power than mainframes of ten years ago. And as servers increasingly acquire several processors, they will leap in power beyond what mainframes have. 3. Servers are typically manufactured from off-the-shelf, standard components that are usually available from several manufacturers. As a result, there is constant competition and constant improvement in quality and features. 4. Servers are much more flexible tools to design networks. You can start with one baby network containing one server and several workstations (aka clients) and confined to one floor of one small building and grow to a huge, complex network containing thousands of workstations, dozens of servers and spanning the globe.

To most people, downsizing is not only swapping out the "big iron" (the mainframe) and bringing in servers and local area networks. It's also a new way of thinking about the way corporations are organized. Downsizing is often accompanied by re-engineering, which is basically re-organizing for a greater focus on the customer — a focus which means responding faster to customer needs. See SERVERS.

DOWNSTREAM CHANNEL The frequency multiplexed band in a CATV channel which distributes signals from the headend to the users. Compare with UPSTREAM CHANNEL, the band of frequencies on a CATV channel reserved for transmission from the user to the CATV company's headend.

DOWNTIME The total time a telephone system is not working due to some software or hardware failure. You know your vendor is about to lie when he begins to answer a question about "downtime."

DP Dial Pulse (as in dialing a phone) or Data Processing. Also called EDP for Electronic Data Processing. Now more commonly called Management Information Systems — or MIS.

DPA Digital Port Adapter. A Northern Telecom word.

DPLB Digital Private Line Billing.

DPMI An acronym for DOS Protected Mode Interface. DPMI is an industry standard that allows MS-DOS applications to execute code in the protected operating mode of the 80286 or 80386 processor. The DPMI specification is available from Intel Corporation. It is a superset of the VCPI (Virtual Control Program Interface) specification for controlling multiple programs inside a PC, as well as programs that use protected mode.

DPN LANSCOPE A Northern Telecom software package for remote management of local area networks over wide area networks based on Northern's DPN-100 digital data packet networking system. DPN Lanscope provides fault and performance monitoring, resource management, software distribution and usage tracking for geographically dispersed LANs. Network configuration, status, alarms and performance information are presented to a centralized LAN administrator through a graphics interface.

DPBX Digital PBX. Not a common term. Most PBXs these days are digitals.

DPN Northern Telecom term for Data Packet Network.

DPP Distributed Processing Peripheral.

DPU Dynamic Path Update. Allows IBM networks to add new network nodes or change backup routing paths while the front-end is still operating.

DPX DataPath loop eXtension.

DQDB Distributed Queue Dual Bus. The metropolitan area network technology that operates by maintaining a queue at each station to determine when the station may access its dual buses. The dual buses provide bidirectional transmission between each station. DQDB is IEEE's standard 802.6 for MANs (Metropolitan Area Networks). Formerly called QPSX (Queued Packet and Synchronous Exchange).

DRAFT PROPOSAL An ISO standards document that has been registered and numbered but not yet approved.

DRAG Dragging is a way of moving an item on the screen using your mouse. To drag a window in Windows 3.1, for example, move the mouse pointer onto a window's title bar, then hold down the mouse button while moving the mouse across your desktop. When you release the mouse button, the window will remain in its new location. Apply this technique to drag any data object, such as icons or list box items.

DRAG AND DROP The "drag and drop" definition defines how objects from one desktop application can be "dragged" out of that application, through clicking on the object with a mouse, across the desktop and "dropped" on another application. Most of the graphics operating systems, like Windows, Apple's Mactinosh and Sun Sparc use Drag and Drop.

DRAG LINE A length of rope or string used to pull wire and cable through conduit or inaccessible spaces. Drag lines are often inserted in wall and ceilings during construction to ease future wire installation.

DRAIN WIRE In a cable, an uninsulated wire laid over the component or components and used as a ground connection.

DRAM 1. Dynamic Random Access Memory chip. See MICROPROCESSOR for an full explanation. See also DYNAMIC RANDOM ACCESS MEMORY. 2. Digital Recorder Announcer Module.

DRAWING In the manufacture of wire, pulling the metal through a die or series of dies in order to reduce the diameter to a specified size.

DRAWING TOOLS A computer imaging term. The means of creating freehand lines or basic geometric shapes. Paint packages often provide an ellipse-drawing function as a variation of the circle (or vice versa) and a square drawing function as a variation of the rectangle. Virtually all packages offer filled geometric figures, the fill item being either a solid color or a pattern.

DRESSING CABLE You "dress" cable by taking multiple cables and joining them together neatly with cable ties. A nicely-dressed, clean installation is a sign of telephony professionalism. It still exists.

DRIFT A slow change in a normally constant signal. The term typically applies to movements in the signal's frequency.

DRIVE MAPPINGS A Novell NetWare term. Drive mappings provide direct access to particular locations in the directory structure. They are a "shorthand" method for accessing directories on a disk. Instead of typing in the complete pathname of a directory that you want to access, you can simply enter a drive letter that has been assigned to that directory. Netware recognizes two types of drives (physical drives and logical drives) and three types of drive mappings (local, network, and search drive mappings).

DRIVER A driver (which is always software) provides instructions for reformatting or interpreting software commands for transfer to and from peripheral devices and the central processor unit (CPU). Many printed circuit boards which you drop into a PC require a software driver in order for the other parts of the computer and the software you're running to work correctly. In other words, the driver is a software module that "drives" the data out of a specific hardware port. The port in question will usually have another device connected, such as a printer or modem, and the driver will be organized in software (i.e. configured) to communicate with the device.

DROP 1. A wire or cable from a pole or cable terminal to a building. 2. That portion of a device that looks toward the internal station facilities, e.g., toward an AUTOVON 4-wire switch, toward a switchboard,or toward switching center. 3. The central office side of test jacks. 4. To delete, intentionally or unintentionally, part of a signal for some reason, e.g., dropping bits.

DROP AND INSERT That process wherein a part of the information carried in a transmission system is demodulated (dropped) at an intermediate point and different information is entered (inserted) for subsequent transmission.

DROP CABLE 1. The outside wire pair which connects your house or office to the transmission line coming from the phone company's central office. See also DROP WIRE, which is different. 2. In local area networks, a cable that connects perpendicularly to the main network cable or bus, and attaches to the DTE equipment.

DROP CHANNEL OPERATION A type of operation where one or more channels of a multichannel system are terminated (dropped) at any intermediate point between the end terminals of the system.

DROP LOOP The segment of wire from the nearest telephone pole to your home or business.

DROP OUTS Drop outs are one major cause of errors in data communications circuits. The technical definition is that the signal level drops more than 12 dB (decibels) for more than 4 milliseconds. It means some of your data will not arrive. A four millisecond drop out in a transmission at 2,400 bits per second will lose about ten bits. A "drop out" is similar to a person's voice fades away in a telephone conversation. To correct the problem of drop out,we will ask the person (or computer) at the other end to repeat what they just said. "Huh?" This is called retransmission of data. In telephony, drop outs are defined as incidents when signal level unexpectedly drops at least 12 dB for more than 4 milliseconds. (Bell standard allows no more than two drop outs per 15 minute period.)

DROP REPEATER A repeater that is provided with the necessary equipment for local termination (dropping) of one or more channels of a multichannel system.

DROP SET All parts needed to complete connection from the drop (wall plate, coupling, MOD-MOD) to the terminal equipment. This would typically include a modular line cord and interface adapter.

DROP SIDE Defines all cabling and connectors from the terminal equipment to the patch panel or punch down block designated for terminal equipment at the distribution frame.

DROP WIRE Wires going from your phone company to the 66 Block or protector in your building. See also DISTRIBUTION CABLE.

DROPOUTS See DROP OUTS.

DROPPED CALL A call in which the radio link between the cellular customer and the cell site is broken. Dropped calls can happen often, and for many reasons, including terrain, equipment problems, atmospheric interference, and traveling out of range.

DRU DACS Remote Unit.

DRUM FACTOR In facsimile systems, the ratio of drum length to drum diameter. Where drums are not used, it is the ratio of the equivalent dimensions.

DRUM SPEED The angular speed of the facsimile transmitter or recorder drum, measured in revolutions per minute.

DRUNKEN SWEDE A way of describing the sound of a computer doing text-to-speech conversion. "Why, he sounds like a drunken swede." This great definition from Stuart Segal of Phone Base Systems, Inc in Vienna, VA. Says Stuart, "Our people think that a drunken swede has recorded this message."

DRY CELL A type of primary cell in which the electrolyte is in the form of a paste rather than that of a liquid.

DRY CIRCUIT A circuit over which voice signals are transmitted and which carries no direct current.

DRY CONTACT An electrical contact made by a pair of metallic contacts. You might close a metallic contact, thus operating a relay which might turn something of higher power on or off. For example, a low voltage signal in a key system might cause a dry contact to close, thus causing much higher voltage to flow to a bell, a klaxon, a strobe light. Wheelock Signals makes lots of dry contact devices. There is no such animal as a "wet contact," except maybe an acquaintance who's crying or a phone system under water.

DRY ELECTROLYTIC CONDENSER An electrolytic condenser in which the electrolyte is in the form of a paste or jelly rather than that of a liquid.

DRY LOOP POWERING Refers to local (not span) plowering, and a transmission medium other than copper wire (microwave/fiber optic).

DRY T-1 A T-1 line with an unpowered interface. A T-1 line with a power is called "Wet."

DRY TWISTED PAIR A normal telephone twisted pair without loading coils. It carries only data, not data and voice.

DS Danske Standardiseringsrad (Danish Standards Institution).

DS- A hierarchy of digital signal speeds used to classify capacities of lines and trunks. The fundamental speed level is DS-0 (64-kilobits per second) and the highest is DS-4 (about 274 million bits per second. Here are the definitions: DS-1, DS-1C, DS-2, DS-3, DS-4. They correspond to 1.544, 3.152, 6.312, 44.736, and 274.176 Mbps. DS-1 is also called T-1.

DS-0 Digital Service, level 0. It is 64,000 bps, the worldwide standard speed for digitizing one voice conversation using pulse code modulation (PCM). There are 24 DS- channels in a DS-1.

DS-1 Digital Service, level 1. It is 1.544 Mbps in North America, 2.048 Mbps elsewhere. Why there's no consistency is one of those wonderful, unanswered, questions. The 1.544 standard is an old Bell System standard. The 2.048 standard is a CCITT standard. Standard for 1.544 Mbps is 24 voice conversations each encoded at 64 Kbps. Standard for 2.048 megabits is 30 conversations.

DS-1C Digital Service, level 1C. It is 3.152 Mbps in North America and is carried on T-1.

DS-2 Digital Service, level 2. It is 6.312 Mbps in North America and is carried on T-2.

DS-3 Digital Service, level 3. Equivalent of 28 T-1 channels, and operating at 44.736 Mbps. Also called T-3.

DS-4 Digital Signal, level 4. 274,176,000 bits per second. 168 T1s. 168 DS1s. 4032 standard voice channels.

DS0 Digital Signal, level Zero. Pronounced "D-S Zero." DS0 is 64,000 bits per second. It is equal to one voice conversation digitized under PCM. Twenty-four DS0s (24x64 Kbps) equal one DS1, which is T-1 or 1.544 million bits per second. See DS-0.

DS0-A Refers to a process where a subrate signal (2.4, 4.8, or 9.6 Kbps) is repeated 20, 10 or 5 times, respectively to make a 64 Kbps DS-0 channel.

DS0-B Refers to a process performed by a subrate multiplexer where twenty 2.4 Kbps, ten 4.8 Kbps, or five 9.6 Kbps signals are bundled into one 64 Kbps DS-0 channel.

DS1 Digital Signal, level One. A 1.544 Mbps digital signal carried on a T-1 transmission facility. See DS-1.

DS2 Digital Signal, level Two. 6,312,000 bits per second. Four T1s. Four DS1s. 96 standard voice channels.

DS3 Digital Signal, level Three. 44,736,000 bits per second. 28 T1s. 28 DS1s. 672 standard voice channels.

DS4 Digital Signal, level Four. 274,176,000 bits per second. 168 T1s. 168 DS1s. 4032 standard voice channels.

DSA Distributed Systems Architecture, the network architecture developed by Honeywell.

DSAT Digital Supervisory Audio Tones. A supervisory signaling scheme used in NAMPS — a new form of digital cellular radial called Narrow-band Advanced Mobile Phone service. See also NAMP.

DSC Digital Selecting Calling. A synchronous system developed by the International Radio Consultative Committee (CCIR), used to establish contact with a station or group of stations automatically by radio. The operational and technical characteristics of this system are contained in CCIR Recommendation 493.

DSDC Direct Service Dialing Capability. Network services provided by local switches interacting with remote data bases via CCIS.

DSE Data Switching Equipment.

DSI Digital Speed Interpolation. A technique for squeezing more voice conversations onto a line. DSI digitizes speech so it can be cut into slices, such that no bits are transmitted when no one is speaking. As soon as speech begins, bits flow again. See DIGITAL SPEECH INTERPOLATION.

DSL See DIGITAL SUBSCRIBER LINE.

DSN 1. Distributed Systems Network, the network architecture developed by Hewlett-Packard. 2. Double Shelf Network.

DSP Display System Protocol or Digital Signal Processor. A Digital Signal Processor is a specialized computer chip designed to perform speedy and complex operations on digitized waveforms. Useful in processing sound and video.

DSP MODULE An internal module of the National Sensor Conductor NS32FX16 processor that handles vector operations on complex variables, enhancing DSP performance of the device.

DSR Data Set Ready. This signal is on pin 6 of the RS-232-C connector. It means the modem (which some telephone companies call a "data set") is ready to send data from the terminal. Some modems use Data Set Ready. Some don't. Modems that are snooty enough to give you the DSR signal, are obnoxious enough to not work until they receive the DTR (Data Terminal Ready) signal from the terminal on pin 20. By bridging pins 6 and 20 on the connector at the modem, you can usually get it to work. If it doesn't, bridge in pin 8 (carrier detect) as well.

DSS Direct Station Select. A piece of key telephone equipment usually attached to an operator's phone set. When the operator needs to call a particular extension he/she simply touches the corresponding button on the Direct Station Select equipment. Typically DSS equipment/feature is part of a Busy Lamp Field (BLF), which shows with lights what's happening at each extension. Is it busy? Is it on hold, etc.?

DSS is also Decision Support Systems. Computerized systems for transforming data into useful information, such as statistical models or predictions of trends, usually in a graphical format, which is used by management in the decision-making process. See DECISION SUPPORT SYSTEMS.

DSRR Digital Short Range Radio.

DSTN Double Super Twisted Nematic. A display technology which uses two layers of crystal to correct distortions caused by the first layer and so improve readability.

DSU Digital Service Unit, also called Data Service Unit. Converts RS-232-C or other terminal interface to DSX-1 interface. See DATA SERVICE UNIT.

DSU/CSU The devices used to access digital data channels channels are called DSU/CSUs (Data Service Unit/Channel Service Units). At the customer's end of the telephone connection, these devices perform much the same function for digital circuits that modems provide for analog connections. For example, DSU/CSUs take data from terminals and computers, encode it, and transmit it down the link. At the receive end, another DSU/CSU equalizes the received signal, filters it, and decodes it for interpretation by the end-user.

DSX Digital System Cross-connect frame. A bay or panel to which T-1 lines and DS1 circuit packs are wired and that permits cross-connections by patch cords and plugs. A DSX panel is used in small office applications where only a few digital trunks are installed. See also DACS.

DSX-1 Digital Signal Cross-connect Level 1. The set of parameters for cross connecting DS-1 lines.

DSX-3 The designation for the DS3 point of interface (cross-connect).

DTC 1. Digital Trunk Controller. 2. Digital Transmit Command.

DTE 1. Data Terminal Equipment. In the RS-232-C standard specification, the RS-232-C is connected between the DCE (Data Communications Equipment) and a DTE. The main difference between a DCE and a DTE is that pins two and three are reversed. See also DCE and the Appendix. 2. Defense Technology Enterprise.

DTE-DCE RATE Data terminal equipment/data communications equipment rate. A designation for the maximum rate at which a modem and a PC can exchange information, expressed in kilobits per second (kbps). For maximum performance, a modem must support a DTE-DCE rate in excess of its maximum theoretical throughput.

DTLU Digital Trunk and Line Unit. Provides system access for T1-carrier lines used for interoffice trunks or remote switching module umbilicals.

DTMF Dual Tone Multi-Frequency. A fancy term describing push button or Touchtone dialing. (Touchtone is a registered trademark of AT&T.) In DTMF, when you touch a button on a pushbutton pad, it makes a tone, actually a combination of two tones, one high frequency and one low frequency. Thus the name Dual Tone Multi Frequency. In U.S. telephony, there are actually two types of "tone" signaling, one used on normal business or home pushbutton/touchtone phones, and one used for signaling within the telephone network itself. When you go into a central office, look for the testboard. There you'll see what looks like a standard touchtone pad. Next to the pad there'll be a small toggle switch that allows you to choose the sounds the touchtone pad will make — either normal touchtone dialing (DTMF) or the network version (MF).

The eight possible tones that comprise the DTMF signaling system were specially selected to easily pass through the telephone network without attenuation and with minimum interaction with each other. Since these tones fall within the frequency range of the human voice, additional considerations were added to prevent the human voice from inadvertantly imitating or "falsing" DTMF signaling digits. One way this was done to break the tones into two groups, a high frequency group and a low frequency group. A valid DTMF tone has only one tone in each group. Here is a table of the DTMF digits with their respective frequencies. One Hertz (abbreviated Hz.) is one cycle per second of frequency.

Digit	Low frequency	High frequency
1	697 Hz.	1209 Hz.
2	697	1336
3	697	1477
4	770	1209
5	770	1336
6	770	1477
7	852	1209
8	852	1336
9	852	1477
0	941	1336
*	941	1209
#	941	1477

There are four other digits defined in the DTMF system and usable for specialized applications that cannot be generated by standard telephones. They are:

A	697 Hz.	1633 Hz.
B	770	1633
C	852	1633
D	941	1633

Normal telephones (yours and mine) have 12 buttons, thus 12 combinations. Government Autovon (Automatic Voice Network) telephones have 16 combinations, the extra four (those above) being used for "precedence," which in Federal government parlance is a designation assigned to a phone call by the caller to indicate to communications personnel the relative urgency (therefore the order of handling) of the call and to the called person the order in which the message is to be noted.

DTMF AUTOMATIC ROUTING This is a term relating to a fax server operating on a Novell file server. In this system, the fax software assigns a four-digit number to each user. A fax sender dials the fax line, and after the fax server answers, it sends a special autorouting request signal. The sender dials the four-digit number for the correct user, and the fax is automatically sent to the user's workstation on the LAN.

DTMF CUT-THROUGH The capability of a voice response system to receive DTMF tones while the voice synthesizer is delivering information, i.e. during speech playback. This capability of DTMF cut-through saves the user waiting until the machine has played the whole message (which typically is a menu with options). The user can simply touchtone his response anytime during the message — when he first hears his selection number, when the message first starts, etc. When the voice processor hears the touchtoned selection (i.e. the DTMF cut-through), it stops speaking and jumps to the chosen selection. For example, the machine starts to say, "If you know the person you're calling, touchtone his extension in now." But before you hear the "If you know" you pushbutton in 230, which you know is Joe's extension. Bingo, the message stops and Joe's extension starts ringing.

DTMF REGISTER A printed circuit card in a switch that converts the DTMF signals coming from the phone into signals which can be used by the switch's stored program control, central computer to do its switching, etc.

DTMF TO DIAL PULSE CONVERSION A PBX feature. DTMF (pushbutton) phones are very popular. But sometimes you install a PBX with pushbutton phones in an area which doesn't have a central office which will respond to pushbutton tones. It's old. In this case, anyone dialing on a pushbutton phone will find that the PBX converts that dialing to rotary pulsing when the PBX accesses a trunk which can't handle pushbutton dialing. All this doesn't speed up the time the call takes to get through. It just speeds up the user's dialing and makes him or her feel she is dealing with a more modern phone system.

DTP DeskTop Publishing.

DTR Data Terminal Ready. A control signal sent from the DTE to the DCE that indicates that the DTE is powered on and ready to communicate. DTR can also be used for hardware flow control.

DTS Digital Termination Systems. Microwave based transmission technology designed for bypass functions for short-hop, line-of-sight applications. It never converts to analog. Is useful in high-volume, pure-data applications in urban settings where line costs are high. It requires FCC license and is referred to formally by FCC as Digital Electronic Message Service, or DEMS.

DTSR Dial Tone Speed Recording.

DTU Digital Test Unit.

DU Fiber Optic Connector developed by Nippon Electric Group.

DUAL CABLE A two-cable system in broadband LANs in which coaxial cable provides two physical paths for transmission, one for transmit and one for receive, instead of dividing the capacity of a single cable.

DUAL COAT An optical fiber coating structure consisting of a soft inner coating and a hard outer coating.

DUAL FIBER CABLE A type of optical fiber cable that has two single-fiber cables enclosed in an extruded overjacket of polyvinyl chloride with a rip cord for peeling back the overjacket to access the fibers.

DUAL HEADSET Also known as an integrated headset. A special type of headset for the blind. One jack plugs into a telephone and another jack plugs into a telephone and another jack plugs into a specially configured PC. This PC provides voice synthesized output. The dual headset allows a visually impaired TSR (Telephone Sales Representative) hands-free capability. Example: The Social Security Administration has numerous blind TSRs handling incoming public calls. Dual headsets allow these blind TSRs to perform their duties with no deterioration in public service. This definition provided by Matt Gottlieb, telecommunications specialist for the Social Security Administration.

DUAL MODE Dual mode is the cellular industry's term for a cellular phone which will work for both analog and digital cellular phone systems. The cellular phone industry is going digital. Today's analog phones won't work on tomorrow's digital systems. But some phones — dual mode — will work on both. You need to buy them over today's analog phones. You also need to be careful that the digital mode which you get in your dual mode cellular phone will work with the digital technology of your local carrier. That's not as standard, as yet, as today's analog technology, which works universally in North America.

DUAL NAM Allows a cellular phone user to have two phone numbers with the same or separate carriers. Very useful for someone who spends half his life in one place and half in another. For example, a friend of mine lives in

LA, but works weekdays in Phoenix. His handheld cellular has phone numbers from LA and Phoenix carriers.

DUAL TONE MULTI-FREQUENCY DTMF. A way of signaling consisting of a pushbutton or touchtone dial that sends out a sound which consists of two discrete tones, picked up and interpreted by telephone switches — either PBXs or central offices. See DTMF.

DUCT A pipe, tube or conduit through which cables or wires are passed. Duct space is always at a premium. If you ever install a duct, make sure it's twice the diameter you think you need. If you're lucky, it will last a couple of years. The cost of putting in thicker or extra ducts is peanuts compared to the cost of having to install additional ones later. Digging up places is getting very expensive, despite Ditch Witch, a company that makes the greatest backhoe trenching equipment. And also has the greatest name.

DUCT LINER A small diameter pipe or tubing placed inside conventional underground conduit so you can install fiber optic or cables. Its main purpose is to provide a clean, continuous path with known frictional characteristics.

DUCTILE Capable of being drawn out, hammered thin or being flexed or bent without failure.

DUE DATE The date an event is to occur, i.e. an installation, a change or a connection. Some vendors give accurate due dates. Penalty clauses work most effectively in ensuring due dates are met.

DUMB SWITCH A slang word for a telecommunications switch that contains only basic switching software and relies on instructions sent it by an outside computer. Those instructions are typically fed the "dumb" switch through a cable from the computer to one or more RS-232 serial ports which the dumb switch sports. The switch makes no demands on what type of computer it talks to, but simply insists that it be able to feed the computer questions and promptly receive responses in a form that it (the switch) can understand. Plain ASCII is OK. For example, the dumb switch might signal the computer, "A call is coming in on port 23, what do I do now?" The computer might reply "Answer it and transfer it to extension 23." Or it might say "answer it and put it on hold," or "answer it, put it on hold and play it recording number three." In essence, a dumb switch is anything but. It is in reality an empty cage containing whatever network interface cards the user has chosen. Each of these network interface cards is designed to "talk" to one type of telephone line. That line might be a T-1 line. It might be a normal tip and ring loop start line. It might be a tie trunk with E&M signaling. The card may handle one or many lines, but always of the same type. The card knows how to answer a call or pulse out a call on that particular type of line. It has all the telephony smarts. What it lacks is the intelligence of what to do with the calls. That is provided by the outside computer. Well, almost. Most "dumb" switches do contain rudimentary intelligence — a small computer and some memory. That computer is usually programmed to handle "default" calls — and to handle calls should the link to the outside computer fail, or the outside computer itself fail. Dumb switches come in flavors all the way from residing in their own cabinet to being printed circuit cards which reside in one or more of the personal computer's slots. Dumb switches are programmed to do "specialized" telecom applications, for example emergency 911, added value 800 services, cellular switching, automatic call distributors, predictive dialers, etc. They can, of course, be programmed to be "normal" PBXs. The question increasingly being asked is "If I want to program a specialized telecom application should I use a dumb switch or should I use an open PBX?" And the answer is "It depends." Depends on what you want to do. Depends on what software is available, etc. See also OAI.

DUMB TERMINAL A computer terminal with no processing or no programming capabilities. Hence, it derives all its power from the computer it is attached to — typically over a local hardwire or a phone line. A dumb terminal does not employ a data transmission protocol and only sends or receives data one character at a time, sequentially. There are many reasons for "dumb" terminals. They're cheap. They're foolproof. Operators don't have to mess with floppy disks, etc. The require minimal training. Dumb terminals are typically used for simple data entry and data retrieval tasks. Their disadvantage is that everything must come from the central computer — not only the information (data record) but also the form in which to put it. This has led to the creation of "intelligent" terminals, which have a modicum of capabilities — such as an inbuilt (with software) form, some smart function keys and perhaps, a modicum of processing power, etc.

DUMMY LOAD A dissipative impedance-matched network, used at the end of a transmission line to absorb all incident power, usually converted to heat.

DUMP To copy the entire contents of something — memory, a file on a disk, a complete disk — to a printer or another magnetic storage medium.

DUOBINARY SIGNAL A pseudobinary-coded signal in which a "O" ("zero") bit is represented by a zero-level electric current or voltage; a "1" ("one") bit is represented by a positive-level current or voltage if the quality of "O" bits since the last "1" bit is even. and by a negative-level current or voltage if the quantity of "O" bits since the last "1" bit is odd. Duobinary signals require less bandwidth than NRZ. Duobinary signaling also permits addition of error-checking bits.

DUPLEX 1. Simultaneous two-way transmission in both directions. A data communications term. 2. Two-sided printing.

DUPLEX CIRCUIT A telephone line or circuit used to transmit in both directions at the same time. Also referred to as full duplex as opposed to half duplex which allows transmission in only one direction at one time.

DUPLEX OPERATION The simultaneous transmission and reception of signals in both directions.

DUPLEX SIGNALING DX. A direct current signaling system that transmits signals directly on the cable pair.

DUPLEX TRANSMISSION The simultaneous transmission of two series of signals by a single operating communicating device. A data communications term.

DUPLEXER A device which splits a higher speed source data stream into two separate streams for transmission over two data channels. Another duplexer at the other end puts the two slower speed streams back together into one higher-spread stream.

DUTY CYCLE The ratio of operating time to total elapsed time for a device that operates intermittently. Usually expressed as a percentage.

DV-1 As in Northern Telecom's PBX/computer product called the Meridian DV-1.

DVI Digital Video Interactive. A name for including still and moving video pictures in material shown on a PC's screen. DVI is part of multimedia. DVI is also Intel's scheme for digitizing and compressing video and audio for storage, editing, playback and integration into PC applications. Theoretically with DV-I, you'll be able to compress about 70 minutes of video onto a standard CR-ROM. See DIGITAL VIDEO INTERACTIVE.

DX SIGNALING A form of DC (direct current) signaling in which the differences in voltage on two pairs of a four-wire trunk indicates the supervision information, i.e. the call's beginning, its end, etc. See DUPLEX SIGNALING.

DXI Data eXchange Interface. A specification developed by the SMDS (Switched Megabit (or Multi-megabit) Data Services) Interest Group to define the interaction between internetworking devices and CSUs/DSUs that are transmitting over an SMDS access line. SMDS is a way for a corporate network to dial up switched data services as fast as 45 megabits per second.

DYE SUBLIMATION a spectacular printing process that works by turning the color toner briefly into gas, which "seeps" into the paper. The colors merge, yielding a nearly continuous tone image. You literally can't distinguish the output from a photograph with your bare eye. You do need special paper, however.

DYNAMIC Events are constantly changing.

DYNAMIC ANSWER This a term typically used in Automatic Call Distributors. The ability to dynamically assign the number of ring cycles (interrupt, more or less) to the queue period when agents are unavailable. The implication of being able to assign this number allows return supervision to the calling in person to be delayed and thus not allow billing on 800 INWATS lines to begin. This is a money saving feature. But it can cost you some customers if they get bored waiting for your phones to pick up.

DYNAMIC BACKUP A backup made while the database is active.

DYNAMIC BANDWIDTH ALLOCATION The capability of subdividing large, high-capacity network transmission resources among multiple applications almost instantaneously, and providing each application with only that share of the bandwidth that the application needs at that moment. Dynamic bandwidth allocation is a feature available on certain high-end T-1 multiplexers that allows the total bit rate of the multiplexer's circuits to exceed the bandwidth of the network trunk. This works because the multiplexer only assigns channels on the network trunk to circuits that are transmitting.

DYNAMIC BEAM FOCUSING When you have a curved cathode ray tube, the distance between the gun which shoots the electrons and all the parts of the screen are equal. When you have a flat screen, the distance varies slightly. Some beams have to travel further. When some have to travel not so far, Dynamic beam focusing, a term I first heard used by NEC, focuses each electron to the precise distance it must travel, thus ensuring edge-to-edge clarity on the screen.

DYNAMIC CAPACITY ALLOCATION The process of determining and changing the amount of shared communications capacity assigned to nodes in the network based on current need.

DYNAMIC DATA EXCHANGE DDE. A form of interprocess communication in Microsoft Windows and OS/2. When two or more programs that support DDE are running simultaneously, they can exchange information and commands. In Windows 3.1, this capability is enhanced with Object Linking and Embedding (OLE).

DYNAMIC-LINK LIBRARY DLL. An executable code module for Microsoft Windows that can be loaded on demand and linked at run time, and then unloaded when the code is no longer needed.

DYNAMIC LOAD BALANCING A technique where a switching system, particularly multiple connected ACDs, apportion incoming calls (the load) to balance the workload. This is done dynamically in real time.

DYNAMIC LOUD SPEAKER A loud speaker in which the diaphragm is driven by means of a small "voice coil" suspended in a powerful magnetic field.

DYNAMIC MEMORY The most common form of memory, used for RAM, with an access speed ranging from about 60 to 150 nanoseconds. (A nanosecond is thousandth of a second.) Dynamic memory is an inexpensive but relatively complicated form of semiconductor memory with two states: presence and absence of electrical charge. Dynamic memory requires a continuous electrical current. All data is lost when the power is cut. Frequent saving files to disk helps preserve your data.

DYNAMIC MICROPHONE A microphone, the coil of which is moved in a strong magnetic field by vibrations striking the diaphragm to which it is attached. Electrical currents are thus generated in the moving coil.

DYNAMIC NODE ACCESS A high-speed bus invented by Dialogic to join together multiple voice processing PEB-based systems. PEB stands for PCM Expansion Bus. See PEB.

DYNAMIC OVERLOAD CONTROL DOC. The feature of a switch which uses its translation tables and intelligence to allow the switch to adapt to changes in traffic loads by re-routing and blocking call attempts.

DYNAMIC RAM RAM memory that requires data to be refreshed periodically to prevent its loss in memory.

DYNAMIC RANDOM ACCESS MEMORY RAM which requires electronic refresh cycles every few milliseconds to preserve its data. See also RANDOM ACCESS MEMORY.

DYNAMIC RANGE In a transmission system, the ratio of the overload level to the noise level of the system, usually expressed in decibels. The ratio of the specified maximum level of a parameter (e.g., power, voltage, frequency, or floating point number representation) to its minimum detectable or positive value, usually expressed in decibels.

DYNAMIC RESOURCE ALLOCATION The assignment of network capacity to specific users and specific services as required on a moment-to-moment basis.

DYNAMIC STORAGE ALLOCATION The allocation of memory space while a program is running. The memory is released when the program is complete.

DYNAMIC VARIATION A short time variation outside of steady-state conditions in the characteristics of power delivered to communication equipment.

DYNAMICALLY ADAPTIVE ROUTING An algorithm, used for route determination in packet-switched networks that automatically routes traffic around congested, damaged, or destroyed switches and trunks and allows the system to continue to function over the remaining portions of the network.

DYNAMO An electrical machine which generates a direct current.

DYNAMOTOR A direct current machine having two windings on its armature: one acting as a motor, the other as a generator.

E

E (ECHO) CHANNEL 16 kbps ISDN basic rate channel echoing contents of DCEs to DTEs. Used in bidding for access to multipoint link.

E & M LEADS The pair of wires carrying signals between trunk equipment and a separate signaling equipment unit. The "M" lead transmits a ground or battery conditions to the signaling equipment. The "E" lead receives open or ground signals from the signaling equipment. These leads are also known as Ear and Mouth Leads. The Ear lead typically means to receive and the Mouth lead typically means to transmit. Changes of voltage on these leads convey such information as seizure of circuit, recognition of seizure, release of circuit, dialed digits, etc. In the old days it was the PBX operators who originated trunk calls by asking the long distance carrier for free trunks using their mouth or M lead. If the carrier had a free trunk, the PBX heard about it through its ear or E lead. See also E & M SIGNALING.

E & M SIGNALING In telephony, an arrangement that uses separate leads, called respectively the "E" lead and "M" lead, for signaling and supervisory purposes. The near end signals the far end by applying -48 volts dc (vdc) to the "M" lead, which results in a ground being applied to the far end's "E" lead. When -48 vdc is applied to the far end "M" lead, the near-end "E" lead is grounded. The "E" originally stood for "ear," i.e., when the near-end "E" lead was grounded, the far end was calling and "wanted your ear." The "M" originally stood for "mouth," because when the near-end wanted to call (i.e., speak to) the far end, -48 vdc was applied to that lead.

When a PBX wishes to connect to another PBX directly or to a remote PBX or extension telephone over a leased voice grade line, a channel on T-1, the PBX uses a special line interface which is quite different from that which it uses to interface to the phones it's attached directly to (i.e. with in-building wires). The basic reason for the difference between a normal extension interface and the long distance interface is that the signaling requirements differ — even if the voice signal parameters such as level and two-wire, 4-wire remain the same. When dealing with tie lines or trunks it is costly, inefficient and too slow for a PBX to do what an extension telephone would do, i.e. go off hook, wait for dial tone, dial, wait for ringing to stop, etc. The E&M tie trunk interface device is the closest thing there is to a standard that exists in the PBX, T-1 multiplexer, voice digitizer telco world. But even then it comes in at least five different flavors. See E & M LEADS.

E-1 Another name given to the CEPT digital telephony format devised by the CCITT that carries data at the rate of 2.048 Mbps (DS-1 level). CEPT format consists of 30 voice channels, one signaling channel, and one framing (synchronization) channel. Since robbed-bit signaling is not used (as it is for T-1 in North America) all 8 bits per channel are used to code the waveshape sample. E-1 is the European version of North American T-1, though T-1 is 1.544 Mbps. See T-1.

E-911 SERVICE Enhanced 911 service. Dial 911 in most major cities and you'll be connected with an emergency service run typically by a combination of the local police and local fire departments. 911 service becomes enhanced 911 emergency reporting service when there is a minimum of two special features added to it. E-911 provides ANI (Automatic Number Identification) and ALI (Automatic Location Information) to the 911 operator. Picture: A call comes in. Someone is dying. The 911 operator's screen comes alive as his phone rings. The number calling is on the screen. The caller is dying and needs an ambulance. The operator punches a button or two and his screen immediately indicates the location of the ambulance dispatch center nearest the caller. The operator contacts the dispatch center and an ambulance gets there in short order. (Remember, this is a book, not the real world.)

E-BEND A smooth change in the direction of the axis of a waveguide, throughout which the axis remains in a plane parallel to the direction of electric E-field (transverse) polarization.

E-MAIL Electronic Mail.

E-TDMA Extended Time Division Multiple Access. A proposed, new, standard for cellular. Other standards are TDMA (Time Division Multiple Access), CDMA (Code Division Multiple Access) and NAMPS (Narrow Advanced Mobile Phone Service). Refers to the extended (digital cellular) transmission technology developed by Hughes Network Systems. E-TDMA is alleged to have 15 times the capacity of today's analog cellular phone systems — in other words to allow the simultaneous use of 15 times as many cellular phones as today's analog cellular phone system.

E.164 A scheme to assign numbers to phone lines.

EA SEE EQUAL ACCESS.

EADAS Engineering and Adminstrative Data Acquistion System.

EADAS/NWM EADAS NetWork Management.

EARLY TOKEN RELEASE This is a method of token passing which allows for two tokens to exist on the network simultaneously. It is used primarily in 16-Mbps token ring LANs. On a regular 4-Mbps token ring LAN, the token is passed on only after the sending computer receives its message back from the destination computer. With early token release, the sending computer does not wait for its message to return before passing the token. This means there are two tokens on the network at the same time. This is done to take advantage of the idle time created on the faster token ring. While the message is moving to its destination and back the sending computer is idle. On the 4-Mbps token ring, this is not much of a problem since most of the time the message is on the ring. On the 16-Mbps token ring less of this idle time is transmission time and more is taken by copying the message to the token ring card. That is, on the faster ring, there is more of a window for a second token. Early token release is especially helpful when traffic is heavy.

EAROM An acronym for Electrically Alterable Read-Only Memory. A type of ROM chip which can be erased and reprogrammed without having to be removed from the circuit board. An EAROM is reprogrammed electrically faster and more conveniently than an EPROM (Erasable Programmable Read-Only Memory). An EAROM chip does not lose its memory when power is turned off.

EARTH GROUND The connection of an electrical system to earth. This connection is necessary to provide lightning and static protection as well as to establish the zero-voltage reference for the system. See EARTH GROUNDING.

EARTH GROUND ELECTRODE The conducting body in contact with the earth. The grounding electrode may be a metallic cold water pipe when used in conjunction with a driven rod, a mat, a grid, etc. Earth should never be used as the sole equipment grounding conductor.

EARTH GROUNDING The purpose of earth grounding is essentially threefold:

1.   Lightning protection; 2. Static protection; and 3. Establish a zero voltage reference. See GROUND and GROUNDING.

EARTH STATION The antenna and associated equipment used to receive and/or transmit telecommunications signals via satellite.

EARTHING There are two distinct and unique categories in the broad area called grounding. One is earthing, which is designed to guard against the adverse effects of lightning, assist in the reduction of static and bring a zero-voltage reference to system components in order that logic circuits can communicate from a known reference. The other category of grounding is known as equipment grounding. This is the primary means of protecting personnel from electrocution. According to the Electric Power Research Institute, "electrical wiring and grounding defects are the source of 90% of all equipment failures." Many telephone system installer/contractors have found that checking for and repairing grounding problems can solve many telephone system problems, especially intermittent "no trouble found" problems. As electrical connections age, they loosen, corrode and become subject to thermal stress that can increase the impedance of the ground path or increase the resistance of the connection to earth. Equipment is available to test for proper grounding. One of our favorite devices is made by Ecos Electronics in Oak Park, Il. Before you attach any equipment (computer, telephone, hi-fi set, etc.) to an improperly grounded electrical outlet, you should have the problems corrected. See also GROUND and GROUNDING.

EAS Extended Area Service. A novel name for a larger than normal local telephone calling area. The local phone company extends its subscribers the option of paying less per month for a small calling area and paying extra per individual call outside that area (i.e. the extended area), or paying more per month flat rate but having a larger calling area (i.e. having extended area service).

EASE A voice processing applications generator from Expert Systems, Inc. in Atlanta GA.

EAX Electronic Automatic eXchange. Term used throughout the non-Bell telephone industry to refer to an electronic central office. Similar to ESS (Electronic Switching System), the term used by AT&T and the Bell operating telephone companies.

EBCDIC (Pronounced Eb-si-dick.) Extended Binary Coded Decimal Interexchange Code. It is the way IBM codes characters, letters and numbers into a digital binary stream for use in its larger computers. EBCDIC codes characters into eight bits. This gives it 256 possible characters, 2 x 2 x 2 x 2 x 2 x 2 x 2 x 2 = 256. See also EXTENDED CHARACTER SET.

EBCDIC is mainly used in IBM mainframes and minicomputers, while ASCII is used in IBM and non-IBM desktop microcomputers. EBCDIC is not compatible with ASCII, meaning that a computer which understands EBCDIC will not understand ASCII. But there are many real-time and non-real time translation programs that will convert text files back and forth. A good program is Word-For-Word from MasterSoft. See ASCII.

EBS 1. Electronic Business Set. 2. Enhanced Business Service (also known as P-Phone) is an analog Centrex offering provided by Northern Telecom. It operates over a single-pair subscriber loop., providing normal full duplex audio conversations and a secondary 8 KHz half-duplex amplitude shift-keyed signal, which is used to transmit signaling information to and from the Northern Telecom-equipped central office.

EC European Community.

ECCENTRICITY Like concentricity a measure of the center of a conductor's location with respect to the circular cross section of the insulation. Expressed as a percentage of center displacement of one circle within the other.

ECHELON The name of a startup company in Palo Alto that is making a microprocessor chip destined for mundane household appliannces like toasters, air conditioners, ovens, etc. The idea is that chip will be used by these devices to talk to other devices and thus coordinate their coming on and going off and doing things. The chips are destined to be networked together. Early uses for the chip includes smoke detectors which call you when they detect smoke and wall switches that detect when you come into a room and turn the lights on.

ECHO 1. European Commission Host Organization. 2. Exactly what you expect it to mean. You hear yourself speak. Echoes happen in both voice and data conversation. Echoes are good and bad. In voice, an echo happens when the equipment meant to amplify the voice of the party at one end, picks up the signals from the party at the other end, and amplifies them back to that party. Some echo is acceptable (in fact, almost a necessity) in voice conversations. It's called SIDETONE. When the speaker can hear himself speak through the receiver, sidetone gives the speaker some feeling his conversation is actually going through. But too much (i.e. too loud) echo is unacceptable. There are devices called echo suppressors, which do exactly that.

In low speed or on-line data conversations, an echo is positively vital. An echo in a data conversation is where I send my words to the distant computer which "echoes" them back to me and my screen displays them. This way I can visually check if the distant computer received my words/data accurately. In some software programs there's a command called ECHO or ECHOPLEX. Switch it one way, the distant computer echoes the words to my screen. Switch it the other, the words I'm typing on my keyboard are put on my screen.

There are two basic transmission modes in data communications — full duplex and half duplex. In full duplex, I have simultaneous two-way data flowing. In full duplex, I therefore have the capacity to "echo" back the data I am sending and have it displayed on my screen. But this "echoing" depends on the capability and/or programming of the computer at the other end. All dial-up services — Tymnet, GTE Telenet, MCI Mail, etc. — will echo my data back to me so I can check it.

Some computers, such as the extremely dumb Compugraphic typesetter which typeset the first edition of this book, won't send an echo. In this case, if I want to see the data I am sending, I can change the parameters on my communications software to "half duplex." This way I will see what I am sending, but I will not see what the computer is receiving. Which may be very different. (And with our Compugraphic often is.) Of course, watching characters being echoed across your screen is a very poor method of data transmission and only useful in on-line transmissions. Some form of error-checking protocol is much better.

An echo is also a public discussion group that extends over more than one BBS (bulletin board system) via echomail.

ECHO ATTENUATION In a communications circuit (4- or 2-wire) in which the two directions of transmission can be separated from each other, the attenuation of echo signals that return to the input of the circuit under consideration. Echo attenuation is expressed as the ratio of the transmitted power to the received echo power in decibels. See also ATTENTUATION.

ECHO CANCELLATION Technique used in higher-speed modems that allows for the isolation and filtering of unwanted signal energy caused by echoes from the main transmitted signal.

ECHO CHECK A technique for verifying data sent to another location by returning the received data (echoing it back) to the sending end.

ECHO RETURN LOSS ERL. The difference between a frequency signal and the echo on that signal as it reaches its destination.

ECHO SUPPRESSOR Used to reduce the annoying effects of echoes in telephone connections. The worst echoes occur on satellite circuits. An echo suppressor works by turning off transmission in the reverse direction while a person is talking, thus effectively making the circuit one way. An echo suppressor obviously impedes full-duplex data — data flowing both ways simultaneously. Echo suppressors are turned off by the high-pitched tone (typically 2025 Hz) in the answering modem, which it uses to signal it's answered the phone and is ready for a data conversation.

ECHO SUPPRESSOR DISABLER An echo suppressor disabler is a device which causes an echo suppressor to be disabled (i.e. turned off). Echo suppressors are turned off by the high-pitched tone (typically 2025 Hz) in the answering modem, which it uses to signal it's answered the phone and is ready for a data conversation. A disabled echo suppressor stays disabled until the circuit is disconnected and restored to its "ready" connection. Because an echo suppressor hinders full duplex transmission in data communications, it is necessary to disable the echo suppressor.

ECHOMAIL A system by which public discussion group is transmitted via an electronic bulletin board system.

ECHOPLEX A way of checking the accuracy of data transmitted whereby the data received are returned to the sender for comparison with the original data. Somewhat time consuming. Used typically in slowspeed transmissions. See ECHO.

ECITC European Committee for Information Technology testing and Certification.

ECL Emitter Coupled Logic.

ECM Error Correction Mode. An enhancement to Group 3 fax machines. Encapsulated data within HDLC frames providing the received with an opportunity to check for, and request retransmission of garbled data.
See
FACSIMILE and V.17.

ECMA European Computer Manufacturers Association. See also CEPT.

ECOC European Conference on Optical Communication.

ECONOMIC BANDWIDTH An AT&T term for the maximum bandwidth that a physical medium can support without a significant increase in its cost.

ECONOMY OF SCALE As throughput gets bigger, so the per unit cost comes down. This is the argument used by economists to justify monopolies — namely that the per unit costs of one supplier are far lower than having two suppliers. The economy of scale argument is used to justify having only one water company in town. It makes more sense in that industry than in the telephone industry.

It was once used in the telephone industry to justify one combined local phone company/long distance phone company/one supplier of terminal equipment. This argument does not really apply to telephony as technological breakthroughs have brought down the cost of getting into the telephone industry and have allowed smaller, competitive companies to become cost effective. Some large telecommunications monopolies, in fact, are experiencing diseconomies of scale. In this case, their cost of per unit business starts to rise as they get very large. Diseconomies of scale are caused by bloated bureaucracies and inertia in management decision making.

ECONOPATH CALLING PLANS Discount plans for New York City businesses to make calls in their regional calling area. For example, Econopath offers a Manhattan business a discount for calls to the East Suffolk region.

ECP Enhanced Call Processing. An Octel term for an interactive customized menu in its voice mail system which provides levels of call routing. See ENHANCED CALL PROCESSING.

ECPA Electronic Communications Privacy Act.

ECS Energy Communications Services.

ECSA Exchange Carriers Standards Association. See EXCHANGE CARRIERS STANDARDS ASSOCIATION.

ECTUA European Council of Telecommunications Users Association.

EDA Electronic Design Automation.

EDDY CURRENT LOSSES Losses in electrical devices using iron, due to the currents set up in it by magnetic action.

EDF Erbium-Doped Fiber.

EDFA Erbium-Doped Fiber Amplifier. A form of fiber optical amplification where the transmitted light signal passes through a section of erbium-doped fiber and is amplified by means of a laser pump diode. EDFA is used in transmitter booster amplifiers, in-line repeating amplifiers, and receiver preamplifiers.

EDGE CONNECTOR A connector made of strips of brass or other conductive metal found at the edge of a printed circuit board. The connector plus into a socket of another circuit board to exchange electronic signals.

EDH Electronic Document Handling.

EDI Electronic Data Interchange. A series of standards which provide computer-to-computer exchange of business documents between different companies' computers over phone lines. These standards allow for the transmission of purchase orders, shipping documents, invoices, invoice payments, etc. between an enteprise and its "trading partners." A trading partner in EDI parlance is a supplier, customer, subsidiary, or any other organization with which an enterprise conducts business. EDI software translates fixed field or "flat" files that are extracted from applications into a standard format and hands off the translated data to communications software for transmission. EDI standards are supported (i.e. have been adopted) by virtually every computer company in the country and increasingly, by every packet switched data communications company. For example, you can use IBM VAN — IBM's Value Added Network for Electronic Data Interchange. The formats used to convert the documents into EDI data are defined by international standards bodies and by specific industry bodies. See also IES.

EDISON BATTERY A type of storage battery in which the elements are nickel and iron and the electrolyte is potassium hydroxide. An old type of battery.

EDISON EFFECT The phenomenon attributed to Edison, that when a filament is incandescent a current will flow between it and another electrode in the tube. In other words, the light bulb.

EDITING Editing is a familiar process of changing the content of files to achieve more effective communication by cutting, pasting, cropping, resizing, or copying. Multimedia editing can be done on all types of media: voice annotations, music, still images, motion video, graphics and text. Tools for editing vary from simple tools for email voice annotations to more sophisticated tools for video manipulation. See also ELECTRONIC MAIL.

EDITOR A software program used to modify programs or files while they are being prepared or after they are (allegedly) complete. An editor is really a very rudimentary word processing program. When you buy MS-DOS, one of the programs you get is a rudimentary editing program called EDLIN. Most programmers, however, now prefer more advanced editors, like ZEdit. This dictionary was written in ZEdit.

EDLIN The MS-DOS line editor that comes with DOS and which you can use to create and edit batch files and other small text files. It's not very good. There are far better editors around, including QEdit.

EDLS Extended Digital Subscriber Line. The ISDN EDSL combines 23 B-channels and one 64-Kbps D-channel on a single line. Also called the Primary Access Rate.

EDMS An imaging term. Engineering Document Management System.

EDP Electronic Data Processing. Also DP, as in Data Processing. Basically, a machine (also called a computer) that receives, stores, operates on, records and outputs data. The word "electronic" was added to Data Processing when the industry moved away from tab cards — the 80 column "do not spindle," etc. — and was able to accept data electronically, instead of electromechanically as with the tab cards. People in the industry used to be called EDPers. Now the term MIS — Management Information System — is more common.

EDSL See EXTENDED DIGITAL SUBSCRIBER LINE.

EDTV See EXTENDED DEFINITION TV.

EDUTAINMENT Unpopular answer to the question "What do you get when you cross educational material with interactive video?" A term coined by "someone who obviously knows nothing about either education or entertainment," says Laura Buddine, president of multimedia games maker Tiger Media.

EEC European Economic Community.

EEHLLAPI Entry Emulator High Level Language Applications Programming Interface. An IBM API subset of HLLAPI.

EEHO Either End Hop Off. In private networks, a switch program that allows a call destined for an off-net location to be placed into the public network at either the closest switch to the origination or the closest switch to the destination. The choice is usually by time of day and is usually done to take advantage of cheaper rates.

EEPROM Electronically Erasable Programmable Read Only Memory. A read only memory device which can be erased and reprogrammed. Typically, it is programmed electronically (not electromagnetically) with ultraviolet light. EEPROMs don't lose their memory when you lose power. EEPROM used to be often used in PBXs and were the way manufacturers of older style PBXs upgraded their software. Im other words, every time they sent you a software upgrade, they'd send you a bunch of chips. You'd pull out a bunch of chips on one of the main boards in the your PBX. And you'd replace them with the new chips. When you don't have a disk drive (and in the olden days disk drives were very expensive), EEPROMs were the only way to go. EEPROM Setup in a computer allows it to recognize certain system board configurations during initialization. You, the user, can then choose options such as the type of memory chips installed and base memory size without changing jumpers on the system board.

EETDN End-to-End Transit Delay Negotiation.

EF&I Engineer, Furnish and Install.

EFFICIENCY FACTOR In data communications, the ratio of the time to transmit a text automatically and at a specified modulation rate, to the time actually required to receive the same text at a specified maximum error rate.

EFOC European Fiber Optics and Communications conference.

EFT Electronic Funds Transfer. The moving of bits of data from one bank to another. Done in place of moving little green pieces of paper, called money.

EFTA European Free Trade Association.

EFTPOS Electronic Funds Transfer Point Of Sale.

EGA Enhanced Graphics Adapter. Second color video interface standard established for IBM PCs. Maximum resolution is 640 x 350 pixels. See MONITOR.

EHz Exahertz (10 to the 18th power hertz). See also SPECTRUM DESIGNATION OF FREQUENCY.

EI Refers to Europe's 2.048 Mbps (T-1 type) digital carrier system.

EIA Electronic Industries Association. A trade organization of manufacturers which sets standards for use of its member companies, conducts educational programs and lobbies in Washington for its members' collective prosperity. In April 1988, a new association called the Telecommunications Industry Association was formed by a merger of the US Telecommunications Suppliers Association (USTSA) and the Electronics Industries Association's Information and Telecommunications Technologies Group (EIA/ITG). TIA and EIA exist separately, each with its own President and governing board. TIA does, however, represent the telecommunications sector for EIA and works with EIA industry groups and divisions and develops technical standards and does market data gathering. See EIA INTERFACE.

EIA-232-D New version of RS-232-C physical layer interface adopted in 1987.

Each pin on an EIA cable transmits or receives a specific signal. For proper communication, your cable must extend the lines that support *every* signal your equipment needs to operate.

Pin 1   Pin 13

Pin 14   Pin 25

You can be sure of proper transmission with Inmac cables. Our pin configuration conforms strictly to the standards set by the Electronic Industries Association (EIA).

Our chart, right, indicates which pins support a particular function.

Pin	Name	To DTE	To DCE	Function	4	9	25
1	FG		→	Frame Ground	•	•	•
2	TD		→	Transmitted Data	•	•	•
3	RD	←		Received Data	•	•	•
4	RTS		→	Request to Send		•	•
5	CTS	←		Clear to Send		•	•
6	DSR	←		Data Set Ready		•	•
7	SG	←		Signal Ground	•	•	•
8	DCD	←		Data Carrier Detect		•	•
9		←		Positive DC Test Voltage			•
10		←		Negative DC Test Voltage			•
11	QM	←		Equalizer Mode			•
12	(S)DCD	←		Sec. Data Carrier Detect			•
13	(S)CTS	←		Sec. Clear to Send			•
14	(S)TD		→	Sec. Transmitted Data			•
15	TC	←		Transmitter Clock			•
16	(S)RD	←		Sec. Received Data			•
17	RC	←		Receiver Clock			•
18				Unassigned			•
19	(S)RTS		→	Sec. Request to Send			•
20	DTR		→	Data Terminal Ready		•	•
21	SQ	←		Signal Quality Detect			•
22	RI	←		Ring Indicator			•
23			→	Data Ready Selector			•
24	(TC)		→	Ext. Transmitter Clock			•
25				Unassigned			•

*Lines 8 and 20 are jumpered at each connector.

EIA INTERFACE A set of signal characteristics (time, duration, voltage and current) set up by the Electronic Industries Association to standardize the transfer of information between different electronic devices, like computers, modems, printers, etc. The most famous EIA interface is the RS-232-C (now called the RS-232-D and shortly to be called the RS-232-E). EIA-232 specifies three things: the functions of the interchange circuits, the electrical characteristics, AND the connector (EIA-232-E includes two different connectors).

In contrast, the CCITT's V.24 specifies ONLY the interchange circuit FUNCTIONS. V.28 specifies electrical characteristics compatible with EIA-232. ISO 2110 is the internal standard that defines the 25-pole D-shell connector compatible with EIA-232. Following the merger of EIA and the ITG part of EIA, all formed EIA telecommunications standards are now EIA/TIA publications and the standard referred to is now known as EIA/TIE-232-D, edition D, being the most recent. See EIA, EIA/TIA-RS-232-E and RS-232-E.

EIA/TIA-232-E The latest version of the familiar RS-232-C serial data transfer standard for communicating between Data Terminal Equipment (DTE) and Data Circuit Terminating equipment employing serial binary data interchange. (EIA/TIE's exact words.) This standard defines the serial ports on computers, which communicate with such things as external modems, serial printers, data PBXs, etc. You can get your very own copy of the 36-page standard from the EIA Standard Sales Office, 2001 Pennsylvania Avenue, NW, Washington D.C. 20006 202-457-4966. See also the APPENDIX.

EIA/TIA 568 EIA/TIA 568 Commercial Building Wiring Standard. This telecommunications standard in early 1991 was out for industry review under draft specification SP-1907B. Its purpose is to define a generic telecommunications wiring system for commercial buildings that will support a multi-product, multi-vendor environment. It covers topics such as:

- ●.Recognized Media
- ●.Cable Lengths/Performance
- ●.Interface Standards
- ●.Wiring Practices
- ●.Hardware Practices
- ●.Administration

EIGHT HUNDRED SERVICE 800-Service. A generic and common (and not trademarked) term for AT&T's, MCI's, US Sprint's and the Bell operating companies' IN-WATS service. All these IN-WATS services have "800" as their "area code." Dialing an 800-number is free to the person making the call. The call is billed to the person or company being called.

800 Service works like this: You're somewhere in North America. You dial 1-800 and seven digits. Your local central office sees the "1" and recognizes

the call as long distance. It ships that call to a bigger central office (or perhaps processes the call itself). At that central office it's processed, a machine will recognize the 800 "area code" and examine the next three digits. Those three digits will tell which long distance carrier to ship the call to.

Until 800 portability, happened in May, 1993 each 800 provider (local and long distance company) was assigned specific 800 three digit "exchanges." For example, MCI had the exchange 999. AT&T had the exchange 542. If you wanted a phone number beginning with 800-999, then you had to subscribe to MCI 800 service. If you wanted a phone number beginning with 800-542, you had to subscribe to AT&T 800 service. With 800 Portability that is no longer the case.

Here is a history of what the phone industry calls 800 Data Base Access Service. It comes courtesy Bellcore:

"After divestiture (1984), the seven regional telecommunications companies began to provide limited 800 Service on their own as well as in conjunction with interexchange carriers. The regional companies transported 800 calls only within their own calling areas. The 800 number — containing 10 digits in accordance with the North American Numbering Plan (NANP) — was routed onto the long distance carrier's networks.

"The Common Carrier Bureau of the Federal Communications Commisson (FCC) endorsed an incremental approach that would ultimately give the seven companies the right to create their own 800 Service architecture and eliminate reliance on the only existing signaling system (AT&T's). That approach involved assigning to 800 service providers one or more special numbers from the NANP. These numbers, known as "NXX codes," allowed carriers (MCI, Sprint, NY Telephone, etc.) to identify their own 800 numbers and offer their customers 800 numbers.

"Bellcore — Bell Communications Research — began to develop a new network architecture that would allow an 800 Service subscriber to change to another carrier without changing their existing 800 number (full number portability), in accordance with a September 1991 FCC order. That order declared that 800 data base service should be implemented by March 1993 (later extended to May, 1993) and that the old NXX plan be eliminated as long as access times met certain FCC standards.

"In September 1991, the FCC endorsed the plan initially set forth by the Bell operating companies, which provided that the administration of the Number Administration and Service Center (NASC) be transferred from Bellcore to an independent third party outside the telecommunications industry. Lockheed Information Management Systems Company (IMS) was selected by competitive bid to succeed Bellcore as NASC administrator.

"How 800 data base service works: The telecommunications network architecture that supports 800 Data Base Access Service is considered "intelligent" because data bases within the network supplement the call processing function performed by network switches. The Service uses a Common Channel Signaling (CCS) network and a collection of computers that accept message queries and provide responses. When a caller dials an 800 number, a Service Switching Point (SSP) recognizes from the digits "8-0-0" that the call requires special treatment and processes that call according to routing instructions it receives from a centralized database. This database, called the Service Control Point (SCP), can store millions of customer records.

"Although each regional company maintains whatever number of SCPs it needs to provide 800 Data Bases Access Service, information about how an 800 call should be handled is entered into the SCP through the off-line Bellcore support system called the Service Management System (SMS). SMS is a national computer system which administers assignment of 800 numbers to 800 service providers. It is located in Kansas City, maintained by Southwestern Bell Telephone Company, and administered by Bellcore with information received from 800 Number Administration and Service Center (NASC). The NASC provides user support and system administration for all 800 Service providers who access the SMS/800."

Because 800 service is essentially a data base lookup service, there are a endless "800 services" you can create. Here are the variables that can be used to influence how an 800 phone call is handled and where an 800 phone call ultimately gets sent:

● The number calling. Virtually all 800 calls in North America (excepting Mexico) now come with the information as to from which number the call came.

● The number being called.

● The time of day, week, month etc.

● The instructions given at that particular moment. A computer might say "Sorry, our phone system is busy. We can't take any more calls in New York. Please send this one and all subsequent ones — until informed otherwise — to our phone system in Kansas City.

Here are a few examples of the services 800 providers have created using the above variables:

● TIME OF DAY ROUTING: Allows you to route incoming calls to alternate, predetermined locations at specified days of the week and times of the day.

● PERCENTAGE ALLOCATION ROUTING: Allows you to route pre-selected percentages of calls from each Originating Routing Group (ORG) to two or more answering locations. Allocation percentages can be defined for each ORG (typically an area code), for each day type and for each time slot.

● SINGLE NUMBER: The same 800 number is used for intrastate and interstate calling.

- CALL BLOCKAGE: You can block calling areas by state or area code. The caller from a blocked area hears the message: "Your 800 call cannot be completed as dialed. Please check the number and dial again or call 1- 800-XXX-XXXX for assistance." (You may want to block callers from areas which didn't see your special commercial, for example.)

- POINT OF CALL ROUTING: Allows a customer to route calls made to a single 800 number to different terminating locations based on the call's point of origin (state or area code.) You establish Originating Routing Groups (ORGs) and designate a specific answering location for each ORG's call.

- CALL ATTEMPT PROFILE: A special service that allows subscribers to purchase a record of the number of attempts that are made to an 800 number. The attempts are captured at the Network Control Point, and from this data a report is produced for the subscriber.

- ALTERNATE ROUTING: Allows a customer to create alternate routing plans that can be activated by the 800 carrier upon command in the event of an emergency. Several alternate plans can be set up using any features previously subscribed to in the main 800 routing plan. Each alternate plan must specify termination in a location previously set up during the order entry process.

- DIALED NUMBER IDENTIFICATION SERVICE: DNIS. Allows a customer to terminate two or more 800 numbers to a single service group and to receive pulsed digits to identify the specific 800 number called. DNIS is only available on dedicated access lines with four-wire E & M type signaling or a digital interface. The customer's equipment must be configured to process the DNIS digits.

- ANI: The carrier will deliver to you the incoming 800 call plus the phone number of the calling party. See also ANI, COMMON CHANNEL INTEROFFICE SIGNALING and ISDN.

- COMMAND ROUTING: Allows the customer to route calls differently on command at any time his business requires it.

- FOLLOW ME 800: Allows the customer to change his call routing whenever he wants to.

Now to the question of how to complete an 800 call. There are essentially two ways to terminate an 800 call. You can end the call on your normal phone line — business or residence. This is the phone line you use for normal in and out calling. That's called not having a dedicated local loop. Or you can end the call on a dedicated phone line. By "dedicated," we mean there's a leased line between your office and the local office of your 800 provider, local or long distance carrier. There are several ways this dedicated "line" might be installed. It could be part of a T-1 circuit. It could be one circuit on one single copper pair. It could even be a phone number dedicated to your 800 number — a phone number you can't make an outgoing call on.

There is one major problem with 800 lines. They're hard to test. You may have bought an 800 number to cover the country, but you may be unreachable from certain parts of the country for weeks on end and not know it. That's part of the problem of a service which uses multiple databases lookup tables and relies on many exchanges to carry the calls. Many companies — like the airlines — recruit their distant employees to call their 800 number regularly. The only part of your 800 IN-WATS line you can test is your local loop (assuming you have one) from the local central office to your office. If you have a dedicated, leased line, you may have local Plant Test Numbers — standard seven digit numbers. You can call these numbers. If they work, you know that the end parts of your lines are working. One of our WATS lines is 1-800-LIBRARY. When it had a dedicated local phone number, it had a plant test number of 212-206-6870. So we could call this and all the subsequent hunt-on numbers every day first thing. Just to check. And when we go traveling, we call our own numbers. Just to check. Now we don't have any dedicated local phone numbers, we rely on prayer. The most common problem we have with our 800 numbers is at our local central office. Seems that it crashes every so often for very short amounts of time. When it starts up, it's meant to load all the tables to give us the features we're paying for — like hunting. Sadly, it doesn't always do this. We then report the trouble to our local phone company. It's usually fixed within an hour or so. Depends on how busy they are. See also 800 at the front of this dictionary.

EISA Extended Industry Standard Architecture. EISA is the independent computer industry's alternate to IBM's Micro-Channel data bus architecture which IBM uses in some of its high end PS/2 line of desktop computers. EISA, like Micro-Channel (also called MCA), is a 32-bit channel. But, unlike IBM's Micro-Channel, plug-in boards which work inside the XT and AT-series of IBM and IBM clone desktop computers will work within EISA machines. They won't work in Micro-Channel machines. EISA expands the original 16-bit ISA (Industry Standard Architecture) to 32-bit. EISA technology is useful in computing environments where multiple high performance peripherals are operating in parallel. The intelligent bus master can share the burden on the main CPU by performing direct data transfers into and out of memory. EISA capabilities are valuable when the system is being used as a server on a local area network or is running a multi-user operating system such as UNIX or OS/2. As of writing, over 200 manufacturers had endorsed EISA. Broader, wider buses than EISA are now available. 64-bit is not uncommon, especially among servers. See VESA for an example of a newer bus.

EITHER END HOP OFF EEHO. In private networks, a switch program that allows a call destined for an off-net location to be placed into the public network at either the closest switch to the origination or the closest switch to the destination. The choice is usually by time of day and is usually done to take advantage of cheaper rates.

EITHER WAY OPERATION Same as half-duplex.

EIU Ethernet Interface Unit

EKTS Electronic Key Telephone System.

ELASTIC BUFFER A variable storage device having adjustable capacity and/or dealay, in which a signal can be temporarily stored.

ELASTICITY OF DEMAND The relationship between price and the quantity sold. The theory is the lower the price, the more you'll sell. In telecommunications, this has traditionally been true, though sometimes it has taken time for demand to catch up with dramatic price cuts.

ELECTRIC BANANA Telecom installers' slang for TONE PROBE.

ELECTRIC LOCK A cellular phone feature that provides security by locking a cellular phone so it can't be used by unauthorized persons.

ELECTRICALLY POWERED TELEPHONE A telephone in which the operating power is obtained either from batteries located at the telephone (local battery) or from a telephone central office (common battery).

ELECTRODEPOSITON The deposition of a conductive material from a plating solution by the application of electric current.

ELECTROLUMINESCENCE The direct conversion of electrical energy into light.

ELECTROLYSIS The production of chemical changes by passage of current through an electrolyte.

ELECTROLYTE A chemical solution used in batteries, chemical rectifiers, and certain types of fixed condensers.

ELECTROLYTIC PROCESS A printing process where paper is treated with an electrolyte and a stylus passes the signal current through the paper to produce an image. Paper is roll-fed past the stylus and changes color depending on the intensity of current passing through the stylus.

ELECTROMAGNETIC EMISSION CONTROL The control of electromagnetic emissions. e.g., radio, radar, and sonar transmissions, for the purpose of preventing or minimizing their use by unintended recipients. A military term.

ELECTROMAGNETIC INTERFACE EMI. The interference in signal transmission or reception caused by the radiation of electrical and magnetic fields.

ELECTROMAGNETIC LINES OF FORCE The lines of force existing about an electromagnet or a current carrying conductor.

ELECTROMAGNETIC WAVE The electric wave propagated by an electrostatic and magnetic field of varying intensity. Its velocity is 186,300 miles per second.

ELECTROMECHANICAL RINGING The traditional bell or buzzer in a telephone which announces incoming calls.

ELECTRON The smallest known particle of matter assumed to be a particle or charge of negative electricity.

ELECTRON GUN Device in a television picture tube from which electrons are emitted toward screen.

ELECTRON TUBE RECTIFIER A device for rectifying an alternating current by utilizing the flow of electrons between a hot cathode and a relatively cold anode.

ELECTRONIC BLACKBOARD This is a teleconferencing tool. At one end there's a large "whiteboard." Write on this board and electronics behind the board pick up your writing and transmit it over phone lines to a remote TV set. The idea is that remote viewers can hear your voice on the phone and see the presentation on the electronic blackboard. The product has not done well because it is expensive — typically several hundred dollars a month just for rent, plus extra hundreds for transmission costs. In Japan, there are similar boards called OABoards — Office Automation Boards. They do one thing differently — they will print a copy on normal letter-size paper of what's written on the board. This takes about 20 seconds. Some of these Japanese OABoards will also transmit their contents over phone lines. So far, neither the OABoards nor the electronic blackboards have found a sizeable market in the United States.

ELECTRONIC BULLETIN BOARD A computer, a modem, a phone line and a piece of software. Load communications software in your computer, dial the distant electronic bulletin board. The system will answer and present you with a menu of options. Typically those options will include leave messages, pick up messages, find out information, fill in a survey and upload and download a file. For a graphic demonstration of an electronic bulletin board call TELECONNECT Magazine's bulletin board. The phone number is 212-989-4675.

ELECTRONIC CALL DISTRIBUTION Another term for Automatic Call Distribution. See AUTOMATIC CALL DISTRIBUTOR.

ELECTRONIC CUSTOM TELEPHONE SERVICE Provides deluxe key telephone features and simplified access to certain AT&T Dimension PBX phones.

ELECTRONIC DATA INTERCHANGE See EDI.

ELECTRONIC DATA PROCESSING See EDP.

ELECTRONIC FUNDS TRANSFER EFT. A system which transfers money electronically between accounts or organizations without moving the actual money.

ELECTRONIC IMAGE MAIL The transmission of slow scan TV or facsimile via "Store and Forward." Not a common term.

ELECTRONIC KEY SYSTEM A key telephone system in which the electromechanical relays and switches have been replaced by electronic devices — often in the phone and in the central cabinet. The innards of the central cabinet of an electronic key system more resemble a computer than a conventional key system. These days, virtually all key systems are electronic. Production of electromechanical key systems (such as 1A2) has been severely curtailed and most manufacturers have ceased making it.

ELECTRONIC LOCK Lets you lock your cellular phone so no one can use it. If you use Electronic Lock, you'll have to punch in some extra digits — like a password — to unlock the lock.

ELECTRONIC MAIL A term which usually means Electronic Text Mail, as opposed to Electronic Voice Mail or Electronic Image Mail. Sometimes electronic mail is written as E-Mail. Sometimes as email. These days electronic mail is everything from simple messages flowing over a local area network from one cubicle to another, to messages flowing across the globe on an X.400 network. Such messages may be simple text messages containing only ASCII or they may be complex messages containing embedded voice messages, spreadsheets and images. See ELECTRONIC TEXT MAIL, ELECTRONIC VOICE MAIL, ELECTRONIC IMAGE MAIL and WINDOWS, WINDOWS TELEPHONY.

ELECTRONIC MESSAGE REGISTRATION A system to detect and count a phone user's completed local calls and then tell the central office the number of message units used. Also used in hotels.

ELECTRONIC ORDER EXCHANGE EOE. Inter-company transactions between buyers and sellers handled electronically via standard data communications protocols. EOE can be employed to send purchase orders, price and product listings and order-related information.

ELECTRONIC PHONE General description for most phones designed after about 1980, where many mechanical and electrical parts are replaced by smaller, lighter, and cheaper electronic parts. Features such as mute, redial and memory became popular with these phones, which range in price from $5 to hundreds of dollars.

ELECTRONIC RECEPTIONIST A fancy name for a voice processing automated attendant, except that in addition to all the normal auto attendant features, it also sends messages to personal PCs on LANs telling the owner who's calling and giving the owner (the called party) the choice of doing something with the call — like answering it or putting it into voice mail.

ELECTRONIC RINGER A substitute for the conventional telephone bell, that uses music synthesizer circuitry to generate an attention-getting signal played through a speaker. Typical sounds include warbles, chirps, beeps, squawks, and chimes. The writer of this entry, Michael Marcus, once installed a phone with a chirp sound. A few days later, the customer complained that she had not been receiving any calls, and the birds in her yard were chirping much more than usual.

ELECTRONIC SERIAL NUMBER ESN. A unique ID number of a cellular phone that has been embedded in its circuits by the manufacturer. See ESN.

ELECTRONIC SWITCHING SYSTEM A telephone switch which uses electronics or computers to control the switching of calls, their billing and other functions. The term is now vaguely defined, with each manufacturer defining it as something somewhat different. In fact, every telephone switch sold today is electronic. The term originally came about because early telephone switches were entirely electro-mechanical. The switch consisted entirely of a moving switch. Devices like relays physically moved in order to send the call through the exchange and on its way. These things moved in direct response to the digits dialed by the telephone subscriber. These switches contained no "intelligence" — i.e. no ability to deviate from a set number of very simple tasks which could be accomplished by electromechanical relays.

Then someone said: it would be more efficient if the "instruction part" of the process were divorced the switching mechanism. This lead to the creation of the "electronic" switch in which the "brains" of the switch are separated from the switching mechanism itself. Thus the "brains" can do simple things like collect the dialed digits as they are slowly dialed and pulse them out quickly to the switch — as fast as it can handle them. Now, the "brains" are typically a digital computer.

ELECTRONIC TANDEM NETWORK Two or more switching systems operating in parallel as part of providing network services (usually voice) to large users.

ELECTRONIC TELEPHONE DIRECTORY SERVICE A PBX feature which stores and produces, on demand, a directory of all extension phone numbers. The directory may include all users in a network. A CRT with keyboard and/or printer is usually required for input and retrieval. In some systems, the CRT or another type of alphanumeric display is part of the Attendant Console. In some systems, the directory may also include names and telephone numbers of frequently called outside people, especially those in the speed calling system. The directory may also be enhanced to include SMDR data such as client codes, account codes and client telephone numbers.

ELECTRONIC TEXT MAIL A "Store and Forward" service for the transmission of textual messages transmitted in machine readable form from a computer terminal or computer system. A message sent from one computer user to another is stored in the recipient's "mailbox" until that person next logs onto the system. The system then can deliver the message. Telex, in which a machine readable form of message transmission takes place, is also considered an Electronic Text Mail medium, albeit a very slow one. For an example of electronic mail, please dial our electronic mail system on 212-989-4675. It's free. Parameters are 300, 1200 or 2400 baud, 8 data bits, one stop bit, and no parity.

ELECTRONIC VOICE MAIL A system which stores messages usually spoken over a telephone. These messages can be retrieved by the intended recipient when that person next calls into the system. Also called Voice Mail, it operates just like a touch-tone controlled answering machine.

ELECTRONIC WARFARE See EW.

ELECTROPHOTOGRAPHIC PRINTING A printing method that uses light to modify electrostatic charges on a photoconductive substrate.

ELECTROSTATIC CHARGE An electric charge at rest.

ELETROSTATIC DISCHARGE ESD. Discharge of a static charge on a surface or body through a conductive path to ground. Can be damaging to integrated circuits.

ELECTROSTATIC PRINTING A method of printing, very common in photocopying, in which charges are beamed onto the surface of paper. The charges attract particles of a very fine (typically black powder) which sticks to the charges. The black powder is fused permanently on the paper by great heat. "XEROXing" is electrostatic printing. In xeroxing, the black powder is called toner.

ELEGANT An elegant program is one that is efficiently written to use the smallest possible amount of main memory and the fewest instructions.

ELEVATOR SEEKING Organizes the way data is read from hard disks and logically organizes disk operations as they arrive at the Novell NetWare local area network server for processing. A queue is maintained for each disk driver operating within the server. As disk read and write requests are queued for a specific drive, the operating system sorts incoming requests into a priority based on the drive's current head position. As the disk driver services the queue, subsequent requests are located either in the vicinity of the last request or in the opposite direction. Thus, the drive heads operate in a sweeping fashion, from the outside to the inside of the disk. Elevator seeking improves disk channel performance by significantly reducing disk head thrashing (rapid back-and-forth movements of the disk head) and by minimizing head seek times. Imagine how inefficient an elevator would be if the people using it had to get off the elevator in the order they got on.

ELIU Electrical Line Interface Unit.

ELONGATION The fractional increase in length of a material stressed in tension.

ELOT Hellenic Organization for Standardization (Greece).

EMAG ETSI MIS Advisory Group.

EMAIL A colloquial term for electronic mail.

EMAIL GATEWAY An email gateway is typically a PC on LAN. The PC has one or more modem and/or fax/modem cards. Its job is to send and receive e-mails and/or send and receive faxes for everyone on the LAN. To pick up emails, it might dial once an hour into various mail systems, like MCI Mail, CompuServe, and download all the messages for all the people on the LAN. Once it has those messages, it brings them onto its hard disk and then alerts the recipients that they now have an e-mail. See SERVER.

EMAIL SERVER See EMAIL GATEWAY.

EMBARC Motorola's company which does wireless electronic mail to people carrying laptops and palmtops. Embarc, according to Motorola, stands for Electronic Mail Broadcast to A Roaming Computer. Actually Embarc does more than mail. It also broadcasts snippets of news.

EMBEDDED BASE EQUIPMENT All customer-premises equipment that has been provided by the Bell Operating Companies (BOCs) prior to January 1, 1984, that was ordered transferred from the BOCs to AT&T by court order.

EMBEDDED-CODE FORMATTING ECF. A NetWare definition. This is something of a programming language, in which faxing commands or other program that automatically generates information, formats it, and faxes it without user intervention.

EMBEDDED CUSTOMER-PREMISES EQUIPMENT Telephone-company-provided premises equipment in use or in inventory of a regulated telephone utility as a December 31, 1982.

EMBEDDED SCSI A hard disk that has a SCSI (Small Computer System Interface) and a hard disk controller built into the hard disk unit. See also SCSI.

EMBEDDED SQL SQL statements embedded within a source program and prepared before the program is executed.

EMBEDDED SYSTEM PROCESSORS National Semiconductor's line of high-performance microprocessors used in dedicated systems, such as fax machines and laser printers.

EMBOSSING A means of marker identification by thermal indentation leaving raised lettering on a cable's sheath material.

EMC ElectroMagnetic Compatibility.

EMERGENCY ACCESS An alarm system built into some PBXs. In an emergency it rings all phones.

EMERGENCY BROADCAST SYSTEM EBS. The EBS is composed of AM, FM, and TV broadcast stations; low-power TV stations; and non-Government industry entities operating on a voluntary, organized basis during emergencies at national, state, or operational (local) area levels.

EMERGENCY DIALING A variation on speed calling to call numbers for police, fire department, ambulance, etc. Typically found as special buttons on an electronic phone.

EMERGENCY HOLD "Emergi-hold" allows a 911 caller's line to be held open in the event that a caller attempts to hang up. This gives the PSAP (Public Service Answering Position) agent full control of the call. It will not be released until the agent finishes the call.

EMERGENCY RINGBACK This feature enables the 911 PSAP (Public Service Answering Position) attendant to signal a caller who has either hung up or left the phone off hook. Emergency Ringback enables the PSAP agent to ring a phone which has been hung up or issue a loud "howling" sound from the customer's phone if it has been left off hook.

EMERGENCY TELEPHONE A single line telephone that becomes active when there is no commercial AC power to the Key Service Unit.

EMI ElectroMagnetic Interference. Leakage of radiation from a transmission medium due to high-frequency energy. EMI is reduced by copper shielding.

EMISSION 1. Electromagnetic energy propagated from a source by radiation or conduction. The energy thus propagated may be either desired or undesired and may occur anywhere in the electromagnetic spectrum. 2. Radiation produced, or the production of radiation, by a radio transmitting station. For example, the energy radiated by the local oscillator of a radio receiver would not be an emission but a radiation.

EMISSIVITY Ratio of flux radiated by a substance to the flux radiated by black body at the same temperature. Emissivity is usually a function of wavelength.

EMITTER The source of optical power.

EMM An acronym for Expanded Memory Manager, the software that controls expanded memory on an IBM PC or clone. Drivers written for the 80386 microprocessors usually allow you to use extended memory to simulate expanded memory. See EXPANDED MEMORY.

EMOTICON From Emotional Icon, one of a growing number of typographical cartoons used on BBSs (Bulletin Board Systems) to portray the mood of the sender, or indicate physical appearance. They are meant to be looked at sideways. Some examples:

    :-D writer talks too much

    :-# writer's lips are sealed

    :-o writer is surprised

    :-& writer is tongue-tied

ALL CAPS writer is shouting

:) is a smiley face

;) is a smile with a wink

;(is a frown with a wink

(:(is very sad

;? is a bad guy

[:0 is a wide-open mouth and a crewcut

(:{>X is bald with a handlebar mustache and bowtie

:-| is Wayne Newton {8")# is Michael Marcus, the writer of this entry: balding, glasses, mustache, smiling, beard.

EMP A large and fast-moving electromagnetic pulse caused by lightning.

EMPHASIS In FM transmission, the intentional alteration of the amplitude-versus-freqeuncy characteristics of the signal to reduce adverse effects of noise in a communication system. The higher frequency signals are emphasized to produce a more equal modulation index for the transmitted frequency spectrum, and therefore a better signal-to-noise ratio for the entire frequency range.

EMS Expanded Memory Specification. Several years ago, three computer companies — Lotus, Intel and Microsoft — jointly developed EMS. This standard defines how an MS-DOS program can access memory beyond 640KB while running under MS-DOS. Applications that conform to EMS (sometimes called LIM-EMS for Lotus/Intel/Microsoft Expanded Memory Specification) can take advtange of the computer's memory beyond 640KB of RAM. LIM-EMS uses a portion of the reserved memory area (between 640KB and 1MB) to access RAM beyond 1MB. Software that supports expanded memory uses this window to pass pages of data to and from expanded RAM as needed. See also EXPANDED MEMORY.

EMULATE To duplicate one system with another. To imitate a computer or computer system by a combination of hardware and software that allows programs written for one computer or terminal to run on another. The most common data terminal is a DEC VT-100. Our communications program, Crosstalk, allows us to "emulate" a DEC-VT100 on our IBM PCs and PC clones.

EMULATION What happens one gadget emulates another. See EMULATE.

EMULATOR A device or computer program which can act as if it is a different device or program, that is Emulate (i.e. pretend to be) another device. Certain computer terminals are necessary in specific systems and a terminal that is not that type may be able to act as if it was. If it can, it is an Emulator. This is not a common term. See also the verb EMULATE.

ENABLE To make something happen. Or, in more complex language, to set various hardware and software parameters so that the central computer will recognize those parameters and start doing what you want.

ENABLING SIGNAL A signal that permits the occurrence of an event.

ENCAPSULATING BRIDGE A LAN/WAN term. A special bridge type usually associated with backbone/subnetwork architectures. Encapsulating bridges place forwarded packets in a backbone-specific envelope — FDDI, for example - and send them out onto the backbone LAN as broadcast packets. The receiving bridges remove the envelope, check the destination address and, if it is local, send the packet to the destination device.

ENCAPSULATION 1. Encasing a splice or closure in a protective material to make it watertight. 2. In object-oriented programming, the grouping of data and the code that manipulates it into a single entity or object. Encapsulation refers to the hiding of most of the details of the object. Both the attributes (data structure) and the methods (procedures) are hidden. Associated with the object is a set of operations that it can perform. These are not hidden. They constitute a well-defined interface — that aspect of the object that is externally visible. The point of encapsulation is to isolate the internal workings of the object so that, if they must be modified, those changes will also be isolated and not affect any part of the program. See OBJECT-ORIENTED PROGRAMMING.

ENCODING The process of converting data into code or analog voice into a digital signal. See also PCM and ADPCM.

ENCRYPTION In security, the ciphering of data by applying an algorithm to plain text in order to convert it to ciphertext.

END DELIMITER ED. Sequence of bits used by IEEE 802 MAC to indicate the end of a frame. Used in token bus and ring networks, with nondata bits making ED easy to recognize.

END DISTORTION In start-stop teletypewriter operations, the shifting of the end of all marking pulses except the stop pulse from their proper positions in relation to the beginning of the next pulse. Shifting of the end of the stop pulse would constitute a deviation in character time and rate rather than being an end distortion. Spacing end distortion is the termination of marking pulses before the proper time. Marking end distortion is the continuation of marking pulses past the proper time. Magnitude of the distortion is expressed in percent of a perfect unit pulse length.

END FINISH Surface conditon at the optical fiber face.

END INSTRUMENT A communication device that is connected to the terminals of a circuit.

END OF FILE EOF. A control character or byte used in data communications that indicates the last character of the last record of a file has been read.

END OF MESSAGE EOM. A control character used in data communications to indicate the end of a message.

END OF TEXT MESSAGE ETX. A control character used in data communications to indicate the end of a text message. See ETX.

END OF TRANSMISSION BLOCK A communications control character indicating the end of a block of Bisync data for communication purposes.

END OF TRANSMISSION BLOCK CHARACTER A control character used in data communications to indicate the end of a block where data are divided into blocks for transmission purposes.

END OFFICE A central office to which a telephone subscriber is connected. Frequently referred to as a Class 5 office. The last central office before the subscriber's phone equipment. The central office which actually delivers dial tone to the subscriber.

END TO END LOSS The loss of an installed transmission path. The loss consists of the loss of the transmission cable or fiber, splices and connectors.

END TO END SIGNALING A signaling system capable of generating and transmitting signals directly from the originating station to the terminating end after the connection is established, without disturbing the connection. Touchtone dialing is such a system, allowing the user to send tones to a remote computer for data or other access. See POINT TO POINT.

END USER A high-falutin' term for a user. It's actually the occupant of the premises who uses and pays for the telephone service received and does not resell it to others. Bellcore's definition: A user who uses a loop-start, ground-start, or ISDN access signaling arrangement. Definition from Bellcore is part of its concept of the Advanced Intelligent Network.

ENDURABILITY The property of a system, subsystem, equipment, or process that enables it to continue to function within specified performance limits for an extended period of time, usually months, despite a potentially severe natural or man-made disturbance, e.g., nuclear attack, and a subsequent loss of external logistic or utility support.

ENERGY COMMUNICATIONS EC. A PBX feature which communicates with energy consuming and monitoring devices and perform functions like dimming the lights or turning down the heat in a vacant hotel room. See also ENERGY CONTROL.

ENERGY CONTROL Indicates that phone system has software and hardware necessary to control and regulate the energy consuming devices in a user's facility (heating, ventilating, air conditioning, electrical machinery etc.). The system's processor transmits control signals, over existing telephone wiring where possible, to control units at each power-consuming device. This feature always includes user reconfiguration of the system's control parameters in response to operational and/or environmental changes. At one stage, AT&T and some other telephone equipment manufacturers sold energy control as a integral feature of their phone systems. The idea didn't take off for a lot of reasons.

ENERGY DENSITY A beam's energy per unit area, expressed in joules per square meter. Equivalent to the radiometric term "irradiance."

ENGINEERING ORDEREWIRE EOW. A communication path for voice or data, or both, that is provided to facilitate the installation, maintenance, restoral, or deactivation of segments of a communication system by equipment operators, attendants, and controllers.

ENFIA Exchange Network Facilities for Interstate Access. A tariff providing a series of options for connecting long distance carriers with local exchange facilities of the local telephone company.

ENHANCED 800 SERVICES A name MCI uses for a family of 800 services with additional features added to them. It includes time of day and day of week routing.

ENHANCED 911 Enhanced 911 is an advanced form of 911 service. With E-911, the telephone number of the caller is transmitted to the Public Safety Answering Point (PSAP) where it is cross-referenced with an address database to determine the caller's location. That information is then displayed on a video-monitor for the emergency dispatcher to direct public safety personnel responding to the emergency. This enables police, fire departments and ambulances to find callers who cannot orally provide their precise location. See also E-911.

ENHANCED CALL PROCESSING An Octel term for the interactive voice response option in its voice mail system. Here's how Octel defines the term: "Companies and departments that receive a heavy volume of calls can use ECP to create menus that are presented to callers. When the system answers a call, a recorded voice instructs the caller how to use a touch-tone telephone to send call routing instructions to the system. Depending on which option is chosen, ECP's customized call routing feature allows a caller to press a single key to reach a predetermined extension, a voice messaging mailbox where he can leave a message, an Information Center Mailbox where he can listen to a series of recordings giving frequently requested information or additional levels of ECP menus. ECP menus are easily custom-built by the customer to meet its specific needs. Each menu can offer as many as ten options."

ENHANCED PARALLEL PORT EPP. A new hardware and software innovation (and now a standard) which allows computers so equipped to send data out their parallel port at twice the speed of present parallel ports. There's no difference in the shape of the plug or the number of conductor.

ENHANCED PRIVATE SWITCHED COMMUNICATIONS SERVICE EPSCS (pronounced EP-SIS). A private line networking offering from AT&T which provides functions similar to CCSA. Big companies are its customers.

ENHANCED SERIAL INTERFACE ESI. A new, broader serial interface announced by Hayes Microcomputer Products, Norcross, GA, and placed in the public domain. The ESI is an extension of the familiar COM card used in personal computers. ESI includes the definition of I/O, control registers, buffer control, Direct Memory Access (DMA) to the system and interaction with attached modem devices. ESI specification is available from Hayes Customer Service at no charge. Combined with Hayes' announcement of ESI was their announcement of new Enhanced Serial Port hardware products for the IBM microchannel and IBM XT/AT or EISA bus personal computers. According to Hayes, the ESI spec and the supporting ESP hardware provide a "cost-effective' communication co-processor to manager the flow of data between an external high speed modem and PC. This technology prevents loss of data resulting from buffer overflow errors and provides maximum data throughput for high speed modems. Hayes says that the combination of ESP and ESI will allow through-the-phone modem speeds of up to 38.4 kbps.

ENHANCED SERIAL PORT See ENHANCED SERIAL INTERFACE.

ENHANCED SERVICE PROVIDER ESP. An ESP is a company that provides enhanced or value-added services to end users. An ESP typically adds value to telephone lines using his own software and hardware. Also called an IP, or Information Provider. An example of an ESP is a public voice mail box provider or a database provider, for example, one giving the latest airline fares. An ESP is an American term, unknown in Europe, where they're most called VANs, or Value Added Networks. See also OPEN NETWORK ARCHITECTURE and INFORMATION PROVIDER.

ENHANCED SERVICES Services offered over transmission facilities which may be provided without filing a tariff. These services usually involve some computer related feature such as formatting data or restructuring the information. Most Bell operating companies (BOCs) are prohibited from offering enhanced services at present. But the restrictions are disappearing.

The FCC defines enhanced services as "services offered over common carrier transmission facilities used in interstate communications, which employ computer processing applications that act on the format, content, code, protocol or similar aspects of the subscriber's transmitted information; provide the subscriber additional, different or restructured information; or involve subscriber interaction with stored information." In other words, an enhanced service is a computer processing application that messes in some way with the information transmitted over the phone lines. Value-Added Networks, Transaction Services, Videotex, Alarm Monitoring and Telemetry, Voice Mail Services and E-Mail are all examples of enhanced services.

ENHANCED SMALL DEVICE INTERFACE An interface which improves the rate of data transfer for hard disk drives and increases the drive's storage capacity.

ENHANCED UNSHIELDED TWISTED PAIR EUTP. UTP (Unshielded Twisted Pair) cables that have enhanced transmission characteristics. Cables that fall under this classification include Category 4 and above.

ENQ enquiry character.

ENQ/ACK PROTOCOL Hewlett-Packard communications protocol in which the HP3000 computer follows each transmission block with ENQ to determine if the destination terminal is ready to receive more data. The terminal indicates its readiness by responding with ACK.

ENRICHED SERVICES PROVIDERS Those third-party service providers (other than Network Providers) who provide value-added services that are accessed through telecommunications networks.

ENSO ETSI National Standardization Organizations (ETSI).

ENTELEC ENergy TELECommunications and electrical association, the oldest nationwide user group in telecommunications. It is an association of communications managers and engineers in the oil, gas, pipeline and utility industries. ENTELEC played an important role in the early opening of competition in the telecommunications industry, including the famous "Above 890" decision, which allowed private companies to build their own long distance microwave system. The decision was called "Above 890" because electromagnetic waves in the radio frequency spectrum above 890 Megahertz (million cycles per second) and below 20 Gigahertz (billion cycles per second) are typically called microwave. Microwave is a common form of transmitting telephone, facsimile, video and data conversations used by common carriers as well as by private networks. Microwave signals only travel in straight lines. In terrestrial microwave systems, they're typically good for 30 miles, at which point you need another repeater tower. Microwave is the frequency for communicating to and from satellites. ENTELEC was formerly known as the Petroleum Industry Electrical Association.

ENTERPRISE NETWORK The word Enterprise was invented by IBM. It means the whole corporation. An enterprise-wide network is one covering the whole corporation. Local PBXs. Local area networks. Inter-networking bridges. Wide area networks, etc, etc. See also CORPORATE NETWORK.

ENTERPRISE NUMBER A service provided by AT&T and the Bell operating companies (a.k.a. the Bell System) years ago which allowed people to make collect calls and have their calls automatically accepted by the company at the other end. It was very expensive. It has largely been replaced with 800 IN-WATS service, which is much more successful.

ENTRANCE FACILITY Point of interconnection between the Network Demarcation Point and/or campus backbone and intrabuilding wiring. The Entrance Facility includes overvoltage protection and connecting hardware for the transition between outdoor and indoor cable.

ENVELOPE The boundary of the family of curves obtained by varying a parameter of a wave.

ENVELOPE DELAY Circuit characteristics which result in some frequencies arriving ahead of others, even though they were transmitted at the same time.

ENVELOPE DELAY DISTORTION The distortion that results when the rate of change of phase shift with frequency over the bandwidth of interest is not constant. It is usually stated as one-half the difference between the delays of the two frequency extremes of the band of interest.

ENVIRONMENT The place your telephone system's main cabinet and main electronics live. While most PBX vendors will specify the room's characteristics, the ultimate responsibility for the room is yours, the user. Not designing your telephone system's environment correctly is tantamount to jinxing your telephone system from the start.

Here are some things to watch out for (your vendor has a more comprehensive list): 1. Sufficient air conditioning? Telephone systems give off heat. You need some way of getting rid of the heat. If you don't, you will blow some of your phone system's delicate electronic circuitry. 2. Sufficient space? Is there room for technicians to get in and around your telephone system so they can repair it? Will you have room for additional cabinets when you need to grow your phone system? 3. Sufficient and correct power? Will you have sufficient clean commercial AC power? Will you require isolation regulators? Or you will require extensive wet cell batteries? Will you have space? 4. Will you have a solid electrical ground? Can you find somewhere solid to ground your telephone system to — other than the third wire on the AC power, which is not suitable for most telephone systems? Beware of cold water pipes which end in PVC plastic pipes.

EO EO is a well-funded startup in Mountain View, CA which does wireless data. It makes a device called EO Personal Communicator 440 and 880. It uses GO's PenPoint operating system and the Hobbit microprocessor made by AT&T, which is "optimized" for telecommunications.

EOW Engineered OrderWire.

EPABX Electronic Private Automatic Branch eXchange. A fancy name for a modern PBX. Other fancy names include CBX, Computerized Branch Exchange.

EPHEMERIS The predictions of current satellite position that are transmitted to the user in the data message of a GPS (Global Positioning System) satellite message.

EPOXY A liquid material that solidifies upon heat curing, ultraviolet light curing, or mixing with another material. Epoxy is sometimes used for fastening fibers to other fibers or for fastening fibers to joining hardware.

EPP Enhanced Parallel Port. A new hardware and software innovation (and now a standard) which allows computers so equipped to send data out their parallel port at twice the speed of present parallel ports. There's no difference in the shape of the plug or the number of conductor. Xircom puts out the best technical definition of EPP.

EO 1. End Office. Typically your own central office. 2. Erasable Optical drive. EO drives act like hard drives yet offer virtually unlimited storage because their cartridges are removable. Each cartridge sports at least 650 MB. Some sport 1 gigabyte.

EOA End Of Address. A header code.

EOB End Of Block. A control character or code that marks the end of a block of data.

EOE See ELECTRONIC ORDER EXCHANGE.

EOF The abbreviation for End Of File. MS-DOS files and some programs often mark the end of their files with a Ctrl Z — or ASCII 26.

EOM End of Message (indicator).

EOT End of Transmission, End of Tape.

EOTC European Organization for Testing and Certification.

EPLANS Engineering, PLanning and ANalysis Systems. Software offered by Western Electric (now called AT&T Technologies) to help operating telephone company people run their business better.

EPROM Erasable Programmable Read Only Memory. A read only memory device which can be erased and reprogrammed. Typically, it is programmed electronically (not electromagnetically) with ultraviolet light. EPROMS are typically returned to the vendor or factory for reprogramming. An Eprom on a graphics card might contain the default or ROM character set.

EPS Encapsulated PostScript. A desktop publishing and imaging term.

EPSCS (Pron. Ep-Sis.) Enhanced Private Switched Communications Service. An AT&T offering for large businesses with offices scattered all over the country. This service allows such businesses to rent space on AT&T electronic switches and join that switching capacity to leased lines. EPSCS customers get a network control center in their offices which gives them information on the continuing operation of their network and allows them some limited options for changing their services.

EPSN Enhanced Private Switched Network.

EQ Abbreviation for EQUALIZATION.

EQUAL ACCESS All long distance carriers must be accessible by dialing 1 — and not a string of long dialing codes. This is laid down in Judge Green's Modified Final Judgment (MFJ), which spelled out the terms of the Divestiture of the Bell Operating phone Companies (BOCs) from their parent, AT&T. Under the terms of this Divestiture, all long distance common carriers must have Equal Access for their long distance caller customers. City by city telephone subscribers are being asked to choose their primary carrier who they will reach by dialing 1 before their long distance number. All other carriers (including AT&T, if not chosen as primary) can be reached by dialing a five digit code (10XXX), thus providing Equal Access for all carriers. Not all long distance companies will opt for full equal access since this involves considerable expense to the local phone companies. See also FEATURE GROUP A, B, C and D.

EQUAL ACCESS END OFFICE A central office capable of providing equal access. See also EQUAL ACCESS.

EQUAL GAIN COMBINER A diversity combiner in which the signals on each channel are added together. The channel gains are all equal and can be made to vary equally so that the resultant signal is approximately constant.

EQUALIZATION The process of reducing distortion over transmission paths by putting in compensating devices. The telephone network is equalized by the spacing and operation of amplifiers along the way. In recording, equalization is frequency manipulation to meet the requirements of recording; also the inverse manipulation in playback to achieve uniform or "flat" response. Also called Compensation.

EQUATORIAL ORBIT An orbit with a zero degree inclination angle, i.e. the oribital plane and the Earths' equatorial plane are coincident.

EQUIPMENT CABINET The metal box which houses relays, circuit boards or other phone apparatus. Usually also contains the power supply, which converts the 120 volt AC current into the low voltage direct current necessary to run the telephone system.

EQUIPMENT COMPATIBILITY One computer system will successfully do the same thing that another computer will do with the same data. There are many levels of "equipment compatibility." The only true compatibility, however, is identical machinery. And identical means "identical" down to the very last chip and very last integrated circuit. We have found that some computers — even those consecutively numbered — do not always perform the same. We have empirically proven this for both IBM and AT&T computers.

EQUIPMENT WIRING SUBSYSTEM The cable and distribution components in an equipment room that interconnect system-common equipment, other associated equipment, and cross connects.

EQUIPPED FOR CAPACITY The maximum number of lines and trunks that can be supported by the available hardware. It is not a totally effective measure of the size of a PBX. See WIRED-FOR-CAPACITY.

EQUIVALENT FOUR-WIRE SYSTEM Transmission using frequency division to get full duplex transmission over only one pair of wires. Normally two pairs are needed for full duplex.

EQUIVALENT NETWORK 1. A network that may replace another network without altering the performance of that portion of the system external to the network. 2. A theoretical representation of an actual network.

EQUIVALENT PCM NOISE Through comparative tests, the amount of thermal noise power on an FDM or wire channel necessary to approximate the same judgment of speech quality created by quantizing noise in a PCM channel.

ERASABLE PROGRAMMABLE READ-ONLY MEMORY See EPROM.

ERASABLE STORAGE A storage device whose contents can be changed, i.e. random access memory, or RAM. Compare with read-only storage.

ERASE HEAD On a magnetic tape recorder — voice or video — this is the "head" which erases the tape by demagnetizing it immediately before a new recording is placed on the tape by the adjacent record head.

ERBIUM A rare earth element that when added to fiber optic cabling could obviate the need for repeaters every 20 miles on undersea cables and expand fiber optic cabling to capacities of trillions of bits a second.

ERGONOMICS The science of determining proper relations between mechanical and computerized devices and personal comfort and convenience; e.g., how a telephone handset should be shaped, how a keyboard should be laid out.

ERLANG A measurement of telephone traffic. One Erlang is equal to one full hour of use (e.g. conversation), or 60 x 60 = 3,600 seconds of phone conversation. You convert CCS (hundred call seconds) into Erlangs by multiplying by 100 and then dividing by 3,600 (i.e. dividing by 36). Numerically, traffic on a trunk group, when measured in erlangs, is equal to the average number of trunks in use during the hour in question. Thus, if a group of trunks carries 12.35 erlangs during an hour, a little more than 12 trunks were busy, on the average.

Erlang gets its name from the father of queuing theory, A. K. Erlang, a Danish telephone engineer, who, in 1908, began to study congestion in the telephone service of the Copenhagen Telephone Company. A few years later he arrived at a mathematical approach to assist in designing the size of telephone switches. Central to queuing theory are basic facts of queuing life. First, traffic varies widely. Second, anyone who designs a telephone switch to completely handle all peak traffic will find the switch idle for most of the time. He was also find that he's built a very expensive switch. Third, it is possible, with varying degrees of certainty to predict upcoming "busy" periods. See also ERLANG, A.K., ERLANG B, ERLANG C and POISSON.

ERLANG B A probability distribution developed by A.K. Erlang to estimate the number of telephone trunks needed to carry a given amount of traffic.

Erlang B assumes that, when a call arriving at random finds all trunks busy, it vanishes (the blocked calls cleared condition). Erlang B is also known as "Lost Calls Cleared." Erlang B is used when traffic is random and there is no queuing. Calls which cannot get through, go away and do not return. This is the primary assumption behind Erlang B. Erlang B is easier to program than Poisson or Erlang C. This convenience is one of its main recommendations. Using Erlang B will produce a phone network with fewer trunks than one using Poisson formulae. See also ERLANG, ERLANG A. K., ERLANG C, and TRAFFIC ENGINEERING.

ERLANG C A formula for designing telephone traffic handling for PBXs and networks. Used when traffic is random and there is queuing. It assumes that all callers will wait indefinitely to get through. Therefore offered traffic (see ERLANG) cannot be bigger than the number of trunks available (if it is, more traffic will come in than goes out, and queue delay will become infinite). Erlang C is not a perfect traffic engineering formula. There are none are.

ERLANG, A. K. In 1918, A. K. Erlang, a Danish telephone engineer, published his work on blocking in "The Post Office Electrical Engineers' Journal," a British publication. Like E.C. Molina, an AT&T engineer, Erlang assumed a Poisson distribution of calls arriving in a given time. Molina had assumed a constant holding time for all calls, whereas Erlang assumed an exponential distribution for holding times. That means that longer calls occur less frequently than shorter calls. Erlang assumed that blocked calls are immediately cleared and lost and do not return. A formula that Erlang worked out based on these assumptions (Erlang B) is still in use in telephone engineering. See ERLANG, ERLANG B, ERLANG C and POISSON.

ERMES European Radio MEssaging System.

ERP Effective Radiated Power.

ERROR BURST A sequence of transmitted signals containing one or more errors but regarded as a unit in error in accordance with a predefined measure. Enough consecutive transmitted bits in error to cause a loss of synchronization between sending and receiving stations and to necessitate resynchronization.

ERROR CONTROL PROTOCOLS Besides high-speed modulation protocols, all current models of high-speed dial-up modems also support error control and data compression protocols. There are two standards for error control protocols: MNP-4 and V.42. The Microcom Networking Protocol, MNP, was developed by Microcom. MNP 2 to 4 are error correction protocols. V.42 was established by CCITT. V.42 actually incorporates two error control schemes. V.42 uses LAP-M (Link Access Procedure for Modems) as the primary scheme and includes MNP-4 as the alternate scheme. V.42 and MNP-4 can provide error-free connections. Modems without error control protocols, such as most 2400 bps Hayes-compatible modems, cannot provide error-free data communications. The noise and other phone line anomalies are beyond the capabilities of any standard modem to deliver error-free data. V.42 (and MNP 2-4) copes with phone line impairments by filtering out the line noise and automatically retransmitting corrupted data. The filtering process used by V.42 (and MNP 2-4) is similar to the error correction scheme used by file transfer protocols (such as XMODEM). The two modems use a sophisticated algorithm to make sure that the data received match with the data sent. If there is a discrepancy, the data is re-sent.

What is the difference between error control protocols (such as V.42) and file transfer protocols (such as Xmodem)? For one thing, file transfer protocols provide error detection and correction only during file transfers. File transfer protocols do not provide any error control when you are reading e-mail messages or chatting online. Even though an error control protocol is "on" all the time, we still need file transfer protocols when two modems establish a reliable link. A modem works with bit streams, timing and tones. It does not understand what a file is. When you download or upload a file, your communications software needs to take care of the details related to the file: the filename, file size, etc. This is handled by the file transfer protocol which does more than error-checking.

The other benefit of V.42 (or MNP 4) is that it can improve throughput. Before sending the data to a remote system, a modem with V.42 (or MNP 4) assembles the data into packets and during that process it is able to reduce the size of the data by stripping out the start and stop bits. A character typically takes up 1 start bit, 8 data bits and 1 stop bit for a total of 10 bits. When two modems establish a reliable link using V.42 or MNP 4, the sending modem strips the start and stop bits (which subtracts 20% of the data) and sends the data to the other end. The receiving modem then reinserts the start and stop bits and passes the data to the computer.

Therefore, even without compressing the data you can expect to see as much as 1150 characters per second on a 9600 bps connection. Although the modem subtracts 20% of the data, the speed increase is less than 20% due to the overhead incurred by the error control protocol.

The above definition with great thanks to modem expert Patrick Chen.

ERROR CORRECTING PROTOCOL A method of transmitting bit streams in a mathematical way such that the receiving computer verifies to the sending computer that all bits have been received properly. SNA and XMODEM protocols, in the mainframe and microcomputer environments respectively, are Error Correcting Protocols. See ERROR CONTROL PROTOCOL.

ERROR CORRECTION CODE In computers, rules of code construction that facilitate reconstruction of part or all of a message received with errors.

ERROR CORRECTION MODE A method of transmitting and receiving data that eliminates errors.

ERROR LEVEL A numeric value set by some programs that you can test with the errorlevel option of the "If" batch command. It works as follows. Some programs set the DOS errorlevel to a certain number depending on a certain input or response to an event. Let's say when you type the letter "Y" in response to a question the errorlevel is set to 32. Once this is done, you may condition other events based upon this number using an If command in a batch file. You can say "IF ERRORLEVEL = 32 THEN GOTO END." That way, when you type "Y" you will get whatever is at END. This can be very helpful in batch files and other programs for providing "branching" from one event to another based on certain inputs.

ERROR RATE In data transmission, the ratio of the number of incorrect elements transmitted to the total number of elements transmitted.

ERROR SUSPENSE An MCI definition. An automated process which allows billable MCI calls on switch tapes to be processed for billing, while calls with errors are held in the Error Suspense File (a separate file for each switch).

ERROR TRAPPING In software programming, an exception is an interruption to the normal flow of a program. Common exceptions are division-by-zero, stack overflow, diskful errors and I/O (input/output) problems with a file that isn't open. The quality of a software program depends on how completely it checks for possible errors and deals with them. Code used for trapping errors can be excessive. Some programming languages have error trapping built in. Others don't and you have to program it in.

ERSTWHILE An English word meaning previous. I define this word because I use it in this dictionary and lots of readers have told me they don't know it.

ES Errored-Second.

ES/9000 IBM Enterprise System/9000: mainframe computer family.

ESA Emergency Stand Alone.

ESC The ESC key on the keyboard. Often used to leave (escape) a program. Appears on the upper left of some keyboards on the IBM or compatibles but moves around with IBM's latest keyboard redesign whim. See also ESCAPE.

ESCALATION A formal word for taking your trouble up through the levels of management at the vendor — until you get your problem resolved. Some users have formal Escalation Charts, which detail action to be taken depending on how many hours the problem persists, etc. Escalation sometimes works and sometimes doesn't, depending on the vendor. Usually it does. The rule in telecommunications (and we guess most other industries) is that "the squeaky wheel gets the most attention." Escalation works well with honey and flowers and chocolates.

ESCAPE 1. The button on many computer keyboards which allows you to "escape" the present program. ESCape is the ASCII control character — code 27. It is often used to mark the beginning of a series of characters that represent a command rather than data. So called "ESCAPE" because it escapes from the usual meaning of the ASCII code and allows commands to be interspersed in a file of data, especially for data transmission to peripheral devices such as printers and modems. See ESCAPE SEQUENCE. 2. A means of aborting the task currently in progress. 3. A code used to force a smart modem back to the command state from the on-line state.

ESCAPE GUARD TIME An idle period of time before and after the escape code sent to a smart modem, which distinguishes between data and escapes that are intended as a command to the modem.

ESCAPE SEQUENCE A series of characters, usually beginning with the escape character, that is to be interpreted as a command, not as data. Escape sequences are used with ANSI.SYS to change the color of a screen. They are mostly used to send print commands to printers. The name Escape is due to the fact that it "escapes" from the usual meaning of the ASCII code, letting characters be commands instead of data, yet interspersed with data in a transmission.

ESCROW BUCKET A hopper at the outlet of a coin phone's acceptor/rejector that is tipped electrically to return money through the Coin Return or to send the money to the Cash Box as a collection for a completed call.

ESD Electrostatic Discharge.

ESDI 1. Enhanced Small Device Interface. An interface which improves the rate of data transfer for hard disk drives and increases the drive's storage capacity. 2. Northern Telecom term for Enhanced Serial Data Interface.

ESF Extended Super Frame or Extended Superframe Format. A T-1 format that uses the 193rd bit as a framing bit. ESF provides frame synchronization, cyclic redundancy checking and data link bits. Frames consist of 24 bits instead of the previous standard 12 bits as in the D4 format. The standard allows error information to be stored and retrieved easily, facilitating network performance monitoring and maintenance. Electronic Tandem Network

ESI See ENHANCED SERIAL INTERFACE.

ESMR Enhanced Specialized Mobile Radio.

ESN 1. Emergency Service Number. An ESN is a "list" of emergency numbers that corresponds to a particular ESZ (Emergency Service Zone). This list has to do with 911 service. Usually this ESN list is unique and contains a listing of the corresponding police, figure and ambulance dispatch centers for the caller's area. This "list" is used for selective routing and one button transfer to secondary PSAPs — Public Safety Answering Positions. The ESN/ESZ concept is especially useful in fringe areas.

2. Electronic Serial Number. Each cellular phone is assigned a unique ESN, which is automatically transmitted to the base station every time a cellular call is placed. The Mobile Telephone Switching office checks the ESN to make sure it is valid, that the phone has not been reported stolen, that the user's monthly bill has been paid, etc., before permitting the call to go through. At least that's the theory. It doesn't always work this way on calls made from roaming cellular phones.

ESOs European Standardization Organizations.

ESP 1. Enhanced Serial Port. The Hayes Enhanced Serial Port (ESP) adapter, introduced in late 1990, replaces and extends the traditional COM1/COM2 serial port adapter. The ESP combines dual 16550 UARTS with an on-board communications co-processor. The ESP has two distinct modes of operation to provide both old and new standards in the same package: Compatability Mode and Enhanced Mode. Each ESP port can be independently operated in either mode. Default modes are configured via DIP switches and can be modified by ESP commands. The MCA-bus version of the ESP uses Programmable Option Selection (POS) rather than DIP switches. See ENHANCED SERIAL INTERFACE.

2. Enhanced Service Provider — a vendor who adds value to telephone lines using his own software and hardware. Also called an IP, or Information Provider. An example of an ESP is a public voice mail box provider or a database provider, say one giving the latest airline fares. An ESP is an American term, unknown in Europe, where they're most called VANs, or Value Added Networks. See also OPEN NETWORK ARCHITECTURE and INFORMATION PROVIDER.

ESPRIT European Strategic Program for Research and development in Information Technology. A $1.7 billion research and development program funded by the European Community.

ESS 1. Electronic Switching System. ESS was originally a designation for the switching equipment in Bell System central offices but has slightly more general use now. In the independent telephone company industry, the abbreviation for the same thing is EAX. 2. European Standardization System.

ESS NO 4 AT&T's large toll telephone switch. It will handle over 100,000 trunks and over 500,000 attempts at making a call each hour. It's large and sophisticated and can probably be configured to be the largest telephone switch in the world.

ESS NO 5 AT&T's Class 5 digital central office. See also END OFFICE.

ESSENTIAL SERVICE 1. A service provided by a telecommunications provider, such as an operating telephone company or a carrier, for delivery of priority dial tone. Generally, only up to 10 percent of the customers may request this type of service. 2. A service that is recommended for use in conjunction with NS/EP (national emergency) telecommunications services.

ESSX ESSX (pronounced essex) is some local phone companies' name for Centrex. See CENTREX.

ESZ Emergency Service Zone. This term is used in conjunction with 911 emergency service. An ESZ is a geographic area that is served by a unique mix of emergency services. Each ESZ has a corresponding ESN (a list of Emergency Service Numbers) which enables 911 service to properly route incoming calls.

ET Exchange Termination. Refers to the central office link with the ISDN user.

ETACS Extended TACS. The cellular technology used in the United Kingdom and other countries. It is developed from the U.S. AMPS technology. See also AMPS, TACS, NTACS and NAMPS.

ETB End of Transmission Block.

ETERNITY HOLD Our own creation for what happens when someone puts you on long-term hold. Governmental agencies, airlines and police departments (especially when you need them) tend to be firm believers in placing their callers on Eternity Hold. A new service adjunct to Eternity Hold is Conference Hold. Here everyone on Eternity Hold can speak to each other. We made this up. It doesn't exist, but we think it would be great if it did.

ETHER The medium which, according to one theory, permeates all space and matter and which transmits all electromagnetic waves.

ETHERNET A local area network used for connecting computers, printers, workstations, terminals, etc., within the same building. Ethernet operates over twisted wire and over coaxial cable at speeds up to 10 Mbps. For LAN interconnection, Ethernet is a physical link and data link protocol reflecting the two lowest layers of the DNA/OSI model. The theoretical limit of Ethernet, measured in 64 byte packets, is 14,800 packets per second (PPS). By comparison, Token Ring is 30,000 and FDDI is 170,000.

Ethernet specifies a CSMA/CD (Carrier Sense Multiple Access with Collision Detection). CSMA/CD is a technique of sharing a common medium (wire, coaxial cable) among several devices. As Byte Magazine explained in its January, 1991 issue, Ethernet is based on the same etiquette that makes for a polite conversation: "Listen before talking." Of course, even when people are trying not to interrupt each other, there are those embarrassing moment when two people accidentally start talking at the same time. This is essentially what happens in Ethernet networks, where such a situation is

AN ETHERNET FRAME					
Preamble 8 bytes	Destination address 6 bytes	Source address 6 bytes	Type 2 bytes	Data up to 1500 bytes	Frame check sequence 4 bytes (contains CRC check)

called a collision. If a node on the network detects a collision, it alerts the other nodes by jamming the network. Then, after a random pause, the sending nodes try again. The messages are called frames (see the diagram).

The first personal computer Ethernet LAN adapter was shipped by 3Com on September 29, 1982 using the first Ethernet silicon from SEEQ Technology. Bob Metcalfe who created the original Ethernet specification at Xerox PARC and later went on to found 3Com. Thin Ethernet cable and silicon dropped from about $5,000 to $750 and 3Com went off like a rocket ship. Compare with TOKEN RING.

ETHERNET IDENTIFICATION NUMBER This is a unique, hexadecimal Ethernet number that identifies a device, such as a PC/AT with a SpeedLink/PC16 network interface card installed, on an Ethernet network.

ETHERNET SWITCH A new device that connects local area networks. Here's a definition of the capabilities which an Ethernet switch must have from a company called Kalpana Inc in Santa Clara CA. "What capabilities must a device have to be an Ethernet Switch? Ethernet switching is being embraced as the next milestone solution for bandwidth-constrained Ethernets. To qualify as an Ethernet Switch, the device must: Be capable of switching packets from one Ethernet segment to another "on-the-fly;" Avoid using slower store-and-forward technologies to route packets from one segment to another; Exhibit very low port-to-port latency (the elapsed time between receiving and transmitting a LAN packet is measured in 10s of microseconds, not 100s); Offer a busless, scalable architecture that increases network carrying capacity as switched connections are added; Support all higher-level products; Provide the technology for creating a massively parallel system with a tens-of-gigabits per second capacity."

ETHERTALK AppleTalk protocol governing Ethernet local area network transmissions. Also the Apple Computer Ethernet adapter and drivers. Apple's implementation of Ethernet is compliant with IEEE specification 802.3.

ETHERTYPE A two-byte code indicating protocol type in an Ethernet local area network packet.

ETI Electronic Telephone Interface.

ETN Electronic Tandem Network.

ETS See ELECTRONIC TANDEM SWITCHING.

ETSI European Telecommunications Standards Institute, counterpart to ANSI, the American National Standards Institute. ETSI is based in Sophia Antipolis, near Nice, France. ETSI's task is to pave the way for telecommunications integration in the European community as part of the single European market program.

ETX End of Text. Indicates the end of a message. If multiple transmission blocks are contained in a message in Bisynch systems, ETX terminates the last block of the message. ETB is used to terminate preceding blocks. The block check character is sent immediately following ETX. ETX requires a reply indicating the receiving station's status.

EUCL End User Common Line charge. An amount added by your local phone company to your monthly phone charges for the privilege (it seems) of providing you phone service. No one seems to understand the reason for this charge. EUCL is (or was) an FCC idea. And the FCC seems to mandate what the local operating phone companies should charge each subscriber for EUCL each month.

EURESCOM EUropean institute for REsearch and Strategic studies in TeleCOMmunication.

EUROSINET-EUROTOP International ISDN pilot project for travel agents.

EUROTELDEV EUROpean TELecommunications DEVelopment. An organization involved in telecommunications standardization.

EUTELSAT EUropean TELecommunications SATellite organization.

EUTP Enhanced Unshielded Twisted Pair. UTP Cables that have enhanced transmission characteristics. Cables that fall under this classification include Category 4 and above.

EVEN PARITY In data communications there's something called a PARITY BIT that's used for error checking. The transmitting device adds that parity bit to a data word to make the sum of all the "1" ("one" bits) either odd or even. If the sum is odd, the result is called ODD parity. If it's even, it's called EVEN PARITY. See also PARITY.

EVENT An unsolicited communication from a hardware device to a computer operating system, application, or driver. Events are generally attention-getting messages, allowing a process to know when a task is complete or when an external event occurs.

EVENT DRIVEN A style of programming under which programs wait for messages to be sent to them and react to those messages. See EVENT DRIVEN ALARMS/TRIGERS/TICKLETS.

EVENT DRIVEN ALARMS/TRIGGERS/TICKLERS In a parallel

process, an event trigger can be set to move the processing forward when a set of criteria is met (ex. the last piece of documentation is added to the file). Alarms can also be time-driven, as when a folder is automatically routed to exception processing if no action is taken within a specified time frame. This term is often found in worflow management.

EVENT MASK The set of events that the SLEE (Service Logic Execution Environment) designates the ASC (AIN Switch Capabilities) to report for a particular connection segment, and an indication for each event if the ASC should suspend processing events for that connection segment until the SLEE sends a message back. Definition from Bellcore in reference to its concept of the Advanced Intelligent Network.

EW Electronic Warfare. The military use of radar, electronic counter measures and electronic counter-counter measures to keep an enemy from finding invading forces, on land or in the air. It covers such methods as sending planes equipped with equipment which transmit thousands of signals purporting to be signals that an enemy radar might see on locating an incoming plane. By sending thousands of such signals, the enemry's radar becomes a myriad of "radar" signals, of bright spots. Thus it's impossible for the enemy to read any intelligent information. There are also anti-radiation missiles which home in on and destroy air-defense radar facilities. the only defense against such anti-radiation missiles is to turn off the radar. Electronic warfare also covers such techniques as jamming radio frequencies, anti-jamming. It is not the state of Judge Greene's courtroom or the boardroom at the FCC.

EWOS European Workshop for Open Systems.

EXABYTE An exabyte is equal to 10th the 18th power. An exabyte is equal to 1,000 petabytes.

EXALTED CARRIER RECEPTION A method of receiving either amplitude- or phase-modulated signals in which the carrier is separated from the sidebands, filtered and amplified, and then combined with the sidebands again at a higher level prior to demodulation.

EXCA Exchangeable Card Architecture. ExCA is a hardware and software architectural implementation of PCMCIA 2.0 from Intel that allows card interoperability and exchangeability from system to system, regardless of manufacturer. See PCMCIA.

EXCEPTION 1. In telecom, when something happens that's "unusual," it's an exception. The key is to define what's "unusual." For example, you might define that every phone call of longer than 15 minutes is an "exception." Now you have defined an "exception," the question is how to use that information. You might ask the phone system to print out each "exception" call on a printer next to your desk immediately after the call is over. Or you might ask the machine to print "Exceptions" reports at the end of the month listing all the calls over 15 minutes. These reports might be by perpetrator.

Or in chronological order, or order of phone number called, etc. In short, any event you define by certain strict parameters can be an "exception." Management reports printed in full are almost useless because they contain so much information, so much paper. Management reports which list only previously-defined "exceptions" are more useful. They show you where to focus your attention so as to improve you or your company's performance.

2. In software programming, an exception is an interruption to the normal flow of a program. Common exceptions are division-by-zero, stack overflow, diskful errors and I/O (input/output) problems with a file that isn't open. The quality of a software program depends on how completely it checks for possible errors and deals with them. Code used for trapping errors can be excessive. Some programming languages have error trapping built in. Others don't and you have to program it in.

EXCEPTION CONDITION In data transmission, the condition assumed by a device when it receives a command that it cannot execute.

EXCEPTION REPORTS Reports generated by "exceptions," often detailing extra long calls or indications of bad circuits. See EXCEPTION.

EXCESS INSERTION LOSS In a optical fiber coupler, the optical loss associated with that portion of the light which does not emerge from the operational ports of the device.

EXCESSIVE ZEROS More consecutive zeroes received than are permitted for the selected coding scheme. For AMI-encoded T-1 signals, 16 or more zeroes are excessive. For B8ZS encoded serial data, 8 or more zeroes are excessive.

EXCHANGE 1. Sometimes used to refer to a telephone switching center — a physical room or building. 2. An area in which there is a uniform set of charges for telephone service. Outside North America, telephone central offices are called "Public Exchanges."

EXCHANGE ACCESS In the telephone networks, the provision of exchange services for the purpose of originating or terminating interexchange telecommunications. Such services are provided by facilities in an exchange area for the transmission, switching, or routing of interexchange telecommunications originating or terminating within the exchange area.

EXCHANGE AREA Geographic area in which telephone services and prices are the same. The concept of exchange is based on geography and regulation, not equipment. An exchange might have one or several central offices. Anyone in that exchange area could get service from any one of those central offices. It's good to ask which central offices could serve your home or office and take service from the most modern. There will be no difference in price between being served by a one-year old central office, or a 50-year old step-by-step central office.

EXCHANGE CARRIER ASSOCIATION An organization of long distance telephone companies with specific administrative duties relative to tariffs, access charges and payments.

EXCHANGE CARRIERS STANDARDS ASSOCIATION ECSA. According to their literature ECSA is "the national problem-solving and standards-setting organization where local exchange carriers, interexchange carriers, manufacturers, vendors and users rationally resolve significant operating and technical issues such as network interconnection standards and 800 database trouble reporting guidelines. The Association was created in 1983. The major committees sponsored by ECSA are The Carrier Liaison Committee (to coordinate and resolve national issues related to provision of exchange access); the Telecommunications Industry Forum (TCIF) (to respond to the growing need for voluntary guidelines to facilitate the use of new technology that offers cost savings throughout the telecommunications industry — e.g. EDI, bar coding, automatic number identification); and the Information Industry Liaison Committee (IILC) (an interindustry forum for discussion and voluntary resolution of industry-wide concerns about the provision of Open Network Architecture (ONA) services and related matters and Committee T1-Telecommunications (an accredited standards group under ANSI to develop technical standards and reports for US telecommunications networks.

EXCHANGE FACILITIES Those facilities included within a local access and transport area.

EXCHANGE NETWORK FACILITIES FOR INTERSTATE ACCESS See ENFIA.

EXCHANGE, PRIVATE AUTOMATIC BRANCH (PABX) A private telephone exchange which transmits calls internally and to and from the public telephone network.

EXCHANGE SERVICE A name that BellSouth gives to its local phone services, which it also calls Plain Old Telephone Service (POTS).

EXCLUDE A memory management command-line option that tells the memory manager in an MS-DOS machine not to use a certain segment of memory. For example, you may exclude upper memory locations D200 through D800 (hexadecimal) because your network adapter card uses that space. The reciprocal term — include — specifically directs the memory manager to use an area of memory.

EXCLUSION A PBX feature that prevents the attendant from silently monitoring a call once he/she has extended it.

EXCLUSIVE HOLD Only the telephone putting the call on hold can take it off. This feature assures that the call on hold will not be picked up by someone at another telephone who can then listen to your call.

EXCLUSIVE HOLD RECALL When a call is placed on "Exclusive Hold" and is not picked up after a predetermined amount of time, you will hear a beeping at that phone, which indicates the call is still on hold.

EXCLUSIVE OR PRIVATE UNIT A circuit card installed in each key telephone set sharing the same line or intercom path that causes the first caller on the line to lock out (exclude) all other stations from using or listening in, until the line is released (or privacy feature is defeated by the active caller).

EXECUNET An intercity switched telephone service introduced by MCI in 1975. Execunet was the first dial-up switched service introduced by a long distance phone company in competition with AT&T. At that time, all of AT&T's competitors, including MCI, were selling full-time private lines and shared private lines. The service was named by Carl Vorder-Bruegge, MCI's VP marketing at that time and introduced and made successful by Jerry Taylor, who was MCI's regional manager in Texas and is now one of the company's most senior executives. The service was the forerunner of what is today a $10 billion plus industry — the non-AT&T provided switched long distance business. MCI no longer uses the word Execunet to describe its switched long distance service. It's just plain long distance. Jerry Taylor started Execunet using a 104-port Action WATSBOX in Dallas, Texas. He deserves a place in the history books, not a crummy dictionary.

EXECUTE To complete a task.

EXECUTION TIME The time needed to complete a task.

EXECUTIVE BARGE-IN See EXECUTIVE OVERRIDE.

EXECUTIVE BUSY OVERRIDE See EXECUTIVE OVERRIDE.

EXECUTIVE CAMP-ON A feature for use by executives or other privileged people. When they call a someone lowly, that low person hears a special distinctive tone or or sees a special light or sees a special signal that their phone has been camped on by someone significant. These days many PBXs let you know who's calling — even though you're on the phone. So executive camp-on is not that useful.

EXECUTIVE OVERRIDE A feature of some telephone systems which permits certain users to intrude on conversations on other extensions. In some systems, executive barging-in will not be heard by the person outside the office, only the one inside the office. In some systems, such as the Mitel SX series with the Mitel Superset 4 phones, this feature activates the hands-free speakerphone of the called party, who is using his other line to speak on a normal phone conversation.

EXIT EVENT An event occurring in an ASC (AIN Switch Capabilities) that causes call processing to leave a PIC (Point in Call). Definition from Bellcore in reference to its concept of the Advanced Intelligent Network.

EXM Exit Message. The seventh ISUP message. It's a message sent in the backward direction from the access tandem to the end office indicating that call setup information has successfully proceeded to the adjacent network. See ISUP and COMMON CHANNEL SIGNALING.

EXOS Abbreviation for EXtension OutSide; a phone connected to a key system based in another building. The wiring belongs to the telephone company, even though the phone equipment may not. Unlike an OPX, the circuit between the two locations does not pass through a central office.

EXPANDED MEMORY MS-DOS running on the Intel 80286, 80386 and 80486 family of microprocessors can only address one megabyte at one time. Expanded memory is memory located between base memory (either 512K or 640K) and one megabyte. Expanded memory is reserved by MS-DOS for "housekeeping" tasks such as managing output to the screen. As programs got larger and more hungry for memory (640K was no longer enough), people started jealously eyeing the memory between 640K and 1024K (one megabyte). The first technique was a standard called LIM-EMS, named after the three companies which developed it — Lotus, Intel and Microsoft. Essentially LIM grabs 64K of the 640-1024 memory and uses it to swap pages of other memory in and out quickly. This fools DOS into thinking that it has actually more memory. LIM-EMS lets you work on bigger spreadsheets, and do other jobs faster.

There are many ways of using expanded memory, including special memory management application program or DOS 5.0. 80386, 80386SX, and 80486 computers can create expanded memory readily by using the EMS (expanded memory specification) driver provided with DOS, through Microsoft Windows, or through a memory manager such as Quarterdeck QEMM or Qualitas 386. To use expanded memory, a program must be EMS-aware or run under an environment such as Microsoft Windows. 8088 and 80286-based computers often need special hardware to run expanded memory. See also EXTENDED MEMORY, which is memory above 1MB.

EXPANDED SPECTRUM A cellular telephone term for having the full 832-channel analog cellular spectrum currently available to you, the user of the cellular phone.

EXPANDER That device in a transmission facility which expands the amplitude of received compressed signals to their approximate normal range. The receiving side of a compandor.

EXPANDOR See EXPANDER.

EXPANSION The switching of a number of input channels, such as telephone lines onto a larger number of output channels.

EXPANSION SLOTS In a computer there are card slots for adding accessories such as internal modems, extra drivers, hard disks, monitor adapters, hard disk drivers, etc. Most modern PBXs are actually cabinets with nothing but expansion slots inside. Into these slots we fit trunk cards, line cards, console cards, etc. Some phone systems have "universal" slots, meaning you can put any card in any slot. Some phone systems have dedicated expansion slots, meaning that they expect only a certain card in that slot. In the PC industry, many manufacturers make cards for IBM and IBM compatible slots. In the phone industry, nobody makes cards for expansion slots in anyone else's phone system. See also EISA and MCA.

EXPERT SYSTEM A very sophisticated computer program consisting of three parts. 1. A stock of rules or general statements, e.g. Some long distance phone calls are free. These rules are generally based on the collective wisdom of human "experts" who are interviewed. 2. A set of particular facts, e.g. Three companies provide the bulk of long distance service in the United States. 3. Most importantly, a "logical engine" which can apply facts to rules to reach all the conclusions that can be drawn from them — one of which might be "Three companies give away long distance phone calls." (Which would be wrong.) The idea of expert systems is to help people solve problems. For example, Compaq is trying to improve its customer service by installing automated assistants that work on the principle that reasoning is often just a matter of remembering the best precedent. The simplest expert systems, according to the Economist Magazine, assume that their rules and facts tell them everything there is to know. Any statement that cannot be deduced from the system's rules and facts is assumed to be false. This can lead machines to answer "YES" or "NO," when they should say "I don't know." Slowly we are beginning to find ways of dealing with the inflexibility of machines. One such gadget is a "truth maintenance machine" invented by Dr. Jon Doyle of MIT. As each fact is fed into the system, Dr. Doyle's program checks to see if it (or the deductions derived from it) contradict any of the facts or deductions already in the system. If there is a contradiction, the machine works backward along its chain of reasoning to find the source and dispose of that troublesome fact or deduction. So the system maintains one consistent set of beliefs.

EXPORT Imagine you have a software program, like a spreadsheet or a database. And you have information in that program. Let's say it's Microsoft Word or Lotus 123. And you want to get it into a different program, say to give it to a workmate who uses WordPerfect or Excel. You have to convert it from one format to another. From Word to Wordperfect or from Lotus to Excel. That process is typically called "exporting." And you'll typically see the word "EXPORT" as a choice on one of your menus. The opposite is called importing. See IMPORT.

EXPORT SCRIPT First read my definition of EXPORT. An export script is a series of specifications which control the export process. It contains the fields to be sent, which records to be sent, the name of file to send as well as the name of the import script (if there is one) located at the receiver's end which will control the merge. See EXPORT.

EXPRESS CALL COMPLETION Someone calls an information operator. "What is the name?" the operator answers. "Here is the number. Would you like me to get that number for you now? If so, please hit 1." Express Call Completion lets the operator complete the call for you while you're on line.

Express Call Completion was begun in the September of 1990 by Pacific Bell using a Northern Telecom central office. Express Call Completion is part of Northern Telecom's Automated Directory Assistance Call Completion (ADACC) software and Traffic Operator Position Systems Multipurpose (TOPS MP).

EXPRESS ORDERWIRE A permanently connected voice circuit between selected stations for technical control purposes.

EXT See EXTENSION.

EXTEND A verb used by the phone industry to describe an operator transferring a call to a telephone extension. The word is used thus: The operator extended the call to Mr. Smith on extension 200. "Putting a call through" is a clearer way of saying "extending" a call. The word "extend" probably comes from the old days when the operator extended her arm to plug you in on her cordboard.

EXTENDED ADDRESSING In many bit-oriented protocols, extended addressing is a facility allowing larger addresses than normal to be used. In IBM's SNA, the addition of two high-order bits to the basic addressing scheme.

EXTENDED AREA SERVICE An option offered by local telephone companies where a subscriber can pay a higher rate and reach more areas as local calls (no long distance charges).

EXTENDED BINARY CODED DECIMAL INTERCHANGE CODE EBCDIC. (Pronounced Eb-Si-Dick.) An IBM standard of coding characters. It's an 8-bit code and can represent up to 256 characters. A ninth bit is used as a parity bit. See PARITY and EBCDIC.

EXTENDED BIOS DATA AREA In PCs, extended BIOS data area is 1KB of RAM located at 639KB. It is used to support extended BIOS functions including support for PS/2.

EXTENDED CALL MANAGEMENT A Northern Telecom term for a collection of features being added to its DMS Meridian central office Automatic Call Distribution (ACD) service. Using Switch-to-Computer Applications Interface (SCAI), ECM will work with user-provided computer equipment to integrate call processing, voice processing (recorded announcements, voice mail and voice response) and data processing. For example, ECM will allow an outboard computer device to coordinate the presentation of customer data on the ACD agent's computer screen with an incoming call. The D channel of an ISDN Basic Rate Interface (BRI) serves as the transport mechanism from the DMS-100 central office switch to an outboard computing device. Communication is peer-to-peer, meaning that neither the switch or the computer is in a "slave" relationship to the other. The application layer messaging — i.e. layer 7 messaging as defined by the Open Systems Interconnection (OSI) reference model — is in the Q.932 format and is designed to conform to the T1S1 SCAI message protocol.

EXTENDED CHARACTER SET The characters assigned to ASCII codes 128 through 255 on IBM and IBM-compatible microcomputers. These characters are not defined by the ASCII standard and are therefore not "standard." See EXTENDED GRAPHICS CHARACTER SET.

EXTENDED DIGITAL SUBSCRIBER LINE The ISDN EDSL combines 24 B-channels and one 64-Kb/s D-channel on a single line, ISDN primary rate interface.

EXTENDED-DEFINITION TELEVISION EDTV. Television that includes improvements to the standard NTSC television system, which improvements are receiver-compatible with the NTSC standard, but modify the NTSC emission standards. Such improvements may include (a) a wider aspect ratio, (b) higher picture definition than distribution-quality definition but lower than HDTV, and/or (c)any of the improvements used in improved-definition television. When EDTV is transmitted in the 4:3 aspect ratio, it is referred to simply as "EDTV." When transmitted in a wider aspect ratio, it is referred to as "EDTV-Wide."

EXTENDED GRAPHICS CHARACTER SET The characters assigned to ASCII codes 128 through 255 on IBM and IBM-compatible microcomputers. These characters are not defined by the ASCII standard and are therefore not "standard." The original ASCII code used a seven bit one-or-zero code. There are two to the seventh power, or 128 possible combinations. The IBM PC uses a 16-bit CPU with an eight bit data bus and thus transmits data internally in eight big bytes. Instead of using the seven bit ASCII code, the PC uses the equivalent eight bit code, by simply making the left most digit, a zero. In seven bit code, an R is 1010010. In 8-bit, it's 01010010. The only difference between the first 128 characters and the second 128 characters is that in the second, the first bit is a 1.

EXTENDED KEY CODE The two digit code that represents pressing a key outside the typewriter portion of the keyboard, such as a function key, cursor-control key or combinations of CTRL (control) and ALT keys with another key. The first number is always 0 (zero) and is separated from the second number by a semicolon.

EXTENDED MEMORY Memory above 1Mb in 80286 and higher computers. Can be used for RAM disks, disk caches, or Microsoft Windows, but requires the processor to operate in a special mode (protected mode or virtual real mode). With a special driver, you can use extended memory to create expanded memory. See also EXPANDED MEMORY.

EXTENDED SUPER-FRAME FORMAT ESF. A new T1 framing standard used in Wide Area Networks (WANs). With this format 24 frames — instead of 12 — are grouped together. In this grouping, the 8,000 bps frame is redefined as follows:

❽ 2,000 bps for framing and signaling to provide the functions generally defined in the D-4 format.

Ⓢ 2,000 bps are CRC-6 (Cyclic Redundancy Check-code 6) to detect logic errors caused by line equipment, noise, lightning and other interference. Performance checking is done by both the carrier and the customer without causing any interference with the T-1 traffic.

Ⓢ 4,000 bps are used as a data link. This link is to perform functions such as enhanced end-to-end diagnostics, networking reporting and control, channel or equipment switching, and/or optional functions or services. See also T-1 FRAMING and D-4 FRAMING.

EXTENDED SUPERFRAME MONITORING UNIT ESFMU. An MCI definition. Placed on customer data circuits to provide performance monitoring throughout MCIs Digial Data Network.

EXTENDED TEXT MODE Standard text mode is 80 columns wide. So-called extended text mode is 132 columns wide. This mode allows you to view more text on-screen when using such applications as Lotus 1-2-3.

EXTENSION 1. An additional telephone connected to a line. Allows two or more locations to be served by the same telephone line or line group. May also refer to an intercom phone number in an office. 2. The optional second part of an PC computer filename. Extensions begin with a period and contain from one to three characters. Most application programs supply extensions for files they create. Checking a file's extension often tells you what the file does or contains. For example, most BASIC files use a filename extension of .BAS. Most backup files have an extension of .BAK. MS-DOS programs have .EXE or .COM. dBASE database files have the extension .DBF and .DBT. Paradox files have the extension .DB. Files of sounds have their own extensions. Here are the typical extensions on sound files of various computers:

Microsoft Windows — .wav

Apple — .aif

NeXT — .snd

MIDI — .mid and .nni

Sound Blaster — .voc

Here are the typical extensions on graphics formats:

.TIFF, .EPS, .CGM, .PCX, .DRW, .WMF, and .BMP

EXTENSION CORD A multi-conductor, male/female modular line cord generally used to permit greater separation between the Communications Outlet and the telephone equipment. Available in various lengths up to 25 feet. May be of tinsel or stranded wire construction.

EXTERNAL MEMORY Storage devices, such as magnetic disks, drums or tapes which are outside (externally attached) to the main telephone or computer system.

EXTERNAL MODEM A modem external to the computer, it sits in its own little box connected to a computer through the computer's serial port. Compare with an internal modem, which typically comes on one printed circuit card and is placed into one of the computer's expansion slots and thus connects to the computer through the computer's "backplane." Internal modems cost less because they don't need any external housing and separate power supply. But because they're mounted inside the computer, it's harder to see what they're doing. You can't see the various status lights, like OH (for Off-Hook) and CD (for Carrier Detect). They also take up valuable slots instead of a serial port.

EXTERNAL PHOTOEFFECT In fiber optics, an exernal photoeffect consists of photon-excited electrons that are emitted after overcoming the energy barrier at the surface of a photo-emissive surface.

EXTERNAL STORAGE See also EXTERNAL MEMORY.

EXTERNAL TIMING REFERENCE A timing reference obtained from a source external to the communications system such as one of the navigation systems. Many of which are referenced to Coordinated Universal Time (UTC).

EXTN Extension.

EXTREMELY HIGH FREQUENCY EHF. Frequencies from 30 GHz to 300 GHz.

EXTREMELY LOW FREQUENCY ELF. Frequencies from 30 Hz to 300 Hz.

EXTRINSIC JOINT LOSS For an optical fiber, that portion of a joint loss that is not intrinsic to the fibers, e.g., loss caused by end separation, angular misalignment, or lateral misalignment.

EXTRUSION Method of continuously forcing plastic, rubber or elastometer material through an orifice to apply insulation or jacketing over a conductor or cable core.

EYE PATTERN An oscilloscope display used to visually determine the quality of an equalized transmission line signal being received. So called because portions of the pattern appearing on the scope resemble the elliptical shape of the human eye.

EYE PHONE Several researchers are studying something they call "virtual reality." One version of it, a system developed by a company called VPL Research, Redwood City, CA, is based around three things: a three-dimensional glove worn on the head (called an Eye Phone), an electronic glove (the Data Glove) and a high-speed computer. The whole system cost $250,000 in the fall of 1990.

F TYPE CONNECTOR A low cost connector used by the TV industry to connect coaxial cable to equipment.

FAC See FORCED AUTHORIZATION CODE.

FACEPLATE A cover that fits around the pushbuttons or rotary dial of a telephone. Hotels and motels put instructions on them. More businesses should also.

FACILITIES A stupid, imprecisely defined word that means anything and everything. To me it sounds like toilets. But it's not. It can mean the equipment and services which make up a telecom system. It can mean offices, factories, and/or building. It can be anywhere you choose to put telecom things. Oop, I nearly said telecom facilities. So "facilities" means practically anything you want it to mean so long as it covers a sufficiently broad variety of "things" which you haven't got a convenient name for. "Facilities" sounds better than things. Especially if you want to sound pompous.

FACILITIES ADMINISTRATION AND CONTROL A PBX feature which allows you, the subscriber, to assign to your users features and privileges like authorization codes, restriction levels and calling privileges.

FACILITIES ASSURANCE REPORTS This feature allows a subscriber to get an audit trail of the referrals produced by the automatic circuit assurance feature of some PBXs. The audit trail will identify the trunk circuit, the time of referral, the nature of the problem and if a test was performed, the outcome of the test.

FACILITIES BASED CARRIER Long distance carriers which own call switching equipment and transmission lines regionally or nationally are called facilities-based carriers. The major national facilities based carriers are AT&T, MCI and Sprint. Facilities-based carriers other than AT&T along with resellers also are known as Other Common Carriers. The national facilities-based long distance carriers have switching offices in all service areas of the country and provide originating service nationwide. Major facilities-based carriers sell their services to business and residential users and other long distance companies which resell those services.

FACILITIES MANAGEMENT Also called Outsourcing, facilities management is having someone else (another company) run your computers or your telecommunications system. The concept is that you're a great bank and you should concentrate on that. And your outside facilities manager should concentrate on running your computers or telecom. Moreover, they were, allegedly, cheaper. Ross Perot's Electronic Data Systems (EDS) probably started facilities management. Mr. Perot incorporated EDS on June 27, 1962. At that time he was a leading IBM salesman. See also OUTSOURCING.

FACILITIES RESTRICTION LEVEL Which types of calls a PBX user is entitled to make.

FACILITY A telephone industry term for a phone or data line. Sometimes (but rarely) used to describe equipment.

FACILITY GROUNDING SYSTEM The electrically interconnected system of conductors and conductive elements that provides multiple current paths to the earth electrode subsystem. The facility grounding system consists of the earth electrode subsystem, the lightning protection subsystem, the signal reference subsystem, and the fault protection subsystem. Faulty grounding causes more phone and computer problems than any other single factor.

FACILITY WORK ORDER An order to a phone company to rearrange things.

FACSIMILE EQUIPMENT FAX. Equipment which allows hard copy (written, typed or drawn material) to be sent through the switched telephone system and printed out elsewhere. Think of a fax machine as essentially two machines — one for transmitting and one for receiving. The sending fax machines typically consists of a scanner for converting material to be faxed into digital bits, a digital signal processor (a single chip specialized microprocessor) for reducing those bits (encoding white space into a formula and not an endless series of bits representing white), and a modem for converting the bits into an analog signal for transmission over analog dial-up phone lines. The receiving fax consists of a modem and a printer which converts the incoming bits into black and white images on paper. More modern and more expensive machines also have memory — such that if the machine runs out of paper, it will still continue to receive incoming faxes, storing those faxes into memory until someone fills the machine with paper and it prints the faxes out.

There are five internationally accepted specifications for facsimile equipment. Group 1, 2, 3, 3 Enhanced and 4. Only 1, 2, 3 and 3 Enhanced will work on "normal" analog dialup phone lines. Group 4 is designed for digital lines running at 56/64 KBps. Among the analog line-usable fax machines, Group 2 is faster than Group 1. Group 3 is faster than Group 2, etc. Virtually all machines sold today are Group 3. They send an 8-1/2 x 11 inch page over a normal phone line in about 20 seconds. How much time it actually takes depends on how much stuff is actually on the paper. Unlike older machines, Group 3 machines are "intelligent." They only transmit the stuff that's on the paper. They do not transmit white space, as earlier machines did. Group 3 fax machines are now available in "slimy" (i.e. chemically coated) paper and plain paper. When a fax machine calls a phone line and the phone line answers, the calling fax machine emits a standard CCITT-defined, "CNG tone" (calling tone) — 1100 Hz tone every three seconds. When the receiving fax machine hears this tone, it knows it's an incoming call and it can automatically connect. With this tone it is possible to insert a "fax switch," which would "listen" for an incoming fax call and switch it to a fax machine if it heard the tones or to something else —

like a phone — if it didn't. It is not possible to do this with a modem. A modem works backwards — when the receiving machine answers the phone, it emits a tone.

Typically, a Group 3 machine can speak to a Group 2 and a Group 1 machine. A Group 2 can speak to a Group 1. Speaking down means slowing down. Fax machines are dropping in price. "Personal" fax machines are emerging. Most fax machines today at Group 3 or Group 3 enhanced. A Group 4 standard has been promulgated by the CCITT. Group 4 facsimile machines are 100% digital and directly attach to the B (bearer channel) of a digital ISDN line. They will transmit a sheet of 8 1/2 x 11 paper in under six seconds. The author of this dictionary has seen a working Group 4 fax machine. It's mighty impressive.

Some warnings on fax machines:

1. All fax machines pose a security risk. Anyone can attach a normal audio cassette recorder to a phone line, record the incoming or outgoing fax "tones" of an analog fax machine. By playing back to another fax machine at a later time, you'll get a perfect reproduction of the fax. There are now fax encryption devices which make the fax transmission unintelligible to any machine other than the one it's intended for — i.e. the one that has a similar un-encryption device.

2. Some plain paper fax machines present a different security risk. Some (not all) use a carbon ribbon the width of their paper. As a result, if you want to read what came in, you simply read the carbon ribbon, which you open like a scroll, which the cleaning lady finds in the trash. These machines are increasingly less common, as plain paper fax machines acquire lasser printing engines.

3. Most fax machines record all the digits dialed into them which were used to set up a fax call. If a fax machine is sitting behind a PBX (as many are these days) it will capture all the confidential authorization codes of all the company's employees. To get those codes all you need do is ask the machine to print out a report. There is no easy solution to this problem as at the time of writing this dictionary, except that some fax makers have told me they intend to obscure these numbers on their reports, at some stage. Some may, by the time you read this.

4. Slimy paper fades. How long it takes to fade depends on a bunch of factors — from what's sitting on top of the fax, to the temperature in the room, to whether it's exposed to sunlight, etc. Recommendation: If you want to retain a slimy fax, make a xerox of it the moment you get it and throw out the original.

5. Poor quality slimy fax paper can abrade the fax machine's drum and cause a costly repair. Don't buy cheap slimy fax paper. See FAX/DATA MODEM and FACSIMILE SWITCH.

6. Plain paper fax machines cost more to buy, but less to run. Some

plain paper fax machines have a tendency, like photocopiers, to jam. Plain paper fax machines typically use cut paper. Slimy fax machines use roll paper. You can buy a second tray for some plain paper fax machines which will hold 8 1/2" wide x 14" long paper, which is useful for receiving faxes from outside the US where they use longer paper.

7. It makes sense to have banks of fax machines attached to phones which roll over — also called "hunt" in some places. It makes absolutely no sense to have multiple fax machines on separate phone lines that don't hunt. Two fax machines in rotary can receive and transmit more than twice the number of faxes that two machines on separate, non-hunting phone lines can send and receive. "Personal" fax machines are out. Banks of fax machines are in.

8. The paper feed mechanism on plain fax machines has a tendency to jam — just as the paper feed mechanism on plain paper xerox machines have a tendency to jam. Slimy paper fax machines don't jam because their paper typically comes in rolls. And roll paper typically doesn't jam.

9. Plain paper fax machines, like laser printers (which many are) use supplies, like toner, which run out. When the supplies run out, such machines usually accept incoming faxes into memory — until that runs out. Then they just ring and ring and ring. Which means that incoming faxes don't get through and don't roll over to the next machine. There is no simple solution since the fax industry is convinced that it should not make a fax machine that returns a busy to the central office if it runs out of supplies or paper. We have a separate machine that automatically busies out a line if it failed to answer on the fifth ring. But so far, the device is not commercially available. I don't know the answer to this problem except to make sure your fax machine is always stuffed with supplies. Especially check every Friday night. A final note: If your plain paper fax machine is mising supplies, but stuffed with incoming messages in memory, don't turn it off, since you'll lose the messages. Simply replace the supplies and pray your messages will emerge.

10. Some slimy fax paper rolls are coated on the inside of the paper. Others are coated on the outside. When you put one in a fax machine and images don't appear on the paper, then turn the roll over and feed it from underneath. In short, ignore what the instruction book says.

11. Fax-modem switches only work when they're called by a fax machine — not by a person using a phone who's awaiting the sound of the distant fax prior to pushing the "Send" button. Make sure you warn your senders. It's remarkable how many people manually dial their faxes and thus can't get through fax-modem switches.

12. Think about putting your fax machine on "fine." You'll transmit better quality faxes and may only cost yourself 10% more in transmission time. But that savings depends on the quality of the fax machine at the other end. If

it's an older machine, it may cost you as much as double the transmission time. Here are the numbers: Standard is 203 x 98 dpi. Fine is 203 x 196 dpi. "Fine" faxes obviously look much better.

13. Printed circuit cards which slide into slots of PCs and allow you to transmit and receive faxes work well — when transmitting faxes. They work far less well when receiving faxes — largely because of the difficulty of reading faxes. Faxes conform to one type of digital encoding and PC screens conform to another. Moreover a PC screen is landscape (i.e. horizontal), while a fax message is portrait (i.e. vertical). Here is a comparison of how fax machines and how personal computer screens encode their images. Obviously, the more digits or pixels, the clearer the end picture. Notice that the encodings are completely dissimilar:

FAX ENCODING

Standard, Group III	203 x 98
Fine, Group III	203 x 196
Superfine, Group III	203 x 391
Standard, Group IV	400 x 400

PC SCREEN ENCODING

CGA	320 x 200
Enhanced CGA	640 x 400
EGA	640 x 350
Hercules	720 x 348
VGA	640 x 480
Super VGA	800 x 600
8514/A (also called XGA)	1,024 x 768

See also 1966, 1978, 1980, AT WORK, DEMODULATION, FACSIMILE CONVERTER, FACSIMILE RECORER, FACSIMILE SIGNAL LEVEL, FACSIMILE SWITCH, FAX, FAX AT WORK, FAX BACK, FAX BOARD, FAX DATA MODEM, FAX DEMODULATION, FAX MAILBOX, FAX MODEM, FAX PUBLISHING, FAX SERVER, FAX SWITCH, FAXBIOS, GROUP 1, 2, 3, 3 BIS AND 4, PHASE A thru E, and WINDOWS TELEPHONY.

FACSIMILE CONVERTER 1. (Receiving). A facsimile device that changes the type of modulation from frequency shift to amplitude . 2. (Transmitting). A facsimile device that changes the type of modulation from amplitude to frequency shift.

FACSIMILE RECORDER That part of the facsimile receiver that performs the final conversion of the facsimile picture signal to an image of the original subject copy on the record medium.

FACSIMILE SIGNAL LEVEL The facsimile signal power or voltage measured at any point in a facsimile system. It is used to establish the operating levels in a facsimile system, and may be expressed in decibels with respect to some standard value such as 1 milliwatt.

FACSIMILE SWITCH A new breed of "black box." Its purpose is to avoid having to lease a separate phone line for your facsimile machine, for your phone and for your modem. You buy this box, connect it to an incoming line, connect it to your fax machine, your phone and, possibly, your modem. When a call comes in, the fax switch answers the call, listens if the call coming in is from a fax machine (it can hear the fax machine's CNG tone) and switches the call to the fax machine, or switches the call to a phone or to your modem if a computer is calling. It knows if a computer is calling because the calling computer will, when it hears the fax switch answer, send out some ASCII characters — e.g. 22. (You have to put those numbers in your dialing stream.)

These are the basics of how fax switches work. There are variations on this theme. Some fax switches work automatically. Some work by the incoming caller punching in digits. Some allow you to switch from fax machine to modem to phone and back again. And some fax switches will answer and connect to three modems and one fax or other combinations. The major problem with fax switches is that they typically send a DC ringing tone to whatever device they're trying to connect you (the incoming caller with). Sometimes some devices — for example, high-speed 9600 baud modems — have difficulties responding to low power, DC ringing signals. And they just sit there not answering. In short, before you buy a fax/modem/phone switch, test it on your favorite 9600 or 14,400 bps modem. The more expensive switches tend to work better.

FADE A reduction in a received signal which is caused by reflecting, refraction or absorption. See also FADING.

FADE MARGIN The depth of fade, expressed in dB, that a microwave receiver can tolerate while still maintaining acceptable circuit quality.

FADING The reduction in signal intensity of one or all of the components of a radio signal.

FADS Force Administration Data System. A system which takes basic statistics on telephone traffic and gives hints as to how many operators should be employed to answer the incoming calls and when they should be present.

FAIL SAFE A specially designed system that continues working after a failure of some component or piece of the system. There are precious few, genuinely fail safe systems. To be genuinely fail safe, a system needs to be completed duplicated. It is prohibitively expensive for most commercial users to duplicate every part of their system. But you can duplicate selectively and bring yourself closer to "fail safe." The extent of the duplications you choose (and thus the cost of your telephone equipment and transmission system) depends on how important it is that your system function as close to 100% as possible. The idea is to identify those things most likely to break and to duplicate them. Power is clearly the first area to focus on. These days, the words "FAIL SAFE" are increasingly being replaced with "FAULT TOLERANT." Given the number of times your local, friendly airline has told you that its "computer is down," you can understand the reason for the wording change.

FAIR MARKET VALUE See FMV.

FALL.COM An early virus which made the characters on a screen fall to the bottom.

FALSE RINGING False ringing is a recording of a telephone ringing signal (two seconds on, four seconds off, which is played while a call is transferred or while a switching device listens for modem for facsimile CND (calling) tones.

FALSING In telecom signaling, DTMF tones are created using specific combinations of frequencies to prevent the possibility of "falsing." Falsing is the condition where a DTMF detector incorrectly believes a DTMF is present when in fact it is actually a combination of voice, noise and/or music.

FAKE ROOT A subdirectory on the file server of a local area network that functions as a root directory, where you can safely assign rights to users. Fake roots only work with NetWare shells included with NetWare v2.2 and above. If you use older versions of the workstation shell, you will not be able to create fake roots.

FAN ANTENNA An aerial consisting of a number of wires radiating upwards from a common terminal to points on a supporting wire.

FANATIC Someone who's overly enthusiastic about something in which you have zero interest.

FAP Formats And Protocols. The set of rules that specifies the format, timing, sequence and/or error checking for communication between clients and servers.

FAR TALK In voice recognition, far talk is an arrangement where a microphone is more than four inches from the speaker's mouth. The opposite is CLOSE TALK, where the microphone is closer than four inches.

FARAD The practical unit of capacity. A capacity which retains a charge of one coulomb with a potential difference of one volt. See FARADAY and FARADAY CAGE.

FARADAY As a Faraday shield: refers to the protection a material or container provides to electronic devices to keep them from exposure to electrostatic fields. Named after M. Faraday, the English physicist.

FARADAY CAGE A structure designed to isolate a sensitive electronic system or device from outside interference, usually constructed of metal screens. Named for 19th century inventor Michael Faraday, whose name also gave us the FARAD, the unit of measuring capacitance.

FAR-END CROSSTALK Crosstalk which travels along a circuit in the same direction as the signals in the circuit. The terminals of the disturbed channel at which the far-end crosstalk is present and the energized terminals of the disturbing channel are usually remote from each other.

FAR-FIELD PATTERN Synonym for Far-Field Radiation Pattern.

FARMS OF MAINFRAMES Picture a hall full of large mainframe computers. Picture a hall full of American Airline mainframe computers, lined one after another. Now you have the concept of a farm of mainframes.

FAST BUSY A busy signal which sounds at twice the normal rate (120 interruptions/minute vs. 60/minute). A "fast busy" signal indicates all trunks are busy.

FAST ETHERNET A way to run Ethernet at 100 million bits per second, up tenfold from today's Ethernet, which runs at 10 mbps. Fast ethernet, running on one or two pairs of standard unshielded telephone copper wire, is positioned as an alternative to CDDI and FDDI, which is also delivering 100 Mbps on unshielded twisted pairs. We'll see.

FAST NETWORK An AT&T term for a network with low delay relative to the needs of the application.

FAST PACKET MULTIPLEXING Multiplexing is putting more than one "conversation" onto one circuit. You can do this in either of two ways — by splitting the channels sideways into subchannels of narrower frequency. This is called Frequency Division Multiplexing. Or you could split it by time. Like a railroad train. The first car carries "Conversation 1." The second carries "Conversation 2." And split them apart at the other end.

Fast packet multiplexing is a combination of three techniques — time division multiplexing, packetizing of voice and other analog signals and computer intelligence. Here are the main advantages fast packet multiplexing has over today's industry standard time division multiplexing:

1. Fast packet multiplexing doesn't blindly slot in "information" from devices if there's no information to send. Most other multiplexing techniques, including the most common — time division and frequency division — slot in capacity, whether the device is "talking" or not.

2. The fast packet multiplexor can start sending a packet before it has completely received the packet. This speed of movement is critical to voice, for example, which must move ultra-fast. Delays are devastating. (No one can afford to replace the phone instruments broken in anger.)

3. Fast packet multiplexing can interrupt the delivery of one packet in favor of sending another. It's OK to delay a packet of data by several milliseconds. It's not OK to delay a packet of voice or video.

FAST PACKET SWITCHING Packet switching that transports a dynamically varying combination of voice, fax, asynchronous and synchronous data, video and LAN traffic. See FAST PACKET MULTIPLEXING.

FAST SELECT In packet switched networks, a calling method which allows the user to send a limited amount of information along with a "call request packet" rather than after the packet. A more technical explanation: An optional user facility in the virtual call service of CCITT X.25 protocol that allows the inclusion of user data in the call request/connected and clear indication packets. An essential feature of the CCITT X.25 (1984) protocol.

FAST STAT MUX MICOM's advanced statistical multiplexor that uses data compression, priority echoplex handling and fast packet technology to improve throughput.

FAST SWITCHING CHANNEL A single channel on a GPS (Global Positioning System) which rapidly samples a number of satellite ranges. "Fast" means that the switching time is sufficiently fast (2 to 5 milliseconds) to recover the data message.

FAT File Allocation Table. The FAT is an integral of the MS-DOS operating system. It is like an index of a hard or floppy disk. It keeps track of where the various pieces of each file on a disk are stored. A hard disk's directory and file allocation tables are extremely important because they contain the address and mapping information the operating system needs to figure where to store and retrieve data. If any of the data storage blocks containing these tables is damaged, some or all of the data may be lost. For a much longer explanation, see MS-DOS. Novell's Netware maintains duplicate copies of directory entries and file allocation tables on separate areas of the hard disk, thus reducing the chance of a catastrophic loss of data.

FATBITS A computer imaging term. Extreme magnification of individual pixels to allow easy pixel-by-pixel editing of images.

FAULT MANAGEMENT Detects, isolates and corrects network faults. It is also one of five categories of network management defined by the ISO (International Standards Organization).

FAULT TOLERANT A method of making a computer or network system resistant to software errors and hardware problems. A fault tolerant LAN system tries to ensure that even in the event of a power failure, a disk crash or a major user error, data isn't lost and the system can keep running. Cabling systems can also be fault tolerant, using redundant wiring so that even if a cable is cut, the system can keep running. True fault tolerance is very difficult to achieve.

FAX An abbreviation for FACSIMILE. See FACSIMILE and FACSIMILE SWITCHES.

FAX AT WORK Fax At Work is a subset of Microsoft's office equipment architecture called At Work which it announced on June 9, 1993. Microsoft's idea is to put a set of software building blocks into both office machines and PC products, including:

● Desktop and network-connected printers.

- Digital monochrome and color copiers.
- Telephones and voice messaging systems.
- Fax machines and PC fax products.
- Handheld systems.
- Hybrid combinations of the above.

According to Microsoft, the Microsoft At Work architecture focuses on creating digital connections between machines (i.e. the ones above) to allow information to flow freely throughout the workplace. The Microsoft At Work software architecture consists of several technology components that serve as building blocks to enable these connections, including

- Microsoft At Work operating system. A real-time, pre-emptive, multitasking operating system that is designed to specifically address the requirements of the office automation and communication industries. The new operating system supports Windows-compatible application programming interfaces (APIs) where appropriate for the device.

- Microsoft At Work communications. Will provide the connectivity between Microsoft At Work-based devices and PCs. It will support the secure transmission of original digital documents, and it is compatible with the Windows Messaging API and the Windows Telephony API of the Windows Open Services Architecture (WOSA).

- Microsoft At Work rendering. Will make the transmission of digital documents, with formatting and fonts intact, very fast and, consequently, cost-effective; will ensure that a document sent to any of these devices will produce high-quality output, referred to as "What You Print Is What You Fax Is What You Copy Is What You See."

- Microsoft At Work graphical user interface. Will make all devices very easy to use and will make sophisticated features accessible; will provide useful feedback to users. Leveraging Microsoft's experience in the Windows user interface, Microsoft At Work-based products will use very simple graphical user interfaces designed for people who are not computer users.

- Microsoft At Work desktop software for Windows-based PCs. Will provide Windows-based PC applications the ability to control, access and exchange information with any product based on Microsoft At Work. Desktop software is the one piece of the Microsoft At Work architecture that will reside on PCs.

Despite the dramatic growth in fax usage in recent years, the fax machine, according to Microsoft (and it's right) is still a fairly primitive communications tool. Difficulty using machine features, low-quality printing, lack of integration with the work environment and lack of security are all commonly identified problems. Microsoft At Work-based fax capabilities will address these deficiencies with a broad spectrum of fax solutions that will transform the fax from an independent tool to a powerful, integrated part of the modern communications process. Microsoft At Work-based fax products include the following:

● Microsoft At Work-based departmental fax machines. A standalone multifunctional machine (fax, print, scan, copy) will be able to be used by a single person or an entire department of people. In addition to being great standalone devices, they will be able to be integrated completely with PCs. They will also be sharable via direct network connection or via direct PC connection.

● Microsoft At Work-based fax servers. High-volume, LAN-connected fax solutions will offer the ideal platform for automating wide-area communication tasks, such as forms automation, billing and invoicing with suppliers, distribution of information to a field organization, etc. A host of new applications will be possible when users and developers can count on a widely deployed, secure, anywhere-to-anywhere messaging platform that will be provided by Microsoft At Work-based systems that are also integrated with Windows-based PCs.

● Microsoft At Work-based PC faxes. Any user of Windows with an industry-standard fax board will benefit from rich document transmission through Microsoft At Work desktop software that will become a standard part of the Windows operating system and other Microsoft At Work-based products and services.

● Microsoft At Work-based fax-enabled network. Public networks will be adding support for Microsoft At Work communications, allowing users to benefit from their high-volume broadcasting capabilities and the ability to access integrated, public mailboxes from any location.

Key benefits of Microsoft At Work-based faxes (as implemented in any of the above products or services) will include the following:

+ Far Greater Ease of Use

While today's fax machines have dozens of advanced features, few are ever used. In fact, many users do not even know these features exist. The problem is that the small, cryptic display on today's fax machines makes these features inaccessible to users. To compound the problem, owners' manuals are rarely available when a problem occurs.

Microsoft At Work-based fax machines will use a graphical, touch-sensitive display to make every feature simple to use. Context-sensitive features will help guide users through tasks. For example, if a jam occurs, a picture showing users how to clear it will be displayed.

+ Ability to Send Original-quality "Published" and Editable Documents

Today's fax machines send fuzzy pages that are often difficult to read. As a result, people either don't use a fax when the document has to look professional, or they send another "good copy" via courier. Today's machines also don't allow users to send editable documents, which would enable wide-area joint authoring and the automation of many communication tasks.

Using Microsoft At Work rendering technology, a fax machine will become a remote publishing tool, allowing users to distribute final, laser-quality versions of documents directly from PC applications. Users will also be able to send editable versions of documents to reviewers and co-authors so that changes can be made directly without re-keying information, and then be returned to the author.

+ Full Document Security

The most frequently faxed documents include contracts, internal correspondence and purchase orders. Despite the sensitive nature of these documents, anyone can walk by and read or pick up received faxes, and there's no guarantee that the document will even get to the proper recipient. Some fax machines advertise security features, but these machines are not really secure. Passwords are included in the message, but the encryption method is easy to break. Moreover, all of these methods require both sending and receiving machines to be from the same manufacturer, a rare occurrence in today's market.

Microsoft At Work-based faxes will have strong built-in security that will allow users to encrypt messages so that documents aren't read by others. It will also be able to ensure that documents are delivered to intended recipients and verify document contents as authentic. By implementing Microsoft At Work security in both Windows-based applications and in devices from a broad base of manufacturers, secure messaging could become as commonplace in the future as regular fax transmissions are today.

+ Strong PC Connectivity

While the vast majority of all documents today are created on PCs, most users still print documents and manually feed them into fax machines. Users who choose to investigate PC fax alternatives find them unreliable and not well-integrated into their PC environment.

The Microsoft At Work-based fax is designed to fully integrate faxes with the rest of a PC's messaging environment by integrating this functionality into the operating system. Users will be able to send fax messages in the same way they send other messages, simply by selecting "Send" from their mail package or their favorite application. Received faxes will be automatically delivered into the user's mailbox - the same mailbox where e-mail and voice-mail messages are received. They will be able to forward and reply to the message with a single button click.

+ MIS Support

Today's fax machines are a nightmare for MIS professionals. They can't be centrally managed, so someone has to walk around to every machine to update fax numbers, change settings, collect activity reports and fix problems. Most machines don't support "default settings," so they can't set up machines to do things such as automatically send faxes when telephone rates are lowest. Users frequently can't enter accounting codes to track costs, and even when they can, the resulting reports can only be printed out, so the data must be manually entered into the accounting system. Finally, fax machines represent a network entirely distinct from the advanced data networks that they pay every month to maintain. MIS professionals should rightly wonder why they can't send all that "charged-per-minute" fax traffic over the data lines for which they pay a fixed monthly fee. Microsoft At Work-based fax machines are designed to let MIS manage fax services in the same way as other corporate communication resources. They will be centrally administrable so that any settings can be changed directly, and common resources such as address books will be able to be maintained and downloaded automatically. They are programmable so that faxes queued up after 4 p.m., for example, will be able to automatically be sent at discount rates, saving between 25 percent and 40 percent on toll charges. Activity reports will be able to automatically be sent in binary format to accounting, where they could be entered into accounting systems directly. They will automatically send trouble reports when problems occur. They will easily route traffic over existing corporate data networks, saving 95 percent of the transmission costs.

+ Features to Reduce Fax Costs

Long-distance charges and the employee time required to send and receive faxes account for more than three-fourths of total fax costs, while the cost of the fax machine accounts for only 15 percent. Yet today's fax machines do little to address these costs. Moreover, the few features that manufacturers have added are virtually unused because they are so difficult to access. For example, while most mid- to higher-end machines offer the ability to delay fax transmissions until rates decrease, few people know how to use this feature today.

Microsoft At Work-based fax machines will have features to dramatically reduce fax costs. In addition to making cost-saving features easy to find and use, Microsoft At Work rendering will reduce file sizes and, as a result, transmission times. Digital cover sheets can decrease the cost of a typical four-page fax by up to 25 percent. Cost savings assumes that digitally transmitted header eliminates the majority of cover sheet data that is currently sent in bitmap form. . As noted above, simple access to discount transmissions can reduce toll charges by 25 percent to 40 percent and integration with corporate networks would reduce toll charges by as much as 95 percent.

FAX BACK A computer-based system that lets a caller in and, using voice prompts, allows them to select information (e.g., price lists) that they would like to receive. The system either asks the caller to key in their fax number for a return call with the information, or to call from a fax machine, press the "start" key when they're ready and just receive the information directly.

FAX BOARD A specialized synchronous modem for designed to transmit and receive facsimile documents. Many fax boards also allow for binary synhcronous file transfer and V.22 bis communication. See also FAX SERVER.

FAX DATA MODEM See FAX MODEM.

FAX DEMODULATION A technique for taking a Group III fax signal and converting it back to its original 9.6 Kbps. It works like this: When a sheet of paper is inserted into a fax machine, the fax machine scans that paper into digital bits — a stream of 9600 bps. Then, for transmission over phone lines, that 9.6 Kbps is converted into an analog signal. But if you wish to transmit the fax signal over a digital line, then it makes sense to convert it back to its original 9.6 Kbps. That means you can put several fax transmissions on one 56 Kbps line — the capacity you'd normally need if you transmitted one voice conversation, or one erstwhile analog fax transmission. See FAX/DATA modem.

FAX MAILBOX Companies can send facsimiles of documents to be stored for later retrieval to a fax mailbox — a cousin to a voice mailbox. Travelers can check their fax mailboxes and have the faxes sent to convenient locations, like a hotel front desk.

FAX MODEM A combination facsimile machine/modem. A device which lets you send documents from a computer to a fax machine. It typically comes as a card which you slip into a vacant slot in your desktop or laptop PC. But it may also come as a small self-contained package about the size of a cigarette package. There are big advantages in such a device: First, faxes sent are cleaner because they're not scanned but computer generated. Second, sending faxes directly from your computer is faster than printing the document, then sliding it in a fax machine and dialing and sending it. Third, a fax modem may be cheaper than a fax machine. Fourth, because a fax modem uses computer software it may have some neat features, like the ability to send faxes when phone costs are low, like running the fax software in the background.

There are two main disadvantages:

1. You may still have to print the incoming faxes. If you don't have a decent quality printer, having to buy one will kill the economic advantages of buying a combination fax/modem.

2. Viewing the incoming fax on your PC's screen is not easy. It's not easy to translate an incoming fax into the pixels on your computer screen. Here's why:

FAX ENCODING

Standard, Group III	203 x 98
Fine, Group III	203 x 196
Superfine, Group III	203 x 391
Standard, Group IV	400 x 400

PC SCREEN ENCODING

CGA	320 x 200
Enhanced CGA	640 x 400
EGA	640 x 350
Hercules	720 x 348
VGA	640 x 480
Super VGA	800 x 600
8514/A (also called XGA)	1,024 x 768

See also FAX DEMODULATION, FAX SERVER AND FAX SWITCH.

FAX PUBLISHING Fax publishing allows a caller to have electronically stored information automatically faxed to them via a touch-tone telephone. By pressing touch-tone keys, callers can have timely information, including product brochures, business forms and benefits information, automatically faxed to them anytime, anywhere.

FAX SERVER 1. A relatively high-powered computer which sits on a LAN and has one or more PC fax boards in its slots. The fax server receives incoming faxes over phone lines, stores them on its hard disk and, if it knows for whom the faxes are meant, it will alert that person. If it doesn't, it may send the faxes to a printer or alert a supervisor to manually check the incoming faxes and distribute them — electronically or on paper. The fax server also accepts from workstations on the LAN, stores them and gets them ready for sending out over phone lines. It might send the faxes immediately or wait until later, when the phone lines are cheaper.

2. A fax server is also a specialized interactive voice response system which you call. It answers, gives you a menu of options — various documents it can send you. You choose which documents you want by touchtoning in numbers. Then you designate to which fax machine you want the documents sent. The fax machine you designate might be the one you're calling from, or another one. There are two types of interative voice response fax servers. One is a one-call machine. The caller calls from his fax machine. When he's chosen his faxes and he's ready to receive a fax, he simply hits the "Send" button on his fax machine and his machine receives (a well-named button). Or it might be a two-call machine. The caller will call from a phone and touchtone in the phone number of a fax machine he wants the fax of his desired documents sent. One-call IVR fax servers are the newer breed, harder to build than the older two-call machines.

FAX SWITCH A device which allows you to share one phone line with a fax machine, a phone and a modem. Here's how it works. A call comes in.

The device answers the call. The switch listens for the distinctive CNG (Calling) tone which a calling fax machine emits (the "cry" of the fax machine). When it hears this sound, it switches the call to the fax machine. If it doesn't and hears nothing (or at least nothing it can recognize) it switches the call to the phone. If it hears some touchtones — e.g. 44, or *6 — it will switch the call to the modem (and therefore the attached computer). The advantage of a fax switch is that it saves on having to buy several phone lines. Phone lines are expensive compared to fax switches. There are disadvantages to a fax switch — it typically must hear an incoming CNG tone to switch the call to the fax machine. This means if your friend wanting to send you a fax is dialling manually (i.e. not letting his fax machine do it), your fax switch may not ever send the call to your fax machine. Also you have to set up to dial those extra digits for your distant computer to "dial through" your fax switch. And finally, some fax switches don't send the "right" ringing signal to their attached devices. Some 9600 baud modems, for example, are very sensitive and won't answer certain fax switches' ringing signals. All this can be solved, however, with intelligence, checking and proper programming. I use a fax modem switch every day. It saves me money and is convenient.

FAXBIOS The FaxBios Association is an organization of fax printed circuit card manufacturers who have formed an association in order to promulgate a standard applications programming interface (API) which they are calling FaxBios. Contact is 801-225-1850. Or 2625 Alcatraz Avenue, Berkeley CA 94705.

FAXED The past tense of the new verb "to fax," as in "I faxed the document to him."

FB Framing bit.

FBT Fused Biconic Tape.

FC 1.Fiber optic Connector (developed by NTT). 2. Frame Control. On Token Ring networks, this data supplies the frame type.

FC AND PC Face Contact and Point Contact. Designations for fiber optic connectors designed by Nippon Telegraph and Telephone which feature a movable anti-rotation key allowing good repeatable performance despite numerous matings.

FCB The abbreviation for File Control Block. FCBs are used by older MS-DOS application programs to create, open, delete, read, and write files. One FCB is set up for each file you open.

FCC Federal Communications Commission. See FEDERAL COMMUNICATIONS COMMISSION.

FCC REGISTRATION NUMBER A number assigned to specific telephone equipment registered with the FCC, as set forth in FCC docket 19528, part 68. The presence of this number affixed to a device indicates that the FCC has approved it as being a compatible device for direct connection to telephone line facilities.

FCC TARIFF #9 The FCC tariff for private line services including Accunet T-1.5, DDS, Voice Grade circuits, and Accunet T45.

FCC TARIFF #11 The FCC tariff for local private line services.

FCC TARIFF #12 The FCC tariff for custom-designed integrated services. A special tariff that allows AT&T to develop custom network solutions, including allowing customers to install their networking multiplexers in AT&T central offices and letting AT&T manage the network.

FCC TARIFF #15 The proposed FCC tariff that allows AT&T to lower rates after all bids are placed to be competitive with other carriers.

FCFS A silly abbreviation for First Come First Served. See FIFO (First In, First Out).

FCOS Fully programmable classes of service that control user (Feature Class of Service) access to mailbox features, operations and options. Feature Classes of Service (FCOS) are entirely independent of Limits Classes of Service (LCOS).

FCS 1. Frame Check Sequence. In bit-oriented protocols, a 16-bit field that contains transmission error checking information, usually appended to the end of the frame. See FRAME CHECK SEQUENCE. 2. Federation of Communications Services. 3. An MCI term for Fraud Control System.

FDD Floppy Disk Drive.

FDDI Fiber Distributed Data Interface. FDDI is a 100 Mbps fiber optic LAN. It is an ANSI standard. It uses a "counter-rotating" token ring topology. It is compatible with the standards for the physical layer of the OSI model. FDDI is an expensive LAN. Cards for devices on the LAN cost $5,000 to $6,000 in the fall of 1991. An FDDI LAN is typically known as a "backbone" LAN. It is used for joining file servers together and for joining other LANs together. The theoretical limit of Ethernet, measured in 64 byte packets, is 14,800 packets per second (PPS). By comparison, Token Ring is 30,000 and FDDI is 170,000 pps. FDDI LANs also work on twisted copper pairs. See FDDI-II and FDDI TERMS.

FDDI TERMS DAC Dual Attachment Concentrator DAS Dual Attachment Station ECF Echo Frames ESF Extended Service Frames LER Link Error Rate LLC Logical Link Control MAC Media Access Control MIC Media Interface Connector NIF Neighborhood Information Frame NSA Next Station Addressing PDU Protocol Data Unit PHY Physical Protocol PMD Physical Media Department PMF Parameter Management Frames RAF Resource Allocation Frames RDF Request Denied Frames SAC Single Attachment Concentrator SAS Single Attachment Station SDU Service Data Unit SIF Station Information Frames SMT Station Management SRF Status Report Frame THT Token Holding Timer TRT Token Rotation Timer TTRT Target

Token Rotation Timer TVX Valid Transmission Timer UNA Upstream Neighbor Address

FDDI-II Fiber Distributed Data Interchange II is proposed to be an update (i.e. faster, somewhere in the gigabit per second range) of FDDI. See FDDI.

FDM Frequency Division Multiplexing. A technique in which the available transmission bandwidth of a circuit is divided by frequency into narrower bands, each used for a separate voice or data transmission channel. This means you can carry many conversations on one circuit. The conversations are separated by "guard channels." FDM is still the most used method of multiplexing long-haul conversations. It is typically used in analog transmission.

FDMA Frequency Division Multiple Access. One of several technologies used to separate multiple transmissions over a finite frequency allocation. FDMA refers to the method of allocating a discrete amount of frequency bandwidth to each user to permit many simultaneous conversations. In cellular telephony, for example, each caller occupies approximately 25 kHz of frequency spectrum. The cellular telephone frequency band, allocated from 824 MHz to 849 MHz and 869 MHz, consists of 416 total channels, or frequency slots, available for conversations. Within each cell, approximately 48 channels are available for mobile users. Different channels are allocated for neighboring cell sites, allowing for re-use of frequencies with a minimum of interference. This technique of assigning individual frequency slots, and re-using these frequency slots throughout the system, is known as FDMA. See CDMA, TDMA.

FDS Frequency Division Switching. Seldom used for voice switching. Primarily used for radio and TV broadcasting.

FDX See FULL DUPLEX.

FE Extended Framing ("F sub E"). An old name for ESF, also known as Extended SuperFrame, a T-1 carrier framing format that provides a 64 Kbps clear channel, error checking, 16 state signaling and some other nice data transmission features.

FE D4 SUPERFRAME EXTENDED Another designation for AT&T's ESF.

FEATHER An imaging term. An effect in which the edges of a pasted selection or paint tool fade progressively at the edges for a seamless blend with the background.

FEATURE BUTTONS Pushing a feature button replaces the need for the user to hit the switch hook and to hit the pushbutton pad to activate a feature of the telephone system. For example, hitting the call forward Feature Button sets the system up to forward calls. Think of a Feature Button as just a collection of numbers stored in a bin. When you hit the button, the bin quickly disgorges all the numbers one after another. This button is the first button pressed on a Northern Telecom Norstar telephone before you reprogram the things your phone can do.

FEATURE CARTRIDGE A replaceable software cartridge containing features. The Feature Cartridge is inserted into the Key Service Unit. Several small phone systems (under 100 lines) use cartridges to upgrade their software.

FEATURE CODE This is a number that is used to activate a particular feature on a phone system.

FEATURE CREEP A term to show how features tend to get added to telecom equipment as time passes and new models appear. The term "feature creep" makes no judgments about whether the new features are actually useful.

FEATURE GROUP A, B, C, D FGA, FGB, FGC, FGD, Four separate switching arrangements available from local exchange carrier (LEC) end central offices to interexchange (long distance) carriers for accessing the LEC end-users who wish to make toll calls. Feature groups are described in a tariff filed by the National Exchange Carrier Association with the FCC. The feature group used by each IX carrier together with any special access surcharge determines the service they can provide their customers and the carrier common line access fee they will pay to the local exchange carrier involved. See the next four definitions. See FEATURE GROUP A, FEATURE GROUP B, FEATURE GROUP C, FEATURE GROUP D

FEATURE GROUP A Offers access to the local exchange carrier's network through a subscriber-type line connection rather than a trunk. It is a continuation of the ENFIA arrangement used in the early days of OCCs, until equal access using an access tandem central office is available. Remember, without equal access the IX carrier had to require its customers to dial a local number to reach their OCC's facilities, then dial an identification number, then dial long distance numbers of the called party desired. This service handicap, compared to AT&T's superior connections, qualifies the OCC for a discount off the FGA rate until access is equal. The IX carrier is billed by the LEC based upon actual monthly use rather than the ENFIA method of projected "minutes of use" rate.

FEATURE GROUP B Is similar to FGA, but provides a higher quality trunk line connection from end CO to the IX carrier's facilities, instead of the subscriber-type line. The IX customer can originate a call from anywhere within the LATA, while FGA requires customers to initiate the call from within the local exchange of the exchange carrier connecting to the IXC. FGB billings to the IX are on a flat usage basis, and a discount is applicable.

FEATURE GROUP C Is the traditional toll service arrangement offered by LECs to AT&T prior to breakup of the Bell System. Quality is superior, and the service includes automatic number identification of the calling party, answerback, and disconnection supervision, and the subscribers can use either a dial or touch-tone pad. This FGC service is offered only to AT&T without a discount.

FEATURE GROUP D Is the class of service associated with equal access arrangements. All IX carriers enjoy identical connections to the local exchange carrier. All customers dial the same number of digits, and can reach the predetermined IX of their choice by dialing 1 plus the telephone number being called. When equal access is implemented, all other feature groups convert to FGD and the IX is billed for actual measured use, without discount. In some cases an IX carrier may desire to maintain FGA or FGB arrangements, but the FGD equal access rates will apply.

FEATURE KEYS See FEATURE BUTTONS. A key is to a telephone man what a switch is to an electrical man.

FEATURE PHONE A generic name for a telephone that incorporates extra features (typically one button speed dial buttons) designed to simplify and speed operation.

FEC Forward Error Correction. A technique used by a receiver for correcting errors incurred in transmission over a communications channel without requiring retransmission of any information by the transmitter. Typically involves a convolution of the transmitter using a common algorithm. See FORWARD ERROR CORRECTION.

FECN Forward Explicit Congestion Notification. This bit notifies the user that congestion-avoidance procedures should be initiated where applicable for traffic in the same direction as the received frame. It indicates that this frame, on this logical connection, has encountered congested resources.

FED Field Emission Display. A new way of making TV and computer screen displays. FED screens are flat and potentially cheap. Like conventional glass screens, they emit light. LCDs, by comparison, don't. A typical FED screen packs millions of tiny individual emitters between two ultra-thin glass layers. Each emitter fires electrons simultaneously across a miniscule vacuum gap onto a phoasphor coating very much like a CRT's. See also FIELD EMISSION DISPLAYS.

FED-STD A system of standards numbered FED-STD-1001 to 1008 which set modulation specifications for data transmission.

FEDERAL COMMUNICATIONS COMMISSION The federal organization in Washington D.C. set up by the Communications Act of 1934. It has the authority to regulate all interstate (but not intrastate) communications originating in the United States. The FCC is run by a seven member board appointed by the President. Stripped of all the extensive regulatory and legal mumbo jumbo, the FCC essentially does three things: 1. It sets the prices for interstate phone, data and video service. 2. It determines who can or cannot get into the business of providing telecommunications service or equipment in the United States. 3. It determines the electrical and physical standards for telecommunications equipment. The FCC's powers, although strong, are tempered (limited) by (a) The Federal Courts. Anyone who disagrees with FCC rulings can appeal them to a Federal Court. (b) The Justice Department. The Justice Department changed the industry with Divestiture. (c) Congress and (d) The 50 state public service commissions.

FEDERAL TELECOMMUNICATIONS SYSTEM FTS. The private network used primarily by the civilian agencies of the federal government to call other government locations and to place calls to phones connected to the public network.

FEDERAL-STATE JOINT BOARD An organization with representatives from the FCC and the state public service commissions which tries to resolve Federal and State conflicts on telecommunications regulatory issues. Sometimes successfully and sometimes not successfully.

FEEDBACK The return of part of an output signal back to the input side of the device. Think of the high-pitched squeal you hear when someone brings a microphone too close to the loudspeaker. Not all feedback is as obvious or as irritating. Some feedback is good. See SIDETONE, which is what happens when you hear a little in the receiver of you're saying in the transmitter of a phone.

FEEDER CABLE A group of wires, usually 25-pair or multiples of 25-pair, that supports multiple phones in a single cable sheath. These cables may or may not be terminated with a connector on one or both ends. Feeder cable typically connects an intermediate distribution frame (IDF) to a main distribution frame (MDF). But the term "feeder cable" is also used in backbone wiring.

FEEDHOLES Holes punched in paper or papertape which allow the paper or paper tape to be driven by sprocket wheels.

FEFO First Ended, First Out. A rule for dealing with things in a queue. For example, higher priority messages will be sent before lower priority messages.

FEMTOSECOND One-millionth of a billionth of a second. Femtoseconds are used in laser transmission and in other measures of very small happenings. It's 10 to the minus 15. There are as many femtoseconds in one second as there are seconds in thirty million years. There are 1,000,000,000,000,000 femtoseconds in one second. How small is a femotsecond? In a little more than a second, light can travel from the moon to the earth, but in a femtosecond it only travels one hundredth the width of a human hair.

FEP Front End Processor. The "traffic cop" of the data communications world. Typically sits in front of a computer and is designed to handle the telecommunications burden, so the computer can concentrate on handling the processing burden. Here's a more technical definition: A dedicated communications system that intercepts and handles activity for the host.

Can perform line control, message handling, code conversion, error control, and such applications functions as control and operation of special-purpose terminals. Designed to offload from the host computer all or most of its data communications functions.

FERNSPRECHVERMITTLUNGSSTELLE A central office in German. In Europe, they call a central office a "public exchange," or just plain "exchange." They look at you kinda strange when you say the North American word, namely "central office."

FERREED ASSEMBLY A glass enclosed reed relay switch in which the reeds are made of some metal which can be opened or closed by an external magnetic field.

FERRI CHROME A tape comprising a layer of ferric oxide particles and a layer of chromium dioxide particles and combining the attributes of both.

FERRIC OXIDE A tape whose coating is of red iron oxide, the original material used for magnetic recording tapes.

FERRULE A component of a fiber optic connection that holds a fiber in place and aids in its alignment.

FET Field Effect Transistor. Very thin and small transistors are used to control pixels in a TFT (Thin Film Transistor) display.

FEWER A smaller number. The word "fewer" is always confused with the word "less." According to the Oxford American Dictionary, the word "less" is used of things that are measured by amount (for example, eat less butter, use less fuel). Its use with things measured by numbers is regarded as incorrect (for example in "we need less workers;" correct usage is fewer workers.)

FF Form Feed. A printer function used to skip to the top of the next page or form.

FFDI Fast Fiber Data Interface. A proprietary 100 megabit per second local area network that uses fiber optic, coax, shielded twisted pair or unshielded twisted pair. It is manufactured by PlusNet, Phoenix, Arizona.

FGB See FEATURE GROUP B.

FGC See FEATURE GROUP C.

FGC-EA See FEATURE GROUP C and EQUAL ACCESS.

FGD See FEATURE GROUP D.

FGD-EA Feature Group D - Equal Access. See FEATURE GROUP D, also See EQUAL ACCESS.

FIAT Fix It Again Tony.

FIBRE The European, Australian, Canadian and British spelling. See FIBER.

FIBER Dielectric waveguide that guides light. See also FIBER OPTICS.

FIBER AXIS In an optical fiber, the line connecting the centers of line circles that circumscribe the core, as defined under "tolerance field."

FIBER BUFFER The material surrounding and immediately adjacent to an optical fiber that provides mechanical isolation and protection. Buffers are generally softer than jackets.

FIBER BUNDLE An assembly of parallel unbuffered optical fibers, in intimate contact with one another and secured, usually with an epoxy or other adhesive. Each endface of the bundle is typically finished to a flat or other optical surface, usually at right angles to the axis of the bundle. Such bundles are used to transmit optical power or images. Bundles used to transmit images must maintain spatial coherence amongst the relative positions of the respective fibers at each end (aligned bundles). There is no requirement for this if the bundle is used to transmit optical power only. Fiber bundles were employed in early, short-distance communication applications, but have become obsolete in modern telecommunications.

FIBER DISTRIBUTED DATA INTERFACE FDDI. A set of ANSI/ISO standards that, when taken together, define a 100 Mbps, timed-token protocol, Local Area Network that uses fiber optic cable as the transmission medium. The standards define Physical Layer Medium Dependent, Physical Layer, Media Access Control, and Station Management entities. The standard specifies: multi-mode fiber, 50/125, 62.5/125, or 85/125 core-cladding specification; and LED or laser light source; and 2 kilometers for unrepeated data transmission at 40 Mbps.

FIBER IDENTIFIER A test instrument that can differentiate between live and dead fibers in a working cable and can identify a preselected fiber to which a special transmitter has been attached.

FIBER LOSS The attenuation (deterioration) of the light signal in optical fiber transmission.

FIBER OPTIC WAVEGUIDE A relatively long thin strand of transparent substance, usually glass, capable of conducting an electromagnetic wave of optical wavelength (visible region of the frequency spectrum) with some ability to confine longitudinally directed, or near-longitudinally directed, lightwaves to its interior by means of internal reflection.

FIBER OPTICS A technology in which light is used to transport information from one point to another. More specifically, fiber optics are thin filaments of glass through which light beams are transmitted over long distances carrying enormous amounts of data. Modulating light on thin strands of glass produces major benefits in high bandwidth, relatively low cost, low power consumption, small space needs, total insensitivity to electromagnetic interference and great insensitivity to being bugged. All these benefits have great attraction to anyone who needs vast, clean transmission capacity, to the military and to anyone who runs a factory with lots of electronic machinery.

The first field trial of an AT&T lightwave system took place in Chicago in

1977. There has been a rapid improvement in cost effectiveness of fiber systems, expressed as cost per bit per kilometer. A one hundredfold decrease in cost in one five year period — from about 1980 to 1985! Some versions of fiber optics new carry two billion pulses of light a second to carry more than 30,000 times the information of electronical signals over copper wire. See LEDs.

FIBER PIGTAIL A short length of optical fiber, permanently fixed to a component, used to couple power between the component and the transmission fiber.

FIBEROPTICHEAD Slang expression to describe a customer who thinks he knows everything about cable. Usage: "That fiberoptichead wouldn't know a drop from a fish job."

FIBERPHONE A battery-powered device that connects to both ends of a fiber optic cable allowing people (typically craftspeople) to talk over the cable. The complete device (two ends) costs $1,000 to $2,000 and often comes with a headset.

FIBERWORLD In simultaneous media events in Washington and Montreal on October 12, 1989, Northern Telecom and Bell Northern Research (BNR) unveiled "FiberWorld," which they referred to "as a vision and commitment to deliver the world's first completely family of fiber-optic access, transport, and switching products."

FIDONET An electronic bulletin board technology for transfer and receipt of messages. According to PC Magazine, the origins of FidoNet date back to the early 1980s, when the two authors of the BBS software Fido, who lived on opposite coasts, needed an easy way to exchange modifications they made to the source code. They designed a system where, as a nightly event, the board would shut down and run utilities that automatically transferred the changed files between the author's BBSs. The logical next step was to permit the exchange of private mail messages called NetMail, between the sysops. The author found these capabilities so useful that they include them as part of the Fido BBS (Bulletin Board Software) package. It didn't take long for an informal network of Fido nodes to come into existence, all running the Fido software and exchanging various utility and program files and NetMail among sysops. Like other BBSs, the FidoNet BBSs had their own SIGs, or Special Interest Groups, where users with similar interests could exchange messages in a way similar to what on-line services call conferences or forums. By 1986 a Fido sysop had extended the NetMail concept to allow SIGs to share public messages among the BBSs, and EchoMail was born. In the years since, BBS authors and FidoNet users and sysops extended these capabilities to other BBS packages, and FidoNet grew. It currently has over 11,000 nodes covering most of the world. Many of the existing public and private networks go through FidoNet gateways into the Internet Mail system, which carries e-mail over a group of interconnected networks to universities, government agencies, military branches, and corporations. FidoNet technology uses store-and-forward messaging and is based on point-to-point communications between nodes.

FIELD 1. One half (every other line) of a television picture "frame". There are 60 fields per second in American television. 2. A place with no phones or other communications capability where an important person inevitably is when you need some vital information, service or device that only he or she can provide. "I'm sorry, the chief technician is in the field today, and can't be reached." Few "fields" are actually fields. They're usually downtown office buildings. 3. The specific location of data within a record. In the jargon of database management systems, many fields make up one record Many records make up one file. Here's another explanation. A field is one of the basic subdivisions of a data record. The record on you in your company's database might include your name, your address, your salary, etc. A field is simply one of these — e.g. your salary, your last name, or your street address. All the records of all the employees in your company make up a file, also called a database. 4. The name given to that part of an electrical system in which electromagnetic lines of force are established.

FIELD EMISSION DISPLAYS FED. Another way of making thin, flat, light-weight computer displays for laptops, planes, etc. The other way is called "active matrix liquid crystal display." In field emission displays, a tiny color cathode ray tube sits behind each of the many pixels in the screen. This results in a brighter picture that uses less energy than the active matrix LCD displays. See also FED.

FIELD INTENSITY The irradiance of an electromagnetic beam under specified conditions. Usually specified in terms of power per unit area, e.g., watts per square meter, milliwatts per square centimeter.

FIELD PROGRAMMABLE The ability of a system to have changes made in its program while it is installed — without having to be returned to the factory.

FIELD REPAIRABLE A characteristic of an unfortunately-decreasing number of electronic devices, that allows users or technicians to fix them where they are used ("in the field"), instead of having to send them to a centralized repair facility where esoteric parts and tools are available.

FIELD RHEOSTAT A variable resistance used in the field circuit of a generator or motor to control the field current and consequently the strength of the electromagnetic field, thereby regulating the speed or power of the motor, or the output of the generator.

FIELD STRENGTH The intensity of an electric, magnetic, or electromagnetic field at a given point. Normally used to refer to the rms value of the electric field, expressed in volts per meter, or of the magnetic field, expressed in amperes per meter.

FIELD STRENGTH METER Electronic instrument that measures the intensity of the magnetic field.

FIELD UPGRADABLE A desirable characteristic of telecom equipment, computers, etc., that allows new features to be added and other improvements to be made, where the device is used, rather than having to return it to the manufacturer or a repair facility.

FIELD WIRE A flexible insulated wire used in field telephone and telegraph systems. WD-1 and WF-16 are types of field wire. Usually contains a strength member.

FIFO First In, First Out. All telephone networks are a tradeoff. It's simply too expensive to build a phone network which will be ready to give everyone dial tone and a circuit — if everyone picked up the phone simultaneously and tried to make a call. There are basically two ways of handling calls which cannot be sent on their way — i.e. for which there's no present available capacity. First, you can "block" the call. This means giving the caller a busy or a "nothing" (also called "high and dry"). Second, you can put the call into a queue. Now you have people waiting in queue, how do you handle them? The most equitable — the way most queues work — is to handle the calls on the basis of First In, First Out. (First call to come in is handled first.) There are other ways of handling calls in a queue — including First In, Last Out, by priority (e.g. which line you came in on and how much it cost, or how high you are in the corporation, etc.)

FIFO also is a term used in data communications. It is a buffering scheme in which the first byte of data that enters the buffer is also the first byte retrieved by the CPU. This scheme is used in the 16550 (the UART chip which controls the serial port on most PCs and most other serial-buffering designs, because it closely mimics the way serial data is actually transmitted; that is, one bit at a time.

FIFTH GENERATION Fifth generation computers and telephone systems will be based on artificial intelligence. A fifth generation phone system may make far more sophisticated decisions about routing calls across networks. Those decisions may be made on how many calls have already happened so far that month, the choice of carrier by the likely quality of his connection, etc.

FIGS FIGure Shift. A physical shift in a terminal using Baudot Code that enables the printing of numbers, symbols and upper-case letters.

FILAMENT An electrically heated wire in an evacuated glass bulb, forming one element (the cathode) of a vacuum tube.

FILE A set of similarly structured data records (such as personnel records using a standardized form). See FIELD.

FILE ALLOCATION TABLE MS-DOS' method of storing and keeping track of files on a disk (hard or floppy) is referred to as the File Allocation Table (FAT) file system. It's a map that DOS uses to store and retrieve files on disk. The FAT's map also shows available and used disk space. See FAT.

FILE CACHING A Novell local area network NetWare file server can service requests from workstations up to 100 times faster when it reads from and writes to the file server's cache memory (in RAM) rather than executing direct reads from and writes to the file server's hard disks.

FILE EXTENSIONS MS-DOS files can have an 8-character filename followed by a period and a 3-character file extension. While most extensions are arbitrarily assigned by users or companies, some extensions are reserved for special purposes or circumstances. Many local area networks follow the MS-DOS naming conventions:

EXE	DOS executable file
BAT	DOS executable batch file
DAT	ASCII text file (usually)
COM	DOS executable command file
ERR	Error log file
OVL	Overlay file used often to contain
HLP	Help screens which appear by pressing F1
SYS	Operating system file

FILE LOCKING Picture a cabinet of file folders. Now I remove a folder to work on it. I make a photocopy of the folder in the cabinet and leave the original. You come along and remove the original because you want to work on it. You make changes and replace the changed copy in the cabinet. Ten minutes later I pull your file out and replace it with mine. Bingo, all your changes are lost. But let's say when I remove the file to work on it, I staple the remaining folder shut. That's a message to anyone else — including you that you shouldn't mess with the file. When I return, I unstaple the file, and add my changes. Now it's ready for you to do your thing. File locking ensures that a file will be updated correctly before another user, applications, or process will be allowed to write to the file. When a file is locked, no one else can write to it. Without file locking, one user could overwrite the file update of another user. In contrast to file locking, record locking allows many users to access the same file at once, but have only one access the record. See also RECORD LOCKING.

FILE MAINTENANCE The job of keeping your data base files up to date by adding, changing or deleting data.

FILE MANAGEMENT The system of rules and policies for maintaining a set of files — including how files can be created, accessed, retrieved and deleted.

FILE SERVER A file server is a device on a local area which "serves" files to everyone on that local area network (LAN). It allows everyone on the network to get to files in a single place, on one computer. It typically is a combination computer, data management software, and large hard disk drive. A file server directs all movement of files and data on a multi-user communications network, namely the LAN. It allows the user to store information, leave electronic mail messages for other users on the system and access application software on the file server — e.g. word processing, spreadsheet. A file server should also stop more than one user accessing (and potentially changing) a file at the same time — a capability called file locking. This means that certain files are "locked" to certain users, i.e. those users cannot access those files.

FILE SERVER CONSOLE OPERATOR A user or a member of a group to whom a Novell NetWare SUPERVISOR delegates certain rights in managing the file server. A file server console operator has rights to use FCONSOLE to broadcast messages to users, to change file servers, to access connection information, to monitor file/lock activity, to check LAN driver configurations and to purge all salvagable files.

FILE SHARING A topology-independent feature of Apple Macintosh's System 7 operating system which allows users to share files and folders on their disks with other users across the LAN. File sharing is slow but acceptable for sharing small numbers of files among small groups. For larger networking, the user must consider AppleShare, Netware, Vines, etc.

FILE TRANSFER PROTOCOLS One problem with transmitting information over phone lines is the noise on the phone line. One way to overcome the problem of noise is a file transfer protocol. The idea is simple: send your information in bundles (called packets). Accompany those packets with a special number derived in some way from the information in the packet. Send it all to the other end. Have the computer at the other check the number and see if corresponds to the packet. If not, send a signal back, saying "Something went wrong. Please send the packet of information back again."

Most asynchronous file transfer protocols use some form of error detection, typically checksum or cyclic redundancy check (CRC). Both the checksum and the CRC are values derived from the data being sent (or received) according to mathematical algorithms. The protocol sends the value long with the information (the bits) in in the packet. The receiving program compares with the check values with the values it calculates. If the check values do not match, the receiver asks the sending computer to retransmit the packet. Older protocols required a positive acknowledgement (an ACK) before they sent another packet. But newer protocols allow transmission of several packets before they receive an acknowledgement. This is particularly useful for circuits with long delays, especially satellites. See also XMODEM.

FILL Bit Stuffing

FILLS A computer imaging term. Designated areas that are flooded with a particular color. Most paint packages let you create geometric shapes in filled form. All packages also let you fill irregular closed regions. Two types of such fills exist: A seed fill floods all connected regions with the color specified by the mouse or stylus pointer; a boundary fill floods a color until the algforithm encounters a specified boundary color.

FINDER The user interface portion of the Apple Macintosh operating system. Unlike running Windows on top of DOS, tight integration of the finder and system requires both to be running.

FINGER A standard protocol specified in RFC-742. A program implementing this protocol lists who is currently logged in on another host. In short, finger is a computer command that displays information about people using a particular computer, such as their names and their identification numbers.

FILTER 1. A device which transmits a selected range of energy. An electrical filter transmits a selected range of frequencies, while stopping (attenuating) all others. It is used to suppress unwanted frequencies or noise, or to separate channels in communications circuits. Such a filter might be called a BANDPASS filter. You can also use a filter to remove certain characters you might be receiving over a data communications channel, for example control characters or higher-order nonstandard ASCII bits. 2. An operating parameter used in LAN bridges and routers that when set will cause these devices to block the transfer of packets from one LAN to another. Filters can be set to prevent the internetworking of several types of messages. They may be set to block all packets originating from a specific destination, called source address filtering, or all packets heading for a particular destination, called destination address filtering. Filters may also be set to exclude packet of a particular protocol or any particular filed in a LAN packet.

FIPS Federal Information Processing Standard. See also FIPS PUBS nn.

FIPS PUBS nn Various standards for data communications.

FIREWALL A LAN term. A barrier set up to contain designated LAN traffic within a specified area. Routers and other internetworking devices use their access control capabilities to build firewalls that can, for example, keep fault from propagating throughout the entire internet.

FIRM ORDER CONFIRMATION FOC. The form the local Telco submits to MCI indicating the date ordered circuits will be installed.

FIRMWARE Software kept in semi-permanent memory. Firmware is used in conjunction with hardware and software. It also shares the characteristics of both. Firmware is usually stored on PROMS (Programmable Read Only Memory) or EPROMs (Electrical PROMS). Firmware contains software which is so constantly called upon by a computer or phone system that it is "burned" into a chip, thereby becoming firmware. The computer program is written into the PROM electrically at higher than usual voltage, causing the bits to "retain" the pattern as it is "burned in." Firmware is non-volatile. It will not be "forgotten" when the power is shut off. Hand-held calculators contain firmware with the instructions for doing their various mathematical operations. Firmware programs can be altered. An EPROM is typically erased by using intense ultraviolet light.

FIRST OFFICE APPLICATION The first Ericsson AXE central office to put a new feature into service.

FIRST IN, FIRST OUT See FIFO.

FISH To push a stiff steel wire or tape through a conduit or interior wall. Pull through wires, cable or a heavier pulling-in is then attached to one end of the steel wire. The other end is then pulled until the wire or cable appears.

FISH JOB Running cables inside walls. Usage: "That fish job is too tough for a rookie."

FISH TAPE Non-conductive tape with a reinforced fiberglass core and slippery outer nylon coating which slides easily through conduit without jamming. The idea is to push the tape through, attach it to cable and pull the cable back. You might use something called wire pulling lubricants, which come in various formulations — for use in different temperatures, for pulling different cable, etc.

FITH Fiber to The Home. (I kid you not. That's what it stands for.)

FITL Fiber In The Loop.

FIVE BY FIVE Slang expression meaning satisfactory transmission in both directions.

FIXED CONDENSER A condenser, the plates of which are stationary and the capacity of which cannot be changed.

FIXED FORMAT A way of communicating in which everything to be sent follows a predetermined sequence, i.e. it fits into a specific length and format. The idea is to allow you to predict message length, the location of the message, where the control characters are, etc.

FIXED LENGTH RECORDS A set of data records all having the same number of characters in them. Think of a database of name, address, city, state, zip. Clearly, not everyone's record will be the same length. In order to make a fixed length record, the computer will pad the record with "padding characters" which the computer will ignore when it reads the record. But by including the padding characters it has effectively given everyone the same fixed length record.

FIXED LOOP A services feature available in some switching systems that permits an attendant on an assisted call to retain connection through the attendant position for the duration of the call. The attendant will normally recieve a disconnect signal when the call has been completed.

FIXED PRIORITY-ORIENTED-DEMAND ASSIGNMENT FPODA. Medium access technique in which one station acts as master and controls channel based on requests from stations.

FIXED RATE A fixed monthly price. See also FLAT RATE.

FIXED SATELLITE SERVICE A radiocommunication service between Earth stations as specified fixed points when one or more satellites are used; in some cases this service includes satellite-to-satellite links, which may also be effected in the inter-satellite service, the fixed-satellite service may also include feeder linker for other space radiocommunication services.

FL Fault Locating.

FLAG 1. A variable in a program to inform the program later on that a condition has been met. 2. In synchronous transmission, a flag is a pattern of six consecutive 1 bits used to mark the beginning and end of a "Frame" (IBM jargon for a packet). The character representation of the six consecutive "1" bits is 01111110. See ZERO STUFFING.

FLAME An outpouring of verbal abuse that network users write about other users who break the rules. Also a wonderful term for getting mad via electronic mail. See FLAME MAIL.

FLAME MAIL Slang term for rude electronic mail. Bill Gates, Microsoft chairman, is said to be famous for the flame mail he sends to employees who don't perform according to his likings. Mr. Gates is famous for flame mail sent by him between midnight and 2:00 AM.

FLAME-RESISTANT Insulated wire which has been chemically treated so it will not aid the spread of flames.

FLAME-RETARDANT Constructed or treated so as not be able to convey flame.

FLAMMABILITY Measure of a material's ability to support combustion.

FLASH Quickly depressing and releasing the plunger in or the actual handset-cradle to create a signal to a PBX or Centrex that special instructions will follow such as transferring the call to another extension.

FLASH BUTTON A button on a phone which performs the same thing as quickly pressing the switch hook on a phone. See FLASH, FLASH HOOK and FLASHPHONE.

FLASH CUT The conversion from an old to a new phone system occurs instantly as one is removed from the circuit and the other is brought in. There are advantages and disadvantages to Flash Cuts. For one, they're likely to be much more dangerous than the opposite view, known as a Parallel Cut, in which the two phone systems run side by side for a month or so. Also known as Hot Cut.

FLASH EPROM A type of EPROM that can be electronically erased. It differs from EEPROM in that generally the entire memory must be erased at once.

FLASH HOOK Another name for Switch Hook. The little button on the telephone that you place your receiver into. It obviously hangs the phone up, releasing that line to receive another call. If you push the flash hook quickly, you can signal the switch at the other end (central office or PBX) to do something, such as place a call on hold and switch to the incoming one (call waiting), or transfer the call to another phone. See FLASH and FLASH BUTTON above.

FLASH MEMORY Intel's new form of computer memory. Flash memory occupies little space and doesn't need continuous power to retain its memory. Some laptop companies, like Toshiba, are using flash memory as non-volatile storage for the BIOS (Basic Input/Output System) and the instructions that start the company (the bootstrap loader). See also MEMORY CARDS.

FLASH ROM Flast Read Only Memory. See FLASH MEMORY.

FLASHPHONE A Rolm single line analog phone that has a "flash" button. If you pushed this button, it gave the PBX the same signal as if you had flicked the touch hook up and down. The PBX would then give you a dial tone and you could pushbutton in codes to get access to the PBX's features, like transfer, etc. See FLASH.

FLAT RATE SERVICE An erstwhile common method of pricing local phone calls in the United States. The concept was that for a fixed amount of money — say $10 a month — you received a plain old desk telephone and an unlimited number of local calls. For years, most residential and most business phones were on a flat rate service. The first thing to go was the phone instrument. You had to pay a dollar or so a month to continue renting it, or you could send it back and buy your own. Second to go was the size of the local calling area you could call. It got smaller.

Third to go were the phone calls themselves. This happened first with businesses and now increasingly with residential service. Under this new "pay-per-call" you get charged a "message unit" for each local calls. A message unit is typically eight to ten cents. But psychologically, "message units" sound better than dimes. Fourth to go was the definition of local calls. What was now a "local" call got smaller, i.e. you could call less far for the price of a local call. And what was now a "local" long distance call changed. Calls which, years ago, were free (i.e. on flat rate service) have now become long distance calls. You can witness this phenomenon of changing local pricing in California, New York and Jersey. In other states, it's taking a little longer. There are cities where flat rate service still exists. Treasure them. They're disappearing, too.

FLAT TOP ANTENNA An aerial consisting of one or more parallel horizontal wires supported between masts. The "T" type and the inverted "L" type belong in this class.

FLATTERY The art of telling someone exactly what he thinks of himself.

FLEX LIFE The measurement of the ability of a conductor or cable to withstand repeated bending.

NEWTON'S TELECOM DICTIONARY

FLEXIBLE DIALING PATTERN A PBX dialing pattern that allows you to set your PBX so it can have one, two, three or four digit numbers for its extensions. See also FLEXIBLE NUMBERING OF STATIONS.

FLEXIBLE DRILL BIT A long drill bit that bends and is used for pulling cable and wire through walls in one operation. This means you drill the hole and then reverse the drill and it pulls the cable through the hole, while the drill bit is still inserted. Diversified Manufacturing of Graham, NC makes such a marvelous product.

FLEXIBLE INTERCEPT Allows you to assign "operator intercept" service to those extensions you wish for whatever reason, unassigned number, temporary disconnect, etc.

FLEXIBLE LINE RINGING A PBX feature which allows different phones to have different ringing for incoming calls from inside the building and from outside. Different ringing for intercom calls, different for inter-net calls, different ringing for outside calls, etc.

FLEXIBLE NUMBERING OF STATIONS A PBX feature which allows you some flexibility in the way you number the extensions off your PBX. How much flexibility depends on the particular PBX and the number of extensions you have. Hotels like giving their hotel phones the same number as the rooms. Makes sense. See FLEXIBLE STATION NUMBERING.

FLEXIBLE PRICING TARIFFS A regulatory procedure which permits rates for certain services to be changed quickly to meet market conditions, i.e. competition.

FLEXIBLE RELEASE The ability of the switching system to release a connection when either party hangs up.

FLEXIBLE ROUTING The ability to choose different physical paths through a network for different calls as circumstances warrant.

FLEXIBLE STATION NUMBERING A feature that allows telephone extensions to be numbered according to their physical location or departmental location, etc. No rewiring is required for in-place telephones. It's all done in software. See FLEXIBLE NUMBERING OF STATIONS.

FLEXIBILITY The quality of a cable or cable component which allows for bending under the influence of outside force, as opposed to limpness which is bending due to the cable's own weight..

FLEXPATH FLEXPATH service provides a 1.544 Mbps interface between a digital PBX and a New York Telephone central office (or New England Telephone central office) and supports Direct Inward Dialing (DID) and Direct Outward Dialing (DOD). In short, it allows an incoming call to be dialed directly to a phone associated with a digital PBX on the user's premises. It also allows outgoing phone calls to be dialed directly (i.e. dial 9), without using a PBX attendant.

FLICKER The wavering or unsteady image sometimes seen on monitors. A major cause can be low refresh rate or use of interlacing. Above 60 Hz, flicker disappears completely. See MONITOR.

FLINK A FLash and a wINK makes a flink signal.

FLIP FLOP A device or circuit which can assume either of two stable states. Flip flop devices are used to store one bit of information.

FLOATING POINT Arithmetical computations which use a form of scientific notation that allows the representation of very large numbers using a small number of bits. The speed of scientific computers is often rated in the Millions of FLoating Operations Per Second (MFLOPS) they can perform.

FLOATING SELECTION An imaging term. A selected area that is conceptually floating above the image, allowing it to be manipulated without affecting the background (for example, the contents of the Clipboard).

FLOOD PROJECTION In facsimile, the optical method of scanning in which the original is floodlighted and the scanning spot is defined by a masked portion of the illuminated area.

FLOOD SEARCH ROUTING A routing method that employs an algorithm that determines the optimum route for traffic within a network, avoiding failed and congested links.

FLOPPY DISK A thin, flexible plastic disk resembling a phonograph record upon which computer data is stored magnetically. Called a floppy disk because it is flexible and can (and will) flop inside a drive as it is being turned. And it may sound as though it is flopping. Floppy disks were never designed as the permanent storage many people are using them for at present. Floppy disks were designed by IBM as a way of having its sellers and engineers carry programs and program updates to its customers. Floppy disks were lighter and less cumbersome than carrying heavy spools of magnetic tape. IBM designed its floppy disks to be thrown away once their information was loaded into the mainframe computer. The moral of this story is that floppy disks are NOT permanent reliable storage. Anything stored on floppy disks should be backed up at least once and, if possible, twice. Floppy disks come in three diameter sizes — 3 1/2, 5 1/4 and 8 inches. Floppy disks can be now safely put through X-ray machines at US airports.

FLOPPY MINI A floppy disk smaller than the traditional 5 1/4 inch diameter floppy disk. Now most commonly the 3 1/2 inch size invented by Sony, and used by the Apple Macintosh, among others. All MS-DOS laptop computers have 3 1/2 inch disks.

FLOPTICAL TECHNOLOGY The combination of optical servo track positioning and magnetic read-and-write technologies used in 3 1/2-inch Very High Density floppy disk drives. Floptical is a registered trademark of Insite Peripherals.

FLOW CONTROL 1. The hardware, software and procedure for controlling the transfer of messages or characters between two points in a data network — such as between a protocol converter and a printer — to prevent loss of data when the receiving device's buffer begins to reach its capacity. 2. The process of protecting network service by denying access to additional traffic that would further add to congestion. (Think about flow control and the airlines.) See FLOW CONTROL PROCEDURE.

FLOW CONTROL PARAMETER FACILITY X.25 facility that allows the negotiation of packet and window sizes in both directions of transmission.

FLOW CONTROL PROCEDURE The procedure for controlling the rate of transfer of data among elements of a network, e.g., between a DTE and a data switching exchange network, to prevent overload.

FLOWCHART A graphic or diagram which shows how a complex operation, such as programming, takes place. The flowchart breaks that operation down into its smallest, and easiest-to-understand events.

FLUSH OUTLET A Communication Outlet recessed into the wall. This type of outlet may be positioned approximately 12" above the floor level for the connection of portable communications devices or at shoulder height to accept permanent wall telephone installations.

FLUTTER A rapid change in an electrical signal. The change may be in strength, frequency or phase. Distortion due to variation in loss resulting from the simultaneous transmission of a signal to another frequency.

FLY-BY-WIRE In traditional airplanes, the controls pilots moved were attached to heavy cables and hydraulic systems which themselves physically moved the rudder or the flaps, etc. Fly-by-wire replaced these wires and the hydraulic systems with computers and thin electrical wires. There are two main advantages to fly-by-wire. The computers can continuously adjust the aircraft's controls without the input of the pilot, trimming control surfaces so that the plane slides through the air with a minimum of air drag. Second, by eliminating heavy control cables and cutting down on hydraulic lines you can cut several hundred pounds off the the weight of plane, thus saving huge amounts of fuel over the life of the plane.

FLUX In soldering, a substance used to remove oxides from metal so the metal can be wet with molten solder for soldering.

FLYWHEEL A flywheel is a large heavy wheel used in electrical power generation. It's connected to an electrical power generator and will keep the generator spinning after the power source (a waterfall, or whatever) is unavailable.

FM See FREQUENCY MODULATION.

FMAS Facility Maintenance and Administration System.

FM BLANKETING That form of interference to the reception of other broadcast stations, which is caused by the presence of an FM broadcast signal of 115 dBu (562 mV/m) or greater signal strength in the area adjacent to the antenna of the transmitting station. The 115-dBu contour is referred to as the "blanking area."

FM STEREO SEPARATION A measure of a radio tuner's ability to separate the left and right hand channels of a stereo broadcast. The higher the number, the greater the separation. The unit of measure is the Decibel (dB), a logarithmic unit which expresses the ratio between two voltage, current or power levels, usually relating to a standard reference level, or a background noise level.

FMS Fraud Management System. An MCI term.

FMV Fair Market Value. A special lease for IRS purposes. Be careful. With Fair Market Value (FMW) leases, there is a catch to having the lessor guarantee the dollar amount or the percentage of your buyout. In order to be a FMV lease there must be a risk. That is why you are paying a lower rate of interest. If you agree on an amount up front, make sure it is not in writing, otherwise it does not meet the IRS test for a FMV lease. With A FMV lease, the lessor owned the asset and depreciates it; lessee expenses monthly payments and deducts them for tax purposes. If the buyout is determined in writing and the IRS can prove it, then it is a financing lease and lessee owns asset and depreciates it. Beware of this. This advice from Jane A Blank, telecom consultant, Westerville OH

FNA A Brussels-based strategic alliance, which exists to facilitate global communications connnections for companies in the financial services sector. The 12 founding FNA companies are Stentor of Canada, AOTC of Australia, RTT-Belgacom of Belgium, France Telecom, Deutsche Bundespost Telekom of Germany, Hong Kong Telecom, Italcable of Italy, KDD of Japan, Singapore Telecom, Telefonica of Spain, Mercury Communications of the United Kingdom, and MCI of the United States.

FNF Future of Numbering Forum. This definition, according to Lee Goeller: A series of meetings which Bellcore hopes will allow the industry to decide numbering issues without resorting to violence or the FCC.

FNR Fixed Network Reconfiguration

FO Fiber Optics.

FOCUS A measure of the clarity of a color monitor. Focus relates to the sharpness of a monitor's electron beam as it paints the face of a cathode ray tube (CRT). The other measures are convergence and dot pitch.

FOD Fax On Demand.

FOIL A slang term for an overhead transparency. The express "he gives good foil" reflects an executive's ability to make great presentations using overhead transparencies. the 1970s and early 1980s, so many managers at

IBM made presentations that some senior executives actually got overhead projectors built into their desks.

FOIRL Fiber Optic Inter Repeater Link.

FOLDER The equivalent on an Apple Macintosh of an MS-DOS sub-directory.

FOLLOW ME 800 SERVICE Basically, Follow Me 800 Service is call forwarding of your personal 800 line. MCI announced this service in the Spring of 1991. It differs from local call forwarding in that you can dial into MCI from anywhere in the world and change the number your 800 line will send its calls to. Your 800 number always stays the same. What changes is the number it calls. A simple explanation: We buy a personal 800 line from MCI. The number is 800-555-6534. When someone calls that number, MCI looks up a database, checks where to send the number and sends it to my office at 212-691-8215. However, one day I go traveling. So I call another MCI 800 number, punch in my identification number and then give it the new number I will be at — namely 212-206-6660. From then on, MCI will send all my calls to that number — until I call and change the number again.

FOLLOW-ME CALL FORWARDING ROLM's way of saying Progressive Call Forwarding. Allows a previously forwarded call to be forwarded from that to another extension.

FONLINE 800 Sprint's inbound service for small to medium-sized customers with applications up to 500 hours per month.

FONT Alphanumeric and other characters in a distinctively shaped type style or type face. The words you are now reading are in the Helvetica normal type font, also called Helios by some people. In Windows 3.1 terminology, font includes the type size.

FONT FAMILY A group designation that describes the general look of a font. For example, in Windows 3.1 the Times New Roman font family contains proportionally spaced fonts with serifs.

FONT SIZE See point size.

FONVIEW A Sprint term for a combination of analytical software and monthly usage data diskettes which allow small and medium sized customers to perform traffic analysis, summarize usage, analyze historical usage, allocate cost to departments or clients and perform accounting functions on an IBM compatible personal computer.

FOOTPRINT 1. The area on the earth's surface where the signals from a specific satellite can be received. A footprint is shown as a series of concentric contour lines that show the area covered and the decreasing power of the signal as it spreads out from the center. 2. The area on a desk a computer will occupy, i.e. the computer's footprint.

FORCE ADMINISTRATION DATA SYSTEM See FADS.

FORCED ACCOUNT CODE BILLING A telephone feature which prevents call from being completed if the user does not pushbutton in a billing code. That billing code may correspond to the department within the company. Or it may conform to the client and to the client's matter number the call must be billed to.

FORCED AUTHORIZATION CODE FAC. A PBX feature which requires all or certain users to enter a code before dialing an outside number.

FORCED RELEASE/DISCONNECT The switching center's automatic hang-up if the calling party fails to do so at the end of a conversation.

FORCED ROUTE OVERRIDE Allows a PBX user to automatically redirect an outgoing call to a different trunk if the first trunk is busy or the connection is poor.

FORD Fixed Or Repaired Daily. Found On the Road Dead.

FORECASTING Taking historical data (what happened in the past) from your ACD and using that information to predict what might happen in the future. Has your call volume always doubled on Tuesday? It will probably double next Tuesday too. A very important function of call center management software.

FOREGROUND PROCESSING Automatic execution of computer programs designed to preempt the use of the computing facilities. Usually a real time, urgent program. Contrast this with Background Processing, which might be something less urgent, for example, diagnostics of the system.

FOREIGN AREA TRANSLATION Translating the office codes of a distant (foreign) area to codes that make sense to a PBX which has more than one way of completing the call to that area.

FOREIGN CENTRAL OFFICE SERVICE Getting telephone service in a multi-office exchange from a central office other than the one you are normally served by. Not a common term any longer. Foreign central office service is the same price as normal local telephone service. It typically just involves asking for service off another central office. For example, our main number in New York City is 212-691-8215. Our 691- central office is in the 18th Street Exchange, a tall building on 18th Street. There is another central office in the same building. It is 206- and it is a more modern central office. When we ordered additional lines, we ordered them from this central office. You can now also call us on 212-206-6660. Don't trust my definition, however. Ask you local telephone company. See also FOREIGN CENTRAL OFFICE.

FOREIGN EMF Any unwanted voltage on a telecommunications circuit.

FOREIGN EXCHANGE SERVICE FX. Provides local telephone service from a central office which is outside (foreign to) the subscriber's exchange area. In its simplest form, a user picks up the phone in one city and receives a dial tone in the foreign city. He will also receive calls dialed to the phone in the foreign city. This means that people located in the foreign city can place a local call to get the user. The airlines use a lot of foreign exchange service. Many times, the seven digit local phone number for the airline you just called will be answered in another city, hundreds of miles away.

FOREIGN PREFIX SERVICE Getting dial tone in a multi wire center exchange from a foreign wire center other than the one you are normally served by. Similar to Foreign Central Office Service, except that you may get charged extra for Foreign Prefix Service. Don't trust my definition, however. Ask you local telephone company. See also FOREIGN CENTRAL OFFICE.

FORKLIFT UPGRADES There is some telecom equipment that can be upgraded and expanded by simply inserting a card or two and perhaps swapping out a power supply. And there's some equipment that needs to be almost completely replaced — cabinet and all. These sorts of upgrades are called "Forklift Upgrades."

FORM 230 Form 730 Application Guide is a collection of literature you'll need to register your telephone/telecom equipment under Part 68 of Title 47 at the Federal Communications Commissions. To get this material (it's free) drop a line or call the Federal Communications Commission, Washington DC 20554. As I write this edition, the person at the FCC in charge is William H. Von Alven, who also puts out a newsletter for Part 68 applicants. See PART 68 for a much larger explanation.

FORM FACTOR Fancy way of saying shape and size (width, depth, height).

FORMAT 1. Arrangement of bits or characters within a group, such as a word, message, or language. 2. Shape, size and general makeup of a document. As a verb, its most common usage is in "to format this disk."

FORTRAN FORmula TRANslating system. A computer programming language.

FORTUITOUS CONDUCTOR Any conductor that may provide an unintended path for intelligible signals, e.g., water pipes, wire or cable, metal structural members.

FORWARD BUSYING That feature of a telecommunications system wherein supervisory signals are forwarded in advance of address signals to seize assets of the system before attempting to establish a call.

FORWARD CHANNEL The communications path carrying data or voice from the person who made the call. The Forward Channel is the opposite of the Reverse Channel.

FORWARD ECHO An echo propagating in the same direction as the original wave in a transmission line, and formed by energy reflected back from one irregularity and then onward again by a second. Forward echoes can occur at all irregularities in a length of cable, and, when they add systematically, can impair its performance as a transmission medium.

FORWARD ERROR CORRECTION FEC. A system of data transmission in which redundant bits generated at the transmitted end are used at the receiving terminal to detect, locate and correct any transmission errors before delivery to the local data communications link. The idea of forward error correction is to avoid having to retransmit information sent incorrectly. This technique is consuming of bandwidth and can make the transmission take longer.

FOSSIL Fido/Opus/Seadog Standard Interface Layer. This is the interface used as an add-on to mailer software packages to connect them to PCs that are not 100% IBM-compatible.

FOTS Fiber Optics Transmission Systems. Not the same as POTS. But a neat acronym, nevertheless.

FOUNDATION GRAPHICS A set of graphics libraries or imaging models that form the lowest level graphics programmer's interface in Sun's OpenWindows. Examples: a graphics sub-routine library that a program could call to draw graphics primitives like arcs, circles, rectangles, etc.

FOUR HORSEMEN OF THE APOCALYPSE War, Plague, Famine and Death.

FOUR-WIRE CIRCUIT A path in which four wires are presented to the terminal equipment (phone or data), thus allowing for simultaneous transmission and reception. Two wires are used for transmission in one direction and two in the other direction.

FOUR-WIRE REPEATER A repeater consisting of two amplifiers, used a four-wire circuit.

FOURIER'S THEOREM In the early 1800s, the French mathematician Emile Fourier proved that a repeating, time-varying function may be expressed as the sum of a (possibly infinite) series of sine and cosine waves. Digital data is a bit stream, which can be sent as a sequence of square waves. Fourier's Theorem shows that to send a square wave (digital signal), a series of sine waves (analog signals) are actually summed together. If 1,000 square waves are to be sent every second, for example, the frequency components of the sine waves that are summed together are 1 kHz, 3 kHz, 5 kHz, 7 kHz, etc. The point of this analysis is to show that high frequency signals are required to form a stable, recognizable square wave.

As the bit rate increases, the square wave frequency increases and the width of the square waves decrease. Thus, narrower square waves require sine waves of even higher frequencies to form the digital signal. Note, then, that there is insufficient bandwidth in the 3 kHz voiceband to send square waves due to the absence of frequency components above 3,300 Hz. Even low frequency square waves cannot be sent because sine waves below 300 Hz are also absent. Thus, the local loop, according to Fourier's Theorem, cannot be used for the transmission of digital signals! The last paragraph is, in fact, no longer totally correct, as the increasingly successful ISDN trials are proving.

FOUR-WIRE A transmission path that allows physical separation of transmit and receive channels. At one time, 4-wire was the only method for implementing full-duplex transmission.

FOUR-WIRE ADAPTER A device which allows the connection of two-wire telephone equipment to a four-wire line. See FOUR-WIRE CIRCUITS.

FOUR-WIRE CIRCUITS Telephone lines using two wires for transmitting and two wires for receiving, i.e. four altogether. All long distance circuits are four-wire. Almost all local phone lines are two-wire. All analog phones are two-wire. Four-wire circuits offer much higher quality.

FOUR-WIRE REPEATER A repeater with two amplifiers, one used to amplify the signal going. The other used to amplify the signal coming. See FOUR-WIRE CIRCUITS.

FOUR-WIRE TERMINATING SET An electrical device which takes a four-wire circuit — one pair coming and one pair going — and turns it into the "normal" tip and ring circuit you need for a typical telephone, key system or PBX. See FOUR-WIRE CIRCUITS.

FOURTH UTILITY The non-vendor specific communications premise wiring system which you use for integrated information distribution (voice, data, video, etc.) Leviton in Bothell, Washington has trademarked the term Fourth Utility. They make a broad range of premise wiring products.

FOX MESSAGE A standard sentence for testing teletypewriter circuits because it uses all the letters on the keyboard. That sentence is The quick brown fox jumped over the lazy sleeping dog.

FP File Processor.

FP Feature Package. A software release for a telephone system. Originated with AT&T's Dimension PBX, now manufacturer discontinued.

FPS Fast Packet Switching.

FR-1 A flammability rating established by Underwriters Laboratories for wires and cables that pass a specially designed vertical flame test. This designation has been replaced by VW-1.

FRACTAL COMPRESSION A developing and as yet unproven technology for image compression based on principles of fractal geometry. It promises high-resolution and impressive compression ratios., i.e. substantially reduced storage of images.

FRACTIONAL T-1 Fractional T-1 refers to any data transmission rate between 56 kbps (DSO rate) and 1.544 megabits per second (Mbps), which is a full T-1. Fractional T-1 is simply a digital line that's not as fast as a T-1. Fractional T-1 is popular because it's typically provided by a phone company (local or long distance) at less money than a full T-1. FT-1 is typically used for LAN interconnection, videoconferencing, high-speed mainframe connection and computer imaging. Fractional T-1 is typically provided on four-wire (two-pair) copper circuits. See also ASDS.

FRAD Frame Relay Access Devices.

FRAGMENTATION A condition that affects data stored on a disk. Adding and deleting records in a file, creates what is sometimes called the Swiss cheese effect. The operating system stores the data for an individual file in many different physical locations on the disk, leaving large holes between records. Fragmented files slow system performance because it takes time to locate all parts of a file.

FRAME 1. Generally, a group of data bits in a specific format, with a flag at each end to indicate the beginning and end of the frame. The defined format enables network equipment to recognize the meaning and purpose of specific bits. The group of bits are sent serially (one after another). Generally a frame is a logical transmission unit. A frame usually contains its own control information for addressing and error checking. A frame is the basic data transmission unit employed in bit-oriented protocols. In this way, a frame is similar to a block. In video transmission, a frame is usually 525 electron scan lines that comprise one TV picture. 2. One complete cycle of events in time-division multiplexing. The frame usually includes a sequence of time slots for the various sub-channels as well as extra bits for control, calibration, etc. 3. A distributing frame. A rectangular steel bar framework having "verticals and horizontals" which is used to place semipermanent wire cross connections to permanent equipment. Found in telephone rooms and central offices. See FRAME RELAY and DISTRIBUTION FRAME.

FRAME ALIGNMENT The extent to which the frame of the receiving equipment is correctly phased with respect to that of the received signal.

FRAME BUFFER A large section of memory used to store an image to be displayed on-screen as well as parts of the image that lie outside the limits of the display.

FRAME CHECK SEQUENCE Bits added to the end of a frame for error detection. Similar to a block check character (BCC). In bit-oriented protocols, a frame check sequence is a 16-bit field added to the end of a frame that contains transmission error-checking information. In a token ring LAN, the FCS is a 32-bit field which follows the data field in every token ring packet. This field contains a value which is calculated by the source computer. The receiving computer performs the same calculation. If the receiving computer's calculation does not match the result sent by the source computer, the packet is judged corrupt and discarded. An FCS calculation is made for each packet. This calculation is done by plugging the numbers (1's and 0's) from three fields in the packet (destination address, source address, and data) into a polynomial equation. The result is a 32-bit

NEWTON'S TELECOM DICTIONARY

number (again 1's and 0's) that can be checked at the destination computer. This corruption detection method is accurate to one packet in 4 billion.

FRAME, DATA An SCSA term. A set of time slots which are grouped together for synchronization purposes. The number of time slots in each frame depends on the SCbus or SCxbus Data Bus data rate. Each frame has a fixed period of 125us. Frames are delineated by the timing signal FSYNC.

FRAME DURATION The sum of all the unit time intervals of a frame. The time from the start of one frame until the start of the next frame.

FRAME ERROR An invalid frame identified by the Frame Check Sum (FCS). See also FRAME ERRORS.

FRAME ERRORS In the 12-bit, D4 frame word, an error is counted when the 12-bit frame word received does not conform to the standard 12-bit frame word pattern.

FRAME GRABBER A device in a visual display unit which allows you to store and display one frame of information.

FRAME GROUND FGD. Frame Ground is connected to the equipment chassis and thus provides a protective ground. Frame Ground is usually connected to an external ground such as the ground pin of an AC power plug.

FRAME, MESSAGE A SCSA term. A data link layer frame the encapsulates control and signaling data transmitted on hte SCbus or SCxbus Message Bus. The form of a Message Bus frame is fully compliant with ISO HDLC UI (Unnumbered Information) Frame specifications.

FRAME RELAY Frame relay switching is a form of packet switching, but uses smaller packets and requires less error checking than traditional forms of packet switching. Frame Relay is very good at efficiently handling high-speed, bursty data over wide area networks. It offers lower costs and higher performance for those applications in contrast to the traditional point-to-point services. With frame relay, a pool of bandwidth is made instantly available to any of the concurrent data sessions sharing the circuit whenever a burst of data occurs. An addressed frame is sent into the network, which in turn interprets the address and sends the information to its destination at up to 2.048 Mbps.

Like traditional X.25 packet networks, frame relay networks use bandwidth only when there is traffic to send. Frame relay is often provided to the end user at three speeds — 56/64 kbits per second, 256 kbps and 1,024 mbps. Frame relay does not support voice, because voice traffic is highly sensitive to variations in the transmission delay introduced by the packet networks, while such small variations are usually not as critical to data traffic. For voice to be supported satisfactorily in packet a network, each packet must have a time-stamp which is monitored by the network. Frame relay lacks such a mechanism.

The American National Standards Institute (ANSI) describes frame relay service in the following documents:

ANSI T1.602 — Telecommunications - ISDN — Data Link Layer Signaling Specification for Application at the User Network Interface.

ANSI T1.606 — Frame Relaying Bearer Service — Architectural Framework and Service Description.

ANSI T1S1/90 — 175 - Addendum to T1.606 - Frame Relaying Bearer Service — Architectural Framework and Service Description.

ANSI T1S1/90-214 — DSS1 - Core Aspects of Frame Protocol for Use with Frame Relay Bearer Service.

ANSI T1S1/90-213 — DSS1 — Signaling Specific for Frame Relay Bearer Service.

Sprint devoted an edition of its TeleNotes newsletter to "The Frame Relay Solution." See FRAME RELAY IMPLEMENTORS FORUM. See also its faster cousin, called SMDS, for SWITCHED MULTIMEGABIT SERVICE.

FRAME RELAY IMPLEMENTORS FORUM A group of companies which have announced their support for a common specification for frame relay connections to link customers premises equipment to networking equipment. The common specification was originally announced on September 4, 1990. The common specification is based on the standard frame relay interface proposed by the American National Standards Institute (ANSI). The common specification supports the proposed ANSI standard and defines the extensions to that standard, including a local management interface that allows the exchange of control information between the user device and the frame relay network equipment. The specification is available for review from cisco Systems, Digital Equipment Corporation, Northern Telecom and StrataCom. See FRAME RELAY.

FRAME SLIP That condition under which a received digital signal loses frame synchronization. The dropping or repeating of a full frame by a transmission or switching facility without the loss of frame synchronization.

FRAME SYNCHRONIZATION The process whereby a given digital channel (time slot) at the receiving end is aligned with the corresponding channel (time slot) of the transmitting end as it occurs in the received signal. Usually extra bits (frame synchronization bits) are inserted at regular intervals to indicate the beginning of a frame and for use in frame synchronization.

FRAMING An error control procedure with multiplexed digital channels, such as T-1, where bits are inserted so that the receiver can identify the time slots that are allocated to each subchannel. Framing bits may also carry alarm signals indicating specific alarms. In TDM reception, framing is the process of adjusting the timing of the receiver to coincide with that of the received framing signals. In video reception, the process of adjusting the timing of the receiving to coincide with the received video sync pulse. In facsimile the adjustment of the facsimile picture to a desired position in the direction of line progression

FRAMING BIT 1. A bit used for frame synchronization purposes. A bit at a specific interval in a bit stream used in determining the beginning or end of a frame. Framing bits are non-information-carrying bits used to make possible the separation of characters in a bit stream into lines, paragraphs, pages, channels etc. Framing in a digital signal is usually repetitive.

FRAMING ERROR An error occurring when a receiver improperly interprets the set of bits within a frame.

FRANCHISE The exclusive right to operate telephone service in a community. This right — also called the franchise — is granted by some government agency. Some phone companies existed before the appropriate regulatory authority, so they're "grandfathered" in their exclusivity. Some phone companies have an exclusive area to serve more because of their presence than because of the legal right conferred on them. The question of who has a franchise to serve what community with what service is becoming increasingly unclear as competition penetrates all aspects of the phone industry.

FRD Fire RetarDant. A rating used for cable within duPont's Teflon or equivalent fluorpolymer material. FRD cable is used when local fire codes call for low flame and low smoke cable. FRD cable is typically run in forced air plenums as an alternative to metal conduits.

FREE SPACE COMMUNICATIONS Any form of telecommunications that doesn't use cable or fiber optic. In other words, free space communications is radio, microwave, satellite, wireless LANs, cellular, etc. Free space communications is in great demand today because of its use as a method of disaster prevention — when cables get sliced, etc.

FREEPHONE The overseas name for what we know as 800 IN-WATS service, international 800 service. And it means you can now have your overseas customers call you for free on an 800 line, just as your domestic customers do. The service is available from companies including Australia, Brazil, France, Hong Kong, Israel, Italy, Japan, Sweden, Switzerland and the United Kingdom. See EIGHT HUNDRED SERVICE.

FREEZE FRAME The transmission of discrete video picture frames at a data rate which is too slow to provide the psychopath perception of natural motion, referred to as "full-motion." An uncompressed, digitized full-motion video signal is typically transmitted at a rate of 90 Mbps. Freeze frame can be carried on anything from a simple voice grade phone line operating at 9.6 Kbps (the same speed as a Group 3 facsimile machine) or a DDS channel at 64 Kbps.

FREQ Also known as File REQuest; the ability in FidoNet to transfer files back and forth between BBSs (bulletin board systems) automatically. Equivalent to file transfer in PCRelay.

FREQUENCY The rate at which an electrical current alternates, usually measured in Hertz. Hertz is a unit of measure which means "cycles per second." So, frequency equals the number of complete cycles of current occurring in one second.

FREQUENCY AGILE MODEM A modem used on some broadband systems that can shift frequencies to communicate with stations in different dedicated bands.

FREQUENCY AGILITY The ability of a cellular mobile telephone system to shift automatically between frequencies.

FREQUENCY BAND The portion of the electromagnetic spectrum within a specified upper- and lower-frequency limit. Also known as Frequency Range.

FREQUENCY DIVERSITY A way of protecting a radio signal by providing a second, continuously operating radio signal on a different frequency, which will assume the load when the regular channel fails. Here's another way of saying the same thing: Frequency diversity is a any method of diversity transmission and reception wherein the same information signal is transmitted and received simultaneously on two or more independently fading carrier frequencies.

FREQUENCY DIVISION MULTIPLE ACCESS A technique for sharing a single transmission channel (such as a satellite transponder) among two or more users by assigning each to an exclusive frequency band within the channel.

FREQUENCY DIVISION MULTIPLEXING FDM. An older technique in which the available transmission bandwidth of a circuit is divided by frequency into narrower bands, each used for a separate voice or data transmission channel. This means you can carry many conversations on one circuit.

FREQUENCY FROGGING 1. Alternate use of frequencies at repeater sites of line-of-sight microwave systems. 2. The interchanging of the frequency allocations of carrier channels to prevent singing, reduce crosstalk, and to correct for a transmission line frquency-response slope. It is accomplished by having the modulators in a repeater translate a low-frequency group to a high-frequency group, and vice versa. Because of this frequency inversion process, a channel will appear in the low group for one repeater section and will then be translated to the high group for the next section. This results in nearly constant attenuation with frequency over two successive repeater sections, and eliminates the need for large slope equalization and adjustment. Also, singing and crosstalk are minimized because the high-level output of a repeater is at a different frequency from the low-level input to other repeaters.

FREQUENCY HOPPING Another name for spread spectrum transmission. A technique developed by Hedy Lamarr, the actress, in the early part of the second world war to prevent the enemy from jamming or eavesdropping on conversations and on commands to steer torpedoes, etc. The idea is to hop from one frequency to another in split-second intervals as you transmit information. Attempts to jam the signal succeed only in knocking out a few small bits of it. So effective is the concept that it is now the principal antijamming device in the US military. Ms. Lamarr never got paid for the invention. But it was definitely hers. And she invented it because of her patriotism for the United States. She had fled Austria in 1937. And she received a U.S. patent in 1940. See also SPREAD SPECTRUM.

FREQUENCY MODULATION A modulation technique in which the carrier frequency is shifted by an amount proportional to the value of the modulating signal. The amplitude of the carrier signals remains constant. The deviation of the carrier frequency determines the signal content of the message. Commercial TV and FM radio use this technique, which is much less sensitive to noise and interference.

FREQUENCY RESPONSE The variation (dB) in relative strength between frequencies in a given frequency band, usually the voice frequency band of an analog telephone line.

FREQUENCY REUSE The ability to use the same frequencies repeatedly within a single system, made possible by the basic design approach used in cellular. Since each cell is designed to use radio frequencies only within its boundaries, the same frequencies can be reused in other cells not far away with little potential for interference. The reuse of frequencies is what allows a cellular system to handle a huge number of calls with a limited number of channels.

FREQUENCY SHIFT KEYING FSK. A modulation technique for data transmission. It shifts the frequency above the carrier for a 1 and below the carrier for a 0 (zero). See also FSK.

FREQUENCY TOLERANCE The maximum permissible departure by the center frequency of the band occupied by an emission from the assigned frequency or by the characteristic frequency of an emission from the reference requency. By international agreement, frequency tolerance is expressed in parts per 10 (6) or in hertz. This includes both the initial setting tolerance and excursions related to short- and long-term instability and aging. In the United States, frequency tolerence is expressed in parts per 10(n), in hertz, or in percentages.

FRESNEL LOSS The loss at a joint that is caused by a portion of the light being reflected.

FRESNEL RELFECTION In optical physics, fresnel reflection is the reflection of a portion of incident light at a planar interface between two homogeneous media having different reflective indices. Fresnel reflection occurs at the air-glass interfaces at entrances at entrance and exit ends of an optical fiber. Resultant transmission losses (on the order of 4 percent per interface) can be virtually eliminated by using antireflection coatings or index-matching materials. Fresnel reflection depends upon the index difference and the angle of incidence. In optical elements, a thin transparent film is sometimes used to give an additional Fresenel reflection that cancels the original one by interference. This is called an antireflection coating.

FRESNEL REFLECTIVE LOSSES For optical fiber communication, the losses incurred at the terminus interface that are due to refractive index differences.

FRESNEL REGION In radio communications, the region between the near field of an antenna and the Fraunhofer region. The boundary between the two is generally considered to be at a radius equal to twice the square of antenna length divided by wavelength.

FRICTIONAL ELECTRICITY Static electricity produced by friction (e.g., by rubbing a hard rubber rod with a silk cloth.)

FRIESEN, GERRY Mr. Friesen is half the operation which published this dictionary. Call him if you find any mistakes in this dictionary. He didn't write it. But he should take the blame. He's good at handling blame. His phone number is 215-355-2886.

FRL Facility Restriction Level. A term created by AT&T for its Dimension PBX. These levels define the calling privileges associated with a line; for example, intragroup calling only in the warehouse, but unrestricted calling from the boardroom.

FROGGING Frogging is the process of inverting line frequencies of a carrier system so that incoming high-frequency channels leave at low frequencies and vice versa. Frogging equalizes the transmission loss between high and low frequency channels.

FRONT END CONTROLLER See FRONT END PROCESSOR.

FRONT END EQUIPMENT The equipment positioned between a computer and the communications line(s). Its purpose is to organize data being sent and received.

FRONT END PROCESSOR FEP. An FEP is a computer under the control of another, larger computer in a communications network. The FEP does simple, basic "housekeeping" operations on the data streams as they arrive to be processed by the bigger computer. The FEP acts as a sort of intelligent traffic cop. It relieve the bigger, host computer of some of its telecommunications Input/Output burden, so that the host computer can concentrate on handling the processing burden. Depending on its sophistication, the front end processor might also perform serial to parallel conversion, protocol conversion, block or message assembly, etc. Here's a more technical definition: A dedicated communications system that intercepts and handles activity for the host. Can perform line control, message handling, code conversion, error control, and such applications functions as control and operation of special-purpose terminals. Designed to offload from the host computer all or most of its data communications functions. IBM 3705, 3725 and 3745 are Front End Processors.

FSK Frequency Shift Keying. A modulation technique for translating 1's and 0's into something that can be carried over telephone lines, like sounds. A "1" will be assigned a certain frequency of tone, and a "0" will be assigned to another tone. The transmission of the bits keys the sounds to shift from one frequency to the other. See also FREQUENCY SHIFT KEYING.

FT-1 Fractional T-1. Any part of a T-1 circuit that's smaller than a full T-1 circuit. Fractional T-1 circuits are cheaper than full T-1 circuits. That's their reason for existing. See FRACTIONAL T-1 for a bigger explanation.

FT1 Fractional T1.

FTAM File Transfer and Access Management. An OSI protocol that provides access to files stored on dissimilar systems. FTAM is also an international standard.

FTTC Fiber To The Curb.

FTP File Transfer Protocol. In local area networking technology, file-sharing protocol that operates at layers 5 through 7 of the Open Systems Interconnection (OSI) model. As specified in RFC-959, FTP provides full authentication of the user by requiring login on the remote host. It lets users transfer text and binary files to and from a PC, list directories on the foreign host, delete and rename files on the foreign host, and perform wildcard transfers between hosts.

FTS Federal Telecommunications System is a private telephone network sometimes shared enthusiastically by all federal government agencies. And sometimes not.

FUBAR Fouled Up Beyond All Recognition. A total disaster with no chance of recovery. Your new phone system is supposed to go on-line in ten minutes, and a vital component is in a UPS truck that was just hijacked by crack-crazed gang of Albino Liberation Front terrorists. See SNAFU.

FUGITIVE GLUE Glue used by printers to affix stuff into magazines. The glue is designed to stick until the magazine is delivered. At that point, the stuck-in thing becomes easier to remove and/or falls into your lap.

FUGITIVE ODOR A smell that leaks out of a composting plant or landfill.

FULL AVAILABILITY Idealized condition which exists when your phone system can provide connections for every telephone connected to it. Also called NON-BLOCKING.

FULL DUPLEX Transmission in two directions simultaneously, or, more technically, bidirectional, simultaneous two-way communications. The best two-way phone conversations take place on four-wire circuits, two for transmission in one direction and two for transmission in the other. All long distance circuits are four wire. Most local lines are two wire, which means they're a compromise. Most speakerphones are half-duplex, meaning they only transmit in one direction at one time. The speakerphone flips its direction based on who's talking, or, more precisely, who's talking the loudest. Full duplex speakerphones are the best, but they're expensive. See SPEAKERPHONES and FOUR-WIRE CIRCUITS.

FULL ECHO SUPPRESSOR An echo suppressor in which the speech signals on each path are used to control the suppression loss in the other path of a 4-wire circuit. Used for long-distance communications. Compare with split echo compressor.

FULL MOTION VIDEO Television transmission where images are sent and displayed in real-time and motion is continuous. Compare with freeze frame. See FREEZE FRAME VIDEO.

FULL SYSTEM BATTERY BACKUP This means there's sufficient battery power backing the phone system so that during a power outage, the telephone system will continue to work, i.e. you won't even know the commercial power has gone out. All programming will be intact. Calls will get through, etc. Full System Battery Backup is critical to many businesses, especially those in the "life or death" business, such as hospitals, police, fire departments, etc. Other businesses who depend heavily on the phone for their revenues — airlines, brokerage companies, hotel/motels, etc. — often also use full system battery backup.

FULLY CONNECTED NETWORK A network topology in which each node is directly connected by branches to all other nodes. This architecture becomes impractical as the number of nodes in the network increases in complexity. Such networks normally go to distributed nodes.

FULLY PERFORATED Paper tape on which information is represented by the holes punched through the paper.

FULLY RESTRICTED STATIONS In a PBX, fully restricted stations (also called phones) can't place any outside calls. They can make intercom calls as well as receive incoming calls.

FUNCTION KEY 1. A key on a computer keyboard that has a defined function, such as the DELETE or BACK SPACE key. 2. An undefined key that can be defined to perform one function, which would normally require the user hitting one or several keys in succession. For example, one function key might move a block of data from one point in a file to another point.

FUNCTIONAL ENTITY FE. A set of functions that provides one or more specified capabilities. Seven FEs have been identified for the Advanced Intelligent Network Release 1 architecture: Network Access, Service Switching, Service Logic and Control, Information Management, Service Assistance, Automatic Message Accounting and Operations. Definition from Bellcore in reference to its concept of the Advanced Intelligent Network.

NEWTON'S TELECOM DICTIONARY

FUNCTIONAL GROUP A collection of FEs (Functional Entities) that reside together in a system.

FUNCTIONAL RESOURCE An abstraction of physical entities (e.g., voice synthesizers) that the Service Assistance FE (Functional Entities) can manipulate.

FUNCTIONAL SIGNALING In an ISDN circuit, function signaling provides messages with unambiguous, defined meanings known to both the sender and receiver of the messages. Signaling is generated by the terminal.

FUNCTIONAL SPECIFICATION A description of a system from a working point of view. It differs from a precise technical description which includes each piece of equipment precisely spelled out. A system can often work the same using different hardware and software configurations. By functionally describing a system, a user allows sellers to use their imagination to solve the problem in the most creative, cost-effective way. Most sellers prefer functional descriptions.

FUNCTIONAL SPLIT A division within an automatic call distributor (ACD) which allows incoming calls to be directed from a specific group of trunks to a specific group of agents.

FUNCTIONAL TEST A test carried out under normal working conditions to verify that a circuit or particular part of the equipment works properly.

FUNCTIONAL TRANSPARENCY The ability of a network to carry any user information regardless of its form, so that user applications can operate through the network.

FUNCTIONAL USER An entity external to the functional architecture that uses the functional architecture capabilities to exchange information with other functional users. Definition from Bellcore in reference to its concept of the Advanced Intelligent Network.

FUNCTIONAL-MANAGEMENT LAYER A communications layer in SNA that formats presentations.

FUSE 1. Verb: To blend together through melting. 2. Noun: An electrical device typically consisting of a wire or strip of fusible metal that melts to interrupt an electrical circuit when current exceeds the rated level of the fuse. The idea is that in any electrical circuit, the fuse should be the weakest point — thus the point that heats up when things go wrong and melts. Better the fuse melts than your expensive PBX.

FUSED QUARTZ The precise term for glass made by melting natural quartz crystals.

FUSIBLE LINKS Short lengths (about 25 feet) of fine-gauge wire pairs inside metallic sheath cable that melt to interrupt an electrical circuit and to prevent overheating in building wiring and equipment.

FUSION SPLICING In optical transmission systems using solid transmission media, the joining together of two media by butting them, forming an interface between them, and then removing the common surfaces so that there be no interface between them. Thus, no reflection or refraction at the former interface occurs.

FUZZY LOGIC Fuzzy logic is the newest wrinkle in the ancient science of controlling processes that involve constantly changing variables. Contrary to its name, fuzzy logic is a very precise subdiscipline in mathematics. It was invented in the 1960s by University of Berkeley's Russian-born Iranian computer science professor Lotfi Zadeh. It enables mathematicians and engineers to simulate human thinking by quantifying concepts such as hot, cold, very far, pretty close, quite true, most usually, almost impossible, etc. It does this by recognizing that measurements are much more useful when they are characterized in linguistic terms that when taken to the fourth decimal point. Fuzzy logic reduces a spectrum of numbers into a few categories called membership groups. Within five years virtually all consumer goods will come with fuzzy logic. Already fuzzy logic is inside video camcorders (to reduce the motion of the camera), in washing machines (to figure the optimum mix of washing conditions for that weight and filth). Fuzzy logic chips are made by companies such as InfraLogic Inc. of Irvine, CA.

FWIW Abbreviation for "For What It's Worth;" commonly used on E-mail and BBSs (Bulletin Board Systems).

FYI SERVICE An MCI International service that provides a summary of the latest news on business, current events, and sports in the USA via Telex.

FX See FOREIGN EXCHANGE.

FZA Fernmeldetechnisches Zentralamt. Telecom approval authority Austria, literally translated "long distance communications technical central office." All that in two words. Not bad!

G 1. Giga, meaning billion or thousand million. In computers it is 1024 times mega and is actually 1,073,741,824. One thousand gigas are a tera. One thousand teras one peta, which is equal to 10 to the 15th.

2. Abbreviation of "Grin," commonly typed within pointy brackets as <G>, at the end of an item uploaded to a BBS (Bulletin Board System), where the sender wants to make sure that readers realize that the message was meant to be humorous or sarcastic, and not to be taken literally. Example: "If my wife makes meatloaf one more time, I'm going to cut her fingers off <G>." Usage is similar to appending Wayne's-World usage of "Not" to reverse the meaning of a sentence.

G-STYLE HANDSET A G-style handset is a standard round handset, as compared to the K-style handset, which is the newer square handset with the two screws in the middle.

G,D&R Abbreviation for "Grinning, Ducking and Running;" commonly used on E-mail and BBSs (Bulletin Board Systems).

GA 1. Generally Available. A vague term manufacturers use to refer to when their new product will be generally available. 2. Abbreviation for "Go Ahead," used in real-time computer communications to indicate that you have finished a sentence and are awaiting a reply.

GAFF The spur on a telephone lineman's climbing iron.

GAIN The increase in signaling power that occurs as the signal is boosted by an electronic device. It's measured in decibels (dB).

GAIN HITS A cause of errors in data transmission over phone lines. Usually the signal surges more than 3dB and lasts for more than four milliseconds. AT&T's standard calls for eight or fewer gain hits in a 15-minute period.

GALLIUM ARSENIDE A substance from which microprocessor and memory chips are made. Compared with silicon, GaAs

- is three to ten times faster or, depending on its speed, uses as little as one-tenth the power,

- can detect, emit and convert light into electrical signals, opening the possibility of providing optoelectronic properties on a single chip.

- can resist up to 10,000 times the radiation.

- can withstand operating temperatures of 200 degrees Centigrade, and

- has a higher electron mobility.

GALVANOMETER A delicate instrument used for measuring minute currents.

GALVO MAN Telco-talk for Galvanometer Man, a technician who uses a galvanometer to find and repair circuit faults. It's common for the phone company rep to tell you that your new lines can't be installed when promised because the galvo man hasn't finished his work.

GAMMIC FERRIC OXIDE The type of magnetic particle used in conventional floppy disks.

GAN Global Area Network.

GAP An open space in a circuit through which a condenser discharges for producing electric oscillations.

GAP LOSS That optical power loss caused by a space between axially aligned fibers. For waveguide-to-waveguide coupling, it is commonly called "longitudinal offset loss."

GARAGE Silicon Valley, according to contemporary lore, started in a garage in Palo Alto in 1939. In that year Bill Hewlett and Dave Packard started Hewlett Packard with $538. Hewlett was the inventor and Packard the manager. Their first product, an audio oscillator, was an immediate success. Walt Disney used it in making Fantasia.

GARBAGE COLLECTION Routine that searches memory for program segments or data that are no longer active in order to reclaim that space.

GARBAGE IN, GARBAGE OUT GIGO. If the input data is wrong or inaccurate, the output data will be inaccurate or wrong. GIGO is problem with data entered by hand into computer systems. Ask yourself how many times you've received "junk" mail with the wrong spelling of your name? That's called Garbage In, Garbage Out.

GARBITRAGE Sending garbage from one city to another, usually organized by garbitrageurs on the phone.

GAS PRESSURIZATION A method for preventing water from entering openings in splice closures or cable sheaths by keeping the cables under pressure with dry gas.

GAS TUBE A method of protecting phone lines and phone equipment from high voltage caused by lightning strikes. See CARBON BLOCK (another protection technology) for a more detailed explanation.

GASEOUS CONDUCTORS The gases which, when ionized by an electric field, permit the passage of an electric current.

GATE This term is typically used in Automatic Call Distributors, devices used for handling many incoming telephone calls. Gate refers to a telephone trunk or business transaction grouping that may be handled by one group of telephone answerers (called attendants, operators, agents or telemarketers). That one group of telephone answerers is called "the gate." All calls coming into that gate can, theoretically, be handled by any of the telephone answerers. A telephone call is homogeneous throughout the gate. An automatic call distributor may have one gate — all calls coming in can be handled by everyone. Or it may have many gates, each one consisting of the line (or lines) bringing the call in — e.g. Band 5 WATS, New York City foreign exchange line. Or it may have two gates — one for orders and one for service. ACDs with multiple gates will establish rules for moving the calls between the gates, should one gate become overloaded.

GATE ARRAY A circuit consisting of an array of logic gates aligned on a substrate (a piece of silicon) in a regular pattern.

GATE ASSIGNMENTS Used in context of ACD (Automatic Call Distribution) equipment. Gates are made up of trunks that require similar agent processing. Individual agents can be reassigned from one gate to another gate by the customer via the supervisory control and display station. Also called splits.

GATEWAY A gateway is what it sounds like. It's an entrance and exit into a communications network. Gateways exist at the point where AT&T Communications ends and Comsat begins — for taking my call overseas. Gateways also exist between data networks. In data communications, they're typically referred to as a node on a network that connects two otherwise incompatible networks. For example, PC users on a local area network may need a gateway to gain access to a mainframe computer since the mainframe does not speak the same language (protocols) as the PCs on the LAN. Thus, gateways on data networks often perform code and protocol conversion processes. Gateways also eliminate duplicate wiring by giving all users on the network access to the mainframe without having a direct, hard-wired connection. Gateways also connect compatible networks owned by different entities, such as X.25 networks linked by X.75 gateways. Gateways are commonly used to connect people on one network, say a token ring network, with those on a long distance network. According to the OSI model, a gateway is a device that provides mapping at all seven layers of the model. A gateway may be used to interface between two incompatible electronic mail systems or for transferring data files from one system to another. Electronic mail systems that sit on local area networks often have gateways into bigger e-mail systems, like Internet or MCI Mail. For example, I might use MCI Mail to send a e-mail to someone's internal LAN e-mail. It might travel from MCI Mail to Internet via a gateway and then from Internet via another gateway to the company's e-mail on its own LAN.

GATEWAY CITY A city where international calls must be routed. New York, Washington, DC, Miami, New Orleans, and San Francisco are the five gateway cities in the United States.

GATING 1. Enabling or disabling a signal through applied logic. If it's turned on, the signal gets through. If not, the signal doesn't get through. 2. The process of selecting only those portions of a wave between specified time intervals or between specified amplitude limits.

GAUGE A term for specifying the thickness (diameter) of cables. Thicker cables have a lower number in the American Wire Gauge (AWG) scale. (It doesn't make sense. But that's the way it is.) Thicker gauge cables can carry phone conversations further and more cleanly than thinner gauge cable. But thicker cables cost more and take up more room, especially when you bundle them together and put them in a duct. When buying a phone system it is good to specify the thickness of the cables that will be installed — especially if some of your extensions will be a great distance from the central telephone switch, if you intend to carry high-speed data on them or you intend to live with your cabling scheme for more than a few months. You should, of course, not only specify the cable's thickness, but also whether it's stranded or solid core, coax, etc. Gauge is but one part of a cable description. See AWG.

GAUGE, WIRE The method of specifying the size of wire. The two important American gauges are the American Wire Gauge (Brown and Sharpe) and the Steel Wire Gauge.

GAUSS The unit of magnetic field intensity in terms of the lines of force per square centimeter.

GAUSSIAN NOISE Gaussian noise is white noise uniform across the whole range of frequencies. "Gaussian" refers to the measurement of the noise. It is essentially the assumption you make when working on the problem of noise mathematically.

GBH Group Busy Hour.

GBCS AT&T Global Business Communications Systems. The new name for the merger of two divisions into one division now responsible for all the business telephone system sales of AT&T worldwide. The two divisions that were merged into GBCS were called General Business Systems (office systems 80 lines and smaller) and Business Communications Systems (systems bigger than 80 lines). The merger happened during the summer of 1992.

GCT Greenwich Civil Time.

GDF Group Distribution Frame.

GDDM An SNA definition: Graphical Data Display Manager (GDDM) system software used for graphics display and printer devices and performs the same functions as QuickDraw in Macintosh computers.

GDMO Guidelines for the Definition of Managed Objects.

GENERAL CALL The letter CQ in the international code and used as a general inquiry call.

GENERAL MAGIC An alliance of Apple, AT&T, Matsushita, Motorola, Philips and Sony based in Mountain View, CA to establish a new class of personal communication products and services. Magic Cap and Telescript technologies are at the core of the company's offerings. The company's first public announcement was February 8, 1993. General Magic started in

January 1989. Apple Computer established a project led by Marc Porat to develop business opportunities beyond traditonal personal computing. The team examined how people will need to deal with the complexities of everyday life in the coming century. Code-named Paradigm and Pocket Crystal, the project evolved into a set of comprehensive plans, including products and services that would require expertise in computing, communications and consumer electronics. It became clear that no one company could deliver all the components of personal intelligent communications. In February 1991, Sony and Motorola joined Apple, becoming investors in General Magic and licensees of its technology. AT&T joined the alliance in January of 1992, Philips in November of 1992 and Matsushita in January of 1993. Sony, Motorola and Philips are building devices using Magic Cap to support personal intelligent communications. AT&T is providing a new kind of public messaging service based on Telescript. Apple will incorporate General Magic technologies into its products. See TELESCRIPT.

GENERAL PURPOSE NETWORK An AT&T term for a network suitable for carrying many forms of communication — voice and data, circuit and packet, image, sensor or signaling, for example.

GENERATIONS, COMPUTER As computers have improved, so the industry's pundits have assigned "generations" to those improvements. The concept of generations is not perfect nor finite. Here's our best shot on generations in computers:

● First generation: 1951-1958, core memory 8Kbytes to 32 Kbytes.

● Second generation: 1958-1964, transistor technology, memory 32Kbytes to 64 Kbytes.

● Third generation: 1964-1975, integrated circuitry.

● Fourth generation: 1975-date, nonprocedural languages, software driven.

● Fifth generation: into the 1990s, natural language programming, parallel processing and supercomputing.

● Sixth generation: in the 2000, will process knowledge rather than data.

GENERATIONS, PBX As PBXs have improved, so the industry's pundits have assigned "generations" to those improvements, as they did in computers. The concept of generations is not perfect nor finite. Here's our best shot on generations in PBXs:

● First generation: 1920s to the late 1960s. Step-by-step mechanical equipment. The first and the last of the step-by-step Bell PBXs switches was called a 701. Lee Goeller says the 701 "was the best PBX ever built. It was infinitely flexible. It was just too BIG. In fact, it was usually bigger than the office it served. This era of the stepper will be remembered as the era the Bell System was intact and had the gaul to rent operator chairs."

NEWTON'S TELECOM DICTIONARY

● Second Generation: Late 1960s: Bell 801 reed relay switch. Stromberg Carlson 800 series reed relay switch. GTE had a series, also. Reed relay switches were not very popular.

● Third Generation: 1974 and 1975: Rolm introduces its first CBX, an electronic, solid-state PBX. AT&T introduces Dimension. Digital Telephone Systems introduced the D1200. Northern introduced its first stored-program controlled SL-1. Some of these PBXs switched voice digitally, though they used different techniques, including PCM, PAM, and Delta Modulation. The codecs were in the switch, not in the instruments.

● Fourth generation: early 1980s. Distributed processing. Northern, Rolm and NEC and others introduced remote modules — slaves to the master switch at headquarters. These switches also added the capability of handling data without using modems. Switches like Lexar and InteCom were designed from the beginning to handle data without modems, thus requiring digital capability out to the set.

● Fifth generation: CXC, Anderson Jacobson and Ztel and others called themselves "fourth generation." When they started to fail, some people called them the "fifth generation." It wasn't clear exactly what that generation was. But they all got lots of publicity and the PBXs from CXC, Anderson Jacobson and Ztel ultimately failed.

● Sixth generation: Networked PBXs. Sit in New York. Operate your national network as if it were in the same building. Bingo, you can transfer calls across the country. All your messaging is the same wherever you sit on the network. Lee Goeller, however, says you can network stepper PBXs. In fact, in 1971 he says he managed one of the biggest integrated voice and data networks in the US using step-by-step electromechanical PBXs (701s made by AT&T). It was the world's largest dial tandem network. He had 63 different locations and three hubs.

● Seventh generation: Open Architecture. You can now program your own PBX. For more, see the NORSTAR COMMAND SET.

● Eighth generation: Dumb swiches. You can now buy completely dumb phone systems which are just basically switches. To get them to do anything they require an external computer (and software programming that computer) to drive the dumb switch. Often the "driving" is done through one or more serial ports.

In reality, the concept of generations amongst PBXs is very flimsy. But it's the stuff dictionaries are made of.

GENERATOR A machine which converts mechanical energy, such as the power from a piston engine into electrical energy.

GENERIC PROGRAM A set of instructions for an ESS or electronic PBX that is the same for all installations of that equipment. Detailed differences for each individual installation are listed in a separate parameter table.

GEOGRAPHIC INFORMATION SYSTEMS GIS. Computer applications involving the storage and manipulation of electronic maps and related data. Applications include resource planning, commercial development, military mapping, etc.

GEOMETRIC DILUTION OF PRECISION The multiplicative factor that modifies the ranging error. It is caused solely by the geometry between the user and his set of GPS (Global Positioning System) satellites. Known as DOP (Dilution Of Precision) or GDOP. See GPS.

GEOSTATIONARY ORBIT An orbit, any point on which has a period equal to the average rotational period of the Earth, is called a synchronous orbit. If the orbit is also circular and equatorial, it is called a stationary or geostationary orbit.

GEOSTATIONARY SATELLITE A satellite in geostationary orbit, also called geosynchronous orbit. A satellite placed in an geosynchronous orbit — 22,300 miles (or 42,164 kilometers)) directly over the earth's equator — will appear to be stationary in the sky, turning synchronously with the earth. This means you can plant a satellite receiving/transmitting antenna on the ground, and point it at that one place in the sky to receive signals from and transmit signals to "the bird", as satellites are sometimes called. Most communications satellites are in geostationary or geosynchronous orbit. The Russians have some satellites that orbit the earth and require antennae which move. These satellites are used to transmit to far northern communities which are difficult to reach with normal geosynchronous satellites.

GEOSYNCHRONOUS ORBIT Synchronous with the Earth. An orbit above the earth's equator where satellites circle at the same rate as the earth's rotation, thereby appearing stationary to an earth-bound observer. See also GEOSTATIONARY ORBIT.

GFCI. Ground Fault Circuit Interrupter. A device intended to interrupt the electrical circuit when the fault current to ground exceeds a predetermined value (usually 4 to 6 milliamps) that is less than required to operate the overcurrent protection (fuse or breaker) for the circuit. This device is intended to protect people against electrocution. It does not protect against fire from circuit overload. GFCI outlets are typically installed in bathrooms, kitchens and garages because the presence of water in these area increases the possibility of electric shock. Sometime GFCI circuits are incorrectly wired. The way to find out if your GFCI is wired correctly is to press the test button on its face. This should shut off power to the GFCI outlet and to those outlets connected to it.

GFI Group Format Identifier. In packet switching, refers to the first four bits in a packet header. Contains the Q bit, D bit and modulus value.

GFLOPS One billion FLoating point Operations Per Second. (G stands for GIGA, meaning billion). Today's fastest supercomputers are able to maintain a sustained throughput of over one billion floating point operations per second (GFLOPS) while performing real-world applications. By contrast, a 25-MHz 486 personal computer can sustain about one million floating operations per second (one MFLOP), or about one-thousandth the throughput of a supercomputer. See also G.

GIF GIF stands for Graphics Interface Format, which is pronounced "Jiff." It is a format for encoding images (pictures, drawings, etc.) into bits so that a computer can "read" the GIF file and throw the picture up on on a computer screen. (Other graphics formats include PCX, TIFF, etc.) CompuServe pioneered the bit-graphics format titled Graphics Interface Format. The format has become a standard in the electronic bulletin board world and it is used primarily to carry pornographic photographs. According to Jack Rickard, publisher of Boardwatch Magazing, "some of the photographs are reasonably good, but most feature strikingly plain women rather artlessly photographed by those whose higher calling is probably more aptly found in the building trades or automotive repair."

GIGA Prefix meaning one billion, which is one thousand million. 1,000,000,000. See also GFLOPS.

GIGABITS One thousand million bits. One billion bits. Or more precisely 1,073,741,824 bits.

GIGABYTE GB. One thousand million bytes. One billion bytes. More precisely, 1,073,741,824 bytes.

GIGAHERTZ A measurement of the frequency of a signal equivalent to one billion cycles per second, or one thousand million cycles per second.

GIM Group Identification Mark. The Group ID mark is a two-digit number used by cellular sites other than your home system to determine if your cellular phone should be allowed access on "roam" status. This feature is not yet fully implemented.

GIS Geographic Information Services. Computer applications involving the storage and manipulation of electronic maps and related data. Applications include resource planning, commercial development, military mapping, etc. Raw input comes often from satellite photographs.

GL Graphics Library.

GLARE Glare occurs when both ends of a telephone line or trunk are seized at the same time for different purposes or by different users. Most embarrassing. See GLARE RESOLUTION.

GLARE RESOLUTION Ability of a system to ensure that if a trunk is seized by both ends simultaneously, one caller is given priority and the other is switched to another trunk.

GLASGAL COMMUNICATIONS Glasgal publishes one of the best networking and data communications catalogs around. Their annual catalog contains the best technical explanations. Their president and founder, Ralph Glasgal, is an absolutely wonderful person. When he first started, he used to peddle datacom equipment out of catalogs he carried in a used shopping bag, peddling from door to door on Wall Street. He was, thus, one of the original shopping bag men. He's authored a number of books on data communications. And once he authored a column called Baudy Bits. These days he likes music, professionalism and success. He's good at all three. 201-768-8082.

GLASS INSULATORS Glass insulators were widely used in the 1800s to fasten open wire to telephone poles and to protect insulator pins from moisture so they couldn't conduct electricity. This was a technique developed by the telegraph industry over a 40-year period of experimentation and was one of the few basic telegraph practices carried over into telephone line construction. Insulators are found in a variety of different shapes and colors depending on the time period they were developed and on their application. Most have a greenish color from traces of iron oxide from the sand used to make the glass. When insulator design was in its heyday in the mid-to-late 1800s, hundreds of patents to improve the product were issued. For example, the double petticoat, a second lip on the bottom of the insulator, was added to reduce the amount of moisture that could travel up the inside of the cap. The above explanation courtesy Tellabs of Lisle, IL.

GLASS TERMINAL A keyboard and screen that conveys data generated by the user directly to a computer or network without buffering or otherwise acting upon the data, and also returns data unchanged from the computer to the user. This terminal type does not provide for cursor addressing or escape sequences.

GLITCH A problem or a delay. Can be a noun. "What's the glitch?" Or a verb: "Who glitched this thing up?" Glitch is also a momentary interrurption in electrical power.

GLOBAL Universal. An adjective meaning the whole world. See GLOBAL SEARCH.

GLOBAL ACCESS A new service of MCI Mail. It allows you, an MCI Mail user, to use your computer and its modem to dial a local number in a foreign (i.e. non-North American city) and reach a port of a packet switched operation called InfoNet. When you reach InfoNet you will then punch in a few letters and reach MCI Mail in the U.S. You can then leave MCI Mail messages, send telexes, send faxes and send paper mail, i.e. do all the normal services MCI Mail allows you to do. The advantage of Global Access is that you don't have to dial back to the U.S. (which usually doesn't work because of all the garbage on the line) or subscribe to a foreign packet switched operation (they have them in all industrialized countries). Sadly, it usually takes weeks to subscribe to a foreign packet switched operator.

GLOBAL POSITIONING SYSTEM See GPS.

GLOBAL SATELLITE SYSTEM A new breed of high-power satellite systems that propose to offer global telecom services. According to the Economist, they will offer three basic services:

• Voice: Satellite telephones will be able to make calls from anywhere on earth to anywhere else. That could make them especially useful to remote, third-world villages (some of which already use stationary satellite telephones), explorers and disaster-relief teams. Today's mobile telephones depend on earth-bound transmitters, whose technical standards vary from country to country. So business travelers cannot use their mobile phones on international trips. Satellite telephones would make that possible.

• Messaging: Satellite messagers have the same global coverage as satellite telephones, but carry text alone, which could be useful for those with laptop computers. Equipped with a small screen like today's pagers, satellite messagers will also receive short messages.

• Tracking: Voice and messaging systems will also tell their users where they are to within a few hundred meters. Combined with the messaging service, the location service could help rescue teams to find stranded adventurers, the police to find stolen cars, exporters to follow the progress of cargoes, and haulage companies to check that drivers are not detouring to the pub. America's military Global Positioning System (GPS) satellites will provide better positioning information to anyone who has a receiver for their signals, but GPS does not carry messages, so such a receiver cannot be used on its own for tracking or rescue. By the mid-1990s GPS receivers will be able to tell people where they are to within 70 metres anywhere in the world, and to within a metre or so in areas where the service is supplemented by a ground-based transmitter.

GLOBAL SEARCH A word processing term meaning to automatically find a character or group of characters wherever they appear in a document.

GLOBAL SEARCH AND REPLACE A word processing term meaning to automatically find a character or group of characters wherever they appear in a document and replace them with something else.

GLOBAL SOFTWARE DEFINED NETWORK AT&T's international virtual private network. It provides business customers with point-to-point, two-way voice and voiceband data communications between the US and various overseas countries. Features include:

• International two-way on-net calling.

• Abbreviated user defined 7-digit dialing.

• Usage sensitivity.

• SDN call screening.

GMD Gesellschaft fur Mathematik und Datenverarbeitung: a German government computer science research institute.

GMDSS Global Maritime Distress and Safety System.

GNE Gateway Network Element. A SONET Network Element (NE) that provides a direct OS/NE interface. The GNE provides an indirect OS/NE interface. The GNE provides an indirect OS/NE interface for other NEs in its own management subnetwork.

GNX DEVELOPMENT TOOLS A set of fax software development tools offered by National Semiconductor.

GO LOCAL A command typically given in a microcomputer asynchronous data communications program to tell the computer that it will connect to something without a modem over a null modem cable. The command "Go Local" also refers to modem connections and can tell one modem to overlook some of the handshaking and assume it's already taken place.

GOLD CODES Named after Robert Gold, Gold codes are used in direct-sequence spread spectrum transmission. Each transmitted signal is assigned to unique Gold code, which correlates the original information signal into a pseudo-random sequence. This sequence is then modulated and transmitted as a spread spectrum signal. The receiver, which uses the same Gold code, is able to de-correlate the spread spectrum signal and recover the original information. Gold codes possess two very desirable qualities which are important in a high quality communications system. The first quality is called "auto-correlation." When a receiver is subjected to several spread spectrum signals, it must extract the desired information and reject the remainder. Auto-correlation allows for an excellent signal recovery when the transmitted code matches the reference code in the receiver.

The second quality is called "cross-correlation." Cross-correlation simply means that an undesired transmitted code cannot produce a false match at the receiver. The advantage of Gold codes is that they consistently exhibit superior cross-correlation performance, which is critical in an environment with multiple transmitters, each representing a potential interfering source. See SPREAD SPECTRUM.

GOLD NUMBER Also called vanity number. A service of New York Telephone. It's a phone number that's easy for your customers to remember, e.g. 555-LIMO. But occasionally hard for them to dial. Tip: If you buy a vanity number, make sure it doesn't have numbers in it. 555-LIMO is harder to remember than CAR-RENT.

GOPHER Programmers at the University of Minnesota — home of the Golden Gophers — developed a kind of menu to "go for" items on Internet, bypassing complicated addresses and commands. If you want to connect to the State Library in Albany you select that option off the menu.

GORIZONT The Russian geostationary telecommunications satellite.

GOS Grade of Service. Telecom traffic term. The probability that a random call will be delayed, or receive a busy signal, under a given traffic load.

GOSIP Government Open Systems Interconnection Profile. The U.S. government's version of the OSI protocols. GOSIP compliance is typically a requirement in government networking purchases. GOSIP addresses communication and interoperation among end systems and intermediate systems. It provides specific peer-level, process-to-process and terminal access functionality between computer system users within and across government agencies.

GOVERNMENT RADIO PUBLICATIONS Publications on radio subjects by the Bureau of Standards and Signal Corps and sold by the superintendent of Documents, Government Printing Office, Washington D.C.

GPA General Purpose Adapater. An AT&T Merlin device that connects an analog multiline telephone to optional equipment such as an answering machine or a FAX machine.

GPI GammaFAx Programmers Interface. C-level programming language. Real-time applications for fax switched and gateways.

GPIB An interconnection bus and protocol that allows connection of multiple instruments in a network under the direction of a controller. Also known as the IEEE 488 bus, it allows test engineers to configure complete systems from off-the-shelf instruments and control those systems with a single, proven interface.

GPS Global Positioning System. A system to allow us all to figure out precisely where we are anywhere on earth. The GPS will eventually consist of a constellation of 21 satellites orbiting the earth at 10,900 miles — they circle the earth twice a day. In a way, you can think of them as "man-made stars" to replace the stars that we've traditionally used for navigation. The US Government is investing over $10 billion to build and maintain the system. Applications are almost limitless: Delivery vehicles will be able to pinpoint destinations. Emergency vehicles will be more prompt. Cars will have electronic maps that will instantly show us the way to any destination. Planes will be able to land in zero visibility. GPS is based on satellite ranging. That means we figure our position on earth by measuring our distance from a group of satellites in space. The satellites act as precise reference points. To get your precise position, latitude, longitude and altitude (and in some applications velocity), you need to get a "fix" off at least four satellites. That's the main reason for the 21 satellites.

Each GPS satellite transmits on two frequencies: 1575.42 MHz referred to as L1, and 1227.60 MHz referred to as L2. It transmits a host of somewhat complicated data occupying about 20 MHz of the spectrum on each channel. But basically, it boils down to three items. The satellite transmits its own position, its time, and a long psuedorandom noise code (PRN). The noise code is used by the receiver to calculate range. If we know precisely where a satellite is located and our precise range from it, and if we can obtain similar readings from other satellites, we can calculate precisely our own location and even altitude by triangulation. Satellite position and time are derived from on-board celestial navigation equipment and atomic clocks accurate to one second in 300,000 years. But the ranging is the heart of GPS. Both in the receiver, and in the satellite, a very long sequence of apparently random bits are generated. By comparing internal stream of bits in the receiver to the precisely duplicate received bits from the satellite, and "aligning" the two streams, a shift error or displacement can be calculated representing the precise travel time from satellite to receiver. Since the receiver also knows the precise position of the satellite, and its range from the receiver, a simple triangulation calculation can give two dimensional position (lat/long) from three satellites and additional elevation information from a fourth.

There are actually two PRN strings transmitted: a course acquisition code (C/A code) and a precision code (P code). The coarse code sequence consists of 1023 bits repeated every 266 days. But each satellite transmits a seven day segment re-initialized at midnight Saturday/Sunday of each week. By using both codes a very accurate position can be calculated. By transmitting them at different frequencies, even the signal attenuating effects of the ionosphere can to some degree be factored out. At the present time, civilian users are only authorized to use the coarse acquisition code and this is referred to as the GPS Standard Positioning Service (SPS), a best accuracy of about 5 meters. Military users use both the coarse acquisition code and the precision code in what is referred to as the Precise Positioning Service or PPS accuracy to centimeters. The Department of Defense (DOD) can at any time encrypt the precision code with another secret code on demand. This is referred to as "anti-spoofing" and ensures that no hostile military forces can also use the GPS service. The DOD can also purposely degrade the accuracy of the coarse acquisition code referred to as "selective availability" to about a 100 meter accuracy. But other than during brief test periods and national emergencies, the service is generally available to all. New techniques now make the civilian use of GPS almost as accurate as the military use.

By the mid-1990s GPS receivers will be able to tell people where they are to within 70 metres anywhere in the world, and to within a metre or so in areas where the service is supplemented by a ground-based transmitter.

GRACEFUL CLOSE Method terminating a connection at the transport layer with no loss of data.

GRACEFUL DEGRADATION A condition in which a system continues to operate, providing services in a degraded mode rather than failing completely.

GRADE 1 CABLE Twisted pair cables specifically designed for analog voice circuits and data transmissions up to 1 Mbps. Applications — Key systems, analog and digital PBX, low speed data, RS-232, etc.

GRADE 2 CABLE Twisted pair cables designed to meet the IBM Type 3 specification. These cables are capable of data transmissions at 4 Mbps, IBM 3270, STAR-LAN I, IBM PC Network, ISDN, etc.

GRADE 3 CABLE Twisted pair grade 3 LAN cables have performance characteristics that permit data transmissions at 10 Mbps. Each have been tested to insure they meet the EIA/TIA 568 emerging standard. Applications — 802.3 10BASE-T at 10 Mbps, STARLAN 10 and 802.5 token ring at 4 Mbps.

GRADE 4 CABLE The highest quality twisted pair cables available. Super grade cables have been tested up to speeds of 20 Mbps, 802.5 token ring at 4 Mbps and 802.3 10Base-T at 10 Mbps.

GRADE 5 CABLE These are the IBM-type individually shielded 2 pair twisted data cables. They're currently being tested for data rates at 100 Mbps. Applications — IBM Cabling System, 802.5 token ring at 16 Mbps and FDDI at 100 Mbps.

GRADE OF SERVICE GOS. A term associated with telephone service indicating the probability that a call attempted will receive a busy signal, expressed as a decimal fraction. Grade of service may be applied to the busy hour or to some other specified period. A P.01 Grade of Service means the user has a 1% chance of reaching a busy signal.

GRADED INDEX FIBER Graded index fiber is a multimode fiber optic cable that is made with progressively lower refractive index fiber toward the outer core. This reduces dispersion, which is fiber's equivalent of fading.

GRADIENT FILL A computer imaging term. A fill composed of a smooth blend from a starting color to an ending color. There are many variations on this theme. Most programs let you apply textures, and others have "smart" gradient fill routilnes that lend a three-dimensional appearance.

GRANDFATHERED Something that has a right to be a thing or own a thing by reason of it being or owning that thing before laws or rules were introduced to formalize the process. The derivation of term goes back to the Civil War. Grandfathering was a provision in several southern state constitutions designed to enfranchise poor whites and disfranchise blacks by waiving voting requirements for descendants of men who voted before 1867. The word derives from a "grandfather clause." Grandfather clauses stated that the right to vote was only available to those Americans whose grandfathers had been eligible to vote. These clauses were used, primarily in the South, to discriminate against blacks and immigrants shortly after Lincoln's issuance of the Emancipation Proclamation and congressional ratification of the Fourteenth Amendment. As a result, "grandfather" has come to mean something allowable because it was allowable before prohibitive legislation. See also GRANDFATHERED EQUIPMENT.

GRANDFATHERED EQUIPMENT Non-FCC registered telephone equipment that was directly connected to the telecommunications network without a phone company-provided protective connecting arrangement (PCA) prior to the formalized FCC registration program. See GRANDFATHERED.

GRAPHIC CHARACTER A character, other than a character representing a control function (like Ctrl G being, in WordStar and dBASE nomenclature, to delete the character on the right) that has a visual representation normally handwritten, printed, or displayed, and that has a coded representation consisting of one or more bit combinations.

GRAPHIC EQUALIZER A device that permits altering the tonal balance of an audio component/system at several frequency levels.

GRAPHICAL USER INTERFACE GUI. A fancy name probably originated by Microsoft which lets users get into and out of programs and manipulate the commands in those programs by using a pointing device (often a mouse). Microsoft's own definition is more elaborate. Namely that GUI puts visual metaphor that uses icons representing actual desktop objects that the user can access and manipulate with a pointing device.

GRAPHICS COPROCESSOR A programmable chip that speeds video performance by carrying out graphics processing independently of the computer's CPU. Among the coprocessor's common abilities are drawing graphics primitives and converting vectors to bitmaps.

GRAPHICS INTERFACE FORMAT Graphics Interface Format (GIF) is pronounced "Jiff." GIF is a format for encoding images (pictures, drawings, etc.) into bits so that a computer can "read" the GIF file and throw the picture up on on a computer screen. CompuServe pioneered the bit-graphics format titled Graphics Interface Format. The format has become a standard in the electronic bulletin board world and it is used primarily to carry pornographic photographs. According to Jack Rickard, publisher of Boardwatch Magazing, "some of the photographs are reasonably good, but most feature strikingly plain women rather artlessly photographed by those whose higher calling is probably more aptly found in the building trades or automotive repair."

GRAPHICS MODE PCs work in two modes — text and graphics. In graphics mode, the pixels are individually addressable. In text mode, the graphics card inside your PC throws a type font on your screen. And that's it. You can't change it. In graphics mode, you can. Graphics and text modes are mutually exclusive.

GRASSHOPPER FUSE A fuse that indicates that it has been blown by the movement of a piece of sringy metal.

GRATING LOBES Secondary main lobes.

GRAVITY CELL A closed circuit cell used where a continuous flow of current is desired. This type consists of copper and zinc electrodes with copper sulfate and zinc sulfate electrolyte. These are separated because of difference in their specific gravity.

GRAY Elisha Gray was an inventor who filed for a patent on his own telephone design a few hours after Alexander Graham You-know-who. Gray was involved in a number of lawsuits with the young AT&T, and ultimately co-founded (with Enos BARTON) electrical equipment maker Western Electric, which was later sold to AT&T.

GRAY SCALE An optical pattern consisting of discrete steps or shades of gray between black and white. Early facsimile machines could only receive black and white images and print them in black or white. Now they can print 16 shades of gray. This way if they receive a photo, it will look like a photo.

GRAY WHALE One of the first non-Bell key systems sold in North America. It was a 1A2 electro-mechanical key system from TIE/communications. TIE was a shortening of the words Telephone Interconnect Equipment. It was a wonderfully reliable phone system. A gray whale is now a prized possession.

GRAYBAR Probably the oldest distributor of phone equipment, as well as various electrical products. Named for Elisha GRAY and Enos BARTON, who formed Western Electric. The company is headquartered in St. Louis, though there is a famous Graybar building in Manhattan, attached to Grand Central Terminal. A plaque in the terminal near stairs leading into the Graybar building shows Gray and Barton (if it hasn't been defaced or stolen).

GREAT CIRCLE A circle defined by the intersection of the surface of the Earth and any plane that passes through the center of the Earth. The shortest distance, over the idealized surface of the Earth, between two points, lies along a great circle.

GREEK PREFIXES Remember the word "chronous?" It's used to mean the process of adjusting intervals or events of two signals to get the desired relationship between them. Here are the Greek prefixes that describe different timing conditions:

- asyn — not with
- hetero — different
- homo — the same
- iso — equal
- meso — middle
- piesio — near
- syn — together

GREENWASHER A business that uses the fact that it recyles to promote itself.

GREENWICH MEAN TIME GMT. Mean solar time at the meridian of Greenwich, England; formerly used as a basis for standard time throughout the world. also called Zulu time and World Time. Normally expressed in 24-hour time. GMT is an obsolete term. Because the second is no longer defined in terms of astronomical phenomena, "Universal Time" (which is defined in terms of cesium-133 transitions) is the most accurate measure of time, and the primary term name for time is "Coordinated Universal Time."

GREETING ONLY MAILBOXES Mailboxes that deliver a message to incoming callers but do not allow a message to be left. The Greeting Only mailbox may transfer a caller to a designated telephone number.

GRID 1. That element in a vacuum tube having the appearance of a grid and which controls the flow of electrons from the filament to the plate. "Grid" generally refers to the control grid. 2. Global Resource Information Database: part of the United Nations environment program.

GROOM/FILL In telephony, terms associated with more efficient use of T-1 trunks by combining partially filled input T-1 trunks into fully filled outgoing T-1 trunks.

GROUND 1. A problem that exists when a circuit is accidentally crossed with a grounded conductor. 2. Connecting equipment by some conductor (wire) to a route that winds up in the earth (Ground) for electrical purposes. One purpose of a "ground" wire is to carry spurious voltage (e.g. lightning strikes) away from the electrical and electronic circuits it can cause harm to. Incorrect grounding is probably the major cause of telephone systems problems. See GROUNDING (the major explanation), GROUND RETURN and GROUND START.

GROUND ABSORPTION The loss of energy in transmission of radio waves due to dissipation in the ground.

GROUND BUTTON A button needed on phones used for power failure transfer behind a PBX. You need the button because many trunks behind a PBX are ground start (as compared to loop start).

GROUND CONSTANTS The electrical constants of the earth, such as conductivity and dielectric constant. The values vary with frequency, and also with local moisture content and chemical composition of the earth.

GROUND FAULT In AC electricity, a ground fault is any unintended connection between a supply conductor and ground (ie: hot conductor in contact with the metal case of a piece of equipment). A ground fault will cause a high current flow and should operate the overcurrent protection (fuse or breaker provided such devices are functionally adequate) only if the ground path impedance is sufficiently low — but under no circumstances greater than two ohms.

GROUND FAULT CIRCUIT INTERRUPTER GFCI or GFI. A device intended to interrupt the electrical circuit when the fault current to ground exceeds a predetermined value (usually 4 to 6 milliamps) that is less than required to operate the overcurrent protection (fuse or breaker) for the circuit. This device is intended to protect people against electrocution. It does not protect against fire from circuit overload.

GROUND FAULT PROTECTOR GFP. A device designed to protect electrical service equipment from arcing ground faults. A GFP does not provide protection for people.

GROUND LEAD The conductor leading to the ground. Connection.

GROUND LOOP This occurs when a circuit is grounded at one or more points. It can cause telephone system problems.

GROUND PLANE The surface existing or provided, that serves as the near-field reflection point for an antenna.

GROUND POTENTIAL The electrical potential of the earth with respect to another body or region. The ground potential of the earth will vary with locality and also as a function of certain phenomena such as meteorological disturbances.

GROUND RETURN If a battery is connected to a closed electrical circuit, an electric current will flow in the circuit. In the early days of the telegraph, the circuit consisted of a long wire, the telegraph key, the electromagnet of a telegraph sounder and a return path through the ground, which served as a conductor. Thus the current flowed from one terminal of the battery through the wire, through the electromagnet, to a metal stake driven into the ground (a "ground" electrode), back through hundreds of miles of earth to the distant stake at the distant telegraph office and then to the other terminal of the battery. In later telecommunications, the ground return path was replaced by a second wire.

GROUND RETURN CIRCUIT A circuit in which the earth serves as one conductor. A circuit in which there is a common return path, whether or not connected to earth ground.

GROUND START A way of signaling on subscriber trunks in which one side of the two wire trunk (typically the "Ring" conductor of the Tip and Ring) is momentarily grounded (often to a cold water pipe) to get dialtone. There are two types of switched trunks typically for lease by a local phone company — ground start and loop start. PBXs work best on ground start trunks, though many will work — albeit intermittently — on both types. Normal single line phones and key systems typically work on loop start lines. You must be careful to order the correct type of trunk from your local phone company and correctly install your telephone system at your end — so that they both match. In technical language, a ground start trunk initiates an outgoing trunk seizure by applying a maximum local resistance of 550 ohms to the tip conductor. See LOOP START.

GROUND START SUPERVISION Telephone circuitry developed to prevent Glare.

GROUND STATION A cluster of communications equipment, usually including signal generator, transmitter, receiver and antenna that receives and/or transmits to and from a communications satellite. Also called a satellite earth station.

GROUND WAVE In radio transmission, a surface wave that propagates close to the surface of the Earth. The Earth has one refractive index and the atmosphere has another, thus constituting an interface. These refractive indices are subject to spatial and temporal changes. Ground waves do not include ionospheric and troposperic waves.

GROUNDING There are two distinct and unique categories in this broad area called grounding. One is earth grounding. The purpose of an earth grounding system is essentially threefold: 1. To guard against the adverse effects of lightning, 2. To assist in the reduction of static and 3. To bring a zero-voltage reference to system components in order that logic circuits can communicate from a known reference. The other category of grounding is known as equipment grounding. The purpose of equipment grounding is threefold: 1. To maintain "zero volts" on all metal enclosures under normal operating conditions. This provides protection from shock or electrocution to personnel in contact with the enclosure.. This is the safety aspect. This is the primary means of protecting personnel from electrocution. 2. To provide an intentional path of high current carrying capacity and low impedance to carry fault current under ground fault conditions; and 3. To establish a zero voltage reference for the reliable operation of sensitive electronic equipment. Effective equipment grounding is defined in the National Electrical Code, Article 250-51 and the Canadian Electrical Code Article 10-500. These Codes read almost identically. They say, "The path to ground from circuits, equipment and metallic enclosures for conductors shall;

1. Be permanent and continuous.

2. Have the capacity to conduct safely any fault current likely to be imposed on it, and

3. Have sufficiently low impedance to limit the voltage to ground and to facilitate the operation of the circuit protective devices in the circuit.

The Earth shall not be used as the sole equipment grounding conductor."

According to the Electric Power Research Institute, "electrical wiring and grounding defects are the source of 90% of all equipment failures." Many telephone system installer/contractors have found that checking for and repairing grounding problems can solve many telephone system problems, especially intermittent "no trouble found" problems. As electrical connections age, they loosen, corrode and become subject to thermal stress that can increase the impedance of the ground path or increase the resistance of the connection to earth. Equipment is available to test for proper grounding. (Ecos Electronics of Oak Park, IL makes some.) Before you install power conditioning equipment such as voltage regulators, surge arrestors, etc. you should test for and correct any problems you have with grounding and wiring. See also AC, AC POWER and BATTERY.

GROUNDING STRAP A device worn on the wrist or on the shoe when handling a static-sensitive component to prevent static shocks (sparks) which could damage the component. Don't even think of touching a printed circuit card without wearing a grounding strap.

See GROUNDING.

GROUP 1. In automatic call distributors, the same as GATE or SPLIT. 2. A collection of voice channels, typically 12. In AT&T jargon, a group is 12 channels. A supergroup is 60 channels. A mastergroup is 10 supergroups or 600 voice channels.

GROUP 1, 2, 3, 3 bis & 4 These relate to the facsimile machine business. They are essentially standards of speed and sophistication. They were created by the CCITT in Geneva, Switzerland to make sure facsimile machines from one maker could speak to facsimile machines of another maker.

● Group 1 transmits an 8 1/2 by 11-inch page in around six minutes. It conforms to CCITT Recommendation T.2.

● Group 2 transmits an 8 1/2 by 11-inch page in around three minutes. It conforms to CCITT Recommendation T.3.

● Group 3 — the most common fax in the world today — transmits an 8 1/2 by 11-inch page (also called A4)in as little as 20 seconds. It is a digital machine and includes a 9,600 baud modem. It transmits over dial up phone lines. Group 3 standards for facsimile devices were developed by CCITT adopted in 1980 and modified in 1984 and 1988. Group 3 defines a resolution of 203 x 98 dots per inch and 203 x 196 for "fine." Group 3 uses modified Huffman code to compress fax data for transmission. For example, a white line with no text, called a run, extending across an 8.5" page equals 1728 bits. Modified Huffman Code compresses the 1728 bits into a 17-bit code word. The lengths for all possible white runs are grouped together into 92 binary codes that will handle any white run length from 0 to 1728.

● Group 3 bis. This is an update to Group 3. It includes an image resolution of 406 x 196 dpi and a transfer rate of 14,400 bits per second.

● Group 4 Fax. The latest and fastest international standard for facsimile machines. It specifies a machine which operates at 64 Kbps, which can only work on a digital channel and which takes six seconds to transmit a 8 1/2 x 11 inch page. The Group 4 standard was promulgated in January, 1987. Group 4 fax machines are designed to use one of the 64,000 bit per second B (Bearer) channels on ISDN.

Most Group 3 machines will transmit and receive from Group 1, Group 2 and Group 3 machines (but at their slower speeds). Group 1, 2, 3 & 4 are international standards. Group 3 is now by far and away the most common.

All Group 3 machines will transmit and receive from each other. Some manufacturers have improved on the standards by offering Group 3 "fine," for example. These "fines" can talk to the same machines. But often can't talk to other "fines." If you're buying a facsimile machine and want super-quality transmission, check its compatibility with other machines. Or, easier, buy all identical machines. See FACSIMILE.

GROUP ADDRESSING In transmission, the use of an address that is common to two or more stations. On a multipoint line, where all stations recognize addressing characters but only one station responds.

GROUP BUSY HOUR GBH. The busy hour offered to a given trunk group.

GROUP CALL A special type of station (i.e. extension) hunting that requires a special access number to permit a call to the special access number and ring the first available phone in that group.

GROUP DISTRIBUTION FRAME GDF. In frequency-division multiplexing, a distribution frame that provides terminating and interconnecting facilities for the modulator output and demodulator input circuits of the channel transmitting equipment and modular input and demodulator output circuits for the group translating equipment operating in the basic spectrum of 60 kHz to 108 kHz.

GROUP HUNTING Automatically finds free telephones in a designated group. See HUNT

GROUP VELOCITY 1. The velocity of propagation of an envelope produced when an electromagnetic wave is modulated by, or mixed with, other waves of different frequencies. The group velocity is the velocity of information propagation. In optical fiber transmission, for a particular mode, the reciprocal of the rate of change of the phase constant with respect to angular frequency.

GROUPING A facsimile term for periodic error in the spacing of recorded lines.

GROUPWARE A term for software which runs on a local area network and which allows people on the network (typically a team) to participate in a joint (often complex) project. According to Fortune Magazine, March 23, 19992, using groupware, "Boeing has cut the time needed to complete a wide range of team projects by an average of 91%, or to one-tenth of what similar work took in the past." Groupware can be used in a meeting, with everyone sitting around a conference table and typing their ideas into the PC in front of them. Groupware can also be used off-line, with members of the "team" in different cities adding their comments. The "bellwether" of groupware software is Lotus' program called notes.

GRSU Generic Remote Switch Unit.

GS TRUNK Ground-Start Trunk. A trunk on which the communications system, after verifying that the trunk is idle (no ground on tip), transmits a request for service (puts ground on ring) to a telephone company. The other and more common type of trunk is called a Loop-Start Trunk.

GSA General Services Administration.

GSDN See GLOBAL SOFTWARE DEFINED NETWORK.

GSM Groupe Speciale Mobile, now Anglicized Global Standard for Mobile Communications. Pan-European cellular digital system Global System for Mobile communication. GSM is a new digital European cellular phone system that will let European travelers use a single cellular phone in more than 20 countries (by the end of 1993, allegedly) — and have every call billed to one account. Because of Europe's immense size, GSM has the potential to be the world's largest cellular system. See also BSS, which stands for Base Station System.

GSTN General Switched Telephone Network. Same as public telephone network.

GTA 1. Government Telecommunications Association. An association of local, state and federal telecommunications professionals in Washington, D.C.

2. Government Telecommunications Agency. Specialized agency which provides telecom service to Canadian federal government departments.

GTE General Telephone and Electronics. A major telecommunications company, whose main business is owning and operating "independent" (i.e. non Bell) telephone companies. In 1990 it bought Continental Telephone. GTE also has a small part of a long distance company called US Sprint, a packet switched operation called Telenet and various equity interests in various manufacturing operations making most things in telecommunications — from central offices to PBXs. Its partners in these joint ventures include Fujitsu and Siemens. See also GTE SPRINT and GTE TELENET.

GTE SPRINT A long distance service once provided by GTE, then a 50-50 joint venture of GTE and United Telecom. Now majority owned (80%) by United Telecom and 20% orf so by GTE. Now, GTE Sprint is just called Sprint.

GTE TELENET A public data network which operates by using the CCITT approved X.25 packet switching protocol. The new name for GTE TELENET is SPRINTNET. It's owned and run by Sprint, whis is 80% owned by United Telecom and 20% by GTE.

GTP General Telemetry Processor. An E-telemetry remote for use in terminal offices as the interface to ()Ss. (???) It provides AS&C, PM, and FL for several systems, including DDM-1000.

GTT Global Title Translations.

GUARD BAND A narrow bandwidth between adjacent channels in a communications amplifier which serves to reduce interference between adjacent channels. That interference might be crosstalk. Guard bands are typically used in frequency division multiplexing.

GUARDING The process of holding a circuit busy for a certain interval after its release to assure that a necessary minimum disconnect interval will occur between calls.

GUEST MAILBOX A mailbox used by a hotel or motel to set up temporary mailboxes for their guests.

GUI Graphical User Interface. A generic name for any computer interface that substitutes graphics for characters. GUIs usually work with a mouse or trackball. Windows 3.0 and Windows 3.1 are the most famous GUIs. Second most famous is the Apple Macintosh. See GRAPHICAL USER INTERFACE.

GUIDED RAY In an optical waveguide, a ray that is completely confined to the core.

GUIDED WAVE A wave whose energy is concentrated near a boundary or between substantially parallel boundaries separating materials of different properties and whose direction of propagation is effectively parallel to these boundaries.

GUY WIRE A wire used to support a radio mast.

H

H-CHANNEL The packet-switched channel on an ISDN BRI which is designed to carry user information streams at varying rates, depending on type: H11 - 1.536 kbps; HO - 3.84 kbps; and H12 - 19.20 kbps.

H.R.nnnn A proposed law introduced into the House of Representatives by a Congressman. Typically, four digits follow the H.R., signifying the proposed bill's number. The reason for including this definition in this dictionary is that every few months since divestiture some Congressman has attempted to introduce a bill into the House of Representatives changing the Communications Act of 1934. Such a bill is generally supported by a bevy of Bell telephone companies trying to use the proposed bill to remove those restrictions placed on them by Divestiture — manufacturing, creating information content and getting into long distance.

HACK The output of a hacker. Usually good programs, but sometimes just something clever of no discernible use. Just a "good hack", or something done for the "hack value."

HACKER A person who "hacks" away at a computer until his program works. The term has been wrongly used by the press to mean people who break into computer systems. See CRACKER.

HAL 1. The computer from the movie 2000: A Space Odyssey. It derived its name from a one-shift in letters from IBM. The I became H. The B became A. The M became L. 2. Hardware Abstraction Layer. See Windows NT.

HALF-DUPLEX A circuit designed for data transmission in both directions, but not at the same time. Telex is an example of a half duplex system, as is speaking on with most speakerphones. (The best speakerphones are full duplex. They're rare and expensive.)

HALFTONE Any photomechanical printing surface or the impression therefrom in which detail and tone values are represented by a series of evenly spaced dots in varying size and shape, varying in direct proportion to the intensity of tones they represent.

HALF-WAVE ANTENNA An antenna which is half as long as the wave being received.

HAMMING CODE An error correcting code named after R. W. Hamming of Bell Labs. The code has four information bits and three check bits per character.

HAND-OFF The process of transferring cellular-based calls from one cell site to another as the mobile or portable moves through the service area.

HANDHOLE A buried box whose lid is even with the surface of the ground. It provides a space for splicing and terminating cables.

HANDOFF The process by which the mobile telephone switching office passes a cellular phone conversation from one radio frequency in one cell to another radio frequency in another cell. It is performed so quickly (allegedly 250 milliseconds) that callers don't notice. Or we hope they don't notice.

HANDOVER WORD The word in the GPS (Global Positioning System) message that contains synchronization information for the transfer of tracking from C/A to P code.

HANDSET The part of a phone held in the hand to speak and listen, it contains a transmitter and receiver. In the old days, the transmitter was a carbon mike. Now it's mostly electronic. Some electronic mikes are awful. Some phone makers are going back to carbon mikes. There are two basic types of telephone handsets in North America: the G-style handset, which has round, screw-in ear and mouthpiece, and the new K-style handset, which has square ear and mouthpieces and has the two screws in the middle. I prefer the older G-style one. I think it's sturdier.

HANDSFREE A feature that's included with most of today's car phones. It permits the driver to use his cellular car phone without lifting or holding the handset to his ear. This is an important safety feature. See also HANDSFREE DIALING.

HANDSFREE ANSWERBACK This feature, when activated, automatically turns ON the microphone at a telephone receiving a Call so that the person receiving the call can respond without lifting the receiver. Handsfree answerback is typically used on intercom calls.

HANDSFREE DIALING A telephone feature which allows the user to place outside calls and listen to the progress of those calls without lifting the handset of his telephone. This feature is unbelievably useful when calling airlines which inevitably put you on "eternity hold." (We made that term up.)

HANDSFREE MONITORING You can dial an outside call and hear the call's progress without having to lift your handset. Similar to hands-free dialing. With hands-free monitoring, you can only listen. To speak, you must pick up the handset. To be able to speak, you need a full speakerphone. Be careful of the distinction. Many people have been caught.

HANDSFREE TELEPHONE Could be another word for a speakerphone or for a phone that does hands-free dialing.

HANDSHAKE The series of signals between a computer and another peripheral device (for example, a modem) that establishes the parameters required for passing data.

HANDSHAKING The initial exchange between two data communications systems prior to and during data transmission to ensure proper data transmission. A handshake method is part of the complete transmission protocol. A serial (asynchronous) transmission protocol might include the handshake method (XON/XOFF), baud rate, parity setting, number of data bits and number of stop bits.

HANDSHAKE IN HIN. A general purpose control signal sent from the

DTE to DCE in a Newbridge Networks RS-232-C connection. HIN can be used in place of Request to Send (RTS), Carrier Detect (CD) or Ring Indicator (RI).

HANDSHAKE OUT HOUT. A general purpose control signal sent from the DCE to the DTE. For example, in the case of a Newbridge Networks Mainstreet Data Controller with ports configured as DCE, HOUT is sent from the Data Controller to an attached device. HOUT can be used in place of Clear to Send (CTS), Carrier Detect (CD) or Ring Indicator (RI).

HANDSHAKING The electrical exchange of predetermined signals when a connection is made between two modems or other devices carrying data. Just as people shake hands, and go through a perfunctory "Hi, how are ya?", computers must go through a procedure of greeting the opposite party, verifying the identity of the other party, and other functions that can be described by this "humanizing term". As with human contacts, once the Handshaking is complete, the business of communications begins.

HANDWRITING RECOGNITION A system for taking handwritten generated with a stylus on a computer pad or directly onto the computer screen, and converting then into machine-readable text.

HANG UP Hang up lets you disconnect from an ISDN call. To hang up from the phone set you must depress and hold the receiver button for a specified amount of time. By default, the time is set for 0.8 of a second.

HARD COPY Anything on paper. It is all well and good to have information flash by on your CRT or video display terminal, but there are times when you want to take a Hard Copy with you. This dictionary was written on a computer screen. Now you have a hard copy in your hands. In this case, that's a lot more useful than having a disk.

HARD DISK ASSEMBLY A sealed mass storage unit used for storing large amounts of data. Now available on personal computers.

HARD DRAWN COPPER WIRE Copper wire that has been drawn to size and not annealed.

HARD RAM Carve some memory out of a computer's RAM; power it continuously and bingo you have Hard RAM, also called a Virtual disk. Setting up a RAM disk lets you use your computer's conventional, extended or expanded memory to simulate a disk drive (or drives). The primary advantages of a RAM disk are its very fast access speed and its battery power-saving properties. It has not mechanical element to slow it down or use additional power. Hard RAM exists in memory beyond 640KB.

HARD RUBBER A hard insulating material made of rubber, and having a dielectric constant of from two to four.

HARD SECTORING Physically marking the sector boundaries of a magnetic disk by punching holes in the disk where there's space available to store data. Hard sectored disks are not very common these days. Most disks — like those used on the IBM PC — are soft-sectored.

HARD TUBES Vacuum tubes having a high vacuum.

HARD WIRED 1. Describes a circuit designed to do one task (e.g. a leased line). 2. A person with a very narrow and rigid view of his or her job. "That security guard is really hard-wired."

HARDENED Resistant to disaster. Facilities with protective features that have been designed to withstand an explosion, a natural disaster, or ionizing radiation.

HARDWARE The actual physical computing machinery, as opposed to Software which is the list of instructions to operate the hardware, or the Firmware which is combination hardware/software that is "burned into" a Programmable Read Only Memory chip or chips. See FIRMWARE and SOFTWARE.

HARDWARE INTERRUPT See INTERRUPT.

HARDWIRE To permanently connect by wire two or more devices rather than to connect them temporarily through connectors or switches. Hardwire is a term also used to represent a leased line.

HARDWIRE SERVICES An MCI definition. Services providing intercity communications facilities dedicated to the use of a specific customer, and provided through a dedicated access line from the customer to the MCI switch.

HARDWIRE TERMINATING CITY City of circuit termination for hardwire services.

HARM See NETWORK HARM.

HARMONIC A frequency which is an exact multiple of a fundamental frequency.

HARMONIC DISTORTION A problem caused when the nonlinearities in communication channel cause the harmonics of the input frequencies to appear in the output channel.

HARMONIC RINGING A way of stopping users on a party line from hearing other than their own ring. We do this by tuning the ringer in their phone to a given ringing frequency, so it only rings when their frequency comes down the line.

HARMONICA A device attached to the end of a connectorized feeder cable that converts the 25 pair into individual 4, 6 or 8 wire modular channels.

HASH TOTAL Adding up one or more information fields in order to provide a check number for error control. The addition is not intended to have any meaning other than for checking.

HASP Houston Automatic Spooling Program. A control protocol adopted by IBM for transmitting data processing files and jobs to IBM 360 and 370 computers. An early job control language still in limited use.

HAYES AT COMMAND SET Before 1981, the modem was a dumb device. It had no memory or ability to recognize commands. It simply modulated and demodulated signals between the telephone line and the computer or terminal. In 1981, Hayes Microcomputer Products, Inc. in Norcross, GA produced the first "smart" modem, appropriately named the Smartmodem 300. It was "smart" because it understood commands, such as "ATD" which means "ATention, Dial the phone." The Hayes Standard AT Command Set (its full name) — a language for modems — has been accepted as a standard by the modem industry. And now many modems claim to be 100% Hayes compatible, which may mean they are and may mean they aren't. As in all cases of claimed compatibility, one should check. You'll find the complete Hayes AT Command Set spelled out in virtually every manual of every modem which purports to be "100% Hayes Compatible." See also CLASS 1.

HAYES MICROCOMPUTER PRODUCTS, INC. The company that made modems for PCs affordable and intelligent. Continues to make great modems. Still the standard against which most PC modems are measured. Based in Norcross, GA. See also HAYES COMMAND SET.

HAYES ULTRA 96 New Hayes 9600 bps modem with CCITT V.32, V.42 error correction and V.42 bis data compression. 9600 bps communications does not require data compression, although most modem manufacturers do have compression at 9600 bps. What happens is two 9600 bps modems will first negotiate modulation, then they'll negotiate error-control, and finally, they'll negotiate data compression. Hayes' ULTRA 96 has "Automatic Feature Negotiation" which means this whole process occurs automatically without the user's help. All this means is that two Hayes Ultras talking to each other can "talk" as fast as 38,400 bps.

HBA Host Bus Adapter. A printed circuit board that acts as an interface between the host microprocessor and the disk controller. The HBA relieves the host microprocessor of data storage and retrieval tasks, usually increasing the computer's performance time. A host bus adapter (or host adapter) and its disk subsystems make up a disk channel.

HCI Host Command Interface. Mitel SX-2000 PBX to computer link. HCI is designed to work with Digital Equipment Corporation computers. See OPEN APPLICATION INTERFACE.

HCS 1. Hundred Call Seconds. One hundred seconds of telephone conversation. See CCS. 2. Hard Clad Silica.

HDB3 High Density Bipolar 3. A bipolar coding method that does not allow more than 3 consecutive zeroes.

HDD Hard Disk Drive.

HDLC High level Data Link Control. A standard bit-oriented protocol developed by the International Standards Organization (ISO). In HDLC, control information is always placed in the same position. And specific bit patterns used for control differ dramatically from those used in representing data, so that errors are less likely to occur. SDLC and ADCCP are similar protocols. See also HIGH LEVEL DATA LINK CONTROL.

HDMAC Another potential high definition TV standard. HDMAC was spawned by Britain's Independent Broadcasting Authority. Unlike Japan's Hi-Vision, HDMAC has the attraction of being compatible with existing TV sets, i.e. those in Europe.

HDSL High bit rate Digital Subscriber Line. A technology to put two-way T-1 on a normal unshielded twisted pair (the stuff common in local loops) without using repeaters. See also ADSL.

HDT Host Digital Terminal.

HDTP Hoofddirectie Telecommunicatie en Post (Directorate for Telecommunications and Posts, The Netherlands).

HDTV High Definition TeleVision. Today's typical TV set in North America contains 336,000 pixels. A high definition TV set — one giving at least the definition of a movie theater, or 35 mm slide — will require at least two million pixels. Researchers are pursuing at least two dozen technologies to achieve this level of quality. The ideal HDTV would be flat screen, cheap, reliable and require very little electrical power.

HD Half Duplex circuit.

HDX Half DupleX.

HEAD A device that reads, writes, or erases data on a storage medium. The device which comes in contact with or comes very close to the magnetic storage device (disk, diskette, drum, tape) and reads and/or writes to the medium. In computer devices, it performs the same function as the head on a home cassette tape recorder.

HEAD END 1. The originating point of a signal in cable TV systems. At the head-end, you'll often find large tall TV and dish satellite receiving antennae. 2. A central control device required within some LAN/MAN systems to provide such centralized functions as remodulation, re-timing, message accountability, contention control, diagnostic control, and access.

HEAD THRASHING A term for rapid back and forth movements of the disk head of a hard drive.

HEADER The portion of a message that contains information that will guide the message to the correct destination. This information contains such things as the sender's and receiver's addresses, precedence level, routing instructions, and synchronization pulses.

HEADSET A telephone transmitter and receiver assembly worn on the head. Headsets are becoming very light and very comfortable and are no longer worn only by switchboard attendants and airline clerks. Northern Telecom says the following are traditional applications for headset use:

Receptionists. Console attendants. Telemarketers. Customer service reps. Order entry reps. Financial Service professionals. Stockbrokers. Sales reps and reservation agents.

HEADSET JACK A place on a phone or console into which you can plug a headset.

HEARING AID COMPATIBLE A hearing aid compatible phone may be used with inductively coupled hearing aid devices. You can find hearing aid compatible coin phones by looking for the blue grommet between the handset and the cord.

HEAT Electromagnetic waves of a frequency between that of light waves and radio waves. A form of energy.

HEAT COIL An electrical protection device used to prevent equipment from overheating as a result of foreign voltages that do not trigger voltage limiting devices. It typically consists of a coil of fine wire around a brass tube that encloses a pin soldered with a low-melting alloy. When abnormal currents occur, the coil heats the brass to soften the solder, allowing the spring-loaded pin to move against a ground plate directing currents to ground.

HEC Header Error Control - a CRC code located in the last byte of an ATM (Asynchronous Transfer Mode) cell header used for checking integrity only.

HEHO Head-End Hop Off. You have a private network. You overflow a long distance call to WATS or DDD at the originating end (the end the call is coming from). This HEHO (Head-End Hop Off) is done because it's usually cheaper than carrying the call part way through the network, then jumping off the network at that point (because the network is busy or it won't reach the end point). The opposite of HEHO is TEHO — Tail-End Hop Off. In TEHO, you carry the call as far as possible through the network, then pass it off to WATS or DDD as close to its destination as possible. The decision to go HEHO or TEHO has to do with economics, primarily which is cheaper.

HELD CALL A held call is a call to which you are connected but which is on hold.

HELD ORDERS A telephone company term for requests for telephone lines which the phone company cannot fill. Thus it is "holding" the orders. The reasons for holding customer orders might range from lack of capacity at the serving central office to a lack of local cable plant.

HELICAL ANTENNA An antenna that has the form of a helix. When the helix circumference is much smaller than one wavelength, the antenna radiates at right angles to the axis of the helix. When the helix circumference is one wavelength, maximum radiation is along the helix axis.

HELICAL SCAN Storage method that increases media capacity by laying data out in diagonal strips. Used in video tape recorders, etc.

HELICAL STRIPE A continuous, colored, spiral stripe applied over the outer perimeter of an insulated conductor for circuit identification purposes.

HELIX A spiral. The shape of screw.

HELLO When the phone was first invented, no one was sure how to begin the conversation. Thomas Edison saw the telephone as being used by businesses with permanently open lines. How would anyone know that the other party wanted to speak? A letter was found from Thomas Edison, dated August 15, 1877 to TBA, David, president of the Central District and Printing Telegraph Co. in Pittsburgh. "Friend David, I don't think we need a call bell as Hello! can be heard 10 to 20 feet away. What do you think? " Edison. At that time Alexander Graham Bell insisted on answering the telephone with "Ahoy." Hello! became the standard as the first telephone exchanges were set up across the country. Hello first appeared in the Oxford English Dictionary in 1883. In September of 1880, the first National Convention of Telephone Companies was held in Niagara Falls. "Hello" was used on everyone's name tag for the first time. Besides electricity, the phonograph and hundreds of other inventions, we can thank Edison for the "Hello" greeting. The above from New Pueblo Communications in Tucson, AZ.

HELP DESK A centralized location where queries about product usage, installation, problems or services are answered. Sometimes help-desks are provided by the mannufacturer of the product. Sometimes help desks are provided by outside companies — systems integrators and integrators, independent software developers and third party companies.

HENRY The inductance in a circuit in which the electromotive force induced is one volt when the inducing current varies at the rate of one ampere per second. It is 1,000,000.000 electromagnetic units, and is the unit of inductance.

HERCULES GRAPHICS Hercules graphics adheres to the Hercules standard of monochrome graphics on a monochrome PC monitor. That standard is 720 x 348 pixel resolution and 64K screen memory. This encoding was never adopted as a color standard and is now pretty well obsolete. See also MONITOR and FACSIMILE.

HERMATICITY TEST A fine and gross leak test of a hermetically sealed IC to see if there are any leaks in the seal. The gross leak test uses a fluorocarbon fluid, and the fine leak uses a light gas such as helium.

HERMETIC COATING A coating applied over the cladding of a fiber that retards the permeation of moisture and hydrogen into the fiber.

HERTZ Abbreviated Hz. A measurement of frequency in cycles per second. A hertz is one cycle per second.

HERTZIAN WAVE A name sometimes given to electromagnetic waves.

HETERO The Greek prefix meaning different.

HETERODYNE To generate new frequencies by mixing two or more signals in a nonlinear device such as a vacuum tube, transistor, or diode mixer. A superheterodyne receiver converts any selected incoming frequency by heterodyne action to a common intermediate frequency where amplification and selectivity (filtering) are provided. A frequency produced by mixing two or more signals in a nonlinear device. See HETERODYNING.

HETERODYNE REPEATER A repeater for a radio system in which the received signals are converted to an intermediate frequency, amplified, and reconverted to a new frequency band for transmission over the next repeater section.

HETERODYNING Here is an explanation from James Harry Green's book, the Dow Jones Handbook of Telecommunications: Analog microwave repeaters use either of two techniques to amplify the received signal for retransmission: HETERODYNING or BASEBAND. In a baseband repeater, the signal is demodulated to the multiplex (or video) signal at every repeater point. In heterodyne repeaters the signal is demodulated to an intermediate frequency, typically 70 MHz, and modulated or heterodyned to the transmitter output frequency. Heterodyne radio is reduced to baseband only at main repeater stations where the baseband signal is required to drop off voice channels. The primary advantage of baseband radio is that some carrier channel groups can be dropped off at repeater stations. Heterodyne radio has the advantage of avoiding the distortions caused by multiple modulation/demodulation and amplification of a baseband signal. Therefore, heterodyne radio is employed for transcontinental use with drop-off points only at major junctions.

HETEROGENEOUS NETWORKS Networks composed of hardware and software from multiple vendors usually implementing multiple protocols.

HETEROJUNCTION A junction between semiconductors that differ in their doping level conductivities, and also in their atomic or alloy compositions.

HEURISTIC Using much trial and error to arrive at a solution to a problem.

HEXADECIMAL A numbering system of 16 characters, ten digits and six letters. It is used to condense the long strings of zeros and ones in large binary numbers. This base-16 numeric notation system is frequently used to specify addresses in computer memory. It makes life simpler for programmers. In hexadecimal notation, the decimal number numbers 0 through 15 are represented by the decimal digits 0 through 9 and the alphabet "digits" A through F (A=decimal 10, B=decimal 11, and so forth).

HFAI Hands Free Answer on Intercom

HFU Hands Free Unit

HGC Hercules Graphic Card; long the standard monochrome graphics adapter for PCs and compatibles. Maximum resolution is 720 x 348 pixels.

HI-LO TARIFF A long distance private line tariff filed by AT&T whereby private lines between major cities were priced lower than private lines between smaller cities. In effect, those "larger" cities were those MCI operated in and those "smaller" cities were those MCI didn't operate it. Eventually the tariff was thrown out by the FCC and it figured in anti-trust suits by MCI and the Federal Government against AT&T.

HIBERNATION A term Compaq made up to describe a very useful laptop feature they finally copied from Toshiba after only seven years or so of being told to. (But they did finally listen.) The way Compaq describes Hibernation is that it "saves all open files to the hard drive and turns the unit off, either upon request or as an automatic feature. Power up the Compaq machine with Hibernation and you're back exactly where you left off. Or drifted off, as the case may be." However, hibernation has some problems. According to PC Magazine, unhibernating under Windows 3.0 took about 30 seconds. In contast, Toshiba's auto-resume feature is instantaneous.

HIDDEN MARKOV METHOD HMM. A common algorithm in voice recognition which uses probabilistic techniques for recognizing discrete and continuous speech.

HIERARCHY A set of transmission speeds arranged to multiplex successively higher numbers of circuits. See also HIERARCHICAL NETWORK.

HIERARCHICAL NETWORK A network that includes two or more different classes of switching systems in a defined homing arrangement, meaning to home in on the telephone you wish to be connected to. This is a fancy Bell System (Oops, I mean AT&T - Old habits die hard) term meaning that when direct circuits between two switches are busy or too far apart to be directly connected, the machinery will seek a higher level of switches to route the call through.

HIGH AND DRY What happens when you dial into a long distance network and nothing happens. You don't hear anything. Your call doesn't go anywhere. You're simply left High and Dry!

HIGH CAPACITY SERVICE Generally refers to tariffed, digital-data transmission service equal to, or in excess of T1 data rates (1,544 Mbit/s.)

HIGH DEFINITION TV HDTV. A system for transmitting a TV signal with far greater resolution than the standard NTSC standards. NTSC is the National Television System Committee and the standard for TV broadcast and reception in North America. HDTV has approximately twice the horizontal and twice the vertical emitted resolution specified by the NTSC standard. HDTV employs a wide aspect ratio. The total number of pixels is therefore more than four times that of NTSC. HDTV may include any or all IDTV and EDTV improvements. Several standards have been proposed in North America and, as of writing, the FCC had not agreed on one. Here are some of the proposed HDTV systems for North America:

Firms:	GI-MIT	GI	ATT-Zenith	ARTC	NHK
Systems:	CC-DigiCipher	DigiCipher	DSC	DSC	Narrow
		HDTV	HDTV	MUSE	
Lines:	787.5	1,050	787.5	1,050	1,125
Screens:	16:9	16:9	16:9	16:9	16:9
Transmission:	Digital	Digital	Digital	Digital	Analog

HIGH FIDELITY Systems of radio transmission and reception which permit a wide band of audio frequencies to be transmitted and/or reproduced.

HIGH LEVEL DATA LINK CONTROL HDLC. A communications protocol that is bit oriented in which control codes differ according to their bit positions and patterns.

HIGH LEVEL LANGUAGES Essentially any of the computer languages whose code is not unique to the hardware or architecture of a particular computer. High level languages are more like human language than the machine language which computers talk. High level languages translate human instructions into the machine language computers can understand, but which humans don't have to (in order to tell the computer what to do). Computer languages such as BASIC, FORTRAN, COBOL and Pascal are high level languages. They are a number of levels (at a High Level) away from the actual bit manipulation (machine language, also called "bit twiddling" by the Hackers). Compare with LOW LEVEL.

HIGH LOW TARIFF A tariff in which two prices are given for something — a high price and a low price. The first high/low tariff from AT&T was for leased voice lines where a lower charge was made per mile for connections between routes that have much traffic (High Density) and greater charges per mile are made for all other (Low Density) routes. The High/Low tariff was significant because it was AT&T's response to competition from long distance carriers like MCI and it was one of the first moves away from nationwide rate averaging, which was the way things were done under monopoly.

HIGH MEMORY AREA HMA. High Memory Area is the first 64KB of extended memory. If you're using MS-DOS 5.0, you can save some conventional memory by loading the operating system into HMA. Add the line DOS=HIGH to your CONFIG.SYS to use HMA for the operating system.

HIGH PASS FILTER A filter which passes frequencies above a certain frequency and stops (attenuates) those below.

HIGH PERFORMANCE COMPUTING ACT An Act passed by Congress in 1991 to foster the creation of computer "superhighways" linking computers at universities, national laboratories and industrial organizations. One objective of the High Performance Computing Program is the establishment of a gigabit/second National Research and Education Network (NREN) that will link the government, industrial and higher education communiities involved in general research acitivities. Such a gigabit network would provide a significant increase in bandwith compared with the existing National Science Foundation network, which is evolving from a 1.5 megabit per second (T-1) backbone to 45 megabit per second (T-3).

HIGH POWER AMPLIFIER HPA. A device which provides the high power needed to shoot signals 22,000 miles plus from an earth station to a satellite.

HIGH REJECTION The ability of a voice recognition system active vocabulary words and reject those sounds that do not match closely with those words.

HIGH RESOLUTION TV Television with over 1000 lines per screen, about double the resolution of present systems. Sometimes called HDTV, for high-definition television. We're still awaiting standards for high resolution TV.

HIGH SPEED PRINTER Any printer which can print at over 100 lines a minute. Like many definitions, this one is arbitrary. Some people claim a dot matrix is "high speed" and a letter quality, daisy wheel is a "low speed" printer. Laser printers could be classed as high speed printers, maybe.

HIGH SPEED SIGNAL An AT&T defintion for a signal traveling at the DS3 rate of 44.736 mbs (million bits per second) or at either 90 mbs or at 180 mbs (Optical mode).

HIGH SPEED REGISTER SET Registers are storage locations within the CPU that are used to hold both the data to be operated on and the instructions to accomplish the operations.

HIGH SPLIT A broadband cable system in which the bandwidth used to send toward the head-end (reverse direction) is about 6 MHz to 180 MHz, and the bandwidth used to send away from the head-end (forward direction) is about 220 MHz to 400 MHz. The guardband between the forward and reverse directions (180 MHz to 220 MHz) provides isolation from interference.

HIGH USAGE GROUPS Trunk groups established between two central office switching machines to serve as the first choice path between the machines and thus, handle the bulk of the traffic.

HIGHWAY Another word for BUS. A common path or set of paths over which many channels of information are transmitted. The channels of the highway are separated by some electrical technique.

HIPPI High Performance Parallel Interface. It's ANSI X3T9.3. HIPPI was originally developed as the interface to move data between supercomputers and peripherals such as disk arrays and frame buffers. More recently HIPPI has been extended and is used to network supercomputers, high-end workstations and peripherals using crossbar-type circuit switches. HIPPI provides for transfer rates of 800 megabits a second over 32 twisted pair copper wires (single HIPPI) and 1600 megabits a second over 64 paids (double HIPPI). HIPPI connections are limited to 25 meters, although a serial HIPPI standard is being developed to extend this range fo more than 10 kilometers. HIPPI is currently the most common interface in supercomputing environments.

HISTOGRAM An imaging term. A display plotting the density of the various colors and/or values in an image.

HIT Electrical interference that causes the loss or introduction of spurious bits into a data stream.

HIVR Host Interactive Voice Response. Tieing a voice response unit into a mainframe computer which has lots of data. Applications which can be produced include bank-by-phone, reservations-by-phone, etc.

HKSW Abbreviation for HOOK SWITCH, the actual electrical switch inside a phone that is controlled by the motion of the SWITCH HOOK.

HLC High Level Committee of ITU (International Telecommunication Union).

HLF High Level Function.

HLLAPI High Level Language Applications Programming Interface. An IBM API.

HMA See HIGH MEMORY AREA.

HMM Hidden Markov Method. A common algorithm in voice recognition which uses probabilistic techniques for recognizing discrete and continuous speech.

HOBIC HOtel Billing Information Center used by hotels for getting immediate charges for long distance calls placed by their guests. A service of AT&T and the local telephone operating company delivered through a distinct and separate trunk and usually terminating on a telex machine, which prints guest long distance charges.

HOBIS HOtel Billing Information System.

HOLD To temporarily leave a phone call without disconnecting it. You can return to the call at any time, sometimes from other extensions. There are several types of "HOLD" on a telephone system. How they work and what lamping they put on instruments varies from phone system to phone system.

● Exclusive Hold: Prevents every other telephone from picking up the call. Only the telephone instrument that put the call on hold can retrieve it.

● I-Hold: Effectively the same as Exclusive Hold.

● Line Hold: The call is on hold. Anyone with a phone with the held line appearing on it can pick up the phone.

HOLDING TANK A queue in which a call is held until it can either use its assigned route or overflow into the next available route.

HOLDING TIME The total time from the instant you pick up the handset, to dialing a call, to waiting for it to answer, to speaking on the phone, to hanging up and replacing the handset in its cradle. You are never billed for holding time. You are always billed for conversation time which is shorter than holding time. But holding time is an important figure to know when you're trying to determine how many circuits you need. For you will need sufficient circuits to take care of dialing, etc. — even though you're not being billed for that time.

HOLD RECALL A telephone system feature which reminds you periodically that you've put someone on hold.

HOLDING TIME The total length of time that a call makes use of a trunk or channel. Holding time is usually measured in call-seconds.

HOLLERITH CARD A punched-hole 80 column card used for storing information for input into a computer. Remember the cards you got telling you "not to fold, bend, punch, spindle, etc."? They were Hollerith Cards. They're now falling into disfavor as other, less tamper-proof methods appear.

HOLLERITH CODE Twelve level punched card code.

HOLLOW PIPELINE Jargon for a broad bandwidth circuit that has no framing. See T-1.

HOME The beginning place of a cursor on a CRT screen. Usually it's the top left hand corner. The function key on an IBM PC or clone marked "Home" will take the cursor to the home position, namely the top left hand corner.

HOME RUN Phone system wiring where the individual cables run from each phone directly back to the central switching equipment. Home run cabling can be thought of as "star" cabling. Every cable radiates out from the central equipment. All PBXs and virtually all key systems work on home run cabling. Some local area networks work on home run wiring. See LOOP THROUGH.

HOME SCREEN An AT&T Merlin term. The "home base" of the display screen on digital telephones, which shows time, date, and call information, and when a feature is in use.

HOMEOSTASIS The state of a system in which the input and output are exactly balanced, so there is no change.

HOMING When you dial a long distance number, your central office will choose a special set of trunks to send your call onto the next switching center for movement through the nationwide toll system. Those trunks are said to be the homing trunks for your central office. In other words, your central office is said to home on these trunks. If you're consistently encountering lousy long distance lines (and so are others on your central office), then ask your telephone company to check these trunks out.

HOMO The Greek prefix meaning the same.

HONEYCOMB COIL A type of inductance in which the turns do not lie adjacent to each other.

HOOKFLASH Momentarily depressing the hookswitch (up to 0.8 of a second) can signal various services such as calling the attendant, conferencing or transferring calls. In ISDN a hookflash signals the System Adapter to perform an operation, such as placing such as placing a call on hold. To hookflash, simply depress and release the receiver button. By default, the Hayes ISDN System Adapter recognizes a hookflash when the receiver button is depressed less than 0.8 of a second. You can change the default.

HOOK-UP WIRE A wire used for low current, low voltage (under 1000 volts) applications within enclosed electronic equipment.

HOOKEMWARE Free software that contains a limited number of features designed to entice the user into purchasing the more comprehensive version.

HOOKING SIGNAL An on-hook signal of 0.1 to 0.2 seconds duration used to indicate that a subscriber intends to initiate a new process such as "add-on."

HOOKSWITCH Also called SWITCHHOOK or switch hook. The place on your telephone instrument where you lay your handset. A hookswitch was originally an electrical "switch" connected to the "hook" on which the handset (or receiver) was placed when the telephone was not in use. The hookswitch is now the little plunger at the top of most telephones which is pushed down when the handset is resting in its cradle (on-hook). When the handset is raised, the plunger pops up and the phone goes off-hook. Momentarily depressing the hookswitch (up to 0.8 of a second) can signal various services such as calling the attendant, conferencing or transferring calls. See HOOKING SIGNAL.

HOOKSWITCH DIALING You can make phone calls by depressing the hookswitch carefully. If you push it five times, you dial five. Push it ten times you dial 0. Some coin phones discourage hookswitch dialing. Some don't.

HOP COUNT A LAN definition. The number of nodes (routers or other devices) between a source and a destination. In TCP/IP networks, hop count is recorded in a special field in the IP packet header and packets are discarded when the hop count reaches a specified maximum value.

HORIZONTAL CROSS-CONNECT A cross-connect in the telecommunications closet or equipment room to the horizontal distribution cabling.

HORIZONTAL DISTRIBUTION FRAME Located on the floor of a building. Consists of the active, passive, and support components that provide the connection between inter-building cabling (i.e. cabling coming from outside the building) and the intra-building cabling for a building.

HORIZONTAL SCAN RATE The frequency in Hz (hertz) at which the monitor is scanned in a horizontal direction; high horizontal scan rates produce higher resolution and less flicker. Thus, the EGA horizontal scan rate is 21.5Hz, while the VGA standard scan rate is 31.4Hz. Some displays now offer even higher scan rates, as much as 70 Khz. See MONITOR.

HORIZONTAL WIRING The portion of the wiring system extending from the workstation's outlet to the BHC (Backbone to Horizontal Cross-Connect) in the telecommunications closet. The outlet and cross-connect facilities in the telecommunications closet are considered part of the horizontal wiring. See HORIZONTAL WIRING SUBSYSTEM.

HORIZONTAL WIRING SUBSYSTEM The part of a premises distribution system installed on one floor that includes the cabling and distribution components connecting the riser subsystem and equipment wiring subsystem to the information outlet via cross connects, components of the administration subsystem.

HORN In radio transmitting, a waveguide section of increasing cross-sectional area used to radiate directly in the desired direction or to feed into a reflector that forms the desired beam.

HORN ALERT A cellular car phone feature that automatically blows the car's horn if a call is coming in.

HORSEPOWER A unit of power equivalent to 550 foot pounds per second or to 746 watts.

HOST BUS ADAPTER HBA. A printed circuit board that acts as an interface between the host microprocessor and the disk controller. The HBA relieves the host microprocessor of data storage and retrieval tasks, usually increasing the computer's performance time. A host bus adapter (or host adapter) and its disk subsystems make up a disk channel.

HOST COMPUTER A computer attached to a network providing primarily services such as computation, database access or specific programs of special programming languages.

HOST INTERACTIVE VOICE RESPONSE A voice response system that can communicate with a host computer, typically a mainframe. Applications which can be produced include bank-by-phone, reservations-by-phone, etc.

HOST NAME RESOLUTION A mechanism that provides static and dynamic mechanisms for resolving host names into numeric addresses. The Internet Name Server Protocol accesses an Internet name server that provides dynamic name-to-number translation (this process is specified in

IEN 116). The Domain Name Protocol accesses a Domain Name Server that provides dynamic name-to-number translation (this process is specified in RFC-1034 and RFC-1035). A static local host table can also be accessed for name-to-number translation.

HOST PROCESSOR Same as HOST COMPUTER.

HOST SITE In the transfer of files, the host site is the location receiving a file. When two individuals are exchanging files, the one who receives the file first would be the host, the other would be considered the remote.

HOST SWITCH A central office switching system which provides certain functions to a smaller switch located remotely.

HOST TABLE An ASCII text file where each line is an entry consisting of one numeric address and one or more names associated with that address. Host tables are used to resolve hostnames into numeric addresses.

HOT Live wire. A conductor carrying a signal is said to be a hot conductor, i.e. the wire carrying the signal or the ground as opposed to the neutral or ground wire.

HOT AND GROUND REVERSED In AC electrical power, the correct connection of the Hot and Ground wires is reversed. This is an extremely dangerous condition because the GROUND path will rise to 129 Volts and can present a lethal shock hazard to anyone in contact with equipment powered from this outlet or any outlet using the same ground path.

HOT AND NEUTRAL REVERSED Also called reversed Polarity. A symptom of poor AC electrical wiring. In this case the correct connection of the Hot and Neutral conductors is reversed. Dangers include increased leakage current, and damage to electronic equipment or motors and appliances requiring correct polarity.

HOT CUT The conversion from an old to a new phone system which occurs instantly as one is removed from the circuit and the other is brought in. There are advantages and disadvantages to Hot Cuts. For one, they're likely to be much more dangerous than a Parallel Cut, in which the two phone systems run side by side for a month or so. Also known as Flash Cut.

HOT FIX A feature of Novell's Netware LAN (local area network) operating system in which a small portion of the hard disk's storage area is set aside as a "Hot Fix Redirection Area." This area is set up as a table to hold data that are "redirected" there from faulty blocks in the main storage area of the disk. It's a safety feature.

HOT KEY COMBINATION A combination of keys on the keyboard that are pressed down simultaneously to make the computer perform a function. For example, the Ctrl, Alt, Del hot-key combination will warm boot an MS-DOS computer.

HOT LINE A private line dedicated between two phones. When you pick up either phone or do some act of signaling (like push a button), the other phone rings instantly. Hot lines are useful in emergencies and other areas where time is of the essence — e.g. trading currencies.

HOT LINE SERVICE When you pick up the phone, you're automatically connected with a phone number. Such Hot-Line Service on a PBX typically gets you emergency service, etc. See also HOT-LINE.

HOT LINKS A methodology that references and can connect information from one document to another, regardless of the type of application used.

HOT ON NEUTRAL, HOT UNWIRED In AC electrical power, the HOT wire is connected to the NEUTRAL terminal of the outlet and the HOT terminal in UNWIRED. Dangers include shock hazard from excessive leakage current and fire hazard. Depending on other conditions, equipment may or may not operate.

HOT REDUNDANCY A term used in conjunction with 911 service. With Hot Redundancy, the component or the system runs in parallel with an identical "twin." Should one twin fail, the other is already running and provides full service without interruption. See also WARM REDUNDANCY.

HOT STANDBY Backup equipment kept turned on and running in case some equipment fails.

HOTEL/MOTEL CONSOLE A specialized PBX console or a normal console programmed to work specifically in hotels and motels. The console will often show room status information.

HOTFIX A Novell program that dynamically marks defective blocks on the hard disk so they will not be used. See HOT FIX.

HOTLINE VIRTUAL PRIVATE LINE SERVICE A New York Telephone offering that simulates private line service. HotLine lets you automatically dial a predetermined line within the HotLine network, just by picking up the handset. Hotline uses facilities, switches and programmed intelligence of the public network to create a closed network of simulated private lines.

HOUSE CABLE Communication cable within a building or a complex of buildings. House cable owned before divestiture by the Bell System and after divestiture by the Regional Bell Operating Companies will eventually be fully depreciated and will then belong to the customer.

HOWLER A device which produces a loud sound to a subscriber's phone or private branch exchange (PBX) extension to indicate that the handset is off-hook and it ought to be put back on hook.

HOWLER TONE A tone which gets increasingly louder over a short period of time. It is used to notify a user that his phone handset is off its hook.

HOWLING Howling is typically heard in a speakerphone or conferencing unit when there is "Acoustic coupling" between the microphone and the speaker. This is due to putting the microphone too near the speaker. New circuits called acoustic echo cancellers allow you to operate the microphone and the speaker simultaneously and much closer to each other.

HPA See HIGH POWER AMPLIFIER.

HPAD Host Packet Assembler/Disassembler. The HPAD can link to a host or FEP with native protocol data, or if the host can accept it, with X.25 input. The 4400 PAD functions as either an HPAD or a TPAD See TPAD.

HPFS OS/2 can use any file system it wants, thanks to its installable file system (IFS) architecture. Two choices available are the FAT file system, used by MS-DOS, and the High Performance File System (HPFS). You can mix and match each and select one at boot time, thanks to OS/2's Dual Boot option. IBM, which created OS/2, claims HPFS is much more efficient than FAT. It tries to store all files on disk contiguously and uses its own built-in cache. However, HPFS' most notable attribute is the long, 254-character file names and case preservation. OS/2 remembers file names as upper and lower case (though it's not case-sensitive to commands).

HPO High Performance Option. A way of improving equipment transmission characteristics. For instance, the upgrading of a voice-grade line to meet standards for data transmission.

HSCS High-Speed Circuit Switched

HSDA High Speed Data Access.

HSDL High-speed Subscriber Data Line. A Bellcore idea for a two pair phone line coming into a house or business that is a full-duplex T-1 line. See also ADSL.

HSDU High Speed Data Unit.

HSL A computer imaging term. A color model based on hue, saturation, and luminance. Hue is the attribute that gives a color its name (e.g., red, blue, yellow, or green). In this model, saturation refers to the strength, or purity, of the color. If you mix watercolors, saturation would specify how much pigment you added to a given amount of water. Luminance identifies the brightness of a color. For example, full luminance yields white, while no luminance yields black. See also HSV.

HSSI High Speed Serial Interface.

HSV A computer imaging term. A color model based on hue, saturation, and value. Hue specifies the color, as in the HSL model. In this model, saturation specifies the amount of black pigment added to or subtracted from the hue. Value identifies the addition or subtraction of white pigment from the hue.

HTR Hard-To-Reach.

HUB The point on a network where a bunch of circuits are connected. Also, a switching node. In Local Area Networks, a hub is the core of a star as in ARCNET, StarLAN, Ethernet, and Token Ring. Hub hardware can be either active or passive. Wiring hubs are useful for their centralized management capabilities and for their ability to isolate nodes from disruption.

HUB POLLING A polling system in which a polled station sends its traffic and passes the polling message (after it's sent its message) to the next station.

HUB JUNCTION BOX A box used to connect a Hub Interface when a node is placed at a remote location.

HUFFMAN ENCODING A popular loss-less data compression algorithm that replaces frequently occurring data strings with shorter codes. Some implementations include tables that predetermine what codes will be generated for a particular string. Other versions of the algorithm build the code table from the data stream during processing. Huffman encoding is often used in image compression.

HUNDRED CALL SECONDS Known by the initials CCS where C is the roman numeral for Hundred. One CCS is 36 times the traffic expressed in Erlangs. See CCS.

HUNT Refers to the progress of a call reaching a group of lines. The call will try the first line of the group. If that line is busy, it will try the second line, then it will hunt to the third, etc. See also HUNT GROUP.

HUNT GROUP A series of telephone lines organized in such a way that if the first line is busy the next line is hunted and so on until a free line is found. Often this arrangement is used on a group of incoming lines. Hunt groups may start with one trunk and hunt downwards. They may start randomly and hunt in clockwise circles. They may start randomly and hunt in counter-clockwise circles. Inter-Tel uses the terms "Linear, Distributed and Terminal" to refer to different types of hunt groups. In data communications, a hunt group is a set of links which provides a common resource and which is assigned a single hunt group designation. A user requesting that designation may then be connected to any member of the hunt group. Hunt group members may also receive calls by station address.

HUNTING See ROLLOVER LINES.

HVQ Hierarchical Vector Quantization — a method of video compession introduced by PictureTel in 1988 which reduced the bandwidth necessary to transmit acceptable color video picture quality to 112 kbps.

HYBRID A device used for converting a conversation coming in on two pairs (one pair for each direction of the conversation) onto one pair and vice versa. This is necessary because all long distance circuits are two pairs, while most local circuits are one pair. Here is a longer explanation from "Signals, The Science of Telecommunications," by John Pierce and Mike Noll:

The telephone instrument in your home is connected to a single pair of wires called the subscriber loop or local loop, which carries both the outgoing voice signal and the incoming one. This pair of wires creates an electrical circuit for each of the two signals. A device in your phone called a hybrid or hybrid coil keeps the two signals separate, more or less, so that what you say into your phone's transmitter doesn't blast into your ear from the receiver.

In contrast, all multiplex systems provide separate talking paths in two directions. Separate paths are necessary because the amplifiers placed along the lines between terminals amplify signals traveling in one direction only. When two people talk between New York and San Francisco the call goes from one phone through a local two-wire voice circuit to a multiplex terminal. There the call is transferred to a four-wire long distance circuit that consists of two separate one-way circuits. At the end of the system, a hybrid reconverts each four-wire circuit into a two-wire circuit.

HYBRID CABLE A communication cable that contains two or more types of conductors that bear electrical signals, a mixture of signal-bearing electrical conductors and optical fibers, and/or two or more different types of optical fibers. A communication cable containing signal-bearing media and electric power conductors.

HYBRID COIL Transformer used in a balancing network to connect a 4-wire line to a 2-wire line.

HYBRID COMMUNICATION NETWORK A communication system that uses a combination of trunks, loops, or links, some of which are capable of transmitting (and receiving) only analog or quasi-analog signals and some of which are capable of transmitting (and receiving) only digital signals.

HYBRID CONNECTOR A connector containing both optical fiber and electrical conductors.

HYBRID COUPLER In antenna work, a hybrid junction forming a directional coupler. The coupling factor is normally 3 dB.

HYBRID JUNCTION A waveguide or transmission line arrangement having four ports that, when terminated in their characteristic impedance, have the property that energy entering any one port is transferred (usually equally) to two of the remaining three ports. Widely used as a mixing or dividing device.

HYBRID KEY SYSTEM Term used to describe a system which has attributes of both Key Telephone Systems and PBXs. The one distinguishing feature these days is that a hybrid key system can use normal single line phones in addition to the normal electronic key phones. A single line phone behind a hybrid works very much like a single line phone behind a PBX. The second distinguishing feature of a hybrid is that it's "non-squared." This means that not every trunk appears as a button on every phone in the system — as occurs on virtually every electronic key system manufactured today.

HYBRID MODE A mode possessing components of both electrical and magnetic field vectors in the direction of propagation.

HYBRID NETWORK 1. A communications network which has some links capable of sending and receiving only analog signals and other links capable of handling only digital signals. The current public switched telephone network is Hybrid. 2. An amalgam of public and private network transmission facilities.

HYBRID SET Two or more transformers interconnected to form a network having four pairs of accessible terminals to which may be connected four impedances so that the branches containing them may be made interchangeable.

HYDRA A 25-pair cable that at one end has an amphenol connector (typical of what 1A2 phone systems were connected with) and at the other has many individual 2, 4, 6 and 8 wire connectors, typically male RJ-11s. It's more commonly called an octopus cable. The reason it's called an octopus is that it looks a bit like an octopus — one body and many arms.

HYDROGEN LOSS Increases in optical fiber attenuation that occur when hydrogen diffuses into the glass matrix and absorbs some light.

HYDROMETER Instrument for determining the density of liquids. Formerly in wide use for testing radio storage "A" batteries.

HYGROSCOPIC Capable of absorbing moisture from the air.

HYPERCHANNEL An SCSA term. A data path on the SCbus or SCxbus Data Bus made up of more than one time slot. By bundling time slots into a hyperchannel, data paths with a bandwidth greater than 64 Kbps can be created.

HYPERMEDIA A way of delivering information that provides multiple connected pathways through a body of information. Hypermedia allows the user to jump easily from one topic to related or supplementary material found in various forms, such as text, graphics, audio or video.

Another definition we found is: Non-linear media, of which multimedia can be a form. Just as hypertext is a non-sequential, random-access arrangement of text, hypermedia is a non-sequential, random-access arrangement of multiple media such as video, sound and computer data.

A third definition: Hypermedia is a type of authoring and playback software through which you can access multiple layers of multimedia information related to a specific topic. The information can be in the form of text, graphics, images, audio, or video. For example, suppose you received a hypermedia document about the Sun file system. You could click on a hotspot (such as the words file system) and then read a description. You could then click an icon to see an illustration of a file structure, and then click the file icon to see and hear information in a video explaining the file system.

HYPERSTREAM A name for frame relay service from Stentor and MCI.

HYPERWARE New hardware that has been announced and perhaps even publicly demonstrated, but is not being shipped to commercial customers. Vaporware is software which has been announced, but is not yet shipping to commercial customers. Years can pass between public announcement and actual commercial shipment. Be wary.

HZ See Hertz.

I

I Used sometimes on switches to mean "ON." The comparable "OFF" setting is "O."

I&R Installation and Repair. The telephone company department responsible for these jobs.

I-CF ISDN Call Forwarding.

I-CFDA ISDN Call Forwarding Don't Answer.

I-CFDAIO ISDN Call Forwarding Don't Answer Incoming Only.

I-CFIB ISDN Call Forwarding Interface Busy.

I-CFIBIO ISDN Call Forwarding Interface Busy Incoming Only.

I-CFIG ISDN Call Forwarding IntraGroup only.

I-CFIO ISDN Call Forwarding Incoming Only.

I-CFPF ISDN Call Forwarding over Private Facilities.

I-CFV ISDN Call Forwarding Variable.

I-CFVCG ISDN Call Forwarding Variable facilities for Customer Groups.

I-CNIS ISDN Calling Number Information Services.

I-ETS Interim European Telecommunications Standard.

I-HC ISDN Hold Capability.

I-HOLD INDICATION A telephone system feature. If I put someone on hold at my phone, all the other phones which have the same line appearing on them will start flashing — indicating that the call is on hold.

I-SERIES RECOMMENDATIONS CCITT recommendations on standards for ISDN services, ISDN networks, user-network interfaces, and internetwork and maintenance principals.

I-USE Shows a user which line the phone is connected to when the receiver is off-hook. It does this by illuminating a small light below that line button. Most key sets and PBX sets have I-Use buttons. Most of the newer two-line phones do also.

I.122 CCITT description of the general "bearer" services offered by ISDN networks, including both packet-switched and frame relay data services.

I.430 Basic rate physical layer interface defined for ISDN.

I.431 Primary rate physical layer interface defined for ISDN.

I/G BIT Bit in IEEE 802 MAC address field distinguishing between individual and group addresses.

I/O Input/Output.

I/O BOUND When a computer systems spend much of its time waiting for periperals like the hard disk or video display, it is said to be I/O bound. If your computer is I/O Bound, going to a faster CPU (like a 386 or 486) might make little perceived difference. What you need is a faster hard disk or faster video card, etc.

I/O CHANNEL Equipment forming part of the input/output system of a computer.

I/O CONTROLLER Provides communications between the central processor and the I/O devices.

iXXX The little i stands for Intel and the numbers that follow refer to the particular microprocessor chip. For example, i386 refers to the 80386 chip.

i386SL One version of Intel's '386 family of microprocessors. The i386SL's special feature is that it can be slowed to 0 megabhertz and still maintain register integrity (memory) practically indefinitely. This results in significant power savings for computers (especially laptops) that advantage of this feature.

IA5 International Alphabet No. 5

IAB Internet Activities Board. A policy-setting and decision-review board for the TCP/IP-based Internet.

IAM Initial Address Message in the ISUP call set up messages. A mandatory message sent in the forward direction to initiate seizure of an outgoing circuit and to transmit address and other information relating to the routing and handling of a call. See also ISUP and COMMON CHANNEL SIGNALING.

IAO IntrAOffice SONET Signal. Standard SONET signal used within an Operating Company central office, remote site, or similar location.

IBM International Business Machines. Also known affectionately as I've Been Moved, International Big Mother, Itty Bitty Machines, It's Better Manually, along with others not suitable for printing (but used in the back of better computer rooms all across the North American continent). IBM dominates parts of the computer industry. This is why many of the IBM terms in this book are described as how IBM defines them.

IBM 8514/A Graphics standard introduced by IBM with 1,024 x 768 resolution. Many current monitors are 8514/A-compatible. 8514/A is also called XGA, or eXtended Graphics Array, which is IBM's high-resolution extension to its VGA adapter. It provides a resolution of 1,024 horizontally x 768 vertically, yielding 786,432 possible bits of information on one screen, more than two and a half times what is possible with VGA.

IBM PC Introduced in the summer of 1981 using the 16-bit Intel 8088 processor.

IBM TOKEN RING A local area network using star wiring architecture of two pair cabling to each drop location — one pair from the hub to the workstation and one pair from the workstation back to the hub to continue the ring. The IBM 8228 Multiple Access Unit (MAU) will support communications for eight PCs (workstations). Up to 33 IBM 8228 MAUs may be connected together into a single ring, supporting up to 260 data devices. MAU to MAU connection is accomplished with data connectors equipped with Type 1 cables from a MAU's RO (Ring Out) connection to the next MAU's RI (Ring In). The final MAU's RO connects back to the initial MAU's RI to complete the ring. See also TOKEN PASSING and TOKEN RING.

IBND Interim Billed Number Database

IBR Bellcore spec 54019, which covers specs on delivering fractional T-1.

IBX Integrated Business eXchange. Another name for a PBX. This is the name InteCom uses for their PBX family. InteCom is now owned by Matra, a French company.

IC 1. InterCom. 2. Integrated Circuit. 3. Iintermediate Cross-connect. An interconnect point within backbone wiring. for example, the interconnection between the main cross-connect and telecommunications closet or between the building entrance facility and the main cross-connect.

IC DRAM Integrated Circuit Dynamic Random Access Memory.

ICA International Communications Association. ICA is the biggest trade association of the largest corporate telecommunications users — the people whose companies spend the most. In 1992, ICA has more than 700 corporate members, representing $23.7 billion in combined annual purchasing power. It was founded in 1949 as the National Communitee of Communications Supervisors. The ICA holds an annual telecommunications trade show. It happens every May. A schedule is published in the back of TELECONNECT Magazine. The ICA is based in Dallas, TX. The other large user association is called the TCA — TeleCommunications Association. They're West Coast oriented. See BIRTHDAYS.

ICEA Insulated Cable Engineers Association.

ICFA International Computer Facsimile Association. The mission of this new organization is to create awareness of the benefits and uses of computer fax to increase worldwide market size.

ICI Interexchange Carrier Interface. The interface between carrier networks that supports SMDS.

ICIT International Center for Information Technologies. A part of MCI.

ICM See INTEGRATED CALL MANAGEMENT.

ICMP Internet Control Message Protocol. As specified in RFC-792, ICMP provides a number of diagnostic functions and can send error packets to hosts. ICMP uses the basic support of IP and is an integral part of IP.

ICON An icon is a picture or symbol representing an object, task, or choice you can select from a piece of software.

ICP 1. Intelligent Call Processing. The ability of the latest ACDs to intelligently route calls based on information provided by the caller, a database on callers and system parameters within the ACD such as call volumes within agent groups and number of agents available. 2. Instituto das Communicacoes de Portugal (The Portuguese Institute of Communications).

ICV Integrity Check Value is a digest of a message which provides a high level of assurance that the message has not been tampered with. Also referred to as Message Authentication Code.

IDA Integrated Data Access or Integrated Digital Access.

IDC Insulation Displacement Connection. A type of wire connection device in which the wire is "punched down" into a double metal holder and as it is the metal holders strip the insulation away from the wire, thus causing the electrical connection to be made. The alternate method of connecting wires is with a screw-down post. There are advantages and disadvantages to both systems. The IDC system, obviously, is faster and uses less space. But it requires a special tool. The screw system takes more time, but may produce a longer-lasting and stronger, more thorough (more of the wire exposed) electrical connection. The most common IDC wiring scheme is the 66-block, originally invented by Western Electric.

IDCMA Independent Data Communications Manufacturers Association, a lobbying and education group based near Washington, DC.

IDDD International Direct Distance Dialing. The capability to directly dial telephones in foreign countries from your own home or office telephone.

IDDS Installable Device Driver Server. A Dialogic term.

IDE Integrated Drive Electronics. IDE is a hard disk drive standard interface for microcomputers. It appeared in 1989 as a low-cost answer to two other standard hard disk interfaces, ESDI and SCSI. The distinguishing feature of the IDE interface is that it incorporates the drive controller functions right on the drive. Instead of connecting to a controller card, an IDE drive attaches directly to the motherboard. IDE drives offer a data transfer rate similar to the RLL ST506 (Seagate interface) type of drives, or about 7.5 megabits per second, which is not very fast. Several methods of data encryption can be used with the IDE interface, including MFM and RLL. Many laptops use IDE drives.

IDENTIFICATION FAILURE Automatic Number Identification (ANI) equipment in the originating office failed to identify the calling number. See ANI.

IDENTIFIED OUTWARD DIALING Same as AIOD. It's a PBX feature which provides identification of the PBX extension making outward toll calls. This identification may be provided by automatic equipment or by attendant identification of the extension.

IDENTIFIER The name of a database object (table, view, index, procedure, trigger, column, default, or rule). An identifier can be from 1 to 30 characters long.

IDF INTERMEDIATE DISTRIBUTION FRAME.

IDLE 1. Not being used but ready. 2. An SCSA term. A state of the SCbus or SCxbus Message Bus where no information is being transmitted and the bus line is pulled high.

IDLE CHANNEL NOISE Noise which exists in a communications channel when no signals are present.

IDLE LINE TERMINATION An electronic network which is switch controlled to maintain a desired impedance at a trunk or line terminal when that terminal is in an idle state.

IDLING SIGNAL Any signal that indicates no data is being sent.

IDN Integrated Digital Network.

IDT Inter-DXC Trunk

IDTV Improved Definition TeleVision. See IMPROVED DEFINITION TELEVISION.

IEC Inter Exchange Carrier. Also called an IXC. Any common carrier authorized by the FCC to carry customer transmissions between LATA's. In practice this means anyone and his brother who print up stationery, rent a few lines and proclaim themselves to be in the long distance phone business. Except for AT&T, regulation of long distance carriers by the FCC is perfunctory. It is less perfunctory by the local state authorities, some of whom still think competition is a mild form of insanity.

IEEE Institute of Electrical and Electronic Engineers, a publishing and standards-making body responsible for many telecom and computing standards, including those standards used in LANs — e.g. the 802 series.

IEEE 488 IEEE 488 is the most widely-used international standard for computer-to-electronic instrument communication. It is also known as GPIB and HPIB.

IEEE 802.1 This IEEE committee defines the LAN Management and bridging standards.

IEEE 802.2 A data link layer standard used with the IEEE 802.3, 802.4 and 802.5 standards. For more on the 802 series, see the numbers definitions at the front of this dictionary.

IEEE 802.3 A physical layer standard specifying a linear bus network LAN (local area network) with a CSMA/CD access method on a bus topology. Ethernet and Starlan both follow the 802.3 standard. Typically they transmit at 10 megabits per second. This is the most common local area network specification.

IEEE 802.3 10 BASE-T This is the standard for Ethernet over twisted pair cabling using home runs. See 802.3

IEEE 802.3 10Broad36 This IEEE standard describes a long-distance type of Ethernet cabling with a 10-megabit-per-second signaling rate, a broadband signaling technique, and a maximum cable-segment distance of 3,600 meters.

IEEE 802.4 A physical layer standard specifying a LAN with a token-passing access method on a bus topology. Used with Manufacturing Automation Protocol (MAP) LANs. Arcnet can work this way. Typical transmission speed is 10 megabits per second.

IEEE 802.5 A physical layer standard specifying a LAN with a token-passing access method on a ring topology. Used by IBM's Token Ring hardware. Typical transmission speed is 4 or 16 megabits per second.

IEEE 802.6 This IEEE standard for metropolitan-area networks (MANs) describes what is called a Distributed Queue Dual Bus (DQDB). The DQDB topology includes two parallel runs of cable-typically fiber-optic cable-linking each node (typically a router for a LAN segment) using signaling rates in the range of 100 megabits per second.

IEEE 802.9 This committee deals with integrated voice and data LANs.

IEEE 802.10 This committee deals with LAN security.

IEN Internet Experimental Note. A standards document similar to an RFC, and is available from the Network Information Center (NIC). IENs contain suggestions and proposals for Internet implementations or specifications.

IES 1. Inter-Enterprise Systems is EDI (Electronic Data Interchange) and inter-company electronic mail, fax, electronic funds transfer, videotex/online databases and the exchange of CAD/CAM graphics. See also EDI. 2. Information Exchange Services.

IETF Internet Engineering Task Force. One of two technical working bodies of the Internet Activities Board. The IETF is the primary working body developing new TCP/IP (Transmission Control Protocol/Internet Protocol) standards for the Internet.

IF Intermediate frequency.

IFRB International Frequency Registration Board.

IG 1. AT&T's ISDN Gateway. A set of specs for hooking up an outside computer to an AT&T switch. Under IG, information travels in one direction — from the switch to the host. See also ITG (which is two-directional), ASAI and OPEN APPLICATION INTERFACE. 2. Isolated Ground. In AC electricity, an isolated ground is a type of outlet characterized by the following features and uses:

● It may be orange and must have a Greek "delta" on the front of the outlet. (A delta looks like a triangle.)

● It must be grounded by an insulated green wire.

● It must have an insulator between the ground terminal and the mounting bracket.

● It is used primarily to power electronic equipment because it reduces the incidence of electrical "noise" on the ground path.

IGNITION KEY A rod arranged to strike the arc in an arc generator of high frequency currents.

IGT Ispettorato Generale delle Telcomunicazioni (General Inspectorate of Telecommunications, Italy).

IILC Information Industry Liaison Committee. See EXCHANGE CARRIERS STANDARDS ASSOCIATION.

IIW The ISDN Implementors Workshop, a group within the North American ISDN Users Forum.

ILAN A protocol independent router for token ring and Ethernet networks from CrossComm Corporation, Marlboro, MA.

ILS Input buffer Limiting Scheme. A flow control scheme used in data communications that blocks overload by limiting the number of blocks arriving at a buffer.

IMAGE ANTENNA A hypothetical, mirror-image antenna considered to be located as far below ground as the actual antenna is above ground.

IMAS Intelligent Maintenance Administration System. Northern Telecom software which is a menu-driven PC-based program that provides enhanced maintenance and administrative capabilities for DMS-10 central offices.

IMHO Abbreviation for "In My Humble Opinion;" commonly used on E-mail and BBSs (Bulletin Board Systems).

IMMEDIATE RINGING A PBX feature which makes the called telephone begin ringing the instant the phone has been dialed. Normally there's a small wait between dialing the number and having the phone ring.

IMO Abbreviation for "In My Opinion;" commonly used on E-mail and BBSs (Bulletin Board Systems). See IMHO.

IMPACT STRENGTH A test designed to ascertain the abuse a cable configuration can absorb, without physical or electrical breakdown. Done by impacting with a given weight, dropped from a given height, in a controlled environment.

IMPACS An MCI International packets switching service that is useful to firms with overseas remote computing needs, and to scientific, educational or commerical organizations that need periodic access to U.S. database facilities. IMPACS also provides overseas users with communications links to their own computers in the USA for applications such as order entry, inventory control, billing, payroll, and sales statistics.

IMPAIRED When an individual circuit exceeds the transmission limits or its signaling functions (e.g., seizure, disconnect, ANI) are experiencing failures.

IMPEDANCE The total opposition (i.e. resistance and reactance) a circuit offers to the flow of alternating current. It is measured in ohms and the lower the ohmic value, the better the quality of the conductor. Low impedance will help provide safety and fire protection and a reduction in the severity of common and normal mode electrical noise and transient voltages. For telecommunications, impedance varies at different frequencies. Ohm's law says that voltage equals the product of current and impedance at any single frequency. The unit of impedance is the ohm.

IMPEDANCE MATCHING The connection of additional impedance to existing impedance one in order to improve the performance of an electrical circuit. Impedance Matching is done to minimize distortion, especially to data circuits.

IMPORT Imagine you have a software program, like a spreadsheet or a database. And you have information in that program. Let's say it's Microsoft Word or Lotus 123. And you want to get it into a different program, say to give it to a workmate who uses WordPerfect or Excel. You have to convert it from one format to another. From Word to Wordperfect or from Lotus to Excel. That process is typically called "exporting" and the process of your workmate getting it into his computer is called "importing." And you'll typically see the words "EXPORT" and "IMPORT" as choices on one of your menus.

IMPORT SCRIPT First read my definition of IMPORT. An import script is a series of specifications which control the merging processes. It contains a series of merge rules which specify how the fields are to be merged and a record precedence rule which governs which records to merge of the ones received.

IMPROVED DEFINTION TELEVISION IDTV. Television that includes improvements to the standard NTSC television system, which improvements remain within the general parameters of NTSC television emission standards. These improvements may be made at the transmitter and/or receiver and may include enhancements in parameters such as encoding, digital filtering, scan interpolation, interlaced scan lines, and ghost cancellation. Such improvements must permit the signal to be transmitted and received in the historical 4:3 aspect ratio.

IMPROVED MOBILE TELEPHONE SERVICE IMTS. In the beginning, there was dispatch mobile service. The base operator broadcast a message to you. Everyone could hear it. You responded. Then they had mobile telephone service. You picked up the phone in your car, the operator responded. You asked for the number you wanted and she/he dialed it and connected you. You had the channel to yourself but others could still tune in.

Then came Improved Mobile Telephone Service (IMTS). Now you could dial from your car without using an operator with some assurance of privacy. The latest development is cellular mobile telephone service. See CELLULAR.

IMPULSE A surge of electrical energy usually of short duration, of a nonrepetitive nature.

IMPULSE HITS Errors in telephone-line data transmission that are caused by voltage surges lasting from 1/3 to 4 milliseconds and at a level within 6 dB of the normal signal level (Bell standard allows no more than 15 impulse hits per 15 minute period).

IMPULSE NOISE High-level, short duration noise that comes on a circuit. You can get impulse noise from electromechanical relays. These noise "spikes" have little effect on voice transmission but can be devastating to data. You can get a piece of test equipment called an impulse noise measuring set. Such a machine establishes a threshold and counts the number of impulses (hits) above that threshold. IMS/VS Information Management System/Virtual Storage. An IBM host operating environment.

IMPURITY LEVEL An energy level outside the normal energy band of the material, caused by he presence of impurity atoms. Such levels are capable of making an insulator semiconductor.

IMT InterMachine Trunk. A circuit which connects two automatic switching centers, both owned by the same company.

IMTS See IMPROVED MOBILE TELEPHONE SERVICE.

IN Intelligent Network.

IN-BAND SIGNALING Signaling made up of tones which pass within the voice frequency band and are carried along the same circuit as the talk path that is being established by the signals. Virtually all signaling — request for service, dialing, disconnect, etc. — is in-band signaling. Most of that signaling is MF — multi-frequency dialing. The more modern form of signaling is out-of-band. Several local and long distance companies provide ANI (Automatic Number Identification) via in-band signaling. Some long distance companies provide it out-of-band, using the D-channel in a PRI ISDN loop. See ISDN and SS7 (CCITT Signaling System Number 7).

INA Information Networking Architecture.

INCENTIVE REGULATION Prices of services provided by the local regulated phone company are fixed or capped but incentives are provided to improve earnings through cost savings. Earning levels are flexible, within a range of rates, allowing opportunity for earnings improvement.

INCC Internal Network Control Center

INCIDENT ANGLE The angle between an incident ray and a line perpendicular to an optical surface.

INCLINED ORBIT Any nonequatorial orbit of a satellite. Inclined orbits may be circular or elliptical and may be synchronous or nonsynchronous. Incliner orbits are used for many reasons — for photographing, for reaching places in the extreme north and south which normal geo-synch satellites can't reach.

INCOHERENT LIGHT A random form of light whereby the phase of the light is unpredictable. LEDs emit incoherent light.

INCOMING CALL IDENTIFICATION ICI. Some way of telling the user who's calling. It might be the caller's extension number on an LCD screen or even the caller's name spelled out, e.g. "KATE BRODIE-DAVID CALLING." Today, most "incoming call identification" is done totally within one PBX. However, the days of ISDN and CCITT Signaling System Number 7 are arriving. They promise to deliver to us the phone number of everyone calling us — from within the PBX or key system and from the outside world.

INCREMENT A small change in the value of a quantity.

INCREMENTAL CURSOR CONTROL The user-controlled function that moves the focus in increments dictated by the application. In character-based text editing, the increment is typically one character in the horizontal direction and one line in the vertical direction.

INDEPENDENT CLOCKS A communication network timing subsystem using precise free-running clocks at the nodes for synchronization purposes. Variable storage buffers installed to accommodate variations in transmission delay between nodes are made large enough to accommodate small time (phase) departures among the nodal clocks that control transmission. Traffic is occasionally interrupted to reset the buffers.

INDEPENDENT-SIDEBAND TRANSMISSION ISB. That method of double-sideband transmission in which the information carried by each sideband is different. The carrier may be suppressed.

INDEPENDENT SOFTWARE VENDOR ISV. Typically a company which writes and sells software, but not hardware. Manufacturers of hardware and operating systems, i.e. IBM or Northern Telecom, often contract with ISVs to produce specialized software to make their hardware and operating system more attractive.

INDEPENDENT TELEPHONE COMPANY A telephone company not affiliated with one of the "Bell" telephone companies. There are about 1,400 independent phone companies. They serve more than half the geographic area of the United States, but only around 15% of its telephones. The independent phone companies used to be represented by the United States Independent Telephone Association (USITA). But once Divestiture happened, the association dropped the word "Independent" from its name, accepted membership of the Bell operating companies (but not AT&T) and became USTA.

INDEX Think of a filing cabinet. It contains oodles of information. Think of a computer hard disk. Same thing as a filing cabinet. Oodles of information. Now think of putting everything in the filing cabinet into filing folders and putting them in alphabetical order. Makes finding things a lot easier. Now think of a computer. You ask it to find you the name of a file folder. Nothing sophisticated here. Except it's dumber than you. It starts at the top and searches down. Of course, it searches fast. But it still searches from the top down. The fastest way for it to search is to give it less stuff to search through. Thus you make an index. Just as you do in a book. Only, compared to you and me, a computer is willing to do more stupid work. It will index in alphabetical order. It will index in date order. It will index in order of how much you sold the guy recently. It will index in any order you ask it to. And many database software programs will let you keep several indexes concurrently, thus allowing you to find things quickly. The rules of database are simple: The more indexes you keep concurrently, the more time your computer will take to update its indexes every time you enter a new record or update an old record.

INDEX OF REFRACTION The ratio of the speed of light in vacuum to the speed of light in a material.

INDEX DIP In an optical fiber, a decrease in the refractive index at the center of the core, caused by certain manufacturing techniques.

INDEX MATCHING MATERIAL In fiber optics, a material (liquid, gel, or cement) whose refractive index is nearly equal to the fiber core index. It is used to reduce Fresnel reflections from a fiber end face.

INDEX OF COOPERATION In facsimile, the product of the total line length in millimeters times the lines per millimeter divided by r. For rotating devices, the index of cooperation is the product of the drum diameter times the number of lines per unit length.

INDEX PROFILE In an optical fiber, the refractive index as a function of radial distance from the optical axis.

INDICATION CIRCUIT X.21 circuit used to send control information from DCE to DTE.

INDICATION OF Lights, bells and buzzers indicating that something has or is about to happen. For example, indication of camp-on to a station: short bursts of tone are periodically transmitted to the busy phone to indicate that another call is camped on and waiting.

INDIRECT CONTROL In digital data transmission, the use of a clock at a higher standard modulation rate, e.g., 4, 8, 128 times the modulation rate, rather than twice the data modulation rate, as is done in direct control.

INDIUM GALLIUM ARSENIDE InGaAs, a semiconductor material used in lasers, LEDs, and detectors.

INDIVIDUAL LOAD CYCLING FEATURE This is one feature of

AT&T's Dimension Energy Communications Service Adjunct. Individual Load Cycling reduces energy consumption by turning devices on and off (e.g. airconditioning) on an hourly basis.

INDIVIDUAL SPEED CALLING A key system or PBX feature by which a user can dial a longer number by punching one or two buttons on his phone. Sometimes this speed dial ability is programmed into the phone. Sometimes it's programmed into the system. Whichever it is, each user has a bunch of numbers he/she can speed dial. These are his/her own. No one else can speed dial them.

INDUCTANCE Inductance is the property of an electric force field built up around a conductor. Inductance allows a circuit to store up electrical energy in electromagnetic form. When current flows through a wire, lines of force are built up around the wire. The field created by DC current is steady. When AC flows through a wire, the lines of force are constantly building and collapsing. An inductor is formed by winding a conductor into a coil. In long local loops, conversation gets difficult because the long wires encounter capacitive resistance. To counter this, inductors known as load coils are connected in series, increasing the inductance. When load coils, or inductors are connected in parallel, they reduce the inductance. See also INDUCTIVE CONNECTION.

INDUCTION Electromagnetic transfer of energy from one coil to another.

INDUCTION COIL A coil having a high turn ratio used for raising the voltage. A step-up transformer.

INDUCTIVE CONNECTION A connection between a telephone instrument and another device by means of the electromagnetic field generated by the telephone instrument. No direct electrical connection is established between the two. See INDUCTANCE.

INDUCTIVE COUPLING The transfer of energy from one circuit to another by means of the mutual inductance between the circuits, i.e. energy jumping from one circuit to another without actually touching it copper wire to copper wire. The coupling may be deliberate and desired as in an antenna coupler or may be undesired as in powerline inductive coupling into telephone lines. See also INDUCTANCE.

INDUCTIVE PICKUP A coil used to tap phone lines without direct connection.

INDUCTIVE TAP Wiretap that is not physically connected to the telephone wires. A voltage proportional to the varying line current is induced into a coil.

INDUCTIVELY COUPLED RECEIVER A radio receiver in which the energy in the antenna circuit is transferred to the secondary circuit by induction.

INDUCTIVITY A term sometimes used to denote the dielectric constant or the specific inductive capacity.

INDUCTOR See INDUCTANCE and INDUCTIVE CONNECTION.

INFERENCE ENGINE The AI (Artificial Intelligence) heart of a knowledge base system. The inference engine is the technology which directs the reasoning process.

INFORMATION AT YOUR FINGERTIPS This is a concept dreamed up by Bill Gates, chairman of Microsoft. Bill's idea is simple. Here's an example: You sit in front of your PC. You want to create a spreadsheet comparing sales of your five geographic divisions. to do the spreadsheet, you need to get five numbers — each of which is located in five computers in different parts of the country. Fortunately, they're all connected by local and wide area networks and your computer (but not you) knows how to retrieve all the information from all those distant computers. Thus you have "Information at your fingertips." See AT WORK and WINDOWS TELEPHONY.

INFORMATION FRAME Frame in HDLC, DDCMP, or related protocols containing user data.

INFORMATION TECHNOLOGY IT. A fancy name for data processing, which became management information systems (MIS), which became information technology. All the same thing, essentially. See also IT.

INFORMATION TO GO A term coined by Digital Equipment Corporation to refer to the transmission of data over airwaves instead of fixed wires.

INFINITE LOOP A state in which specific steps of a program are executed repeatedly, not allowing the program execution to advance further.

INFO-LOOK GATEWAY SERVICE A NYNEX service. Use your PC, modem and communications software to dial Info-Look and check on news, weather, health, finance, sports. Do some shopping. Info-Look connects you to many computer services and databases, none of which are provided by NYNEX, New York Telephone or New England Telephone. That's why Info-Look is called a "gateway." It's a gateway to a myriad of services. As of writing there was talk NYNEX was closing Info-Look down. And it eventually did.

INFOMERCIAL A short segment shown on the video system of a plane purporting to be informational/newsy and educational. In fact, the segment is a commercial paid for by the company whose products and/or services are featured.

INFONET A consortium of about 10 European telephone companies and MCI. InfoNet has built a worldwide packet switched network that is great for data communications. It offers one major advantage over packet switched networks owned by the individual phone companies — You don't have to separately sign up to use InfoNet in all the countries it operates. You just dial Infonet up, punch in and communicate. Not having to sign up is a big savings in time, since it can take weeks to sign up for European packet switched networks and cost minimum monthly fees. For MCI Mail subscribers, using Infonet means you only get one bill — directly from MCI. See also MCI Mail and MCI FAX.

INFOPATH PACKET SWITCHING SERVICE A New York and New England Telephone service using a switched data network, where users share all network facilities. Offered for only the NY Metropolitan RCA. Its Low Throughput (private dial access) is dedicated to one customer, Medium Throughput uses a Data Over Voice channel and High Throughput uses a Digipath Digital Service facility.

INFORMATION AT YOUR FINGERTIPS At Fall Comdex 1990 Bill Gates, Microsoft chairman, suggested the idea. With Information at your fingertips, he said, PC users can easily access companywide information "anywhere at anytime" through an icon-based graphical user interface. In the speech, Gates demonstrated applications that used Object Linking and Embedding (OLE), Dynamic Data Exchange (DDE), handwriting recognition, cellular communications and multimedia. See OLE.

INFORMATION-BEARER CHANNEL 1. A channel provided for data transmission that is capable of carrying all the necessary information to permit communication, including user's data, synchronizing sequences, control signals, etc. It may therefore, operate at a greater signaling rate than that required solely for the user data. 2. A basic communication channel made available by the circuit provider with no enhanced or value-added services included other than the bandwidth transmission capability.

INFORMATION CENTER MAILBOXES An Octel term for a voice bulletin board on a voice mail system. Here's their explanation: Multiple callers can access, directly or indirectly, recorded announcements containing information that would otherwise have been given live by employees. Callers are frequently "outside" users of the system. One type of "listen only" mailbox simply plays the messages to the callers. This technology, sometimes known as audiotex, makes it possible to create a verbal database so callers can select which information they want to hear. Another type of Information Center Mailbox prompts callers to reply to announcements. Callers wanting further information can be given the opportunity to leave their names and phone numbers after listening to a product description. They can also be transferred to a designated employee who can immediately take an order. If desired, a password can be required before confidential or controlled access information can be heard.

INFORMATION ELEMENT The name for the data fields within an ISDN Layer 3 message.

INFORMATION ENGINEERING Coined by James Martin, the most prolific writer in data processing, the term refers to systems within data processing and their impact on giving the corporation a greater competitive edge. In short, a fancy term for Management Information Systems (MIS), which itself was a fancy term for DP, namely Data Processing.

INFORMATION OUTLET IO. Sort of like an AC power outlet, but a little more cerebral. A connecting device designed for a fixed location (usually a wall in the office) on which horizontal wiring subsystem cable pairs terminate and which receives an inserted plug; it is an administration point located between the horizontal wiring subsystem and work location wiring subsystem. Although such devices are also referred to as jacks, the term information outlets encompasses the integration of voice, data, and other communication services that can be supported via a premises distribution system.

INFORMATION PAGE MAPPING See ADSI.

INFORMATION PROVIDER A business or person providing information to the public for money. The information is typically selected by the caller through touchtones, delivered using voice processing equipment and transmitted over tariffed phone lines, e.g., 900, 976, 970. Typically, billing for information providers' services is done by a local or long distance phone company. Sometimes the revenues for the service are split by the information provider and the phone company. Sometimes the phone company simply bills a per minute or flat charge. A typical "information provider" is American Express, which provides a service — 1-900-WEATHER. By dialing that number you can touchtone in city names and find out temperatures, weather forecasts, etc. Calling 1-900-WEATHER costs several dollars a minute.

INFORMATION TECHNOLOGY MANAGEMENT An AT&T term used to encompass telecommunications and data management.

INFRARED The band of electromagnetic wavelengths between the extreme of the visible part of the spectrum (about 0.75 um) and the shortest microwaves (about 100 um). This portion of the electromagnetic spectrum is used for fiber-optical transmission and also for short-haul through-the-air data transmission.

INFRARED FIBER Optical fibers with best transmission at wavelengths of 2 um or longer, made of materials other than silica glass.

INHERITANCE A term from object oriented programming. Data abstraction can be carried up several levels. Classes can have super-classes and subclasses. In moving to a level of greater specificity, the application developer has the option to retain some attributes and methods of the super-class, while dropping or adding new attributes or methods. This allows greater flexibility in class definition. It is even possible in some languages to inherit from more than one parent. This is referred to as multiple inheritance. See OBJECT ORIENTED PROGRAMMING.

INIT An INIT is the Mactinosh System 7 equivalent of a terminate and stay resident (TSR) program . An init might load to initialize a fax modem, screen saver, etc. Similar to the DOS environment, some inits conflict. When troubleshooting operating system problems, remove inits first.

INITIAL PERIOD The minimum billing period on a call. For interstate or inter-LATA AT&T calls, the initial period is one-minute. Some non-AT&T long distance companies have initial periods under one-minute. This also applies to local calls in Measured areas.

INITIAL PROGRAM LOAD The initial loading of generic and/or configuration software into a PBX or other phone system. The Initial Program Load is a pain in the rear end. But an even bigger pain is what happens when you lose your programming and you've forgotten to back it all up.

INITIAL SEQUENCE NUMBER ISN. Generated at each end of TCP connection to help to uniquely indentify that connection.

INITIALIZATION STRING A group of commands sent to the modem by a communications program at start-up — before the number has been dialed. Such a string tells the modem to set itself up in a way that will make it easy to correctly communicate with a distant modem.

INITIATING EVENT An event that causes the ASC (AIN Switch Capabilities) to assign an ID to a connection segment for a certain user ID and to communicate with a SLEE (Service Logic Execution Environment) for the first time with respect to the combination of the specific user ID and connection segment ID.

INJECTION LASER Another name for a semiconductor or diode laser.

INL See INTERNODE LINK.

INMAC International Network Management Center

INMARSAT The INternational MARitime SATellite service that provides mobile communications to ships at sea, aircraft in flight and vehicles on the road. Comsat runs this service. Inmarsat provides dial-up telephone, telex, fax, electronic mail and data connections to more than 14,000 customers. Typically you buy a small earth station and install it on your ship and pay Comsat a per minute charge for the use of the single phone and single telex service most customers subscribe to. As of writing, a ship earth station cost $50,000 and a minute of calling was $10 anywhere in the world. Not cheap!

INN See InterNode Network.

INP BOARD Intelligent Network Processor board for synchronous transmission on an Hewlett Packard 3000 system.

INPA Interchangeable Numbering Plan Area. An area code that looks like an office code. There is no particular name for an office code that looks like an area code, according to Lee Goeller.

INPUT A signal fed into a circuit.

INPUT BUFFER LIMITING Buffering strategy that divides buffer at a mode into two classes, both available to transit packets but only one available to packets input at the node.

INPUT CIRCUIT The grid circuit of an electron tube.

INQUIRY A request for specific information.

IN-SAFE An inbound store-and-forward MCI International Telex service that automatically answers a subscriber's incoming calls, provides an answerback, and accepts the messages.

INSERTION GAIN The gain resulting from the insertion of a device in a transmission line, expressed as the ratio of the power delivered to that part of the line following the device to the power delivered to that same part before insertion. If more than one component is involved in the input or output, the particular component used must be specified. If the resulting number is negative, an "insertion loss" is indicated. This ratio is usually expressed in decibels. See INSERTION LOSS.

INSERTION LOSS The difference in the amount of power received before and after something is inserted into the circuit (viz. another telephone instrument) or a call is connected. In an optical fiber, insertion loss is the optical power loss due to all causes, usually expressed as decibel/kilometer. Causes of insertion loss may be absorption, scattering, diffusion, dispersion, microbending, or methods of coupling power outside the fiber. In lightwave transmission systems, the power lost at the entrance to a waveguide due to causes, such as fresnel reflection, packing fraction, limited numerical aperture, axial misalignment, lateral displacement, initial scattering, or diffusion.

INSIDE DIAL TONE A tone users hear when they are connected to an intercom line.

INSIDE PLANT 1. The portion of a cable network that resides inside buildings. 2. Everything inside a telephone company central office. See also INSIDE WIRING.

INSIDE WIRING That telephone wiring located inside your premises or building. Inside Wiring starts at the telephone company's Demarcation Point and extends to the individual phone extensions. Traditionally, Inside Wiring was installed and owned by the telephone company. But now you can install your own wiring. And most companies installing new phone systems are installing their own new wiring because of potential problems with reusing the old telephone company cable. See also INSIDE PLANT.

INSPECT SCREEN An AT&T Merlin term. A display screen on digital telephones that allows users to preview incoming calls and see a list of the features programmed on line buttons.

INSTABUS1080 and INSTABUS1480 Trademarks for MICOM's direct host attachment products.

INSTALINK 1. An MCI International service that allows access to a host computer in the U.S.A. from a Telex machine anywhere overseas. This allows easier retrieval of information from a U.S. database. 2. A trademark for MICOM's data-over-voice products.

INSTANET Trademark for MICOM's family of local data distribution and data private automatic branch exchange (PABX) products.

INSTANT ON Buy a PC (Personal Computer). Turn it on. Bingo, it's already loaded with Windows or OS/2. Instant On is a new term for preloading software onto hard disks of new computers and shipping those computers already pre-loaded with that software.

INSTANTANEOUS OVERRIDE ENERGY FUNCTION IOEF. A feature of the AT&T PBX Dimension Energy Communications Service Adjunct (ECSA), which allows the user to turn all the ECSA energy functions ON or OFF. IOEF is most often used for periodic maintenance, or to adjust to sudden changes in weather.

INSTATRUNK and INSTATRUNK480 Trademarks for MICOM's local T1 multiplexor products.

INSTRUCTION REGISTER The register which contains the instruction to be executed and functions as the source for the subsequent operations of the arithmetic unit.

INSULATED WIRE Wire which has a non-conducting covering.

INSULATING MATERIALS Those substances which oppose the passage of an electric current through them.

INSULATION A material which does not conduct electricity but is suitable for surrounding conductors to prevent the loss of current.

INSULATION DISPLACEMENT CONNECTION IDC. A type of wire connection device in which the wire is "punched down" into a double metal holder and as it is, the metal holders strip the insulation away from the wire, thus causing the electrical connection to be made. The alternate method of connecting wires is with a screw-down post. There are advantages and disadvantages to both systems. The IDC system, obviously, is faster and uses less space. But it requires a special tool. The screw system takes more time, but may produce a longer-lasting and stronger, more thorough (more of the wire exposed) electrical connection. The most common IDC wiring scheme is the 66-block, invented by Western Electric. See IDC.

INSULATION RESISTANCE That property of an insulating material which resists electrical current flow through the insulating material when a potential difference is applied.

INSULATOR A material which does not conduct electricity and is traditionally used to separate or protect wiring used for carrying signals.

INT14 A software interrupt designed to communicate with the comm (serial) port in a PC. Communications programs use interrupt 14h to talk to a modem physically attached to another computer on the network.

INTEGER A computing procedure for solving or finding the optimum solution for complex problems in which the variables are based on integers.

Integers include all the natural numbers, the negatives of these numbers, or zeros.

INTEGRATED ACCESS An AT&T term for the provision of access for multiple services such as voice and data through a single system built on common principles and providing similar service features for the different classes of services.

INTEGRATED CALL MANAGEMENT ICM. A family of Rolm networking products and services for single-site and multi-site CBX installations.

INTEGRATED CIRCUIT IC. A single electronic device that contains hundreds or thousands of previously separate (discrete) components. The so-called "computer on a chip" is a special purpose integrated circuit.

INTEGRATED DEVELOPMENT ENVIRONMENT IDE. A Windows program within which a developer may perform all the essential tasks of development including editing, compiling and debugging.

INTEGRATED PERSONAL COMPUTER INTERFACE IPCI. A ROLM-designed communications printed circuit card designed to provide an IBM PC with asynchronous data transmission over two-strand wiring to and from a Rolm CBX PBX.

INTEGRATED SERVICES DIGITAL NETWORK See ISDN and SIGNALING SYSTEM 7.

INTEGRATED SERVICES DIGITAL NETWORK USER PART ISDN-UP. The part of SS7 (Signaling System Number 7) that encompasses the signaling functions required to provide voice and non-voice services in ISDN and pre-ISDN architectures. The basic service offered by the ISDN-UP is the control of circuit-switched connections between subscriber line exchange terminations. Definition from Bellcore in reference to its concept of the Advanced Intelligent Network.

INTEGRATED SOLUTION-II/III Integrated Solution II is an AT&T Product that combines Audix Voice Power (Voice Mail), Call Accounting and System Administration Software. Integrated Solution Systems with Audix includes a tape drive that backs up all of the information on the computer's hard disk, including voice messages, auto attendant greetings, system programming, and call accounting records.

INTEGRATED VOICE DATA There are many different meanings to this concept. The most common (we'll get arguments on this) is that a workstation or a combination telephone/personal computer on a desk can combine voice and data signals over a single communications channel. That channel might be carried digitally on one pair of wires. That is "the most integrated" voice/data. Less integrated is when you carry voice and data digitally on two pairs — one pair for transmitting and one pair for receiving. Even less integrated are some systems which use three pairs of cabling set up as one voice analog pair, one digital data pair and one power/signaling pair. In short, "integrated voice/data" means different things to different people and depends on the technology. See also ISDN.

INTEGRATED VOICE DATA WORKSTATION See ISDN, IVDT and INTEGRATED VOICE/DATA.

INTEL i860 MICROPROCESSORS FAMILY Intel Corporation's RISC-based microprocessor line, introduced in 1989, incorporates many firsts, including more than 1 million transistors on a single chip. The line currently comprises the i860 XR, with 1.2 million transistors, and the i860 XP, with 2.5 million transistors.

INTELESYS A voice processing applications generator from Telephone Response Technologies in Roseville CA.

INTELLIGENCE The part of a computer which performs the arithmetic and logic functions. Also, the information impressed or modulated on a transmission carrier — either voice or data.

INTELLIGENT AGENTS A software product that can search through incoming material on networks and find what you're looking for.

INTELLIGENT NETWORK IN. A network that allows functionality to be distributed flexibly at a variety of nodes on and off the network and allows the architecture to be modified to control the services; (In North America) an advanced network concept that is envisioned to offer such things as (a) distributed call-processing capabilities across multiple network modules, (b) real-time authorization code verification, (c) one-number services, and (d) flexible private network services (including (1) reconfiguration by subscriber, (2) traffic analyses, (3) service restrictions, (4) routing control, and (5) data on call histories). Levels of IN development are:

● IN/1. A protocol intelligent network targeted toward services that allow increased customer control and that can be provided by centralized switching vehicles serving a large customer base.

● IN1+. A protocol intelligent network targeted toward services that can be provided by centralized switching vehicles, e.g., access tandems, serving a large customer base.

● N/2. A proposed, advanced intelligent-network concept that extends the distributed IN/1 architecture to accommodate the concept called the "service independence." Traditionally, service logic has been localized at individual switching systems. The IN/2 architecture provides flexibility in the placement of service logic, requiring the use of advanced techniques to manage the distribution of both network data and service logic across multiple IN/2 modules. See ADVANCED INTELLIGENT NETWORK.

INTELLIGENT PERIPHERAL IP. A network system in the Advanced Intelligent Network Release 1 architecture containing an Resource containing an Resource Control Execution Environment (RCEE) functional group that enables flexible information interactions between a user and the network.

INTELLIGENT PHONE When the Bell operating companies get bored they occasionally fantasize about applications for the networks they provide. Here are some of their ideas for what intelligent phones could, if motivated, do:

Select entertainment on demand (movies, music, video); Order groceries or other services or products; Record customized news and sports programming; Enroll and participate in education programs from the convenience of subscribers' living rooms; Find up-to-minute medical, legal and encyclopedic information; Pay bills and manage finances; Make airline, rental car and hotel reservations and buy Buy sports and entertainment tickets.

INTELLIGENT ROUTING A voice call comes in. Your voice mail machine recognizes it as being urgent, so it gives the caller a message, "Please hold. Harry is away from his desk. I'll find Harry for you." Meantime, it dials several numbers looking for me. It also beeps me. Eventually I call in. It tells me, "John Smith is calling for you. You want him?" Yes, I say and we're connected. This is a simple form of a broad concept that many are beginning to call intelligent routing. See also AT WORK and WINDOWS TELEPHONY.

INTELLIGENT TERMINAL A terminal is an input/output device to a distant computer. The terminal may communicate with the computer over a dedicated collection of wires or over phone lines. In the early days, terminals contained no processing power. They simply reflected what the user typed in and what the distant computer responded. As computers became cheaper and with the advent of the "computer on a chip," so it was economically possible to put computing power into a terminal. This reduced the load on the main computer and cut down on communications costs. There are levels of "intelligence" in terminals. An intelligent terminal might perform simple arithmetic functions or it might check the accuracy of input data (does the zip code match the state?). It may perform far more comprehensive processing — as doing virtually all the local processing, and only transmitting summary results to corporate headquarters once a day. A personal computer can be used and act as an Intelligent Terminal. Many personal computer communications software can emulate terminals, the most common being the DEC VT-100.

INTELLIDIAL Intellidial is basically a New York Telephone Centrex service for small offices of big businesses or small businesses. You can get from two to nine lines. And you get to buy "packages" of features. Features in the packages include touch-tone, three-Way calling, call transfer, call hold, call pick-up, intercom, call forward-variable, call forward busy, call forward-don't answer, speed calling and call waiting.

INTELLIGIBLE CROSSTALK 1. Crosstalk giving rise to intelligible signals. 2. Crosstalk from which information can be derived.

INTELLIHUB A New York Telephone and New England Telephone service which offers its larger customers large, local bandwidth. The service was developed primarily as a response to the threat of bypass. INTELLIHUB integrates and modifies FLEXPATH Digital PBX Service, INTELLIPATH, INTELLIPATH II Digital Centrex Service and INFOPATH Packet Switching Service for large multi-location business customers within an regional calling area.

INTELLIMUX A new service from Bell Atlantic. This service allows Bell Atlantic's customers to do real-time reconfigurations of of their network. Changes may be made to specific individual voice grade and digital grade services within a T-1 and/or individual channels of a T-1 service connected at digital cross connect systems.

INTELLIPATH DIGITAL CENTREX SERVICE Intellipath Digital Centrex Service is a New York Telephone and New England Telephone digital Centrex service for smaller businesses with fewer than 99 lines. It has the basic features — such as call transfer, hold and three-way calling. One nice feature: each user can have his own 30-number speed calling list.

INTELLIPATH II DIGITAL CENTREX SERVICE INTELLIPATH II Digital Centrex Service is a New York Telephone and New England Telephone service for businesses needing over 100 lines. It has voice and data features. It has over 100 voice features — from automatic call back, to call pickup, to intercept and three-way calling. Its data features let you plug computers and terminals directly into a digital circuit.

INTELSAT INternational TELecommunications SATellite organization. A worldwide consortium of national satellite communications organizations. As of writing Intelsat is owned by 119 governments and Intelsat itself owns 15 satellites worldwide. Comsat acts as the exclusive manager for Intelsat. Comsat is also the exclusive U.S. representative. Comsat stands for Communications Satellite Corporation.

INTENSITY MODULATION IM. In optical communication, a form of modulation in which the optical power output of a source is varied in accordance with some characteristic of the modulating signal. In intensity modulation, there are no discrete upper and lower sidebands in the usually understood sense of these terms, because present optical sources lack sufficient coherence to produce them. The envelope of the modulated optical signal is an analog of the modulating signal in the sense that the instantaneous power of the envelope is an analog of the characteristic of interest in the modulating signal. Recovery of the modulating signal is by direct detection, not heterodyning.

INTER- Means between two things, as opposed to INTRA-, which means inside one thing. INTERSTATE means communications between states. INTRASTATE means communications inside one state.

INTERACTIVE The ability to interact with a computer or to be in a conversational mode with a computer. Interactive processing is very time dependent since a user is waiting for the computer to ask him/her questions. The opposite of Interactive processing is batch processing. See BATCH.

INTERACTIVE DATA TRANSACTION A single (one-way) message, transmitted via a data channel to which a reply is required for work to proceed logically.

INTERACTIVE VOICE RESPONSE IVR. Think of Interactive Voice Response as a voice computer. Where a computer has a keyboard for entering information, an IVR uses remote touchtone telephones. Where a computer has a screen for showing the results, an IVR uses a digitized synthesized voice to "read" the screen to the distant caller. Whatever a computer can do, an IVR can too, from looking up train timetables to moving calls around an automatic call distributor (ACD). The only limitation on an IVR is that you can't present as many alternatives on a phone as you can on a screen. The caller's brain simply won't remember more than a few. With IVR, you have to present the menus in smaller chunks.

INTERAXIAL SPACING Center to center conductor spacing between any two wires.

INTERBUILDING CABLE The communications cable that is part of the campus subsystem and runs between buildings. There are four methods of installing interbuilding cable: in-conduit (in underground conduit), direct-buried (in trenches), aerial (on poles), and in-tunnel (in steam tunnels).

INTERBUILDING CABLE ENTRANCE The point at which campus subsystem cables enter a building.

INTERBUILDING WIRING Consists of underground or aerial telephone wire/cables used on the premises to connect structures remote from the primary building to the premises telephone system.

INTERCEPT Calls which cannot reach their destination may be intercepted and diverted to a station attendant, a recording or some other place. See INTERCEPT RECORDING and INTERCEPT SERVICE.

INTERCEPT RECORDING You make a phone call. It doesn't go through. The phone company intercepts that call and sends it somewhere. Intercept Recording is a recording telling you your call cannot be completed and has been intercepted on its way to the destination number for some reason that will be explained by the recording. The most common voice you hear on intercept announcements is Jane Barbie's. See BARBIE, JANE and INTERCEPT SERVICE.

INTERCEPT SERVICE A service of the local phone in which a phone call is redirected by an operator or a recording to another phone number or a message.

INTERCOM INTERCOMmunication. An internal communication system which allows you to dial another phone in your building, office complex, factory or home. There are three types of intercom: 1. Dial: It allows you to dial or pushbutton another extension; 2. Automatic: One phone goes off hook and automatically dials another; and 3. Manual: The user can manually signal another phone by pushing a button for that phone. An example is a buzzer between a boss and a secretary.

INTERCOM BLOCKING A PBX feature by which phones with a particular Class Of Service (COS) are blocked from calling certain phones. A rare feature.

INTERCONNECT A circuit administration point, other than a cross connect or an information outlet, that provides capability for routing and re-routing circuits. It does not use patch cords or jumper wires, and typically is a jack-and-plug device used in smaller distribution arrangements or that connects circuits in large cables to those in smaller cables.

INTERCONNECT COMPANIES Companies which sell, install and maintain telephone systems for end users, typically businesses. AT&T coined the word "interconnect" as a pejorative word — to indicate that these companies "interconnected" to AT&T's telephone network — but didn't really belong there. These "interconnect" companies contrasted with true-blue companies belonging to AT&T which did a sterling job — such as AT&T itself or its local operating companies. Anyway, the term stuck but the nasty associations went away. Now the irony is that the CPE (Customer Premise Equipment) equipment subsidiaries and divisions of both AT&T and the local Bell operating telephone companies are, in fact, interconnect companies, though they don't call themselves that. The industry is looking for a better word.

We at TELECONNECT Magazine started a campaign to make "TELECONNECT" a better replacement for interconnect. But our lawyers and the lawyers for a manufacturing/interconnect company called Teleconnect told us to lay off and stop trying to make the word generic. We rather like the terms "Telecommunications Systems Integrator," "Telecommunications VAR" or "Telecom Developer." They seem to be catching on.

INTERDRIVE The name of the FTP Software client impelmentation of the Sun NFS protocol.

INTERENTERPRISE COMMUNICATIONS Communications exchanged between multiple organizations, e.g., between business trading partners, collaborators, affiliates or a business and its customers.

INTEREXCHANGE CARRIER IXC. A telephone company that is allowed to provide long-distance telephone service between LATAs but not within any one LATA. See IXC.

INTEREXCHANGE CUSTOMER SERVICE CENTER ICSC. The Telephone Company's primary point of contact for handling the service needs of all long distance carriers.

INTEREXCHANGE CHANNEL IXC. A communications channel or path between two or more telephone exchanges.

INTERFACE 1. A mechanical or electrical link connecting two or more pieces of equipment together. 2. A shared boundary. A physical point of demarcation between two devices where the electrical signals, connectors, timing and handshaking are defined. The procedures, codes and protocols that enable two entities to interact for a meaningful exchange of information. 3. To bring two things or people together to allow them to talk. 4. A poorly-defined word often used when the speaker is incapable of figuring precisely what he means. 5. An annual data communications trade show organized by Shelly Adelson. See also INTERFACE DEVICE.

INTERFACE DEVICE A device which meets a standard electrical interface on one side and meets some other nonstandard interface on the other. The purpose of the device is to allow a device with a nonstandard interface to connect to a device with a standard interface.

INTERFACE FUNCTIONALITY The characteristic of interfaces that allows them to support transmission, switching, and signaling functions identical to those used in the enhanced services provided by the carrier. As part of its comparably efficient interconnection (CEI) offering, the carrier must make available standardized hardware and software interfaces that are able to support transmission, switching, and signaling functions identical to those used in the enhanced services provided by the carrier.

INTERFACE MESSAGE PROCESSOR IMP. A processor-controlled switch used in packet-switched networks to route packets to their proper destination.

INTERFACE OVERHEAD the interface overhead is the remaining portion of the bit stream after deducting the information payload. The interface overhead may be essential (e.g. framing for an interface shared by users) or ancillary (e.g. performance monitoring).

INTERFACE PAYLOAD The portion of the bit stream which can be used for telecommunications services. Any signaling is included in the interface payload. See also INTERFACE OVERHEAD.

INTERFACE SHELVES Shelves in a Rolm PBX cabinet containing the printed circuit card groups that connect telephones, terminals, lines and trunks to CBX interface channels. These shelves also contain shared electronics cards.

INTERFERENCE Energy you receive with a signal. You don't want the energy. You want the signal. Getting rid of the interference may be a pain. The interference may be manmade (e.g. elevator motors) or it may be GOD-made, e.g. lightning, thunderstorms. Some media (fancy word for cabling) may be more immune to interference than other. Media immune to interference, in order 1. Optical fiber 2. Coax 3. Shielded twisted pair 4. Unshielded twisted pair 5. Unshielded untwisted pair

INTERFERENCE EMISSION Emission that results in an electrical signal being propagated into and interfering with the proper operation of electrical or electronic equipment. The frequency range of such interference may be taken to include the entire electromagnetic spectrum.

INTERFEROMETER An instrument that employs the interference of light waves for measurement.

INTERFLOW The ability to establish a connection to a second ACD and overflow a call from one ACD to the other. This provides a greater level of service to the caller.

INTERFRAME ENCODING A way of video compression that transmits only changed information between successive frames. This saves bandwidth.

INTERLACING Regular TV signals are interlaced. In the US there are 525 scanning lines on the regular TV screen. This is the NTSC standard. Interlaced means the signal refreshes every second line 60 times a second and then jumps to the top and refreshes the other set of lines also 60 times a second. Non-interlaced signals, which are used in the computer industry, means each line on the entire screen is refreshed X times. X times depends on what the video card is outputting to the color monitor. The more expensive the card and the monitor, the more often the monitor will be refreshed. The more it's refreshed, the better and more stable it looks — the less perceived flicker. For example, text on an NTSC United States TV set tends to "flicker." It doesn't on a non-interlaced monitor. Typical non-interlaced computer monitors refresh at 60 to 72 times a second. But good ones refresh at higher rates. Generally, anything over 70 Hz (i.e. 70 times a second) is considered to be flicker-free and therefore preferred, if you can afford it. In short, buy an non-interlaced monitor. You'll like it better.

INTERLATA Telecommunications services that originate in one and terminate in another Local Access and Transport Area (LATA). Under provisions of Divestiture, the Bell operating companies cannot provide Inter-LATA service, but can provide Intra-LATA service. Some LATAs are very large. So some "local" phone companies provide the equivalent of long distance service. And some of these phone companies have different pricing packages. Some of these packages are cheap, but not highly-publicized. See also LATA.

INTERLATA CALL A call that is placed within one LATA (Local Access Transport Area) and received in a different LATA. These calls are currently carried by a long distance company.

INTERLATA COMPETITION Currently being considered by the Public Utility Commission (PUC) in ARF (Alternative Regulatory Framework) Phase III. Would allow long distance phone companies to compete with local monopolies to carry intraLATA toll calls.

INTERLEAVE 1. The transmission of pulses from two or more digital sources in time-division sequence over a single path. 2. A data-communication technique, used in conjunction with error-correcting codes, to reduce the number of undetected error bursts. In the interleaving process, code symbols are reordered before transmission in such a manner that any two successive code symbols are separaed by I-1 symbols in the transmitted sequence, where I is called the degree of interleaving. Upon reception, the interleaved code symbols are reordered into their original sequence, thus effectively spreading or randomizing the errors (in time) to enable more complete correction by a random error-correcting code. 3. Interleaving also refers to the way a computer writes to and reads from a hard disk. Understanding interleaving is critical if you want to get your hard disk to work at its maximum speed (without in any way damaging the disk). Let's look at the way MS-DOS reads information from a hard disk. All hard disks are controlled by a special card called a hard disk controller card. Let's say your computer wants a file. It tells the hard disk controller card it wants the file. The controller searches the disk for the first sector of the requested file, reads that sector (usually 512 bytes) to your computer's RAM and then transfers the information to the CPU to be processed. When this is complete, the controller goes back to the hard disk and searches for the file's second sector. The process continues in this way until the file is completely read.

The problem is that while the controller and the CPU are doing their things, the hard disk itself is spinning 3,600 times a minute. By the time the controller reads one sector and it is ready to return to the disk, the next consecutive file sector has spun past the read/write head. If the file is stored in contiguous sectors, the controller must wait for the disk to complete its revolution before it can read the next file sector. To solve this problem, hard drive makers developed a concept called interleave setting, which tells the hard drive controller to skip a certain number of sectors when it writes a file to disk. Thus, when the file is later read back, the appropriate file sectors should fall under the read/write heads at the appropriate time.

If the controller reads or writes one sector and then skips a sector, the interleave is 2 (every other sector is used to store logically consecutive blocks). The interleave is sometimes written as 2:1. If the controller writes to one sector and then skips two, the interleave is 3 or 3:1. The interleave factor is usually established by the manufacturer or reseller of the hard disk/controller combination. If someone else assembles the hard disk/controller combination, that person may need to experiment to determine the correct interleave factor — i.e. the one that works fastest without messing up.

Setting the "correct" interleave settings on your hard disk is critical to getting maximum performance out of your hard disk. Here's a test that a writer for PCResource Magazine did. He copied the same files from one part of his hard disk to another part using different interleave settings:

Interleave	Time to copy file Setting
3	1 min 15 seconds
4	1 min 17 seconds
5	1 min 1 second
6	35 seconds
7	41 seconds
8	1 min 10 seconds

Clearly his best interleave setting is six. There are two ways of choosing the correct interleave setting. You can do it by trial and error as the writer did. His test took three hours. Or buy a program and do it in seconds. The best program is called Disk Technician. It's from a company called Prime Solutions in San Diego. Sadly, the program doesn't work on certain laptops and on certain controller card/hard disk combinations.

INTERMEDIATE ASSIST A method for pulling cables into conduits or duct liners in which manual labor or machines are used to assist the pulling at intermediate manholes.

INTERMEDIATE CROSS-CONNECT an interconnect point within backbone wiring. for example, the interconnection between the main cross-connect and telecommunications closet or between the building entrance facility and the main cross-connect.

INTERMEDIATE DISTRIBUTION FRAME IDF. A metal rack designed to connect cables and located in an equipment room or closet. Consists of bits and pieces that provide the connection between inter-building cabling and the intra-building cabling, i.e. between the Main Distribution Frame (MDF) and individual phone wiring. There's usually a permanent big, fat cable running between the MDF and IDF. The changes in wiring are done at the IDF. This saves confusion in wiring. See also FEEDER CABLE and CONNECTING BLOCK.

INTERMEDIATE FREQUENCY TRANSFORMER A transformer designed to amplify the intermediate frequencies generated in a superheterodyne radio receiver. These are normally sharply tuned to a single frequency band.

INTERMEDIATE REACH Intermediate reach refers to optical sections from a few km to approximately 15 km. An AT&T SONET term.

INTERMODULATION IM. The production, in a nonlinear element of a system, of frequencies corresponding to the sum and difference frequencies of the fundamentals and integral multiples (harmonics) of the component frequencies that are transmitted through the element.

INTERMODULATION DISTORTION IMD. Nonlinear distortion characterized by the appearance of frequencies in the output, equal to the sum and difference frequencies of integral multiples (harmonics) of the component frequencies present in the input. Harmonic components also present in the output are usually not included as part of the intermodulation distortion.

INTERNAL MODEM A modem on a printed circuit card which is inserted into one of the slots on a PC (personal computer). The other type of modem for a PC is an external modem — essentially a modem with the same circuitry as an internal modem but with a metal or plastic case. An internal modem costs slightly less than an external one. Internal modems are good if you're short of deskspace and afraid your external modem will be stolen. External modems have lights so it's easier to tell what's going on. Everybody has their theories on which type of modem is best. We prefer the external ones — largely for their lights and ease of moving around.

INTERNATIONAL 800 SERVICE You can now have your customers overseas call you for free on an 800 line, just as your domestic customers do. The service is available from countries including Australia, Brazil, France, Hong Kong, Israel, Italy, Japan, Sweden, Switzerland and the United Kingdom. Overseas 800 service is often known as "Freephone."

INTERNATIONAL ALPHABET NO. 5 IA5. Internationally standardized alphanumeric code with national options. ASCII is United States version.

INTERNATIONAL AMPERE The current which will in one second deposit 0.001118 gram of silver from a neutral solution of silver nitrate.

INTERNATIONAL CENTER FOR INFORMATION TECHNOLOGIES A Washington "think tank" whose mission is to bring together discussion on new telecommunications and computer technologies. Targeted at senior executives who are looking for ways to apply new technologies to gaining competitive edges for their company.

INTERNATIONAL DIRECT DISTANCE DIALING IDDD. Being able to automatically dial international long distance calls from your own phone.

INTERNATIONAL GATEWAYS The switches in the various domestic long distance networks (e.g. MCI, AT&T and Sprint) which interface their networks with International telecommunications networks. All US International calls are routed through an international gateway.

INTERNATIONAL ORGANIZATION FOR STANDARDIZATION ISO. An organization established to create standards. See ISO.

INTERNATIONAL TELECOMMUNICATIONS UNION ITU. The specialized agency of the United Nations which tries to establish standardized communications procedures and practices. Its most successful work is done in the allocation of radio frequencies worldwide — including satellites, etc. See ITU.

INTERNATIONAL TELEPHONE ADDRESS A four-part code specifying a unique address for any telephone company in the world.

INTERNET Internet is a computer network which joins many government and university and some private computers together over phone lines (mostly T-1s). Internet traces its origins to a network set up in 1969 by the Defense Department. In 1991 it was running off $20 million a year in federal subsidies and managed by the National Science Foundation. An IBM/MCI venture known as Advanced Network and Services manages a network called NSFnet, which connects hundreds of research centers and universities. NSFnet also manages links to dozens of other countries. All these networks are collectively known as Internet. NSFnet was founded by the National Science Foundation, a Federal Government agency and is composed of leased telephone lines that link special computers called routers, which transmit packages of data to three million users in 33 countries.

INTERNET ADDRESS A unique, 32-bit identifier for a specific TCP/IP host on a network. Also called an Internet Protocol or IP address. IP addresses are normally printed in dotted decimal form, such as 128.127.50.224.

INTERNET MIB SUBTREE A tree-shaped data structure in which network devices on a local area network and their attributes can be identified within the confines of a network management scheme. The name of an object or attribute is derived from its location on this tree.

For example, an object in MIB-I might be named 1.2.1.1.1.0. the first 1 indicates the object is on the Internet. The 2 denotes that it falls within the Management category. The second 1 shows the object is part of the first fully defined MIB, known as MIB-I. The third 1 indicates which of the eight object groups is being referenced. And the fourth 1 is a textual description of the network component. The O indicates there is only one object instance. An object instance links a particular object to a specific node on the network. The numbering system is infinitely extendible to accommodate additions to this base identification scheme. This common naming structure permits equipment from a variety of vendors to be managed by a single management station that uses SNMP. The four main categories of the tree are Directory, Management, Experimental and Private/Enterprises.

INTERNET PACKET EXCHANGE IPX. Novell NetWare's native LAN communications protocol, used to move data between server and/or work-station programs running on different network nodes.

INTERNET PROTOCOL IP. Part of the TCP/IP family of protocols describing software that tracks the Internet address of nodes, routes outgoing message, and recognizes incoming messages. Used in gateways to connect networks at OSI network Level 3 and above.

INTERNET WORM This software program caused a major part of the Internet network to crash by replicating and generating spurious data.

INTERNETWORK See INTERNETWORKING.

INTERNETWORK ROUTER In local area networking technology, an internetwork rourter is a device used for communications between networks. Messages for the connected network are addressed to the internetwork router, which chooses the best path to the selected destination via dynamic routing. Internetwork routers function at the network layer of the Open Systems Interconnection (OSI) model. Also known as a network router or simply as a router.

INTERNETWORKING 1. Communication between two networks or two types of networks or end equipment. This may or may not involve a difference in signaling or protocol elements supported. And, in the narrower sense — to join local area networks together. This way users can get access to other files, databases and applications. Bridges and routers are the devices which typically accomplish the task of joining LANs. Internetworking may be done with cables — joining LANs together in the same building, for example. Or it may be done with telecommunications circuits — joining LANs together across the globe.

INTERNODE Communication paths which originate in one node and terminate in another.

INTERNODE LINK A data line for high-bandwidth connections between PBXs.

INTEROFFICE Between two telephone company switching offices.

INTEROFFICE CHANNEL A transmission path between two AT&T serving offices.

INTEROFFICE TRUNK A trunk circuit connecting two local telephone company central offices.

INTEROPERABILITY The ability to operate software and exchange information in a heterogeneous network, i.e. one large network made up of several different local area networks.

INTERPBX Calls coming into one PBX can be transferred to extensions on another PBX using direct tie lines between the two PBXs.

INTERPOSITION CALLING One operator in a multi-position system calling another.

INTERPOSITION TRANSFER Transfer of a call from one operator to another.

INTERPOSITION TRUNK 1. A connection between two positions of a large switchboard so that a line on one position can be connected to a line on another position. 2. Connections terminated at test positions for testing and patching between testboards and patch bays within a technical control facility.

INTERPROCESS COMMUNICATIONS this is the capability of programs to share information. At the most basic level, it consists of cutting and pasting information between two programs. Above that ranks the "live" paste, in which information shared between two documents is updated whenever one of the documents is modified. This is referred to as Dynamic Data Exchange (DDE). In advanced DDE, programs can send messages as well as data to other programs running locally or remotely. Beyond DDE is Object Linking and Embedding (OLE), which lets one program borrow the specialized capabilities of another program loaded on the machine (say, advanced chart creation) rather than having to implement that capability redundantly.

INTERROGATE To determine the state of a device or unit.

INTERRUPT A temporary suspension of a process caused by an event outside of that process. More specifically, an interrupt is a signal or call to a specific routine. An interrupt setting allows the hardware in a file server, router, workstation or PC to send an interrupt signal to the processor. The interrupt signal temporarily suspends the other station tasks while the processor performs the task requested by the interrupting device. After the routine is completed, the processor then continues with the original tasks. Each piece of hardware (serial and parallel ports and network boards) installed in the same computer needs a unique interrupt. Interrupts are divided into two general types, hardware and software. A hardware interrupt is caused by a signal from a hardware device, such as a printer. A software interrupt is created by instructions from within a software program.

TIP: When you slide a new card into one of the empty slots on your PC and things go awry, check that the new card's Interrupt is not the same as one of the other cards in your bus. An interrupt is also called a hardware interrupt or an InteRupt reQest (IRQ). For a listing of normal IRQs see IRQs. See also INTERRUPT REQUEST and POLLING.

INTERRUPT HANDLING ROUTINE This program, which is often part of a device driver, handles all requests from a particular interrupt line. Interrupt-handling routines are defined in the CPU's Interrupt Descriptor Table (IDT). When the CPU (the Central Processing Unit of your PC) receives an interrupt request, it looks up the matching interrupt-handling routine in the IDT, then transfers control to the routine until it (the CPU) gives an interrupt return call (IRET), indicating the task is complete.

INTERRUPT LATENCY The delay in servicing an interrupt request is known as interrupt latency. It is not a problem with devices that are not sensitive to timing inconsistencies (such as hard-disk controllers or video boards). But it is a problem with high-speed, asynchronous communications (9,600 bps and above), which are highly time-sensitive operations.

INTERRUPT OVERHEAD The cumulative demand on your computer's central microprocessor by peripheral devices that generate interrupt requests is referred to as interrupt overhead. Such devices include hard-disk controllers, network interface cards, parallel and serial ports.

INTERRUPT REQUEST IRQ. This is the communications channel through which devices issue interrupts to the interrupt handler of an IBM PC or IBM compatible PC's microprocessor. It's the channel through which these devices get the microprocessor's attention. Different IRQs are assigned to different devices. This assignment pattern differs from PC to PC. Many LAN interface cards use an IRQ to get to the microprocessor. You must be sure that your LAN interface card is not trying to use the IRQ assigned to another peripheral, like the hard disk controller or EGA card. See also IRQ for a different and longer explanation.

INTERRUPTER An automatically operated electromechanical device used to turn lights, bells or other signals on and off in timed sequences. An interrupter makes lights wink on and off on a key system. Or did, when everything was electromechanical. It was used on 1A key telephone systems.

INTERRUPTING EQUIPMENT Motor-driven mechanical devices used to break the ringing generator's output into ringing and silent periods, creating the busy and ringback tone pulses.

INTERSPAN The full name is InterSpan Frame Relay and it's AT&T's new frame relay data communications service, announced in the late fall of 1991.

INTERSPUTNIK A Russian satellite system similar in concept to the West's Intelsat, except that it's set up by Russia and the Eastern bloc countries. Two US carriers, AT&T and IDB Communications, once used Intersputnik to alleviate their shortage of US-Russia circuits. See INTELSTAT.

INTERSTATE Between states (crossing a state line).

INTERSTICES In cable construction, the spaces, valleys or voids between or around the cable's components.

INTERSYMBOL INTERFERENCE Distortion of signals due to preceding or following pulses affectng desired pulse amplitude at time of sampling.

INTERTOLL TRUNKS Trunks connecting Class 4 and higher switching machines in the AT&T long distance network.

INTERVAL Time. Pulse interval, for example, means the time from the start of one pulse to the start of the next.

INTFC Interface.

INTERSWITCH TRUNK A circuit between two switching machines.

INTRA- Intra- means inside. Intrastate means inside the state. Interstate means between states.

INTRACALLING This is an outside plant term. Intracalling refers to the ability of a remote line concentrator to interconnect users served by the same concentrator without providing two trunks directly back to the central office.

INTRAENTERPRISE COMMUNICATIONS Communications that are exchanged within a single organization (including multiple sites of the organization).

INTRAFLOW This is an automatic call distribution term. It refers to the ability to select a second or subsequent group of agents to backup the primary agent group. This is designed to allow the caller to be serviced more efficiently and less expensively.

INTRAFRAME ENCODING A way of video compression that divides the TV picture into blocks and transmits only changed blocks between successive frames.

INTRALATA Telecommunications services that originate and end in the same Local Access and Transport Area.

INTRAMODAL DISTORTION In an optical fiber, the distortion resulting from dispersion of group velocity of a propagating mode. It is the only form of multimode distortion occurring in single-mode fibers.

INTRANODE Communications path which originates and terminates in the same node.

INTRAOFFICE TRUNK A telephone channel between two pieces of equipment within the same central office.

INTRASTATE Remaining entirely within the boundaries of a single state and, therefore, if related to telephone, falling under the jurisdiction of that state's telephone regulatory procedures.

INTRINSIC JOINT LOSS That loss in optical power transmission, intrinsic to the optical fiber, caused by fiber parameters, e.g., dimensions, profile parameter, mode field diameter, mismatches when two nonidentical fibers are joined.

INTRINSICS Intrinsics are a component of many windows toolkits. The windows toolkit intrinsics definition has been developed by the MIT X Consortium. The intrinsics define the function of specific graphical user interface and window objects. They do not define any particular look or feel, just the function. Example: A pull-down menu intrinsic would define the function of a pull-down menu within a toolkit but not the appearance of it.

INVERSE FOURIER TRANSFORM Inversion of Fourier transform to convert frequency representation of signal to time representation.

INVERSE MULTIPLEXER Because inverse multiplexers are so new, we have two definitions: First, the older definition: An inverse multiplexer is the opposite of a "normal" multiplexer, which takes many small circuits and makes one big one out of them. An inverse multiplexer takes a big circuit — e.g. a T-1 — and pulls smaller ones out of it. A "classic" inverse multiplexer is a device which takes a T-1 circuit and lets you pull one, two or three DS-0s (56 Kbps or 64 Kbps) circuits out of it. The reason you use an inverse multiplexer is that it is cheaper to buy a T-1 circuit for a particular installation than to buy multiple digital channels.

Second, an inverse multiplexer will dial up, combine and synchronize non-contiguous 56/64 kbps channels in any multiple up to an aggregate bandwidth (what the device is capable of, but typically 2.048 megabits per second, which is European T-1). An inverse multiplexer under this definition gives users bandwidth on demand for high-speed applications such as LAN-to-LAN connnectivity and videoconferencing.

INVERTER A device which converts direct current electricity to alternating current electricity, often used to power AC devices in a car.

INVITATION TO SEND A character or sequence of characters which calls for a station to begin transmission. Usually this is part of a polling arrangement.

INWARD RESTRICTION A Centrex service feature which stops Centrex lines from receiving certain incoming calls.

INWARD TRUNK Used only for incoming calls, these trunks cannot dial out. "800" lines, for example, can only be used to receive calls.

INWATS INward Wide Area Telephone Service. A service of AT&T, MCI, Sprint, the Bell operating companies and the independent phone companies in North America which allows subscribers to receive calls from specified areas (depending on the rate band chosen) with no charge to the person who's calling. See 800 SERVICE for a much bigger explanation.

IOC Inter-Office Channel

IOD Identified Outward Dialing. See also AIOD and CALL ACCOUNTING SYSTEM.

ION EXCHANGE TECHNIQUE A method of fabricating a graded-index optical fiber by an ion exchange process.

IONIZATION The process of breaking up molecules into positively and negatively charged carriers of electricity called ions.

IONOSPHERE 1. That part of the atmosphere in which reflection and/or refraction of electromagnetic waves occurs. 2. That part of the atmosphere, extending from about 70 to 500 kilometers, in which ions and free electrons exist in sufficient quantities to reflect electromagnetic waves.

IONOSPHERIC DISTURBANCE An increase in the ionization of the D region of he ionosphere, caused by solar activity, which results in greatly increased radio wave absorption. See IONOSPHERE.

IONOSPHERIC REFRACTION The change in the propagation speed of a signal as it passes through the ionsophere.

IOP Input/Output Processor.

IP 1. Internal Protocol. 2. Internetwork Protocol in ISO or in ARPA. A standard describing software that keeps track of the Internetwork address for different nodes, routes outgoing messages, and recognizes incoming messages. 3. Intelligent Peripheral. A device in an IN (Intelligent Network) that provides capabilities such as voice announcements and help guidance.

IPARS The International Passenger Airline Reservation System. An IBM-originated term.

IPC Interprocess Communications. A system that lets threads and processes transfer data and messages among themselves; used to offer services to and receive services from other programs. Supported IPC mechanisms under MS OS/2 are semaphores, signals, pipes, queues, shared memory, and dynamic data exchange.

IPCH Initial Paging CHannel is the channel number used by your cellular provider to "page" the phones on the system. The term "paging" refers to notifying a particular phone that it has an incoming call. All idle, turned-on phones on a system monitor the data stream on the IPCM. Non-wireline cellular carriers use channel 0333 as the IPCH, while wireline providers (those operated by a telephone company use channel 0334.

IPCI See INTEGRATED PERSONAL COMPUTER INTERFACE.

IPDS Intelligent Printer Data Stream. It's IBM's host-to-printer page description protocol for printing. You can now buy kits which let you use your present printer to emulate an IBM printer.

IPL Initial Program Load.

IPM Interruptions Per Minute or Impulses Per Minute.

IPNS International Private Network Service. It actually international private line service and it's typically a circuit from 9.6 Kbit/sec up to T-1 or E-1. Domestically you would simply call it "Private line data service."

IPS Internet Protocol Suite.

IPX Internet Packet eXchange. NetWare's native LAN communications protocol, used to move data between server and/or workstation programs running on different network nodes. IPX packets are encapsulated and carried by the packets used in Ethernet and the similar frames used in Token-Ring networks. See also IPX.COM.

IPX/SPX Internetwork Packet Exchange/Sequenced Packet Exchange. Two network protocols. IPX is NetWare protocol for moving information across the network; SPX works on top of IPX and adds extra commands. In the OSI model, IPX conforms to the network layer and SPX is the transport layer.

IPX.COM The Novell IPX/SPX (Internetwork Packet eXchange/Sequenced Packet eXchange) communication protocol that creates, maintains, and terminates connections between network devices (workstations, file servers, routers, etc.). IPX.COM uses a LAN driver routine to control the station's network board and address and to route outgoing data packets for delivery on the network. IPX/SPX reads the assigned addresses of returning data and directs the data to the proper area within a workstation's shell or the file server's operating system. See also NETWARE.

IR Infrared. The band of electromagnetic wavelengths between the extreme of the visible part of the spectrum (about 0.75 um) and the shortest microwaves (about 100 um).

IRC International Record (i.e. non-voice) Carrier. One of a group of common carriers that, until a few years ago, exclusively carried data and text traffic from gateway cities in the U.S. to other countries. The distinction between international companies providing "record" and data has eroded and now both types of companies provide voice and data services internationally.

IREQ The Interrupt Request signal between a PCMCIA Card and a socket when the I/O interface is active.

IRIDIUM The name for Motorola's ambitious satellite project "to bring personal communications to every square inch of the earth." According to Motorola, "for the first time, anyone, anywhere, at any time can communicate via voice, fax, or data." Motorola has targeted the band 1610 to 1626.5 MHz. Motorola estimates the service costing $3 a minute. The idea is that we carry an Iridium handset — a device larger than today's cellular phone — and that we talk directly from the phone to the satellite (one of 77) and then down to the satellite closest to the called person, then down to an Iridium phone on the ground or to a satellite dish, through landlines to the phone of the called person. The big benefit is that the system knows who you are and where you are the moment you turn on your phone. This way it can always complete calls from somewhere calling you who doesn't know — or doesn't need to know — where you precisely are. It's called Iridium after the element called Iridium which has 77 electrons. In November of 1992, Business Week estimated that putting up the full Iridium system would cost $3.4 billion.

IROB 1. In Range of Building. An Underwriters Laboratories term to define where the protection of UL 1459 will apply. See UL 1459. 2. An AT&T Merlin term. In-Range Out-of-Bulding Protector. A surge protection device for ott-premises telephones at a location within 1000 ft (305 m) of cable distance from the communications system control unit.

IRQs Interrupt ReQuests. IRQs are found in PCs. IRQs are also called hardware interrupts. They are the way a device signals the data bus and the CPU that it needs attention. In more technical terms, an IRQ is a signal sent to the central processing unit (CPU) to temporarily suspend normal processing and transfer control to an interrupt handling routine. Interrupts may be generated by conditions such as completion of an I/O process, detection of hardware failure, power failures, etc. Devices that use hardware interrupts include the serial and parallel ports, mouse interface cards, modems, game ports, and even the hard disk on XTs. The original IBM PC and PC-XT had only seven hardware interrupts. The bigger AT bus extended that to 15. Until the advent of the 32-bit PS/2 micro-channel and the 32-bit EISA buses, hardware interrupts could not be shared by two or more devices within the PC. Thus if one device had a specific hardware interrupt, even though you weren't using it that time, nothing else could use it. When you start filling your PC with devices (and remember most PCs still use the old AT bus) — like serial ports, modems and mice, you may suddenly find your modem no longer works. There are two solutions — change the interrupts (either in software or using jumpers), making sure no two devices are trying to share the same interrupt — or simply remove one of the printed circuit devices you're not using from the bus. (That's typically my solution.) These are the "normal" IRQs used by current hardware devices in PCs

Device	IRQ
ARCnet card	2
Bus Mouse	2
CD-ROM drive	5
COM1	4
COM2	3
COM3	4
COM4	3
Diskette Controller	6
Ethernet card	3
hard disk drive	14
LPT1 (PARALLEL)	7
LPT2 (PARALLEL)	5
Math Coprocessor	13
Reserved	10
Reserved	11
Reserved	15
Sound Card	7
Take backup card	2

See also INTERRUPT and INTERRUPT REQUEST.

IRRADIATION In insulations, the exposure of the material to high energy emissions for the purpose of favorably altering the molecular structure by crosslinking.

IRU Indefeasible Right of User. A measure of currency in the underseas cable business. Someone owning An IRU means he has the right to use the cable for the time and bandwidth the IRU applies to. An IRU is to a submarine cable what a lease is to a building.

IS Information Separator. A type of control character used to separate and qualify data logically. Its specific meaning has to be defined for each application.

IS-III An AT&T Merlin term. Integrated Solution. One or more UNIX-based applications for improving voice and data communications and automating office operations.

IS-54 Standard for the analog cellular phone service in North America. It is a TIA and CTIA standard.

IS-55 Standard for TDMA digital cellular service, which is three times the capacity of today's analog cellular service. IS-55 is a fully digital cellular system.

ISA Industry Standard Architecture. The most common bus architecture on the motherboard of MS-DOS computers. The ISA bus was originally pioneered by IBM on its PC, then its XT and then its AT. ISA is also called classic bus. It comes in an 8-bit and 16-bit version. Most references to ISA mean the 16-bit version. Many machines claiming ISA compatibility will have both 8- and 16-bit connectors on the motherboard. Later IBM introduced a 32-bit bus which it called MCA for Micro Channel Architecture, which is the internal bus inside some of IBM's line of PS/2 MCA machines. But MCA isn't popular because it is incompatible with ISA, so the industry (excluding IBM) invented a 32-bit bus called EISA which stands for Extended Industry Standard Architecture, which is compatible with ISA. See also EISA.

ISAM Indexed Sequential Access Method. It is a procedure for storing and retrieving data from a disk file. When the programmer designs the format of the file, a set of indexes is created which describes where the records of the file are located on the disk. This provides a quick method of retrieving the data, and eliminates the need to read all the data from the beginning to find the desired information. The indexes can be stored as part of the data file or in a separate index file.

ISARITHMIC FLOW CONTROL Approach to flow control in which transmission permits circulate throughout network. Node wishing to transmit must first capture permit and destroy it, then recreate permit after transmission finished.

ISB InterShelf Bus.

ISDN Integrated Services Digital Network. A totally new concept of what the world's telephone system should be. According to AT&T, today's public switched phone network has the following limitations: 1. Each voice line is only 4 kHz, which is very narrow. 2. Most signaling is in-band signaling, which is very consuming of bandwidth (i.e. it's expensive and inefficient). 3. The little out-of-band signaling that exists today runs on lines separate to the network. (This includes signaling for PBX attendants, hotel/motel, Centrex and PBX calling information.) 4. Most users have separate voice and data networks (which is inefficient, expensive and limiting). 5. Premises telephone and data equipment must be separately administered from the network it runs on. 6. There is a wide and growing variety of voice, data and digital interface standards, many of which are incompatible.

ISDN's "vision" is to overcome these deficiencies in four ways: 1. By providing an internationally accepted standard for voice, data and signaling. 2. By making all transmission circuits end-to-end digital. 3. By adopting a standard out-of-band signaling system. 4. By bringing significantly more bandwidth to the desk top. An ISDN central office will deliver to the user's office or factory four basic ISDN services, also called interfaces.

1. The 2B+D "S" interface (also called the "T" interface). The 2B+D is called the Basic Rate Interface (BRI). The "S" interface uses four unshielded normal telephone wires (two twisted wire pairs) to deliver two "Bearer" 64,000 bits per second channels and one "data" signaling channel of 16,000 bits per second. An S-interfaced phone can be located up to one kilometer from the central office switch driving it. Each of the two 64 kpbs "bearer" or B channels can be used to carry a voice conversation, or one high speed data or several data channels, which are multiplexed into one 64 kbps high speed data line. The "D" channel of 16 kbps will carry control and signaling information to set up and break down the voice and data calls. The "D" channel can also carry data up to 9600 bits per second in addition to the control and signaling information. Signaling and control on the D channel conforms to a protocol (LAPD) and a messaging structure (Q.931). These two allow intelligent endpoints and switching nodes from different vendors to talk a common language and thus be able to transfer features across a network, from one switch to another, e.g. to transfer a Centrex call across town through several switches and to have it arrive at the end phone with the calling party's name.

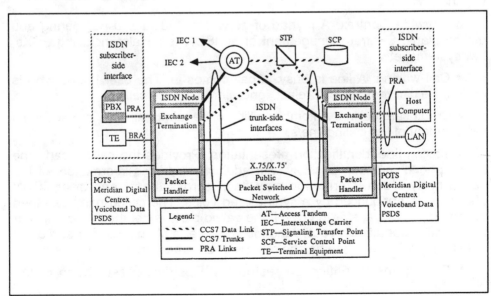

2. The 2B+D "T" interface. This "T" interface delivers the same two 64 kbps bearer channels and one 16 kbps data channel, except that it uses 2-wires (one pair) and can work at 5-10 kilometers from the central office switch driving it.

3. The 23B+D or 30B+D. This is called the Primary Rate Interface (PRI). At 23B+D, it is 1.544 megabits per second. At 30B+D, it is 2.048 megabits per second. The first, 23B+D is the standard T-1 line in the U.S. which operates on two pairs. The second 30B+D is the standard T-1 line in Europe, which also operates on two pairs.

4. A standard single line analog phone. A 2500 or a 500 set. (A connection to tradition?) Integral to ISDN's ability to produce new customer services is CCITT Signaling System 7. This is a CCITT recommendation which does two basic things: First, it removes all phone signaling from the present network onto a separate packet switched data network, thus providing enormous economies of bandwidth. Second, it broadens the information that is generated by a call, or call attempt. This information — like the phone number of the person who's calling — will significantly broaden the number of useful new services the ISDN telephone network of tomorrow will be able to deliver.

Here are some sample ISDN services which the various vendors have publicized. They are "mind-blowing." Most are possible in some way today. They reflect early ISDN "thinking," not ISDN "doing." They remind us of the applications we thought were possible with PCs when we only had CP/M eight bit machines — before the 16-bit IBM PC machine debuted in 1983:

● Simultaneous Data Calls: Two users can talk and exchange information over the D packet and/or the B circuit or packet switched channel.

● Citywide Centrex: A myriad of services: Specialized numbering and dialing plans. Central management of all ISDN terminals, including PBXs, key systems, etc.

● Call waiting: A line is busy. A call comes in. The user knows who is calling. He can then accept, reject, ignore, transfer the call.

● Credit card calling: Automatic billing of certain or all calls into accounts independent of the calling line/s.

● Calling line identification presentation: Provides the calling party the ISDN "phone" number, possibly with additional address information, of the called party. Such information may flash across the screen of an ISDN phone or be announced by a synthesized voice. The called party can then accept, reject or transfer the call. If the called party is not there, then his/her phone will automatically record the incoming call's phone number and allow automatic callbacks when he/she returns or calls back in from elsewhere.

● Calling line identification restriction: Restricts presentation of the calling party's ISDN "phone" number, possibly with additional address information, to the called party.

- Closed user group: Restricts conversations to or among a select group of phone numbers, local, long distance or international.

- E-Mail (aka Personal mailbox): ISDN can carry information to and from unattended phones as long as they're equipped with proper hardware and software.

- Multi-location ringing: An ISDN subscriber can specify several locations where an incoming call should ring simultaneously.

In the summer of 1990 Southwestern Bell issued a press release announcing their signing up of several ISDN customers. In that release, they also included a small listing of what they felt were ISDN benefits:

Most people who use the telephone or a personal computer probably don't care why ISDN works, but they may be very interested in what it can do for them. A few examples:

- Selective Call Screening — Within a business, this application displays the phone number of the calling party before the phone is answered. If two people call simultaneously, the person answering can choose which call is the higher priority to answer by seeing both calling numbers.

- Shared Screen — Switched data services provided via ISDN lets two people in remote locations, both equipped with a computer terminal, to view the same information on their screens and discuss its contents while making changes — all over one telephone line.

- Network Access — Most large companies have many computer networks and databases, but only those workers who regularly use those databases have easy access to them. ISDN allows a person at a personal computer to gain access to virtually any database.

- Less Down Time/Cost Savings Moves — When a company moves an employee within an office, there can be hours or days of lost production while a computer terminal and phone set are being installed. In some cases, the terminal is connected to a network via coaxial cable. ISDN virtually eliminates down time, as well as the need for coaxial cable.

The first ISDN call in North America was placed in Phoenix, Arizona on November 18, 1986. For more on ISDN capabilities, see ISDN STANDARDS, ISDN TELEPHONE, ISUP, NETWORK TERMINATION 1, PERSONAL COMPUTER TERMINAL ADAPTER, Q.931, ROBBED-BIT SIGNALING, SIGNALING SYSTEM 7 and TCAP.

ISDN has produced more than its fair share of scepticism, as reflected in its many "definitions" — e.g. I Still Don't Know; I'm Still Doing Nothing; Improvements Subscribers Don't Need; I'm Spending Dollars Now.

There are two major problems to the widespread acceptance of ISDN in

North America: First, the cost of ISDN terminal equipment is too high. Second, the cost of ISDN central office hardware and software is also too high. Both end users and telco executives simply don't see the persuasive benefits to spending the high amounts of money needed.

ISDN STANDARDS The path of a call in an ISDN network is based on standards:

1. ISDN User A signals the public network over a standard interface. The 2B1Q protocol is used by the terminal as well as the line card in the telephone company central office. The 2B1Q arranges the bits of a digital ISDN signal in a standard manner over the twisted pair connecting the user and the central office. Bellcore TR268 establishes protocols for signaling between the caller and the network.

2. TR444 and TR448 define the standard protocols that allow ISDN services to be carried by the SS7 network.

3. TR317 defines the protocols for standard SS7 networking between the LEC's intraLATA switches that, when combined with TR444 and TR448, can deliver ISDN services.

4. TR394 defines the protocols for standard SS7 networking of the interLATA switches that, when combined with TR444 and TR448, provide the interface for ISDN services and the interexchange network.

5. ISDN UserB, equipped with the standard network interface and using the 2B1Q and TR268 protocols, is prepared to receive the ISDN call from User A. The network delivers the ISDN call information carried over SS7 from User A to User B in the call set-up message.

ISDN TELEPHONE An ISDN phone can attach to an ISDN basic rate interface. It typically has one digital voice (at 64 kbps) channel and two data options — one for packet switched services (up to 9600 bps) and another for circuit switched data (up to 64 kbps). It will also have an RS-232-C connector on its back and a two line, 48-character LCD adjustable display. It will also have a bunch of dedicated buttons for standard stuff — last number redial, speed dial, on-hook dialing, listen-on-hold, etc. Some ISDN phones work behind most ISDN central offices — e.g. the Telrad phones. Most don't. They have to work behind the central office they were designed for. Or did have to. In February, 1991, Bellcore issued a technical specification for a standard ISDN phone line. The idea of National ISDN-1 is that it be a set of standards which every manufacturer can conform to. A consumer can buy an ISDN phone (one conforming to National ISDN-1) at his local Radio Shack (or other store) take it home, plug it in and know it will work, irrespective of whose central office he's connected to. At time of writing most ISDN phones cost over $600. Some cost nearly $1,000. Some cost more than a personal computer. In late fall of 1992 there was increasing talk that PCs will soon come with telecom ports — able to accept the ISDN signal directly from the central office, without the need for a separate (and expensive ISDN) phone instrument. The PC and the software within it, will then become the phone (presumably with a handset, headset or earset attached to the back of the PC). See ISDN.

ISDN TERMINAL ADAPTERS As the integrated services digital network (ISDN) use becomes more widespread, data communications users will need techniques that enable them to connect to this new digital network without abandoning their existing communications equipment. The device that allows this is the ISDN terminal adapter. Terminal adapters offer users a way to take advantage of ISDN's benefits (e.g. high-speed throughput, error-free transmission, multiple line-sharing, local access to packet-switched networks, automatic number identification, and sophisticated diagnostics) without buying ISDN-type terminals and computers. Terminal adapters are essentially similar to modems, with the following difference. Modems connect terminals to the traditional analog network, and terminal adapters connect those analog-network (non-ISDN) terminals to the ISDN network. In this sense, terminal adapters will replace many modem installations, as users gradually convert from analog telephone lines to ISDN lines.

ISDN.ISO 8877 CCITT is the standards group responsible for ISDN-Integrated Services Digital Network. ISDN is an international standard that provides end-to-end digital connectivity to support a wide range of voice, data, and video services. It uses a single communications channel for all forms of information transfer. The ISDN interface connector is specified as an 8-position connector (plug and jack). The four center contacts are assigned to transmit and receive pairs. The four outer contacts are for power.

ISDN/AP Northern Telecom's host to SL1 PBX protocol, which supports NT's Meridian Link. See MERIDIAN LINK and ISDN.

ISE Integrated Switching Element.

ISG Incoming Service Grouping. A fancy name for hunting or rollover. You receive many incoming calls. You don't want to miss a call, so you set your phone lines up to roll over, also called hunt, also called ISG in telephonese. You order five lines in hunt. The calls come into the first. If the first one is busy, the second rings. If it's busy, the third rings. If they're all busy, then the caller receives a busy.

There are two types of hunting — Sequential and Circular hunting. Sequential hunting starts at the number dialed and ends at the last number in the group. Circular hunting hunts all the lines in the hunting group, regardless of the starting point. Circular hunting, according to our understanding, circles only once (though your phone company may be able to program it circle a couple of times). The differences between sequential and circular are subtle. Circular seems to work better for large groups of numbers.

You don't need consecutive phone numbers to do rollovers. Nowadays you can roll lines forwards, backwards and jump around. Rollovers are now done in software. This also has its downside, since software fails. Our recommendation: Test your rollovers at least twice a day. In particular, test that your callers ultimately get a busy if all your lines are busy. Nothing worse your customer should receive a ring-no-answer.

ISL Northern Telecom term for ISDN Signaling Link.

ISM Industrial Scientific Medical. A term the FCC uses to name several of the frequency bands in the spectrum. The 902-928 Mhz is in the ISM band, for example.

ISN AT&T's Information Systems Network.

ISO 1. The Greek prefix which means equal. 2. The International Standards Organization in Paris, devoted to figuring standards for international and national data communications. The U.S. representative to the ISO is ANSI. 3. The initials also stand for Independent Service Organizations or Independent Sales Organizations in the computer sales community.

ISOCHRONOUS Data transmission where timing is derived from the signal carrying the data. No timing or clock lead is provided at the customer interface. In isochronous data transmission, data has no embedded timing - send it slower and it is still valid, just late. Voice and video are intimately tied to timing. Send voice slower and it sounds very different. With TDM services there is a direct relationship between the signal rate used to digitize the voice samples and the bearer channel rate, allowing accurate reconstruction of the voice (or other signals) at the far end. With packet technologies no such relationship exists. Services like ATM must use care in transferring such signals so timing can be recovered since it cannot be derived from the ATM bearer channel.

ISOLATED GROUND IG. In AC electricity, an isolated ground is a type of outlet characterized by the following features and uses:

● It may be orange and must have a Greek "delta" on the front of the outlet. (A delta looks like a triangle.)

● It must be grounded by an insulated green wire.

● It must have an insulator between the ground terminal and the mounting bracket.

● It is used primarily to power electronic equipment because it reduces the incidence of electrical "noise" on the ground path.

ISOLATION See POWER CONDITIONING.

ISP ISDN Signal Processor.

ISPBX Integrated Services Private Branch eXchange.

ISPT Istituto Superiore delle Poste e delle Telcomunicazioni (Superior Institute for Posts and Telecommunications, Italy).

ISSI InterSwitching Interface. An interface between two SMDS switching systems within a LATA.

ISSN Integrated Special Services Network.

ISTF Integrated Services Test Facility.

ISUP Integrated Services Digital Network User Part. The call control part of the SS7 protocol. ISUP determines the procedures for setting up, coordinating, and taking down trunk calls on the SS7 network. ISUP is defined by CCITT recommendations Q.761 and Q.764. ISUP also provides:

- Calling party number information (including privacy indicator).

- Call status checking, to keep trunks in consistent states at both ends.

- Trunk management, and

- Relates of trunks and the application of tones and/or announcements in the originating switch upon encountering error, blockage or busy conditions.

There are seven ISUP Messages: Initial Address Message (IAM), Continuity Check Message (COT), Address Complete Message (ACM), Answer Message(ANM), Release Message (REL), Release Complete Message (RLC) and Exit Message (EXM). For you to benefit from these capabilities, your phone equipment must first be able to access the CCS7 network. One suggested way (but not the only way) is through the ISDN primary rate access (PRA) standard, which supports Q.931 protocol. See IAM, ISDN and COMMON CHANNEL SIGNALING.

ISV Independent Software Vendor. Typically a company which writes and sells software, but not hardware. Manufacturers of hardware and operating systems, i.e. IBM or Northern Telecom, often contract with ISVs to produce specialized software to make their hardware and operating system more attractive.

IT Information Technology. A fancy name for data processing, which became management information systems (MIS), which became information technology. All the same thing, essentially. IT may have come from Europe. I heard it first from Siemens and Nixdorf who merged in 1989.

IT&T Information Technology and Telecommunications.

IT'S A shortened form of "It is." Not to be confused with ITS, which is the possessive of it. Its house. It's a house.

ITB Intermediate Block Character. A transmission control character that terminates an intermediate block. A Block Check Character (BCC) usually follows. Using ITBs allows for error checking of smaller blocks in data communications.

ITC 1. International Teletraffic Congress. 2. Japan's Telecommunications Technology Committee.

ITERATIVE PROCESS The process of repeatedly processing a bunch of instructions. Each repetition, theoretically, comes progressively closer to the desired result, the "correct" answer, etc.

ITG AT&T's Integrated Telemarketing Gateway. This is a set of specs for hooking up an outside computer to an AT&T switch. Under ITG, information travels in both directions — from the switch to the host computer and from the host computer to the switch. See also IG (one-directional link), ASAI and OPEN APPLICATION INTERFACE.

ITI Idle Trunk Indicator.

ITM See Information Technology Management.

ITSEC The European Information Technology Security classification and evaluation initiative.

ITT International Telephone and Telegraph. A company that once was the largest manufacturer of telecommunications equipment outside the U.S.

ITU International Telecommunications Union. An organization established by the United Nations with membership from virtually every government in the world. ITU's objective is to set telecommunications standards, allocate frequencies to various uses and hold trade shows every four years. As satellites have become more important as a method of long distance communications, so the ITU's allocation of scarce satellite frequencies among countries has become a hot bed of controversy. There are many who believe the ITU to be the most important telecommunications organization in the world.

ITUSA Information Technology Users' Standards Association.

IUW The ISDN Users Workshop.

IVDM Integrated Voice and Data Multiplexer. A device that Northern Telecom uses to provide DIALAN, a central office provided local area network offering completely digital, full duplex data transmission at speeds of 300 bps through 19.2 asynchronous and 1,200 bps through 64 kbps synchronous. DIALAN users use existing telephone sets and an Integrated Voice and Data Multiplexer (IVDM) that plugs into a telephone jack.

IVDT Integrated Voice/Data Terminal. A device with a terminal keyboard/display and a voice telephone with or without its own processing power. See INTEGRATED VOICE/DATA TERMINAL.

IVR Interactive Voice Response. Think of IVR as a voice computer. Where a computer has a keyboard for entering information, an IVR uses remote touchtone telephones. Where a computer has a screen for showing the results, an IVR uses a digitized synthesized voice to "read" the screen to the distant caller.

Whatever a computer can do, an IVR can too, from looking up train timetables to moving calls around an automatic call distributor (ACD). The only limitation on an IVR is that you can't present as many alternatives on a phone as you can on a screen. The caller's brain simply won't remember more than a few. With IVR, you have to present the menus in smaller chunks.

IX IntereXchange. Any service which crosses exchange boundaries.

IXC IntereXchange Channel, or IntereXchange Carrier — as contrasted to the LEC — the Local Exchange Carrier, a new word for a local phone company. InterExchange Carriers used to be called "Other Common Carriers," except that didn't include AT&T. Now, AT&T, MCI, U.S. Sprint and all the long distance carriers are called InterExchange Carriers.

J

JABBER To jabber. In local area networking technology, continuously sending random data (garbage). Normally used to describe the action of a station (whose circuitry or logic has failed) that locks up the network with its incessant transmission.

JACKS A receptacle used in conjunction with a plug to make electrical contact between communication circuits. Jacks and their associated plugs are used in a variety of connecting hardware applications including cross connects, interconnects, information outlets, and equipment connections. Jacks are used to connect cords or lines to telephone systems. A jack can be female or male.

JACK CONTACTS Metallic elements of telephone jacks that carry the central office currents/voltages to the CPE plus contacts.

JACK PINS See JACK CONTACTS.

JACK POSITIONS A numbering scheme to permit consistent identification of the Jack Contact(s) position. Position identification helps assure compatibility between the wiring system and the associated terminal equipment.

JACKET The protective and insulating housing of a cable.

JAM SIGNAL A signal generated by a printed circuit card to ensure that other cards know that a packet collision on a local area network has taken place.

JAMMING The interference with through-the-air radio transmission, the object being to hinder the receiver's ability to pick up and understand the signal. An example is the Russians' jamming Radio Free Europe.

JANE BARBIE The electronic "Voice With A Smile" on most telephone company intercept recordings. Ms. Barbie does her work for the Audichron Company of Atlanta, GA. See BARBIE, JANE.

JATE The Japanese equivalent of the U.S. FCC part 68 certification for equipment to be attached to the Japanese telephone network. Getting JATE approval is expensive, complex, and immensely time-consuming.

JCL Job Control Language.

JEDEC Joint Electronic Devices Engineering Council. An organization of the U.S. semi-conductor manufacturers and users that sets package outline dimension standards for packages made in the U.S.

JEOPARDY A wonderful AT&T word meaning anything occurring during the course of accomplishing scheduled work which might cause the scheduled completion date to slip.

JES Job Entry Subsystem. Control protocol and procedure for directing host processing of a task in an IBM host environment. Also the specific IBM software release, host-based, that performs job control functions.

JITTER A tendency towards lack of synchronization caused by mechanical or electrical changes. Technically, the phase shift of digital pulses over a transmission medium. According to Information Gatekeepers, jitter in fiber optical cables is a type of signal distortion. Three forms of jitter exist: Data Dependent Jitter (DDJ), Duty Cycle Distortion (DCD), and Random Jitter (RJ). Data Dependent Jitter is caused by limited bandwidth characteristics and imperfections in the optical channel components as it relates to the transmitted symbol sequence. This jitter results from less than ideal individual pulse responses and from variation in the average value of the encoded pulse sequence which may cause baseline wander and may change the sampling threshold level in the receiver. DCD Jitter is caused by propagation delay differences between low-to-high and high-to-low transitions. DCD is manifested as a pulse width distortion of the nominal baud time. RJ is the result of thermal noise.

JOB A file, typically sent in batch mode. Specifically a set of data, including programs, files and instructions to a computer, that together amount to a unit of work to be done by a computer.

JOIN A basic operation in a relational system that links the rows in two or more tables by comparing the values in specified columns.

JOINT COSTS A regulatory concept. Joint costs are essentially overhead costs. They cover the costs of providing more than one service. Most costs in the telecommunications industry are joint. And being "joint" they give regulators enormous pleasure trying to allocate those costs to various services and therefore trying to figure what prices for those services should be.

JOINT USER SERVICE An arrangement whereby a corporation, association, partnership or individual whose telecommunications needs do not warrant the provision of separate leased service, is permitted to use the service of another customer by mutual agreement. The primary objective of joint user service is to save money by buying circuits in bulk.

JOULE The unit of work or energy. The energy expended when a current of one ampere flows through a resistance of one ohm for one second. Joule's Law says the heat produced in a circuit in joules is proportional to the resistance, to the square of the current and to the time.

JOURNAL PRINTERS These are special purpose printers which provide hard-copy output for audit trail and demand printing functions associated with hotel/motel management features.

JPEG Proposed worldwide standard for image compression devised by the Joint Photographic Experts Group, experts sanctioned by the International Standards Organization (ISO) and the CCITT. The JPEG compression standard works this way, according to the New York Times: A color image is converted into rows of dots, called pixels, each with a numerical value that represents brightness and color. The picture is then broken down into blocks, each 16 pixels x 16 pixels and then reduced to 8 pixels by 8 pixels by subtracting every other pixel. The software uses a formula that computes an average value for each block, permitting it to be represented with less data. Further steps subtract even more information from the image. To retrieve the data, the process is simply reversed to decompress the image. A specialized chip decompresses the images hundreds of times faster than is possible on a standard desktop computer. See also MPEG — a proposed standard for compression of full motion digital video.

JPEG++ Storm Technology's proprietary extension of the JPEG algorithm. It lets users determine the degree of compression that the foreground and background of an image receive; for example, in a portrait, you could compress the face in the foreground only slightly, while you could compress it in the background to a much higher degree. See JPEG.

JUDGE HAROLD GREENE Judge Greene presided over the 1982 AT&T Antitrust settlement, enforcing its provisions and making decisions about requests from the participants to modify or reinterpret the provisions of the settlement. As long as he doesn't allow AT&T to be completely free of regulation, Judge Greene will probably always be involved in figuring the future of the telecommunications industry.

JUKEBOX A jukebox is a piece of hardware that holds storage media, such as optical disks or cartridge tapes. Jukeboxes are typically designed to hold as few as five and as many as 120 devices. Like oldfashioned record playing jukeboxes, media is moved by a robot-like device from the storage slot to the drive reading it. This lets the user share one drive among several cartrdiges or disk. Jukeboxes are typically used for secondary and archival storage. Access to information is not fast.

JUMBO GROUP A 3,600 channel band of frequencies formed from the inputs of six master groups. See MASTERGROUP and SUPERGROUP.

JUMP HUNTING See NONCONSECUTIVE HUNTING.

JUMPER 1. A wire used to connect equipment and cable on a distributing frame. 2. A patch cable or wire used to establish a circuit, often temporarily, for testing or diagnostics. 3. Jumpers are pairs or sets of small prongs on adapters and motherboards. Jumpers allow the user to instruct the computer to select one of its available operation options. When two pins are covered with a plug, an electrical circuit is completed, When the jumper is uncovered the connection is not made. The computer interprets these electrical connections as configuration information. 4. When errors are found on printed circuit boards, a Jumper cable is sometimes soldered in to correct the problem.

JUMPER WIRE A short length of wire used to route a circuit by linking two cross connect points.

JUNCTION BOX Metal box inside which cables are connected.

JUNCTOR A connection or circuit between inlets and outlets of the same or different switching networks.

JUNIPER A Rolm/IBM product that consists of a digital phone and a printed circuit for dropping into an IBM PC or clone.

K

K 1. See K-STYLE HANDSET below. 2. In metric terms it means one thousand (1,000), taken from the Greek word kilo. It is often appended to a measurement such as KHertz or kHz, which means 1,000 Hertz. In data communications, a kilobit means a thousand bits per second. In computer memory terms, it means 1,024, which is the figure for two raised to the 10th power, i.e. $2 \times 2 \times 2 \times 2 \times 2 \times 2 \times 2 \times 2 \times 2 \times 2$.

K Band That portion of the electromagnetic spectrum in the high microwave/millimeter range — from 10.9 GHz to 36 GHz. See also Ka BAND.

K PLANS Also call keysheets. When designing a phone system, you need to assign features and line assignments to each extension. A keysheet or a K Plan is an organized way of figuring and keeping track of those features and assignments. Typically it's one page per extension. These days, keysheets are often done on computer.

K PLANT Old Bell System lingo for equipment used in key systems.

K STYLE HANDSET A K-style handset is the newer, square telephone handset. The older, round handset is called the G-style handset.

K10 Old Bell-Speak for 10-button (9-lines) key telephone.

K20 Old Bell-Speak for 20-button (19 lines) key telephone.

K30 Old Bell-Speak for 30-button (29 lines) key telephone.

Ka BAND That portion of the electromagnetic spectrum in the high microwave/millimeter range — approximately 33 to 36 GHz.

KALEIDA The joint venture between Apple and IBM to make multimedia products. Multimedia is the bringing together of textual, graphical, video and audio material.

KBIT/S KiloBITs per Second. Standard measure of data rate and transmission capacity. See K.

KBPS KiloBits Per Second. One thousand bits per second.

KDD Kokusai Denshin Denshin Denwa Co, Ltd. The Japanese supplier of international telecom service.

KEARNEY SYSTEM An AT&T numbering scheme for telecom parts. See KS NUMBER.

KEEP-ALIVE SIGNAL A generic term for a T-1 signal transmitted when a DTE detects a loss of input from the customer's equipment for 150 msec. (sometimes called a blue signal or AIS).

KERMIT An asynchronous file transfer protocol designed for PC communications at Columbia University. The protocol has become popular because of its flexibility. Kermit is found most frequently on DEC VAX computers, IBM mainframes and other minicomputers. One of the clearest advantages of Kermit is its ability to be tailored for virtually any equipment. Protocols break a file into equal parts called blocks or packets. These packets are sent and the receiving computer checks the arriving packet and sends an acknowledgement (ACK) back to the sending computer. Because modems use phone lines to transfer data, noise or interference on the line will often mess up the block. When a block is damaged in transit, an error occurs. The purpose of a protocol is to set up a mathematical way of measuring if the block came through accurately. And if it didn't, ask the distant end to re-transmit the block until it gets it right. Because of Kermit's emphasis on flexibility, Kermit is very slow and should not be used when faster options (i.e. Zmodem) are available.

KERNEL The part of a computer operating system that performs basic functions such as switching between tasks. See KERNET-BASED WINDOW SYSTEM.

KERNEL-BASED WINDOW SYSTEM Kernel-based window systems are those in which the software application executes and displays in the same physical machine. Examples include personal computers and Macintoshes. The advantage is speed. The disadvantage is that applications are closely tied to the system environment and are therefore not portable. Kernel-based window systems also do not allow users/developers to use the network as a means of sharing computer resources.

KERR EFFECT When polarized light is shined onto a magnetized surface, the light is reflected back at an angle and in a different direction, depending on the polarity of the magnetism. This quirk of nature is called the Kerr Effect and it is the basis of magneto-optical (eraseable) discs.

KEVLAR A strong synthetic material used in cable strength members. The name is a trademark of the Dupont Company. Kevlar is also used in bulletproof vests worn by police.

KEY 1. One or more characters or perhaps a field within a data record used to identify the data and perhaps control its use. 2. The physical button on a telephone set. (What normal people call a "Switch," telephone people call a "Key.") 3. The device which unlocks your front door or perhaps your terminal or computer.

KEY ILLUMINATION A lamp under a button (called a "key" in telephony) which flashes at different rates to signal an incoming call, a steady busy and "wink" (fast) hold.

KEY MAP A MIDI patch-map entry that translates key values for certain MIDI messages, for example, the keys used to play the appropriate percussion instrument or a melodic instrument in the appropriate octave.

KEY PAD The touch-tone dial pad on a pushbutton phone. Touchtone is a registered trademark of AT&T, so most people use the word "pushbutton." But there's really no difference.

KEY PAD STATE An AT&T enhanced fax term. The KEYPAD state can be: NULL: The the keypad is in use by a feature and is not available for use on a call. NON-NULL. The keypad is available for use in originating a call or for sending DTMF tones on an existing call.

KEY PULSE In multifrequency (MF) tone signaling, a signal used to prepare the distant equipment to receive digits.

KEY PULSING A pulsing system in which digits are transmitted using pushbuttons. Each button corresponds to a digit and generates a unique set of tones.

KEY SERVICE PANEL An old 1A2 key telephone term. Wired or unwired connector panel for modular expansion of key system service by allowing the installation of additional Line Cards and/or other KTUs. Typically, Key Service Panels are available in different jack configurations to accommodate 18-, 20-, 36- and 40-pin KTU's. Commonly abbreviated as KSP. Most KSPs are supplied as rack-mount equipment.

KEY SERVICE UNIT KSU. This is a small metal cabinet which contains all the switching electronics of a business key telephone system. The KSU fits between the lines coming in from the central office and the lines going to the individual phones. Be careful where you place the Key Service Unit. That place should be well-ventilated as the KSU gets hot. It should be near a power outlet (it needs one). Unless it's a very small phone system, it should be plugged into a power outlet dedicated to it (other devices, such as typewriters, plugged into the same electrical circuit could affect it). And the power outlet should be above the reach of the mops and brooms of the local cleaning lady. Otherwise the plug will get knocked out and the phone system won't work the next day. See KEY TELEPHONE SYSTEM.

KEY SET Also called Key Telephone Set. A telephone set having several buttons which can be used for call holding, line pick-up, auto-dialing, intercom and other features. Ericsson calls a keyset a touchtone telephone.

KEY STRIP The row(s) of additional buttons on key telephone sets used for call hold, intercom and other KTU function control.

KEY SYSTEM POWER SUPPLY The local source for all DC voltages required for talking and lamp signaling within the Key Telephone System. The power supply may or may not also provide an AC voltage output for ringing. If it does, a separate Ringing Generator will normally not be required.

KEY TELEPHONE SYSTEM A system in which the telephones have multiple buttons permitting the user to select outgoing or incoming central office phone lines directly. With a key system you don't have to dial 9 to get obtain an outside line. With a PBX, you have to dial "9" to make a call outside the building. Dialing 9 is the major difference these days between a key telephone systems and PBXs. PBXs are usually, but not always, larger.

KEY TELEPHONE UNIT A modular 1A2 Key Telephone System building block that plugs into a KSU or KSP. Commonly abbreviated as KTU. Typical KTU examples include 4000 Series Line Cards, 4448 Delayed Ring Transfer Card, 6606 Interrupter, etc.

KEY TO DISK A method of entering data whereby it's sent directly from the keyboard to a disk, usually a hard disk.

KEYBOARD A series of switches, arranged somewhat like a standard "QWERTY" typewriter that allows you to send information to a computer. There is no such animal as a "standard" computer keyboard. For speed typists, this is a terrible pity. If you are buying multiple computers for your office, check out your peoples' preference for keyboards. Getting the right one can make a big difference. You can often buy PCs without keyboards and buy third party differently-designed keyboards.

KEYBOARD BUFFER A temporary storage area in memory that keeps track of keys that you typed, even if the computer did not immediately respond to the keys when you typed them.

KEYBOARD CALL SETUP Allows you to set up a data call using the buttons of a telephone, or it allows you to set up a voice call using the keyboard of your PC. Which definition you choose — setting up a voice or a data call — depends on which manufacturer you're working with.

KEYED A term used in data communications whereby the RJ-45 male plug has a small, square bump on its end and the female RJ-45 plug is shaped to accommodate the plug. A keyed RJ-45 plug will not fit into a female, non-keyed (i.e. normal) RJ-45. The purpose of keying a plug is to differentiate it from a "normal" non-keyed plug. Keyed RJ-45 plugs are typically used for data communications. See also RJ-11, RJ-22 and RJ-45.

KEYING Modulation of a carrier signal, usually by frequency or phase, to encode binary (digital) information, (as in FSK or Frequency Shift Keying).

KHz KiloHertz. One thousand hertz. See K.

KILL MESSAGE A recorded message played at the beginning of a call to a 900 (or other pay-per-call) number that warns the caller of the charges and gives him the option to hang up before it starts.

KILLER APP Killer Application. The high-tech industry's lifelong dream. That dream is to discover a new application that is so useful and so persuasive that millions of customers will rush in, and throw money at you to buy your killer app. The first PBX killer app was probably being able to dial out without an operator (i.e. dial 9). The second was probably least cost routing. The third was probably call accounting. The next may be some form of hookup to PCs, with desktop and LAN connectivity. In the PC industry, killer apps have been spreadsheets, word processing and databases. Finding that one killer app that will make them wealth beyond their wildest dreams is what drives many software programmers and entrepreneurs. See WINDOWS TELEPHONY.

KILO One thousand.

KILOBYTE 1,024 bytes. Roughly the amount of information in half a typewritten page.

KILOCHARACTER One thousand characters. Used as a measure of billing for data communications by some overseas phone companies. See also KILOSEGMENT.

KILOSEGMENT 64,000 characters. Used as a measure of billing for data communications by some overseas phone companies. See also KILOCHARACTER.

KINGSBURY COMMITMENT December 13, 1913: A letter from Nathan C. Kingsbury, VP AT&T, to the Attorney General of the United States committed AT&T to dispose of its stock in Western Union Telegraph Company. It also promised to provide long distance connection of Bell System lines to independent phone companies (where there was no local competition) and further agreed not to purchase any more independent telephone companies, except as approved by the Interstate Commerce Commission which regulated the phone industry at that time. See also DIVESTITURE.

KITTYHAWK A trade name for a line of very small hard disks manufactured by Hewlett Packard.

KLUDGE A hardware solution that has been improvised from various mismatched parts. A slang word meaning makeshift. A kludge can also be in software. It may not be elegant and is probably only a temporary fix. As in, "That patch to the software is a real kludge." See KLUGE.

KLUGE Another way of spelling kludge. We don't know which is correct. See KLUDGE.

KNOWLEDGE BASE SYSTEM In its most simple term, it means knowledge that is known by the system. Software in which application specific information is programmed into something called the "knowledge base" in the form of rules. The system uses artificial intelligence (AI) procedures to mimic human problem-solving. It applies the rules stored in the knowledge base and the facts supplied to the system to solve a particular business problem.

KNOWLEDGE WORKER A person who uses a computer. John Perry Barlow thinks the expression was created by the "droids" who run Microsoft and Apple. Mr. Barlow is a cattle rancher, computer hacker, poet, and a lyricist for the rock band The Grateful Dead.

KNOWBOTS Intelligent computer programs that automate the search and gathering of data from distributed databases. The creation of knowbots is part of a research project headed up by the Corporation for National Research Initiatives, Reston, VA. Two knowbot-based databases for the medical field are expected to be available in 1991. Knowbots could become more widespread for general use, according to networking experts.

KONEXX A modem to telephone connection product made by Unlimited Systems in San Diego, CA. This is the only device which lets you connect your laptop modem to a screwy phone system you encounter in travels. That screwy phone system might be a digital one, or a proprietary electronic one, or anything that isn't plain old tip and ring. With the Konexx, you simply unplug your handset, plug in the Konnexx and plug in your modem. You can dial, connect and transfer e-mails and faxes. A most useful device.

KS NUMBER Abbreviation for Kearney System number. AT&T's Western Electric division had a major manufacturing and distribution facility in Kearney, New Jersey. Thousands of items were assigned part numbers with KS prefixes. KS numbers still appear on certain basic telecom hardware items made by various manufacturers. AT&T now uses both a Code number which reflects standard industry numbering and a different "Comcode" number on most products. The Code No. 259C modular-to-Amphenol adapter is Comcode No. 103339396, and KS No. 21997L15. Very confusing. Kearney, by the way, is pronounced "carny."

KSR Keyboard Send Receive. A combination teleprinter/transmitter/receiver with transmission capability from the keyboard only, i.e. there is no punch paper tape device and no magnetic memory device, such as a floppy disk.

KSU Key Service Unit. The main cabinet containing all electronics necessary to run a key telephone system. See also KEY SERVICE UNIT.

KTA Key Telephone Adapter. A Rolm multiplexing unit which connects a standard 1A2 key telephone to a three-pair cable coming in from the Rolm CBX.

KTI Key Telephone Interface.

KTILA Development Centre for Telecommunications (Greece).

KTS Key Telephone System.

KTU Key Telephone Unit. The circuit cards found in a KSU that control telephone sets and their features in a key system.

KU BAND Portion of the electromagnetic spectrum in the 12 to 14 GHz range. Used for satellites.

KV Old Bell-Speak for key telephone. K apparently stands for Key; V is a mystery.

KVW Old Bell-Speak for a a key telephone that's designed specifically for wall-mounting. Most modern key telephones can be used on a desk or wall.

KWH KiloWatt Hour. One thousand WATTS of electricity used for one hour.

L

L BAND Portion of the electromagnetic spectrum commonly used in satellite and microwave applications, with frequencies in the 390 MHz to 1550 Mhz. The GPS (Global Positioning System) frequencies are in the L-Band. GPS uses 1227.6 MHz and 1575.42 MHz.

L CARRIER A long haul frequency division multiplexed coax-cabled long haul carrier system. It was first introduced just before the second World War. Eventually it grew to a capacity of 13,300 voice channels over a pair of coaxial tubes. L Carrier systems are still used today. They are the most widely-used analog long distance transmission system.

L MULTIPLEX A system of analog multiplexers built up through groups, supergroups, master groups and jumbo groups of circuits. See L CARRIER.

L-to-T CONNECTOR A device that mates two FDM (Frequency Division Multiplexed) groups with one TDM (Time Division Multiplexed) digigroup to allow 24 voice conversations in analog form to talk to (tie into) a DS-1 line — a T-1 line.

LABEL A set of symbols used to identify or describe an item, record, message or file. It can also be the same as the address in storage.

LABELING ALGORITHM Algorithm for shortest path routing or similiar problems which labels individual nodes, updating labels as appropriate to reach a solution.

LAD LATA Architecture Database

LADT Local Area Data Transport. A method by which customers will send and receive digital data over existing customer loop wiring.

LAMA Local Automatic Message Accounting. A process using equipment in the central office which records the information necessary to bill your local phone calls by your local phone company.

LAMBDA The greek letter used as a symbol for wave length.

LAMINATE The whole structure in the mould, consisting of several piles. A layer in a composite is called a "ply."

LAMINATIONS Thin sheets of steel used as the magnetic core in electrical apparatus, (e.g., the core of an audio frequency transformer is normally composed of laminations).

LAMP The technically-correct term for light bulb, which non-technical folks put into their lamps.

LAMP BATTERY A steady (unpulsing) 10 volt AC source of power to operate the lamps in key telephone sets; usually one of the outputs of the local Key System Power Supply.

LAMP FLASH A pulsed 10 VAC source of lamp power sent to a key telephone set to indicate a CO or PBX line is ringing in. Pulse repetition rate is normally 60 Hertz with a duty cycle of .5 sec on and .5 sec off. This signal is usually provided by the local Interrupter KTU.

LAMP LEADS Lamp and Lamp Ground (L&LG) wires connected to all lamps in the key telephone set over which steady and pulsed 10 VAC signals from the Line Card KTU are sent.

LAMP STEADY A steady (unpulsed) 10 VAC source of lamp power sent to a key telephone set to indicate that the line is in use. See also Lamp Battery.

LAMP WINK A pulsed 10 VAC source of lamp power sent to a key telephone set to indicate that the line is on Hold status; pulse repetition rate is normally 120 Hertz with a duty cycle of .4 sec on and .1 sec off. This signal is usually provided by the local Interrupter KTU.

LAMs Line Adaptor Modules.

LAN Local Area Network. A short distance data communications network (typically within a building or campus) used to link together computers and peripheral devices (such as printers) under some form of standard control. For a longer, more detailed explanation, See LOCAL AREA NETWORK.

LAN ADAPTER A PC-compatible circuit card that provides the PC-to-LAN hardware connection. In addition, LAN software drivers and LAN operating systems need to be run on the PC for it to function as a LAN station.

LAN AWARE Applications that have file and record locking for use on a network.

LAN IGNORANT Applications written for single users only. These are not recommended for use on LANs (local area networks).

LAN INTRINSIC Applications written for client-server networks.

LAN MANAGER 1. A person who manages a LAN. Duties can includes adding new users, installing new hardware and software, diagnosing network problems, helping users, performing backup and setting up a security system. Unlike MIS managers, LAN managers are rarely formally trained in LAN management. Sometimes they're called LAN Network Managers. 2. The multiuser network operating system co-developed by Microsoft and 3Com. LAN Manager offers a wide range of network-management and control capabilities. As yet, it is taking a decidedly second place to Novell's NetWare. It has largely been superseded by Windows NT Advanced Server.

LAN NETWORK MANAGER An IBM-developed network management tool. It is a software program that runs under OS/2 and which provides management and diagnostics tools needed to manage a Token Ring LAN. A PS/2 running LAN Network Manager collects vital statistics and special management data packets on the ring to which it is connected. When multiple rings are involved, the LAN Network Manager relies on the token ring bridges and routers to help in managing those token ring LANs that are not directly connected to the LAN Network Manager station. IBM has installed software in its bridges called the LAN Network Manager Agent. The agent software acts as the eyes and ears for the LAN Network Manager station so that the station can manage the remote rings as if it were connected directly to them. If there were no such agents, managers of networks would be blind to what's going on these LANs. Remote management with LAN Network Manager includes the ability to perform ring testing, analyze traffic and error statistics, and force adapters off the network.

LAN SERVER IBM's implementation of LAN manager, now largely superceded by OS/2 2.1.

LAND LINE A telephone circuit that travels over terrestrial circuits, be they wire, fiber or microwave. A call may originate from a source not connected to the "terrestrial" network, as from a car telephone or a ship to shore radio, and the call be completed via a Landline.

LANDA The Local Area Network Dealers Association. It runs a number of excellent trade shows each year. Its members are LAN resellers, distributors, manufacturers, and consultants. It's based at Suite 260, 360 West Butterfield Road, Elmhurst, IL. 708-279-2255. In 1993 it merged with NOMDA, the National Office Machine Dealers Association.

LANDSCAPE Most computer screens are horizontal, i.e. they are wider than they are high. In the new language of computer screens, such screens are called "landscape." When a computer screen is higher than it is wide, it's called "portrait." Some computer screens can actually work both ways. Some even have a small mercury switch in them that determines which way the screen is standing (portrait or landscape) and will adjust their image accordingly.

LANGUAGE Computer software that allows you to write programs.

LANGUAGE INTERPRETER Any processor, assembler or software that accepts statements in one software language and then produces equivalent statements in another language.

LAP Link Access Procedure.

LAP-B LAPB. Link Access Procedure Balanced, the most common data-link control protocol used to interface X.25 DTEs with X.25 also specifies a LAP or link access procedure (not balanced). Both LAP and LAP-B are full-duplex, point-to-point bit-synchronous protocols. The unit of data transmission is called a frame. Frames may contain one or more X.25 packets. LAP-B is the data link level of X.25 in a packet switched network. Same as a subset of the asynchronous balanced mode of HDLC. It is the link initialization procedure that establishes and maintains communications between the data terminal equipment (DTE) and data communications equipment (DCE). All public packet data networks (PDNs) support LAPB.

LAP-D Or LAPD. Link Access Procedure-D. Also called Link Access Protocol for the D channel. Link-level protocol devised for ISDN connections, differing from LAPB (LAP-Balanced) in its framing sequence. Likely to be used as basis for LAPM, the proposed CCITT modem error-control standard.

LAPTOP COMPUTER A portable computer you can use on your lap. Usually weighing less than 15 pounds. Probably the most useful gadget to come along in years. I wrote much of this dictionary in planes, trains, airports, etc. on a laptop computer — initially on a Toshiba T1200HB, sporting one megabyte of RAM, one 21 megabyte drive, one 3 1/2 inch disk drive with a capacity of 730K and a 1200 baud modem, then later on a more modern laptop called the Toshiba T1200XE, sporting five megabytes of RAM, one 42 megabyte hard drive, one 3 1/2 inch disk drive with a capacity of 1.4 megs, and one 2400 baud modem, then later on a Toshiba T2000SX with four megs of RAM and a 60 meg hard disk and now on a Toshiba T3300SL sporting 8 megs of RAM, a 386SL 25 MHz processor and a 130 meg hard disk. There's a new term for a laptop computer, namely a notebook computer. A notebook laptop weighs less than eight pounds and is roughly the shape of a 8 1/2" x 11" sheet of paper. Subnotebooks are under 4 lbs.

LARGE SQUARING CAPABILITY A feature on the AT&T Merlin key system which permits all lines to appear on all telephone sets.

LASER An acronym for Light Amplification by Stimulated Emission of Radiation. It is a device which produces a single frequency light. By turning on and off the laser light signal quickly, you can transmit the ones and zeros of a digital communications channel. Lasers carried through glass fiber are ideal for telecommunications transmission for two major reasons. 1. Glass fiber of such purity has now been developed that only a very minute portion of the laser light traveling through it is lost. In telecom terms, this means very little of the laser signal is attenuated. The signal maintains its strength and thus reduces the need for frequent and expensive repeaters (the digital word for "amplifiers.") Laser transmission systems can now carry thousands of voice conversations for hundreds of miles without repeaters on two fibers no thicker than a human hair. (You need two fibers — one for the conversations coming and one for them going.) 2. Laser fiber optic telecom systems are totally immune to electromagnetic interference of any kind. There's no humming from electrical motors. You can't pick up the local TV station in the background. You can't pick up any interference from adjacent cables.

In recent years, laser fiber optic transmission has been getting cheaper, more reliable and more powerful at roughly the same rate as computers, and like computers, nobody believes there is an end in sight. As we were writing this dictionary, Russell Dewitt of Contel delivered a paper entitled Evolution of fiber optics in rural telephone networks. In it, he talked about "Fiber Optics Progress" and said:

"In 1860, the Pony Express could deliver a letter from St. Louis to San Francisco in ten days. For three typed pages the data transmission rate was about three bits per minute. In comparison, today in Contel we are transmitting at the rate of 565 Mbps (million bits per second) over single mode fiber. This is a capacity of 8064 voice channels. Gigabit per second systems will be available for use this year (a gigabit is a million million) and a 20 Gbps system has been demonstrated in the laboratory. For the future, the ultimate potential of a single mode fiber has been estimated. It is about 25,000 Gbps (25,000,000,000,000,000 bits per second). At that rate you could transmit all the knowledge recorded since the beginning of time in 20 seconds. See also LASER FAX, LCD and FIBER OPTICS.

LASER FAX A conventional laser printer that is also capable of being used as a FAX machine when combined with an optional plug-in cartridge and used with a personal computer.

LASER OPTICAL System of recording on grooveless discs using a laser-optical-tracking pickup. Originally, the technology was WORM — Write Once (i.e. not erasable) Read Many. It's now erasable.

LASER PRINTER A high speed nonimpact dot matrix printer which uses a laser beam to electrostatically form characters on paper. The printer then heats the paper which melts a metallic dust attracted to the electrostatic areas which form the inked images on the paper. Laser printers are fast and the quality of their printing beautiful, rivalling that produced by conventional photo-typeset (the way this book was produced).

LASHING Attachment of a cable to a support strand by wrapping steel wire or dielectric filament around the cable.

LASS See LOCAL AREA SIGNALING SERVICES

LAST DIGIT DIALED SIGNAL Allows the use of the # sign on Touchtone telephones to indicate that the last digit has been dialed on outgoing calls. This signal enables the PBX to process calls more rapidly, since some PBXs count the time after a digit was dialed. If nothing else is dialed within a certain time, it assumes that the dialing is complete and then pulses out the call.

LAST EXTENSION CALLED Same as LAST NUMBER REDIAL.

LAST IN FIRST OUT LIFO. The last phone call (or data) arriving is the first call (or data) to leave — to be processed, to be saved, whatever. The term LIFO comes from accounting. It's one of several ways to value an inventory.

LAST NUMBER REDIAL Most modern electronic phones have a button on them called "Last Number Redial." When you touch this button, your phone will automatically dial the last number you dialed. If you also have speed dial numbers on your phone, any number you dialed with a Speed Dial button will not appear in Last Number Redial. Most Last Number Redial buttons on electronic phones attached to a PBX will only recognize completely-dialed numbers. Last Number Redial buttons are useful. Also useful — but less common — is a stored number dial button. Dial a number, punch in "save," then that number will be saved to that button, ready to be dialed later, even though you might dial some other numbers in the meantime.

LAT Local Area Transport. A proprietary communications protocol developed by DEC for terminal-to-host communications. LAT allows terminal emulators to access VAX and VMS systems over Ethernet. See LAT PROTOCOL.

LAT PROTOCOL The LAT protocol, announced by Digital Equipment Corporation in the mid-80s, is today one of the industry's most widely used protocols for supporting character terminals over Ethernet networks. LAT is currently licensed by more than 40 third-party hardware and software developers, and is compatible with the products of more than 30 major system vendors, from Apollo, and Apple to IBM, Tandem and Wang. The basic function of the LAT protocol is to permit a terminal server to connect multiple asynchronous devices — video display terminals, printers or plotters — to a host timeshare computer. To do this, LAT (or any other terminal server protocol) puts data into packets that can be understood by both the asynchronous device and the host. Essentially, a terminal server protocol is responsible for establishing lower level communications connections, and for routing appropriate transmissions to their destinations.

LATA Local Access and Transport Area. One of 161 local geographical areas in the US within which a local telephone company may offer telecommunications services — local or long distance. AT&T is expressly prohibited from offering intra-LATA calls by the terms of the Divestiture. Other competitors, such as MCI and Sprint, are not, though rules vary by state, according to state regulation.

LATENCY The time interval between when a network station seeks access to a transmission channel and when access is granted or received. Same as waiting time. In a bridge or a router, it is the amount of time elapsed between receiving and retransmitting the LAN packet. The length of time the packet is stuck in a bridge or router. See INTERRUPT LATENCY.

LAUNCH A new term for starting a program from within another. Typically what might happen is you're working in a messaging program, which has individual lines showing you've just received several faxes, voice mails, electronic mail documents. You click on one of the lines. Your program recognizes that it's an electronic mail message and says "quickly open the electronic messaging software and get it to read the message." So it "launches" the messaging software.

LAY A term used in cable manufacturing to denote the distance of advance of one member of a group of spirally twisted members, in one turn, measured axially.

LAYER In the seven layered OSI model, it refers to a collection of network processing-functions that together comprise a set of rules and standards for successful data communication. See OSI MODEL.

LAYERED NETWORK ARCHITECTURES Currently the basis of all telecommunication network architecture standards, with functions allocated to different layers and standardized interfaces between layers. The OSI Model is a layered network architecture.

LAYERED NETWORK SALES STRATEGY An AT&T sales strategy which involves segmenting customer network needs into four usage levels or layers, then pursuing sales opportunities at these various entry points. The layers are Premises Networks, Office Networks, "metropolitan" or " campus" networks and Wide Area Networks.

LAYS The twists in twisted pair cable. Two single wires are twisted together to form a pair; by varying the length of the twists, or lays, the potential for signal interference between pairs is reduced.

LBA An abbreviation for Logical Block Address. See Logical Block Address.

LBO Electrical Line Build Out

LBRV, LOW BIT RATE VOICE Digitized voice that requires a bandwidth of less than 32 kbps. LBRV digitizing techniques include packetized voice, APV, DSI, and LPC.

LCD Liquid Crystal Display. An alphanumeric display using liquid crystal sealed between two pieces of glass. The display is divided into hundreds or thousands of individual dots, which are charged or not charged, reflecting or not reflecting external light to form characters, letters and numbers. LCD displays have certain advantages. They use little electricity and react reasonably quickly — though not nearly as quickly as a glass cathode ray tube or a gas plasma screen. They are reasonably legible. They require external light to reflect their information to the user. The newer so-called "supertwist" LCDs are much more readable. You see LCDs on computer laptops and telephone screens. The reason computer laptop LCD screens are brighter than phone screens is that laptops use fluorescent or other light sources to illuminate the LCD (typically from the back or the side). Phones typically don't have the power. The only way for a phone to get the power is to plug the phone and its screen into an AC outlet. Most users, however, don't want to have to plug their phone into both AC and phone outlets. It's cumbersome. In newer LCDs, called active matrix displays, the circuit board contains individual transistors for each pixel, or dot on the screen. The enables the crystals to shift quickly, resulting in a higher quality image and the ability to display full-motion video. Active matrix displays in color are hard to manufacture. Low production yields are common, though improving.

LCM Line Control Module.

LCR Least Cost Routing. A telephone system feature that automatically chooses the lowest cost phone line to the destination. What actually is the "lowest cost" is determined by algorithms, equations and decision trees programmed into the PBX. Least Cost Routing typically works with "look-up" tables in the PBX's memory. These tables are put into the PBX by the user. The PBX does not automatically know how to route each call. It must be told so by the user. That "telling" might be as simple as saying "all 312 area codes will go via the AT&T FX line."

Or it might be as complex as actually listing which exchanges in the 312 area code go by which method. LEAST COST ROUTING tells the calls to go over the lines which are perceived by the user to be the least cost way of getting the call from point A to point B. There are typically two types of "least cost routing" translation — that which examines the first three digits of the phone number (i.e. just the area code) and the first six digits of the phone number (i.e. the area code and the three digits of the local central office). Six digit translation is preferred because it allows you more flexibility in routing — particularly to big area codes, like 213 in LA, where there are long distance calls within the area code. See also AUTOMATIC ROUTE SELECTION, ALTERNATE ROUTING and SIX DIGIT TRANSLATION.

LD 1. Long Distance. 2. Loop Disconnect.

LDM See LIMITED DISTANCE MODEM.

LDN Listed Directory Number. Your main phone number. The one you list in the telephone directory and Directory Assistance.

LEAD AGENT The first agent in an ACD group. See also AUTOMATIC CALL DISTRIBUTOR.

LEAD IN 1. Wire or cable from antenna to TV set. 2. The conductor from the antenna to the radio receiver.

LEADER The section at the beginning of a roll of magnetic tape which holds no data and often is not even magnetic tape. A leader is used to feed the magnetic tape through the tape mechanism and secure it onto the roll.

LEADING CURRENT The phrase difference in a capacitive alternating current where the current leads the E. M. F.

LEAKY BRIDGE A type of LAN bridge that forwards packets from one LAN to another even though the packet should not be forwarded. Usually due to poor engineering.

LEAKY PBX One of those really silly terms the phone industry is famous for. Picture this. You dial a distant PBX. If you can dial on — either locally or make a long distance call, that distant PBX is referred to as "leaky." All PBXs are, of course, "leaky," or at least capable of being made leaky. But there are some tariffs which the FCC insists on you paying more for if your PBX is being used as a "leaky" PBX. So, to avoid the extra surcharge, almost everyone lies on the little form the carrier sends you.

LEAS LATA Equal Access System.

LEASED CIRCUIT Same as LEASED LINE or PRIVATE LINE.

LEASED LINE Same as a LEASED or DEDICATED CIRCUIT, PRIVATE LINE, LEASED CHANNEL. A telephone line rented for exclusive use 24-hour a day, seven days a week from a telephone company — a local phone company (like New York Telephone) or a long distance company like AT&T or MCI.

LEAST COST ROUTING LCR. A telephone system feature which automatically chooses the "least cost" long distance line to send out a long distance call. The user typically dials "9" and then his 10-digit long distance number which is routed over the least costly service. See also LCR.

LEAVE WORD CALLING For AT&T System 75 and 85 users for internal messages. The caller's name, time of call and extension number are taken and can be retrieved on a Digital Display Monitor or BCT. The service is accompanied by an Integrated Directory — a simple electronic listing of employee names and extension numbers, access by a terminal equipped with a DDM or via the attendant console.

LEC Local Exchange Carrier. The local phone companies, which can be either a Bell Operating Company (BOC) or an independent (e.g. GTE) which provide local transmission services. Prior to divestiture, the LECs were called telephone companies or telcos.

LED Light Emitting Diode. A semiconductor diode which emits light when a current is passed through it. In lightwave transmission systems, light emitting diodes or lasers are used as sources of light. These devices are fabricated from multilayered structures of compound semiconductors epitaxially grown on a single-crystal substrate. LEDs are used as sources for optical data link applications in which the data rates are less than about 500 megabits per second and the transmission distances do not exceed a few kilometers. LEDs are also used in alphanumeric displays on calculators and computer devices. LEDs use less power than normal incandescent light bulbs, but more power than LCDs (Liquid Crystal Displays).

LEG My definition: A segment of a multipoint circuit which lies between any two of the points. Bellcore's definition: An object within a connection view that represents a communication path toward some addressable entity.

LEN Line Equipment Number.

LENGTH The number of bits or bytes in a computer word, a field, a record, etc.

LEOS Low Earth Orbiting Satellites. Motorola's proposed Iridium is one of these.

LEP Large Electron Positron Collider.

LERG The Local Exchange Routing Guide.

LESS THAN Of smaller quantity. Of less importance. The word "less" is always confused with the word "fewer." According to the Oxford American Dictionary, the word "less" is used of things that are measured by amount (for example, eat less butter, use less fuel). Its use with things measured by numbers is regarded as incorrect (for example in "we need less workers;" correct usage is fewer workers.)

LETTER OF AGENCY A letter sent by an end user to a telephone company — local or long distance — authorizing the end user's equipment vendor to deal on the end user's behalf with the phone company. A letter of agency is actually a specialized Power of Attorney.

LETTERS SHIFT A physical shift in a teletypewriter, specifically Telex, which enables the printing of alphabetic characters.

LEVEL 1. The power of a signal measured at a certain point in the circuit. 2. Your management position (i.e. "level" in the management structure) in a telephone company. In AT&T and members of the operating Bell telephone companies, employees are identified by their "Levels." At the bottom of the totem pole are craftspeople, the installers, the repair people, the trench diggers, etc. They do not have a level. They are often unionized. Management begins one level above the union. They are called first level. They are often called supervisors. Above them are second level managers. Above them are third level managers. They are called district managers. Above them are fourth level managers. They are division managers. Fifth level managers are assistant vice presidents. Sixth level managers are vice presidents. Above vice presidents, levels get fairly vague. Salary is contingent upon level. There are several levels with different salary levels within each level. It is not uncommon for AT&T or for a Bell operating company company to have as many as 16 different management levels. At one stage, there was talk about eliminating the fourth level altogether. 3. As wiring got to carry faster and faster data flows, so the quality of wiring has become increasingly important. Thus more and more companies have started specifying cabling standards. Here is a series of standards, which Anixter has promoted:

● Level 1 VOICE

Level 1 cables are MADE to meet minimum telecommunication cable requirements. Typical uses include analog and digital voice plus low speed data (20 kbps). Plenum constructions are available in shielded and unshielded designs while PVC constructions are available in shielded designs only.

● Level 2 ISDN & LOW SPEED DATA

Cables support the IBM Type 3 Media requirement. Most uses are defined through the IBM Cabling System guidelines. This specification defines electrical requirements through 1 MHz. These products are available in both plenum and PVC UTP (unshielded twisted pair) constructions. There are no shielded options in Level 2.

● Level 3 LAN & MEDIUM SPEED DATA

These products support the ANSI/EIA/TIA-568 Commercial Building Telecommunications Wiring Standard specification horizontal cable (also known as Category 3). This standard defines cable performance through 16 MHz and thus supports high speed LAN applications. Shielded constructions are available.

● Level 4 EXTENDED DISTANCE LAN

Level 4 identifies the first 100 ohm premises cables specifically designed for LAN applications. Most UTP LANs require a higher degree of performance than the standard telecommunications design offers. Level 4 cables require performance testing through 20 MHz and provide outstanding crosstalk isolation and attenuation. They are ideal for extended distance 10BaseT and 16 Mbps Token Ring. The specification for Level 4 is referenced from TIA TR41.8.1 Category 4 and NEMA "Low Loss."

● Level 5 HIGH SPEED LAN 100 OHM

This level requires the ultimate design for 100 ohm UTP cable. TIA TR4 and the NEMA Premises Wiring Task Force have recently defined this new specification for 100 ohm cable tested through 100 MHz. These cables are intended to be used up to and including 100 Mbps CDDI applications.

● HIGH SPEED LAN 150 OHM - DGM

The 150 ohm shielded twisted pair (STP) data grade media is the cornerstone of the IBM Cabling System. In addition to the many IBM applications, this cable is now supported by a consortium of five system vendors for 100 Mbps twisted pair transmission until the ANSI X3T9.5 standard is complete.

LEVEL MODE INTERRUPT A method of transmitting an Interrupt Request from a PCMCIA Card to a socket using the IREQ signal. In this mode, the IREQ signal is asserted when the Card initates an interrupt and is negated when the Host acknowledges to the PC Card that the interrupt has been serviced. The method of acknowledgment is specific to devices on the PCMCIA Card.

LEVEL SENSITIVE INTERRUPT A host system interrupt which causes repeated interrupts as long as the interrupt request signal is in the asserted state and the interrupt request is not disabled. Used in Micro Channel Architecture bus hosts and available in EISA hosts.

LEVEL-SENSITIVE INTERRUPT TRIGGER These adjustable triggers are the key to the operation of the new UART chip, called the 16550. They determine both the amount of data (in bytes) that the UART can receive before generating an interrupt request and the remaining buffer space available to store additional, incoming data. See 16550 and UART.

LF Line Feed. ASCII character 10. This character is now identified in the ASCII code set as New Line. See NEW LINE.

LGC Line Group Controller.

LIBERATION A Northern Telecom line of headsets designed for use with Meridian telephones and attendant consoles. The Liberation product line includes monaural and binaural styles. Northern Telecom says the following are traditional applications for headset use:

Receptionists. Console attendants. Telemarketers. Customer service reps. Order entry reps. Financial Service professionals. Stockbrokers. Sales reps and reservation agents.

LIBRARY 1. A file that stores related modules of complied code. 2. As in TELECOM LIBRARY Inc. the source of all good books on telecommunications, voice processing and local area networks. Ask for your FREE catalog today. Call 212-691-8215 or 1-800-LIBRARY.

LIDB Line Information Data Bases which are being developed by the Regional Bell Operating Companies and all the local phone companies will include such services as Originating Line number Screening, Calling Card Validation, Billing Number Screening, Calling Card Fraud and Public Telephone Check. The LIDB systems contain all valid telephone and calling card numbers in their regions, and have the necessary information to perform billing validation. The LIDB systems operational. A national system connecting them all together started working at the beginning of 1992.

LIFE CYCLE A test performed on a material or configuration to determine the length of time before failure in a controlled, usually accelerated, environment.

LIFELINE SERVICE A minimal telephone service designed for the poor and elderly to assure they can be reached by phone and have a "Lifeline" to the world in case of emergency. The basic rate for this limited service is less than standard rates and varies by state. Typically, Lifeline Service entitles you to a phone line, a listing in the directory and a minimal number of outgoing local calls, e.g. 10. Some people who are neither poor nor elderly, subscribe to Lifeline Service and use it for incoming calls — for an answering machine or a computer electronic mail or bulletin boards. There's no difference in the quality of service provided by Lifeline Rates and normal phone lines.

LIFO Last In First Out. A method of organizing queues. See LAST IN FIRST OUT.

LIGHT Technically, light is electromagnetic radiation visible to the human eye. The term is also applied to electromagnetic radiation with properties similar to visible light, including the invisible near-infrared "light" (or more technically correct, radiation) that carries signals in most fiber optic communication systems. Light consists of electro-magnetic waves ordinarily applied to those having a wave length of from .000075 cm. (the red ray) to .000038 cm. (the violet ray).

LIGHT EMITTING DIODE See LED.

LIGHT PEN A video terminal input device which is a light sensitive stylus connected by a cable to the video terminal. The user brings it to the desired point on the screen surface and presses a button. A light pen is used to select options from a menu on the screen or to draw images by dragging the cursor around the screen on a graphics terminal.

LIGHT PIPING Use of optical fibers to illuminate.

LIGHTGATE SERVICE A BellSouth INtraLATA optical fiber-based private line services that allows high-volume customers integrated voice, data and video transmission. Lightgate is the equivalent of 672 voice or data, private line or dial up circuits.

LIGHTWAVE COMMUNICATIONS (Fiber Optic) Communications using light to carry information.

LIGHTWAVE TRANSMISSION This term now means laser communications systems shot through the air (as opposed to glass fiber). Also called "free space lightwave communications." Typically, a signal is radiated directly from a light transmitter to a receiver less than a mile away. Advantages to lightwave transmission: easy to install, no digging of cables, wide bandwidth, reliable, cheap, no FCC frequency clearance approvals required and the receiving and transmitting equipment occupy little space. Disadvantages: only works for a mile or so and is subject to attenuation (fading) from fog and dust. It's perfect for between downtown buildings, where installing cables is too expensive, too cumbersome, too slow, etc. See LASER.

LIKE NEW REPAIR AND UPDATE LNRU. A term in the industry which repairs telecom equipment. It means all equipment is repaired and updated to the current manufacturer's specifications. New plastic is used to refurbish to a "like new" status. Also added are a new coil cord, line cord and address tray. Included is a full diagnostic test with a burn-in (if required) and an operational system test. Definition courtesy Nitsuko America. See also REPAIR AND QUICK CLEAN and REPAIR, UPDATE AND REFURBISH.

LIM-EMS The abbreviation for Lotus Intel Microsoft-Expanded Memory Specification. A software technique that allows MS-DOS to access memory beyond one megabyte by mapping the memory into a window in an area that MS-DOS can access. LIMS-EMS is one of the greatest techniques for speeding up getting in and out of programs. For example, when my calendar program called Maxi-Calendar is not running, it occupies only 7K of normal RAM and 350K of expanded RAM. When I need it, it swaps itself quickly out of expanded RAM into normal RAM, taking less than half a second. If I didn't have expanded memory, it would take as long as 15 seconds to swap the program onto and off my hard disk, which is the other alternative. LIM stands for Lotus/Intel/Microsoft, the founding organizations that developed the Expanded Memory Specification. AST Research was also part of the driving force behind EMS, though its name doesn't appear in the acronym.

LIMITED DISTANCE MODEM LDM. A special-purpose conversion device designed to connect two DTEs (data communications devices) over a relatively short distance, typically up to several miles. An LDM is not really a modem since it does not perform a digital-to-analog conversion, but transmits a special type of digital signal to the other LDM on the circuit. Also called a line driver, local dataset or short-haul modem.

LIMITER A circuit which shapes a signal sent through it to conform to certain preset tolerances, used in both audio and video to regulate signal flow and prevent overloading, which would lead to distortion and the introduction of spurious noise.

LINE An electrical path (two wires) between a phone company central office and a subscriber, usually with an individual phone number that can be used for incoming and outgoing calls.

LINE BUILD OUT Because T-1 circuits require the last span to lose 15-22.5 dB, a selectable out put attenuation is generally required of DTE equipment (typical selections include O.O, 7.5, and 15 dB of loss at 772 KHz).

LINE CARD A plug-in electronic Printed Circuit (PC) card that operates lamps, ringing, holding and other features associated with one or several telephone lines or telephones in a telephone system.

LINE CIRCUIT The sensor in the CO which detects and advises the switching system that one of its subscribers has gone off-hook and wishes to make a call. One line circuit is dedicated to each line of each subscriber.

LINE CONDITIONING A service offered by telephone companies to reduce envelope delay, noise and amplitude distortion. By doing this, you allow for transmission of higher speed data than over a traditional dial-up phone line.

LINE CORD The connecting cord between the phone and the jack in the wall.

LINE CURRENT Electrical current measured on an idle telephone line. Typical range is 20 - 100 ma DC, with 40 - 50 ma considered optimum for proper operation of phone equipment.

LINE DISCIPLINE Archaic term for communications protocol.

LINE DRIVER A short haul communications device used when cable lengths between RS-232 devices begin to the alleged 50-foot RS-232 limit. A line driver is a signal converter that conditions the digital signal transmitted by an RS-232 interface to ensure reliable transmission beyond the 50-foot RS-232 limit and often up to several miles; it is a baseband transmission device. Also called baseband modem, limited distance modem, or short-haul modem. See also LIMITED DISTANCE MODEM.

LINE EQUIPMENT Equipment in a central office which is there to serve one phone line. That line equipment includes a line relay or equivalent which starts to work when the customer's telephone goes off-hook.

LINE FEED The act of moving a cursor or the head or a printer or telex machine down one line. These days, on the keyboards of most equipment — Personal Computers, etc. — there's no single key that says "Line Feed." There's usually a key that's labelled "Enter" or "Return." This key does two functions — a line feed and a carriage return (i.e. sending the print head or cursor to the left hand side of the carriage or the screen). In many (but not all) programs, a line feed is control J or ASCII character 10. The name for this character has been changed to New Line. See NEW LINE.

LINE FINDER The first switching element of a step-by-step phone system which recognizes a calling party is waiting for dial tone to make a call, identifies the party, and connects that party to the switching system so that the processing of the call may begin. Normally line finders serve 100 or 200 subscriber lines.

LINE HIT Electrical interference that causes a hit, that is, a loss or introduction of spurious bits into a data stream.

LINE HOLD Provides a winking, blinking flash on the line lamp at every telephone which has the line appearing on it.

LINE INSULATION TEST LIT. A test performed from the central office, which measures resistance and voltages on local lines to find faults.

LINE LINK FRAME LLF. An arrangement that permits a crossbar office to transmit dial pulse information over a line to a PBX for switching Direct Inward Dial (DID) calls to the indicated phone. See CROSSBAR SWITCHING

LINE LOCKOUT When a phone stays off-hook for longer than a predetermined time, line lockout provides some loud noise and then puts the phone line out of service — until someone puts the phone back on hook again.

LINE NOISE Spurious signals introduced into a line by static, or other imbalances in the circuit. Line Noise is the most common cause of "Hits" or problems in data calls.

LINE OF SIGHT Some through the air transmission media — such as microwave, infrared, and laser — operate at a frequency which transmit in a perfectly straight line. Or in "line of sight." In other words, the area between a transmitter and a receiver must be clear of obstructions.

LINE POOL A Line Pool is a specific group of lines in certain key systems used for making outside calls. In Northern Telecom's Norstar, three Line

Pools give phone access to outside lines without taking up too many Line buttons on each phone instrument.

LINE POWERED Telephone equipment that is powered solely by the CO talk battery supplied in a standard phone line.

LINE PREFERENCE User selects the line to be used simply by pressing the button associated with that line.

LINE PRINTER A type of printer which prints an entire line of text at one time. This printer is obviously a high speed printer. It is used, for example, to print TELECONNECT Magazine's monthly mailing list

LINE PROTOCOL Rules for controlling transmission on a synchronous data transmission line. Includes rules for bidding for the line, for positive and negative acknowledgements, requests for retransmission, and transmitter time-outs.

LINE QUEUING Dial an outside line (typically a long distance line). It's busy. Your phone system will put you in queue for that line. The queue might involve your waiting a few seconds on hold; or it might involve your hanging up and having the phone system call you back. There are thus two types of Line Queuing — hold-on and callback queuing.

LINE RINGING Provides the user with an audible indication of a call on a specific line that appears on his/her telephone.

LINE SIDE CONNECTION A connection of a transmission path to the customer side of a local exchange switching system.

LINE SPEED The maximum number of bits you can transmit over a line in a certain defined time, say one second.

LINE STATUS INDICATION Provides a visual indication on an ECTS (electronic telephone set) telephone of the idle, busy, ringing or held state for each line appearing on the telephone.

LINE SWITCHING Another term for circuit switching. See CIRCUIT SWITCHING and SWITCHING.

LINE TURNAROUND TIME The delay in a circuit as the direction of communications changes, usually in half duplex communications. When one side of the communications stops sending, there is a delay before the other party stars sending in return. This is the Line Turnaround delay.

LINE VOLTAGE Voltage measured on a telephone circuit; typically 48 volts DC when phone is idle. Voltage may be lower at great distance from the central office, or when carrier equipment is used to multiplex several phone lines on one pair of wires. Line voltage on PBX systems is typically 24 volts.

LINEAR DISTORTION Amplitude distortion wherein the output signal envelope is not proportional to the input signal envelope. This distortion is often caused by part of the signal being bounced off something, while part arrives free and clear. Thus the receiver hears the same signal but bits of it arrive earlier and later than other bits, causing distortion. Anyone coming across a more understandable definition, please send it to the editors for the next edition.

LINEAR PREDICTIVE CODING A speech coding method that analyzes a speech waveform to produce a time-varying filter as a model of the human vocal tract. See also Digital Signal Processing.

LINEAR PROGRAMMING Techniques in Operations Research (OR) to find an optimum solution to a linear function, given certain restrictions and typically expressed in many equations. A typical linear programming problem might be to find the least expensive, most efficient route between various pick-up and drop-off points in a transportation route.

LINEARITY The straightness of a frequency response curve as an indication of true or accurate sound reproduction. In an A/D (Analog to Digital) or D/A (Digital to Analog), linearity measures the precision with which the digital output/input tracks the analog input/output.

LINEARLY POLARIZED A mode of operation of fiber optics for which the field components in the direction of propagation are small compared to components perpendicular to that direction.

LINEMAN'S CLIMBERS Telephone pole climbing irons which are strapped to the telephone lineman's legs, allowing him or her to climb a wooden telephone line. You can tell when a pole has been climbed by the holes left in it by the lineman's climbers.

LINES A computer imaging term. The line tool draws straight lines, typically from point to point. Most paint packages let you continue lines in a fashion that permits rapid creation of polygons.

LINES OF FORCE The directional lines of magnetic or static field which represent the stresses.

LINES PER MINUTE The way of measuring the speed of a line printer. Like any measure of speed, the speed you will get from your printer may be different from what the manufacturer says. Your speed will depend on how fast you feed the printer from your computer — a function of how fast you're transmitting, what software you're running, how fast that software can get the information to be printed off your disk, etc.

LINK 1. Another name for a communications channel or circuit. 2. A Windows command that takes several programs and subprograms that were meant to be used together, but were written separately, and combines them into one. Usually used to create an executable program out of modules that were not themselves directly executable.

LINK ATTACHED Describing devices that are connected to a network, a communications data link, or telecommunications circuit; compare with channel-attached.

LINK CONVERTER A device for an InteCom S/80 which connects distributed switching modules to the centralized switching equipment through a coaxial cable or a fiber optic cable.

LINK LAYER ACCESS METHOD The algorithm that determines when any given network interface in a PC/TCP local area network is allowed to transmit. It is also known as the access method. CSMA/CD is the access method for the Ethernet.

LINK PROTOCOL The set of rules by which a logical data link is set up and by which data transfers across the link. It includes formatting of the data.

LINK SET A group of signaling links directly connecting two signaling points.

LINK TIME This is a specific time delay that allows access to PBX or Centrex features through a telephone system. Link Time is also referred to as a Hookswitch Flash or Recall.

LINKS The transmission portion of the local loop.

LIQUID CRYSTAL DISPLAY LCD. A low power display that aligns material suspended in a liquid under the influence of a low voltage so it reflects ambient light and displays alphanumeric characters. LCD displays are finding great use as methods of displaying information on new electronic telephones, especially those positioned behind PBXs. The advantage of putting such displays on telephones is that the power to drive the display is very small. The display can be line powered — i.e. powered by the one or two pairs coming from the PBX. This avoids the necessity and cost of a transformer/rectifier — the little black box you plug into the wall to run your answering machine or to power up your rechargeable calculator/laptop computer. Such LCD displays on electronic phones can perform many functions. The most useful is that of "walking" the user through the phone call — showing him/her how to transfer a call, to make a conference call, to split a conference, etc. An LCD can also alert you as to who's calling you.

LISTED DIRECTORY NUMBER LDN. Incoming exchange network calls to the PBX via assigned listed local telephone directory number are directed to the attendant.

LIT See LINE INSULATION TEST.

LIVE BUG Colloquialism used to refer to a leaded integrated circuit package when the leads are down, like a bug that is alive and standing upright.

LIVELOCK A request for an exclusive lock that is repeatedly denied because a series of overlapping shared locks in a shared database keeps interfering. A SQL server will detect the situation after several denials, and refuse further shared locks.

LIVEWARE People.

LLB Line LoopBack. A maintenance and/or diagnostic mode of operation whereby a CSU regenerates a signal received from a span line and retransmits that signal back onto the span towards its point of origin.

LLC Logical Link Control. A protocol developed by the IEEE 802.2 committee for data-link-level transmission control. It is the upper sublayer of the IEEE Layer 2 (OSI) protocol that complements the MAC protocol. IEEE standard 802.2 includes end-system addressing and error checking. It also provides a common access control standard and governs the assembly of data packets and their exchange between data stations independent of how the packets are transmitted on the LAN. See 802 STANDARDS.

LLF 1. Line Link Frame. See CROSSBAR SWITCHING. 2. Low Layer Functions.

LMDS LEC Message Distribution System.

LMI Local Management Interface. A specification for the use of frame-relay products that define a method of exchanging status information between devices such as routers.

LMOS Loop Maintenance Operations System.

LMSS Land Mobile Satellite Service.

LMU Line Monitor Unit.

LNA Low Noise Amplifier.

LNRU Like New Repair and Update. A term in the industry which repairs telecom equipment. It means all equipment is repaired and updated to the current manufacturer's specifications. New plastic is used to refurbish to a "like new" status. Also added are a new coil cord, line cord and address tray. Included is a full diagnostic test with a burn-in (if required) and an operational system test. Definition courtesy Nitsuko America. See also REPAIR AND QUICK CLEAN and REPAIR, UPDATE AND REFURBISH.

LOAD 1. The act of taking a program or data from external storage — a cassette, a floppy or hard disk, etc. and storing it in the computer's main RAM memory. 2. The load is any electric or electronic appliance or gadget plugged into an AC electrical outlet. It completes the circuit from the transformer through the hot conductor, to the load, through the neutral conductor and back to the utility transformer. See AC, AC POWER, GROUND and GROUNDING.

LOAD BALANCING The practice of splitting communication into two (or more) routes. By balancing the traffic on each route, communication is made faster and more reliable. In telephone systems, you can change phone and trunk terminations in order to even out traffic on the network. An example: You have a PBX of three separate cabinets, each of which are joined by tie lines. Instead of having each cabinet serve anyone in the building, you might figure which groups talk to each other the most and concentrate them into specific cabinets. The objective is to maximize the number of calls that can be handled inside each cabinet and reduce the number of calls that need to travel between the cabinets. This makes the calls go faster and reduces the need for inter- cabinet lines.

In data internetworking, bridges and routers perform load balancing by splitting LAN-to-LAN traffic among two or more WAN links. This allows for the combination of several lower speed lines to transmit higher-speed LAN data simultaneously. In local area networking, load balancing is a function performed by token ring routers.

LOAD COIL An inductor used to increase the inductance of a pair of metal wires in a local loop. The use of the inductor improves the voice transmission characteristics of the loop, but it must be removed if you are running digitally over the line. See LOADING and LOADING COIL.

LOAD LEVELING Distributing traffic over more than one route.

LOAD NUMBER Load number is the Canadian equivalent of the U.S. concept of Ringer Equivalence. The idea is that each phone or "phone thing" you buy (e.g. answering machine) comes with a number. You add the numbers together and if you get above a certain number, you are drawing too much current and none of the bells on the phones will ring. In Canada, single line phones are typically rated at 10 for the newer ones with electronic "bells" or 20 for the older electro-mechanical ones with real metal bells. In Canada, the rule is not more than 100 points on a line. In the U.S., phones are typically one and the rule is not more than five points on a line.

LOAD SHARING In data processing, load sharing is the technique of using two computers to balance the processing normally assigned to one of them. In local area networking, load sharing is performed by token ring routers when connecting remote LANs. It allows combining Ethernet and Token Ring traffic over a common WAN (Wide Area Network) link such as T1 or 56 kbps circuit. Loads sharing eliminates the need for duplicate WAN links (and bridges or routers) each serving a different type of LAN.

LOADED LINE A telephone line equipped with loading coils to add inductance in order to minimize amplitude distortion. See LOADING and LOADING COIL.

LOADING A method of improving the voice quality of a phone line. Telephone companies put load coils on local lines. What this loading does is to insert inductance in a local loop circuit to offset the effect of capacitance in the cable. Loading "tunes" the circuit to the voice frequency band (500 to 2500 Hz) and thus improves the quality at the expense of overall bandwidth. You usually have to ask that the loading coils be removed if you're planning to transmit high-speed data exclusively on that circuit. See LOADING COIL.

LOADING COIL An induction device employed in local loops exceeding 18,000 feet in length, that compensates for wire capacitance and boosts voice grade frequencies. Loading coils are often removed for higher speed data services, as distortion will occur at frequencies higher than those used for voice. See LOADING.

LOADING HIGH A memory management verb for loading a device driver or TSR (Terminate and Stay Resident) program into upper memory, out of conventional memory. Under DOS, the loading high commands are DEVICEHIGH for device drivers and LOADHIGH (or LH) for TSRs. Third-party memory managers use their own routines to load high, though they can sometimes borrow DOS commands.

LOCAL ACCESS TRANSPORT AREA LATA. The geographical area within which a Local Exchange Company (a local phone company) can provide communications services. California is divided into 10 LATAs. Currently, local phone companies, such as Pac Bell, have a monopoly on all calls, including toll calls, made within a LATA.

LOCAL AREA AND TRANSPORT AREA See LATA.

LOCAL AREA DATA TRANSPORT LADT. A service of your local phone company which provides you, the user, with synchronous data communications.

LOCAL AREA NETWORK LAN. A short distance data communications network (typically within a building or campus) used to link computers and peripheral devices (such as printers, CD-ROMs, modems) under some form of standard control. Older data communications networks used dumb terminals (devices with no computing power) to talk to distant computers. But the economics of computing changed with the invention of the personal computer which had "intelligence" and which was cheap. LANs were invented as an afterthought — after PCs — and were originally designed to let cheap PCs share peripherals — like laser printers — which were too expensive to to dedicate to individual PCs. And as time went on, what LANs were used for got broader and broader. Today, LANs have four main advantages: 1. Anyone on the LAN can use any of the peripheral devices connected to the LAN. 2. Anyone on the LAN can access databases and programs running on client servers (super powerful PCs) attached to the LAN; and 3. Anyone on the LAN can send messages to and work jointly with others on the LAN. 4. While a LAN does not use common carrier circuits, it may have gateways and/or bridges to public telecommunications networks. See LAN MANAGER, TOKEN RING and ETHERNET.

LOCAL AREA SIGNALING SERVICES LASS is a group of central office features provided now by virtually all central office switch makers that uses existing customer lines to provide some extra features to the end user (typically a business user). They are based on delivery of calling party number via the local signaling network. LASS can be implemented on a stand-alone single central office basis for intraoffice calls or on a multiple central office grouping in a LATA (what the local phone companies are allowed to serve) for interoffice calls. Local CCS7 (Common Channel Signaling Seven) is required for all configurations. The following features typically make up LASS:

● Automatic Callback: Lets the customer automatically call the last incoming call directory number associated with the customer's phone when both phones become idle. This feature gives the customer the ability to camp-on to a line.

● Automatic Recall: Lets the customer automatically call the last outgoing call currently associated with the customer's station when both stations become idle. This feature gives the customer the ability to camp-on to a line.

● Customer-Originated Trace: Lets the terminating party request an automatic trace of the last call received. The trace includes the calling line directory number and time and date of the call. This information is transmitted via an AM IOP channel to a designated agency, such as the telephone company or law enforcement agency.

● Individual Calling Line Identification: Consists of two distinct features: 1. Calling Number Delivery which transmits data on an incoming call to the terminating phone. 2. Directory Number Privacy which prevents delivery of the directory number to the terminating phone.

Also, LASS has some selective features:

● Selective Call Acceptance: Allows users to restrict which incoming voice calls can terminate, based on the identity attribute of the calling party. Only calls from parties identified on a screening lists are allowed to terminate. Calls from parties not specified on a screening list are rerouted to an appropriate announcement or forwarded to an alternate directory number.

● Selective Call Forwarding: Allows a customer to preselect which calls are forwarded based on the identity attribute of the calling party.

● Selective Call Rejection: Allows a customer to reject incoming voice calls from identity attributes which are on the customer's rejection list. Call attempts from parties specified on the rejection list are prevented from terminating to the customer and are routed to an announcement which informs the caller that his/her call is not presently being accepted by the called party.

● Selective Distinctive Alert: Allows a customer to preselect which voice calls are to be provided distinctive alerting treatment based on the identify attributes of the calling party.

Users can, at their convenience, activate or modify any of these features by sending commands to the central switch from their existing touchtone telephones.

LOCAL AUTOMATIC MESSAGE ACCOUNTING LAMA. A combination of automatic message accounting equipment and automatic number identification equipment in your telephone company's central office and used by them to bill your local phone calls.

LOCAL BATTERY Having "local battery" means the telecom equipment — the telephone, the PBX, the key system, etc. — has its own source of power and does not draw from the power coming down the phone line. The term came from telegraphy and was used to distinguish the battery which provided power to the telegraphic station as against the power that went to drive the line and the signal traveling down it. See BATTERY.

LOCAL BUS A Local Bus is a new type of motherboard which allows your display card to have direct access to the microprocessor and permits the transfer of data at the same speed as the system clock. Local Bus is an emerging standard. Computers that do not have Local Bus capability are hobbled with an 8 MHz transfer speed for ISA and EISA machines and 10 MHZ for MicroChannel (PS/2) machines. See VESA.

LOCAL CALL Any call within the local service area of the calling phone. Individual local calls may or may not cost money. In many parts of the US, the phone company bills its local service as a "flat" monthly fee. This means you can make as many local calls per month as you wish and not pay extra. Increasingly this luxury is dying and individual calls are costing money.

LOCAL CALL ACCOUNTING Computes the dollar amount for local calls based on the total message units stored for each phone.

LOCAL CALL BILLING Computes the dollar amount for local calls placed by guests based on total message units.

LOCAL CENTRAL OFFICE Switching office in which a subscriber's lines terminate.

LOCAL CHANNEL CONTROLLER An AT&T name for its family of 3270 compatible cluster controllers.

LOCAL COMPOSITE LOOPBACK In network management systems. Composite loopback test that forms the loop at the output of the local multiplexor that returns transmitted signals to their source. See also loopback.

LOCAL DATASET Signal converter that conditions the digital signal transmitted by an RS-232 interface to ensure reliable transmission over a dc continuous metallic circuit without interfering with adjacent pairs in the same telephone cable. Normally conforms with Bell 43401. Also called baseband modem, limited distance modem, local modem, or short-haul modem. See also line driver.

LOCAL DISTRIBUTION FRAME LDF. Another word for an Intermediate Distribution Frame. It's a device for cross connecting cables — from one thing to another. On one side of the LDF are the pairs from individual phones in that part of the building or area. On the other side are trunks coming in from a central office or cables coming in from the central, larger PBX. LDFs typically help with the organization of cables in a building or area. See also INTERMEDIATE DISTRIBUTION FRAME.

LOCAL EXCHANGE The telephone company exchange where subscribers lines are terminated. Also called an "End Office."

LOCAL EXCHANGE CARRIER A local phone company. See also LEC.

LOCAL HEAP A memory storage area limited to 64K in size.

LOCAL LOOP The physical wires that run from the subscriber's telephone set, or PBX or key telephone system, to the telephone company central office. Increasingly, the local loop now goes from the main distribution frame in the basement to the phone company. And the subscriber is responsible for getting his/her wires from the box in the basement to his phone, PBX or key system.

LOCAL MANAGEMENT INTERFACE LMI. A specification for the use of frame-relay products that define a method of exchanging status information between devices such as routers.

LOCAL MEASURED SERVICE LMS. Years ago virtually all phone lines in the United States were FLAT RATE. That meant that for a fixed amount of money each month, you, the customer (a.k.a. subscriber) were allowed to make as many local calls as you wanted. For many reasons, the U.S. phone industry has progressively moved to LOCAL MEASURED SERVICE for local calls. Typically this means that for a fixed amount of money each month, you, the customer, can receive as many calls as you want and can make a finite number of outgoing local calls — typically 50. Each additional call beyond the 50 (or whatever the number is) costs extra. How much that call costs depends on the distant the call travels, the time of day, the day of the week, and the local company's tariffs.

LOCAL NET The broadband architecture used in Sytek's work. Also the product name of their network. Sytek is in Sunnyvale, CA.

LOCAL ORDER WIRE A communications circuit between a technical control center and selected terminal or repeater locations.

LOCAL PRINTER A printer that is directly connected to one of the ports on your computer.

LOCAL SERVICE AREA The geographic area that telephones may call without incurring toll charges. A flat rate calling area. Increasingly rare.

LOCAL TANDEM A central office, usually in large metropolitan areas, serving as a transit switch between noncontiguous class 5 exchanges. It connects end office trunks.

LOCAL TEST DESK A testing system that is used to test local loops and central office subscriber line equipment from a central point, typically a central office.

LOCAL TRUNK Trunks between Class 5 offices (local central offices)

LOCALTALK Apple Computer's proprietary local area network for linking Macintosh computers and peripherals, especially LaserWriter printers is called Appletalk. AppleTalk's LAN hardware is called LocalTalk. Appletalk is a CSMA/CD network that runs at 230.4 kilo bits per second and is therefore, incompatible with any other local area network. It is also a lot slower than the present top speeds of Ethernet (10 Mbps) and Token Ring (16 Mbps). Outside manufacturers, however, make gateways which will connect an Appletalk LAN to other local area and telecommunications networks — LANs, WANs and MANs. See also APPLETALK.

LOCATION One definition is the place where a telephone jack is located. This location is given a number. The wire going to that location is given a number. All this in hope of being organized for installation, moves, changes and maintenance.

LOCK ON The process by which an earth station initially acquires the signal from a satellite.

LOCK OUT In a satellite telephone circuit controlled by an echo suppressor, one or both subscribers can't get through because of excessive noise at one end. You get this also with speakerphones. The person with the speakerphone can simply hog the conversation because his speakerphone keeps transmitting his voice. There are weird variations on this. Sometimes you might call someone on your speakerphone and wait for them to pick up. They do. They shout into the phone "I'm here." All they can hear is you at the other end talking or typing. The sound at your end is hogging the channel and thus locking out the person at the other end. The solution? Turn the "mute" button on your speakerphone. This will stop your end transmitting and allow the other end to say "Hello, I'm here."

LOCKER Telco-speak for a storage area, often an urban storefront, where phone company installers and repairman can pick up and drop off tools and installation material such as phones, wire and hardware. These places are prime targets for burglary and robbery, and often have no identification to show their valuable contents.

LOCKING Preventing several people getting to and changing the same data in a shared database simultaneously. Locks may be permanent and prevent access completely, or they may be "advisory." A user is warned the data is being used by someone else and that the data is not presently available. Locks prevent the destruction of data that can occur if two people access a file at the same time. In any data base or other computer system, there are typically two types of "locks" — record and file locks. A record lock occurs when an airline agent pulls up your travel plans. No other travel agent can access those records at that time. A file lock occurs when the whole file is locked up. This might occur in a centralized word processing program. The whole document will be locked when it is being used by someone.

LOCKOUT A PBX feature. Denies the attendant the ability to re-enter an incoming central office connection directly terminated or held on her position, unless specifically recalled by the phone user.

LOG IN The process of identifying and authenticating oneself to a computer system. Used to control access to computer systems.

LOG OFF To type in the needed keystrokes for ending a session that's on-line with a computer. Often those keystrokes are "Logoff." Usually it's very easy to Log Off. It's more difficult to Log On.

LOG ON To enter the needed keystrokes to start an on-line session with a computer. "Logging On" may be done with a computer that's local or one that's long distance and your work is done over communications lines.

LOGICAL BLOCK ADDRESS A logical block address is a sequential address for accessing blocks on storage media. The first block of the media is addressed as block O and succeeding blocks are numbered sequentially until the last block is encountered. This is the traditional method for accessing peripherals on a SCSI bus.

LOGIC BOMB Program routine that destroys data. For example, a logic bomb may reformat the hard disk or insert random bits into data files. It may be brought into a personal computer by downloading a corrupt public-domain program. Once executed, it does its damage right away and then stops, whereas a virus keeps on destroying.

LOGICAL BUS A LAN topology, such as Ethernet, which shares a common communications channel.

LOGICAL CHANNEL X.25 concept referring to a virtual connection operated over a physical connection that can support one or more virtual connections simultaneously.

LOGICAL CHANNEL NUMBER Virtual circuit identified at the packet level of X.25. See LOGICAL CHANNEL.

LOGICAL DRIVE A drive that has been created by the disk operating system (DOS). This is done either at the preference of the user or because the DOS version does not allow a formatted capacity in excess of 32Mb. A user with a 100Mb hard disk will want to use more than 32Mb so a program will tell DOS there are a bunch of "logical" drives that add up to 100 megabytes. DOS 5.0 eliminates this need.

LOGICAL FORMATTING The third step in structuring a data medium so that data may be written to it. Logical formatting must follow physical formatting (also called low-level formatting) and partitioning (figuring into how many drives you wanted to slice the one drive into).

LOGICAL ID An AT&T Merlin term. A numbering sequence used to identify station and trunk locations on the communications system control unit.

LOGICAL LINK A virtual circuit concept of DNA, existing at the End communications and Session control layer above.

LOGICAL LINK CONTROL LLC; A protocol developed by the IEEE 802 committee, common to all of its LAN standards, for data link-level transmission control; the upper sublayer of the IEEE Layer 2 (OSI) protocol that complements the MAC protocol; IEEE standard 802.2; includes end-system addressing and error checking.

LOGICAL PROVISIONING An AT&T term for the establishment of network services by changing software controls, rather than by physically installing or rearranging hardware.

LOGICAL RING A network which is treated logically as a ring even though it maybe cabled as a physical star topology.

LOGICAL UNIT INTERFACE See LU 6.2.

LOGICIEL French for software.

LOGIN SCRIPT When users log into a local area network, they may wish to do many things or the network supervisor may wish them to do several things. These commands are part of something called a "login script." In computerize (Novell's words), a login script contains commands that initialize environmental variables, map network drives, and/or control the user's program execution. Login scripts are similar to batch files. The familiar AUTOEXEC.BAT can be thought of as an MS-DOS login script.

LOI Letter of Intent

LONG DISTANCE Any telephone call to a location outside the local service area. Also called toll call or trunk call.

LONG HAUL COMMUNICATIONS That type of phone call which reaches outside a local exchange or serving area.

LONG REACH Long reach refers to optical sections of approximately 25 km or more in length and is applicable to all SONET rates.

LONG WAVELENGTH Light whose wavelength is greater than about 1 um.

LONGEST AVAILABLE This is a method of distributing incoming calls to a bunch of people. This method selects an agent based on the amount of time that each agent has been on the phone. This allows for an equitable distribution of calls to each agent. See also TOP DOWN and ROUND ROBIN.

LONGITUDINAL BALANCE A measure of the electrical balance between the two conductors (tip and ring) of a telephone circuit; specifically, the difference between the tip-to-ground and ring-to-ground AC signal voltages, expressed in decibels.

LONGITUDINAL REDUNDANCY CHECK LRC. 1. An error checking

technique based on an accumulated collection of transmitted characters. An LRC character is accumulated at both the sending and receiving stations during the transmission of a block. This accumulation is called the Block Check Character (BCC) and is transmitted in the last character in the block. The transmitted BCC is compared with the accumulated BCC character at the receiving station for an equal condition. When they're equal, you know your transmission of that block has been fine. 2. A method of error detection that collects and clocks parity for each code level. Traditionally, magnetic tape recording is done in a number of tracks equivalent to the number of bits per character; LRC then collects parity for each track. Parity is a two-level (odd/even) information element.

LONGITUDINAL TRANSMISSION CHECK LTC. An even or odd parity check at fixed intervals during data transmission.

LONGITUDINAL WRAP A tape applied longitudinally with the axis of the core being covered, a opposed to a helical, or spiral, tape wrapped core.

LONG LINES AT&T Long Lines. The department of AT&T which operates long distance toll service. It is no longer called Long Lines. It is called AT&T Communications.

LOOK-UP TABLE 1. A translation table. You dial a certain number. But the number is meaningless. For the phone system to complete the call, it needs routing instructions. It gets that by "looking up" that number in a table, which translates that number to another number that is now meaningful to the switching network. There are lots of applications for Look-up Tables. Least Cost Routing tables are essentially look up tables. IN-WATS dialing works by looking up the 800 number and finding its real ten digit normal number. Most private networks use look up tables to translate the number dialed by the internal user into a number that the network can recognize. 2.A set of addresses (source and destination) used by a bridge or router to determine what should be done with a packet. As the packet comes in, its address information is read and compared with the information in the look-up table. Depending on the information, the bridge may forward the packet, or discard it, leaving it for the local lan. Many bridges and routers can build their look-up tables as they operate. See also 800 SERVICE, EIGHTHUNDRED SERVICE, BRIDGE, PERSONAL 800 NUMBER and ROUTER.

LOOP 1. Typically a complete electrical circuit. 2. The loop is also the pair of wires that winds its way from the central office to the telephone set or system at the customer's office, home or factory, i.e. "premises" in telephones. 3. In computer software. A loop repeats a series of instructions many times until some prestated event has happened or until some test has been passed.

LOOP ANTENNA An antenna consisting of one or more complete turns of wire, both ends of which are to be connected to the input circuit of the radio receiver.

LOOP BACK A diagnostic test in which a signal is transmitted across a medium while the sending device waits for its return. See LOOKBACK.

LOOP CHECKING A method of checking the accuracy of transmission of data in which the received data are returned to the sending end for comparison with the original data.

LOOP CIRCUIT Generally refers to the circuit connecting the subscriber's set with the local switching equipment.

LOOP CURRENT DETECTION When a modem, telephone or fax card (etc.) seizes the line (i.e. completes the connectio between tip and ring terminals of the telephone cable) current flows from the positive battery supply in the telephone central office, through the twisted pair in the loop, through the card (or phone) and back to the central office negative terminal where it is detected, showing that this telephone or telephone device is off hook. The fax card or modem can detect problems such as disconnnects, shutting down the connection or a busy signal.

LOOP EXTENDER Device in the central office that supplies augmented voltage out to subscribers who are at considerable distances. It provides satisfactory signaling and speech for such subscribers.

LOOP PLANT Telco-talk for all the wires and hardware and poles and manholes used to connect their central offices to their customers.

LOOP SIGNALING SYSTEMS Any of three types of signaling which transmit signaling information over the metallic loop formed by the trunk conductors and the terminating equipment bridges.

LOOP START LS. You "start" (seize) a phone line or trunk by giving it a supervisory signal. That signal is typically taking your phone off hook. There are two ways you can do that — ground start or loop start. With loop start, you seize a line by bridging through a resistance the tip and ring (both wires) of your telephone line.

LOOP TEST A way of testing a circuit to find a fault in it by completing a loop and sending a signal around that loop. See LOOPBACK.

LOOP THROUGH A type of phone system wiring that allows phones to connect to one cable in parallel going to the common central switching equipment. The most common type of Loop Through wiring is that which you have in your home. You have one cable with two conductors — a red and a green — winding through your home. Whenever you want to connect a phone, you simply attach it to the red and green conductors. The other way of connecting phones is called HOME RUN. In that system, every phone has its own one, two or three pairs of conductors which wind their lonely way back to the central PBX or key system cabinet. In Loop Through wiring, many phones share one set of cables. In Home Run Cabling, only one phone sits on that line.

LOOP TIMING A way of synchronizing a circuit that works by taking a synchronizing clock signal from incoming digital pulses.

LOOP UP/LOOP DOWN In T-1, there are generally two loopback types, LLB (line loopback) and TLB or DLB (terminal or DTE loopback). Loop Up refers to activating one of these loop backs, where as Loop Down refers to deactivating one of these loopbacks.

LOOPBACK Type of diagnostic test in which the transmitted signal is returned to the sending device after passing through a data communications link or network. This allows a technician (or built-in diagnostic circuit) to compare the returned signal with the transmitted signal and get some sense of what's wrong. Loopbacks are often done by excluding one piece of equipment after another. This allows you to figure out logically what's wrong. (It's called Sherlock Holmes deductive reasoning.) See LOOPBACK TEST.

LOOPBACK TEST A test typically run on a four-wire circuit. You take the two transmit leads and join them to the two receive leads. Then you put a signal around the loop and see what happens. Measuring differences between the sent and the received signal is the essence of a loopback test. See LOOPBACK.

LOOPING Problem encountered in distributed datagram routing in which packets return to a previously visited node.

LOOSE TUBE BUFFER A cable construction in which the optical fiber is placed in a plastic tube having an inner diameter much larger than the fiber itself. The loose tube isolates the fiber from the exterior mechanical forces acting on the cable. The space between the tube and the fiber is often filled with a gel to cushion the fiber.

LOOSELY COUPLED A computer system architecture consisting of multiple computer systems, each with its own dedicated memory and its own copy of the operating system, connected over a communications link. See also TIGHTLY COUPLED.

LORAN A radio-navigation system which helps you find where you are. It works by timing times the difference in reception of pulses from one or more fixed transmitters, usually on land. It's a radio based systems that's pretty good for coastal waters where there are LORAN transmitters. But it won't work further than 1,000 miles offshore. And it doesn't cover much of the rest of the earth and its accuracy varies depending on electronic interference and geographic variations. For a better system, see GPS.

LOSS The drop in signal level between two points on a network. It is important to distinguish between LOSS and LEVEL. Level is measured at a finite point. Loss is the difference between levels. Loss occurs constantly throughout telephony — from long distance circuits to switches. Loss is usually measured in dB — decibels. Loss is cumulative. Add two circuits each with a loss of 10 dB. You will have 20 dB loss in the total circuit. The human ear can detect a 3 dB loss.

LOSS BUDGET A loss budget is the maximum amount of signal degradation a data communications network can withstand before it

NEWTON'S TELECOM DICTIONARY

becomes susceptible to errors and/or loss of data. The idea is a establish a "loss budget" by consulting your equipment vendors for recommended wire types and maximum allocable lengths of cable before you build the network. We first heard the idea of a loss budget from The Siemon Company, Watertown CT.

LOSSLESS Image- and data-compression applications and algorithms, such as Huffman Encoding, that reduce the number of bits a picture would normally take up without losing any data. In this way, no information is lost or altered in the compression and/or transmission process.

LOSSY Methods of image compression, such as JPEG, that reduce the size of an image by disregarding some pictorial information.

LOST CALL ATTEMPT A call attempt that cannot be further advanced to its destination due to an equipment shortage or failure in the network.

LOST CALLS CLEARED Traffic engineering assumption used in Erlang C that calls not satisfied on the first attempt are held (delayed) in the system until satisfied.

LOST CALLS HELD Traffic engineering assumption used in Poisson that calls not satisfied on the first attempt are held in the phone system for a period not exceeding the average holding time of all calls.

LOTUS EXPRESS An e-mail communications software program for PC users of MCI Mail that allows the user to automatically send and recieve messages, as well as binary files, such as spreadsheets or documents.

LOUDSPEAKER PAGING ACCESS Interface to customer-provided paging equipment.

LOVELACE, ADA AUGUSTA Ada Augusta Lovelace was the daughter of Lord Byron, the English poet. Miss. Lovelace is regarded as the first computer programmer because she worked for the computer pioneer Charles Babage. A computer language was named after her. That language is called ADA.

LOW ENTRY NETWORKING LEN. A peer-oriented extension to SNA, first implemented on IBM's System/36, that allows networks to be more easily built and managed by such techniques as topology database exchange and dynamic route selection.

LOW FREQUENCY The band of frequencies between 30 and 300 kilohertz.

LOW LEVEL FORMATTING See PHYSICAL FORMATTING.

LOW LEVEL LANGUAGE A programming language that uses symbols — one step away from the machine language of a computer. Low level computer languages, such as Assembler and C, actually manipulate the bits in computer registers. Higher level languages such as Basic and Fortran will take care of the piddling details of doing specific functions when you give it a broad command like "PRINT". In a lower level language, you must provide all the details of instruction necessary in the code (program) to perform the operation. It is possible to do this by calling standard routines, but still takes up the programmers' time in deciding which routines, and keeping the registers straight as he designs the program.

LOW NOISE AMPLIFIER LNA. Typically a parametric amplifier in a satellite earth station.

LOW PASS A specific frequency below which a filter will allow all frequencies to pass. Opposite of high pass.

LOW SPEED LOOPBACK A closed circuit feature useful for maintenance or testing.

LOW SPEED SIGNAL Signal traveling at the DS1 rate of 1,544 Mb/s or at the DS1C rate of 3,152 Mb/s.

LOW VOLTAGE A low voltage condition exist when fewer than 105 volts AC is present at a 120 VAC outlet or HOT conductor. This figure was chosen by many manufacturers of electronic and telephone equipment. It is also the test of "low voltage" tested by a wonderful AC electric outlet-testing product called the Accu-Test II made by Ecos Electronics Corporations of Oak Park, Illinois. Below 105 volts, motors deteriorate and electronic circuits overheat. Long-term damage can occur to most gadgets plugged into an electrical outlet which consistently delivers below 105 volts. Also 105 volts is below the stated tolerance levels of all North American power utilities who state that their acceptable power is 120 volts plus or minus 10 percent. If your power is consistently below 105 volts, you should contact your local power utility.

LPC Linear Predictive Coding. Low bit rate voice (LBRV) digitizing technique that requires a bandwidth of only 2.4 or 4.8 kbps. This technique may result in poor quality voice signals.

LPDA-2 IBM's protocol under NetView for monitoring of dial-up modems for error correction.

LPI Lines Per Inch. The number of lines both horizontal and vertical, that a facsimile machine will print in a square inch.

LPP Link Peripheral Processor or Link Peripheral Processing.

LPT PORT A logical designation for a series of I/O (Input/Output) addresses that allows the computer to communicate with a parallel printer.

LPT1 The first or primary parallel printer port on the IBM PC or clone. LPT2 is the second parallel port. COM1 is the first serial port. LPT1 is usually the default printer port, i.e. the one your computer will print to, if you don't tell it something else.

LQA Link Quality Analysis. See AUTOMATIC LINK ESTABLISHMENT.

LRC Longitudinal Redundancy Check.

LS TRUNK Loop-Start Trunk. A trunk on which a closure between the tip and ring leads is used to originate or answer a call. High-voltage 20-Hz AC ringing from the telephone company signals an incoming call. See LOOP START.

LS1A-A Single Mode, Single-Fiber Interconnection Cable. An AT&T defintion.

LSB Least Significant Bit and Least Significant Byte. That portion of a number, address or field which occurs rightmost when its value is written as a single number in conventional hexadecimal or binary notation. The portion of the number having the least weight in a mathematical calculation using the value.

LSCIE Lightguide Stranded-Cable Interconnect Equipment.

LSCIM Lightguide Stranded-Cable Interconnect Module.

LSCIT Lightguide Stranded-Cable Interconnect Terminal.

LSI Large Scale Integration. Refers to microelectronic components which combine many hundreds of transistors on an integrated circuit. See CHIP.

LSL Link Support Layer. A layer within the Novell Open Data-Link Driver specification. This layer lets multiple protocol stacks access a network card simultaneously.

LSSGR LATA Switching System General Requirements.

LT Logical Terminal

LTB Last Trunk Busy.

LTE Line Terminating Equipment. Network elements which originate and/or terminate line (OC-N) signals. LTEs originate, access, modify, and/or terminate the transport overhead.

LTRS Letters Shift. 1 Physical shift in a terminal using Baudot Code that enables the printing of alphabetic characters. 2 Character that causes the shift.

LTS Loop Testing System.

LU 1. Line Unit. 2. Logical Unit, access port for users in SNA. In a bisync network, a port through which the user gains access to the network services. A LU can support sessions with the host-based System Services Control Point (SSCP) and other LUs.

LU 6.2 Logical Unit Interface. Version 6.2. An IBM SNA protocol that allows for peer-to-peer or program-to-program communications. The LU 6.2 protocol standard frees application programs from network specific details. On an IBM PC, a LU 6.2 program accepts commands and passes them on to an SDLC card to communicate directly with the mainframe or a token ring handler. LU 6.2 enables users to develop applications programs for peer-to-peer communications between PC's and IBM host systems. It increases the processing power of the PC user without the constraints of mainframe-based slave devices, i.e. 3274/3276 controllers. It creates a transparent environment for application-to-application communications, regardless of the types of systems used or their relative locations. Also referred to as Advanced Program-to-Program Communication (APPC).

LU TYPE 1 LU 1 is the SNA protocol that describes generic input/output devices. (e.g. line printer)

LU TYPE 3 LU 3 is the SNA protocol that describes a print output device that uses 3270 data streams.

LUG Something which sticks out onto which a wire may be connected by wrapping or soldering.

LUMINA A single line telephone adjunct device produced by Northern Telecom. It is called the Lumina 200. It will display the name and number of the calling person, if that information is provided by the local central office. Lumina sits between the incoming central office line and the telephone and records the incoming number and name of the caller delivered via Calling Line IDentification (CLID) services on Custom Local Area Signaling Services (CLASS). Lumina receives the call identification information between the first and second rings. To capture this information, the telephone must be allowed to ring twice before lifting the receiver to answer a call. See LUMINA CALL DISPLAY.

LUMINA CALL DISPLAY A small Northern Telecom device which sits between the incoming central office line and the telephone and records the incoming number and name of the caller delivered via Calling Line IDentification (CLID) services on Custom Local area Signaling Services (CLASS). The Lumina will also store the date and time of the call, whether the call is new or a repeated call, whether the calls comes from an area not equipped for calling number delivery, whether the call has previously been displayed during a review of the caller's list. The Lumina receives the call identification information between the first and second rings. To capture this information, the telephone must be allowed to ring twice before lifting the receiver to answer a call. See also LUMINA and MAESTRO.

LUMINANCE That part of the video signal which carries the information on how bright the TV signal is to be.

LUNS Logical Unit Numbers. An identification number given to devices connected to a SCSI adapter. Each SCSI ID can have eight LUNs. Normally, there is only one device with LUN 0. See DAISY CHAIN and SCSI.

LZW The Lempel-Ziv-Welsh compression algorithm is another way of reducing the number of bits to transfer. Northern Telecom uses this compression algorithm for its Distributed Processing Peripheral (DPP) — the Automatic Message Accounting Transmitter (AMAT) for the DMS-100 family of central office switches. Northern Telecom selected this nonproprietary protocol and helped promote it as an industry standard. The nominal compression ration is 2.8:1, without considering field suppression. Transmitting data compressed at a ratio of 2.8:1 at 9600 bps is equivalent to transmitting noncompressed data at 27 kbps. Compatible compression collectors can poll the DPP in compressed or noncompressed mode. DPPs equipped with the Data Compression feature can transmit in either compressed or noncompressed mode, based on the collector's polling request for a specific polling session. To preserve data integrity, AMA data are still stored in noncompressed form on the DPP disks. LZW is a lossless data-compression algorithm. See LOSSLESS and LOSSY.

M m (small letter) Milli. One-thousandth. M (big letter) Mega. One million, e.g. Mbps or Mbit/s, one million bits per second.

M BIT The More Data mark in an X.25 packet that allows the DTE or DCE to indicate a sequence of more than one packet.

M-PATCH BAY A patching facility designed for patching and monitoring of digital data circuits at rates from 1 Mbps to 3 Mbps.

M-VTS Marconi Video Telephone Standard sends color pictures over regular phone lines at up to 10 frames per second at 14.4 Kbps. The MCI Video Phone, which conforms to this standard, has a resolution of 128 by 96 pixels.

M1 Multiplexer in the U.S. digital signal hierarchy. See M1, which is listed as if it were M-ONE in this dictionary.

M12 A designation for a multiplex which interfaces between four DSIs and one DS2 circuit.

M13 The multiplexer equivalent of T-1. In the U.S. digital hierarchy, multiplexers are called by the digital signal levels they interface with. For example, a multiplexer, which joins DS-1 channels to DS-3 is called a M1-3. A M1-3 takes 28 DS-1 inputs and combines them into a single 45 megabit per second stream. (The bit stream is actually 44.736 megabits.)

M24 A T-1 service that allows a user to multiplex up to 24 voice or data channels into a single T-1 link, compatible with AT&T central office based channel banks (M24 compatability generally refers to compliance with the channelization and coding techniques specified by AT&T TR62411).

M34 A designation for a multiplex which interfaces between six DS3s and one DS4 circuit.

M44 A T-1 service that allows up to 44 voice channels (48 without signaling) to operate over a single T-1 link by using ADPCM, and is compatible with AT&T central office based equipment. MJ44 compatibility generally refers to the ability to accept the 44 channel T-1 aggregate and break out one of the channels individually for routing purposes.

MA Abbreviation for MILLIAMP or MILLIAMPERS, unit of electric current.

MA BELL A term used to refer affectionately to the old AT&T and the old Bell System. Several Women's Lib organizations objected to it some years ago on the basis that there were no women in the higher corporate structure of AT&T, and that women, as over-supervised operators, were the downtrodden majority within the Bell System. There was a movement afoot to change it Pa Bell. But then came Divestiture and the breakup of the Bell System. The term, MA BELL, now largely belongs in the history books. And there are now a handful of women in senior management in the Bell operating companies.

MAC 1. Moves, Adds and Changes. 2. Media Access Control. A media-specific access control protocol within IEEE 802 specifications. Currently includes variations for the token ring, token bus and CSMA/CD. The lower sublayer of the IEEE's link layer (OSI) which complements the Logical Link Control (LLC).

MAC NAME A MAC name (also called a MAC address) is a 48-bit number, unique to each local area network card, that is programmed into the card, usually at the time of manufacture. Unlike Network Layer Addresses, MAC names are location-independent. Destination and source MAC names are contained in the LAN packet and are used by bridges to filter and forward packets. See also NETWORK LAYER ADDRESS.

MACs Moves, Adds and Changes.

MACHINE CODE Same as Machine Language. See MACHINE LANGUAGE below.

MACHINE DEPENDENT Software which will only run (i.e. is dependent) on a certain computer.

MACHINE LANGUAGE A computer language composed of machine instructions that can be executed directly by a computer without further compilation. Instructions and data coded in binary code. Machine language is the native language of computer hardware. Machine language is the only language recognized by the microprocessor that controls all the operations in your PC. All programs and all data to be processed by your computer (PC, mini or mainframe) have to be translated into machine language at some stage.

MACINTOSH A family of Apple microcomputers that represents the first wide-scale PC (personal computer) deployment of icons, windows, "mice" and a consistent user interface, now called a Graphical User Interface (GUI). Apple introduced the Macintosh in January, 1984.

MACMAIL The name of a piece of communications software that makes using MCI Mail very easy. The software was written by Pete Maclean who can be reached on MCI Mail 263-7215.

MACRO LANGUAGE A collection of instructions by which any kind of information in the system can be located and manipulated and by which new information types can be added to the system.

MACROBENDING In an optical fiber, all macroscopic deviations of the fiber's axis from a straight line; distinguished from microbending.

MACROCELL macrocell is a new word for what we used to call a "cell," as in cellular radio. This is what some researchers at Bell Northern Research (BNR) wrote: "Today's cellular networks employ macrocells and are optimized to serve users in automobiles, moving at relatively high speeds. Yet, a growing proportion of cellular traffic is originating from users who are not driving in vehicles, but are on foot... If a portion of the radio frequencies in a geographic area were transferred from macrocell (optimized for cars) to microcell technology (optimized for pedestrians), cellular traffic would increase up to a hundredfold. Microcell networks will entail the deployment of many more transceivers than today's macrocell systems. However, microcell equipment will be less costly because it is low-power, simpler and smaller, say the researchers at Bell Northern Research.

MACROS A common name for a microcomputer software program which lets you alter the definitions of what the keys on your computer keyboard are. With a "macro" software program, you could change the letter "M" on your keyboard to type "Michael" every time you hit it. But this would be stupid. Better to hit a combination of letters to get "Michael." Most personal computers have extra non-alphabetic keys, like Control and Alternate. And some macro software programs typically allow you to define a "Supershift" key. This means you can define one of your keys as a second Shift key. When you hit it (or Control or Alt) and then hit another key on the keyboard that key will type something different.

For example, when we hit ALT T on the macro we've programmed for this dictionary, we get T103 in square brackets, which means to change the typeface to this, which is called Helvetica Bold. When we first started writing this dictionary, we were using Radio Shack Model II machines running an operating system called CP/M. On that machine, we had no ALT key. It had only a control key. So we defined our Macro key to be "Control 6." When we hit the Control Key and the "6" key simultaneously, nothing happened on the screen, but the next character, number or letter was different, depending on how we defined it. For example, if we hit Control 6 and then T, we'd get T103 in square brackets. Our biggest use for macros is typesetting commands.

We have about 40 macro translations loaded on every MS-DOS machine in our office. Macros are among the most useful and, curiously least expensive, of all PC software programs. Increasingly, macro capability is being built into most major word processors. ZEdit, the word processor we used to write this dictionary, has extensive macros. You can pretty well define any key or combination of keys to type out words or executive commands.

MACSTAR An AT&T 3B2 computer-based software system that interfaces with the Remote Memory Administration System (RMAS) to effect customer moves and rearrangements on the 5ESS switch. The user needs only a terminal and printer.

MADN Multiple Appearance Directory Number.

MAGAZINE Hardware unit, mounted in a frame, containing printed board assemblies.

MAGIC ON HOLD A term peculiar to AT&T's Merlin phone system which refers to customized Music-on-Hold that promotes the customer's products and services.

MAGGOTS Telco-slang for B-connectors, which are about the size and shape of fly larvae.

MAESTRO A Northern Telecom telephone designed for the home for CLASS service, in particular the CLID — Calling Line IDentification service available with SS7. Maestro has a 16-character display and logging capability that retains and displays on command the last 15 unanswered incoming directory numbers, and allows return dialing from the unanswered call log. Maestro's ten programmable one-touch memory keys can be used either for storing phone numbers or for one-button access to CLASS and other custom calling features that are otherwise accessed by dialing a code. MAESTRO also has a Call Forwarding Lamp which makes it easy to tell when call forwarding has been activated from the Maestro. List price for the Maestro was set originally at $136. See also CLASS and LUMINA.

MAGIC CAP Magic Cap is a "Communicating Applications Platform," which, according to General Magic of Mountain View, CA, allows developers to build a new class of software and services, centered on communications and easy for users to personalize."

MAGIC WAND One of the devices used by con men when pretending to do TSCM (Technical Surveillance CounterMeasures). A magic wand is typically a field strength meter or box with many fancy lights.

MAGNETIC BUBBLE A device in which information is stored in a magnetic film as a pattern of oppositely directed magnetic fields. Magnetic bubble devices hold their memory even if you lose power.

MAGNETIC INK An ink that contains particles of a magnetic substance whose presence can be detected by magnetic sensors. Typical is the ink on your checks, which carry your name, your account number and the check's number.

MAGNETIC MEDIUM Any data-storage medium and related technology including diskettes and tapes, in which different patterns of magnetization are used to represent the values of stored bits and bytes.

MAGNETIC STRIPE A strip of magnetic material, usually tape, attached to a credit card containing data relating to the card holder. You have a magnetic stripe now on the back of most of your credit cards. That stripe tells a computer who you are, what your account number is, etc.

MAGNETIC TAPE A tape made of magnetic material upon which data may be stored for later retrieval by a computer.

MAGNETO A small hand-cranked AC generator which uses permanent field magnets and can make electricity to ring telephone bells.

MAGNETO OPTICAL DRIVE A computer data storage device that writes data using magnetism (in the form of a magnetic field called the bias field) and light (a laser beam) to write to a disk that resembles a CR-ROM disk. A magneto optical drive holds huge amounts of information — as much as 500 megabytes on a single disk. Introduced in 1988, the magneto optical drive (also spelled with a dash between the magneto and optical), the drive provides the convenience of the removability of floppies and the Bernoulli Box, the random access convenience of hard disk, the reliability of CD-ROMs and the promise of DAT-like capacity. But, according to PC Magazine, before you rush out and buy this ultimate storage solution, note that they're expensive, can't provide as much storage on one side of a disk as the largest hard disks and they're slower than today's hard disks. An explanation of how magneto optical drives work, courtesy PC Magazine: The recording layer on the disk stores the equivalent of binary 1s and 0s on the magnetic domains. The disk is designed so that the bias field by itself is to too weak to change the polarity of the magnetic domains. But when a spot on the disk is heated by a high-powered laser beam, its resistance to changing polarity drops. The bias field can now change the disk area's polarity. To read the disk, the drive uses a laser beam that is not hot enough to allow the bias field to change the disk area's polarity.

MAGNETO-OPTIC Relating to the change in a material's refractive index under the influence of a magnetic field. Magneto-optic materials generally are used to rotate the plane of the polarization. This phenomenon is how magneto optical disk drives work.

MAHR Abbreviation for MILIAMPERE HOUR, 1/1000th of an ampere hour. Term is commonly used with small rechargeable battery packs, such as those used by portable phones and laptop PCs.

MAIL SERVER A computer host and its associated software that offer electronic mail reception and (optionally) forwarding service. Users may send messages to, and recieve messages from, any other user in the system.

MAILER Also known as the front end; a program that allows BBSs (bulletin board systems) using different software to "talk" to each other. The mailer acts as a transfer layer for the messages passed. Some BBSs require mailers to talk to some netmail systems (for example, Spitfire for FidoNet). Seadog is generally acknowledged to be the market leader, according to PC Magazine.

MAILGRAM An overnight electronic mail service of Western Union. The letter is phoned in or sent by computer to a central Western Union computer, from where it is sent to teleprinter machines located in post offices in major cities. When it's printed at the post office, the Mailgram is placed in an envelope and hand-delivered by your friendly, local mailman in next day's mail.

MAIN PBX or Centrex switch into which other PBXs or remote concentration of switching modules are homed. A PBX or Centrex connected directly to an electronic tandem switch (ETS). Also, a power source.

MAIN CROSS-CONNECT The interconnect point where wiring from the Entrance Facility and from the Workstation is connected to telecom equipment.

MAIN DISTRIBUTION FRAME MDF. A wiring arrangement which connects the telephone lines coming from outside on one side and the internal lines on the other. A main distribution frame may also carry protective devices as well as function as a central testing point. See MAIN DISTRIBUTION FRAME FILL, DISTRIBUTION FRAME and FRAME.

MAIN DISTRIBUTION FRAME FILL The central office mainframe is the termination point for outside plant cables. The "fill" is the percentage of pairs used by customers of the total number of pairs on the frame. Optimum fills vary based on the size of the central office and the amount of growth in the area. A low fill means idle lines and wasted investment in outside plant. A high fill, plus unexpected growth, forces budget busting and crisis construction projects.

MAIN FEEDER Feeder cable that transports pairs from the central office to branching or taper points.

MAIN LOBE The main lobe is the area with the maximum intensity in the pattern of radiation produced by an antenna. One presumes it's called "lobe" because the pattern in a microwave signal of the main lobe typically looks like a ear lobe.

MAIN MEMORY The principal random storage area inside the computer. Used for storing data and programs and under the direct control of the CPU — the main processor. Also called RAM memory.

MAIN NETWORK ADDRESS In IBM's SNA, the logical unit (LU) network address within ACF/VTAM used for SSCP-to-LU sessions for certain LU-to-LU sessions. Compare with auxiliary network address.

MAIN SATELLITE SERVICE A PBX feature that allows multi-location customers to concentrate their attendant positions at one location referred to as the Main. Other unattended locations are referred to as Satellites.

MAIN SERVICE ENTRANCE In AC electricity, the main service entrance is the necessary equipment, usually consisting of main circuit breakers or fuses, a switch and branch circuit breakers or fuses, in a grounded enclosure (panel) connected directly to earth. Located in the building at the point of entrance of the supply conductors from the power utility. Other panels in the building are referred to as branch, service or supply panels.

MAIN STATION A subscriber's telephone instrument, terminal or workstation used to originate and receive calls. Very often if two instruments have the same extension number (are bridged), one becomes the Main Station and the other is a bridged station for inventory purposes.

MAINFRAME A powerful computer, almost always linked to a large set of peripheral devices (disk storage, printers, and so forth), and used in a multipurpose environment at the corporate or major divisional level. The term — main frame — derives from the racks that typically hold a large computer and its memory.

MAINFRAME GATEWAY A hardware/software system that allows PCs on a LAN (Local Area Network) to communicate with a mainframe. A single, usually dedicated, PC acts as the gateway. PCs on the LAN share its hardware and its communication link, communicating with it over the LAN cable. The most common mainframe gateway is an SNA gateway, which hooks a LAN into an IBM mainframe.

MAINS Some countries call their normal commercial power outlets — "mains." In Europe the frequency of commercial power is 50 Hz. In the United States, its frequency is 60 Hz. It's hard to convert the frequency of commercial power. It's easier to convert voltage. In Europe and Australia, normal voltage is 240 volts. In the U.S., it's 120 volts.

MAINTENANCE 1. All work needed to keep the telephone system operating properly, including periodic testing, repairs, etc. See PREVENTIVE MAINTENANCE. 2. All work needed to keep a software program operating properly, operating on new machinery and operating with new management needs. Often, software maintenance means substantially re-writing the original software program. Most of the work done by data processing departments in large companies involves maintaining old programs. This is not a put-down.

MAINTENANCE CONTROL CENTER MCC. A central place in a stored program control central office from which system configuration and trouble testing are controlled.

MAINTENANCE CONTROL CIRCUIT MCC. A voice circuit used by maintenance personnel over microwave links for coordination. This is not available to operations or technical control personnel.

MAINTENANCE SERVICES In IBM's SNA, network services performed between a host SSCP and remote physical units (PUs) that test links and collect and record error information. Related facilities include configuration services, management services and session services.

MAINTENANCE TERMINATION UNIT MTU - An MTU is an electronic circuit that is owned and deployed by a telephone company to aid in fault sectionalization and is installed at the network interface. The MTU should meet the requirements of Bellcore Technical Advisory TSY-000324 and be testable with the Mechanized Loop Test System (MLT). The MTU is designed to work on single line residence or business service.

MAKE BUSY To make a communication circuit unavailable for connection. The technical term for taking the phone off the hook and leaving it off hook.

MALICIOUS CALL TRACING An ISDN service which enables to User to Network message to be sent while the call is in progress, ensuring that origination details are captured at the local exchange.

MAN Metropolitan Area Network. High speed intra-city data network. Typically extends as far as 50-kilometers, operates at speeds from 1 Mbit/s to 200 Mbps and provides an integrated set of services for real-time data, voice and image transmission. Two standards are involved with MANs: IEEE 802.3 and ANSI X3T9.5.

MAN MACHINE INTERFACE A term coined by James Martin to designate the ease (or lack of ease) of a person working with a computer.

MANAGEMENT INFORMATION SYSTEM MIS. Management information provided by computer data processing. Once upon a time called data processing.

MANAGEMENT SERVICES In IBM's SNA, network services performed between a host SSCP and remote physical units (PUs) that include the request and retrieval of network statistics.

MANCHESTER ENCODING A digital encoding technique in which each bit period is divided into two complementary halves. A negative-to-positive (voltage) transition in the middle of the bit period designates a binary "1" while a positive-to-negative transition represents a "0". This encoding technique is self-clocking (the receiving device can recover transmitted clock from the data stream).

MANDREL WRAPPING A technique in which excess higher order modes launched into an optical fiber filtered out by wrapping several turns of fiber around a mandrel approximately 1 cm in diameter.

MANUAL EXCLUSION A PBX extension user, by entering a certain code, can block all other phones on that line from entering the call. Assures privacy on the line.

MANUAL GAIN CONTROL MGC. There are two electronic ways you can control the recording of something — Manual or Automatic Gain Control (AGC). AGC is an electronic circuit in tape recorders, speakerphones and other voice devices which is used to maintain volume. AGC is not always a brilliant idea since it attempts to produce a constant volume level. This means it will try to equalize all sounds — the volume of your voice and, when you stop talking, the circuit static and/or general room noise which you undoubtedly do not want amplified. Sometimes it's better to have quiet, when you want quiet. Manual Gain Control is preferred in professional applications. Manual Gain Control is simply an elegant way of saying there's a record volume control. Never record a seminar or speech using AGC. The end result will be decidedly amateurish.

MANUAL HOLD The method of placing a line circuit on "hold' by activating a non-locking "hold" button on the phone, usually one colored red.

MANUAL INTERCOM A crude, single-path communications link between telephones without the ability to signal the receiving party.

MANUAL MODEM ADAPTER An external device for the Merlin key system from AT&T. It allows connection of single line accessories to any Merlin telephone. The device, in effect, draws a standard tip and ring line out of the Merlin proprietary cabling/signaling scheme. Some other key systems have similar devices. Comdial calls theirs a "data port" and their phones contain extra RJ-11 jacks.

MANUAL ORIGINATING LINE SERVICE The attendant must complete all outgoing calls. All other calls are blocked. This "feature" is used to cut down on long distance phone abuse. There's a wonderful story. When many of the PBXs in Europe went from manual originating line service to automatic dial "9" long distance, the number of long distance calls doubled within two months. Some of these calls were legitimate. Some were not. How much abuse there was varied from company to company. Typically, those companies with employees who were more bored suffered (or enjoyed?) more abuse.

MANUAL PBXs Refers to PBXs which are not automatic and which require that all calls, including intercom calls, be placed through the attendant. Such PBXs are still used today, though in limited applications. You can still find manual PBXs in vacation hotels, nursing homes and in the data communications departments of some firms, who use manual PBXs as manual dataPBXs. These are especially useful in places where long data calls and sold metal-to-metal connections are an advantage.

MANUAL RINGDOWN TIE TRUNK A direct talk path between two distant phones. Signaling must be done manually from either phone. Contrast this with Automatic Ringdown Tie Trunk, in which the signaling occurs the moment one of the phones is lifted off hook.

MANUAL SIGNALING Pushing a button on a telephone sends an audible signal to a predetermined phone. Manual signaling can be used for secretary/boss communications.

MANUAL TELEPHONE A telephone without a dial. Taking the receiver off hook automatically rings a predetermined number. A courtesy phone.

MANUAL TERMINATING LINE SERVICE Provides extension lines that require all calls be completed by the attendant. For a better explanation see MANUAL ORIGINATING LINE SERVICE.

MANUFACTURING AND AUTOMATION PROTOCOL See MAP.

MAP 1. A new term for multiplexing, implying more visibility inside the resultant multiplexed bit stream than available with conventional asynchronous techniques. 2. Maintenance and Administration Position. See MAP/MAAP below. 3. Manufacturing Automation Protocol. A protocol initially developed as an internal specification for its own factory floor equipment and now championed by General Motors as the industry standard to facilitate communications among the diverse automation devices found in production environments. AT&T, IBM and DEC have endorsed this standard and have already or will introduce MAP-compatible products. TOP

(Technical and Office Protocol) was initiated by Boeing Computer Services (one of the nine companies that helped form the MAP Users Group in 1984) and is designed for use in the engineering and office environment and to move information from the factory floor to other parts of the company. Implementation of these protocols would lead to GM's factory of the future concept.

MAP/MAAP Maintenance and Administration Panel. A device attached to a PBX to allow you to maintain and administer the system — to change phone features, etc.

MAPI Microsoft's Windows Messaging Application Programming Interface, which is part of WOSA (Windows Open Services Architecture). When Microsoft announced its At Work architecture on June 9, 1993, it said one At Work's benefits was its integration with Windows messaging. Microsoft said the At Work message protocol interfaces with the Windows Messaging API (MAPI). Consequently, users will be able to send and receive messages to and from Microsoft At Work-based devices through any MAPI-enabled e-mail software. Microsoft At Work-based message recipients are just a different recipient type whose address happens to be a name plus phone number. Another important benefit of this integration is that users will be able to send messages to e-mail and Microsoft At Work-based recipients. Finally, integration with MAPI means that all mail-enabled applications will be able to automatically make use of the Microsoft At Work message protocol with no modifications.

The same MAPI technology is implemented on Microsoft At Work-based devices as well, so we will be able to leverage advances in messaging that are added to MAPI on the desktop (e.g., the ability to have multiple communication "transports," or communications methods, operable at the same time) on Microsoft At Work-based devices. In addition, software developers will be able to leverage their understanding of MAPI on the desktop to develop applications for Microsoft At Work-based devices, according to Microsoft. See AT WORK, FAX AT WORK, WINDOWS TELEPHONY and WOSA.

MAPPING 1. In network operations, the logical association of one set of values, such as addresses on one network, with quantities or values of another set, such as devices on another network (e.g. name-address mapping, internetwork-route mapping). 2. A Novell NetWare term. To assign a drive letter to a chosen directory path on a particular volume of a particular file server. For example, if you map drive F to the directory SYS:ACCTS\RECEIVE, you will access that directory every time you enter "F:" at the DOS prompt. See also DRIVE MAPPINGS.

MARATHON A family of products that are combination fast packet multiplexer, data compression, voice compression and fax de-modulation devices that fit many, voice, data, fax and LAN "conversations" onto one leased circuit — analog or digital. The idea of Marathon is to save money on long distance telecommunications charges. The Marathon family of products is made by Micom Communications Corporation, Simi Valley CA.

MARCONI, GUGLIELMO Guglielmo Marconi was born in Bologna, Italy in 1874. In 1896, in England, Marconi obtained the first patent on the wireless. By 1897 he had transmitted messages over a distance of nearly 20 kilometers. In 1897 he formed Marconi's Wireless Telegraph Co. Ltd. In 1901 he succeeded in transmitting signals across the Atlantic. In 1909 he received jointly with C. F. Braun the Nobel Prize in Physics. Marconi was made a Marchese and a member of the Italian senate. He died in Rome on July 20, 1937.

MARINE TELEPHONE Marine telephones operate on assigned radiotelephone frequencies much as a radio broadcast does. Marine telephones can be used to contact other marine telephones or to reach land-based telephones through an operator.

MARISAT A satellite for marine use. Conversations on MARISAT are crystal clear. Call Comsat and ask them for a demo call to a ship somewhere in the world. It's very exciting.

MARITIME MOBILE SERVICE A mobile service between coast stations and ship stations, or between ship stations, or between associated on-board communication stations. Survival craft stations and emergency position-indicating radiobeacon stations may also participate.

MARITIME MOBILE SATELLITE SERVICE A mobile satellite service in which mobile earth stations are located on board ships. Survival craft stations and emergency position-indicating radiobeacon stations may also participate in this service.

MARITIME RADIONAVIGATION SERVICE A radionavigation service intended for the benefit and for the safe operation of ships.

MARK A term that originated with the telegraph. It currently indicates the binary digit "1" (one) in most coding schemes.

MARK-HOLD The normal no-traffic line condition where a steady mark is transmitted.

MARKER The logic circuitry in a crossbar central office that controls call processing functions.

MARKER BEACON A transmitter in the aeronautical radionavigation service which radiates vertically a distinctive pattern for providing position information to aircraft.

MARKER TAPE A tape laid parallel to the conductors under the sheath in a cable imprinted with the manufacturer's name and the specification to which the cable is made. Other information such as date of manufacture may also be included.

MARKER THREAD A colored thread lain parallel and adjacent to the strands of an insulated conductor which identifies the cable manufacturer. It may also denote a temperature rating or the specification to which the cable is made.

MARKET PRICE Prices set at market rates but, in most cases, are not permitted to be less than cost.

MARKING BIAS The uniform lengthening of all marking signal pulses at the expense of all spacing pulses.

MASER Microwave Amplification by Stimulated Emission of Radiation. A device that generates electromagnetic signals in the microwave range, known for relatively low noise.

MASK A computer imaging term. The electronic equivalent of placing transparent tape over selected regions of an image, a mask marks pixels tht remain unchanged by subsequent painting operations. For example, you might mask out a mountain range and add background clouds to the sky. In the final image, the clouds will appear between the peaks.

MASQUERADE To pretend to be someone else by using another person's password or Token.

MASS860 An organization of computer system vendors formed to promote open system standards and the writing of applications software for the Intel i860 microprocessor. Members include Intel, Oki Electric Industry Co., Ltd., IBM, Stratus, Olivetti, Alliant, Samsung and Stardent Computer.

MASSIVELY PARALLEL SYSTEMS Tightly coupled multiprocessing computers that house 100 or more CPUs, each with its own memory.

MASTER Term applied to the data communications equipment at one end of a synchronous digital transmission network that supplies the clock timing signal that determines the rate of transmission in both directions.

MASTER CLOCK An electronic timing circuit which synchronizes the entire data communications network. The source of timing signals, or the signals themselves, that all network stations use for synchronization.

MASTER CONTROL UNIT MCU. An InteCom word for the device which controls the main operating functions of the system.

MASTER FREQUENCY GENERATOR In FDM, equipment used to provide system end-to-end carrier frequency synchronization and frequency accuracy of tones over the system.

MASTER GROUP MG. In frequency division multiplexing (the old way of putting many voice conversations onto on communications line) a master group consists of 300 voice-grade (4 kHz) channels.

MASTER NUMBER HUNTING When a call is directed to the pilot number of a hunt group, it will hunt to the first non-busy station in that group. If a call is directed to a specific station in that hunt group it will go directly to that station and not hunt to another station in the group.

MASTER SLAVE SWITCHING SYSTEM A configuration consisting of a central switch and one or more remote switches. The master switch typically controls all I/O (input/output) information. The slave system performs tasks as directed by the master, including switching calls between phones attached to that remote module — without sending those calls back to the central switch. There are enormous savings in wiring since not every remote phone has to have a pair back to the central switch.

MASTER SLAVE TIMING In a communication system, a timing subsystem wherein one station or node supplies the timing reference for all other interconnected stations or nodes.

MASTER STATION 1. The main phone or station in a group. The one controlling the transmission of the others. 2. The unit which controls all the workstations on a LAN, usually through some type of polling. The master station on a token-passing ring allows recovery from error conditions, such as lost, busy or duplicate tokens, usually by generating a new token. Sometimes servers are referred to as master stations. 3. In navigation systems employing precise time dissemination, a station whose clock is used to synchronize the clocks of subordinate stations. 4. In basic mode link control, a data station that has accepted an invitation to ensure a data transfer to one or more slave stations. At a given instant, there can be only one master station on a data link.

MASTERGROUP A mastergroup consists of 600 voice channels, or 10 supergroups. Six mastergroups is equal to one jumbogroup.

MATCHED JUNCTION A waveguide component having four or more ports, and so arranged that if all ports except one are terminated in the correct impedance, there will be no reflection of energy from the junction.

MATEL A Multiplex Automatic TELephone system. Picture one long, up to two miles wire (any decent quality works). You roll it out, then you clip phones anywhere into the wire. Then you have, in effect, a seven channel bus PBX. You have two digit extension dialing between the phones (up to 60). You also have conferencing, broadcast, call back, DID and connection to one central office line and one radio channel. The uses? String it around a rioting prison, a siege, an airport hijack, an emergency in New York City subway, etc. Three advantages: instant communications, communications where radio is bad and radio silence — you keep the press and the bad guys in the dark. This definition from John McCann, general manager of Racal Acoustics Limited, Frederick, MD, which makes the MATEL.

MATERIAL SCATTERING In an optical fiber, that part of the total scattering attributable to the properties of the materials used for fiber fabrication.

MATH COPROCESSOR A coprocessor is a special purpose microprocessor which assists the computer's main microprocessor in doing special tasks. A math coprocessor performs mathematical calculations, especially floating point operations. Math coprocessors are also called numeric and floating point coprocessors. If you do a lot of mathetical tasks on your PC, like recalculating large spreadsheets, then installing a math coprocessor makes huge sense. Intel included a math coprocessor with its 486DX chip, but removed it for the 486SX. No other Intel chip has a math coprocessor built in. When you buy a math coprocessor make sure it's the same speed as your existing processor.

MATR Minimum Average Time Requirement.

MATRIX 1. A switch. A device for moving calls from one input to the desired output. There are many types of switching matrices — from simple step-by-step matrices to complex digital pulse code modulated matrices. Most switching matrices are "blocking." They do not have sufficient capacity to switch every call. There are some switches that are "non-blocking." These have the ability to switch every call simultaneously. By definition, non-blocking matrices are more expensive. They are only needed in special situations of high traffic. 2. The encompassing material in the composite (i.e. the plastic).

MATRIX RINGING Two key system phones picking up the same extensions with different lines ringing on different phones. These days, with electronic phones, matrix ringing is easy. In the old days, with 1A2 phones, you needed to do considerable wiring.

MATV Master Antenna System, such as used in apartment buildings and motels.

MAU 1. Math Acceleration Unit. 2. Multistation Access Unit. A MAU is a wiring concentrator used in Local Area Networks. In token ring networks it's called a Multi-station Access Unit. In Ethernet networks it's called a Medium Attachment Unit. Basically a MAU is a device that allows terminals, PCs, printers, and other devices to be connected in a star-based configuration to Token Ring or Ethernet LANs. MAU hardware can be either active or passive.

Each computer is wired directly to the MAU which then provides the connection to all other computers. MAUs themselves can be connected to expand the network. The MAU is a small box with eight or sixteen connectors and an arrangement of relays that function as bypass switches. When only one MAU is used, its relays and internal wiring arrange themselves so that the MAU and the connected computers form a complete electrical ring. MAUs can be cascaded to create bigger rings. The MAU listens for the "I'm here" signal sent by a computer when the computer is attached to the MAU. If the token ring adapter card in a computer is not working properly or the computer is turned off, the MAU no longer hears the "I'm here" signal and automatically disconnects the computer from the ring using the bypass relay.

A managed MAU contains on-board intelligence which enable it to communicate with network management software. This software can then be used to control the MAU. This type of MAU provides the network administrator with an "out-of-band" (a separate line) method of port control, monitoring, and diagnostics. For example, in the event that a token ring network is down, conventional network management may not be possible as it relies on the network itself to communicate with the various components on the token ring LAN. The out-of-band management provided by the managed MAU gives the administrator the ability to diagnose and reconfigure the network without physically inspecting and reconfiguring each MAU in the network.

MAXIMIZE BUTTON The maximize button in Windows is the up-arrow button at the far right of a title bar in the Windows operating system. Click on the maximize button to enlarge the IMARA Lite window to full size. See also, Minimize button and Restore button.

MAXIMUM ACCESS TIME Maximum allowable waiting time between initiation of an access attempt and successful access.

MAXIMUM BLOCK TRANSFER TIME Maximum allowable waiting time initiation of a block transfer attempt and completion of a successful block transfer.

MAXIMUM CALLING AREA Geographic calling limits permitted to a particular access line based on requirements for a particular line.

MAXIMUM KEYING FREQUENCY In facsimile systems, the frequency in hertz numerically equal to the spot speed divided by twice the X-dimension of the scanning spot.

MAXIMUM MODULATING FREQUENCY The highest picture frequency required for a given facsimile transmission system. The maximum modulating frequency and the maximum keying frequency ae not necessarily equal.

MAXIMUM STUFFING RATE The maximum rate at which bits can be inserted or deleted.

MAXIMUM USABLE FREQUENCY MUF. The upper limit of the frequencies that can be used at a specified time for radio transmission between two points and involving propagation by reflection from the regular ionized layers of the ionosphere. MUF is a median frequency applicable to 50 percent of the days of the month, as opposed to 90 percent cited for the lowest usable high frequency (LUF) and the optimum traffic frequency (OTF).

MAXIMUM USER SIGNALING RATE The maximum rate, in bits per second at which binary information can be transferred (in a given direction) between users over the telecommunication system facilities dedicated to a particular information transfer transaction, under conditions of continous transmission and no overhead information.

MBE Micom Business Exchange. Trademark for MICOM's series of communications processors.

MBPS Mbps. M/bps. MegaBits Per Second. Million bits per second.

MBus A Sun Microsystems definition: An open specification for connecting multiple CPUs (such as those in SPARC modules) with a 64-bit, 320-MB/second data path. Designed by Sun Microsystems; available from SPARC International.

MC Main Cross-connect. The interconnect point where wiring from the entrance facility and from the workstation is connected to telecom equipment.

MCA Micro Channel Architecture. The new internal bus inside IBM's new line of PS/2 MCA machines.

MCCS Mechanized Calling Card Service was formerly known as ABC Service. MCCS is a CO switch facility that automatically bills credit card calls made on DDD without the involvement of an operator.

MCF Message Confirmation Frame. Confirmation by the receiver in a fax transmission that the receiver is ready to receive the next page.

MCI Once upon a time it was called Microwave Communications Inc. Thus the MCI. But now it's just MCI and it stands for nothing. It is the largest long distance phone company in the US after AT&T. In MCI's early days, the initials were said to stand for "Money Coming In." Now MCI is a $10 billion plus corporation and its stock is selling for more than AT&T's (or was at the time of writing). MCI is a full-service long distance company offering every service from switched single channel voice to leased T-1. See also MCI FAX and MCI MAIL.

MCI FAX A way of sending facsimile messages. You can send them directly from fax machine to fax machine. Or you can send them from your personal computer (equipped with a modem) to any fax machine anywhere in the world. If you send faxes from your PC, you don't need a fax machine and you can send the same fax to a lot of people very easily and very quickly. MCI FAX is cheaper than sending faxes by dialing directly. A good service. See also MCI Mail and INFONET.

MCI FIBERLINE An MCI International service that uses TAT-8 (the new trans-Atlantic digital fiber optic cable) to provide private-line channels to major business locations throughout Europe, in a wide range of transmission speeds from 56/64 to 1.544/2.048 Mbps.

MCI INFORMATION MANAGER MIM. A program on the NCS host which allows MCI employees access to the Data Base Adminstator (DBA), primarily for updating, maintaining, and troubleshooting purposes for Vnet services.

MCI INTERNATIONAL This MCI subsidiary handles MCIs International business. MCII, which includes Western Union International and RCA Globecom, provides private-line, Telex, cablegram, MCI Mail and other services to more than 100 overseas countries, and voice service to direct-dialable countries.

MCI MAIL A way of sending electronic messages, fax messages and paper mail through the US Postal Service from your PC instantly to other people who have MCI Mail Mailboxes, to anyone on an electronic mail system connected to MCI Mail (like Internet, AT&T Mail, CompuServe, etc.) to anyone who has a fax machine or to anyone who receives US Mail (i.e. all of us). MCI Mail is the easiest, fastest, least expensive way to keep in touch in North America and in most industrialized countries around the globe. If you want to send us a message, send a message to HARRY NEWTON, who is an MCI Mail subscriber. Harry's MCI Mail number is 101-5032. Some of the definitions in this dictionary came to us via MCI Mail. Here's a quick reference to MCI Mail. Ever subscriber has five "folders." They are INBOX (incoming unread mail), DESK (incoming mail already read), OUTDESK (mail you have sent) and PENDING (unsent mail you have prepared). Here are MCI Mail's most important commands: READ (read incoming messages), CREATE (prepare a message to send), ANSWER (respond to a message), PRINT (dump all my incoming messages to me nonstop), FORWARD (send a message I received to someone else). Typically, you get things done on MCI Mail by combining messages, e.g. PRINT INBOX, which dumps all your incoming, unread messages. See also MCI FAX and INFONET.

MCL Mercury Communications Limited (UK). The second long distance company in England. It is competitor of British Telecom, the erstwhile monopoly local and long distance company in the U.K.

MCNC Microelectronic Center of North Carolina.

MCT ALGORITHM A compression algorithm inroduced in 1986 by PictureTel. MCT reduced the bandwidth necessary to transmit acceptable picture quality from 768 kbps to 224 kbps making two-way videoconferencing convenient and economical at relatively low data rates (for those times).

MCU Multipoint Control Unit. A PBX-like device for switching and conferencing video calls, announced by AT&T on March 22, 1993.

MCVF Multi-Channel Voice Frequency.

MD Mediation Device. A SONET device that performs mediation functions between network elements and OSs. Potential mediation functions include protocol conversion, concentration of NE to OS links, conversion of languages, and message processing.

MDA Monochrome Display Adapter.

MDC Meridian Digital Centrex. A Northern Telecom abbreviation.

MDF See MAIN DISTRIBUTION FRAME.

MDT Mean Down Time.

MEACONING A system for receiving radio beacon signals and retransmitting them on the same frequency to confuse navigation and cause inaccurate bearings to be obtained by aircraft or ground stations.

MEAN BUSY HOUR For a telephone line or group of lines or a switch the Mean Busy hour is the 60 minute period where traffic is the greatest.

MEAN POWER OF A RADIO TRANSMITTER The average power supplied to the antenna transmission line by a transmitter during an interval of time sufficiently long compared with the lowest frequency encountered in the modulation taken under normal operating conditions. Normally, a time of 0.1 second, during which the mean power is greatest, will be selected.

MEAN TIME BETWEEN FAILURE MTBF. The average time a manufacturer estimates before a failure occurs in a component, a printed circuit board or a complete telephone system. One must check, since MTBFs are cumulative.

MEAN TIME BETWEEN OUTAGES MTBO. The mean time between equipment failures or significant outages which essentially render transmission useless. See MEAN TIME BETWEEN FAILURE.

MEAN TIME TO REPAIR MTTR. The vendor's estimated average time required to do repairs on equipment.

MEAN TIME TO SERVICE RESTORAL MTSR. The mean time to restore service following system failures that result in a service outage. The time to restore includes all time from the occurrence of the failure until the restoral of service.

MEASURED RATE A message rate structure in which the monthly phone line rental includes a specified number of calls within a defined area, plus a charge for additional calls. See LOCAL MEASURED SERVICE.

MEASURED SERVICE Also known as USAGE SENSITIVE PRICING (USP). A local phone company method of pricing used to bill local phone calls. Measured service is often charged on the number of calls, the time of day, the distance traveled and the length of the call. See LOCAL MEASURED SERVICE.

MECCA Multiplex Engineering Control Center Activity

MECHANICAL HOLD A very basic line-holding mechanism used on simple two- and three-line phones that operated by placing a short circuit or a resistor across one phone line while talking on another. Chief disadvantage was that a call put on hold at one phone could not be taken off hold at another phone. Inexpensive multi-line phones with electronic holds largely replaced mechanical holds in the 1980s.

MECHANICAL SPLICE A splice in which optical glass fibers are joined mechanically (e.g., glued or crimped in place) but not fused (i.e. melted) together.

MECHANICAL STRIPPING Removing the coating from a fiber using a tool similar to those used for removing insulation from wires.

MECHANIZED CALLING CARD SERVICE MCCS was formerly known as ABC Service. MCCS is a central office switch feature that automatically bills credit card calls made on DDD (direct distance dial) rates without the involvement of an operator.

MECHANIZED LINE TESTING MLT - The system provides computer control of accurate and extensive loop testing functions in the customer contact, screening, testing, dispatch and closeout phases of trouble report handling. It also provides full diagnostic outputs instead of just pass/fail indications.

MEDIA In the context of telecommunications, media is most often the conduit or link that carries transmissions. Transport media include copper wire, radio waves and fiber.

MEDIA COMPATIBLE Usually used to refer to floppy disk media. Even though two different computers (e.g. an AT&T PC 6300 and an Apple IIe) both use 5 1/4 inch floppy disks, the information recorded on them is recorded in a different format and thus, they are not media compatible. You can put one disk in another's machine. But it won't work. You'll get a dumb error message.

MEDIA INTERFACE CONNECTOR An optical fiber connector which links the fiber media to the FDDI node or another cable.

MEDIA PATH Same as wire run. The means by which telephone signals are conveyed from the Network Interface Jack to the Communications Outlet.

MEDIA SERVER A new term for a file server on a local area network which contains files containing voice, images, pictures, video, etc. In short, a media server is a repository for media of all types. Media servers are also called file servers.

MEDIUM Any material substance that can be used for the telecommunications transmission of signals. "Mediums'" (or media) include optical fiber, cable, wire, dielectric slab, water, air or free space.

MEDIUM ACCESS CONTROL MAC. Sublayer in a local area network, that part of the OSI Data Link Layer that supports topology-dependent functions and uses the services of the physical layer to provide services to the logical link control sublayer.

MEDIUM FREQUENCY MF. Frequencies from 300 KHz to 3000 KHz.

MEDIUM INTERFACE CONNECTOR MIC. In LAN/MAN systems, the

connector at the interface point between the bus interface unit and the terminal, termed the medium interface point.

MEET-ME CONFERENCE A conference arrangement by which any telephone can dial a specific access code to join a conference with other users who have dialed the same code. Conference participants may call in at a preset time or may be directed to do so by an attendant or secretary. Some phone systems restrict this to intercom circuits only. In almost all phone systems there is a maximum number of parties that can be connected in such conference at one time.

MEET-ME INTERCOM CONFERENCE Dial a special number ("access code") and any telephone can join an intercom conference call.

MEET-ME PAGE A feature which allows a person to answer an intercom page from any phone in the system.

MEGA A prefix meaning one million, also represented as an M. MEGABIT = one million bits. MEGABYTE = one million bytes. MEGAHERTZ = one million cycles per second. See also MEGABYTE.

MEGABYTE Megabyte. A unit of measurement for data storage equal to 1,048,576 bytes.

MEGACENTER An MCI definition. An MCI facility providing concentrated telemarketing. A megacenter does not handle incoming calls or customer service.

MEGACOM Megacom 800 and Megacom. Two AT&T services which are variations on INWATS and OUTWATS. Both are normal WATS services except that the local lines to and from the customer's office to and from AT&T's serving class 4 central office are the responsibility of the customer. Such lines tend to be

T-1.   And they are usually direct wiring through the local phone company, or short-haul microwave, or leased fiber optic.

MEGAFLOPS Million Floating point Operations Per Second. A measure of computing power usually associated with large computers. Mega means million. Also known as MFLOPS.

MEGAHERTZ MHz. A unit of frequency denoting one million Hz.

MEGALINK Name for BellSouth's leased T-1 service.

MEGOHM A resistance of 1,000,000 ohms.

MEMO A telephone feature that enables the user to store a phone number for calling in the future. For example, while speaking to a Directory Assistance operator, you can put the number she gives you into memory, and then call that number by pushing one or two buttons.

MEMORY The part of a computer or sophisticated phone system which stores information or instructions for use. Memory comes in many variations.

There is memory which is lost when the power is switched off. There is memory which is retained when power is turned off.

MEMORY ADMINISTRATION MA. A set of functions that provide network system database updates, network system database integrity, network system database security and network system database backup and restoration. Definition from Bellcore in reference to its concept of the Advanced Intelligent Network.

MEMORY BOARD An add-on board designed to increase a computer's amount of RAM.

MEMORY CACHING A technology for increasing hardware performance by storing frequently used sequences of instructions in a memory cache separate from the computer's main memory where they can be more quickly accessed by the CPU.

MEMORY CALL SERVICE A family of central office based voice messsaging services from BellSouth.

MEMORY CARDS The memory card is a bunch of memory chips crammed into a small plastic cartridge about the size of a credit card and about three times the thickness. It is is used in several palmtop computers. As this dictionary was being written, we were awaiting the release of a 16 megabyte memory card. In contrast to flash memory, a memory card requires small batteries, typically the same ones as used in watches.

MEMORY INTERFACE A PCMCIA definition. The memory interface is the default interface after power up, PCMCIA Hard Reset and PCMCIA Soft Reset for both PCMCIA cards and sockets. This interface supports memory operations as defined in PCMCIA Release 1.0 and later and is used by both Memory Cards and I/O Cards.

MEMORY MAP An indication of what type of data is stored where in a computer's RAM memory.

MEMORY RESERVE POWER The operating voltage, generally provided by a battery, which supplies power to the memory modules when your commercial power fails. You should check your memory reserve power before it's too late. You should test it even when you don't need it.

MEMORY TECHNOLOGY DRIVER A PCMCIA card definition. A memory technology driver is a memory device specific software that interfaces to Card Services to mask the details of accessing different memory technologies.

MENU Options displayed on a computer terminal screen or spoken by a voice processing system. The user can choose what he wants done by simply choosing a menu option — either typing it on the computer keyboard, hitting a touchtone on his phone or speaking a word or two. There are basically two ways of organizing computer or voice processing software — menu-driven and non-menu driven. Menu-driven programs are easier to use but they can only present as many options as can be reasonably crammed on a screen or spoken in a few seconds. Non-menu driven screens allow more alternatives but are much more complex and frightening. It's the difference between receiving a bland "A" or "C" prompt on the screen — as in MS-DOS and receiving a menu of "Press A if you want Word Processing," "Press B if you want Spread Sheet," etc. It's very easy to write menus in MS-DOS using BATch files. See also AUDIO MENUS and PROMPTS.

MERIDIAN A Northern Telecom name for its family of PBXs. In recent years, Northern's PBXs have evolved from the SL-1 family to the Meridian SL-1 family to the Meridian 1 family, which Northern says will support from 30 to 60,000 lines.

MERIDIAN LINK Northern Telecom's product for linking its Meridian 1 PBX with a variety of host (i.e. external computer) protocols. Meridian Link connects with Digital's CIT, Hewlett-Packard's ACT and IBM's CallPath Services Architecture. As of March 1991, Meridian Link is available in a fully integrated version: Meridian Link Module is a VME based UNIX application processor wholly contained in a Meridan 1 module. See OPEN APPLICATION INTERFACE.

MERIDIONAL RAY In fiber optics, a ray that passes through the optical axis of an optical fiber. This contrasts with a skew ray, which does not.

MERLIN AT&T's first electronic key system, distinguished by futuristic styling, horrible membrane line keys, non-standard 8-conductor wiring scheme, and expensive accessories. Later versions were much better. See below.

MERLIN PLUS Second Generation of AT&T's Merlin electronic key telephone system. It introduced such features as call forwarding, automated attendant, remote system access, auto-busy-redial, and direct station access.

MERLIN II Third generation of AT&T's Merlin electronic key telephone system. Uses digital technology, and either older analog Merlin phones, dedicated single-line phones or newer digital multi-line phones. Programming is menu-driven. Features include hospitality functions and automatic route selection. Accepts Legend circuit boards and phones.

MERLIN LEGEND Fourth Generation of AT&T's Merlin phone system, actually considered an enhancement of previous Merlin II. Maximum size is 90 lines and 144 phones (but not both maximums in same system). Operates in either key system, PBX or "behind switch" mode. T-1 compatible. Works with either older Merlin phones or new line of MLX digital phones, with more conventional styling than older Merlin phones.

MERLIN CLASSIC Term applied to original series of AT&T's MERLIN 206, 410 and 820 electronic key telephone systems.

MERS Most Economical Route Selection. A term used by GTE and some other PBX manufacturers to mean Least Cost Routing. See LEAST COST ROUTING.

MESA ARCHITECTURE Centigram's trademarked brand name for its architecture that stands for Modularly Expandable System Architecture: 1. The capability to expand and/or enhance a VoiceMemo II system hardware and software in a modular fashion. 2. The capability to expand a single module VoiceMemo II into a multi-module system with a single database and centralized control.

MESA-FLEX Centigram's service design utility that allows a VoiceMemo II system to be fully customized through individually designed Feature Class of Service, independent Limits Classes of Service, Group Classes of Service and Network Classes of Service.

MESALINK Centigram's registered trademark for its inter-processor high speed bus that carries control information to the distributed processors.

MESH NETWORK A data network that provides multiple paths between points. Internetworking devices choose the most efficient pathways in moving data from one point to another.

MESO The Greek prefix meaning the middle.

MESOCHRONOUS The relationship between two signals such that their corresponding significant instants occur at the same average rate.

MESSAGE 1. A sequence of characters used to convey information or data. In data communications, messages are usually in an agreed format with a heading which establishes the address to which the message will be sent and the text which is the actual message and maybe some information to signify the end of the message. A Northern Telecom Norstar definition: A message, which appears on the telephone display that informs the recipient to call the person who sent the message. Messages can only be sent within the Norstar system. 2. The Layer 3 information in the OSI model that is passed between the CPE and SPCS for signaling.

MESSAGE ALERT A cellular phone term, also called "call-in-absence" indicator. A light or other indicator announcing that a phone call came in, an especially important feature if the cellular subscriber has VOICE MAIL.

MESSAGE ALIGMENT INDICATOR In a signal message, data transmitted between the user part and the message transfer part to identify the boundaries of the signal message.

MESSAGE CENTER A centralized place within the corporation where messages are taken and (occasionally) delivered. Message centers are good if they are staffed with competent, motivated people and the various phones in the place have message waiting lights (like they do in hotels). If staffed by talented people, message centers work a lot better than the amateur message takers called secretaries and their part-time short-term replacements.

MESSAGE DETAIL RECORDING See CALL DETAIL RECORDING and CALL ACCOUNTING SYSTEMS.

MESSAGE FORMAT The rules for placing information necessary for an electronic message. The format includes where the heading is and how long it will be as well as other control information.

MESSAGE HANDLING SERVICE MHS. A utility for Novell NetWare LANs that provides a common format for exchanging information among applications. MHS is most commonly used for e-mail (electronic mail). Various e-mail programs use the MHS format for exchanging e-mail messages.

MESSAGE HANDLING SYSTEM MHS. The standard defined by CCITT as X.400 and by ISO as Message-Oriented Text Interchange Standard (MOTIS). MHS is the X.400 family of services and protocols that provides the functions for global electronic-mail transfer among local mail systems.

MESSAGE HEADER The header before a string of data containing information regarding the destination of the data, usually in a packet in X.25 format.

MESSAGE MANAGEMENT A new term for managing all your voice mail, fax mail and electronic mail. The major concept is to join the control of the devices that produce voice, fax and e-mail through your desktop PC connected over your LAN. For example, you come into work in the morning, turn your PC on, and immediately see a screenful of messages — one line per message. By clicking on that line with your mouse, your PC would pull up the application that will then let you read or hear your message. The benefit is that you can handle your messages faster and be more discriminating about which ones you pay most and least attention to.

MESSAGE PACKET A unit of information used in network communication. Messages sent between network devices (workstations, file servers, etc.) are formed into packets at the source device. The packets are reassembled, if necessary, into complete messages when they reach their destination. A message packet might contain a request for service, information on how to handle the request, and the data that will be serviced. An individual packet consists of headers and a data portion. Additional headers are appended to the data portion as the packet travels through the layers of the communication protocol. Any message that exceeds the maximum size is partitioned and carried as several packets. When the packet arrives at its destination, the headers are stripped off, the message delivered and the request serviced.

MESSAGE RATE A method of billing local phone calls that varies from one place to another. Phone calls are billed as "message units." Message units are a combination of length of call and distance of the call. In a city like New York you might buy "basic" phone service and be entitled to 50 "message units." That may mean you can call the local pizza house for under 5 minutes 50 times. Or it may mean that you can call from Manhattan to the Bronx 25 times — assuming each call is two message units.

MESSAGE UNIT See MESSAGE RATE.

MESSAGE REGISTER LEADS Terminal equipment leads at the interface used solely for receiving dc message register pulses from a central office at a PBX so that message unit information normally recorded at the central office only is also recorded at the PBX.

MESSAGE REGISTRATION A phone system feature that records the number of message units incurred by each phone. Useful in hotels which bill local calls by message units.

MESSAGE RETRIEVAL The ability of a fax machine to store material already transmitted so it can be retransmitted.

MESSAGE SIGNAL UNIT Signal unit of CCS that carries a message corresponding to the information part or packet of the HDLC frame plus a message transfer part corresponding to the HDLC frame header.

MESSAGE STORE An X.400 electronical mail term: A staging point, similar to a post office, in which messages are temporarily held for later transmission to one or more recipients.

MESSAGE SWITCHING A technique for receiving a message, storing it for a while and then sending it on. Message switching is normally used when the desired recipient is not there. The message switch will keep attempting delivery, freeing the calling party to handle other work. Unlike voice phone calls no direct connection is made in message switching between the incoming and outgoing messages. Each message, like a Western Union telegram, contains a destination address and is recipient through intermediate nodes. Each node along the way receives the message, stores it briefly, and then passes it on to the next node.

MESSAGE SWITCHING NETWORK A public data communications network over which subscribers send primarily text messages to one another.

MESSAGE TELECOMMUNICATIONS SERVICE MTS. The regulatory term for long distance or message toll voice service. Misnamed. Actually there's nothing "message-y" about this service. This is a 100% switched voice service (though it can obviously be used for data).

MESSAGE TELEPHONE SERVICE MTS. Official designation for tariffed long-distance, or toll, telephone service. See MESSAGE TELECOMMUNICATIONS SERVICE.

MESSAGE TRANSFER AGENT An X.400 electronical mail term: Software usually residing in a LAN server or host computer that moves messages between senders and recipients.

MESSAGE UNIT The charge for one unit of local telephone service. How many message units you will find on your bill is a function of how many calls you made, how far the calls traveled, what time of the day or night you called and for how long you talked.

MESSAGE UNIT DETAIL MUD. A service offered by local telephone companies in which they give you a report listing the phone number of all local calls made from each of your billing numbers. The billing number may be the main number for a PBX or the individual extensions if Centrex service is used. MUD reports are usually available to a telephone company customer at additional cost. MUD reports generally have to be requested in advance. Some telephone company central offices cannot generate MUD reports. When available, MUD reports may not be in machine processible form.

MESSAGE WAITING A light on the phone or some letters or characters on the phone's display indicating there's a message waiting somewhere for the owner of the phone. That message might be with a special message center (as in a hotel or a larger company), with the operator or with a computer attached to the phone system or with someone else in the company. Message waiting lights are incredibly useful at hotels. It's amazing more companies don't use them also.

MESSAGE-TO-SLAVE DIRECTORY PROPAGATION In electronic mail on a local area network, message-to-slave directory propagation is a way of updating user addresses where changes in the master post office are sent to the slaves, but changes in the slave post offices are not sent to the master.

MESSAGING APPLICATION PROGRAMMING INTERFACE MAPI. See MAPI.

MESSENGER A piece of heavy metal cabling attached to a pole line to support aerial phone cable.

MET Multibutton Electronic Telephone for an old phone system called AT&T Horizon.

METAL TAPE Recording tape coated with iron particles and noted for its wide dynamic range and wide frequency response.

METALLIC CIRCUIT A circuit completely provided by metallic wire conductors, and not containing any carrier, radio or fiber and in which the ground or earth forms no part.

METALLIC VOLTAGE A potential difference between metallic conductors, as opposed to a potential difference between metallic conductor and ground.

METALLIZATION Metallization is necessary if composites are to be used in antenna applications. Antennas are mainly metallized with copper or gold. Composite systems that lend themselves to metallization are those epoxy and thermoplastic composites with Kevlar, glass or carbon fibre reinforcement.

METAPHOR See DESKTOP METAPHOR.

METEOR BURST COMMUNICATIONS Communications by radio signals reflected by ionized meteor trails.

METER The metric unit of length, equivalent to 39.37 inches. An instrument for measuring quantities of length.

METERING PULSES In virtually all foreign countries, periodic pulses are returned from the distant exchange to the exchange (central office) of the calling number. These pulses determine the cost of the call, local or long distance. Typically, all pulses cost the same. However, the farther you call, the quicker the pulses come. This system contrasts to the North American long distance billing scheme which typically charges a certain amount for the first minute — no matter how much of the minute is actually used in conversation. After the first minute in the U.S., conversations are billed in one minute increments. Overseas pulses can be as short as three or four seconds (especially for international calls).

METROPOLITAN AREA NETWORK MAN. A loosely defined term generally understood to describe a broadband network covering an area larger than a local area network. It typically interconnects two or more local area networks, may operate at a higher speed, may cross administrative boundaries, and may use multiple access methods. It may carry data, voice, video and image.

METROPOLITAN DIAL The common rotary dial or touch-tone pad that contains both numbers and letters. Dials and pads are also available without the letters. Presumably metropolitan areas required the letters because of multiple central office exchanges, but rural areas with few subscribers and only one CO, required just a few digits and no letters.

MF See MULTI-FREQUENCY PULSING.

MFD Abbreviation for Microfarad; one thousandth of a farad, the unit of measuring capacitance. The capacitor is a common electrical device that can store electric charges, and pass AC but not DC. Most phones use capacitors to disconnect the bell during conversations.

MFJ The Modified Final Judgement is the federal court ruling that set up the rules and regulations concerning deregulation and divestiture of AT&T and the Bell system.

MFM 1. Modified Frequency Modulation. An encoding scheme used to record data on the magnetic surfaces of hard disks. It is the oldest and slowest of the Winchester hard disk interface standards. RLL (Run Length Limited encoding) is a newer standard, for example. 2. Multi Function Module. A term in the AT&T Merlin phone system. MLM is an adapter that has a tip/ring mode for answering machines, modems, FAX machines, and tip/ring alerts, and a Supplemental Alert Adapter mode for 48VDC alerts. It supplies the connection of optional equipment such as answering machines, external alerts, and FAX machines to a Merlin MLX telephone. The MFM is installed inside the MLX telephone.

MFOS MultiFunction Operations System. An AT&T term.

MFLOPS Million Floating point Operations Per Second. A measure of computing power usually associated with large computers. Also known as MEGAFLOPS.

MFSK Multiple Frequency Shift Keying.

MIB Management Information Base. A directory listing the logical names of all information resources residing in a network and pertinent to the network's management. Within the Internet MIB employed for SNMP (Simple Network Management Protocol)-based management, ASN.1 (Abstract Syntax Notation One) is used to describe network management variables. These variables, which include such information as error counts or on/off status of a device, are assigned a place on a tree data structure. MIB is used in X.400 electronic mail. See INTERNET MIB TREE.

MIB-I The initial collection of objects and attributes defined by the TCP/IP (Transmission Control Protocol/Internet Protocol) standards community. MIB-I was elevated to Internet standard status in May 1990.

MIC Medium Interface Connnector.

MICR An imaging term. Magnetic Ink Character Recognition. The type of ink they print on checks.

MID-SPAN MEET Sonet's ability to mix the terminal, multiplexing and cross-connect equipment from different vendors. A major accomplishment for standardization. Wish more telecom systems could meet mid-span. Sadly, most can't.

MIDI Musical Instrument Digital Interface, a standard protocol for communication between musical instruments and computers.

MIDSPLIT A broadband cable system in which the cable bandwidth is divided between transmit and receive frequencies. The bandwidth used to send toward the head-end (reverse direction) is about 5 MHz to 100 Mhz, and the bandwidth used to send away from the head-end (forward direction) is about 160 MHz to 300 Mhz. The guard band between the forward and reverse directions (100 MHz to 160 MHz) provides isolation from interference.

MH Modified Huffman data compression method.

MHO The unit of conductivity.

MHS Message Handling Service. A program developed by Action Technologies (and others) and marketed by those firms and Novell to exchange files with other programs and send files out through gateways to other computers and mail networks. It is used particularly to link dissimilar electronic-mail systems. A company running e-mail on their internal LAN will dedicate one computer on the network to be a MHS machine. Every hour or so it will call MCI Mail, CompuServe, etc. and download e-mail messages for people and upload messages from people on the network. Once it has the messages downloaded it will distribute them to the people on the LAN the messages are destined for. See MHS MESSAGE HANDLING SYSTEM.

MHS MESSAGE HANDLING SYSTEM An ISO standard Application Layer protocol that defines a framework for distributing data from one network to several others. It transfers relatively small messages in a store-and-forward manner (defined by CCITT as X.400 and by ISO as MOTIS/Message-Oriented Text Interchange Standard). See MHS.

MHz An abbreviation for Megahertz. One million Hertz. One million cycles per second. A measure of sine waves used for telecommunications. Megabertz is also used by the computer industry more loosely to mean millions of clock cycles per second. Everything that happens in a computer is timed according to a clock which ticks millions of times every second. Higher MHz computers work faster than lower MHz computers, and all the components inside the computer should be able to keep up with the system's clock speed. Slow PCs and Macs run 8MHz. Fast ones run as high as 100 MHz.

MIC A designation for a multiplex which interfaces between two DSIs and one DSIC circuit.

MICHAEL Harry's favorite son. (His only one, in case you hadn't guessed already.)

MICKEY Unit of space that a mouse moves, measured at 1/200th of an inch.

MICOM A manufacturer of data and voice equipment located in Simi Valley, CA.

MICR Magnetic Ink Character Recognition. A process of character recognition where printed characters containing particles of magnetic material, are read by a scanner and converted into a computer-readable digital format.

MICRO One-millionth.

MICRO CASSETTE Miniaturized version of the standard audio cassette.

MICRO CHANNEL A proprietary bus developed by IBM for its PS/2 family of computers' internal expansion cards. Also offered by NCR, Tandy and other vendors. See ISA and EISA.

MICRO COMPONENTS Miniaturized audio components that provide the benefits of traditional sized components in far less space.

MICRO FARAD One millionth of a farad. This is the common unit for designation capacitance in electronics and communications.

MICRO TO MAINFRAME LINK The telecommunications path over which data between a microcomputer and a mainframe computer travels.

MICRO TO MAINFRAME SOFTWARE Software which provides the logic by which data can be transferred back and forth between a microcomputer and a mainframe computer.

MICROBEND LOSS In an optical fiber, that loss attributable to macrobending.

MICROCELL 1. A PacTel technology to improve cellular calling coverage in areas where high quality cellular service has never been available. PacTel MicroCell, according to PacTel, will reach into canyons, freeway underpasses and high-rise areas where it has sometimes been impossible to provide good cellular coverage. MicroCell uses very small antennas that can be mounted on utility poles or billboards or in other inconspicuous places. The microcell technology can direct the cellular signal right into an isolated trouble spot, leaving broader coverage to conventional cellular sites. 2. A cellular radio cell aimed at serving pedestrians, not automobile drivers. Microcells are smaller, lower-powered, simpler and smaller than macrocells. See MACROCELL.

MICROCHANNEL A proprietary bus developed by IBM for its PS/2 family of computers' internal expansion cards. Also offered by Tandy and other vendors. See ISA and EISA.

MICROCODE Programmed instructions that typically are unalterable. Usually synonymous with firmware and programmable read-only-memory (PROM).

MICROCOM NETWORK PROTOCOL. The Microcom Networking Protocol, MNP, is a defacto standard protocol that provides error correction and data compression in dial-up modems. The protocol's design allows for a broad range of services to be implemented, while maintaining compatibility among modems with different levels of MNP capabilities. For example, a modem capable of MNP Class 5 and Class 7 data compression can talk to a modem that lacks MNP data compression.

According to Microcom, "MNP is an error correction protocol accepted by international standards authorities (CCITT Rec. V.42). MNP offers a reliable and widely accepted method of correcting errors in transmissions over dial-up communications lines. MNP incorporates three different data compression methods, including the CCITT recommendation, V.42bis.

Since its original definition, MNP has evolved through nine classes of enhancements. Of those nine classes, the first four provide error control and are in the public domain. Classes 5 through 7 may be licensed from Microcom. Currently MNP error control (Classes 2,3 and 4) has been adopted, along with the LAPM protocol, as mandatory elements of the Consultative Committee on International Telegraphy and Telephony (CCITT) V.42 recommendation for modem error control.

AN OVERVIEW OF MNP SERVICE CLASSES

Class 1. This is the first level of MNP performance. MNP Class 1 uses an asynchronous byte-oriented half-duplex method of exchanging data. MNP Class 1 implementations make minimal demands of processor speeds and memory storage. MNP Class 1 makes it possible for devices with few hardware resources to communicate error-free. Class 1 implementations are no longer included in modems.

Class 2. MNP Class 2 uses asynchronous byte-oriented full-duplex data exchange (i.e., data goes in both directions at once). All microprocessor-based modems are capable of supporting MNP Class 2 performance.

Class 3. This class uses synchronous bit-oriented full-duplex data exchange, eliminating the overhead of start and stop bits used in byte-oriented asynchronous communications. The user still sends data asynchronously to the modem while communications between modems is synchronous.

Class 4. This class introduces two new concepts. Adaptive Packet Assembly and Data Phase Optimization, both of which further enhance performance. Adaptive Packet Assembly means that the size of the packets in which data is sent between modems is altered according to the quality of the physical link. The higher the line quality, the larger the packets. Larger packets, while more efficient (the ratio of user data to control data is higher), are also more susceptible to errors. Data Phase Optimization means that repetitive control information is removed from the data stream to make packets more efficient. Both techniques, when combined with Class 3, yield a protocol efficiency of about 120 percent (A V.22bis 2400 bps modem will realize approximately a 2900 bps throughput).

Class 5. This class implements MNP basic data compression to realize a net throughput efficiency of 200 percent on average. (A 2400 bps modem will realize 4800 bps). Class 5 uses a real-time adaptive algorithm to compress data. The real-time aspects of the algorithm allow the data compression to operate on interactive terminal data as well as file transfer data. The adaptive nature of the algorithm means data compression is always optimized for the user's data. The compression algorithm continuously analyzes the user data and adjusts the compression parameters to maximize data throughput.

Class 6. This class implements Universal Link Negotiation. and Statistical Duplexing. The first feature allows a single modem to operate at a full range of speeds between 300 and 9600 bps, depending on the maximum speed of the modem on the other end of the link. Modems begin operation at a common slower speed and negotiate the use of an alternative high speed modulation technique.

The Microcom AX/9624c modem is an example of a modem that uses Universal Link Negotiation, starting with 2400 bps. V.22bis technology and shifting to 9600 bps V.29 fast train technology, if the other modem has that technology too. Statistical Duplexing allows the modem to simulate full-duplex service on the half-duplex V.29 modem connection.

Class 7. This class implements a more efficient data compression method than the one used in Class 5. The difference between the two classes is that Class 5 realizes an average 200 percent speed improvement over a non-MNP modem, versus an average 300 percent improvement for Class 7. Class 7 data compression uses Huffman encoding with a predictive algorithm to represent user data in the shortest possible Huffman codes.

In addition to Class 5 and Class 7 data compression, MNP also supports V.42bis data compression. Based on the Lempel Ziv data compression model, V.42bis supports an average 400 percent efficiency improvement.

Class 8. Not defined.

Class 9. This class reduces the amount of time required for the modem to perform two frequently-occurring administrative activities: to acknowledge that a message was received- and to retransmit information following an error. Message acknowledgment is streamlined by "piggy-backing" the acknowledgment in its own dedicated packet. Retransmission is streamlined by indicating in the error or Negative Acknowledgment Packet (NAK) the order sequence number of each of the failed messages. Rather then sending all the messages over again (even the good ones) from the point of the error, as is usually done with error correcting protocols, only the failed messages are resent.

Class 10. MNP Class 10 consists of Adverse Channel Enhancements that optimize performance in environments with poor or varying line quality, such as cellular telephones, international telephone calls, and rural telephone service. These enchancements fall into four categories:

1. Multiple aggressive attempts at link setup

2. Adapting packet size to accommodate varying levels of interference

3. Negotiating transmission speed shifts to achieve the maximum acceptable line speed

4. Dynamically shifting to the modem speed most suitable to transmission line conditions.

See ERROR CONTROL PROTOCOLS and LZW.

MICROCOMPUTER The combination of CPU (Central Processing Unit) and other peripherals (I/O, memory, etc.) that form a basic computer system. See MICROPROCESSOR.

MICROFLOPPIES The latest generation of floppy disks at 3 1/2 inches diameter, invented by Sony. The microfloppy is used in the Apple Macintosh and most MS-DOS laptop computers. Used in an MS-DOS machine, a 3 1/2 inch microfloppy diskette will currently format to carry 1.44 million bytes of data — equivalent to about 500 pages of double-spaced text.

MICROFORM Microform means Microfiche and Microfilm.

MICROGRAPHICS Conversion of information into or from microfilm or microfiche.

MICRON One thousandth of a millimeter. Or one millionth of a meter. A unit of measurement corresponding to 1/25,000 of an inch. A micron can be used to specify the core diameter of fiber-optic network cabling. This diameter should match your hardware vendor's requirements; but if you install fiber before you buy the equipment, specify the 62.5-micron size.

MICROPHONE A transducer that changes the air pressure of sound waves into an electrical signal that can be recorded, amplified and/or transmitted to another location.

MICROPROCESSOR An electronic circuit, usually on a single chip, which performs arithmetic, logic and control operations, with the assistance of internal memory. The microprocessor is the fabled "computer on a chip," the "brains" behind all desktop personal computers. Typically, the microprocessor contains read only memory — ROM — (permanently stored instructions), read and write memory — RAM, and a control decoder for breaking down the instructions stored in ROM into detailed steps for action by the arithmetic logic unit — ALU — which actually carries out the numerical calculations. There's also a clock circuitry which connects the chip to an exterior quartz crystal whose vibrations coordinate the chip's operations, keeping everything in step. And finally, the input/output section directs communications with devices on the outside of the chip, such as the keyboard, the screen and the various disk drives.

The Fortune Magazine issue of May 6, 1991 contained a very good explanation of chips and microprocessors (usually used interchangeably). Here is the article, slightly condensed:

Chips today can store and retrieve data, perform a simple mathematical calculation, or compare two numbers or words in a few billionths of a second. And they can carry out tens of thousands of such tasks in the blink of an eye. Today's chips contain millions of transistors, capacitors, diodes, and other electronic components, all connected by metallic threads a fraction of the diameter of a human hair. A single chip the size of a fingernail can store dozens of pages of text or combine circuits that can perform scores of tasks simultaneously.

Most chips fall into one of two categories - memory chips and logic chips. Memory chips have the easier job: They merely store information that will be manipulated by the logic chips, the ones with the smarts. Today's biggest-selling memory chip (mid-1991) is the one-megabit dynamic random access memory, or DRAM. Each DRAM is a slice of silicon embedded with a lattice of 1,000 vertical and 1,000 horizontal aluminum wires that circumscribe one million data cells. The densest DRAM designed so far has 64 million cells.

Think of those wires as streets and those cells as blocks. Each block contains a transistor that can be turned on or off — to signify 1 or 0 — and that can be identified by it's unique "address" in the wire grid, much like a house in a suburban subdivision. Each digit, letter, or punctuation mark is represented by 1's or 0's stored in eight-cell strings. (See ASCII.) The word "chip" takes up 32 cells in a memory chip. Most PCs sold today have at least eight one-megabit DRAMs.

It's the job of the logic chips to turn those transistors in the DRAMs on or off, and to retrieve and manipulate that information once it's stored. The most important and complex logic chips are microprocessors like Intel's 80386DX, the brains of the more powerful IBM-compatible PCs sold today. If the structure of a memory chip is a suburban subdivision, the layout of a microprocessor is more like an entire metropolitan area, with distinct neighborhoods devoted to different activities. A typical microprocessor contains among other things:

● A timing system that synchronizes the flow of information to and from memory and throughout the rest of the chip.

● An address directory that keeps track of where data and program instructions are stored in the DRAMs.

● An arithmetic logic unit with all the circuits needed to crunch numbers.

● On-board instructions that control the sequence of microprocessor operations.

Other logic chips in a computer take their cues from the microprocessor millions of times each second to draw images on the screen, to feed instructions from a spreadsheet program, say, out of the disk drives into DRAMs, or to dispatch data to a modem or a printer. Perhaps most amazing of all, memory and logic chips can accomplish all this with just a trickle of electricity - far less than it takes to light a flashlight bulb.

Ted Hoff at Intel invented the microprocessor in 1971. See also 1971 in the beginning of this dictionary.

MICROSECOND One millionth of a second.

MICROSOFT Founded in 1975 by Bill Gates and Paul Allen, Microsoft is (or was at the time of writing this edition of this dictionary) one of the largest software companies in the world. It is the originator of At Work, MICROSOFT AT WORK, MS-DOS, Windows, Windows NT and Windows Telephony. See AT WORK, MS-DOS, WINDOWS, WINDOWS NT and WINDOWS TELEPHONY.

MICROSOFT AT WORK A new architecture announced on June 9, 1993. It consists of a set of software building blocks that will sit in both office machines and PC products, including:

● Desktop and network-connected printers.

● Digital monochrome and color copiers.

- Telephones and voice messaging systems.
- Fax machines and PC fax products.
- Handheld systems.
- Hybrid combinations of the above.

According to Microsoft, the Microsoft At Work architecture focuses on creating digital connections between machines (i.e. the ones above) to allow information to flow freely throughout the workplace. The Microsoft At Work software architecture consists of several technology components that serve as building blocks to enable these connections. Only one of the components, desktop software, will reside on PCs. The rest will be incorporated into other types of office devices (the ones above), making these products easier to use, compatible with one another and compatible with Microsoft Windows-based PCs. The components, according to Microsoft, are:

- Microsoft At Work operating system. A real-time, pre-emptive, multitasking operating system that is designed to specifically address the requirements of the office automation and communication industries. The new operating system supports Windows-compatible application programming interfaces (APIs) where appropriate for the device.

- Microsoft At Work communications. Will provide the connectivity between Microsoft At Work-based devices and PCs. It will support the secure transmission of original digital documents, and it is compatible with the Windows Messaging API and the Windows Telephony API of the Windows Open Services Architecture (WOSA).

- Microsoft At Work rendering. Will make the transmission of digital documents, with formatting and fonts intact, very fast and, consequently, cost-effective; will ensure that a document sent to any of these devices will produce high-quality output, referred to as "What You Print Is What You Fax Is What You Copy Is What You See."

- Microsoft At Work graphical user interface. Will make all devices very easy to use and will make sophisticated features accessible; will provide useful feedback to users. Leveraging Microsoft's experience in the Windows user interface, Microsoft At Work-based products will use very simple graphical user interfaces designed for people who are not computer users.

- Microsoft At Work desktop software for Windows-based PCs. Will provide Windows-based PC applications the ability to control, access and exchange information with any product based on Microsoft At Work. Desktop software is the one piece of the Microsoft At Work architecture that will reside on PCs. See also FAX AT WORK, VOICE SERVER, WINDOWS, WINDOWS TELEPHONY and WOSA.

MICROSOFT SQL SERVER A Microsoft retail product that provides distributed database managment. Multiple workstations manipulate data stored on a server, where the server coordinates operations and performs resource-intensive calculations.

MICROTAC A Motorola name for a family of small handheld cellular phones.

MICROVAX II DEC's minicomputer operating system which runs on Berkeley UNIX (also known as 4.2).

MICROWAVE Electromagnetic waves in the radio frequency spectrum above 890 Megahertz (million cycles per second) and below 20 Gigahertz (billion cycles per second). (Some people say microwave refers to frequencies between 1 GHz and 30 GHz.) Microwave is a common form of transmitting telephone, facsimile, video and data conversations used by common carriers as well as by private networks. Microwave signals only travel in straight lines. In terrestrial microwave systems, they're typically good for 30 miles, at which point you need another repeater tower. Microwave is the frequency for communicating to and from satellites.

MIF Minimum Internetworking Functionality. A general principle within the ISO that calls for minimum local area network station complexity when interconnecting with resources outside the local area network.

MIGRATION An AT&T marketing strategy designed to encourage all phone equipment month-to-month renters into long-term contracts for AT&T's "flagship products", i.e., System 75, 85 and Definity PBXs.

MIL 1/1000 of an inch.

MILEAGE See AIRLINE MILEAGE.

MILLI One thousandth. Millisecond equals one thousand of a second.

MILLIWATT One thousandth of a WATT. Used as a reference point for signal levels at a given point in a circuit.

MIM Metal-Insulator-Metal. A display technology which uses active matrix technology that uses diodes behind each pixel to produce images. It is an improvement on passive displays but a step behind TFT (thin Film Transistor) technology. See also LCD.

MIMD Multiple Instruction Multiple Data is a type of parallel processing computer, which includes dozens of processors. Each processor can run different parts of the same program and execute those instructions on different data. This makes it more flexible, though more expensive than a computer running SIMD — single instruction multiple data.

MIN Mobile Identification Number. The MIN is the actual seven digit cellular telephone number assigned by the cellular carrier exclusively to your phone.

MINI-FLOPPY A floppy disk that is 3 1/2 inches in diameter. Also called a microfloppy. See MICROFLOPPY.

MINI-MAP Mini-Manufacturing Automation Protocol. A version of MAP consisting of only physical, link and application layers intended for lower-cost process-control networks. With mini-MAP, a device with a token can request a response from an addressed device. Unlike a standard MAP protocol, the addressed Mini-MAP device need not wait for the token to respond.

MINICLAS A service from New York Telephone which allows a small (up to 199 lines) Centrex III user to make certain changes to his own Centrex features and lines with an easy-to-use computer program or a touch-tone phone. See also CLAS.

MIMIMAL REGULATION Regulated local telephone company under limited state regulation has the ability to file price lists for services and those price lists are usually effective on 10-days' notice to local state commission and customers. This means there are no extensive hearings.

MINIMIZE BUTTON The minimize button is the down-arrow button at the immediate right of a title bar in Windows software. Clicking the minimize button will shrink a window to its icon.

MINIMUM INTERNETWORKING FUNCTIONALITY MIF. A general principle within the ISO that calls for minimum local network station complexity when interconnecting with resources outside the local network.

MINITEL French name for videotex. Very popular. See VIDEOTEX and packet switched networks.

MIPS Millions of Instructions Per Second. A measure of computer speed that refers to the average number of machine language instructions performed by the CPU in one second. A typical Intel 80386-based PC is a 3 to 5 MIPS machine, whereas an IBM System 370 mainframe typically delivers between 5 and 40 MIPS. MIPS measures raw CPU performance, but not overall system performance.

MIRRORING A fault tolerance method in which a backup data storage device maintains data identical to that on the primary device and can replace the primary if it fails. Mirroring will typically cost you a 50% performance degradation when your write to disk and 0% performance degradation when you are reading. For a full explanation, see DISK MIRRORING.

MIS 1. Management Information System. A fancy name for Data Processing. MIS are also the first three letters of the word MISanthrope and MISguided and lots of other MIS words. MIS departments are taking over corporate telecommunications departments which is why there's little love lost between the two. 2. IBM-speak for Management Initiated Separation. Translation: You're fired.

MISCELLANEOUS COMMON CARRIER A communications common carrier (typically one using microwave) which is not offering switched service to the public or to companies. A miscellaneous common carrier usually provides video and radio leased line transmission services to TV and radio networks.

MISCELLANEOUS TRUNK RESTRICTIONS Denies preselected lines access to preselected trunk groups (e.g., FX or WATS trunks). A call attempt over a restricted group routes to an intercept tone.

MISSION CRITICAL SYSTEMS Systems on which the future success of an organisation depends.

MIXED CABLE Cables have characteristic impedances which vary according to the cables' physical parameters. When cables of different characteristic impedance are mixed, an impedance imbalance will occur. It is thus bad practice to mix different wire gauges, and twisted or non-twisted pair cables. However, it is accepted practice to combine long runs of twisted pair cable with short lengths of modular patch cords and line cords. Baluns are an exception to this rule.

MIXED MODE An imprecise term which suggests that one digital bit stream can carry voice, data, facsimile and video signals.

MIXED MODE NIGHT SERVICE After-hours answering of incoming calls in which Assigned Night Answer (ANA) is specified for some trunks, and Universal Night Answer (UNA) specified for others.

MIXED STATION DIALING A telephone system feature which allows you to install both rotary and pushbutton phones on your phone system. Most modern PBXs have this feature.

MLHG MultiLine Hunt Group

MLID Mutliple Link Interface Driver. A layer of the Novell Open DataLink Interface specification. The MLID layer controls a specific network interface, and works below the Link Support Layer.

MLL Monthly Leased Lines.

MLPP See MULTILEVEL PRECEDENCE PREEMPTION.

MLT Mechanized Loop Testing.

MMFD Abbreviation for micromicrofarad; one millionth of a farad, the unit of measuring capacitance.

MMJ A six wire modular jack with the locking tab shifted off to the right hand side. Used in the DEC wiring system.

MMR Modified Modified Read data compression method used in newer Group 3 facsimile machines.

MMSU Modular Metallic Service Unit.

MNEMONIC A shorthand label or term that is easy to remember, usually made up from the initials of the words in a term or process. LASER is a mnemonic. See LASER.

MNEMONIC DIAL PLAN Pronounced "nemonic." A way of dialing using characters typed on the keyboard of a terminal. The word Mnemonic comes from the same roots as memory. It's a memory jogging way of remembering something, like a way to dial. See MNEMONIC PROMPTS.

MNEMONIC PROMPTS System commands represented by the appropriate alphabet letter rather than by a number, (for example, "P" to "Play", "A" to Answer"). See MNEMONIC DIAL PLAN.

MNP Microcom Networking Protocol. A proprietary error-correcting and data compression protocol for dial-up modems from 2.4 to 14.4 Kbps. See MICROCOM NETWORKING PROTOCOL and ERROR CONTROL PROTOCOLS for full explanations.

MOBILE CELLULAR PHONE The cellular handset unit permanently mounted in a vehicle. See CAR PHONE.

MOBILE DATA Mobile data is a generic term used to describe data communications through the air from and to field workers — from package deliverers, to car rental companies (to track cars), to field service personnel, to law enforcement officials checking license plates.

MOBILE MOUNTING KIT An optional cellular phone accessory that allows a transportable or portable to be connected to a vehicle's power supply and antenna lead, thereby boosting power and improving reception. Sometimes referred to as a car kit or carmounting kit. Some of these kits are very expensive. Check the price of the kit before you buy your phone.

MOBILE PHONE One term for a cellular phone. There are four main types of cellular phones — mobile (also called car phone), transportable, portable and personal. A mobile phone is attached to the vehicle, the vehicle's battery and has an external antenna. The mobile phone (the car phone) transmits with a standard three watts of power. Mobile telephone service is provided from a broadcast point located within range of the moving vehicle. That range is called a "cell." The broadcast point in turn is connected to the public network so that calls can be completed to or from any stationary telephone, i.e. one connected to a land line. See CELLULAR and CAR PHONE.

MODAL DISPERSION Digital pulse rounding in lightwave communications that takes place because of the slightly different paths followed by the laser light rays as they arrive at the detector slightly out of phase.

MODAL DISTRIBUTION 1. In an optical fiber operating at a single wavelength, the number of modes supported by the fiber, and their propagation time differences. 2. In an optical fiber operating at multiple wavelengths simultaneously, the separation in wavelengths among the modes being supported by the fiber.

MODAL LOSS In an open waveguide, such as an optical fiber, a loss of energy on the part of an electromagnetic wave due to obstacles outside the waveguide, abrupt changes in direction of the waveguide, or other anomalies, that cause changes in the propagation mode of the wave in the waveguide.

MODE Mode is essentially a switch inside a computer that makes it run like another computer, usually an older one.

MODEM Acronym for MOdulator/DEModulator. Equipment which converts digital signals to analog signals and vice-versa. Modems are used to send data signals (digital) over the telephone network, which usually is analog. The Modem modulates the "1's" and "0's" into tones which can be carried by the phone network. At the other end, the demodulator part of the modem converts the tones back into digital 1's and 0's. See MODEM ELIMINATOR, MODEM POOL, MODEM STANDARDS, MODULATION PROTOCOLS and SERIAL PORT.

MODEM ELIMINATOR A wiring device designed to replace two modems; it connects equipment over a distance of up to several hundred feet. In asynchronous systems, this is a simple cable. Here is a specific application using a Modem Eliminator: You can connect a PC to a printer, or a PC to another printer using a cable. But you can only go a certain distance — maybe 100 feet. After that, the traditional solution has been to use a modem and go over traditional phone lines. Instead, you can connect the two devices directly by wire using a Modem Eliminator. There are two advantages of a Modem Eliminator over a normal modem. The eliminator is cheaper and it can often transmit faster. According to Glasgal Communications, there are many cases where it is either unnecessary, cumbersome or too expensive to interconnect terminals using modems or line drivers in an experimental or a very short-haul environment. A modem eliminator functionally resembles two modems back-to-back on a leased line and therefore saves the cost of two modems and a line in many situations.

MODEM FALLBACK When the telephone line quality is not good enough to accommodate the top rated speed of a modem — for example 9,600 bps — the modem drops down to lower speeds — initially to 7,200 bps, then if necessary, to 4,800 bps, or even down to 2,400 bps.

MODEM POOL A collection of modems which a user can dial up from his terminal, access one and use that one to make a data call over the switched telephone network. Modem pools are obviously designed to allow many users to share few modems, thus saving on modems. Now that modems have become less expensive, the advantages of modem pooling are no longer as great. There are also some advantages in having a modem right next to your terminal or computer — namely you can see how it is functioning. And modems have lights to indicate what they're doing. One of the most useful lights on most modems indicates whether the line is "off hook" or not. It is possible for your computer to instruct your modem to hang up the line and for your modem to forget to do it, leaving you with a huge phone bill. One problem with giving people their own modems is they (the modems) have a tendency to get pinched. It's hard to screw down modems. Harder, anyway, than computers and disk drives.

MODEM SERVER A networked computer with a modem or group of modems attached to it that allows network users to share the modems for outbound calls.

MODEM STANDARDS Definitions of electrical and telecommunications characteristics which enable modems from dissimilar manufacturers to speak to each other. Bell 103...US standard for 300 bps; CCITT V.21...International standard for 300 bps; Bell 212A...US standard for 1200 bps; CCITT V.22...International standard for 1200 bps; CCITT V.22 bis...US and international standard for 2400 bps; CCITT V.23...International videotex standard (1200/75 bps or 75/1200 bps). See also HAYES COMMAND SET.

MODEM TURNAROUND TIME The time needed for a half-duplex modem (an old-fashioned one) to reverse its transmission direction.

MODIFIED FREQUENCY MODULATION MFM. An encoding scheme used to record data on the magnetic surfaces of hard disks. It is the oldest and slowest of the Winchester hard disk interface standards. RLL (Run Length Limited encoding) is a newer standard, for example.

MODIFIED HUFFMAN A one-dimensional data-compression scheme that compresses data in a horizontal direction only. Allows no transmission of redundant data.

MODIFIED READ A two-dimensional coding scheme for facsimile machines that handles the data compression of the vertical line and that concentrates on space between the lines and within given characters.

MODULAR Equipment is said to be modular when it is made of "plug-in units" which can be added together to make the system larger, improve its capabilities or expand its size. There are very few phone systems that are truly modular.

MODULAR JACK A device that conforms to the Code of Federations, Title 47, part 68, which defines size and configuration of all units that are permitted for connection to the public telephone network.

MODULAR PLUG A series of connecting devices adopted by the FCC as the standard interface for telephone and data equipment to the public network. The most common is the RJ-11, used to connect a single line phone.

MODULATED WAVES Alternating current waves which have their amplitude varied periodically. The signals transmitted by a radio station are examples of a modulated wave.

MODULATION The process of varying some characteristic of the electrical carrier wave as the information to be transmitted on that carrier wave varies. Three types of modulation are commonly used for communications, Amplitude Modulation, Frequency Modulation and Phase Modulation. And there are variations on these themes called Phase Shift Keying (PSK) and Quadrature Amplitude Modulation (QAM).

MODULATION INDEX In angle modulation, the ratio of the frequency deviation of the modulated signal to the frequency of a sinusoidal modulating signal. The modulation index is numerically equal to the phase deviation in radians.

MODULATION PROTOCOLS Modem stands for MOdulator/ DEModulator. A modem converts digital signals generated by the computer into analog signals which can be transmitted over an analog telephone line and transforms incoming analog signals into their digital equivalents. The specific techniques used to encode the digital bits into analog signals are called modulation protocols. The various modulation protocols define the exact methods of encoding and the data transfer speed. In fact, you cannot have a modem without modulation protocols. A modem typically supports more than one modulation protocol.

The raw speed (the speed without data compression) of a modem is determined by the modulation protocols. A 2400 bps Hayes-compatible modem typically supports the following modulation protocols:

Bell 103	(300 bps U.S. Standard)
Bell 212A	(1200 bps U.S. Standard)
CCITT V.22	(1200 bps standard used outside the U.S.)
CCITT V.22 bis	(2400 bps International Standard)

Some 2400 bps modems also support the following protocols:

CCITT V.21	(300 bps standard used outside the U.S.)
CCITT V.23	(1200/75 and 75/1200 bps, used in Europe)

There are two standard modulation protocols for high-speed modems: V.32 and V.32 bis. Both are standards established by the CCITT. V.32 is the standard for 9,600 (and 4,800) bps modems. V.32 was adopted by the CCITT in 1984.

V.32 bis, established in early 1991, is the CCITT standard for 14,400 bps modems. A V.32 bis modem also can fall back to 12,000, 9,600, 7,200 and 4,800 bps. V.32 bis is downwardly compatible with V.32.

Unlike 2400 bps modems where a single modulation protocol (V.22 bis) is supported by all modem makers, there are several proprietary modulation protocols used by V.32 and V.32 bis modems from different manufacturers. Until the recent surge of V.32 modems, the U.S. Robotics HST (High Speech Technology) was the de facto standard in the PC-based BBS community. The original Courier HST modem ran at 9,600 bps. U.S. Robotics later improved the speed of the Courier HST to 14,400 bps.

Telebit introduced the TrailBlazer in 1985 which used a proprietary modulation protocol called PEP (Packetized Ensemble Protocol). Hayes entered the high-speed modem arena in 1987 with the introduction of the V-series Smartmodem 9600. The modem used a proprietary modulation protocol called Express 96 (also known as Hayes "Ping Pong" protocol). The V-series modems have not been as successful as the U.S. Robotics or the Telebit modems.

Two modems can establish a connection only when they share a common modulation protocol. To connect at high speed, two modems have to support the same high-speed modulation protocol. Therefore, a modem with a proprietary modulation protocol can only establish a high-speed connection with another modem from the same manufacturer. A U.S. Robotics HST modem can only establish a high-speed connection (at 9600 or 14400 bps) with another HST or an USR Dual Standard modem. A Courier HST modem cannot establish a high-speed connection with a Courier V.32 bis modem. They can only connect at 2400 bps. All high-speed modems in the market support the CCITT V.22 bis modulation protocol.

On the other hand, two V.32 modems can talk to each other at 9600 bps. They do not have to be from the same manufacturer. Two V.32 bis modems can talk to each other at 14,400 bps. A V.32 modem can talk to a V.32 bis modem at 9600 bps. This is because these are public standards promulgated by a public body called CCITT.

CCITT is working on a new modem standard, dubbed V.fast. If all goes well, the next modem standard can materialize before 1993. A V.fast modem is expected to reach a raw speed of 19,200-24,000 bps over standard dial-up telephone lines.

This definition on Modulation Protocols with thanks to modem expert, Patrick Chen.

MODULATION RATE The reciprocal of the measure of the shortest nominal time interval between successive significant instants of the modulated signal.

MODULATION SUPPRESSION In the reception of an amplitude-modulated signal, an apparent reduction in the depth of modulation of a wanted signal, caused by presence, at the detector, of a stronger unwanted signal.

MODULATOR A device which converts a voice or data signal into a form that can be transmitted.

MODULO Term used to express the maximum number of states for a counter. Used to describe several packet-switched network parameters, such as packet number (usually set to modulo 8 — counted from 0 to 7). When the maximum count is exceeded, the counter is reset to 0.

MODULO N In communications, refers to a quantity, such as the number of frames or packets to be counted before the counter resets to zero.

Relates to the number of frames or packets that can be outstanding from a transmitter before an acknowledgement is required from the receiver. Also indicates the maximum number of frames or packets stored, in case a retransmission is required (i.e., Modulo 8 or Modulo 128).

MOH Music On Hold.

MOISTURE BARRIER BAG MBB. A three-ply bag with characteristics that allow minmal moisture transmission, thereby preserving plastic surface-mount packages, which are packed into the bag, in a dry state.

MOISTURE RESISTANCE The ability of a material to resist absorbing moisture from the air or when immersed in water.

MOLDING RACEWAY METHOD A cable-distribution method in which hollow metal or wood moldings support cables. Small sleeves of pipe are placed in the wall behind the molding to allow cable to pass through the wall.

MONITOR 1. To listen in on a conversation for the purpose of determining the quality of the attendant's or agent's response and politeness to customers. 2. Video monitor. TV screen and surrounding electronics. IBM personal computer monitors come in monochrome and color. The more you pay the better quality the monitor is. The quality of monitors is typically measured by how monitor's screen resolution, which is measured by pixels, or picture elements. In monochrome monitors, the "standard" is Hercules Graphics, which offers a resolution of 720 pixels horizontally by 348 vertically. The worst color monitor is called CGA, which stands for Color Graphics Adapter. It offers 320 x 200. Most low-end laptops have this resolution screen. Next better is EGA, Enhanced Graphics Adapter. It offers 640 x 350 pixels. Next better is VGA, or Video Graphics Array, which offers 640 x 480. Next up is 8514/A also called XGA, or eXtended Graphics Array, which is IBM's high-resolution extension to its VGA adapter. It provides a resolution of 1,024 horizontally x 768 vertically, yielding 786,432 possible bits of information on one screen, more than two and a half times what is possible with VGA. It will only work on IBM machines with the Micro Channel Architecture (MCA). Here is a chart showing the pixel coding of various PC standard screens.

PC SCREEN ENCODING

CGA	320 x 200
Enhanced CGA	640 x 400
EGA	640 x 350
Hercules	720 x 348
VGA	640 x 480
Super VGA	800 x 600
8514/A (also called XGA)	1,024 x 768

MONITOR ON HOLD A telephone feature. If the person you're speaking with puts you "on hold," you can turn your speaker on your phone and hang up your handset but keep listening until the other person comes back to the phone.

MONOCHROMATIC Consisting of one color or wavelength. Although light in practice is never perfectly monochromatic, it can have a narrow wavelength.

MONOCHROME MONITOR A monitor with 720 x 348 pixel resolution in a single color. Most monochrome monitors display in paper white, green or amber.

MONOSPACED FONT A font in which all characters have uniform widths. See also PROPORTIONAL FONT.

MONTH TO MONTH The standard way of paying for telephone service. Some services now come in "rate stability" packages, which means if you commit to keeping the service for a while — typically three or five years — it's cheaper each month.

MOON Magneto Optical On Network.

MOORE'S LAW First put forth by Intel chairman, Gordon Moore 25 years ago, Moore's Law states that every 18 months the number of transistors on a microprocessor will double. This has proven true for over 25 years. Intel engineers now believe that by the year 2000, a 100-million transistor microprocessor will be possible.

MOPS Millions of operations per second. Refers to a processor's performance. In the case of DVI (Digital Video Interactive) technology, more MOPS translates to better video quality. Intel's video processor can perform multiple video operations per instruction, thus the MOPS rating is usually greater than the MIPS rating.

MORSE CODE The International Morse code, named for Samuel F. B. Morse who invented telegraph, is referred to as International Telegraph Alphabet 1. Mr. Morse first demonstrated the telegraph in 1844. It is still used in radio telegraphy to ships at sea, though many ships now carry satellite antennae and subscribe to MARISAT.

Morse code represents letters by combinations of long and short signals. Morse code can be written in dots and dashes or signaled with flashlights and radio bleeps. In 1912 the easily-memorized letters SOS were chosen as the international distress signal. "Save Our Souls" was the catchphrase devised later.

```
A .-    B -...   C -.-.
D -..   E .      F ..—.
G —.    H ....   I ..
J .—    K -.-    L .-..
```

```
M—    N-.    O—
P.—.   Q—.-  R.-.
S...   T-     U..-
V...-  W.—   X-..-
Y-.—   Z—..
```

See also MORSE, SAMUEL

MORSE, SAMUEL Samuel Finley Breese Morse was born in Charlestown (now a part of Boston) on April 27, 1791. He entered Yale University at the age of 14 and graduated in 1810. Although he attended lectures on electricity while at Yale, after graduation he went to England to study art. He returned to the United States in 1815 and became a well-known painter. In 1832, while returning from Europe, he and a fellow passenger discussed the electromagnet and Morse conceived the idea of his telegraph. He made a working model about 1835 and filed for a patent in 1838 and in 1844 inaugurated public service between Washington and Baltimore with his famous message, "What hath God wrought?" He died in 1872. See MORSE CODE.

MORT AT&T's database of its dead employees.

MOS Metal Oxide Semiconductor. Technology describing a transistor composed of a semiconductor layer including "source" and "drain" regions separated by a channel. Above the channel is a thin layer of oxide and over that a metal electrode called a gate. A voltage applied to this gate controls the current between the source and drain regions, or in another format, stops a flow between the two areas. (Definition courtesy of Bell Labs)

MOST ECONOMICAL ROUTE SELECTION MERS. Used by several phone companies and several manufacturers to mean Least Cost Routing — the feature of a telephone system which automatically chooses the least cost route for a long distance call. See LEAST COST ROUTING.

MOST FAVORED NATION CLAUSE A clause added to a purchase contract with a vendor saying that for a certain period after signing the contract, if the buyer finds out that the product has been bought for less, then the seller will refund the difference. The idea is to give the purchaser the assurance of the least expensive price.

MOTHER OF The largest, greatest, grandest, of something. An expression coined in 1990 by Saddam Hussein, Iraqi dictator. The Mother Of all telephone switches would be the largest, most powerful, most elaborate etc. Such a device doesn't exist, as yet — as, in fact, Saddam Hussein's Mother of all Battles (the one against the Allies in 1990-1991) didn't exist. He lost in a the Mother Of all defeats.

MOTHERBOARD The main circuit board of a computer system. The motherboard contains edge connectors or sockets so other PC (printed circuit) boards can be plugged into it. (Those boards are typically called Fatherboards, because they plug into the Motherboard.) On IBM's new OS series of personal computers, the motherboard is called the PLANAR BOARD. Motherboards are common in key systems and hybrid key/PBXs. They are not common in PBXs, where all the electronics are typically on printed circuit cards which slide into the PBX's cage and which attach to a backplane, which is typically a wiring scheme connecting the PBX's printed circuit cards. See also DAUGHTERBOARD.

MOTIF Motif is the name given to the Open Software Foundation's (OSF) toolkit (Application Programming Interface) and look and feel. The Motif toolkit is based on intrinsics.

MOTOROLA According to the family which founded Motorola in the 1920s, the name Motorola was chosen to mean "Music in motion" to signify one of the company's first products — a car radio.

MOU Memorandum Of Understanding.

MOUNT The method in NFS and other networks by which modes access network resources. The word "mount" is often used as a verb, as in my workstation "mounts" the file server, called DALLAS2.

MOUSE A hand-held computer input device that generates the coordinates of a position indicator on your computer screen (e.g. a hand, an arrow) and is worked by being moved on a flat surface.

MOUSE BLUR Move your mouse quickly across your screen and if you're running an LCD (for example on a laptop), the mouse's pointer will blur — due to the screen's inability to change as fast as you can move the mouse. Another term for mouse blur is Cursor Submarining.

MOV Metal Oxide Varistor. A type of surge suppressor which absorbs voltage and current surges and spikes. Many trunk boards inside PBX are protected by MOVs. This means that the first device a trunk coming in hits on the circuit board is an MOV. If the voltage or current is high, it will blow the MOV, thus protecting the remaining and far more valuable devices on the board.

MPEG An image-compression scheme for full motion video proposed by the Motion Picture Experts Group, an ISO-sanctioned group. MPEG image scheme offers more compression than the JPEG scheme, which is largely for still images, because it takes advantage of the fact that full motion video is made up of many successive frames consisting of large areas that are not changed — like blue sky background. While JPEG compresses each still frame in a video sequence as much as possible, MPEG also performs "differencing," noting differences between consecutive frames. If two consecutive frames are identical, the second can be stored with the appropriate information. MPEG condenses moving images about three times more tightly than JPEG.

MPG Microwave Pulse Generator. A device that generates electrical pulses at microwave frequencies.

MPI Multi-Path Interface. Between a transmitter and receiver, the radio wave can take a direct path and one or more reflected paths. The direct radio wave always arrives prior to the reflected waves. If the reflected waves are of sufficient amplitude, they will interfere with the direct wave. The relationship of the amplitude and time delay between the direct and reflected waves create peaks and nulls at the receiver, causing momentary signal fading or loss. In a digital system, this can result in very significant degradation, as the receiver loses signal acquisition and frame synchronization during each fade. The net effect is an increase in the residual bit error rate.

MPS Multip Page Signal. A frame sent in fax transmission if the sendeer has more pages to transmit.

MR Modified Read. Relative element address differentiation code. A two-dimensional compression technique for fax machines that handles the data commpression of the vertical line and that concentrates on space between the lines and within given characters. See MMR.

MSAU Multi-Station Access Unit.

MSB Abbreviation for Most Significant Bit and Most Significant Byte. That portion of a number, address or field which occurs leftmost when its value is written as a single number in conventional hexadecimal or binary notation. The portion of the number having the most weight in a mathematical calculation using the value.

MS-DOS MicroSoft Disk Operating System. Being dumb, a computer needs to be told from the very basic steps what to do. MS-DOS is the basic command system for IBM and IBM clone personal computers. It explains to the computer how to talk to its keyboard, to its screen, to its various "ports" — serial and parallel — and how to talk to its internal bus — the broadband communications system that sends messages between PC (printed circuit) cards that are slid into the empty slots most personal computers come with.

One critical MS-DOS function is to "talk" to its disk/s — hard and/or soft. Let me explain: In MS-DOS when you format a disk, you actually put temporary dummy data all throughout the disk. The smallest unit of storage on a disk is 512 bytes. When you create a file (say a letter), MS-DOS stores the file in clusters, which are typically groups of sectors. MS-DOS doesn't store these clusters contiguously (i.e. next to each other). Rather, it stores them all over the disk. Each cluster thus contains only a portion of the file. This is efficient, since MS-DOS then doesn't require long uninterrupted areas of space on the disk for each file.

If your files are stored all over the disk, clearly you need an index or roadmap to where the files are. When you format a disk, in addition to laying down dummy data, MS-DOS makes two other things — first, an area of the disk containing the boot-up logic MS-DOS needs to start the machine. And second, two copies of something called the File Allocation Table. The FAT is like an index to what's on the disk. When you make a new file, MS-DOS automatically checks the FAT to figure where the chunks of your new file should be stored. When you do a DIR, you can't see the FAT. It's hidden away. But it's there. And it's duplicated (just in case).

Sometimes the FAT becomes corrupted. This is a nice term for "messed up." When the FAT and the directory entries fall out of synch with each other, you could be in trouble. The most common problem is a lost cluster. MS-DOS wrote a portion of a file to the disk, but didn't connect it with a file. In other words, MS-DOS has simply misplaced the cluster. To solve the problem you must use the CHKDSK command. You do this by typing a C: prompt

CHKDSK /F

That means check the disk and fix it. One more point: How to bring back a file you've erased. MS-DOS doesn't actually "erase" a file. It marks the directory entry of the file as "erased" and frees the sectors (i.e. space) listed in the FAT. When you create a new file or add to an existing one, MS-DOS may then use these freed-up sectors. The key to recovering a file you've erased is not to have written anything to disk after you erased the file. If you erase a file, say "Drat" and then instantly use a program like Norton Utilities' UNERASE program. You'll be able to bring your erased file back to life with absolutely no problem and totally intact. The key is NOT to write anything over it.

According to the Economist Magazine of May 22, 1993, some jealous Microsoft rivals claim that MS-DOS now stands for Microsoft Seeks Domination Over Society. See also DEVICE DRIVER, QDOS and WINDOWS.

MS-NET Microsoft Network, the MS-DOS networking systems software product shipped in 1985. Largely superseded by Microsoft LAN Manager. Now largely superseded by Windows NT Advanced Server.

MSA Metropolitan Statistical Area. When it issued cellular radio licenses, the Federal Communications Commission divided the United States into MSA markets and Rural Service Area (RSA) markets. There are 306 MSAs in the United States, all of which now have cellular service.

MSAT Mobile SATellite. Technology for transmitting and receiving satellite transmissions in moving vehicles.

MSNF Multisystem Networking Facility. An optional feature of certain IBM telecommunications access methods that allows more than one host running ACF/TCAM or VTAM to jointly control an ACF/NCP program.

MSP The name of a general purpose programmable switch made by Redcom Laboratories.

MTA Message Transfer Agent.

MTBF Mean Time Between Failure. The length of time a user may reasonably expect a device or system to work before an incapacitating fault occurs.

MTD Memory Technology Drive.

MTM Maintenance Trunk Monitor.

MTP Message Transfer Part of the SS7 Protocol. It provides functions for basic routing of signaling messages between signaling points.

MTS Message Telecommunications Service. AT&T's name for standard switched telephone service. Also called DDD, for Direct Distance Dial.

MTSO Mobile Telephone Switching Office. This central office houses the field monitoring and relay stations for switching calls between the cellular and wire-based (land-line) central office. The MTSO controls the entire operation of a cellular system. It is a sophisticated computer that monitors all cellular calls, keeps track of the location of all cellular-equipped vehicles traveling in the system, arranges handoffs, keeps track of billing information, etc.

MTTR Mean Time to Repair. The average time required to return a failed device or system to service.

MU-LAW The PCM coding and companding standard used in Japan and North America. See A-LAW.

MUDBOX An unsheltered item of equipment that is sufficiently rugged to withstand adverse environments. It is expected to work perfectly though it sits outdoors in good and bad weather.

MULDEM A contraction for Multiplexer Demultiplexer, referring to a piece of equipment which performs both functions and generally operates between two of the AT&T digital hierarchy rates (i.e., DSI to DS3).

MULTI VENDOR INTEGRATION PROTOCOL See MVIP.

MULTI-ACCESS The ability of several users to communicate with a computer at the same time with each working independently on their own job.

MULTI-ADDRESS CALLING FACILITY A system service feature that permits a user to nominate more than one addressee for the same data. The network may accomplish this sequentially or simultaneously.

MULTI-CARRIER MODULATION MCM. A technique of transmitting data by dividing the data into several interleaved bit streams and using these to modulate several carriers. MCM is a form of frequency division multiplexing.

MULTI-CAST The broadcast of messages to a selected group of workstations on a LAN. See MULTI-CAST PACKETS.

MULTI-CAST PACKETS Multicast packets are addressed to a group of devices on a LAN. LAN stations use multicast packets to deliver information to a specific set of devices such as routers, file servers, and hosts.

MULTI-CAST USER MESSAGE A user message generated at the source node and distributed to two or more destination nodes.

MULTI-CHANNEL The use of a common channel to make two or more channels either by splitting the frequency band of the common channel into several narrower bands (called frequency-division multiplexing) or by allocating time slots in the entire channel (time-division multiplexing).

MULTI-CONDUCTOR More than one conductor within a single cable complex.

MULTI-DROP A communications circuit with multiple terminals and peripherals. Only one may transmit at any time.

MULTI-DROP LINE A communications channel that services many data terminals at different geographical locations and in which a computer (node) controls utilization of the channel by polling one distant terminal after another and asking it, in effect, "Do you have anything for me?"

MULTI-FIBER A fiber that supports propagation of more than one of a given wavelength.

MULTI-FRAME In PCM systems, a set of consecutive frames in which the position of each frame can be identified by reference to a multi-frame alignment signal. The multi-frame alignment signal does not necessarily occur, in whole or in part, in each multi-frame.

MULTI-FREQUENCY MONITORS Also known as multisync or multiscan monitors. They can show images in several resolution standards. Such versatility makes them more expensive than single-resolution monitors (e.g. a standard VGA) but also less prone to instant obsolescence. A multisync monitor showing a VGA may or may not look better than VGA monitor showing a VGA image. That depends on the screen's other attributes.

MULTI-FREQUENCY PULSING An in-band address signaling method in which ten decimal digits (the numbers on the touchtone pad) and five auxiliary signals are each represented by selecting two frequencies and combining them into one "musical" sound.. The frequencies are selected from six separate frequencies — 700, 900, 1100, 1300, 1500 and 1700 Hz. See also CAPTAIN CRUNCH.

MULTI-FUNCTION PERIPHERALS These are devices which take on two or more functions generally associated with individual peripherals and combine these into one product or in a linker series of modules. A multifunction peripheral might combine a fax machine with a copier with a computer printer. The term is not very precise, nor very useful.

MULTI-HOP An example of a single hop system is a microwave system between one building (let's say downtown San Francisco) and another across town (let's say uptown San Francisco). Each with one microwave antenna on its roof. Let's say we wanted to extend that system to Oakland. We'd put a second antenna on the uptown San Francisco building and shoot across to an antenna in Oakland. That building would now have a multi-hop transmission system.

MULTI-LEAVING In communications, the transmission (usually via bisync facilities and using bisync protocols) of a variable number of data streams between user devices and a computer.

MULTI-LEVEL PRECEDENCE PREEMPTION MLPP. A system in which selected customers may exercise preemption capabilities to seize facilities being used for calls with lower precedence levels.

MULTI-LINE HUNT The ability of switching equipment to connect calls to another phone in the group when other numbers in the group are busy.

MULTI-LINE TELEPHONE Any telephone set with buttons which can answer or originate calls on one or more central office lines or trunks. Originally all multi-line telephones were 1A2 and they came in sizes of 2, 3, 5, 9, 11, 17, 19, 29, and 60 lines. Now, skinny wire electronic key systems come in all sizes. See KEY TELEPHONE SYSTEM.

MULTI-LINE TERMINATING SYSTEM Premises switching equipment and key telephone type systems which are capable of terminating more than one local exchange service line, WATS access line, FX circuit, etc.

MULTI-LOCATION BILLING Multilocation Billing is an option whereby a long distance carrier bills separate locations and applies volume discounts pro-rated to each site based on usage, or fixed percentage with pro-rated discounts to sites based on usage.

MULTI-MEDIA Multi-media is the combination of multiple forms of media in the communication of information. Multimedia enables people to communicate using integrated media: audio, video, text, graphics, fax, and telephony. The benefit is more powerful communication. The combination of several media often provides richer, more effective communication of information or ideas than a single media such as traditional text-based communication can accomplish. Multi-media communication formats vary, but they usually include voice communications (vocoding, speech recognition, speaker verification and text-to-speech), audio processing (music synthesis, CD-ROMs), data communications, image processing and telecommunications using LANs, MANs and WANs in ISDN and POTS networks. Multimedia technology will ultimately take the disparate technologies of the computer, the telephone, the fax machine, the CD player, and the video camera and combine them into one powerful communication center. Technologies that were once analog — video, audio, telephony — are now digital. The power of multimedia is the integration of these digital technologies. To many people, "multimedia" (as defined above) is a disparate collection of technologies in search of a purpose. And it's true: most of the merger of media (as above) is taking place in business communications in the moving around of compound documents. Meantime, multimedia has moved into training and in the home for education and entertainment. See AUTHORING, COMPOUND DOCUMENTS, HYPERMEDIA, OLE, SHARED SCREENS, SHARED WHITEBOARDS, and SYNCHRONIZATION.

MULTI-MODE DISTORTION In an optical fiber, a result of different values of the group delay for each individual mode at a single wavelength. It isn't the same as "multi-mode dispersion."

MULTI-MEDIA NETWORK A network capable of carrying multiple forms of user information such as voice text, sounds, etc.

MULTI-MEDIA PROTOCOL A protocol suitable for handling multiple forms of information such as voice, text, pictures, numbers, etc.

MULTI-MEDIA PC The Multimedia PC Council now defines a multimedia PC as a PC having a minimum of two megabytes of memory, a 30 megabyte hard drive, a CD ROM drive, digital sound support and Microsoft's Multimedia Extensions for Windows. See MULI-MEDIA.

MULTI-MODE In fiber-optics, an optical fiber designed to carry multiple signals distinguished by frequency or phase at the same time (contrasts with single- mode). (Also spelled multimode.)

MULTI-MODE DISTORTION In an optical fiber, a result of different values of the group delay for each individual mode at a single wavelength. The term "multi-mode dispersion" is often used as a synonym; such usage, however, is discouraged since the mechanism is not dispersive in nature.

MULTI-MODE FIBER An optical fiber with a core diameter of 25 to 200 microns. The core is much larger than single-mode fiber and allows several beams of light to be passed through it.

MULTI-NAM A cellular telephone term to allow a cellular phone to have two phone numbers, each of which can be on a different cellular system. This lets you register with both carriers in your home city. Wherever you are, you can choose the carrier which provides the best service. Multi-NAM means you could also subscribe to one carrier in your home city and another in a distant city — perhaps one you travel often to. This saves you paying extra roaming charges.

MULTI-PATH Multiple routes taken by RF energy between the transmitter and the receiver. Signal can cancel or reinforce. Varying multipath (at sunset or sunrise) causes varying signal strength that sounds like a train's steam engine starting up.

MULTI-PATH ERROR Errors caused by the interference of a signal that has reached the receiver antenna by two or more different paths. Usually caused by one path being bounced or reflected.

MULTI-POINT A configuration or topology, designed to transmit data between a central site and a number of remote terminals on the same circuit. Individual terminals will generally be able to transmit to the central site but not to each other.

MULTI-POINT CIRCUIT A circuit connecting three or more locations. It is often called a multidrop circuit. See also MULTI-POINT and MULTI-DROP LINE.

MULTI-POINT DISTRIBUTION SERVICE A one-way domestic public radio service rendered on microwave frequencies from a fixed station transmitting (usually in an omnidirectional pattern) to multiple receiving facilities located at fixed points.

MULTI-POINT GROUNDING SYSTEM A system of equipment bonded together and also bonded to the facility ground at the nearest location of the facility ground.

MULTI-POINT LINE A single communications link for two or more devices shared by one computer and or more computers or terminals. Use of this line requires a polling mechanism. It is also called a multidrop line.

MULTI-PROCESSING A type of computing characterized by systems that use more than one CPU to execute applications. Multi-processing is not multi-tasking, which is the abillity to have more one application running on a system at the same time. The technique is not associated with multi-processing, nor does it require multiprocessing to take place. Multi-tasking typically uses a computer with one CPU (e.g. your desktop or laptop). Multi-processing uses a computer with several CPUs, often a server. See MULTI-TASKING.

MULTI-PROGRAMMING Computer system operation whereby a number of independent jobs are processed together.

MULTI-PROTOCOL MESSAGE ROUTERS A device which converts different electronic mail formats. Such a router would be used to move electronic mail from a cc mail equipped-LAN to a Davinci e-mail LAN to a Wang mini-computeer based system.

MULTI-SERVER NETWORK A single local area network (one cabling system) that has two or more file servers attached. Network addresses assigned to the LAN drivers are the same in each file server because the network boards are attached to the same cabling system. On a multiserver network, users can access files from any file server to which they are attached (if they have access rights). A multiserver network should not be confused with an internetwork (two or more networks linked together through an internal or external router).

MULTI-STAGE QUEUING This a term typically used in Automatic Call Distributors. It is the ability to array a number of agent groups in a routing table. The notion of multiple agent groups being addressed may mean that the system may be able to "look-back" and "look forward" as it searches for a free agent in the right group to take the call presently holding.

MULTI-STATION Any network of stations capable of communicating with each other on one circuit or through a switching center.

MULTI-TASKING The concurrent management of two or more distinct tasks by a computer. Although a computer with a single processing unit (as virtually all PCs are) can only execute one application's code at a given moment, a multitasking operating system can load and manage the execution of multiple applications, allocating processing cycles to each in sequence. Because of the processing speed of computers, the apparent result is the simultaneous processing of multiple tasks. Standard mode Windows performs multitasking only in the form of context switching. 386 enhanced mode allows multitasking in the form of timeslicing. See MULTI-PROCESSING.

MULTI-TENANT SHARING The capability of a PBX to serve more than one tenant in a building. This process is a new option for building owners. They now become the Telephone Company for tenants in the building. There is money in this business, but chiefly on the resale of long distance phone calls.

MULTI-TESTER Usually an alternate name for VOLT-OHM-MILLIAMETER, but may also apply to other multiple-function testing devices.

MULTI-THREADING Concurrent processing of more than one message by an application program. One of OS/2's advantages over Windows is that IBM designed it as a multithreaded operating system. Each program in OS/2 can start two or more threads, which carry out various interrelated tasks with less overhead than two separate programs would require. For example, a communications program could have three threads running: one that waits for characters to be received, another that monitors the keyboard, and a third that displays information. This is more efficient than running multiple tasks because it doesn't require the overhead of an operating-system context switch.

In short, a new and complex method of programming. Here is a definition from Sun Microsystems. A traditional UNIX process has a single thread of control. A thread of control, or more simply a thread, is a sequence of instructions being executed in a program. A thread has a program counter (PC) and a stack to keep track of local variables and return addresses. A multithreaded UNIX process is no longer a thread of control of itself; instead, it is associated with one or more threads. Threads execute independently. There is in general no way to predict how the instructions of different threads are interleaved, though they have execution priorities that can influence the relative speed of execution. In general, the number or identities of threads that an application process chooses to apply to a problem are invisible from outside the process. Threads can be viewed as execution resources that may be applied to solving the problem at hand.

Threads share the process instructions and most of its data. A change in shared data by one thread can be seen by the other threads in the process. Threads also share the operating system. Each sees the same open files. For example, if one thread opens a file, another thread can read it. Because threads share so much of the process state, threads can affect each other in sometimes surprising ways. Programming with threads requires more care and discipline than ordinary programming because there is no system-enforced protection between threads. See WINDOWS NT.

MULTI-TIER TARIFFS A way of paying for something (i.e. equipment) from your local phone company. The idea is that one tier of your monthly payments is to pay off the equipment, and after a finite period, this tier payment drops to zero. The next tier is to pay for your monthly service and it is on-going. Other tiers are for other reasons. As this technique was practiced by the Bell System, it was called "two tier." You will no longer find two tier tariffs in common use.

MULTI-USER PC A microcomputer that has several terminals attached to it, so that multiple users can simultaneously use its resources. Multi-user PCs can either slice up the time of a single microprocessor or can give each terminal-based user his own microprocessor. Multi-user PCs are an alternative to LANs and are typically used in specialized, one-application solutions, such as a doctor's office billing system.

MULTI-USER SOFTWARE An application designed for simultaneous access by two or more network nodes, i.e. two or more users on a network. It typically employs file and/or record locking. It is not associated with multiprocessing, nor does it require multiprocessing to implement.

MULTI-VENDOR INTEGRATION PROTOCOL See MVIP.

MULTI-WAY COMMUNICATION A multimedia definition. Multi-way communication goes between two people, or between groups of people in all directions. Multi-way communication can be in real-time, or in store-and-forward mode. Examples of multi-way communication include a video conference, where one individual is giving a presentation to a group of people who listen and ask questions from their workstations; and group conferencing, where several people collaborate, supported by audio, video, and graphics on their workstation screens.

MULTIMEDIA See MULTI-MEDIA.

MULTIMEDIA CAPABILITIES The ability to run simultaneous voice, image, data and video applications on a computer. A technology that requires enormous bandwidth and processing power. See MULTi-MEDIA.

MULTIMEDIA PC The Multimedia PC Council now defines a multimedia PC as a PC having a minimum of two megabytes of memory, a 30 megabyte hard drive, a CD ROM drive, digital sound support and Microsoft's Multimedia Extensions for Windows. See MULTI-MEDIA.

MULTIPLE ACCESS The ability of several personal computers connected to a Local Area Network to access one another through a common addressing scheme and protocol.

MULTIPLE ADDRESS MESSAGE A message to be delivered to more than one destination.

MULTIPLE CONSOLE OPERATION A phone system with this feature can use more than one attendant console. It's good to know the maximum number of consoles your chosen PBX can use.

MULTIPLE CUSTOMER GROUP OPERATION A PBX shared by several different companies, each having separate consoles and trunks.

MULTIPLE DOMAINS A set of domains on a single LAN, each of which has its own domain-wide post office. Hosts within each domain can exchange mail by going through one domain post office. Hosts in different domains must generally send mail though two intermediary post offices: the sender's domain post office and the receiver's domain post office.

MULTIPLE FREQUENCY-SHIFT KEYING MFSK. A form of frequency-shift keying in which multiple codes are used in the transmission of digital signals. The coding systems may use multiple frequencies transmitted concurrently or sequentially.

MULTIPLE HOMING Connecting your phone so it can be served by one or several switching centers. This service may use a single directory number. It may also use several directory numbers (another term for phone numbers). It all depends on how you set the service up with your local phone company. The idea is to give you more ways of reaching the switched network — in case one or more of your local loops breaks.

MULTIPLE LISTED DIRECTORY NUMBER SERVICE Permits more than one listed directory number to be associated with a single PBX.

MULTIPLE NAME SPACES The association of several names or other pieces of information with the same file. This allows renaming files and designating them for dissimilar computer systems such as the PC and the Mac.

MULTIPLE ROUTING The process of sending a message to more than one recipient, usually when all destinations are specified in the header of the message.

MULTIPLE SPOT SCANNING In facsimile systems, the method in which scanning is carried on simultaneously by two or more scanning spots, each one analyzing its fraction of the total scanned area of the subject copy.

MULTIPLE TOKEN OPERATION Variant of token passing for rings in which a free token on a LAN is transmitted immediately after the last bit of the data packet, allowing multiple tokens on ring (but only one free token) simultaneously.

MULTIPLE TUNED ANTENNA An antenna with connections through inductances to ground at more than one point and so determined that the total reactances in parallel are equal to those necessary to give the antenna the desired natural frequency.

MULTIPLEX To transmit two or more signals over a single channel.

MULTIPLEX AGGREGATE BIT RATE The bit rate in a time-division multiplexer that is equal to the sum of the input channel data signaling rates available to the user plus the rate of the overhead bits required.

MULTIPLEX BASEBAND In frequency-division multiplexing, the frequency band occupied by the aggregate of the signals in the line interconnecting the multiplexing and radio or line equipment.

MULTIPLEX HIERARCHY In the U.S. frequency-division multiplex hierarchy,

> 12 channels = 1 group
>
> 5 groups (60 channels) = 1 supergroup
>
> 10 supergroups (600 channels) = 1 mastergroup
>
> 6 mastergroups = 1 jumbo group

In contrast, the CCITT standard says 5 supergroups (i.e. 300 channels) = 1 mastergroup.

MULTIPLEXED CHANNEL A communications channel capable of carrying the telecommunications transmissions of a number of devices or users at one time.

MULTIPLEXER Electronic equipment which allows two or more signals to pass over one communications circuit. That "circuit' may be a phone line, a microwave circuit, a through-the-air TV signal. That circuit may be analog or digital. There are many multiplexing techniques to accommodate both.

MULTIPLEXING EFFICIENCY Figure of merit for multiplexors. The ratio of the aggregate channel input data rate to the composite output data rate. Many statistical multiplexors achieve a multiplexing efficiency of 8 or more.

MULTIPOINT GROUNDING SYSTEM A system of equipment bonded together and also bonded to the facility ground.

MULTIPORT CARD A circuit board with two or more ports for modems or other devices. Useful for enabling one PC to handle multiple incoming or outgoing calls at one time.

MULTIPROCESSING A type of computing characterized by systems that use more than one CPU to execute applications. Multiprocessing is not multitasking, which is the abillity to have more one application running on a

NEWTON'S TELECOM DICTIONARY

system at the same time. The technique is not associated with multiprocessing, nor does it require multiprocessing to take place. Multitasking typically uses a computer with one CPU (e.g. your desktop or laptop). Multiprocessing uses a computer with several CPUs, often a server. See MULTI-PROCESSING, MULTI-TASKING and MULTI-THREADED.

MULTITASKING See MULTI-TASKING.

MULTITHREADED See MULTI-THREADED.

MURIEL Muriel Fullam worked for me for ten years before she worked with me on this dictionary. That had to be the longest apprenticeship ever. It shows. She did great work. Thanks. She is married to Jerry Fullam who will love it when he sees his name here.

MUSIC-ON-CAMP Audio source input for use with attendant camp-on. See also MUSIC-ON-HOLD.

MUSIC-ON-HOLD Background music heard when someone is put on hold, letting them know they are still connected. Some modern phone systems generate their own electronic synthesized music. Most phone systems have the ability to connect any sound-producing device, e.g. a radio or a cassette player. Most companies, unfortunately, devote little attention to the sound source they select. Sometimes competitors will deliberately advertise on the radio station that callers will hear on hold. Thus, Macys is now selling Gimbels. It's better to use pre-recorded music. Better yet are tapes of "specials" and other happenings around your firm. Use the "Music-on-Hold" feature as another method of selling. "Ask the operator about our special on ladies' underwear." "Ask our operator to send you a copy of our latest annual report."

MUSIC SOURCE An external music source such as a radio, can be connected to the Key Service Unit for Music on Hold, Background Music, or both.

MUTE A feature which disconnects the handset microphone or speakerphone microphone so that side conversations won't be heard.

MUTUAL CAPACITANCE The capacitance between two conductors when all other conductors, including the shield, are short circuited to ground.

MUTUALLY SYNCHRONIZED NETWORK A network-synchronized arrangement in which each clock in the network exerts a degree of control on all others.

MUTUAL SYNCHRONIZATION A timing subsystem not employing directed control, by which the frequency of the clock at a particular node is controlled by some weighted average of the timing on all signals received from neighboring nodes.

MUX See MULTIPLEXER.

MVIP Multi Vendor Integration Protocol. Picture a printed circuit card that fits into an empty slot in a personal computer. The slot carries information to and from the computer. This is called the data bus. Printed circuit cards that do voice processing typically have a second "bus" — the voice bus. That "bus" is actually a ribbon cable which connects one voice processing card to another. The ribbon cable is typically connected to the top of the printed circuit card, while the data bus is at the bottom. As of writing (summer, 1993) there were four "standard" communications buses defined and accepted. Three buses were defined by Dialogic Corporation. They are called The Analog Expansion Bus, the PCM Expansion Bus and the SCSA, which stands for Signal Computing System Architecture. The other bus (called MVIP) is from Natural MicroSystems. Both companies have co-opted a number of companies to accept their standard. Both buses can handle voice, data and fax. Here is a writeup on MVIP from Mitel Semiconductor, which has adopted MVIP:

"The MVIP consists of communications hardware and software that allows printed circuit cards from multiple vendors to exchange information in a standardized digital format. The MVIP bus consists of eight 2 megabyte serial highways and clock signals that are routed from one card to another over a ribbon cable. Each of these highways is partitioned into 32 channels for a total capacity of 256 voice channels on the MVIP bus. These serial link from one card to another. They are electronically compatible with Mitel's ST-BUS specification for inter-chip communications. By letting expansion cards exchange data directly, the MVIP bus opens the PC architecture to voice/data applications that would otherwise overburden the PC processor with data transfers. The MVIP bus is equivalent to an extra backplane that is capable of routing circuit switched data.

"MVIP systems generally have two types of cards; network cards and resource cards. They differ by the switching they provide and in the way they are wired to the bus. Network cards almost always provide more flexible switching and can drive either the input or the output side of the bus, although they usually drive the output side of the bus. Resource cards usually provide very little switching and are only able to drive the input side of the bus. Resource cards usually rely on the network cards to do most or all of the switching on the MVIP bus."

According to Charlie Foskett, chairman of Natural MicroSystems of Needham, MA, MVIP's prime mover, separating MVIP switching from resources on the MVIP bus (the separate bus on top of the PC card) simplifies access to the MVIP bus for communication service providers (fax, voice processing, speech recognition,etc.). It also simplifies access for the applications developers. Locating the switching capability on trunk interfaces assigns the switching to modules which connect to the network, and which have sufficient real estate for switching elements and switch control logic, and which also perform trunk signal decoding and/or analog-to-digital conversion. This allows the switching to be digital and totally software controlled. Software controlled digital switching at the application level is a seminal change in voice and call processing systems, and moves application developers into new markets and new levels of value-added contribution. See AEB, PEB and SCSA.

MVS Multiple Virtual Storage.

MW Abbreviation for MILLIWATT.

MX3 A designation for a multiplex which interfaces between any of the following circuit combinations: 28 DSIs to one DS3 (M13), 14 DSICs to one DS3 (MC3), or 7 DS2s to one DS3 (M23).

MXR Multiplexer

MZI Mach Zehnder Interferometer.

N

N SERIES TERMINATORS Most local area networks are bus configurations. This means one long piece of cable (coaxial or fiber) with workstations connected along the way, typically with "T" connectors. For a network to work properly, you need to place resistance at the end of the bus, to terminate it. A thin wire Ethernet typically requires a 50 ohm resistance at either end of the bus. Thin wire Ethernet terminators are commonly called N series terminators. They may also be used with grounding wires to ground the network. Networks don't work well without resistance at the end of their buses.

N-ISDN Narrowband ISDN (Integrated Services Digital Network). Narrowband ISDN is an unkind name for the present form of ISDN presently implemented. According to Professor Michael L. Dertouzos of MIT, narrowband ISDN suffers from the same contraints as classical voice telephony. For example, N-ISDN can carry reasonably be altered to accommodate the great information only in fixed chunks of 64 kilobits per second. This would be like a road system closed to everything except motorcycle. An 18-wheel truck carrying produce or a heating fuel tanker would be "welcome" to use this road as long as it could repackage its cargo into (and out of) motorcycle-size chunks. See also B-ISDN.

N1 The first short-haul multiplex carrier in the U.S. by the Bell System was Western Electric's N1. The N1 transmitted 12 voice frequency channels over separate transmit and receive pairs in a single cable. N carriers have been progressively improving.

N2 In packet data networking technology, parameter used to specify the allowable number of retransmissions before disconnection.

NA See NIGHT ANSWER.

NADF North American Directory Plan. An association of electronic mail providers who are figuring standards and ways of sending mail between their subscribers.

NAILED CONNECTION A permanent circuit of a previously-switched circuit/s. Defined by Fujitsu, their Omni SI PBX provides up to eight dedicated (constant) trunk-to-trunk connections for special applications. See also NAILED DATA CONNECTION and NAILED-UP CIRCUIT.

NAILED DATA CONNECTION A permanently established connection between two InteCom IBM S/80 data interfaces. This connection is defined in the IBM database and the switch paths are established when the call processing software is first brought on line.

NAILED-UP CIRCUIT A circuit semipermanently established through a circuit-switching facility for point-to-point connectivity.

NAK Negative AcKnowledgement. NAK is a control character in ASCII that means a packet arrived with the check digits in error. It is sent from the computer receiving the packets to the sender, implying that the packet should be retransmitted so that all bits will arrive intact in the next go-round. See CHECK DIGITS and ACK.

NAM Numerical Assignment Module. Basically, your cellular telephone number, although it refers specifically to the component or module in the phone where the number is stored. Phones with dual or Multi-NAM features offer the user the option of registering the phone so that it will have two or more phone numbers.

NAMAS NAtional Measurement Accreditation Service.

NAME A name, as opposed to an address, is a location. Independent description of an end-station or node on a network (LAN or WAN) that contains no information about where the name entity is located. Certain protocols, such as IBM NetBIOS, make extensive use of a naming scheme.

NAME SERVER A directory service located in the SLEE (Service Logic Execution Environment) that provides a mapping between a resource's global name and its physical location in the network.

NAMED PIPE A connection used to transfer data between separate processes, usually on seperate computers. Named pipes are the foundation of interprocess communications (IPC). An administrator can set permissions on named pipes, but only LAN Manager and network applications can create them. See also NAMED PIPES.

NAMED PIPES A technique used for communications between applications operating on the same computer or across the local area network. It includes an applications programming interface, providing application programmers with a way to create interprogram communications using routines similar to disk-file opening, reading, and writing. In Microsoft's words, named pipes allow two or more processes to communicate with each other. Any process that knows the name of a named pipe can access it (subject to security checks).

NAMPS Narrow-band Analog Mobile Phone Service. A proposed new standard for cellular radio. NAMPS combines current voice processing with digital signaling. According to Motorola, NAMPS triples the capacity of today's cellular AMPS system, reduces the number of dropped calls and offers a range of new performance enhancements and digital messaging services. The other cellular standards include E-TDMA (Extended Time Division Multiple Access), TDMA (Time Division Multiple Access) and CDMA (Code Division Multiple Access).

NANCY REAGAN DEFENSE Just say No.

NANOMETER One billionth of a meter. Written nm.

NANOSECOND One billionth of a second. Written nsec.

NANP The North American Numbering PlAn (NANPA). It assigns area codes and sets rules for calls to be routed across North America. It is administered by Bellcore.

NAP Network Action Point. An AT&T term describing the switching point through which a call is processed. The NAP switches the call based on routing instructions received from the NCP.

NAPI Numbering/Addressing Plan Identifier.

NAPLPS North American Presentation-Level Protocol Syntax. A protocol for videotex text graphics and screen formats, developed by AT&T and since standardized within ANSI, based on Canada's Telidon videographics protocol.

NARRATIVE TRAFFIC Messages normally prepared in accordance with standardized procedures for transmission via optical character recognition equipment or teletypewriter. In contrast to data pattern traffic, narrative messages must contain additional message format lines.

NARROWBAND 1. An imprecise term. Some people think it's sub-voice grade channels capable of only carrying 100 to 200 bits per second. Others think it means lines or circuits able to carry data up to 2400 bits per second. So as lines get broader, narrowband gets broader. See also N-ISDN and B-ISDN. 2. In cellular radio terminology, narrowband refers to the methodology of gaining more channels (and hence more capacity) by splitting FM channels into channels that are narrower in bandwidth. See NAMPS and NTACS.

NARROWBAND ISDN Any ISDN speed up to 1.544 Mbps, which is called PRI or PRA. But this definition is imprecise. And as speeds get faster, so the definition of narrowband ISDN means faster and faster. See N-ISDN and B-ISDN.

NARROWBAND SIGNAL Any analog signal or analog representation of a digital signal whose essential spectral content is limited to that which can be contained within a voice channel of nominal 4-kHz bandwidth.

NARTE National Association of Radio and Telecommunications Engineers, based in Salem, OR. 800-933-1470.

NARUC National Association of Regulatory and Utility Commissioners. Members are representatives of state regulatory agencies concerned with telephone regulatory and other utility matters.

NAS NAS is Digital Equipment Corporation's implementation of standards-based software for open computing and is the foundation for delivering the Open Advantage through a combination of open technology, open services, and open business practices.

NASA National Aeronautics and Space Administration.

NASC Number Administration and Service Center. Provides centralized administration of the Service Managment System (SMS) database of 800 numbers. The NASC keeps track of the 800 numbers that are in use, or available for use, by new 800 users.

NATA North American Telecommunications Association. A trade association of manufacturers and distributors of telephone equipment and now also telephone companies and, more recently, some computer companies. NATA was founded in 1970, two years after the Carterfone decision. NATA runs an annual tradeshow called UNICOM. It's typically in October or November.

NATIONAL COMMUNICATIONS SYSTEM NCS. The organization established by Section 1(a) of Executive Order No. 12472 to assist the President, the National Security Council, the Director of the Office of Science and Technology Policy, and the Director of the Office of Management and Budget, in the discharge of their national security emergency preparedness telecommunications functions.

NATIONAL COORDINATING CENTER NCC. The joint telecommunications industry-Federal Government operation established by the National Communications System to assist in the initiation, coordination, restoration, and reconstitution of NS/EP telecommunication services or facilities.

NATIONAL ELECTRICAL CODE NEC. A nationally recognized safety standard for the design, construction, and maintenance of electrical circuits. The NEC also gives rules for the installation of electrical and telephone cabling. The NEC is developed by the NEC Committee of the American National Standards Institute (ANSI), sponsored by the National Fire Protection Association (NFPA, Boston) and identified by the desciption ANSI/NFPA 70-1990. This code has been adopted and enforced by many states and municipalities as law.

NATIONAL ISDN-1 National ISDN-1 is a specification for a "standard" ISDN phone line. It is based on technical references (TRs) specified by Bellcore that lay the groundwork for a national ISDN infrastructure. Bellcore issued the National ISDN-1 document, SR-NWT-001937, Issue 1, in February 1991. The idea of National ISDN-1 is that it be a set of standards which every manufacturer can conform to. A consumer can buy an ISDN phone (one conforming to National ISDN-1) at his local Radio Shack (or other store) take it home, plug it in and know it will work, irrespective of whose central office he's connected to. Sadly, National ISDN-1 has been a total bomb. And we are currently awaiting National ISDN-2 which is supposed to do what National ISDN-1 was meant to do — provide "Plug 'N Play" ISDN. See ISDN.

NATIONAL ISDN-2 See NATIONAL ISDN-1.

NATIONAL TELEVISION STANDARDS COMMITTEE STANDARD NTSC. The North American standard for the generation, transmission, and reception of television communication wherein the 525-line picture is the standard. The picture information is transmitted in AM and the sound information is transmitted in FM. Compatible with CCIR Standard M. This standard is used also in Central America, a number of South American countries, and some Asian countries including Japan. See NTSC.

NATIVE MODE Uncompressed.

NATOA The National Association of Telecommunications Officers and Advisors, an affiliate of the National League of Cities. An association based in Washington, DC.

NATURAL A voice recognition term for a language as in normal spoken conversational sentences. The vocabulary would include words like fifty, sixty, hundred etc. and be used in digit recognition.

NATURAL FREQUENCY The natural frequency of an antenna, the lowest frequency at which the antenna resonates without the addition of any inductance or capacitance.

NATURAL MICROSYSTEMS A manufacturer of voice processing componentry based in Natick, MA.

NATURAL MONOPOLY A term used by economists to justify regulation. The idea is that one company can provide certain services (such as gas, water, or telecommunications) considerably cheaper than two or three. Therefore, let one company have the monopoly on the service. But substitute government regulation for free competition and this way keep prices down. How well the theory and the practice of government regulation has worked is the subject of acres of learned prose. Suffice, the theory of "natural monopoly" has evaporated in most areas it was practiced — from airlines to telephones, local and long distance. When regulation is removed, prices have usually fallen.

NAU Network Addressable Unit. SNA term for LU, PU and SSCP. Each unit in SNA has a unique address.

NAUCS Network Access Usage and Cost System.

NAUTICAL MILE 6,076 feet. 15% longer than a normal mile, which is 5,280 feet. A measure of distance equal of one minute of arc on the Earth. An international nautical mile is equal to 1,852 meters or 6,076.11549 feet.

NBI Some people think this famous company's name stood for "Nothing But Initials." Others thought it stood for Nectum Bilinium Inc. It actually stood for "Nothing But Initials."

NBP Name Binding Protocol. AppleTalk protocol for translating device names to addresses.

NBS National Bureau of Standards. A US government agency that produces Federal Information Processing Standards (FIPS) for all other agencies except the Department of Defense (DoD).

NBS/ICST National Bureau of Standards/Institute for Computer Sciences and Technology. The NBS directorate, based in Gaithersburg, MD, is concerned with developing computer and data communications.

NCA Number of Calls Abandoned. The number of calls accepted into the ACD on the trunks only but lost before being connected to a person.

NCC 1. Network Control Center. A central location on a network where remote diagnostics and network management are controlled. 2. National Computer Conference, the erstwhile largest annual conference of the computer industry.

NCD See NET CARD DETECTION.

NCCF Network Communication Control Facility. An IBM term. See NETVIEW.

NCCS Network Control Center System.

NCEO NonCompliant End Office.

NCO Network Control Office.

NCOP Network Code Of Practice.

NCP 1. In AT&T language, Network Control Point. A routing, billing, and call control data base system for DSDC which uses the AT&T 3B2OD computer as the feature processor. 2. In IBM language, Network Control Program, which is a program that controls the operations of the communication controllers, 3704 and 3705 in an IBM SNA network. 3. In Northern Telecom language, it means Network Configuration Process.

NCRA National Cellular Resellers Association. A Washington lobbying organization.

NCTA National Cable Television Association. A trade organization representing U.S. cable-television carriers.

NCTE Network Channel Terminating Equipment. The general name for equipment that provides line transmission termination and layer-1 maintenance and multiplexing, terminating a 2-wire U-interface. Another name for a CSU, a Channel Service Unit. Also called a Data Service Unit. A device to terminate a digital channel on a customer's premises. It performs certain line-conditioning and equalization functions, and responds to loopback commands sent from the central office. A CSU sits between the digital line coming in from the central office and devices such as channel banks or data communications devices. Recent FCC decisions have established that most NCTE is customer premises equipment (CPE) and may therefore, by supplied by third-party vendors as well as the telephone company.

NDA Non Disclosure Agreement. Check carefully before you sign one. There are precious few new ideas in the history of the world.

NDD Network Descriptive Database.

NDIS Network Driver Interface Specification. A device driver specification codeveloped by Microsoft and 3Com and supported by many network card vendors. Besides providing hardware and protocol independence for network drivers, NDIS supports both MS-DOS and OS/2. It offers protocol multiplexing so that multiple protocol stacks can coexist in the same host. NDIS is conceptually similar to ODI.

NDS NetWare Directory Services. A new feature of Novell's NetWare 4.0. Log onto NetWare, you're part of a group. That group gives you various "directories," i.e. access to files. Those dierctories may be on one or many servers.

NDT No Dial Tone.

NE Network Element. A single piece of telecommunications equipment used to perform a function or service integral to the underlying bearer network.

NEAR-END CROSSTALK In wires packed together within a cable, the signals generated at one end of the link can drown out the weaker signals coming back from the recipient.

NEAR-LINE A storage term typically used as "near-line storage." A digital audio tape (DAT) might be considered near-line storage. A DAT would typically store a database of information sequentially. To find a record might take anywhere from three to 23 seconds. That's an eternity in most computer applications, but it may be adequate for finding something you rarely need to find — maybe several times a year. Thus the concept "near-line" storage.

NEBS 1. New Equipment Building Systems. 2. Network Equipment Building Systems requirement. A "standard" of sorts issued by Bellcore. It spells out central office standards for grounding and cabling, power and operations interfaces, as well as techniques for surviving fire and earthquakes. In short, if the equipment is NEBS compliant, it will withstand Armageddon (the final battle). But it won't be cheap.

NEC See NATIONAL ELECTRIC CODE.

NEC REQUIREMENTS The National Electrical Code (NEC) is written and administered by the National Fire Protection Agency (NFPA). The latest 1990 version states that any equipment connected to the telecommunications networks must be listed for that purpose. Listing is acquired through Underwriters Laboratories (UL) or a similar approved lab. Listing requirements for premises wiring between the Network Interface Device and the modular jack at the work area took effect on October 1, 1990.

NECA National Exchange Carrier Association. Nonprofit organization established by the FCC in 1983 to implement the access charge objectives being introduced replacing interstate division of revenue procedures. Membership includes all U.S. local exchange carriers. NECA files interstate access charges with the FCC, and after approval, pools such collections from the LECs and distributes these revenues equitably to the members based on each one's contribution in terms of expenses and capital investment for interstate toll.

NECTAR Nectar is a collaboration among Bell Atlantic/Bell of PA, Carnegie-Mellon University, the Pittsburgh Supercomputing Center and Bellcore.

NEGATED A signal is negated when it is in the state opposed to that which is indicated by the name of the signal. Opposite of Asserted.

NEGATIVE ABSORPTION Amplification. The positive difference between stimulated and absorbed radiation.

NEGATIVE ACKNOWLEDGEMENT NAK. A communications control character sent by a receiving station to indicate that the last message or block received was not received correctly.

NELSON, LORRAINE ROUTH The lady who records the messages on AT&T's Audix voice mail system. She records her timeless messages at the AT&T Bell lab in Denver. She lives in Oregon.

NEMA National Electrical Manufacturers Association.

NEMKO Norwegian Board for Testing and Approval of Electrical Equipment.

NEP See NOISE EQUIVALENT POWER.

NEPER Np. A method of expressing the ratio between two quantities (Q1,Q2). Np=log(n)xQ1/Q2. One Neper equals 8,686 decibels.

NEST To embed a set of instructions or a block data within another.

NET 1. NETwork. 2. Normes Europeenes de Telecommuncation (European Telecommunications Standards).

NET 1000 A data communications network and processing service of AT&T that never got off the ground and was closed down at a cost of about $1 billion. At one stage it was called Advanced Communications Service.

NET ADDRESS The location on a network where an addressee's mail is held, usually in storage until the user logs into the system. The system delivers the message at that time. The Net Address in the header of a message gives the information required by an automated message processing or message switch, to deliver a message to an intended addressee. A net address of RA3Y#SAIL would designate that the message was addressed to the user with the "Net Name" of "RA3Y" (pronounced "Ray". The 3 is silent) located at (signified by the symbol "#") the system in the network called "SAIL", in this case, the Stanford (University) Artificial Intelligence Laboratory.

NET CARD DETECTION LIBRARY NCD. Part of Microsoft's Windows for Workgroups. Its purpose is to determine the network adapted installed in the workstation and minimize mistakes made by the user.

NET LOSS The signal loss encountered in a transmission facility or network, or the sum of all the losses the signal encounters on its way to its final destination.

NET/ONE The family of local area network products, bridges, gateways, network interfaces and software from Ungermann-Bass, Santa Clara, CA.

NETBIOS Network Basic Input/Output System. A layer of software originally developed by IBM and Sytek to link a network operating system with specific hardware. Originally designed as the network controller for IBM's PC Network LAN, NetBIOS has now been extended to allow programs written using the NetBIOS interface to operate on the IBM Token ring. NetBIOS has been adopted as something of an industry standard and now it's common to refer to Netbios-compatible LANs. It offers LAN applications, a variety of "hooks" to carry out inter-application communications and data transfer. Essentially, NetBIOS is a way for application programs to talk to the network. Other applications interfaces are also being used these days, such as IBM's APPC. To run an application that works with NetBIOS, a non-IBM network operating system or network interface card must offer a NetBIOS emulator. More and more hardware and software vendors offer these emulators. They aren't always perfectly compatible, though. Today, many vendors either provide a version of NetBIOS to interface with their hardware or emulate its transport-layer communications services in their network products.

NETBIOS EMULATOR An emulator program provided with NetWare that allows workstations to run applications that support IBM's NetBIOS calls.

NETBEUI NetBIOS Extended User Interface. The transport layer driver frequently used by LAN Manager. NetBEUI implements the OSI LLC2 protocol.

NETI Network Information Table.

NETMAIL Private e-mail sent via the BBS network, either point-to-point (in FidoNet) or hub-routed (in PCRelay). See ECHO.

NETVIEW An IBM product for management of heterogeneous networks that integrates the functions of three formerly separate Communications Network Management (CNM) software programs: 1. NCCF. Network Communication Control Facility. 2. NLDM. Network Logical Data Manager, which uses functions from NCCF and helps pinpoint problems along the logical connection/path of an SNA session. 3. NPDA. Network Problem Determination Application, which displays various alerts using IBM equipment located at strategic points in the network and allows diagnostic information to be displayed. Also, NetView incorporates some of the functions from two other programs: VNCA (Virtual Telecommunications

Access Method/Node Control Application) which monitors the status and current activity of all resources in a domain, and NMPF (Network Management Productivity Facility) which helps the network operator to install, learn and use many network management products. See also NETWORK and NETWORK MANAGEMENT.

NETWARE NetWare is an extremely popular and extremely good operating system for a local area network from Novell, Orem, UT. NetWare is actually its own operating system. This means it is the link between machine hardware (file servers, printers, modems, etc.) and people who want it use that hardware. NetWare is neither DOS nor OS/2 though it can be made to look and act like them. That's part (a small part) of its popularity. Because of NetWare's power, it is not easy to learn. Most of its complexity can easily be insulated from a normal user. See NETWARE MHS, NETWARE WORKSTATION FILES, NETx.COM and NOVELL.

NETWARE MHS Netware MHS, which is software that provides store-and-forward capability. Fax and E-mail systems that support MHS format their message transmissions according to MHS specifications. MHS reads compatible transmissions, determines the intended recipient and his location, and then sends the message to that location, regardless of the type of fax or E-mail system at the different ends. See MHS.

NETWARE WORKSTATION FILES Novell NetWare files that, along with a network board, convert a standalone computer into a network workstation. These files are memory-resident programs — IPX.COM (a protocol/LAN driver file) and NETx.COM (the NetWare shell). When a DOS workstation is booted, NETx.COM loads the NetWare shell into the workstation's RAM as a TSR (Terminate-and-Stay Resident) program that provides an interface between the application and DOS. The shell intercepts application requests and determines whether to route them locally to DOS or to the network file server for service by the NetWare operating system using NCP (NetWare Core Protocol). If the request needs services from the network, the shell makes any necessary protocol conversions.

NETWORK 1. Networks are common in our lives. Think about trains and phones. A networks ties things together. Computer networks connect all types of computers and computer-related things — terminals, printers, modems, door entry sensors, temperature monitors, etc. The networks we're most familiar with are long distance ones, like phones and trains. But there are also Local Area Networks (LANs) which exist within a limited geographic area — like the few hundred feet of a small office, an entire building or even a "campus," such as a university or industrial park. There are also Metropolitan Area Networks (MANs). See also LAN and MAN.

NETWORK ACCESS CONTROL Electronic circuitry that determines which workstation may transmit next or when a particular workstation may transmit.

NETWORK ACD Network ACD allows ACD agent groups, at different locations (nodes), to service calls over the network independent of where the call first entered the network. NACD uses ISDN D-channel messaging to exchange information between nodes.

NETWORK ADDRESS An eight-digit hexadecimal number that uniquely identifies a network. Network addressing concepts can be compared to a postal numbering system. A street number or name identifies a city street, and building numbers identify individual buildings along the street. The combination of a street number or name and a building number tells the post office where to deliver mail within a city.

NETWORK ADDRESSABLE UNIT NAU. In IBM's SNA, a logical unit (LU), physical unit (PU) or system services control point (SSCP), which is host-based, that is the origin or destination of information transmitted by the path control portion of an SNA network.

NETWORK APPLICATION SUPPORT Digital Equipment Corporation's set of open software which allegedly allows its customers to integrate, port and distribute applications across different computer systems, including VMS, UNIX, MS-DOS, OS/2 and Apple MacIntosh.

NETWORK ARCHITECTURE The structure and protocols of a computer network. See ARCHITECTURE.

NETWORK BALANCING 1. Lumped circuit elements (inductances, capacitances and resistances) connected so as to simulate the impedance of a uniform cable or open-wire circuit over a band of frequencies. 2. Moving circuits around in a multi-node switching network such the switching loads on each of similar switching modules are roughly equal.

NETWORK BOARD 1. A circuit board installed in each network station to allow stations to communicate with each other and with the file server. 2. An SCSA term. A board device designed to act as an interface between a computer-based signal processing system and a telephone network.

NETWORK CHANNEL TERMINATING EQUIPMENT NCTE. A device or devices at the user's premises used to amplify, match impedance or match network signaling to the customer's equipment connected to the network. Basically, network channel terminating equipment is a general name for equipment linking the network to a customer's premises. When NCTE connects to digital circuits, it typically consists of DSUs and CSUs. They are used for balancing of signals and providing for loop-back testing.

NETWORK CONTROL POINT In IBM SNA networks, a host-generated program that controls the operation of a communications controller (such as an IBM 3705 or 3725).

NETWORK CONTROL SIGNALING The transmission of signals used in the telecommunications system which perform functions such as supervision, address signaling and audible tone signals to control the operation of switching machines in the telecommunication system.

NETWORK CONTROL SIGNALING UNIT A telephone set that controls the transmission of signals into the telephone system which will perform supervision, number identification and control of the switching machines.

NETWORK CONTROLLER A powerful microprocessor device designed to perform communications protocol translations between various terminals and computers and an X.25 packet switching network.

NETWORK DEMARCATION POINT The network demarcation point is the point of interconnection between the local exchange carrier's facilities and the wiring and equipment at the end user's facilities. The demarcation point is located on the subscriber's side of the telephone company's protector.

NETWORK, DISTRIBUTED See DISTRIBUTED NETWORK.

NETWORK DIVERSITY A simply concept that says if you have a network which is important you need to have multiple ways of moving information around that network. Some of those ways should be provided by circuits from one vendor and some should be be provided by circuits from several vendors. In other words, there should be diversity in both circuits and vendors. As an example of the necessity of taking network diversity very seriously, consider the year 1991. In 1991, nearly 30 million residential and business customers, more than one hundred thousand airline passengers and an alphabet soup of state and federal agencies were temporarily crippled by nine major telephone network outages. Also in a 12-month period, the FAA (Federal Aviation Commission) reported a total of 114 phone-service failures that disrupted air traffic facilities around the nation. Between June 10 and July 1, 1991, six major outages in three states comprised the largest series of network outages in history.

NETWORK DRIVE A disk drive that is available to multiple users and computers on a network. Network drives often store data files for many people in a work group.

NETWORK ELEMENTS NE. Entities defined by the functionality of the functional groups they contain and by their interfaces. Definition from Bellcore in reference to its concept of the Advanced Intelligent Network.

NETWORK EQUALIZING A device connected to a transmission path in order to alter the characteristics of that path in a specified way. Often used to equalize the frequency response characteristic of a circuit for data transmission.

NETWORK EXTENSION UNIT NEU. An AT&T thing which sits in a telephone satellite closet (their words) which links up to 11 Starlan daisy chained clusters of PCs, etc. in a star configuration through standard telephone wiring, modular cords and plugs.

NETWORK FAX SERVER An network fax server is typically a PC on LAN. The PC has one or more fax/modem cards. Its job is to send and receive faxes for everyone on the LAN. As a result it is connected to dial out phone lines. See SERVER.

NETWORK HARM The reasoning behind the Bell System's insistence that the public could not hook its own equipment to the telephone line for fear it would produce "Irreparable Harm To The Network". A Bell System publication quoted the National Academy of Sciences as identifying four areas of potential harm. They were: Excessive signal power, hazardous voltage, improper network control signaling and line imbalance. Since the Carterfone Decision in the summer of 1968, the FCC has seen fit to allow devices, which pass an FCC Registration program, to be connected to the network, and while the quality of the stuff is occasionally poor, the fears of Network Harm have proven groundless. The fears were, of course, raised to preserve the Bell System's erstwhile almost-monopoly on the manufacture of telephone equipment in the U.S.

NETWORK INTERFACE The point of interconnection between Telephone Company communications facilities and terminal equipment, protective apparatus or wiring at a subscriber's premises. The network interface or demarcation point shall be located on the subscriber's side of the Telephone Company's protector, or the equivalent thereof in cases where a protector is not employed, as provided under the local telephone company's reasonable and nondiscriminatory standard operating practices.

NETWORK INTERFACE CARD Electronic circuitry connecting a workstation to a network. Usually a card that fits into one of the expansion slots inside a personal computer. It works with the network software and computer operating system to transmit and receive messages on the network.

NETWORK INTERFACE CONTROLLER Same as a Network Interface Card. See above definition.

NETWORK INTERFACE DEVICE 1. NID. A device wired between a telephone protector and the inside wiring to isolate the customer's equipment from the network. 2. A device that performs, functions such as code and protocol conversion, and buffering required for communications to and from a network. 3. A device used primarily within a local area network to allow a number of independent devices, with varying protocols, to communicate with each other. This communication is accomplished by converting each device protocol into a common transmission protocol.

NETWORK INTERFACE MODULE Electronic circuitry connecting a system (typically a PC) to the telepone network. Network interface modules come in as many versions as there are ways of connecting to the telephone network. They range from a simple loop start telephone line to complex ISDN PRI circuits. Usually the network interface modible slides into one of the expansion slots inside a PC. The card transmits and receives messages from the resource modules and provides access to the telephone network.

NETWORK INWARD DIALING NID. A service feature of an automatically switched telephone network that allows a calling user to dial directly to an extension number at the called user facility without operator intervention.

NETWORK LAYER Third layer of the OSI model of data communications, sometimes called the packet layer. Involves routing data messages through the network on alternate routes. See OSI STANDARDS.

NETWORK LAYER ADDRESS NLA. An address appended to the LAN packet that, unlike a MAC name, indicates exactly where a computing device is located within an internetwork. TCP/IP, DECNet and IPX support network layer addressing and each has its own unique NLA format. Protocol dependent routers use the NLA to make routing decisions.

NETWORK MANAGEMENT A set of procedures, software, equipment and operations designed to keep a network operating near maximum efficiency. Network management generally falls into five areas:

1. CONFIGURATION MANAGEMENT deals with installing, initializing, "boot" loading, modifying and tracking the configuration parameters of network hardware and software.

2. FAULT LOCATION and REPAIR MANAGEMENT tools let you find out what's going wrong with what equipment or lines and give you the ability to fix those resources — by re-routing traffic on different lines or reporting problems to the carrier, or suggesting to whoever that certain equipments should be replaced. Fault location and management tools have strong error and alarm characteristics.

3. SECURITY MANAGEMENT tools allow the network manager to restrict access to various resources in the network. There are devices such as password protection schemes, giving users different levels of access to different network resources.

4. PERFORMANCE MANAGEMENT tools provide real-time and historical statistical information about the network's operation. Such tools show, for example, how many packets are being transmitted at any given moment, the number of users logged into a specific server and use of network lines.

5. ACCOUNTING MANAGEMENT applications help users allocate the costs of the various network resources — from lines to PBXs, from access to a mainframe to time used on printers.

See NETVIEW.

NETWORK MANAGEMENT CONTROL CENTER NMCC. A central place from which the network is maintained and changed and from where statistical information is collected.

NETWORK MANAGEMENT SYSTEM 1. A comprehensive system of equipment used in monitoring, controlling and managing a data communications network. Usually consists of testing devices, CRT displays and printers, patch panels and circuitry for diagnostics and reconfiguration of channels, generally housed together in an operator console unit. 2. An MCI definition. An MCI system that is used for the automated transmission of data billing information is passed from the switches to an AOM sub-system within each division and then passed on to the billing centers to be edited and processed. This automated system of transfer of traffic information is much faster than the "switch tape" method, in which a physical tape is made and then mailed to the Billing Centers.

NETWORK NAME AUTOMATIC ROUTING A system for getting network-delivered faxes deliveered to individual users. The fax network assigns each user a name (usually the user's network login name), and the sender uses this name. The receiving fax system detects this name and routes the fax to the intended recipient.

NETWORK OPERATING SYSTEM NOS. The software side of a LAN. The program that controls the operation of a network. It allows users to communicate and share files and peripherals. It provides the user interface to the LAN, and it communicates with the LAN hardware or network interface card. It is important to note that a network operating system is different from a network interface card: IBM's Token Ring, for example, is an interface card, not a NOS. IBM's NOS is called the PC LAN Support Program. A variety of other vendors also offer NOSs, including Novell and 3Com. Most have drivers to support a variety of network interface cards.

NETWORK OPERATIONS Functions that provide, maintain and administer services supported by the network systems. These functions reside in network systems or network operations applications that interface directly to network systems and include memory administration, surveillance, testing, network traffic management and network data collection. Definition from Bellcore in reference to its concept of the Advanced Intelligent Network.

NETWORK OPERATIONS BUSINESS INFORMATION SYSTEM NOBIS. An MCI definition. An MCI system supporting the construction and operation of MCI's telecommunications network.

NETWORK OPERATIONS CENTER A name for the central place which monitors the status of a corporate network and sends out instructions to repair bits and pieces of the network when they break. In more formal terms, monitoring of network status, supervision and coordination of network maintenance, accumulation of accounting and usage data and user support.

NETWORK OUTWARD DIALING NOD. A service feature of an automatically switched telephone network that allows a calling user to dial directly all network user numbers without operator intervention.

NETWORK PRINTER A printer shared by multiple computers over a network. See also local printer.

NETWORK PROBLEM DETERMINATION APPLICATION NPDA. A host-resident IBM program product that aids a network operator in interactively identifying network problems from a central point.

NETWORK PROTECTION A term used to describe an array of strategies to protect your network from crashing around your ears should a disaster happen. The ultimate network protection means duplicating every item in the network — including the people who operate it. Obviously anything else (which is what we are all forced to do) is a compromise. The typical network protection these days tends to focus on alternate routing and duplication of network lines, including local loops and long distance lines.

NETWORK PROTECTION DEVICE NPD. A device which provides isolation between PBX circuits and CO trunks or tie lines.

NETWORK RECONFIGURATION SERVICE NRS. A New York Telephone service that lets you control, rearrange and switch your private line voice, private line analog data and Superpath 1.544 Mbps lines. You might wish to do this because you want to temporarily join one office to another for a high-speed data dump, or for a videoconference. Or in case something happens and you may want to route yourself around the trouble. You can reconfigure you own network in one of two ways — using a computer terminal or PC to dial in your instructions or call an 800 number and have an NYTel attendant do it for you. Rearrangements can be made in near-real time or scheduled for an appointed time.

NETWORK SERVER A powerful computer on a LAN designed to serve the needs of all the people on the LAN with everything from database, email, fax, images, voice messages, communications, etc. See also EMAIL SERVER and FAX SERVER.

NETWORK SERVICES In IBM's SNA, the services within network addressable units (NAUs) that control network operations via sessions to and from the SSCP.

NETWORK TERMINAL NUMBER NTN. The number assigned to a data terminal under the Data Network Identification Code system. In the CCITT International X.121 format, the sets of digits that comprise the complete address of the data terminal end point. For an NTN that is not part of a national integrated numbering format, the NTN is the 10 digits of the CCITT X.25 14-digit address that follow the Data Network Identification Code (DNIC). When part of a national integrated numbering format, the NTN is the 11 digits of the CCITT X.25 14-digit address that follow the DNIC.

NETWORK TERMINAL OPTION NTO. An IBM program product that enables an SNA network to accommodate a select group of non-SNA asynchronous and bisynch devices via the NCP-driven communications controller.

NETWORK TERMINATING INTERFACE NTI. 1. The point where the network service provider's responsibilities for service begin or end. 2.The interface between DCE and its connected DTE.

NETWORK TERMINATING UNIT NTU. The part of the network equipment which connects directly to the data terminal equipment.

NETWORK TERMINATION 1 The ISDN Network Termination 1 (NT1) provides an interface between the ISDN loop and an S or T interface terminal, such as an ISDN phone, or the PCTA (Personal Computer Terminal Adapter). The PCTA is the device which turns a PC into an ISDN terminal/phone. The NTI is the classic ISDN "black box." It sits on the subscribers premises at the end of the subscriber loop coming in from the phone company. It talks to the ISDN central office. And, in turn, all ISDN terminals, phones and other devices on the subscriber premises are plugged into this black box. The basic NT1 functions are:

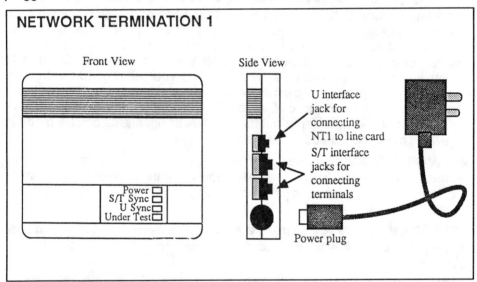

NETWORK TERMINATION 1

Front View Side View

U interface jack for connecting NT1 to line card
S/T interface jacks for connecting terminals

Power
S/T Sync
U Sync
Under Test

Power plug

● Line transmission termination.

● Layer 1 line maintenance functions and performance monitoring.

● Layer 1 multiplexing, and

● Interface termination, including multidrop termination employing layer 1 contention resolution.

See ISDN.

NETWORK TOPOLOGY The geometric arrangement of links and nodes of a network. The geography of a network. Networks are typically of either a star, ring, tree or bus topology, or some hybrid combination.

NETWORK TRAFFIC MANAGEMENT NTM. Functionality that maximizes the traffic throughput of the network during times of overload or failure and minimizes the impact of one service on the performance of others. This is done through centralized surveillance of maintenance conditions and traffic, and centralized control of traffic volumes being originated in network systems. Definition from Bellcore in reference to its concept of the Advanced Intelligent Network.

NETWORK VIRTUAL TERMINAL A communications concept wherein a variety of DTEs, with different data rates, protocols, codes and formats, are accommodated in the same network. This is done as a result of network processing, where each device's data is converted into a network standard format and then converted into the format of the receiving device at the destination end.

NETWORKING SYSTEMS IBM Networking Systems is new name (summer, 1991) for its Communication Systems group, formed in January, 1988.

NETx.COM This Novell NetWare workstation shell file provides an interface between the application and DOS, monitoring all data transmissions that move in or out of either one. When a function request needs network service, such as a call to read a file from the file server, the shell begins the process of protocol conversion and network transmission. Netx intercepts requests by taking over software interrupts 21h (used to call standard DOS functions), 24h (DOS's critical error handler vector), and 17th (used to send data to local printer ports). In general, the shell intercepts all interrupt 21h DOS requests and inspects each one. The "x" typically stands for which version of DOS the workstation is running. NET3.COM would run on a workstation running MS-DOS 3.X, i.e. 3.1, 3.2 and 3.3. (There is no 3.4).

NEURAL NETWORK COMPUTER A very different kind of computer. Neural network computers are built from webs of randomly connected electronic neurons. These machines are designed to be trained, not programmed. In design and in function, they are meant to closely resemble the human brain. As in the brain, the neurons send signals to one another through thousands of adjustable connections, or synapses. As the machine learns, the settings of these controls are automatically turned up or down. And the chaos of connections evolves into a finely tuned machine, one that can read handwritten letters or recognize the spoken words. With a neural network computer, a trainer simply speaks words to the machine, rewarding it if it acts correctly and punishing it when it acts incorrectly. There is hope that neural network computers may perform better than traditional computers in running artificial intelligence software. See NEURAL NETWORKS.

NEURAL NETWORKS Neural networks are computer devices in which bits of silicon pretend to work like the nerve cells in the brain. The hope of neural networks is that by mimicking the brain, machines might develop some of the vague, useful skills at which people excel and computers mostly fail — such as recognizing faces.

NEUTRAL The ac power system conductor that is intentionally grounded on the supply side of the service disconnect. It is the low potential (white) side of a single phase ac circuit or the low potential fourth wire of a three-phase Wye distribution system. The neutral provides a current return path for ac power currents whereas the safety ground (green) conductor should not, except during fault conditions.

NEUTRAL GROUND An intentional ground applied to the neutral conductor or neutral point of a circuit, transformer, machine, apparatus, or system.

NEUTRAL TRANSMISSION Unipolar transmission. A form of signaling which employs two distinct states, one of which represents the existence of a space as well as the absence of current.

NEW LINE ASCII character 10, abbreviated "NL". This character replaced the abbreviation "LF" which meant Line Feed. Newer terminals accept the NL character to mean both CR (Carriage Return) and LF functions for "end of line" sequences. The function of transmitting an "end of line" sequence to a printer or remote computer system is to designate to a computer to print what follows on the next line of a print out. This usually consists of transmitting the characters CR, LF (Carriage Return, followed by Line Feed). On older printing terminals, these two characters would be followed by a number of null characters whose job would be to waste time until the print head got back to the left margin before printing the first letter of the next line on the page. Otherwise, that character would be in the middle of the page, and the second character would start the line. Telex machines usually send the sequence CR, LF, CR as a New Line sequence to give the head enough time to get back.

NEW WAVE New Wave is a user environment available for personal computers from Hewlett-Packard. It includes a look and feel specification, a toolkit and a desktop metaphor set of tools and definition.

NEWBRIDGE NETWORKS A manufacturer of good T-1 muxes, channel banks and other digital communications devices founded by Terry Matthews, co-founder of Mitel and Peter Madsen, who also made his fortune with Mitel. Newbridge is one of our favorite companies. Terry and Peter will be pleased when they see their name in this dictionary.

NEWTON The author of this dictionary, Harry Newton, has reached a pinnacle of achievement. According to Susan, his wife, he has a become a sex symbol for women who no longer care. The photo on the back cover (in case you hadn't already figured) is years old. Maybe decades old.

NEXT 1. Near End Crosstalk. 2. Steve Jobs' "new" computing company — the one he started after leaving Apple. It used to be in hardware. It's now only in software.

NEXTSTATION The name of Steve Jobs' new computer. It is made by his company which is called Next Inc. Nextstation comes with a user interface control panel (also called a user interface) called NextStep, which makes the computer especially easy to use. Next's color computer is called Nextdimension.

NEXTSTEP NextStep is the software development environment shipped by Next Computer. IBM's recently announced RISC System 6000 workstation family will support the NextStep environment for non-networked users. IBM has licensed the technology from Next.

NF Noise Figure.

NFAS Network Facility Associated Signaling. See also D CHANNEL and ISDN.

NFPA National Fire Protection Agency. See NEC REQUIREMENTS.

NFS Network File System. One of many distributed-file-system protocols that allow a computer on a network to use the files and peripherals of another networked computer as if they were local. This protocol was developed by Sun Micro-Systems and adopted by other vendors.

NI Network Interface. Demarcation point between PSTN and CPE.

NIA Network Interface Adapter. An IBM hardware device that with certain software, will allow an SNA device to communicate over a packet switching network.

NIBBLE Four bits or half a byte. Usually described by one hexadecimal digit.

NIBBLE INTERLEAVING/MULTIPLEXING A technique where 4 bit nibbles (one at a time) from each lower speed input a channel are used to build the higher speed frame output of a multiplexer.

NIC 1. Near Instantaneous Companding. This describes the very fast, essentially real-time, process of quantizing an analog signal into digital symbols. 2. Network Interface Card. The attachment that connects a device to a network. The NIC, usually a PC expansion board, executes the code needed by the connected device to share a cable or some other media with other stations.

NICKEL HYDRIDE A new type of rechargeable battery, now becoming used in laptop computers. Most of today's rechargeable batteries are nickel cadmium. These suffer from several problems: 1. They have a "memory." Which means they must be fully discharged once a month or they won't deliver their full potential. 2. They are hard to dispose of. Nickel hydride is a new technology with some benefits: It's easier to dispose of. It can hold twice as much power per unit as a standard nickel cadmium battery. It doesn't have a "memory." (Neither do car or telephone batteries, which are typically lead acid.) But there are some downsides: Nickel hydride batteries lose their charge faster than nickel cadmium. In two months a nickel cadmium battery will lose its charge. Nickel hydride batteries are more expensive than nickel cadmium. The Nickel hydride battery also can not put out power as fast as as a nickel cadmium one can, so it probably won't be suitable for power tools and appliances that drain batteries quickly.

NICNAME A LAN protocol specified in RFC-812. It requests information about a specific user or hostname from the Network Information Center (or NIC) name database service.

NID Network Inward Dialing. A service feature of an automatically switched telephone network that allows a calling user to dial directly to an extension number without operator intervention.

NIF Network Interface Function.

NIGHT ANSWER Incoming calls to a switchboard during evening and weekend hours are automatically rerouted to ring only at designated night answering phones such as the security desk. See the next few definitions.

NIGHT ANSWER — ASSIGNED Night answer going to specific, assigned telephones.

NIGHT ANSWER — OFFSITE Phones being answered after hours by people and machinery located offsite — someplace else.

NIGHT ANSWER — UNIVERSAL Anybody and everybody can answer the incoming calls from any phone. In TELECONNECT, if the phone rings after hours, we simply touch "6" on any phone and we can answer that incoming call — whether it's a local, normal DDD or incoming WATS.

NIGHT AUDIT This feature provides automatic printout of message registration data for all quest rooms at the front desk console.

NIGHT CHIME An auxiliary ringer, usually wall mounted, used to indicate a ringing trunk during night operations or used as a "phantom" extension for overflow applications.

NIGHT CONSOLE POSITION Provides an alternate attendant position which can be used at night in lieu of the regular console. Usually cheaper than buying a second normal console.

NIGHT PATCH Assigned Night Answer, Fixed Night Service, Programmable Night Connections. Provides arrangements (which are prewired into the system) to route incoming central office calls normally answered at the attendant position, to preselected stations within the PBX system when the attendant is not on duty.

NIGHT SERVICE Your operator goes home, puts your phone system into "night service." A call now comes in. The night bell rings. You hear it. You go to a phone and hit a code (such as #6) or hit the flashing "Nigh Answer" button. And you answer the call. Not all phone systems need to be placed in Night Service for you to answer an incoming call from any phone. And you can program the night bell to ring all day.

NIGHT SERVICE AUTOMATIC SWITCHING Should the attendant neglect to place the console in the night answering mode, after a certain period of timed ringing from an incoming central office call, the entire system will automatically jump to the night service.

NIGHT SERVICE — EXPANDED SERVICE Routes calls normally directed to the attendant to preselected station lines within the system when it is arranged for night service. Calls to specific exchange trunks can be arranged to route to specific station lines and can be assigned on a flexible basis. Trunk Answer From Any Station capability is provided for calls which are handled by assigned night stations.

NIGHT SERVICE — FIXED SERVICE Provides arrangements to route calls normally directed to the attendant to preselected station lines within the PBX system when regular attendant positions are not in use. In addition, calls to specific trunks can be arranged to ring on specific phones. The receiving phone can then transfer the call.

NIGHT STATION The phone assigned to automatically handle incoming calls after the main switchboard has shut down for the day.

NIH Not Invented Here. The tendency of organizations to reject ideas and inventions which they didn't think of. A major and continuing problem in the telephone industry.

NIN Network Imaging Server. A local area network based server largely devoted to storing, retrieving and possibly manipulating images. See also SERVER.

NIST The National Institute of Standards and Technology, which is part of the U.S. Department of Commerce. See also the NORTH AMERICAN ISDN USERS' FORUM.

NIOD Network Inward/Outward Dialing.

NIUF North American ISDN Users Forum.

NKT Nederlands Keuringsinstituut voor Telecommunicatieapparatuur (Private laboratory for regulatory testing, The Netherlands).

NL See NEW LINE.

NLA Network Layer Address. An address appended to the LAN packet that, unlike a MAC name, indicates exactly where a computing device is located within an internetwork. TCP/IP, DECNet and IPX support network layer addressing and each has its own unique NLA format. Protocol dependent routers use the NLA to make routing decisions.

NLDM Network Logical Data Manager. An IBM term. See also NETVIEW.

NLM NetWare Loadable Modules. Applications and drivers that run in a server under Novell's NetWare 386 and can be loaded or unloaded on the fly. In other networks, such applications could require dedicated PCs.

NLSP NetWare Link Services Protocol.

NM Network Management.

NMOS N-channel Metal Oxide Semiconductor.

NMP Network Management Protocol. An AT&T-developed set of protocols designed to exchange information with and control the devices that govern various components of a network, including modems and T1 multiplexers.

NMS Network Management System.

NMT Another form of cellular service, common in some overseas countries.

NNI Network Node Interface. An Asynchronous Transfer Mode (ATM) term. The interface between two public network pieces of equipment (contrast that to UNI, which stands for User Network Interface).

NNTP Network News Transport Protocol. An extension of the TCP/IP local area network protocol that provides a network news transport service.

NNX A three-digit code to identify the local central office in which N represents any digit from 2 to 9 and X is any digit. NNX means the first three digits of a North American local telephone number. Originally, only NNX codes were used to identify and number local central offices. Now all subscribers dial 1+ when making a direct distance dialed long distance call. And central offices are being changed to be NXX — which allows local central offices to have numbers which look like area codes, e.g. 206, 210, etc. This gives us more central office numbers.

NO ANSWER TRANSFER A service provided by a cellular carrier that automatically transfers an incoming cellular call to another phone number if the cellular subscriber is unable to answer. Most no-answer transfer systems will automatically transfer an incoming cellular call to another phone number if the cellular subscriber is unable to answer (it's not turned on) or if it's not answered after the third or fourth ring if the phone is turned on.

NO ATTENDANT OPTION CBX systems with Direct Inward Dialing may be designed (configured) without an attendant console.

NO BILL PHONE A name for a cellular phone from which you can make free phone calls — local or long distance. The name "no bill" was given by crooks, largely in Southern California in the Spring of 1992, to phones they had modified to emulate other legitimate cellular phones. Thus all calls made by "no bill" phones are billed to legitimate users, who happen to have other cellular phones with identical codes and now have huge cellular bills. Sorry about that.

NO BUSY TEST A circuit used to connect to a busy subscriber's line number.

NO HOLD CONFERENCE/TRANSFER In the event that a call to 911 is being transferred to a secondary or what they call a downstream PSAP

(Public Service Answering Position), it is important that the caller never be left in disconcerting silence. After all it is an emergency call. "No hold" features allow the conference or transfer to be done while the PSAP 911 agent is in full uninterrupted communication with the caller.

NO LINE PREFERENCE Requires the user to manually select (i.e. punch down) a line for each call.

NO OP Instruction that does nothing. It is used to hold the place for future insertion of a machine instruction.

NOC Networks Operations Center.

NOD Network Outward Dialing. A service feature of an automatically switched telephone network that allows a calling user to dial directly all user numbers on the network without operator intervention. See also DIRECT OUTWARD DIALING.

NODAL CLOCK The principal clock or alternate clock located at a particular node that provides the timing reference for all major functions at that node.

NODE 1. A point of connection into a network. In multipoint networks, it means it's a unit that's polled. In LANs, it's a device on the ring. In packet switched networks, it's one of the many packet switches which form the network's backbone. 2. An SCSA term. An independent SCSA unit in a distributed processing SCSA network, consisting of one or more resource and/or network boards, and one or more SCxbus adapter boards. Communication between nodes take place via the SCxbus. From a device programming point of view, a node is simply an addressable system unit which contains boards connected by an SCbus.

NODE NUMBER A node number identifies a network board on a local area network. Every station on a network must contain at least one network board. Each network board must have a unique node number to distinguish it from all the other network boards in that network. In a file server with more than one network board, the node number in LAN A is designated for all traffic addressed to that server. Node numbers can be set in a variety of ways, depending on which network board you use: (1) with jumpers or switches on boards such as Arcnet, (2) at the factory for Token-Ring and Ethernet boards, or (3) with software.

NODE TYPE In IBM's SNA, the classification of a network device based on the protocols it supports and the network addressable units (NAUs) it can contain. Type 1 and Type 2 nodes are peripheral nodes. Type 4 and 5 nodes are subarea nodes.

NOISE Unwanted electrical signals introduced into telephone lines by circuit components or natural disturbances which tend to degrade the performance of the line. Also known as Line Noise.

NOISE EQUIVALENT POWER At a given data-signaling rate or

NEWTON'S TELECOM DICTIONARY

modulation frequency, operating wavelength, and effective noise bandwidth, the radiant power that produces a signal-to-noise ratio of unity at the output of a given optical detector. Information Gatekeepers defines NEP as a measurement in fiber optics that at a given modulation frequency, wavelength, and for a given effective noise bandwidth, the radiant power that produces a signal-to-noise ratio of 1 at the output of a given detector. Some manufacturers and authors, according to Information Gatekeepers, define NEP as the minimum detectable power per root unit bandwidth; when defined in this way, NEP has the units of watts/(hertz) 1/2. Therefore, the term is a misnomer, because the units of power per watts. Some manufacturers define NEP as the radiant power that produces a signal-to-dark current noise ratio of unity. This is misleading when dark-current noise does not dominate, as is often true in fiber systems.

NOISE MEASUREMENT UNITS A series of terms used to express circuit noise. These units include: -dB RN — Decibel rated noise -dBrnC — C message weighting refers to the noise measured at 1000 Hz.

NOISE SUPPRESSOR Filtering or digital signal-processing circuitry in a receiver or transmitter that automatically eliminates or reduces noise.

NOISE VOLTAGE In optical communication, an rms component of the optical detector electrical output voltage which is incoherent with the signal radiant power.

NOISE WEIGHTING A method of assigning a specific value to the transmission impairment due to the noise encountered by an average user operating a particular telephone. Noise weightings generally in use have been established by regulatory agencies concerned with public telephone service. They are tightened as technology improves.

NOMDA National Office Machine Dealers Association, now merged with LANDA.

NOMINAL BIT STUFFING RATE The rate at which stuffing bits are inserted (or deleted) when both the input and output bit rates are at their nominal values.

NOMINAL LINEWIDTH In facsimile systems, the average separation between centers of adjacent scanning or recording lines.

NON-BLOCKING A PBX is Non-Blocking if all callers can be switched through the PBX even during the busiest time of day. However, the caller may find no trunks are available and thus may not be able to complete the call. The trunk availability is a different problem than the ability of the switch to handle all the traffic it gets. But if your call does not go through do you care? A more technical explanation from InteCom of non-blocking: "Indicates that the internal network of the switching system is such that the total number of available transmission paths is equal to the number of ports. Therefore, all ports can have simultaneous access through the network."

NON-CONCUR IBM-speak for to withhold approval, as in I nonconcur with this proposal.

NON-CONSECUTIVE HUNTING Often referred to as "jump hunting." Nonconsecutive lines, trunks or extensions can be accessed or "searched" by the switching equipment upon dialing the initial number in the hunting group to find a connection to the first non-busy phone. Nonconsecutive hunting can be used on incoming and outgoing lines. For example, you could order four trunks from your local phone company which are to "hunt" on. Should the first be busy, the call will go to the next. If the next is busy, then it will hunt to the next. TELECONNECT Magazine has "consecutive" numbering in its first four phone numbers — 212-691-8215, 8216, 8217 and 8218. But let's say we only started with one number and then, because of growth, we needed three more. It's possible consecutive numbers might be taken. Therefore to get the hunting feature, the phone company might have assigned us NONCONSECUTIVE hunting numbers like 691-8220, 8256, 8678. Sometimes the phone company will also assign us "coded" trunks as part of our trunk group. These are trunks which have no dialable number associated with them. It's best to get real numbers so you can test them by calling them individually. You cannot test coded trunks.

NON-CRITICAL TECHNICAL LOAD That part of the technical load not required for synchronous operation.

NON-DATA BIT Bit with encoding violating normal format: used for special control purposes.

NON-DEDICATED SERVER A node on which user applications are available while network resource maintenance applications execute in the background.

NON-ERASABLE A switch where a through traffic path always exists for each attached phone. Generically, a switch or switching environment designed never to experience a busy condition due to call volume. See NON-BLOCKING, which is a better term.

NON-IMPACT PRINTER Refers to printers that do not strike a hammer to a platen as typewriters do. Usually a heat sensitive paper or laser/xerox type technology is involved.

NON-INTELLIGIBLE CROSSTALK Crosstalk which is not of sufficient level to be understood by a listener but which is more annoying than other crosstalk because you think it's intelligible. Or think it should be intelligible.

NON-INTERLACED There's a good definition on interlacing and non-interlacing under INTERLACING.

NON-ISDN LINE Any connection from a CPE to a central office switch that is not served by D-channel signaling.

NON-ISDN TRUNK In ISDN language, a non-ISDN trunk is any trunk not served by either SS7 or D-channel signaling.

NON-LINEAR DISTORTION Amplitude distortion of a signal in which the output signal does not have a linear relationship to the input signal.

NON-LOADED LINES Cable pairs or transmission lines with no added inductive loading coils. In short, straight, raw copper pairs. See LOAD COILS.

NON-PERSISTENT In local area networking technology, describes a carrier sense multiple access (CSMA) local area network (LAN) in which the stations involved in a collision do not try to retransmit immediately — even if the network is quiet. Compare with persistent and p-persistent.

NON-PRINTING CHARACTER A character in a transmission code which performs a control function but is not reproduced when the transmission is printed.

NON-PROPRIETARY LAN A Local Area Network that can connect the equipment of many vendors. See PROPRIETARY LAN.

NON-PUBLISHED A telephone line with no phone number listed in the telephone company's directory is called an unlisted number. Centrex numbers, for example, are often unlisted, meaning you can't get them from the telephone company even if you pulled the biggest string imaginable. Compare unlisted number to non-published number, where the number is listed in the telephone company's directory. But no one in the world outside the phone company can get their hands on that number. "Published" means "to make public." And that's the one thing the phone company won't do with a non-published number. You won't, for example, find the number in a phone book. You also won't get it from Directory Assistance. Over 25% of many private phone numbers in major metropolitan areas are now non-published — a "service" their subscribers pay extra for.

NON-ROUTABLE PROTOCOLS LAN protocols, such as IBM's NetBIOS, LAN Server and SNA, that use names and not Network Layer Addresses to identify devices and therefore supply no routing information. Internetworking devices must find other ways to route traffic in networks that use nonroutable protocols.

NON-SENT PAID Utility industry term for calls made as third party billings, reversed charges or with a Calling Card.

NON-SESSION A type of synchronous access mode that can exist between an end user and a host computer in an Amdahl packet network. In non-session access, the calling line (PU) is mapped to a specific offering line (LU). The offering line is reserved for that calling line at all times.

NON-SIMULTANEOUS TRANSMISSION Half duplex transmission. Transmission in one direction at a time. This mode of transmission may be the result of limitations of the transmission channel or of the transmitting/receiving equipment.

NON-SYNCHRONOUS COMMUNICATIONS See ASYNCHRONOUS COMMUNICATIONS.

NON-TRAFFIC SENSITIVE PLANT Telephone company facilities which are unaffected by changes in volume of telephone activity.

NON-TRANSPARENT MODE A transmission environment, mainly of bisynch transmission, in which control characters and control-character sequences are recognized through the examination of all transmitted data. Compare with transparent mode. Also called normal mode.

NON-VOLATILE Memory which is not lost (i.e. that does not "forget") when the power is shut off.

NON-WIRELINE Also called the block "A" carrier. The "A" originally stood for "alternate." The FCC, in setting up the licensing and systems in each market. It reserved one for the local wireline telephone company, and opened the second system — the Block A system — to other interested applicants. The distinction between Block A and Block B is meaningful only during the licensing phase at the FCC. Once a system is constructed, it can be sold to anyone. Thus in some markets today, both the A and B systems are owned by a telephone company. One happens to be the local phone company, and the other is a phone company that decided to buy a cellular system outside its home territory. Non-Wireline, or Block A systems, operate on the radio frequencies from 824 to 849 Megahertz.

NORC Network Operators Research Committee.

NORMAL REPONSE MODE NRM. HDLC mode for use on links with one primary and one or more secondaries. Under NRM, a secondary can transmit only after receiving a poll addressed to it by a primary. It may then send a series of responses. But after it sets the F bit in a response, it cannot transmit any more until it receives another poll.

NORMALIZED AVERAGE TRANSFER DELAY Average transfer delay divided by packet transmission time at the clock rate of the medium.

NORMALIZED NETWORK THROUGHPUT Network throughput in packets per second divided by maximum throughput possible at clock rate of medium. Less than one.

NORMALIZED OFFERED TRAFFIC The average number of attempted packet transmissions per second divided by the average number of packet transmissions/second possible at the clock rate of the medium. May exceed one.

NORSTAR A programmable phone system from Northern Telecom which can accommodate up to 100 people. See ACCESS TOOLKIT.

NORSTAR ACCESS TOOLKIT See ACCESS TOOLKIT

NORSTAR MANAGER A feature which permits remote programming and administration of a Norstar telephone system.

NORTH AMERICAN AREA CODES 201 Northern New Jersey; 202 Washington DC; 203 Connecticut; 204 Manitoba, Canada; 205 Alabama;

206 Washington (Seattle); 207 Maine; 208 Idaho; 209 California; 210 San Antonio, Texas; 212 New York (Manhattan, Bronx); 213 California (part of Los Angeles);; 214 Texas (Dallas); 215 Pennsylvania (Philadelphia); 216 Ohio (Cleveland); 217 Illinois (Springfield); 218 Minnesota (Duluth);; 219 Indiana (South Bend);

301 Maryland; 302 Delaware; 303 Colorado; 304 West Virginia; 305 Florida (Miami); 306 Saskatchewan, Canada; 307 Wyoming; 308 Nebraska (North Platte); 309 Illinois (Peoria); 310 Southern California; 312 Illinois (Chicago); 313 Michigan (Detroit); 314 Missouri (St Louis); 315 New York (Syracuse); 316 Kansas (Wichita); 317 Indiana (Indianapolis); 318 Louisiana (Shreveport); 319 Iowa (Dubuque);

401 Rhode Island; 402 Nebraska; 403 Alberta, Yukon, Northwest Territories, Canada; 404 Georgia (Atlanta); 405 Oklahoma (Oklahoma City); 406 Montana; 407 Florida (Boca Raton); 408 California (Silicon Valley, Cupertino); 409 Texas (Beaumont); 410 Maryland; 412 Pennsylvania (Pittsburgh); 413 Massachusetts (Springfield); 414 Wisconsin (Milwaukee); 415 California (San Francisco); 416 Ontario (Toronto) Canada; 417 Missouri (Springfield); 418 Quebec (Quebec City) Canada; 419 Ohio (Toledo);

501 Arkansas; 502 Kentucky (Louisville); 503 Oregon; 504 Louisiana (New Orleans); 505 New Mexico; 506 New Brunswick; 507 Minnesota; 508 Massachusetts (Worcester); 509 Washington (Spokane); 510 Northern California; 512 Texas (San Antonio); 513 Ohio (Cincinnati); 514 Quebec (Montreal) Canada; 515 Iowa (Des Moines); 516 New York (Long Island); 517 Michigan (Lansing); 518 New York (Semi-Upstate); 519 Ontario, Canada;

601 Mississippi; 602 Arizona; 603 New Hampshire; 604 British Columbia, Canada; 605 South Dakota; 606 Kentucky (Covington); 607 New York (Binghamton); 608 Wisconsin (Madison); 609 New Jersey (Trenton); 612 Minnesota (Minneapolis); 613 Ontario (Ottawa) Canada; 614 Ohio (Columbus); 615 Tennessee (Nashville); 616 Michigan (Grand Rapids); 617 Massachusetts (Boston); 618 Illinois (Centralia); 619 California (San Diego);

700 Information and other Services by local and long distance phone carriers; 701 North Dakota; 702 Nevada; 703 Virginia (Arlington); 704 North Carolina (Charlotte); 705 Ontario (North Bay) Canada; 706 Georgia (Atlanta); 707 California (Santa Rosa); 708 Illinois (Chicago); 709 Newfoundland and Labrador, Canada; 712 Iowa (Council Bluffs); 713 Texas (Houston); 714 California (Anaheim); 715 Wisconsin (Eau Claire); 716 New York (Buffalo); 717 Pennsylvania (Harrisburg); 718 New York (Brooklyn, Queens, Staten Island); 719 Colorado

800 IN-WATS Service; 801 Utah; 802 Vermont; 803 South Carolina; 804 Virginia (Richmond); 805 California (Bakersfield); 806 Texas (Amarillo); 807 Ontario (Thunder Bay) Canada; 808 Hawaii; 809 Bermuda, Puerto Rico, Virgin Islands & Caribbean Islands; 812 Indiana (Evansville); 813 Florida

(Fort Meyers); 814 Pennsylvania (Altoona); 815 Illinois (Rockford); 816 Missouri (Kansas City); 817 Texas (Fort Worth); 818 California (Burbank); 819 Quebec (Sherbrooke) Canada;

900 DIAL-IT Services; 901 Tennessee (Memphis); 902 Nova Scotia, Prince Edward Island, Canada; 903 Texas (Dallas suburbs); 904 Florida (Jacksonville); 905 Mexico City, Mexico; 906 Michigan (Escanaba); 907 Alaska; 908 New Jersey; 909 California (as of 1993); 912 Georgia (Savannah); 913 Kansas (Topeka); 914 New York (Westchester County); 915 Texas (Sweetwater); 916 California (Sacramento); 917 New York (Manhattan, The Bronx) (Cellular and Beepers); 918 Oklahoma (Tulsa); 919 North Carolina (Raleigh)

See NPA.

NORTH AMERICAN CELLULAR NETWORK A Craig McCaw idea to join together a bunch of cellular phone companies providers who would provide a painless, simple way for someone making or receiving a cellular call in their territory. Up until now, traveling cellular users — what the industry calls "roamers" — have been forced to pay heavy charges for calling from the territory of a cellular company not theirs. And roamers have been in effect incommunicado from incoming calls. It's impossible to call someone on a cellular phone if they're not in the own territory and you don't know where they are. Craig McCaw is the chairman and founder of McCaw Communications, a large cellular phone company and now partly-owned by AT&T.

NORTH AMERICAN DIRECTORY FORUM NADF. An association of electronic mail providers who are figuring standards and ways of sending mail between their subscribers.

NORTH AMERICAN ISDN USERS FORUM Here is the complete explanation of this important group, as excerpted from their brochure: The barriers to the widespread use of ISDN nationally and internationally is difficult because the technology is complex and developing rapidly. One underlying problem is the lack of standard implementations of ISDN applications. ISDN standards are currently developed by the International Telephone and Telegraph Consultative Committee (CCITT) and by accredited standards committee T-1 under the umbrella of the American National Standards Institute (ANSI). But standards designed to meet many requirements offer multiple options which are open to diverse interpretations. As a result, services and products produced by different manufacturers are incompatible.

To solve this problem, NIST collaborated with industry in 1988 to establish the North American ISDN User's Forum (NIU-Forum). NIST's (the National Institute of Standards and Technology's) Computer Systems Laboratory (CSL) serves as chair of the forum and hosts the NIU-Forum Secretariat. Through support of the forum, CSL advances new uses of computer and telecommunications technology in government and industry. The purpose of the NIU-Forum is to create a strong user voice in the implementation of ISDN applications. The forum provides users of ISDN technology with the opportunity to work with implementors to assure that user's needs are met in the ISDN design process. Through the forum, users and manufacturers concur on ISDN applications, the selection of options from standards, and conformance tests, enhancing the strength of the U.S. telecommunications industry in the world marketplace.

NORTH AMERICAN NUMBERING PLAN The method of identifying telephone trunks in the public network of North America, called World Numbering Zone 1 by the CCITT. The Plan has three ways of identifying phone numbers in North America — a three digit area code, a three digit exchange or central office code and four digit subscriber code. Other countries have much more complicated numbering schemes. There are some countries, for example, where the length of the area code actually exceeds the subscriber code. There are many countries where there is no consistency in the length of phone numbers. Some are nine-digit. Some are 12-digit, etc. All these varying number lengths may be within 100 miles of each other.

NORTH AMERICAN TELECOMMUNICATIONS ASSOCIATION NATA. The national trade association for companies providing customer premise telephone equipment. NATA represents the interests of the industry before the Congress, the FCC and in court actions. See also NATA.

NORSTAR A family of telephone systems from Northern Telecom. See ACCESS TOOLKIT and NORSTAR COMMAND SET.

NORSTAR COMMAND SET A series of standard commands for programming a telephone system. These commands were created by Northern Telecom to program their Norstar telephone system. The Norstar Command Set includes commands such as mDisconnectCall mDialDigits mJoinCalls mOnEvent mOnErrorEvent mTermWrite (which means to write to the phone's screen).

In creating this command set, Northern Telecom saw two types of applications for its Norstar telephone system: 1. Server applications; and 2. Personal telephony applications.

Server applications would include automatic call distribution, dial by name, predictive dialing, dial from a computer and transfer a database record and the call to an agent. Personal telephony applications include on-screen dialing for telemarketing. placing a call in an electronic rolodex by hitting "ENTER."

Under the Norstar Command set, a programmer can take complete control of a phone system away from its central factory-programming. Using the Norstar command set, one moment a phone could be an ACD agent terminal, the next moment a predictive dialer, the next a data input terminal and the third an operator position. For more information on the Norstar Command Set, see page 14 of the December, 1990 issue of TELECONNECT Magazine.

NOTCHED NOISE Noise in which a narrow band of frequencies has been removed. Normally used for testing devices or circuits.

NOTEPHONE One of the first products of a collaboration of Apple Computer and Siemens Private Communications Systems Group. The NotePhone (which I haven't seen) will, according to Apple, Rolm and Siemens, combine Siemens and Rolm Telephony and Apple's Newton technology to provide access to telephone and fax features. Siemens and Rolm are planning to provide NotePhones for standard (analog) telephone lines commonly found in homes and hotels as well as for digital business communications systems (i.e. PBXs) from Siemens and Rolm.

NOTHS Network Operations Trouble Handling System.

NOS Network Operating System. Controlling software for a local area network, which may run on top of DOS, that oversees resource sharing and often provides security and administrative tools.

NOVELL Novell is the reincarnation of NDSI, a computer firm that almost went under in the early 1980s. The then nearly 60-year-old Ray Noorda, who had had 20 years of experience in systems automation with General Electric before striking out for Silicon Valley, was called in to help NDSI prepare for a trade show. He spotted that it had some potentially interesting technology, and bought the ailing company in 1983. He still owns a sufficiently large stake in the company to make him a billionaire and Novell sold more networking software than anyone else in the world. Their software is called NetWare. See NETWARE.

NPA 1. In IBM language, it means Network Performance Analyzer, a product for network tuning, determining performance, degradation and determining the affect of network growth. 2. AT&T's National Pricing Agreement. A multi-year agreement an AT&T customer signs with AT&T which specifies that the customer will buy $xxx of equipment and services from AT&T at a "deep" discount. (This definition from AT&T.) 3. Numbering Plan Area. A fancy way of saying Area Codes. There are over 200 area codes in the United States, Canada, Bermuda, the Caribbean, Northwestern Mexico, Alaska and Hawaii. Within any of these area codes, no two telephone lines may have the same seven digit phone number. The middle number has been either "1" or "0" creating "N 1/0 x" codes. The number of codes available on this basis were nearing depletion. Bellcore has now modified the plan to obtain more area codes. Future area codes will be NXX like the central office numbering scheme. Switching systems in the national network will differentiate between the central office and area codes by recognizing the subscriber always dials 1+ or 0+ preceding an area code when direct dialing such long distance calls.

Here are the special, unassigned and reserved NPAs:

200 Reserved for special services

211 Assigned to local operators

300 Assigned to special services

311 Reserved for special local services

400 Reserved for special services

500 Reserved for special services

511 Reserved for special local services

600 Reserved for special services

700 Assigned special access code for interLATA carriers/resellers

711 Reserved for special local services

See NNX and NORTH AMERICAN AREA CODES.

NPC Network Processing Card.

NPD See NETWORK PROTECTION DEVICE.

NPDA Network Problem Determination Application. An IBM term. See NETVIEW.

NPDU Network Protocol Data Unit

NPM Network Process Monitor.

NREN The National Research and Education Network, an ultragibgabit network established by legislation in 1991 by the U.S. House and Senate. Preliminary steps toward deploying this information superhighway (for talking between University computers) include some gigabit network testbeds and the cutover to a 45 megabit per second backbone for the National Science Foundation Network (NSFnet) used by the scientific research and university community nationwide.

NRUG National Rolm Users Group.

NPSI IBM X.25 NCP Packet Switching Interface. Networking software package that allows Systems Network Architecture (SNA) 3270 traffic to be transmitted over an X.25 packet data network (PDN). See also QLLC. Contrast with DSP.

NRAM Nonvolatile memory. NRAM does not lose its memory when you turn off the computer or phone system. Many modems, for example, use nonvolatile memory to store configuration information (in place of the switches used on other modems). The command &W writes instructions to the NRAM in many PC modems — chiefly those 2400 baud and faster.

NRC Non-Recurring Charge.

NRM NoRMal response of HDLC. See NORMAL RESPONSE MODE.

NRZ Non-Return to Zero. A binary encoding scheme in which ones and zeroes are represented by opposite and alternating high and low voltages and where there is no return to a zero (reference) voltage between encoded bits. NRZ is now used as an encryption scheme for getting data onto and off hard disk fast. It eliminates the need for clock pulses and yields up to 18.5 kilobytes per track and high read/write speeds.

NRZI Non-Return to Zero Inverted. A binary encoding scheme that inverts the signal on a "one" and leaves the signal unchanged for a "zero". Where a change in the voltage signals a "one" bit, and the absence of a change denotes a "zero" bit value. Also called transition coding.

NSC 1. Network Service Center. See NETWORK CONTROL POINT and SDN. 2. Non-Standard facilities Command. A response to the called fax DIS response.

NS/EP TELECOMMUNICATIONS Federal government definition. Telecommunications services that are used to maintain a state of readiness or to respond to and manage any event or crisis (local, national, or international) that causes or could cause injury or harm to the population, damage to or loss of property, or degrade or threaten the national security or emergency preparedness of the United States.

NSFNET National Science Foundation's TCP/IP-based NETwork, funded by the U.S. Government, that links supercomputing centers and over 2500 academic and scientific institutions across the world. See NREN.

NSG National Systems Group. Division of Canadian telcos responsible for multiple accounts — large customers with service in multiple telephone company territories.

NSS Non Standard Facilities Setup command, a response to an NSF frame.

NT New Technology, usually known as Windows NT. It's a new operating system from Microsoft which will let Windows run on high-end machines, such as file servers and workstations. NT has two sets of goals: to provide true multi-tasking, security, network connectivity and 32-bit power. Secondly, it's to provide a smooth upgrade path from Windows and MS-DOS. See WINDOWS NT and WINDOWS NT ADVANCED SERVER.

NT2 Network Termination 2. A unit that provides switching concentration of subscribers lines at the S-interface. This unit performs the functions of a customer-premises switch or multiplexer to multiplex B channel(s) and D channel onto one physical path and to route calls to the appropriate B or D channel.

NT-1 Network Termination type 1. The NT-1 is the first customer premise device on a two-wire ISDN circuit coming in from the ISDN central office. It does several things. It converts the two-write ISDN circuit (called "U" interface) to four-wire so you can hook up several terminals — like a voice phone and a videophone. The NT-1 typiically has several lights on it which indicate if it's working. An ISDN central office can usually "talk" to the NT-1 and do testing and maintenance by instructing the NT-1 to loop signals back to the central office. An NT-1 will support up to eight terminal devices, though I've never seen it work with that many. See NETWORK TERMINATION 1.

NT-2 In ISDN, the Network Termination type 2 is an intelligent customer premise device terminates the 4-wire T interface. The NT-2 can perform switching and concentration, such as a digital PBX. It typically terminates primary rate access lines from the local ISDN CO switch. It may include the Layer 1 functions of a NT-1 and the protocol handling functions of Layers 2 and 3. See NETWORK TERMINATION 1.

NT1 The CCITT name for ISDN NCTE. Provides line transmission termination and layer-1 maintenance and multiplexing, terminating a 2-wire U-interface. See NT-1.

NT2 Terminates the 4-wire T-interface. See NT-2.

NTACS Narrow TACS. Cellular radio system deployed in Japan using narrowband technology to increase capacity by splitting TACs channels into two narrow channels.

NTI 1. Northern Telecom Inc. 2. Network Terminating Interface. A. The point where the network service provider's responsibilities for service begin or end. B. The interface between DCE and its connected DTE.

NTIA National Telecommunications and Information Administration. An agency of the U.S. Department of Commerce concerned with the development of communications (primarily telephony) standards.

NTCA National Telephone Cooperative Association. A trade association representing primarily rural telephone cooperatives and other small telephone companies.

NTN See NETWORK TERMINAL NUMBER.

NTO Network Terminal Option. An IBM program product that enables an SNA network to accommodate a select group non-SNA asynchronous and bisynchronous devices via the NCP-driven communications controller.

NTP Network Termination Point.

NTS 1. Network Test System. 2. Non-Traffic-Sensitive commerical line costs levied on the user.

NTSC National Television Standards Committee. The initials are used to describe the standard method of television transmission in North America. The North American system uses interlaced scans and 525 horizontal lines per frame at a rate of 30 frames per second. The picture information is transmitted in AM and the sound information is transmitted in FM. Compatible with CCIR Standard M. This standard is used also in Central

NEWTON'S TELECOM DICTIONARY

America, a number of South American countries, and some Asian countries including Japan. PAL is the name of the format for color TV signals used in West Germany, England, Holland, Australia and several other countries. It uses an interlaced format with 25 frames per second and 625 lines per frame. The two systems are not compatible. You cannot view an Australian videotape on a US TV.

When TV engineers get together to hoist some brews, however, the initials for the various standards for TV broadcast take on other meanings, such as: NTSC, Never Twice the Same Color. PAL, Peace At Last. PAL-M, Peace At Last — Maybe. SECAM (French system) becomes System Essentially Contrary to the American Method. We bother mentioning it because if you try to take computer terminals outside the country and connect the video outputs to monitors, you will be made aware of the many TV and video monitor "standards" in use.

NTSC SIGNAL National Television System Committee specified signal. De-facto standard governing the format of television transmission signals in the United States.

NUBUS NuBus. (Pronounced "New Bus.") The name of the bus design for most Apple Macintosh computers. See NUBUS CARD.

NUBUS CARD An add-on card that fits inside the NuBus slots of a Modular Macintosh. Often used for video cards and modems.

NUI Network User Identifier. A unique alphanumeric number provided to dial-up users to identify them to packet switched networks around the world. The number is used to get onto the network and for billing.

NULL A dummy letter, letter symbol, or code group inserted in an encrypted message to delay or prevent its solution, or to complete encrypted groups for transmission or transmission security purposes. See also NULL CHARACTERS.

NULL CALL_ID AN ISDN term. A null call_id is the call_id used to convey information that does not pertain to a specific call between the ISDN System Adapter and the central office switch. Null call_ids are primarily used for accessing feature buttons that do not relate to a specific call.

NULL CHARACTERS Characters transmitted to fill space, time or to "pad" something. They add nothing to the meaning of a transmitted message, but the null characters are expected by the system. On older teletype machines, for example, when the type head reaches the end of a line and the New Line sequence is transmitted, it usually includes a number of Null Characters in order to give the mechanical type head enough time to reach the left margin of the page before transmitting the next line to the terminal. In this manner, no characters are lost. MCI Mail uses five null characters at the beginning of every line — unless you tell it otherwise.

NULL MODEM CABLE Special wiring of an RS-232-C cable such that a computer can talk to another computer without a modem (thus "null" modem) or a computer can talk to a printer. Essentially, a null modem cable reverses pins 2 and 3 on an RS-232-C cable. But there are no standard null modem cables. And other pins need changing and jumpering together. Control Cable in Baltimore, MD sells one that works for us.

NUMBER ADMINISTRATION AND SERVICE CENTER NASC. Provides centralized administration of the Service Managment System (SMS) database of 800 numbers. The NASC keeps track of the 800 numbers that are in use, or available for use, by new 800 customers.

NUMBER CRUNCHING A repetitive series of mathematical calculations.

NUMBERING PLAN 1. In Wide Area Networks, the method for assigning NNX codes to provide a unique telephone address for each subscriber, special line or trunk destination. 2. In PBX's, the method of assigning extension numbers and trunk designations at the local premises.

NUMBERING PLAN AREA NPA. A fancy term the Bell System came up with years ago to mean Area Codes. See NPA.

NUMBER PORTABILITY The technology that will allow a telephone number to travel with a customer from place to place and, for 800 numbers, from one long-distance company to another. Number portability for 800 numbers is scheduled to begin March, 1993.

NUMBERS SHIFT A character in the Baudot code which establishes that the characters following in the transmission are to be interpreted as numeric characters. See LETTERS SHIFT.

NUMERIC KEY PAD A separate section of a computer keyboard which contains all the numerals 0 through 9. Sometimes, some special keys are included — a plus sign, a minus sign, a multiplication sign and a division sign. The numeric key pad on a computer is the same as that found on calculators and adding machines. The top row is 789. The second top row is 456. The third top row is 123. The lowest row is typically 0, "." and "+". The numeric key pad is exactly opposite that of the touchtone telephone keypad, which was designed deliberately to be unfamiliar to users, so they may not input digits into the nation's telephone system faster than it could take them. Early touchtone central offices were very slow.

NUMERIS The French name for ISDN.

NXX In a seven digit local phone number, the first three digits identify the specific telephone company central office which serves that number. These digits are referred to as the NXX where N can be any number from 2 to 9 and X can be any number. At one stage, many moons ago, it was not permissible to have a 1 or a 0 as the second digit in an NXX and it was called an NNX. But that was before everyone had to dial a "1" before making a direct distance dialed long distance call, whether within their own area code or outside it. This little trick of forcing everyone to dial "1" for long distance allowed us to introduce telephone exchanges with the same three digits as area codes. For example, one of our company's numbers is 212-206-6660. The "206" elsewhere is an area code for Seattle and other parts of Washington state.

NYNEX CORPORATION One of the seven Regional Holding Companies formed at Divestiture. It includes New England Telephone and New York Telephone Company and sundry other service and cellular radio companies.

NYQUIST THEOREM In communications theory, a formula stating that two samples per cycle is sufficient to characterize an analog signal. In other words, the sampling rate must be twice the highest frequency component of the signal (i.e., sample 4 KHz analog voice channels 8000 times per second.)

O Used sometimes on switches to mean "OFF." The comparable "ON" setting is "I."

O+ CALLS Called "OH PLUS." O+ plus calls are calls made by dialing zero plus the desired telephone number. Calls made this way may be interrupted by a live operator requesting billing information, or a recorded announcement requesting the caller to enter the billing information.

O- CALLS Called "OH MINUS." O- calls are operator-assisted calls. The caller dials zero and waits for the operator to pick up the line and talk to the caller.

O/E Optic to Electric conversion.

O&M Operations and Maintenance

OA Office Automation. Nobody knows what it means. But there are many consultants out there who will tell you for the right amount of money. Actually the early "office automation" seemed to translate into word processing for the masses. When someone discovered that word processing didn't enhance office productivity, office automation fell into disrepute.

OA&M Operations, Administration and Maintenance. See OAM.

OAI Open Application Interface. Basically one or many openings in a telephone system that lets you link a computer to that phone system and lets the computer command the phone system to answer, delay, switch, hold etc. calls. The term is also called PHI — as in PBX-Host-Interface. The term OAI was first used by PBX makers, NEC and InteCom. And now the term has become somewhat generic, like all good things. Essentially every manufacturer of phone systems is evolving towards open application interfaces of their own. According to Probe Research, there are really two separate "markets" for OAI or PHI:

First, there's Horizontal/Office Automation applications. These are applications that support business functions across organizational groups or industry verticals in inter- or intra-department business settings. Examples include voice mail, electronic mail, message centers, corporate telephone directories, automated screen-based dialing, personal productivity tools, conferencing, PBX feature enhancements, ANI interfaces, time clocks, 911 emergency service and compound image (data, text, image and voice) processing. I see these applications as all those useful, productivity-enhancing things I always wished my telephone systems would do if only they would let me program the thing. (Until OAI, all phone systems were totally closed architecture.)

Second, there's transaction applications. These are applications that support an actual business transaction — customer service, inbound telephone order taking, outbound telemarketing, market research, data gathering, inventory inquiry, account time billing, credit collections, locator services with or without transfer to the local dealer. These always require access to a computer database. These applications are generally complicated, time-sensitive and customized for each installation.

A sample OAI arrangement: In early 1993, Novell and AT&T inked a deal to put telephony onto Novell LANs. The Telephony Server NetWare Loadable Module (NLM) will be the first product. It is an AT&T PC-card sitting in the Novell File server. The card connects to the ASAI (Adjunct Switch Applications Interface) port on the AT&T Definity PBX. Anyone with a PC on the network and an AT&T phone on their desk can use telephone features, such as auto-dialing, conference calling and message management (a new term for integrating voice, fax and e-mail on your desktop PC via your LAN). The Novell/AT&T deal intendes to create open Application Programming Interfaces (APIs) that third-party developers can work with. A Novell/AT&T example of what could be developed: A user could select names from a directory on his PC. He could tell the Definity PBX through the PC over the LAN to place a conference call to those names. At the same time, a program running under NetWare would automatically send an e-mail to the people, alerting them to the conference call and giving them the agenda. All participants would have access to both the document and the conference call simultaneously.

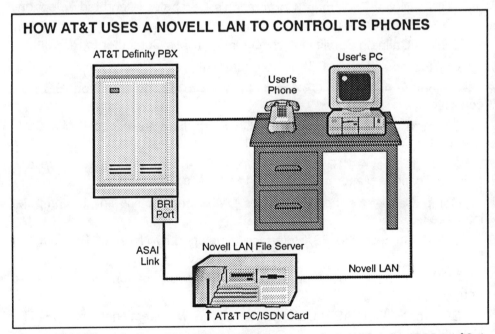

HOW AT&T USES A NOVELL LAN TO CONTROL ITS PHONES

AT&T Definity PBX

User's PC

User's Phone

BRI Port

ASAI Link

Novell LAN File Server

Novell LAN

↑ AT&T PC/ISDN Card

Probe figured that the OAI market will grow from $46 million in 1989 to $2.4 billion by 1993 in computers and applications software and $400 million in direct PBX/ACD enhancements. As a result of this bullishness several things have happened: Virtually every computer manufacturer has jumped in. Virtually every telephone manufacturer is hurrying to open his architecture or introduce a phone system that is open. And the author of this dictionary has started a trade show to concentrated on this area. It's called TELECOM DEVELOPERS. It happens in the Spring of every year. (If you'd like more information on the show, call 1-800-999-0345 or 1-800-LIBRARY). (If you'd like more on OAI, read TELECONNECT Magazine.) Meantime, here are some of the names which manufacturers of PBXs and computers have coined for their open application interfaces, also called PHIs:

ACL — Applications Connectivity Link — Siemens' protocol

ACT — Applied Computer Telephony — Hewlett Packard's generic application interface to PBXs

Application Bridge — Aspect Telecommunications' ACD to host computer link

ASAI — AT&T's Adjunct Switch Application Interface

CAM — Tandem's Call Applications Manager — the name of the Tandem software interface which provides the link between a call center switch telepone switch (either a PBX or an ACD) and all Tandem NonStop (fault tolerant) computers.

CIT — Digital Equipment Corporation's Computer Integrated Telephony (works with major PBXs)

CSA — Callpath Services Architecture — IBM's Computer to PBX link

Call Frame — Harris' PBX to computer link

Callbridge — Rolm's CBX and Siemens to IBM host or non-IBM host computer link

Callpath — IBM's announced, CICS application link to IBM's CSA, available on the AS400 in April of 1991

Callpath Host — IBM and ROLM's CICS-based integrated voice and data applications platform which links to ROLM's 9751 PBX

CompuCall — Northern Telecom's DMS central office link to computer interface

CPI — Computer to PBX Interface developed by Northern Telecom and DEC

CSTA — Computer Supported Telephony Application, RSL standard from ECMA

DECags — DEC ASAI Gateway Services. Two-directional link to AT&T's Definity

DMI — AT&T's Digital Multiplexed Interface, a T-1 PBX to computer interface

HCI — Host Command Interface. Mitel's digital PBX link to DEC computer

IG — AT&T's ISDN Gateway (one direction from the switch to the host)

ITG — AT&T's Integrated Telemarketing Gateway (two directional)

ISDN/AP — Northern Telecom's host to SL1 PBX protocol, which supports NT's Meridian Link

Meridian Link — Northern Telecom's host to PBX link available on the Meridian PBX

ONA — Open Network Architecture (for telephone central offices)

PACT — Siemen's PBX and Computer Teaming, protocols between Siemens PBXs and computers

PDI — Telenova/Lexar's Predictive Dialing Interface

PHI — PBX Host Interface (a generic term coined by Probe Research)

SAI — Stratus Computer Switch Application Interface

SCAI — Switch to Computer Application Interface, one name given by Northern Telecom to PHI

SCIL — Aristacom's Switch Computer Interface Link Transaction Link

Solid State Applications Interface Bridge — Solid's State's PBX to external computer link.

STEP — Speech and Telephony Environment for Programmers; WANG's link

Transaction Link — Rockwell's link from its Galaxy ACD to an external computer

Teleos IRX-9000 — Teleos' Intelligent Call Distribution platform

VoiceFrame — Harris Digital Telephone Systems Division Platform

OAM Operations, Administration and Maintenance. Some switches have computers devoted to OAM. Northern Telecom, for example, uses a Sun Microsystems 3/80 B-4 processor in one of its central office switches.

OAMP Operation, Administration, Maintenance and Provisioning.

OBJECT See OBJECT ORIENTED PROGRAMMING.

OBJECT CODE Instruction code in machine language produced as the output of a compiler or a assembler. The original program, or code, is called the source Code.

OBJECT LINKING AND EMBEDDING OLE. An enhancement to DDE protocol that allows you to embed or link data created in one Windows application in a document created in another application, and subsequently edit that data in the original application without leaving the compound document. See DDE and OLE.

OBJECT ORIENTED FILE SYSTEM A file system, based on object-oriented programming, that allows permanent storage of objects and associated links.

OBJECT ORIENTED PROGRAMMING OOP. Object oriented programming is a form of software development that models the real world through representation of "objects" or modules that contain data as well as instructions that work upon that data. These objects are the encapsulation of the attributes, relationships, and methods of software-identifiable program components. Object-oriented methodology differs from conventional software programming where functions contained in code are found within an application. Although hype about object-oriented technology is fairly recent, the approach was first introduced in the programming language Simula developed in Norway in the late 1960s. The methodology was based on the way children learn (i.e., object + action = result). The idea of object oriented programming is make the writing of complex computer software much easier. The idea is to simply combine objects together to produce a fully-written software application. The work, goes into producing all the objects. They are the building blocks. Theoretically, libraries of objects will be worth a fortune to those companies who develop them.

Object oriented programming is not easy to understand. Here's a definition of object-oriented programming from Business Week, September 30, 1991. "Software objects are chunks of programming and data that can behave like things in the real world. An object can be a business form, an insurance policy or even an automobile axle. The axle object would include data describing its physical dimensions and programming that describes how it interacts with other parts, such as wheels and struts. A system for a human resources department would have objects called employees, which would have data about each worker and the programming needed to calculate salary raises and vacation pay, sign up dependents for benefits, and make payroll deductions. Because objects have 'intelligence,' they know what they are and what they can and can't do. Thus objects can automatically carry out tasks such as calling into another computer, perhaps to update a file when an employee is promoted. The biggest advantage of objects is they can be reused in different programs. The object in an electronic-mail program that places messages in alphabetical order can also be used to alphabetize invoices. Thus, programs can be built from prefabricated, pretested building blocks in a fraction of the time it would take to build them from scratch. Programs can be upgraded by simply adding new objects."

The key concepts of object-oriented programming, according to ComputerWorld are 1. OBJECTS. The basic building block of a program is an object. Objects are software entities. They may model something physical like a person, or they may model something virtual like a checking account. Normally an object has one or more attributes (fields) that collectively define the state of the object; behavior defined by a set of methods (procedures) that can modify those attributes; and an identity that distinguishes it from all other objects. Some objects may be transient, existing temporarily during the execution of a program, i.e., only during run time. Others may be persistent, existing on some form of permanent storage (file, database, programming library) after the program finishes. 2. ENCAPSULATION. This concept refers to the hiding of most of the details of the object. Both the attributes (data structure) and the methods (procedures) are hidden. Associated with the object is a set of operations it can perform. These are not hidden. They constitute a well-defined interface — that aspect of the object that is externally visible. The point of encapsulation is to isolate the internal workings of the object so that, if they must be modified, those changes will also be isolated and not affect any part of the program 3. MESSAGING. One object requests another object to perform its operation through messaging. The client object sends a message to the server object consisting of the identity of the server object, the name of the operation and, in some cases, optional parameters. The names of the operations are limited to those defined for that object. For example, the operations for a checking account object may be defined to be OPEN, DEBIT, CREDIT, COMPUTE INTEREST, ISSUE STATEMENT, SCHEDULE AUDIT, AND CLOSE. 4. DATA ABSTRACTION. An object is sometimes referred to as an instance of an abstract data type or class. Abstract data types are constructed using the built-in data types supported by the underlying programming language, such as integer and date. The common characteristics (both attributes and methods) of a group of similar objects are collected to create a new data type or class. Not only is this a natural way to think about the problem domain, it is a very efficient way to write programs. Instead of individually describing several dozen instances, the programmer describes the class once. Once identified, each instance is complete with the exception of its instance variables. The instance variables are associated with each instance, i.e., each object; methods exist only with the classes. 5. INHERITANCE. Data abstraction can be carried up several levels. Classes can have super-classes and subclasses. In moving to a level of greater specificity, the application developer has the option to retain some attributes and methods of the super-class, while dropping or adding new attributes or methods. This allows greater flexibility in class definition. It is even possible in some languages to inherit from more than one parent. This is referred to as multiple inheritance.

OBJECTVISION FOR WINDOWS A computer program from Borland, with the following explanation: There have been many attempts to create end user-programming tools based on cards and stacks with Basic-like scripting languages such as HyperCard and Toolbook. Yet these have not achieved widespread success because end users do not want to write code in any language. A more appropriate metaphor for business users is based on forms and databases. For many common applications, ObjectVision provides the built-in forms and database management capabilities as well as visual programming tools to handle business decisions. ObjectVision supports the creation of interactive business applications without the need for procedure programming (i.e. code). ObjectVision uses visual programming techniques to allow users to define business rules and directly access Paradox, dBase and BTrieve databases across a network.

OC Optical Carrier. A SONET optical signal. See OC-1.

OC-1 Optical Carrier level-1. The optical counterpart of STS-1 (the basic rate, 51.840 Mbps, on which Sonet is based). Direct electrical-to-optical mapping of the STS-1 signal with frame synchronous scrambling. All higher levels are direct multiples of OC-1 (i.e., OC-3 =3 times OC-1,etc). See OC-N.

OC-12 Sonet channel of 622.08 Mbps.

OC-48 Sonet channel of 2.4 Gbps, the highest level now available. Sonet theoretically can be pushed as high as 13 Gbps.

OC-N Optical Carrier level N. The optical signal that results from an optical conversion of an STS-N signal. N= 1, 3, 9, 12, 18, 24, 36, or 48. See OC-1.

OCC Other Common Carriers. Carriers providing long distance communications service other than AT&T. Nowadays, these companies (including AT&T) are called IXCs — IntereXchange Carriers.

OCCUPANCY The time a circuit or a switch is in use, i.e. occupied. Occupancy is normally expressed as a percentage, occupancy represents the actual usage versus the maximum amount of time available during a 1-hour period.

OCDD On-line Call Detail Data. An AT&T method of accessing ANI (Automatic Number Identification) information from their computer within 48 hours after receiving the telephone call. You access the OCCDD via a DEC VT100 and retrieve the phone numbers of the people who called you.

OCE See OPEN COLLABORATION ENVIRONMENT.

OCIS On-Line Customer Information System. An MCI defniition: OCIS. An MCI customer service and sales system used for on-line access of customer information stored in the MCI Customer Database and for processing information to update the Customer Database.

OCR See OPTICAL CHARACTER RECOGNITION or OUTGOING CALL RESTRICTION.

OCR AUTOMATIC ROUTING Implemented by Optus and others, this technique also assigns a number to each user up to four digits long. The sender types this number within double parentheses anywhere on the cover sheet of a fax transmission, and the LAN-networked fax system uses optical scanning technology to read the number and route the fax to the intended recipient's workstation.

OCTAL A numbering system with the base eight.

OCTATHORP Some people call the tic-tac-toe button on the phone's touchtone pad — namely the # — the octothorpe. Some people believe it's properly spelled "octathorp."

OCTET An eight-bit byte.

OCTOPUS A 25-pair cable that at one end has an amphenol connector (typical of what 1A2 phone systems were connected with) and at the other has many individual 2, 4, 6 and 8 wire connectors, typically male RJ-11s. The reason it's called an octopus is that it looks a bit like an octopus — one body and many arms. It's also called a Hydra.

OCTOTHORPE Some people call the tic-tac-toe button on the phone's touchtone pad — namely the # — the octothorpe. Some people believe it's properly spelled "octathorp."

OCUDP Office Channel Unit Data Port. A channel bank unit used to interface between the channel bank and a customer's DDS CSU or DSU.

ODA Office Document Architecture. ISO's standard 8613-1/8 for document architecture and interchange format adopted by MAP/TOP 3.O, GOSIP, and standardized by ECMA as ECMA-101.

ODD PARITY One of many methods for detecting errors in transmitted data. An extra bit is added to each character sent and that bit is given a value of 0 ("zero") or 1 ("one") such that the total number of ones in the character (including the parity bit) will be odd.

ODI 1. Operational Data Integrator. An MCI term: Combines data from the Customer Information Manager, the MCI Information Manager, and the Management Information Systems to build databases containing network information. 2. Open Data-link Interface. A device driver standard from Novell. ODI allows you to run multiple protocols on the same network adapter card. Interconnectivity strategy that adds functionality to Novell's NetWare and network computing environments by supporting multiple protocols and drivers. ODI's benefits allow you to:

● Expand your network by using multiple protocols without adding network boards to the workstation. ODI creates a "logical network board" to send different packet types over one board and wire.

● Communicate with a variety of workstations, file servers, and mainframe computers via different protocols without rebooting your workstation.

● Configure the LAP driver for any possible hardware configuration with NET.CFG, instead of using limited SHELL.CFG choices.

ODP Open Distributed Processing.

OEM 1. Original Equipment Manufacturer. The maker of equipment marketed by another vendor, usually under the name of the reseller. The OEM may only manufacture certain components, or complete computers, which are then often configured with software and/or other hardware, by the reseller. 2. Operations Enterprise Model. MCI's name for the mass of its internal productvity tools. Covers everything from group calendars to presentation tools.

OES Operations Evaluation System. An MCI internal system, which generates daily, weekly, and monthly switch data reports; used to scan high-level switch degradation problems and to analyze specific switch problems.

OFF-HOOK When the handset is lifted from its cradle it's Off-Hook. Lifting the hookswitch alerts the central office that the user wants the phone to do something like dial a call. A dial tone is a sign saying "Give me an order." The term "off-hook" originated when the early handsets were actually suspended from a metal hook on the phone. When the handset is removed from its hook or its cradle (in modern phones), it completes the electrical loop, thus signaling the central office that it wishes dial tone. Some leased line channels work by lifting the handset, signaling the central office at the other end which rings the phone at the other end. Some phones have autodialers in them. Lifting the phone signals the phone to dial that one number. An example is a phone without a dial at an airport, which automatically dials the local taxi company. All this by simply lifting the handset at one end — going "off-hook."

OFF-HOOK QUEUE There are two types of queuing: ON-HOOK and OFF-HOOK. In On-Hook Queuing, the user dials his number, the switch tells him the outgoing trunks are busy. The user then hangs up. The switch calls him back when a trunk becomes available. In Off-Hook dialing, the user waits with his receiver screwed into his ear until a trunk comes free and the PBX connects him to the next available trunk. Off-Hook queues are usually shorter than on-hook queues. If a trunk doesn't come free quickly in off-hook queuing, the call will often flow over onto the more expensive DDD trunks. Off-hook queuing costs more but keeps the user waiting less. On-hook queuing costs less by waiting for a cheaper trunk but can be tiring and frustrating for the workers waiting for their calls to go through.

OFF-HOOK ROUTING See OFFHOOK and RINGDOWN.

OFF-HOOK VOICE ANNOUNCE A telephone system feature. A telephone has a speaker. If the person is speaking on the phone, another person (inside the building, on the same phone system) can "off-hook voice announce" you and can give you a message or speak with you. You will hear their voice coming through the speaker on your phone. (So may the person on the other end.) Depending on your phone, you may be able to put your hand over your telephone handset and whisper something back to the person who's "off-hook voice announcing" you. Otherwise you'll have to hang up or put the person on hold, and speak to the person on another line.

OFF-LINE Any equipment not actively connected to a phone line but which can be activated to work with that system is Off-Line. This concept also applies to computer systems. For example, a modem attached to or built into a microcomputer can be plugged permanently into a phone line. But the microcomputer can be used for word processing most of the time. While it's doing word processing, it is "off-line." When the user loads the communications software and turns on the modem, the microcomputer is now said to be "on line." Off-line computer storage is a place to put stuff which a computer cannot access "on-line," like a hard-disk. Off-line storage might be microfilm or microfiche.

OFF-LINE STORAGE Storage that is not under the control of a processing unit.

OFF-NET CALLING Phone calls which are carried in part on a network but are destined for a phone not on the network, i.e. some part of the conversation's journey will be over the public switched network or over someone else's network. MCI defines off-net calls as "Billable calls to non-tariffed cities. Can be MCI Off-Net or WATS Off-Net. Classified as Tier 2 for tariff purposes."

OFF-NETWORK ACCESS LINE ONAL. A circuit in a private network which allows the user to go off the private network and complete calls on the public dial network.

OFF PEAK The periods of time after the business day has ended during which carriers offer discounted airtime charges. Usually, OFF-PEAK rates are available for cellular calls between 7:00 p.m. and 7:00 a.m. and on weekends and holidays, but times vary among carriers. Among landline carriers, the business day usually ends at 5 p.m., after which time residential calling builds, and that ends at 11 p.m., after which little happens, except rates drop once again until they rise at the beginning of the next business day at 8 a.m. the next morning.

OFF-PREMISES EXTENSION OPX. Now also called OPS for Off-Premises Station. A telephone located in a different office or building from the main phone system. The OPX is connected by a phone line dedicated to it. It acts as if it were in the same place as the main phone system and can use its full capabilities. Here's another explanation a reader sent in. OPX is the appearance of an actual telephone line (such as 212-691-8215) in two physically separate locations. For example, this line (212-691-8215) could appear and ring in my office and at my home without my home phone being a part of the office telephone system. An OPX is commonly used for answering services or for small businesses. Bell operating phone companies are sharply increasing the charge for dedicated OPS lines — often by several hundred percent per year.

OFF-THE-SHELF When something has already been produced and is available for immediate delivery, it is said to be available "off-the shelf." It is presumably sitting on the shelf in a warehouse waiting for your order.

OFFERED LOAD The total telephone traffic load, including load that results from retries, submitted to a group of servers. See also OFFERED TRAFFIC.

OFFERED TRAFFIC The total attempts to seize a group of servers.

OFFICE CLASS Functional ranking of a telephone central office switch depending on transmission requirements and hierarchical relationship to other switching centers. (Awful mouthful!) There used to be five classes of switches in the U.S. telephone network hierarchy, with the one closest to the end-subscriber being a class 5 central office. But technology and marketing is changing things and, by distributing intelligence closer to the end user, it is diffusing our traditional definitions of network hierarchies and the class of switches. See CLASS 5 central office. See OFFICE CLASSIFICATION.

OFFICE CLASSIFICATION Prior to divestiture, those numbers that were assigned to offices according to their hierarchical function in the U.S. public switched telephone network. The following class numbers are used:

● Class 1: Regional Center (RC)

● Class 2: Sectional Center (SC)

● Class 3: Primary Center (PC)

● Class 4: Toll Center (TC) if operators are present, otherwise Toll Point (TP)

● Class 5: End Office (EO) (local central office)

Any one center handles traffic from one to two or more centers lower in the hierarchy. Since divestiture and with more intelligent software going into telephone switching offices, these designations have become less firm.

OFFICE CODE The first three digits of your seven-digit local telephone number. Also called NNX code.

OFFICE NETWORK A network within an office. An older term for a Local Area Network. User concern is with application sharing, file/database sharing, electronic mail, word processing and circuit switching.

OFFICE TELESYSTEM OTS. An AT&T office automation solution that runs on 3B computers and includes a family of allegedly low-cost, easy-to-use workstations.

OFFICE USER INTERFACE A special shell program which sets up windows with menus of available utilities and applications.

OFFICE WINDOW INTERFACE See OFFICE USER INTERFACE.

OFFICEVISION OfficeVision is a series of IBM applications programs that run 'cooperatively' on PCs and IBM mainframes and performs such tasks as manage electronic mail and extract data from a mainframe for use in a PC spreadsheet. OfficeVision is meant to be a concrete example of one of the benefits of IBM's Systems Application Architecture. OfficeVision was announced in May, 1989. Delivery was scheduled for the following year. See SYSTEMS APPLICATIONS ARCHITECTURE.

OFFSET The offset of a port or a memory location is the difference between the address of the specific port or memory address and the address of the first port or memory address within a contiguous group of ports or a memory window. This term is used when identifying the locations of registers located with respect to the base address of the 16 contiguous I/O ports in a PCMCIA card. It is also used when identifying the location of memory mapped registers with respect to the base address of the memory window.

OFFSET GEOMETRY Shadow-free geometry. The feeder in the primary focus is mounted so that the effect of its shadow on the secondary radiation is negligible.

OFFSITE NIGHT ANSWER This mode allows incoming after-hours calls to be forwarded automatically to an offsite location.

OFTEL OFfice of TELecommunications.

OGM OutGoing Message. The message an answering machine delivers to someone who calls. Sample, "I'm not here. Leave a message after the beep."

OGT OutGoing trunk.

OHD Optical Hard Drive. A term pioneered by Pinnacle Micro, Irvine, CA. OHD technology, according to Pinnacle, combines the advantages of magneto-optical technology with speeds faster than most hard drives.

OHM The practical unit of resistance. The resistance that will allow one ampere of current to pass at the electrical potential of one volt. Ohm's Law dictates the relation between the current, electromotive force and resistance in a circuit:

Amperes	=	Volts divided by Ohms
Volts	=	product of Amperes and Ohms
Ohms	=	Volts divided by Amperes

OHMS Measures of resistance. A resistance of one Ohm allows one Ampere to flow when a potential difference of one volt is applied to the resistance. See OHM'S LAW.

OHM'S LAW The law which relates current measured as Amps (I), voltage (V) and resistance measured as Ohms (R). Ohm's Law is $E = I \times R$. It can also be expressed as $I = V/R$, or $R = V/I$. See OHMS.

OHQ Off-Hook Queue. See OFF-HOOK QUEUING.

OHR Optical Handwriting Recognition. Exactly what it says. Machine reading of handwriting.

OHSA Occupational Health and Safety Act. Specifically the Williams-Steiger law passed in 1970 covering all factors relating to safety in places of employment.

OHVA Off-Hook Voice Anounce. A phone system feature that permits an intercom announcement to be heard thrugh a speaker at a phone where the handset is in use on an outside call.

OLCE On-Line Circuit Engineering. An MCI defniition: A NOBIS subsystem that allows On-Line Circuit Engineering and Circuit Record Sheet (CRS) file storage.

OLE Object Linking and Embedding. It means tying one piece of information in one form into a document in another form, such that a change in one piece of information will be automatically reflected in the other document. Here's an explanation from the New York Times: Business reports may contain information in a variety of formats, including text and numbers, charts, tables, images, graphics, sound and video. Typically, these are created in separate applications programs (e.g. spreadsheet, word processing, charting, database, etc.) and are merged into a single document (i.e. the report). But when the numbers used to create a chart are changed the chart must be updated as well. The executive then has to track down all the various components of the report, call up their respective applications, make the changes and stitch everything back together. OLE promises to keep track of those links and update the various components as they change.

OLIU Optical Line Interface Unit

OLTP OnLine Transaction Processing. A generic concept in the computer industry to cover everything from issuing airline tickets to dispensing money out of street-corner, automated teller machines.

OMAT Operational Measurement and Analysis Tool.

OMEGA A global radio navigation system that provides position information by measuring phase difference between signals radiated by a network of eight transmitting stations deployed worldwide. The transmitted signals time-share transmission on frequencies of 10.2, 11.05, 11.33, and 13.6 Khz. Since the transmissions are coordinated with UTC (USNO), they also provide time reference.

OMNIDIRECTIONAL A microphone with a pickup pattern essentially uniform in all directions.

OMNIDIRECTIONAL ANTENNA An antenna whose pattern is nondirectional in azimuth. The vertical pattern may be of any shape.

OMR Optical Mark Recognition. Refers to machine recognition of filled-in "bubbles" on reader service bingo cards.

ON-HOOK When the phone handset is resting in its cradle. The phone is not connected to any particular line. Only the bell is active, i.e. it will ring if a call comes in. See ON-HOOK DIALING and OFF-HOOK.

ON-HOOK DIALING Allows a caller to dial a call without lifting his handset. After dialing, the caller can listen to the progress of the call over the phone's built-in speaker. When you hear the called person answer, you can pick up the handset and speak or you can talk hands-free in the direction of your phone, if it's a speakerphone. Critical: Many phones have speakers for hands-free listening. Not all phones with speakers are speakerphones — i.e. have microphones, which allow you to speak, also.

ON-LINE When a device is actively connected to a PBX or a computer, it is On-Line. Terminals, PCs, modems and phones are often On-Line.

ON-LINE CIRCUIT ENGINEERING An MCI defniition: OLCE. A NOBIS subsystem that allows On-Line Circuit Engineering and Circuit Record Sheet (CRS) file storage.

ON-NET Telephone calls which stay on a customer's private network, traveling by private line from beginning to end are said to be on-net. Here's MCI's definition: Billable calls to MCI-tariffed cities, including those cities reached via leased lines. Can be MCI On-Net or WATS On-Net. Classified as Tier 1 for tariff purposes.

ONA See OPEN NETWORK ARCHITECTURE.

ONAC Operations Network Administration Center.

ONAL Off Network Access Line.

ONE CALL 1. Fax-back system that requires you to call from your fax machine to send documents on the same line after picking from menu of verbal prompts. the other fax-back system is called a two-call system. You dial from one line and tell the fax-back machine on the other end that you want it to send your requested fax to second number, i.e. one where your fax machine will receive your requested message. 2. A service provided by Centigram which lets its users dial their Centigram voice mail machines and hear their voice mail messages and store and receive their faxes.

ONE DIMENSIONAL CODING A data compression scheme for fax machines that considers each scan line as being unique without referencing it to a previous scan line. One dimensional coding operates horizontally only.

ONE NUMBER PRESENCE This is the consistent use of one telephone number (particularly an 800 number) across all advertising media. The long distance vendors can arrange this for both in-state and national 800 services.

ONE-PLUS PER-CALL RESTRICTION This is the name for a local service provided by a Northern Telecom DMS central office switch. Subscribers can restrict one-plus toll calls from their phones by requiring that a PIN (Personal Identification Number) be dialed prior to a one-plus call. If the PIN is valid, the caller hears a second dial tone, and the one-plus number can then be dialed. When a one-plus call is attempted without the PIN or with a wrong PIN, the caller is routed to a tone or announcement and is not able to place the one-plus call.

ONE-PLUS BULK RESTRICTION This is the name for a local service provided by a Northern Telecom DMS central office switch. One-Plus Bulk Restriction allows subscribers to deny or permit all one-plus calls from their phones simply by dialing a special PIN (Personal Identification Number).

ONE-TIME PROGRAMMABLE OTP. A term describing memory that can be programmed to a specific value once, and thereafter cannot be changed (or can only be revised in a limited way.) OTP EPROMs are typically ordinary EPROMs that have been packaged in such as way that ultra-violet light cannot be used to erase the contents of the EPROM. Such packaging is usually less expensive.

ONE-WAY OPERATION See SIMPLEX.

ONE-WAY SPLITTING When the attendant is connected to an outside trunk and an internal phone, pushing a button on the console allows her to speak privately with the internal extension, thus "splitting" her off from the external trunk.

ONE-WAY TRUNK A trunk between a switch (PBX) and a central office, or between central offices, where traffic originates from only one end. You can, of course, still speak and listen on the trunk. It's just like a normal two-way trunk except that a one-way trunk can only be used for dialing out or only to receive calls.

ONES DENSITY The requirement for digital transmission lines in the public switched telephone network that eight consecutive zeros cannot be in a digital data streams. Ones density exists because repeaters and clocking devices within the network will lose timing after receiving eight zeros in a row. Any number of techniques or algorithms used to insert a one after every seventh-consecutive zero. See BIT STUFFING.

ONI 1. Operator Number Identification. 2. Optical Network Interface. A device which converts photons to electrons and vice versa. It's a device which converts an optical signal into an electrical signal that non-optical telecommunications transmission and switching devices can understand and vice versa.

ONLINE TRANSACTION PROCESSING See OLTP.

ONMS Open Network Management System. Digital Communications Associates architecture for products confirming to ISO's CMIP.

ONP Open Network Provision.

OOF Out Of Frame. A designation for a condition defined as either the network or the DTE equipment sensing an error in framing bits. It's declared when 2 of 4 or 2 of 5 framing bits are missed (the OOF condition existing for 2.5 seconds generally creates a local Red Alarm).

OOP See OBJECT ORIENTED PROGRAMMING.

OPEN Means the circuit is not complete or that the fiber is broken. There is a break in it. A break does not necessarily mean it's malfunctioning, only that it's been turned off.

OPEN AIR TRANSMISSION Referring to a transmission type or associated equipment, that uses no physical communications medium other than air. Most radio communications systems, including microwave, shortwave and FM radio and infrared are open-air (also called "through-the-air") transmission systems.

OPEN APPLICATION INTERFACE See OAI.

OPEN ARCHITECTURE See OAI.

OPEN CIRCUIT A circuit is not complete. There is no complete path for current flow. Electrical current cannot flow in the circuit. In electrical engineering, a loop or path that contains an infinite impendance. In communications, a circuit available for use.

OPEN COLLABORATION ENVIRONMENT O.C.E. Apple's Open Collaboration Environment extends the Macintosh operating system to provide a platform for the integration of fax, voicemail, electronic mail, directories, telephony and agents. From a user's perspective, according to Apple, O.C.E.'s functionality will be seen through:

• System-wide directory services, including a desktop directory browser and electronic business cards.

• A compound mailbox for mail from all sources — fax, voice mail, e-mail, pager, etc.

• Application integration, with all applications having the ability to send documents.

OPEN ENDED ACCESS Term used to describe the ability to terminate a call to any public network destination. For example, on the open end of a foreign exchange circuit, the customer may call any number in the local calling area without being charged for long distance service.

OPEN GROUND, NEUTRAL or HOT In AC electrical power, an "open" is a break, an extremely loose or an unconnected wire in any electrical path. Dangers of an "open" GROUND include serious shock and fire hazard and are life-threatening. Caution: an "open" GROUND will not stop equipment from operating. However it will stop a fuse or circuit breaker from operating should a ground fault occur.

OPEN LINE DEALING This is a term used by British Telecom in its turrets. The system electronically recreates the original "pit" share trading environment in the stock exchange in which everybody could talk to everybody else. In open line dealing, the trader has the ability to program a number of counterparties onto speakers. Full duplex speech is achieved using the associated microphones and all lines receive a simultaneous broadcast.

OPEN LOOP SYSTEM A control system which does not use feedback to determine its output.

OPEN NETWORK ARCHITECTURE ONA. The "network" refers to the public switched network. The FCC wants to encourage companies to get into the value-added telecom business — voice mail, electronic mail, shopping by phone, etc. These companies may be called "value added providers" or "enhanced service providers." The FCC's idea of encouraging companies to add value to phone lines is a nice idea, except that all these companies will rely on phone lines provided by local phone companies who also want to be in value-added telecommunications business. And the local phone companies would prefer that the business be a monopoly (easier to manager, higher prices, etc.) If the FCC is to allow the Bell operating companies and other local phone companies into the value-added business and encourage others in, then it must figure a way the Bell operating companies don't organize things so they have an unfair advantage. The FCC's latest idea is called ONA — Open Network Architecture. Under this concept, the telephone companies are obliged to provide a certain class of service to their own internal value-added divisions and the SAME class of service to nonaffiliated (i.e. outside) valued-added companies. The concept is that the phone company's architecture is to be "open" and that everyone and anyone can gain access to it on equal footing. ONA is only a concept at present and still needs some rigorous defining. There is not much pressure from outside entrepreneurial companies for ONA access. Thus ONA at the FCC and elsewhere drags its feet.

The March 18, 1991 issue of Telephony Magazine said that as conceptualized by the FCC, ONA "is the overall design of a carrier's basic network facilities and services to permit all users of the basic network, including the enhanced services operations of a carrier and its competitors, to interconnect to specific basic network functions on an unbundled and "equal access" "basis." Selected regional Bell holding companies ONA services would include

1. Basic Serving arrangements (BSAs):

A BSA is the basic interconnection access arrangement which offers a customer access to the public network and provides for the selection of available Basic Service Elements (BSEs, see below). Basic serving arrangements are:

- Switched, line side connection
- Switched, trunk side connection
- Dedicated, metallic dedicated

2. Basic service elements (BSEs):

Basic Service Elements are optional basic network functions that are not required for an ESP to have a BSA, but when combined with BSEs can offer additional features and services. Most BSEs allow an ESP to offer enhanced services to their customers in a more flexible manner. BSEs fall into four general categories: Switching, where call routing, call management and processing are required; Signaling, for applications like remote alarm monitoring and meter reading; Transmission, where dedicated bandwidth or bit rate is allocated to a customer application; and Network Management, where a customer is given the ability to monitor network performance and reallocate certain capabilities. The selection of available BSEs is an ongoing process, with new arrangements being developed many times in response to customer demands. ANI, Audiotext "Dial-It" Services, and Message Waiting Notification are all examples of BSEs, which also include:

- Multiline hunt group
- Uniform call distribution
- Central office announcements
- Three-way call transfer

3. Complementary network services (CNSs):

CNSs are basic services associated with end user's lines that make it easier for ESPs (Enhanced Service Providers) to offer enhanced services. Some examples of CNSs include

- Call forwarding Busy/Don't Answer
- Three way calling
- Call waiting
- Virtual dial tone
- Message waiting/indicator
- Speed calling
- Warm line

4. Ancillary services.

Ancillary Services. These are options available to an ESP which support and complement the provision of enhanced services. Examples of ancillary services are protocol conversion, and DID with third number billing inhibited.

In June, 1991, according to Communications Week, the FCC established a tariff structure that will determine how much the telcos can charge enhanced-services providers — and ultimately how much end users will have to pay for those services. FCC Chairman Alfred Sikes called the agency's action "one of our most pivotal steps" in the implementation of ONA. The FCC's idea is that ONA tariffs will be filed with the FCC in November, 1991 and will take effect February 1, 1992. We'll see.

See also COMPUCALL, ENHANCED SERVICES, OAI, and OPEN APPLICATION INTERFACE.

OPEN SKIES When a government or government agency allows virtually anyone to sell satellite telecommunications service, you have "OPEN SKIES." The United States has an Open Skies satellite policy. Virtually anyone can apply to launch and operate a telecommunications satellite and, with a high degree of certainty, you'll be granted your wish. The European community is just now (summer, 1991) beginning to think of opening its skies. They have gone one small step — namely allowing anyone to buy and operate a receive-only satellite earth station not connected to the public network.

OPEN SOLUTIONS DEVELOPERS A Dialogic term for companies which develop and sell end-user voice processing applications. We'd probably call these people value added resellers (VARs).

OPEN SYSTEM INTERCONNECT OSI. An ISO publication that defines seven independent layers of communication protocols. Each layer enhances the communication services of the layer just below it and shields the layer above it from the implementation details of the lower layer. In theory, this allows communication systems to be built from independently developed layers. See OSI.

OPEN SYSTEMS Open systems refers to that best of all possible worlds, where everyone would comply with a set of hardware and software standards. You could buy a server from company A, a client from company B, a networking system from companies C, D or E, and applications software from companies F-Z, and everything would work harmoniously. In real life, some "open" systems are more open than others. Some companies talk, without embarrassment, of their "proprietary open systems." Some things are open and closed. PBXs have many "open" ports on which you can attach things. But there are no PBXs I know of which have open backlanes, meaning you (or someone else) can design a board and plug it into the PBX's backplane. That's closed. The concept of open systems has been more popular in the computer industry.

OPEN SYSTEMS INTERCONNECTION See OSI.

OPEN TOOLKIT DEVELOPERS A Dialogic term for outside developers (outside of Dialogic) who provide applications generators that simply application development and work in a variety of operating systems — including MS-DOS, UNIX, OS/2, Windows, etc.

OPEN WIRE A transmission facility typically consisting of pairs of bare (uninsulated) conductors supported on insulators which are mounted on poles to form an aerial (above ground) pole line. Most basic of all practical types of transmission media. Open wire may be used in both communication and power.

OPENVIEW Hewlett-Packard's suite of a network-management application, a server platform, and support services. OpenView is based on HP-UX, which complies with AT&T's Unix system.

OPERAND That which is being operated on. An operand is usually identified by the address part of an instruction.

OPERATING ENVIRONMENT Referring to the combination of (usually IBM) host software that includes operating system, telecommunications access method, database software and user applications. Some common operating environments include MVS/CICS and MVS/TSO.

OPERATING SYSTEM A software program which manages the basic operations of a computer system. It figures how the computer main memory will be apportioned, how and in what order it will handle tasks assigned to it, how it will manage the flow of information into and out of the main processor, how it will get material to the printer for printing, to the screen for viewing, how it will receive information from the keyboard, etc. In short, the operating system handles the computer's basic housekeeping. MS-DOS, UNIX, PICK, etc. are operating systems.

OPERATING TIME The time required for seizing the line, dialing the call and waiting for the connection to be established.

OPERATION CODE The command part of a machine instruction.

OPERATIONAL DATA INTEGRATOR ODI. An MCI term: Combines data from the Customer Information Manager, the MCI Information Manager, and the Management Information Systems to build databases containing network information.

OPERATIONAL GRAMMAR A voice recognition term. A vocabulary structure where certain word sets activate other word sets.

OPERATIONAL LOAD The total power requirements for communication facilities.

OPERATIONAL SECURITY OPSEC. A thorough on-site examination of an operation or activity to determine if there are vulnerabilities that would permit adversaries and exploitation of critical information during the planning, preparation, execution, and post-execution phases of any operation or activity. A Federal Government definition.

OPERATIONAL SERVICE PERIOD A performance measurement period, or succession of performance measurement periods, during which a telecommunication service remains in an operational service state. An operational service period begins at the beginning of the performance measurement period in which the telecommunications service enters the operational service state, and ends at the beginning of the performance measurement period in which the telecommunications service leaves the operational service state.

OPERATIONS EVALUATION SYSTEM OES. An MCI internal system, which generates daily, weekly, and monthly switch data reports; used to scan high-level switch degradation problems and to analyze specific switch problems.

OTS Operations Technical Support

OPERATOR Employee of telephone company, or an individual business or institution, who aids in the completion of phone calls. Traditionally a woman's occupation, now increasingly the role of men and machines. In some countries, like Germany, the phone company doesn't have operators.

OPERATOR ASSISTANT A software program from TELECONNECT Magazine which allows you to maintain a directory of personnel and their messages on a PC. The program runs on a network and people can pick up their messages from their computers attached to the network — without calling the company's telephone operator. The program is available for free. It is a premium for subscribing to TELECONNECT Magazine.

OPERATOR ASSISTED A phone call placed with the assistance of the carrier's operator. You pay more when you use an operator.

OPERATOR CONSOLE Same as attendant console. See ATTENDANT CONSOLE.

OPERATOR SERVICES Any of a variety of telephone services which need the assistance of an operator. Such services include collect calls, third-party billed calls and person-to-person calls.

OPRE Operations Order Review

OPS 1. Operator Services 2. Off-Premises Station. See OFF PREMISES EXTENSIONS.

OPTICAL AMPLIFIER A device to amplify an optical signal without converting the signal from optical to electrical back again to optical energy. The two most common optical amplifiers are erbium-doped fiber amplifiers (EDFAs), which amplify with a laser pump diode and a section of erbium-doped fiber, and semiconductor laser amplifiers.

OPTICAL ATTENUATOR In optical communications, a device used to reduce the intensity of the optical signal. In some optical attenuators used in optical fiber systems, the amount of attentuation depends on the modal distribution of the optical signal.

OPTICAL BLANK A casting consisting of an optical material molded into the desired geometry for grinding; polishing; or, in the case of some optical fiber manufacturing processes, drawing to the final optical/mechanical specifications.

OPTICAL CAVITY A region bounded by two or more cavity surfaces, referred to as mirrors or cavity mirrors, whose elements are aligned to provide multiple reflections of lightwaves. The resonator in a laser is an optical cavity.

OPTICAL CHARACTER RECOGNITION OCR. Reading data using a machine that visually scans the characters in a document and converts that data into standard form which can be stored on conventional magnetic medium, e.g. floppy or hard disk. See OPTICAL SCANNER.

OPTICAL COMBINER A passive device in which power from several input fibers is distributed among the smaller number (one or more) of output fibers.

OPTICAL COMPUTER A computer that uses photons, not electrons as in today's old-fashioned computers. Scientists think photon computers and photon switches could be a thousand times faster than present computers and switches, and, of course, totally impervious to electromagnetic interference.

OPTICAL CONNECTORS Connectors designed to terminate and connect either single or multiple optical fibers. Optical connectors are used to connect fiber cable to equipment and interconnect cables.

OPTICAL CROSS CONNECT PANEL A cross connect unit used for circuit administration and built from modular cabinets. It provides for the connection of individual optical fibers with optical fiber patch cords.

OPTICAL DISK Peripheral storage disk for programs and information. Optical disks are emerging as computer storage devices because of their tremendous storage capacities in comparison to magnetic disk. Optical disks are WORM — which stands for Write Once, Read Many Times, meaning you write once to the disk, and read that information many times. But with today's technology, you can't erase the information on the optical disk. It is not uncommon to be able to store 600 megabytes of information on an optical disk the size and shape of one you currently buy recorded music on. See OPTICAL STORAGE DEVICE.

OPTICAL FIBER Any filament made of dielectric materials, that guides light, whether or not it is used to transmit signals. An optical fiber not carrying signals is typically called a "dark fiber." Optical fiber is glass fiber for carrying lightwave communications. There are two types of optical fiber: Single Mode and Multimode. In single mode fiber, light can only take a single path through a core that measures about 10 microns in diameter. (A micron is one millionth of a meter.) Multimode fibers have thicker cores — typically 50 to 200 microns. Single mode fiber is more efficient. It offers low dispersion, travels great distances without repeaters and has enormous information carrying capacity. But it's more expensive to make. The relatively large core of multimode fiber lightguide allows light pulses to zig-zag along many different paths. It's also ideal for light sources larger than lasers, such as LEDs (Light Emitting Diodes). Multi-mode fiber is not the preferred method of optical telecommunications.

OPTICAL FIBER CABLE A transmission medium consisting of a core of glass or plastic surrounded by a protective cladding, strengthening material, and outer jacket. Signals are transmitted as light pulses, introduced into the fiber by light transmitter (either a laser or light emitting diode). Low data loss, high-speed transmission, large bandwidth, small physical size, light weight, and freedom from electromagnetic interference and grounding problems are some of the advantages offered by optical fiber cable. There are five common types: single, dual, quad, stranded, and ribbon.

OPTICAL FIBER FACILITY Transmission system which uses glass fibers as the transmission medium.

OPTICAL FIBER PREFORM Optical fiber material from which an optical fiber is made, usually by drawing or rolling.

OPTICAL FIBER RIBBON A cable of optical fibers laminated in a flat plastic strip.

OPTICAL FIBER SPLICE A permanent joint whose purpose is to couple optical power between two fibers.

OPTICAL FIBRE In an optical fibre transmission system, the data is carried by pulses of light along glass fibres. This method of transmission has a much higher bandwidth than copper cables and is less subject to distortion and interference. It is safer than copper because it provides electrical isolation and as it carries no current can be used in flammable areas.

OPTICAL INTERCONNECTION PANEL An interconnection unit used for circuit administration and built from modular cabinets. It provides interconnection for individual optical fibers. Unlike the optical cross-connect panel, the interconnection panel does not use patch cords.

OPTICAL REPEATER In an optical fiber communication system, an optoelectronic device or module that receives a signal, amplifies it (or, in the case of a digital signal, reshapes, retimes, or otherwise reconstructs it) and retransmits it. See also OPTICAL AMPLFIER.

OPTICAL SCANNER A hardware device that recognizes images on paper, film and other media and converts them into digital form which can be stored in a conventional computer readable magnetic medium, such as floppy or hard disk. Optical scanners are getting better and better but are still not perfect. See OCR.

OPTICAL SPECTRUM Generally, the electromagnetic spectrum within the wavelength region extending from the vacuum ultraviolet at 1 nm to the far infrared at 0.1 mm. The term was originally applied to that region of the electromagnetic spectrum visible to the normal human eye, but is now considered to include all wavelengths between the shortest wavelengths of radio and the longest of X-rays.

OPTICAL STORAGE DEVICE Optical storage devices use a source of coherent light — usually a semiconductor laser — to read and write the data. There are three big advantages to using a laser — size, safety and portability. Because you can focus a laser into approximately one micron in size — a far smaller area for encoding a bit of data than conventional drives — you can fit more data in.

Optical media are also more stable than metal-oxide disks. They aren't affected by light, normal temperatures or electromagnetic fields. (You can put through as many airport x-ray machines as you wish.) And best, the read/write head doesn't get as close to the recording medium as it does in conventional disk drives. Optical drives are interchangeable, also. You can remove them and store them. That makes them great for archiving.

OPTICAL TIME DOMAIN REFLECTOMETER OTDR. A device that measures distance to a reflection surface by measuring the time it takes for a lightwave pulse to reflect from the surface. Reflection surfaces include the ends of cables and breaks in fiber. The reflectometer measures the ratio of incident and reflected light power. By using this device you can figure precisely where a fiber optic link is broken. This device operates like Radar. It sends a light pulse down the cable and waits for it to return. It measures the time taken and calculates the distance based on the speed of light through the fiber optic cable. The reflectometer usually also displays the reflected waves on a time axis for precise reading of, e.g., the leading edges of the transmitted and reflected waves. The reflectometer is also capable of launching a light pulse into the fiber optic transmission medium and measuring the time required for its reflection to return by backscattering or end reflection, thus indicating the continuity, crack, fracture, break, or other anisotropic features of the medium.

OPTICAL WAVEGUIDE Technically, any structure that can guide light. Sometimes used as a synonym for optical fiber, it also can apply to planar light waveguides.

OPTICAL WAVEGUIDE CONNECTOR A device whose purpose is to transfer optical power between two optical waveguides or bundles, and that is designed to be connected and disconnected repeatedly.

OPTICALLY ACTIVE MATERIAL A material that can rotate the polarization of light that passes through it. An optically active material exhibits different refractive indices for left and right circular polarizations (circular birefringence).

OPTO-ELECTRICAL TRANSDUCER A device which converts electrical energy to optical energy and vice versa. Used as transmitters and receivers in fiber optic communications systems.

OPTO-ELECTRONICS The range of materials and devices that generate light (lasers and light-emitting devices), amplify light (optical amplifiers), detect light (photodiodes), and control light (electro-optic circuits). Each of these functions requires electrical energy to operate and depends on electronic devices to sense and control this energy.

OPX See OFF PREMISE EXTENSION.

ORANGE BOOK The common name for the U.S. Department of Defense's Trusted Computer System Evaluation Criteria (TSEC).

ORB Office Repeater Bay.

ORDER ENTRY A voice processing application which allows someone with a touchtone phone to buy something, i.e. enter their order.

ORDER WIRE 1. A circuit used by telephone personnel for fixing, installing and removing phone lines. 2. Equipment and the circuit providing a telephone company with the means to establish voice contact between central office and carrier repeater locations.

ORDER WIRE CIRCUIT A voice or data circuit used by telephone company technical control and maintenance personnel for the coordination and control action relating to activation, deactivation, change, rerouting, reporting and maintenance of communication systems and services.

ORIGINATE MODE The "originate mode" sets the modem to begin a data phone call — i.e. dial the phone, listen for a carrier tone from a remote modem and connect to that modem. The modem at the receiving end must be set to "Answer" mode. In any asynchronous data conversation, one side must be set to "Originate" and the other to "Answer." Such settings are usually made in software.

ORIGINATING RESTRICTION A phone line with this restriction cannot place calls at any time. Calls directed to the phone, however, will be completed normally.

ORM Optically Remote Module. A type of switching module made by AT&T which connects directly to the 5ESS switch communications module via optical fibers.

OS 1. Outage Seconds. 2. Operating System, as in MS-DOS (MicroSoft-Disk Operating System) or OS/2. See OPERATING SYSTEM. 3. Operations System. Includes SCOTS, FMAS, etc.

OS/2 Operating System/2. An operating system originally developed by IBM and Microsoft for use with Intel's microprocessors and for use with IBM personal system/2 personal computers. Now OS/2 is the prime responsibility of IBM and it will run on many PCs, inclduing those using the Intel family of PC microprocessors. OS/2 is a multitasking operating system. This means many programs can run at the same time. See OS/2 EXTENDED EDITION.

OS/2 2.0 A 32-bit version of the IBM's OS/2 operating system. Apple Macintosh's operating system is 32-bit.

OSBORNE EFFECT Once there was a personal computer company called Osborne Computer Company. One day, the president announced a revolutionary new computer. It was so good not one of his dealers wanted to (or could) sell the existing product and they sent all their inventory back. Meantime, it was six months before the company could deliver the new product. But without any sales in the meantime, it had no money and Osborne went broke. There is a lesson here for companies who are attempting to manage transition between old and new product lines. Be careful, or suffer the horrible consequences of The Osborne Effect.

OSCILLATOR 1. A device for generating an analog test signal. 2. Electronic circuit that creates a single frequency signal.

OSCILLOSCOPE Electronic testing device that can display wave forms and other information on a TV-screen-like cathode ray tube. A basic fixture in sci-fi movies.

OSI Open Systems Interconnection. The only internationally accepted framework of standards for communication between different systems made by different vendors. ISO's major goal is to create an open systems networking environment where any vendor's computer system, connected to any network, can freely share data with any other computer system on that network or a linked network. OSI was developed by the International Standards Organization. Most of the dominant communications protocols used today have a structure based on the OSI model. Although OSI is a model and not an actively used protocol, and there are still very few pure OSI-based products on the market today, it is still important to understand its structure. The OSI model organizes the communications process into seven different catogories and places these categories in a layered sequence based on their relation to the user. Layers 7 through 4 deal with end to end communications between the message source and the message destination, while layers 3 through 1 deal with network access.

Layer 1 — The Physical layer deals with the physical means of sending data over lines (i.e. the electrical, mechanical and functional control of data circuits).

Layer 2 — The Data Link layer is concerned with procedures and protocols for operating the communications lines. It also has a way of detecting and correcting message errors.

Layer 3 — The Network layer determines how data is transferred between computers. It also addresses routing within and between individual networks.

Layer 4 — The Transport layer defines the rules for information exchange and manages end-to-end delivery of information within and between networks, including error recovery and flow control.

Layer 5 — The Session layer is concerned with dialog management. It controls the use of the basic communications facility provided by the Transport layer.

Layer 6 — The Presentation layer provides transparent communications services by masking the differences of varying data formats (character codes, for example) between dissimilar systems.

Layer 7 — The Applications layer contains functions for particular applications services, such as file transfer, remote file access and virtual terminals.

See also OSI STANDARDS.

OSI MODEL Open Systems Interconnection Model. See OSI.

OSI STANDARDS The International Standards Organization (ISO) has established the Open Systems Interconnection (OSI). The idea of OSI is to provide a network design framework to allow equipment from different vendors to be able to communicate. Codex of Mansfield, MA. has published an excellent booklet called "The Basics Booklet of Local Area Networking". Here is a shortened excerpt of what Codex says about standards. "Standards allow us to buy items such as batteries and bulbs. Many of us have learned "the hard way" that the lack of computer standards can make it impossible for computers from different vendors to talk to each other. Because a major goal of a LAN (Local Area Network) is to connect varied systems, standards are being developed to specify the set of rules networks will follow. The OSI Model is a design in which groups of protocols, or rules for communicating, are arranged in layers. Each layer performs a specific data communications function. The concept of layered protocols is analogous to the steps we follow in making a phone call:

Step 1 — Listen for dial tone.

Step 2 — Dial a phone number.

Step 3 — Wait for a ring.

Step 4 — Exchange greetings.

Step 5 — Communicate message.

Step 6 — Say Good-bye.

Step 7 — Hang up.

Each of these steps, or OSI "layers," builds upon the one below it. Although each step must be performed in preset order, within each layer there are several options. Within the OSI model, there are seven layers. The first three are the PHYSICAL, DATA LINK, and NETWORK layers, all of which are concerned with data transmission and routing. The last three — SESSION, PRESENTATION and APPLICATIONS — focus on user applications. The fourth layer TRANSMISSION provides an interface between the first and last three layers. The X.25 PROTOCOL which created a standard for data transmission and routing is equivalent to the last three layers of the OSI Model. The OSI model is quickly becoming the standard for how LAN products should be built." See also OSI and X.25.

OSINET A test network sponsored by the National Bureau of Standards (NBS) designed to provide vendors of products based on the OSI model a forum for doing interoperability testing.

OSN Operations System Network.

OSP Operator Service Provider. A new breed of long distance phone company. It handles operator-assisted calls, in particular Credit Card, Collect, Third Party Billed and Person-to-Person. Phone calls provided by OSP companies are often more expensive than phone calls provided by "normal" long distance companies, i.e. those which have their own long distance networks and which you see advertised on TV. You normally encounter an OSP only when you're making a phone call from a hotel or hospital phone, or privately-owned payphone. It's a good idea to ask the operator what the cost of your call will be before you make it.

OSPF Open Shortest Path First interior gateway protocol.

OSPS An AT&T word for Operator Services Position System.

OTDR Optical Time Domain Reflectometer, a test and measurement device often used to check the accuracy of fusion splices and the location of fiber optic breakers. See OPTICAL TIME DOMAIN RELFECTOMETER.

OTGR Operations Technology Generic Requirements.

OTHER COMMON CARRIERS Providers of long distance telephone service in competition with AT&T. OCCs often (but not always) have lower rates than AT&T. All long distance carriers — including AT&T — are now called interexchange carriers.

OTOH Abbreviation for "On The Other Hand;" commonly used on E-mail and BBSs (Bulletin Board Systems).

OTS See OFFICE TELESYSTEM.

OUT-OF-BAND NETWORK MANAGEMENT A method of managing LAN bridges and routers that uses telephone lines for communications between the network management station and the managed devices. This type of management is normally in addition to the conventional method which uses the LANs and WANs that are being connected by these devices. The principal advantage is that in the event of a system failure (which may take a LAN or a WAN down), a network supervisor can bypass the failed system and use a telephone link to reach a bridge/router to diagnose a network problem. Bridges and routers must have built-in telephone modems for this to work.

OUT-OF-BAND SIGNALING Signaling that is separated from the channel carrying the information — the voice, data, video, etc. Typically the separation is accomplished by a filter. The signaling includes dialing and other supervisory signals.

OUT-OF-FRAME In T-1 transmission, an OOF (Out Of Frame) error occurs when two or more of four consecutive framing bits are in error. When this condition exists for more than 2.5 seconds a RED alarms is sent by OOF detecting unit. Equipment receiving this RED alarm responds with a YELLOW alarm.

OUT-OF-ORDER TONE A tone which indicates the phone line is broken.

OUT-OF-PAPER RECEPTION The ability to receive a facsimile transmission into memory when the facsimile machine is out of paper. The facsimile paper will be printed when you put in new paper.

OUTAGE Service interrupted.

OUTAGE RATIO The sum of all the outage durations divided by the time period of measurement.

OUTGOING ACCESS The capability of a user in one network to communicate with a user in another network (CCITT).

OUTGOING LINE RESTRICTION The ability of the system to selectively restrict any outgoing line to "incoming only."

OUTGOING STATION RESTRICTION The ability of the system to restrict any given phone from making outside calls.

OUTGOING TRUNK A line or trunk used to make calls.

OUTGOING TRUNK QUEUING OTQ. Extensions can dial a busy outgoing trunk group, be automatically placed in a queue and then called back when a trunk in the group is available. This feature allows more efficient use of expensive special lines such as WATS or FX. Instead of having to redial the trunk access code until a line is free, the caller can activate OTQ. See also OFF-HOOK QUEUING.

OUTLET TELECOMMUNICATIONS A single-piece cable termination assembly (typically on the floor or in the wall) andcontaining one or more modular telecom jacks. Such jacks might be RJ-11, RJ-45, coaxial terminators, etc.

OUTLINE FONT Font is the design of printed letters, like the ones you see on this page. The first type was produced with raised metal or wooden blocks. Put ink on the blocks. Put paper on the inked blocks. Lift paper off. Bingo you have type on paper. Blocks came in fonts — styles of type, which has neat names like Times Roman, Helvetica, Souvenir, etc. Blocks also came in various sizes — 10 point, 12 point, 14 point, 36 point, etc. "Point" is simply the name for a way of measuring the size of type, like miles measure distance. When computers came along, they simply copied this technique. You picked type and you picked the size. Printers with print cartridges still work this way. They have to. They couldn't simply take one size font and enlarge or contract it because type enlarged or contracted doesn't look "right." Then two men, John Warnock and Martin Newell, said there had to be a better way and they came up with the idea of an outline font, originally called JaM, then Interpress and now PostScript. In PostScript letters and numbers become mathematical formulas for lines, curves and which parts of the character are to be filled with ink and which parts are not. Because they are mathematical, outline fonts are resolution independent. They can be scaled up or down in size in as fine detail as the printer or typesetted is capable of producing. PostScript outline fonts contain "hints" which control how much detail is given up as the type becomes smaller. This makes smaller type faces much more readable than they otherwise would be. Before outline fonts can be printed, they have to rasterized. This means that a description of which bits to print where on the page has to be generated.

And this is one reason printing outline fonts is so consuming of computer power (whether the power is in the computer or in the printer — usually it's in both). But it's also the reason why outline fonts, of which PostScript is the most successful and the most common, look so great.

OUTPULSE DIAL A pushbutton dial which allows rotary dial users the convenience of "Touch-Tone" dialing. Pushing the buttons makes the phone pretend to be a rotary dial phone. This is necessary because touch-tones are not recognized everywhere.

OUTPULSING The process of transmitting address information over a trunk from one switching center to another.

OUTPUT Data that flows out of a computer to any device.

OUTPUT DEVICE A device by which a computer transfers its information to the outside world. For example, a printer.

OUTSIDE PLANT The outside plant includes all cables and wires extending outward from the network protectors on the main distribution frame, supporting structures and other associated apparatus necessary to connect the terminal equipment to the outside plant.

OUTSOURCING An allegedly more modern word for the term "facilities management." What outsourcing means is that a company contracts one of its internal functions out to an outside company. Those functions might include running the company's phone systems and telecom networks and/or running the company's computer system. A company might be motivated to do this because they lack the internal resources (typically people) or feel they can bring their phone costs into line and those phone costs (or at least certain of them) might now become able to be budgeted with some precision. This has appeal to senior management, who are trying to reduce their uncertainties. This usually has no appeal to lower level management who might be fired, especially if the new corporate outsourcing manager felt they were useless.

Here are some questions and answers about outsourcing taken from an information brochure from a company called Cyclix Communications Corporations, which does a lot of outsourcing:

Q: What is outsourcing?

A: Outsourcing is the process by which a company arranges for a third party to implement and manage a specific department or function of the company.

Q: Why would a company outsource?

A: A company would outsource for a number of reasons. In a recent Network World "Critical Issues Survey," two-thirds of the respondents noted lack of in-house resources, staff or expertise, while one-third noted cost effectiveness as reasons for outsourcing. Other reasons for outsourcing may include to cope with new technologies, to minimize capital expenses by having a third party provide, manage and maintain hardware and software, to acquire skilled personnel without having to train them or put them on the payroll and to remain focused on what the company can do best.

Q: What is an advantage of outsourcing?

A: The advantages of outsourcing will largely be dependent upon the objectives which were predetermined before the arrangement begins. For example, if a relatively small MIS department is responsible for both data processing and data networking for a national company, outsourcing one of those functions to an experienced vendor will allow the internal department to concentrate more fully on the other function.

Q: What is a disadvantage of outsourcing?

A: Once you decide to outsource, the transition back to managing those functions in-house can be costly. Companies must realize that outsourcing is a long term financial and competitive strategy. To simply try outsourcing creates false expectations and limits the long-term benefits which can be derived from outsourcing.

OUTWARD RESTRICTION Phone lines within the PBX can be denied the ability to access the exchange network without the assistance of the attendant. Restricted calls are routed to intercept tone.

OUTWARD TRUNK QUEUING A process of holding outgoing long distance calls in queue until the appropriate long distance facility is available. See OFF-HOOK QUEUING.

OUTWATS See WATS.

OVERBUILD Adding radio capacity to a telecommunications network.

OVERDRIVE PROCESSOR Intel's name for its line of single-chip performance upgrade chips. Based on Intel486 DX2 "speed doubling" technology, the Intel overdrive processors allow users of Intel486SX systems to double the internal speed of their computer's CPU by adding a single chip, without upgrading or modifying any other system components.

OVERFLOOR DUCT METHOD A distribution method that uses metal or rubber ducts to protect and conceal exposed wiring across floor surfaces.

OVERFLOW Additional traffic beyond the capacity of a specific trunking group which is then offered to another group or line. For example, overflowing calls from WATS lines to (DDD) direct distance dial lines.

OVERHEAD In communications, all information, such as control, routing and error-checking characters, that is in addition to user-transmitted data. Includes information that carries network status or operational instructions, network routing information, as well as retransmissions of user-data messages that are received in error.

OVERHEAD BIT A bit other than one containing information. It may be an error checking bit or a framing bit.

OVERLAY Typically a piece of cut-out carboard, which you place over certain of the keys on a phone or console. When you punch in a certain code, the buttons become what's written on the programming overlay. Also called a Proramming Overlay.

OVERLAY NETWORK A separate network for a particular service covering most of the same geographical locations as the basic telephone network, but operating independently.

OVERLOAD MANAGEMENT An AT&T term for handling peak demands by selectively delaying, degrading, or dropping only those portions of traffic flow that are tolerant of those particular types of impairments.

OVERRIDE When a circuit already in use is seized. For example, when your boss can break into your telephone conversation.

OVERRIDE PROMPTS The ability of callers and users to key over system prompts.

OVERRUN Loss of data because the receiving equipment could not accept the data at the speed at which it was being transmitted.

OVERSAMPLING Time division multiplexing (TDM) technique where each bit from each channel is sampled more than once.

OVERSCAN The image fills the screen from bezel to bezel. The bezel is the metal or plastic part — in short, the frame — that surrounds a cathode ray tube — a "boob" tube. NEC's term for overscan is "full scan."

OVERSPEED Condition in which the transmitting device runs slightly faster than the data presented for transmission. Overspeeds of 0.1% for data PABXs are typical.

OVERTIME PERIOD Those minutes of use of a telephone service beyond the initially defined period for which a basic charge is quoted. The initial period on many calls is one or three minutes. After that, the next minute is overtime.

OVERVIEW Proteon's architecture for products conforming to SNMP.

OWT Operator Work Time.

P

P-CODE The Precise or Protected Code. A very long sequence of pseudo-random binary biphase modulations on the GPS (Global Positioning System) carrier at a chip rate of 10.23 MHz which repeats every 267 days. Each one week segment of this code is unique to one GPS satellite and is reset each week.

P-PHONE Enhanced Business Service (also known as P-Phone) is an analog Centrex offering provided by Northern Telecom. It operates over a single-pair subscriber loop., providing normal full duplex audio conversations and a secondary 8 KHz half-duplex amplitude shift-keyed signal, which is used to transmit signaling information to and from the Northern Telecom-equipped central office.

P/AR Peak to Average Ratio. A standard analog transmission-line test signal of varying frequencies and amplitudes, which is then compared with the received signal. Composite results are a weighted number from 1 to 100 being the maximum. The P/AR is used increasingly as a standard quick test of a telecommunications channel comparative quality. Per Bell standard, the minimal acceptable P/AR rating for medium-speed data transmission is 48.

P01, P.01, Pnn or P.nn The Grade of Service for a telephone system. The digits following the P, i.e. nn, indicate the number of calls per hundred that are or can be blocked by the system. It is a goal or a measure of an event. In this example, P01 means one call in a hundred can be blocked, so the system is designed to meet this criterion. Typically, grade of service is designed for the peak busy hour — the busiest hour of the busiest day of the year.

PA Public Address. Loud speaker system, sometimes used for paging.

PABX Private Automatic Branch eXchange. Originally, PBX was the word for a switch inside a private business (as against one serving the public). PBX means a Private Branch Exchange. Such a "PBX" was typically a manual device, requiring operator assistance to complete a call. Then the PBX went "modern" (i.e. automatic) and no operator was needed any longer to complete outgoing calls. You could dial "9." Thus it became a "PABX." Now all PABXs are modern. And a PABX is now commonly referred to as a "PBX." Some manufacturers have tried to make their PBX appear different by calling it something else. Rolm/IBM calls theirs the "CBX" (Computerized Branch Exchange). Some others call theirs the "EPABX" (the Electronic Private Automatic Branch Exchange. Then there are the special ones, like Wang's WBX, SRX's SRX, NEC's IMS (Information Management System), etc. See PBX.

PAC Personal Activity Center. A combination IBM PC clone, alarm clock, answering machine, speakerphone, fax machine, modem, compact-disk player and AM/FM radio all rolled into one unit sitting on your desk.

PACIFIC TELESIS One of the seven, now-independent Regional Holding

NEWTON'S TELECOM DICTIONARY

Companies formed at the Divestiture of AT&T of 1983. It holds Pacific Bell, Nevada Bell and several non-regulated subsidiaries.

PACING A method of flow control in IBM's SNA. See PACING GROUP.

PACING ALGORITHM The mathematical rules established to control the rate at which calls are placed by an automatic dialing machine.

PACING CONTROL SNA term for flow control. See PACING GROUP.

PACING GROUP In IBM's SNA, the number of data units (Path Information Units, or PIUs) that can be sent before a response is received. An IBM term for window.

PACK To compress data items so they take up less space. A process used by many database programs to remove records marked for deletion.

PACKET A bundle of data, usually in binary form, organized in a specific way for transmission. Three principal elements are included in the packet: 1. Control information — destination, origin, length of packet, etc., 2. the data to be transmitted and 3. error detection and correction bits.

PACKET ASSEMBLER/DISASSEMBLER PAD. A hardware/software combination that forms the interface between an X.25 network such as PDN and an asynchronous device such as a PC. The PAD generates call request, call clear, and other information packets in addition to the ones that contain user data.

PACKET BUFFER Memory set aside for storing a packet awaiting transmission or for storing a received packet. The memory may be located in the network interface controller or in the computer to which the controller is connected. See BUFFER.

PACKET CONTROLLER The hub of the AT&T ISN system. It acts as a fast packet switch providing virtual circuit services to the devices hooked to the system.

PACKET DRIVER The specification developed by John Romkey at FTP Software to allow TCP/IP and other transport protocols to share a common network interface card. Packet Drivers have been written for a variety of network interface cards, and in many cases provide NetWare compatibility.

PACKET FILTER The ability to search a packet to determine its destination and to then route it accordingly. This ability helps to control network traffic.

PACKET FORWARDING Copying the packet to another node without looking at the destination address.

PACKET LEVEL In packet data networking technology, level 3 of X.25. Defines how user messages are broken into packets, how calls are established and cleared over the packet data network (PDN) and how data flows across the entire PDN. The packet level also handles missing and duplicate packets.

PACKET OVERHEAD A measure of the ratio of the total packet bits occupied by control information to the number of bits of data, usually expressed as a percent.

PACKET RADIO Packet Radio is the transmission of data over radio using a version of the international standard X.25 data communications protocol adapted to radio (AX.25). It takes your information, and breaks it up into "packets" which are each sent and acknowledged separately. This assures error-free delivery from sender to receiver. A packet is a stream of characters consisting of a header, the information the user is sending, and a check sequence. The header gives the destination call sign, the call sign of the sender, and any digipeaters (digital repeater) call signs that will be used for relaying the packet. The check sequence makes certain that the data received is what was sent.

PACKET SIZE The length of a packet, expressed in bytes.

PACKET SWITCHING Sending data in packets through a network to some remote location. The data to be sent is subdivided into individual packets of data, each having a unique identification and carrying its destination address. This way each packet can go by a different route. It may also arrive in a different order than it was shipped. The packet ID lets the data be reassembled in proper sequence. Packet switching is a very efficient method of moving digital data around. It is not useful for voice, yet, though experiments are underway.

PACKET SWITCHING NETWORK A network designed to carry data in the form of packets. See PACKET SWITCHING.

PACKET TYPE IDENTIFIER In packet data networking technology, the third octet in the packet header that identifies the packet's function and, if applicable, its sequence number.

PACKET-LEVEL PROCEDURE PLP. A full-duplex protocol that defines the means of packet transfer between a X.25 DTE and a X.25 DCE. It supports packet sequencing, flow control (including maintenance of transmission speed), and error detection and recovery.

PACKETIZED VOICE First read the definition of "Packet Switching" just above. The idea is to digitize voice and then slice it up into packets and sent those packets from the sender by various routes and assemble them as they get to the receiver. Packet switching for data makes sense. Packet switching for voice has not made sense because the voice is too sensitive to small delays. Yet the logic and the economics are there. And experiments continue.

PACKETNET Sprint's internal X.25 Packet Network.

PACT Siemens's PBX And Computer Teaming. It defines protocols between Siemens PBXs and external computers,

PAD 1. A device inserted into a circuit to introduce loss. 2. Packet

Assembler/Disassembler. A device that accepts characters from a terminal or host computer and puts the characters into packets that can be handled by a packet switching network. It also accepts packets from the network, and disassembles them into character streams that can be handled by the terminal or host.

PAD CHARACTERS In (primarily) synchronous transmission, characters that are inserted to ensure that the first and last characters of a packet or block are received correctly. Inserted characters that aid in clock synchronization at the receiving end of a synchronous transmission link. Also called fill characters.

PAD SWITCHING A technique of automatically cutting a transmission loss pad into and out of a transmission circuit for different operating conditions.

PAGER A small one-way receiver you carry with you. When someone wants you, they make your pager receiver sound an alarm. They can activate your pager in a number of ways, including dialing your pager digits directly into a computer, or giving your name and pager number to an operator who then punches out your numbers. Pagers have become small, cheap and very reliable. Monthly service costs have dropped and the area which you can be paged in most areas has widened dramatically. With some pagers you can be reached in most major metropolitan areas of the US. Some pagers also display small alphanumeric messages — like phone numbers to call and names of babies born. All this has made the pager far more useful. See also PAGING.

PAGING To give a message to someone who is somewhere, but where we don't know. Paging can be done with a little "beeper" carried in her purse or on his belt. Paging can also be done through speakers in phones or from speakers in the ceiling. Most phone systems offer a paging channel access. You dial that number and page your party. The system comes "live" and your voice is heard everywhere. Similar to the stuff they have at airline terminals. Paging systems as an accessory to phone systems always cost extra. They're one of the most valuable features on a phone system. Don't skimp, however, on the quality of the speakers or the power of the paging system. If you do, your system will sound awful and people will not use it. See PAGER.

PAGING ACCESS, RAPID Your attendant and you or anybody else with an extension off your PBX can make a page (access the paging equipment) by pushbuttoning one or several digits. Sometimes you can dial one several numbers for different paging alternatives. One number gives you the tenth floor. One number gives you the fourth floor, etc. And one number to page everyone — also called an "ALL CALL" page. See also RAPID PAGING ACCESS.

PAGE ZONE A local area in the office that can receive directed Page announcements independently of the remainder of the office.

PAGING BY ZONE By dialing the appropriate access code, any phone is able to selectively page "groups" of predesignated phones or speakers.

PAGING CODE CALL ACCESS A feature of the ROLM Attendant Console which offers direct, one-touch access to the paging or code call features.

PAGING SPEAKERS Speakers in the telephone. Also external units located in ceilings, on walls, etc.

PAGING TOTAL SYSTEM Upon dialing the appropriate special code, any station may make a paging announcement through all the loudspeakers.

PAID CALL The usual type of a toll telephone call automatically billed to the calling telephone number.

PAIR The two wires of a circuit. Those which make up the subscriber's loop from his office to the central office.

PAIR GAIN The multiplexing of x phone conversations over a lesser number of physical facilities. Pair gain usually refers to electronic systems used in outside plant — from the central office to the subscriber's premises. In "pair gain" you might do something as simple as take one pair of wires and carry two conversations on it. You might also take two pairs and carry 128 conversations. "Pair gain" is actually the number of conversations you get minus the number of wire pairs used by the system.

AT&T Technologies has various subscriber pair gain devices called "SLC" (pronounced "slick" and standing for Subscriber Loop Carrier Systems). Other companies, like Rockwell, have comparable systems. The more circuits these devices produce, i.e. the more cable pairs they save you, the more they cost. The cost of subscriber pair gain equipment — like all electronics — has been dropping in recent years, reducing the phone company's need to install outside cable and thus making better use of the presently installed cable. T-1 is a type of subscriber pair gain equipment.

PAIRED CABLE A cable in which all conductors are arranged in twisted pairs. This form of cable is the most common for communications.

PAL 1. Programmable Array Logic. 2. Proprietary ALgorithm. A designation for a privately designed and owned intelligence-based electronic method for performing a task (such as voice compression). 3 PAL is also the format for color TV signals used in the United Kingdom, West Germany, Holland, much of the rest of western Europe, several South American countries, some Middle East and Asian countries, several African countries, Australia, New Zealand, and other Pacific island countries. It stands for Phase Alternating Line system. It was invented in 1961 and is used in England and many other European countries. With its 625-line scan picture delivered at 25 frames/second (primary power 220 volts), it provides a better image and an improved color transmission over the US system called NTSC, which uses interlaced scans and 525 horizontal lines per frames at a rate of 30 frames per second. SECAM, Sequential and Memory, is used in France and in a modified form in the USSR. SECAM uses an 819-line scan picture which provides better resolution than PAL's 625-line and NTSC's 525. All three systems are not compatible. You cannot view an Australian or English videotape on a US TV.

PAL-M A modified version of the phase-alternation-by-line (PAL) television signal standard (525 lines, 50 hertz, 220 volts primary power), used in Brazil. See also NTSC, PAL, SECAM.

PAM Pulse Amplitude Modulation. Process of representing a continuous analog signal (a voice conversation) with a series of discrete analog samples. This concept is based on the information theory which suggests that the signal can be accurately recreated from a sufficient sample. Why bother? Sampling allows several signals to then be combined on a channel that otherwise would only carry one telephone conversation. PAM was used as part of a method of switching phones calls in several PBXs. It is not a truly "digital" switching system. PAM is the basis of PCM, Pulse Code Modulation. See PCM and T-1.

PAMA Pulse Address Multiple Access. Where carriers are distinguished by their time and space characteristics simultaneously.

PANCAKE COIL A type of inductance having flat spiral windings. An old radio definition.

PANEL, PATCH See PATCH PANEL.

PANNE FATALE An equipment crash in Italian.

PANS Pretty Amazing New Services. PANS is a term coined to describe ISDN Capabilities which should eventually replace POTS. Contrast with POTS.

PAP Packet-Level Procedure. A protocol for the transfer of packets between an X.25 DTE and an X.25 DCE.X.25 PAP is a full-duplex protocol that supports data sequencing, flow control, accountability, and error detection and recovery.

PAPER TAPE A long thin paper roll on which data is stored in the form of punched holes. Usually used as input to other systems. Many old-fashioned telex machines still use paper tape as their storage medium. Punch up the message on the paper tape, rewind the paper tape, call the distant telex machine, then start the paper tape containing the message. The primary benefit of paper tape is that you save on transmission line cost. The paper tape will run through at the maximum speed of the line, while a human operator typing manually would be slower. The disadvantage of paper tape is that you can't change the message once you've typed it. Magnetic medium — floppy disks, hard disks, bubble memory — are much more flexible. They are rapidly replacing paper tape, even on telex machines, or on personal computers, which are replacing telex machines as telex data entry devices.

PAPER TAPE PUNCH A device to physically punch holes in a roll of paper tape in order to store information.

PAPER TAPE READER A device which translates the holes in coded perforated tape into electrical signals suitable for further handling. The reader may be attached to a keyboard-printer or it may be a free standing device.

PARABOLA A shape which can focus a microwave signal into one narrow beam. All satellite and microwave antennae are parabolic, not spherical.

PARABOLIC REFLECTOR The technical name for a dish antenna shaped like a perfect parabola.

PARADIGM An assumption about the ways things work. The word paradigm (pronounced par-a-dime) is typically used by people who want to sound a little more pompous and intellectual than you and I. A yuppie word. If you want to talk about how things are changing you can talk about a "paradigm shift." According to the Economist Magazine, Thomas Kuhn invented the notion of the paradigm shift to explain what happens in scientific revolutions. A revolution happens, his theory goes, not because of startling new facts, but because of a change in the overall way that the universe is seen. After this shift, old knowledges suddenly take on new meaning.

PARALLEL CIRCUIT A circuit in which electricity can take more than one path. Household wiring is the most common type of parallel circuitry. Every outlet is parallel with every other outlet on the same circuit-breaker. So, if a bulb blows in a light fixture on that circuit, all the other devices on that circuit will still function. Another explanation. Imagine three 1.5 volt batteries. With the batteries connected in parallel, the circuit will deliver 1.5 volts. Connected in series it will deliver 3 x 1.5 volts, or 4.5 volts. By contrast, a string of Christmas tree lights is strung in a series circuit, one long continuous circuit. Should one bulb go out, usually the rest will also. See also PARALLEL DATA.

PARALLEL CONNECTION A connection in which the current divides, only a part of the total current passing through each device.

PARALLEL DATA The transmission of bits over multiple wires at one time. This is usually accomplished by having one wire for each bit of an eight-bit byte going from a device, usually a computer, to another device, usually a printer. Thus the word "Parallel." Data transmission in parallel is very fast, but usually happens only over short distances (typically under 500 feet) because of the need for huge amounts of cable. In contrast, the other common method of data transmission, serial transmission, takes place over one pair of wires and is usually slower than parallel transmission, but can happen over much longer distances, especially using phone lines. Parallel data transmission does not happen on phone lines. See SERIAL DATA and see the APPENDIX.

PARALLEL INTERFACING A method of interfacing peripherals to computers, usually printers. Not as common as RS-232-C serial interfacing.

PARALLEL PORT An output receptacle often located on the rear of a computer. Unlike serial, there is no EIA standard for parallel transmission, but most equipment adheres to a quasi-standard called the Centronics Parallel Standard.

PARALLEL PROCESSING 1. A computer technology in which several or even hundreds of low-cost microprocessors are linked and able to work on different parts of a problem simultaneously. 2. A computer performs two or more tasks simultaneously. This contrasts with multi-tasking in which the computer works fast and gives the impression of performing several tasks at once.

PARALLEL SESSIONS In IBM's SNA, two or more concurrently active sessions between the same two logical units (LUs), using different network addresses. Each session can have different transmission parameters.

PARALLEL TRANSMISSION 1. Method of information transfer in which all bits of a character are sent simultaneously as opposed to serial transmission where the bits are sent one after another. 2. Method of achieving higher system reliability through use of completely redundant transmission facilities.

PARAMETERS The record in a stored program control central office's data base that specifies equipment and software and options and addresses of peripheral equipment for use in call processing.

PARAMETRIC EQUALIZER A device for manipulating sound by boosting and cutting selected frequencies by specific amounts. Basically, a much more elaborate and precise version of the bass and treble controls found on stereo systems. See EQUALIZATION.

PARASITE A radio tap that takes its power from the phone line.

PARITY A process for detecting whether bits of data (parts of characters) have been altered during transmission of that data. Since data is transmitted as a stream of bits with values of one or zero, each character of data composed of, say seven bits has another bit added to it. The value of that bit is chosen so that either the total number of one bits is always even if Even Parity error correction is to be obeyed or always Odd if odd Parity error correction is chosen.

Here's an explanation (better, but longer) from The Black Box Corporation in Pittsburgh: Many asynchronous systems append a parity bit following the data bits for error detection. Parity bits trap errors in the following way. When the transmitting device frames a character, it counts either the number of 0s or 1s in the data bits and appends a parity bit that corresponds to whether or not the count in the data bits was even or odd. The receiving end also counts the data bit 0s or 1s as it receives them and then compares the computation to the parity bit. If an error is detected, a flag can be set and retransmission may be requested. When even parity is chosen, the parity bit is set at 0 if the number of 1's in the data bits is even and it is set at 1 if the number of 1's is odd. Conversely, odd parity sets the parity bit at 1 if the number of 1's in the data bits is even, and it is set at 0 if the number of 1's is odd. Other parity selections include mark, space or off. Mark parity always sets parity at 1. Space parity always sets parity at 0, and "off" tells the system to ignore the parity bit.

PARITY BIT A binary bit appended to an array of bits to make the sum of all the bits always odd or always even. See PARITY and ASCII. See PARITY.

PARITY CHECK A method of error-detection in binary data transmission whereby an extra bit is added to each group of bits (usually a character of data). If parity is to be odd, then the extra or parity bit is assigned either a one or zero so the total number of ones in the character will be odd. If the parity is even, the parity bit is assigned a value so that the total number of ones in the character is even. This way errors can be detected. See PARITY.

PARK 1. A telephone system feature that (like many features) may mean different things depending on who created it. One definition of "park" is that I dial another extension and park the call at that extension. It doesn't ring. Then I go over to that extension and pick up the phone and I'll be speaking with whoever I parked over there. This feature is useful if I have to go to another phone to find some information the caller wants. There's another definition of the telephone system meaning of "park." You have a single line phone. You put that call on a variation of hold. Then you or anyone else can pick up any phone in that pickup group and you will have your parked call.

2.   In the language of hard disks, "parking" means moving the read/write head to a safe area of the hard disk when you're ready to turn the disk off. "Parking" places the heads of a hard disk in a locked position so that the storage medium (i.e. the hard disk) will not be damaged during transit. This is useful because it keeps the head from bouncing on data areas of the disk and damaging the disk. Some hard disks have a program called "park" which you run before you turn off the machine. Others do it (self-park) automatically. All hard disks on laptops are self-parking. Most modern disks are. You ought to check. It's very important.

PARK TIMEOUT This is the period of time before an unanswered Call Park call is redirected to the Prime Phone for the line the call is on.

PART 68 REQUIREMENTS Specifications established by the FCC as the minimum acceptable protection communications equipment must provide the telephone network. Meeting these requirements does not certify that equipment performs any task. Part 68 is the section of Title 47 of the Code of Federal Regulations governing the direct connection of telecommunications equipment and premises wiring with the public switched telephone network and certain private line services, e.g., foreign exchange lines (customer premises end), the station end of off-premises stations associated with PBX and Centrex services, trunk-to-station tie lines (trunk end only), and switched service network station lines (common control switching arrangements); and the direct connection of all PBX (or similar) systems to private line services for tie trunk type interfaces, off-premises station lines, automatic identified outward dialing and message registration. These rules provide the technical, procedural and labeling standards under which direct electrical connection of customer-provided telephone equipment, systems, and protective apparatus may be made to the nationwide network without causing harm and without a requirement for protective circuit arrangements in the service provider's network. Form 730 Application Guide is a collection of literature you'll need to register your telephone/telecom equipment under Part 68 of Title 47 at the Federal Communications Commissions. To get this material (it's free) drop a line or call the Federal Communications Commission, Washington DC 20554. As I write this edition, the person at the FCC in charge is William H. Von Alven, (202-634-1833) who also puts out a very useful newsletter for Part 68 applicants. The newsletter is called "The Billboard." You can file Form 730 yourself, but the Form 730 Application Guide also contains a list of Part 68 Certification Laboratories, a list of technical references and a list of reference sources.

PARTIALLY PERFORATED TAPE Same as chadless tape. See CHADLESS TAPE.

PARTITION A division of memory or hard disk. For example, the MS-DOS and MS OS/2 operating systems can allocate hard disk space for one or more partitions, each of which behaves as a physically distinct hard disk.

PARTITIONED EMULATION PROGRAMMING EXTENSION PEP. An IBM special software package that, with the Network Control Program (NCP), allows the same communications controller to operate in split mode, controlling an SNA network while at the same time managing a number of non-SNA communications lines. It was developed by IBM to facilitate migration of users to SNA.

PARTITIONS Sections on a hard disk. You can divide your hard disk into as many as four partitions to run four operating systems. See also 32-MEGABYTE BARRIER.

PARTY A stupid word for the person making or receiving a phone call. Also now used in the airline business, as in "How many people will there be in your Party?"

PARTY IDENTIFICATION Identifying the person who is placing a call on a party line, i.e. phone line with several people sharing it. Often found in rural locations.

PARTY LINE 1. Saying what your company or boss wants you to say; or 2. A telephone line with several subscribers sharing its use.

PARTY LINE SERVICE Telephone service which provides for two or more phones to share the same loop circuit. Party line service, which is becoming less common, is offered in two-party, four-party and eight-party versions. Interestingly, there is a version of ISDN in which several subscribers do share the same ISDN line — but they would rarely be affected by it because of ISDN's specialized signaling and the two phone lines in its 2B+D bandwidth.

PARTY LINE STATIONS Two party phone service can be expanded to support to multi-party service.

PAS A Northern Telecom word for Port Adapter System.

PASCAL A programming language designed for general information processing and noted for its structured design.

PASSAGEWAY The name of the AT&T device which connects to your PC's serial port on the one end and your AT&T proprietary phone on the other and allows you to control your phone and all its incoming and outgoing calls with Windows software on your PC. AT&T's idea behind the name PassageWay is that it unlocks the the hidden PassageWay between your computer and your telephone on your Desk. Stephen Smith of AT&T is credited with creating the term PassageWay.

PASSBAND The range of frequencies that can pass through a filter without being attenuated (i.e. stopped).

PASSIVE BUS ISDN feature which allows up to six terminal devices and two voice devices (also called telephones) to simultaneously share the same twisted pair, each being uniquely identifiable to the switched ISDN telephone network. See ISDN.

PASSIVE CONTRACT In the software business, there are two types of contracts. One you sign and one you don't. A passive contract is the one you don't sign. A passive contract typically comes with an over-the-counter, shrink-wrapped software package and you execute it by breaking the seal on the package. The passive contract spells out terms and conditions you agree to — like not copying the software, not selling, etc.

PASSIVE COUPLER A coupler that divides entering light among output ports without generating new light.

PASSIVE HEAD END A device that connects the two broadband cables of a dual-cable system. It does not provide frequency translation.

PASSIVE HUB A device used in certain network topologies to split a transmission signal, allowing additional workstations to be added. A passive hub cannot amplify the signal, so it must be connected directly to a workstation or an active hub.

PASSIVE LEG A leg of a call representing the communication path toward another user. Definition from Bellcore in reference to its concept of the Advanced Intelligent Network.

PASSIVE SPLICING Aligning the two ends of a fiber without monitoring its splice loss.

PASSIVE STAR In fiber optics, a passive device that accepts a light signal on its input fiber and retransmits it on multiple output fibers with minimal loss (the fibers are actually fused together). Also called a star coupler or a retransmissive star.

PASSTHROUGH Gaining access to one network through another element.

PASSWORD A word or string of characters recognized by automatic means permitting a user access to a place or to protected storage, files or input or output devices.

PASSWORD CONTROL OF CHANGES A feature that makes it impossible to alter the performance of a piece of equipment without first entering a password.

PATCH 1. Instructions added to a software program, usually at the last moment, to get the program to run. The "patch" is usually not part of the original planning or logic of the program. Too many patches make it difficult to effectively manage the program over a long term. Patches, like the main programming, should be extensively documented. 2. To connect circuits temporarily with a jack and a cable. Patching is typically done on devices called PATCH BAYS, PATCHBOARDS or PATCH PANELS. See also PATCHING.

PATCH BAY A collection of hardware put together in such a way that circuits appear on jacks and can be connected together for transmission, monitoring and testing. See PATCH PANEL.

PATCH CORD A short length of wire or fiber cable with connectors on each end used to join communication circuits at a cross connect.

PATCH PANEL A device in which temporary connections can be made between incoming lines and outgoing lines. It is used for modifying or reconfiguring a communications system or for connecting devices such as test instruments to specific lines. A patch panel differs from a distribution frame in that the interconnections on a distribution frame are intended to be permanent.

PATCHBOARD Same as a patch bay. See PATCH BAY.

PATCHING Means of connecting circuits via cords and connectors that can be easily disconnected and reconnected at another point. May be accomplished by using modular cords connected between jack fields or by patch cord assemblies that plug onto connecting blocks.

PATCHMASTER A patch panel in which multiple pair lines can be interconnected as a group.

PATH 1. The route a telecommunications signal follows through a circuit or through the air. 2. A description of the location of an MS-DOS directory or file within your computer. The idea is that the Path command shows DOS a "path" to find a file or command you wish to execute. The path name of a file consists of a drive letter, followed by a directory name, one or more subdirectory names and a filename. You use a backslash to separate each name from the previous one. The MS-DOS command may look like this

path c:\bin;c:\wp;c:\wfw;c:\glite;c:\ccm;c:\bin\compare

In this way, you can find an executable file which might be located in any of the above directories. Writing about Paths, Van Wolverton says "as its name implies, the PATH is essentially a trail that DOS follows to get somewhere. But, unlike trails you find on a map, the DOS Path isn't a trail that someone at Microsoft or IBM to lead DOS to a specific place. Instead, the DOS Path is a trail you define so that DOS can find external commands, program files and batch files.

DOS will always search the current subdirectory for any command you want. Then, if it finds nothing, it will follow the trail set in the path.

PATH CLEARANCE In through-the-air microwave transmission, you must find a line-of-sight path, free of obstruction of buildings, trees, other microwave towers, etc. In microwave line-of-sight communications, the perpendicular distance from the radio-beam axis to obstructions such as trees, buildings, or terrain. The required path clearance is usually expressed, for a particular k-factor, as some fraction of the first Fresnel zone radius. That's the technical definition of path clearance.

PATH CONTROL LAYER In IBM's SNA, the network processing layer that handles primarily the routing of data units as they travel through the network and manages shared link resources.

PATTERN RECOGNITION A small element of human intelligence. The ability to recognize and match visual patterns. (Auditory pattern recognition is the ability to recognize spoken words.) Pattern recognition basically works by having the computer seek out paricular attributes of the character (assuming it's pattern recognition for reading words) and then having the computer compare what it finds to what's in its database of patterns. By a process of breaking down letters into curves and lines, and by a process of elimination, the computer can figure out what it's seeing. As Forbes said, "think of pattern recognition as a kind of super detective, a tireless if unimaginative collector of clues, distinguished not by brilliance, but by ceaseless legwork.

PAUSE This feature on some phone systems — especially the Northern Telecom Norstar — inserts a 1.5 second delay in a dialing sequence on an outside line.

PAX Private Automatic eXchange. Typically an intercom system not joined to the public telephone system. PAXes are more common in Europe, where is it common for business people to have two phones on their desk — one for internal intercom calls and one for external calls.

PAY PHONE See PAYPHONE

PAYLOAD From the perspective of a network service provider: of a data field, block or stream being processed or transported, the part that represents information useful to the user, as opposed to system overhead information. Payload includes user information and may include such additional information as user-requested network management and accounting information.

In Sonet, the STS-1 signal is divided into a transport overhead section and an information payload section (similar to signaling and data). See SPE (Synchronous Payload Envelope) for a description of what would be found in the payload.

PAYPHONE Used to be just a public phone that accepted only coins. Now pay phones can be coinless and can read credit cards. Soon they will be acquiring keyboards, computer screens and dataports for plugging in fax machines and portable computers. The payphone was invented by William Gray, an American whose previous inventions included the inflatable chest protector for baseball players. Mr. Gray's first phone lacked a dial. Its instructions read:

"Call Central in the usual manner. When told by the operator, drop coin in proper channel and push plunger down."

In today's nomenclature, Mr. Gray's original phone is known as a post-pay coin phone. See other entries below.

PAYPHONE-POSTPAY Calls are paid for after they are completed, typically with a credit card or calling card, etc.

PAYPHONE-PREPAY At a coin phone, calls must be paid for before they can de dialed. Virtually all local calls are prepay.

PAYPHONE-PRIVATE Referred to as Customer Owned Coin Operated Telephone Companies (COCOTs). Installed and maintained by companies other than local exchange carriers who are rapidly entering this industry. COCOTs may have access to more than one IXC.

PAYPHONE-PUBLIC A coin phone installed in a "public" place. The local operating Company is totally responsible for its installation. The phone company will typically pay someone — the city, the bus station owner — a commission on the calls made from this phone. Also see PAYPHONE-SEMI-PUBLIC.

PAYPHONE-SEMI-PUBLIC A coin phone installed for public use but installed in a "semi-public" place, such as a restaurant or bar. The proprietor of the establishment is obliged to guarantee that the phone company will receive a minimum amount of money out of the phone. The phone company will typically not pay a commission on this type of phone and takes all the money in the coin box for itself. What is a "public" and what is a "semi-public" phone is a decision made by the local telephone company for whatever reason it chooses. The pay phone business is rapidly deregulating. It is now legal to own your own payphone.

PAYSTATION, POSTPAY Calls are paid for after they are completed, typically with a credit or calling card, etc.

PAYSTATION, PREPAY Calls must be paid for before they can be dialed. Virtually all local calls are prepay.

PAYSTATION, PUBLIC A coin phone installed in a "public" place. The phone company is totally responsible for its installation. The phone company will typically pay someone — the city, the bus station owner — a commission on the calls made from this phone. See PAYSTATION, SEMI-PUBLIC.

PAYSTATION, SEMI-PUBLIC A coin phone installed for public use but installed in a "semi-private" place, such as a restaurant or bar. The proprietor of the establishment is obliged to guarantee that the phone company will receive a minimum amount of money out of the phone. The phone company will typically not pay a commission on this type of phone and takes all the money in the coin box for itself. What is a "Public" and what is a "Semi- Public" phone is a decision made by the local telephone company for whatever reasons it chooses. The pay phone business is rapidly deregulating. So the rules are changing. And it is now legal to own your own payphone.

PBX Private Branch eXchange. A private (i.e. you, as against the phone company owns it), branch (meaning it is a small phone company central office), exchange (a central office was originally called a public exchange, or simply an exchange). In other words, a PBX is a small version of the phone company's larger central switching office. A PBX is also called a Private Automatic Branch Exchange, though that has now become an obsolete term. In the very old days, you called the operator to make an external call, except in Europe. Then later someone made a phone system that you simply dialed nine (or another digit — in Europe it's often zero), got a second dial tone and dialed some more digits to dial out, locally or long distance. So, the early name of Private Branch Exchange (which needed an operator) became Private AUTOMATIC Branch Exchange (which didn't need an operator). Now, all PBXs are automatic. And now they're all called PBXs, except overseas where they still have PBXs that are not automatic.

At the time of the Carterfone decision in the summer of 1968, PBXs were electro-mechanical step-by-step monsters. They were 100% the monopoly of the local phone company. AT&T was the major manufacturer with over

90% of all the PBXs in the U.S. GTE was next. But the Carterfone decision allowed anyone to make and sell a PBX. And the resulting inflow of manufacturers and outflow of innovation caused PBXs to go through five, six or seven generations — depending on which guru you listen to. (See my definition for GENERATIONS in this dictionary). Anyway, by the fall of 1991 when I wrote this fourth edition of this dictionary, PBXs were thoroughly digital, very reliable, and very full featured. There wasn't much you couldn't do with them. They had oodles of features. You could combine them and make your company a mini-network. And you could buy electronic phones that made getting to all the features that much easier. Sadly, by the late 1980s the manufacturers seemed to have finished innovating and were into price cutting. As a result, the secondary market in telephone systems was booming. Fortunately, that isn't the end of the story. For some of the manufacturers in the late 1980s figured that if they opened their PBXs' architecture to outside computers, their customers could realize some significant benefits. (You must remember that up until this time, PBXs were one of the last remaining special purpose computers that had totally closed architecture. No one else could program them other than their makers.) Some of the benefits customers could realize from open architecture included:

* Simultaneous voice call and data screen transfer.

● Automated dial-outs from computer databases of phone numbers and automatic transfers to idle operators.

● Transfers to experts based on responses to questions, not on phone numbers.

And a million more benefits. We discuss them at our annual trade show called TELECOM DEVELOPERS held in May each year. Call 212-691-8215 for more information. For more on open architecture, see OAI.

An alternative to getting a PBX is to subscribe to your local telephone company's Centrex service. For a long explanation on Centrex and its benefits, see CENTREX. Here are some of the benefits of a PBX versus Centrex:

1. Ownership. Once you've paid for it, you own it. There are obvious financial and tax benefits.

2. Flexibility. A PBX is a far more flexible than a central office based Centrex. A PBX has more features. You can change them faster. You can expand faster. Drop another card in, plug some phones in, do your programming and bingo you're live.

3. Centrex benefits. You can always put Centrex lines behind a PBX and get the advantages of both. In some towns, Centrex lines are cheaper than PBX lines. So buy Centrex lines and put them behind your PBX. Make sure you don't pay for Centrex features your PBX already has. (It has most.)

4. PBX phones. There are really no Centrex phones — other than a few Centrex consoles. If you want to take advantage of Centrex features, you have to punch in cumbersome, difficult-to-remember codes on typically single line phones. PBXs have electronic phones, often with screens and dedicated buttons. They're usually a lot easier to work. A lot easier to transfer a call. Conference another, etc. A lot more productive.

5. Footprint savings. Modern PBXs take up room, more than Centrex. But the space they take up is far less than it used to be. PBXs are getting smaller.

6. Voice Processing/Automated Attendants. Centrex's DID (Direct Inward Dialing) feature was always pushed as a big "plus." You saved operators. However, you can now do operator-saving things with PC-based voice processing and automated attendants you couldn't do five years ago. These things work better with on-site standalone PBXs than with distant, central office based Centrex. Moreover, virtually every PBX in existence today supports DID. You can dial directly into PBXs and reach someone at their desk just as easily as you can dial directly using Centrex.

7. Open Architecture. Most PBXs have open architecture. See OAI for the benefits. Central offices don't.

8. Good Reliability. There have been sufficient central office crashes and sufficient improvement in the reliability of PBXs that you could happily argue that the two are on a par with each other today. Both are equally reliable, or unreliable. The only caveat, of course, is that you back your PBX up with sufficient batteries that it will last a decent power outage. Of course, that assumes that your people will be prepared to hang around and answer the phones during a blackout.

9. Expansion. Central offices are big. Allegedly you can grow your lines to whatever size you want. In contrast, PBXs have finite growth. It's true about PBXs. But it's equally true about central offices. I've personally heard too many stories about central office line shortages to believe in the nonsense about "infinite Centrex" growth. Fact is central offices grow out, just like PBXs. Given the tight economy of recent years, local phone companies have not been buying the central offices they should have. And they have been filling central offices up a little too tight for my taste.

10. Technological obsolescence. Allegedly central offices are upgraded faster than PBXs and therefore are always up to date technologically. It's nonsense. The life cycle of a typical central office was 40 years until recently. It's now around 20 years. Think of what's happened to PCs in the past 10 years — the IBM PC debuted only in 1981 — and you can imagine how obsolete many of the nation's central offices are.

PBX EXTENSION A telephone line connected to a PBX.

PBX FRAUD Same as TOLL FRAUD.

PBX GENERATIONS See GENERATIONS, PBX.

PBX LINE ACCESS An AT&T term. Provides for a PBX line to appear in a line access button on 16 ECTS telephones. A single-line telephone may be used for an appearance of a PBX.

PBX STATION LINE A transmission path extending from the station (phone instrument) location to the switching equipment.

PBX TIE LINE A tie line between two PBX's, permitting extensions in one PBX to be connected to extensions in the other without having to dial through the public switched network. See also OPX and OPS, which are different and are lines between PBXs and distant extensions, not tie lines between PBXs.

PBX TRUNK A circuit which connects the PBX to the local telephone company's central office switching center or other switching system center.

PC 1. Personal Computer. 2. Peg Count. 3. Printed Circuit. 4. Product Committee. 5. Politically Correct. PC speaking or writing uses the term He/She, rather than He, which is grammatically correct. PC speaking or writing means also using the passive tense. It means using the word "they." Being "PC" make writing and speaking very boring.

PC CARD A memory or I/O card compatible with the PCMCIA PC Card Standard. This definition from the Personal Computer Memory Card International Association.

PC NETWORK IBM's first LAN (Local Area Network).

PC-DOS What IBM calls a version of the operating system on its older personal computers. If PC-DOS runs on an IBM compatible, it is called MS-DOS, which stands for MicroSoft Disk Operating System. Microsoft of Bellevue, Washington, wrote MS-DOS.

PCA Protective Connecting Arrangement. A device that AT&T and members of the Bell System insisted be connected between a telecommunications device (like a phone) that wasn't made and sold by AT&T and a phone line provided by an AT&T Bell operating company. Many years later, the PCAs were found by the FCC to be totally unnecessary and AT&T and members of the Bell System were ordered to refund all payments received for rental of PCAs. The Bell System insisted on the PCAs as a way of protecting AT&T's effective monopoly of telecommunications equipment. See also PROTECTIVE CONNECTIVE ARRANGEMENT.

PCC Personal Companion Computer. What Intel

PCB Printed Circuit Board.

PCF Physical Control Fields. The AC (Access Control) and FC (Frame Control) bytes in a Token Ring header.

PCI Peripheral Component Interconnect, a local motherboard specification designed by Intel. It will enable high performance, peripheral component level interface to the CPU bus and will be an interconnect strategy for "glueless" I/O subsystems, according to Intel.

PCL Hewlett-Packard's Printer Control Language, developed for the company's line of laser printers. A de facto standard, PCL allows the type of sophisticated page creation generally referred to as "laser quality output." PCL Level 5, resident in the HP Laser Jet Series III family of printers, supports such advanced features as fully scalable typefaces and rotation of text.

PCM Pulse Code Modulation. The most common method of encoding an analog voice signal into a digital bit stream. First, the amplitude of the voice conversation is sampled. This is called PAM, Pulse Amplitude Modulation. This PAM sample is then coded (quantized) into a binary (digital) number. This digital number consists of zeros and ones. The voice signal can then be switched, transmitted and stored digitally. There are three basic advantages to PCM voice. They are the three basic advantages of digital switching and transmission. First, it is less expensive to switch and transmit a digital signal. Second, by making an analog voice signal into a digital signal, you can interleave it with other digital signals — such as those from computers or facsimile machines. Third, a voice signal which is switched and transmitted end-to-end in a digital format will usually come through "cleaner," i.e. have less noise, than one transmitted and switched in analog. The reason is simple: An electrical signal loses strength over a distance. It must then be amplified. In analog transmission, everything is amplified, including the noise and static the signal has collected along the way. In digital transmission, the signal is "regenerated," i.e. put back together again, by comparing the incoming signal to a logical question: Is it a one or a zero? Then, the signal is regenerated, amplified and sent along its way.

PCM refers to a technique of digitization. It does not refer to a universally accepted standard of digitizing voice. The most common PCM method is to sample a voice conversation at 8000 times a seconds. The theory is that if the sampling is at least twice the highest frequency on the channel, then the result sounds OK. (See NYQUIST THEOREM.) Thus, the highest frequency on a voice phone line is 4,000 Hertz. So one must sample it at 8,000 times a second. Many PCM digital voice conversations are typically put on one communications channel. In North America, the most typical channel is called the T-1 (also spelled T1). It places 24 voice conversations on two pairs of copper wires (one for receiving and one for transmitting). It contains 8000 frames each of 8 bits of 24 voice channels plus one framing (synchronizing bit) bit which equals 1.544 Mbps, i.e. 8000 x (8 x 24 + 1) equals 1.544 megabits.

Countries outside of the United States and North America use a different scheme for multiplexing voice conversations. It is based not on 24 voice channels, but on 32. This scheme keeps two of the 32 channels for control, actually transmitting 30 voice conversations at a data rate of 2.048 Mbps. The European system is calculated as 8 bits x 32 channels x 8000 frames per second. European PCM multiplexing is not compatible with North American multiplexing. The two systems cannot be directly connected. Some PBXs in the U.S. conform to the U.S. standard only. Some (very few) conform to both. Both the European and North American T-1 "standards" have now been accepted as ISDN "standards." In addition to PCM, there are many other ways of digitally encoding voice. PCM remains the most common. See T-1 and VOICE COMPRESSION.

PCM-30 Short name of international 2.048 Mbps T-1 (also known as E1) service derived from the fact that 30 channels are available for 64 Kbps digitized voice each using pulse code modulation (PCM).

PCMCIA The Personal Computer Memory Card International Association (an awful mouthful) standardizes credit-card size packages for memory and I/O (modems, LAN cards, etc.) for computers, laptops, palmtops, etc. There are three standards for PCMCIA cards — Type 1, 2 and 3. The cards are 69.2 millimeters (3.37 inches) long x 51.46 millimeters (2.126 inches) wide. All three types use the same 68 female pin edge connector for attachment to the computer, and differ only in thickness. The thickness for Type I, Type II and Type III are 3.3, 5.0, 10.5 millimeters respectively. At time of writing Type 2 cards were out containing full Ethernet thinnet and 10BaseT and Token Ring LAN connection. In Type 3, the thickest, some manufacturers have managed to squeeze hard disks up to 105 megabytes. PCMCIA's first standards were issued in September, 1991. The idea is that small computers will use these cards for modems, fax cards, hard disks, LAN connections, ethernet connections etc.). A PCMCIA card is really the only way to get to a laptop's bus without attaching a docking station. Standards exist so others can make these cards. Some computers — like some pre-summer 1991 notebooks and laptops from Compaq and Toshiba — don't comply because these computers were released before the standards were released. The new PCMCIA 2.0 standard contains a software specification for XIP, the "eXecute In Place" mechanism that maps application software stored on the PCMCIA card into the system address space. This means application software will run directly from the card, start faster and not require precious RAM from the host computer.

A Type I PC Card is typically used for various types of memory enhancements, including RAM, FLASH memory, one-time programmable (OTP) memory, and electronically erasable programmable read only memory (EEPROM). A Type II PC Card is typically used for memory enhancements and/or for I/O features such as modem, LANs and host communications. A Type III PC Card is twice the thickness of the Type II and is typically used for memory enhancements and/or for I/O features that require a larger size, such as rotating mass storage devices (removable hard disk drives) and radio communication devices. Since Type I, Type II and Type III Cards all use the same interface, the size of the card chosen for the application is dependent on the miniaturization of the technology to be implemented.

The key elements of the PCMCIA software architecture are Socket Services and Card Services. Socket Services is a BIOS level software interface that provides a way to access the PCMCIA sockets (slots) of a computer. Socket Services identifies how many sockets are in your computer system and detects the insertion or removal of a PC Card while the system is powered on. Socket Services is part of the PCMCIA Specification and interfaces with Card Services.

Card Services is a software managment interface that allows the allocation of system resources (such as memory and interrupts) automatically, once the Socket Services detects that a PC Card has been added. Card Services also releases these resources when the PC Card has been removed. Furthermore, Card Services provides you with an interface to higher level software to load any needed hardware drivers. Card Services is also part of the PCMCIA Specification.

The combination of PC Card hardware, Card Services software and Socket Services software provides a "plug-and-play" capability in the portable computing environment. Once the software has been installed, it is possible to add and remove PC Cards without powering off the system or opening the covers of the personal computer system unit. For example, it is possible to insert a Modem PC Card to access another computer system, download information into the portable computer's memory, remove the Modem PC Card, replace it with a Flash PC Card, and store the downloaded information - all while your portable computer is still powered on.

As PC Card features are added and removed, it is no longer necessary to worry about what memory blocks, I/O ports, or interrupt levels are available. Card and Socket Services software configures the system automatically.

As of writing (Spring, 1993), Socket and Card services were not fully defined and not implemented fully on any computer. Socket and Card services software is very complex. Expect them to appear commonly in full production models sometime in 1994.

PCMCIA's plus: PC Cards provide the flexibility of adding the necessary features after the base system has been purchased. PCMCIA slots can be added to ISA and EISA, and other standard bus configurations for personal computer systems. The same PC Card can operate in all these machine types with the appropriate Card and Socket Services software.

The PCMCIA has around 300 members, including including manufacturers of semiconductors, connectors, peripherals and systems, as well as BIOS and software developers and related industries. Members include Intel, IBM, Toshiba, Lotus, Epson and Fujitsu. The association is based in Sunnyvale, CA. 408-720-0107. It has an electronic bulletin board — 408-720-9388. Its standards are also recognized by the Japanese Electronic Industry

Development Association (JEIDA). The Association publishes a book listing all the manufacturers making cards which comply to their standards. The book is free. As the first modem and Ethernet PCMCIA cards began to appear, they suffered one minor inconvenience: They have a small "pigtail," a three to four inch device that plugs into the side of the card which is in the computer and allows a user to plug an RJ-11 or RJ-45 or other plug into. By early 1993 some PCMCIA cards were losing their pigtails in favor of proprietary (i.e. non-standard) cables. If you buy a PCMCIA card, make sure you buy a second cable, just in case. See PCMCIA STANDARDS.

PCMCIA STANDARDS The complete set of all of the PCMCIA PC Card Standards. It includes the PC Card Standard Release 2.01, Socket Services Specification Release 2.0, Card Services Specification Release 2.0, ATA Specification Release 1.01, AIMS Specification Release 1.0, and the Recommended Extensions Release 1.0.

PCN Personal Communications Network. A new type of wireless telephone system that would use light, inexpensive handheld handsets and communicate via low-power antennas. When it was originally conceived, PCN was primarily seen as an a city communications system, with far less range than cellular. Subscribers would be able to make and receive calls while they are traveling, as they can do today with cellular radio systems, but at a low price. Now PCN is seen as what Dr. Sorin Cohn of Northern Telecom calls an "enabler of unplanned growth." One idea for PCN is to locate a PCN cell site (transmitter/receiver) in a residential community. When someone wanted a new phone line, they'd simply drop down to their local phone store, pick up a PCN portable phone and, by the time, they got back home, their frequency would be "switched on" and they'd be "live." See also PERSONAL COMMUNICATIONS NETWORK.

PCS Personal Communications Software — available in ROLM Cedar, Cypress and Juniper — makes for easy access to external data bases, rapid transfer of data files and one-touch access to most telephone features. Other PCS features include built-in calculator, small phone list, reminder function and internal clock.

PCSA Personal Computing System Architecture. A PC implementation of DECnet, that lets PCs work in a DECnet environment.

PCTA Personal Computer Terminal Adapter. A printed circuit card that slips into an IBM PC or PC compatible and allows that PC to be connected to the ISDN T-interface. See PERSONAL COMPUTER TERMINAL ADAPTER.

PCTE Portable Common Tool Environment.

PDA Personal Digital Assistant. A consumer electronics gadget that looks like a palmtop computer. Unlike personal computers, PDAs will perform specific tasks — acting like an electronic diary, carry-along personal database, multimedia player, personal communicator, memo taker, calculator, alarm clock. The communications will take place through the phone or through wireless. Apple has announced a PDA, which it has named Newton. When I added this definition in the late fall of 1992, sales of PDAs weren't doing well and some wag in Silicon Valley called them Probably Disappointed Again. IBM prefers to call them Personal Communicators. General Magic prefers to called them PICs, Personal Intelligent Communicators.

PDI Telenova/Lexar's Predictive Dialing Interface which links the Telenova/Lexar PBX and an outboard predictive dialing computer processor. In the Telenova system, the predictive processor talks directly the T-1 card in the Lexar System 2000. By talking directly, Telenova claims certain benefits:

● The system is not load sensitive. This means you've talking to the outside world more than internally.

● The system supports much larger platforms. You can hook up to 16,000 ports.

● The system has an internal T-1 card, instead of relying on call banks.

Sadly, as of writing Telenova was in Chapter 11.

PDL A page description language (PDL) is a is a clever short-cut for transmitting bit-mapped images from a PC application to a printer. They save processing time, by sending only "instructions" to a printer, rather than the entire bitmapped image. They also allow the printer to print any font, any size. PDL is the generic term. Hewlett-Packard has been the major proponent of the concept of PDLs. And they include something called PCL with all their printers. PCL stands for Printer Command Language. Postscript is also a PDL, but different to PCL. HP includes PCL with all its laser printers, but has only included

What we really meant was that HP had never built PostScript into their printers. They still haven't, really. You still have to buy PostScript as either a plug-in cartridge or an add-on "SIM" chip from HP, Adobe or third parties for most of the HP line. The exception is the top-of-the-line LaserJet IIIsi, for which built-in PostScript is an option that you pay extra for.

That may change. For now, if you're using Windows applications, Windows' built-in "True Type" scalable fonts — which do work on HP and other non-PostScript printers — will satisfy most of your printing needs.

PDM See PERSONAL DATA MODULE.

PDN Public Data Network. A public network for the transmission of data, particularly a network compatible with X.25 protocol. A public data network is to data what the Public Switched Voice Network is to voice. To access a public data network, you typically dial a local number, receive a carrier tone and then follow very specific instructions. Public data networks send their digital data in packets over high speed channels. The major reason to use a PDN is that it may be cheaper than dialing directly on a switched voice line. Also, they get you into some databases and services which are hard to get into by dialing direct. There are many public data networks in the United States. The two best-known public data networks are Tymnet and Telenet. But there are probably 30 more. Every industrialized foreign country has at least one, usually owned by the local government phone company.

PDP See POWER DISTRIBUTION PANEL.

PDP-11 On the last day of March, 1970 Digital Equipment shipped its first PDP-11/20 minicomputer to a customer in Tennessee. The PDP-11 family was among the first minicomputer that incorporated open standards into its operations. And the PDP-11 software platform has continued through subsequent generations of hardware.

PDS 1. Premise Distribution System. AT&T's proprietary buildingwide telecommunications cabling system. 2. Processor Direct Slot. Some non-NuBus Apple Macintosh computers have one PDS that allows for expanison cards.

PDU Protocol Data Unit. The unit of data in the OSI Reference Model containing both protocol-control information and user data from the layer above. A block of information that is exchanged between two processes within communicating machines. It contains both data and control (protocol) information that allows the two to coordinate their interactions.

PE Processing Element.

PEAK That part of the business day in which customers expect to pay full service rates. For cellular customers, peak hours are generally 7:00 a.m. to 7:00 p.m. For business landline customers, peak hours are generally 8:00 a.m. to 5:00 p.m.

PEAK EMISSION WAVELENGTH Of an optical emitter, the spectral line having the greatest power.

PEAK HOUR When used with an automatic call disributor, the peak hour is when the number of calls coming into your center are at their highest level. ACDs allow you to track and report on calls by hour. Some allow you to also track peak half-hours, or peak delays of the week or months of the year.

PEAK LOAD A higher than average quantity of traffic. Peak Load is usually expressed for a one-hour period, often the busiest hour of the busiest day of the year. See BUSY HOUR.

PEAK RATE The per-minute price for using a communications device in the "peak" time period. For cellular, "Peak" time generally includes hours such as evenings Monday through Friday, and all day Saturday, Sunday, and certain holidays. For normal landline phone service, peak rates will include workday days.

PEAK TO AVERAGE RATIO P/AR. An analog test that provides a measure of data circuit quality by sending a pulse into one end of a circuit and measuring its envelope at the distant end of the circuit. See P/AR.

PEANUT TUBES A name given to the smaller sizes of vacuum tubes.

PEB PCM Expansion Bus. A standard digital voice bus for connecting different voice processing components. PEB is from Dialogic, Parsippany, NJ. It is an open platform. Many companies make voice processing products connecting via PEB. See also DYNAMIC NODE ACCESS.

PEDESTAL A mounting device used in pay telephone installations where the instrument is not attached to a wall. Pedestals are usually too small and rarely have a shelf big enough to take notes on.

PEEK/POKE Instructions that view and alter a byte of memory by referencing a specific memory address. Peek displays the contents; poke changes it.

PEER-PEER DIRECTORY PROPAGATION A way of updating user addresses in which changes in any post office on a LAN (local area network) are sent to all other post offices.

PEER-TO-PEER NETWORK 1. A network (typically a local area network) in which every node has equal access to the network and can send and receive data at any time without having to wait for permission from a control node. While peer-to-peer resource sharing is effective in small networks, security and reliability issues prevent its widespread use in larger networks.

2.   A new telephony term describing the relationship between a telephone system and the external computer working with it. Picture a telephone switch acting as an automatic call distributor and an outboard computer processor. The idea is to coordinate the call and the screen at the agent. Communication must take place between the switch and the computer. If that communication is peer-to-peer, as it is, for example, in the DMS Meridian ACD, then neither the switch nor the computer is in a "slave" relationship to the other. See EXTENDED CALL MANAGEMENT.

PEER-TO-PEER RESOURCE SHARING An architecture that lets any station contribute resources to the network while still running local application programs. 10-Net Local Area Network allows for peer-to-peer resource sharing.

PEG COUNT A raw count of some event. Because this was originally maintained by moving pegs on a board with units of 1,10s,100, 1000s it became a peg count. A count of the number of calls placed or received at a certain point or over certain lines during a period such as an hour or day or week. A peg count simply tells you how many calls you made or received. It does not tell you how long they were or where they went or anything else. In the old days before we had accurate and relatively inexpensive call accounting equipment, we relied on Peg Counts to figure out how many circuits we needed. No more. The peg count method is too inaccurate.

PEL Picture ELement. A pel is the smallest area on a video screen that can be controlld by software. Pels are arranged on screens in a grid-like fashion.

Sometimes a pel equals a pixel, which is a single point and the smallest unit of area on the screen. Depending on the screen mode selected by your software, a pel ma be a single pixel or several pixels. The pel size determines the screen resolution. On the other hand, if each is smaller, more can fit on the screen, resulting in higher resolution. See also FAX and VGA.

PEN REGISTER Also called a Dialed Number Recorder (DNR). An instrument that records telephone dial pulses as inked dashes on paper tape. A touch-tone decoder performs the same thing for a touch-tone telephone.

PEN WINDOWS A new Microsoft operating system for notebook size computers that uses a stylus instead of a keyboard.

PENPOINT An operating system from Go Corp. for pen computers. Such computers are light, small, portable and have a stylus and a screen which recognizes the words and numbers you write on the screen with the stylus. PenPoint is to pen computers what MS-DOS (or more recently, Windows) is to desktop computers. PenPoint won't run existing MS-DOS software. But Microsoft's new Windows For Pens — what it calls an "operating environment" — promises to. But it also promises to be more difficult to use than PenPoint. As of writing this, (early 1992), I hadn't seen final versions of either operating system. So we'll see.

PENTIUM In the fall of 1992, Intel adopted the name Pentium for its 80586 chip, its successor to the 80486. It introduced the Pentium formally in early April, 1993. The chip is capable of 112 million instructions per second and is 80% faster than the fastest 80486. It contains more than three million transistors and is said to be a superscalar chip, which means it can execute two instructions at a time.

PERCENTAGE ATB Percentage of All Trunks Busy. Percentage of time during a reporting period that all trunks in a group or split were busy. This may be measured in two ways, actual simultaneous busies and call length per event, or backed into statistically. Neither technique is absolutely accurate as each depends on "snap shots" in a environment of random interleaved call events.

PERCENTAGE CA Percentage of Calls Abandoned. Indicates the percentage of calls abandoned by callers after being accepted by the ACD.

PERCENTAGE HLD Percentage of total calls HeLD in queue within a reporting group.

PERCENTAGE NCO Percentage of total of Number of Calls Offered to a particular reporting group.

PERCENTAGE TUT Percentage of Trunk Utilization Time. The percentage of a time during a reporting period that a trunk is in use and not idle.

PERFORATOR An instrument for the manual preparation of a perforated tape, on which telegraph signals are represented by holes punched in accordance with a predetermined code.

PERFORATOR, PAPER TAPE An electromechanical device which converts electrical signals into coded holes in a paper tape. See PAPER TAPE PUNCH.

PERFORMANCE MANAGEMENT Measures and records resource utilization. It is one of the categories of network management defined by the ISO (international Standards Organization).

PERIAPSIS In satellite systems, the point on a satellite's orbit at which it is closest to the center of the primary body about which it is orbiting. Where Earth-based satellite systems are concerned, the term is synonymous with perigee. See also GEOSTATIONARY ORBIT.

PERIGEE The point at which a satellite orbit is the least distance from the center of the gravitational field of the Earth. See also PERIAPSIS.

PERIMETER PROTECTION SYSTEM A field disturbance sensor which uses buried leaky cables isntalled around a facility to detect any unathorized entry or exit.

PERIOD OF A SATELLITE The time elapsing between two consecutive passages of a satellite through a characteristic point on its orbit.

PERIPHERAL DEVICE See PERIPHERAL EQUIPMENT or APPLICATIONS PROCESSOR.

PERIPHERAL EQUIPMENT Equipment not integral to but working with a phone system. An example might be a printer or television screen on which calling traffic statistics are displayed. It might also be a voice mail system. AT&T once called PBX peripheral equipment "applications processors," because they process specific applications. Some people now call them Adjunct Processor or Outboard Processors.

PERMANENT SIGNAL A sustained off-hook supervisory signal originating outside a switching system and not related to a call in progress. Permanent signals can occupy a substantial part of the capacity of a switching system.

PERMANENT VIRTUAL CIRCUIT A virtual circuit that provides the equivalent of a dedicated private line service over a packet switching network between two DTEs. The path between users is fixed. A PVC uses a fixed logical channel to maintain a permanent association between the FTEs. Once a PVC is defined, it requires no setup operation before data is sent and no disconnect operation after data is sent. A new connection between the same users may be routed along a different path. See also VIRTUAL CIRCUIT and SDN for another type of virtual network.

PERMISSIBLE INTERFERENCE Observed or predicted interference which complies with quantitative interference and sharing criteria contained in these [Radio] Regulations or in CCIR Recommendations or in special agreements as provided for in these Regulations. (RR) See also accepted interference, interference.

PERMISSIONS A Northern Telecom Norstar definition to define specific characteristics that can be assigned to an individual telephone. Permissions includes Full Handsfree, Handsfree Answerback, Pickup Group, Page Zone, Auxiliary Ringer, Receive tones, and Priority Call.

PERMUTER TABLE Routing table in TYMNET.

PERSPECTIVE FOR VNET A new service from MCI which allows large companies to analyze long distance billing information electronically or via CD-ROM.

PERPETRATOR Someone who carries out an illegal or malicious act affecting information security.

PERSISTENCE In a CRT, the time a phosphor dot remains illuminated after being energized. Long-persistent phosphors reduce flicker, but generate ghost-like images that linger on screen for a fraction of a second.

PERSISTENT COMMUNICATION A dialogue between an ASC (AIN Switch Capabilities) and a SLEE (Service Logic Execution Environment) that may involve a sequence of messages. Definition from Bellcore in reference to its concept of the Advanced Intelligent Network.

PERSISTENT INFORMATION Information for which a permanent data object exists. Definition from Bellcore in reference to its concept of the Advanced Intelligent Network.

PERSON CALL There will be two types of calls: person calls and place calls. I make a place call when I call a phone number which ends in one designated, fixed RJ-11 jack attached to the wall or floor. I make a person call when I call a phone number which doesn't necessarily end on a fixed place. A typical person call might be a cellular or wireless phone call. It might also be a service like MCI's Personal 800 Service. The major characteristic of a person call is that I am calling a person and I don't know where that person is. As a result, the person I called might answer my call anywhere — from his car, from vacation home, from his wireless phone, etc.

PERSON TO PERSON CALL The most expensive way to make a long distance call. Call the operator. Say "I want to speak to Andy Moore on 212-691-8215." The operator dials Mr. Moore's phone number, gets Mr. Moore on the phone. "Are you Mr. Moore?" Mr. Moore replies: "Yes, I am." The operator bows out of the conversation and sends you, the caller, a hefty bill for that personalized service. Until recently, person-to-person service was only offered by AT&T. Now it's offered by many companies. But prices are not regulated. And some companies charge an arm and a leg. Please be careful.

PERSONAL 800 NUMBER Several long distance companies are now offering Personal 800 numbers, which are basically party line 800 numbers with call routing. The way they work is as follows: You dial a number, e.g. 800-484-1000. A machine answers with a double beep. You punch in four or five digits on your touchtone pad. A voice response unit at the other end hears the digits, says "Thank you for using MCI" and dials out your long distance number which might be 212-691-8215 (mine). The long distance carriers are charging under $5 a month and 15 to 25 cents a minute for the service. The per minute charges are more expensive than normal 800 lines. One company, MCI, is also offering FOLLOW ME 800 which allows you to change the routing of your personal 800 number instantly with one phone line.

PERSONAL CENTRAL OFFICE TRUNK LINE Allows a user to access a central office trunk line dedicated to him. A trunk line can appear in a line access button on his PBX phone or his 16 ECTS telephones on a AT&T PBX.

PERSONAL COMMUNICATIONS NETWORKS PCN. A new type of wireless telephone system that would use light, inexpensive handheld handsets and communicate via low-power antennas. PCN is primarily seen as a city communications system, with far less range than cellular. Subscribers would be able to make and perhaps receive calls while they are traveling, as they can do today with cellular radio systems, but at a low price. There's talk that they'll put PCN antennas in communities and issue everyone in the community with a PCN phone that would hub off the PCN antenna. This would save the phone company wiring up each house. In this way, the PCN phone would resemble the common household cordless phone, but with a larger range. Dr. Sorin Cohn of Northern Telecom calls the new low-power, wireless, personal communications sytems an "enabler of unplanned growth." Nice definition. See PCN amd PERSONAL COMMUNICATIONS SERVICES.

In the fall of 1992 MCI broadened the definition of PCN. It proposed a national consortium of local PCNs joined together by a long distance carrier (namely it). In its release, MCI said that "PCNs are the next generation of digital wireless communications technology. PCNs use less power and are less expensive than the current cellular technology and permit the use of inexpensive pocket telephones with much longer battery life than cellular portables. PCN phones will have many more features than today's cellular or conventional telephones, and unlike cellular phones, will be useable in most areas of the world. PCNs will operate in the same frequency band in most countries, (1850-1990 MHz) while cellular is operating in several different frequency bands in various countries, and thus is not portable from country to country." See also PERSONAL COMMUNICATIONS SERVICES.

PERSONAL COMMUNICATIONS SERVICES PCS are a broad range of individualized telecommunications services that let people or devices to communicate irrespective of where they are. Some of the services include:

- Personal numbers assigned to individuals rather than telephones
- Call completion regardless of location ("find me")
- Calls to the PCS customer can be paid for by the caller, or by the PCS customer
- Call management services giving the called party much greater control over incoming calls.

PCS can both find and complete a call to a person regardless of location, but give that person the choice of accepting or rejecting the call or sending it somewhere else. PCS will possibly use a new category of wireless, voice and data communications — using low power, lightweight pocket telephones and hand-held computers.

PERSONAL COMMUNICATOR IBM's preferred name for what Apple calls a PDA, Personal Digital Assistant. Tandy calls theirs a Personal Information Processor. See PDA.

PERSONAL COMPUTER PC. A computer for personal single-user use, as opposed to other types of computers — mainframes and minis — typically shared by many users.

PERSONAL COMPUTER MEMORY CARD INTERNATIONAL ASSOCIATION See PCMCIA.

PERSONAL COMPUTER TERMINAL ADAPTER PCTA. A printed circuit card that slips into an IBM PC or PC compatible and connects the PC to the ISDN T-interface. As of writing, such devices cost between $1250 and $1750 and are available in almost-commercial form from about six manufacturers. The PCTA basically turns a normal PC into an ISDN phone and ISDN terminal, ready for voice and data communications. According to Northern Telecom, one of the manufacturers of such a device, the PCTA does:

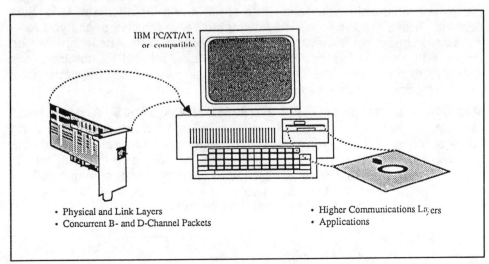

IBM PC/XT/AT, or compatible

- Physical and Link Layers
- Concurrent B- and D-Channel Packets

- Higher Communications Layers
- Applications

- Functional signaling call setup.
- B channel for circuit switched data.
- X.25 packet data services on the B or D channel.
- Simultaneous operation of the B and D channels.
- M5317T digital telephone to PC messaging for integrated voice and data operation.
- NetBIOS interface to applications software, such as Microsoft Networks. For more, see Northern Telecom's brochure ISDN PC Terminal Adapter NetBIOS Interface Description (D307-1).

PERSONAL DATA MODULE A removable module, unique to the ROLM Cypress and Cedar, which stores all information entered by the user. Such items as phone numbers, terminal profiles and log-on sequences are stored in the PDM, which also features battery backup to protect the memory in the event of a power failure. The user can take his personal data module with him, plug it into another Cypress or Cedar and get all his speed dial and other personalized programming on his phone he just moved from.

PERSONAL DIGITAL ASSISTANT PDA. A consumer electronics gadget that looks like a palmtop computer. Unlike personal computers, PDAs will perform specific tasks — acting like an electronic diary, carry-along personal database, multimedia player, personal communicator, memo taker, calculator, alarm clock. The communications will take place through the phone or through wireless. Apple has announced a PDA, which it has code-named, Newton.

PERSONAL IDENTIFICATION NUMBER PIN number. 1. An AT&T term meaning the last four digits of your AT&T, MCI Bell operating company Credit Card — the card you use for making long distance numbers. 2. Some banks and financial institutions issue credit cards for machine, teller-less banking. These machines, called Automated Teller Machines, ask you for a password consisting of several numbers or characters. These are not on your credit card. These numbers or characters, called PIN numbers, are designed to make sure the right person is using your card. It's not a good idea to use your birthday as your PIN number.

PERSONAL INTELLIGENT COMMUNICATIONS What General Magic calls the products and services its alliance members will create using General Magic technologies that will help people remember, communicate and know things in new and powerful ways. According to General Magic, "the alliance's shared long-term vision is to bring personal communications to people who may not use a computer today, to people whose personal technology is a car, a television set and a telephone."

PERSONAL INFORMATION ASSISTANT Tandy's name for what Apple calls a Personal Digital Assistant. See PDA.

PERSONAL LINE A feature which allows specific key telephones to have their own private Central Office line. Sometimes called an AUXILIARY LINE. You can typically receive and make calls on this line. No one else can answer it, since it does not appear on any other phone instrument in the office. You can give this number to your wife or girlfriend. It is not a good idea to give it to both.

PERSONAL PRODUCTIVITY TOOL Another term for a computer. John Perry Barlow thinks the expression was created by the "droids" who run Microsoft and Apple. Mr. Barlow is a cattle rancher, computer hacker, poet, and a lyricist for the rock band The Grateful Dead.

PERSONAL SPEED DIAL Simplified ways of dialing. You do them by dialing a couple of digits. Or you punch in a button at your phone. Personal Speed Dial codes are programmed for each telephone, and can only be used at the telephone on which they are programmed. System Speed Dials, in contrast, can be used from every phone in the system.

PERSONAL SYSTEM/2 PS/2. IBM's current family of microcomputers some of whom sport one major difference from its predecessors, namely the existence of a 32-bit micro-channel bus. This "bus" serves the same purpose as a PBX's backplane — namely to move information from the printed circuit cards and to other printed circuit cards, which may contain their own individual microprocessors (computers on a chip) and which may communicate with the outside world through their own communications ports.

PERSONAL TELEPHONE The category of cellular telephones pioneered by Motorola's Pan American Cellular Subscriber Group with the introduction of the MicroTAC Digital Personal Communicator Telephone. Weighing less than one pound, they are so compact and lightweight, they fit comfortably into a shirt pocket or purse making them "body friendly."

PERSONAL VIDEO SYSTEM A PC-based video system for Windows introduced by AT&T in conjunction with its NCR subsidiary in the spring of 1993.

PERSONALITY MODULE A small motherboard added to a voice board to give it the "personality" of a proprietary electronic PBX telephone. "Personality" means electrical characteristics and the same button configuration and responsiveness, all of which can be recreated on the screen of a PC which has the voice board installed.

PERSONALIZED RINGING A telephone feature which allows you to select different ringing sounds for your telephone. This feature is useful if you work in a big room with lots of other people and it's hard to tell whose phone is ringing.

NEWTON'S TELECOM DICTIONARY

PERT Project Evaluation and Review Technique. A variation on the Critical Path Method of organizing the completion of projects. Projects are examined for the their worst, best, average completion times. A critical path is determined and overall standards for completion times are created. The PERT technique was created by the military. It is used for organizing complex tasks.

PETABYTE A petabyte is equal to 10 to the 15th. A petabyte is equal to 1,000 terabytes.

PF XFER Power Failure Transfer.

PGA Programmable Gain Amplifier, a part of the Analog Front End.

PH Packet Handler, or Packet Handling function.

PHF Packet Handling Function. The switching capability that processes and routes X.25 virtual calls.

PHz Petahertz (10 to the 15th power hertz). See also SPECTRUM DESIGNATION OF FREQUENCY.

PHANTOM CIRCUIT A circuit derived from two suitably arranged pairs of wires, called side circuits, with each pair of wires being a circuit in itself and at the same time acting as one conductor of the phantom.

PHASE A Phase A is the first part of a fax machine's call process. It is the call establishment. It occurs when transmitting and receiving units connect over the phone line, recognizing one another as fax machines. This is the start of the handshaking procedure. See PHASE B.

PHASE B Phase B is the second part of a fax machine's call process. It is the premessage procedure, where the answering machine identifies itself, describing its capabilities in a burst of digital information packed in frames comforting to the HDLC standard. See PHASE C.

PHASE C Phase C is the third part of a fax machine's call process. It is the fax transmission portion of the operation. This step consists of two parts C1 and C2 which take place simultaneously. Phase C1 deals with synchronization, line monitoring and problem detection. Phase C2 includes data transmission. See PHASE D.

PHASE D Phase D is the fourth part of a fax machine's call process. This phase begins once a page has been transmitted. Both the sender and receiver revert to using HDLC packets as during Phase B. If the sender has further pages to transmit, it sends an MPS and Phase C recommences for the following page. See PHASE E.

PHASE E Phase E is the fifth part of a fax machine's call process. This phase is the call release portion. The side that transmitted last sends a DCN frame and hangs up without awaiting a response.

PHASE DELAY See ENVELOPE DELAY.

PHASE DISTORTION An unwanted modification of a transmitted signal caused by the non-uniform transmission of the different frequency components of the signal. Same as Delay Distortion.

PHASE HIT In telephony, the unwanted and significant shifting in phase of an analog signal. As defined by AT&T: any case where the phase of a 1004 HZ test signal shifts more than 20 degrees. Also, error-causing events more severe than phase jitter, especially for data transmission equipment using PSK modulation.

PHASE JITTER In telephony, the measurement, in degrees out of phase, that an analog signal deviates from the referenced phase of the main data-carrying signal. Phase jitter is often caused by alternating current components in a network.

PHASE LOCK LOOP In electronics, a circuit that acts as a phase detector by comparing the frequency of a known oscillator with an incoming signal and then feeds back the output of the detector to keep the oscillator in phase with the incoming frequency.

PHASE MODULATION One of three ways to change a sine wave (or L signal) to let it carry information. In this case, the phase of the sine wave is changed as the information to be carried is changed. See PHASE SHIFT KEYING and MODULATION.

PHASE SHIFT A change in the time or amplitude that a signal is delayed with respect to a reference signal.

PHASE SHIFT KEYING Used for transmitting digital signals over analog phone lines. Some modems use phase shift keying. Picture a sine wave. The sine wave is the carrier. We want to place a digital signal on it. We want the signal to change in some way to reflect the presence of a "1" or the absence of a one, i.e. a zero. In phase shift keying, we simply change the phase of the signal. See the diagrams in the APPENDIX.

PHASING The process of ensuring that both sending and receiving facsimile machines start at the same position on a page.

PHASOR Temporary buffer storage that compensates for slight differences in data rate between TDM I/O ports and devices.

PHENOLIC INSULATING MATERIALS A type of insulating materials, one of which is bakelite. Now no longer used.

PHI 1. PBX-to-Host Interface. The same as CPI (Computer to PBX Interface) but it puts the PBX first, which is the way many telephone manufacturers prefer to see it. It refers to a connection between a telephone system and a computer, such that the computer can signal the telephone system to switch calls and the telephone system can signal the computer when it has switched them. There are major advantages in joining a telephone system to a computer. For a much greater explanation, see OAI, which stands for OPEN APPLICATION INTERFACE. 2. PHI is also a Northern Telecom term for Packet Handler Interface.

PHOENIX MCI's ill-fated order entry system that never rose from the dead, i.e. never worked.

PHONE PHREAKS Communication hobbyists. People, usually kids, who like to figure out how the telephone network works and sometimes make free calls on the network by figuring a way to bypass billing mechanisms. Phone Phreaks have become Computer Phreaks with the boom of microcomputers and the advent of out-of-band signaling, making it a lot more difficult to make long distance calls for free.

PHONEMAIL A ROLM term for Voice Mail. Rolm's PhoneMail is a voice messaging system that provides telephone answering (with the user's own greeting), the capability to store and forward voice messages and the capability to turn on a message waiting light or message on the recipient's phone. PhoneMail can be used positively to speed the flow of information. It can also be used negatively to allow the user to "hide behind" the system and avoid the outside world and anyone in the outside world who might actually want to buy something. See also VOICE MAIL.

PHONEME A voice recognition term. The minimal significant structural unit in the sound system of any language that can be used to distinguish one word from another. For example, the p of pit and the b of bit are considered two separate phonemes, while the p or spin is not. These minimal sound units comprise words.

PHONENET Farallon's twist on Apple's local area network called LocalTalk. PhoneNet uses standard one pair UTP (unshielded twisted pair) wiring for networking. PhoneNet is compatible with LocalTalk.

PHONESMART A name for a bundle of features NY Telephone provides from selected digital central office. They include: Call Return — automatically dials the number of the last person who called. Repeat Dialing — redials the last number called. Call Trace — forwards the number, the date and time of the last call received to New York Telephone's Annoyance Call Bureau.

PHONETIC ALPHABET A list of standard words used to identify letters in a message transmitted by radio or telephone. The following are the authorized words, listed in order, for each letter in the alphabet: Alpha, Bravo, Charlie, Delta, Echo, Foxtrot, Golf, Hotel, India, Juliet, Kilo Lima, Mike, November, Oscar, Papa, Quebec, Romeo, Sierra, Tango, Uniform, Victor, Whiskey, X-ray, Yankee, Zulu.

PHOSPHOR Substance which glows when struck by electrons. The back of a picture tube face is coated with phosphor.

PHOTOCONDUCTIVE EFFECT Some non-metallic materials exhibit a marked increase in electrical conductivity when they absorb photon or light energy. This is called the photoconductive effect. The conductivity increase is due to the additional free carriers generated when photon energies are absorbed in electronic transitions. The rate at which free carriers are generated and the length of time they persist in conducting states (their lifetime) determines the amount of conductivity change.

PHOTOCONDUCTIVITY The conductivity increase exhibited by some nonmetallic materials, resulting from the free carriers generated when photon (i.e. light) energy is absorbed in electronic transistions. The rate at which free carriers are generated, the mobility of the carriers, the length of time they persist in conducting states (their lifetime) are some of the factors that determine the extent of conductivity charge. See PHOTOCONDUCTIVE EFFECT.

PHOTOCONDUCTOR 1. Any transducer that produces a current which varies in accordance with the incident light energy. A fiber optic communications term. 2. Photoconductor is also material, available in many forms (sheets, belts, and drums), which changes in electrical conductivity when acted upon by light. Electrophotography (a form of facsimile machine printing) relies on the action of light to selectively change the potential of a charged photoconductive surface, creating areas receptive to an oppositely charged toner, thus making the latent charged-image visible.

PHOTOCURRENT The current that flows through a photosensitive device (such as a photodiode) as the result of exposure to radiant power. Internal gain, such as that in an avalanche photodiode, may enhance or increase the current flow but is a distinct mechanism.

PHOTODETECTOR In a lightwave system, a device which turns pulses of light into bursts of electricity.

PHOTOELECTRIC EFFECT The emission of electrons by a material when it is exposed to light. Albert Einstein received a Nobel Prize for explaining this phenomenon. Amazingly, he never received one for his brilliant theories of relativity.

PHOTON The fundamental unit of light and other forms of electromagnetic energy. Photons are to optical fibers what electrons are to copper wires. Like electrons they have a wave motion.

PHOTONIC LAYER The lowest of four layers of Sonet capability, which specifies the kind of fiber to be used including sensitivity and laser type. See SONET.

PHOTONICS The technology that uses light particles (photons) to carry information over hair-thin fibers of very pure glass.

PHOTOTRANSISTOR A transistor that detects light and amplifies the resulting electrical signal. Light falling on the base-collector junction generates a current, which is amplified internally.

PHOTOVOLTAIC Adjective to describe material which develops voltage and electrical current when light shines on it.

PHOTOVOLTAIC EFFECT Using light to produce electricity. Shine light on a device, typically a "cell." If the device produces electricity, that's called the photovoltaic effect. It's not very efficient at present. Less than 10% of the light energy emerges as electricity. But it's getting better.

PHYSICAL ADDRESS A six digit number giving the physical location of an extension within the Rolm CBX. The number is in the form of xxyyzz, where xx=shelf, yy=slot and zz=channel.

PHYSICAL COLOCATION A local exchange carrier (LEC) provides space within its the builing housing its central office to other local phone companies, to interconnect companies or to users (interconnectors) to place their equipment. Typically it's done to connect circuits — transmission or switching — to the phone company's central office. The interconnector installs, maintains, and repairs its own equipment, while the LEC provides power, environmental conditioning, and conduit and riser space for the interconnector's cable.

PHYSICAL CONNECTION The full-duplex physical layer association between adjacent PHYs in an FDDI ring.

PHYSICAL FORMATTING The second step in structuring a hard drive so that you may write to it. Physical formatting follows partitioning.

PHYSICAL LAYER The wires, cables, and interface hardware that connect devices on the network. Within the OSI model, the physical layer is the lowest level of network processing, below the link layer, that is concerned with the electrical, mechanical and handshaking procedures over the interface that connects a device to a transmission medium.

PHYSICAL LAYER MEDIUM DEPENDENT The Physical Layer sublayer that defines the media independent portion of the Physical Layer in FDDI. Items defined by PMD include transmit and receive power levels, connector requirements, and fiber optic cable requirements.

PHYSICAL LAYER PROTOCOL The Physical Layer sublayer that defines the media independent portion of the Physical Layer in FDDI. Items defined by the PMD include transmit and receive power levels, connector requirements, and fiber optic cable requirements.

PHYSICAL SIGNALING SUBLAYER PLS. In a LAN or MAN system, that portion of the OSI Physical Layer that interfaces with the medium access control sublayer and performs bit symbol encoding and transmission, bit symbol reception and decoding, and optional isolation functions.

PHYSICAL UNIT PU. In IBM's SNA, the component that manages and monitors the resources of a node, such as attached links and adjacent link stations. PU types follow the same classification as node types.

PHYSICAL UNIT CONTROL POINT PUCP. In SNA, the component that provides a subset of the system-services control point (SSCP) within a node. Types 1, 2 and 4 nodes contain a PUCP, while a Type 5 (host) contains a SSCP.

PIA Personal Information Appliance. A name for a product most people call a Personal Digital Assistant (PDA).

PIC 1. See PRIMARY INTEREXCHANGE CARRIER. 2. Plastic Insulated Conductor. Conductors covered with an extruded coating of plastic. 3. Also an imaging term. Picture Image Compression. Intel-DVI Technology's on-line still image compression algorithm. See DVI. 4. Personal Intelligent Communicator. A General Magic term for a product most other people called a Personal Digital Assistnt. See PDA.

PICK The computer operating system of VMark Computer Inc. Pick is a neat operating system that unfortunately never really caught on.

PICK-AND-PLACE The manufacturing operation in which components are selected and placed in the correct position on a substrate for the purpose of interconnection to the substrate. This is most commonly done with a programmable machine equipped with a robot arm.

PICKUP Means you can answer a call from your phone. There all sorts of "pickups." The most common is GROUP PICKUP. Here you are part of a group and you can answer — from your phone — the call of anybody in that group, usually by punching a digit or a button or two. There's also NIGHT PICKUP, which typically allows anyone to answer an incoming call after hours, again by punching down a digit or a button or two. In TELECONNECT Magazine, we have one GROUP PICKUP. Everybody in the company belongs to that Group and everyone can answer everyone else's phone. We believe this simplifies things. It also allows anyone, anywhere, from any phone, to play telephone attendant, answering any and all incoming calls and transferring them through the system.

PICKUP GROUP A telephone can be placed into one of four Call Pickup Groups. A call ringing at a telephone within a Pickup Group can be picked up by any other telephone within the same Pickup Group.

PICKUP PATTERN A determination of the directions from which a microphone is sensitive to sound waves. It varies with the mike element and mike design. The two most common pickup patterns are omni- and uni-directional.

PICO Prefix meaning one-trillionth.

PICOFARAD One-trillionth of a farad. A unit of capacitance usually used to designate capacitance unbalance between pairs and capacitance unbalance of the two wires of a pair to ground.

PICOSECOND One-millionth of a millionth of a second. NANO is a billionth of a second, (or, for those in England, Australia or New Zealand, one thousand millionth of a second).

PICS Product Inventory Control System.

PICTURE ELEMENT See PIXEL.

PICTUREPHONE AT&T's trademark for a video telephone that permitted the user to see as well as talk with the person at the distant end. It was introduced in 1963 but failed in the marketplace when AT&T discovered no one wanted to pay $100 a month and more for it. AT&T picked up on the name Picturephone and came out with an offering called Picturephone Meeting Service which provided full video Teleconferencing for business available through rented rooms or through equipment sold or rented to corporations. We believe, as of writing, AT&T has abandoned Picturephone, the product, and has closed down the Picturephone Meeting Service rooms it rented to corporations at one stage. In January, 1992 AT&T introduced a product called VIDEOPHONE 2500, which transmitted moving (albeit slowly-moving) color pictures over normal analog phone lines. See VIDEOPHONE 2500.

PICTUREPHONE MEETING SERVICE An AT&T service once provided under experimental tariff. It combined TV techniques with voice transmission. PMS is usually only available between telephone company-located picturephone centers. Most (we think all) have now been closed down. The venture was losing too much money.

PIECE Productivity, Information, Education, Creativity, Entertainment. Microsoft's trick for remembering the big five multimedia computing applications.

PIEPSER The german word for beeper. Also the name of a small beeper made by Swatch and sold by BellSouth.

PIESIO The Greek prefix meaning near.

PIEZO-ELECTRIC CRYSTAL A type of crystal which, when subjected to mechanical stress, generates current; or which, when subjected to varying electrical stresses, generates mechanical movement. Most familiar type is Rochelle Salts crystal. An old radio term.

PIF Program Information File, which contains information about how Windows should run a non-Windows application, such as how much memory it needs. Windows uses this information to run the application in the most efficient way.

PIGTAIL 1. Multiple pieces of short cable with single circuit connectors connected to a multi-conductor cable. 2. A short, permanently attached piece of optical fiber used to link the transmitter and receiver to the transmission fiber.

PIGTAIL ANTENNA The standard cellular antenna for a car. The term "pigtail" refers to the spring-like section in the lower third of the antenna, the phasing coil.

PILOT NUMBER Identifies a Hunt Group or Distribution Group.

PILOT-MAKE-BUSY CIRCUIT A circuit arrangement by which trunks provided over a carrier system are made busy to the switching equipment in the event of carrier system failure, or during a fade of the radio system.

PIN 1. Procedure Interrupt Negative. A fax term. 2. Positive Intrinsic Negative. Type of photodetector used to sense lightwave energy and then to convert it into electrical signals. See PIN DIODE. 3. Pesonal Identification Number. See PERSONAL IDENTIFICATION NUMBER.

PIN DIODE A photodiode made with an intrinsic layer of undoped material between doped P and N layers and used as a lightwave detector.

PIN NUMBER Personal Identification Number. A group of characters entered as a secret code to gain access to a computer system, such as the one that completes long distance calls. See PERSONAL IDENTIFICATION NUMBER.

PIN PHOTODIODE An optical detector that converts light into electricity. This type is the typical diode used in a fiber optic receiver.

PINCUSHION DISTORTION When a video screen is distorted — with the top, bottom and sides pushing in — the screen is said to be suffering pincushion distortion.

PING A program that is useful for testing and debugging networks. It sends an ICMP Echo packet to a specified host, and waits for a reponse. It reports success or failure and statistics about its operation.

PING PONG A method of getting full duplex data transmission over a two wire circuit by rapidly alternating the transmission direction. See PING PONGING.

PING PONGING Routing that causes a packet to bounce back and forth between two modes.

PINK NOISE Noise in which power distribution is logarithmic through the spectrum, with an equal amount of power in each octave.

PINOUTS Pin configurations for cabling. In other words, which pin connects to which cable. Not all pins are always connected. Not all cables always connected.

PINOSECOND One-trillionth of a second. One-millionth of a microsecond.

PIPE A communications process within the operating system that acts as an interface between a computer's devices (keyboard, disk drives, memory, and so on) and an applications program. A pipe simplifies the development of application programs by "buffering" a program from the intricacies of the hardware or the software that controls the hardware; the application developer writes code to a single pipe, not to several individual devices. A pipe is also used for program-to-program communications.

PIPELINING 1. Executing instructions by breaking them into component parts and processing them in parallel to reduce cycle time and increase the computer's performance. 2. In imaging, pipelining lets an imaging card start compessing and writing the image to disk while it is still being scanned.

PITA Abbreviation for "Pain In The Ass;" commonly used on E-mail and BBSs (Bulletin Board Systems).

PITCH CONTROL Variable control for increasing or decreasing the speed of a tape deck or turntable.

PIU Path Information Unit in SNA.

PIXEL PIcture ELement. The smallest unit of area of a video screen image. The single point on a CRT display. The single point in a facsimile transmission. The image you see on your screen is the result of some pixels being on and others off. A pixel is one of the phosphor elements that coat the inside of a CRT tube. Pixels glow when struck by an electron beam. The number of pixels in a monitor display is usually expressed as, say, 640 x 480, with the first number (640) being the number of pixels in each horizontal row and the second number (480) the number of rows displayed. Resolution (crispness and clarity of text and images) improves as the number of pixels displayed increases.

PIXRECTS Pixrects is the primary graphics programming interface in the SunView Window System from Sun Microsystems. It is replaced in the OpenWindows XView toolkit by the Pixwin interface, which is a thin layer on top of Xlib.

PIXWIN Pixwin is the primary graphics programming interface in the XView toolkit from Sun Microsystems. Pixwin is a thin layer on top of Xlib.

PJ-327 A double RCA dipole plug for connecting a headset into a PBX console. When you buy a headset you need to specify — 4-pin modular jack (for connecting to a telephone) or two prong plug (for connecting to a PBX console).

PL Private Line.

PL/1 Programming Language One (IBM).

PLACE CALL There will be two types of calls: person calls and place calls. I make a place call when I call a phone number which ends in one designated, fixed RJ-11 jack attached to the wall or floor. I make a person call when I call a phone number which doesn't necessarily end on a fixed place. A typical person call might be a cellular or wireless phone call. It might also be a service like MCI's Personal 800 Service. The major characteristic of a person call is that I am calling a person and I don't know where that person is. As a result, the person I called might answer my call anywhere — from his car, from vacation home, from his wireless phone, etc.

PLAINTEXT A message which is not encrypted.

PLAN A route to an end or objective usually achieved accidentally and often written in hindsight. Derived from the expression: "Most people spend more time planning their annual vacation than they do planning their careers."

PLANAR BOARD IBM's new name for a motherboard in their new series of System/2 Personal Computers. A motherboard is the main board in a PC on which the main CPU, the main memory, the clock and sundry other things like serial and parallel ports are mounted. Other boards, i.e. graphics boards, are plugged into the motherboard. Thus the expression "motherboard." No one knows why IBM dropped the word. Maybe it was too risque? Maybe they included more on their motherboards in the System/2 series that they would no longer function as motherboards? Maybe a feminist group of mothers objected?

PLANT A general term for all equipment used by a telephone company to provide telecommunications services. Usually divided into outside and inside plant.

PLANT HUMP A very friendly term for a craftsperson in a phone company — installer, splicer, underground cable guy — who works hard with outside phone equipment, often under adverse conditions and whose labors tend to be undervalued, particularly by the white collar, pencil pushers back at headquarters. There is a badge of honor to being a "plant hump." These are the people who bring phone service to your door. This definition contributed by Steve Marcus of New York Telephone, who readily acknowledges he is one of the pencil pushers back at headquarters.

PLANT TEST NUMBERS Virtually every 800 IN-WATS number has a plant test number. This is its equivalent seven digit local number. That number looks like a normal local seven digit number, with a standard three-digit central office exchange code and a four-digit extension. The purpose of plant test numbers is to allow the telephone company to test the local part of the incoming 800 number by simply dialing that number. For example, TELECOM LIBRARY and TELECONNECT Magazine, which published this dictionary have an 800 number — 800-LIBRARY (or 800-542-7279). The plant test number of the first line of that 800-LIBRARY group is 212-206-6870. The second line is 212-206-6871 and so on. It is valuable to know the plant test numbers of your incoming WATS lines so you can test the local loop part of those lines. The local loop part is the part which typically gives the most problem. It is, unfortunately, the only part of your 800 lines you can test yourself — unless you ask someone (or several people) to call you regularly on your 800 lines, just to test them. You can get plant test numbers out of your local and/or your long distance carrier. When they tell you those numbers are "not available," beg a little. They are available and you are entitled to them. Calling plant test numbers costs exactly what a normal long distance IN-WATS call on that line costs. So keep your test calls short. You should call your plant test numbers once a day.

PLANTHUMP A colloquial word for a telephone company craftsperson. It derives from the term "plant," a telephone company word used to describe their "factory" — i.e. everything from their inside plant, their central office switch, to their outside plant, which includes wire strung on telephone poles. In British slang, "hump" means to exert oneself. Planthump is a term of endearment in the telehone industry. Definition courtesy, Steve Marcus, New York Telephone.

PLAR Private Line, Automatic Ringdown. In telecommunications, leased voice circuit that connects two single instruments together. When either handset is lifted, the other instrument automatically rings.

PLASMA An ionized gas with a mixture of positive and negative electrons. See PLASMA DISPLAY.

PLASMA DISPLAY Type of flat visual display device in which selected electrodes, part of a grid of crisscross electrodes in a gas-filled panel, are energized, causing the gas to be ionized and light to be emitted. Some computer use plasma displays. They're fabulous, and quite expensive.

PLASTICIZER A chemical agent added in compounding plastics to make them softer and more flexible.

PLAT An imaging term. When a CAD/CAM plotter prints a large drawing, it's called a plat.

PLATE The anode in a vacuum tube, which collects the electrons emitted by the filament.

PLATE BATTERY The source of E.M.F. connected in the plate circuit to give the plate element its positive charge.

PLATE VOLTAGE The potential applied to the plate of the vacuum tube by the plate voltage supply.

PLATEN A cylinder in a printer or typewriter around which the paper goes and which the printing mechanism strikes to produce an impression.

PLATFORM A loosely-defined word for a software operating system and/or open hardware, which an outsider could write software for. If every phone system were a platform, then every owner of that phone system could buy outside-produced software and have his phone system work more to his liking. That's the objective of creating a "platform." See also OAI and PLATFORM INDEPENDENCE.

PLATFORM INDEPENDENCE A term from IBM and Metaphor Computer Systems. The idea, they say, is to produce a layer of software that would rest atop any operating system on any piece of hardware. The applications developers would write their software just once, rather than start from scratch each time they wanted get their software working on a different computer. If the whole idea sounds rather daunting, you're right.

PLATTER A circular data storage medium located within a hard disk or diskette.

PLAYBACK A multimedia term. Playback is the process of viewing multimedia materials created by an author. Playback can include a range of activities, from viewing a single video clip to participating in a series of interactive multimedia training modules. Some playback applications (for example many training and presentation applications) are sold separately from their authoring applications. However, many developers are selling authoring and playback capabilities in a single product.

PLAYBACK HEAD The part which converts the magnetic information on the tape or disk into an electrical signal. Moving the magnetic fields on the medium (tape or disk) past the playback head generates a tiny voltage, which is picked up in a conductor (a coil) in the payback head and sent onto the electronic equipment where it is amplified or transmitted.

PLCP Physical Layer Convergence Protocol. The part of the physical layer that adapts the transmission facility to handle DQDB functions as defined in IEEE 802.6-1990.

PLENUM In some modern buildings, the ducts carrying the air conditioning are not metal ducts but actually are part of the ceiling. This is called a plenum ceiling. Most cities now have rules and regulations which say that if you run cabling through these plenum ceilings, you must not use cabling sheathed in PVC (polyvinyl chloride), the standard jacketing of most electrical cable. The reason is that PVC burns and emits toxic smoke ferociously. Plenum cable is low smoking so that if it catches fire it won't circulate toxic smoke through the vent system and suffocate everyone. Plenum cabling is often made of teflon. It's much more expensive than normal cabling.

PLENUM AREA The space between the drop ceiling and the floor above. Continuous throughout the length and width of each commercial building floor.

PLENUM CABLE Cable specifically designed for use in a plenum (the space above a suspended ceiling used to circulate air back to the heating or cooling system in a building). Plenum cable has insulated conductors often jacketed with polyvinylidene diflouride (PVDF) material to give them low flame spread and low smoke-producing properties. Plenum cable has fully color coded insulated copper conductors and is available in various pair sizes. It can be either 22 or 24 AWG.

PLESIOCHRONOUS Two signals that are not sourced from the same clock but are nominally at the same frequency to a defined degree of precision. For example, because they are not sourced to the same atomic clock, DS1s (also called T-1s) from MCI and AT&T are plesiochronous. They are arbitrarily close but over the long term will cause slips (frame repeats or deletions due to buffer under or overflow) in digital signals crossing between the two carriers.

PLESIOCHRONOUS NETWORKS Network elements that derive timing from more than one primary reference source. Network elements accommodate minor frequency differences between nodes.

PLMN Public Land Mobile Network.

PLOTTER A type of computer peripheral printer that displays data in two-dimensional graphics form.

PLS Premises Lightwave System.

PLSC Private Line Service Center.

PLUG A male element of a plug/jack connector system. In the Premises Wiring System it provides the means for the user to connect his communications devices to the Communications Outlet as well as the means to disconnect his service at the Network Interface Jack when trouble analysis is required.

PLUG "N" GO A new product IBM introduced in September, 1991. The Plug "N" Go System Solution includes an AS/400 9402 Model DO2, terminals, printers and pre-loaded software, including Operating System/400*, the IBM Application Program Driver and selected Plug "N" Go Applications. The Plug "N" Go System Solution carries a customer satisfaction guarantee. The entire system — hardware, software and application — can be returned within 90 days for a full refund. The guarantee is designed for small businesses and is limited to one per customer. With a pre-loaded Plug "N" Go System Solution, according to IBM, customers can install a Model DO2 and start using the application approximately ten minutes after turning on the system.

PLUG 'N PLAY Manufacturers' concept of how easy it is to install their equipment. "Why it's just plug 'n play," says the manufacturer. In reality, nothing, absolutely nothing, is plug 'n play. It's a fantasy concept.

PLUG-COMPATIBLE Devices made by different manufacturers that are totally interchangeable. The word derives from the fact that the devices are so completely interchangeable that you can simply unplug one device and plug in another device made by different manufacturer and it will work the same, or better.

PLUG-IN STATIONS The telephone need stays constant for all types of phones. For ease in phone "moves" and rearrangements, all phones are provided (and installed) as plug-in instruments.

PLUGBOARD A telephone switchboard on which connections are made by a jack and an attached cord representing a trunk (the male jack and the cord) and a female plug (the telephone extension). Early plugboards needed an operator to place outside calls and connect incoming calls. All calls were completed by the operator. Plugboards were common in the days of "PBXs." Then came PABXs (Private Automated Branch Exchanges) and you could dial out without the help of an operator. Then electronic PABXs came in and you could dial directly in to many internal extensions, using a feature called

DID (Direct Inward Dial). Now PABXs are called PBXs because they're all automatic. Plugboards are rapidly disappearing. They do have two great uses, however. First, operators who grew up with them, still like them. Operators who now live in nursing homes like them. Second, because the jack and plug make a pure metallic connection, they're great for data transmission and occasional data switching.

PLV An imaging term. Production Level Video. DVI Technology's highest quality motion video compression algorithm. It's about 120-1 compression. Compression is done "off-line". i.e. non-real time, and playback (decompression) is real time. Independent of the technology in use, off-line compression will produce a better image quality than real time since more time and processing power is used per frame.

PLY One layer in a composite.

PM Performance Monitoring. Gives a measure of the quality of service and identifies degrading or marginally operating systems (before an alarm would be generated). Digital signal parameters, including errored seconds and out of frame, measure the integrity of a communication channel as defined in AT&T Compatibility Bulletin 149 (CB 149).

PMD Physical Medium Dependant. The bottom half of BISDN Layer 1.

PMMU Paged Memory Management Unit. Macintosh computers equipped with a PMMU may use virtual memory with the System 7 operating system.

PMN Indicates loss of ac power at the far-end terminal.

PMS 1. Picturephone Meeting Service. An AT&T service once provided under experimental tariff. It combined TV techniques with voice transmission. PMS is usually only available between telephone company-located picturephone centers. Most have now been closed down. The venture was losing too much money.

2. Property Management System, a software program and computer that controls all guest billing and guest services functions in a hotel. In short, the guts of a hotel's computer system. Some telephone systems have a PMS Interface, which allows various degrees of integration between the telephone system and the hotel's computer systems. For example, voice mail could be administered through the hotel's Property Management System.

3. The Pantone Matching System, a universal language for solid-color specification and reproductin. Colors defined by PMS receive a unique number and mixing formula. Consequently, when artists specify a PMS number they can be sure that the final printed product will match the chosen color. But, be careful, PMS colors look different when printed on different papers. The biggest perceived difference is when you print on glossy or mat paper.

PMS INTERFACE An interface that allows telephone system functions (like voice mail) to be administered through a hotel's Property Management System.

PNM Public Network Management.

PNS Personal Number Service is a new concept in telecommunications that assigns a telephone number to a person, not a location, effectively allowing a subscriber to use one number for all calls and helping them manage their incoming communications. The service does not require the user to change any existing phone numbers. The subscriber simply provides the various numbers — office, cellular, pager, fax and home — and instructions on where and when the calls should be routed, and the PNS directs the calls in the order requested by the subscriber.

POGO Post Office Goes Obsolete. When MCI Mail was originally being planned, its code name was POGO. The idea was obvious.

POH Path OverHead. Overhead assigned to and transported with the payload until the payload is demultiplexed. It is used for functions that are necessary to transport the payload. These functions include parity check and trace capability. An AT&T SONET term.

POINT IN CALL PIC. A representation of a sequence of activities that the ASC (AIN Switch Capabilities) performs in setting up and maintaining a basic two-party call. PICs occur in Originating and Terminating BCSMs (Basic Call State Model).

POINT OF INTERFACE The physical telecommunications interface between the LATA access and the interLATA functions. This point establishes the technical interface, the test points, and the points of operational responsibility.

POINT OF PRESENCE POP. Physical place within a LATA where a long distance carrier interfaces with the network of the local ·exchange carrier (LEC), also called the local telephone company. The point at which the local telephone company terminates subscribers circuits for long-distance dial-up or leased-line communications.

POINT OF SALE TERMINAL A special type of computer terminal which is used to collect and store retail sales data. This terminal may be connected to a bar code reader and it may query a central computer for the current price of that item. It may also contain a device for getting authorizations on credit cards.

POINT OF TERMINATION The physical telecommunications interface that establishes the technical interface, the test points and the points of operational responsibility.

POINT SIZE The height of a printed character specified in units called points. A point equals 1/72 inch. Also known as font size.

POINT TO MULTIPOINT A circuit by which a single signal goes from one origination point to many destination points. The classic example is a TV signal (say a Home Box Office program) being broadcast from one satellite to many CATV subscribers all around the country. Not to be confused with a multi-drop circuit.

POINT TO POINT A private circuit, conversation or teleconference in which there is one person at each end, usually connected by some dedicated transmission line. See also POINT TO MULTIPOINT.

POINT TO POINT CONNECTION An uninterrupted connection between one piece of equipment and another.

POINT TO POINT SIGNALING A signaling method where signals must be completely received by an intermediate station before that station can set up a call connection. See END TO END SIGNALING.

POINTER PROCESSING Pointer processing accommodates frequency differences by adjusting the starting position of the payload within the frame. A pointer keeps track of the starting position of the payload.

POISSON See POISSON DISTRIBUTION.

POISSON DISTRIBUTION A mathematical formula named after the French mathematician S. D. Poisson, which indicates the probability of certain events occurring. It is used in traffic engineering to design telephone networks. It is one method of figuring how many trunks you will need in the future based on measurements of past calls. Poisson distribution describes how calls react when they encounter blockage (see QUEUING THEORY for a detailed explanation of blockage). There are two main formulas used today in traffic engineering: Erlang B and Poisson. The Erlang B formula assumes all blocked calls are cleared. This means they disappear, never to reappear. The Poisson formula assumes no blocked calls disappear. The user simply redials and redials. If you use the Poisson method of prediction, you will buy more trunks than if you use Erlang B. Poisson typically overestimates the number of trunks you will need, while Erlang B typically underestimates the number of trunks you will need. There are other more complex but more accurate ways of figuring trunks — Erlang C (blocked calls delayed or queued) and computer simulation. Poisson has been used extensively by AT&T to recommend to its customers the number of trunks they needed. Since AT&T was selling the circuits and preferred its customers to have excellent service, it made sense to use the Poisson formula. As competition in long distance has heated up, as circuits have become more costly and as companies have become more economically-minded (more aware of their rising phone bills), Poisson has become widely ignored.

After I wrote the above definition, Lee Goeller, a noted traffic engineering expert contributed the following definition of Poisson Distribution: A probability distribution developed by E.C. Molina of AT&T in the early 1900s for use in solving problems in telephone traffic (see TRAFFIC

ENGINEERING), although it has many other uses and is widely applied in many fields. When made aware of Poisson's prior effort (circa 1820), Molina gave him full credit and even taught himself French so he could read Poisson in the original. The Poisson distribution assumes a call is in the system for one holding time, whether it is served or not (blocked calls held); the first form of the distribution estimates the probability that exactly X calls will be in the system, while the second estimates the probability that X or more calls will be present. If there are only X trunks to serve the calls, the second form gives the probability of blocking. Although limited tabulations of the Poisson distribution had been made earlier, Molina published an extensive set of tables in 1942. The Poisson distribution slightly overstates the number of trunks needed when compared to the Erlang B distribution (see ERLANG B).

POISSON PROCESS A kind of random process based on simplified mathematical assumptions which makes the development of complex probability functions easier. In traffic theory, the arrival of telephone calls for service is considered a Poisson process. Calls arrive "individually and collectively at random," and the probability of a new call arriving in any time interval is independent of the number of calls already present. A Poisson process should not be confused with the Poisson Distribution, which gives the probability that a certain number of calls will be present if certain additional assumptions are made. See POISSON DISTRIBUTION.

POKE-THROUGH METHOD A distribution method that involves drilling a hole through the floor and poking cables through to terminal equipment from the ceiling space of the floor below. See also CEILING DISTRIBUTION SYSTEMS and NEWTON.

POLAR KEYING A transmission technique for digital signals in which the current flows in opposite directions for 1s and 0s or marks and spaces. It is used in telegraph signaling. It is also known as polar transmission.

POLAR RELAY A relay containing a permanent magnet that centers the armature. The direction of movement of the armature is governed by the direction of current flow.

POLARITY Which side of an electrical circuit is the positive? Which is the negative? Polarity is the term describing which is which. Knowing polarity is not critical with rotary phones. They will work irrespective of which way the telephone circuit's polarity is. Touchtone phones, however, need correct polarity for their touchtone pads to work. How to tell? If you can receive an incoming call, can speak on the phone clearly, but can't "break" dial tone by touching a digit on your touchtone pad, then the polarity of your line is reversed. Simply reverse the red and green wires. Some electronic phones behind PBXs and key systems are also sensitive to polarity. If in doubt, simply reverse the wires. In video, reversed polarity results in a negative picture.

POLARIZATION Characteristic of electromagnetic radiation (e.g. lightwave, radio or microwave) where the electric-field vector of the wave energy is perpendicular to the main direction, or vector, of the electromagnetic beam.

POLISHING Preparing a fiber end by moving the end over an abrasive material.

POLITENESS The most acceptable hypocrisy. Mostly seen before the sale.

POLITICS A clash of interests masquerading as a clash of principles. Also, the technique by which most telephone systems are bought in large corporations.

POLL In data communications, an individual control message from a central controller to an individual station on a multipoint network inviting that station to send if it has any traffic to send. See POLLING.

POLL CYCLE The complete sequence in which stations are polled on a polled network.

POLL/FINAL BIT Bit in HDLC frame control field. If frame is a command, bit is a poll bit asking station to reply. If frame is a response, bit is a final bit identifying last frame in message.

POLLING Refers to some form of data or fax network arrangement whereby a central computer or fax machine asks each remote location in turn (and very quickly) whether they want to send some information. The purpose is to give each user or each remote data terminal an opportunity to transmit and receive information on a circuit or using facilities which are being shared. Polling is typically used on a multipoint or multidrop line. Polling is done to save money on telephone lines.

POLLING DELAY Communications control procedure where a master station systematically invites tributary stations on a multipoint circuit to transmit data. Polling delay is a measure of the time to transmit and receive on a polled network versus a direct point-to-point circuit.

POLSK POLarization Shift Keying.

POLYETHYLENE A family of insulating (thermoplastic) materials derived from polymerization of ethylene gas. They are basically pure hydrocarbon resins with excellent dielectric properties. Used extensively in cables.

POLYMER A material having molecules of high molecular weight formed by polymerization of lower molecular weight molecules.

POLYMERIZATION A chemical reaction in which low molecular weight molecules unite with each other to form molecules with higher molecular weights.

POLYOLEFIN Any of the polymers and copolymers of the ethylene family of hydrocarbons.

POLYPROPYLENE A thermoplastic similar to polyethylene but stiffer and having a higher softening point (temperature) and excellent electric properties.

POLYVINYLCHLORIDE PVC. A thermoplastic material composed of polymers of vinyl chloride. A tough, water and flame-retardant thermoplastic insulation material that is commonly used in the jackets of building cables when fire retardant, but not smoke retardant properties are required. Unfortunately, it burns and gives out noxious gases which kill. PVC can't be run in air return ducts, also called plenum ducts and most towns, therefore, don't allow PVC to be run in their plenum ceilings. See PLENUM.

POLYVINYLIDENE DIFLUORIDE PVDF. A fluoropolymer material that is resistant to heat and used in the jackets of plenum cable.

PONY EXPRESS Out of the summer haze bursts a horse and rider, swiftly approaching a lonely sod building on the prairie. Arriving in a cloud of dust, the rider leaps from his horse and heads for a water barrel to quench his thirst. Meanwhile, a leather sack filled with mail is whisked off the tired horse and thrown over the saddle of a fresh mount. Within two minutes, the rider is gone, galloping toward the far horizon. This young man in a hurry was one of some 200 Pony Express riders who carried the mail in a giant relay between St. Joseph, Missouri, and Sacramento, California, a distance of 1,966 miles, in ten days or less. Changing horses every ten to fifteen miles at swing stations, and switching riders at home stations after a run of 75 miles or more, the riders averaged 250 miles a day. During the short time the Pony Express was in operation — from April 1860, through October, 1861 — its rider defied hostile Indians, blazing desert heat, and bone-chilling blizzards to travel a total of 650,000 miles with 34,753 pieces of mail. To save weight the letters they carried were written on tissue-thin paper as postage cost $10 an ounce, later cut to $2. The best time ever achieved was in March 1861, when Lincoln's inaugural address was carried from Missouri to California in seven days, 17 hours.

The Pony Express was organized by stagecoach operator William Hepburn Russell, who had been convinced by a group of prominent Californians that an overland mail route to their state was feasible. Russell's business partners opposed the venture because it was not protected by a U.S. mail contract. (They had competition and de-regulation even in those days.) But Russell went ahead, building stations and purchasing 500 top quality Indian horses. In advertising for riders, he hinted at the hazardous nature of the job by asking for "small, daring young men, preferably orphans." The riders received board and keep and were paid $100 to $150 a month. Their average age was 19, but one rider, David Jay, was 13, and William F. Cody, who became famous as "Buffalo Bill," was 15. In a further effort to save weight, a rider usually carried only a pistol and a knife. He was expected to out-run the Indians, not out-fight them.

The Pony Express days of glory ended abruptly in 1861 following completion

NEWTON'S TELECOM DICTIONARY

of the transcontinental telegraph. Russell's firm lost more than $200,000 in the venture, but the daring of the Pony Express riders caught the imagination of every American, and their exploits became an important part of the legend and lore of the nation.

The above, copyright 1979 by Panarizon Publishing Corp.

POOL A collection of things available to all for the asking or the dialing. A modem pool is a collection of modems typically attached to a PBX. Dial a special extension and you can use the modem, which answers that extension (or one of the extensions in the hunt group) to make a data call. Pooling is sharing. The purpose of having a "pool" is to avoid buying everybody one of whatever it is you're pooling. Actually, "pooling" is a fancy word for something we've been doing in the telephone business for the past 100 years — sharing. We started sharing lines, then sharing switches, then sharing voice mail devices, now we're sharing equipment, like modems.

POP 1. Point-Of-Presence. A long distance carrier's office in your local community (defined as your LATA). A POP is the place your long distance carrier, called an IntereXchange Carrier (IXC), terminates your long distance lines just before those lines are connected to your local phone company's lines or to your own direct hookup. Each IXC can have multiple POPs within one LATA. All long distance phone connections go through the POPs. 2. Short for "population." One "pop" equals one person. In the cellular industry, systems are valued financially based on the population of the market served.

POPS A cellular industry term for its customers or its potential customers. (It varies with usage.) Pops refers to members of the population.

POPULATED Occupied by chips on printed circuit boards.

POP-UP PROGRAM A memory-resident program that is loaded into memory but isn't visible until you press a certain key combination or until a certain event occurs, such as receiving a message. See also TSR.

PORT 1. An entrance to or exit from a network. 2. The physical or electrical interface through which one gains access. 3. The interface between a process or program and a communications or transmission facility. 4. A point in the computer or telephone system where data may be accessed. Peripherals — like call accounting devices — are connected to ports. The two most common ports are the paralle and serial ports. 5. To move a process, program or subroutine from one processor to controller to another ("port it over").

PORT SELECTOR Another name for a dataPBX. Since the advent of LANs (local area networks) these devices have been getting a bad rap. Not fair. These gadgets are really great at transmitting and switching huge number of low-speed asynchronous lines. If you put this sort of traffic on a LAN, you could severely mess up its performance. Some port selectors have data throughputs in excess of 20 million bits per second.

PORT SHARING DEVICE A system which connects multiple lines to a single port by means of a manual or automatic line selection method.

PORTABILITY 1. The ability of a customer to take his telephone number from place to place and, for 800 numbers, from one long-distance company to another. 2. The ability of software designed for one computer system to be used on other systems. Little software outside MS-DOS software for IBM and IBM clone computers is portable. UNIX software is portable to an extent.

PORTABLE A one-piece, self-contained cellular telephone — easily carried in a brief case or purse. Portables normally have a built-in antenna and rechargeable battery and operate with six-tenths of one watt (0.6 watt) of power. Car cellular phones operate with three watts.

PORTABLE CELLULAR PHONE Also known as a "hand-held phone". Refers to a lightweight, compact cellular handset that incorporates a battery power supply, and can be used without any peripheral power or antenna. See PORTABLE.

PORTRAIT Most computer screens are horizontal, i.e. they are wider than they are high. In the new language of computer screens, this is called "landscape." When a computer screen is higher than it is wide, it's called "portrait." Some computer screens can actually work both ways. Some even have a small mercury switch in them that determines which way the screen is standing (portrait or landscape) and will adjust their image accordingly. See also PORTRAIT MODE.

PORTRAIT MODE 1. In facsimile, the mode of scanning lines across the shorter dimension of a rectangular original. CCITT Group 1, 2 and 3 facsimile machines use portrait mode. 2. In computer graphics, the orientation of a page in which the shorter dimension is horizontal. The opposite is called landscape mode. See also PORTRAIT.

POS Point Of Service. Also called Point of Presence. See POINT OF PRESENCE.

POSITION A telephone console at a switchboard manned, er, staffed by an attendant, or operator, or agent, or whatever the latest fashionable word is.

POSITIVE ACTION DIGIT A digit that must be dialed before a PBX will advance a call to a higher-cost route. The WATS lines are busy. Time on the queue is over. It's time to move the call to the more expensive direct distance dial. Before it can go that route, the caller must punch in a positive action digit. This affirms that the user knows he is now making a more expensive call. It causes him to think twice, allegedly.

POSIX Portable Operating Systems for computer environments. See WINDOWS NT.

POST Power-On Self-Test

POST DIAL DELAY PDD. The time from when the last digit is dialed to the moment the phone rings at the receiving location.

POST OFFICE Any part of an e-mail system that directors or delivers mail. But, says PC Magazine's David Stone, to refer to a particular level of mail handling, the term post office needs a modifier. A local post office or host post office is the module on a LAN that users directly interact with to send and receive mail. A domain post office is the module that controls the mail delivery within a domain of multiple hosts on a single network.

POST PAY A method of coin phone operation characterized by the operation of a lever or button that causes the collection of deposits after the called party answers. This method of "A" and "Buttons" is still used on coin phones overseas, especially in Great Britain.

POSTALIZE To structure rates or prices so that they are not distance sensitive, but depend on other factors (such as duration of a call, etc.) See also POSTALIZED.

POSTALIZED Long distance phone calls are traditionally billed by the distance they travel. The longer they travel, the more they cost. However, to be competitive (and different) some long distance companies started charging a flat rate per minute — irrespective of how far you called. They called this "postalized" charging — from the fact that Post Office also charges a flat rate irrespective of how far it carries the mail (within the country).

POSTSCRIPT PostScript by Adobe Systems Inc. is the standard page description language for desktop computer systems. It describes type, graphics and halftones as well as the placement of each on the page. The big advantage of PostScript is that it is device independent. Thus if you create a postscript image (text and/or photo and/or drawing), you can print it to a relatively cheap, low quality printer like a laser printer or a magazine quality printer like a Linotronics. PostScript is a printer language, much the same that BASIC is a computer language. By sending your PostScript printer a series of commands, you can make it do almost anything from printing text in a circle to printing foot-high letters to printing halftones. If you need PostScript, buy a printer that has built-in PostScript. If your printer doesn't have built-in PostScript, you may be able to get an external software interpreter but that interpreter will slow down your printer and tie up your computer while printing. See OUTLINE FONT.

POT Techie-slang for POTENTIOMETER.

POTENTIAL The difference in voltage between one point and another. One point is usually ground.

POTENTIOMETER A variable RESISTOR, such as the ubiquitous volume control.

POTS Plain Old Telephone Service. The basic service supplying standard single line telephones, telephone lines and access to the public switched network. Nothing fancy. No added features. Just receive and place calls. Nothing like Call Waiting or Call Forwarding. They are not POTS services. Pronounced POTS, like in pots and pans.

PANS Pretty Amazing New Stuff is a term coined to describe ISDN Capabilities eventually to replace POTS, which is Plain Old Telephone Service.

POWER The term which describes the amount of work an electric current can do in a unit of time. We measure power in WATTS (note we spell it with two "T"s.) A WATT measures the amount of work done in lifting a quarter-pound weight a distance of one yard in one second. Metric WATTS are a little more powerful. They go the distance of one meter. Power is the product of the current in amperes times the voltage, i.e. P = IV. See OHM's LAW.

POWER CONDITIONING Power conditioning is a generic concept to encompass all the methods of protecting sensitive hardware against power fluctuations. When electricity leaves a commercial power generating plant, it is very clean. In fact, most power companies make sure the power they put out is a pure sine wave. Unfortunately, nearly all devices connected to power lines — and the worst are things with motors, like elevators, airconditioners, etc. — create disturbances that pollute the sine wave. As power travels through a wire away from the power plant, it picks up more of these interferences. A pure AC power sine wave appears as a smooth wave. The height of the wave is measured in volts. The wave starts at zero volts and moves to the highest point of 120 volts. The wave then cycles through a low point of -120 volts and back to zero. The speed at which it travels through this cycle is the frequency. Normal frequency in North America is 60 cycles per second (Hz). (In other places it's often 50 cycles per second.) Anything that disrupts this wave can cause hardware or data problems and needs to be regulated.

Power disturbances can be categorized in several ways. A transient, sometimes called a spike or surge, is a very short, but extreme, burst of voltage. Noise or static is a smaller change in voltage. Brownouts and blackouts are the temporary drop in or loss of electrical power. Three types of protection against these three events are available: suppression, isolation, and regulation.

Suppression protects against transients. The most common suppression devices are surge protectors that include circuitry to prevent excess voltage. Although manufacturers originally designed surge protectors to prevent large voltage changes, most have also added circuitry to reduce noise on the line. Isolation protects against noise. Ferro-resonant isolation transformers use a transformer within the circuitry to envelop the sine wave at a slightly higher and lower voltage. Any voltage irregularity that extends beyond this envelope is clamped. Isolation transformers are usually expensive.

Regulation protects against brownouts and blackouts. Regulation modifies the power wave to conform to a nearly pure wave form. The Uninterruptible Power Supply (UPS) is the most commonly used form of regulation. A UPS comes in two varieties, on-line and off-line. An on-line UPS actively modifies the power as it moves through the unit. This is closer to true regulation than the off-line variety. If a power outage occurs, the unit is already active and continues to provide power. The on-line UPS is usually more expensive but provides a nearly constant source of energy during power outages. The off-line UPS monitors the AC line. When power drops, the UPS is activated. The drawback to this method is the slight lag before the off-line UPS jumps into action. That lag is getting shorter as electronics improves. So it's rarely a problem any longer.

Because UPS systems are expensive, most companies attach them only to the most critical devices, such as phone systems, network file servers, routers, and hard disk subsystems. Attaching a UPS to a local area network file server enables the server to properly close files and rewrite the system directory to disk. Sadly, most programs run on the workstation and data stored in their RAM is not saved during a power outage unless each workstation has its own UPS. If the UPS doesn't have its own form of surge protection, it is a good idea to install a surge protector to protect the UPS from transients. Proper use of power conditioning devices greatly reduces telephone system and network maintenance costs. Make sure that proper amperage is available for each system and that all outlets are grounded. Power conditioning devices connected to poorly-grounded outlets offer very little protection.

Studies have shown that total local area network maintenance costs are higher with line-surge suppressors and ferro-resonant isolation transformers alone, than with uninterruptible power supplies.

POWER DISTRIBUTION PANEL A part of the Rolm CBX power distribution system that receives voltages from the main power supply and distributes them to the cabinet shelves.

POWER DOWN The sequence of things you to have to do to turn off a computer or telephone system. Not following the correct power down procedures can cause a loss of data.

POWER FAIL BYPASS A feature that allows analog trunks to be answered if your commercial AC power or your telephone system crashes.

POWER FAILURE BACKUP If your AC power fails, your telephone system can still operate by switching to a backup battery power supply, often called a UPS — Uninterruptible Power Supply.

POWER FAILURE TRANSFER When the commercial AC power fails and there is no backup power source — such as a battery or a generator — this feature switches some of the trunks connected to the phone system to several single line phones, which don't need external power and can draw their power from the phone lines.

POWER LEVEL The measure of signal power at some point. The measure can be referenced to some power level in which case the measurement is expressed in dB (decibels). It may also be referenced to 1 milliwatt in which case the measurement is expressed in dBm.

POWER LINE CARRIER An AC power line can be made to carry high frequency radio waves, which can carry "information," which could be a voice or data call. Over the years many companies have tried power line carrier — a seductively easy method of not having to install conventional phone lines. The results have been poor-to-awful. One day someone will figure a reliable, cheap method.

POWER ON See POWER UP.

POWER OPEN A new operating system which is planned to run on a new super-powerful PC manufactured by a joint IBM-Apple alliance. The idea of the IBM-Apple alliance is make a super-powerful PC that runs virtually every PC operating system imaginable, including MS-DOS, UNIX, Windows, OS/2, Macintosh. The new, all powerful operating system, would be called "Power Open."

POWER PC A goal of a joint IBM-Apple alliance to make a super-powerful PC that runs virtually every PC operating system imaginable, including MS-DOS, UNIX, Windows, OS/2, Macintosh. And the PC would run under a new operating system called "Power Open."

POWER REGULATOR Equipment that regulates the power delivered to a system. Designed to mitigate transients in the commercial electric power source.

POWER SUPPLY That part of a phone system or a computer which converts the normal 120 or 240 volts AC power to AC and DC at the various voltages and frequencies as needed by the components and circuits of a system. Power supplies are usually the least reliable part of modern electronic gadgetry. This is because they take the hits and the garbage power the local utility sends in and also, many manufacturers skimp on the quality of their power supplies. A cheap power supply is not evident immediately. It may take time to break down. Whenever you're having intermittent problems with your phone system or computer, suspect the power supply. Most often you'll be right.

POWER UP The sequence of things you have to do in order to turn a computer or telephone system on. You can't cut corners starting up electronic equipment. It must be done carefully and in the correct order. Always count to ten after turning something off before turning it back on again. See also POWER DOWN.

POWERBOOK Apple's name for a line of laptop Macintosh computers it introduced in late 1991.

POWER, PEAK In a pulsed laser, the maximum power emitted.

PPDN Public Packet Data Network.

PPI Pixels Per Inch. See RESOLUTION.

PPM Northern Telecom term for Periodic Pulse Metering.

PPS 1. Pulses Per Second. 2. Precise Positioning Service. The most accurate dynamic positioning possible with GPS (Global Positioning System), based on the dual frequency P-code. 3. Packets Per Second. 4. The Path Protection Switched ring defined by Bellcore TA-496. PPS is really a fancy name for a duplicated SONET signal traveling over diverse (i.e. different) routes. When one route of network crashes, the other will take over. This enables it to survive service outages caused by cable cuts, earthquakes, lightning strikes and equipment failures. The PPS ring gives a SONET route a greater degree of survivability than other Sonet transmission paths that don't have route diversity.

PPSN Public Packet Switched Network

PRA PRIMARY RATE ACCESS. A Canadian term for ISDN's PRI, which is Primary Rate Interface or 23 64 kbps channels and one 64 kbps D (data) channel. See also PRIMARY RATE INTERFACE.

PRACTICE The technical and installation manuals often used by Bell Operating Companies. A poor use of the word. A better word would be procedure.

PRBS Pseudo-Random Bit Sequence/pattern. A test pattern having the properties of random data (generally 511 or 2047 bits), but generated in such a manner that another circuit, operating independently, can synchronize on the pattern and detect individual transmission bit errors.

PRE-AMPLIFIER An electronic circuit which maintains or establishes an audio or video signal at a predetermined signal strength, prior to that signal being amplified for reproduction through a monitor or speaker.

PRE-EMPTIVE, REAL TIME SUPPORT When Microsoft released its At Work operating system, it said it had a number of key features, one of which was "pre-emptive, real-time support." Here's Microsoft's description:

● Pre-emptive, real-time support. Communication devices such as fax machines and phones are distinct from personal computers in that they have critical real-time needs. Consequently, the software in these devices must attend to communication hardware such as modems very frequently, so that pieces of the communication are not lost. To support this need, the operating system was designed to be able to put other processes "on hold" temporarily in order to service the communication hardware before continuing other functions. See AT WORK and WINDOWS TELEPHONY.

PRE-SUBSCRIPTION A local Bell or local independent operating telephone company service that encourages each subscriber to select one long distance carrier he may use without having to dial a multiple digit access code. If you pre-subscribe to MCI, you will simply reach MCI by dialing "1" plus the 10-digit long distance number.

PRE-TRIP A central office malfunction that causes a phone to ring only once, and then stop, as if it had been answered. IT can be very confusing and difficult to get repaired, because most telco repair people have never heard of the problem and will insist your phone is at fault. Often fixed by replacing a faulty heat coil.

PRE-WIRING The practice of concealing telephone wiring or cable in the wall of a building while the building is being constructed.

PREAMPLIFIER See PRE-AMPLIFIER.

PRECEDENCE Precedence is Federal government parlance to mean a designation assigned to a phone call by the caller to indicate to communications personnel the relative urgency (therefore the order of handling) of the call and to the called person the order in which the message is to be noted. Autovon phones which have "precedence" have an additional four touchtone buttons. You can find frequencies for those buttons under the definition for DTMF.

PRECEDENCE PROSIGN An introductory character or set of characters which indicate how a message is to be handled by the receiving unit.

PRECISE POSITIONING SERVICE The most accurate dynamic positioning possible with GPS (Global Positioning System), based on the dual frequency P-code.

PREDICTIVE DIALER See PREDICTIVE DIALING.

PREDICTIVE DIALING An automated method of making many outbound calls without people and then passing answered calls to a person as the calls are answered. Here's the story: Imagine a bunch of operators having to call a bunch of people. Those calls may be for collections. They may be for employee callups. They may be for alumnae fund raising. When it's done manual, here's how it works: Before each call operators spend time reviewing paper records or computer terminal screens, selecting the person to be called, finding the phone number, dialing the numbers, listening to rings, listening to phone company intercepts, busy signals and answering machines. Operators also spend time updating the records after each call. Predictive dialing automates this process, with the computer choosing the person to be called and dialing the number and only passing it to an operator when a real live human being answers. There are enormous productivity gains made by screening out answering machines, busy signals, network busy signals, non-completed calls, operator intercepts etc. The result is productivity increases of 200% to 300%. According to generally accepted industry lore, a well-run manual dialing center can get its people talking on the phone for 25 minutes an hour. With a predictive dialer you can get them on the phone making sales, collecting money, etc. for 55 minutes an hour. It's a major productivity gain.

True predictive dialing should not be confused with automated dialing. True predictive dialing has complex mathematical algorithms that consider, in real time, the number of available telephone lines, the number of available operators, the probability of getting no answer, a busy signal, a disconnected number, operator intercept or an answering machine, the time between calls required for maximum operator efficiency, the length of an average conversation and the average length of time the operators need to enter the relevant data. Some predictive dialing systems constantly adjust the dialing rate by monitoring changes in all these factors.

Some people don't like the term "predictive dialing," since they think it's getting "a bad rap" in Washington, DC by being associated with junk phone calls. As a result some people would prefer to call it Computer Aided Dialing. See also PREVIEW DIALING.

PREFERRED CALL A local phone company services which lets you forward calls from a bunch of numbers you have pre-selected. The service uses the calling number ID as the basis for choosing which calls to forward.

PREFIX One or several digits dialed or touchtoned in front of a phone number, usually to indicate something to the phone system. For example, dialing a zero in front of a long distance number in the United States would indicate to the phone company you wanted operator assistance on the call.

PREFORM Optical fiber source material. Preform is glass rod formed and used as source material for drawing an optical fiber. The glass structure is a magnified version of the fiber to be drawn from it.

PREMISE A thesis. a proposition supposed or proved as a basis of argument or inference. Often misused to mean the space occupied by a customer or authorized or joint user in a building or buildings on continuous or contiguous property (except railroad rights of way, etc.) not separated by a public road or highway. See PREMISES.

PREMISES the space occupied by a customer or authorized or joint user in a building or buildings on continuous or contiguous property (except railroad rights of way, etc.) not separated by a public road or highway.

PREMISES DISTRIBUTION SYSTEM PDS. There are two meanings for premises distribution system — a general one and a specific one, specific to AT&T. Here, first, is the general definition. A PDS is the transmission network inside a building or group of buildings that connects various types of voice and data communications devices, switching equipment, and other information management systems to each other, as well as to outside communications networks. It includes cabling and distribution hardware components and facilities between the point where building wiring connects to the outside network lines and back to the voice and data terminals in your office or other user work location. The system consists of all the transmission media and electronics, administration points, connectors, adapters, plugs, and support hardware between the building's side of the network interface and the terminal equipment required to make the system operational.

Here is the specific definition — A multi-functional distribution system from AT&T to support voice, data, graphics and video communications on premise. PDS includes cables, adapters, electronics, eight pin universal wall jacks and protective devices, all arranged in a logically coherent and economic fashion. It uses fiber optic cable and twisted pair copper wire and is suitable for single building, multi-tenant high rise or campus environment.

PREMISES LIGHTWAVE SYSTEM The fiber optic part of the Premises Distribution System (PDS) from AT&T. PDS, which can replace the coaxial cables linking IBM terminals and printers, consists of two fiber optic interface units, one at a controller-end and the optic interface units and one at a terminal-end linked by a fiber optic pair. The fiber optic interface units connect to the terminals through four-pair building wiring and balun adaptors. Balun adaptors also enable direct connections of the terminals to the cluster controller through building wiring.

PREMISES WIRE The twisted-pair, quad or other wire installed at the user's location to provide telephone service. Includes both intra-building and inter-building wiring.

PREMISES WIRING SYSTEM The entire wiring system on the user's premises, especially the supporting wiring that connects the communications outlets to the network interface jack.

PREPAY The industry standard for coin phone operation which requires that the full cost of a call be deposited before a connection is attempted through the Central Office.

PREPROCESSOR A device or information handling system which converts raw data into a form more easily processed with standard equipment.

PRESENTATION LAYER The sixth layer of the OSI model of data communications. It controls the formats of screens and files. Control codes, special graphics and character sets work in this layer. See OSI STANDARDS.

PRESENTATION MANAGER Presentation Manager is a look and feel specification and kernel-based toolkit development environment. It was developed for IBM by Microsoft with input from IBM. Presentation Manager is the standard graphical user interface and toolkit for the OS/2 operating system, which is a multitasking operating system for personal computers. The screens are similar to those of Microsoft Windows.

PRESET The "programming" of radio station frequencies on a tuner or receiver or musical selections on a tape, for instant recall at the push of a button.

PRESET CALL FORWARDING Incoming calls will be re-routed to a pre-determined secondary number.

PRESS-TO-TALK Telephone circuits are two way. Some circuits, such as mobile dispatch services for taxis, etc., are one-way. They use a microphone or handset with a button you must press-to-talk and release to listen. You can also buy a normal telephone handset with a press-to-talk button. Such a handset is useful in noisy places.

PRESSURIZATION Pumping inert gas into a heavy casing in which a couple of thick cables will be joined. The pressure is usually maintained at a few pounds above the surrounding atmospheric pressure. The idea is that the higher pressure inside keeps moisture out of the splice and thus improves the quality of phone service.

PRESTEL A videotex system used only in Britain.

PRESUBSCRIPTION A process where a customer choose a long distance carrier and then is able to access that carrier by dialing 1+. Other carriers are accessed by 1-0-XXX calling. AT&T's code is 1-0-288 (as in 1-0-ATT). MCI's is 1-0-222. Sprint's is 1-0-333. See PRE-SUBSCRIPTION.

PRETRIP See PRE-TRIP.

PREVAIL An office automation UNIX software package which combines functions usually available only in individual programs, such as spreadsheet, a word processor, a database management system, communication capabilities and more.

PREVENTIVE MAINTENANCE The periodic inspection, cleaning, adjusting and repair to eliminate problems before they affect service. Usually ignored.

PREVIEW DIALING Preview dialing is a term used to describe an automatic dialer. Preview dialing is also called "screen dialing" or "cursor dialing." Typically the prospect's account information and/or phone number appears on the screen BEFORE the call is made. Thus the agent can "preview" the number, the screen, the customer. If the agent wants to make the call, the agent hits a key, such as "Enter" and the computer dials the number. In some preview dialing equipments, the agent must hit a key if he/she DOESN'T want the the number dialed. Contrast preview dialing with Predictive Dialing where the computer makes all the dialing decisions and presents the calls to the agent only after they are connected. Predictive dialing is a lot faster than preview dialing. See PREDICTIVE DIALING and ANTICIPATORY DIALING.

PREWIRING The practice of concealing telephone wiring or cable in the wall of a building while the building is being constructed.

PRI See PRIMARY RATE INTERFACE and ISDN.

PRI-EOP A fax signal. PRocedure Interrupt-End of Page.

PRI-MPS A fax signal. PRocedure Interrupt-PultiPage Signal.

PRICE CAP The phone industry has always been regulated on the basis of the profits it earns compared to the investment it had. That was called Rate of Return Regulation. How you figure profits — since you also have to figure what are allowable expenses — has been the subject of on-going debate for over 100 years. The latest idea in regulation is to replace the rate of return regulation with something called "Price caps" which allow the price of phone company services to rise by x% at maximum — the so-called price cap.

PRIMARY AGENT GROUP An automatic call distributor term: Primary agent group for which the inbound calls are intended. Intraflow goes to secondary and tertiary groups if the primary group does not have an agent available after the time or after overflow parameters are exceeded. Different ACD systems label this process differently.

PRIMARY BUFFER A part of a computer's memory where fast incoming or outgoing data is kept until the computer has a chance to process it.

PRIMARY CENTER A control center connecting toll centers — a Class 3 Central Office. It can also serve as a toll center for its local end offices.

PRIMARY GROUP A group of basic signals which are combined by multiplexing. The lowest level of the multiplexing hierarchy.

PRIMARY INSULATION The first layer of non-conductive material applied over a conductor to act as electrical insulation.

PRIMARY INTEREXCHANGE CARRIER A primary Interexchange Carrier is the long distance company to which traffic from a given location is automatically routed when dialing 1+ in equal access areas. The PIC is identified by a code number which is assigned by the local telephone company to the telephone numbers of all the subscribers to that carrier to ensure the calls are routed over the correct network. When a subscriber switches long distance carriers, it often is referred to as a PIC change.

PRIMARY LINK The active LAN connection. When it fails the LAN is switched to the Backup link.

PRIMARY PARTITION A portion of a physical disk that can be marked for use by an operating system. Under MS-DOS, there can be up to four primary partitions (or up to three, if there is an extended partition) per physical disk. A primary partition cannot be subpartitioned.

PRIMARY RATE INTERFACE The ISDN equivalent of a T-1 circuit. The Primary Rate Interface (that which is delivered to the customer's premises) provides 23B+D (in North America) or 30B+D (in Europe) running at 1.544 megabits per second and 2.048 megabits per second, respectively. There is another ISDN interface. It's called the Basic Rate Interface. It delivers 2B+D over either one or two pairs. In ISDN, the "B" stands for Bearer, which is 64,000 bits per second, which can carry PCM-digitized voice or data. See ISDN for a much better explanation.

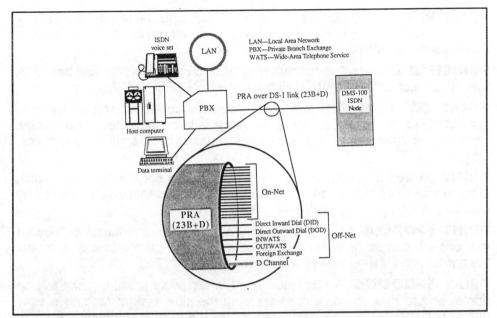

PRIMARY STATION A network node that controls the flow of information on a communications link. Also, the station that, for some period of time, has control of information flow on a communications link (in this case primary status is temporary).

PRIMARY STORAGE The main internal storage.

PRIMARY WIRE CENTER A switching center in the AT&T/Bell system hierarchy of exchange classes. The primary center is a Class 3 exchange. It is used to connect toll offices and less frequently to connect a toll center with a local end office. Primary centers are capable of connecting toll centers through sectional centers and then to local end offices to establish communication connections when simple routing possibilities are busy.

PRIME LINE A telephone can be programmed to automatically select a certain line type whenever a call is made by lifting the receiver.

PRIME LINE PREFERENCE When you pick up the handset on your key system or hybrid key, you are automatically connected to your preferred line (central office or intercom), rather than having to punch down an extra line button. Some phone systems tout this as a feature. Some have it set up where you simply leave one of the line buttons depressed and it doesn't pop up when you put your handset back into its cradle. Most 1A2 phone systems have this feature. Not all electronic phone systems do.

PRIMITIVES Abstract representations of interactions across the service access points indicating information is passed between the service user and service provider. There are four types of primitives in the OSI Reference Model — request, indication, response and confirm.

PRINCIPAL First or highest in importance. An owner or part-owner of a business. A person who authorizes another, as an agent, to represent him. Often confused with principle. See PRINCIPLE.

PRINCIPLE A general or fundamental truth on which others are based. A rule of conduct. Often confused with principal. See PRINCIPAL.

PRINT CONTROL CHARACTER A coded control character used to instruct the receiving unit on how a message is to be formatted in hard copy. Print control characters include carriage returns, back spaces, line feeds, tabs, etc.

PRINT SERVER A networked computer, usually consisting of fixed-disk storage and a CPU, that controls one or more printers that can be shared by users.

PRINT SPOOLER An application that manages print requests or jobs so that one job can be processed while other jobs are placed in a queue until the printer has finished with previous jobs. See PRINT SPOOLING.

PRINT SPOOLING A technique used to schedule printing tasks to one printer and to free up computer time from the slow task of feeding a slow printer (Any printer is slow compared to the speed of a computer). A small program or program/machine called the spooler does the scheduling. A user loads the print task to the spooler and when the print task's turn comes, the job is printed. Print spooling is handled several ways: You can allocate part of the computer's main memory to become a print spooler. You can allocate part of the company's disk memory to become a print spooler. You can get an external device called a print spooler. It will have all the storage space and software necessary. There are two primary advantages to Print Spooling: 1. You can use the spooler to save your and your computer's time. Dump the report to a print spooler at thousands of bits per second. Get on with something else on the computer. 2. You can use a print spooler to schedule several users' printing requests. This is particularly good in multi-user environments — for example, where the printer is a laser printer (and therefore expensive) and is attached to a LAN (Local Area Network).

PRINTED CIRCUIT BOARD PCB. Flat material (fiberglass/epoxy) on which electronic components are mounted. A PCB also provides electrical pathways called traces, that connect components. Printed circuit boards are what PBXs and computers are made of these days. Be careful when you're replacing PCBs. They're usually very sensitive to static electricity. Handle them only when you're attached to a static electricity strap that is properly grounded. Lay them down only on a surface you're sure is static electricity free. And don't touch the components on PCBs whatever you do.

PRINTER A device which takes computer information and prints it on paper.

PRINTER DRIVER A program that controls how your computer and printer interact. A printer driver file supplies information such as the printing interface, description of fonts, and features of the installed printer.

PRINTER EMULATION A fax term for mimicking a printer-generated document. This way, the outgoing fax will look as if it has come from the printer attached to the computer. This can include full formatting, as well as letterhead, signature and graphic images.

PRINTER FONT A font stored in your printer's memory, or soft fonts that are sent to your printer before a document is printed.

PRINTER SERVER A computer and/or program providing LAN (Local Area Network) users with access to a centralized printer. A person using the LAN will send a message to the printer server computer. This computer will then assign it a piece of memory or disk space to store its file while it waits to be printed. With a printer server, users can send to the printer any time. Their print jobs are usually handled in the order they are received. But "big bosses" can be given priority and can be bumped to the top of the queue. Print servers allow fewer printers to satisfy more users. Print servers are also especially useful for expensive, laser or high speed printers because they (the print servers) spread the cost of these expensive machines over many users, making them more affordable. See PRINT SPOOLING.

PRINTER, WIRE A matrix printer which prints using a set of wire hammers which strike the page through a carbon ribbon to generate the matrix characters.

PRIORITIZATION The process of assigning different values to network users, such that a user with higher priority will be offered access or service before a user with lower priority. Increasingly available as an added option with network operation. Any procedure where different levels of precedence exist.

PRIORITY A ranking given to a task which determines when it will be processed.

PRIORITY BUMPING The process during a link, trunk or facility failure where lower priority user access to network services is interrupted in order to offer those services or bandwidth to a predesignated higher priority user.

PRIORITY CALL Emergency calls to the attendant bypass the normal queue and alert the attendant with some special signal.

PRIORITY INDICATOR A character or group of characters which determine the position in queue of the message in relation to the urgency of other messages. Priority indicators control the order in which messages are to be delivered.

PRIORITY RINGING A name for a Pacific Bell (and possibly other local telephone companies') service which alerts you to have calls from selected numbers ring at another number.

PRIORITY TRANSPORT The capability of a network for certain classes of traffic to have priority over others and thus have lower delay or otherwise better performance.

PRIORITY TRUNK QUEUING Through user-chosen trunk access level, this PBX feature places any caller with this or higher level in the class of service assignment ahead of callers waiting for the same trunk group (or Agent Group in the case of incoming ACD calls).

PRIVACY Privacy usually means that once a caller "seizes" a line, no other user can access that same line even though it appears on his/her key set. Privacy can be automatic or selected for each call.

PRIVACY AND PRIVACY RELEASE All other extensions of a line are unable to enter a conversation in progress unless the initiating telephone releases the feature.

PRIVACY LOCKOUT Privacy automatically splits the connection whenever an attendant would otherwise be included on the call, i.e. the attendant can't listen in to a call she's just extended to someone. A tone warning is generated when the attendant bridges into a conversation in progress.

PRIVACY OVERRIDE Activation of a special pushbutton allows the phone user to access a given busy line, even though the automatic exclusion facility is being used by the station on that line. This privilege of Privacy Override is usually only given to Big Bosses.

PRIVATE AUTOMATIC BRANCH EXCHANGE PABX. A private telephone switch for a business or an organization in which people have to dial "9" to access a local line. In the old days, private branch exchanges were manual, meaning that operators/attendants were needed to manually place calls. Then the systems improved and you were able to dial the outside world from your extension without the help (or hindrance?) of an operator. Thus they became known as private automatic branch exchanges. But then all PBXs became Automatic. So these days, PABXs are all called PBXs, except in some countries outside North America, where they're still called PABXs. See also the next definition and PBX.

PRIVATE BRANCH EXCHANGE PBX. Term used now interchangeably with PABX. PBX is a private telephone switching system, usually located on a customer's premises with an attendant console. It is connected to a common group of lines from one or more central offices to provide service to a number of individual phones, such as in a hotel, business or government office. For the biggest definition, see PBX. See also PABX.

PRIVATE DIAL-IN PORTS. A packet network term. For customers who have many calls, the packet network operator provides dedicated, unpublished phone numbers. The idea is to give the preferred user better service.

PRIVATE EXCHANGE PX. A telephone switch serving a particular organization and having no means of connection with a public exchange. In other words, a phone system just for intercom calls.

PRIVATE LINE A direct channel specifically dedicated to a customer's use between specified points. A line leased from a carrier, local or long distance. A non-switched circuit. One end of the line is directly connected to the other end. Here's the AT&T definition of a private line. "A dedicated, nonswitchable link from one or more customer-specified locations to one or more customer-specified locations..."

PRIVATE LINE SERVICE An outside telephone number separate from the PABX, can be set up to appear on one of the buttons of a key telephone. Also called an Auxiliary Line.

PRIVATE MANAGEMENT DOMAIN PRMD. An X.400 electronical mail term: A private domain to which MTAs (Message Transfer Agents) send mail. PRMDs are connected to ADMDs (Administrative Management Domains) for message routing over wide area links.

PRIVATE MESSAGE A message designation which prevents that message from being given to another mailbox.

PRIVATE NETWORK A series of offices connected together by leased and non-leased phone lines with switching facilities and transmission equipment owned and operated by the user or by the carrier and leased to the user. This is a broad definition. But these days with SDN and other virtual private networks, it's hard to see the difference between using a private network and using the public network except that you hope your private network will be cheaper, better quality and perhaps offer a little more flexibility in the types of traffic — voice, video, data and fax — you carry on it. See PRIVATE VOICEBAND NETWORK.

PRIVATE NETWORKS MARKETING A Northern Telecom term which defines their organization for making and selling all telecom switches, except central offices. These products include the Meridian 1 PBX family, residential and business telephone sets, including Norstar and data communications.

PRIVATE VOICEBAND NETWORK A network that is made up of voice band circuits, and sometimes switching arrangements, for the exclusive use of one customer. These networks can be nationwide in scope and typically serve large corporations or government agencies.

PRIVATE WIRE A private line. Derives its name from the old telegraph days when messages were carried on wires that strung across the nation.

PRIVILEGES The access rights to a directory, file or program. Typically read, write, delete, create and execute.

PRO WATS PRO WATS I is AT&T's discount long distance service for companies which spend over $120 a month on long distance. AT&T PRO

WATS II and III are designed for companies with higher calling volumes. Charges and discounts increase with plan size.

Pro750 An imaging term. A DVI product family introduced in 1989 consisting of Application Development Platform, boards and software.

PROACTIVE Taking the initiative. Doing it before someone (most likely your competition) forces you to do it. The word is currently in vogue among those people who believe the telephone companies should do all the positive, forward-looking actions before the competition does them and gets the public kudos. The word has no real meaning, but serves a purpose as a cry to action. The word actually is grammatically incorrect. The real word is "active." It is the opposite of "reactive." The person who told us this is Norm Brust, a wonderful man and one of the more active (not proactive) people in our industry.

PROBE A sensing device, typically about the size and shape of a pencil, that is used to sense various physical conditions such as temperature, humidity, current flow, speed. Usually connected to a meter or oscilloscope which displays the condition being monitored.

PROCESS A software application. Any activity or systematic sequence of operations that produces a specified result. Typically, a computer function that consists of, or involves, procedure code, data storage and an interface for communicating with other processes.

PROCESS MANUFACTURING The making of things. This contrasts with flow manufacturing which is working on something — like oil — that flows through a production process.

PROCESSING GAIN In a spread spectrum transmission system, the original information signal is combined with a pseudo-random correlating, or spreading code. The more random and the greater the length of the code, the more robust the resulting spread spectrum signal is against interference and interception. A measure of this robustness is referred to as processing gain. The FCC requires a minimum of 10 dB processing gain for non-licensed equipment operating in the Part 15 902-928 MHz, 2400-2483 MHz, and 5725-5850 MHz frequency bands. See also CDMA.

PROCESSING, BATCH A method of computer operation in which a number of similar input items are accumulated and sorted for processing. Compare with ON-LINE or INTERACTIVE PROCESSING.

PROCESSOR The intelligent central element of a computer or other information handling system. Also called the Central Processing Unit (CPU).

PROCESSOR DATA MODULE AT&T's PDM performs conversion between the EIA signal protocol and the System 85 Digital Communications Protocol (DCP).

PROCESSOR OCCUPANCY The time the telephone system processor is in use. There are two typical demands on the central processor in a telephone system, moving calls around and running self-diagnostics. Be sure you factor in the second when you're trying to figure out how many calls your telephone system processor will handle before it dies.

PROCUREMENT LEAD TIME The interval in months between the initiation of procurement action and receipt into the supply system of the production model (excludes prototypes) purchased as the result of such actions, and is composed of two elements, production lead time and administrative lead time.

PROCR Processor.

PROD A device that resembles a pencil, but containing a metal tip in an insulated handle with a wire to connect it to a piece of test equipment, such as a VOM (volt-ohm-milliameter). the metal tip is touched to various points in an electrical circuit for measurements and trouble-shooting.

PRODIGY A joint venture of IBM and Sears Roebuck & Company, Prodigy offers on-line computer services, at last count, roughly 800. These services are offered for a largely flat monthly fee — probably the only on-line service offering unlimited usage for one monthly price. The fees are kept low by allowing companies to run commercials on the bottom of subscriber screens. children get a kick out of Prodigy.

PROFILE A set of parameters defining the way a device acts. In the LAN world, a profile is often used by one or more workstations to determine the connections they will have with other devices and those devices they will offer for use by other devices. Often called a login file. Profiles and login files usually work like batch files, automatically executing a number of commands when you turn on the machine.

PROFS PRofessional OFfice System. Interactive productivity software developed by IBM that is part of the Virtual Machine (VM) Productivity System and runs under the VM/CMS mainframe system. PROFS is frequently used for electronic mail and is said to give a user an edge in productivity in three areas: business communications (including electronic mail), time management and document handling.

PROGRAM Instructions given to a computer or automated phone system to perform certain tasks. Most vendors improve (update) their software programs continuously. It's a good idea to ask what the deal is with getting updates.

PROGRAM CIRCUIT A voice circuit used for the transmission of radio program materials. It is a telephone circuit which has been equalized to handle a wider range of frequencies than are required for ordinary speech signals.

PROGRAM COUNTER A device inside a computer which keeps track of which instruction in the program is next, etc.

PROGRAM EVALUATION REVIEW TECHNIQUE PERT. A

management tool for graphically displaying projected tasks and milestones, schedules and discrepancies between tasks.

PROGRAM LOGIC The particular sequence of instructions in a program.

PROGRAMMABLE In telephony, the ability to change a feature or a function or the extension assigned to a telephone without rewiring.

PROGRAMMABLE CALL FORWARDING This feature of a telephone system allows a user to instruct his phone to send all his calls to another phone. That phone might be another extension in the same phone system or it might be another phone number altogether in a different part of the country. This feature is great. You're going to a meeting but don't want to miss that one special call. You can send your calls to a person close to the meeting and ask them to interrupt you if that "special" call comes in. The problem with this feature is that often people forget their phone is on "forwarding" and when they return to their office, they sit around all afternoon waiting for that special call, which got call forwarded elsewhere. There are two ways to overcome this. Some phones have lights or messages on their screens which indicate all calls are being forwarded. Also, some telecom managers program their total phone systems so that twice a day, all call forwarding shall cease and all calls shall return to their original phone.

PROGRAMMABLE CONFIGURATION SELECT Refers to the EEPROM setup routine which allows jumperless configuration of the system board.

PROGRAMMABLE MEMORY Memory that can be both read from and be written into by the processor. Synonym for RANDOM ACCESS MEMORY — RAM.

PROGRAMMABLE TERMINAL A user terminal that has some limited processing power. Also, intelligent terminal.

PROGRAMMING LANGUAGE A language used by a programmer to develop instructions for the computer. It is translated into machine language by language software called assemblers, compilers and interpreters. Each programming language has its own grammar and syntax.

PROGRAMMING OVERLAY Typically a piece of cut-out carboard, which you place over certain of the keys on a phone or console. When you punch in a certain code, the buttons become what's written on the programming overlay.

PROGRAM SHARING The ability of several users or computers to use a program simultaneously.

PROGRAM STORE Permanent memory in a stored program control central office that contains the machine's generic software program, parameters and translations.

PROGESSIVE CONFERENCE A PBX feature. Allows the extension user to create conferences of more than three people using the consultation hold and add-on conference features. To create a conference, an extension user typically uses the consultation hold, dials the desired internal or external number and effects an add-on conference. The conference may then be progressively expanded, in this same fashion, to the maximum capability of the phone system offering this feature. A good question to ask before you get sold this feature is "does the conferencing have amplification and balancing?" Without these features, the conferencing conversation will simply get more and more difficult to hear on.

PROGRESSIVE DIALING A form of predictive dialing, progressive dialing is slightly more automated than preview dialing. The customer data is not displayed until the number is dialed, giving the agent less time to review it and a shorter time between calls. See also PREDICTIVE DIALING and PREVIEW DIALING.

PROGRESSIVE TUNING A method of painting pictures on computer monitors or TV screens in which the picture is painted line by line. It is today's most common way of painting a picture or an image on a computer screen.

PROJECT EVALUATION REVIEW TECHNIQUE PERT. A technique for managing a project — say the installation of a PBX — which produces a guess at the project's critical path (longest task to complete) and of project milestone completion dates. See PERT.

PROM Programmable Read Only Memory. A PROM is a programmable semiconductor device in which the contents are not intended to be altered during normal operation. PROM acts like non-volatile memory. When you install an autoboot PROM on a LAN network board, the workstation can boot up from the network server. This is particularly useful for diskless workstations.

PROMPT An audible or visible signal to the system user that some process is complete or some user action is required. Also used to signify a need for further input and/or location of needed input. See also PROMPTS.

PROMPTS 1. Recorded instructions delivered by voice processing units. Prompts may include MENUS or other information that is played each time you get into the system. 2. Messages from the computer instructing the user on how to use the system. See MENU and AUDIO MENU.

PRONET A family of token-passing local area networks from Proteon, Natick, MA. The fastest of Proteon's networks is an extremely fast 80 Mbps. See the next two definitions also.

PRONET-4/16 An IEEE 802.5 Token-Ring network sold by Proteon Inc.

PRONET-10 A proprietary star-shaped Token-Ring network operating at 10 Mbit/sec, and sold by Proteon Inc.

PROPAGATION DELAY The time it takes for a signal to travel from one point on a circuit to another.

PROPAGATION TIME Time required for an electrical wave to travel between two points on a transmission line.

PROPERTY MANAGEMENT INTERFACE PMI. A telephone system's ability to talk to a hotel's computer system.

PROPORTIONAL FONT A font in which different characters have varying widths. All magazines and newspapers are printed in proportional characters, which make reading easier. By contrast, in a monospaced font, such as one on an old typewriter, all characters have the same widths.

PROPRIETARY If something is proprietary it means it will only work with one vendor's telephone system. There are many telephones that are proprietary to one telephone system or one manufacturer. These Proprietary phones are usually the electronic and multi-line instruments. For example, Rolm's Cedar, Juniper and Cypress phones will only work connected to a Rolm PBX. Similarly with the CXC Rose TeleTerminal which will only worked connected to a CXC Rose PBX. However, the Mitel SuperSet 4s will work with Solid State PBXs and ACDs.

PROPRIETARY LAN A LAN that runs the equipment of only one vendor. A proprietary LAN, for example, cannot join IBM PC's to DEC minicomputers. DEC and Wang both make proprietary LANs. Some people say such LANs are more "bug-free" because they have only one vendors' wares to deal with. They also tend to be more expensive. They also tend to tie you to one vendor, although some makers are now coming out with bridges which connect proprietary LANs to non-proprietary LANs.

PROSODY Intonation. In text to speech, prosody refers to how natural it sounds — the ups and downs of the sentence.

PROSPECTIVE The opposite of Retrospective or Retroactive. Most regulatory commission rate cases are prospective, which means they relate to prices and things in the future. Some rate cases, however, are retroactive or retrospective, which means they apply to prices and things in the past. Most of these decisions involve forcing the company to return money to its subscribers in the form of a refund. Interestingly — try this one — most retroactive commission decisions are prospectively retroactive. In other words, they only take effect some time in the future, when the decision is voted upon by all the commission members.

PROTECTED DISTRIBUTION SYSTEM PDS. This is a US Federal Government definition: A wireline or fiber-optics telecommunication system which includes adequate acoustic, electrical, electromagnetic, and physical safeguards to permit its use for the unencrypted transmission of classified information. A complete protected distribution system includes the subscriber and terminal equipment and the interconnecting lines.

PROTECTED MODE An operating mode for the Intel 80286 and higher processors that supports multitasking, data security, and virtual memory. The 80286 processor can run in either of two modes: real or protected. In real mode, it emulates an 8086 (it accesses a maximum of 640KB of RAM and runs only one software application at a time). Protected mode allows the 80286 processor to access up to 16MB of memory. It uses a 24-bit address bus. Since a bit can have one of two values, raising the base number of 2 to the power of 24 is equal to 16,777,316 unique memory addresses. Each memory address can store one byte of information (16,777,216 bytes equals 16MB).

Protected mode operation also makes it possible to run more than one application at once and to handle more processes because more memory is available. Processes can be requests from an operating system or an application to perform disk I/O, memory management, printing, or other functions. Processes are assigned priority numbers in protected mode. The processor gives priority to those with higher numbers. Operating system processes always have higher priority than application processes. See also REAL MODE and VIRTUAL 8086 MODE.

PROTECTIVE CONNECTING ARRANGEMENT PCA. A device leased from the telephone company and placed between your own (customer-provided) telephone equipment and the lines of the telephone company. The idea was to protect their lines from your junky equipment. No instance/case was ever proven of harm occurring to the network from faulty customer-provided equipment and the PCAs were thrown out and replaced by the FCC's Part 68 Registration Program. Under this program, customer-owned equipment which passes FCC tests can be registered and connected directly to the phone network without these devices. The phone industry eventually refunded most of the fees it charged on the PCAs. NATA and many manufacturers claimed the PCAs were designed to prevent the growth of the interconnect or customer-owned phone industry. They were probably right. The question is now moot, since the charges and the devices no longer exist, except in a museum or attached to very old equipment. See also PROTECTIVE COUPLING ARRANGEMENT and PCA.

PROTECTIVE COUPLING ARRANGEMENT PCA. A device placed between the phone company's trunks and your particular telephone gadget. The objective of the PCA is to isolate the telephone company's lines from your equipment and thus protect their lines from your equipment. The device is not needed if your equipment has passed FCC approval — under Part 68 of the FCC's rules. See also PROTECTIVE CONNECTIVE ARRANGEMENT, which is another term for the same thing.

PROTECTOR BLOCK A device interconnected to an exchange access line to protect the connected equipment from over-voltage and/or over-current of 600 volts or greater. Hazardous voltages and currents are shunted to ground.

PROTN Protection.

PROTOCOL A specific set of rules, procedures or conventions relating to format and timing of data transmission between two devices. A standard procedure that two data devices must accept and use to be able to understand each other. Sort of like us both speaking English so we can communicate. The protocols for data communications cover such things as framing, error handling, transparency and line control. There are three basic types of protocol: character-oriented, byte-oriented and bit-oriented.

Protocols break a file into equal parts called blocks or packets. These packets are sent and the receiving computer checks the arriving packet and sends an acknowledgement (ACK) back to the sending computer. Because modems use phone lines to transfer data, noise or interference on the line will often mess up the block. When a block is damaged in transit, an error occurs. The purpose of a protocol is to set up a mathematical way of measuring if the block came through accurately. And if it didn't, ask the distant end to re-transmit the block until it gets it right. See PROTOCOLS for a list of the more common prototypes.

PROTOCOL ANALYZER A specialized computer and/or program that hooks into a LAN and analyzes its traffic. Good protocol analyzers can record and display data on all levels of traffic on a LAN cable, from the lowest media access control packets to NetBIOS commands and application data. They are excellent for diagnosing network problems, but they require some expertise, as their data output can be obscure.

PROTOCOL CONVERSION A data communications procedure which permits computers operating with different protocols to communicate with each other. See PROTOCOL and PROTOCOL CONVERTER.

PROTOCOL CONVERTER A device which does protocol conversion. It's your classic "black box." Glasgal Communications defines a protocol converter as any device which translates a binary data stream from one format to another according to a fixed algorithm. Compare with bridge and gateway, which are different animals and may contain protocol converters...and more.

PROTOCOL DEPENDENT ROUTING Any routing method in which routing decisions are made on the basis of information provided by the specific LAN protocol used by the communicating devices. TCP/IP and DECnet routers are protocol dependent routers. So are so-called multiprotocol routers, because they must support each protocol running in the network. See also PROTOCOL INDEPENDENT ROUTING.

PROTOCOL INDEPENDENT ROUTER A routing device that provides the functionality of protocol specific routers such as TCP/IP or DECnet routers but is independent of protocols. In addition to routing "routable" protocols like TCP/IP, DECnet or XNS, it routes IBM protocols which are not routable. The protocol independent router combines the latest in computer hardware with the new advanced routing technologies such as SPF (Shortest Path First) and IS-IS (OSI routing standard). It represents an alternative to conventional routers that use old routing technologies and are protocol dependent. Protocol independent routers provide easy-to-install-and-use enterprise-wide networks in a token ring or Ethernet environment.

PROTOCOL INDEPENDENT ROUTING A routing method in which routing decisions are made without reference to the protocol being used by the communicating devices. Protocol independent routers provide the functionality of protocol specific routers such as TCP/IP or DECnet routers, but can also route non-routable protocols. See also PROTOCOL INDEPENDENT ROUTER.

PROTOCOL STACK A group of drivers that work together to span the layers in the network protocol hierarchy.

PROTOCOL SUITE A hierarchial set of related protocols.

PROTOCOLS For an explanation of protocols, see PROTOCOL. Here are the more common PC protocoal types:

MODULATION PROTOCOLS

Bell 103: Low Speed	(300 baud)
Bell 212: Low Speed	(1200bps)
CCITT V.22bis: Medium	(2400bps)
CCITT V.32 High Speed	(9600bps)
CCITT V.32bis: High Speed	(1440bps)

ERROR CONTROL PROTOCOLS

Microcom Network Protocol	(MNP)
CCITT V.42	(Includes LAP-M & MNP)

DATA COMPRESSION PROTOCOLS

MNP/5

CCITT V.42bis

All data compression requires an underlying error control protocol.

FILE TRANSFER PROTOCOLS

Kermit: 7-bit data path, quotes control characters.

XMODEM: 8 bit data path, ACK/NAK protocol.

YMODEM: 8-bit data path, batch capability.

ZMODEM: 8-bit data path, quotes some control characters.

PROVISIONING The act of supplying telecommunications service to a user, including all associated transmission, wiring, and equipment. In NS/EP telecommunication services, "provisioning" and "initiation" are synonymous and include altering the state of an existing priority service or capability.

PRX Program.

PS/2 IBM Personal System/2 personal computer.

PSAI AT&T's Processor-to-Switch Applications Interface. See also ASAI and SCAI.

PSAP Public Safety Answering Position. PSAPs are customarily segmented as "primary," "secondary" and so on. The primary PSAP is the first contact a 911 caller will get. Here, the PSAP operator verifies or obtains the caller's whereabouts (called locational information), determines the nature of the emergency and decides which emergency response teams should be notified. In some instances, the primary PSAP may dispatch aid. In most cases, the caller is then conferenced or transferred to a secondary PSAP from which help will be dispatched. Secondary PSAPs might be located at fire dispatch areas, municipal police force headquarters or ambulance dispatch centers. Often the primary PSAP will answer for an entire region.

PSC/PUC Public Service Commission. Also known as Public Utility Commission. It's the state agency charged with regulating the local phone company utility. In reality, there are only two things the PSC can do: 1. Allow the phone company to increase its prices, and 2. Restrict competition to the phone company by creating all sorts of restrictive rules and regulations. As competition in the telecommunications industry grows — chiefly because of Federal rulings — the state PSCs are losing their power. This bothers them.

PSDS Public Switched Digital Service. A BOC service. AT&T Circuit Switched Digital Capability (CSDC), also known commercially as AT&T's Accunet Switched 56 service. It allows a full-duplex, dial up, 56-kbit/s digital circuits on an end-to-end basis.

PSEUDO CODE P-CODE. A code which must be translated before it can be executed or acted upon. Here's a more technical explanation. Pseudo Code is a compiled program written for a hypothetical processor and interpreted at runtime by a P-code interpreter written for a native environment. P-code has many objectives in its different implementations, most often portability and space savings.

PSEUDO RANDOM BIT PATTERN Test message consisting of 511 or 2,047 bits ensuring that all possible bit combinations can pass through a network without error.

PSEUDOLITE A ground based differential GPS (Global Positioning System) which transmits a signal like that of an actual GPS satellite, and can be used for ranging.

PSEUDORANGE A distance measurement based on the correlation of a GPS (Global Positioning System) satellite transmitted code and the local receiver's reference code, that has not been corrected for errors in synchronization between the transmitter's clock and the receiver's clock.

PSEUDOTERNARY A term used in ISDN Basic rate interface data coding. Refers to three encoded signal levels representing two-level binary data (binary "1"s are represented by no line signal, and binary "O"s by alternating positive and negative pulses).

PSI Packet Switching Interface.

PSK Phase Shift Keying. A method of modulating the phase of a signal to carry information. See PHASE MODULATION.

PSPDN Packet Switched Public Data Network.

PSOPHOMETER An instrument arranged to give visual indication corresponding to the aural effect of disturbing voltages of various frequencies. A psophometer usually incorporates a weighting network, the characteristics of which differ according to the type of circuit under consideration; e.g., high-quality music or commercial speech circuits.

PSTN Public Switched Telephone Network. An abbreviation used by the CCITT. See PUBLIC SWITCHED TELEPHONE NETWORK and PUBLIC DATA NETWORK.

PSU Packet Switch Unit.

PSYCHIC ANI A term created by Howard Bubb from Dialogic to designate what happens when you call someone on one line while they're calling you on the other.

PTC Personal Telecommunications Center. Infocorp's name for a product most people call a PDA, Personal Digital Assistant.

PTE Path Terminating Equipment. Network elements that multiplex and demultiplex the payload and that process the path overhead necessary to transport the payload. An AT&T SONET term.

PTN Public Telecommunications Network.

PTS Public Telecommunications Systems.

PTT Post Telephone & Telegraph administration. The PTTs, usually controlled by their governments, provide telephone and telecommunications services in most foreign countries. In CCITT documents, these are the Administrations referred to as Operating Administrations. The term Operating Administrations also refers to "Private Recognized Operating Agencies" which are the private companies that provide communications services in those very few countries that allow private ownership of telecommunications equipment.

PTY Party.

PU Physical Unit. In IBM's SNA, the component that manages and monitors the resources of a node, such as attached links and adjacent link stations. PU types follow the same classification as node types.

PU 2.0 & 2.1 IBM protocols which allow applications written to APCC and interpreted by LU 6.2 to access the mainframe (2.0) and token ring LAN (2.1).

PU TYPE 2 A physical unit (PU) refers to the management services in SNA node always contains one physical unit (PU), which represents the device and its resources to the network. PU Type 2 is often referred to as a cluster controller.

PUBLIC ACCESS TERMINAL A kiosk (SK series), enclosure (TK series) or a system for special enclosures and custom applications (XE Series) which provides the public access to service. Contains a color monitor and keypad for customer interaction.

PUBLIC ANNOUNCEMENT TRUNK GROUP A trunk group used to provide multiple types of announcements, such as the weather, time and sports results.

PUBLIC ASYNCHRONOUS DIAL-IN PORT A term used in packet switching networks referring to the local phone number of a port into the packet switched network. Some networks provide different numbers for different speeds. Some provide different speeds on the same numbers. See also PRIVATE DIAL-IN PORTS.

PUBLIC DATA NETWORK A network available to the public for the transmission of data, usually using packet switching under the CCITT X.25 packet switching protocol. See PACKET SWITCHED NETWORK.

PUBLIC DIAL-UP PORT A port on a computer system or on a communications network which is accessible to devices operating over the public switched telephone network.

PUBLIC EXCHANGE A British word for Central Office. Outside North America, central offices are all called "public exchanges." In the US, a public exchange is typically a local telephone switch. TELECONNECT's phone number in North America is 212-691-8215. The 212 is our area code. The 691 designates the central office or public exchange which serves us. That public exchange belongs to New York Telephone Company. See also CENTRAL OFFICE and CO.

PUBLIC NETWORK A network operated by common carriers or telecommunications administrations for the provision of circuit-switched, packet-switched and leased-lined circuits to the public. Compare with private network.

PUBLIC SERVICE COMMISSION PSC. The state regulatory authority responsible for communications regulation. Also known as Public Utility Commission, Corporate Commission and in some states, the Railway Commission.

PUBLIC SWITCHED NETWORK Any common carrier network that provides circuit switching between public users. The term is usually applied to the public telephone network but it could be applied more generally to other switched networks such as Telex, MCI's Execunet, etc.

PUBLIC SWITCHED TELEPHONE NETWORK Usually refers to the worldwide voice telephone network accessible to all those with telephones and access privileges (i.e. In the U.S., it was formerly called the Bell System network or the AT&T long distance network).

PUBLIC TELEPHONE STATION Coin phone. Pay phone.

PUBLIC UTILITY COMMISSION PUC. State body charged with regulating phone companies. Also called Public Service Commissions. See PUBLIC SERVICE COMMISSION.

PUBLICATIONS, COMPUTER & TELECOM

Alcatel's Electrical Communication, a quarterly technical journal from Alcatel NV, 33 rue Emeriau, 75725 Paris Cedex 15, France

Boardwatch, 5970 S. Vivian St., Littleton, CO 80127

Business Communications Review, 950 York Rd., Hinsdale, IL 60521

BYTE, One Phoenix Mill Lane, Peterborough, NH 03458

CALL CENTER Magazine, 12 West 21 Street, New York, NY 10010

Communications News, 2504 N. Tamiami Trail, Nokomis, FL 34275

Communications Week, 600 Community Dr., Manhasset, NY 11030

Computerworld, P.O. Box 9171, 375 Cochituate Rd., Framingham, MA 01701

Data Communciations, 1221 Avenue of the Americas, New York, NY 10020

DEC Professional, 921 Bethlehem Pike, Spring House, PA 19477

Dr. Dobb's Journal, 501 Galveston Dr., Redwood City, CA 94063

Electronic Business, Cahners Building, 275 Washington St., Newton, MA 02158

Federal Computer Week, 3110 Fairview Park Dr, # 1040, Falls Church VA 22042

IEEE Spectrum, 345 E. 47th St., New York, NY 10017

IMAGING Magazine, 12 West 21 Street, New York, NY 10010

InfoWorld, 1060 Marsh Rd., Menlo Park, CA 94025

Inform, 1100 Wayne Ave., Suite 1100, Silver Spring, MD 20910

Information Week, 600 Community Dr., Manhasset, NY 11030

InfoText, 34700 Coast Highway, Suite 309, Capistrano Beach, CA 92624

LAN Magazine, 500 Howard St., San Francisco, CA 94105

LAN Technology, 501 Galveston Dr., Redwood City, CA 94063

MacWEEK, P.O. Box 1763, Riverton, NJ 08077-9763

Marketing Computers, 49 E. 21st St., New York, NY 10010

Mobile Office, 21600 Oxnard St., Suite 480, Woodland Hills, CA 91367

Network Computing, 600 Community Drive, Manhasset, NY 11030

Network World, 161 Worcester Rd., Framingham, MA 01701-9172

NeXTWORLD, P.O. Box 56430, Boulder, CO 80322-6430

Payphone Magazine, P.O. Box 42371, Houston, TX 77242

PC Magazine, One Park Avenue, New York, NY 10016

PC Resource, 80 Elm St., Peterborough, NH 03458

PC Sources, P.O. Box 53297, Boulder, CO 80322-3297

PC WEEK, One Park Avenue, New York, NY 10016

PC World, 501 Second St. #600, San Francisco, CA 94107

PC/Computing, 950 Tower La., Foster City, CA 94404

Phone+, 4141 N. Scottsdale Rd., Suite 316, Scottsdale, AZ 85251

Procomm Enterprises, 901 A Street, Suite E-2, San Rafael, CA 94901

Public Communications Magazine, P.O. Box 42371, Houston, TX 77242

Satellite Comms, 6300 S. Syracuse Way, Suite 650, Englewood, CO 80111

Telecom Gear, 15400 Knoll Trail, Dallas, TX 75248

TELECOM LIBRARY Inc, Central Source of All Books on Telecommunications, 12 West 21 Street, New York, NY 10010 212-691-8215. Ask for a free catalog.

TeleManagement, 1400 Bayly St., Office Mall 2, Suite 3, Pickering, Ont., Canada L1W 3R2

Telemarketing. 1 Technology Plaza, Norwalk, CT 06854

Telecommunications, 685 Canton St., Norwood, MA, 02062

TELECONNECT Magazine, 12 West 21 Street, New York, NY 10010

Telephone Engineer & Management, 233 N. Michigan Ave., Chicago, IL 60601

Telephony, 55 E. Jackson, Chicago, IL 60604

TeleProfessional, 209 West Fifth Street, Suite N, Waterloo, IA 50701

The Office, 1600 Summer St., Stamford, CT 06905

UnixWorld, P.O. Box 571, Hightstown, NJ 08520-9331

VARBusiness, 600 Community Dr., Manhasset, NY 11030

Voice Processing Magazine, P.O. Box 42382, Houston, TX 77242

PUBLISHING Making resources available to network users.

PUC See PUBLIC UTILITY COMMISSION.

PULL BOX A box with a cover inserted in a long conduit run, particularly at a corner. It makes it easier to pull wire or cable into the conduits.

PULLING EYE A device on the end of a cable to which a pulling line is attached for pulling cable into conduit or duct liner.

PULLING STRENGTH Expressed in lbs. The maximum force which may be applied to strength members of a cable. Pulling strength limits are specified for all Belden Fiber Optic cables in the General Line and Fiber Optic catalogs. Affects pulling methods, pulling tension and operation tension.

PULP A type of older telephone twisted-pair cable whose wood-pulp "paper" insulation is formed on the cable during manufacture.

PULSE A quick change in the current or voltage produced in a circuit used to operate an electrical switch or relay or which can be detected by a logic circuit.

PULSE ADDRESS MULTIPLE ACCESS PAMA. The ability of a communication satellite to receive signals from several Earth terminals simultaneously and to amplify, translate, and relay the signals back to Earth, based on the addressing of each station by an assignment of a unique combination of time and frequency slots. This ability may be restricted by allowing only some of the terminals access to the satellite at any given time.

PULSE AMPLITUDE MODULATION PAM. A technique for placing binary information on a carrier to transmit that information. PAM is a technique for analog multiplexing. The amplitude of the information being modulated controls the amplitude of the modulated pulses. Samples of each input voltage are placed between voltage samples from other channels. The cycle is repeated fast enough so the sampling rate of any one channel is more than twice the highest frequency transmitted. See also PAM and PCM.

PULSE CABLE A type of coaxial cable constructed to transmit repeated high voltage pulses without degradation.

PULSE CODE MODULATION PCM. The most common and most important method a telephone system in North America can use to sample a voice signal and convert that sample into an equivalent digital code. PCM is a digital modulation method that encodes a Pulse Amplitude Modulated (PAM) signal into a PCM signal. See PCM and T-1.

PULSE DENSITY In T-1, since "O"s are represented by no pulse and "1"s by alternating pulses, pulse density refers to the number of no pulse ("O") periods allowed before a pulse ("1") must occur. Typically, no more than 15 no pulse periods ("O"s) are allowed before a pulse ("1") must occur.

PULSE DIALING One or two types of dialing that uses rotary pulses to generate the telephone number.

PULSE DISPERSION The spreading out of pulses as they travel along an optical fiber.

PULSE DURATION MODULATION PDM. That form of modulation in which the duration of the pulse is varied in accordance with some characteristic of the modulating signal.

PULSE LINK REPEATER A signaling set that interconnects the E and M leads of two circuits. In E & M signaling, a device that interfaces the signal paths of concatenated trunk circuits. Such a device responds to a ground on the "E" lead of one trunk by applying -48Vdc to the "M" lead of the connecting trunk, and vice versa. This function is a built-in, switch-selectable option in some commercially available carrier channel units.

PULSE OVERSHOOT In T-1, the amount of signal voltage that can remain at the trailing end of a pulse. It can be no more than 10-30% of the pulse amplitude. Also called afterkick.

PULSE-POSITION MODULATION PPM. That form of modulation in which the positions in time of the pulses are varied in accordance with some characteristic of the modulating signals, without modifiying the pulse width.

PULSE REPETITION FREQUENCY PRF. In radar, the number of pulses that occur each second. Not to be confused with transmission frequency which is determined by the rate at which cycles are repeated within the transmitted pulse.

PULSE STUFFING When timing signals on digital circuits get out of whack, some method of allowing mismatches must be provided. In time division multiplexing, this is called pulse stuffing. One stream of data has bits added to it so its final rate is the same as the master clock.

PULSE TRAIN The resulting electronic impulses that transmit encoded information.

PULSE WIDTH In T-1, refers to the width (at half amplitude) of the bipolar pulse (typically 324 + or -45 nsec).

PULSE WIDTH MODULATION Another but not very common method of modulating a signal, in which an analog input signal's DC level controls the pulse width of the digital output pulses. See PULSE CODE MODULATION and PULSE AMPLITUDE MODULATION.

PULSENET ALERT TRANSPORT SERVICE A service from New York Telephone, PULSENET Alert Transport Service lets monitoring agencies use a business or residence customer's existing POTS telephone line to transport information (burglar, fire, medical, alert, etc.) without interfering with their basic voice telephone service.

PULSING The method used for transmitting the phone number dialed to a telephone company switching office.

PUNCH 1. The process of perforating a paper tape or card in order to code information into machine readable form. 2. The process of connecting jumper interconnection wires on a distribution frame. It is called punching because of the tool which places the wire on the metal post of the frame. It is called a PUNCH and requires a heavy "punch" to make it strip its wires, then connect into the PUNCH-DOWN BLOCK.

PUNCH DOWN A term used to describe the connection of twisted pair wires to an insulation displacement block. (eg patch panel).

PUNCHDOWN BLOCK A device used to connect one group of wires to another. Usually each wire can be connected to several other wires in a bus or common arrangement. A 66-type block is the most common type of punchdown block. It was invented by Western Electric. Northern Telecom has one called a Bix block. There are others. These two are probably the most common. A punchdown block is also called a a terminating block, a connecting block, a punch-down block, a quick-connect block, a cross-connect block. A punchdown block will include insulation displacement connections (IDC). In other words, with a connecting block, you don't have to remove the plastic shielding from around your wire conductor before you "punch it down."

PURE ALOHA A random access technique developed by the University of Hawaii in the early 1970's. In this scheme, a user wishing to transmit does so at will. Collisions are resolved by retransmitting after a random period of time.

PURGED CUSTOMER ACCOUNT An MCI definition. MCI customer account information removed from both A/R and OCIS.

PUSH Mechanism in TCP for ensuring immediate transmission of data.

PUSH-DOWN FILE Last-in, first-out

PUSH-TO-TALK 1. In telephone or two-way radio systems, you have to push a button to talk and stop pushing to listen. Typically you say "over" to indicate it's the other person's turn to talk. In radio, it is used where the same frequency is employed by both transmitters. 2. A method of payphone operation in which a push button switch is touched by the caller when the called party answers. Once pushed, money is collected and handset microphone turned on. This system deprives the phone company of revenues for calls to 976 numbers, answering machines or answering services.

PUSHBUTTON DIALING Instead of rotary dialing, buttons are pushed to generate the tones needed to place a phone call. Also called Touchtone and

NEWTON'S TELECOM DICTIONARY

Touch-call. Some pushbutton phones do not produce tones, but generate the dial pulses of rotary dials. Some phones and phone systems will generate both rotary dial pulses and tone signaling.

PUSHBUTTON DIALING TO STATIONS A special attendant console feature in which the switching system is served by rotary dial central office trunk circuits. A ten-button keyset is provided on the console which allows fast dialing of extension numbers to complete incoming calls.

PUSHBUTTON ORIGINATING REGISTER A register used to store information about originating calls with pushbutton signals.

PUT-UP Refers to the packaging of wire and cable. The term itself refers to the packaged product that is ready to be stored or shipped.

PVC 1. Premises Visit Charge. 2. PolyVinyl Chloride, a common type of plastic used for cladding telephone cable (except that to be run in plenum ceilings). Or, 3. Permanent Virtual Circuit, a permanent association between two DTEs established by configuration. A PVC uses a fixed logical channel to maintain a permanent association between the DTEs. Once a PVC is defined, it requires no setup operation before data is sent and no disconnect operation after. A new connection, i.e. new information to be sent between the same users may be routed along a different path.

PVDF See POLYVINYLIDENE DIFLUORIDE.

PVN Private Virtual Network.

PWB Printed Wire Board.

PWM Pulse Width Modulation. In communications, encoding information based on variations of the duration of carrier pulses. Also called Pulse Duration Modulation or PDM.

PWR Power.

Px64 Informal name for CCITT video algorithm (formal name is H.261) proposed by CCITT for teleconferencing. Targeted for ratification as a standard for telephony soon.

PYRAMID CONFIGURATION A communications network in which the data link(s) of one or more multiplexers are connected to I/O ports of another multiplexer.

Q Queue.

Q BIT The qualifier bit in an X.25 packet that allows the DTE to indicate that it wishes to transmit data on more than one level.

Q.921 Q.921 defines the ISDN frame format at the data link layer of the OSI/ISDN Model. It contains address information. The CCITT/OSI Layer 2 protocol used in the D channel. It is synonymous with LAPD.

Q.931 Q.931 is the powerful message-oriented signaling protocol in the PRI ISDN D-channel. It is also referred as CCITT Recommendation I.451. This protocol describes what goes into a signaling packet and defines the message type and content. Specifically, Q.931 provides:

● call setup and take down.

● called party number, with type of number indication (private or public).

● calling party number information (including privacy and authenticity indicators).

● bearer capability (to distinguish, for example, voice versus data for compatibility check between terminals.

● status checking (for recovery from abnormal events, such as protocol failures or the manual busying of trunks), and

● release of B-channels and the application of tones and/or announcements in the originating switch upon encountering errors.

Q.931 makes it possible to interwork PBX features with features in the public network. In addition to offering users more access to a wider range of services, this interaction, according to Northern Telecom, will improve the revenue potential of service providers. Service provided over PRA, using Q.931, include:

● access to the public network, such as equal access, WATS, DDD, international DDD, dial-800 and other special number services and operator assisted calls.

● access to and from such private networks as Northern Telecom's Meridian Switched Network (previously call Electronic Switched Network — ESN), tandem tie networks, and extension dialing network, and

● integration of voice and circuit-switched data traffic (up to 64 kbps).

The Q.931 protocol also enables corporations to use B-channels — that is voice and data channels — in ways currently not possible. Today, for example, a separate trunk from the PBX to the central office is often required for each different service, such as voice, data, foreign exchange, 800-service. With PRA, one common trunk between the PBX and the central office can carry multiple call types. Moreover each B-channel within the PRA trunk can be assigned dynamically to carry whatever service is needed at the moment.

QA Quality assurance

QAM, QSAM Quadrature Amplitude Modulation, Quadrature Sideband Amplitude Modulation. A sophisticated modulation technique, using variations in signal amplitude, that allows data-encoded symbols to be represented as any of 16 or 32 different states. Some QAM modems allow dial-up data rates of up to 9600 bits per second.

QBE Query By Example. A database front-end that requests the user to supply an example of the type of data to be retrieved.

QBF A test message containing the "Quick Brown Fox" text. Used to test data terminals. The text is "The Quick Brown Fox jumped over the lazy dog." It contains every letter of the alphabet. Check it out.

QDOS In 1980 IBM showed up on Bill Gates' doorstep seeking an operating system for its upcoming personal computer. Mr. Gates did not have one. But he knew someone that had one. A little firm down the road (in Seattle) had developed QDOS — the Quick and Dirty Operating System. It looked just right for IBM's PC. Mr. Gates bought QDOS for $100,000 and renamed it MS-DOS — Microsoft Disk Operating System. According to the Economist Magazine of May 22, 1993, some jealous Microsoft rivals claim that MS-DOS now stands for Microsoft Seeks Domination Over Society.

QDU Quantizing Distortion Units. CCITT Recommendation G.113 defines one QDU as the amount of degradation introduced into a voice channel by a single conversion from analog to PCM and back to analog (analog-PCM-analog). Where several voice channels are connected in tandem, the end-to-end QDU rating for the whole circuit is calculated by adding the number of conversions from analog to PCM and back. For example: analog - PCM - analog - PCM - analog introduces 2QDUs.

QLLC Qualified Logical Link Control. Software package that allows Systems Network Architecture (SNA) commands to be transmitted over an X.25 packet data network (PDN). See also NPSI. Contrast with DSP.

QoS Quality of Service.

QPSK Quaternary Phase Shift Keying. Another way of sending data through a modem over an analog phone line.

QPSX Queued Packed and Synchronous Exchange. Technology used in Institute of Electrical and Electronic Engineers (IEEE) standard 802.6 for metropolitan area networks (MANs).

QSAM Quadrature Sideband Amplitude Modulation. A sophisticated modulation technique, using variations in signal amplitude, that allows data-encoded symbols to be represented as any of 16 or 32 different states.

QUAD Term used to describe the four-wire cable used in homes. Typically, one pair is used for "tip and ring," also called positive and negative. These two wires carry the phone conversation and the ringing. Typically these wires are red and green. The other pair of the quad is usually black and yellow and is used as a spare, as a second line or to carry power to a lamp in the dial of the phone, etc.

QUAD-FIBER CABLE A cable consisting of four single optical fiber cables placed inside a polyvinyl chloride jacket with a rip cord to peel back the jacket and gain access to each single cable.

QUADDED CABLE A cable in which at least some of the conductors are arranged in the form of a quad.

QUALITY OF SERVICE A measure of the telephone service quality provided to a subscriber. It's not easy to define "quality" of telephone service. It's very subjective. Is the call easy to hear? Is it "clear?" Is it loud enough, etc.? The state public service commissions have various measures which they insist phone companies conform to. They tend to be more measurable. They include the longest time someone should wait after picking up the handset before they receive dial tone (three seconds in most states).

QUANTIZATION Take an analog voice signal, sample it and put numbers on those samples. That's called quantization. Here's an explanation from Understanding Telephone Electronics: "A circuit called a quantizer takes in the analog signal and produces an equivalent number. Threshold levels are established and numbers are assigned to the analog samples as their amplitudes fall within the bands formed by the threshold numbers. (For example, everything within the range 1000.05 and 1000.06 Hz is given the number 14568.) The assigned number in most costs is an approximation rather than a true value because the true value would require many more bits (i.e. more threshold limits) in the binary code...This approximation causes an error which is the difference between the approximate number and the true sample. This quantization error adds noise to the signal, called quantization noise, which is heard in the telephone as hissing. Quantization noise can be reduced by making the threshold bands narrower...However, providing more intervals requires more bits in the binary code. Therefore, more bandwidth is needed. There is a tradeoff between small quantizing intervals (higher bandwidth, lower noise), and fewer intervals (lower bandwidth, higher noise)."

QUANTIZATION NOISE Signal errors which result from the process of digitizing (and therefore ascribing finite quantities to) a continuously variable signal. See QUANTIZATION.

QUANTIZE The process of encoding a PAM signal (Pulse Amplitude Signal) into a PCM signal (Pulse Code Modulation). See QUANTIZATION.

QUANTIZING The second stage of pulse code modulation (PCM). The waveform samples obtained from each communication channel are measured to obtain a discrete value of amplitude. These quantized values are converted to a binary code and transmitted to a distant location to reconstruct the original waveform. See QUANTIZE and QUANTIZATION.

QUANTIZING NOISE Noise caused by the inability of an analog signal to be exactly replicated in digital form.

QUANTUM In physics, quantum means a very small indivisible piece of energy. This word is widely misused by people who refer to "a quantum leap," meaning a big leap.

QUARTER SPEED An international leased teletype line capable of transmitting one quarter of Telex speed of 16 2/3 words per minute.

QUARTER WAVE ANTENNA An antenna, the length of which is 1/4 that of the wave length received.

QUARTZ CRYSTAL A small piece of quartz which is cut to a precise size. When electricity is applied to the crystal, it vibrates at a specific and precise frequency. Quartz crystals are often used in watches. They vibrate quickly and make the watch far more accurate than a timing device which vibrates far more slowly, like a pendulum, for example, or a tick tock watch.

QUENCHED GAP A spark gap so arranged that the spark is quenched quickly by a cooling effect. A method used to give impluse exitation. An old radio term.

QUERY 1. In data communications, it's the process by which a master station (or mainframe or boss computer) asks a slave station to identify itself and tell its status, i.e. is it busy, alive, OK, waiting, etc.? 2. In database, a query is a for the retrieval of data.

QUERY LANGUAGE A programming language designed to make it easier to specify what information a user wants to retrieve from a database.

QUEUE A stream of tasks waiting to be executed. A series of calls or messages waiting for connection to a line. See QUEUING.

QUEUED MODE Calls entering an Automatic Call Distributing system wait in a queue are presented, one at a time, to the first idle trunk in the chosen group.

QUEUED TELECOMMUNICATIONS ACCESS METHOD QTAM. A program component in a computer which handles some of the communications processing tasks for an application program. QTAM is employed in data collection, message switching and many other teleprocessing applications.

QUEUING The act of "stacking" or holding calls to be handled by a specific person, trunk or trunk group. There are two reasons to queue telephone calls:

1. Because you simply don't have enough trunks.

2. Because you want to save money.

You can queue calls mechanically using your telephone switch or manually using a human operator or attendant. There are two ways you can queue calls — hold-on or call-back. In "hold-on" queuing, you dial, you get some queuing tone (or the operator tells you you're being queued), then you wait on-line until a line becomes free and you're connected. In "call-back" queuing, you tell the operator or the machine you want to dial a call. And you hang up. When the line becomes free you are called back and connected. There are advantages and disadvantages to both systems. In "hold-on" queuing, you waste your time but save on phone time. In call-back queuing, you waste less of your time, but more phone line time. In call-back queuing, the operator or the phone system has to grab the line you want and simultaneously call you. By then, you may have left your desk. The call may be wasted, etc. The line given to you could have been used by someone else, etc. Queuing calls as a method to save money on long distance calling makes sense ONLY:

1. IF you are out of trunks because of a temporary surge in telephone traffic — perhaps at your peak, peak busy time and it's very expensive to buy sufficient "cheap long distance" trunks to handle every conceivable peak, and

2. IF you never plan on having a queue longer than 20 seconds for a hold-on queue and 60 seconds for a call-back queue and

3. IF you are queuing calls into an expensive fixed-cost line. For example a tie-line between New York and London. If you queue calls into a variable cost line, like an interstate WATS line, you will save money over throwing the call onto DDD, but the pennies you save usually won't be worth it — considering the aggravation you're going to cause your people. Queuing is a very sensitive subject in corporate telecommunications departments. People don't like to wait for telephone lines. They consider that insulting to them personally, damaging to their "productivity" and to heck with the cost. Queues do, however, make enormous sense. Even a queue as short as ten seconds can save big amounts of money. Queues of a maximum length of ten seconds are rarely noticed. These days some of the more modern PBXs will allow you to offer "selective" queuing, or levels of queuing. Upper management doesn't have to queue for the cheap long distance lines before it's bounced to the expensive ones. While lower management has to wait up to 30 seconds. And the worker bees (non-management) have to wait even longer. Queuing is also used on incoming trunks. See ACD and QUEUING THEORY.

QUEUING THEORY The study of the behavior of a system that uses queuing, such as a telephone system. Much of queuing theory derives from the science of Operations Research (OR). Dr. Leonard Kleinrock has written the authoritative books on the subject. He is probably a genius. His books are very difficult to understand for laymen. Here is an explanation of Queuing Theory from James Henry Green's Dow Jones-Irwin Handbook of Telecommunications (you can get a copy from Telecom Library at 1-800-LIBRARY or 1-212-691-8215.):

"The most common (telephone) network design method involves modeling the (phone) network according to principles of queuing theory, which describes how customers or users behave in a queue. Three variables are considered in network design. The first is the arrival or input process that describes the way users array themselves as they arrive to request service...The second variable is the service process, which describes the way users are handled when they are taken from queue and admitted into the service providing mechanism. The third method is the queue discipline, which describes the way users behave when they encounter blockage in the network...Three reactions to blockage are possible:

● Blocked calls held (BCH). When users encounter blockage, they immediately redial and reenter the queue.

● Blocked calls cleared (BCC). When users encounter blockage, they wait for some time before redialing.

● Blocked calls delayed (BCD). When users encounter blockage, they are placed in a holding circuit until capacity to serve them is available. (See QUEUE.)

"Traffic engineers have different formulas or tables to apply, corresponding to the assumption about how users behave when they encounter blockage." See POISSON.

After I wrote the above definition, Lee Goeller, a noted traffic engineering expert contributed the following definition:

The study of systems in which customers wait in line for servers to become available, the "blocked calls delayed" condition in telephony (see TRAFFIC ENGINEERING). Although seldom used in designing voice networks (other techniques are usually more cost-effective), queuing is very important in the design of packet networks where speed of transmission more than offsets the delay of waiting for a transmission facility to become available, and in staffing Automatic Call Distributors.

QUICK CONNECT BLOCK Also called a 66-block or punch-down block. It's a two foot piece of metal and plastic which allows you to connect telephone wiring coming from two remote points. The quick-connect block has multiple metal "jaws" ranging horizontally and vertically. To connect up, you "punch" (or push) a wire between the two metal teeth of the "jaws." This both holds it firm and strips the wire's insulation, thus allowing for a good electrical connection. (There are special "punch-down" tools for punching wires into 66-blocks.) On a 66-block, one horizontal row of "jaws" is always the same conductor. To connect other wires to it, you simply punch those wires down along the row. Some 66-blocks have a gap between one side of the 66-block and the other. To connect one wire on one side to the wire on the other side, you have to use a BRIDGING CLIP. This is a small metal clip about one inch long. The bridging clip has one purpose: you can slip it off easily and thus cut one side of the circuit from the other. For example, if you connected central office trunks on one side of the 66-block and a PBX on the other, by removing the bridging clips, you can tell instantly if the trouble is in the PBX or in the central office. Two conductors on a 66-block makes a circuit — a trunk or a line. Therefore, the trunk 212-691-8215 (our main number) takes up the first two horizontal rows on our 66-block. The second two horizontal rows are taken up with 212-691-8216, and so on.

It is good to learn where your main 66-block is — the one that connects you to the telephone company's central office lines. The 66-block is what the telephone company calls the "demarcation point." And they (the phone company) usually install the 66-block. On one side (the trunk side) of their block, they're responsible. On the other (the PBX, key system or phone side), you're responsible. By knowing how to test your lines at this point, you can know whose fault it is — the phone company's or your equipment's. This can avoid having to wait until the phone company arrives, discovers it's not their problem and then sends you a hefty bill. Or the interconnect company arrives, finds out it's not their problem, and sends you a hefty bill, etc.

Quick Connect Blocks or 66-blocks are found in the Main Distribution Frame — where lines coming out of the PBX are connected to the individual wires going to the phones, or to big cables going to clumps of phones in other parts of the building. They're also found in Satellite Distribution Frames where they take big cable coming in from the main distribution frame and connect it to the individual cable pairs going to the individual phones. See CONNECTING BLOCK.

QUICK FORMAT A DOS program which deletes the file allocation table and root directory of a disk but does not scan the disk for bad areas.

QUIESCENT A fancy word for quiet. No noise. No activity. Quiescent time is the best time to write this dictionary. Sadly, it wasn't always to be.

QUORUM A family of teleconferencing products linked in a system designed to meet a customer's teleconferencing needs.

QWERTY A standard typewriter keyboard. The left side top row of letter keys on the keyboard spell QWERTY. In reality, the last "standard" keyboard was IBM's Selectric keyboard. And even then there were variations to suit different tasks, languages, etc. Computer keyboards typically have 20 to 30 extra keys more than "standard" typewriter keyboards. Many of the keys on computer keyboards are called "function" keys. If you hit one of them, they might perform a complete function on the computer, e.g. save a file, move to the end of the file, etc. There is absolutely no such thing as a standard computer keyboard.

QZ Special billing arrangement provided by your local telephone company. Before there was automatic call accounting and before there was Centrex, the phone company would give you "time and charges" on every outgoing call. This service was called "QZ" billing. It was used by engineers, lawyers, accountants, consultants and other service people who had to bill their calls back to their clients.

R INTERFACE The 2-wire physical interface which is used for a single customer termination between the TE2 and TA.

R REFERENCE Non-ISDN (TE2) terminal equipment connects to ISDN at the R-reference point through a terminal adaptor.

R2 A whole series of CCITT specs which refers to European analog and digital trunk signaling. It refers to a type of a loop start trunk found in Europe which uses compelled handshaking on every MF (multi-frequency) signaling digit.

RACE An association in the European Economic Community. RACE stands for Research and development for Advanced Communications in Europe.

RACEWAY Metal or plastic channel used for loosely holding electrical and telephone wires in buildings. A raceway is usually located in the floor and is encased on three or four sides by concrete. A raceway is used for interior wiring and performs the same job as a conduit but is typically larger.

RACEWAY METHOD A ceiling distribution method in which open or closed metal trays are suspended in false ceilings from the structural floor above. The raceway method is generally used in large buildings or for complex distribution systems that demand extra support. When closed metal trays are embedded in the floor, this distribution method is often called underfloor raceways. See also CEILING DISTRIBUTION SYSTEMS and UNDERFLOOR DUCT METHOD.

RACK An open structure typically made of aluminum or steel, onto which equipment is mounted. A rack is typically attached to a building ceiling or wall. Cables are laid in and fastened to the rack. Sometimes a rack is called a tray. What a rack is to equipment, so a frame is to wiring. See also DISTRIBUTION FRAME.

RACON A radionavigation system transmitting, automatically or in response to a predetermined received signal, a pulsed radio signal with specific characteristics.

RAD The unit used to measure the absorption of ionizing radiation.

RADAR RAdio Detection And Ranging. See RADAR DETECTOR.

RADAR DETECTOR Picture a trooper sitting in his car airiming his radar gun down the highway. The gun emits a beam of electrons at microwave frequency. Those beams bounce off approaching vehicles and reflect back to the trooper's radar at an altered frequency (the Doppler Effect). By measuring the change in frequency, the trooper calculates the speed of the oncoming vehicle. The trouble is the radar beam fans out like a searchlight. At a distance of 1,000 feet, the beam is about as wide as the highway itself. That makes it difficult for the trooper to know which vehicle he's tracking.

Also, his reading can be thrown off by any number of operating errors or by interference from power lines, neon lights or even the fan motor in the trooper's car. According to some estimates, Esquire Magazine reported, as many as 30% of all radar-generated speeding tickets were given in error. In 1979 a Miami TV station showed a police radar clocking a house going 28 miles per hour and a hanyan tree doing 86! Radar detectors are very much like FM receivers. They can pick up radar signals more than a mile from the source. At that distance the beam is too weak to bounce all the way back to the trooper's car but strong enough to make the detector beep.

RADIANT ENERGY Energy as measured in joules which is transferred via electromagnetic waves. There is no associated transfer of matter. And typically the giver or energy and the receiver of energy are not touching.

RADIO The science of communicating over a distance by converting sounds or signals to electromagnetic waves and radiating them through the air or through space. Also called Wireless by the British and the Australians.

RADIO BROADCAST DATA SYSTEM RBDS. A new system designed to let radio stations braodcasters send text messages, such as emergency warnings and traffic alerts to radios equipped with special LCD screens. The system is designed ultimately to replace the Emergency Broadcast System

RADIO COMMUNICATION Any telecommunication by means of radio waves.

RADIO FREQUENCY That group of electromagnetic energy whose wavelengths are between the audio and the light range. Electromagnetic waves transmitted usually are between 500 KHz and 300 GHz.

RADIO FREQUENCY FILTER FIT A Northern Telecom Norstar device designed to alleviate problems associated with radio frequency interference that may be experienced when a headset or external Auxiliary Ringer is used with a telephone.

RADIO FREQUENCY INTERFERENCE The disruption of radio signal reception caused by any source which generates radio waves at the same frequency and along the same path as the desired wave.

RADIO FREQUENCY INTERFERENCE SHIELD RFI Shield. A metal shield enclosing the printed circuit boards of the printer or computer to prevent radio and TV interference.

RADIO PAGING ACCESS Provides attendant and phone user dial access to customer-owned radio paging equipment to selectively tone-alert, or voice-page individuals carrying pocket radio receivers. The paged party can answer by dialing an answering code from a phone within the PBX.

RADIO PAGING ACCESS WITH ANSWER BACK Allows access to customer-provided paging systems and provides the capability in the PBX to connect the paged party when the former answers the radio page by dialing a special code from any PBX.

RADIO WAVE Electromagnetic waves of frequencies between 10 KHz and 3MHz, propagated without guide in free space (air).

RADIOGRAM A telegram sent by radio. Totally obsolete term, but cute.

RADIOPHONE Apparatus for transmitting and/or receiving speech or music by radio. Totally obsolete term, but cute.

RADIOSONDE An automatic radio transmitter in the meterological aids service usually carried on an aircraft, free ballon, kite, or parachute, and which transmits meterological data.

RADIOTELEPHONY The science, art, and act of transmitting speech by means of radio. Now probably called telecommunications.

RADOME A plastic cover for a microwave antenna. It protects the antenna from awful weather, but has little effect on the radiation pattern of the antenna.

RAID Redundant Array of Inexpensive Disks. A method of backing up computer data. At its simplest, the technique mirrors data to two drives. Mirroring is convenient because it requires absolutely no user action. It's brainless. Data backup is continuous. Once a failure occurs, the system can be up and running with little delay, theoretically. In practice, disk mirroring is an old art on bigger computers, but still a very new "art" on PCs and LAN file servers and doesn't work as well as it should on this newer equipment. See also REDUNDANT ARRAY OF INEXPENSIVE DISKS for a much more detailed explanation.

RAIN ATTENUATION Signal losses due to absorption are common when radio signals encounter a heavily moisture laden atmosphere. Generally, the higher the radio frequency, the more attenuation (i.e. the more losses). Since microwave signals for satellite and for land line are essentially line-of-sight, microwave radio is very susceptible to signal attenuation in heavy rain. Modern microwave paths are engineered with weather patterns in mind. In areas where heavy rainfalls occur, microwave links may be closer together or more attention is paid to diverse routing.

RAIN BARREL EFFECT Signal distortion of a voice telephone line caused by the under-attenuated echoes on the return path.

RAISED FLOOR METHOD A floor distribution method in which square, steel and wood-laminated plates resting on aluminum locking pedestals are attached to the building floor. The plates are usually covered with cork, carpet, or vinyl tiles, and each plate can be removed for easy access to the cables below. Also referred to as access floor.

RAM Random Access Memory. The primary memory in a computer. Memory that can be overwritten with new information. The "random access" part of its name comes from the fact that the next "bit" of information in RAM can be located — no matter where it is — in an equal amount of time. This means that access to and from RAM memory is extraordinarily fast. By contrast, other storage media — like magnetic tape — have their information stored serially, one bit after another. Therefore you have to search for them. And your search time will depend on how far from the bit you're searching for you are. Floppy disks are faster than magnetic tape because their information is readily at hand, though the read/write head will have to search for it. Hard disks are even faster because there are multiple heads and because the disks spin faster and everything moves faster. RAM memory is the fastest of all. The problem with RAM memory is that it's volatile. This means when power is turned off (or power glitches occur) RAM memory is erased. RAM memory can be protected with rechargeable batteries — just remember to charge the batteries.

RAM BASE ADDRESS Random Access Memory Base Address. Starting address for memory dedicated to a specific task.

RAM BIOS BIOS transferred to RAM so things go faster.

RAM DISK A logical device made from semiconductor (i.e. chip) memory which emulates the functioning of a disk drive as closely as possible. Since most semiconductor memory (RAM) is volatile, most RAM disks are also volatile, i.e. they lose their memory when you turn off power.

RAM MOBILE DATA A public data communications wireless network that allows people carrying handheld devices to send and receive short data messages. Such messages might be from sheriff standing in the street searching his department's data base for unpaid parking tickets. A competitor to RAM Mobile Data is Ardis.

RAMBUTAN A symmetric cryptographic algorithm developed by Marconi.

RAMDAC Random access memory digital-to-analog converter. The chip on a VGA board that translates the digital representation of a pixel into the analog information needed for display on the monitor.

RAN Return Authorization Number. A number you need for returning busted equipment to the factory.

RANDOM ACCESS Usually refers to computer memory or storage. Random Access is the ability to reach any piece of data in the memory directly without having to pass by other pieces of data. In telephony, this means the ability to reach any other subscriber through the telco switching network. See SEQUENTIAL ACCESS.

RANDOM ACCESS MEMORY See RAM.

RANDOM NOISE Interference to telephone communications occurring at irregular intervals.

RANGE EXTENDER A device that increases the length of a local loop by boosting battery voltage being sent out from the telephone company central office.

RARE EARTH DOPING Here is an article on rare earth doping from The

NEWTON'S TELECOM DICTIONARY

Economist Magazine of July 6, 1991: Optical fiber is the darling of the telecommunications world. Because light waves can be superimposed on one another, fiber can carry thousands of laser-generated messages at the same time, over longer and longer distances. The longest fibers were once those which doctors use to explore their patients innards. Now they can stretch 70 km (40 miles). But even that does not get you across a sea much bigger than the English Channel without the messages fading. So today's transatlantic and transpacific optical cables are interrupted about every 70 km so that the messages can be sorted out, passed through an electronic amplifier, and then, turned into light again. These amplifiers are costly. Soon, though, they may be replaced.

The key technique is called rare earth doping, which was developed not by crooked bookmakers but by scientists at Southampton University in England, and AT&T Bell laboratories in New Jersey. The rare earths are a group of chemical elements with particularly restless electrons in their atoms. If these electrons are stirred up by a laser, they rise to higher energy levels inside their atoms. When they fall back again, they emit light. The frequency of the light emitted depends on the element. The trick is to pick one which emits at frequency used for telecommunications. By adding the right rare earth to a stretch of fiber, you can make it amplify signals. You can also make a laser out of the fiber itself.

In the optical amplifier developed at Southampton University, a laser is used to lift electrons in the rare earth atoms in a stretch of fiber up to higher energy levels. When a light signal comes along, it may knock one of these electrons off its perch. The falling electron gives off light, which boosts the signal. The enhanced signal then knocks down more electrons, gathering strength as it goes. Rare earths in the cable can be used for other things, as the team at Bell Labs has found. Normal light waves, even those in laser beams, spread out and dissipate as they travel.

Solitons, a special kind of wave, do not. Tidal bores, the best known form of soliton, can move up rivers for miles without losing their shapes. Light that travelled in solitons could travel much farther along an optical fiber between boosts. Solitons are created either by pumping the initial signal through an optical amplifier, or by using a laser made from doped fiber. The soliton holds its shape because the passage of light through the fiber temporarily increases the speed of light in that part of the fiber, so the back of the wave is always trying to travel faster than the front. The stronger the light, the stronger the effect.

Rare earth doping, with metals called erbium and praseodymium, has resulted in fibers which can handle billions of bits of data per second, and carry them thousands of kilometers. AT&T hopes to use erbium amplifiers in its new trans-oceanic cables in the 1990s. Other companies — such as British Telecom and NTT — also like praseodymium, which is harder to handle, but emits light at a more commonly used frequency.

RARP Reverse Address Resolution Protocol. A TCP/IP protocol governing the translation of a DLC (Data-Link Control) address to an IP (Internet Protocol) address.

RASTER A pattern of horizontal scanning lines on a TV screen. Input data causes the beam of the TV tube to illuminate the correct dots to produce the required characters. See RASTER SCANNING.

RASTER SCANNING The method of scanning in which the scanning spot moves along a network of parallel lines, either from side to side or top to bottom.

RATE The price of a particular service or piece of equipment from a telephone company. Telephone companies don't use the word "price." They use the word "rate." No one knows why, except that if they didn't cultivate their own jargon, there'd be no job for telecommunications dictionary writers. God forbid!

RATE ARRANGEMENTS Telephone customer prices charged by tariffs for specified telephone services.

RATE AVERAGING Telephone companies' method for establishing uniform pricing by distance rather than on the relative cost (to them) of the particular route. The theory is that some routes are more heavily trafficked, have huge transmission equipment and achieve great economies of scale. Some routes, on the other hand, have little traffic, small transmission equipment and achieve no economies of scale. Therefore, it costs more to provide calls on these less-trafficked routes. But the phone industry doesn't charge more to call small towns than big cities. The phone industry simply charges by distance, averaging its costs. This is called rate averaging.

RATE BASE A regulated telephone company's plant and equipment which forms the dollar base upon which a specified rate of return can be earned. The total invested capital on which a regulated company is entitled to earn a reasonable rate of return.

RATE CENTER Telephone company-designated geographic locations assigned vertical and horizontal coordinates between which airline mileages are determined for the charging of private lines. See AIRLINE MILEAGE.

RATE CHIP A standard, nonvolatile memory device used to retain data base information on call pricing by Area Code and Central Office. Typically used in call accounting equipment.

RATE DESIGN Utilities have a specific rate for every service provided. The rates must be approved by the PUC. In a major rate case, rates for many services will be changed in tandem. In a rate design hearing, different proposals as to rate levels are considered. The level of one rate can have an impact on what the level of another rate should be. The inter-relationship between rates and the impact of demand must all be considered in "designing" a rate structure.

RATE ELEMENTS The pricing structure of various telecommunications service offerings usually described in tariffs.

RATE OF RETURN The percentage of net profit which a telephone company is authorized (by a regulatory commission) to earn on its rate base. See RATE BASE.

RATE PERIOD Dividing a day into various slices of time for the purpose of charging differently for long distance and local calls. There are three rate periods in force today in North America for intra-North America calls. One rate period is from 11:00 P.M. to 8:00 A.M.; one is from 8:00 A.M. to 5:00 P.M. and one is from 5:00 P.M. to 11:00 P.M. If you call outside the United States, there are different rate periods.

RATE REALIGNMENT In California's Alternative Regulatory Framework Phase III, rate realignment refers to redesigning telephone rates to reduce intraLATA toll rates and increase rates for other services to make up for the phone companies lost revenues. The Public Utility Commission (PUC) must approve all rate realignment proposals in the rate design stage of the proceeding.

RATE STABILITY PLAN Commit yourself to keeping a New York Telephone service for several years and you'll pay less than if you keep it only from month to month. Other phone companies have similar schemes, typically by other names.

RATE TABLE A data base that contains the cost of calls referenced to the Area Code and/or number dialed plus time of day considerations. See RATE PERIOD.

RATE ZONE A defined geographic division of an exchange area used as the primary basis for figuring toll rates.

RATED TEMPERATURE The maximum temperature at which an electric component can operate for extended periods without loss of its basic properties.

RATED VOLTAGE The maximum voltage at which an electric component can operate for extended periods without undue degradation or safety hazard.

RAYLEIGH SCATTERING Scattering due to tiny impurities in the optical fiber which are fractions of the wavelength of the infrared rays.

RB Reverse Battery.

RBDS Radio Broadcast Data System. A new system designed to let radio stations braodcasters send text messages, such as emergency warnings and traffic alerts to radios equipped with special LCD screens. The system is designed ultimately to replace the Emergency Broadcast System

RBOC Regional Bell Operating Company. There are seven RBOCs each of which own two or more BOCs (Bell Operating Companies). The RBOCs were carved out of the old AT&T/Bell System by Judge Harold Greene when he signed off on the divestiture of the Bell operating companies from AT&T at the end of 1984. There is nothing magical about seven — nor the grouping of BOCs into RBOCS — except the Judge wanted to keep them all roughly the same size.

RBS Robbed-Bit Signaling. See ROBBED-BIT SIGNALING.

RCA 1. Regional Calling Area. The geographical area covered by a telephone company. 2. Once it stood for Radio Corporation of America.

RCA GLOBCOM An International Telex and high-speed data communications company acquired by MCI from RCA in 1987. The acquisition of RCA Globecom gave MCI approximately 40% of the International Telex market and helped strengthen MCI's role in International data.

RCC Radio Common Carrier.

RCL ReCaLl.

RCP The Berkeley UNIX remote copy program.

RDF Radio Direction Finding.

RDT Recall Dial Tone.

RDY ReaDY.

RE-422 A high-speed electrical interface defined by the CCITT, supporting data rates of up to 768 Kbit/s over up to 300 feet of cable.

RE-ENGINEERING A term probably invented by Michael Hammer in the July-August, 1990 issue of Harvard Business Review. In that issue, he wrote "It is time to stop paving the cowpaths. Instead of embedding outdated processes in silicon and software, we should obliterate them and start over. We should 're-engineer' our business: use the power of modern information technology to radically redesign our business processes in order to achieve dramatic improvements in their performance." The term re-engineering now seems to me mean taking tasks presently running on mainframes and making them run on file servers running on LANs — Local Area Netwotks. The idea is to save money on hardware and make the information more freely available to more people. More intelligent companies also redesign their organization to use the now, more-freely available information. Also called VALUE DRIVEN RE-ENGINEERING.

RE-INITIATION TIME The time required for a device or system to restart (usually after a power outage).

RE-INSTALLED CUSTOMER An MCI customer who is installed again with the same customer account number after having been previously canceled either at their, MCI's, or a third party's request.

REA Rural Electrification Administration. A federal agency which makes loans to extend telephone service into rural areas. The REA has been one of the most successful federal government programs ever.

REACTANCE The opposition offered to the flow of an alternating current which is due to the presence of inductance or capacity or both, in the circuit.

READ To glean information from a storage device, like a floppy disk. The opposite of READ is to WRITE. That's when you put information onto that storage device. Some storage devices can only be READ, but not written to. On a floppy disk that's called being "WRITE PROTECTED." See also WORM, which stands for Write Once, Read Many.

READ ONLY FILE A PC computer term. A read only file is a file that you can read but cannot make changes to. The read-only attribute specifies whether a file is read-only. To remove the read-only attribute, you would type the following command

ATTRIB -R FILENAME

READ ONLY MEMORY ROM. A memory device which is programmed at the factory and whose contents thereafter cannot be altered, even by a power breakdown, or being written to, or anything else. ROM memory is also random-access, which means accessing its information is very fast. See also MICROPROCESSOR and RAM.

READ WRITE CYCLE Time of reading and writing data onto a memory device. See READ.

READER 1. A device which converts information into a format recognized by a machine as input. 2. A device which interprets coded data in the process of transferring that data from one coded state of storage to another.

READYLINE 800 A toll-free service designed for the small business. Receive "800" dialed calls over your existing telephone lines and equipment — no new lines to install, no new equipment needed. You can still use those same lines to make and receive local and long distance calls. Choose the geographic areas you want to cover — from a single area code to an entire state or the whole country. Even decide when you want your toll-free number to be available. You pay a one-time start-up charge and a low monthly fee. Calling prices are based on the market coverage you choose. There are time-of-day and day-of-week discounts, and a volume usage discount. Calls are priced on a mileage/distance-sensitive basis.

REAL MODE Originally there was the first IBM PC and it was powered by an Intel 8086 chip which addressed a maximum of 1MB (megabyte of RAM). Real mode is the term that later generations of Intel chips came to call their ability to run programs written for the 8086. Real mode allows 80286, 80386, or 80486 processors to emulate an 8086 processor but perform better than the 8086 because they operate at a faster clock rate. Real mode is limited to a maximum of 1MB of addressable memory because the 8086 processor uses a memory address bus of 20 bits. This is calculated thus: Since a bit can have one of two values, raising the base number of 2 to the power of 20 is equal to 1,048,576 unique memory addresses. Each memory address can store 1 byte of information (1,048,576 bytes equal 1MB). See also PROTECTED MODE.

REAL TIME A voice telephone conversation is conducted in Real Time. That is, there is no perceived delay in the transmission of the voice message or in the response to it. This concept often applies to interaction between a computer and a terminal. See also REAL TIME CAPACITY. In data processing or data communications, real time means the data is processed the moment it enters a computer, as opposed to BATCH processing where the information enters the system, is stored and is operated on a later time.

REAL TIME CAPACITY The capacity of the central computer processor of a stored program control telephone system to process the instructions coming at it. Real Time Capacity is probably the most important measure of the size of a telephone system relying on a single main processor.

REARRANGEMENT A fancy word for moving phone extensions around.

REASONABLENESS CHECKS Tests made on information reaching a real-time system or being transmitted from it to ensure that the data lie within a given range.

REASSERTING STATUS An ISDN term. When the ISDN phone is being directly controlled by the application program, the set's physical status may be different from the status that has been received from the network. When direct control ends, the ISDN set reasserts the status received from the network to bring its physical condition back into conformity with the network status.

REASSIGNMENT Here is an explanation by Bill Etling, a senior planner for GTE. "Under the assigned plant concept, a pair is dedicated from the central office to the subscriber home and maintained at that address, even when idle. The likelihood of such a pair being reused, thus eliminating a field visit and extra assignment work, more than makes up for lost revenue while the pair is vacant. In areas of high cable fills, such a pair, when vacant, is often used to fill an order at a different address. Reassignment quickly snowballs, generating many installation field visits and assignment changes, increasing paperwork and the chance of errors."

REBILLER A rebiller, also called a switchless reseller, buys long distance service in bulk from a long distance company, such as AT&T, and resells that service to smaller users. It typically gets its monthly bill on magnetic tape, then rebills the bulk service to its customers. A rebiller owns no communications facilities — switches or transmission. It has two "assets" — a computer program to rebill the tape and sales skills to sell its services to end users. The profit it makes comes from the difference between what it pays the long distance company and what it is able to sell its services at. It's not an easy business to be in, since you are selling a long distance company's services to compete against itself.

REBOOTING Repeating a Boot. Turning on or resetting the telephone system or the computer. The word derives from "boot-strapping." Starting from scratch. Pulling oneself up by one's own bootstraps. Booting a telephone system or a computer means starting it from scratch, usually by turning its AC power on. Rebooting a telephone system is done by simply turning it off, counting to ten and turning it back on again.

Rebooting is done to clear the volatile part of the telephone system's or computer's memory and its various processing and clock chips. You reboot typically when your PC "locks" inexplicably or when your telephone system does something you can't explain logically — like ring phones randomly or give strange error messages on the console. On a computer, "Lock" means that no matter which key or combination of keys you touch on your keyboard, you can't get your computer to do anything. In addition to "unlocking" your computer, you also reboot to clear RAM or RAM-resident programs. On an IBM or an IBM clone, rebooting is done by pressing the CONTROL, ALT and DELETE keys simultaneously. You can also reboot by pressing the reset button if your computer has one. (Not all do.)

You can reboot any computer by turning its power off, then turning it back on. This is usually not a good idea, since the surge of power that accompanies a computer being turned on and off will reduce the life of many of its electronic components. Some experts recommend leaving computers running full-time, though turning their hard disks off. They also recommend turning your screen off, or at least running a public domain program such as SCRNSAVE.COM or SCRN.COM which turn off your screen after several minutes of doing nothing (inactivity).

RECALL The recall button on many phones provides a fresh dial tone without physically putting down and picking up the handset. Don't confuse it with REDIAL, which is a feature of a phone or phone system that allows a user to call the previously-dialed number by pressing one or a few buttons.

RECALL DIAL TONE A stutter or interrupted dial tone indicating to the extension user that the hookswitch flash has been properly used to gain access to system features.

RECALL KEY Used to get dial-tone or to transfer calls on a key system installed within a PBX. See also RECALL.

RECEIVE INTERRUPTION The interruption of a transmission to a terminal to receive or send a higher priority message from the terminal.

RECEIVE ONLY RO. Describing operation of a device, usually a page printer, that can receive transmissions but cannot transmit.

RECEIVED LINE SIGNAL DETECTOR Modem interface signal defined in RS-232-C EIA interface which indicates to the attached data terminal equipment that it is receiving a signal from the distant modem.

RECEIVED SIGNAL LEVEL RSL. The strength of a radio signal received at the input to a radio receiver.

RECEIVER 1. Any device which receives a transmission signal. 2. Any portion of a telecommunications device which decodes an encoded signal into its desired form. 3. The earpiece portion of a telephone handset, which converts an alternating electric current into sound waves, usually through an electromagnet moving a diaphragm. 4. An electronic component capable of collecting radio frequency broadcasts and reproducing them in their original audio and/or video form, e.g. a TV or radio receiver.

RECEIVER OFF-HOOK TONE The loud tone sent by the central office to tell the telephone user that his/her phone is off the hook.

RECEIVER SENSITIVITY The magnitude of the received signal necessary to produce objective BER or channel noise performance.

RECEIVING PERFORATOR REPERFORATOR. A telegraph instrument in which the received signals cause the code of the corresponding characters or functions to be punched in a tape.

RECENT CHANGE Changes to line and trunk translations in a stored program control switching machine that have not been merged with the permanent data base.

RECOGNIZER A voice recognition term. A system that attempts to classify speech (input utterances) as words from an active vocabulary.

RECONFIGURATION A fancy word for rearranging equipment, features and options.

RECORD In a database, a record is a group of related data items treated as one unit of information — for example, your name, address and phone number. Each Record is made up of several fields. A field is simply your last name.

RECORD COMMUNICATIONS Any form of communication which produces a "written" record of the transmission. Teletypewriter and facsimile are examples or record communications. Companies such as RCA Globecom, ITT Worldcom, TRT and MCI, which provide international telex, are known as international record carriers. Before deregulation, that business was exceptionally profitable.

RECORD HEAD The electromagnetic device which magnetizes the surface of a magnetic recording — tape, disk, etc. — in proportion to an electrical signal.

RECORD LENGTH The number of bytes in a record. See RECORD.

RECORD LOCKING Think about an airline reservation. You call up. You want to change your reservation. While the airline has your record open, your travel agent calls up to change it. You change your reservation. Your travel agent changes it. Which one ends up in the "permanent" record? Confusion reigns. Clearly it makes sense to only allow one person to access one record at once and lock everyone else out. Record locking is the most common and most sophisticated means for multi-user LAN applications to maintain data integrity. In a record locking system, users are prevented from working on the same data record at the same time. That way, users don't overwrite other users' changes and data integrity is maintained. But though it doesn't allow users into the same record at the same time, record locking does allows multiple users to work on the same file simultaneously. So multi-user access is maximized. Contrast with file locking, which only allows a single user to work on a file at a time.

RECORDED ANNOUNCEMENT INTERCEPT Provides a recorded message to an intercepted call indicating why the call cannot be completed, as an alternative to attendant intercept or intercept one for DID and CCSA calls to restricted or unassigned numbers.

RECORDED ANNOUNCEMENT SERVICE A special type of central office trunk which when dialed, will connect the caller to a prerecorded message.

RECORDED TELEPHONE DICTATION Phone users can dial into centralized telephone dictation equipment. The dictation equipment is usually handled as a trunk connection or it can be wired on an extension level.

RECORDER A device many large phone users use to record conversations with their callers. Recording truck dispatches can help a company gain the upper hand in customer service. Purchasing departments may use the recorder to remind vendors of their promises. The financial department can document money transfer orders and investments. Recorders come in several sizes. There are cassette recorders with standard speed and slow extended play speed. Open or reel-to-reel recorders have features similar to cassette recorders. Cassette recorders may be voice-operated (VOX) or started by a recorder coupler. Channel capacities available today include 7, 10, 14, 20, 28, 30, 40, 56 and 60 channels, depending on the manufacturer. Some recorders can search for and recall conversations recorded with an option called "autosearch."

RECORDER WARNING TONE A one-half second burst of 1400 Hz applied to a telephone line every 15 seconds to indicate to the called party that the calling party is recording the conversation. This tone is required by law to be generated as an integral part of any recording device used for the purpose and is required to be not under the control of the calling party. The tone is recorded together with the conversation.

RECOVERY The way a computer or telephone system resumes operation after overcoming a problem with the hardware (say a power failure) or a program error. Some phone systems recover quickly by themselves. Some recover slowly by themselves. Some need human intervention. These are the slowest. Check yours out. If your recovery is slow, and if you local power company is unreliable, you might consider backing your computer up with an uninterruptible power supply.

RECTIFIER A device for converting Alternating Current (AC) into Direct Current (DC). AC current comes out of the commercial power supply — 120 volts, 60 Hz. DC power is what drives telephone systems and the circuits that move the transmission around. Typically that DC power ranges from 5 to 48 volts.

RED ALARM In T-1, a red alarm is generated for a locally detected failure such as when a condition like loss of synchronization exists for 2.5 seconds, causing a CGA, (Carrier Group Alarm). See T-1.

RED BLACK CONCEPT The separation of electrical and electronic circuits, components, equipment, and systems that handle classified plain text (RED) information in electrical signal form from those that handle encrypted or unclassified (BLACK) information.

RED BOX A device that produces tones similar to those produced by dropping coins into a pay phone to inform the operator or automatic machinery that money has been deposited. The red box is used to defraud telephone companies. It is so named because they are usually built small enough to be placed in the "crush proof box" of a packet of Marlboro cigarettes. Red boxes are illegal.

REDIRECTOR A LAN software module loaded into every network workstation. It captures application programs requests for file- and equipment-sharing services and routes them through the network for action.

REDUCE A Windows term. To minimize a window to an icon at the bottom of the desktop by using the Minimize button or the Minimize command. A minimized application continues running, and you can select the icon to make it the active application.

REDUNDANCY 1. That part of any message which can be eliminated without losing the important information. 2. Having one or more "backup" systems available in case of failure of the main system.

REDUNDANCY CHECK A technique of error detection involving the transmission of additional data related to the basic data in such a way that the receiving terminal, by comparing the two sets of data, can determine to a high degree of probability whether there has been an error in transmission.

REDUNDANT ARRAY OF INEXPENSIVE DISKS RAID. RAID is a new concept in the use of disk storage that gives the user greater control of three of the more important storage variables—cost, availability and performance. RAID is a concept first defined in 1987 by Patterson, Gibson and Katz of the University of California, Berkeley. As defined, RAID has three attributes:

1. It is a set of physical disk drives viewed by the user as a single logical device. 2. The user's data is distributed across the physical set of disk drives in a defined manner. 3. Redundant disk capacity is added so that the user's data can be recovered even if a drive fails.

The Berkeley engineers described five levels of RAID configurations called RAID-1 through RAID-5. RAID-0 and RAID-6 have since been added by industry usage. The distinguishing features among the various RAID levels are the way data is distributed and the way redundant capacity is implemented. Each RAID level represents very different tradeoffs in terms of cost, availability and performance. Here's a simple explanation of the various levels of RAID:

Level O: Disk striping without parity information.

Level 1: Disk mirroring or shadowing.

Level 2: Disk striping at bit level and parity information.

Level 3: Disk striping at the byte level and one disk per set for parity information.

Level 4: Similar to RAID-3, but stripes data in large chunks.

Level 5: Disk striping in sequential blocks across all disks with parity data.

Level 6: RAID-5, plus redundant disk controllers, fans buses,etc.

REDUNDANT BITS The extra bits included in a transmission for purposes of detecting and/or correcting errors. See REDUNDANCY CHECK.

RE-ENGINEER To redesign a business process. Re-engineering aims to use the power of information technology to radically redesign business processes to improve speed, service and quality. See DOWNSIZING.

REED RELAY Two tiny pieces of metal encapsulated in a tiny nitrogen-filled glass tube. When a current is passed through a magnet around the nitrogen-filled glass capsule, one arm of the metal reed relay moves and makes contact with the other. In this way it acts as a "switch." Reed relay switches are reliable. Because they are metal, they can carry great amounts of data. They are rapidly becoming obsolete.

REENGINEER See RE-ENGINEER.

REFERENCE CLOCK A clock of high stability and accuracy that is used to govern the frequency of a network and mutually synchronize clocks of lower stability.

REFERENCE LEVEL The measure of a value used as a starting point for further measurements. In communications applications this term usually refers to a power level of a signal or a noise. A common reference level is 0 dBm, that is, 1 milliwatt.

REFERENCE LINE In faxing, the reference line is the first scanning line in memory. The location of each black pixel of this line is kept in memory for the next scanned line. Depending on the compression technique used, more or fewer scan lines are necessary.

REFERENCE NUMBER PROMPTING An AT&T Enhanced Fax Mail term. Reference number prompting is an option that allows you to prompt anyone sending a fax message to your mailbox for a reference number of up to 16 digits.

REFERENCE TRACK A special magnetic track placed on Floptical diskettes used by the drive to calibrate the optical tracking system with respect to the magnetic recording tracks.

REFERENCE NOISE RN. A reference level of noise power.

REFERENTIAL INTEGRITY Refers to a database's ability to link data in two or more files, so that adding data to a record in one file automatically updates data in another file.

REFLECTANCE The ratio of reflected light power to incident light power. Synonym for "return loss."

REFLOW SOLDERING A surface-mounting process for electronic components in which a solder paste is applied to the solder lands on the PCB and the components are properly aligned and placed on them. Upon heating the solder, it melts and forms a solder bond with the component terminals, electronically and mechanically bonding the component to the board.

REFRACTIVE INDEX A ratio of the velocity of light in a vacuum to the velocity of light in another medium, like glass.

REFRESH RATE Also called Vertical Scan Frequency or Verticial Scan Rate. The phosphor coating on a monitor tube must be repainted or "refreshed" periodically. Typically, color displays use a low-persistence phosphor that must be refreshed 60 times per second, or a rate of 60Hz to 70 Hz or more for VGA and higher resolution monitors. Generally, the faster the refresh rate, the less the flicker. Monochrome displays use a phosphor coating with longer persistence and typically are refreshed at a rate of 50 hertz; this difference accounts for the flicker sometimes seen on color monitors operating in a monochrome mode.

REFURBISHED Refurbishing means that telephone equipment has been cleaned, polished, resurfaced or whatever else it takes to return the equipment to a "like-new" appearance. Refurbishing does not necessarily mean that it has been tested or repaired or certified. See USED, CERTIFIED and REMANUFACTURED.

REGENERATE To restore a signal to its original shape. Signals need to be restored because they become distorted and acquire noise during transmission. Analog signals cannot be regenerated because it is very hard for telecommunications equipment to distinguish between unwanted noise and wanted noise (i.e. your voice) in an analog signal. Digital signals can be more easily regenerated since they consist of "ones" and "zeros." If digital signals are flattened or distorted, a simple logic circuit — "Is it a zero or a one?" — can restore the signal to its original clean squared shape.

REGENERATIVE REPEATER A device which regenerates incoming signals and retransmits these signals on an outgoing circuit. See REGENERATE.

REGENERATOR A receiver and transmitter combination used to reconstruct signals for digital transmission. In an optical regenerator, the receiver converts incoming optical pulses to electrical pulses, decides whether the pulses are "1s" or "0s," generates "cleaned up" electrical pulses, and then converts them to squared off pulses for transmission.

REGIONAL CENTER A control center (Class 1 office) connecting sectional centers of the telephone system together.

REGISTER A temporary-memory device used to receive, hold, and transfer data (usually a computer word) to be operated upon by a processing unit. The register holds the information for manipulation by the telephone system or a computer. In an automatic telephone system, a register receives dialed pulses or pushbutton tones and then uses that information to control the switch. Computers typically contain a variety of registers. General-purpose registers perform such functions as accumulating arithmetic results. Other registers hold the instruction being executed, the address of a storage location, or data being retrieved from or sent to storage. Other words associated with "register" include buffer, fetch protection, M-sequence, read-only storage, permanent storage, random-access memory and shift register.

REGISTERED JACK RJ. Any of the RJ series of jacks, described in the Code of Federal Regulations, Title 47, part 68 used to provide interface to the public telephone network. See also RJ-11, RJ-45.

REGISTERED TERMINAL EQUIPMENT Terminal equipment which is registered for connection to the telecommunications network in accordance with Subpart C of Part 68 of the FCC's Rules. If a terminal device has been properly registered it will have an identification number permanently affixed to it.

REGISTERS An ISDN term. Registers are named storage areas for numbers or strings of characters that control the operation of the ISDN set.

REGISTRATION NUMBER (FCC PART 68) Approval number given to telephone equipment to certify that a particular device passes the tests defined in Part 68 of the FCC Rules. These tests certify the phone won't cause any harm to the public network. They do not attest to the commercial value of the product, nor whether it will (or won't) sell. See REGISTRATION PROGRAM.

REGISTRATION PROGRAM The Federal Communications Commission program and associated directives intended to assure that all connected terminal equipment and protective circuitry will not harm the public switched telephone network or certain private line services. The program requires the registering of terminal equipment and protective circuitry in accordance with Subpart C of part 68, Title 47 of the Code of

Federal Regulations. This includes the assignment of identification numbers to the equipment and the testing of the equipment. The registration program contains no requirement that accepted terminal equipment be compatible with, or function with, the network. In other words, a product registered under Part 68 doesn't mean that the product will actually work — i.e. make and receive phone calls (or whatever). Part 68 simply says it won't cause any harm to the network. See REGISTRATION NUMBER and PART 68.

REGRESSION ANALYSIS A method of forecasting the future by plotting events in the past and assuming there'll be some similarity in the future. About as accurate as any other pseudoscientific method.

REGULATED 1. Controlled for uniformity. Many aspects of telecom are regulated — from the input voltage powering a telecom system to the output signal of a microwave system. 2. Adhering to the rules, and sundry whims of a government agency. Most aspects of the telephone business are under the control of a government agency to some degree. Their rules cover everything from certifying of expenses which may be capitalized to specifying how many seconds the subscriber can be forced to wait for dial tone (three seconds). Stripped to bare essentials, a regulatory agency can only do two things. First, it can allow the regulated entity to raise its prices to a point where nobody wants to buy anymore. Second, it can stop competitors coming into the business. The first (high price) is the reason no one (or few people, anyway) send telegrams. The second (keep out the competition) reason gets stymied because new technology — e.g. cheap local microwave — comes along to force the regulatory agency's hand. In the long run, no regulated entity survives because it has a regulated monopoly. It survives because it provides good service at a fair price.

REGULATION See POWER CONDITIONING.

REGULATORY GROUPS Refers to local, State or Federal entities that issue orders, findings, etc. that are binding upon providers and users of telecommunications and services.

REHOMING An MCI definition. A major MCI network change which involves moving the appropriate customer service from a working switching center to a different switching center and establishing the necessary facilities. Rehomes can be any of the following: switch upgrade, switch move/decommission, off-to-on-net conversion.

REJ Abbreviation for REJect.

REJECTION A word used in voice recognition to mean a type of recognition classification where the input utterance did not meet the criteria necessary to be classified as a word in the active vocabulary. Usually the speaker is asked to repeat the utterance.

REL RELease message. The fifth of the ISUP call set-up messages. A message sent in either direction indicating that the circuit identified in the message is being released due to the reason (cause) supplied and is ready to be put into the idle state on receipt of the Release Complete Message. See ISUP and COMMON CHANNEL SIGNALING.

RELATION Synonym for table.

RELATIONAL DATABASE A database that is organized and accessed according to relationships between data items. A relational database consists of tables, rows and columns. In its simplest conception, a relational database is actually a collection of data files that "relate" to each other through at least one common field. For example, one's employee number can be the common thread through several data files — payroll, telephone directory, etc. One's employee number might thus be a good way of relating all the files together in one gigantic data base management system (DBMS). A relational database consists of tables, rows and columns. Most mini-computers and mainframes today have relational database systems available for business use. Typical examples are DB2 from IBM and RDB from Digital Equipment Corp. Relational databases differ from nonrelational databases in that there are no system dependencies stored within the data; for example, hierarchial databases are not relational because they contain pointers to other data.

RELATIVE TRANSMISSION LEVEL The ratio of the test-tone power at one point to the test-tone power at some other point in the system chosen as a reference point.

RELAX A release tool for an Ericsson AXE.

RELAY An electrically activated switch used to operate a circuit. It connects one set of wires to another. Usually, the relay is operated by low voltage electric current and is used to open or close another circuit, which is of much higher voltage. Older telephone switches used many relays to switch (i.e. complete) their calls. Relays come in many forms. There are hermetically-sealed relays, in which thin metal contacts are sealed in an airtight glass or metal enclosure. There are also mercury relays in which a small tube of mercury tilts and completes or breaks a circuit. See also REED RELAY.

RELAY RACK Open ironwork designed to mount and support electronic equipment. A relay rack is to electronic equipment what a distribution frame is to wire. See DISTRIBUTION FRAME.

RELEASE 1. A call comes into a switchboard. The operator calls you to tell you it's for you. Then he/she "releases" the call to you. On most switchboards there's a button labelled "RLS." That's the release button. 2. The ending of an inbound ACD call by hanging up. 3. The feature key on most ACD instruments labelled Release.

RELEASE 1.0 A monthly newsletter from PC guru, Esther Dyson and her knowledgeable staff at EDventure Holdings on Park Avenue, New York City.

RELEASE BUTTON The release button — found always on operator consoles and occasionally on some phones — ends a call in the same way that hanging up the receiver does.

RELEASE LINK CAPABILITY The ability for an originating switching system, on receipt of a new destination address from the current terminating switching system, to release the transmission link to that terminating switching system and continue call processing using the new destination address. Definition from Bellcore in reference to its concept of the Advanced Intelligent Network.

RELEASE LINK TRUNK RLT. Telecommunications channel used with Centralized Attendant Service to connect attendant-seeking calls from a branch location to a main location.

RELEASE WITH HOWLER If a phone stays off-hook without originating a call (or the receiver is accidentally knocked off), the system transmits a loud tone over the line and then disconnects the line and the phone. The central office effectively then ignores them (the line and the phone) until someone puts the receiver back on-hook again.

RELIABILITY A measure of how dependable a system is once you actually use it. Very different from MTBF (Mean Time Between Failures). And very different from availability. See MTBF.

RELOCATABLE CODE Machine language programs that can reside in any portion of memory.

REMANUFACTURED Equipment, parts and/or systems that have been repaired and upgraded to the latest higher revision level. The remanufacturing process makes the telecom equipment (used or new) into a finished product that is the latest release and ready for resale.

REMAPPING The practice of redefining the meaning of keys on the keyboard.

REMISSION IBM-speak to change the mission of a product or a facility.

REMOTE ACCESS Sending and receiving data to and from a computer or controlling a computer with terminals or PCs connected through communications (i.e. phone) links.

REMOTE ACCESS TO PBX SERVICES Allows a user outside the PBX to access the PBX by dialing it over a normal phone line. You dial the number. It answers. It may or may not say anything. It may just give you dial tone. You now punch in an authorization code. If your code is acceptable, the PBX gives you another dial tone. That dial tone is effectively the one all users within the PBX get. Once you have this dial tone, you can dial another extension, jump on the company's WATS network, get into the dictation unit, access its voice mail, or whatever. Suffice, you are inside the PBX. You can do whatever anyone else inside the PBX can do.

REMOTE BATCH PROCESSING Processing in a computer system in which batch programs and batch data are entered from a remote terminal or a remote PC (personal computer) over phone lines.

REMOTE CALL FORWARDING RCF. This is a neat service. It allows a customer to have a local telephone number in a distant city. Every time someone calls that number, that call is forwarded to you in your city. Remote call forwarding is very much like call forwarding on a local residential line, except that you have no phone, no office and no physical presence in that distant city. Remote Call Forwarding exists purely in the central office. You can also think of it as measured Foreign Exchange. Companies buy Remote Call Forwarding for three reasons: 1. To encourage distant customers to call them by giving them a local number in their own city to call. (This the most obvious reason for an IN-WATS line, a FX or a RCF line); 2. They buy RCF over IN-WATS or FX lines because they don't have the volume to justify these potentially more expensive lines. 3. Companies buy RCF lines as overflow lines from IN-WATS and FX lines. They use their RCF lines when the other lines (FX and IN-WATS) get busy during peak busy periods. Remote Call Forwarding calls are typically charged at the same price as normal DDD calls (i.e. the most expensive to call). And you can't, as yet, reprogram RCF calls easily. You have to place an order with your friendly telco and wait...

REMOTE CONCENTRATOR A remote multiplexer. A device which places more than one distant user on two cable pairs. The idea of a remote concentrator is to substitute electronics for cable. It's simply cheaper to put electronics on either end of two cable pairs and drive many conversations through those wires, than running extra cables (digging streets, erecting poles, etc.)

REMOTE DIAGNOSTICS You own a phone system. You have a service company. There's some problem with it. Instead of sending a technician out, your service company dials your PBX from a data terminal or PC and "asks" your PBX in computerese what's wrong with it. If it isn't too broken, it will come back and give you some indication. This is called remote diagnostics. Some service companies call all their customers' phone systems every morning and run routine remote diagnostics on their switch. It's like going to the doctor for a daily physical. Sometimes this test may find a problem before the user is even aware. Sometimes the problem can be repaired on-line. If not, the service company will have to dispatch a technician. Remote diagnostics is a good idea. More phone systems should have it. To do remote diagnostics on a telephone system, you will typically need a phone line dedicated to the PBX and a modem on either end.

REMOTE JOB ENTRY RJE. Remote Job Entry occurs in computer operations where work or input is sent in remotely over phone lines. That "work" might include the day's sales of a distant store.

REMOTE LINE CONCENTRATOR A multiplexer. A device that "concentrates" several users' lines on a fewer number of trunks. Typically, a remote line concentrator is used because it's cheaper, easier or more flexible to substitute electronics for cable. See REMOTE CONCENTRATOR.

REMOTE LINE SWITCH A line unit mounted near a cluster of users and equipped with intracalling capability.

REMOTE LINE UNIT A remote line concentrator without intracalling capability. See REMOTE CONCENTRATOR and REMOTE LINE SWITCH.

REMOTE MAINTENANCE FACILITY See REMOTE DIAGNOSTICS.

REMOTE OFFICE TEST LINE ROTL. A testing device that acts in conjunction with a central controller and a responder to make two-way transmission and supervision measurements.

REMOTE OPERATIONS SERVICE ELEMENT ROSE. An application layer protocol that provides the capability to perform remote operations at a remote process. Definition from Bellcore in reference to its concept of the Advanced Intelligent Network.

REMOTE ORDER WIRE An order wire is a line on which maintenance and monitoring is done. A remote order wire is an order wire that has been extended to a distant point that may be more convenient.

REMOTE PROGRAMMING Dial your phone system with your friendly personal computer, modem and a communications software package and you can change the telephone system's programming remotely. This feature is great for companies with telephone systems in many locations. They can all be run from one central point. This feature is also great if you want some changes made on your system. It's obviously a lot cheaper for your vendor to make those changes from his office rather than have to visit yours. It's also a lot faster. See REMOTE DIAGNOSTICS.

REMOTE SITE The remote site is the person or location doing the sending in a file transfer operation. An example: Sales reps in the field typically update the central database on a periodic basis. The central database location is known as the host and the sales reps in the field are doing so from remote locations.

REMOTE SITE LOCATION A location for a DCE device which is not at the central or control site. A typical application would have a terminal at the remote site and the host computer at the central or control site.

REMOTE STATION Any piece of equipment attached to a LAN by a telephone company supplied link. Technically, that includes all devices that aren't servers. Usually it refers to a workstation at a distant location, linked to the main LAN by a modem and connected through a serial port "gateway." See MODEM.

REMOTE STATION LAMP FIELD For use at multi-line phones, usually manned by secretaries who answer many phone lines.

REMOTE SWITCHING SYSTEM A technique of handling the switching functions of a remote location by relaying the calls through a more sophisticated switching system in a central location. See also REMOTE CONCENTRATOR.

REMOTE TERMINAL A terminal connected to a computer over a phone line.

REMOTE TRAFFIC MEASUREMENT Traffic and feature usage data can be transmitted by the system to a distant service technician.

REMOTE WORKSTATION A terminal or personal computer connected to the LAN (local area network) by a modem. A remote workstation can be either a standalone computer or a workstation on another network.

REMOVABLE CARTRIDGE SYSTEM A high-capacity storage system that can be removed from the PC. A removable cartridge systems consists of a drive mechanism and the cartridges used to store data. The most well-known removable cartridge system is the Bernoulli Box by Iomega Corp.

REMOVABLE MEDIA Diskettes or cartridges that can be removed from a computer drive. For example, a Bernoulli box uses removable cartridges.

REMS Remote Electronic Mail System.

REN Ringer Equivalency Number. Part of the FCC certification number approving a telephone terminal product for direct sale to the end user as not doing harm to the network. The REN consists of a number and a letter which indicates the frequency response of that telephone's ringer. "A" = 20 Hz or 30 Hz "B" = a range from 15.3 Hz to 68 Hz. The remaining letters represent ringers that will work on very narrow ranges such as "C" = 15.3 Hz to 17.4 Hz, etc. The number indicates the quantity of ringers which may be connected to a single telephone line and still all ring. The total of all RENs of the telephones connected to the one line must not exceed the value 5 or some or all of the ringers may not operate.

REORDER TONE The Reorder tone sounds like a busy signal but is twice as fast. It means that all switching paths are busy. A busy signal means that the line called is in use. A reorder (or fast busy) tone means all the circuits are busy. But you have a much better chance of getting one out of many than one out of one. So if you hear a reorder signal, dial back immediately.

REPAIR AND QUICK CLEAN RQC. A term in the industry which repairs telecom equipment. It means all equipment is repaired and fully tested with a burn-in (if required) and an operational systems test. It also includes minor cosmetic cleaning of the unit. Definition courtesy Nitsuko America. See also LIKE NEW REPAIR AND UPDATE and REPAIR, UPDATE AND REFURBISH.

REPAIR, UPDATE AND REFURBISH RUR. A term in the industry which repairs telecom equipment. It means equipment is repaired and updated to current manufacturer's specifications. Also includes minor cosmetic cleaning of metal cabinets, a full diagnostic test with burn-in (if required) and an operational test. Definition courtesy Nitsuko America. See also LIKE NEW REPAIR AND UPDATE and QUICK CLEAN.

REPAIR SERVICE ANSWERING RSA. Functions that support the initial handling and entry of subscriber reported troubles. They enable subscribers to request trouble verification tests, to to initiate a trouble report and to obtain information on the status of an open trouble report. Definition from Bellcore in reference to its concept of the Advanced Intelligent Network.

REPEAT The act of a station receiving a code-bit stream (frame or token) from an upstream station and placing it onto the ring to its downstream neighbor. The repeating station may examine, copy to a buffer, or modify control bits in the code-bit stream as appropriate.

REPEAT DIALING A name for a Pacific Bell (and possibly other local telephone companies') service which automatically checks a busy number and when the line is free, it rings you back and completes the call.

REPEATER 1. An opto-electronic device inserted at intervals along a circuit to boost, and amplify an analog signal being transmitted. A repeater is needed because the quality and strength of a signal decays over distance. You will find repeaters in cables and in microwave systems. Repeaters may also regenerate a digital signal — "squaring it" and "cleaning" it up — but not changing it. Regenerating the signal removes noise and thus reduces the likelihood of errors. You can only regenerate digital signals. You cannot regenerate analog signals. You can regenerate digital signals because a machine can tell what's a signal and what's noise in a digital signal. But no machine exists to do that with an analog signal. 2. The simplest type of LAN interconnection device. A repeater moves all received packets or frames between LAN segments. The primary function of a repeater is to extend the length of the network media, i.e. the cable.

REPEATING COIL A transformer which connects one telephone circuit with another without any DC connection between the circuits. Here's a more technical explanation: A voice-frequency transformer characterized by a closed core, a pair of identical balanced primary (line) windings, a pair of identical but not necessarily balanced secondary (drop) windings, and a low transmission loss at voice frequencies. It permits transfer of voice currents from one winding to another by magnetic induction, matches line and drop impedances, and prevents direct conduction between the line and the drop.

REPERFORATOR In teletypewriter systems, a device used to punch a tape in accordance with arriving signals, permitting reproduction of the signals for retransmission. See also CHAD.

REPERFORATOR/TRANSMITTER RT. A teletypewriter unit consisting of a reperforator and a tape transmitter, each independent of the other.

REPERTORY DIALING Sometimes known as "memory dialing" or "speed-calling." A feature that allows you to recall from nine to 99 (or more) phone numbers from a phone's memory with the touch of just one, two or three buttons.

REPLY A transmitted message which serves as a response to an original message. (What else?)

REPORT PROGRAM GENERATOR A computer language for processing large data files.

REPORT-ONLY EVENT An event that the ASC (AIN Switch Capabilities) reports to a SLEE (Service Logic Execution Environment) but the ASC does not suspend processing events for the connection segment. Definition from Bellcore in reference to its concept of the Advanced Intelligent Network.

REQUEST TO SEND RTS. One of the control signals on a standard RS-232-C connector. It places the modem in the originate mode so it can begin to send.

RESALE CARRIER A long distance company that does not own its own transmission lines. It buys lines from other carriers and then resells them to its subscribers. Some resale carriers have their own switches. Some don't. Some have a mix of their own lines and leased lines. Most long distance carriers — including MCI and US Sprint — have a mix of their own lines and leased lines.

RESAMPLING Reducing or increasing the number of pixels in an image to conform to a new size or resolution.

RESELLER See AGGREGATOR.

RESERVE POWER A telephone system may be equipped with storage batteries to provide primary power during a commercial power failure. No loss of service will occur during transition to battery power. All this is a long way of saying your phone system is backed by batteries, typically lead acid (the same ones used in your car).

RESET PACKET A packet that identifies error conditions on an X.25 communications circuit. The reset packet does not clear the session but rather notifies the communicating DTEs of error conditions at a known point in the data-packet transfer sequence.

RESIDENT COMMAND A command located in the personal computer's operating system itself, contained in the file COMMAND.COM.

RESIDENT PROGRAM See RAM-RESIDENT PROGRAM.

RESIDENTIAL AND LIGHT COMMERCIAL WIRING Refers to the wiring system and all of its appurtenances required to provide convenient and useful telephone services to residences and light commercial buildings.

RESIDUAL ERROR RATE The ratio of the number of bits, unit elements, characters or blocks incorrectly received but undetected or uncorrected by the error-control equipment to the total number of bits, unit elements, characters or blocks sent.

RESISTANCE Any electrical conductor will resist the flow of electrical current. As it resists the flow of current, so the current becomes weaker. Resistance generates heat and occasionally light. It is technically defined as a property or a characteristic of a conductor, i.e. the metal through which the electricity flows. It is measured in Ohms.

RESISTOR A unit designed to oppose but not completely obstruct the passage of electrical current.

RESOURCE 1. Any facility of a computing system or operating system required by a job or task, including memory, input/output devices, processing unit, data files, and control or processing programs. 2. A network component such as a file, printer, or serial device that is shared by other components of the network. 4. An SCSA term. A voice processing technology, such as voice store and forward, fax processing, voice recognition, or text to speech. 5. A Windows term. A resource is a program object, such as a button, menu or dialog box, that Windows treats differently than normal programs. Resources are developed either in a special resource language or using interactive tools. They can be loaded from separate files or bound directly to the executable file.

RESOURCE GROUP An SCSA term. A resource group is a dynamically formed group of resource units that can be made to work together as if they were a single device.

RESOURCE MODULE A resource module is a card that slides into a PC and does everything from text-to-speech, to fax, to voice recognition, etc. Everything except interfacing to the network, which is done by another card or another part of the resource module card called the Network Interface Module. See NETWORK INTERFACE MODULE.

RESOLUTION 1. The minimum difference between two discrete values that can be distinguished by a measuring device. High resolution does not necessarily imply high accuracy. 2. The degree of precision to which a quantity can be measured or determined. 3. A measurement of the smallest detail that can be distinguished by a sensor system under specific conditions. 4. A measure of the quality of a transmitted image. Beginning with the scan processing in the transmitter and ending with the display and/or printing process in the receiver, resolution is a basic parameter of any image transmission system. It affects the design of all its subsystems. In the scanner, the resolution is a function of the spot size which the scanner optics and associated electronics "look" at the scene and through which the system can uniquely identify the smallest distance along the scan line. Resolution is measured in picture elements (pixels) and is the total number of pixels (horizontal x vertical) used to display alphanumeric characters of graphic images on the screen. High resolution images are composed of more dots per inch and appear smoother than low-resolution images. The higher the resolution, the better the display of details. See also MONITOR.

RESONANCE The condition that exists when inductive reactance equals capacitive reactance. In a series circuit it results in maximum current at the resonant frequency. In a parallel circuit it results in maximum voltage at the resonant frequency.

RESONANT CAVITY Closed metal container which has the characteristics of a parallel resonant circuit.

RESPONDER A test line that can make transmission and supervision measurements through its host switch under control of a remote computer.

RESPONSE An answer to an inquiry. In IBM's SNA, the control information sent from a secondary station to the primary station under SDLC.

RESPONSE TIME The time it takes a system to react to a given input. In voice recognition, response time typically refers to the amount of time required for a word (or utterance) to be recognized once the end of the word is detected. True response time is longer because silence often must occur before the end of the word can be declared. When operating a terminal connected to a computer, response time would be the time between the operator pressing the last key of a series of keys and the appearance of a response on the operator's display. In a data communications system, response time includes the transmission time, the processing time, the searching for records time and the transmission time back to the originator. Response time is very critical in applications like airline reservation systems. Here the customer is on the phone awaiting a reply. That time is critical in whether the customer perceives he's getting good or bad service. Response times of more than three seconds are not acceptable in situations where the customer is waiting on the phone to buy something. Response time is a function, inter alia, of the number of phone lines you lease or use. You can save a lot of phone line costs by cutting back on lines. But you'll extend response time. Life, as always, is a trade-off.

RESPONSIBLE ORGANIZATIONS RespOrgs. Telecommunications providers that have responsibility for obtaining 800 Service numbers from the Service Mangement System and building and maintaining customer records. See EIGHTHUNDRED SERVICE.

RESTART A central office word or Apple Macintosh word for the rebooting a personal computer. In telephony, a system initiated action designed to restore overall service capacity.

RESTART PACKET A block of data that notifies X.25 DTEs that an irrecoverable error exists within X.25 network. Restart packets clear all existing SVCs and resynchronize all existing PVCs between X.25 DET and X.25 DCE.

RESTORE 1. Typically, to put a telephone system back into full operation.

RESTORE BUTTON A Windows term. The small button containing both an up and down arrow at the right of the title bar. The Restore button appears only after you have enlarged a window to its maximum size. Mouse users can click the Restore button to return the window to its previous size. Keyboard users can use the Restore command on the Control menu.

RESTRICTION Phone systems can disallow people or extensions from making certain calls. If they're not allowed to make long distance calls, this is called toll restriction. See TOLL RESTRICTION. There are other forms of restriction, like being able to only use the company's internal network.

RESTRICTION FROM OUTGOING CALLS Phone users may be restricted from placing outgoing calls. See CLASS OF SERVICE.

RESTRICTION SERVICES These features allow the attendant to control the restriction of phones or groups of phones. It can be very useful in hotels and motels to turn off service to room phones during the time between check out and check in of quests. Here are some examples of restriction services:

● CONTROLLED OUTWARD RESTRICTION: Phones can be restricted from making dialed outgoing calls while inward calls are completed normally.

● CONTROLLED STATION-TO-STATION RESTRICTION: Originating phone calls to other extensions in the system are blocked, however, normal incoming and outgoing calls can be completed.

● CONTROLLED TERMINATION RESTRICTION: Phones can complete outgoing calls normally, but incoming calls are directed to either the attendant or an intercept tone or recording.

● CONTROLLED TOTAL RESTRICTION: Restricted phone lines cannot make or receive any calls.

RETARD COIL A coil having a large inductance which retards sudden changes of the current flowing through its winding.

RETRACTILE CORD A coiled cord that springs back to its original length when you let it go. Telephone handset cords are the most common retractile cords. There are wide quality variations among retractile cords. Western Electric (oops AT&T Technologies) has set a very good standard for retractile cords. But not everyone conforms to it. If you want to quickly see the quality difference among various coil cords, take six from different manufacturers and hang them over your office door and come back in a week. You'll see a bunch touching the floor. Others will still be taut. Another way is simply to connect them to your phone, one by one, and listen to the differences. Some simply sound weaker. Cheaper ones tend to sound worse. (So what's new?)

RETRAINING Training is a feature of some modems which adjust to the conditions including amplitude response, delay distortions, timing recovery, and echo characteristic, of a particular telecommunications connection by a receiving modem. Retraining occurs after modems have been successfully transmitting and receiving data. Usually due to a change in line conditions.

RETRANSMISSION A method of error control in which hosts receiving messages acknowledge the receipt of correct messages and either do not acknowledge, or acknowledge in the negative, the receipt of incorrect messages. The lack of acknowledgment, or receipt of negative acknowledgment, is an indication to the sending host that it should transmit the failed message again.

RETRANSMISSIVE STAR In optical fiber transmission, a passive component that permits the light signal on an input fiber to be retransmitted on multiple output fibers. The signal comes in on one fiber, hits a star-type connector which splays the transmission out. A retransmissive star is formed by heating together a bundle of fibers to near their melting point. Such a device is used mainly in fiber-based local networks. It's also called star coupler. When you see one you'll be surprised how crude this device looks, despite its fancy name.

RETRIAL After failing to complete a call, a person tries again. This is called a "retrial." The term is used in traffic engineering. It's critical in figuring needed trunking capacity. See QUEUING THEORY, POISSON and TRAFFIC ENGINEERING.

RETROFIT KIT A conversion kit which makes a standard pay phone into one which will accept credit cards.

RETRY In the bisynchronous protocol, the process of resending the current block of data a prescribed number of times until it is accepted.

RETURN A carriage return. This key on some keyboards is also called "Enter." Touching the CR (Carriage Return) gives you two functions: a "line terminating function" and a "new line function", abbreviated "NL". Simply put, a Return at the end of a line, terminates that line and begins a new one.

RETURN LOSS A measure of the similarity of the impedance of a transmission line and the impedance at its termination. It is a ratio, expressed in decibels, of the power of outgoing signal to the power of the signal reflected back from an impedance discontinuity.

RETURN TO ZERO. RZ. Method of transmitting binary information such that, after each encoded bit, voltage returns to the zero level.

RETURN-TO-ZERO CODE A code form having two information states called "zero" and "one" in which the signal returns to a rest state during a portion of the bit period.

REVENUE ACCOUNTING OFFICE RAO. A telephone company center using mainframe computers for billing other data processing. Functions performed include receipt and processing of AMA (Automatic Message Accounting) data and preparation of the subscriber's bill. Definition from Bellcore in reference to its concept of the Advanced Intelligent Network.

REVENUE VOLUME PRICING PLAN AT&T's Revenue Volume Pricing Plan gives discounts based on total monthly 800 and 900 billing after all other term discounts have been taken. One of two plans used by aggregators to resell 800 services, the other is Customer Specific Term Plan.

REVENUE REQUIREMENT How much money a regulated phone company is allowed to earn is typically determined by its rate base (depreciated value of its assets). It is allowed to earn a percentage on its rate rate — just as you earn interest on your rate base (what you have deposited in the bank). So how the regulation works is (in principle) simple: Figure what the phone company's assets are. Figure what percentage you want the phone company to earn on its assets. Figure the calculation. Bingo you have the revenue requirement. Except you have to allow it to pay its expenses. So that gets added onto the revenue requirement. The formula is amount of return (rate base times rate of return — ROR) plus operations expenses. See also ROE.

REVERSE BATTERY SIGNALING A type of loop signaling in which battery and ground are reversed on the tip and ring of the loop to give an "off-hook" signal when the called party answers. Some systems employ reverse battery, either for a short period or until the call is finished, to indicate that it is a toll call. In some PBXs this is used to provide toll diversion.

REVERSE BATTERY SUPERVISION A way of telling the originating central office that the called telephone has been answered (i.e. it has gone off-hook). The voltage of the line at the originating end is reversed. Reverse battery supervision, which puts a signal at the user's premises, is very useful for devices like call accounting systems (knowing precisely when to begin the billing cycle) and telemarketing systems (knowing precisely when to transfer the machined-dialed call over to the operator). See also ANSWER SUPERVISION.

REVERSE CHANNEL 1. A (typically) small-bandwidth channel used for supervisory or error-control signaling. Signals are transmitted in the opposite direction to the data that is sent. 2. The channel in a dial-up telephone circuit from the called party to the calling party.

REVERSE INTERRUPT In Bisync, a control character sequence (DLE) sequence sent by a receiving station instead of ACK1 or ACK0 to request premature termination of the transmission in progress.

REVERSE MATCHING Attaching the name and address to a phone number. A It's a job usually done by a specialized service bureau. Called "reverse" matching because the service bureaus started in business by attaching phone numbers to lists containing names and their addresses. With ANI (Automatic Number Identification), we get the phone numbers of people calling us. But we don't get their names and addresses. We need to get this information for many reasons. The obvious being that getting this information on-line and fast saves asking the caller for it and typing all the stuff in. That saves time on the phone — as much as 20 seconds. And fewer questions about boring stuff like phone number, address, city, state, zip means less typing time (also called data entry time, less clerking time) and more time to explain the specials we're selling today. In short, the fewer questions we ask, the less we type and the more stuff we can sell. Reverse matching can be done instantly on-line via a direct data hookup to a distant specialized service bureau or it can be done at the end of the month when we receive our 800 phone bill containing the phone numbers of the people who called us that month.

REVERSE OPERATION Briefly running a shredder in reverse to clear jams.

REVERSE TRANSFER An Inter-Tel term for a phone feature in which a call on common hold at any phone may be retrieved from any phone anywhere in the phone system.

REVERSE VIDEO A video display with all the characters reversed. Characters which are normally white on the screen appear black. And blacks appear white. Reverse video is used to emphasize or enhance things — like those characters to be printed in italics or bold.

REVERTIVE PULSE Ground pulses sent back to the sender in the orignating panel office from the various selector frames to control the selection process.

REVERTIVE PULSING In telephone networks, a means of controlling distant switching selections by pulsing, in which the near end receives signals from the far end.

REVISABLE-FORM DOCUMENT An electronic document with its formatting information intact, readable and modifiable.

REWRITABLE OPTICAL DISKS They look like CD-ROMS but they're not. On one side you can store 284 megabytes or 335 megabytes depending on how large you make the sectors — either 512-byte sectors or 1,024-byte, respectively. All the optical disks conform to standards set up by ISO. They fit between Winchester hard drives and tape drives. Compared with hard drives, they are very very slow. And the optical drives are not cheap — at least $4,000 at this writing. However, the optical disks are cheap and make reasonably good secondary storage devices.

RF Radio Frequency. Electromagnetic waves operating between 10 kHz and 3 MHz propagated without guide (wire or cable) in free space. If you have a home computer that lets you use your home TV set as a video display device, then the computer has an RF Generator. This means that this device is generating an RF carrier to carry the video signal information.

RFC Request For Comment. A document from the Network Information Center (NIC). The contents of an RFC may range from an official standardized protocol specification to research results or proposals.

RFI 1. Request For Information. General notification of an intended purchase of equipment or equipment and lines sent to potential suppliers to determine interest and solicit general descriptive product materials, but not prices or a formal request. See RFQ for a detailed explanation. 2. Radio Frequency Interference. All computer equipment generates radio frequency signals. The FCC regulates the amount of RFI a computing device can leak past its shielding. A Class A device is sufficient for office use. A Class B is a more stringent classification for home equipment use. See RADIO FREQUENCY INTERFERENCE.

RFP Request For Proposal. A detailed document prepared by a buyer defining his requirements for service and equipment sent to one or several vendors. A vendor's response to an RFP will typically be binding on the vendor, i.e. he will be obliged to deliver what he says in his RFP at the prices and following the conditions explained in that RFP. See RFQ for a detailed explanation.

RFQ Request For Quotation. A document prepared by a buyer defining his needs for service and equipment in fairly broad terms and sent to one or several vendors. The RFQ is much less detailed than the RFP. Let's start at the beginning of the buying process. We have a buyer who wants a phone system. His first step may be to issue a formal or informal RFI — Request For Information. In effect, the RFI says "Please tell me what you have. I have a vague idea of what I want but I don't know exactly what is available to suit my needs. Please send me some information."

After a buyer gets his responses to his RFI's, he may issue an RFQ — Request For Quotation. An RFQ may include a tentative configuration of the type of phone system the user wants, plus some listing of features the buyer is interested in. In the RFQ, the buyer asks for a "ballpark" (approximation) of the possible price for such a system. Usually the "price" is within plus or minus 10% of where it will eventually be in the final configuration. In short, an RFQ's purpose is not to buy, but to find out what's out there and what it might cost. The purpose may be to allocate a budget or to put aside some money for the forthcoming purchase.

An RFP — Request For Proposal — is much more formal and definitive. Its purpose is simple. The buyer wants to buy something. The RFP contains a list of what the buyer wants, when he wants it, how it should be installed, how it should delivered, what financing may be necessary. It is now up to the vendor/s to respond with their configuration, their precise prices and their terms and conditions of sale. Whatever the vendor responds with — called a Response to an RFP — constitutes a definite offer. At this point, the buyer can negotiate the terms of the vendor's Response to his RFP. This will lead to the writing, and eventual signing of a contract. Or the buyer may simply decide to accept the Vendor's Response. Often that Response may have a line at the back of it — "I accept the terms and conditions of this response." If the buyer signs this, then the Response to the RFP becomes a valid contract.

RFS Ready for Service.

RG-58 Coaxial cable with 50-ohm impedance used by Thinnet.

RG-62 Coaxial cable with 93-ohm impedance used by ARCnet.

RG/U RG is the military designation for coaxial cable. U stands for general utility.

RGB A color model based on the mixing of red, green, and blue - the primary colors used by color monitor displays and TVs.

RH Request Header or Response Header.

RHEOSTAT A variable resistor.

RHETOREX A manufacturer of voice processing componentry based in Campbell, CA. Inspiration for the company's name came from the word rhetoric, which is the art of effectively using speech and language.

RHOMBIC ANTENNA An antenna composed of wire radiators describing the sides of a rhombus. It is usually terminated and unidirectional; when unterminated, it is bidirectional.

RIBBON CABLE Multi-wire cable that is flat instead of round. In ribbon cable, the conductors are laid side by side. Ribbon cable can be more easily laid under carpeting because it is flat and thus, can extend phone and computer services to places otherwise hard to reach. There are disadvantages to ribbon cable. Because ribbon cable is flat, it's hard to twist its individual wire conductors around each other (thus humming can be a problem). It is hard to put a metal shielding around the twisted wire pairs. It is hard to put coax cable into ribbon cable. It is hard to make ribbon cable sufficiently strong to withstand thousands of high heels trampling it. It is hard to make ribbon cable which turns a corner... But there has been enormous progress in ribbon cable. And ribbon cable is finding greater use in buildings. These days it even carries commercial A.C. power.

RIBBON FIBER CABLE A cable that accommodates one to 12 ribbons, each ribbon having 12 fibers for a cable size range of 12 to 144 fibers. Ribbon cables are designed for use in larger distribution systems where small cable size and high pulling strength are important.

RIGHT HAND RULE A rule for indicating the direction of magnetic effect. Grasp the wire with the right hand and with the thumb extended along the wire in the direction of current. The curved fingertips will indicate the direction of magnetic flow. Not totally relevant for including in this dictionary. But cute.

RIGHT TO USE See RTU.

RIGHTSIZING Another term for re-engineering. See RE-ENGINEERING.

RING 1. As in Tip and Ring. One of the two wires (the two are Tip and Ring) needed to set up a telephone connection. 2. Also a reference to the ringing of the telephone set. 3. The design of a Local Area Network (LAN) in which the wiring loops from one workstation to another, forming a circle (thus, the term "ring"). In a ring LAN, data is sent from workstation to workstation around the loop in the same direction. Each workstation (which is usually a PC) acts as a repeater by re-sending messages to the next PC in the ring. The more PC's, the slower the LAN. Network control is distributed in a ring network. Since the message passes through each PC, loss of one PC may disable the entire network. However, most ring LANs recover very quickly should one PC die or be turned off. If it dies, you can remove it physically from the network. If it's off, the network senses that and the token ignores that machine. In some token LANs, the LAN will close around a dead workstation and join the two workstations on either side together. If you lose the PC doing the control functions, another PC will jump in and take over. This is how the IBM Token-Passing Ring works. See TOPOLOGY, BYPASS CABLE and TOKEN RING.

RING AGAIN The PBX remembers the last number called by a phone and will redial it when the feature is activated.

RING BACK TONE The sound you hear when you're calling someone else's phone. The tone you hear is generated by a device at your central office and may bear no relationship to the sound the phone at the other end is emitting — or not emitting. If your call didn't go through the first time, always call back at least once. See RINGING TONE.

RING BANDING A method of color coding insulated conductors by means of a small band of colored ink applied circumferentially at regular intervals along the axis of the insulated conductor.

RING BATTERY Commonly unfiltered - 24 VDC source that supplies operating power to all local KSU components. Also called the B Battery.

RING CONDUCTOR One conductor of a phone line.

RING CYCLE A ring cycle in North America is typically six seconds long, two of ringing, four of silence, then repeated.

RING GENERATOR A component of virtually all phone sustems, ranging from large central offices to small key systems, that supplies the power to ring the bells inside phones, typically 90 volts AC at 20 Hz.

RING INDICATOR Modem interface signal defined in RS-232-C which indicates to the data terminal equipment that a call is coming in.

RING ISOLATOR A device placed on a telephone line to disconnect the ringer when it is an idle state. It is used for noise prevention.

RING LATENCY In a token-ring network, the time measured in bits at the data transmission rate, required for a signal to propagate once around the ring. Ring latency includes the signal propagation delay through the ring medium, including drop cables, plus the sum of propagation delays through each data station connected to the token-ring network. See also TOKEN-RING NETWORK.

RING NETWORK A network that links PBXs, computers, terminals, printers and other devices in a circular communications link. See RING.

RING SIGNAL The pulse ringing voltage output of the local Interrupter KSU. Typically, this signal is 105 VAC with a duty cycle of 2 seconds on and 4 seconds off.

RING TOPOLOGY A network topology in which nodes are connected to a closed loop, no terminators are required because there are no unconnected ends.

RING TRIP The process of stopping the AC ringing signal at the central office when the telephone being rung is answered.

RINGDOWN CIRCUIT A tie line connecting phones in which picking up one phone automatically rings the other phone. In a ringdown circuit, a ringing current (AC) is sent down the line. That current may light a lamp, set off a bell, buzz a buzzer. The idea is to alert the person at the other end to the incoming call.

RINGDOWN INTERFACE A private line two-wire interface also called Loop Start Trunk.

RINGER A bell in a telephone which indicates if a phone call is coming in. These days "ringers" are electromechanical and clunky (old-style) or small and electronic (new style). The new electronic ones are cheaper, but less interesting to listen to. Most sound like bleating sheep in heat.

RINGER EQUIVALENCE NUMBER REN. A number required in the U.S. for registering your telephone equipment with the phone company. Add together the REN's of all the telephones on a single line. The sum of those numbers should never exceed five otherwise none of your bells will work and you won't hear an incoming call. (Your central office simply doesn't send sufficient current down the line.) The alphabetic character after the number refers to the ringing frequency of the alternating current sent down the line to ring the bell. If the letter is "A", the ringer frequency is about 20 Hertz. Most single line phones have a Ringer Equivalence of 1.0A. If the letter is "B", the ringer will respond to any current coming down the line. Any other letter, and you are probably on a party line where the ringer frequency is used for party selection. In Canada, they use the term "Load Number" instead of Ringer Equivalence. The numbers are different, but the concept is the same. See LOAD NUMBER.

RINGER ISOLATOR A device in the phone which disconnects the ringer when ringing voltage is not present.

RINGING Alternating Current (AC) sent out from the central office along the local loop to the subscriber. It's typically 70 to 90 volts at 17 Hz to 20 Hz. You can get a mild shock if you have your hands on a telephone circuit when ringing current comes along. The rest of the time, the lines are harmless.

RINGING GENERATOR An optional KTU facility that generates the AC ringer voltage from the 24 VDC local Key System Power Supply source. Typically, this voltage is 90 to 115 (nominally 105) VAC at 30 Hertz.

RINGING KEY A key that sends a ringing current.

RINGING SIGNAL Any AC or DC signal transmitted over a line or trunk for the purpose of alerting someone or some thing at the distant end of an incoming call.

RINGING TONE A low tone which is one second ON and three seconds OFF. It indicates that ringing current is being sent by the central office to the person receiving the call. Ringing tone is not produced by the calling party's central office — but by the called party's central office. Thus, it is possible for you to hear ringing tone but for the person you are calling not to hear anything. As a general rule, if the person doesn't answer, call them a second time. Often, they'll say "The phone never rang." This will not be a lie, but simply a temporary glitch in their central office.

RINGING TRANSFER A PBX feature which allows you to choose which bells in a group of phones will ring when a call is coming in for that group.

RINGING VOLTAGE In addition to talk battery, a Central Office provides ringing signaling. Ring Voltage is generally 70 to 90 volts at 17 Hz to 20 Hz. See also RINGING.

RINGMATE A New York Telephone and New England Telephone service which allows you to add one or two additional numbers to your existing phone number. You can tell which phone is ringing by the sound of the ringing. You can, of course, only speak on one line at once. The purpose of the service is to help you identify who's calling you and decide whether or not to answer.

RIP Routing Information Protocol. RIP is based on distance-vector algorithms that measure the shortest parth between two points on a network in terms of the number of "hop" between those points.

RIP-CORD A cord placed directly under the jacket of a cable in order to facilitate stripping (removal) of the jacket.

RISC Reduced Instruction Set Computer. Computers based on an unusual high speed processing technology that uses a far simpler set of operating commands. These commands greatly speed a computer's performance, especially for calculation-intensive operations such as those performed by scientists and computer-aided design (CAD) and computer-aided manufacture (CAM) engineers. RISC is a design that achieves high performance by doing the most common computer operations very quickly. In contrast, the microprocessors used in most PCs are based on a design called CISC (Complex Instruction Set Computing). CISC does not execute instructions as quickly as RISC but it has more commands and accomplishes more with each command. Programs written for RISC are typically not compatible with those written for CISC processors. RISC is the prevailing technology for workstations today. The RISC semiconductor was an IBM baby, born in its Yorktown Heights, NY lab in 1974. But internal arguments over, and even whether the chip should be used kept IBM fiddling while Sun and other companies decisely powered ahead. IBM got its first good RISC product, the RS/6000, to market in 1990.

RISC SYSTEM/6000 An IBM family of workstations and servers designed to run applications developed for the UNIX operating system.

RISER The conduit or path between floors of a building into which telephone and other utility cables are placed to bring service from one floor to another. Your risers should be twice the size you ever think you'll need in the next 30 years. It's expensive to build risers after the building is built. Very expensive.

RISER CABLE High strength cables intended for use in vertical shafts between floors in multi-story buildings. Such shafts are called riser shafts. (What else would they be called?)

RISER CLOSET The closet where riser cable is terminated and cross connected to either horizontal distribution cable or other riser cable. The riser closet houses cross connect facilities, and may contain auxiliary power supplies for terminal equipment located at the user work location. See also SATELLITE CLOSET.

RISER SUBSYSTEM The part of a premises distribution system that includes a main cable route and facilities for supporting the cable from an equipment room (often in the building) to the upper floors, or along the same floor, where it is terminated on a cross connect in a riser closet, at the network interface, or other distribution components of the campus subsystem. The subsystem can also extend out on a floor to connect a satellite closet or other satellite location.

RISK A potential liability, caused by a threat.

RISK ASSESSMENT The process of quantifying the potential impact on an organisation from various security threats.

RISLU Remote Integrated Services Line Unit. One of the remoting arrangements that the AT&T 5ESS switch architecture permits. The RISLU terminates DSLs and connects to the switch DLTU via T-1.

RIT Rate of Information Transfer. The amount of information that can be communicated from a sender to a receiver in a given length of time.

RJ Registered Jacks. They're telephone and data plugs registered with the FCC. RJ-XX (where X is a number) are probably the most common plugs in the world. Here is a table of the most common registered jacks, courtesy the FCC. Following the table are descriptions of the most common RJ jacks.

RJICX   Single Tie Trunk, Type I or II E&M interface, 8 position.

RJIDC	Single-line, 4-wire, T/R, T1/R1, 6-position.
RJ11C/W	Single-line, 2-wire, T/R, 6 position.
RJ14C/W	Two-line, 2-wire, T/R, T(MR)/R(MR), T(OPS)/R(OPS) 6-position.
RJ14X	Two-line, T1/R1, T2/R2, with sliding cover, 6-position.
RJ15C	Single-line, T/R, weatherproof, 3-position.
RJ17C	Single-line, T/R, used in hospital critical care areas,
RJ18C/W	Single-line, T/R, with Make Busy leads, 6 positions.
RJ2DX	12 lines, 4 wire, T/R, T1/R1, 50 positions.
RJ2EX	12 Tie trunks, 2-wire, T/R, E&M Type I, 50 position.
RJ2FX	8 Tie trunks, 2-wire, T/R, E&M SG/SB Type II 50 position.
RJ2GX	8 Tie trunks, 4-wire, T/R, T1/R1, E&M, Type I 50 position.
RJ2HX	6 Tie trunks, 4-wire, T/R, T1/R1, E&M, SG/SB, Type II, 50 positions.
RJ2MB	12 lines, 2-wire, T/R, Make Busy leads, 50 position.
RJ21X	25 lines, 2-wire, T/R, 50 position.
RJ25C	3 lines, 2-wire, T/R, T (MR)/R(MR), T(OPS)/R(OPS), 6 position.
RJ26X	8 lines, 2-wire, T/R, FLL, or Programmed data, 50 position.
RJ27X	8 lines, 2-wire, T/R, Programmed Data, 50 position.
RJ4MB	Single-line, 2-wire, T/R, MB/MB1, PR/PC, with Make Busy. 8 position, keyed and programmed.
RJ41M	Up to 8 multiple installations of FLL or Programmed Data. 8 positon, keyed.
RJ41S	Single-line, 2-wire, T/R, FLL or Programmed Data, 8 position, keyed.
RJ45M	Up to 8 multiple installations of Programmed Data. 8 -position, keyed.
RJ45S	Single-line, 2-wire, T/R, PR/PC, programmed data, 8 positon, keyed.
RJ48C	Single-line, 4-wire, T/R, T1/R1, 1.544 Mbps, 8 position.
RJ48H	Up to 12 lines. 4-wire, T/R, T1/R1, 1.544 Mbps, 50 position.

RJ48M	Up to 8 lines, 4-wire, T/R, T1/R1, 1.544 Mbps, 50 position.
RJ48S	One or two lines. T/R or T/R, T1/R1, LADC or subrate. 8-position, keyed.
RJ48T	Up to 25 (2-wire) or 12 (4-wire), T/R OR T/R, TI/R1; LADC or Subrate,50-position.
RJ48X	Single-line, 4-wire, T/R, T1/R1, 1.544 Mbps, 8-position with shorting bar.
RJ61X	Up to 4 lines, T/R, 8-position.
RJM8	Single private line, 2/4 wire, T/R or T/R, T1/R1, Non-registered service, 8-position, keyed, w/wo loopback.

RJ-11 RJ-11 is is a six conductor modular jack that is typically wired for four conductors (i.e. four wires). Occasionally it is wired for only two conductors — especially if you're only wiring up for tip and ring. The RJ-11 jack (also called plug) is the most common telephone jack in the world. The RJ-11 is typically used for connecting telephone instruments, modems and fax machines to a female RJ-22 jack on the wall or in the floor. That jack in turn is connected to twisted wire coming in from "the network" — which might be a PBX or the local telephone company central office. RJ-22 wiring is typically flat. None of its conductors (i.e. wires) are twisted. You cannot use flat cable for high-speed data communications, like local area networks. See also RJ-22 and RJ-45.

RJ-14 A jack that looks and is exactly like the standard RJ-11 that you see on every single line telephone. Whereas the RJ-11 defines one line — with the two center, red and green, conductors being tip and ring, the RJ-14 defines two phone lines. One of the lines is the "normal" RJ-11 line — the red and green conductors in the center. The second line is the second set of conductors — black and yellow — on the outside.

RJ-21 Same as an RJ-21X. See RJ-21X.

RJ-21X An Amphenol connector under a different name. Here's the explanation: Amphenol is a manufacturer of connectors. They make many connectors, many of which are made by other companies. Their most famous connector was the 25-pair connector used on 1A2 key telephones and for connecting cables to many electronic key systems and PBXs. The telephone companies call the 25-pair Amphenol connector the RJ21X. The RJ21X connector is made by other companies including 3M and TRW.

RJ-22 RJ-22 is a four position modular jack that is typically used for connecting telephone handsets to telephone instruments. It is always wired with four conductors (also called wires). It is different to the more common RJ-11 which is typically used for connecting telephone instruments, modems and fax machines to a female RJ-22 jack on the wall or in the floor. That jack in turn is connected to twisted wire coming in from "the network" — which might be a PBX or the local telephone company central office. RJ-22 wiring is typically flat. None of its conductors (i.e. wires) are twisted. You cannot use flat cable for high-speed data communications, like local area networks. See RJ-11 and RJ-45.

RJ-45 The RJ-45 is the 8-pin connector used for data transmission over standard telephone wire. That wire could be flat or twisted. And it's very important that you know what you're working with. You can easily use flat wire for serial data communications up to 19.2 Kbps. Up to that speed you're connecting with your wire to a dataPBX, a modem, a printer or a printer buffer. If you wish to connect to a 10BaseT local area network, which you also do with a RJ-45, you must use twisted wire. You can typically tell the difference by looking at the cable. If it's flat grey satin (like a typical phone wire, only bigger) than it's probably untwisted. If it's circular, then it's probably twisted and therefore good for LANs. RJ-45 connectors come into two varieties — keyed and non-keyed. Keyed means that the male RJ-45 plug has a small, square bump on its end and the female RJ-45 plug is shaped to accommodate the plug. A keyed RJ-45 plug will not fit into a female, non-keyed (i.e. normal) RJ-45. See RJ-11 and RJ-22.

RJE Remote Job Entry. A Remote Job Entry terminal is used for the transmission of "batch" data to a remote computer system. Processed information is then returned to the printer in the terminal. This type of processing from a remote site is a standard method of data transmission. See IBM.

RJXXX Registered Jack.

RLC ReLease Complete message. The sixth ISUP call set-up message. A message sent in either direction in response to the receipt of a Release Message, or if appropriate to, a Reset Circuit Message when the circuit concerned has been brought into the idle condition. See ISUP and COMMON CHANNEL SIGNALING.

RLCM Remote Line Concentrating Module.

RLL Run Length Limited. A type of data coding used for disk drives. The term Run Length Limited derives from the fact that the techniques limit the distance (run length) between magnetic flux reversals on the disk platter. An RLL certified hard drive can use an MFM controller card but the storage capacity and the data transfer rate will be reduced.

RLR Receive Loudness Rating.

RLT Release-Link Trunks.

RMA Returned Merchandise Authorization.

RMAS Remote Memory Administration System.

RMATS Remote Maintenance and Test System. That equipment and programming used to run, maintain and test a telephone system remotely — usually by dialing in on a special phone line.

RMS Root Mean Square. Method of measuring amplifier power.

RMS-D1 Remote Measurement System Digital 1.

RMU Remote Mask Unit.

RNR Abbreviation for not ready to receive.

RO Receive Only.

ROAMING Using your cellular phone in a city besides the one in which you live. Roaming usually incurs extra charges.

ROBBED-BIT SIGNALING This explanation from Gary Maier of Dianatel: ISDN is the key to future sophisticated telephone network services with its dynamic, highly configurable T-1 connection (also called PRI connection). Since T-1 is a common method of carrying 24 telephone circuits, many wonder about the uses for ISDN, especially when they learn ISDN signaling requires an entire voice channel, reducing today's T-1 from 24 voice channels to 23. But the popular signaling mechanism of "robbed bit" signaling in T-1 has serious limititations. Robbed bit signaling typically uses bits known as the A and B bits. These bits are sent by each side of a T-1 termination and are buried in the voice data of each voice channel in the T-1 circuit. Hence the term "robbed bit" as the bits are stolen from the voice data. Since the bits are stolen so infrequently, the voice quality is not compromised by much. But the available signaling combinations are limited to ringing, hang up, wink, and pulse digit dialing. In fact, the limitations are obvious when one recognizes DNIS and ANI information are sent as DTMF tones.

This introduces a problem: time. Each DTMF tone requires at least 100 milliseconds to send, which in a DNIS and ANI situation with 20 DTMFs will take at least two full seconds. There is also a margin for error in transmission or detection, resulting in DNIS or ANI failures. With the explosion of telephone related services, the telephone companies are turning to ISDN PRI to provide the more complicated and exact signaling required for new services. ISDN employs a more robust method of signaling. ISDN uses a T-1 circuit as 23 voice channels and one signaling channel. The term 23B plus D refers to 23 bearer (voice) channels and 1 Data (signaling) channel. The data channel carries the signaling information at a rate of 64 kilobits per second. This speed is many times greater than some of the most powerful modems available. Because of this high speed, telephone calls can be placed more quickly, and because of the protocol used, DNIS or ANI transmission failures are impossible.

Additionally, since no bits are "robbed" from the voice channels, the voice quality is better than that of Robbed Bit signaling on today's T-1 circuits. Also, computer modems and high speed faxes can use the voice channel for sending digital data instead of the traditional analog bit "noise." Therefore, ISDN PRI offers the end user countless new service capabilities. One channel could be used for faxing, another for modem data, several for video, another for a LAN and the remainder for voice. Suddenly, the average T-1 circuit becomes a pipeline for all communications! Increasingly long distance carriers are using ISDN PRI to provide inbound 800 calls with ANI and DNIS and re-routing skills. Dianatel makes some of the most sophisticated ISDN interface equipment around.

ROE Regulatory commission authorized allowed rate of return on equity. See REVENUE REQUIREMENT.

ROFL Abbreviation for "Rolling On the Floor, Laughing;" commonly used on E-mail and BBSs (Bulletin Board Systems).

ROH Receiver Off Hook.

ROI Return On Investment.

ROLL-CALL POLLING A technique in which every station is interrogated sequentially by a central computer system.

ROLLOVER LINES You receive many incoming calls. You don't want to miss a call, so you set your phone lines up to roll over, also called hunt, also called ISG in telephonese. You order five lines in hunt. The calls come into the first. If the first one is busy, the second rings. If it's busy, the third rings. If they're all busy, then the caller receives a busy.

There are two types of hunting — Sequential and Circular hunting. Sequential hunting starts at the number dialed and ends at the last number in the group. Circular hunting hunts all the lines in the hunting group, regardless of the starting point. Circular hunting, according to our understanding, circles only once (though your phone company may be able to program it circle a couple of times). The differences between sequential and circular are subtle. Circular seems to work better for large groups of numbers.

You don't need consecutive phone numbers to do rollovers. Nowadays you can roll lines forwards, backwards and jump around. Rollovers are now done in software. This also has its downside, since software fails. Our recommendation: Test your rollovers at least twice a day. In particular, test that your callers ultimately get a busy if all your lines are busy. Nothing worse your customer should receive a ring-no-answer.

ROLM A telephone equipment manufacturer based in Santa Clara, CA and owned by Siemens.

ROLMNET II ANALYSIS AND SUPPORT A service provided by the Rolm Analysis Center (RAC) that analyzes current call patterns and trunking facilities, chooses alternative facilities, and recommends the most cost effective long distance network based on the customer's needs. It also compares the present facilities to the proposed network and calculates cost savings.

ROLMPHONE DATA RPD INTERFACE A group of printed circuit cards forming the interface between Rolm digital desktop products and the CBX (Rolm's name for its PBX) for transmission of digital data. It accommodates ROLMphone telephones equipped with DataCom Modules, as well as Cedar, Cypress and Juniper desktop products. Compare with ROLMPHONE INTERFACE.

ROLMPHONE INTERFACE RPI. A group of printed circuit cards forming the interface between Rolm digital desktop products and the CBX for transmission of digitized voice signals. In addition to the ROLMphones, the RPI also accommodates connections to Cypress, Cedar and Juniper. Compare with ROLMPHONE DATA INTERFACE.

ROLMPHONES A family of electronic telephones which only work on the Rolm line of PBXs (which Rolm calls CBXs). As of writing, these phones include the ROLMphone 400, ROLMphone 240 and ROLMphone 120. In addition, Rolm has telephone/workstation devices called Cypress, Cedar and Juniper and will probably have more by the time you read this.

ROM Read Only Memory. Computer memory which can only be read from. New data cannot be entered and the existing data is non-volatile. This means it stays there even when power is turned off. A ROM is a memory device which is programmed at the factory and whose contents thereafter cannot be altered. In contrast is the device called RAM, whose contents can be altered. See READ ONLY MEMORY and MICROPROCESSOR.

ROM FONT The ROM Font is your PC's type font. It consists of a set of 256 characters which cannot be edited — unless you are running in video mode, in which case you can design your own type font.

ROOFING FILTER A low-pass filter used to reduce unwanted higher frequencies.

ROOM CUT-OFF Hotel/motel guest telephones restricted from outgoing calls when the guest room is unoccupied.

ROOM STATUS AND SELECTION Provides the capability to store and display the occupancy and cleaning status and the type number of each guest room. This helps housekeeping management, maid locating and room selection. Also, communications between the front desk and the housekeeper are speeded up via real-time maid activity and checkout audit printouts to indicate which rooms need cleaning next. The occupancy status is normally changed by the maid or inspector dialing from the room telephone.

ROOT DIRECTORY The top-level directory of a PC disk, hard or floppy. The root directory is created when you format the disk. From the root directory, you can create files and other directories.

ROSE 1. Remote Operations Service Element. An application layer protocol that provides the capability to perform remote operations at a remote process. Definition from Bellcore in reference to its concept of the Advanced

NEWTON'S TELECOM DICTIONARY

Intelligent Network. 2. As in Bodin. The very thoughtful lady who helps us, our friends and customers. We couldn't survive without Rose. Call her and tell her that you also can't survive without Rose. 1-212-691-8215.

ROTARY DIAL The circular telephone dial. As it returns to its normal position (after being turned) it opens and closes the electrical loop sent by the central office. Thus it generates pulses for each digit dialed. You can hear the "clicks". The number "seven," for example consists of seven "opens and closes," or seven clicks. You can dial on a rotary phone without using the rotary dial. Simply depress the switch hook quickly, allowing pauses in between to signify that you're about to send a new digit. It's a good party trick.

ROTARY DIAL CALLING The telephone system will accept dialing from conventional rotary dial sets, although pushbutton dial sets offer faster calling and greater reliability.

ROTARY HUNT You buy several phone lines. Let's say 212-691-8215, 212-691-8216, 212-691-8217, 212-691-8218. Someone dials you on your main number — 212-691-8215. It's busy. (That's our number.) The central office slides the call over to 212-691-8216. If that number is busy, it slides it over to 212-691-8217, and so on. This is called rotary hunt. It hunts to the next line in the rotary group. In the old days, the phone lines you could rotary hunt to had to be in numerical sequence. But now with modern stored program control central offices, your lines in rotary hunt can be very different as long as they're all on the same exchange.

ROTARY OUTPUT TO CENTRAL OFFICE Most central offices are equipped to provide tone dial service. In cases where the telephone company central office trunks are not designed to accept tone signaling, your on-premise phone system (PBX, key system or single line phone) will translate the number entered by a phone in tones into rotary dial pulses which can be processed by the central office.

ROTARY REGISTER A Rolm CBX printed circuit card that converts offhook bits corresponding to dial pulses into digital words suitable for computer processing.

ROTARY SENDER A Rolm CBX printed circuit card that receives digital code words from the computer and converts them into digital pulses. These are routed to an interface card which performs the proper outpulsing conversion.

ROTATING CYLINDER (DRUM) SCANNER A scanning technique using a drum and a photocell scan head. The original is attached to the drum, enabling the scan head to travel along the length of the document. Reflected light from the document is concentrated on the scanner photocell, which causes an analog signal.

ROTATING HELICAL APERTURE SCANNER Original is illuminated by a lamp when fed onto the platen, via a mirror and lens system, the document's image is focused first through a fixed horizontal slot, then through a rotating spiral slit disk series, and finally onto a photocell to generate an analogous electrical current.

ROTATIONAL MAILBOXES Information only mailboxes whose information is automatically changed on a time-sensitive or usage-sensitive basis.

ROTL Remote Office Test Line. Provides the capability to originate automatic interoffice trunk transmission test calls under the automatic control of CAROT from a remote location.

ROTOR The rotating part of a motor or other electrical machines.

ROTS Rotary Out-Trunk Switches.

ROUND ROBIN This is a method of distributing incoming calls to a bunch of people. This method selects the next agent on the list following the agent that received the last call. See also TOP DOWN and LONGEST AVAILABLE.

ROUNDTRIP PROPAGATION DELAY Roundtrip propagation delay from a burst modem to a burst modem will be about 470 milliseconds to 570 milliseconds (About half a second). See SATELLITE TRANSMISSION DELAY.

ROUTABLE PROTOCOLS Protocols, such as TCP/IP, DECnet, and XNS, that support Network Layer addressing. Packets constructed using these protocols contain information about how data should move through a network. This information, carried in the NLA (Netork Layer Address) field of the packet, is used by internetworking devices to make routing decisions.

ROUTE ADVANCE This feature routes outgoing calls over alternate long distance lines when the first choice trunk group is busy. The phone user selects the first choice route by dialing the corresponding access code. The phone equipment automatically advances to alternate trunks and trunk groups, based on the user's class of service. Route advance is a more primitive form of least cost routing. See LEAST COST ROUTING.

ROUTE DISCOVERY Process through which a brouter can learn LAN topology by passing information about its address and the LANs it connects and receiving the same information from others.

ROUTE LIST A sequence of trunk groups that can be searched for a particular route. This list is comprised of trunk groups and configuration attributes (e.g. Class of Service) governing the use of a particular trunk group.

ROUTE INDICATOR An address or group of characters in the heading of a message defining the final circuit or terminal to which the message is to be delivered.

ROUTE OPTIMIZATION The Rolm way of saying Least Cost Routing. See LEAST COST ROUTING and ROUTE OPTIMIZATION II.

NEWTON'S TELECOM DICTIONARY

ROUTE OPTIMIZATION II A Rolm product which offers automatic long distance cost control through Least Cost Routing, Queuing, Toll Restriction and the use of alternate long distance carriers. See also LEAST COST ROUTING, QUEUING and TOLL RESTRICTION.

ROUTER An interface between two networks. While routers are like bridges, they work differently. Routers provide more functionality than bridges. For example, they can find the best route between any two networks, even if there are several different networks in between. Routers provide network management capabilities such as load balancing, partitioning of the network, use statistics, communication priority, and troubleshooting tools that allow network managers to detect and correct problems even in a complex network of networks. Given these capabilities, routers are often used in building wide area or enterprise-wide networks.

There are two types of routers, protocol dependent and protocol independent. Protocol dependent routers rely on the end stations (computers on a LAN) for routing information. Computers tell the routers where (on which network) the destination computer is located and the routers find the best way to get there. This means that routers must understand the language (LAN protocol) the computers are talking, this makes them protocol dependent. Protocol independent routers discover the location of the destination device on their own and without any assistance from the communicating computers. They therefore, do not need to understand the language the computers are using which makes them protocol independent.

Protocol independent routers are easier to install and use. Most importantly, they can route nonroutable protocols, like those used by IBM networks. See also INTERNETWORKING and BRIDGES.

ROUTINE A program, or a sequence of instructions called by a program, that has some general or frequent use.

ROUTING The process of selecting the correct circuit path for a message.

ROUTING CODE The combination of characters or digits required by the switching system to route a transmission to its desired destination.

ROUTING DATA BASE Distance table in DNA.

ROUTING FLEXIBILITY The ability to send information over various network paths to avoid congestion and use portions of a total network that would otherwise be idle.

ROUTING LABEL The part of a signaling message identifying its destination.

ROUTING TABLE 1.Incoming Calls: A routing table is a user definable list of steps which are treatment instructions for an incoming call. Ideally these steps should be addressed and the call treatment begun before the call is answered. A routing table should consist of a minimum of steps that include

NEWTON'S TELECOM DICTIONARY

agent groups, voice response devices, announcements (delay and informational) music on hold, intraflow and interflow steps, route dialing (machine based call forwarding). A significant issue in the structure of routing tables is "look-back" capability, where no one previously interrogated resource is abandoned by the system (i.e. an agent group is now ignored, even though an agent is now available, because the ACD does not consider previous steps in the routing table).

2. Outgoing Calls: For a specific calling site, this table lists the long distance routing choices for each location to be dialed. There may be only one choice (route) listed for some or all destinations or there may be several choices for some destinations. (It depends how many outgoing lines and how many outgoing trunk groups you have.) If there are several choices then they will be ranked by some criteria (least cost, best quality, etc.).

RPC Remote Procedure Call. 1. A protocol governing the method with which an application activates processes on other nodes and retrieves the results. 2. A mechanism defined by Sun Microsystems and described in RFC-1057 that provides a standard for initiating and controlling processes on remote or distributed computer systems.

RPD See ROLMPHONE DATA INTERFACE.

RPI See ROLMPHONE INTERFACE.

RPG Report Program Generator. A computer language for processing large data files.

RPL ROLM Processing Language. A high-level programming language that gives the programmer access to the underlying CBX II 9000 processor architecture so that real-time communications capabilities of the processor microcode can be used.

RPM Remote Packet Module.

RPOA Recognized Private Operating Agency. A term used by the CCITT to describe those companies designated as operating telephone companies — if the country's phone networks are not run by government-owned administrations, such as the PTT's in Europe.

RPQ Request for Price Quotation. Solicitation for pricing for a specific component, software product, service or system. See also RFQ.

RQC Repair and Quick Clean. A term in the industry which repairs telecom equipment. It means all equipment is repaired and fully tested with a burn-in (if required) and an operational systems test. It also includes minor cosmetic cleaning of the unit. Definition courtesy Nitsuko America. See also LIKE NEW REPAIR AND UPDATE and REPAIR, UPDATE AND REFURBISH.

RR Abbreviation for Ready to Receive.

RS 1. Recommended Standard, as in RS-232. See the next definition. 2. Record Separator, in data processing terms.

RS-232-C Also known as RS-232 and in its latest version EIA/TIA-232-E. A set of standards specifying various electrical and mechanical characteristics for interfaces between computers, terminals and modems. The RS-232-C standard, which was developed by the EIA (Electrical Industries Association), defines the mechanical and electrical characteristics for connecting DTE and DCE data communications devices. It defines what the interface does, circuit functions and their corresponding connector pin assignments. The standard applies to both synchronous and asynchronous binary data transmission.

Most personal computers use the RS-232-C interface to attach modems. Some printers also use RS-232-C. You should be aware that despite the fact that RS-232-C is an EIA "standard," you cannot necessarily connect one RS-232-C equipped device to another one (like a printer to a computer) and expect them to work intelligently together. That's because different RS-232-C devices are often wired or pinned differently and may also use different wires for different functions. The "traditional" RS-232-C plug has 25 pins. The new IBM PC AT, most AT compatibles and the Toshiba T1100 Plus have a "new" RS-232-C plug with only nine pins. This smaller plug does essentially the same thing as its bigger cousin, but you need an adapter cable to connect one to another. They're widely available. See also interface and the RS-232-C diagram. See EIA/TIA-232-E and the APPENDIX for description of the pins and what they do.

RS-232 FAX SERVER A RS-232 fax server is software which connects a network server to a fax machine via an RS-232 port attached to the fax machine. There are not many fax machines with R2-232 so you need to chose carefully. The idea of this arrangement is to let users send faxes directly from their own PC via the fax server via the attached fax machine, or directly from the fax machine. Users can also use the fax machine as a scanner.

RS-328 October, 1966 the Electronic Industries Association issues its first fax standard: the EIA Standard RS-328, Message Facsimile Equipment for Operation on Switched Voice Facilities Using Data Communications Equipment. The Group 1 standard, as it later became known, made possible the more generalized business use of fax. Transmission was analog and it took four to six minutes to send a page.

RS-422 A standard operating in conjunction with RS-449 that specifies electrical characteristics for balanced circuits (circuits with their own ground leads).

RS-422-A Electrical characteristics of balanced-voltage digital interface circuits.

RS-423 A standard operating in conjunction with RS-449 that specifies electrical characteristics for unbalanced circuits (circuits using common or shared grounding techniques). Another EIA standard for DTE/DCE connection which specifies interface requirements for expanded transmission speeds (up to 2 Mbps), longer cable lengths, and 10 additional functions. RS-449 applies to binary, serial, synchronous or asynchronous communications. Half- and full-duplex modes are accommodated and transmission can be over 2- or 4-wire facilities such as point-to-point or multipoint lines. The physical connection between DTE and DCE is made through a 37-contact connector; a separate 9-connector is specified to service secondary channel interchange circuits, when used.

RS-423-A Electrical characteristics of unbalanced-voltage digital interface circuits.

RS-449 Another "standard" data communications connector. This one uses 37-pins and is designed for higher speed transmission. Each signal pin has its own return line, instead of a common ground return and the signal pairs (signal, return) are balanced lines rather than a signal referenced to ground. This cable typically uses twisted pairs, while a RS-232-C cable usually doesn't.

RS-499-1 Addendum 1 to RS-449. (What else?)

RSA Rural Service (or Statistical) Area. The FCC designated 428 rural markets across the country and is still in the process of licensing cellular operators for them. See also MSA.

RSC Remote Switching Center.

RSL Request and Status Links. A generic term for linking computers and PBXs. Every manufacturer of phone systems is evolving towards open architecture and their own "RSL." The term RSL, which is too passive, is being replaced with PHI (PBX Host Interface), a term coined by Probe Research. Manufacturer PHI names include:

ACL — Applications Connectivity Link — Siemens' PHI link protocol

ACT — Applied Computer Telephony — Hewlett Packard's generic application interface to PBXs

Application Bridge — Aspect Telecommunications' ACD to host computer link

ASAI — AT&T's Adjunct Switch Application Interface

CIT — Digital Equipment Corporation's Computer Integrated Telephony (works with major PBXs)

CSA — Callpath Services Architecture — IBM's Computer to PBX link

Call Frame — Harris' PBX to computer link

Callpath Host — IBM and ROLM's CICS-based integrated voice and data applications platform which links to ROLM's 9751

Callpath — IBM's announced, CICS application link to IBM's CSA, available on the AS400 in April of 1991

Callbridge — Rolm's CBX and Siemens to IBM host or non-IBM host computer link

CompuCall — Northern Telecom's DMS central office link to computer interface

CPI — Computer to PBX Interface developed by Northern Telecom and DEC

CSP — Nabnasset's Communications Services Platform

CSTA — Computer Supported Telephony Application, PHI standard from ECMA

DECags — DEC ASAI Gateway Services. Two-directional link to AT&T's Definity

DMI — AT&T's Digital Multiplexed Interface, a T-1 PBX to computer interface

HCI — Host Command Interface. Mitel's digital PBX link to DEC computer

IG — AT&T's ISDN Gateway (one direction from the switch to the host)

ITG — AT&T's Integrated Telemarketing Gateway (two directional)

ISDN/AP — NT's PHI SL1 protocol supports NT's Meridian Link PHI

Meridian Link — NT's PHI product available on the Meridian PBX

OAI — Open Application Interface. InteCom's and NEC's PHI

ONA — Open Network Architecture (for telephone central offices)

PACT — Siemen's PBX and Computer Teaming, protocols between PBXs and computers

PDI — Telenova/Lexar's Predictive Dialing Interface

SAI — Stratus Computer Switch Application Interface

SCAI — Switch to Computer Application Interface, the name given by T1S1 to PHI

SCIL — Aristacom's Switch Computer Interface Link Transaction Link

STEP — Speech and Telephony Environment for Programmers; WANG's link

Transaction Link — Rockwell's link from its Galaxy ACD to an external computer

Solid State Applications Interface Bridge — Solid's State Systems' PHI

Teleos IRX-9000 — Teleos' Intelligent Call Distribution platform

For more information, see OAI (Open Architecture Interface.)

RSM Remote Switching Module. An AT&T 5ESS switch stand-alone switching module that supports all line features and routes intro-RSM calls. It is either a single module or a multimodule and can be situated up to 150 miles from the 5ESS switch host.

RT 1. Reorder Tone. 2. Remote Terminal.

RTAN Real Time ANI.

RTFM Read The F...ing Manual.

RTM Ready To Manfacture.

RTO-IS Ready To Order - In Service.

RTS Request To Send. One of the control signals on a standard RS-232-C connector. It places the modem in the originate mode so it can begin to send. See the APPENDIX.

RTTU Remote Trunk Test Unit.

RTU Right To Use. A term manufacturers have invented to stiffle the used/secondary market in their equipment. Basically, the manufacturer says "Fine, you can sell your no-longer-needed product to some used equipment dealer. But if someone buys it from the dealer and wants to use it, they have to pay me a Right To Use fee." Without payment of this fee, the manufacturer won't contract to maintain the customer's equipment and certainly won't sell the customer software updates, etc. The right to use fee is exhorbitant — typically considerably more than what the product actually sells on the used market for. A better approach for a manufacturer would be to innovate a little more and make the customer wants his new product more than his old price (despite the old product's lower price).

RTV An imaging term. Real-Time Video. DVI software that implements quick-and-dirty, realtime video compression. Once called "edit-level video," it stores video as only 10 frames per second. Meant for use while developing DVI applications.

RU Request Unit or Response Unit. A basic unit of data in SNA.

RULE-BASED SYSTEM The most popular way to represent knowledge in an expert system. In general, a rule-based system's knowledge base contains both facts and IF..THEN production rules.

RUN To start a software program.

RUN/STOP On a Northern Telecom Norstar phone, this feature inserts a delay in a dialing sequence. The delay can be any length of time.

RUN LENGTH ENCODING A facsimile encoding process that converts an expanse of white or black to a code corresponding to the length of the run.

RUN TIME The time it takes to execute a software program. See RUNTIME.

RUNTIME A runtime environment is the software that plays back multimedia materials. The runtime material is created by the author. Examples of runtime applications are presentations are training, where the material cannot be edited but only viewed. The runtime software could be a slide show viewer, a software-only video playback application, or a hypermedia runtime document.

RUR Repair, Update and Refurbish. A term in the industry which repairs telecom equipment. It means equipment is repaired and updated to current manufacturer's specifications. Also includes minor cosmetic cleaning of metal cabinets, a full diagnostic test with burn-in (if required) and an operational test. Definition courtesy Nitsuko America. See also LIKE NEW REPAIR AND UPDATE and QUICK CLEAN.

RVVP See REVENUE VOLUME PRICING PLAN.

RZ Return to Zero. A method of transmitting binary information where voltage returns to a zero (reference) level after each encoded bit.

RZ CODE Return to zero code. A code form having two information states called "zero" and "one" in which the signal returns to a rest state during a portion of the bit period.

S

S Designation the sleeve or control leads in electromechanical Central Offices which are used to make busy circuits, trunks and subscriber lines, as well as to test for busy conditions. It also designates the sleeve wire on a switchboard cord.

S INTERFACE For basic rate access in ISDN, the S interface denotes a user-to-network interface reference point characterized by a four-wire, 144-kbps (2B+D) user rate. As a universal interface between ISDN terminals or terminal adapters and the network channel termination, the S interface allows a variety of terminal types and subscriber networks (e.g., PBXs, LANs, and controllers) to be connected to this type of network. At the S interface, there are 4,000 frames of 48 bits each, per second, for 192 kbps. The user's portion is 36 bits per frame, or 144 kbps. See also ISDN.

S-SEED Symmetric Self Electro-optic Effect Device. A switching device in which signals enter and exit as beams of light, not through electrical contacts. In 1990 AT&T Bell Labs built a general purpose digital optical processor/computer. The device contained 2,048 S-SEED chips which could be accessed simultaneously with separate beams of light. That means, that ultimately, such a computer could process huge amounts of information in parallel.

S/DMS SONET DMS is a family of products for Northern Telecom's DMS family of central office switches. There were three initial members of the family as we went to press:

S/DMS TransportNode — a transport vehicle which provides SONET connectivity and bandwidth management for long-haul, inter-offce and local applications. It includes elements for the transport of SONET over fiber or radio, including integrated bandwidth management functions.

S/DMS AccessNode — a business service access vehicle which delivers switched and special services to the customer's premises, with bandwidth ranging from narrowband to broadband.

S/DMS SuperNode — an evolution of the DMS SuperNode system, which also supports the narrowband capabilities of a SONET network, while adding future broadband switching and network management capabilities.

S10 REGISTER Hayes, the modem people, invented their "Command Set." This command set lets you control your Hayes compatible modem. In the Command Set there are "S" registers which set how the modem responds to events like anwsering. Should it answer on the first, second, third, etc. ring. There are 27 registers. The most important S register is S10. This register sets the time between loss of carrier and internal modem disconnect. The factory setting is 1.3 seconds. Drop carrier for 1.3 seconds and your modem will turn itself off. This is long enough for all conditions, except the awful "call waiting" signal you get at hotels and at home. There is a solution: Get your communications software to "go local." Then type

ATS10=20. That will increase your S10 register to two seconds. If you have a 300 or 1200 baud you'll have to do this every time you turn on your modem. If you have a 2400 baud modem (the only one to get), you type ATS10=20&W only once. The "&W" writes it into your 2400 baud's non-volatile memory. If you want to check to see if you did it right, type ATS10? That will reply by saying 020. That means 20 tenths of a second, or two seconds. If that still doesn't work for you, increase S10 to three seconds. Other S registers control how long your modem waits for the other end to answer, how long its dialing "pause" is, how quickly it outpulses tones for dialing, etc.

SA SOURCE ADDRESS The MAC (Media Access Control, the lower part of ISO layer two) address of the IEEE 802.10 security committee.

SAA 1. Systems Application Architecture. A set of specifications written by IBM describing how users should interface with applications and communications programs. The idea is to give all software "a common feel" so that training will be less burdensome. According to IBM advertising, "SAA will make it possible for everyone in an organization to access information regardless of its location. What's more, all software written to SAA specifications will provide similar screen layouts, menus and terminology." For a fuller explanation, see SYSTEMS APPLICATIONS ARCHITECTURE. 2. An AT&T Merlin term. Supplemental Alert Adapter. A device that permits 48VDC alerting equipment to be connect to an analog multiline telephone jack so that people working in noisy or remote areas of a building can be alerted to incoming calls.

SADL Synchronous Auto Dial Language. Created by Racal Vadic, SADL is a public domain auto-dialing protocol which defines procedures in BSC, SDLC (SNA) and HDLC for PCs and larger computers that wish to control synchronous modems directly under program control. SADL does for synchronous dialing systems what the Hayes "AT" command set has done for the async PC dialing world.

SAFE A store-and-forward MCI International message-switching system that provides customers with control of their Telex messages by enabling them to create messages, then specify the message-handling parameters in a unique customer reference file. Customers can send and receive messages from the MCI Safe computer at speeds up to 9600 bps.

SAG The downward curvature of a wire or cable due to its weight.

SAI Stratus Computer's PBX Switch to Stratus Computer Application Interface.

SALES AGENT See AGGREGATOR.

SALES AUTOMATION See SALES FORCE AUTOMATION.

SALES FORCE AUTOMATION The use of computers and computer software by salespeople to boost their sales. There are two types of sales force automation — those totally self-contained on the computers of salespeople (mostly laptops) or those which communicate with headquarters computer over phone lines. There are many purposes of the phone communication — sending orders in, finding out about backorders, getting updates on "specials," dropping letters and memos in, getting new prices, new products, new technical specs, etc. Salespeople routinely show 10% to 20% sales gains armed with a laptop PC and sales automation software (also called "personal contact") software.

SAMPLING Converting continuous signals, like voice or video, into discrete values, e.g. digital signals. See also PCM and DIGITAL SIGNAL PROCESSING.

SAMPLING RATE The number of times per second that an analog signal is measured and converted to a binary number — the purpose being to convert the analog signal to a digital analog. The most common digital signal — PCM — samples 8,000 times a minute.

SANITY CHECK A check to confirm the service capability of a switching system. This test has not been applied to the author of this dictionary.

SAP In local area networks, SAP is Service Access Point. The part of an IEEE 802 frame that identifies the frame's protocol type. IBM defines SAP as a logical point made available by an interface card where information can be received and transmitted.

SAR Segmentation And Reassembly. The lower half of BISDN Layer 3.

SAPI Service Access Point Identifier. The SAPI identifies a logical point at which data link layer services are provided by a data link layer entity to a Layer 3 entity. ISDN jargon.

SAS Simple Attachment Scheme.

SASG Special Autonomous Study Group. These CCITT study groups are chartered to produce handbooks on basic telecommunications technical or administrative subjects for developing countries.

SASI Shugart Associates System Interface. The first SCSI interface specification defined by Shugart, a disk drive manufacturer. Later it was modified and renamed as the Small Computer System Interface (SCSI), pronounced Scuzzy. See also SCSI.

SASS Shared Access for Switched Services. An AT&T offering combining MEGACOM WATS and MEGACOM 800 to enable both outgoing and incoming MEGACOM service on the same T-1 circuit.

SATELLITE 1. A microwave receiver, repeater, regenerator in a geosynchronous orbit 22,300 miles above the earth. 2. Something distant to the main something. See MAIN DISTRIBUTION FRAME and SATELLITE TRANSMISSION.

SATELLITE BUSINESS SYSTEMS SBS. A satellite long distance carrier originally owned jointly by IBM, Aetna Insurance and Comsat, but now owned by MCI (which acquired it in 1986). SBS started out to serve the data communications transmission marketplace but found that marketplace too small to be profitable. It then started to serve the voice transmission marketplace and did somewhat better. Satellite Business Systems no longer exists as a separate entity. It has been merged into MCI. See SBS.

SATELLITE CABINET Surface-mounted or flush-type wall cabinets for housing circuit administration hardware. Satellite cabinets, like satellite closets, supplement riser closets by providing additional facilities for connecting horizontal wiring subsystem cables from information outlets in user locations. Sometimes referred to as satellite location.

SATELLITE CLOSET A walk-in or shallow wall closet that supplements a backbone or riser closet by providing additional facilities for connecting riser subsystem cables to horizontal wiring subsystem cables from information outlets. Also referred to as satellite location. See also RISER CLOSET and BACKBONE CLOSET.

SATELLITE COMMUNICATIONS The use of geostationary orbiting satellites to relay information.

SATELLITE COMMUNICATIONS CONTROL SCC. The earth station equipment that controls such communications functions as access, echo suppression, forward error correction and signaling.

SATELLITE CONSTELLATION The arrangement in space of a set of satellites.

SATELLITE DELAY COMPENSATOR A device that compensates for the absolute delay in a satellite circuit communicating with data terminal equipment (DTE) with the DTE's own protocol.

SATELLITE DISTRIBUTION FRAME An intermediate point for connecting wires running between a group of phones and the Main Distribution Frame located elsewhere in the building. A fat multi-conductor cable comes from the main distribution frame to the satellite distribution frame, where it splits into individual cables to individual phones or workstations. The satellite distribution frame is usually located in a satellite wiring closet or cabinet. These wires are ultimately connected to the telephone system. See DISTRIBUTION FRAME.

SATELLITE FACILITY A transmission system using a satellite in a geostationary orbit above the earth and a number of earth stations.

SATELLITE LINK Microwave link using a satellite to receive, amplify and retransmit signals. Typically that satellite is in a geosynchronous orbit.

SATELLITE OPERATION A configuration of multiple PBXs or one big PBX and several smaller PBXs. The configuration gives a company with several nearby locations a unified system of centralized trunks, centralized attendants, overall call detail recording and many of the advantages of a private network. The key advantage of satellite operation is that one big centralized telephone system can contain most of the intelligence and computer smarts for the total system. This advantage is heavily economic. A variation on satellite operation is called CENTRALIZED ATTENDANT SERVICE (CAS).

SATELLITE PREMISES CHANNEL This is the cable connecting arrangement between a dedicated earth station and the Customer Provided Equipment.

SATELLITE PROCESSOR A computer with little computing power used for operations that do not require the full processing power of the main machine.

SATELLITE TRANSMISSION A form of transmission which sends signals to an orbiting satellite which receives them, amplifies them and returns those signals back to earth. Satellite transmission provides great clarity but suffers from delay. See SATELLITE TRANSMISSION DELAY.

SATELLITE TRANSMISSION DELAY Referring to the time it takes a signal to travel from one satellite earth station to the satellite in the sky then to the satellite earth station at the other end. Since most communications satellites orbit the earth at a distance of approximately 22,300 miles, the total distance the signal travels is 44,600 miles. Since radio waves travel at the speed of light (186,000 miles per second), simple arithmetic will show a delay of approximately one-quarter of one second thus, 44,600 divided by 186,000 = 0.239 second. If you are waiting for a reply, double this time. (You double the distance.)

SATURN A family of excellent digital PBXs made by Siemens and sold by Siemens Information Systems of Boca Raton, FL.

SAVE A telephone feature that allows the user to put a phone number into memory for future calls, by pressing one or two buttons after dialing it the first time. See also SNR.

SAVE AND REPEAT Another way of saying "Autodial." Electronic phones may be able to save a number so you can dial it later by simply hitting one button on the phone. This feature is similar to a "Last Number Redial" button, except that button just dials the last number called. "Save and Repeat" puts a number into temporary storage for dialing at another time. Phones should have both auto-redial and save-and-repeat buttons.

SBS Satellite Business Systems. A long distance satellite company that started out as a joint venture between Lockheed and MCI, was sold to IBM Aetna and Comsat and then eventually was given to MCI in exchange for shares issued to IBM. SBS never made any money. But that was irrelevant. Its job was to help IBM sell computer networks. See SATELLITE BUSINESS SYSTEMS.

SCA Supplemental Communications Authority. The authority granted by the Federal Communications Commission to transmit on a subcarrier.

SCAI Switch to Computer Applications Interface. A protocol that defines how switches talk to outboard computers, i.e. computers which are external to the switch and contain such a database of customer buying information. Using SCAI, calls and data screens about a calling customer can be presented to the agent simultaneously. See OPEN APPLICATION INTERFACE.

SCALABLE Something that can be made larger or smaller relatively easily and painlessly. And the cost to grow is straight-line, not stair-step, as in the old days of mainframes. At least that was the earlier, accepted definition. Then Microsoft started referring to Windows NT as "scalable," namely that it runs on everying from Intel to RISC processors and single to multiprocessor systems.

SCALABLE TYPEFACE A font that can be enlarged or reduced to virtually any size.

SCAN 1. Switched Circuit Automatic Network. 2. To examine sequentially, part by part. 3. To examine every reference or every entry in a file routinely as part of a retrieval scheme. 4. In electromagnetic or acoustic search, one complete rotation of an antenna. 5. The motion of an electronic beam through space searching for a target. Scanning is produced by the motion of the antenna or by lobe switching.

SCAN TIME The time between two successive polls to a workstation on a data communications network.

SCANNER A device used to input graphic images into the computer. Scanners look at or "scan" a piece of paper and put the image's information into digital form. The information can then be recognized by the computer. A scanner is also in a fax machine that "looks" at the original document and determines the brightness level of each pixel to be transmitted. See also Optical Character Recognition.

SCANNS Multiplexers which perform the vital functions of monitoring and control within System 75s and 85s Automated Building Management feature. The SCANNS continuously scan sensors and send the resulting data to local control units.

SCapi SCSA Application Programming Interface. A high-level, object-oriented hardware independent, technology independent programming model that permits the design and implementation of call processing applications.

SCATTERING A cause of lightwave signal loss in optical fiber transmission. The diffusion of a light beam caused by microscopic variations in the material density of the transmission medium. Scattering is a physical mechanism in fibers that attenuates light by changing its direction.

SCbus The standard bus for communication within an SCSA node. The SCbus features a hybrid bus architecture consisting of a serial Message Bus for control and signaling, and a 16-wire TDM data bus.

SCC Specialized Common Carrier. Another term for a long distance carrier in competition with AT&T. The word "Specialized" came about because these long distance carriers purported to provide "specialized" circuits for business customers. At one stage they were also known as OCCs, or Other Common Carriers (i.e. other than AT&T). These days, both terms have fallen into disrepute. All long distance carriers — including AT&T — are called IntereXchange Carriers (IXCs).

SCCP Signaling Connection Control Part. Part of the CCITT #7 signaling protocol. and of the SS7 protocol. It provides additional routing and management functions for transfer of messages other than call set-up between signaling points. See also SIGNALING SYSTEM 7 and COMMON CHANNEL SIGNALING.

SCCS Switching Center Control System.

SCdpi SCSA Device Programming Interface: A set of callable functions that allow SCSA application software to control SCSA hardware. The SCdpi consists of both common call processing services and technology-specific modules for the application of particular resources to call processing tasks.

SCE Service Creation Environments. A term used in the jargon of intelligent networks (IN) to allow outside developers to define and create new value-added (i.e. intelligent) services.

SCEPTRE A consumer videotex interactive terminal which, when used with a TV set and a phone line, allows the consumer to interact with a videotex data base service.

SCHEDULING Making the timetable of agent hours and shifts for your call center. Includes vacation days, breaks, training time, lengths of shifts and should take into account forecasting information. A call center software management package helps you with this.

SCHEMATIC Diagram which details the electrical elements of a circuit or system.

SCHLEPP Jewish word meaning to carry around, to drag around, as in "This machine is heavy. Schlepping it is a pain."

SCIL Aristacom's Switch Computer Interface Link. Aristacom is an external software company that has developed software for linking programs on an external computer to a PBX and having that computer control the movement of calls within the PBX. See also OPEN APPLICATION INTERFACE.

SCINTILLATION In electromagnetic wave propagation, a random fluctuation of the received field strength about its mean value, the deviations usually being relatively small. The effects of this phenomenon become more significant as the frequency of the propagating wave increases.

SCM Station Class Mark. A two-digit number that identifies certain capabilities of your cellular phone. How the cellular network handles your call is based on these digits. The SCM tells the system if your phone transmits at standard power levels or low power levels, if it can use the full 832 channels or only the original 666 frequencies. The last attribute identified is whether your phone uses voice-activated transmission (VOX).

SCO An AT&T specialized network maintenance organization providing a single point of contact for resolving customer network faults.

SCOPE A slang term for cathode ray oscilloscope.

SCOTS 1. Surveillance and COntrol of Transmission Systems. 2. Switched Circuit Ordering and Tracking System. MCI's automated tracking and order processing system for Dial-Up products, IMTs, and the MCI switched network.

SCP 1. Service Control Point. Also called Signal Control Point. A remote database within the System Signaling 7 network. The SCP supplies the translation and routing data needed to deliver advanced network services. The SCP translates an 800-IN-WATS number to the required routing number. It is separated from the actual switch, making it easier to introduce new services on the network. See also TCAP. 2. Northern Telecom term for a Satellite Communications Processor.

SCR Abbreviation for Silicon Controlled Rectifier, a semiconductor device that allows one electric circuit to control another; often replaces electromechanical relays.

SCRAMBLER A device which deliberately distorts a voice or data conversation so that only another like device can figure out the content of the message. Analog scramblers invert the frequencies of speech. Digital scramblers first convert speech to digital form and then encrypt. Both types also perform the reverse process. The sophistication (i.e. complexity) of a scrambler determines its price.

SCRATCHPAD A part of the random access memory of a computer or telephone system which can be used to temporarily store data. In a cellular phone system, scratch pad allows storage of phone numbers in temporary memory during a call. Silent scratch pads allows number entry into scratch pad without making beep tones. See also REGISTER.

SCREEN FONT The font that is displayed on your screen. It is, hopefully, designed to match the printer font so that documents look the same on the screen as they do when printed. You typically need a graphics interface on your company — like Windows or X-Windows — to make the font you see on your screen the same as what you see when you print it out.

SCREEN REFRESH RATE The rate at which your computer screen is redrawn every second by a horizontal beam that scans from the top left hand corner to the bottom right hand corner. Screen refresh rates differ by the graphics standard you're running.

SCREENED TRANSFER You are transferring a call from your phone to your boss. You dial a code for transfer, then dial your boss. The caller you're transferring is automatically put on hold. You speak to your boss, tell her who you're putting through. She okays the transfer, then you hit another digit and the call goes right through. This is called screened transfer. An unscreened transfer occurs when you simply dial your boss's office and send the call through without announcing it. Most PBXs have the ability to do both screened and unscreened calls.

SCRIPT FILES Some communications programs had script files that automate loging onto communications services, such as MCI Mail. The files are saved on your disk and read by your communications software when connecting to a remote service. Newer communications programs will "write" their own scripts by recording what you do in response to what questions from the remote service. This typically happens using a program feature called "Learn."

SCRIPT LANGUAGE A software language that contains English-statements for commands. A statement might be as simple as WrapPara() for wrap paragraph. Typically a script language contains commands that are specific to the type of task it's doing. For example, VOS from Parity Software in San Francisco is a script language for voice processing using Dialogic voice processing cards. A script language is more flexible than an Applications Generator, but is more difficult to program.

SCROLLING Browsing through information at a video terminal. Scrolling is the continuous movement of information either vertically or horizontally on a video screen as if the information were on a paper being rolled under it.

SCSA Signal Computing System Architecture. A generalized open-standard architecture describing the components and specifying the interfaces for a signal processing system for the PC-based voice processing, call processing and telecom switching industry. SCSA describes all elements of the system architecture from the electrical characteristics of the SCbus and SCxbus to the high level application programming interfaces (APIs). SCSA was first made public in early Spring 1993. According to TELECONNECT Magazine, this SCSA standard is remarkable for several things:

1. On the day of its announcement over 60 telecom and voice processing companies publicly endorsed SCSA, committed to work with it and are clearly planning to work it.

2. With SCSA — a standard for PC/LANs and VME-backplaned computers — you can build much larger telecom switches and much larger call and voice processing boxes. Previous standards, like AEB, PEB and MVIP, were basically limited to what you could do with one PC. Now PCs can be joined together. With SCSA, you can put 16 T-1 lines, or 512 voice lines in one PC and join together 16 PCs, for a total of 16 x 16 x 24 = 6,144 lines! That's a central office built out of networked PCs. A mainframe built out of a LAN. The SCSA joining is not via LAN or LAN-emulation. That

would be too slow and the transmission too bursty (great for data, lousy for voice). It's via an SCbus — something that looks and works like a PBX backplane.

3. SCSA incorporates virtually every other standard in PC-based swiching — including the most popular ones, Mitel's ST-Bus, MVIP, Siemens PCM Highway, AEB and PEB.

4. It's a lot faster and more reliable. All signaling is out of band. There's clock fall-back and time slot bundling. It's more modular, meaning you can start with one PC and grow one at a time. That makes it more "modular" (scalable is the new word). It's also hot pluggable. You don't have to turn off to upgrade.

5. It has applications portability. Tandem, the highly-successful fault-tolerant mini-computer maker, has an SCSA application in a call center. They call it the Tandem Non-Step Call Center. It uses the Tandem 2400 VRU and the 4800 VRU.

SCSA is open, truly open. All its specs and all levels of its specs are available. To that extent, SCSA represents a remarkable gamble by its creator, Dialogic, a telecom/voice processing hardware company. It is encouraging competing manufacturers to build hardware to its specs and gambling that it won't be left in the dust, as IBM was with its PC. (Compaq, not IBM, built the first '386 PC.)

SCSA, as an idea, is revolutionary (for telecom). No one in telecom has ever promolgated an open standard everyone can adopt — hardware and software vendors. Dialogic has done it to create opportunities by providing great economies of scale for the developers. Write one application, create one applications generator, design one piece of hardware. Erector set telecom/voice processing! Build small. Build large. Just join the bits and pieces together. See also AEB, PEB and MVIP.

SCSA-COMPATIBLE An SCSA term. Able to function in an SCSA environment in its native mode.

SCSI Small Computer System Interface. (Pronounced Scuzzie.) SCSI is a new and faster way for a PC to communicate with and control as many as seven different devices — such as magnetic hard disks, optical disks, tape drives, printers and scanners — without siphoning excessive power away from the computer's main processor. SCSI disk drives also work fast, typically faster than a "normal" IDE drive. ANSI (American National Standards Institute) has set several guidelines for SCSI connection. There is SCSI-1 and SCSI-2. The SCSI specifications are available from ANSI, 1430 Broadway, New York NY 10018 212-642-4900.

All Apple Macintosh machines come with built-in SCSI ports to which you can daisy chain one periperhal after another another, until you have a total of seven. This is fairly easy job. If you've removed the hard drive in your Macintosh (and replaced it with one or more SCSI-attached drives) your

Macintosh may require a hard disk terminator. Some (not all) Macintoshes require a hard disk terminator (A $5 device) if their hard disk has been removed.

To add SCSI devices to an IBM or clone, you must first place a SCSI adapter card in your PC's bus and connect the devices to that card. Sadly, for the IBM clone, SCSI is not a universal plug-n-play standard. According to Keith Comer of Toshiba, when asked why Toshiba's computers didn't come with SCSI ports as they came with parallel and serial ports, said, "I an unconvinced of SCSI's universal compatibility. It's a non-trivial task to connect SCSI devices. All devices need their own drivers. And each need to be configured for the particular SCSI card you have. Further, many of the SCSI drivers are incompatible with memory managers. In short, for us it would be a support nightmare."

The problem is slowly lessening. Corel has been pushing their SCSI Interface kit and it makes connecting things less of a pain. You can also connect some SCSI devices to a computer's parallel port, using a parellel/SCSI interface. But the throughout is slow. See SCSI-2.

SCSI-2 SCSI-2 (pronunced Scuzzie-Two) is a 16-bit implementation of the 8-bit SCSI bus. Using a superset of the SCSI commands, the SCSI-2 maintains downward compatibility with other standard SCSI devices while improving upon reliability and data throughput.

SCVF Single Channel Voice Frequency.

SCxbus An SCSA term. The standard SCSA bus for communication between nodes. The SCxbus features the same hybrid architecture as the SCbus.

SDE 1. Synchronization Distribution Expander. 2. Secure Data Exchange as defined by the IEEE 802.10 security committee.

SDEC Northern Telecom term for Satellite Data Exchange Controller.

SDH Synchronous Digital Hierarchy. Term used by the International Telegraph and Telephone Consultative Committee to refer to Sonet.

SDI Northern Telecom term for Serial Data Interface.

SDF Sub Distribution Frame. Intermediate cross connect points, usually located in wiring or utility closets. A trunk cable or LAN backbone is run from each SDF to the MDF (Main Distribution Frame).

SDH Synchronous Digital Hierarchy. SDH is a CCITT defined standard technically consistent with SONET. In short, another name for SONET.

SDK Software Development Kit.

SDL Signaling Data Link.

SDLC Synchronous Data Link Control. A bit-oriented synchronous communications protocol developed by IBM where the message may contain any collection or sequence of bits without being mistaken for a control character. SDLC is used in IBM's SNA — System Network Architecture. See HDLC and IBM.

SDM Subrate Data Multiplexing. A European term. In North America, it's called SRDM.

SDMA Station Detail Message Accounting. See CALL ACCOUNTING.

SDN Software Defined Network. See SOFTWARE DEFINED NETWORK, SDN SERVING OFFICE, VIRTUAL NETWORK and the APPENDIX.

SDN SERVING OFFICE One of many AT&T-supplied switching nodes in an SDN network. See also SOFTWARE DEFINED NETWORK and the APPENDIX.

SDRM Sub-rate Data Multiplexing. Refers to a service where a DSO (64 Kbps) channel may contain one 56 Kbps signal, five 9.6 Kbps signals, ten 4.8 Kbps signals or twenty 2.4 Kbps signals. Although speeds may be mixed, the highest speed determines the number of signals supported.

SDS IS Switched Digital Service Integrated Systems. A new (Spring, 1993) service of Pacific Bell which provides ISDN over one single business line, rather than the minimum two lines required previously.

SDSAF Switched Digital Services Applications Forum, a group of manufacturers and carriers whose objective to standardize the interconnection of switched 56 kilobit and n x switched 56 channel local and long distance services. The group is based in Reston, VA. Today a switched 56 kbps "phone" call between multiple carriers probably wouldn't get through. In short, this group is trying to bring the simplicity of the voice dial up phone system into the switched data world.

SDU-SMDS DATA UNIT The user payload in an SMDS L3PDU packet. The SDU can contain up to 9,188 bytes.

SE Systems Engineering

SEALING CURRENT A designation for a powering situation that consists of a wet loop without span power.

SEALINK Sealink is an error-correcting file transfer, data transmission protocol for transmitting files between PCs. It is a variant of Xmodem. It was developed to overcome the transmission delays caused by satellite relays or packet-switching networks.

SEALS A way of telling if a device has been tampered with.

SEAMLESS In a LAN environment, it means that what takes place between the user and the application accessed is transparent. The user doesn't perceive he's on a network because his programs run as though they were on his personal computer.

SEARCH DRIVE A drive that is automatically searched by the operating system when a requested file is not found in the current (default) directory. A search drive allows a user working in one directory to transparently access an application or data file that is located in another directory.

SEATFONE GTE's name for air-to-ground telephones which it installs in some airplanes. GTE is investing millions to make its service useful. It needs to.

SECAM Acronym for Systeme Electronique Couleur Avec Memoire. A television signal standard (625 lines, 50 hertz, 220 volts primary power) used in France, eastern European countries, the USSR and some African countries. Sequential and memory color TV system adopted by France and most Eastern European and Middle Eastern countries, the USSR and some African countries. SECAM uses an 819-line scan picture which provides a better resolution than PAL's 625-lines and NTSC's 525-lines (the US standard). All three two systems are not compatible. You cannot view an Australian, English or French videotape or through-the-air broadcast on a US TV.

SECONDARY EQUIPMENT Used telecommunications equipment. See also USED, CERTIFIED, REFURBISHED and REMANUFACTURED.

SECONDARY MARKET The market for used business telecommunications and computer equipment. The magazine serving this market is called TELECOM GEAR. It's a monthly. You can get your free subscription by calling 1-800-322-5156.

SECONDARY PROTECTION Primary protection is a device that sits at your building entrance between your phone line coming in from outside and your line going into and up your building. The phone company is responsible for installing primary protection. Secondary protection sits on your floor just next to your phone system. Secondary protection is designed to protect your phone equipment from spikes, surges and high electricity that might affect your phone lines between the primary protection downstairs and the secondary protection upstairs. Secondary protection typically costs $20 to $30 a line. It's worth every penny.

SECONDARY RADAR A radiodetermination system based on the comparison of reference signals with radio signals retransmitted from the position to be determined.

SECONDARY RADIATION Particles (such as photons, Compton recoil electrons, delta rays, secondary cosmic rays, and secondary electrons) that are produced by the action of primary radiation on matter.

SECONDARY SERVICE AREA The service area of a broadcast station served by the skywave and not subject to objectionable interference and in which the signal is subject to intermittent variations in strength.

SECONDARY STATION In a data communication network, the secondary station responsible for performing unbalanced link-level operations, as instructed by the primary station. A secondary station interprets received commands and generates responses.

SECONDARY WINDING The minor winding on a relay having two windings. The winding on a transformer that is not connected to a AC source.

SECORD SEcure voice CORD board.

SECRETARIAL HUNTING The secretary's station number is programmed as the last number in one or more hunt groups. If all phones within a hunt group are busy the call will hunt to the secretary.

SECRETARIAL INTERCEPT A PBX feature. Causes calls for an executive to ring his/her secretary — even if the executive's direct extension number was dialed. The executive's phone will ring only if the secretary's phone is placed on "Do Not Disturb" or the secretary transfers the call in.

SECTEL Acronym for SECure TELephone.

SECTIONAL CENTER A control center connecting primary telco switching centers. A Class 2 office. The next to the highest rank (Class 2) Toll Switching Center which homes on a Regional Center (Class 1).

SECTOR A pie-shaped portion of a hard disk. A disk is divided into tracks and sectors. Tracks are complete circuits and are divided into sectors. Under MS-DOS a sector is 512 bytes.

SECTORING The process of dividing a mobile cellular radio cell into 180-, 120- or 60-degree assigned to the cell.

SECURE KERNEL The core of a secure operating system.

SECURE TELEPHONE UNIT STU. A U.S. Government-approved telecommunication terminal designed to protect the transmission of sensitive or classified information — voice, data and fax.

SECURE VOICE Voice signals that are encoded or encrypted to prevent unauthorized listening.

SECURE VOICE CORD BOARD SECORD. A desk-mounted patch panel that provides the capability for controlling 16 wideband (50 kbps) or narrowband (2400 bps) user lines and five narrowband trunks to AUTOVON or other DCS narrowband facilities.

SECURENET A service from Southwestern Bell in which customers' dedicated circuits are routed through a serving central office to a "primary" hub. In addition, a secondary path is routed via a SWBT-designated alternate serving central office and an alternate hub. The service is designed to give Southwestern Bell customers better reliability.

SECURITY A way of insuring data on a LAN is protected from unauthorized use. Network security measures can be software-based, where passwords restrict users' access to certain data files or directories. This kind of security is usually implemented by the network operating system. Audit trails are another software-based security measure, where an ongoing journal of what users did what with what files is maintained. Security can also be hardware-based, using the more traditional lock and key.

SECURITY ACCESS MANAGER SAM. An AT&T computer-based building access security system.

SECURITY BLANKING The ability of a switch to blank out the called digits for certain extensions so no called number detail is printed. Senior executives in serious takeover negotiations find this feature useful. There have been instances of people figuring out which company another company is about to buy based on telephone calling records. If you have this information, you can buy the company's stock before the bid is announced and make a lot of money. This feature — security blanking — is designed to avoid such occurrences.

SECURITY CABINET A cabinet, usually on casters, used to store confidential materials under lock and key prior to shredding.

SECURITY CODE 1. A user identification code required by computer systems to protect information or information resources from unauthorized use. 2. A six-digit number used to prevent unauthorized or accidental alteration of data programmed into cellular phones. The factory default is 000000.

SECURITY EQUIVALENCE A security equivalence allows one user to have the same rights as another. Use security equivalence when you need to give a user temporary access to the same information or rights as another user. By using a security equivalence, you avoid having to review the whole directory structure and determine which rights need to be assigned in which directories.

SECURITY MANAGEMENT Protects a network from invalid accesses. It is one of the management categories defined by the ISO (International Standards Organization).

SECURITY STUD A cylindrically shaped metal finger that holds open the door to a Cash Box until the box is removed for collection.

SEEK TIME The time it takes to find some information on a disk (hard or soft) in a computer. Average seek time is a critical measure of the speed of a computer disk drive.

SEF Source Explicit Forwarding. Security feature that allows transmissions only from specified stations to be forwarded by bridges.

SEGMENT 1. 64 characters. Use as a method of data communications billing by some overseas phone companies. 2. An electronically continuous portion of a network, usually consisting of the same wire.

SEIZE To access a circuit and use it, or make it busy so that others cannot use it.

SEIZURE SIGNAL A signal used by the calling end of a trunk or line to indicate a request for service.

SELECT CALL FORWARDING A name for a Pacific Bell (and possibly other local telephone companies') service which allows you to have calls from selected numbers ring at another number.

SELECTIVE CALLING The ability of the transmitting phone to specify which of several phones on the a line is to receive a message.

SELECTIVE FADING Fading in which the components of the received radio signal fluctuate independently.

SELECTIVE PAGING TO STATION A phone can page to individual phone instruments.

SELECTIVE RINGING A method of ringing only the desired party on a party line.

SELECTIVE SIGNALING A method of in-band signaling used on private networks to tell switches to switch the call.

SELECTIVITY Ability of a tuner or receiver to get only a desired station while rejecting other adjacent stations. The higher the figure expressed in decibels (dB), the better the selectivity.

SELF DIAGNOSTICS Your phone system tells you when something is wrong with it by sending you a "message" via the operator console or through one of the data ports on the phone system.

SELF ELECTRO-OPTIC EFFECT DEVICES SEEDs. Switches guided by light.

SELF EXTINGUISHING The characteristic of a material whose flame is extinguished after the igniting flame is removed.

SELF INDULGENCE The author's writing of occasional irrelevant "definitions" in this dictionary.

SELF TEST The capability of a PBX to run programs at regular intervals to test its own operation and signal when failures have occurred or are about to occur without human intervention.

SEMAPHORE A message sent when a file is opened to prevent other users from opening the same file at that time. Its purpose is to preserve the integrity of data (i.e. stop it from being messed with) while you're using it.

SEMI-AUTOMATIC MESSAGE SWITCHING A network control technique whereby an operator manually switches a message to a destination according to the address information contained in the message header.

SEMI-RIGID A cable containing a flexible inner core and a relatively inflexible sheathing material, such as a metallic tube but, which can be bent for coiling or spooling and placing in duct or cable run.

SEMICONDUCTOR Material which has a resistance to electricity somewhere between a conductor (e.g. a copper wire) and an insulator (e.g. plastic). Hence the word "semi" conductor. Silicon and germanium are the two most commonly-used semiconductor materials. The flow of current in a semiconductor can be changed by light or the presence or absence of an electric or magnetic field.

SENDER Equipment in the originating telephone system which outpulses (sends out) the routing digits and the called person's number. Senders are necessary in computerized (stored program control) switches because the switch needs to know all the digits of the numbers you are calling before it chooses and seizes a trunk.

SENSITIVITY 1. The input signal level required for a tuner, amplifier, etc., to produce a stated output. The lower the required input, the higher the sensitivity. Measured in mV (microvolts). 2. The degree to which a radio receiver responds to the wave to which it is tuned.

SENSITIVITY ANALYSIS The process of rerunning a financial study to figure the degress to which changing the assumptions changes the result of the analysis.

SENSOR APPLICATIONS Services involving the remote monitoring of instruments including burglar alarms, fire alarms, meter reading, energy management and load shedding.

SENSOR GLOVE An interface device for experiencing virtual reality with the hand. Wired with sensors, it detects changes in finger, hand and arm movements and relays them to the computer, allowing users to manipulate and move things in a virtual environment. See VIRTUAL REALITY.

SENT PAID A utility industry term that describes all calls charged to the originating number or collected as coins in a pay telephone.

SEPARATION Extent to which two stereo channels are kept apart. Expressed in decibels, the larger the number, the better the separation and stereo effect.

SEPARATIONS AND SETTLEMENTS A complex set of accounting procedures developed by the traditional telephone industry. The procedures classify telephone plant as intrastate or interstate, and return revenues from long distance phone calls to local telephone companies. As part of Deregulation and Divestiture, this procedure is being replaced by per minute access charges.

SEPARATOR Pertaining to wire and cable, a layer of insulating material such as textile, paper, etc. placed between a conductor and its insulation, between a cable jacket and the components it covers or between various components of a multi-conductor cable. It can be utilized to improve stripping qualities and/or flexibility, or can offer additional mechanical or electrical protection to the components it separates.

SEPT Signaling End Point Translator, part of Signaling System 7. See SIGNALING SYSTEM 7.

SEQUENCING Sequencing is the process of dividing a data message into smaller pieces for transmission, where each piece has its own sequence number for reassembly of the complete message at the destination end. Sequencing is thus also the process of properly ordering the receipt of packet data at their destination, regardless of the time they have taken to travel the X.25 network. It's similar to packetizing. See PACKET.

SEQUENCING RECEIVERS All GPS (Global Positioning System) receivers must receive information from at least four satellites to calculate accurately where they (and thus you) are. Sequencing receivers use a single channel and move it from one satellite to the next to gather this data. They usually have less circuitry so they're cheaper and they consume less power than receivers which work on four satellites simultaneously. Unfortunately the sequencing can interrupt positioning and can limit their overall accuracy.

SEQUENTIAL Pertaining to events occurring in a specific time or code order.

SEQUENTIAL ACCESS The need to read data — one record after another in sequence — before getting to the information you want. Magnetic tape, for example, requires you to read the entire tape up to where your information is. This is because the computer cannot tell where on the tape your information is because records on tape files are often of variable length. Most Random Access files, usually kept on a disk drive, require records to be of a fixed length, such as 80 characters per record. Then when you seek record 23, the computer seeks character 1840 in the file (23 x 80), and takes the next 80 characters as the record you want. Using the analogy of music recorded on records and magnetic tape, a phonograph record needle has the capability of random access because the needle can be set down in the spaces between cuts on the record. With mag tape, you must fast forward past all the music you don't want before you get to the music you want to hear. Also, if the computer tape drive is fast forwarding, it cannot count characters to find the record, and must read in the data you don't want (and throw it away), before it gets to the data you need. Random access is much faster than sequential access.

SEQUENTIAL LOGIC ELEMENT A device that has at least one output channel and one or more input channels, all characterized by discrete states, such that the state of each output channel is determined by the previous states of the input channels.

SEQUENTIAL PACKET EXCHANGE SPX. Novell's implementation of SPP for its NetWare local area network operating system.

SERIAL CALL Telephone system feature set up by the attendant when an incoming calling party wishes to speak with more than one person internally. When the first party hangs up, the call automatically moves to the second person the outside party wants to speak with. When that person hangs up, then the call automatically goes to the third person, etc.

SERIAL COMMUNICATION Networks (local and long distance) use the RS-232 serial communications standard to send information to serial printers, remote workstations, remote routers, and asynchronous communication servers. The RS-232 standard uses several parameters that must match on both systems for information to be transferred. These parameters include baud rate, character length, parity, stop bit, and XON/XOFF.

Baud rate is the signal modulation rate, or the speed at which a signal changes. Since most modems or serial printers attached to personal computers send only one bit per signaling event, baud can be thought of as bits per second. However, higher-speed modems may transfer several bits per signal change. Typical baud rates are 300, 1200, 2400, 4800, 9600 and 19,200. The higher the number, the greater the number of signal changes and, therefore, the faster the transmission.

Character length specifies the number of bits used to form a character. The standard ASCII character set (including letters, numbers, and punctuation) consists of 128 characters and requires a character length of 7 bits for transmissions. Extended character sets (containing line drawings or the foreign characters used in IBM's extended character set) contain an additional 128 characters and require a character lengths of 8 bits. Parity error checking can only be used with character lengths of 7 bits.

Parity is a method of checking for errors in transmitted data. You can set parity to odd or even, or not use parity at all. When the character length is set to 8, parity checking cannot be done because there are no "spare" bits in the byte. When the character length is 7, the eighth bit in each byte is set to 0 or 1 so that the sum of bits (Os and 1s) in the byte is odd or even (according to the parity setting). When each character is received, its parity is checked again. If it is incorrect (because a bit was changed during transmission), the communications software determines that a transmission error has occurred and can request that the data be retransmitted.

Stop bit is a special signal that indicates the end of that character. Today's modems are fast enough that the stop bit is always set to one Slower modems used to require two stop bits.

XON/XOFF is one of many methods used to prevent the sending system from transmitting data faster than the receiving system can accept the information. See also EIA/TIA-232-E, RS-232-C and the APPENDIX.

SERIAL INTERFACE The "lowest common denominator" of data communications. A mechanism for changing the parallel arrangement of data within computers to the serial (one bit after the other) form used on data transmission lines and vice versa. At least one serial interface is usually provided on all computers for the connection of a terminal, a modem or a printer. Sometimes also called a serial port. See EIA/TIA-232-E, RS-232-C, SERIAL INTERFACE CARD and the APPENDIX.

SERIAL INTERFACE CARD A printed circuit card which drops into one of the expansion slots of your computer and changes the parallel internal communications of your computer into the one-bit-at-time serial transmission for sending information to your modem or to a serial printer.

SERIAL MEMORY Memory medium to which access is in a set sequence and not at random.

SERIAL PORT An input/output port (plug) that transmits data out one bit at a time, as opposed to the parallel port which transmits data out eight bits, or one byte at a time. Most personal computers (PCs) have at least one serial and one parallel port. In a typical configuration, the serial port is used for a modem while the parallel port is used for a printer. For a diagram of a typical 25-pin RS-232-C serial port, see the APPENDIX at the back of this book.

SERIAL PROCESSING Method of data processing in which only one bit is handled at a time.

SERIAL TRANSMISSION Sending pulses one after another rather than several at the same time (parallel). When transmitting data over a telephone line there is only one set of wires. Therefore, the only logical way to transmit it is to send the data in serial mode. It is possible to use eight different frequencies to transmit a character all at once (parallel), but these modems are ridiculously expensive. See SERIAL PORT and PARALLEL.

SERIALIZE To change from parallel-by-byte to serial-by-bit.

SERIES 11000 An AT&T private line long distance tariff created in the 1970s and designed expressly to reduce MCI's chances of selling any private lines and thus of surviving. It was thrown out by the FCC and the tariff figured in MCI's and the Federal Government's anti-trust against AT&T.

SERIES CONNECTION A connection of electrical apparatus or cicuits in which all of the current passes through each of the devices in succession or on after another. See also PARALLEL.

SERIES RF TAP A bugging device. It is a radio transmitter which is installed in series with one wire of the telephone circuit. Normally a parasite (i.e. takes power from the phone line). Transmits both sides of the conversation. It transmits only when the phone is off-hook.

SERVER A server is a shared computer on the local area network that can be as simple as a regular PC set aside to handle print requests to a single printer. Or, more usually, it is the the fastest and brawniest PC around. It may be used as a repository and distributor of oodles of data. It may also be the gatekeeper controlling access to voice mail, electronic-mail, facsimile services. At one stage, a local area network had only one server. These days networks have multiple servers. Servers these days have multiple brains, large arrays of big disk drives (often in redundant arrays) and other powerful features. New powerful servers are called superservers. A $35,000 superserver today can match the performance of a $2 million mainframe of ten years ago. Then again, according to Peter Lewis of the New York Times, the lowliest client today has more computing power than was available to the entire Allied Army in World War II. See DOWNSIZING for some of the benefits of running servers as against mainframes.

SERVER API A SCSA term. A communications protocol that allows a call processing application running on one computer to control SCSA hardware residing in another computer.

SERVER APPLICATION A Windows NT application that can create objects for linking or embedding into other documents.

SERVER TELESCRIPT A General Magic term. Telescript deployed on a server, enabling Telescript clients to participate in smart messaging.

SERVICE AREA The geographic area served by a supplier. The area in which the supplier, theoretically, stands ready to provide his service. The service area of New York Telephone is most (not all) of New York State.

SERVICE BUREAU A data processing center that does work for others. There are many ways of bringing work to a service bureau, including mailing it and transmitting it over phone lines. If it comes over phone lines, the service is likely to be called "time sharing."

SERVICE CHARGE The amount you pay each month to receive cellular service. This amount is fixed, and you pay the same fee each month regardless of how much or how little you use your cellular phone. It usually ranges from about $10 to $65 per month, depending on the carrier's tariffs and the particular plan of service you select. In addition you page air time. Service Charge doesn't usually include any air time.

SERVICE CHARGE DETAIL A listing of all the telephone equipment installed as part of a specific telephone system. Usually provided by the vendor or maintenance organization.

SERVICE CONTROL POINT SCP. The local versions of the national SMS/800 number database. SCPs contain the intelligence to screen the full ten digits of an 800 number and route calls to the appropriate, customer-designated long distance carrier. Bellcore defines SCP as the network system in the Advanced Intelligent Network Release 1 architecture that contains SLEE (Service Logic Execution Environment) functionality and communicates with AIN Release 1 Switching Systems in processing AIN Release 1 calls.

SERVICE CREATION The set of activities that must be performed to create a new service to be offered to subscribers and the associated service-specific operations capabilites to support the new service. Definition from Bellcore in reference to its concept of the Advanced Intelligent Network.

SERVICE DISPLAY Displays a specific service being presently in effect.

SERVICE ENTRANCE The point at which network communications lines (telephone company lines) enter a building.

SERVICE FUNCTION A primary or secondary service function.

SERVICE IDENTIFICATION The information uniquely identifying an NS/EP telecommunications service to the service vendor and/or service user. NS/EP is a federal government definition. It refers to telecommunications services that are used to maintain a state of readiness or to respond to and manage any event or crisis (local, national, or international) that causes or could cause injury or harm to the population, damage to or loss of property, or degrade or threaten the national security or emergency preparedness of the United States.

SERVICE INDEPENDENT BAF The finite set of BAF structures and modules needed to record usage of Advanced Intelligent Network Release 1 services. The set is said to be robust because it will be designed to record future AIN Release 1 services that have not yet been identified. Definition from Bellcore in reference to its concept of the Advanced Intelligent Network.

SERVICE LEVEL Usually expressed as a percentage of a statistical goal. For example, if your goal is an average speed of answer of 100 seconds or less, and 80% of your calls are answered in 100 seconds or less, then your service level is 80%.

SERVICE LINE An exchange line associated with multiple data station installations to provide monitoring and testing of both customer and Telco data equipment.

SERVICE LOGIC EXECUTION ENVIRONMENT SLEE. A functional group residing in an SCP (Service Control Point) or Adjunct that contains the Service Logic and Control, Information Management, AMA (Automatic Message Accounting) and Operations FEs (Functional Entity). This composite set of capabilities, which includes FC routines, provides a functionally consistent interface to SLPs (Service Logic Program) independent of the underlying operating system. Definition from Bellcore in reference to its concept of the Advanced Intelligent Network.

SERVICE NEGOTIATION The functionality needed to gather subscriber Advanced Intelligent Network Release 1 business needs; provide answers, AIN Release 1 service/feature descriptions, prerequisite non-AIN services, availability and costs; reserve AIN Release 1 resources (e.g. 800 number and 900 number); identify required network resources; and identify available AIN Release 1 services/features by wire center. Definition from Bellcore in reference to its concept of the Advanced Intelligent Network.

SERVICE OBJECTIVE Goal statement referring to the quality of service you provide a customer. You, the vendor, are not guaranteeing that service — just stating it as your objective.

SERVICE OBSERVATION 1. A generic word used by telephone companies to check the quality of the service they're providing. Some of it is done automatically with machinery. Some of it is done by senior operators who listen in on the conversations of other operators dealing with their subscribers. In short, the senior operators "observe" the service the junior operators are providing. 2. As a feature of some telephone systems, the Service Observation (SOB) command provides the capability to automatically record data about completed calls, incomplete calls and abnormal calls for the purpose of qualitative supervision of call traffic conditions.

SERVICE ORDER Document or system-generated group of information requesting installation or disconnection of, moving, or changing circuits.

SERVICE PERIOD The time during which the telephone company furnishes a circuit.

SERVICE POINTS The points on the customer's premises where such channels or facilities are terminated in switching equipment used for communications with phones or customer-provided equipment located on the premises.

SERVICE PROFILE IDENTIFIER SPID. The Service Profile Identifier is used to identify a specific ISDN set when more than one ISDN set has been attached to the same central office line. In most cases, only one ISDN set will be assigned to a line, and the SPID is not used by the switch.

SERVICE PROVIDER A Windows Telephony Applications standard which lies between Windows Telephony and the network. It defines how the network — anything from POTS to T-1, from a Northern Telecom to an AT&T PBX — shall interface to Windows Telephony, which in turn talks to the Applications Programming Interface, which talks to the Windows telephony applications software. See WINDOWS TELEPHONY.

SERVICE TERMINAL The equipment needed to terminate the channel and connect to the phone apparatus or customer terminal.

SERVICE TRAFFIC MANAGEMENT STM. The SLEE (Service Logic Execution Environment) functionality for detecting overloads associated with a specific service and for sending Automatic Code Gap messages to the appropriate entities. The SN&M (Service Negotiation and Management) OA (Operations Application) also provides STM(Service Traffic Management)-related capabilities.

SERVICE NET-2000 A AT&T umbrella name for family of digital products and services.

SERVICES MANAGEMENT SYSTEM SMS. Administers 800 Data

Base Service numbers on a national basis. Customer records for 800 Service are entered into the SCP through this system. See EIGHT HUNDRED SERVICE.

SERVICES ON DEMAND An AT&T term for the immediate provision of almost any network service through universal ports, whenever required by a user; as opposed to provision via an expensive, time-consuming, inflexible service order process.

SERVING CLOSET The general term used to refer to either a riser or a satellite closet; Satellite Cabinet; Satellite Closet.

SERVING OFFICE An office of AT&T or its Connecting or Concurring Carriers, from which interstate communications services are furnished.

SERVING WIRE CENTER The wire center from which service is provided to the customer.

SES 1. Satellite Earth Stations. 2. Severly Errored Seconds. Errored seconds during which the error rate exceeded 10.

SESSION An active communications connection, measured from beginning to end, between computers or applications over a network. Often used in reference to terminal-to-mainframe connections. Also a data conversation between two devices, say, a dumb terminal and a mainframe. It is possible to have more than one session going between two devices simultaneously.

SESSION LAYER The fifth layer — the network processing layer — in the OSI Reference Model, which sets up the conditions whereby individual nodes on the network can communicate or send data to each other. The session layer is responsible for binding and unbinding logical links between users. It manages, maintains and controls the dialogue between the users of the service. The session layer's many functions include network gateway communications.

SET Set is another name for a telephone.

SET-ASSOCIATIVE MAPPING A caching technique where each block of main computer memory is assigned to a location in each cache set where the cache is divided into multiple sets.

SETA SouthEastern Telecommunications Association, a user group.

SF Single Frequency. A method of in-band signaling. Single frequency signaling typically uses the presence or absence of a single specified frequency (usually 2,600 Hz). See SIGNALING.

SFG Simulated Facility Group

SFT System Fault Tolerance. The capability to recover from or avoid a system crash. Novell uses a Transaction Tracking System (TSS), disk mirroring, and disk duplexing as its system recovery methods. System Fault Tolerance as a Novell NetWare term means data duplication on multiple storage devices; if one storage device fails, the data is available from another device. There are several levels of hardware and software system fault tolerance; each level of redundancy (duplication) decreases the possibility of data loss.

SGML Standard Generalized Markup Language. SGML was adopted by the International Standards Orgaanization in 1986. SGML allows organizations to structure and manage information in a cross-platform, application-independent way. It tags documents as a series of data objects rather than storing them as huge files. Theoretically SGML can reduce errors, slice costs and speed work. SCML attempts to separate the informational content of a document from the information needed to present it, either on paper or on screen.

SHADOW BIOS ROM Shadow Bios ROM is a concept I first found in Toshiba laptops which use Flash ROM to hold the machine's BIOS. When you start the machine, the BIOS copies itself from the flash ROM to the Shadow BIOS area. Accessing the BIOS from the Shadow BIOS is much faster than from flash ROM.

SHADOW MASK The most common type of color picture tube in which the electron beam is directed through a perforated metal mask to the desired phosphor color element.

SHADOW ROM A process used in many 386 machines to map ROM BIOS activities into faster 32-bit RAM memory. Shadow memory must be loaded with BIOS routines each time the computer boots.

SHANNON A measurement of the quality of information in a message represented by one or the other of two equally probable, exclusive and exhaustive states. See SHANNON'S LAW.

SHANNON'S LAW A statement defining the theoretical maximum rate at which error-free digits can be transmitted over a bandwidth-limited channel in the presence of noise.

SHAPING NETWORK A network inserted in a circuit for improving or modifying the wave shape of the signals.

SHARED LOCK In a database a shared lock is created by nonupdate (read) operations. Other users can read the data concurrently, but no transaction can acquire an exclusive lock on the data until all the shared locks have been released.

SHARED LOGIC Simultaneous use of a single computer by multiple users.

SHARED MEMORY Portion of memory accessible to multiple processes.

SHARED SCREENS A multimedia concept. Shared screen applications enable two or more workstations to display the same screen simultaneoulsy. For example, two users sharing a screen can work on the same spreadsheet. Changes made by one user can be seen by the other as they are made. Shared screens can be implemented in two ways. One way

NEWTON'S TELECOM DICTIONARY

enables people to view each other's screen while one person makes changes. The other way enables people to run the same application on both screens so that both users can make changes simultaneously.

SHARED SERVICES Providing PBX-based communications and processing services to the unaffiliated tenants and/or the building manager/owner of a commercial building in a standalone or campus environment.

SHARED TENANT SERVICES Providing centralized telecommunications services to tenants in a building or complex.

SHARED WHITEBOARDS A multimedia concept. Shared whiteboards enable you to "mark-up" a screen using a mouse or stylus input device and have the results show on other screens, often commmunicating over long distance telephone lines. The concept is similar to a traditional whiteboard mark-up process where everyone has a different color marking pen to circle, write, or cross out items. The background board can be a window from the workstation such as a spreadsheet, image, or blank canvas, or it can be the entire workstation screen. The shared whiteboard can be used for either real-time or store-and-forward collaboration. In the store-and-forward scenario, the mark-ups can be implemented in a time-delayed fashion so everyone can follow the entire step-by-step process.

SHEAR A computer imaging term. A tool for distorting a selected area vertilcally or horizontally.

SHEATH The outer jacket (usually metal or plastic) surrounding copper and fiber cables that prevents water damage to the cables inside.

SHEATH MILES The actual length of cable in route miles.

SHELF LIFE The useful life of components when not in use — such as being stored on a shelf as spare parts or in a warehouse awaiting shipment. Batteries tend to have the shortest shelf life of most telecommunications components. Today, the shelf life is less a problem of shelf decay and more a problem of technological obsolescence.

SHELL An outer layer of a program that provides the user interface, or the user's way of commanding the computer. Instead of presenting the user with a bland C prompt, i.e. C:> the shell presents a list of programs that the user can choose from, making it easier, allegedly, to figure out which program to run. The problem with shells is that they often take up precious memory. That memory might better be used in actually running a program faster, or more efficiently.

SHIELD A metallic layer consisting of type, braid, wire or sheath that surrounds insulated conductors in shielded cable. The shield may be the metallic sheath of the cable or the metallic layer inside a nonmetallic sheath. Shields reduce stray electrical fields and provide for safety of personnel. See SHIELD EFFECTIVENESS.

SHIELD EFFECTIVENESS The relative ability of a cable shield to screen our undesirable radiation. Frequently confused with the term shield percentage, which it is not.

SHIELDED PAIR Two insulated wires in a cable wrapped with metallic braid or foil to prevent the wires acting as antennas and picking up external interference (e.g. a local TV station).

SHIELDING 1. The metal-backed mylar, plastic, teflon or PVC that protects a data-communications medium such as coaxial cable from Electromagnetic Interface (EMI) and Radio Frequency Interference (RFI). 2. The process by which electrical conductors are wrapped with metallic foil or braid to insulate them from interference and thus provide high quality transmission. Many devices can cause interference to cables (i.e. multiple conductors) carrying telecommunications conversations. Such things include high voltage AC power lines, machinery with motors, machines which make rays of some type (X-Ray systems, TV sets etc.). By wrapping conductors around the cable cores, these cables are less likely to be affected by these outside forces and the noise they create on telephone lines. Shielding will also lessen the chance that the information movement along the cable will interfere with signals on other, adjacent cables. The need for shielding stems from this phenomenon: If you send an electrical signal along one pair of cables, those cables will give off a small amount of electrical energy — called magnetic radiation. That radiation will cause electromagnetic interference with a cable close by. If you "shield" the pair carrying the electrical signal, you will cut down the susceptibility of those cables to interference from other cables. LANs should always be installed with the best quality shielded cable. They will run better with shielded cable. Never skimp on the quality of the cable you're installing for LANs. Most telephones don't require shielded cable unless the cable serving them is passing through some area of high electro-mechanical interference.

SHIFT 1. The movement of data to either the right or the left of an existing position in a data field. 2. The code control function of converting the characters from upper to lower case, or vice versa.

SHIFT BUTTON This button acts exactly like a Shift button on a typewriter or computer. It gives the key you're touching a second meaning — either a capital letter or a second set of speed dial buttons, etc.

SHIFT CHARACTER The control character which defines the shift function.

SHIFT REGISTER A register in which a clock pulse causes the stored data to move to the right or left one bit position. See ZERO STUFFING.

SHIP TO SHORE TELEPHONE See MARINE TELEPHONES.

SHOCK A sudden stimulation of the nerve and convulsive contraction of the muscles caused by a discharge of electricity through the body. The severity depends on the amount and duration of the current and whether the path of the current is through a vital organ.

SHOEBOX A shoebox is a housing device with a power supply to support external peripherals. When the user's main computer case is filled to capacity, an external device is needed to handle the overflow. Hence a shoebox.

SHORT A circuit impairment that exists when two conductors of the same pair, which normally make up an operating electrical circuit, touch or are connected.

SHORT BUS A high-speed common channel in the AT&T ISN packet controller over which all messages between sending and receiving devices pass.

SHORT CIRCUIT A near zero resistance connection between any two wires that disrupts transmission where two pairs are involved usually called a "cross." It disrupts transmission and may cause an excessive current flow. In AC electficity, a short circuit is an unintended connection between two supply conductors (ie: HOT and Neutral conductors.) A short circuit will usually cause high current flow and will operate the over current protection (fuse or breakers) to interrupt the circuit.

SHORT HAUL Between a few hundred yards and 20 miles. Many people would argue with this definition.

SHORT HAUL MODEM A data set designed for use in communicating data up to distances of 25 miles over a dedicated unloaded copper pair. Many people would argue with this definition.

SHORT REACH Short Reach refers to optical sections of approximately 2 km or less in length. The sections may be interoffice or intraoffice sections. A SONET term.

SHOULDER SURFING You're standing at a payphone. You punch in your credit card numbers to make your long distance call. There's a fellow standing behind who. He's carefully watching what you're doing. He is memorizing the digits you have punched in. When you are through, he will write them down and sell them to someone else, who will use them to make fraudulent long distance phone calls. Our friend is indulging in a new "occupation." It's called "shoulder surfing."

SHP Signaling Handoff Point, a type of equipment which acts as a gateway between two dissimilar Signaling System 7 networks, allowing information exchange between the two networks.

SHT Short Hold Time.

SHUNT CIRCUIT An arrangement of apparatus or circuits in which the total current is subdivided. Same as Parallel Circuit.

SI Shift In.

SIA Securities Industries Association.

SIBB Service Independent Building Blocks, a term coined by Bellcore for the Intelligent Network. Creation of SIBBs will in theory make it easier for non-software specialists to create new services by mixing and matching SIBBs.

SID System IDentification number. A five digit number that has been assigned to identify the particular cellular carrier from whom you are obtaining seervice. This number identifies your "home" system.

SIDE CIRCUIT A metallic, single pair circuit arranged to derive a phantom circuit. The phantom circuit is derived by center tapping a repeating coil in each of two side circuits.

SIDE HOUR Any hour that is not the Busy Hour.

SIDEBAND The frequencies on either side of the main frequency in a telecommunications signal. In the early days these sideband frequencies were not used because they were too "noisy," unreliable and were not needed. Now, technology has improved and frequencies are in short supply, more and more transmission vendors are making use of their sidebands, and thus substantially broadening the throughput of their existing transmission paths. Sideband technology has made great strides especially in through-the-air microwave transmission.

SIDETONE A part of the design of a telephone handset which allows you to hear your own voice while speaking. The idea is to let you know that the telephone you're speaking on is working. Too much sidetone becomes an echo and is bad. Too little sidetone makes the channel unerring.

SIG Special Interest Group. A SIG is an ongoing discussion group held electronically via PCs. A SIG focuses on one area of interest. Members phone in with their PCs, read messages posted, contribute their wisdom, ask questions, etc. SIGs are ways people get up-to-date accurate information on a subject. SIGs are run on most BBS (Bulletin Board Systems). SIGs are to bulletin boards what on-line services call conferences or forums.

SIG-SMDS INTEREST GROUP A consortium of vendors and consultants who are committed to advancing worldwide SMDS as an open, interoperable solution for high-performance data connectivity.

SIGN-ON To go through the process of beginning a working session between you, your data terminal or PC and a computer system.

SIGN ON/SIGN OFF The process of identifying oneself to a machine so as to gain access. In the case of an ACD system this process allows statistics to be kept for this person individually. It also allows for the movement of the person around the system while statistics are accumulated in one logical file.

SIGNAL 1. An electrical wave used to convey information. 2. An alert. 3.

An acoustic device (e.g. a bell) or a visual device (e.g. a lamp) which calls attention. To transmit an information signal or alerting signal.

SIGNAL CONDITIONING The amplification and/or modification of electrical signals to make them more appropriate for transmission over a certain medium — cable, microwave, etc.

SIGNAL CONVERTER The equipment which changes the data signal into a form suitable for the transmission medium, or the reverse. The converter can also work with DC/AC current. The signal converter comprises a modulator and/or demodulator.

SIGNAL GROUND SGD. In RS-232-C signaling, Signal Ground establishes a common reference level for the voltages of all other signals (such as RXD/TXD), except Frame Ground.

SIGNAL LEVEL The strength of a signal, generally expressed in either absolute units of voltage or power, or in units relative to the strength of the signal at its source.

SIGNAL TO NOISE RATIO The ratio of the usable signal being transmitted to the noise or undesired signal. Usually expressed in decibels. This ratio is a measure of the quality of a transmission.

SIGNAL TRANSFER POINT The packet switch in the Common Channel Interoffice Signaling (CCIS) system. The CCIS is a packet switched network operating at 4800 bits per second. CCIS replaces both SF (Single Frequency) and MF (Multi-frequency) by converting dialed digits to data messages. See SIGNALING SYSTEM 7.

SIGNALS INTELLIGENCE SIGINT. A federal government term. A category of intelligence information comprising, either individually or in combination, all communications intelligence, electronics intelligence, and foreign instrumentation signals intelligence, however transmitted.

SIGNALING Pertains to the transmission of electrical signals to and from the user's premises and the telephone company central office. Examples of central office signals to the user's premises are ringing (audible alerting) signals, dial tone, speech signals, etc. Signals from the user's telephone include off-hook (request for service), dialing (network control signaling), speech to the distant party, on-hook (disconnect signal), etc. See SIGNALING SYSTEM 7.

SIGNALING CONNECTION CONTROL PART SCCP. Part of the SS7 protocol that provides communication between signaling nodes by adding circuit and routing information to the signaling message. The ISDN-UP (Integrated Services Digital Network User Part) and TCAP (Transaction Capabilities Application Part) use the SCCP (Signaling Connection Control Part) and the MTP (Message Transfer Part) to transport information. Definition from Bellcore in reference to its concept of the Advanced Intelligent Network.

SIGNALING POINTS SPs are located at each switch in a Signaling System 7 network. They interface the switch with the Signal Transfer Points (STPs). See SIGNAL TRANSFER POINTS and SIGNALING SYSTEM 7.

SIGNALING SYSTEM 7 SS7. All phone systems need signaling. According to James Henry Green, author of the Dow Jones-Irwin Handbook of Telecommunications, signals have three basic functions:

1. SUPERVISING. Monitoring the status of a line or circuit to see if it is busy, idle or requesting service. Supervision is a term derived from the job telephone operators perform in manually monitoring circuits on a switchboard. On switchboards, supervisory signals are shown by a lit lamp indicating a request for service on an incoming line or an on-hook condition of a switchboard cord circuit. In the network (i.e. the automated part of the network), supervisory signals are indicated by the voltage level on signaling leads, or the on-hook/off-hook status of signaling tones or bits.

2. ALERTING. Indicates the arrival of an incoming call. Alerting signals are bells, buzzers, whoofers, tones, strobes and lights.

3. ADDRESSING. Transmitting routing and destination signals over the network. Addressing signals are in the form of dial pulses, tone pulses or data pulses over loops, trunks and signaling networks.

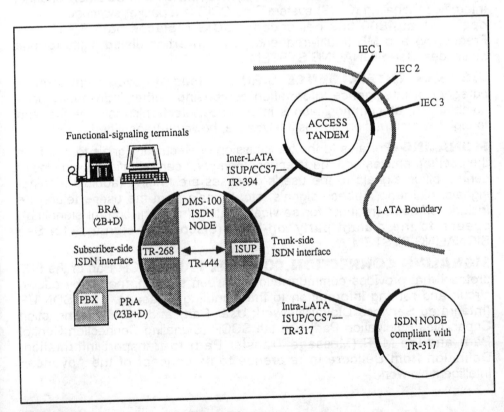

Most signaling today is MF (multi-frequency) and SF (single frequency) and is in-band. This means that it goes along and occupies the same circuits as those which carry voice conversations. There are two problems with this. First, about 35% of all toll calls are not completed because the phone doesn't answer or is busy, or there are equipment problems along the way. The circuit time used in signaling is substantial, expensive and wasteful. Second, in-band signaling is vulnerable to fraud. So the idea of out-of-band signaling came about. It got the name of Common Channel Interoffice Signaling (CCIS) because it used a communications network totally separate from the switched voice network. In North America, CCIS started out as an AT&T packet switched network operating at 4800 bits per second. Each of the packet switches in this network (they are no longer exclusively AT&T's) are called Signal Transfer Points — STPs. CCIS has the following advantages over SF/MF signaling:

Fraud is reduced. "Talk-off" is reduced. (Talk-off occurs when your voice contains enough 2600 Hz energy to activate the tone-detecting circuits in the central office.) Signaling is faster allowing circuits and conversations to be set up and torn down (i.e. disconnected) faster. Signals can be sent in both directions simultaneously and during voice conversation if necessary. Network management information is routed over the CCIS network. For example, when trunks fail, switching systems can be told with CCIS data messages to reroute traffic around problem areas.

The older CCIS signaling is being replaced with a newer out-of-band signaling system called CCITT Signaling System 7. According to an AT&T technical paper delivered at the International Switching Symposium in Spring, 1987, CCITT Signaling System 7 is being required by telecommunications administrations worldwide (i.e. all the local country-owned telephone companies) for their networks. AT&T continued with the introduction of digital switches and transmission equipment with 56 kbps and 64 kbps transmission rates, the International Telegraph and Telephone Consultative Committee (CCITT in French) in 1980 approved the CCITT 7 recommendations optimized for digital networks. This new protocol uses destination routing, octet oriented fields, variable length messages and a maximum message length allowing for 256 bytes of data. Addition of flow control, connectionless services and Integrated Services Digital Network (ISDN) capabilities were approved by CCITT in 1984. A major characteristic of CCITT #7 is its layered functional structure. Its transport functions are divided into four levels, three of which constitute the Message Transfer Part (MTP). The fourth consists of a common Signaling Connection Control Part (SCCP).

The SS7 protocol consists of four basic sub-protocols:

● Message Transfer Part (MTP), which provides functions for basic routing of signaling messages between signaling points.

● Signaling Connection Control Part (SCCP), which provides additional routing and management functions for transfer of messages other than call set-up between signaling points.

● Integrated Services Digital Network User Part (ISUP), which provides for transfer of call set-up signaling information between signaling points.

● Transaction Capabilities Application Part (TCAP), which provides for transfer of non-circuit related information between signaling points.

Signaling System 7 provides two major capabilities:

1. Fast call set-up, via high-speed circuit-switched connections.

2. Transaction capabilities which deal with remote data base interactions. What this means in its simplest terms and in one simple application is that Signaling System 7 information can tell the called party who's calling and, more important, tell the called party's computer. A scenario: when you call a direct mail order business, Signaling System 7 will send a signal as to which phone is calling. The agent's CRT screen will pop the caller's name and perhaps the caller's most recent buying information. The agent may answer the phone "Good morning, Mr. Newton. Did you enjoy the three khaki pants we sent you last week?..." Signaling System 7 will be an integral part of ISDN. It will enable us to extend full PBX and Centrex-based services like call forwarding, call waiting, call screening, call transfer, etc. outside the switch to the full international network. In effect, with Signaling System 7, the entire network will acquire the "smarts" of today's smartest electronic digital PBX. See also CAPTAIN CRUNCH, ISUP, MTP, SCCP, and TCAP.

SIGNIFICANT HOUR Any hour that influences the sizing of a trunk group.

SILENCE SUPPRESSION A term used in voice compression for transmission whereby silence in the voice conversation is filled with other transmissions — e.g. data, video, imaging, etc. According to AT&T, the average voice conversation is 62% quiet and 38% not quiet (i.e. actual conversation). You can figure that for yourself: One person is speaking at a time. That's 50% of the circuit silent. The person who's speaking doesn't speak continuously. He pauses, takes a breath, thinks, etc. That's another 12%. Thus 62% in silence. A company like Micom in Simi Valley, CA makes a product called Marathon which uses the 62% silence between syllables, words and sentences to transmit data, fax and video. Micom tells me that the typical talk spurt sequence is 300 milliseconds. And it can use very small time (as short as 300 milliseconds) between talk spurts to stuff data, fax or video into and transmit.

SILICON A dark gray, hard, crystalline solid. Next to oxygen, the second most abundant element in the earth's surface. Transistor chips are made from silicon, and it is the basic material for most integrated circuits and semiconductor devices. Silicon, a neutral element, is found primarily in raw form as sand. See SEMICONDUCTOR.

SILICON AVALANCHE DIODE A fast-acting surge protector which features a narrow voltage clamping range.

SILICON VALLEY Silicon Valley in Santa Clara County, California, south of San Francisco Bay, is known for its microelectronics innovation. It is one of the two places (the other being Dallas, Texas) where the microchip was invented and produced. There are over 3,000 microelectronic hardware and software firms within a radius of about 30 miles. Silicon Valley owes its good fortune to:

The fact that W. Shockley, one of the three inventors of the transistor, being a native of Palo Alto, went there in 1955 after he left Bell Laboratories, to start his own industrial research center;

The proximity of technology universities, such as Stanford University;

A very active financial market in California and the enterprising attitude of capitalists willing to enter into "joint ventures," often very profitable;

The West Coast orientation to Japan.

The above information courtesy of Electronics, Computers and Telephone Switching by Robert J Chapuis Amos E Joel, Jr.

SILS A Standard being formulated for Interoperating LAN Security.

SIMD Single Instruction Multiple Data is a type of parallel processing computer, which inclues dozens of processors. Each processor runs the same instrucions but on different data and one chip provides central coordination. See also MIMD.

SIMM Single In line Memory Module. Used on Macs and PCs. The most common SIMM is the 30-pin, 9-bit wide "1 by 9", which is the standard memory upgrade for PCs.

SIMM SOCKET The connector inside the Macintosh that holds the SIMM and connects it to the rest of the computer electronically.

SIMPLE MAIL TRANSFER PROTOCOL SMTP. The TCP/IP protocol governing electronic mail transmissions and receptions.

SIMPLE NETWORK MANAGEMENT PROTOCOL SMNP. The protocol governing network management and monitoring of network devices and their functions. SNMP came out of the TCP/IP environment.

SIMPLEX 1. Operating a channel in one direction only with no ability to operate in the other direction. For example one side of a telephone conversation is all that could be carried by a Simplex line. 2. One-sided printing.

SIMPLEX LOOP POWERING In T-1, refers to the powering of the digital signal pairs that are simplex in nature (Tip or Ring) and that may have voltage applied to maintain the required 60 mA dc current to control repeater signal regeneration, loopbacks, keep alive signals and alarms.

SIMULATOR A program in which a mathematical model represents an external system or process. For example, an engineer can simulate the forces that act on a building during an earthquake to find out how much damage is likely to be incurred.

SIMULTANEOUS PERIPHERAL OPERATIONS ON LINE SPOOL. Temporarily storing programs, data or output on magnetic tape or in RAM for later output or execution. Many PCs use a small software spooling program which accepts material to be printed very quickly, stores it in a portion of RAM, then feeds that material to the printer at a speed the printer can handle. See SPOOLING.

SIMULATION A technique, often involving a computer, to guess the outcome of various events in the future. Where multitudes of complex events interact, simulation may well be the only way to deal with a given problem. Simulation is often used in traffic engineering instead of or in addition to the proven formula. Many people believe that simulation should NEVER be used when standard, proven formulas (such as Poisson, Erlang B and Erlang C) are appropriate. The difficulty with simulation is actually finding out what rules to use and then programming them correctly. Once this is done, it takes time, even on a fast computer, to run thousands of simulations to get a stable statistical estimate; a single run of simulation, like a single roll of the dice, is worse than useless. Simulators were built into hardware to predict the overall behavior of AT&T's No. 5 Crossbar switch when it was developed in the late 1940s; 1ESS behavior was simulated with software in the 1960s. These were major efforts involving many people and several years, but they dealt with problems far beyond the capabilities of standard traffic equations.

SINGING An undesirable whistle or howl on a transmission circuit. Singing is usually caused by feedback, excessive gain, or unbalance of hybrid coils, or by some combination. Singing is the same effect observed when you increase the volume on a public address system until the system squeals or "sings."

SINGING RETURN LOSS The loss at which a circuit oscillates or sings at the extreme low and high ends of the voice band.

SINGLE ADDRESS MESSAGE A message which is to be transmitted to only one specific terminal, as opposed to a broadcast or group message.

SINGLE DIGIT DIALING Provides for single-digit dialing to reach a preselected phone or group of phones.

SINGLE ENDED TERMINAL DEVICE A device which terminates only one line at a given time.

SINGLE FIBER CABLE A plastic-coated fiber surrounded by an extruded layer of polyvinyl chloride, encased in a synthetic strengthening material and enclosed in an outer polyvinyl chloride sheath.

SINGLE FREQUENCY SIGNALING The use of one tone — typically 2600 Hz — to indicate if the phone line is busy or idle (supervision) and to convey dial pulse signals from one end of a trunk or line to the other, using the presence or absence of a single specified frequency.

SINGLE-FREQUENCY (SF) SIGNALING In telephone communications, a method of conveying dialing or supervisory signals, or both, with one or more specified single frequencies. Note: The DCS transmits dc signaling pulses or supervisory signals, or both, over carrier channels or cable pairs on a 4-wire basis using a 2600-Hz signal tone. The conversion into tones, or vice versa, is done by SF signal units. See also FREQUENCY, IN-BAND SIGNALING, SIGNAL.

SINGLE IN LINE MEMORY MODULES Basically memory packaged so it can be slipped into a PC or laptop PC much easier than present methods of installing memory — which typically consist of pushing memory chips with legs into printed circuit boards. The problem with memory with legs is that you're likely to bend one of the legs and thus have the installation go awry.

SINGLE LINE INSTRUMENT A telephone set normally used to access only one line. However when used with advanced telephone systems, additional lines can be accessed by dialing specific codes rather than by depressing keys.

SINGLE MODE FIBER An optical waveguide which is constructed to propagate (i.e. carry) only the single wavelength selected for transmission.

SINGLE NUMBER SERVICE An optional feature for 800 IN-WATS Services which allows a subscriber who has or wants to have both intrastate and interstate 800 service to use the same 1-800 number for both services. If you'd like to buy another copy of this dictionary, call 1-800-LIBRARY. That phone number will be answered at our office in New York City. It will work for calls from inside and from outside New York State.

SINGLE SIDEBAND TRANSMISSION A system of transmission which suppresses one side-band of the carrier frequency at the source. Also applied to receiving systems designed to reproduce such transmissions.

SINGLE SLOT Current standard for coin phone construction that uses one slot for the deposit of all acceptable coins.

SINGLE USE BATTERIES Batteries that aren't rechargeable — in other words, the Duracell and Everyready batteries at your local supermarket.

SINGLE WIRE LINE A transmission path which uses a single conductor and a ground return to complete a circuit. Used a lot in rural areas.

SINK That part of a communications system which receives information.

SIO Serial Input/Output. The electronic methodology used in serial data transmission.

SIP 1. Single Inline Module with pins. 2. An SMDS term meaning Standard Interface Protocol. 2. Simple Internet Protocol.

SIP-SMDS INTERFACE PROTOCOL An SMDS term. The protocol defined at the interface between the SMDS network and the end user.

SIP L2PDU-SMDS Standard Interface Protocol Layer 2 protocol data unit. The 53-octet unit of information processed by the second layer of the SIP.

SIP L3PDU-SMDS An SMDS term. Standard Interface Protocol layer 3 protocol data unit. A variable-length (up to 9,220 octets long) unit of information processed by the third layer of the SIP.

SIR 1. Speaker Independent Recognition. See SPEAKER INDEPENDENT RECOGNITION. 2. An SMDS term meaning Sustained Information Rate. Determined at time of subscription, the SIR defines the long term average throughout an SMDS access line can carry. SIR is enforced through a Credit Manager resident of the SMDS network switches, and the Access Class-4 Mbps, 10 Mbps, 16 Mbps, 25 Mbps or 34 Mbps- the subscriber selects.

SIT TONES 1. Standard Information Tones. These are tones sent out by a central office to a pay phone to indicate that the dialed call has been answered by the distant phone, etc. 2. Special Information Tones. These are tones for identifying network provided announcements. Here's Bellcore's explanation: Automated detection devices cannot distinguish recorded voice from live voice answer unless a machine-detectable signal is included with the recorded announcement. The CCITT, which specifies signals that may be applied to international circuits, has defined Special Information Tones for identifying network provided announcement. The SIT used to preceed machine-generated announcements also alerts the calling customer that a machine-generated announcement follows. Since SIT consists of a sequence of three precisely defined tones, SIT can be machine-detected, and therefore machine-generated announcements preceded by a SIT can be classified. At least four SIT encodings have been defined: Vacant Code (VC), Intercept (IC), Reorder (RO) and No Circuit (NC). With the exception of some small stored Program Control Systems (SPCSs) and some customer negotiated announcements, Bell operating companies in North America now precede appropriate announcements with encoded SITs to detect and classify announcements.

SITA Society of International Aeronautical Telecommunications. The international data communications network used by many airlines.

SITE CONTROLLER An industrial grade PC located at MCI terminals and junctions. It provides the operator local visibility into alarm and performance information from the Extended Superframe Monitoring Unit and 1/0 DXC, as well as enabling the operator to interact with both devices.

SITE LICENSE Companies that buy software for multiple computers typically buy one copy of the program and a license to reproduce it up to a certain number of times. This is called a site license, though it may apply to its use throughout an organization. Site licenses vary. Some require that a copy be bought for each potential user — the only purpose being to indicate the volume discount and keep tabs. Others allow for a copy to be placed on a network server but limit the number of users who can gain simultaneous access. This is called a concurrent site license. And many network administrators prefer this concurrent license, since it gives them greater control. For example, if the software is customized, it need be customized only once.

SIVR Speaker Independent Voice Recogntion. See SPEAKER INDEPENDENT VOICE RECOGNITION.

SIX DIGIT TRANSLATION We have a long distance number 212-691-8215. The ability of a switching system to do six digit translation means that it can "look at" 212-691 and figure how to route the phone call. The criterion of choosing which way to send the call is, most often, the least expensive way. Six digit translation is often an integral part of Least Cost Routing programs within the phone system which tell the calls to go over the lines perceived by the user to be the least cost way of getting the call from point A to point B. There are typically two types of "least cost routing" translation — that which examines the first three digits of the phone number (i.e. just the area code) and the first six digits of the phone number (i.e. the area code and the three digits of the local central office). Six digit translation is preferred because it allows you more flexibility in routing, particularly to big area codes, like 213 in LA, where there are long distance calls within the area code. See also LEAST COST ROUTING and ALTERNATE ROUTING.

SKEW 1. The deviation from synchronization of two or more signals. 2. A computer imaging term. A tool that slants a selected area in any direction. 3. In parallel transmission, the difference in arrival time of bits transmitted at the same time. 4. For data recorded on multichannel magnetic tape, the difference in time of reading bits recorded in a single line. 5. In facsimile systems, the angular deviation for the received frame from rectangularity due to asynchronism between scanner and recorder. Skew is expressed numerically as the tangent of the angle of deviation.

SKEW RAY In a multimode optical fiber, any bound ray that in propagating does not intersect the fiber axis (in contrast with a meridional ray). In a straight, ideal fiber, a skew ray traverses a helical path along the fiber, not crossing the fiber axis. A skew ray is not confined to the meridian plane.

SKIN Surface layer in a sandwich structure.

SKIN EFFECT The tendency of a current to pass through the outer portion rather than through the center of a conductor.

SKIP ZONE a ring-shaped region within the transmission range wherein signals from a transmitter are not received. It is the area between the farthest points reached by the ground wave and nearest points at which reflected sky waves come back to earth.

SKYTEL The company which provides SkyPager, SkyTalk and SkyWord, nationwide paging voice messaging services and alphanumeric text messaging. The company's primary services run at 931 MHz, which is the frequency of the SkyTel pager.

SLAMMING The practice of switching a telephone customer's long distance company without obtaining permission from the customer. A long distance company might do this to get itself some easy revenues. After a bitter court battle, AT&T and MCI settled on some proposed standards to allow a long distance to switch a customer's service under the following circumstances:

1. The customer initiates the switch by calling either their local telephone company, their current long distance company or the the long distance company they want to switch to;

2. Someone outside the long distance company's sales department verifies the request to switch; or

3. The customer submits written authorization to the company.

SLAVE A device which operates under the control of a master — another device or system. Slave switching systems are common in rural areas. The master central office might be in town A. Twenty miles away there's a smaller town. It makes no economic sense to serve those subscribers each on single local dedicated loops from Town A. Best solution: place a "slave" central office in that distant town and drive its software, diagnostics and changes from the main central office in Town A. See also REMOTE CONCENTRATOR.

SLC-96 Pronounced "Slick 96." A product of AT&T Technologies. It's a short haul multiplexing device which enables up to 96 telephone customers to be served on three pairs of wires. SLC stands for Subscriber Loop Carrier.

SLCC Abbreviation for Subscriber Line (or Loop) Carrier Circuit, and pronounced "slick." It's a system that allows one pair of wires, that would normally provide one phone line, to carry multiple conversations. Various models are available, with capacity ranging from 2 to 96 lines. A SLCC is used between phone company central offices and areas where there are too many customers for the cable that is in place. It's much less expensive to install SLCCs than new cable, but the SLCC provides lower-than-normal line voltage, which may cause some phones to malfunction.

SLEE Service Logic Execution Environment.

SLEEVES Short lengths of conduit, usually made from rigid metal pipes, used to protect cables entering a premises through a building wall or running through concrete floors between vertically aligned riser closets. Sleeves also provide for easy pulling of cable.

SLIC An AT&T term for Subscriber's Line Interface Circuit, a device that interfaces the SLC series of AT&T products of local subscriber pair gain or multiplexing devices. See SLC-96.

SLIDEWARE Slideware is hardware or software whose reason for existing (eventually) has been explained in 35-mm slides, foils, charts and/or PC presentation programs. Vaporware is software which has been announced, perhaps even demonstrated, but not delivered to commercial customers. Hyperware is hardware which has been announced but has not yet been delivered. Slideware is usually less real than vaporware or hyperware, though some people would argue with this. Some slideware has actually been delivered as a product, which customers have paid real money for.

SLIP/SLIP RATE The loss (or rate of loss) of a data bit on a T-1 link due to a frame misalignment between the timing at a transmit node and timing at a receive node.

SLOTS Openings, typically rectangular, in the floor of vertically aligned riser closets that enable cable to pass through from floor to floor. A slot accommodates more cables than an individual sleeve.

SLOTTED ALOHA A random access technique extending pure ALOHA to the case in which messages may only be transmitted in slotted intervals of time.

SLOTTED RING A LAN architecture in which a constant number of fixed-length slots (packets) circulate continuously around the ring. A full/empty indicator within the slot header indicates when a workstation or PC attached to the LAN may place information into the slot. Think of a slotted ring LAN as an empty train that constantly travels in a circle, being filled and emptied at different terminals (workstations).

SLOW SWITCHING CHANNEL A sequencing GPS (Global Positioning System) receiver channel that switches too slowly to allow the continuous recovery of the data message.

SLR Send Loudness Rating.

SLSA Single Line Switching Apparatus.

SLT Single-Line Telephone, as opposed to a phone that has buttons to select from several lines.

SMA 905/906 (Subminature type A). A former microwave connector modified by Amphenol to become the "standard" fiber optic connector. The 905 version is a straight ferrule design, where as the 906 is a stepped ferrule design and uses a plastic sleeve for alignment.

SMALL VOCABULARY A voice recognition term. Vocabularies containing fewer than 50 words.

SMB Server Message Block. A protocol defined by Microsoft and Intel to provide access to server-based files and print queues. SMB operates above the session layer, and usually works over a network using a NetBIOS application program interface. SMB is similar in nature to a remote procedure call (RPC) that is specialized for file systems.

SMART CARD A credit card-sized card which contains electronics, including a microprocessor, memory and a battery. The card can be used to store the entire repair and maintenance history on the family automobile or any member of the family. There is no direct contact between the "smart card" and the device which reads it. This avoids the problem of wear that afflicts traditional credit cards — both their embossed numbers on the front and their magnetic strip on the back.

SMART PHONE 1. A microcomputer-controlled electronic telephone with lots of features. Typically a single line phone with a simple tip and ring interface (i.e. not proprietary to any special key system or PBX). 2. A phone created by AT&T Network Systems and due out some time in 1992 or 1993. The phone has no buttons but simply a touch sensitive screen. From one moment to another the image on the screen will change, requesting information from the user — the number or person to call, the letters you'd like to transmit to an electronic mail system, the amount of money you'd like to transfer to your checking account, etc. AT&T has announced the phone, but not its price nor precise availability.

SMARTCALL Smartcall is a name registered by GTE for services more advanced than conventional Custom Calling call enhancement services, such as speed calling or call waiting. Calling Number Identification is a GTE Smartcall service. Other services include Automatic Call Return, Automatic Busy Redial, Call Tracing Service, Protected Number Service, VIP Alert, Call Block, etc.

SMARTHOUSE The National Society of Home Builders has registered SmartHouse. BellSouth has trademarked SuperHouse. And GTE has registered SmartPark. One day, fiber optic will snake to everyone's house, bringing the potential of immense information services. Until that day comes they'll be lots of interesting demonstrations at distant trade shows.

SMARTPARK GTE's registered trademark for a fiber-optic wired industrial park offering a wide variety of voice, data and video transmission and switching services. "The GTE SmartPark services help protect tenants from communications obsolescence and eliminates the need for relocation when their telecommunications requirements expand," says Harrison Coleman, national SmartPark product manager.

SMARTRING Self-Healing Multi-Nodal Alternate Route Topology which BellSouth describes as a dedicated ring-type special access DS3 service.

SMAS Switched Maintenance Access System.

SMC Standard Management Committee. Directs specialized working groups of the Architecture and Standards Steering Council.

SMDA Station Message Detail Accounting. Another name for telephone call accounting. See CALL ACCOUNTING SYSTEM.

SMDI Station Message Desk Interface or Simplified Message Desk

Interface. The SMIS is the data link from the central office if you have ESSX, Centrex or Centron (etc.) that gives you your stutter dial tone or message waiting light. In essence, SMDI is a data line from the central office containing information and instructions to your on-premises voice mail box. With SMDI, the calling person is not required to re-enter the called phone number (or in any other way identify the called party) once the call terminates to the messaging system.

SMDR Station Message Detail Reporting. Another name for telephone call accounting. See SMDR PORT and CALL ACCOUNTING SYSTEM.

SMDR PORT Modern PBXs and some larger key systems have an Station Message Detail Recording (SMDR) electrical plug, usually an RS-232-C receptacle, into which one plugs a printer or a call accounting system. The telephone system sends information on each call made from the system to the outside world through the SMDR port. That information — who made the call, where it went, what time of day, etc. — will be printed by the printer or will be "captured" by the call accounting system on a floppy or a hard magnetic disk and later processed into meaningful management reports. See CALL ACCOUNTING SYSTEM.

SMDS Switched Megabit (or Multi-megabit) Data Services. A way for a corporate network to dial up switched data services as fast as 45 megabits per second.

SMDS INTEREST GROUP A non-profit industry consortium chartered to promote interoperability among SMDS products, applications and services.

SMI Structure of Management Information. The set of rules and formats for defining, accessing and adding objects to the Internet MIB. SMI was elevated to full standard status in May 1990.

SMNP Simple Network Management Protocol. The protocol governing network management and monitoring of network devices and their functions. SNMP came out of the TCP/IP environment.

SMOKE TEST Test of new or repaired equipment by turning it on. If there's smoke, it doesn't work!

SMOKEWARE When manufacturers announce new products, sometimes the products are not ready. Humorists have various words for these products — smokeware, slideware, foilware, vaporware and hyperware.

SMRT Single Message-unit Rate Timing. USA telephone company tariff under which local calls are timed in 5-minute increments — with a single message unit charge applied to each complete or partial increment.

SMS Service Management System, a term coined by Bellcore for the Intelligent Network. The SMS allows provision and updating of information on subscribers and services in near-real time for billing and administrative purposes.

SMS/800 The national database Service Management System that retains all 800 records. This database provides long distance carriers a single interface for 800 number reservations and record maintenance. Developed by Bellcore, the database has been in use by various Regional Bell Operating Companies (RBOCs) since 1988. The FCC has mandated that a neutral third party administer the database after portability.

SMSA Standard Metropolitan Statistical Area. A metropolitan area consisting of one or more cities as defined by the Office of Management and Budget and used by the FCC to allocate the cellular radio market.

SMT Surface Mounting Technology.

SMTA Single-line Multi-extension Telephone Apparatus.

SMTP Simple Mail Transfer Protocol. In local area networking technology, protocol that operates at layers 5 through 7 of the Open Systems Interconnection (OSI) model. This TCP/IP protocol governs electronic mail transmissions and receptions.

SNA Systems Network Architecture. An IBM product. The most successful computer network architecture in the world. See IBM and SYSTEMS NETWORK ARCHITECTURE.

SNADS SNA Distribution Services. An IBM protocol that allows the distribution of electronic mail and attached documents through an SNA network.

SNAFU Situation Normal All Fouled Up. World War II military slang, that often describes frustrating facets of the telecom industry. See FUBAR.

SNAKE A flexible strip of metal, typically 1/4 to 1/2" wide and 10 to 100' long, used to pull or push wire and cable through conduit, ceilings, walls or crawl spaces where it is difficult or impossible for a human to fit.

SND Cellular language for SEND. You punch your digits into your phone. Check them the screen. If they're fine, hit the SND button. The calls goes through.

SNEAK CURRENTS Unwanted but steady currents which seep into a communication circuit. These low-level currents are insufficient to trigger electrical surge protectors and therefore are able to pass them undetected. They are usually too weak to cause immediate damage, but if unchecked could potentially create harmful heating effects. Sneak currents may result from contact between communications lines and AC power circuits or from power induction, and may cause equipment damage due to overheating.

SNEAK FUSE A fuse operated by a low-level current and capable of preventing sneak currents on communication lines. See also SNEAK CURRENTS.

SNIGLET Any word that does not appear in the dictionary, but should. A term invented by Rich Hall of the HBO Television program "Not Necessarily The News". An example of a sniglet is the definition of "Hozone." It's obviously where socks go when they don't come back from the laundry.

SNMP Simple Network Management Protocol. In 1988, the Department of Defense and commercial TCP/IP implementors designed a network management architecture for the needs of the average internet (a collection of disparate networks joined together with bridges or routers). Although SNMP was designed as the TCP's stack network management protocol, it can now manage virtually any network type and has been extended to include non-TCP devices such as 802.1 Ethernet bridges. SNMP is widely deployed in TCP/IP (Transmission Control Protocol/Internet Protocol) networks, but actual transport independence means it is not limited to TCP/IP. SNMP has been implemented over Ethernet as well as OSI transports. SNMP became a TCP/IP standard protocol in May 1990. SNMP operates on top of the Internet Protocol, and is similar in concept to IBM's NetView and ISO's CMIP. In 1991, Microsoft started refering to SNMP as SubNetwork Access Protocol.

SNR Abbreviation for SAVED NUMBER REDIAL, a phone system memory feature that allows the user to store a number for as long as it is useful, as opposed to other numbers that are stored more permanently. Some phones have two buttons — one for REDIAL and one for SNR. Redial will dial the last phone number you called. Saved Number Redial will dial one you dialed earlier and chose to save because you're going to call it back. Both buttons are very useful.

SO Serving Office. Central office where IXC (IntereXchange Carrier) has POP (Point Of Presence).

SOAK A means of uncovering problems in software and hardware by running them under operating conditions while they are closely supervised by their developers.

SOCIAL CONTRACT An arrangement between the local telephone company and its local regulatory authority whereby the telephone company's services are detariffed, but cannot be priced at less than cost. Quality of service standards apply.

SOCKET 1. A synonym for a port. 2. The socket in a PC which is responsible for accepting a PCMCIA Card and mapping the host's internal bus signals to the PCMCIA interface signals.

SOCKET SERVICES The software layer directly above the hardware that provides a standardized interface to manipulate PCMCIA Cards, sockets and adapters. Socket Services is a BIOS level software interface that provides a method for accessing the PCMCIA slots of a computer. For PCMCIA cards to operate correctly you also need Card Services, which is (not are) a software management interface that allows the allocation of system resources (such as memory and interrupts) automatically once the Socket Services detects that a PC Card has been inserted. See PCMCIA.

SOCKETS An application program interface (API) for communications between Unix and TCP/IP.

SOFT COPY A copy of a file or program which resides on magnetic medium, such as a floppy disk, or any form that is not a hard copy — which is paper.

SOFT FONT A font, usually provided by a font vendor, that must be installed on your computer and sent to the printer before text formatted in that font can be printed. Also known as downloadable font.

SOFT KEY There are three types of keys on a telephone: hard, programmable and soft. HARD keys are those which do one thing and one thing only, e.g. the touchtone buttons 1, 2, 3, * and # etc. PROGRAMMABLE keys are those which you can program to do produce a bunch of tones. Those tones might be "dial mother." They might be "transfer this call to my home for the evening." They might be "go into data mode, dial my distant computer, log in and put in my password." SOFT keys are the most interesting. They are unmarked buttons which sit below or above on the side of a screen. They derive their meaning from what's presently on the screen. And what's on the screen will change based on where the call is at that moment — in a conference call, about to set up a conference call, about to go into voice mail, into voice mail, programming a speed dial number, etc.

SOFT SECTORED A floppy disk whose sector boundaries are marked with records instead of holes. Soft-sectored disks have typically one hole. Hard sectored disks have many holes. A soft-sectored disk won't work on disk drives which use hard-sectored drives and vice versa — even though the disks might be the same size. Soft-sectored disks are now much more common.

SOFT SELECTABE/SOFT STRAPPABLE Refers to an option that is controllable throught software rather than hardware.

SOFTKEY See SOFT KEY.

SOFTKEY MAPPING See ADSI.

SOFTWARE The detailed instructions to operate a computer. The term was created to differentiate instructions (i.e. the program) from the hardware. See PROGRAM, HARDWARE and FIRMWARE.

SOFTWARE DEFINED NETWORK SDN. Generically, a software defined network refers to a virtual private network. Specifically, it refers to AT&T's Software Defined Network Service, which was introduced in 1985 for AT&T's largest customers and provided only dedicated access services. In 1989, AT&T extended its SDN Network to switched access. Currently, SDN is the most commonly resold of all long distance services. The AT&T Software Defined Network Service Description of July 1986 describes SDN as a service developed for multi-location businesses which allows network managers to tailor their network to their own specific communications needs. Call processing information is stored in a database that is accessed during a call. Calls are transferred over AT&T facilities to either a location that is a dedicated part of the network (for "on-net calling") or to non-dedicated facilities that are part of the network ("on-net" calling). Any company location can become part of a network through SDN dedicated access lines to an AT&T SDN serving office. Here is further explanation of SDN by Siemens Information Systems, whose Saturn PBX has the capability to interface to and mesh neatly with an AT&T SDN network. Here is Siemens' explanation (it's good): When a company establishes an SDN, each phone on the network has a unique seven digit number. This number may or may not be the same as the Listed Directory Number (LDN). When a call is placed at one PBX, it is sent over a dedicated access line to the long distance network. The call is received by the SDN Serving Office and digits are sent via a CCIS (Common Channel Interoffice Signaling) link to the Network Control Point (NCP) for analysis and routing. There is one NCP per SDN network. The NCP contains the unique database for the company using the SDN. The NCP analyzes the digits received against the database, determines whether it is an on-net or off-net call, and sets up the path over which the call will be rerouted on the long distance network. If it is an on-net call, the NCP translates the unique seven digit locator code to one that will be recognized by the AT&T network, sends the call over the network to another SDN Serving Office, and completes the call over dedicated lines to the PBX being called. There is a discount for any call which remains on-net throughout. If the call is off-net, the digits dialed are sent over the long distance network to a Central Office that is not part of the SDN. The call is then completed to the corporate PBX over DID (Direct Inward Dial) lines. Since the introduction of route selection features in PBXs, the caller now has the ability to dial the 10-digit LDN (Long Distance Number) and have the PBX make the decisions on the route and make the decisions on any digit translation or deletion that is necessary to route the call. The CCIS network which carries SDN call signaling is a packet switching network operating at 4,800 bits per second. It will eventually be replaced by CCITT 7 Signaling, a more powerful internationally-accepted signaling system. See SIGNALING SYSTEM 7.

SOFTWARE ENGINEERING A broadly defined discipline that integrates the many aspects of programming, from writing code to meeting budgets, to produce affordable software that works.

SOFTWARE INTERFACES Language between programs which allows one program to call upon another for assistance in processing.

SOFTWARE-ONLY VIDEO PLAYBACK A multimedia term. Video software playback displays a stream of video without any specialized chips or boards. The playback is done through a software application. The video is usually compressed to minimize the storage space required.

SOFTWARE SUPERVISION "Answer Supervision" is knowing when the person at the other end answers the phone. The main reason for wanting to know this is so that a phone company can start billing the call. There are two ways of doing answer supervision. You can get it from the nation's phone system, i.e. the distant office signals back across the country when the called person picks up the phone. Or you can fake it with "software supervision." Essentially this means there's electronics which "listens" to the call. If it "hears" voice or something like voice, it assumes the conversation has started and it's time to start billing the call. Software supervision is not accurate. But when you haven't got access to real answer supervision (for whatever reason) it's better than the previous alternative, which was "timeout." In timeout answer supervision, the carrier simply assumed the call had begun after a certain number of seconds — like 30 — had elapsed with the calling person hanging up. This meant, for example, if you called Grandma and she wasn't there, but you left it ringing, 'cause you knew she took time to answer the phone, then you'd be charged for the call — even though she didn't answer phone!

SOH Start Of Header. A transmission control character used as the first character of the heading of an information message.

SOHO Small Office Home Office. An acronym for a new market opening up. In New York City, there's an area called SOHO. It stands for South of Houston Street.

SOLDER 1. An alloy of lead and tin having a low melting point. 2. To unite or join by solder.

SOLENOID A coil consisting of a number of turns in cylindrical form.

SOLID STATE Any semiconductor device that controls electrons, electric fields and magnetic fields in a solid material — and typically has no moving parts.

SOLID STATE APPLICATIONS INTERFACE BRIDGE Solid's State Systems' PBX to external computer link. See OPEN APPLICATION INTERFACE.

SOLITONS See RARE EARTH DOPING.

SOLUTION IBM-speak to solve, as in "We've got to solution this problem if we're going to make the sale."

SONET Synchronous Optical NETwork. A family of fiber-optic transmission rates from 51.84 Mbps to 13.22 Gbps, created to provide the flexibility needed to transport many digital signals with different capacities, and to provide a standard for manufacturers to design from. Sonet is an optical interface standard that allows interworking of transmission products from multiple vendors (i.e. mid-span meets). It defines a physical interface, optical line rates known as Optical Carrier (OC) signals, frame format and an OAM&P protocol (Operations, Administration, Maintenance, And Provisioning). The OC signals have electrical called Synchronous Transport Signals (STSs). The base rate is 51.84 Mb/s (OC-1/STS-1) and higher rates are direct multiples of the base rate.

SONET was created by the Exchange Carriers Standards Association for the American National Standards Institute (ANSI). The standard is being defined in phases — Phase 1, adopted in March of 1988 by ANSI, and

Phase 2, planned or completion by February of 1990. SONET has also been adopted by the Consultive Committee for International Telephone and Telegraph (CCITT).

SONET was initiated by Bellcore on behalf of the Regional Bell Operating Companies to attain these goals: Multi-vendor interworking, to be cost effective for existing services on an end-to-end basis, to create an infrastructure to support new broadband services and for enhanced operations, administration, maintenance and provisioning (OAM&P).

SONET, according to Northern Telecom, offers many advantages over asynchronous transport including: Opportunity for back-to-back multiplexing, digital cross-connect panels; Easy evolution to broadband transport; Compatibility with evolving operations standards; Enhanced performance monitoring and Extension of OAM&P capabilities to end users.

SONET transmission equipment interleaves STSs in simple integer multiples to form a synchronous high speed signal. This permits easy access to low speed signals (e.g. DS-O, DS-1, etc.) without multi-stage multiplexing and demultiplexing. The low speed signals are mapped into sub-STS-1 signals called Virtual Tributaries (VTs).

SONET uses a 51.84 Mb/s STS-1 signal as the basic building block. Higher rate signals are multiples of STS-1 (e.g. the STS-12/OC-12 signal has a rate of 12 x 51.84 Mb/s or 622.080 Mb/s). The frame format consists of 90 x 9 bytes. The SONET frame format is divided into two main areas: Synchronous Payload Envelope (SPE) and Transport Overhead (TOH). The SPE contains the information being transported by the frame. The TOH supports the OAM&P functions of SONET, and includes a data communication channel that provides an OAM&P communication path between multiple interconnected SONET network elements.

The SPE can handle payloads in any of three ways:

1. As a continuous 50.11 Mb/s envelope for carrying asynchronous DS-3, and other payloads requiring up to 50.11 Mb/s capacity in asynchronous (byte invisible) or byte visible format;

2. In a VT structured envelope to accommodate DS-1, DS-1C, DS-2, European CEPT1, or future VT based services (see chart below). These signals can have either an asynchronous or byte visible format; and

3. As concatenated payloads to accommodate services requiring more than 50.11 Mb/s capacity. For example, three STS-1 SPEs may be concatenated (combined) to transport a broadband ISDN signal of 135 Mb/s.

According to AT&T, the main Sonet characteristics are a family of rates at N x 51.84 Mb/s; Optical interconnect allowing mid-span meet; Intraoffice mixed vendor interconnects; Overhead channels for OAM & P functions and Synchronous networking.

SONET RATES ARE

OC Level	Line Rates	Capacity
OC-1	52 Mb/s	28 DS1s or 1 DS3
OC-3	155 Mb/s	84 DS1s or 3 DS3s
OC-9	466 Mb/s	252 DS1s or 9 DS3s
OC-12	622 Mb/s	336 DS1s or 12 DS3s
OC-18	933 Mb/s	504 DS1s or 18 DS3s
OC-24	1.2 Gb/s	672 DS1s or 24 DS3s
OC-36	1.9 Gb/s	1008 DS1s or 36 DS3s
OC-48	2.5 Gb/s	1344 DS1s or 48 DS3s

See also SONET INTERFACE LAYERS.

SONET INTERFACE LAYERS The SONET standards define four optical interface layers. While conceptually similar to layering within the Open System Interconnection (OSI) reference model, SONET itself corresponds only to the OSI Physical Layer. The SONET interface layers are:

1. Photonic Layer: Handles bit transport across the physical medium; primarily responsible for converting STS (electrical) signals to OC (optical) signals. Electro-optical devices communicate at this layer;

2. Section Layer: Transports STS-N frames and Section Overhead (SOH) across the medium; functions include framing, scrambling, and error monitoring. Section Terminating Equipment (STE) communicate at this layer;

3. Line Layer: Responsible for the reliable transport of the Synchronous Payload Envelope (SPE) (i.e., user data) and Line Overhead (LOH) across the medium; responsibilities include synchronization and multiplexing for the Path Layer and mapping the SPE and LOH into an STS-N frame. An OC-N-to-OC-M multiplexer is an example of Line Terminating Equipment (LTE); and

4. Path Layer: Handles transport of services (e.g., DS-1, DS-3, E-1, or video) between Path Terminal Equipment (PTE); the main function is to map the services and Path Overhead (POH) information into the PTE includes SONET-capable switches with an interface to a non-SONET network, such as a T1-to-SONET multiplexer.

SONY MINI DISC A 2 1/2 inch silvery CD (compact Disc) that can record and play 74 minutes of sounds, almost as much as its five-inch forebear. To record on this disc, a laser momentarily heats a tiny spot on the disk to 400 degrees Fahrenheit, while a magnetic head writes the signal into the heated part of the magnetic layer. To play the disk an optical pickup analyzes the polarity of the light reflected from each spot.

SOP Standard Operating Procedure.

SOUND FILES Files on PCs have their own extensions — the three letters which follow the name of the file. For example, a sound file of jungle noises might be called jungle.wav. Here are the typical extensions on sound files of various computers:

Microsoft Windows	—	wav
Apple	—	aif
NeXT	—	snd
MIDI	—	mid and .nni
Sound Blaster	—	voc

SOUND POWERED TELEPHONE A telephone in which the operating power is derived from the speech input only.

SOUND WAVES The waves given off by a vibrating body, which are transmitted by an elastic material medium (such as the air) and which can be detected by the ear.

SOURCE That part of a communications system which transmits information.

SOURCE ADDRESS The part of a message which indicates who sent the message. Just like the top left-hand address on the envelope.

SOURCE CODE A set of instructions, written in a programming language, that must be translated to machine instructions before the program can be run on a computer. The program which finally runs on that computer is known as the object code.

SOURCE EXPLICIT FORWARDING A feature that allows MAC-layer bridges on local area networks to forward packets from only source address specified by the network administrator.

SOURCE ROUTING A method used by a bridge for moving data between two networks. Originally developed by IBM's token ring network, it relies on information contained within the token to route the packet between the two networks. Since the information in the token is supplied by the computer that sent the data packet, that computer must know on which network the destination computer is located. IBM developed a special protocol that lets computers discover that information. For source routing to work, every computer and every bridge on all networks must support this protocol. If some computers do not use this protocol, they will not receive packets from bridges that use source routing. See BRIDGE. Compare to TRANSPARENT ROUTING.

In IBM's method of routing local area network data across bridges, IBM's bridges can be configured as either single-route broadcast or all-routes broadcast. The default is single-route broadcast. Single-route broadcasting means that only one designated single-route bridge will pass the packet and only one copy of the packet will arrive at its destination. Single-route broadcast bridges can transmit both single-route and all-routes packets. All-routes broadcasting sends the packet across every possible route in the network, resulting in as many copies of the frame at the destination as there are all-routes broadcasting bridges in the network. All-routes broadcast bridges only pass all-routes broadcast packets.

SORT To order a collection of records — for example, a telephone directory — in some specified way, say, in alphabetical order. Computers can sort in virtually any way you ask them to. Most companies don't produce sufficient "sorts" on their telephone directories.

SOUTHWESTERN BELL CORPORATION One of the seven Regional Holding Companies formed at Divestiture. It includes Southwestern Bell and other companies.

SP 1. Support Processor. 2. Sending Program. 3. Signal Present. 4. Signal Processor. 5. Signaling Point.

SPACE In digital transmission, the space is equated to the zero (0) and the mark is equated to the one (1). In telecommunications, space is the absence of a signal. Equivalent to a binary "O".

SPACE DIVERSITY Protection of a radio signal by providing a separate antenna located a few feet below the regular antenna on the same tower to assume the load when the regular transmission path on the same tower fades because of rain, a bird flying through it, etc.

SPACE DIVISION MULTIPLEXING Each distinct signal or message travels over a separate physical path such as its own wire or wire pair within a cable.

SPACE DIVISION SWITCHING Method for switching circuits in which each connection through the switch takes a physically separate path.

SPACE HOLD A no traffic line condition where a steady space is transmitted.

SPACE SEGMENT 1. The part of a satellite system that is in space. 2. This is also the imprecise term used to describe the band of frequency purchased by the satellite customer. The customer can purchase a portion of the bandwidth of a single transponder or the customer can purchase one or more entire transponder bandwidths.

SPACECRAFT SWITCHED TIME DIVISION MULTIPLE ACCESS SSTDMA. A method of sharing the capacity of a communications satellite by on-board switching of signals aimed at earth stations.

SPADE LUG A metal connector attached to the end of a piece of wire, typically by soldering or by pressure. The metal spade lug is shaped like a "U." The idea is to slide the flat "U" shaped metal piece under a screw and then tighten the screw, thus making a connection. In the old days, all phones came with spade lug connectors. These days, there are other faster, more efficient ways of connecting phones — including modular jacks and punchdown tools.

SPAG Europe's Standards Promotion and Application Group.

SPAGHETTI CODE A program written without thought, logic or structure. And whose "logic" is therefore very difficult to follow. Some would say this definition covers most software written today. That's unfair.

SPAN 1. Refers to that portion of a high speed digital system than connects a C.O. (Central Office) to C.O. or terminal office to terminal office. 2. Also called a T-Span Line. A repeatered outside plant four-wire, two twisted-pair transmission line.

SPAN LINE A T-1 link.

SPAN POWERED In T-1, refers to the application of a varying voltage (+130V to -130V) to the digital cable pairs to maintain a 60mA DC current at each repeater and at the customer premises (this power is generally used for regeneration, loop backs, keep alive signals and alarms).

SPANNING TREE ALGORITHM STA. A technique based on an IEEE 802.1 standard that detects and eliminates logical loops in a bridged network. When multiple paths exist, says PC Magazine's Frank Derfler, STA lets a bridge use only the most efficient one. If that path fails, STA automatically reconfigures the network to make another path become active, sustaining network operations. This algorithm is used mostly by local bridges; it is not economical for use over leased telephone circuits connecting remote bridges.

SPANNING TREE PROTOCOL STP. Inactivation of links between networks so that information packets are channeled along one route and will not search endlessly for a destination.

SPARC A proprietary RISC microprocessor designed and marketed by Sun Microsystems and included in all Sun SPARCstations.

SPARE PAIRS In existing distribution systems, twisted pairs that are not being used and can be used to serve new communications devices. Spare pairs are exactly what they sound like — spare pairs of cables. Best to install as many spares as you can when you initially wire up a building or office. Remember Newton's Rule: You'll always need twice as much cabling as you ever dreamed in your wildest dreams you'd need.

SPARK An arc of very short short duration.

SPARK GAP Terminals or electrodes designed to permit spark discharges to take place across a gap.

SPARK TEST A test designed to locate pin-holes in a wire's insulation by application of an electrical potential across the material for a very short period of time while the wire is drawn through an electrode field with one end of the wire grounded.

SPATA SPeech And daTA. Watch for this expression to pick up steam once true integration of voice and data occurs. The expression does not come from the sentence: "Spata to integrate today than tomorrow."

SPATIAL DATA MANAGEMENT A technique which allows users access to information by pointing at picture symbols on the screen.

SPC Stored Program Control. All phone systems these days are SPCs. There's stored software, which is the program, which controls the computer or microprocessor which in turn controls the operation of the switch. Thus switches are stored program control.

SPCS Stored Program Controlled Switch. A digital switch that supports call control, routing, and supplementary services provision under software control. Pretty well switches made after 1970 in North America are SPCSs.

SPCL SPectrum CeLlular error-correction protocol.

SPE 1. Switch Processing Element. 2. Synchronous Payload Envelope. In Sonet, three different payload structures are defined to address different input requirements: 1. Direct-to-STS-1 line rate multiplexing takes 28 DS-Is, 14 DS-ICs or 7 DS-2s directly into the 51.84 Mbps rate. Each is uniquely transported within the SPE; 2. Asynchronous DS-3 Multiplexing takes a complete asynchronous DS-3 bundle (the output of an M13 for example) into the SPE; 3. Synchronous DS-3 Multiplexing maps a Syntran DS-3 signal to the SPE.

SPEAKER DEPENDENT VOICE RECOGNITION Technology capable of recognizing speech from a given user or others who sound like this user after completion of an enrollment procedure. It is not voice verification although it is sometimes confused with this technology.

SPEAKER INDEPENDENT VOICE RECOGNITION SIR or SIVR. Technology capable of recognizing any user without prior training or knowledge of the user. SIR converts speech to accurate and meaningful textual information (typically ASCII). SIR is used to accept input from callers to voice processors where the callers are using rotary dial phones instead of touchtone phones. SIR can substitute for the numbers on the DTMF keypad and can add the benefit of a few basic voice commands, e.g., Yes, No, Help, etc.

Because computer processing demands are formidable with speaker independent recognition, accurate speaker independent products are created with limited vocabularies. In contrast, trainable or speaker dependent recognizers can feature larger vocabularies at lower prices. SIR has been slowly gaining acceptance in telephone applications. SIR is increasingly used in automated operator assistance applications. SIR will see increased use as system builders respond to pressures to provide voice processing functions to the enormous rotary phone installed base domestically and abroad.

SPEAKERPHONE A telephone which has a speaker and microphone for hands free, two-way conversation.

SPECIAL ACCESS A dedicated line from a customer to a long distance company provided by a local phone company.

SPECIAL BILLING NUMBER A phone number assigned to certain customers for billing purposes. It cannot be called. It may be given to an operator as the calling number on an outgoing paid call, or it may be used as a "third number billed" number. It's designed as a measure of security and accounting convenience.

SPECIAL CHARACTERS 1. Microsoft calls special characters that ones not found on your computer's keyboard. In Windows 3.1 these characters are accessible through Character Map, an application in the Accesssories group. 2. An AT&T Merlin term. A pause, stop, or end-of-dialing signal in a programmed dialing sequence such as an Auto Dial or Personal Speed Dial number.

SPECIAL GRADE ACCESS LINE An AUTOVON access line specially conditioned, usually by providing amplitude and delay equalization, to give it characteristics suitable for handling special services; e.g., lower signaling rates of 600 to 2400 bits per second.

SPECIAL NIGHT ANSWERING POSITION Provides either a console or a pre-assigned single extension phone to answer all incoming night calls.

SPECIAL SERVICES A variety of services that are separate from the public switched network.

SPECIALIZED COMMON CARRIER A company providing domestic long distance telecommunications services other than AT&T. See OTHER COMMON CARRIERS.

SPECIFIC GRAVITY The ratio of the weight of any volume of substance to a weight of an equal volume of some substance taken as a standard, usually water for liquids and hydrogen for gases.

SPECIFIC INDUCTIVE CAPACITY The direct measure of the ability of a substance to store up electrical energy when used as a dielectric material in a condenser.

SPECKLE The bright and dark spots on the end face of a fiber caused by the interference of modes.

SPECTRAL EFFICIENCY The efficiency of a microwave system in its use of the radio spectrum, usually expressed in bits per Hz for digital radios and KHz per voice channel in analog radios.

SPECTROGRAM A basic research tool for the speech scientist which provides a three-dimensional visual representation of speech.

SPECTRUM A continuous range of frequencies, usually wide in extent within which waves have some specific common characteristics. See SPECTRUM DESIGNATION OF FREQUENCY.

SPECTRUM ANALYZER Tuneable RF instrument which displays a portion of the RF spectrum with amplitude of signals on the vertical axis and frequency on the horizontal axis on a screen. Used in TSCM to analyze transmissions for the characteristics of an illegitimate transmitter (radio bug).

SPECTRUM DESIGNATION OF FREQUENCY A method of referring to a range or band of communication frequencies. In American practice the designator is a two- or three-letter abbreviation for the name. In ITU practice, the designator is numeric. These ranges or bands are:

FREQUENCY RANGE	ITU FREQUENCY BAND DESIGNATOR
3 - 30 THz	13
30 -300 THz	14
300- 3000 THz	15
3 - 30 PHz	16
30 - 300 PHz	17
300 - 3000 PHz	18
3 - 30 EHz	19
30 - 300 EHz	20
300 - 3000 EHz	21

FREQUENCY RANGE	TYPICAL AMERICAN DESIGNATOR	ITU FREQUENCY BAND DESIGNATOR
30 - 300 Hz	ELF (Extremely Low Frequency	2
300 - 3000 Hz	ULF (Ultra Low Frequency	3
3 - 30 kHz	VLF (Very Low Frequency)	4
30 - 300 kHz	LF (Low Frequency)	5
300 - 3000 kHz	MF (Medium Frequency)	6
3 - 30 MHz	HF (High Frequency)	7
30 - 300 MHz	VHF (Very High Frequency)	8
300 - 3000 MHz	UHF (Ultra High Frequency)	9
3 - 30 GHz	SHF (Super High Frequency)	10
30 - 300 GHz	EHF (Extremely High Frequency)	11
300 - 3000 GHz	THF (Tremendously High Frequency)	12

THz = Terahertz (10 to the 12th power hertz)
PHz = Petahertz (10 to the 15th power hertz)
EHz = Exahertz (10 to the 18th power hertz)

SPECTRUS Name for BellSouth's general tariff service specifically for video, such as broadcast and commercial quality.

SPEECH CONCATENATION A term used in voice processing for economical digitized speech playback that uses independently recorded files of phrases or file segments linked together under application program control to produce a customized response in natural sounding language. For example, order status, bank balances, bus schedules or lottery results, etc. Concatenation is done for speed and economy. It lends itself to limited and structured vocabularies that are best stored in RAM (Random Access Memory) or speedily accessible from disk. Concatenation does not replace Text-To-Speech (TTS) as a method of getting the voice processer to deliver its responsese. Concatenation, however, can be an excellent complement to TTS when a voice application demands broad, real time vocabulary production. See TEXT-TO-SPEECH.

SPEECH DIGIT SIGNALING Signaling in which digit time slots used primarily for encoded speech are periodically used for signaling (as, optionally, in ISDN). See also ISDN.

SPEED DIAL A feature that enables a PBX or PBX phone to store certain telephone numbers and dial them automatically when a code is entered. See SPEED DIALING.

SPEED DIALING Permits fast dialing of frequently used numbers. A repertory of numbers may be stored in the instrument and/or in the telephone switch. Usually a button or one, two or three digits are dialed to activate speed dialing.

SPEED OF LIGHT IN A VACUUM 299 x 106 meters per second. Used in computing index of refraction.

SPI Service Provider Interface. See SERVICE PROVIDE INTERFACE and WINDOWS TELEHONY.

SPID The Service Profile Identifier is used to identify a specific ISDN set when more than one ISDN set has been attached to the same central office line. In most cases, only one ISDN set will be assigned to a line, and the SPID is not used by the switch.

SPIE Society of Photometric Industry Engineers.

SPIKE MIKE Contact microphone for listening through walls.

SPIKES Electrical anomalies represented as short duration, instantaneous, very high voltage fluctuations on an electrical service.

SPILL-FORWARD FEATURE A service feature, in the operation of an intermediate office, that, acting on incoming trunk service treatment indications, assumes routing control of the call from the originating office. This increases the chances of completion by offering the call to more trunk groups than are available in the originating office.

SPIN STABILIZATION A method of preventing a satellite from tumbling by spinning it about its axis.

SPIRAL WRAP A term given to describe the helical wrap of a tape or thread over a core.

SPIRIT COMMUNICATIONS SYSTEM A small electronic key system from AT&T. A SPIRIT telephone system supports as few as three outside lines and eight telephones (or, with an expansion unit, up to 24 outside lines with 48 phones).

SPLANCH SPlit Level rANCH.

SPLASH TONE Distinctive sound used on some phone systems to indicate that a command has been received, or that something has to be done. Vaguely resembles water being splashed.

SPLASHING A "splash" happens when an Alternate Operator Service (AOS) company, located in a city different to the one you're calling from, connects your call to the long distance carrier of your choice in the city the AOS operator is in. Splashing does not imply backhauling, but it often happens. For example, let's say you're calling from Hotel Magnificent in Chicago. You ask AT&T to handle your call. The AOS, located in Atlanta, "splashes" your call over to AT&T in Atlanta. But you're calling Los Angeles. Bingo. Your AT&T call to LA is now more expensive than it would be if you had been connected directly to AT&T from Hotel Magnificent in Chicago.

SPLICE Verb. The joining of two or more cables together by splicing the conductors pair-to-pair.

SPLINT A perjorative word for US Sprint, a long distance company now owned largely (80%) by United Telecom, Kansas City and 20% by GTE and now called just Sprint.

SPLIT Same as Group. See ACD or AUTOMATIC CALL DISTRIBUTOR.

SPLIT ACCESS TO OUTGOING TRUNKS Two separate trunk groups provided for direct outward dialing which can be accessed by dialing the same trunk access code. Controlled on class of service basis.

SPLIT CHANNEL MODEM A modem which divides a communications channel into separate send and receive channels. Most modems which use the dial-up phone network are split channel — meaning they can transmit and receive simultaneously over a two wire circuit. See also SPLIT STREAM MODEM, which is another term for the same thing.

SPLIT LINK When one multiplexer uses two links to communicate to two separate multiplexers.

SPLIT PAIR Something that happens in cable splicing when one wire of a pair gets spliced to the wire of an adjacent pair. You could call it a split pair. It's more accurate to call it a mistake.

SPLIT STREAM MODEM A modem which can handle multiple, independent channels over a single transmission path.

SPLITTING Permits operator to consult privately with one party on a call without the other party's hearing. Or permits a three-party telephone conference user to consult privately with one side of the conference while the other is effectively put on hold. Jumping from one party to the other is called "Swapping."

SPM 1. Subscriber Private Meter. 2. An AT&T Merlin term. System Programming and Maintenance. A DOS- or UNIX-based application for programming and maintaining the Merlin communications system.

SPN Subscriber Premises Networks.

SPOI Signaling Point Of Interface.

SPOOFING 1. In COMSEC applications, the interception, alteration, and retransmission of a cipher signal or data in such a way as to mislead the receiver. 2. In automated-information-systems applications, an attempt to gain access to an automated information system by posing as an authorized user.

SPOOL Simultaneous Peripheral Operation On Line. A program or piece of hardware that controls a buffer of data going to some output device, including a printer or a screen. A spool allows several users to send data to a device such as a printer at the same time, even when the printer is busy. The spool controls the transmission of data to the device by using a buffer or creating a temporary file in which to store the data going to the busy device. See SPOOLING.

SPOOLING Simultaneous Peripheral Operations On Line. Spooling means temporarily storing programs or program outputs on magnetic tape, RAM or disks for output or processing. The word "Spooling" is mostly associated with printers. Here's an example: Pretend that a lot of people on your Local Area Network all want to send their reports to the printer today. Instead of each person having control of the printer and relinquishing it only when they're through, each user tells the print Spooler what file they want printed. The program, called the spooler, places the print request in the print queue. When your request reaches the top of the queue, your report is printed out. Using a PC as print spooler slows it down. Best not to use it for much else.

SPOT BEAM ANTENNA A satellite antenna capable of illuminating or focussing on a narrow portion of the earth's surface.

SPP Sequenced Packet Protocol. XNS (Xerox Network Systems) protocol governing sequenced data.

SPREAD SPECTRUM Also called frequency hopping, spread spectrum is a modulation technique in which the information content is spread over a wider bandwidth than the frequency content of the original information. Spread spectrum takes an input signal, mixes it with FM noise and "spreads" the signal over a broad frequency range, hopping from frequency to frequency at split-second intervals. The spread signal has greater bandwidth than the original message. Spread spectrum receivers recognize a spread signal, acquire and "de-spread" it and thus return it to its initial form (the original message). Spread spectrum is highly secure. Would-be eavesdroppers hear only unintelligible blips. Attempts to jam the signal succeed only at knocking out a few small bits of it. So effective is the concept that it is now the principal antijamming device in the U.S. Government's Milstar defese communications satellite system. Hedy Lamarr, the actress, created the concept of spread spectrum in 1940 and, two years later, received a U.S. patent for a "secret communication system." The patent was issued to her and George Antheil, a film-score composer, to whom Ms. Lamarr had turned for help in perfecting her idea. Spread spectrum was never of used during the World War II and did not come into use until 1962 when Sylvania installed it on ships sent to blockade Cuba. Ms. Lamarr never received one penny for her invention.

SPRINGBOARD Dialogic's term for a general purpose computing engine designed for a wide range of powerful voice processing applications. It contains two Motorola 56001 DSPs (Digital Signal Processors) and one Intel 80286 12.5 MHz microprocessor. It allows Dialogic's Technology Partners to extend D/12x functions.

SPRINT A long distance telephone company now owned 80% by United Telecom, Kansas City and 20% by GTE. It used to be called GTE Sprint and once was called US Sprint. But now it's just called Sprint. Here are some of the services Sprint provides (MCI and AT&T provide similar services, though under different names):

SPRINT DATACALL PLUS: offers global dial-up access to host computers, using the SprintNet data network (once called Telenet), for asynchronous and X.25 applications at 300 to 9600 bps, with end-to-end error protection.

SPRINT DAY PLUS: Sprint switched service for small business customers.

SPRINT EXPRESS: Using Sprint Express, you may call the United States from a number of overseas locations simply by dialing a toll-free number direct to a Sprint operator in the U.S. You do not have to contact a foreign operator or pay excessive local surcharges. You can bill the call to your FONCARD, local exchange carrier card or call collect. You will receive one consolidated bill, in U.S. currency.

SPRINT FAX: Send faxes. Broadcast Distribution allows a fax to be sent to multiple locations simply by making one phone call. Document on Demand automates information retrieval via fax from an 800 or 900 number.

SPRINT FONCARD: Sprint's name for its credit card.

SPRINTMAIL MESSAGING SERVICES: Allows you to send, receive

and file messages 24 hours a day from a terminal, PC or communicating word processor via fax, telex or hard copy, anywhere in the world. SprintMail Fax allows messages to be sent directly from a desktop PC to virtually any fax machine in the world. SprintMail Post delivers electronically input messages from a desktop PC as laser-printed mail, in two days or less, anywhere in the continental U.S.

SPRINT MEETING CHANNEL: Allegedly the world's largest two-way digital videoconferencing network with over 950 locations in 30 countries world-wide. It's organized and run by Sprint.

SPRINT PLUS: Sprint PLUS is the name for Sprint's basic switched telephone service.

SPRINT QUICKCONFERENCE: A three-way conferencing capability, using Sprint's FONCARD when you're away from the office.

SPRINT VISA: Sprint VISA is a multi-functional credit card that combines a traditional VISA card with the Sprint FONCARD. It allows you to buy goods and services, access the VISA ATM network for cash and place a FONCARD call all with a single card. All FONCARD calls are billed to the VISA account.

SPRINT WORLD: Sprint WORLD gives residential customers flat rates to a designated number of countries during discount and economy time periods for a monthly fee.

SPS 1. Signalling Protocols and Switching. 2. Standard Positioning Service. The normal civilian positioning accuracy obtained by using the single frequency C/A code in the GPS (Global Positioning System) system.

SPUD A special long-handled shovel used to loosen soil in a hole into which you're going to put a telephone pole.

SPURIOUS A term used in voice recognition. A spurious error is said to occur when a sound that is not a valid spoken input is incorrectly accepted as an input speech utterance.

SPURIOUS EMISSION Emission on a frequency or frequencies which are outside the necessary bandwidth and the level of which may be reduced without affecting the corresponding transmission of information. Spurious emissions include harmonic emissions, parasitic emissions, intermodulation products and frequency conversion products, but exclude out-of-band emissions.

SPURS 1. The sharp metal devices on the climbers used by telephone line-persons (people who climb telephone poles). Such climbing spurs make a mess of telephone poles. 2. The cowboy devices awarded by US WEST to privileged persons who have done US WEST some nice favor or are otherwise deserving of honor.

SPUTNIK Sputnik was the world's first artificial satellite. It was launched by the Russians on October 4, 1957.

SPX Sequenced Packet eXchange. 1. An enhanced set of commands implemented on top of IPX to create a true transport-layer interface. SPX provides more functions than IPX, including guaranteed packet delivery. 2. Novell's implementation of SPP for its NetWare local area network operating system.

SQL Structured Query Language. Invented by IBM, SQL is a powerful database language used for creating, maintaining and viewing database data. It is becoming somewhat of a standard in the mainframe and minicomputer world, and it is on its way to becoming a PC standard. When it is a fully-accepted standard, different computer systems running different DBMSs will easily be able to communicate and exchange data with each other by simply trading SQL commands. SQL is commonly used with database servers. There is now an ANSI standard SQL definition for all computer systems. The largest purveyors of SQL databases are Oracle, Sybase, Informix, Microsoft and Gupta. See SQL SERVER.

SQL SERVER Microsoft SQL Server. A Microsoft retail product that provides distributed database managment. Multiple workstations manipulate data stored on a server, where the server coordinates operations and performs resource-intensive calculations.

SQUARE OPERATION If there are fewer than eight lines in a Merlin system, all users can access all lines. See SQUARED KEY SYSTEM.

SQUARED KEY SYSTEM What is a squared key system? No one knows where the word "squared" came from. So if our explanation bears no relation to the word "squared," sorry. But it goes like this (we think): In the old days there were 1A2 phone systems. These 1A2 phones had buttons on them. These buttons could correspond to trunks — any trunk. These were called non-squared systems. Then came electronic key systems. Each trunk had to "appear" (i.e. be) the same button on each phone. These electronic key systems were called squared systems. There are advantages and disadvantages. Squared systems are portrayed as having one advantage: You can go to any phone anywhere in the system and punch any button for any trunk and know it to be the same button for the same trunk. Thus less confusion. But this means you can only have as many trunks on your key system as you have trunk buttons on your key telephones. In a non-squared system — a 1A2, the newer hybrids or some of the newer programmable key systems — you can have more trunks than you have buttons on each phone. Some phones will have trunks that others don't have and vice versa. Thus you can have more trunks on your phone system than you have buttons on your phones. This means, for example, that four executives can have each have private lines and access to four trunks on a six button phone. (The other button is for Hold.)

SQUELCH A circuit function that acts to suppress the audio output of a receiver.

SRAM See STATIC RAM.

SRC Strategic Review Committee (ETSI).

SRDC SubRate Digital Cross-connect.

SRDM SubRate Data Multiplexer. The Europeans call it SDM.

SRT 1. Station Ringing Transfer. 2. Source Routing Transparent, a token ring bridging standard that is jointly sponsored by the IEEE and IBM. It combines IBM Source Routing and Transparent Bridging (IEEE 802.1) in the same unit. This provides a way for universal bridging of token ring LANs supporting IBM and all non-IBM LAN protocols. An SRT bridge examines each data packet on the ring to discover whether the packet is using a source routing or non-source routing protocol. It then applies the appropriate bridging method. See also BRIDGE, SOURCE ROUTING and TRANSPARENT ROUTING.

SS7 Signaling System 7. See SIGNALING SYSTEM 7.

SSB Single SideBand. See SINGLE SIDEBAND.

SSB-SC Single-SideBand Suppressed Carrier.

SSCP System Services Control Point. A host based network entity in SNA that manages the network configuration, coordinates network operator and problem determination requests, maintains network address and mapping tables and provides directory support and session services.

SSP Service Switching Point. A switch that can recognize IN (Intelligent Network) calls and route and connect them under the direction of an SCP (Service Control Point. A computer database that holds information on IN (Intelligent Network) services and subscribers. The SCP is separated from the actual SCP switch, making it easier to introduce new services on the network.

ST 1. STart signal to indicate end of outpulsing. 2. Straight Tip. A fiber-optic connector designed by AT&T which uses the bayonet style coupling rather than screw-on as the SMA uses. The ST is generally considered the eventual replacement for the SMA type connector.

ST CONNECTOR See STRAIGHT-TIP CONNECTOR.

STA Spanning Tree Algorithm. A technique based on an IEEE 802.1 standard that detects and eliminates logical loops in a bridged network. When multiple paths exist, STA lets a bridge use only the most efficient one. If that path fails, STA automatically reconfigures the network so that another path becomes active, sustaining network operations.

STACK A set of data storage locations that are accessed in a fixed sequence.

STAGGER In facsimile systems, periodic error in the position of the recorded spot along the recorded line.

STAKO An Ericsson committee for component standardization.

STAND ALONE Any device that can perform independently of something else.

STANDARD JACK The means of connecting Customer premises equipment to a circuit as specified in the FCC Registration Program.

STANDARD METROPOLITAN STATISTICAL AREA SMSA. A metropolitan area consisting of one or more cities as defined by the Office of Management and Budget and used by the FCC to allocate the cellular radio market.

STANDARD TEST ZONE A single-frequency signal with a standardization level generally used for level alignment of single links in tandem.

STANDARDIZED TEST TONE A single frequency signal at a standardized power level.

STANDARDS Agreed principles of protocol. Standards are set by committees working under various trade and international organizations. RS standards, such as RS-232-C are set by the EIA, the Electronics Industries Association. ANSI standards for data communications are from the X committee. Standards from ANSI would look like X3.4-1967 which is the standard for the ASCII code. The CCITT does not put out standards, but rather, publishes "recommendations", owing to the international egos involved. "V" series recommendations refer to data transmission over the telephone network, while "X" series recommendations, such as X.25 (properly pronounced "Eks dot twenty five"), refer to data transmission over public data networks. Notice that the ANSI standards have the year they were approved as part of the name of the standard, while CCITT recommendations do not. The placement of the "dot" is another clue as to whose confusing standard belongs to whom.

When you're buying a phone system, at minimum it should conform to four standards:

● Emmissions compliance according to the FCC Part 15.

● Telephone compliance according to the FCC Part 68.

● Safety standards set by the National Electric Code, OSHA and the Underwriters Laboratories 1459.

● Bellcore compliance (from the Network Equipment Building System publication and their Generic Physical Design Requirements for Telecommunications Products and Equipment publication. See STANDARDS BODIES.

STANDARDS BODIES Here is a list of the major standards bodies in telecom and computing:

ANSI, American National Standards Institute, 1430 Broadway, New York, NY 10018. 212-642-4900

Bellcore, 445 South Street, Morristown NJ 07962, 201-829-2410

CSA, Canadian Standards Association, 178 Rexdale Road, Rexdale (Toronto), Ontario Canada M9W 1R3, 416-747-4044;

DOC, Government of Canada, Department of Communications, 1241 Clyde Avenue, Ottowa K2C 1Y3 (613)998-5968;

EIA, Electronics Industry Association, 17221 I Street, NW, Suite 300, Washington, D.C. 20006. 202-457-4931;

Global Engineering Documents, 2805 McGraw Avenue, P.O. Box 19539, Irvine, CA 92714, 714-261-1455;

ICEA, Insulated Cable Engineers Association, P.O. Box 440, South Yarmouth, MA 02664, 508-394-4424;

NFPA, National Fire Protection Association, Batterymarch Park, Quincey, MA 02169, 617-770-3000;

OFR, Office of the Federal Register, National Archives & Records Administration Washington, D.C. 20408 202-523-3117;

TIA, Telecommunications Industry Association, 1722 I Street NW Suite 300, Washington, DC 20006, 202-457-4912;

UL, Underwriters Laboratory, 333 Pfingsten Road, Northbrook, IL 60062, 708-272-8800.

STANDBY PROCESSOR A spare computer exists which can direct PBX operations if the primary one fails. Some standbys are just sitting there, installed but not turned on. They require someone to turn them on. Some standbys are actually running all the time, as the main one is. If the main one crashes, the standby processor is ready to take over.

STANDBY TIME The amount of time you can leave your fully charged cellular portable or transportable phone turned on to receive incoming calls before the phone will completely discharge the batteries. See TALK TIME.

STANDING WAVE When you look at it on an oscilloscope the pattern of the wave is perfectly flat, i.e. horizontal. It's caused by two sine waves of the same frequency moving in opposite directions. In transmission line theory the accepted definition is simply the superposition of two waves traveling in opposite directions.

STANDING WAVE RATIO SWR. The ratio of the amplitude of a standing wave at an anti-node to the amplitude at a node.

STAR 1. A topology in which all phones or workstations are wired directly to a central service unit or workstation that establishes, maintains and breaks connections between the workstations. Virtually all phone systems are stars configurations. ISDN BRI bus will be the first phone system to operate on a bus. In datacom language, the center of a star is called the hub. The advantage of a star is that it is easy to isolate a problem node. However, if the central node fails, the entire network fails. The star network we're all most familiar with is our local telephone exchange. At the center (the hub) rests the central office. Spanning out in a star are the lines going to the individual workstations (telephones) in peoples' houses and offices. 2. Advanced telecommunications for the industrially less advanced regions of the European Community.

STAR COUPLER A device that couples multiple fibers at a central point and distributes the signal from one fiber into all others simultaneously.

STAR NETWORK A computer network with peripheral nodes all connected to one or more computers at a centrally located facility.

STAR QUADDED CABLE Spiral-four cable. See STAR NETWORK.

STARCONTROLLER Farallon's controller allowing users to build Apple Macintosh LocalTalk networks in star configurations.

STARLAN A local area network developed by AT&T which uses twisted pair telephone wires in a star configuration. StarLan is AT&T's proprietary CSMA/CD product line, and includes a network operating system and Network Interface Cards (NICs). The original StarLan transmitted data at 1Mbps using the CSMA/CD access method, over unshielded twisted pair; it now offers standard 10Mbps CSMA/CD (also known as Ethernet) capabilities. It is compatible with AT&T's Premises Distribution System, a large cabling system. StarLan connects to the Information Systems Network, a larger data communications switching system for high-speed terminal-to-host and host-to-host connectivity. StarLan software provides transparency and ease of use to the end-user through the AT&T menu program. AT&T is based in Bridgewater, NJ.

START BIT In asynchronous data communications, characters are sent at arbitrary intervals, i.e. when the operator hits a key. In order for the computer to make heads or tails of what's coming in, each character starts its transmission with a Start Bit. This way, if the first bit of the character to be transmitted is a 0, the fact of receiving a Start Bit (always a 1) tips off the computer that the next bit is part of a transmitted character and not just part of the inter-character gap. See STOP BIT.

START ELEMENT 1. The start pulse of a transmission character. It is used for synchronization of the following bits in a serial transmission process. 2. One of the input or output points in a communications system. This would include a telephone set, a data terminal, a computer communications port.

START OF HEADING SOH. A control character used in data communications that designates the beginning of the message header.

START OF HEADING CHARACTER SOH. A transmission control character used as the first character of a message heading.

START OF MESSAGE SOM. A control character used in data communications that designates the beginning of the message.

START OF TEXT STX. A control character used in data communications that designates the beginning of the information being transmitted.

START STOP TRANSMISSION The technique of asynchronous data transmission wherein each character is comprised of a start element at its beginning and a stop element at its end. Start-stop elements allow the receiving device to determine where the transmitted bits for one character ends and the next begins.

STAT MUX Informal for STATistical MUltipleXor.

STAT V Trademark for MICOM's series of combined statistical multiplexor and APV products.

STATE MACHINE PROGRAMMING To control multiple telephone lines in a single voice processing program, a new program structure is required. Dialogic calls this technique state machine programming. Computer Science called state machines "Deterministic Finite State Automata."

STATE PUBLIC SERVICE COMMISSION PSC. The State legislative body responsible for among other things, regulating the operation of telephone companies and other persons involved in the furnishing of telephone service. Some states' PSCs are called Public Utilities Commissions. See the next definition.

STATE UTILITY COMMISSIONS Each state has a utility commission responsible for the regulation of telephone service provided wholly within that state. Regulation extends to introduction of new services, their prices, who will provide them, as well as discontinuance of existing services.

STATEMENT 1. In computer programming languages, a language construct that represents a set of declarations or a step in a sequence of actions. 2. In computer programming, a meaningful expression or generalized instruction represented in a source language.

STATIC Interference caused by natural electric disturbances in the atmosphere, in your office, in your home. Static electricity can play havoc with telephone systems. Properly grounding your phone system to a true cold water pipe (not one that connects to a PVC plastic piper) is the most minimal protection.

STATIC OBJECT Information that has been pasted into a document. Unlike embedded or "linked" objects, static objects cannot be changed from within the document. The only way you can change a static object is to delete it from the document, change it in the application used to create it, and paste it into the document again.

STATIC POSITIONING Location determination when the GPS (Global

Positioning System) receiver's antenna is presumed to be stationary in the earth. This allows the use of various averaging techniques that improve the accuracy of figuring where you are by factors by over 1000.

STATIC RAM Static Random Access Memory chips do not require a refresh cycle like Dynamic RAM chips and thus can be accessed well over twice as quickly. The system must have power present to maintain the data being held in SRAM. Static RAM chips cost more than Dynamic RAM chips, also called D-RAM.

STATION A dumb word for a telephone. Also called an instrument, or a telephone instrument. An extension station is one connected "behind" a PBX or key system. In other words, the PBX or key system is between the station and the telephone central office. We tried to remove the word "station" from this dictionary, but failed. We suspect the word comes from the very old days when the telephone industry was regulated by the Interstate Commerce Commission, (the ICC) which also regulated the railroad industry.

STATION ADAPTERS Cables and interface assemblies for connecting Dialogic network interface and switching products to telephones or analog telephone lines.

STATION APPARATUS The equipment which is installed on the customer's premises, including phones, ancillary electronics and small hardware.

STATION AUXILIARY POWER SUPPLY This device is used to provide power to an electronic phone that is connected more than 300 meters (or 1,000 feet) or so away from the Key Service Unit.

STATION BATTERY A separate power source which provides the necessary DC power to drive a telephone system. Individual telephones are usually powered by a central source, i.e. their PBX or central office. The batteries may also power radio and telephone equipment as well as provide emergency lighting and controls for equipment. See BATTERY.

STATION BUSY LAMPS Lamps located on a station instrument, providing visual indication of each busy phone in the system. Busy Lamp Fields (BLFs) often come on key systems and sometimes on smaller PBXs. They're very handy.

STATION BUSY OVERRIDE Preselected phones have the privilege and ability to preempt busy circuits and override a private conversation.

STATION CALL TRANSFER A phone user can transfer incoming and outgoing calls to another phone without attendant assistance.

STATION CAMP-ON Phones can camp-on to a busy extension. The camped-on phone will be notified of the camp-on by a special beep signal. The person at the other end may or may not hear the signal.

STATION CLOCK The principal clock or alternative clock located at a particular station providing the timing reference for all major telecommunications functions at that station. A station clock may also be used to provide timing or frequency signals to other equipment.

STATION CODE The final four digits of a standard seven or 10 digit telephone number.

STATION DIRECT STATION SELECTION The phone user places a call to an extension within the PBX by pushing a single pushbutton on his phone.

STATION EQUIPMENT Telephone instruments and associated equipment furnished to subscribers. We suspect that the word "station" came from early telephone industry which was regulated by the same government agency which regulated the railroad business.

STATION HUNTING This feature allows a calling phone which places a call to a busy phone to proceed to the next idle phone in the hunt group. This jump is done automatically. See also ROTARY HUNT, which is the same thing for trunks.

STATION KEEPING The process on board a satellite for keeping it at its assigned longitude and inclination.

STATION LOAD The total power requirements of the integrated station facilities.

STATION MESSAGE DETAIL RECORDING Now refers to the RS-232-C "port" or plug found on the back of most modern PBXs and some larger key systems. See CALL ACCOUNTING SYSTEM and CALL DETAIL RECORDING.

STATION MESSAGE REGISTERS Message unit information centrally recorded on a per-station basis for each completed outgoing call.

STATION MESSAGE WAITING Special light on a phone to alert hotel/motel guests of messages waiting at the front desk.

STATION MONITORING Selected phones can monitor (i.e. listen in on) any other phones in the system.

STATION OVERRIDE SECURITY Designated phones can be shielded against executive busy override (presumably other executives).

STATION PROTECTOR A gas discharge, carbon block or other device that short circuits harmful voltages to ground in the event of lightning strikes on the phone line.

STATION REARRANGEMENT AND CHANGE Allows a user to move phones, change the features and/or restrictions assigned to phones and administer features associated with telephones.

STATION REVIEW A study of how people in an organization use the telephones and what communications needs are not being satisfied.

STATION RINGER CUTOFF Allows the ringer on the telephone to be turned off. Not always a good idea, since calls may still come in for that phone, but no one may pick them up because they don't hear it ring.

STATION TO STATION CALL A directly dialed call. No operator is used. Most calls are now directly dialed. Some long distance companies don't even have operators to help complete calls. AT&T still does.

STATION TONE RINGING Electronic tone ringer that replaces the bell.

STATION TRANSFER SECURITY If trunk call is transferred from one phone to another, and the second phone does not answer within a predetermined time, the trunk call will automatically go to the attendant.

STATION VISUAL SIGNALING Lamp on a phone which indicates flashing incoming, steady busy, and "wink" hold visual conditions associated with that phone.

STATIONARY ORBIT An orbit, any point on which has a period equal to the average rotational period of the Earth, is called a synchronous orbit. If the orbit is also circular and equatorial, it is called a stationary or geostationary orbit.

STATISTICAL MULTIPLEXING A way of multiplexing a channel so that many data communications conversations may fit on the channel simultaneously. In statistical multiplexing a channel is only assigned to communicating devices when they actually have data to send or receive. See also FAST PACKET MULTIPLEXING.

STATISTICS Numbers looking for an argument. The best statistics are those for which you are the sole source or those which are repeated sufficiently often for them to become an integral part of society's conventional wisdom.

STATISTICS PORT In network management systems, interface for reporting events and status.

STATMUX A statistical multiplexer. See STATISTICAL MULTIPLEXING.

STATUS INFORMATION Information about the logical state of a piece of equipment.

STATUS SIGNAL UNIT Signal unit of CCS used to initiate transmission on a link or to recover from loss of transmission.

STATUTE MILE A unit of distance equal to 1.609 km, 0.869 nmi, or 5,280 ft.

STC Society of Telecommunications Consultants. A professional society for telecommunications consultants. They endeavor to set standards of behavior for the consulting community.

STD Subscriber Trunk Dialing. An non-North American term for direct distance dialing, i.e. dialing long distance calls directly without an operator's assistance.

STDM Statistical Time Division Multiplexer. STDMs are TDMs with an added microprocessor that provides more intelligent data flow control and enhanced functionality, such as error control and more sophisticated user diagnostics. The major difference between TDMs and STDMs is that stat muxes dynamically allocate time slots on the link to inputting devices on an as-needed basis (rather than in round-robin fashion where all devices are polled in preordained order). Therefore, there is no idle time on the link because a device does not have information to send. Unlike TDMs, STDMs have buffers for holding data from attached devices. They can handle a combined input speed (aggregate speed) that exceeds the speed of the communications link.

STE Section Terminating Equipment. Network elements which perform section functions such as facility performance monitoring. The section is the portion of a transmission facility between a lightwave terminal and a line repeater or between two line repeaters. An AT&T SONET definition.

STEADY-STATE CONDITION 1. In a communication circuit, a condition in which some specified characteristic of a condition, such as value, rate, periodicity, or amplitude, exhibits only negligible change over an arbitrarily long period of time. 2. In an electrical circuit, a condition, occurring after all initial transients or fluctuating conditions have damped out, in which currents, voltages, or fields remain essentially constant or oscillate uniformly without changes in characteristics such as amplitude, frequency, or wave shape. 3. In fiber optics, synonym for equilibrium mode power distribution.

STENTOR A new name for the long distance network of nine regional Canadian phone companies. Inspiration for the name came from the Greek poet Homer. He had immortalized Stentor, a warrior in the Trojan war, "whose voice was as powerful as the voices of 50 other men." And so the adjective "stentorian" survived to be applied to someone with a powerful voice, often a politician.

STEP 1. One movement of an electromechanical switch which typically corresponds to one impulse from a rotary dial or one impulse from a touch tone phone which has been converted to a rotary dial. 2. Wang's name for its telephony link is STEP, which stands for Speech and Telephony Environment for Programmers.

STEP BY STEP SXS. An automatic dial-telephone system in which calls go through the switching equipment by a succession of switches that move a step at a time, from stage to stage, each step being made in response to the dialing of a number. SXS is electromechanical switching. It was invented in the 1920s.

STEP CALL The phone user can, upon finding that the called phone is busy, call an idle nearby phone by merely dialing an additional digit.

STEP DOWN 1. Reduce the voltage. 2. A feature of fax machines that makes them drop their transmission speed when the quality of the phone lines they are transmitting over begins to deteriorate. Dropping the transmission speed is the major way of getting the faxes through on "dirty" lines. All Group III fax machines have "step-down" as a built in feature, or should have.

STEP DOWN TRANSFORMER A transformer wound to give a lower voltage on the secondary side than that impressed on the primary. The current, however, will be stepped up. A step down (often spelled step-down) transformer has more primary than secondary turns.

STEP INDEX FIBER An optical fiber with a core having a uniform refractive index.

STEP INDEX PROFILE For an optical fiber, a refractive index profile characterized by a uniform refractive index within the core and a sharp decrease in refractive index at the core-cladding interface.

STEP UP TRANSFORMER A transformer wound to give a higher voltage on the secondary side than that impressed on the primary. The current, however, will be stepped down. It has fewer primary than secondary turns.

STEPPED INDEX Referring to a type of optical fiber which exhibits a uniform refractive index at the core and a sharp decrease in the refractive index at the core-cladding interface.

STEREOPHONIC CROSSTALK An undesired signal occurring in the main channel from modulation of the stereophonic channel or that occurring in the stereophonic channel from modulation of the main channel.

STEREOPHONIC SOUND SUBCARRIER A subcarrier within the FM broadcast baseband used for transmitting signals for stereophonic sound reception of the main broadcast program service.

STEREOPHONIC SOUND SUBCHANNEL The band of frequencies from 23 kHz to 99 kHz containing sound subcarriers and their associated sidebands.

STG An imaging term. Scale To Gray. STG uses gray pixels to fill in jagged edges of document images. STG improves readability. According to a study commissioner by Cornerstone and done by Dr. Jim Sheedy, the ability to read STG images was improved between 4% and 19%, depending on the resolution, and symptoms such as headaches, tired back, blurred vision were cut way down.

STFS Standard Time and Frequency Signal.

STICKY A sticky shift key lets you access the shifted functions (such as capital A) by pressing the shift key first and then pressing the second key. Sticky keys may stay down for a second or two. Or you may have to hit them again to unstick them — somewhat like the CapsLock key.

STIMULATED EMISSION Radiation emitted when the internal energy of a quantum mechanical system drops from an excited level to a lower level when induced by the presence of radiant energy at the same frequency. An example is the radiation from an injection laser diode above lasing threshold.

STL 1. Standard Telegraph Level. 2. Studio-To-Transmitter link — typically through the air microwave.

STM Synchronous Transfer Mode. A transport and switching method that depends on information occurring in regular and fixed patterns with respect to a reference such as a frame pattern. A time-division multiplex-and-switching technique to be used across the user's network interface for a broadband ISDN. It gives each user up to 50 million bits per second simultaneously — regardless of the number of users.

STN 1. Statens Telenamd (Swedish National Telecommunications Council). 2. Super Twist Nematic is a passive matrix technology now used in screens in some laptop computers. In a passive matrix color screen the current travels along transparent electrodes printed on the glass screen. These electrodes are driven by transistors placed around the edges of the display. Horizontal and vertical electrodes form a grid-like matrix, with a pixel at every intersection. A major problem with passive technology arises when current is lost in crosstalk as the electrodes criss-cross each other. This crossing over effect greatly diminishes overall display quality.

STOP BIT The Stop Bit is an interval at the end of each Asynchronous Character that allows the receiving computer to pause before the start of the next character. The Stop Bit is always a 0. See START BIT.

STOP ELEMENT The last element of a character in asynchronous serial transmission, used to ensure recognition of the next start element.

STOP/START TRANSMISSION A method of transmission in which a group of bits are preceded by a start bit and followed by a stop bit. Also called asynchronous transmission. See ASYNCHRONOUS.

STOP-RECORD SIGNAL In facsimile systems, a signal used for stopping the process of converting the electrical signal to an image on the record sheet.

STORAGE UNIT A device in which information can be recorded and retained for later retrieval and use.

STORE AND FORWARD In communications systems, when a message is transmitted to some intermediate relay point and stored temporarily. Later the message is sent the rest of the way. Not very convenient for voice conversations, but useful for telex type, and other one-way transmission of messages. Telephone answering machines, as well as voice mailboxes are considered forms of Store and Forward message switching.

STORED PROCEDURES Compiled code on a database server that reduces the processing burden on clients.

STORED-PROGRAM COMPUTER A computer controlled by internally stored instructions, that can synthesize and store instructions, and that can subsequently execute those instructions. See also STORED PROGRAM CONTROL.

STORED PROGRAM CONTROL SPC. The routing of a phone call through a switching matrix is handled by a program stored in a computer-like device, which may well be a special-purpose computer. Before SPC switches came along, the rotary dialing of the phone caused the elements of the switch to directly "step" through their dialing path. This was slow and cumbersome, since dialing can be slow. Also subscribers can abort half way (they made a mistake) and this can mess up the switch's efficiency. Thus the move to stored program control switches was very significant. These days virtually all switches as stored program control. Nothing happens in the switching matrix until the stored program control receives all the dialing digits and decides what to do with them.

STP 1. Shielded Twisted Pair. Twisted pair (TP) wiring with a metal sheath around it to prevent interference. 2. Signal Transfer Point. The packet switch in the nation's emerging Common Channel Interoffice Signaling (CCIS) system. The CCIS is a packet switched network operating at 4800 bits per second. CCIS replaces both SF (Single Frequency) and MF (Multi-frequency) by converting dialed digits to data messages. It will run at 56,000 bps with the introduction of Signaling System 7. See SIGNALING SYSTEM 7.

STS Synchronous Transport Signal. A SONET electrical signal rate. See STS-1.

STS-1 Synchronous transport signal level 1, an electrical signal that is converted to or from Sonet's optically based signal; equivalent to the OC-1 signal of 51.84 Mbps. STS-1 was designed to allow mapping in a DS3 channel of 454 Mbps.

STRAIGHT-THROUGH When wiring up phone and some data extensions, there are basically two ways of doing it — straight-through and crossover. Straight-through occurs when you wire both ends identically so the signals pass straight through. This is typically done with patch panels and modular EIA adapters. Crossover wiring has a reverse order of wiring. As an example, let's take a four conductor, RJ-11. In a crosscover wiring (e.g. an RJ-11 phone extension cord), conductor 1 would be connected to hole 1 on one plug and one 4 on the other end. Conductor 2 would be connected to 4. And 3 would be connected to hole 2.

STRAIGHT-TIP CONNECTOR ST Connector. An optical fiber connector used to join single fibers together at interconnects or to connect them to optical cross connects.

STRAIGHTFORWARD OUTWARD COMPLETION Operator can place an outgoing call for phone user. Also called "Through Supervision."

STRAND A single uninsulated wire.

STRAND LAY The distance of advance of one strand of a spirally stranded conductor, in one turn, measured axially.

STRANDED CONDUCTOR A conductor composed of groups of wires twisted together.

STRANDED COPPER A type of electrical wire conductor comprised of multiple copper wires twisted together forming a single conductor and then covered with an insulating jacket.

STRANDED FIBER CABLE A fiber cable in which individual optical fibers are twisted around strength members. Both campus and building versions are used. The campus version, unlike the one for buildings, is environmentally protected for outside use.

STRAY CURRENT Current through a path other than the intended path. See also SPURIOUS EMISSION.

STREAM An SCSA term. One of 16 physical data lines making up the SCbus or SCxbus Data Bus.

STREAMER Streaming tape drive.

STREAMING TAPE BACKUP A device to back up files and programs. A streaming tape backup looks very much like a large audio cassette. It records data sequentially.

STREAMING TAPE DRIVE A magnetic tape unit especially designed to make a nonstop dump or restore magnetic disks without stopping at interblock gaps.

STREAMS An architecture introduced with Unix System V, Release 3.2 that provides for flexible and layered communication path between processes (programs) and device drivers. Many companies market applications and devices that can integrate through Streams protocols.

STREETSWEEPER A heavy machine gun. This word crept into a story the Wall Street Journal ran on cellular fraud. When the Feds rang a cellular phone store as a sting operation, one customer offered to trade his steetsweeper in on a phone. That's how dependent Detroit's drug-traffickers have become on cellular phones and beepers.

STREET PRICE The real or typical selling price of computers, hardware, and software. Most laptop and desktop computers sell for about 25 percent below list price. Software may be discounted even more.

STREET TALK The Banyan-developed protocol for discovering and maintaining resource information distributed among the servers connected to Banyan's VINES network operating system. Also known as a global naming service.

STRING A sequence of elements of the same type, such as characters, considered as a unit (a whole) by a computer. A data structure composed of a sequence of characters, usually in human-readable text.

STROBE An electrical pulse used to call for the transfer of information.

STROKE A straight line or arc that is used as a segment of a graphic character.

STROKE EDGE An imaging and OCR term. In character recognition, the line of discontinuity between a side of a stroke and the background, obtained by averaging, over the length of the stroke, the irregularities resulting from the printing and detecting processes.

STROKE SPEED In facsimile systems, the number of times per minute that a fixed line perpendicular to the direction of scanning is crossed in one direction by a scanning or recording spot. In most conventional mechanical systems, this is equivalent to drum speed. In systems in which the picture signal is used while scanning in both directions, the stroke speed is twice the above figure.

STROKE WIDTH In character recognition, the distance measured perpendicularly to the stroke centerline between the two stroke edges.

STROWGER, ARMOND The man who invented the telephone dial and the earliest automatic telephone switch as a method of allowing the user to complete calls without using the Operator. In Kansas City in the late 1800's, 'Ol Armond was an undertaker who wasn't getting much business. That's because the girlfriend of a rival undertaker was a telephone operator, and when she got a call asking for the local undertaker, she forwarded the calls to her boyfriend. This story may or may not be apocryphal. But it's a great story.

STRUCTURED QUERY LANGUAGE SQL. A relational database language (ANSI Standard) that consists of a set of facililties for defining, manipulating and controlling data.

STRUCTURED PROGRAMMING A technique for organizing and coding (computer) programs in which a heirarchy of modules is used, each having a single entry and a single exit point, and in which control is passed downward through the structure without unconditional branches to higher levels of the structure. Three types of control flow are used: sequential, test, and iteration.

STRUCTURED WIRING As data flows sped up in recent years, so the erstwhile idea of wiring up a building with plain old analog voice telephone wire became increasingly not viable. The idea then came up of defining wiring standards and schemes so that a user could feel comfortable about choosing a complete solution for wiring phones, workstations, PCs and other communicating devices throughout the building, the campus, the network, the company. Consistency of design, layout and logic are the keys to structured wiring systems. A structured cabling system will improve performance in five ways, according to Anixter, a leading supplier of structured wiring systems:

1. It eases network segmentation, the job of dividing the network into pieces to isolate and minimize traffic, and thus congestion.

2. It ensures that proper physical requirements, such as distance, capacitance, and attenuation are met.

3. It means adds, moves, and changes are easy to make without expensive and cumbersome rewiring.

4. It radically eases problem detection and isolation.

5. It allows for intelligent, easy and computerized tracking and documentation.

"Structure" brings order to what has often been an afterthought — wiring. The main pieces of a structured wiring system are:

1. Drop cable. The cable that runs from the computer to a network outlet.

2. Cable run. The cable that runs from the outlet to the wiring closet.

3. Patch panel. A board that collects all the cable runs in one place and "patches" them to different parts of the wiring concentrator. Network managers (users or their secretaries, it's that simple) change the LAN layout by plugging and unplugging "patch cables" between the patch panel and the wiring concentrators. No rewiring is necessary to move one user from one network segment to another.

4. Wiring concentrator. It makes the network connections. Some wiring concentrators are dumb, making only physical connections between network segments. Others are intelligent, making networking decisions and providing network diagnostics. A wiring concentrator can have bridges and routers that divide the network into segments. It can have the hardware necessary to change from one media, say twisted pair, to another, say fiber optic. And it can contain the hardware to change from one network type to another, say from Ethernet to Token Ring.

Here is a glossary of structured wiring words, with thanks to Anixter.

Access Method — The method of "communicating" on the wire. Examples include Ethernet, Token Ring, AppleTalk, AS400 and 3270.

Cable Type (Media) — The type of cable used in the system. Examples are coaxial, UTP, STP and fiber. Factors including cost, connectivty and bandwidth are important in determining cable type.

Data Speeds — Different interconnect products (cables and connectors) are capable of supporting different data rates. For instance, Level 3 cable supports data rates up to 10 Mbps. (See LEVEL).

Environment — Where the structured wiring system is found. The large majority of systems are located in office environments as opposed to factory or industrial environments.

Life Cycle — How long the cable is physically anticipated to be in place.

NEWTON'S TELECOM DICTIONARY

For example, if a customer intends to be in a large office for 10 years, fiber installation may be considered.

Methodology — The physical means of getting the wiring system to the user (its distribution path). Examples include modular furniture, surface mounts, fixed wall, recessed wall, raised floor and undercarpet wiring.

Topology — The way the cable is physically laid out or configured. Examples include star, ring, daisy chain and backbone.

STS Synchronous Transport Signal

STS-1 Synchronous Transport Signal Level - 1. The basic rate (51.840 Mbps) and associated byte interleaved multiplex structure that all Sonet products/offerings are based (i.e.,n times the STS-1 rate).

STS-N Synchronous Transport Signal level N. A signal obtained by interleaving N STS-1 signals together. A SONET term.

STU Secure Telephone Unit.

STUDIO-TO-TRANSMITTER LINK STL. Any communication link used for transmission of broadcast material from a studio to the transmitter. It's typically microwave radio but it may also be a conventional landline link.

STUNT BOX A device to 1. control the nonprinting functions of a teletypewriter terminal, such as a carriage return and line feed and 2. a device to recognize line control characters.

STYLUS A pen-shaped instrument that is used to enter text, draw images, or point to choices on a computer desktop.

SUB Substitute Character. A control character used in the place of a character that has been found to be invalid or in error.

SUBADDRESSING A name for an ISDN service which enables many different types of terminals — phones, fax machines, PCs, etc. — to be connected to the ISDN user interface and uniquely identified during a call request. See ISDN.

SUBCARRIER A carrier which modulates a main carrier so that two different modulating signals can be transmitted simultaneously, one on the main carrier and one on the subcarrier.

SUBMARINING Same as CURSOR SUBMARINING. When you drag your cursor across a screen and the cursor disappears as you move it. That's called Cursor Submarining. It happens most on LCD screens because they change slowly — much slower than CRTs or VDTs (glass screens).

SUBNETWORK A token ring LAN that is used to serve the communication needs of a department. Subnetworks are normally connected to token ring backbones via token ring bridges or routers so that they can communicate with other subnetworks via the backbone or with computers directly connected to the backbone.

SUBROUTINE A functionally isolated progam or sequence of instructions for a specific function that is often called by a program. A piece of software that performs a useful function that will be needed often. The code for the subroutine is stored on disk (like a letter, etc.) and dropped into a larger program as needed. A nicely-written subroutine saves you "re-inventing the wheel" and allows you to re-use your code in many programs.

SUBSCRIBER A person or company who has telephone service provided by a phone company. In other industries, subscribers are called customers. Some telephone companies are beginning to call their subscribers customers. Thank goodness.

SUBSCRIBER LINE The telephone line connecting the local telco central office to the subscriber's telephone instrument or telephone system.

SUBSCRIBER LINE CHARGE A monthly charge on subscribers created by the Federal Communications Commission and paid to the local telephone company. The logic for this charge has something to do with reimbursing the local phone companies for some costs which it is not recovering elsewhere. In reality, it's just another rate increase.

SUBSCRIBER LOOP The circuit that connects the telephone company's central office to the demarcation point on the customer's premises. The circuit is most likely a pair of wires. But it could be three wires if some external signaling is being used. It could also be four wires if the circuit was a four-wire full duplex leased line.

SUBSCRIBER LOOP CARRIER See SLC-96.

SUBSCRIBER NUMBER The number that permits a user to reach a subscriber in the same local network or numbering area (same as Directory Number or DN).

SUBSCRIBER PLANT FACTOR A planning factor used by common carriers to allocate investment in phone equipment, subscriber lines and the nontraffic sensitive portion of the central office equipment.

SUBSCRIBER'S DROP Wire which runs from a cable terminal or distribution point to the subscriber's premises.

SUBSET A contraction for Subscriber Set, or telephone set.

SUBSTATION An additional phone which has been established as an extension to the main phone or primary line.

SUBSTITUTION A word used in voice recognition to mean a type of error that occurs when a word within the active vocabulary is spoken correctly but classified as another word within the vocabulary. This error is usually dealt with during a verification stage in an application, i.e. " you said, 1,2,3...correct?"

SUBVOICE-GRADE CHANNEL A communications channel of bandwidth narrower than a standard 3Hz voice line. A subvoice-grade

NEWTON'S TELECOM DICTIONARY

channel is usually used for slow data transmission such as teletype or telemetry.

SUITE A collection. A suite of software tools is a collection of software tools.

SUMMARY BILLING New York Telephone will give you one monthly consolidated phone bill — no matter how many New York Telephone number accounts you have in your billing area.

SUMMATION CHECK A check based on the formation of the sum of the digits of a numeral. The sum of the individual digits is usually compared with a previously computed value.

SUN TRANSIT OUTRAGE Satellite circuit outrage caused by direct radiation of the sun's rays on an earth station receiving antenna.

SUNOS SunOS is Sun Microsystems' implementation of UNIX.

SUNVIEW SunView is Sum Microsystems' kernel-based window system.

SUPER SPEED CALLING A feature of Northern Telecom's DMS line of central offices. Subscribers can use a four-letter dialable name, preceded by an octothorpe (#), to speed-call up to 14 digits. For example, "#WORK" or "#HOME" could be used as a code for a longer number. Dialing is faster, and subscribers have the added convenience of using easier-to-remember names instead of forgettable numbers on their speed calling list. The list size can be set by the telephone operating company at initial set-up on a per-system basis. Northern's default is 12 names per list.

SUPERCOMPUTING A term applied to a class of high-speed computers employing advanced technologies such as simplified instruction sets, wide data paths and pipelining.

SUPERCONDUCTORS Superconductors are materials which have no resistance to the flow of electricity. They are widely believed to have great potential for dramatically faster telecommunications switches and computers. In the past, the superconducting state — zero resistance to the flow of electricity — could be achieved only by cooling certain metal allows to temperatures of near absolute zero, or about 460 degrees below zero. Starting in 1986, researchers discovered that ceramic materials could reach superconductivity at temperatures as high as 235 degrees below zero.

SUPERDRIVE The name for Apple's 1.44 Mb floppy that can read and write MS-DOS formatted floppies and Mac formatted disks. DOS floppies require Apple File Exchange or a third party product to read the DOS format.

SUPERGROUP Sixty voice channels. In more technical terms: the assembly of five 12-channel groups occupying adjacent bands in the spectrum for the purpose of simultaneous modulation or demodulation.

SUPERHETERODYNE A type of radio receiver operating on the heterodyne or beat principle. See HETERODYNE.

SUPERHOUSE The National Society of Home Builders has registered SmartHouse. BellSouth has trademarked SuperHouse. And GTE has registered SmartPark. One day, fiber optic will snake to everyone's house, bringing the potential of immense information services. Until that day comes they'll be lots of interesting demonstrations at distant trade shows.

SUPERIMPOSED RINGING A way of stopping party line phone users from hearing each other's ring by superimposing a DC (direct current) voltage over the ringing signal and using it to alert a vacuum tube or semiconductor device in only the phone instrument that we want to ring. See also SUPERPOSED RINGING.

SUPERPATH New York and New England Telephone's Superpath services offer dedicated end-to-end digital transmissions at 1.544 Mbps (T-1) or 44.736 Mbps (T-3).

SUPERPOSED CIRCUIT An additional channel obtained from one or more circuits, normally provided for other channels, in such a manner that all the channels can be used simultaneously without mutual interference.

SUPERPOSED RINGING Party-line telephone ringing in which a combination of alternating and direct currents is used, the objective being to only ring the bell in the phone of the one whose call is coming in. See also SUPERIMPOSED RINGING for a better explanation.

SUPERTRUNK A cable that carries several video channels between facilities of a cable television company. A trunk between the master and the hub headends in a hub CATV system.

SUPERVISED TRANSFER A call transfer made by an automatic device such as voice response unit which attempts to determine the result of the transfer — answered, busy, ring no answer — by analyzing call progress tones on the time.

SUPERVISION Supervision of a phone call is detecting when a called party has picked up his phone and when that party has hung up. Supervision is used primarily for billing purposes. Not all long distance carriers have supervision capability. It depends on how "equal accessed" they have chosen to be. See ANSWER SUPERVISION, SOFTWARE SUPERVISION and SIGNALING SYSTEM 7.

SUPERVISORY CALL This service feature allows the attendant, after connecting an incoming CO line or tie line call to the wanted phone, to continuously supervise the call in progress.

SUPERVISORY CONTROL Characters or signals which automatically actuate equipment or indicators at a remote terminal.

SUPERVISORY LAMP A lamp which shows the operator whether the person is speaking (off-hook) or is not speaking (on-hook). These days such lamps are called BUSY LAMP FIELDS. In some smaller key systems, all phones have them. Busy lamp fields are an operator's best friend.

SUPERVISORY PROGRAM 1. A program, usually part of an operating system, that controls the execution of other computer programs and regulates the flow of work in a data processing system. 2. A computer program that allocates computer component space and schedules computer events by task queueing and system interrupts. Control of the system is returned to the supervisory program frequently enough to ensure that demands on the system are met.

SUPERVISORY RELAY A relay which, during a call, is controlled by the transmitter current supplied to a subscriber line to receive from the associated phone signals that control the actions of operators or switching mechanisms.

SUPERVISORY ROUTINE A routine that allocates computer component space and schedules computer events by task queueing and system interrupts. Control of the system is returned to the supervisory program frequently enough to ensure that demands on the system are met.

SUPERVISORY SIGNAL 1. A signal which indicates whether a circuit is in use, or not in use, and which indicates change in use, and/or 2. A signal used to indicate the various operating states of circuit combinations.

SUPPLEMENTARY SERVICE A service that provides the network user with additional capabilities over and above elementary call control. An ISDN term.

SUPPORT HARDWARE The racks, clamps, cabinets, brackets, trays, and other equipment that provide the physical means to hold the transmission media and connecting hardware. An AT&T definition.

SUPPRESSED CARRIER SINGLE-SIDEBAND EMISSION A single-sideband emission in which the carrier is virtually suppressed and not intended to be used for demodulation.

SUPPRESSED CARRIER TRANSMISSION A transmission technique in which only the sidebands (one or both) are transmitted and the main carrier is not transmitted and thus not used.

SUPPRESSORS, ECHO Echo is controlled in long distance circuits with devices called echo suppressors. These devices automatically insert loss in the return path of a four-wire circuit. All long distance circuits are four-wire — two wires for each of the two paths (receiving and transmitting). The echo suppressor jumps back and forth between the two transmission paths. Properly adjusted, an echo suppressor puts only sufficient loss in a circuit so a listener can interrupt the talker. With very long circuits — 22,300 miles — in satellites, a better way is needed. They're called echo cancellers.

SURCHARGE A charge imposed in accordance with the Commission's Access Reconsideration decision in CC Docket 78-72, Phase 1, FCC 83-356. released August 22, 1983 and updated too many times since. The monthly charge is about $2.00 and is going up to $3.50. This charge is said to compensate the local phone company for long distance commissions (called settlements and separations) lost and now replaced with per minute access charges.

SURFACE MOUNT With surface mount technology, Components sit on the surface of printed circuit boards and are soldered to conductive pads. In the "thru-the-hole" process, component leads are placed through holes in the boards and are sent through wave soldering for attachment. Surface mount technology is more cost-effective, as it allows for denser packaging on the board and components can be mounted on both sides of the surface.

SURFACE OUTLET A Communications Outlet (modular jack) that is installed on the surface of the mounting location. The premises wire serving such an outlet may or may not be concealed behind the mounting surface.

SURFACE WAVE A wave that is guided along the interface between two different media or by a refractive index gradient. The field components of the wave diminish with distance from the interface. Optical energy is not converted from the surface wave field to another form of energy and the wave does not have a component directed normal to the interface surface. In optical fiber transmission, evanescent waves are surface waves. In radio transmission, ground waves are surface waves that propagate close to the surface of the Earth, the Earth having one refractive index and the atmosphere another, thus constituting an inerface surface.

SURGE A sudden voltage rise and fall in an electrical circuit.

SURGE PROTECTOR A device which plugs between the phone system and the commercial AC power outlet. It is designed to protect the phone system from high voltage spikes (also called surges) which might damage the phone system. When a surge occurs on the power line, the surge protector sends the overload to ground. How fast it sends it to ground is a subject that could fill a book. The type of surge protector that you buy will be determined mostly by the speed you need to protect your equipment.

SURGES The increased flow of current through an electrical device brought about by an instantaneous change in its resistance or impedance.

SURVIVABILITY A property of a system, subsystem, equipment, process, or procedure that provides a defined degree of assurance that the device or system will continue to work during and after a natural or man-made disturbance; e.g. nuclear attack. This term must be qualified by specifying the range of conditions over which the entity will survive, the minimum acceptable level or post-disturbance functionality, and the maximum acceptable outage duration.

SUSAN A nice name for a wife. Everyone should have such a good one. She is the mother of my two children, Claire and Michael.

SUSCEPTIVENESS In telephone systems, the tendency of circuits to pick up noise and low frequency induction from power systems. It depends on telephone circuit balance, transpositions, wiring spacing, and isolation from ground.

SUSPENDED CUSTOMER An MCI definition. An MCI customer who has requested service but has not yet been installed due to insufficient network capacity or some other operational/administrative constraint.

SVC Switched Virtual Circuit. A connection across a network. It is established on an as-needed basis and can provide connection to any other user in the network. The connection lasts only for the duration of the transfer. It is the datacom equivalent of a dialed phone call.

SVD Simultaneous Voice Data.

SWAP FILE Some operating systems and applications let you use more memory than what you have in RAM. They do this by pretending that part of your hard disk is RAM memory. They do this by creating a swap file on your hard disk and swapping memory back and forth. Some computer systems call this virtual memory. You need to be careful with swap files. Never turn your machine off when you have applications running. If you do you're likely to leave a huge swap on your hard disk, which you may not find (it's hidden) and which your system may not dispose of. To get back the space on your hard disk, you'll need to erase it separately.

SWEDAC Swedish Board for Technical Accreditation. They have established two standards, which effectively limit radiation emmissions, MPR1 and MPR2. These standards specify maximum values for both alternating electric fields and magnetic fields and provide monitor manufacturers with guidelines in creating low emission monitors. There is, as yet, no definite proof of harm from normal computers monitors. But the argument goes that they weren't so sure about nicotine 30 years ago.

SWEEP ACQUISTION A technique whereby the frequency of the local ocillator is slowly swept past the reference to assure that the pull-in range is reached.

SWHK Abbreviation for SWITCH HOOK. Originally referred to an actual hook on older phones that held the receiver, and sprang upward to close a switch and activate the phone when the receiver was picked up. Today the term refers to any of various buttons and plungers that are pressed down and released when the handset is put down (physically "hung up" in the old days) and picked up.

SWIM Slow, graceful, undesired movements of display elements, groups, or images about their mean position on a display surface, such as that of a monitor. Swim can be followed by the human eye, whereas jitters usually appears as a blur.

SWISS ARMY KNIFE The one tool to have when you can't have more than one. Be sure it has a normal screwdriver, a phillips head screwdriver and a pair of scissors. A corkscrew also is useful.

SWITCH A mechanical, electrical or electronic device which opens or closes circuits, completes or breaks an electrical path, or selects paths or circuits.

946

SWITCH BASED RESELLERS Switch-based resellers lease facilities from national carriers or large private line networks. They resell services provided over those facilities under their own name and provide sales, customer service, billing and technical support. Switch-based resellers own or lease their own switching equipment and, in some cases, own their transmission facilities. they typically provide originating service on a regional basis.

SWITCH BUSY HOUR The busy hour for a single switch.

SWITCH HOOK It is also called the Hook Switch. A switch hook or hook switch was originally an electrical "switch" connected to the "hook" on which the handset (or receiver) was placed when the telephone was not in use. The switch hook is now the little plunger at the top of most telephones which is pushed down when the handset is resting in its cradle (on-hook). When the handset is raised, the plunger pops up (the phone goes off-hook). Momentarily depressing the switch hook (under 0.8 of a second) can signal various services such as calling the attendant, conferencing or transferring calls.

In ISDN, the AT&T ISDN sets have several switchhooks; one for the handset, one for the speakerphone, a "virtual" switchhook, and if an adjunct is attached, an adjunct switchhook. If all switchhooks are "on-hook" or hung up, the ISDN set is on-hook. If any switchhook is "off-hook," then the ISDN set is off-hook. If more than one switchhook is off-hook, the ISDN set uses a complex algorithm to determine whether the handset, the speakerphone, or the adjunct has precedence (only one can be used at a time).

SWITCH HOOK FLASH A signaling technique whereby the signal is originated by momentarily depressing the switch hook. See SWITCH HOOK.

SWITCH OVER When a failure occurs in the equipment, a switch may occur to an alternative piece of equipment.

SWITCH ROOM The room in which you put phone equipment. Also called the Phone Room. (What else?) The Phone Room should be large, clean and should stay at roughly seventy degrees and 50% humidity. You, the customer, are responsible for the quality and condition of your phone room. The messier it is, the hotter it is, the dirtier it is, the poorer your phone system (and its technicians) will function.

SWITCH TRAIN In a telecom circuit (typically a step-by-step central office), the series of switching devices which a call moves through in sequence.

SWITCHBOARD The attendant position of a PBX. Most of them don't actually have "boards" (they were big), they have consoles (they're much smaller and they fit on desks). Switchboards are desks.

SWITCHBOARD CABLE A cable used within and between the central office main frames and the switchboard.

SWITCHED ACCESS A method of obtaining test access to telecommunications circuits by using electromechanical circuitry to switch test apparatus to the circuit.

SWITCHED CARRIER In data terms, physical line specification selection indicating a half duplex line in a bisync network.

SWITCHED CIRCUIT AUTOMATIC NETWORK SCAN. A service arrangement at certain Telco premises to interconnect private line telephone service channels of a switched service network provided to certain agencies of the federal Government.

SWITCHED CIRCUIT ORDERING AND TRACKING SYSTEM SCOTS. MCI's automated tracking and order processing system for Dial-Up products, IMTs, and the MCI switched network.

SWITCHED DIGITAL SERVICES APPLICATIONS FORUM See SDSAF.

SWITCHED LINE A circuit which is routed through a circuit switched network, such as the telephone or telex network.

SWITCHED LOOP In telephony, a circuit that automatically releases connection from a console or switchboard, once connection has been made, to the appropriate terminal. Loop buttons or jacks are used to answer incoming listed directory number calls, dial "O" internal calls, transfer requests , and intercepted calls. The attendant can handle only one call at a time.

SWITCHED LOOP OPERATION Each call requiring attendant assistance is automatically switched to one of several switched loops on an attendant position.

SWITCHED MULTI-MEGABIT DIGITAL SERVICE SMDS. A 1.544 Mbps public data service with an IEEE 802.6 standard user interface. It can support Ethernet, Token Ring and FDDI (OC-3c) LAN-to-LAN connections.

SWITCHED NETWORK See PSTN.

SWITCHED PRIVATE LINE NETWORK A network which results from combining point-to-point circuits with switches.

SWITCHED SERVICE NETWORK A private line network that uses scan and/or CCSA type common control switching.

SWITCHED TRANSPORT A name for telephone traffic between the local exchange carriers' Central Offices and an interexchange carrier's point of presence (POP). Switched transport is enerally provided on a monopoly basis as part of a LEC's network.

SWITCHED VIRTUAL CIRCUIT A call which is only established for the duration of a session and is then disconnected.

SWITCHHOOK See SWITCH HOOK.

SWITCHING Connecting the calling party to the called party. This may involve one or many physical switches.

SWITCHING ARRANGEMENT A circuit component which enables a Customer to establish a communications path between two phones on a network.

SWITCHING CENTERS There are four levels in the North American switching hierarchy run at AT&T. They are: Class 1 — Regional Center, Class 2 — Sectional Center, Class 3 — Primary Center, Class 4c — Toll Center and Class 4P — Toll Point. In addition, the local Bell operating companies run a fifth level in the hierarchy, called the Class 5 — End Office.

SWITCHING EQUIPMENT Premises equipment which performs the functions of establishing and releasing connections on a per call basis between two or more circuits, services or communications systems.

SWITCHLESS RESELLERS A switchless reseller buys long distance service in bulk from a long distance company, such as AT&T, and resells that service to smaller users. It typically gets its monthly bill on magnetic tape, then rebills the bulk service to its customers. A switchless reseller owns no communications facilities — switches or transmission. It has two "assets" — a computer program to rebill the tape and some sales skills to sell its services to end users. The profit it makes comes from the difference between what it pays the long distance company and what it is able to sell its services at. Switchless resellers are also called rebillers. It's not an easy business to be in, since you are selling a long distance company's services to compete against itself. See also AGGREGATOR.

SWITCHWAY New York and New England Telephone's Switchway is switched 56 Kbps service. Switchway lets you dial up and transmit data at up to 56,000 bits per second. It is a totally digital service — from one end to the other. Think of it as a dial-up service for computers. It's billed like a voice line — a monthly charge plus so much per minute. Switchway lines are assigned normal telephone numbers. SWITCHWAY lines require either a 2-wire or 4-wire non-loaded metallic connection. You can dial in and around New York City using Switchway. You can call further across the country by using Switchway to connect to long distance companies, like AT&T, MCI and Sprint. Switchway was constructed as a separate data network overlaid on top of the normal voice network. It is thus far more expensive to use than a voice call, though it is largely carried digitally.

SX A family of excellent PBXs made by Mitel of Kanata, Ontario Canada. There's the analog SX-10, SX-20, SX-50, SX-100 and SX-200, and the digital SX-2000.

SXS Step by Step switching system. An automatic dial-telephone system in which calls go through the switching equipment by a succession of switches that move a step at a time, from stage to stage, each step being made in response to the dialing of a number.

SYMBOL An abbreviated, predetermined representation of any relationship, association or convention.

SYMBOLIC LANGUAGE A computer programming language used to express addresses and instructions with symbols convenient to humans rather than machines.

SYMBOLIC LOGIC The discipline in which valid arguments and operations are dealt with using an artificial language designed to avoid the ambiguities and logical inadequacies of natural languages.

SYMMETRICAL CHANNEL A channel in which the send and receive directions of transmission have the same data signaling rate.

SYMMETRICAL PAIR A balanced transmission line in a multipair cable having equal conductor resistances per unit length, equal impedances from each conductor to earth, and equal impedances to other lines.

SYN, SYN CHARACTER, SYNCHRONOUS IDLE In synchronous transmission. Control character in character-oriented protocols used to maintain synchronization and as a time-fill in the absence of data. The sequence of two SYN characters in succession is used to maintain synchronization following each line turnaround. Contrast with flag.

SYN(C) Synchronization character.

SYNC BITS Synchronizing bits (more properly bytes or characters) used in synchronous transmission to maintain synchronization between transmitter and receiver.

SYNCHRONET SERVICE Dedicated point to point and multipoint digital data transmission service offered by BellSouth at speeds of 2.4, 4.8, 9.6, 19.2, 56 and 64 kbps.

SYNCHRONIZATION A multimedia term. Synchronization is very precise real-time processing, down to the milli-second. Some forms of multimedia, such as audio and video, are time-critical. Time delays that might not be noticeable in text or graphics delivery,, but are unacceptable for audio and video. Workstations and networks must be capable of transmitting this kind of data in a synchronized manner. Where audio and video are combined, they must be time-stamped so that they can both play back at the same time.

SYNCHRONIZATION BIT A binary digit used to acheive or maintain synchronism. The term "synchronization bit" is usually applied to digital data streams, whereas the term "synchronization pulse" is usually applied to analog signals.

SYNCHRONIZATION CODE In digital systems, a sequence of digital symbols introduced into a transmission signal to achieve or maintain synchronism.

SYNCHRONIZATION PULSE A pulse used to achieve or maintain synchronism. The term "synchronization pulse" is usually applied to analog signals, whereas the term "synchronization bit" is usually applied to digital data streams.

SYNCHRONIZING Achieving and maintaining synchronism. In facsimile, acheiving and maintaining predetermined speed relations between the scanning spot and the recording spot within each scanning line.

SYNCHRONIZING PILOT In FDM, a reference frequency used for acheiving and maintaining syntonization of the oscillators of a carrier system or for comparing the frequencies or phases of the currents generated by those oscillators.

SYNCHRONOUS 1. The condition that occurs when two events happen in a specific time relationship with each other and both are under control of a master clock. 2. Synchronous transmission means there is a constant time between successive bits, characters or events. The timing is achieved by the sharing of a single clock. Each end of the transmission synchronizes itself with the use of clocks and information sent along with the transmitted data. Synchronous is the most popular communications method to and from mainframes. In synchronous transmission, characters are spaced by time, not by start and stop bits. Because you don't have to add these bits, synchronous transmission of a message will take fewer bits (and therefore less time) than an asynchronous transmission. But because precise clocks and careful timing are needed in synchronous transmission, it's usually more expensive to set up synchronous transmission. See ASYNCHRONOUS

SYNCHRONOUS DATA LINK CONTROL SDLC. A data communications line protocol associated with the IBM Systems Network Architecture. See SYSTEMS NETWORK ARCHITECTURE.

SYNCHRONOUS DATA NETWORK A data network in which synchronism is acheived and maintained between data circuit-terminating equipment (DCE) and the data switching exchange (DSE), and between DSEs. The data signaling rates are controlled by timing equipment within the network.

SYNCHRONOUS DIGITAL HIERARCHY SDH. Term used by the International Telegraph and Telephone Consultative Committee to refer to Sonet.

SYNCHRONOUS IDLE CHARACTER A transmission control character used in synchronous transmission systems to provide a signal from which synchronism or synchronous correction may be achieved between data terminal equipment, particularly when no other character is being transmitted.

SYNCHRONOUS NETWORK A network in which all the communication links are synchronized to a common clock.

SYNCHRONOUS ORBIT An orbit, any point on which has a period equal to the average rotational period of the Earth. If the orbit is also circular and equatorial, it is called a stationary (geostationary) orbit.

SYNCHRONOUS SATELLITE A satellilte in a synchronous orbit. See SYNCHRONOUS ORBIT.

SYNCHRONOUS TDM A multiplexing scheme in which timing is obtained from a clock that in turn controls both the multiplexer and the channel source.

SYNCHRONOUS TRANSFER MODE A proposed transport level, a time-division multiplex-and-switching technique to be used across the user's network interface for a broadband ISDN. See STM.

SYNCHRONOUS TRANSMISSION Transmission in which the data characters and bits are transmitted at a fixed rate with the transmitter and receiver synchronized. Synchronous transmission eliminates the need for start and stop bits. See SYNCHRONOUS and ASYNCHRONOUS.

SYNCHRONOUS TRANSPORT SIGNAL LEVEL. STS-1. The basic logical building block signal in its electronic form with a rate of 49.92 Mbps.

SYNCHRONIZATION BIT A binary bit used to synchronize the transmission and receipt of characters in data communications.

SYNCHRONIZE To cause two systems to work at the same speed.

SYNCORDIA A subsidiary of British Telecommunications which specializes in telecom outsourcing.

SYNDROME Basic element of decoding procedure. Identifies the bits in error.

SYNTAX The rules of grammar in any language, including computer language. Specifically, it is the set of rules for using a programming language. It is the grammar used in programming statements.

SYNTAX ERROR An error caused by incorrect programming statements according to the rules of the language being used. Sometimes the computer will throw up "SN" to indicate a syntax error.

SYNTHESIZED VOICE Human speech approximated by a computer device that concatenates basic speech parts (or phonemes) together. Usually has a metallic, germanic sound.

SYNTONIZATION The process of setting the frequency of one oscillator equal to that of another.

SYNTRAN SYNCHRONOUS TRANSMISSION A restructured DS-3 signal format for synchronous transmission at the 4.736 Mbps DS-3 level of the North American Hierarchy.

SYSGEN Acronym for SYStem GENeration.

SYSOP The SYStem OPerator of a PC-based electronic bulletin board/mail service. SYSOPs (pron. sis-ops) typically put computers and modems on phone lines, then published the phone number, then invited people with computers to call them and leave them messages and interesting software programs which they had written. These programs then became "public domain," or freeware. And other callers were invited to download these programs for their own use. I'm the SYSOP of TELECONNECT's bulletin board — which is 212-989-4675. See also BBS.

SYSREQ System request; the seldom-used key used to get attention from another computer.

SYSTEM An organized assembly of equipment, personnel, procedures and other facilities designed to perform a specific function or set of functions.

SYSTEM 25 The System 25 PBX from AT&T is a digital phone system for businesses with 20 to 150 telephones.

SYSTEM ADMINISTRATOR The person or persons responsible for the administrative and operational functions of a computer and a telecom system that are independent of any particular application. The system Administrator is likely to be a person with the best overview of all the applications. The System Administrator advises application designers about the data that already exists on the various services, makes recommendations about standardizing data definitions across applications, and so on.

SYSTEM BUILD This is the original manufacturer system building that occurs when the order is placed by the buyer with the vendor. The basic configuration is set up to reflect the users needs at that point in time. Thereafter, if any changes occur to reflect changes in the operating environment, the manufacturer must reconfigure the system to reflect this change. There is usually a reprogramming charge and a delay associated with the change.

SYSTEM CLOCK The clock designated as the reference for all clocking in a network of eleconic devices such as a multiplexer or transmission facilities management system.

SYSTEM COMMON EQUIPMENT The equipment on a premises that provides functions common to terminal devices such as telephones, data terminals, integrated work station terminals, and personal computers. Typically, the system-common equipment is the PBX switch, data packet switch, or central host computer. Often called common equipment.

SYSTEM CONNECT The method by which connection is physically made to the cost computer or local area network.

SYSTEM COORDINATOR This is the title assigned to the person responsible for administration programming and the training of workers on your phone system.

SYSTEM DISK A disk that has been formatted as a system disk. MS-DOS system disks have two hidden files and the COMMAND.COM file. You can start the computer using a system disk.

SYSTEM GAIN The amount of free space path loss that a radio can overcome by a combination of enhancing transmitted power and improving receiver sensitivity.

SYSTEM RELOAD A process allowing stored data to be written from a tape into the system memory. Picture: your telephone system goes dead. For whatever reason it loses all memory of its generic programming and your specific programming (whose extension gets what, etc.). You have to quickly grab the backup (hopefully you have it on tape or magnetic disk) and load it back into your telephone system's memory. This is called system reload. Sometimes it's done automatically. Sometimes you have to do it manually.

SYSTEM RENUMBERING An AT&T Merlin term. A process used to change the extension numbers assigned to telephones, adjuncts, Calling Groups, Paging Groups, Call Park Zones, Remote Access, and lines/trunks.

SYSTEM SEGMENT A conceptual subset of a system, usually referring to one which can be functionally replaced without damaging the capability of the system.

SYSTEM SIDE Defines all cabling and connectors from the host computer or local area network to the cross connect field at the distribution frame.

SYSTEM SPEED DIAL Simplified ways of dialing. You do them by dialing several digits. System speed dial numbers can be used by everyone on the phone system — whether they are on an electronic phone or just a simply single line phone.

SYSTEM/36 The System/36 is a small computer that IBM calls a "departmental computer". It is designed to satisfy computing needs of a department whereas the mainframe is designed to fill the computing needs of the entire company. System/36 computers can be directly connected to a Token Ring LAN using TIC cards.

SYSTEM/370 IBM's flagship mainframe computer is very popular in large corporations. It is used to store and manipulate very large amounts of information such as airline reservation applications or banking transaction processing. System/370 computers can be attached to token ring LANs via intermediate Communications Controllers such as 3720 or 3725.

SYMMETRIC MULTIPROCESSING A type of multiprocessing in which more than one processor can execute in can execute kernel-level code at the same time. The degree of symmetry can vary from limited, where there is very little concurrency of execution, to the theoretically ideal fully symmetric system where any function can be executed on any processor at any time.

SYSTEMS ANALYSIS Analysing an organization's activities to figure the best way of applying computer systems to its organization.

SYSTEMS ANALYST A person who performs systems analysis and who follows through with methods, techniques and programs to meet the need.

SYSTEMS APPLICATION ARCHITECTURE SAA. An ambitious IBM plan to create software to weave together its incompatible computers. According to IBM advertising, "SAA will make it possible for everyone in an organization to access information regardless of its location. What's more, all software written to SAA specifications will provide similar screen layouts, menus and terminology." IBM announced SAA in March 1987 and told its customers, according to Business Week, that they would be able to share programs and shuttle information easily among mainframes, minicomputers and desktop systems. Business Week said "The initial (SAA) concept was admittedly sketchy. But IBM committed massive monies to SAA and eventually it assigned an estimated 30,000 programmers to SAA. In May 1989 IBM showed a concrete example of how SAA could work. It introduced OfficeVision, which is series of IBM applications programs that run 'cooperatively' on PCs and IBM mainframes and performs such tasks as manage electronic mail and extract data from a mainframe for use in a PC spreadsheet. OfficeVision is meant to be a concrete example of one of the benefits of IBM's Systems Application Architecture. Delivery of OfficeVision was scheduled for 1990. But didn't make that year. See SYSTEMS APPLICATIONS ARCHITECTURE.

SYSTEMS INTEGRATOR A systems integrator is a company that specializes in planning, coordinating, scheduling, testing, improving and sometimes maintaining a computing operation (sometimes companywide, sometimes just locally). In the old days, this was done almost exclusively by the International Business Machines Corporation. Somewhere along, companies discovered they could get more flexibility and computing power at a lower cost by shopping around. Today, hundreds of companies contribute various components — hardware, software, wiring, communications and so on — to a company's computer operation. But the added flexibility can bring stunning complexity. Systems integrators try to bring order to the disparate suppliers.

SYSTEMS NETWORK ARCHITECTURE SNA. IBM's successful computer network architecture. At one stage the most successful computer network architecture in the world. In the days of mainframe computers, it was as successful in the computer networking world as AT&T's telephone network design was in telecommunications. The best explanation we've ever read of SNA is in James Henry Green's Dow Jones-Irwin Handbook of Telecommunications. (You can get a copy of this great book by calling the Telecom Library at 1-800-LIBRARY.) Here is an excerpt:

"SNA is a tree-structured architecture, with a mainframe host computer acting as the network control center. The boundaries described by the host computer, front-end processors, cluster controllers and terminals are referred to as the network's domain. Unlike the switched telephone network that establishes physical paths between terminals for the duration of a session, SNA establishes a logical path between network nodes, and it routes each message with addressing information contained in the protocol. The network is therefore incompatible with any but approved protocols. SNA uses the SDLC data link protocol exclusively. Devices using asynchronous or binary synchronous can access SNA only through protocol converters...SNA works in seven layers roughly analogous to ISO's seven level OSI model. Unlike OSI, however, SNA is fully defined at each level. SNA was first announced in 1974 and is the basis for much of the OSI model, but it differs from OSI in several significant respects." For more on these differences, see page 96 in Green's Handbook.

The following is a description we received from IBM's PR department: "What is SNA?" In general, SNA is the description of the rules that enable IBM's customers to transmit and receive information through their computer networks. SNA may also be viewed as three distinct but related entities: a specification, a plan for structuring a network and a set of products. First, SNA is a specification governing the design of IBM products that are to communicate with one another in a network. It is called an architecture because it specifies the operating relationships of those products as part of system. Second, SNA provides a coherent structure that enables users to establish and manage their networks and, in response to new requirements and technologies, to change or expand them. Third, SNA may be viewed as a set of products: combinations of hardware and programming designed in accordance with the specification of SNA. In addition to a large number of computer terminals for both specific industries and general applications, IBM's SNA product line includes host processors, communication controllers, and adapters, modems and data encryption units. The SNA product line also includes a variety of programs and programming subsystems. Telecommunications access methods, network management programs, distributed applications programming and the network control program are examples.

SYSTEMS SOFTWARE A type of program used to enhance the operating systems and the computer systems they support.

SYSTEMVIEW The network management program that purports to let UNIX-based computers be managed along with other IBM systems.

SYSTIMAX A structured cabling system from AT&T. Described by AT&T, Systimax is a modular system comprised of unshielded twisted-pair copper and fiber optic cables, connectors and components that provides integrated, efficient signal transport.

SYSTIMAX SCS Systimax Structured Cabling System. See SYSTIMAX.

T 1. Tip. 2. Tera, which is 10 raised to the 12th power, or 1,000,000,000,000.

T 1 See T-1

T CARRIER Generic name for any of several digitally multiplexed carrier systems. The designators for T carrier in the North American digital hierarchy correspond to the designators for the digital signal (DS) level hierarchy. T carrier systems were originally designed to transmit digitized voice signals. Current applications also include digital data transmission. The table below lists the designators and rates for current T carrier systems. If an "F" precedes the "T", it's an optical fiber cable system, but the same rates.

North American Designator (DS LEVEL)

T1 (DS 1)	1.544 Mbps	24 voice channels
T1C	3.152 Mbps	48 voice channels
T2 (DS 2)	6.312 Mbps	96 voice channels
T3 (DS 3)	44.736 Mbps	672 voice channels
T4 (DS 4)	274.176 Mbps	4032 voice channels

JAPANESE HIERARCHY

DS 1	1.544 Mbps	24 voice channels
DS 2	6.312 Mbps	96 voice channels
DS 3	32.064 Mbps	480 voice channels
DS 4	97.728 Mbps	1440 voice channels
DS 5	400.352 Mbps	5760 voice channels

EUROPEAN HIERARCHY (CEPT)

DS 1	2.048 Mbps	30 voice channels
DS 2	8.448 Mbps	120 voice channels
DS 3	34.368 Mbps	480 voice channels
DS 4	139.268 Mbps	1920 voice channels
DS 5	565.148 Mbps	7680 voice channels

T CONNECTION T-shaped three-way conductor for distributing an incoming signal in two outgoing ways. Same shape as a T-connection in the road.

T CONNECTOR A T-shaped device with two female connectors and one male BNC connector used with Ethernet coaxial cable and used on local area networks.

T INTERFACE 4-wire ISDN circuit. The T Interface (more properly the T-Reference Point) performs the same function as the S-interface but uses an

NT1 rather than an NT2. A more common ISDN circuit is called the "U" interface. See U INTERFACE and ISDN.

T-REFERENCE POINT See T INTERFACE.

T TAP A passive line interface used for extracting data from a circuit. Also, for extracting optical signals from a fiber cable or electrical signals from a coaxial cable.

T-1 Also spelled T1. A digital transmission link with a capacity of 1.544 Mbps (1,544,000 bits per second). T-1 uses two pairs of normal twisted wires, the same as you'd find in your house. T-1 normally can handle 24 voice conversations, each one digitized at 64 Kbps. But, with more advanced digital voice encoding techniques, it can handle more voice channels. T-1 is a standard for digital transmission in North America. (For the complete T Carrier hierarchy see the definition for T Carrier above.)

T-1 lines are used for connecting networks across remote distances. Bridges and routers are used to connect LANs over T-1 networks. There are faster services available. T-1 links can often be connected directly to new PBXs and many new forms of short-haul transmission, such as short-haul microwave systems. It is not compatible with T-1 outside the United States and Canada. In Europe T-1 is called E-1 or E1.

Outside of the United States and Canada, the "T-1" line bit rate is usually 2,048,000 bits per second. Japan, France and West Germany impose slight variations that make their formats unique. Only one element remains constant — the DS-0. The 64 kilobit per channel is universal. Most often it represents a PCM voice signal sampled at 8,000 times per second. However, the form of PCM encoding differs between T-1 (mu-law) and E-1 (A-law companding). According to Bill Flanagan's book, the differences are not so great that a multiplexer cannot convert between them. Conversion of E-1 to T-1 involves both the compression law and the signaling format.

At the higher rate of 2,048,000, 32 time slots are defined at the CEPT interface, but two are used for signalling and other housekeeping chores. Typically 30 channels are left for user information — voice, video, data, etc. CEPT is the Conference of European Postal and Telecommunications administrations. Standards-setting body whose membership includes European Post, Telephone, and Telegraphy Authorities (PTTs).

For a full explanation of T-1 see Bill Flanagan's book The Guide to T-1 Networking. (Call 1-800-LIBRARY or 212-691-8215 for your copy.) See also PRI, PRA and T CARRIER and the the following five definitions.

T-1 FRAMING Digitization and coding of analog voice signals requires 8,000 samples per second (two times the highest voice frequency of 4,000 Hz) and its coding in 8-bit words yields the fundamental T-1 building block of 64 Kbps for voice. This is termed a Level 0 Signal and is represented by DS-0 (Digital Signal at Level 0). Combining 24 such voice channels into a serial bit stream using Time Division Multiplexing (TDM) is performed on a frame-by-frame basis. A frame is a sample of all 24 channels (24 x 8 = 192) plus a synchronization bit called a framing bit, which yields a block of 193 bits. Frames are transmitted at a rate of 8,000 per second (corresponding to the required sampling rate), thus creating a 1.544 Mbps (8,000 x 193 = 1,544 Mpbs) transmission rate, the standard North American T-1 rate. This rate is termed DS-1. See also D-4 FRAMING and EXTENDED SUPER-FRAME FORMAT. See also T CARRIER, T2, T3 and T4.

T-1 SPAN LINE See SPAN.

T-I CHANNEL Either of the two external ports of a TDI or RDI which provides for transmitting or receiving eight TDM channels.

T-SPAN A telephone circuit or cable through which a T-carrier runs. Also called a Span line. See T-SPAN LINE and T-1.

T-SPAN LINE Also called a Span line. A repeatered outside plant four-wire, two twisted-pair transmission line.

T.30 CCITT standard. Handshake protocol. This standard describes the overall procedure for establishing and managing communication between the two fax machines. There are five phases of operation covered: call set up, premessage procedure (selecting the communication mode), message transmission (including phasing and synchronization), post-message procedure (end-of-message and confirmation) and call release (disconnection). See CCITT.

T.35 CCITT recommendation proposing a procedure for the allocation of CCITT members' country or area codes for non-standard facilities in telematic services.

T.4 CCITT standard for Group 3 fax machines, using T.30 and various V series standards. It also describes the data compression methods MH and MR.

T.6 CCITT recommendation for Group 3 fax machines using T.30 and various V series standards. It also describes comrpession methods (Modified Huffman and Modified READ).

T.611 Also known as Appli/Com. A messaging standard proposed by France and Germany defining a Programmable Communication Interface (PCI) for Group 3 fax, Group 4 fax, teletex and telex service.

T1 See T-1 above (as in T-ONE).

T1-606/T1-6ac/T1-gfr ANSI's frame relay service specifications.

T1C 3.152 million bits per second. Capable of handling 48 voice conversations. T1C is further up the North American digital carrier hierarchy. See T-1.

T1M1 T1M1 is a technical subcommittee to T-1 responsible for standards related to services, architectures, and signaling.

T1S1 T1S1 is a technical subcommittee to T1 responsible for standards related to services, architectures, and signaling.

T1X1 T1X1 is a technical subcommittee to T-1 responsible for standards pertaining to synchronous interfaces and hierarchical structures relevant to interconnection of network transport signals.

T2 6.312 million bits per second. Capable of handling at least 96 voice conversations depending on the encoding scheme chosen. T2 is four times the capacity of T1. T2 is further up the North American digital carrier hierarchy. See T-1.

T3 28 T1 lines or 44.736 million bits per second. Commonly referred to as 45 megabits per second. Capable of handling 672 voice conversations. T3 runs on fiber optic and is typically called FT3. T3 is further up the North American digital carrier hierarchy. See T1.

T4 274.176 million bits per second. Capable of handling 4032 voice conversations. T4 has 168 times the capacity of T1. T4 can run on coaxial cable, waveguide, millimeter radio or fiber optic. T4 is further up the North American digital carrier hierarchy. See also T1.

TA 1. A Terminal Adapter allows existing non-ISDN terminals to operate on ISDN lines. It provides conversion between a non-ISDN terminal device and the ISDN user/network interface. 2. Technical Advisory. These publications are documents describing Bellcore's preliminary view of proposed generic requirements for products, new technologies, services, or interfaces.

TABLE DRIVEN Describing a logical computer process, widespread in the operation of communications devices and networks, in which a user-entered variable is matched against an array of predefined values. Frequently used in network routing, access security and modem operation. It involves a table lookup that is a reference to a collection of predefined values.

TABLE HOOK-UP METHOD An information retrieval system in which the input information and the related output information are stored as a pair. When a particular input is given, the table is accessed and the output data which coincides with the input is taken out.

TABLES A collection of data in which each item is arranged in relation to the other items. Many telephony functions use "lookup tables" to determine the routing of calls. These tables solve the problem, "If the call is going to this exchange in this area code, then use this trunk and this routing pattern." See TABLE DRIVEN.

TABS AT&T's Telemetry Asynchronous Block Serial protocol. A polled point-to-point or multipoint "master-slave" (remote-monitored equipment) communication protocol that supports moderate data transfer rates over intraoffice wire pairs. The remotes send "requests" or "polls" to monitored equipment. The monitored equipment answers the request with "responses."

Defines two physical interfaces for direct connection between the telemetry remote and the monitored equipment:

- R5422 Point-to-Point
- RS485 Point-to-Point or Multi-Point.

Four wire, two Tx (remote to monitored) and two to Tx (monitored to remote), 22 or 21 gauge twisted pair, max 4 kft remote-to-monitored.

TAC Total Access Communications systems.

TACT TransACtive Cordless Telephony, a new idea being developed by company in the personal communications field called American Telezone, based in Houston, TX.

TACTICAL AUTOMATIC DIGITAL SWITCHING SYSTEM TADSS. A transportable store-and-forward, message-switching system designed for rapid deployment in support of tactical forces. A military definition.

TACTICAL COMMAND AND CONTROL (C2) SYSTEMS The equipment, communication, procedures, and personnel essential to a commander for planning, directing, coordinating, and controlling tactical operations of assigned forces pursuant to the missions assigned. A military definition.

TACTICAL COMMUNICATION A military term. A method or means of conveying information of any kind, especially orders and decisions from one command, person, or place to another within the tactical forces, normally by means of electronic equipment (including communications security equipment). Excluded from this definition are communications provided to tactical forces by DCS, to nontactical forces by DCS, to tactical forces by nontactical military commands, and to tactical forces by civil organizations.

TACTICAL COMMUNICATION SYSTEM A system configured by various types of fixed-size, self-contained assemblages, such as radio terminals and repeaters; switching, transmission, and terminal equipment; and interconnect and control facilities, that are used within or in support of tactical military forces. The system provides securable voice and data communications and among mobile users to facilitate command and control within, and in support of, tactical forces.

TACTICAL DATA INFORMATION LINK TADIL. A military term. A Joint-Chiefs-of-Staff-approved standardized communication link suitable for transmission of digital information. A TADIL is characterized by its standardized message formats and transmission characteristics.

TACTICAL DATA INFORMATION LINK — A TADIL—A. A military term. A netted link in which one unit acts as a net control station and interrogates each unit by roll call. Once interrogated, that unit transmits its data to the net. This means that each unit receives all the information transmitted. This is a direct transfer of data and no relaying is involved.

TACTICAL DATA INFORMATION LINK — B TADIL—B. A military term. A point-to-point data link between two units which provides for simultaneous transmission and reception of data (duplex).

TACTICAL LOAD A military term. That part of the operational load required by the host service consisting of weapons, detection, command control systems, and related functions.

TAD Telephone Answering Device.

TADIL Tactical Data Information Link.

TADSS Tactical Automatic Digital Switching System.

TAFAS Trunk Answer From Any Station. The ability to answer an incoming phone call from any telephone attached to the system.

TAI inTernational Atomic tIme.

TAIL CIRCUIT A feeder circuit or an access line to a network.

TAIL-END-HOP-OFF TEHO. In a private network with several nodes (locations), TEHO occurs when a call placed from one location on the network to a location not on the network leaves the network at the node closest to its destination.

TALK BATTERY The DC voltage supplied by the central office to the subscriber's loop so as to allow you to have a voice conversation. Also known as A BATTERY. Typically somewhere between 5 and 25 volts. See B BATTERY.

TALK PATH The tip and ring conductors of a telephone circuit.

TALK TIME 1. The amount of time agents spend on the phone, as opposed to the time between calls spent updating records, sending out literature or going to the bathroom. 2. The length of time you can talk on your portable or transportable cellular phone from a fully charged battery without standby time. The battery capacity of a cellular portable or transportable is usually expressed in terms of so many minutes of talk time or so many hours of standby time. When you are talking, the phone draws more power from the battery.

TALK, SET, OPTICAL An instrument for talking over fibers — used when installing and testing the cable.

TALK-OFF Talk-off is one hazard of in-band signaling. Talk-off occurs when your voice has enough 2600 Hz energy to activate the 2600 Hz tone-detecting circuits in the central office. The 2600 Hz tone is used for in-band signaling. See SIGNALING SYSTEM #7.

TANDEM The connection of networks or circuits in series. That is, the connection of the output of one circuit to the input of another. See TANDEM SWITCH.

TANDEM CALL A call processed by two or more switches. Also used to designate this type of call at a switch where a connection is established from one trunk to another (tandem trunking). See TANDEM SWITCH.

TANDEM CENTER In a communication system, an installation in which switching equipment connects trunks to trunks, but not any customer loops.

TANDEM DATA CIRCUIT A data channel passing through more than two data circuit-terminating equipment (DCE) devices in series.

TANDEM OFFICE A major phone company switching center for the switched telephone network. It serves to connect central offices when direct interoffice trunks are not available.

TANDEM SWITCH Tandem is a telephony term meaning to "connect in series." Thus a tandem switch connects one trunk to another. A tandem switch is an intermediate switch or connection between an originating telephone call location and the final destination of the call. The tandem point passes the call along. A PBX can often handle tandem calls from other/to other locations as well as process calls to, from and within its own location.

TANDEM TIE TRUNK SWITCHING The PBX permits tie lines to "tandem" through the switch. This means an incoming tie line call from a distant PBX receives a dial tone instead of automatically connecting with the operator. The caller can then dial a connection with either a phone on the PBX or an outgoing line. The outgoing line can be a local trunk in which case the distant PBX has access to a form of foreign exchange service, or another tie line which links a third system. This system of tie lines is widely used to form a corporate communications system, allowing economical connections between distant offices. To provide tie line tandeming ability, the PBX must be able to detect when either tie line goes on-hook at the distant end so that it can break its tandem connection and allow the tie lines to be used for other calls.

TANDEM TRUNKS Trunks between an end office and a tandem switching machine or between tandem switching machines. Tandem trunks can provide direct routing or alternate routing capability when direct trunks are occupied.

TANK TEST A voltage dielectric test in which the wire or cable test sample is submerged in water and voltage is applied between the conductor and water as ground.

TAP An electrical connection permitting signals to be transmitted onto or off a bus. The link between the bus and the drop cable that connects the workstation to the bus. Also a device used on CATV cables for matching impedance or connecting subscriber drops.

TAP BUTTON A button found on single line phones behind a PBX or Centrex. The tap button gives a precisely measured Hookswitch flash. The purpose of this button is to signal the PBX that it is about to receive a command — typically a transfer. To transfer a call on a single line phone,

NEWTON'S TELECOM DICTIONARY

you typically depress the hookswitch, then punch out the extension you want to transfer the call to, announce the call when someone answers, then hang up and the PBX or Centrex transfers the call. The problem with using a hookswitch to make this transfer is that if you depress the hookswitch for too long you will cut the call off. As a result, some manufacturers put a tap button on their single line phones. This button gives the precise hookswitch signal for the precise length of time necessary — no more, no less. The Tap Button is also called a Flash button or a Tap Key.

TAP KEY Also called Tap Button or Flash Key. A button on a phone that accomplishes the same function as a switch-hook but is not a switch-hook. See TAP BUTTON.

TAPAC Terminal Attachment Program Advisory Committee. Body which recommends telecom standards to the Canadian Federal Government.

TAPE DRIVE The physical unit that holds, reads and writes magnetic tape.

TAPE READER A device which reads information recorded on punched paper tape or magnetic tape.

TAPE RELAY A method of retransmitting TTY traffic from one channel to another, in which messages arriving on an incoming channel are recorded in the form of perforated tape, this tape then being either fed directly and automatically into an outgoing channel, or manually transferred to an automatic transmitter for transmission on an outgoing channel.

TAPERED RATE 1. A proposal by New York Telephone to give discounts to large customers who might be considering bypass. 2. Prices drop as usage increases.

TARGA Truevision Advanced Raster Graphics Adapter.

TARIFF Documents filed by a regulated telephone company with a state public utility commission or the Federal Communications Commission. The tariff, a public document, details services, equipment and pricing offered by the telephone company (a common carrier) to all potential customers. Being a "common carrier" means it (the phone company) must offer its services to everybody at the prices and at the conditions outlined in its public tariffs. Tariffs do not carry the weight of law behind them. If you or the telephone company violate them, no one will go to jail. The worst that can happen to you, as a subscriber, is that your service will be cut off, or threatened to be cut off. Regulatory authorities do not normally approve tariffs. They accept them — until they are successfully challenged before a hearing of the regulatory body or in court (usually Federal Court). Many tariffs were accepted by regulatory commissions only to be struck down in court as unlawful, discriminatory, not cost-justified, etc. Monies collected under the tariff have been refunded and unnecessary equipment removed. In these new, competitive days, many telephone companies are violating their own tariffs by charging less money than their tariffs say they should, or bundling services together at a discount. They are also providing service and

964

equipment on terms less onerous than outlined in their tariffs. Many users now regard tariffs as starting bargaining points, rather than ending bargaining points.

TARIFF 12 A user-specific long distance tariff of AT&T. Tariff 12 gives AT&T the ability to price its long distance services for one company practically any which way it feels — giving them a mix of services at stable prices over the long term with significant volume discounts. As this dictionary was going to the printer, a federal appeals court overturned the Federal Communications Commission's April 1989 decision allowing AT&T to offer custom networks and ordered the FCC to reopen its investigation into the legality of the Tariff 12 deals. There are still some users. They are "grandfathered" until we get a final say on the tariff. And, as we go to press, AT&T can offer Tariff 12 customized services to any company — but cannot include 800 services in its Tariff 12 pricing.

TARIFF 15 A user-specific long distance tariff of AT&T. Tariff 15 gives AT&T the ability to price its long distance services for one company practically any way it feels. Tariff 15 is single-customer discounting. Some of AT&T competitors claim the tariff is "illegal."

TARM Telephone Answering and Recording Machines.

TAS Telephone Answering Service.

TASC Telecommunications Alarm, Surveillance, and Control system. Expands the scope of maintenance from the traditional alarm monitoring and control functions to include performance monitoring and fault locating.

TASI Time Assignment Speech Interpolation. A money-saving analog multiplexing procedure which keeps the connection to the circuit as long as someone is speaking and lets other conversations use the circuit during the intervals (measured in microseconds) when there's no speaking. Since a long distance circuit is usually only half used — one person speaking, one person listening — at least 50% of the circuit can be used by someone else. TASI is typically used by long distance companies on submarine cable across the Atlantic and the Pacific. Unfortunately, the flip-flopping around of circuit allocation by TASI means that the first tiny bit of a conversation is often lost. This can be disastrous for data. The key in data is to keep transmitting. The key in voice is to say something like "Ah" to seize the channel and then say what you want. TASI is very much like a very fast version of mobile dispatch radio. A modern version of TASI is called DIGITAL SPEECH INTERPOLATION. TASI is somewhat comparable to statistical multiplexing of data.

TASK MANAGEMENT Allocating resources and overseeing the sequence of tasks completed by the computer.

TASK SWITCHING You have a computer and you want to have it do several tasks at once. There are two ways. One is multitasking. The computer will keep working on several tasks at once, though you may not see them on your screen. For example, you pay start a spreadsheet recalculating. And then you may call your electronic mail system. While you're receiving your mail, your spreadsheet is still recalculating. When you're through, you can switch back to your spreadsheet and see the final results. That's called multitasking and MS-DOS doesn't have it. MS-DOS 5.0 through its Shell has something called task switching, whose idea is that you can load several programs into your computer and switch quickly between them. But the programs you put in background won't run. They stop the moment you put them in background. When you cycle back to them, they will start running again. Sadly, MS-DOS 5.0 Shell's task switching capabilities are very weak. Your programs will lock up and you will lose your data. I do not recommend using Task Switching in MS-DOS 5.0. Windows 3.1 is alleged to have a form of multitasking. I don't trust it either yet. Windows has locked up on me on several occasions.

TAT TransAtlantic Telephone cable.

TB/S TeraBits per Second.

TBA To Be Announced. Pricing of a product that may exist and that may, one day, be priced. You often see TBA after products which are hyperware, vaporware, mirrowware or smokeware.

TBB Transnational Broadband Backbone.

TBBS The Bread Board System. A proprietary name for one of the earliest and still one of the best electronic bulletin boards. From a company called eSoft in Aurora CO. The president is Phil Becker. He's great. Tell him, Harry says Hello.

TBOS Telemetry Byte Oriented Serial protocol. TBOS is a protocol for transmitting alarm, status, and control points between NE and OS. TBOS defines one physical interface for direct connection between telemetry remote and the monitored equipment. This is a point-to-point communication, RS 422A modified four wire, two to Tx (remote to monitored) and two to Tx (monitored to remote), 26 gauge, max 4 kft remote-to-monitored. Remote sees a 100 to 180 ohms resistor at monitored terminal.

TBR Timed BReak.

TC 1. Transmission Control. 2. Transmission Convergence. The upper half of BISDN Layer 3. Telecommunications Closet. a closet which houses telecommunications wiring and telecom wiring equipment. contains the BHC (Backbone to Horizontal Cross-connect). may also contain the network demarcation, or MC (Main Cross-connect). the telecommunications closet is used to connect up telecom wiring. the closet typically has a door. It's a good idea to lock the door and not put anything else in the closet, like mops, buckets and brooms.

TCA TeleCommunications Association. A major association of West-of-the-

Rockies telecommunications management professionals. Every September, TCA runs the TCA Show in September each year in San Diego.

TCAM TeleCommunications Access Method. A popular telecommunications software package to run on IBM 370 computers. See IBM.

TCAP Transactional Capabilities Application Part. Provides the signaling function for network data bases. TCAP is an ISDN application protocol. In addition to PRA and ISUP, the third major ISDN protocol in the delivery of advanced network services is TCAP, a CCS7 application protocol that provides the platform to support non-circuit related, transaction-based information exchange between network entities. This capability is required by transaction-based services that must exchange information between a pair of signaling nodes in a CCS7 network. Examples of these services include enhanced dial-800 service, automated credit card calling and virtual private networking. The TCAP protocol enables these services to access remote databases called service control points (SCPs) to process part of the call. The SCP supplies the translation and routing data needed to deliver advanced network services — like translating a dial calls into the required routing number. TCAP is useful also in coordinating some enhanced call-related services. For example, network ring again requires the connection of two users when both stations become idle. In this case, TCAP is used to coordinate between the users' switches while waiting for each line to become idle. And it can do this without tying up network trunks.

One of the major advantages of TCAP is that it provides a set of protocol building blocks for use in a variety of service definitions. The TCAP building blocks are subdivided into the transaction sublayer and the component sublayer. For more on TCAP, see the 1988-3 issue of Northern Telecom's Telesis publication.

TCAS T-Carrier Administration System. Provides mechanized support for the facility maintenance and administration center to achieve centralized administration and control of the digital network.

TCF Training Check Frame. Last step in a series of signals in a fax transmission called a training sequence, designed to let the receiver adjust to telephone line conditions.

TCHOTCHKE A New York Jewish word meaning trinkets, best emplified by the giveaway junk we often pick up at telecommunications trade shows.

TCIF The TeleCommunications Industry Forum, a major committee sponsored by the ECSA, the Exchange Carriers Standards Association. See EXCHANGE CARRIERS STANDARDS ASSOCIATION.

TCM 1. Traveling Class Mark. 2. Trellis Coding Modulation. 3. Time-Compression Multiplexing. A digital transmission technique that permits full duplex data transmission by sending compressed bursts of data in a "ping-pong" fashion.

TCNS Thomas Conrad Networking System is a 100 million bit per second proprietary networking system (LAN) based on ARCnet that can use most standard ARCnet drivers on any network operating systems.

TCP Transmission Control Protocol. ARPAnet-developed transport layer protocol. Corresponds to OSI layers 4 and 5, transport and session. TCP is a transport layer, connection-oriented, end-to-end protocol. It provides reliable, sequenced, and unduplicated delivery of bytes to a remote or local user. TCP provides reliable byte stream communication between pairs of processes in hosts attached to interconnected networks. It is the portion of the TCP/IP protocol suite that governs the exchange of sequential data. See also TCP/IP.

TCP/IP Transmission Control Protocol/Internet Program. A set of protocols developed by the Department of Defense to link dissimilar computers across many kinds of networks, including unreliable ones and connected to dissimilar LANs. Developed in the 1970s by the U.S. Department of Defense's Advanced Research Projects Agency (DARPA) as a military standard protocol, its assurance of multivendor connectivity has made it popular among commerical users as well, who have adopted TCP/IP as an interim step while awaiting the availability of OSI products. Consequently, TCP/IP now is supported by many manufacturers of minicomputers, personal computers, mainframes, technical workstations and data communications equipment. It is also the protocol commonly used over Ethernet (as well as X.25) networks. It has been implemented on everything from PC LANs to minis and mainframes. Although committed to an eventual migration to an OSI architecture, TCP/IP currently divides networking functionality into only four layers:

A Network Interface Layer that corresponds to the OSI Physical and Data Link Layers. This layer manages the exchange of data between a device and the network to which it is attached and routes data between devices on the same network.

An Internet Layer which corresponds to the OSI network layer. The Internet Protocol (IP) subset of the TCP/IP suite runs at this layer. IP provides the addressing needed to allow routers to forward packets across a multiple LAN internetwork. In IEEE terms, it provides connectionless datagram service, which means it attempts to deliver every packet, but has no provision for retransmitting lost or damaged packets. IP leaves such error correction, if required, to higher level protocols, such as TCP.

IP addresses are 32 bits in length and have two parts: the Network Identifier (Net ID) and the Host Identifier (Host ID). Assigned by a central authority, the Net ID specifies the address, unique across the internet, for each network or related group of networks. Assigned by the local network administrator, the Host ID specifies a particular host, station or node within a given network and need only be unique within that network.

A Transport Layer, which corresponds to the OSI Transport Layer. The Transmission Control Protocol (TCP) subset runs at this layer. TCP provides end-to-end connectivity between data source and destination with detection of, and recovery from, lost, duplicated, or corrupted packets — thus offering the error control lacking in lower level IP routing. In TCP, message blocks from applications are divided into smaller segments, each with a sequence number that indicates the order of the segment within the block. The destination device examines the message segments and, when a complete sequence of segments is recieved, sends an acknowledgement (ACK) to the source, containing the number of the next byte expected at the destination.

An Application Layer, which corresponds to the session, presentation and application layers of the OSI model. This layer manages the function required by the user programs and includes protocols for remote log-in (Telnet), file transfer (FTP), and electronic mail (SMTP). See OSI.

TCR Transaction Confirmation Report. A report from a fax machine listing the faxes received and transmitted. It provides details about each fax, including date, time, the remote fax's number, results, total pages.

TDC Time Division Controller.

TDF Trunk Distributing Frame.

TDI Transmit Division Intertie.

TDM See TIME DIVISION MULTIPLEXING.

TDM NETWORK A Rolm term: The assembly of interface cards and buses for connecting phones to each other, to outside trunks, etc., and to certain shared electronics within the CBX (Rolm term for PBX).

TDMA Time Division Multiple Access. One of several technologies used to separate multiple conversation transmissions over a finite frequency allocation of through-the-air bandwidth. As with FDMA (Frequency Division Multiple Access), TDMA is used to allocate a discrete amount of frequency bandwidth to each user, in order to permit many simultaneous conversations. However, each caller is assigned a specific timeslot for transmission. A newly proposed digital cellular telephone system assigns 10 timeslots for each frequency channel, and cellular telephones send bursts, or packets, of information during each timeslot. The packets of information are reassembled by the receiving equipment into the original voice components. TDMA promises to significantly increase the efficiency of cellular telephone systems, allowing a greater number of simultaneous conversations. See CDMA, FDMA.

TDMS 1. Technical Document Management Systems. 2. Time Division Multiplex System. 3. Transmission Distortion Measuring Set.

TDR Time Domain Reflectometer.

TDSAI Transit Delay Selection And Indication

NEWTON'S TELECOM DICTIONARY

TE ISDN Terminal Equipment. See the next two definitions.

TE1 Terminal Equipment Type 1. ISDN-compatible terminals.

TE2 Terminal Equipment Type 2. Non-ISDN terminal equipment linked at the RS-232, RS-449, or V.35 interfaces.

TEI Terrminal Endpoint Identifier. The TEI is used to identify a specific connection endpoint within a service access point.

TEC NIS Telecommunications and Electronics Consortium in the Newly Independent States. An organization based in Moscow and administered by TIA (Telecommunications Industry Association) to assist US telecommunications and telecommunications-related electronics companies with doing business in the region.

TECHNICAL CONTROL CENTER A testing center for telecommunications circuits. The center provides test access and computer-assisted support functions to aid in circuit maintenance.

TECHNICAL CONTROL FACILITY A federal government term . A term plant, or a designated and specially configured part thereof, containing the equipment necessary for ensuring fast, reliable, and secure exchange of information. This facility typically includes distribution frames and associated panels, jacks, and switches; and monitoring, test, conditioning, and orderwire equipment.

TECHNICAL LOAD A military term. The portion of the operational load required for communications, tactical operations, and ancillary equipment including necessary lighting, air conditioning, or ventilation required for full continuity of communications.

TECHNICAL OFFICE PROTOCOL TOP. A version of the Open Systems Interconnection (OSI) model for use in the office, developed by Boeing, the people who make the planes.

TECHNOLOGY PARTNERS Dialogic term for companies which make specialized voice processing devices which can be used with Dialogic products to build end user products. Technology partners include those with skills in facsimile, voice recognition and text-to-speech. Their products will work with Dialogic products.

TED Trunk Encryption Device.

TEDDY BEAR A stuffed animal named after President "Teddy" Roosevelt, a keen hunter who once took pity on a baby bear.

TEDIS Trade Electronic Data Interchange Systems.

TEEN SERVICE A feature of some central offices which allows two telephone numbers to be assigned to a single party phone line. Each number has a distinctive ringing pattern so that the called parties can recognize which line is ringing. The inventor of this service named it after the fact that his teenage children were always receiving phone calls. And he wanted a way for them to recognize when the calls were for them and when they were for the parents. Sadly, this phenomenon now begins earlier in life, with children as young as six receiving their own calls. We speak from experience.

TEHO See TAIL END HOP-OFF (traffic engineering).

TEI Northern Telecom term for Terminal Endpoint Identifier.

TEK Traffic Encryption Key.

TELABUSE A term coined by John Haugh of Telecommunications Advisors in Portland, OR to include "insider" toll fraud, waste and abuse.

TELBANKING Banking transactions conducted through telecommunications.

TELCO The local telephone company. Often a term of endearment. Americanism for telephone company.

TELEACTION SERVICE In ISDN applications, a telecommunications service using very short messages with very low data transmission rates between the user and the network.

TELECOM DEVELOPERS An annual trade show devoted to the notion that users ought to have the ability to program, control and build their own telephone systems. The logic is simple: If you can program, control and build your own phone system, you can customize it for you and your customers' needs. And since nothing is more important than your customers, being able to program your phone system is absolutely critical. One key benefit: the ability to have a screen of information on your customer pop up as the call comes in. TELECOM DEVELOPERS Conference and Exposition is held every year in the Spring. For more information, call 212-691-8215 or 800-999-0345 or 800-LIBRARY or 212-206-6660. See ERECTOR SET TELECOM.

TELECOMMUNICATIONS 1. The art and science of "communicating" over a distance by telephone, telegraph and radio. The transmission, reception and the switching of signals, such as electrical or optical, by wire, fiber, or electromagnetic (i.e. through-the-air) means. 2. A fancy word for "telephony," which it replaced and which many thought meant only analog voice, but didn't.

TELECOMMUNICATION ARCHITECTURE The governing plan showing the capabilities of functional elements and their interaction, including configuration, integration, standardization, life-cycle mangement, and definition of protocol specifications, among these elements.

TELECOMMUNICATIONS BROKER A person or an organization which buys telecommunications services at bulk rates and resells these services at below "normal" i.e. retail prices.

TELECOMMUNICATIONS CLOSET A closet which houses telecommunications wiring and telecom wiring equipment. Contains the BHC (Backbone to Horizontal Cross-connect). May also contain the Network Demarcation, or MC (Main Cross-connect). The telecommunications closet is used to connect up telecom wiring. The closet typically has a door. It's a good idea to lock the door and not put anything else in the closet, like mops, buckets and brooms.

TELECOMMUNICATION FACILITIES The aggregate of equipment, such as telephones, teletypewriters, facsimile equipment, cables, and switches, used for various modes of transmission, such as digital data, audio signals, image and video signals.

TELECOMMUNICATIONS LINES Telephone and other communications lines used to transmit messages from one location to another.

TELECOMMUNICATIONS NETWORK The public switched telephone exchange network.

TELECOMMUNICATION SERVICE Any service provided by a telecommunication provider. A specified set of user-information transfer capabilities provided to a group of users. The telecommunication service provider has the responsibility for the acceptance, transmission, and delivery of the message.

TELECOMMUTING Working off-site. The process of commuting to the office through a communications link rather than transferring one's physical presence. In short, working at home on a computer, a modem and maybe a facsimile machine, rather than going into the office. There are benefits: you can live somewhere charming. There are disadvantages, especially accentuated if you work with others: "When you're getting data frm afar, you're not in touch with the soul of the business, anymore," according to one telecommuter interviewed by the New York Times. He went on to say, "All the electronic communications are simply back-up, I just hadn't factored the importance of personal loyalty and contact into the equation. And I was very wrong."

TELECONFERENCE A conference between persons remote from one another but linked by a telecommunications system.

TELECONFERENCING A conference of more than two people linked by telecommunications. Can be audio only; can be video one-way and audio the other; can be video both ways. For years, teleconferencing has been heralded as a great coming event, and a significant replacement for travel. The death of travel has not happened because teleconferencing remains expensive, cumbersome, lacking in the human touch and difficult to initiate. Few companies have teleconferencing facilities in their offices. So, to hold a teleconference you often have to travel somewhere — a local hotel ballroom, the local AT&T office, etc. Teleconferencing will not displace travel. But it is growing and growing rapidly. It is developing its own special niche in the telecommunications travel-continuum. That niche is increasingly for events like new product announcements, price changes, new Vision statements — happenings which need to be broadcast quickly to many people, and which often generate questions from the dispersed audience.

TELECONNECT MAGAZINE TELECONNECT is a monthly magazine covering developments in telecommunications equipment. Its the largest monthly telecommunications magazine. Its job is to help its readers choose, install and maintain telecom equipment. TELECONNECT Magazine contains critical reviews of new products and product comparisons. Subscriptions are available from 1-800-999-0345 and 212-691-8215 for $15 a year.

TELECOPIER A fancy word for a facsimile machine.

TELEFAX 1. European term for fax. 2. A high-speed, 64 kilobit per second facsimile service that uses Group 4 fax machines and one Bearer channel of an ISDN circuit, or any other 64 kbps circuit. Group 4 fax machines take about six seconds to transmit a page. They're fast and impressive.

TELEGRAM Hard-copy information, in written, printed or pictorial form, routed to the general telegraph service for transmission and delivery to the addressee. Telegrams are dying due to the high cost of delivery.

TELEGRAPH A system employing the interruption of, or change in, the polarity of DC current signaling to convey coded information.

TELEGRAPH KEY A type of switch for making and breaking a circuit at will for the purpose of transmitting dots and dashes.

TELEGRAPHY Aging data transmission technique characterized by maximum data rates of 75 bits per second and signaling where the direction, or polarity, of DC current flow is reversed to indicate bit states.

TELEMAGIC Our very favorite contact management software program. It's from Remote Control in Carlsbad, CA. Check it out. You won't be disappointed.

TELEMANAGEMENT A new term which involves using computer technology and techniques to better manage the telephone and telecommunications expenses of a corporation. Telemanagement includes every function the corporate telecommunications manager does today — from call accounting to ordering of new circuits, from managing the corporate inventory of phones, lines and other equipment, to choosing the right number of operators to man the phones at the right time, etc. Increasingly, you now see personal computers sitting on top of telephone systems, collecting and processing information. That's part of telemanagement, too.

TELEMARKETING Marketing and sales conducted via the telephone. There are two sides to telemarketing — incoming and outgoing. Incoming telemarketing is largely run through 800 toll-free IN-WATS numbers and local FX (foreign exchange) lines. Outgoing telemarketing is organized over OUT-WATS lines. An expanding range of telecom gadgetry is being developed to automate telemarketing — including automated outbound dialers, voice processing technology and automatic call distributors. The tone recognition, voice detection and transaction audiotex and transaction processing capabilities of voice processing gear can be used to enhance all telemarketing applications.

TELEMETRY A communications system for the transmission of digital or analog data which represents status information on a remote process, function or device.

TELEOS IRX-9000 Teleos' Intelligent Call Distribution platform. Teleos makes a programmable switch which can be controlled by an external computer. It calls the switch the IRX-9000 and the ability to write software for it, its intelligent call distribution platform.

TELEPARENTS Parents who equip their children with pagers before allowing them to go out.

TELEPHONE 1. An invention of the devil. 2. The most intrusive device ever invented. 3. The biggest time waster of all time, as in: "What did you do all day?" "Nothing. Just spent the day on the phone." 4. Also a truly remarkable invention. Here's a list of the eight things a telephone does, according to Understanding Telephone Electronics:

1. When you lift the handset, it signals you wish to use the worldwide phone system.

2. It indicates the phone system is ready for your wish by receiving a tone, called a dial tone.

3. It sends the number of the telephone to be called.

4. It indicates the progress of your call by receiving tones — ringing, busy, etc.

5. It alerts you to an incoming call.

6. It changes your speech into electrical signals for transmission to someone distant. It also changes the electrical signals it receives from the distant person to speech so you can understand them.

7. It automatically adjusts for changes in the power supplied to it.

8. When you hang up, it signals the phone system your call is finished.

And, most remarkably, most simple telephones cost under $50. Wait until you see what ISDN phones will cost.

TELEPHONE AMPLIFIER A device to amplify the sound of the receiver. Something no phone should be without. Some devices work strictly on line power. They can only increase volume by 10 dB, which is often not enough (especially if you're over 40). The best telephone amplifiers are powered by

AC/DC adapters. Newer ones are powered by nicad batteries. They will amplify to 20 dB.

TELEPHONE ANSWERING A feature of some voice mail systems in which incoming callers are immediately directed to the called party's voice mailbox where they hear a personalized greeting in the called party's voice and are prompted to leave a detailed message.

TELEPHONE CHANNEL A transmission path suitable for carrying voice signals. Defined by its ability to transmit signals in a frequency range of about 300 to 3000 Hz.

TELEPHONE CIRCUIT Electrical connection permitting the establishment of telephone communication in both directions between two telephone exchanges.

TELEPHONE EXCHANGE A switching center for connecting and switching phone lines. A European term for what North Americans call central office.

TELEPHONE FREQUENCY Any frequency within that part of the audio frequency range essential for the transmitting speech, i.e. 300 to 3000 Hz.

TELEPHONE MANAGEMENT SYSTEM The term originally meant a system for controlling telephone costs by:

1. Automatically selecting lower-cost long distance routes for placed calls; 2. Automatically restricting certain people's abilities to make some or all long distance calls; and 3. Automatically keeping track of telephone usage by extension, time of day, number called, trunk used and sometimes by person calling and client or account to be billed for call.

These days the terms means those three functions plus a whole lot more, typically those associated with professionally managing the corporate or government telecommunications expenses, including (but not limited to):

● Computerized inventory monitoring,

● Computerized traffic engineering and network design,

● Departmental telephone bill allocation and invoicing,

● Automated telephone directory, etc.

● Project tracking,

● Automated equipment and service ordering.

In short, all the functions of professional telecommunications management that can be automated or organized in some way on a computer. The telecommunications management system thus refers to the computer hardware and the software. For more on this subject see the latest June issue of TELECONNECT Magazine. See also CALL ACCOUNTING SYSTEM.

TELEPHONE MESSAGE MANAGEMENT SYSTEM TMMS. This IBM

software product permits detailed personalized call answering in the CBX II 9000 environment. Which sounds like voice mail to us. We stole this definition from a glossary Rolm supplied us.

TELEPHONE RECEIVER Telephone earpiece. Device that converts electrical energy into sound energy, designed to be held to the ear.

TELEPHONE SERVICE REPRESENTATIVE TSR. Another word for agent — the person who answers the phone on an automatic call distributor. See AGENT.

TELEPHONE SET A fancy name for a telephone.

TELEPHONE SET EMULATION The concept is simple: Emulate the proprietary electronic phone on a printed circuit card inside a PC. Let the PC do everything a human using the phone could do. Only the PC will do it more efficiently and the human will find it easier to use all his phone's features because the PC's screen is bigger and the PC's keyboard easier to use than the phone's keyboard. Attach the phone emulation card to voice and call processing cards, like voice synthesis, voice recognition, voice mail, touchtone generation and recognition, etc. And bingo, phone systems acquire all the benefits of integrated voice and call processing. It's powerful concept. As I wrote this, a handful of telephone phone emulation cards had appeared. Within a little while, there won't be a phone worldwide that you won't be able to emulate on a printed circuit card you can drop into a vacant slot inside your PC.

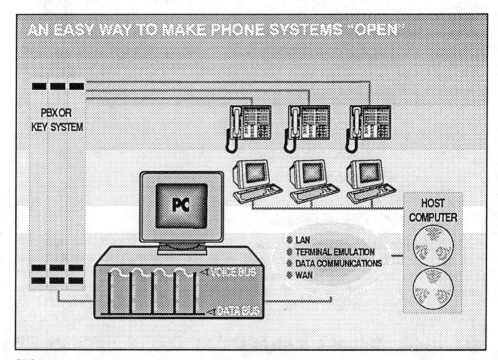

TELEPHONE SIGNALING DEVICE A gadget which indicates that the phone is ringing. May also be hooked up to lamps or overhead lighting to cause those lights to flash when the phone is ringing.

TELEPHONE TAG I call you. But you're not there. I leave a message. You call call me back. But I'm not there. You leave a message. And so on. We're now playing telephone tag.

TELEPHONY Here's one definition: The science of converting or transmitting voice or other signals over a distance, and the re-converting them to an audible sound at the far end (Greek for " far sound"). Here's another: Converting voices and other sounds into electrical impulses for transmission by wire or other means over distances greater than what you can hear by shouting.

Here's a third. It comes from a white paper on Multimedia from Sun Microsystems: Telephony refers to the integration of the telephone into the workstation. For instance, making or forwarding a call will be as easy as pointing to an address book entry. Caller identification (if available from the telephone company) could be used to automatically start an application or bring up a database file. Voicemail and incoming faxes can be integrated with email. Users can have all the features of today's telephones accessible through their workstations, plus the added benefits provided by integrating the telephone with other desktop functions.

TELEPHONY SERVER NLM Telephony Server NetWare Loadable Module. A product announced in early 1993 by AT&T. The Telephony Server NLM is an AT&T-made card sitting in a file server on a Novell LAN. The card connects directly to the ASAI (Adjunct Switch Applications Interface) port on the AT&T Definity PBX. Anyone with a PC on the network and an AT&T phone on their desk will be able to use telephone features, such as auto-dialing, conference calling and message management (a new term for integrating voice, fax and e-mail on your desktop PC). Novell/AT&T have announced that they intend to create open Application Programming Interfaces (APIs) third-party developers can work with. A Novell/AT&T example of what could be developed: A user could select names from a directory on his PC. He could tell the Definity PBX through the PC over the LAN to place calls to them. At the same time, a program running under NetWare would automatically send an e-mail to the people in the conference call. All participants would have access to both the document and the conference call simultaneously.

A Novell White Paper in Spring of 1993 said "Telephony Services represents a significant piece of NetWare's overall strategy of providing a comprehensive set of integrated network services. Through the combining of Telephony Services for NetWare with the functionality of other network services such as fax, video, messaging and others, further gains are easily demonstrated. Today, organizations view the telephone and computer as essential parts of conducting daily business. In fact, they rely so heavily on the technology of these two instruments that productivity can often be jeapordized when access is interrupted. With such heavy reliance, the next stop in the technology evolution is to merge and integrate the capabilities of these two technologies to improve the return and benefits provided to customers.

"Telephony Services for NetWare provides benefits to three main customer segments. First, applications are being developed to provide increased productivity to everyday computer desktop users. Second, call-centers take advantage of this technology as it provides a right-sizing cost-effective solution. Finally, benefits will be available to telecommunications/IS administrators by providing the ability to reduce administrative costs through easier management of user databases.

"Computer-Telepone Integration (CTI) combines telephone and computer technology to provide access and control telephone functionality from a computer terminal. It combines the easy access and usable graphical interface of the computer desktop with the features of the telephone. CTI is not a new concept. Traditionally, however, CTI has only been available in a mini and mainframe computer environments. These solutions are expensive and can be cost-justified only in large call-center applications. Consequently, the penetration of CTI solutions has been very small.

"However, providing CTI in NetWare environment brings this technology mainstream. Not only does this solution provide a more cost-effective implementation, it also allows integration with the rich set of NetWare services. In the simplest example, a Telephony Services for NetWare application allows users to make a phone call by clicking on a name from a calling list displayed on a desktop computer and having the desktop computer dial the number. Possibilities exist for applications that will allow similar functionality with the addition of conference calling capability. Instead of clicking on a single name, the user can highlight a number of names, click on a conference-call icon and have the system place the calls to all parties. The benefits which are derived from the integration of telephony with other NetWare services is far reaching. As part of continued development efforts, applications are becoming available which allow desktop video phone calls. Callers can see each other and talk on the phone, while simultaneously viewing and editing image documents.

"Other capabilities include integrating voice-mail, fax and e-mail into a single message-management application. Possiblities also exist utilizing number recognition technology to integrate computer database records with caller-id. Administrators can manage a single user database utilized by the computer network, the PBX and the voice-mail system.

"Telephony Services for NetWare takes advantages of client/server technology to provide a broad framework for creating first-party and third-party call-control applications. These applications answer the customer demand for integrated business tools and solutions. This technology provides a logical connection between the desktop computer and the telephone. The only physical connection is established between the PBX and a NetWare server. This architecture is cost-effective and efficient by utilizing a company or organization's existing equipment. The initial product deliverables include the following components:

- Client/Server API
- Telephony Server NLM
- PBX Driver
- PBX Link Hardware
- Passageway Application

"The Telephony Server NLM is the merchanism for passing information between the PBX and the NetWare server. As part of the NLM, an open PBX Driver Interface allows PBX manufacturers to write drivers which communicate with their respective PBX models. The client/server API provides support across multiple desktop operating systems. It also allows call control at either the client or the server. The Passageway application provides the user with basic autodialing and notes capability.

"Telephony Services for NetWare provides a key opportunity for developers. Open APIs which support multiple desktop operating systems provide a development platform for both traditional telecommunications developers and new or experienced NetWare developers.

TELEPHONY SERVICES See TELEPHONY SERVER NLM

TELEPORTS The definition written by Gary Stix in the August 12, 1986 issue of Computer Decisions reads, "High bandwidth telecommunications distribution systems that allow major local users to obtain local, private services and long distance services. The most notable example is the New York Teleport," which is located on Staten Island. Teleports traditionally consist of two things — a fiber optic/coaxial cable network around a city and a collection of nearby satellite antennas. The cable network collects transmissions from larger customers and takes them to the antennas for shipping to and from distant offices. Teleport companies are now more successful as local communications companies than they are as long distance gateways. Which is understandable, since the cost of local calls has gone up, while the cost of long distance calls has gone down.

TELEPRESENCE In 1985 a team of researchers at NASA invented the notion of telepresence — projecting yourself into someone else's virtual reality. In one version of telepresence, according to Discover Magazine, a computer prompts a robot to mimic your movements. As you manipulate objects in your virtual world a robot somewhere else does the same thing to real objects. Telepresence will be especially useful for hazardous jobs like repairing a nuclear reactor or satellite. Or going on a blind date? See VIRTUAL REALITY.

TELEPRINTER A teletypewriter. Also called a telex machine.

TELEPROCESSING An IBM term for data communications.

TELESCRIPT Trademark name of General Magic's communications language technology. An interpreted, object-oriented language that creates and manages intelligent agents as they move through a network of computers and personal communicators. Telescript is implemented as a portable interpreter, called Telescript engine. Programs written in Telescript are called scripts. General Magic says that it expects Telescript to become an industry standard, licensed by major suppliers of personal intelligent communicators, computers, communication networks, and information services. See GENERAL MAGIC.

TELETEX A new CCITT standard for text and message transmission which is replacing Telex. Teletex operates at 2400 baud, about 50 times faster than telex. Teletex uses ASCII to encode its characters for transmission.

TELETEXT A data communications information service used to transmit information from remote data banks to viewers. It was transmitted over the air in the vertical blanking interval of the TV signal of the BBS (British Broadcasting Service). Teletext was originally designed for public consumption. It gave out weather information, sports results, headlines, etc. Teletext is proving somewhat more successful among corporations for the internal dissemination of information.

TELETRAFFIC OPTIMIZER PROGRAM Derives data by processing actual calls instead of using an analytical model based on estimates or summaries.

TELETRAINING Education and training through telecommunications.

TELETYPE A specific type of teletypewriter.

TELETYPEWRITER TTY. A telegraph device capable of transmitting and receiving alphanumeric information over communications channels. It may also contain a keyboard similar to that of a typewriter or computer but usually with fewer keys. See TELETYPE.

TELETYPEWRITER CONTROL UNIT TCU. A device that serves as the control and coordination unit between teletypewriter devices and a message switching center when controlling teletypewriter operations.

TELETYPEWRITER EXCHANGE SERVICE TWX. A switched teletypewriter service in which suitably arranged teletypewriter stations are provided with lines to a central office for access to other such stations. TWX and Telex are commerical teletypewriter exchange services. They are currently both owned by AT&T. These days their revenues are in decline. A computer with a modem is a lot faster than TWX or telex.

TELETYPEWRITER SIGNAL DISTORTION The shifting of signal-pulse transitions from their proper positions relative to the beginning of the start pulse. The magnitude of the distortion is expressed in percent of a perfect unit pulse length.

TELEVISION A standard TV channel today fits into a frequency bandwidth of six megahertz.

TELEWATCH New York Telephone's Telewatch is a maintenance service which periodically tests NYTel analog DID trunks for transmission loss, noise and trouble.

TELEX A worldwide switched message service. Telex service is offered in the United States by the Western Union Telegraph Company, MCI, ITT, RCA, FTCC and TRT. Telex has one gigantic advantage: Overseas it's very popular and widely used. Contacting overseas businesses by telex is often far more reliable and faster than contacting them by telephone. Telex is good for overseas time zone differences because you can send a message to an unattended telex machine. It also delivers a printed record. Telex is relatively inexpensive usually costing a little less than a phone call. Telex has one disadvantage: It's very slow and not very accurate with virtually no data communications error checking procedures. Telex is being rapidly displaced by faster, more accurate forms of data communications, including the public packet switched networks and the various electronic mail services, and most recently by massive competition from low-cost facsimile machines. See TELETEX.

TELNET The process by which a person using one computer can sign on to a computer in another city, state or country. Terminal-remote host protocol developed for ARPAnet. Using Telnet, you can work from your PC as if it were a terminal attached to another machine by a hard-wired line. The TCP/IP protocol governing the exchange of character-oriented terminal data.

TELPAK A discontinued AT&T service that gave large customers discounts on purchases of multiple analog private lines. Telpak was to discourage users from building their own private microwave systems. Users who bought Telpak, however, were not allowed to resell any of the circuits, though they were allowed to share them. The FCC ruled Telpak as being discriminatory against competition. (It was too cheap.) It may still exist on an intrastate basis in some states. Telpak typically came in bundles of 12, 24, 60 and 240 voice lines. The bigger the bundle, the cheaper the per circuit cost.

TELSTAR 1 Telstar 1 was the world's first active communications satellite. It was launched on July 10, 1962. Sputnik was launched on October 4, 1957.

TELSTRA OTC Telstra OTC is Australia's largest local and overseas phone company. It was formed in February of 1992 by the merger of national (Telecom) and international (OTC) carriers. According to a press release of June 1993, the company has 76,000 employees, 8 million customers and 120 products and services. It claims to be the sixth largest user of Intelsat and the third largest owner of submarine cable in the world.

TEMA Telecommunication Engineering and Manufacturing Association limited.

TEMPERATURE RATING The maximum temperature at which the insulating material may be used in continuous operation without loss of its basic properties.

TEMPEST Unclassified short name referring to the investigation, study, and control of compromising emanations from electrical and electronic equipment. Devices which are tempest-secure mean they do not send emanate electromagnetic signals which can, potentially, be received by others, i.e. enemies.

TEMPLATE 1. A voice processing term. A pattern of information as a function of time, which is intended to represent an entire word. 2. A Northern Telecom Norstar definition: A system-wide setting assigned during System Startup. The most important effects of a template are the number of lines assigned to the telephones, and the assignment of Line Pool Access. Templates will also assign other system-wide defaults, such as Prime Line and Ringing Line assignment. It is important to understand that a template is only provided as a convenience, and that any settings effected by the template can be changed.

TEMPORARY STATION DISCONNECTION Allows the attendant to completely remove selected phones from service at any time on a temporary basis.

TENANT SERVICE Some businesses acquire a telephone system too large for their needs so they sell parts of the service to smaller offices in their own building or in the surrounding community. There are two ways to make money on tenant service — renting phone equipment or re-selling long distance lines. There's more money on re-selling long distance lines.

TENSILE STRENGTH A term denoting the greatest longitudinal tensile stress a substance can bear withour tearing apart or rupturing.

TERA- A million million, or a thousand giga-. Megabytes is one million bytes. Gigabytes is one thousand million bytes. And terabytes is one thousand gigabytes, or one million megabytes. A petabyte is equal to 1,000 exabytes. An exabyte is equal to 1,000 terabytes. A terabyte is equal to 1,000 gigabytes, or one million megabytes, or one million million, or ten to the 12th power.

TERABYTE A million million bytes. One terabyte is equal to 10 to 12th. See TERA-.

TERAFLOP A trillion floating point instructions per second. A measure of a computer's speed.

TERAHERTZ THz. A unit denoting one trillion (10 to the 12th) hertz. See TERA-

TERMINAL 1. The point at which a telephone line ends, or is connected to other circuits of a network. 2. An input/output device for communicating with computers. Typically has a keyboard and a CRT (TV screen) display. See TERMINALS.

TERMINAL ADAPTER An interfacing device employed at the "R" reference point in an ISDN environment that allows connection of a non-ISDN terminal at the physical layer to communicate with an ISDN network. Typically, this adapter will support standard RJ-11 telephone connection plugs for voice and RS-232C, V.35 and RS-449 interfaces for data.

TERMINAL BLOCK A device used to connect one group of wires to another. Usually each wire can be connected to several other wires in a bus or common arrangement. A 66-type block is the most common type of connecting block. It was invented by Western Electric. orthern Telecom has a terminal block called a Bix block. There are others. A terminating block is also called a connecting block, a punch-down block, a quick-connect block, a cross-connect block. A connecting block will include insulation displacement connections (IDC). In other words, with a connecting block, you don't have to remove the plastic shielding from around your wire conductor before you "punch it down."

TERMINAL CONFIGURATION The functional interconnection of the components of a terminal. For example, a keyboard-printer may be configured to transmit keystrokes without printing them. Printing is only performed on data retrieved from the communication line. Terminals with multiple components can be configured in a variety of ways.

TERMINAL EMULATION An application that allows an intelligent computing device such as a PC to mimic or emulate the operation of a dumb terminal for communications with a mainframe or minicomputer. It does this with special printed circuit boards inserted into its motherboard and/or special software. For example, TELECONNECT uses the communications software program called Crosstalk to emulate a DEC VT-100, a Digital Equipment Corporation VT-100 terminal. We do this because emulating a DEC VT-100 works better with certain software programs we call up remotely.

TERMINAL EQUIPMENT Terminal Equipment usually refers to the telephones and other equipment at the end of telephone lines.

TERMINAL IMPEDANCE The impedance as measured at the unloaded output terminals of transmission equipment or a line that is otherwise in normal operating condition. The ratio of voltage to current at the output terminals of a device, including the connected load.

TERMINAL NODE In IBM's SNA, a peripheral node that is not user-programmable, having less intelligence and processing capability than a cluster node.

TERMINAL REPEATER A repeater for use at the end of a trunk line.

TERMINAL SERVER A device that allows the input/output of a variety of terminals to be multiplexed onto a LAN cable. A terminal server has a single network interface and several ports for terminal connections. The advantage of a terminal server is it allows many terminals to be connected to a host via a single existing LAN cable, rather than a variety of point-to-point cables. Digital Equipment's DECnet makes heavy use of terminal servers.

TERMINAL TABLE An ordered collection of information that identifies each line, phone, component or application program from which a message can be sent.

TERMINALS The screws or soldering lugs to which an external circuit can be connected.

TERMINALS TO LONG DISTANCE OPERATOR Commonly known as "toll terminals", they provide special trunks directly to the long distance telephone company operators. Upon completion of long distance calls, the toll operator will ring the attendant (or hotel operator) and give them "time and charges" for the phone call just ended.

TERMINATE 1. To connect a wire conductor to something, typically a piece of equipment. 2. To end one's telecommunications service or equipment rental.

TERMINATED 1. The condition of a wire or cable pair which is connected to (terminated on) binding posts or a terminal block. 2. The condition of a circuit connected to a network which has the same impedance the circuit would have if it were infinitely long.

TERMINATED LINE A telephone circuit with a resistance at the far end equal to the characteristic impedance of the line, so no reflections or standing waves are present when a signal is entered at the near end. Compare with bridge tap.

TERMINATING CHANNEL The name for the circuit in a private line channel that connects a local central office with the CBX/PBX or telephone instrument at the customer's premises.

TERMINATING OFFICE The switching center (i.e. the central office) of the person you're calling (the "called party").

TERMINATING RESISTOR A grounding resistor placed at the end of a bus, line, or cable to prevent signals from being reflected or echoed. Sometimes shortened to terminator.

TERMINATION Termination involves the placement of impedance matching circuits on a bus to prevent signals from being reflected or echoed.

TERMINATION RESTRICTION Prevents a user from receiving any calls on the phone line. A DID call to the restricted termination routes to an attendant, an announcement or intercept tone at customer option. All other calls route to intercept tone.

TERMINATION OF SERVICE The end of service of a line or equipment. All pursuant to the regulations set forth in the tariff.

TERMINATOR Most local area networks are bus configurations. This means one long piece of cable (coaxial or fiber) with workstations connected along the way, typically with "T" connectors. For a network to work properly, you need to place resistance at the end of the bus, to terminate it. A thin wire Ethernet typically requires a 50 ohm resistance at either end of the bus. You can buy these Ethernet terminators already included in a connector.

TERMINUS A device used to terminate an optical fiber that provides a means to locate and contain an optical fiber within a connector.

TERRESTRIAL Long distance facilities which are entirely on land and do not use satellites. This includes microwave, coaxial cable, optical fiber, normal cable, etc. There are reasons to prefer terrestrial facilities over satellite facilities, though satellites also have many advantages:

1.No echo or delay in voice conversation. Some people find satellite conversations disturbing because of the delay; and 2. No significant reduction in data throughput. Most data communications protocols send their data in "chunks" and require an acknowledgement from the other end when one chunk has been received before the next chunk can be sent. When it takes a long time for an acknowledgement to be received (as in a satellite circuit), the effective throughput of data becomes very slow.

When you're trying to send one one-way signal to many locations, satellites often do a better and cheaper job.

TEST AND VALIDATION Physical measurements taken to verify conclusions obtained from mathematical modeling and analysis.

TEST ANTENNA An antenna of known performance characteristics used in determining transmission characteristics of equipment and associated propagation paths.

TEST BOARD A switchboard equipped with testing apparatus.

TEST CENTER Equipment for detecting and diagnosing faults and problems with communications lines and the equipment attached to them. If centralized, a facility where a network manager or technician can gain access to (almost) any circuit in a network for the purpose of running diagnostic testing. Also called a network control center.

TEST DESK A desk equipped with equipment to test and repair subscriber lines. See also TEST CENTER.

TEST SET A telephone handset with extra electronics designed to test telephone circuits. Also called a butt set, since it typically hangs on the technician's tool belt near the wearer's butt... Well, that's one explanation. Another is that it's called a "butt" set because it allows the use to "butt in" to a conversation and listen to its quality, etc.

TEST SHOE A device that is applied to a circuit at a distributing frame to gain test access to circuit conductors.

TEST TONE A tone used to find trouble on phone lines. A more technical explanation: A tone sent at a predetermined level and frequency through a transmission system to facilitate measurement and/or alignment of the gains and/or losses of devices in the transmission circuit.

TEST, FRIENDLY BUSY A test to see if a line is busy. The subscriber does not know the line is being tested. Such a test is usually performed if someone calling that number requests it.

TETRODE A four-element vacuum tube, consisting of filament (or cathode), grid, screen grid and plate.

TEXT Transmitted characters which make up the body of a message.

TEXT FILE A file containing only letters, numbers, and symbols. A text file contains no formatting information (like bolding and underlining and type fonts and sizes), except possibly line feeds and carriage returns. A text file is an ASCII file. A text file can be read by every word processor and editor. A text file the lowest common denominator in the word processing world. I wrote this file with an editor called ZEdit, which produces only text files. I did this because this dictionary has to be sent to a Macintosh for "typesetting" and to a DEC for distribution on CD-ROM. And a text file is the form both most easily recognize.

TEXT-TO-SPEECH SYNTHESIS TTS. Technologies for converting textual (ASCII) information into synthetic speech output. Used in voice processing applications requiring production of broad, unrelated and unpredictable vocabularies, e.g., products in a catalog, names and addresses, etc. This technology is appropriate when system design constraints prevent the more efficient use of speech concatenation alone. See SPEECH CONCATENATION.

TFT Thin Film Transistor. A display technology which uses modern active matrix technology that operates by assigning a tiny transistor to each pixel, making it possible to control pixels independently of each other. TFT screens are very fast, have a high contrast ratio and a wide viewing area.

TFTP Trivial File Transfer Protocol. A simplified version of FTP that transfers files but does not provide password protection or user-directory capability. It is associated with the TCP/IP family of protocols.

TFTS Terrestrial Flight Telephone System.

TGB Trunk Group Busy.

TGC Transmission Group Control in IBM's SNA.

TGW Trunk Group Warning.

TH Transmission Header, an SNA term.

THE PHONE COMPANY Also known by the initials TPC. In the 1966 James Coburn movie "The President's Analyst", the evil worldwide conspiracy was run by TPC, which turned out to be The Phone Company. Some people believe the movie was not fiction.

THERMAL NOISE Noise created in an electronic circuit by movement and collision of electrons.

THERMIONIC EMISSION The emission of electrons or ions under the influence of heat, as in a vacuum tube cathode.

THERMISTOR A device made from mixtures of metal oxides that exhibits large negative coefficient of resistance changes as the temperature increases.

THERMOCOULE Two dissimilar wires joined together that generate a voltage proportional to temperature when their junction is heated.

THERMOPLASTIC Material that will resoften and distort from its formed shape when heated above a critical temperature peculiar to the material.

THERMOSET A plastic material which is crosslinked by a heating process known as curing. Once cured, thermosets cannot be reshaped.

THERMOSTAT Device responding to temperature changes, used to control heating and cooling equipment.

THF Tremendously High Frequency.

THI Telephone Headset Integrator. A new form of headset manufacturer who will make headsets that do new tasks, like take a phone off hook without physically having to lift the receiver off the phone.

THICK ETHERNET CABLE Thick Ethernet cable is 0.4-inch diameter, 50-ohm coaxial cable. Thick Ethernet cable can be bought in pre-cut lengths, with standard N-Series male connectors installed on each end. It also is available in bulk cable without connectors. Any of the following types of connectors will work:

Belden 9880 or Belden 89889

Montrose CBL5688 or Montrose CBL5713

Malco 250-4315-0004 or Malco 250-4314-0003

Inmac 1784 or Inmac 1785

THICKNET Jargon used to describe thick Ethernet coaxial cable.

THIN ETHERNET A coaxial (0.2-inch, RG58A/U 50-ohm) that uses a smaller diameter coaxial cable than standard thick Ethernet. Thin Ethernet is also called "Cheapernet" due to the lower cabling cost. Thin Ethernet systems tend to have transceivers on the network interface card, rather than in external boxes. PCs connect to the Thin Ethernet bus via a coaxial "T" connector. Thin Ethernet is now the most common Ethernet coaxial cable, though twisted pair is gaining. Thin Ethernet is also referred to as ThinNet, ThinWire or Cheapernet. See also 10BASE-T.

THINNET Jargon used to describe thin Ethernet coaxial cable. Referred to ThinNet, ThinWire or Cheapernet.

THINWIRE See ThinNet.

THIRD PARTY CALL Any call charged to a number other than that of the origination or destination party. It's not a good idea to let your employees make third party calls to one or more of your phone numbers. Best to ask them to place the calls on their personal phone credit cards. This way, they will spend a modicum of time justifying their exorbitant phone calls.

THIRD WIRE TAP The activating of a telephone handset microphone by using a third wire, thus bypassing the hook switch.

THREAD A sequence of computing instructions that make up a program. A multi-threaded process can have multiple threads, each executing independently and each executing on separate processors. A multi-threaded program, if running on a computer with multiple processors, will run much faster than a single-threaded program running on a single processor machine. Windows NT is scheduled to be the first generally-available multi-threaded PC operating system.

THREADED CODE Threaded code is also known as Threaded Pseudo Code, or threaded p-code. It was first popularized in a software language called Forth. Eventually Microsoft fixed Forth and changed it into Basic. See THREAD, THREADS and MULTITHREADING.

THREADS Individual processes within a single application.

THREE FINGER SALUTE Ctrl Alt Delete.

THREE SLOT An obsolete pay phone that is identified by three separate coin slots.

THREE-WAY CALLING A local phone company feature that allows a phone user to add another user to an existing conversation and have a three party conference call.

THREE-WATT BOOSTER Optional equipment for use with a cellular phone car-mounting kit that raises a portable phone's maximum transmission power from 0.6 watts to 3.0 watts.

THREE-WAY CONFERENCE TRANSFER A PBX feature. By depressing the switchhook, a user can dial another extension and either hang up and transfer the call, get information from the called party and then resume the first call or bridge all parties together for a three-way conference call.

THRESHOLD The minimum value of a signal that can be detected by the system or sensor under consideration.

THRESHOLD OF PAIN 1. The present price of local telephone service. 2. Unbearable noise.

THROUGH DIALING Allows the attendant on a phone system to select a trunk and pass dial tone to a restricted phone user so that user may directly dial an outside call.

THROUGHPUT The actual amount of useful and non-redundant information which is transmitted or processed. Throughput is the end result of a data call. It may only be a small part of what was pumped in at the other end. The relationship of what went in one end and what came out the other is a measure of the efficiency of that communications link — a function of cleanliness, speed, etc.

THZ Terahertz (10 to the 12th power hertz). See also SPECTRUM DESIGNATION OF FREQUENCY.

TIA Telecommunications Industry Association. A new Washington lobbying and trade association, the result of the merger of the USTA (United States Telephone Association) and the EIA (Electronic Industries Association. See also EIA/TIA-232-E.

TIC 1. An AT&T term for a digital carrier facility used to transmit a DS-1 formatted digital signal at 3.152 Mbps. 2. Token-Ring Interface Coupler. An IBM device that allows a controller or processor to attach directly to a Token-Ring network. This is an optional part of several IBM terminal cluster controllers and front-end processors.

TIC CARD Token Ring Interface Coupler is the IBM name for a variety of token ring adapter cards used to connect IBM controllers to token ring LANs. See TIC.

TICK TONE Clicking noise heard on some PBX lines indicating that the digits dialed will shortly be repeated to the central office.

TICKER A one-way telex machine used to typically report stock or commodity prices. The machine prints on ticker tape, which is about one inch wide and perfect for throwing out windows at passing celebrities. Thus the term "Ticker Tape Parade."

TICKET A telephone industry term for a filled-out form, usually a form for billing someone for a call. There are all sorts of tickets, including ones on paper, ones on computer and ones automatically generated without human intervention.

TIE 1. Joining cables and/or wires together. 2. Time Interval Error. 3. Trusted Information Environment, an encryption scheme.

TIE/communications A large PBX and key system distributor to end users based in Seymour, CT. TIE was one of the original manufacturers of interconnect equipment in the US. TIE stood for Telephone Interconnect Equipment. The company fell on hard times in the late 1980s. It ceased manufacturing equipment and ceased acting as a wholesaler of others' equipment. Now it's simply a distributor and Nitsuko, its primary Japanese supplier, has taken over the sale of its own equipment directly.

TIE DOWN Verb meaning to terminate a wire on a main, intermediate or satellite distribution frame.

TIE LINE A dedicated circuit linking two points without having to dial the normal phone number. A tie line may be accessed by lifting a telephone handset or by pushing one, two or three buttons.

TIE TRUNK A dedicated circuit linking two PBXs.

TIE TRUNK ACCESS Allows a phone system to handle tie lines which can be accessed either by dialing a trunk group access code or through the attendant.

TIFF Tagged Image File Format. TIFF provides a way of storing and exchanging digital image data. Aldus Corp., Microsoft Corp., and major scanner vendors developed TIFF to help link scanned images with the popular desktop publishing applications. It is now used for many different types of software applications ranging from medical imagery to fax modem data transfers, CAD programs, and 3D graphic packages. The current TIFF specification supports three main types of image data: Black and white data, halftones or dithered data, and grayscale data. Some wags think TIFF stands for "Took It From a FotograF." It doesn't.

TIES Time Indpendent Escape Sequence, a feature of modems.

TIGHT JACKET BUFFER A buffer construction which uses a direct extrusion of plastic over the basic fiber coating. This construction serves to protect the fiber from crushing and impact loads and to some extent from the microbending induced during cabling operations. See also LOOSE TUBE BUFFER.

TIGHTLY COUPLED Describing the interrelationship of processing units that share real storage, that are controlled by the same control program and that communicate directly with each other. Compare with loosely coupled.

TIGHTLY COUPLED CPUs Term used to describe multiple-processor computers in which several processors share the same memory and bus.

TIME ASSIGNMENT SPEECH INTERPOLATION See TASI.

TIME CONGESTION The time resources (outgoing trunks) are busy.

TIME DIVERT TO ATTENDANT A system feature which automatically transfers a phone to the attendant if the phone has been left off-hook too long.

TIME DIVERSITY A method of transmission wherein a signal representing the same information is sent over the same channel at different times. Often used over systems subject to burst error conditions and with the spacing adjusted to be longer than an error burst.

TIME DIVISION CONTROLLER TDC. A device which commands functions, monitors status and connects channels of TDM cards.

TIME DIVISION MULTIPLE ACCESS TDMA. A technique originated in satellite communications to interweave multiple conversations into one transponder so as to appear to get simultaneous conversations. A variation on TASI. A technique now used in cellular and other wireless communications. See TDMA.

TIME DIVISION MULTIPLEX TDM. A technique for transmitting a number of separate data, voice and/or video signals simultaneously over one communications medium by quickly interleaving a piece of each signal one after another. Here's our problem. We have to transport the freight of five manufacturers from Chicago to New York. Each manufacturer's freight will fit into 20 rail boxcars. We have three basic solutions. First, build five separate railway lines from Chicago to New York. Second, rent five engines and schlepp five complete trains to New York on one railway track. Or, third, join all the boxcars together into one train of 100 boxcars and run them on one track. The train might look like this: Engine, Boxcar from Producer A, Box Car from Producer B, Producer C, Producer D, Producer E, and then the order begins again...Boxcar from Producer A, Producer B...Moving one large train of 100 boxcars is likely to be cheaper and more efficient than moving five smaller trains each of 20 boxcars on five separate railway tracks. Time Division Multiplexing, thus, represents substantial savings over have five separate networks (five separate tracks) and sending five separate transmissions (five separate trains).

This is what Time Division Multiplexing is all about. And the analogy is perfect. Take one large train (fast communications channel) and interleave pieces (boxcars) from each conversation one after another. If you do this fast enough, you'll never notice you've broken the conversations apart, moved them separately, and then put them back together at the distant end. In TDM, you "sample" each voice conversation, interleave the samples, send them on their way, then reconstruct the several conversations at the other end. There are several ways to do the sampling. You can sample eight bits (one byte) of each conversation, or you can sample one bit. The former is called word interleaving; the latter bit interleaving. The basic goal of multiplexing — whether it be time division multiplexing, or any other form — is to save money, to cram more conversations (voice, data, video or facsimile) onto fewer phone lines. To substitute electronics for copper. See MULTIPLEXING.

TIME DIVISION MULTIPLEXER TDM. A device which derives multiple channels on a single transmission facility by connecting bit streams one at a time at regular intervals. It interleaves bits or characters from each terminal or device using the time. See TIME DIVISION MULTIPLEX.

TIME DIVISION SIGNALING Signaling over a time-division multiplex system in which all voice channels share a common signaling channel, with time division providing the separation between signaling channels. See SIGNALING SYSTEM 7.

NEWTON'S TELECOM DICTIONARY

TIME DIVISION SWITCHING The connection of two circuits in a network by assigning them to the same time slot on a common time division switched bus.

TIME DOMAIN REFLECTOMETER TDR. A testing device that acts on radar-like principles to determine the location of metallic circuit faults.

TIME GUARD BAND A time interval left vacant on a channel to provide a margin of safety against interference in the time domain between sequential operations, such as detection, integration, differentiation, transmission, encoding, decoding, or switching.

TIME JITTERS Short-term variation or instability in the duration of a specified interval.

TIME MARKER A reference signal, often repeated periodically, enabling the correlation of specific events with a time scale. markers are used in some systems for establishing synchronization.

TIME MULTIPLEXED SWITCH The space switch of which the cross point settings are changed in each time slot.

TIME OF DAY DISPLAY The time and date displays on phones. Actually, it's very useful information. Sometimes it's not displayed on the operator's console. As a result, the operator may never know that every phone in the office is showing the wrong time and date.

TIME OF DAY ROUTING 1. This feature automatically changes access to certain types of lines at times when the lines change from being expensive to cheap, or vice versa. For example, it's cheaper to use WATS lines before 8:00 AM in the morning. A company has offices in New York and Los Angeles. It might be cheaper to route calls to Chicago in the morning over the tie lines to LA and then out the LA WATS lines to Chicago, than to go directly out the New York WATS lines. 2. This is a way to allocate bandwidth for LAN traffic over corporate T1 Networks. By programming T1 multiplexers, customers can allocate the amount of T1 bandwidth that can be used by voice, data, and LAN traffic on a time of day basis. For example, during the day, most of the T1 bandwidth can be allocated for voice. At night, after employees go home, more bandwidth can be allocated to LAN and other computer data traffic so that file transfers can be done faster. This is particularly useful in IBM mainframe environments where large amounts of data needs to be transferred form remote offices/divisions to the headquarters.

TIME OUT In telecommunications and computer networks, an event which occurs at the end of a predetermined interval of time is called Time Out. For example if you lift the phone off the cradle and do not proceed to dial, after a certain number of seconds you will hear either a voice telling you to get on with it or a howling sound of some sort. Data networks have the same thing. Don't do anything for x minutes and the system will knock you off the air, i.e. hang up on you. In more technical terms, time out is the amount of time that

992

hardware or software waits for an expected event before taking corrective action. In its most common form, time out is the amount of time an OCC or telephone system waits after your call goes through before it begins billing or timing the call. Also see ANSWER SUPERVISION.

TIME SHARING A mode of operation that provides for the interleaving of two or more independent processes on one functional unit. Its most common use is the interleaved use of time on a computing system enabling two or more users to execute computer programs concurrently. Time sharing of computer resources is now relatively obsolete. See also TIMESHARING below.

TIME SLICE In a multitasking environment, each task is allotted a portion of the CPU's overall processing power. This portion is called a time-slice. The CPU switches between tasks, and those with higher priority receive more time-slices than lower-priority tasks.

TIME SLICING The term used to describe the dividing of a computer resource so multiple applications or tasks requesting the resource are allocated some amount of the resource's time. See TIME SLICE.

TIME SLOT 1. In time division multiplexing or switching, the slot belonging to a voice, data or video conversation. It can be occupied with conversation or left blank. But the slot is always present. You can tell the capacity of the switch or the transmission channel by figuring how many slots are present. 2. An SCSA term. The smallest switchable data unit on the SCbus or SCxbus Data Bus. A time slot consists of eight consecutive bits of data. One time slot is equivalent to a data path with a bandwidth of 64 Kbps.

TIME SPACE TIME SYSTEM TST. The most common form of switching matrix for small digital telephone exchanges in which a space switch is sandwiched between two time switches.

TIME SWITCH A device incorporating a clock which arranges to switch equipment on or off at predetermined times.

TIMED DETECTION As a substitute for answer supervision, some long distance phone companies use call timing and estimate that a call is completed if the caller remains off-hook for 30 seconds or more. This is not necessarily accurate, of course. The caller might be holding, thinking the person is in the shower, out in the garden, etc. Little does the caller know he is now being charged to listen to ringing signals. A long distance phone company that is "equal accessed" doesn't have this problem. A long distance company that isn't equal accessed — one that you have to dial directly with a local call — might well have this problem. Rule: When in doubt, don't wait too long on the phone listening to endless ringing. Hang up. Count to ten. Then redial.

TIMED RECALL Your PBX can be instructed to place a call at a designated time. When the time comes, your PBX rings your phone. When you answer your phone, the PBX places the call.

TIMED REMINDERS At 20-second intervals, timed reminders will alert an attendant that a call is still waiting, a called line has not yet been answered or a call is still on hold. Timed reminders can be made longer or shorter. They can alert attendants to all sorts of events and non-events.

TIMEOUT If a device is not performing a task, the amount of time the computer should wait before detecting it as an error.

TIMESHARING The use of one computer by many users at one time. Each user is typically sitting in front of a data terminal and connected to the master computer through communications lines — local or long distance. The user asks the computer to work on his task, whether it be a simple as looking up some stock prices, checking an airline reservation or doing some accounting calculations. It appears to each user as if he/she has a computer dedicated to his own task, but the computer is large and powerful, and is moving rapidly from one user's task to the next. Timesharing's advantages are twofold: 1. The user may find it cheaper to time share a computer than to buy his own. 2. The computer may have valuable and extensive information in it, which would be virtually impossible to duplicate or handle in many stand-alone computers. Timesharing was more popular when computers were more expensive.

TIMING JITTER In digital carrier systems, an accumulative relative timing discrepancy between digital signal elements.

TIMING RECOVERY The derivation of a timing signal from a received signal.

TIMING SIGNAL The output of a clock. A signal used to synchronize connected equipment.

TINNED WIRE Copper wire coated with tin to make soldering easier.

TINSEL A component of some phone line cord conductors. Tinsel is made by rolling copper into very thin, narrow rolls and then winding several strands of tinsel around a non-metallic core (a string) and then placing an insulating cover over the resulting conductor. A cord is then built up of two or more conductors encased in a plastic jacket. The essential reason for this type of construction is to obtain good cord flexibility and long life.

TIP 1. The first wire in a pair of wires. The second wire is called the "ring" wire. 2. A conductor in a telephone cable pair which is usually connected to positive side of a battery at the telephone company's central office. It is the phone industry's equivalent of Ground in a normal electrical circuit. See TIP & RING.

TIP & RING An old fashioned way of saying "plus" and "minus," or ground and positive in electrical circuits. Tip and Ring are telephony terms. They derive their names from the operator's cordboard plug. The tip wire was connected to the tip of the plug, and the ring wire was connected to the slip ring around the jack. A third conductor on some jacks was called the sleeve. That's it. Nothing more sinister. Nothing more interesting.

TIP CABLE A small cable connecting terminals on a distributing frame to cable pairs in the cable vault.

TIP CONDUCTOR The first conductor of a customer line.

TIP SIDE That conductor of a circuit which is associated with the tip of a plug, or of a telephone circuit.

TIPI Telephone Industry Price Index.

TIS Technical Information Sheets.

TITLES In the language of multimedia, when an author sells what he or she has created, it is called a title. The encyclopedias, dictionaries, musical works, and games available on CD are all "titles." Someone authors the material, and sells it to users who can play it back but not change the content.

TJF Test Jack Frame.

TL Tie Line.

TL1 Transaction Language 1. A machine to machine communications language which is a subset of CCITT's man machine language.

TLA Three Letter Acronym. A form and usage common to our acronym-happy industry.

TLB Test LoopBack. A CSU (Channel Service Unit) operating mode that loops the telco's T-1 transmission facility back towards itself at itself at the same time it loops the CPE back toward itself.

TLF Trunk Link Frame.

TLP Transmission Level Point.

TMA Telecommunication Managers Association.

TMS Time Multiplexed Switch. In the AT&T 5ESS switch CM, the TM provides switch paths between switching modules and passes control messages to and from the message switch, and functions as the hub for clock distribution to the switching modules.

TN Twisted Nematic. Most used display technology for calculators, watches and measuring equipment. TN uses liquid crystals sandwiched between two plates of glass with integrated transparent electrodes which can be made transparent and non-transparent by applying an electric current to them. See LCD.

TNC A small connector used on coaxial cable, commonly used for cellular antennas, and some data and test equipment.

TNL Terminal Net Loss.

TOA/NPI Type Of Address/Numbering Plan Identifier.

TOGGLE 1. A flip-flop switch that changes for every input pulse. 2. Any simple two-position switch.

TOKEN 1. In networking, a unique combination of bits used to confer transmit privileges to a computer on a local area network. It also carries important information for routing messages over the network, such as source and destination addresses, access control information, route control information, and date checking information. When a LAN-attached computer receives a token, it has been given permission to transmit. On a token ring network, the token is 24 bits long. See TOKEN PASSING and TOKEN RING. 2. Here is a Rolm definition: The floating master message which coordinates use of the CBX control packet network among the nodes connected to it. See TOKEN PASSING, TOKEN BUS and TOKEN RING.

TOKEN BUS A local network access mechanism and topology in which all phones or workstations attached to the bus listen for a broadcast token or supervisory frame. That token confers on them the right to communicate over the share channel, the token bus. An example of a Token-Bus is IEEE 802.4. See TOKEN PASSING.

TOKEN LATENCY The time it takes for a token to be passed around the local area network ring.

TOKEN PASSING A method whereby each device on a local area network receives and passes the right to use the single channel on the LAN. The key to remember is that a token passing, or token ring LAN has only one channel. It's a high-speed channel. It can move a lot of data. But it can only move one "conversation" at a time. The Token acts like a traffic cop. It confers the privilege to send a transmission. Tokens are special bit patterns or packets, usually several bits in length, which circulate from node to node when there is no message traffic. Possession of the token gives exclusive access to the network for transmission of a message. The token is generated by one device on the network. If that device is turned off or fails, another device will assume the token creation task. When the package of token and message reaches its destination, the computer copies the message. The package is then put back on the network where it continues to circulate until it returns to the source computer. The source computer then releases the token for the next computer in the sequence.

With token passing it is possible to give some computers more access to the token than others. Usually one device on the network is designated the token manager. It generates the token. If that device is turned off or fails, another device will assume management of the token. There is a complicated sequence of events that result in the generation of a token and that deal with the eventuality of token loss or destruction. The logic for this process is built into token ring cards that fit inside computers. In some manufacturers' products, the logic is slightly different and can cause incompatibilities. See TOKEN, TOKEN RING and TOKEN RING PACKET

TOKEN RING A ring type of local area network (LAN) in which a supervisory frame, or token, must be received by an attached terminal or workstation before that terminal or workstation can start transmitting. The workstation with the token then transmits and uses the entire bandwidth of whatever communications media the token ring network is using. A token ring is a baseband network. Token ring is the technique used by IBM, Arcnet, and others. A token ring LAN can be wired as a circle or a star, with all workstations wired to a central wiring center, or to multiple wiring centers. The most common wiring scheme is called a star-wired ring. In this configuration, each computer is wired directly to a device called a Multi-station Access Unit (MAU). These are usually grouped together in a wiring closet for convenience. The MAU is wired in such a way as to create a ring between the computers. If one of the computers is turned off or breaks or its cable to the MAU is broken, the MAU automatically recreates the ring without that computer. This gives token ring networks great flexibility, reliability, and ease of configuration and maintenance.

Despite the wiring, a token ring LAN always works logically as a circle, with the token passing around the circle from one workstation to another. The advantage of token ring LANs is that media faults (broken cable) can be fixed easily. It's easy to isolate them. Token rings are typically installed in centralized closets, with loops snaking to served workstations. Some other LANs require your going up in the ceiling or into walls and finding coax taps. All the work on a token ring can be done on one or several panels. These panels allow you to isolate workstations, and thus isolate faults.

Token Ring LANs can operate at transmission rates of either 4M bits per second or 16M bits per second. The number of computers that can be connected to a single Token Ring LAN is limited to 256. The typical installation is usually less than 100. Large installations connect multiple token ring LANS with bridges. The theoretical limit of Ethernet, measured in 64 byte packets, is 14,800 packets per second (PPS). By comparison, Token Ring is 30,000 and FDDI is 170,000. See FDDI-II and FDDI TERMS. Help on this definition courtesy Tad Witkowicz of Crosscom, Marlboro, MA, Tim Becker, Lanquest Group, Santa Clara, CA and Elaine Jones, VP Marketing, Coral Network Corporation, Marlborough, MA. See also BRIDGE. IBM TOKEN RING, MAU, TOKEN PASSING, TOKEN RING, TOKEN RING CARD and TOKEN RING PACKET.

TOKEN RING CARD Name given to the circuit board inserted into a computer device for connection to a token ring LAN. This board provides the physical connection to the LAN. It also participates in the collective management of the token by sending various messages to other token ring cards. Usually, one token ring card on the network is designated the token manager. It automatically generates a token as soon as it discovers one is missing, often with the help of other token ring cards. The sending of messages between token ring cards can be used to gather information about what is taking place on the network. Statistics may be collected. These may indicated that the network should be altered in some way to improve performance. This management capability is a distinct advantage of token ring LANs. One possible drawback is that various manufacturers' token ring cards may differ slightly in how they implement token management, thereby making them incompatible in certain management features. Virtually all token ring cards will work together in basic token passing.

TOKEN RING PACKET Packets on a token ring network are made up of nine fields: starting delimiter, access control, frame control, destination address, source address, routing information, the data, frame check sequence, and ending delimiter.

Starting Delimiter (SD): This is an 8-bit binary (1s and 0s) sequence which marks the beginning of a data packet.

Access Control (AC) and Frame Control (AC): These are two 8-bit sequences that are used by the computers for maintenance purposes.

Destination Address (DA): This is a 48-bit sequence that uniquely identifies the physical name of the computer to which the data packet is being transmitted. Each computer on a ring examines this field to determine if the packet is for it.

Source Address (SA): This is a 48-bit sequence that uniquely identifies the physical name of the computer that send the data packet. This is used by the receiving computer to formulate its acknowledgement.

Routing Information (RI): This is a variable-length sequence used if the data packet is being sent to a computer located on another token ring LAN. (This information can make it impossible for some bridges to route some packets. See BRIDGE.)

Data: This is a variable-length sequence (up to 17,800 bytes) that is the actual data being sent from source to destination.

Frame Check Sequence (FCS): This 32-bit sequence is used to protect the contents of the packet from being corrupted during transmission. See FRAME CHECK SEQUENCE.

Ending Delimiter (ED): This is an 8-bit sequence that signals the end of a packet.

TOKENTALK The Apple Macintosh implementation of the Token Ring local area network.

TOLL CALL A call to any location outside the local service area. A long distance call.

TOLL CENTER A Class Four central office.

TOLL CONNECTING TRUNK A trunk used to connect a Class 5 office (local central office) to the direct distance dialing network.

TOLL DENIAL Permits phone user to make local calls but denies completion of toll calls or calls to the toll operator without the assistance of the attendant. See TOLL RESTRICTION.

NEWTON'S TELECOM DICTIONARY

TOLL DIVERSION A system service feature by which users are denied the ability to place toll calls without the assistance of a human attendant. Toll diversion affects the entire switching system instead of discriminating between individual extensions.

TOLL FRAUD Theft of long distance service. Today's most common forms of toll fraud are DISA, voice mail and shoulder surfing. According to John Haugh of Telecommunications Advisors in Portland, OR, there are three distinct varieties of toll fraud:

"First Party" Toll Fraud, which is helped along by a member of the management or staff of a user. An example would be the telecommunications manager at the Human Resources department of New York City (an "insider") who sold his agency's internal code to the thieves, who in turn ran up unauthorized long distance charges exceeding $500,000.

"Second Party" Toll Fraud, which is facilitated by a staff member or subcontractor of a long distance carrier IXCs, vendor or local exchange telephone company selling the information to the actual thieves, or their "middlemen." An example would be a "back office clerk" working for one of these concerns who sells the codes to others.

"Third Party" Toll Fraud is facilitated by unrelated "strangers" who, though various artifices, either "hack" into a user's equipment and learn the codes and procedures, or obtain the needed information through some other source, to commit Toll Fraud.

TOLL OFFICE A central office used primarily for supervising and switching toll traffic.

TOLL RESTRICTION To curb a telephone user's ability to make long distance calls. Toll restriction capability on modern PBXs and key telephone systems has been increasing in sophistication. Some PBXs now allow selective restriction based on specific extensions, users or geography. In other words, Joe Smith, the president, could call everywhere. John Doe in accounting might only be allowed to call Chicago and Houston, where our two factories are located. Mary Johnson, the seller for the western U.S., might only be allowed to call Denver and points west. There's considerable debate as to how useful toll restriction really is.

TOLL STATION A Telco phone from which established long distance message rates are charged for all messages sent over company lines.

TOLL SWITCHING TRUNK A trunk connecting one or more end offices to a toll center as the first stage of concentration for intertoll traffic. Operator assistance or participation may be an optional function. In U.S. common carrier telephony service, a toll center designated "Class 4C" is an office where assistance in completing incoming calls is provided in addition to other traffic; a toll center designated "Class 4P" is an office where operators handle only outbound calls, or where switching is performed without operator assistance.

TOLL TESTBOARD Manual test position at which toll circuits are tested and repaired.

TOLL TERMINAL A phone only furnished with long distance service.

TOLL TERMINAL ACCESS Allows hotel/motel guest phones to access toll calling trunks.

TOLL TICKET Ticket is the telephone company term for a bill. A toll ticket is a bill containing the calling number, called number, time of day, date and call duration. Some phone systems generate their own bills automatically. Some still need an operator. It depends on the equipment and the type of call.

TOLL TRUNK A communications channel between a toll office and a local central office.

TONE ALTERNATOR A motor-driven AC generator that produces audio-frequency tones.

TONE DIAL A pushbutton telephone dial that makes a different sound (in fact, a combination of two tones) for each number pushed. The correct name for tone dial is "Dual Tone MultiFrequency" (DTMF). This is because each button generates two tones, one from a "high" group of frequencies — 1209, 1136, 1477 and 1633 Hz — and one from a "low" group of frequencies — 697, 770, 852 and 841 Hz. The frequencies and the keyboard, or tone dial, layout have been internationally standardized, but the tolerances on individual frequencies vary between countries. This makes it more difficult to take a touchtone phone overseas than a rotary phone.

You can "dial" a number faster on a tone dial than on a rotary dial, but you make more mistakes on a tone dial and have to redial more often. Some people actually find rotary dials to be, on average, faster for them. The design of all tone dials is stupid. Deliberately so. They were deliberately designed to be the exact opposite (i.e. upside down) of the standard calculator pad, now incorporated into virtually all computer keyboards. The reason for the dumb phone design was to slow the user's dialing down to the speed Bell central offices of early touch tone vintage could take. Today, central offices can accept tone dialing at high speed. But sadly, no one in North America makes a phone with a sensible, calculator pad or computer keyboard dial. On some telephone/computer workstations you can dial using the calculator pad on the keyboard. This is a breakthrough. It a lot faster to use this pad. The keys are larger, more sensibly laid out and can actually be touch-typed (like touch-typing on a keyboard.) Nobody, but nobody can "touch-type" a conventional telephone tone pad. A tone dial on a telephone can provide access to various special services and features — from ordering your groceries over the phone to inquiring into the prices of your (hopefully) rising stocks.

TONE DISABLING A method of controlling the operation of communications equipment by transmitting a certain tone over the phone line.

TONE DIVERSITY A method of voice frequency telegraph (VFTG) transmission wherein two channels of a 16-channel VFTG carry the same information. This is commonly achieved by twinning the channels of a 16-channel VFTG to provide eight channels with dual diversity.

TONE PROBE A testing device used to detect signals from a TONE GENERATOR to identify phone circuits, often the size of a fat pencil or skinny banana. Some models contain speakers; others must be used with a HEADSET or BUTT SET.

TONE RINGING Either a steady or oscillating electronic tone at the phone to tell you someone is calling.

TONE SENDER 1. A printed circuit card in Rolm CBX which supplies the data bus with the digital representations of the following tones: dial, ring, busy, error, howler (off-hook timeout) and pulse (after flashing). 2. A printed circuit card which generates the following tones: dial, ring, busy, error, howler (off-hook timeout) and pulse (after flashing).

TONE SIGNALING The transmission of supervisory, address and alerting signals over a telephone circuit by means of tones. Typically in-band. See also SIGNALING SYSTEM #7.

TONE TO DIAL PULSE CONVERSION Converts DTMF (Dual Tone Multiple Frequency) signals to dial pulse signals when trunks going to carry outgoing calls are not equipped to receive tone signals. A lot of electronic phones with touchtone dials have a sliding switch that allows you to choose whether the phone will outpulse in rotary, or whether it will touchtone out. You choose whichever your trunk line will accept.

TOOL In some computer languages, a small program executed as a shell command. In other computer languages, such as BASIC, it is called a "utility."

TOOLKIT A Dialogic word for an Applications Generator.

TOOLKIT DEVELOPER PROGRAM A strategic alignment by Dialogic with suppliers of voice processing applications development software to provide high-level application development tools.

TOP Technical Office Protocol. A version of the Open Systems Interconnection (OSI) model for use in the office, developed by Boeing, the people who make the planes.

TOP DOWN This is a method of distributing incoming calls to a bunch of people. It always starts at the top of a list of agents and proceeds down the list looking for an available agent. See also ROUND ROBIN and LONGEST AVAILABLE.

TOPOLOGY Network Topology. The geometric physical or electrical configuration describing a local communication network — the shape or arrangement of the system. The most common distribution system topologies are the bus, ring, and star.

TOPS Traffic Operator Position System. A system to help a telephone company operator complete toll calls.

TOPS MPX Northern Telecom's Traffic Operator Position System designed on a token ring for interface between operator positions and the IBM Directory Assistance system database.

TORN TAPE RELAY An antiquated tape relay system in which the perforated tape is manually transferred by an operator to the appropriate outgoing transmitter. In short, it's a torn tape relay is a store and forward message switching system which uses punched paper as the storage medium.

TOTAL HARMONIC DISTORTION The ratio of the sum of the powers of all harmonic frequency signals (other than the fundamental) to the power of the fundamental frequency signal. This ratio is measured at the output of a device under specified conditions and is expressed in decibels.

TOTAL INTERNAL REFLECTION The reflection that occurs when light strikes an interface at an angle of incidence (with respect to the normal) greater than the critical angle.

TOWER A name for a PC in a vertical or upright case. Tower PCs (if they're correctly designed) have a big benefit. Heat rises and escapes more easily than in traditional horizontal machines. Heat and power surges are the most damaging threats to PC.

TOUCHTONE A trademark owned by AT&T for Tone Dialing. The author apologizes to AT&T for using this word throughout this dictionary. It's simply a nicer word than the alternative, pushbutton. For a full explanation of touchtone, see DTMF.

TP Abbreviation for Transport Protocol or Twisted Pair.

TP-4 Transport Protocol 4. An OSI layer-4 protocol developed by the National Bureau of Standards.

TP-PMD Twisted-Pair Physical Media Dependent, Technology under review by the ANSI X3T9.5 working group that allow 100 Mbps transmission over twisted-pair cable. Also referred to as CDDI or TPDDI.

TPAD Terminal Packet Assembler/Disassembler linked to a cluster controller or terminal device, taking native protocol input and converting it to X.25 for transmission over a packet network.

TPDDI Twisted Pair Distributed Data Interface. Iso known as ANSI X3T9.5.-TPDDI. TPDDI is a new technology that allows users to run the FDDI standard 100 Mbps transmission speed over twisted-pair wiring. Unshielded twisted-pair has been tested for distances over 50 meters (164 ft.). TPDDI is designed to help users make an earlier transition to 100 Mbps at the workstation. Also known as CDDI, Copper Distributed Data Interface.

TPDU Abbreviation for Transport Protocol Data Unit.

TPI Tracks Per Inch. A measurement of how much data can be stored on a disk.

TPON Telephone Passive Optical Network.

TR 1. Trouble Report or Technical Reference (BELLCORE). 2. Technical Requirement. These publications are the standard form of Bellcore-created technical documents representing Bellcore's view of proposed generic requirements and standards for products, new technologies, services, or interfaces. See ISDN.

TR-303 A defacto standard published by Bellcore. It amounts to an industry standard high level control interface to dumb switches. It also applies to Fiber In The Loop (FITL).

TR-444 A defacto standard published by Bellcore which spells out how the Bell regionals want long distance companies to connect to the Bell regionals' local networks. Several observers compare the TR-444 specs to simple direct dial long distance voice phone service.

TRA The Telecommunications Resellers Association is an organization representing the interests of more than 100 companies involved in the switchless resale of long distance telecommunications services. TRA can be reached at P.O. Box 8361, McLean, Va, 22106-8361, 703-734-1225, Fax 703-734-8572.

TRAC Northern Telecom term for Technical Recommendations Approval Committee.

TRACE AGENT This is a command used in the Infoswitch product line to report all the events and transactions an agent has been involved in over a defined period of time.

TRACE PACKET A special kind of packet in a packet-switching network which functions as a normal packet but causes a report of each stage of its progress to be sent to the network control center.

TRACE PROGRAM A computer program that performs a check on another computer program by showing the sequence in which the instructions are executed and usually the results of executing the instructions.

TRACER STRIPE When more than one color coding stripe is required, the first or widest stripe is the base stripe. The other, usually narrower stripes are the tracer stripes.

TRACK 1. A storage channel on a disk or tape which can be magnetically encoded. 2. On a data medium, a path associated with a single read/write head as data move past the head.

TRACK ACCESS TIME The time it takes to move the pickup head on a disk drive from one track to another.

TRACK DENSITY The number of tracks per unit length, measured in a direction perpendicular to the tracks.

TRACK SPEED The maximum speed which a train can travel over a section of railway tracks.

TRACKBALL An upside-down MOUSE; a rotatable ball in a housing used to position the cursor and move images on a computer screen. A mouse needs desktop room to work, a trackball stays in one place, and can even be part of a keyboard or built into a laptop computer. It's hard to see why anyone uses a mouse instead of a trackball. This dictionary was typeset by a fine lady called Jennifer Cooper-Farrow, who used a trackball and a Macintosh computer.

TRACKING 1. Figuring where a satellite is and keeping track of it. This is not an easy job, given the vastness of space. 2. The effect created in compressed video when the speed of the transmission is not great enough to keep up with the speed of the action. Tracking creates a tearing effect on the video picture.

TRACTOR FEEDER A device which attaches to a computer printer and allows the printer to use continuous, sprocket-fed, paper. Such paper has a row of evenly spaced holes on both sides. Those holes coincide with the pins on the tractor feeder. In all tractor-fed printers, the tractor moves the paper, not the printers's platen.

TRADER TURRET A very large key telephone used by traders of commodities, securities, etc. Turrets typically have many line buttons. Each one corresponds to a trunk, an autodial or tie-line circuit to another trader or a financial institution. The objective of turrets is to allow the trader to be in instant communication with others who might want to buy or sell that which he is trying to sell or buy. See the June issue of TELECONNECT for an annual roundup of turrets.

TRAFFIC The amount of activity during a given period of time over a circuit, line or group of lines, or the number of messages handled by a data communications switch. There are many measures of "traffic." Typically it's so many minutes of voice conversation, or so many bits of data conversation. See also TRAFFIC ENGINEERING and QUEUING THEORY.

TRAFFIC CAPACITY The number of CCS (hundred call seconds) of conversation a switching system is designed to handle in one hour. This is the simple definition. See TRAFFIC ENGINEERING.

TRAFFIC CARRIED See TRAFFIC OFFERED AND CARRIED.

TRAFFIC CONCENTRATION The average ratio of the traffic during the busy hour to the total traffic during the day.

TRAFFIC DATA TO CUSTOMER The owner of a call accounting system can poll his PBXs daily or hourly and get traffic measurements, including peg counts, usage and overflow data. Summary reports, exception reports and complete traffic register outputs can be obtained.

TRAFFIC ENGINEERING The science of figuring how many trunks, how much switching equipment, how many phones, how much communications equipment you'll need to handle the telephone, voice, data, image and video traffic you're estimating. Traffic engineering suffers from several problems:

1. You are basing your future needs on past traffic.

2. Most traffic engineering is based on one or more mathematical formulas, all of which approach but never quite match the real world situation of an actual operating phone system. Computer simulation is the best method of predicting one's needs, but it's expensive in both computer and people time.

3. Many people in the telecommunications industry do not understand traffic engineering, have not worked with it sufficiently and make dumb and costly mistakes.

4. Since there are now several hundred long distance companies in the United States and several thousand different-priced ways of dialing between major cities (most at different prices), traffic engineering has become very complex.

After I wrote the above definition, Lee Goeller, disagreed with me and contributed this definition.

Traffic Engineering: The application of probability theory to estimating the number of servers required to meet the needs of an anticipated number of customers. In telephone work, the servers are often trunks, and the customers are telephone calls, assumed to arrive at random (see POISSON PROCESS). When arriving calls, upon finding all trunks busy, vanish, a "blocked call cleared" situation obtains (see ERLANG B). When a call stays in the system for a given length of time, whether it gets a trunk or not, "blocked calls held" applies (see POISSON DISTRIBUTION). If a call simply waits around until a trunk becomes available and then uses the trunk for a full holding time, the correct term is "blocked calls delayed" (See ERLANG C and QUEUING THEORY). Like any form of predicting the future on the basis of past behavior, traffic engineering has its limitations; however, when used by those who have taken the trouble to learn how it works, its track record is surprisingly good, and vastly better than most forms of simulation (see SIMULATION).

TRAFFIC INTENSITY A measure of the average occupancy of a facility during a period of time, normally a busy hour, measured in traffic units (erlangs) and defined as the ratio of the time during which a facility is occupied continuously or cumulatively) to the time this facility is available. A traffic intensity of one traffic unit (one erlang) means continuous occupancy of a facility during the time period under consideration, regardless of whether or not information is transmitted. See also TRAFFIC ENGINEERING.

TRAFFIC LOAD Total traffic carried by a trunk during a certain time interval.

TRAFFIC MEASUREMENT Memory and other software in a telephone system which collect telephone traffic data such as number of attempted calls, number of completed calls and number of calls encountering a busy. The objective of traffic measurement is to enter the results into traffic engineering and so arrange one's incoming and outgoing trunks to get the best possible service. See TRAFFIC ENGINEERING.

TRAFFIC MONITOR PBX feature that provides basic statistics on the amount of traffic handled by the system.

TRAFFIC OFFERED AND CARRIED People pick up the phone and try to place their calls. This is "Traffic Offered" to the switch. The calls that get through the switch and onto lines is called "Traffic Carried." The difference between traffic offered and carried is the traffic that was lost or delayed because of congestion. There are two basic ways of measuring traffic — erlangs and CCS (or hundred call seconds).

TRAFFIC OVERFLOW Occurs when traffic flow exceeds the capacity of a particular trunk group and flows over to another trunk group.

TRAFFIC PATH A path over which individual communications pass in sequence.

TRAFFIC RECORDER A device which measures traffic activity on a transmission channel. It's a recorder, not a processor. It's dumb.

TRAFFIC TABLE A computer database into which a PBX enters a count of feature activity. Certain detected operating errors are also entered in the traffic table.

TRAFFIC USAGE RECORDER A device for measuring and recording the amount of telephone traffic carried by a group, or several groups, of switches or trunks.

TRAILER A nonstandard way of standard way of sending data. Trailers are used on some networks by 4BSD UNIX and some of its derivatives.

TRAIN The creation of word reference data by presenting words to a recognizer. A voice recognition term.

TRAINING A feature of some modems which adjust to the conditions including amplitude response, delay distortions, timing recovery, and echo characteristic, of a particular telecommunications connection by a receiving modem.

TRANSACTION It is a completed event that can be assembled in chronological sequence for an audit trail.

TRANSACTION CAPABILITIES APPLICATION PART TCAP. The application layer protocol of SS7. Transaction capabilities in the SS7 protocol are functions that control non-circuit related information transferred between two or more signaling nodes. Definition from Bellcore in reference to its concept of the Advanced Intelligent Network.

TRANSACTION DETAIL The detail of a transaction record.

TRANSACTION FILE A collection of transaction records. A transaction data entry program allows for the creation of new transaction files used to update the data base.

TRANSACTION LINK Rockwell's link from its Galaxy ACD to an external computer. See OPEN APPLICATION INTERFACE.

TRANSCEIVER 1. A combination transmitter and receiver providing both output and input interfaces with a device. In sending and receiving information, it often provides data packet collision detection as well. 2. A device to connect workstations to standard thick Ethernet-style (IEEE 802.3).

TRANSCEIVER CABLE External transceivers on a thick-cable network need special cables to connect them to the network interface boards. Each transceiver generally is shipped with its own cable. See TRANSCEIVER.

TRANSCODER A device that combines two 1.544 megabit per second bit streams into a single 1.544 megabit per second bit stream to enable transmission of 44 or 48 voice conversations over a DS-1 medium.

TRANSDUCER A device which converts one form of energy into another. The diaphragm in the telephone receiver and the carbon microphone in the transmitter are transducers. They change variations in sound pressure (your voice) to variations in electricity, and vice versa.

TRANSFER A telephone system feature which provides the ability to move a call from one extension to another. It is probably the most commonly used and misused feature on a PBX. Before you buy a PBX, check out how easy it is to transfer a call. If you have a single line phone, you should simply hit the touch-hook, hear a dial tone and then dial the chosen extension number and hang up. This sounds easy in principle, but many people find it difficult since they associate the touch-hook with hanging up the phone. Some companies have gotten around this by putting a "hookflash" button on the phone itself. Such a button is like having an autodial button which just makes the exact short tone you make when you quickly hit the hookflash button. An even better solution is an electronic phone with a button specially marked "transfer," or a button next to a screen which lights up "transfer." Failing to efficiently transfer a call is the easiest way to give your customers the wrong impression of your firm. Think of how many times have you called a company only to be told it wasn't the fellow's job and he will transfer the call, but "If we get cut off, please call Joe back on extension 2358." There are typically four types of Transfer: Transfer using Hold, Transfer using Conference, and Transfer with and without Announcement.

TRANSFER CALLBACK After a specified number of rings, an unanswered transferred call will return to the telephone which originally made the transfer.

TRANSFER DELAY A characteristic of system performance that expresses the time delay in processing information through a data transmission system.

TRANSFER RATE The speed of data transfer — in bits, bytes or characters per second — between devices.

TRANSFORMER An electrical device used to reduce or increase the voltage in a circuit or to transfer energy from one circuit to another. One reason for using a transformer is that commercial power is typically 120 or 240 volts while many phone systems (and other computer-type "things") work best on 48, 24 or lower voltage.

TRANSHYBRID LOSS The transmission loss between opposite ports of a hybrid network, that is between the two ports of the four-wire connection.

TRANSIENTS Intermittent, short-duration impairments in signal strength caused by "junk" on the line. Transients can interrupt or halt data exchange on a network. See HIT.

TRANSIENT MOBILE UNIT A mobile unit communicating through a foreign base station.

TRANSIT DELAY In ISDN, the elapsed time between the moment that the first bit of a unit of data (such as a frame) passes a given point and the moment that bit passes another given point plus the transmission time of that data unit.

TRANSITION PROBABILITIES Probabilities of moving from one state to another.

TRANSITION ZONE The zone between the far end of the near-field region and the near end of the far-field region. The transition is gradual.

TRANSISTOR The transistor was invented in 1947 by John Bardeen, Walter H. Brattain and William Shockley of Bell Laboratories. Here is an explanation of how a transistor works, taken from "Signals, The Science of Telecommunications" by John Pierce and Michael Noll:

"To understand how a transistor works, we must look at the laws of quantum mechanics. We commonly picture an atom as a positive nucleus surrounded by orbiting electrons ... Vacuum tubes rely on the ability of electrons to travel freely with any energy through a vacuum. Transistors rely on the free travel of electrons through crystalline solids called semiconductors ... Semiconductors (such as silicon or gallium arsenide) differ from pure conductors, such as metals, in how full of electrons are the energy bands that allow free travel."

And depending on their design, transistors can act as amplifiers or switches. See TRANSISTOR RADIO.

TRANSISTOR MILESTONES

Point-contact transistor	1948
Single-crystal Germanium	1950
Grown junction transistor	1951
Alloy junction transistor	1952
Zone melting and refining	1952
Single-crystal Silicon	1952
Diffused-base transistor	1955
Oxide masking	1957
Planar transistor	1960
MOS transistor	1960
Epitaxial transistor	1960
Integrated circuits	1961

TRANSISTOR RADIO Sony unveiled the first transistor radio in 1955.

TRANSLATE To change the digits dialed on your phone into digits necessary for routing the call across the country. See TRANSLATIONS.

TRANSLATING BRIDGE A special bridge that interconnects different LAN types using different protocols at the physical and data link layers, such as Ethernet and Token Ring. A translating bridge supports the physical and data link protocols of both LAN types. When they forward packets from one LAN to another, they manipulate the packet envelope to conform to the physical and data link protocols of the destination LAN.

TRANSLATIONS Translations are changes made by the network to dialed telephone numbers to allow the call to progress through the network. Sometimes the translations are made automatically. Take one series of dialed numbers; convert them to another. Sometimes, translations are done with the help of "lookup" tables, also called databases. Here's an example of translations done with the help of a database. TELECONNECT Magazine has a WATS line, 1-800-LIBRARY. If you dial it on the phone, you'll see it is really 1-800-542-7279. But this is not its real number. When someone in California dials 1-800-LIBRARY, AT&T's long distance network recognizes the "1-800" portion of the call and sends it to a special AT&T central office in Utah. When the call arrives, a computer looks up the number 542-7279 in its database and translates that to 1-212-206-6871 and puts the call back into the network. Within seconds, that number in New York, 212-206-6871, which we think is our IN-WATS line, rings.

TRANSLITERATE To convert the characters of one alphabet to the corresponding characters of another alphabet.

TRANSLATOR 1. A device that converts information from one system into equivalent information in another system. 2. In telephone equipment, it is the device that converts dialed digits into call-routing information. 3. In computers, it is a program that translates from one language into another language and in particular from one programming language into another programming language. 4. In FM and TV broadcasting, a repeater station that receives a primary station's signal, amplifies it, shifts it in frequency, and rebroadcasts it.

TRANSLITERATE To convert the characters of one alphabet to the corresponding characters of another alphabet.

TRANSMISSION Sending electrical signals carrying information over a line to a destination.

TRANSMISSION BLOCK A group of bits or characters transmitted as a unit, with an encoding procedure for error control purposes.

TRANSMISSION BUS The circuits mounted on the backplane of the AT&T ISN packet controller that carry data packets from sending device interface modules into the switch and back to the receiving device interface modules. See also BACKPLANE.

TRANSMISSION CHANNEL All of the transmission facilities between the input (to the channel) from an initiating node and the output (from the channel) to a terminating node. In telephony, transmission channels may be of various bandwidths: e.g. nominal 3-kHz, nominal 4-kHz, or nominal 48-kHz (group). "Transmission channel" should not be confused with the more general term "channel."

TRANSMISSION CODE A code by which information is sent and received on a transmission system.

TRANSMISSION COEFFICIENT The ratio of the transmitted field strength to the incident field strength when an electromagnetic wave is incident upon an interface surface between media with two different refractive indices. In a transmission line, the ratio of the complex amplitude of the transmitted wave to that of the incident wave at a discontinuity in the line. A number indicating the probable performance of a portion of a transmission circuit. The value of a transmission coefficient is inversely related to the quality of the link or circuit.

TRANSMISSION CONTROL Category of control characters intended to control or help transmission of information over telecommunication networks.

TRANSMISSION CONTROL PROTOCOL TCP. A specification for software that bundles outgoing data into packets (and bundles incoming data), manages the transmission of packets on a network, and checks for errors. TCP is the portion of the TCP/IP protocol suite that governs the exchange of sequential data.

TRANSMISSION ELECTRONICS Any of the various devices used in conjunction with different transmission media to convert from one transmission method to another. Transmission electronics devices typically include multiplexing equipment and Asynchronous Data Units.

TRANSMISSION FACILITY A piece of a telecommunications system through which information is transmitted.

TRANSMISSION FRAME A data structure, beginning and ending with delimiters, that consists of fields predetermined by a protocol for the transmission of user and control data.

TRANSMISSION LEVEL The power of a transmission signal at a specific point on a transmission facility. See DECIBEL.

TRANSMISSION LEVEL POINT TLP. A designated point on a circuit where the transmission level has been specified by the designer. Referencing this point in relation to others in the network can determine the performance of the network.

TRANSMISSION LIMIT The wavelengths above and below which the fiber ceases to be transparent and therefore, can no longer transmit information.

TRANSMISSION LOSS Total loss encountered in transmission through a system.

TRANSMISSION MEDIA Anything, such as wire, coaxial cable, fiber optics, air or vacuum, that is used to carry an electrical signal which has information. Transmission media usually refers to the various types of wire and optical fiber cable used for transmitting voice or data signals. Typically, wire cable includes twisted pair, coaxial, and twinaxial. Optical fiber cable includes single, dual, quad, stranded, and ribbon.

TRANSMISSION OBJECTIVES A stated set of desired performance characteristics for a transmission system.

TRANSMISSION SECURITY KEY TSK. A key that is used in the control of transmission security processes such as frequency hopping and spread spectrum.

TRANSMISSIVE The way many LCD (liquid crystal display) screens on laptops reflect light.

TRANSMIT BUS In AT&T's Information Systems Network (ISN), the circuit on the backplane of the packet controller that transports message packets from sending device interface modules to the switch module.

TRANSMIT DIGITAL INTERTIE TDI. A 16-channel serial converter which converts the TDM Data Bus from parallel format to serial format for transmission between nodes.

TRANSMITTANCE The ratio of transmitted power to incident power. In optics, frequently expressed as optical density or percent; in communications applications, generally expressed in decibels.

TRANSMITTER The device in the telephone handset which converts speech into electrical impulses for transmission.

TRANSMITTER DISTRIBUTOR A device in a teletypewriter system which converts the information from the parallel form in which it is used in the keyboard-printer to and from the serial form which it is transmitted on the transmission line.

TRANSMITTER START CODE A coded control character or code sequence transmitted to a remote terminal instructing that terminal to begin sending information.

TRANSMOBILE The transmobile (not to be confused with a TRANSPORTABLE) is another type of cellular phone. It is essentially a standard 3-watt mobile unit — without an external battery pack — that can be quickly and easily moved from one vehicle to another. It draws its power from the vehicle's battery via a cigarette lighter plug.

TRANSMULTIPLEXER A device that takes a bunch of voice analog phone conversations and converts them directly into a T-1 1.544 megabit per second bit stream — without the need for de-multiplexing the bunches down to individual conversations, then digitizing them, then bundling them up into a T-1 digital bit stream. A transmultiplexer does it all in one go.

TRANSPARENCY 1. A data communications mode that allows equipment to send and receive bit patterns of virtually any form. The user is unaware that he is transmitting to a machine that receives faster or slower, or transmits to him faster or slower, or in a different bit pattern. All the translations are done somewhere in the network. He is unaware of the changes occuring — they are transparent. ISDN is planned to be transparent.

TRANSPARENCY/OPACITY An imaging term. A setting available in many image-processing functions that allows part of the underlying image to show through. 80 percent opacity is equivalent to 20 percent transparency.

TRANSPARENT When applied to telephone communications, the provision of a feature or service such as Automatic Route Selection in a such a way that the user is unaware of it and it has no affect on the way he uses the telephone. It's "transparent" to him. Translations are transparent to the telephone user. See TRANSLATIONS and TRANSPARENCY.

TRANSPARENT MODE 1.The operation of a digital transmission facility during which the user has complete and free use of the available bandwidth and is unaware of any inter- mediate processing. Generally implies out-of-brand signaling (also called Clear Channel). 2.In BSC data transmission, the suppression of recognition of control characters, to allow transmission of raw binary data without fear of misinterpretation.

TRANSPARENT ROUTING A method used by a bridge for moving data between two networks. With this type of routing, the bridge learns which computers are operating on which network. It then uses this information to route packets between networks. It does not rely on the sending computers for its decision-making routine. A special kind of bridge combines the practice of transparent routing with source routing. It is called a source routing transparent (SRT) bridge. It examines each packet that comes by to see if it is using IBM's special source routing protocol. If so, this protocol is used to forward the packet. If not, the transparent method is used. Thus, the SRT bridge will support both IBM and non-IBM network protocols. See also BRIDGE and SRT. Compare with SOURCE ROUTING.

TRANSPONDER There are two meanings: 1. A transponder is a fancy name for radio relay equipment on board a communications satellite. Just like its domestic microwave counterpart (which you see along highways), a transponder will receive a signal, amplify it, change its frequency and then send it back to earth. Transponders typically have 36 MHz bandwidth. Full motion, full color TV video requires a 6 MHz analog channel. 2. A transponder on an airline is a slightly different kettle of fish. When a radar signal strikes a airline, it activates an electronic transmitter called a transponder. The transponder sends out a coded signal to the ground radar. The code appears next to the radar image of the plane, allowing the controller to identify each plane under his control.

TRANSPORT EFFICIENCY An AT&T term for the ability to carry information through a network using no more resources than necessary. Transport efficiency is achieved, for example, by statistical transport, which removes silent intervals from voice, data or other traffic and carries only the bursts of meaningful user information.

TRANSPORT LAYER Layer 4 in the Open Systems Interconnection (OSI) data communications reference model that, along with the underlying network, data link and physical layers, is responsible for the end-to-end control of transmitted information and the optimized use of network resources. Layer 4 defines the protocols governing message structure and portions of the network's error-checking capabilities. Also serves the session layer. Software in the transport layer checks the integrity of and formats the data carried by the physical layer (layer 1, the network wiring and interface hardware), managed by the data link layer (layer 2) and possibly routed by the network layer (layer 1, which has the rules determining the path to be taken by data flowing through a network). See OSI.

TRANSPORT PROTOCOL A protocol that provides end-to-end data integrity and service quality on a network.

TRANSPORT MEDIUM The actual medium over which transmission takes place including copper wire, fiber optics, microwave and satellites, to name a few.

TRANSPORTABLE CELLULAR PHONE The transportable cellular phone is a standard 3-watt mobile phone that can be removed from the car and used by itself with an attached battery pack. The entire unit is generally mounted or built into a custom carrying case to make it easy to carry on your shoulder. Although technically "portable," the transportable should not be confused with the true portable one-piece cellular phone. Also known as a "bag phone" or "briefcase phone"; refers to a cellular handset that is packaged with a larger carrying case containing a full-scale power supply.

TRANSPOSITION 1. In data transmission, a transmission defect in which, during one character period, one or more signal elements are changed from one significant condition to the other, and an equal number of elements are changed in the opposite sense. 2. Interchanging the relative position of conductors at regular intervals to reduce crosstalk.

TRANSVERSE INTERFEROMETRY The method used to measure the index profile of an optical fiber by placing it in an interferometer and illuminating the fiber transversely to its axis. Generally, a computer is required to interpret the interference pattern.

TRANSVERSE PARITY CHECK Type of parity error checking performed on a group of bits in a transverse direction for each frame. See PARITY CHECK.

TRANSVERSE SCATTERING The method for measuring the index profile of an optical fiber or preform by illuminating the fiber or preform coherently and transversely to its axis, and examining the farfield irradiance pattern. A computer is required to interpret the pattern of the scattered light.

TRAP A mechanism permitting a device to automatically send an alarm for certain network events to a management station. Typically, network management information is gained by polling network nodes on a regular basis. This strategy can be modified when a trap is set from a network node. With traps, a node alerts the management station of a catastrophic problem. The management station can then immediately initiate a polling sequence to the node to determine the cause of the problem. This strategy is often called trap-directed polling.

TRAP AND TRACE An old telephone company term. Equipment and procedures for determining the source of an incoming call.

TRASHWARE Software that is so poorly designed that it winds up in the garbage can.

TRAVELING CLASS MARK TCM. A code that accompanies a long distance call. When Automatic Route Selection (ARS) or Uniform Numbering/Automatic Alternate Routing (UN/AAR) selects a tie trunk to a distant tandem PBX, the traveling class mark (TCM) is sent over the tie trunk. It is then used by the distant system to determine the best available long distance line consistent with the user's calling privileges. The TCM indicates the restriction level to be used based on the phone, trunk or attendant originating the call or the authorization code, if dialed.

TRAY See RACK.

TREE 1. A network topology shaped like a branching tree. (What else?) It is characterized by the existence of only one route between any two network nodes. Most CATV distribution networks are tree networks. 2. In MS-DOS, a tree describes the organization of directories, subdirectories, and files on a disk.

TREE HUGGER IBM-speak for an employee who resists a move or any other change.

TREE MAILBOX A special function mailbox that provides the caller with a menu and allows selections from the menu using single digit commands.

TREE SEARCH In a tree structure, a search in which it is possible to decide, at each step, which part of the tree may be rejected without further search.

TREE STRUCTURE Describes the organization of directories, subdirectories, and files on a disk.

TREE TOPOLOGY A network cabling architecture in which nodes are connected by cables to a central, or trunk, cable with a central retransmission capability.

TRELLIS CODING A method of forward error correction used in certain high-speed modems where each signal element is assigned a coded binary value representing that element's phase and amplitude. It allows the receiving modem to determine, based on the value of the preceding signal, whether or not a given signal element is received in error. See V.32 and V.32 bis.

TRELLIS CODING MODULATION TCM. A modem modulation technique in which sophisticated mathematics are used to predict the best fit between the incoming signal and a large set of possible combinations of amplitude and phase changes. TCM provides for transmission speeds of 14,400 bps and above on single voice grade phone lines. See V.32 and V.32 bis.

TREMENDOUSLY HIGH FREQUENCY Frequencies from 300 GHz to 3000 GHz.

TRFR TRansFeR.

TRIAXIAL CABLE A cable construction having three coincident axes, such as a conductor, first shield and second shield all insulated from one another.

TRIBUTARY CIRCUIT A circuit connecting an individual phone to a switching center.

TRIBUTARY OFFICE A local office, located outside the exchange in which a toll center is located, that has a different rate center from its toll center.

TRIBUTARY PBX An exchange within the main PBX configuration but with its own listed number.

TRIBUTARY STATION In a data network, a station other than the control station. On a multipoint connection or a point-to-point connection using basic mode link control, any data station other than the control station.

TRIGGER The combination of the occurrence of an event and the satisfaction of trigger criteria. Definition from Bellcore in reference to its concept of the Advanced Intelligent Network.

TRIGGERING The process of detecting a word (or utterance) and capturing the speech data associated with that word (or utterance) for subsequent processing.

TRIGGERS Uncompiled code residing on an intelligent database server.

TRIODE A combination of a heated cathode, a relatively cold anode, and a third electrode for controlling the current flowing between the other two; the whole enclosed in an evacuated bulb. Variously called, audion, pliotron, radiotron, oscillion, audiotron, aerotron, electron tube, vacuum tube, etc.

TRIP '92 TRanscontinental ISDN Project '92.

TRL Transistor Resistor Logic.

TROPOSPHERE The lower layers of the earth's atmosphere. You can bounce certain frequency radio signals off it and use it as an elementary transmission reflector. The troposhere is the region where clouds form, convection is active, and mixing is continuous and more or less complete. The lower layers of the Earth's atmosphere, between the surface and the stratosphere, in which about 80 percent of the total mass of air is located and in which temperature normally decreases with altitude. The thickness of the troposphere varies with season and latitude; it is usually 16 km to 18km over topical regions and 10 km or less over the poles. See TROPOSHERIC SCATTER and TROPOSHERIC WAVE.

TROPOSPHERIC SCATTER The propagation of radio waves by scattering as a result of irregularities or discontinuties in the physical properties of the troposphere. The propagation of electromagnetic waves by scattering as a result of irregularities or discontinuities in the physical properties of the troposphere. A method of transhorizon communications using frequencies from approximately 350 MHz to approximately 8400 MHz. The propagation mechanism is still not fully understood, though it includes several distinguishable but changeable mechanisms such as propagation by means of random reflections and scattering from irregularities in the dielectric gradient density of the troposphere, smooth-Earth diffraction, and diffraction over isolated obstacles (knife-edge diffraction).

TROPOSPHERIC WAVE A radio wave that is propagated by reflection from a place of abrupt change in the dielectric constant or its gradient in the troposphere. In some cases, the ground wave may be so altered that new components appear to arise from reflection in regions of rapidly changing dielectric constant. When these components are distinguishable from the other components, they are called "tropospheric waves."

TROUBLE NUMBER DISPLAY The operator will know what the trouble is with the phone system by seeing a number pop up on her/his console. That number may pop up automatically or the operator may have to hit the ALM (for ALARM) or similar button.

TROUBLE TICKET Form used to report problems. Often incorrectly filled-in. Check.

TROUBLE UNIT A weighting figure applied to telephone circuit or circuits to indicate expected performance in a given period.

TROUBLES PER HUNDRED Troubles per hundred is a criterion for acceptable customer service which telephone companies and public utility commissions have agreed upon. It's measured in terms of the number of complaints received per hundred telephones in one month. Six complaints per hundred is considered the maximum for acceptable service. See QUALITY OF SERVICE.

TRU SYSTEM PC-based call accounting software from the fine people at Telco Research Nashville, TN. Includes call recording and polling, directory, ISDN recording, Centrex call detail capture, cost allocation, traffic statistics, network optimization, bill verification, client billback, inventory management, hospitality and toll fraud detection applications.

TRUETYPE TrueType is a new feature of Windows 3.1. It offers fonts which are scalable and available from many vendors. Using TrueType, you'll be able to create documents that retain their format and fonts on any Windows 3.1 machines — even if the fonts aren't installed on that computer. This makes Windows 3.1 documents portable.

TRUNCATION In data processing, the deletion or omission of a leading or a trailing portion of a string in accordance with specified criteria.

TRUNK A communication line between two switching systems. The term switching systems typically includes equipment in a central office (the telephone company) and PBXs. A tie trunk connects PBXs. Central office trunks connect a PBX to the switching system at the central office.

TRUNK ACCESS NUMBER The number of the trunk over which a call is to be routed.

TRUNK ANSWER FROM ANY PHONE When a call comes in, something rings. You can now answer the incoming call from any phone. To do so, you must dial a special code or hit a special feature button on your phone. When TELECONNECT'S PBX bells ring, all we have to do is to touch "6" on any phone and we can answer the incoming call.

TRUNK DATA MODULE TDM. Provides the interface between the DCP signal and a modem or Digital Service Unit (DSU).

TRUNK DIRECT TERMINATION An option on switchboards which terminates a trunk group on one key (or button) on the console.

TRUNK ENCRYPTION DEVICE TED. A bulk encryption device used to provide secure communication over a wideband digital transmission link. It is usually located between the output of a trunk group multiplexer and a wideband radio or cable facility.

TRUNK EXCHANGE A telephone exchange dedicated primarily to interconnecting trunks.

TRUNK GROUP A group of essentially like trunks that go between the same two geographical points. They have similar electrical characteristics. A trunk group performs the same function as a single trunk, except that on a trunk group you can carry multiple conversations. You use a trunk group when your traffic demands it. Typically, the trunks in a trunk group are accessed the same way. You dial your Band 5 WATS trunk group by dialing 62, for example. If the first trunk of that group is busy, you choose the second, then the third, etc. See TRUNK HUNTING.

TRUNK GROUP MULTIPLEXER TGM. A time-division multiplexer whose function is to combine individual digital trunk groups into a higher rate bit stream for transmission over wideband digital communication links.

TRUNK GROUP WARNING Alerts the attendant when a preset number of trunks in a group are busy. See TRUNK GROUP.

TRUNK HUNTING Switching incoming calls to the next consecutive number if the first called number is busy.

TRUNK MAKE BUSY A fancy name for saying that, by punching a few buttons on the console, you can make any trunks in your PBX or key system busy, effectively putting the trunk out of service. You may want to do this if your trunk is acting up. By busying it out at the console, you are effectively denying its use to anyone in the company. Thus you are protecting yourself from further complaints. Hopefully, it will be repaired promptly.

TRUNK MONITORING Feature which allows individual trunk testing to verify supervision and transmission. You dial an access code and then the specific trunk number from the attendant console. You want the ability to test a specific trunk because normally you might be only accessing a trunk group when you dial an access code. Thus, each time you dial into the trunk group, you might end up on another individual trunk. Some PBXs have a variation of trunk monitoring, whereby if a user encounters a bad trunk, he can dial a specific code, then hang up. The PBX recognizes these digits and makes a trouble report on that specific trunk, possibly reporting it to the operator, keeping it in memory for later analysis or dialing a remote diagnostic center and reporting its agony.

TRUNK NUMBER DISPLAY The specific trunk number of an incoming call can be displayed on the attendant console, enabling your attendant to instantly identify the origin of certain calls. For example, if you have several tie lines to branch offices, your attendant knows immediately which office is calling. Many newer PBXs have displays on individual telephones, which show the actual trunk being used for outgoing and incoming calls. This provides an additional measure of control. You might, for example, speak faster if you knew the call was coming in on your INWATS line. You might also answer the call differently if you know what trunk it's coming in on. For example, you might be running several, totally-separate businesses from the same console. Each business has a different number. The only way you know what to answer — Joe's Bakery or Mary's Real Estate — is by the trunk.

TRUNK ORDER A document (or data system equivalent) used in an operating telephone company to request a change to a trunk group.

TRUNK QUEUING A feature whereby your phone system automatically stacks requests for outgoing circuits and processes those requests on, typically, a first-in/first-out basis. See QUEUING THEORY.

TRUNK RESERVATION The attendant can hold a single trunk in a group and then extend it to a specific phone. This means, for example, that a WATS line can be held for someone special — a heavy caller, the president of the firm, etc.

TRUNK RESTRICTION Some people may not be allowed to use certain trunks at certain times. The sophistication of trunk restriction depends on the switch and the way it's programmed.

TRUNK SEGMENT The main segment of cable in an Ethernet network is called the trunk segment.

TRUNK TYPE TT. Trunks that use the same type of equipment going to the same terminating location.

TRUNK TYPE MASTER FILE TTMF. An MCI definition. A comprehensive listing of all trunk assignments on the MCI network for shared and dedicated services, necessary for processing and billing MCI customer calls.

TRUNK TO TIE TRUNK CONNECTIONS The ability of the switching system to provide the attendant with the capability of extending an incoming trunk call to a tie trunk terminating some place else.

TRUNK TO TRUNK BY STATION A PBX feature which permits the user who established a three-way conference involving himself and two trunks to drop from the call without disconnecting the trunk-to-trunk connection.

TRUNK TO TRUNK CONNECTIONS The attendant can establish connections between two outside parties on separate trunks. Call your office on your IN-WATS. Ask the operator to extend that call to the VP who happens to be at his home. The operator must place an outside call to the

VP on an outside trunk and join that call to the incoming call. Sometimes it works.

TRUNK TO TRUNK CONSULTATIONS Allows a phone connected to an outside trunk circuit to gain access to a second outside trunk for "outside" consultation. No conference capability is available with this feature.

TRUNK TRANSFER BY STATION Permits the user who established a three-way conference involving two lines to drop from the call without disconnecting the trunk-to-trunk connection.

TRUNK VERIFICATION BY CUSTOMER Provides the attendant or phone user access to individual lines in a trunk group to check their condition. See also TRUNK MONITORING.

TRUNK VERIFICATION BY STATION Provides a warning tone if a phone user enters a busy trunk.

TRUTH TABLE An operation table for a logic operation. A table that describes a logic function by listing all possible combinations of input values and indicating, for each combination, the output value.

TRXXX Various Bellcore standards. See ISDN.

TSAP Abbreviation for Transport Service Access Point in the OSI transport protocol layer.

TSCM Technical Surveillance CounterMeasures. Commonly called debugging, sweeps or electronic sweeping.

TSI 1. Time Slot Interchange or Interchanger. A way of temporarily storing data bytes so they can be sent in a different order than they were received. Time Slot Interchange is a way to switch calls. 2. Transmitting Subscriber Information. A frame that may be sent by the caller, with the caller's phone number, which may be used to screen calls, etc.

TSIU Time Slot Interchange Unit. Switching module hardware unit that provides the digital time switching function.

TSK Transmission Security Key.

TSO Time Share Operation.

TSP Telecommunication Service Priority.

TSPS Traffic Service Position System permits operator positions serving public phones and HOBIC operations to be located remotely from the CO which services the pay phone or the hotel, or the hospital, etc.

TSR 1. Telephone Service Representative. See also AGENT. 2. Terminate and Stay Resident. A term for loading a software program in an MS-DOS computer in which the program loads into memory and is always ready for running at the touch of a combination of keys, e.g. Alt M, or Ctrl ESC. Here's some information from Jackie Fox writing in PC Today: You can't load TSRs willy-nilly and expect them to work with each other. Some will get along with each other. Others won't. When you install a TSR, it goes to a location in RAM (Random Access Memory) called the Interrupt Vector Table.

The interrupt vector table is like a hotel lobby, and TSRs are like guests waiting for messages. The TSR watches every incoming keystroke to see if it's the special hot key combination (message), the TSR is waiting for. If it isn't, the TSR passes it back to the regular program. What if you have four or five TSRs loaded? The one you loaded last has seniority. It checks the incoming keystrokes first. If the TSR recognizes the keystroke combination as its own hot-key combination, it takes over. If not, it passes it along to the next TSR. This process is called interrupt handler chaining.

If none of the TSRs recognize that particular combination, they pass it along to DOS so it can process it as a regular keystroke combination. Not all TSRs pass instructions along the way they should. Some TSRs intercept keystrokes and never pass them on. Some TSRs never restore their original addresses. Sometimes two TSRs fight over the same hot key combination. Then you end up with a frozen keyboard. The basic problem is there are no rules for loading and running TSRs.

TSRM Telecommunication Standards Reference Manual.

TST Time-Space-Time system.

TSTN Triple Super Twisted Nematic. A display technology often used on laptop computers which uses three layers of crystal to give better contrast and more grey scales.

TTD Temporary Text Delay. The TTD control sequence (STX ENQ) is sent by a sending station in message transfer state when it wants to retain the line but is not ready to transmit.

TTI Transmit Terminal Identification. A fax machine's stupid term for its telephone number and the name of its owner. When you receive a fax from someone, the top line of the fax typically will have a phone number and a name on it. That phone number and name does NOT come from the phone or the phone company. It comes from what the person who owns the machine programmed into his machine. He typically did that by punching buttons on his fax machine. He'll do that if he can understand the instruction booklet which came with his fax (which he probably won't). The point of all this is twofold: First, don't forget to put your name and phone number into your fax machine. Second, don't assume that what you read at the top of any fax you receive is accurate.

TTL Transistor Transistor Logic.

TTR Touch Tone Receiver. A device used to decode touch-tones dialed from single-line telephones or Remote Access telephones.

TTS 1. Text To Speech. A term used in voice processing. See TEXT-TO-SPEECH. 2. Transaction Tracking System. A Novell NetWare feature that protects database applications from corruption by backing out incomplete transactions that result from a failure in a network component. When a transaction is backed out, data and index information in the database are returned to the state they were in before the transaction began.

TTTN Tandem Tie Trunk Network.

TTY A teletypewriter. Typewriter-style device for communicating alphanumeric information over telecom networks.

TTY/TDD A unique telecommunication device for the deaf, using TTY principles.

TUA Telecommunications Users Association (UK).

TUG Telecommunication User Group.

TUNABLE OPERATING SYSTEM PARAMETERS Tuning an operating system is the same as optimizing it, in that you rewrite commands and programs so they operate faster and more efficiently. Any new operating system needs to be tuned to the specific machine on which it is running.

TUNGSTEN A metallic element used in ceramic IC packaging to provide the traces within the package that connect the device circuitry to the external terminals pads or leads.

TUNNELING RAY Leaky ray.

TUR Traffic Usage Recorder.

TURING MACHINE A mathematical model of a device that changes its internal state and reads from, writes on, and moves a potentially infinite tape, all in accordance with its present state, thereby constituting a model for computer-like behavior.

TURNAROUND TIME On a half-duplex channel, the time during which the transmission flow is stopped each time the direction of transmission is reversed.

TURBO FAT Turbo Fat is an index Netware v2.2 creates to group all the FAT (File Allocation Table) entries corresponding to a file larger than 262,144KB. The first entry in the turbo FAT index table consists of the first FAT number of the file. The second entry consists of the second FAT number of the file, etc. The turbo FAT enables a large file to be accessed quickly.

TURN Toward Utility Rate Normalization. A non-profit education organization that gets it funding from the California Public Utilities Commission. Turn's goal is "to help consumer organizations better educate their clients or members about the changes taking place in the telecommunications industry and in the way the industry is regulated. It's based in San Francisco.

TURNAROUND TIME The actual time required to reverse the direction of transmission from sender to receiver or vice versa when using a half-duplex circuit. The turnaround time is needed for line propagation effects, modem timing and computer reaction.

TURNKEY SYSTEM An entire phone system with hardware and software assembled and installed by a vendor and sold as a total package. The term "turnkey" means the buyer is presented with the key to the thing he has just bought. He turns the key and the system will do everything it is supposed to do, including work. Most telephone systems are purchased Turnkey. An integral part of a contract to buy a turnkey phone system is the terms and conditions for the acceptance of the system. Someone has to define what it means for the thing to work, what you expect from it — so you, the buyer, can formally accept the system and thus incur an obligation to pay for it. Defining Acceptance Conditions is no small task on bigger phone systems.

TURRET A very large key system for financial traders, emergency teams at nuclear power stations and others who need single phone button access to hundreds of people. By simply pushing one button, the user can dial one of hundreds of people. These buttons may be connected to tie lines, foreign exchange lines. They may even be DDD lines with autodial capability. Like all good key systems, the buttons have a lamping display which shows if the particular line is idle, busy, ringing, on hold, etc.

TVC See TRUNK VERIFICATION BY CUSTOMER.

TVS See TRUNK VERIFICATION BY STATION.

TWAIN A cross-platform application interface standard for image capturing, announced in October 1991. Spearheaded by Hewlett-Packard Co., Logitech, Eastman Kodak, Aldus, Caere and other imaging hardware and software vendors. Previously known as CLASP and "Direct Connect" during development stage.

TWIN CABLE A cable composed of two insulated conductors laid parallel and either attached to each other by the insulation or bound together with a common covering.

TWINAX Twinaxial Cable made up of two central conducting leads of coaxial cable. See TWINAXIAL CABLE.

TWINAXIAL CABLE Two insulated conductors inside a common insulator, covered by a metallic shield, and enclosed in a cable sheath. Because it carries high frequencies, twinaxial cable is often used for data transmission and video applications, especially for cable television.

TWINPLEX A frequency-shift-keyed, carrier telegraphy system in which four unique tones (two pairs of tones) are transmitted over a single transmission channel (such as one twisted pair). One tone of each tone pair represents a "mark," and the other, a "space."

TWIST 1. In telephony, a change, as a function of temperature, in the response characteristic of a transmission line. 2. Signals at different frequencies are transmitted with differing response by the transmission system. Usually refers to distortion of DTMF signals.

TWISTED PAIR Two insulated copper wires twisted around each other to reduce induction (thus interference) from one wire to the other. The twists, or lays, are varied in length to reduce the potential for signal interference between pairs. Several sets of twisted pair wires may be enclosed in a single cable. In cables greater than 25 pairs, the twisted pairs are grouped and bound together in a common cable sheath. Twisted pair cable is the most common type of transmission media. It is the normal cabling from a central office to your home or office, or from your PBX to your office phone. Twisted pair wiring comes in various thicknesses. As a general rule, the thicker the cable is, the better the quality of the conversation and the longer cable can be and still get acceptable conversation quality. However, the thicker it is, the more it costs.

TWO DIMENSIONAL CODING A data compression scheme in facsimile transmission that uses the previous scan line as a reference when scanning a subsequent line. Because an image has a high degree of correlation vertically as well as horizontally, two-dimensional coding schemes work only with variable increments between one line and the next, permitting higher data compresson. See ONE DIMENSIONAL CODING.

TWO ELECTRODE VACUUM TUBE A vacuum tube having a hot cathode and a relatively cold anode, i.e., one with filament and plate only.

TWO HOTS IN OUTLETS In AC electrical power, more than one HOT conductor has been incorrectly connected to the terminals in the outlet being tested. Dangers include extreme fire hazard and/or major damage to equipment plugged into the outlet.

TWO-OUT-OF-FIVE CODE A decimal code system in which each decimal digit is represented by five binary bits, two of which are ones and three are zeroes.

TWO-PARTY HOLD ON CONSOLE Allows an attendant to hold a call with both a calling and a called phone (or trunk) connected. Such a feature is required for activation of Attendant Lockout, Serial Call and Trunk-to-Trunk connections features.

TWO-PARTY STATION SERVICE PBX system with two internal phones, each with selective ringing. Resembles rural two party service of old.

TWO-PILOT REGUALTION In FDM systems, the use of two pilot frequencies within a band so that the change in attenuation due to twist can be detected and compensated for by a regulator.

TWO-TIER PRICING A complex and now largely obsolete AT&T pricing plan which imposed two monthly "rate elements" on every hardware piece of an AT&T telephone system. Tier A was a fixed rate, not subject to rate increases. It was fixed for a certain number of months, say 60. It was, allegedly, to pay for the system. At the end of the 60 months, Tier A disappeared, as though it were a full-payout lease and you now owned the equipment (which you didn't.) Tier B is the second element in this pricing scheme. It covers maintenance, and it is subject to rate increases. AT&T doesn't offer two-tier pricing any longer. Many two-tier contracts are now finding their Tier A payments ceasing. Remember, the equipment still belongs to AT&T.

TWO-TONE KEY Same as frequency shift keying.

TWO-TONE KEYING In telegraphy systems, a system employing a transmission path composed of two channels in the same direction, one for transmitting the "space" binary modulation, the other for transmitting the "mark" of the same modulation; or that form of keying in which the modulating wave causes the carrier to be modulated with a single tone for the "marking" condition and modulated with a different single tone for the "spacing" condition.

TWO-WAY SIMULTANEOUS OPERATION Duplex operation.

TWO-WAY SPLITTING PBX feature. Allows a telephone user to jump back and forth between two calls. Try this: Someone calls you. You both decide you want to speak to a third person. You call that person and conference the three of you together. Then you decide you want to consult with one of the people confidentially. So you "split" one from the other and you speak to one. Then you swap back and forth between the two, speaking to one and then the other in complete privacy. It's easier to do this sort of complicated phone transaction on a phone with a LCD screen. Fortunately, these are becoming more common these days.

TWO-WAY TRUNK A trunk which can be seized from either end. Can be used to carry conversations into or out of a telephone system, i.e. most trunks. Some trunks are set up as one-way only. A classic one-way trunk is a IN-WATS line. It is designed to only receive calls.

TWO-WIRE CIRCUIT A transmission circuit composed of two wires — signal and ground — used to both send and receive information. In contrast, a four wire circuit consists of two pairs. One pair is used to send. One pair is used to receive. All trunk circuits — long distance circuits — are four wire. A four wire circuit costs more but delivers better reception. All local loop circuits — those coming from a Class 5 central office to the subscriber's phone system — are two wire, unless you ask for a four-wire circuit and pay a little more.

TWT Traveling Wave Tube.

TWX (Pronounced TWIX.) Teletype Writer eXchange. An automatic teletypewriter (i.e. telex-like) switching service where subscribers may dial any other subscriber and send and receive a message. Formerly owned by AT&T and sold to Western Union in 1972. It differed from Telex in that TWX used AT&T's normal long distance phone network, was thus more ubiquitous, was faster than Telex and was incompatible with Telex, which Western Union owned. However, Western Union, in a major accomplishment, got them to talk to each other.

TYMNET A packet switched company, offering its services to the public.

TYPE APPROVAL A concept in which a design is approved by an agency and all devices subsequently manufactured according to that design are automatically approved.

TYPE 3 CABLE An unshielded twisted-pair wire that meets IBM specifications for use in 4-megabit-per-second Token-Ring networks.

TYPE 66 PUNCHDOWN BLOCK A standard, solderless terminal wiring block used today. Invented by Western Electronic.

TYPE I PC CARD The thinnest PCMCIA Card from factor at 3.3 mm thick. The Type I format is typically used for various memory enhancements, including RAM, Flash, OTP, SRAM, and EEPROM.

TYPE II PC CARD A PCMCIA Card which is 5 mm thick. This card is typically used for I/O such as modem, LAN, and host communications.

TYPE III PC CARD The thickest PCMCIA Card type at 10.5 mm thick, the Type III Format is primarily used for memory enhancements or I/O capabilities that require more space, such as roatating media and wireless communication devices.

TYPEBAR Linear type element in a printer containing the printable symbols.

TYPING REPERFORATOR Same as receive only typing reperforator.

U INTERFACE Two wire ISDN circuit — essentially today's standard one pair telephone company local loop made of twisted-wire. The "U" interface is the most common ISDN interface. It carries 160,000 bits per second from the central office to your home or office. Of those 160,000 bits, two are used for 64,000 bps Bearer (B) channels and one is used by the subscriber for 16,000 bps of data (the D channel). The other 16,000 bps is used by the network for signaling between the black box on the subscriber premises and the central office. The idea is to get the ISDN "U" interface working to 18,000 feet — the average length of a North American subscriber local loop. You screw the two "U" wires (local loop pair) coming in from your local ISDN CO into a black box about the size of desk printing calculator, called an NT-1. Out the side of the black box comes four wires, which are called the "S Bus." Onto these four wires you can attach, in a loop configuration (also called single bus), as many as eight ISDN terminals — telephones, fax machines, etc. See ISDN.

UART Universal Asynchronous Receiver/Transmitter. PCs have a serial port, which is used for bringing data into and out of the computer. The serial port is used for data movement on a channel which requires that one bit be sent (or received) after another, i.e. serially. The UART is a device, usually an integrated circuit chip that performs the parallel-to-serial conversion of digital data to be transmitted and the serial-to-parallel conversion of digital data that has been transmitted. The UART converts the incoming serial data from a modem (or whatever else is connected to the serial port) into the parallel form which your computer handles. UART also does the opposite. It converts the computer's parallel data into serial data suitable for asynchronous transmission on phone lines. UART chips control the serial port/s on personal computers. See INTERRUPT, INTERRUPT LATENCY, INTERRUPT OVERHEAD, INTERRUPT REQUEST, UART OVERRUN and 16550.

UART OVERRUN UART overrun occurs when the UART's receive buffer is not serviced quickly enough by the CPU, and the next incoming byte of data crashes into the previous byte. The previous byte is then lost, forcing the communications driver to report and error. Your communications software must then ask for a retransmission of the lost data. High interrupt overhead is the most common cause of a UART overrun. The easiest way of solving UART overrun is to get yourself a UART with a 16 byte buffer (like the 16550), not today's typical one byte buffer UART. See 16550 and UART.

UCD Uniform Call Distributor. A device for allocating incoming calls to a bunch of people. Less full-featured than an Automatic Call Distributor. For a bigger explanation see UNIFORM CALL DISTRIBUTOR.

UDI Unrestricted Digital Information.

UDK A dumb GTE abbreviation, for Universal Dialing Keyset, a key pad that is switchable for either TONE or PULSE dialing. Outside GTE's private world, a keyset would mean a KEY TELEPHONE, not part of a phone.

UDP User Datagram Protocol. A TCP/IP protocol describing how messages reach application programs within a destination computer. This protocol is normally bundled with IP-layer software. UDP is a transport layer, connectionless mode protocol, providing a (potentially unreliable, unsequenced, and/or duplicated) datagram mode of communication for delivery of packets to a remote or local user.

UG UnderGround.

UHF The Ultra High Frequency part of the radio frequency spectrum ranging between 300 MegaHertz and 3 GigaHertz.

UI UNIX International is a consortium of computer hardware and software vendors which is interested in the development of open software standards for the UNIX industry. Prominent members include AT&T, Sun, UNISYS and Fujitsu.

UIS Universal Information Services. AT&T's vision of a single fully-integrated, user-defined digital network with a universal port of entry. Very similar to ISDN, now aggressively adopted by AT&T.

UL Underwriters Laboratories, a privately-owned company that charges manufacturers a stiff fee to make sure their products meet the safety standards which UL itself develops. A UL label on a product has a very specific message. It says the product confirms to the safety standards UL has developed — nothing more. It does not affirm that the product will work. UL is now beginning to concern itself with adopting and promulgating standards (which have nothing to do with safety standards) including those relating to cabling. See UL APPROVED, UL CABLE CERTIFICATION PROGRAM and UL NNNN.

UL 1449 A method of rating and aproving surge supprssors. This Underwriters Laboratories measurment is important as it tells if you're buying a true surge suppressor or just an extension cord. This listing measures how much voltage actually reaches the attached equipment after going through the surge suppressor. It's on a scale from about 330 volts to 6,000 volts. The lower the rating, the greater the protection. Decent surge suppressors tend to be rated around 400 volts for the basic units and 340 for the advanced and superior models. In short, check for UL 1449 rating on your surge arrestor before you buy it.

UL 1459 Effective 7/1/91, telephone equipment manufacturers will be required to provide protection from current overloads and power line crosses on equipment systems. Equipment systems covered under this listing requirement include single- and multi-line telephones, PBXs, key systems and central office switches. In general, the UL 1459 requirements apply to any location where wires enter a building from the public network, as well as in most IROB (In Range Out of Building) situations. See also NEC REQUIREMENTS and UNDERWRITERS LABORATORIES.

UL 1863 This requirement covers miscellaneous accessories intended to be electrically connected to the telecommunications network. The listing requirement applies to components that comprise the premises communications wiring system from the point of demarcation up to and including the final outlet providing modular plug and jack connection (or equivalent). Requirements are listed under Communication Circuit Accessories, UL 1863. Listing equipment for all other equipment will be covered under UL 1459, effective July 1, 1991. See also NEC REQUIREMENTS and UNDERWRITERS LABORATORIES.

UL 497 & 497A According to the National Electrical Code, primary and secondary protection systems that will be used on a telephone circuit must be listed for that purpose. The listing requirements are UL 497 for primary protection systems and UL 497A for secondary protection systems. See also NEC REQUIREMENTS and UNDERWRITERS LABORATORIES.

UL APPROVED Tested and approved by the Underwriters Laboratories. The Underwriters Laboratories, Inc. was established by the National Board of Fire Underwriters to test equipment affecting insurance risks of fire and safety. Most phone systems are tested and approved. Most of the testing focuses on the power supply feeding the phone system. The power supply is that little black box that plugs into the AC wall outlet at one end, takes 120 volt AC and converts it to low voltage DC power that the phone system typically runs on. If the power supply tests OK, then that's usually sufficient UL testing. For it is the power supply — and what happens to the commercial AC power that feeds into the power supply — that determines the potential fire hazard of your phone system. After many fire deaths in recent years, most local communities are a lot more concerned about UL Approval of installed telephone equipment. Fire departments have been known to zealously enforce these rules. In addition to the UL approval, the other major fire concern is the use of proper wire in new building construction, with especial emphasis on teflon-covered cable in plenum ceilings. See also UL, an entry which talks about UL's expanding certification business. See also UL CABLE CERTIFICATION PROGRAM.

UL CABLE CERTIFICATION PROGRAM United Laboratories, in conjunction with companies such as Anixter, has developed a Data-Transmission Performance-Level Marking Program that covers UL Listed communications cable or power-limited circuit cable. The UL program identifies five levels of performance. UL evaluates cable samples to all of the tests required for each level. Only Levels II through V require testing.

LEVEL I: Level I cable performance is intended for basic communications and power-limited circuit cable. There are no performance criteria for cable at this level.

LEVEL II: Level II cable performance requirements are similar to those for Type 3 cable (multi-pair communications cable) of the IBM Cabling System Technical Interface Specification (GA27-3773-1). These

NEWTON'S TELECOM DICTIONARY

requirements apply to both shielded and unshielded cable constructions. Level II covers cable with two to 25 pair twisted pairs of conductors.

LEVEL III: Level III data cable complies with the transmission requirements in the Electrical Industries Association/Telecommunications Wiring Standard for Horizontal Unshielded Twisted-Pair (UTP) Cable and with the requirements for Category 3 in the proposed EIA/TIA Technical Systems Bulletin PN-2841. These requirements apply to both shielded and unshielded cables.

LEVEL IV: Level IV cable complies with the requirements in the proposed National Manufacturer Association (NEMA) Standard for Low-Loss Premises Telecommunications Cable. Level IV requirements are similar to Category 4 requirements of the proposed Electronic Industries Association/Telecommunication Industry Association (EIA/TIA) Technical Systems Bulletin PN-2841. These requirements apply to both shielded and unshielded cable constructions.

LEVEL V: Level V cable complies with the requirements in the proposed National Electrical Manufacturers Association (NEMA) Standard for Low-Loss Extended-Frequency Premises Telecommunications Cable. Level V requirements are similar to Category 5 requirements of the proposed Electronic Industries Association/Telecommunication Industry Association (EIA/TIA) Technical Systems Bulletin PN-2841. These requirements apply to both shielded and unshielded cable constructions.

UL evaluates communications and data transmission cable to one of two UL Safety Standards: UL 444, the Standard for Safety for Communications Cable; and UL 13, the Standard for Safety for Power-Limited Circuit Cable.

ULP Abbreviation for Upper Layer Protocol. Layer above TCP.

ULSI Ultra Large Scale Integration, the technique of putting millions of transistors on a single integrated circuit. Compare with LSI (Large Scale Integration) and VLSI (Very Large Scale Integration).

ULTIMEDIA IBM's word for the ultimate in multimedia — combining sound, motion video, photographic imagery, graphics, text and touch into a unified, natural interface representing, in IBM's words, the ultimate in multimedia solutions. Coined in the Spring of 1992.

ULTRA 800 Sprint service for large users of 800 service. Access is provided over a T-1.

ULTRA HI-RES Ultra high resolution. Properly speaking, the term should be for monitors with resolutions of 1,200 x 800, 1,024 x 1024 or better, but it is sometimes used to describe monitors with 800 x 600 resolution and above.

ULTA HIGH FREQUENCY Frequencies from 300 MHz to 3000 MHz.

ULTRA WATS PLUS Sprint's Ultra WATS PLUS is a packaging of Sprint Dial 1 WATS, Ultra WATS, and FONCARD services.

ULTRASONIC BONDING The use of ultrasonic energy and pressure to join two materials.

ULTRAVIOLET That portion of the electromagnetic spectrum in which the wavelength is just below the visible spectrum, extending from approximately 4 nanometers to approximately 400 nanometers. Some scientists place the lower limit at values between 1 and 40 nanometers, 1 nm being the upper wavelength limit of X-rays. The 400-nm limit is the lowest visible frequency, namely violet. "Light" in the ultraviolet spectrum is used for erasing EPROMS.

ULTRAVIOLET FIBER Special fiber which extends the usable range into the UV region of the spectrum.

ULTRIX Ultrix is Digital Equipment Corporation's proprietary implementation of the UNIX operating system. It runs on DEC's RISC-based workstations.

UM Micron (10-6 meters).

UMA See UPPER MEMORY AREA.

UMB An acronym for Upper Memory Block, an area of upper memory (the area between 640KB and 1MB of RAM) in an MS-DOS PC that has been remapped with usable RAM. This allows device drivers and TSRs to be loaded high, into the UMB and out of conventional memory. See UPPER MEMORY AREA.

UMTS Universal Mobile Telecommunications Systems.

UNATTENDED Equipment working without a human attendant or operator. There are pros and cons to operators. On the pro side, they offer a personalized service that's absolutely critical to customer goodwill. On the con side, they can be slow and cumbersome. They can be very irksome when you know you could do that task yourself, but have to wait for the operator. Some companies have only one main number. Some companies use a main number and DID — on their Centrex and their PBX. Some companies use an automated attendant and an operator. There's more flexibility with DID and a main number, or Centrex DID and a main number. Customers without knowledge dial the main number. Customers with knowledge can dial direct DID numbers. See also AUTOMATED ATTENDANTS.

UNATTENDED CALL Calls placed by a computerized dialing system in anticipation of an agent being available to answer the call. A called party is detected answering the phone and no agent is available to serve the call. The system hangs up on the party so as not to create any greater nuisance than has already occurred. The telemarketing industry does not believe that an unattended call can be queued for the next available agent.

UNBALANCED LINE A telephone circuit in which the voltages on the two conductors are not equal with respect to ground. Unbalanced lines give poor phone service. Lines can become unbalanced when they come from the central office or when they are in the PBX or the on-site phone system. Problems can and should be repaired for decent quality results.

UNBUNDLED Services, programs, software and training sold separately from the hardware.

UNDERFILL A condition for launching light into a fiber in which not all the modes that the fiber can support are excited (i.e. turned on).

UNDERFLOOR DUCT METHOD A floor distribution method using a series of metal distribution channels, often embedded in concrete, for placing cables. This method uses one or two levels depending on the complexity of the system. Sometimes referred to as underfloor raceways. See also RACEWAYS METHOD.

UNDERFLOW In computing, a condition occurring when a machine calculation produces a non-zero result that is smaller than the smallest non-zero quantity that the machine's storage unit is capable of storing or representing.

UNDERGROUND Cable installed in buried conduit. Does not typically include cables buried directly in the ground.

UNDERLAP In facsimile, a defect that occurs when the width of the scanning line is less than the scanning pitch.

UNDERLYING CARRIER A common carrier providing facilities to another common carrier which then provides services to end users.

UNDERWRITERS LABORATORIES, INC A non-profit laboratory which examines and tests devices, materials and systems for safety, not for satisfactory operation. It also has begun to establish safety standards. See also UL APPROVED.

UNDESIRED SIGNAL Any signal that tends to produce degradation in the operation of equipment or systems.

UNDETECTED ERROR RATIO The ratio of the number of bits, unit elements, characters, or blocks incorrectly received and undetected, to the total number of bits, unit elements, characters, or blocks sent.

UNDISTURBED DAY A day in which the sunspot activity or ionospheric disturbance does not interfere with radio communications.

UNEQUAL ACCESS Refers to long distance phone companies who do not take advantage of Judge Harold Greene's Equal Access divestiture provisions. Rather than a carrier selection code, unequal access carriers require you to dial a local seven digit number and punch in an authorization code. If the carrier elected to pay for Equal Access, you would just dial directly the same 10 digits you do today, and your local telephone company would give your billing number to your long distance company.

UNERASE A command for getting back files you've accidentally erased. See MS-DOS.

UNGROUNDED Not connected to ground. PBXs, key systems and other phone systems will not work well when not connected to a solid ground because they have no place to send high voltage spikes (static electricity, lightning strikes, etc.) Improper grounding is probably the most common cause of phone system faults. Our feeling: the better the ground, the better the phone system performance. One way of grounding is the third wire of an electrical outlet. This may be OK if you check where that wire is ultimately connected to. You can ground to the metal cold water pipe. But that may connect to a plastic PVC pipe one floor below. Best to check. A ground ultimately ending firmly routed a dozen feet below the ground is best. Books have been written on the subject of grounding for telephony. See Lees abc Teletraining books, available from the Telecom Library at 1-800-LIBRARY or 212-691-8215.

UNI User-Network Interface. The physical and electrical demarcation point between the user and the public network service provider. An Asynchronous Transfer Mode (ATM) term.

UNIBOL A UNIX version of COBOL.

UNIDIRECTIONAL The transmission of information in one direction only.

UNIFORM ACCESS NUMBER See UNISERV.

UNIFORM CALL DISTRIBUTION See UNIFORM CALL DISTRIBUTOR.

UNIFORM CALL DISTRIBUTOR A device for distributing many incoming calls uniformly among a group of people (typically called "agents" because of the early use of these machines by the airline, hotel and car reservation industry). These days the term Uniform Call Distributor is falling into disrepute as the newer term, Automatic Call Distributor comes in. According to incoming call experts, a Uniform Call Distributor is generally less "intelligent," and therefore less costly than an ACD. A UCD will distribute calls following a predetermined logic, for example "top down" or "round robin." It will not typically pay any heed to real-time traffic load, or which agent has been busiest or idle the longest. Also, a UCD's management reports tend to be rudimentary, consisting of simple pegs counts, as opposed to an ACD, which can produce reports on the productivity of agents.

UNIFORM ENCODING An analog-to-digital conversion process in which, except for the highest and lowest quantization steps, all of the quantization subrange values are equal.

UNIFORM LINEAR ARRAY An antenna composed of a relatively large number of usually identical elements arranged in a single line or in a plane with uniform spacing and usually with a uniform feed system.

NEWTON'S TELECOM DICTIONARY

UNIFORM NUMBERING PLAN A uniform seven-digit number assignment made to each phone in a private corporate network. Such a plan allows routing of calls to distant phones from any on-net telephone without any differences in the dialed number. Without a uniform numbering plan, you would dial your boss in New York differently if you were in the company's Chicago office and differently again if you were in your company's San Francisco office. With a uniform numbering plan, it would be the same from all locations. The nation's long distance network has, obviously, a uniform numbering plan.

UNIFORM SERVICE ORDER CODE See USOC.

UNIFORM SPECTRUM RANDOM NOISE Noise distributed over the spectrum in such a way that the power per unit bandwidth is constant. Also known as "white" noise.

UNINTELLIGENT CROSSTALK Crosstalk giving rise to unintelligent signals.

UNINTERRUPTIBLE POWER SUPPLY UPS. (Pronounced "UPs.") An auxiliary power unit for a telephone system that provides continuous power in case you lose commercial power. An UPS is typically a bank of wet cell batteries (similar to automobile batteries) engineered to power a phone system up to eight hours without any re-charging. A UPS system can also include a gasoline-powered generator. And if the generator works (make sure it has gas), you can power your phone system for much longer. According to Bell Labs, however, over 90% of all power outages last less than five minutes.

UNIPOLAR SIGNAL A two-state signal where one of the states is represented by voltage or current and the other state is represented by no voltage or no current. The current flow can be in either direction.

UNIQUE ADDRESSING The addressing of a node by using the software-programmable address assigned to each one upon system initialization. For example, TELECONNECT's LAN has a "unique" addressing scheme. Each workstation is known by the operator's first name.

UNISERV SERVICE A BellSouth service which provides a seven-digit local phone number that a subscriber may use in multiple LATAs or local calling area. The subscriber's clients will be able to dial one number from all locations within the calling area, and the call will then be routed to one specified location within the calling area. The service was formerly called Uniform Access Number.

UNIT INTERVAL In a system using isochronous transmission, that interval of time such that the theoretical durations of the significant intervals of a signal are all whole multiples of this interval. The unit interval is the shortest time interval between two consecutive significant instants.

UNITED STATES TELEPHONE ASSOCIATION USTA. The largest

trade association of telephone companies. Based in Washington, its primary role is to ensure no regulation or legislation is passed that is unfavorable to the telephone industry. Its secondary aim is to hold trade shows/conventions each year. Its third aim is education. It has a sister organization, the United States Telephone Suppliers Association, which is now merged with the EIA, forming the TIA. See the next definition.

UNITED STATES TELEPHONE SUPPLIERS ASSOCIATION USTSA. This is the association of suppliers — manufacturers and wholesalers — affiliated with the United States Telephone Association (USTA). It is based in Chicago. Its aims are to promote sales of its members' products to international and domestic telephone companies through conventions. It has merged with the Electronic Industries Association to become the TIA — Telecommunications Industry Association.

UNITED TELECOM Local operating telephone holding company which changed its name to Sprint Corporation in February, 1992 after it became the sole owner of Sprint, the long distance company.

UNITY GAIN Refers to the balance between signal loss on a broadband network and signal gain through amplifiers.

UNIVERSAL ACCESS NUMBER A single number dialed from anywhere in the country which will route a customer to one or several locations for service, advice, etc. The definition varies depending on whose networking scheme you're dealing with.

UNIVERSAL ADDRESSING The addressing of a node by the use of the universal addresses which all nodes recognize.

UNIVERSAL ASYNCHRONOUS RECEIVER-TRANSMITTER UART. A device that converts outgoing parallel data from your computer to serial transmission and converts incoming serial data to parallel for reception. See UART for a bigger explanation.

UNIVERSAL DEVICE A SCSA device. A call processing device which has every conceivable resource for the handling of calls. The SCSA programming applies resources from many different physical devices to a call processing task. These then act as if they were a single universal device.

UNIVERSAL SERVICE FUND There is money somewhere in Washington in something called the Universal Service Fund, whose goal is to provide telephone service to every household in the U.S. with at least one access line for basic telephone service. This fund gets money from a surcharge on phone lines. The fund's goal is to offset operating costs of small telcos.

UNIVERSAL INFORMATION SERVICES UIS. AT&T's vision for the future of the telecommunications industry, where network providers everywhere can give any customer any kind of voice, data or image service in any place, at any time, in any combination and with maximum convenience and economy. UIS is very much like ISDN. The word UIS seems to be disappearing as AT&T embraces ISDN.

UNIVERSAL INTEGRATED SERVICES See UNIVERSAL INFORMATION SERVICES.

UNIVERSAL MAILBOX Allows a user of unified messaging services to have single access to all messages from internal and external electronic mail systems. A nice idea given today's lack of standardization among electronic mail services. Not yet a reality.

UNIVERSAL NIGHT ANSWER A feature of telephone systems that permits any phone to pick up any incoming trunk call when the Attendant's console is unmanned (unpersonned?) and the phone system is set up (typically at the console) for "Night Answer."

UNIVERSAL PAY PHONE Description for a coin-and-credit-card phone.

UNIVERSAL PORTS A modern telephone system is typically an empty cabinet into which you slide printed circuit cards. Those cards have an edge connector and they slide into a connector at the rear of the cabinet. That connector connects via wires to other connectors in what is typically called the phone system's bus. In the old days, phone systems had dedicated slots — meaning you could only slide one type of printed circuit card into that particular slot. As phone systems got more advanced, they acquired "universal ports." Our definition of a universal port is that all the slots are totally flexible — namely that you can slide any trunk or phone card (either electronic or single line phone) into any slot in the phone system. The advantage of this is obviously a far more flexible phone system, able to accommodate lots of phones and few trunks or vice versa.

UNIVERSAL SENDER Allows the dialed number to be sent out by the user.

UNIVERSAL SERVICE Originally conceived by the first chairman of the Bell System, Theodore Vail, universal service has been the goal of the entire telephone industry, including its Federal and state regulators, since the 1920s. The idea of universal service is to have residential telephone service priced sufficiently low so anyone in the United States can afford it. Keeping residential service low has been the reason why local business service is usually priced much higher — though the two services are usually identical. Universal Service is now effectively accomplished. It has become a political rallying cry, used to justify the strange and wonderful pricing schemes the phone industry and its regulators create with little regard for the actual costs of providing those services.

UNIVERSAL TURRET A very large key system for financial traders, emergency teams at nuclear power stations and others who need single phone button access to hundreds of people. By simply pushing one of the button in front of them, the user can dial one of hundreds of people. These buttons may be connected to tie lines, foreign exchange lines. They may even be DDD lines with autodial capability. Like all good key systems, the buttons have a lamping display which shows if the particular line is idle, busy, ringing, on hold, etc.

UNIVERSAL WALL JACK There's really no such animal. Every manufacturer of installation gadgetry is trying to propagate the idea that their jack is universal, when it really isn't. The "universal" wall jack we installed in our new offices is actually four jacks — 1. Four pairs for two PBX voice lines (one electronic two-pair phone and one tip and ring phone) and one spare. 2. One RS-232-C 12-conductor shielded cable for connecting to centralized printers, for connecting to a dataPBX and for permanent null-modem connection of computers. 3. One for connecting to our high-speed, one megabit per second LAN, and 4. One spare twisted, shielded, stranded pair for a second LAN, or whatever comes along.

UNIX An immensely powerful and complex operating system for computers for running data processing and for running telephone systems. UNIX provides multitasking, multiuser capabilities that allow both multiple programs to be run simultaneously and multiple users to use a single computer. On a single-user system, such as MS-DOS, only one person at a time, on an individual task basis, can use a computer's files. programs, and other resources. UNIX works on many different computers. This means you can often take applications software which runs on UNIX and move it — with little changing — to a bigger, different computer, or to a smaller, computer. This process of moving programs to other computers is known as "porting." Today, the UNIX operating system is available on a wide range of hardware, from small personal computers to the most powerful mainframes, from a multitude of hardware and software vendors. UNIX was developed in 1969 by Ken Thompson of AT&T Bell Laboratories.

UNLISTED NUMBER A telephone line with no phone number listed in the telephone company's directory. Centrex numbers, for example, are often unlisted, meaning you can't get them from the telephone company even if you pulled the biggest string imaginable. Compare unlisted number to non-published number, where the number is listed in the telephone company's directory. But no one in the world outside the phone company can get their hands on that number. "Published" means "to make public." And that's the one thing the phone company won't do with a non-published number. You won't, for example, find the number in a phone book. You also won't get it from Directory Assistance. Over 25% of many private phone numbers in major metropolitan areas are now non-published — a "service" their subscribers pay extra for.

UNLOADED LINE A telephone line with its loading coils removed to increase the distance and speed with which data may be transmitted over the line. A fee is usually charged for removing the coils.

UNLOCK CODE This is a three-digit number required to unlock a cellular phone when you have electronically locked it to prevent unauthorized use. You might lock it when you park your car in a hotel. The factory default is 123.

UNMA AT&T's Unified Network Management Architecture.

UNMR Universal Network Management Record.

UNNUMBERED COMMAND In a data transmission, a command that does not contain sequence numbers in the control field.

UNRESTRICTED DIGITAL INFORMATION An ISDN term. An information sequence of bits is transferred at its specified bit rate without alteration.

UNSHIELDED Wiring not protected by a metal sheathing from electromagnetic and radio frequency interference, but covered with plastic and/or PVC.

UNSHIELDED TWISTED PAIR UTP. A cable medium with one or more pairs of twisted insulated copper conductors bound in a single plastic sheath. Now becoming the most common method of bringing telephone and data to the desktop. There is now a strong belief that twisted pair cables carrying data over 16 megabits per second should definitely be carried on unshielded twisted wire — since at such speeds, such cables emanate radiation which should be allowed to escape (otherwise it would interfere with itself). Hence the unshielded cables.

UNSUCCESSFUL CALL A call attempt that does not result in the establishment of a connection.

UP-CONVERTER A device for performing frequency translation in such a manner that the output frequencies are higher than the input frequencies.

UPCS Universal Personal Communications Services.

UPLINK 1. In satellites, it's the link from the earth station up to the satellite. The link from the satellite down to the earth station is called the downlink. The two are differentiated because customers often buy uplinks and downlinks from different suppliers — especially in international telecommunications. 2. In data transmission, an uplink is from a data station to the head-end or mainframe.

UPLOAD To transmit a data file from your computer to another computer. The opposite of download, which is receiving a file on your computer from another computer. Upload means the same as TRANSMIT, while DOWNLOAD means the same as receive. Before you upload or download, check at least three times you're going the direction you want. It's very easy to erase files (weeks of work) if you make a mistake and confuse uploading and downloading. (Don't laugh. We've done it several times. Dumb!)

UPPER MEMORY AREA In an IBM compatible PC, upper memory is the area between 640KB and 1MB of RAM. This area is made up of Upper

Memory Blocks (UMBs) of various sizes. Access to this area is possible only with a special memory drive such as MS-DOS's EMM386.EXE.

UPPER MEMORY BLOCKS See UPPER MEMORY AREA.

UPS 1. See UNINTERRUPTIBLE POWER SUPPLY. 2. United Parcel Service, a package deliverer that regularly lives up to its self-imposed, relatively speedy delivery schedule.

UPS MONITORING UPS monitoring allows a local area network file server to monitor an attached Uninterruptable Power Supply (UPS). When a power failure occurs, NetWare notifies users. After a timeout specified with SERVER.CFG and ROUTER.CFG, the server logs out any remaining users, closes any open files, and shuts itself down. If you install a Novell-approved UPS, you must also install a printed circuit board in the file server to monitor the UPS. If you have a file server with a microchannel bus (as compared to the more common AT bus), the UPS is monitored through the mouse port and does not require a board.

UPSTREAM In a broadband network, the signal from the transmitting stations to the headend. See UPSTREAM CHANNEL.

UPSTREAM CHANNEL A collection of frequencies on a CATV channel reserved for transmission from the terminal next to the user TV set to (upstream to) the CATV company's computer. Such signals might be requests for pay movies.

UPSTREAM OPERATIONS Functions that provide a BCC (Bellcore Client Company) control of features and service configurations and subject to BCC control, some service management capabilities for subscribers. These functions include Service Negotiation and Management, Service Provisioning and Repair Service Answering/Work Force Administration. Definition from Bellcore in reference to its concept of the Advanced Intelligent Network.

UPT Universal Personal Telecommunications.

UPTIME Colloquial expression for the uninterrupted amount of time that network or computer resources are working and available to a user. In short, time between failures or periods of nonavailability (as for maintenance).

UPWARD COMPATIBLE Any device that can be easily organized, fixed or configured to work in either a different, expanded operating environment or some enhanced mode. Software is said to be upward compatible if a computer larger than the one for which it was written can run the program.

URBAN SERVICE Any of the grades of service regularly furnished inside base or locality rate areas, or outside base or locality rate areas at base or locality rates plus zone connection charges or incremental rates. Another way of saying expanded metropolitan phone service.

US SPRINT An old name for Sprint, the long distance carrier.

US WEST One of the seven Regional Holding Companies formed at divestiture. It includes Mountain Telephone, Northwestern Bell and Pacific Northwest Bell among other service entities and entrepreneurial adventures.

USA DIRECT An AT&T service designed for those calling the U.S. from overseas. Callers in foreign countries dial a toll-free number in that country. That call gets them to an AT&T operator in the U.S. who lets them make calls to the U.S. with their AT&T calling card or by making a collect call. AT&T calls the service USADirect — one word. It would look like a mistake if I spelled it that way in this dictionary. MCI has a similar service called "Call USA."

USACII See ASCII. The name change was a result of the name change of the standards organization. When the name changed again to ANSI, most people simply reverted to ASCII.

USAGE BASED Usage-Based refers to a rate or price for telephone service based on usage rather than a flat, fixed monthly fee. Until a few years ago, most local phone service in the United States was charged on a flat rate basis. Increasingly, phone companies are switching their local charging over to usage-based. Flat-rate calling will probably disappear within a few years. Allegedly, usage based phone service pricing is fairer on those phone subscribers who don't use their phone much. Usage based pricing is not consistent throughout the U.S. Typically, you get charged for each call. And the charging is very much like that for long distance — by length of call, by time of day and by distance called. See also FLAT RATE.

USAGE SENSITIVE A form of Measured Rate Service. See USAGE BASED.

USART Universal Synchronous/Asynchronous Receiver/Transmitter. An integrated circuit chip that handles the I/O (input/output) functions of a computer port. It converts data coming in parallel form from the CPU into serial form suitable for transmission, and vice versa.

USED Equipment which was previously in service (i.e. used someplace else) and may not have been tested, refurbished or remanufactured before you bought it. Used simply means it's no longer new. No more, no less. See also CERTIFIED and REFURBISHED.

USER ACCESSIBLE TABLES There are many tables (databases) inside a phone system. They include the extensions with privileges and long-distance dialing selections (see LEAST COST ROUTING). In the old days, most PBX and phone system tables were not accessible to the user, on the assumptions that 1. The user would screw the tables up, and/or 2. Really didn't care about getting access. Things have changed. Users now want faster and greater control over their own destiny. So, many manufacturers are making their tables user accessible.

USER ACCOUNT Each user has a user account that is part of local area network security and controls the user environment. Some account features are assigned to each user automatically, some must be assigned, some are optional.

USER AGENT 1. Generally refers to the windows and menus used to make interfacing to UNIX easier. 2. An X.400 electronical mail term: Software that prepares the message for transmission to the Message Transfer Agent. The user can be an individual or a distribution list. Users are known by their originator/recipient (O/R) addresses.

USER CONTEXT A user session created by an operating system in response to a logon request, and typically characterized by privilege sets that strictly define the user's authority to access system resources and information on a LAN. Contexts restrict unauthorized access to facilities and data and protect the system itself from user and applications interference, accidental or otherwise. Contexts are a feature of most multiuser operating systems, usually integrated with the security system.

USER DATA X.25 call control field used to transfer information concerning layers above X.25 between the originating and terminating DTEs.

USER ID Persistent information in an ASC (AIN Switch Capabilities) that the ASC communicates to the SLEE (Service Logic Execution Environment) as a parameter in a message to the SLEE. The SLEE uses this parameter to identify the set of information related to the user (e.g., customer record) that service logic needs to perform its task. If a user does not subscribe to any Advanced Intelligent Network Release 1 feature but invokes an AIN Release 1 feature, the user ID in the ASC may correlate in the SLEE to a set of default information to be used by service logic.

USER LOOP A 2- or 4-wire circuit connecting a user to a PBX or other phone system.

USER MESSAGE Part of a CPN message directing a destination node to accomplish some task.

USER SEGMENT The part of a satellite system that includes the receivers on the users' premises.

USER TO USER MESSAGING An ISDN service enabling voice and computer data to be transmitted simultaneously — for example, enabling one person to transmit a spreadsheet file to another so both can examine it on their individual screens, and for each to have the ability to change the spreadsheet and have the changes appear instantly on the other person's screen, and then discuss the changes.

USER'S SET Apparatus located on the premises of a communications user. Designed to work with other parts of his system.

USITA United States Independent Telephone Association, the old name for the United States Telephone Association. See USTA.

USOC Universal Service Order Code. (Pronounced "U-Sock.") An old Bell

System term identifying a particular service or equipment offered under tariff. There was nothing "Universal" or consistent about USOC codes. Many services and equipment were called different things by different Bell operating companies. Since Divestiture, there is absolutely no consistency and little relevance left in USOC codes. Each Bell operating company is busily creating its own billing codes and terms.

USOS Universal Operations Services. A software application that supports UIS by providing traditional network operations functions.

USP Usage Sensitive Pricing. A tariff for local service under which the subscriber only pays for the telephone service he uses. This is done for gas and electric service.

USRT Universal Synchronous Receiver/Transmitter. Integrated circuit that performs conversion of parallel data to serial for transmission over a synchronous data channel.

USTA See UNITED STATES TELEPHONE ASSOCIATION.

USTSA See UNITED STATES TELEPHONE SUPPLIERS ASSOCIATION.

UT Universal Time.

UTC Coordinated Universal Time as kept by the "i" laboratory, where i is any laboratory cooperating in the determination of UTC. In the United States, the official UTC is kept by the U.S. Naval Observatory and is referred to as UTC.

UTDR Universal Trunk Data Record.

UTILITY PROGRAM A computer program in general support of the processes of a computer; for example, a diagnostic program.

UTILITY ROUTINE A routine in general support of the processes of a computer; for example, an input routine.

UTILIZE An absolutely awful word created the people who believe that speaking or writing in big words is a demonstration of their superior intelligence.

UTILITY In some computer languages, a small program executed as a shell command is called a "tool." In other computer languages, such as BASIC, it is called a "utility."

UTILITY PROGRAM A program which performs generalized functions.

UTILITY ROUTINE A routine in general support of the operation of a computer, including input/output, diagnostic, tracing or monitoring.

UTP Unshielded Twisted Pair. A cable medium with one or more pairs of twisted insulated copper conductors bound in a single plastic sheath. Now becoming the most common method of bringing telephone and data to the desktop. There is now a strong belief that twisted pair cables carrying data over 16 megabits per second should definitely be carried on unshielded twisted wire — since at such speeds, such cables emanate radiation which should be allowed to escape (otherwise it would interfere with itself). Hence the unshielded cables.

UTR Universal Tone Receiver.

UTS Universal Telephone Service.

UTTERANCE A word used in voice recognition to mean a vocalized sound that is typically a word.

UV 1. UltraViolet. 2. A microvolt.

V Abbreviation for VOLT.

V & H Vertical and Horizontal grid coordinates. AT&T Bell Labs assigned pair of numbers that locates each telephone company's central office or rate center on a grid of the North American Continent. The V & H numbers are used to determine the "airline distance" between any two rate centers. Long distance phone calls are priced on the basis of airline distance between two rate centers or telephone central offices. You calculate airline distance based on Pythagoras' theorem. The formula is thus:

Step One. Calculate the sum of V1 minus V2 all squared plus H1 minus H2 all squared.

Step Two. Divide the answer by 10.

Step Three: Take the square root of this number.

Example: San Diego to Boston.

(V1 = 9,468) - (V2 = 4422) = 5046

(5046 x 5046) = 25,462,116

(H1 = 7629) - (H2 = 1249) = 6380

6038 x 6038 = 40,704,400

25,462,116 + 40,704,400 = 66,166,516

Divide 66,166,516 by 10 = 6,616,652

The square root of 6,616,652 = 2,572 airline lines

V & H COORDINATES OF MAJOR CONTINENTAL US CITIES

	V coordinates	H		V coordinates	H		V coordinates	H
ALABAMA			Redwood City	8556	8682	**DELAWARE**		
Birmingham	7518	2304	Sacramento	8304	8580	Wilmington	5326	1485
Huntsville	7267	2535	San Bernadino	9172	7710	**DISTRICT OF COLUMBIA (D.C.)**		
Mobile	8167	2367	San Diego	9468	7629	Washington	5622	1583
Montgomery	7692	2247	San Francisco	8492	8719			
			San Jose	8583	8619	**FLORIDA**		
ARIZONA			Santa Monica	9227	7920	Clearwater	8203	1206
Flagstaff	8746	6760	Santa Rosa	8354	8787	Daytona Beach	7791	1052
Phoenix	9135	6748	Sunnyvale	8576	8643	Fort Lauderdale	8282	0557
Tucson	9345	6485	Van Nuys	9197	7919	Jacksonville 7649 1276		
Yuma	9385	7171				Miami	8351	0527
			COLORADO			Orlando	7954	1031
ARKANSAS			Denver	7501	5899	Tallahassee	7877	1716
Fayetteville	7600	3872	Fort Collins	7331	5965	Tampa	8173	1147
Hot Springs	7827	3554	Grand Junction	7804 6	438			
Pine Bluff	7803	3358	Greeley	7345	5895	**GEORGIA**		
			Pueblo	7787	5742	Atlanta	7260	2083
CALIFORNIA						Augusta	7089	1674
Anaheim	9250	7810	**CONNECTICUT**			Macon	7364	1865
Bakersfield	8947	8060	Bridgeport	4841	1360	Savannah	7266	1379
Fresno	8669	8239	Hartford	4687	1373	**IDAHO**		
Long Beach	9217	7856	New Haven	4792	1342	Boise	7096	7869
Los Angeles	9213	7878	New London	4700	1242			
Oakland	8486	8695	Stamford	4897	1388	Pocatello	7146	7250

	V coordinates	H
ILLINOIS		
Chicago	5986	3426
Joliet	6088	3454
Peoria	6362	3592
Rock Island	6276	3816
Springfield	6539	3518
INDIANA		
Bloomington	6417	2984
Fort Wayne	5942	2982
Indianapolis	6272	2992
Muncie	6130	2925
South Bend	5918	3206
Terre Haute	6428	3145
IOWA		
Burlington	6449	3829
Cedar Rapids	6261	4021
Des Moines	6471	4275
Dubuque	6088	3925
Iowa City	6313	3972
Sioux City	6468	4768
KANSAS		
Dodge City	7640	4958
Topeka	7110	4369
Wichita	7489	4520
KENTUCKY		
Danville	6558	2561
Frankfort	6462	2634
Madisonville	6845	2942
Paducah	6982	3088
Winchester	6441	2509
LOUISIANA		
Baton Rouge	8476	2874
New Orleans	8483	2638
Shreveport	8272	3495
MAINE		
Augusta	3961	1870
Lewiston	4042	1391
Portland	4121	1384
MARYLAND		
Baltimore	5510	1575
MASSACHUSETTS		
Boston	4422	1249
Framingham	4472	1284
Springfield	4620	1408
Worcester	4513	1330
MICHIGAN		
Detroit	5536	2828
Flint	5461	2993
Grand Rapids	5628	3261
Kalamazoo	5749	3177
Lansing	5584	3081
MINNESOTA		
Duluth	5352	4530
Minneapolis	5777	4513
St. Paul	5776	4498

	V coordinates	H
MISSISSIPPI		
Biloxi	8296	2481
Jackson	8035	2880
Meridian	7899	2639
MISSOURI		
Joplin	7421	4015
Kansas City	7027	4203
St. Joseph	6913	4301
Springfield	7310	3836
MONTANA		
Billings	6391	6790
Helena	6336	7348
Missoula	6336	7650
NEBRASKA		
Grand Island	6901	4936
Omaha	6687	4595
NEVADA		
Carson City	8139	8306
Las Vegas	8665	7411
Reno	8064	8323
NEW HAMPSHIRE		
Concord	4326	1426
Manchester	4354	1388
Nashua	4394	1356
NEW JERSEY		
Atlantic City 5284 1284		
Camden	5249	1453
Hackensack	4976	1432
Morristown	5035	1478
Newark	5015	1430
New Brunswick	5085	1434
Trenton	5164	1440
NEW MEXICO		
Albuquerque	8549	5887
Las Cruces	9132	5742
Santa Fe	8389	5804
NEW YORK		
Albany	4639	1629
Binghamton	4943	1837
Buffalo	5076	2326
Nassau	4961	1355
New York City	4977	1406
Poughkeepsie	4821	1526
Rochester	4913	2195
Syracuse	4798	1990
Troy	4616	1633
Westchester	4912	1330
NORTH CAROLINA		
Asheville	6749	2001
Charlotte	6657	1698
Fayetteville	6501	1385
Raleigh	6344	1436
Winston-Salem 6440 1710		
NORTH DAKOTA		
Bismarck	5840	5736
Fargo	5615	5182

	V coordinates	H
Grand Forks	5420	5300
OHIO		
Akron	5637	2472
Canton	5676	2419
Cincinnati	6263	2679
Cleveland	5574	2543
Columbus	5872	2555
Dayton	6113	2705
Toledo	5704	2820
OKLAHOMA		
Lawton	8178	4451
Oklahoma City	7947	4373
Tulsa	7707	4173
OREGON		
Medford	7503	8892
Pendleton	6707	8326
Portland	6799	8914
PENNSYLVANIA		
Allentown	5166	1585
Altoona	5460	1972
Harrisburg	5363	1733
Philadelphia	5257	1501
Pittsburgh	5621	2185
Reading	5258	1612
Scranton	5042	1715
RHODE ISLAND		
Providence	4550	1219
SOUTH CAROLINA		
Charleston	7021	1281
Columbia	6901	1589
Spartanburg	6811	1833
SOUTH DAKOTA		
Aberdeen	5992	5308
Huron	6201	5183
Sioux Falls	6279	4900
TENNESSEE		
Chattanooga	7098	2366
Johnson City	6595	2050
Knoxville	6801	2251
Memphis	7471	3125
Nashville	7010	2710
TEXAS		
Amarillo	8266	5076
Austin	9005	3996
Corpus Christi	9475	3739
Dallas	8436	4034
El Paso	9231	5655
Fort Worth	8479	4122
Houston	8938	3563
Laredo	9681	4099
Lubbock	8596	4962
San Antonio	9225	4062
UTAH		
Logan	7367	7102
Ogden	7480	7100
Provo	7680	7006

NEWTON'S TELECOM DICTIONARY

	V coordinates	H		V coordinates	H		V coordinates	H
Salt Lake City	7576	7065	WASHINGTON			WISCONSIN		
VERMONT			Bellingham	6087	8933	Appleton	5589	3776
Burlington	4270	1808	Kennewick	6595	8391	Eau Claire	5698	4261
			North Bend	6354	8815	Green Bay	5512	3747
VIRGINIA			Seattle	6336	8896	La Crosse	5874	4133
Blacksburg	6247	1867	Spokane	6247	8180	Madison	5887	3796
Leesburg	5634	1685	Yakima	6533	8607	Milwaukee	5788	3589
Lynchburg	6093	1703				Racine	5837	3535
Norfolk	5918	1223	WEST VIRGINIA					
Richmond	5906	1472	Clarksburg	5865	2095	WYOMING		
Roanoke	6196	1801	Morgantown	5764	2083	Casper	6918	6297
			Wheeling	5755	2241	Cheyenne	7203	5958

V INTERFACE The 2-wire ISDN physical interface used for single-customer termination from a remote terminal. See ISDN and U INTERFACE.

V PATH CUSTOM NETWORK SERVICE V PATH is a network service from New York Telephone for voice and data transmissions specifically designed for large, multi-location business customers within a regional calling area. V PATH is designed to provide the features of a private network using public switched lines.

V REFERENCE POINT The proposed interface point in an ISDN environment between the line termination and the exchange termination.

V SERIES RECOMMENDATIONS CCITT standards dealing with data communications operation over the telephone network. The idea of standards is simple. If you have them and if every manufacturer conforms, then every modem can talk to every other one. That's the idea. But it's not always that simple. Sometimes you have to conform to several standards. For example, in the higher speed modems, for example those at 9,600 bps, you have to conform to speed (that's one standard). You have to conform to error control. That's another standard. And you also have to conform to data compression — if you are using data compression. ISDN terminal adapters are V series recommendations, too. CCITT uses the term "bis" to designate the second in a family of related standards and "ter" designates the third in a family.

V.110 AND V.120 Terminal rate adaption protocols for the ISDN B channel.

V.13 CCITT standard for simulated carrier control. Allows a full-duplex modem to be used to emulate a half-duplex modem with interchange circuits changing at appropriate times.

V.14 CCITT standard for asynchronous-to-synchronous conversion without error control. Allows a modem that is actually synchronous to be used to carry start/stop (async) characters. If a V.42 modem connects with another modem that doesn't have error-control, it falls back to V.14 operation to work without error-control.

V.17 New CCITT standard for simplex (one-way transmission) modulation

1046

technique for use in extended Group 3 Facsimile applications only. Provides 7200, 9600, 12000, and 14400 bps trellis-coded modulation (the modulation scheme is similar to V.33), MMR (Modified Modified Read) compression and error-correction mode (ECM).

V.21 CCITT standard for 300 bit per second duplex modems for use on the switched telephone network. V.21 modulation is used in a half-duplex mode for Group 3 fax negotiation and control procedures (CCITT T.30).

V.21 CH 2 CCITT standard for 300 bps modem, describing the operation of modems at 300 bps, and used for critical control and handshaking functions. This low speed is highly tolerant of noise and impairments on the phone line. Fax machines use only Channel 2 of the V.21 recommendations (half duplex channel).

V.22 CCITT standard for 1,200 bit per second duplex modems for use on the switched telephone network and on leased circuits.

V.22 bis CCITT standard for 2,400 bit per second duplex modems for use on the switched telephone network. V.22 bis also provides for 1200bps operation for V.22 compatibility. Bis is used by the CCITT to designate the second in a family of related standards. "ter" designates the third in a family. See V SERIES.

V.23 V.23 is the standard for a modem with a 600 bps or 1200 bps "forward channel" and a 75 bps "reverse" channel for use on the switched telephone network.

V.24 CCITT definitions for interchange circuits between data terminal equipment (DTE) and data communications equipment (DCE) equipment.

V.25 Automatic calling and/or answering equipment on the general switched telephone network, including disabling of echo suppressors on manually established calls.

V.25 bis V.25 bis is an automatic calling and answering command set including ability to work with async, bisync, and HDLC devices. Provides a small subset of the functions of the Hayes Standard AT Command Set.

V.26 V.26 is the CCITT standard for 2400 bps modem for use on 4-wire leased lines.

V.26 bis CCITT standard for 1.2/2.4 kbps modem. It is important to note that V.26 bis is a half-duplex modem (1200 or 2400 bps in only one direction at a time); it provides an optional 75 bps reverse channel as well.

V.26 ter V.26 ter is a FULL DUPLEX 2400 bps modem, like V.22 bis. The difference is that V.26 ter uses echo cancellation (like V.32) instead of frequency division (like V.22 bis), making it more expensive than V.22 bis. It was intended to serve as a fallback mode from V.32, but most manufacturers ignored it and provide V.22 bis as a fallback instead (V.26 ter is used only in a few installations in France, as far as we know).

V.27 CCITT standard for 4,800 bits per second modem with manual equalizer for use on leased telephone-type circuits. May be full-duplex on four-wire leased lines, or half-duplex on two-wire lines.

V.27 bis CCITT standard for 2.4/4.8-kbit/s modem with automatic equalizer for use on leased telephone-type circuits. 2.4 Kbps modem for 4-wire leased circuits. Either speed (2400 is a fallback) can be used on either 4-wire leased lines (full duplex) or 2-wire leased lines (half-duplex). It also provides an optional 75 bps reverse channel.

V.27 ter CCITT standard for 2.4/4.8-kbit/s modem for use on the switched telephone network. Half-Duplex only. V.27 ter is the modulation scheme used in Group 3 Facsimile for image transfer at 2400 and 4800 bps. 4800 bps is a common "fallback" speed.

V.28 V.28, entitled "Electrical Characteristics for Unbalanced Double-Current Interchange Circuits" provides the CCITT equivalent of the electrical characteristics defined in EIA-232.

V.29 CCITT standard for 9,600 bits per second modem for use on point-to-point leased circuits. Virtually all 9,600 bps leased line modems adhere to this standard. V.29 uses a carrier frequency of 1700 Hz which is varied in both phase and amplitude. V.29 also provides fallback rates of 4800 and 7200 bps. V.29 can be full-duplex on 4-wire leased circuits, or half-duplex on two-wire and dial-up circuits. V.29 is the modulation technique used in Group 3 fax for image transfer at 7200 and 9600bps.

V.32 CCITT standard for 9,600 bit per second two-wire full duplex modem operating on regular dial-up lines or 2-wire leased lines. If you're buying a 9,600 bps modem for use on the normal dial-up switched phone lines, make sure it conforms to V.32. If your modem also conforms to V.42 bis, you should be able to transmit and receive at up to 38,400 bps with other modems that conform to these two specifications. I personally use a number of V.32/V.42 bis modem and they work wonderfully fast. V.32 also provides fallback operation at 4,800 bps. See also V.32 bis, V.42 bis ERROR CORRECTION and V.42 bis DATA COMPRESSION and MODULATION PROTOCOLS.

V.32 bis New higher speed CCITT standard for full-duplex transmission on two-wire leased and dial-up lines at 4,800, 7,200, 9,600, 12,000, AND 14,400 bps. Provides backward compatibility with V.32. Modems running at V.32 bis at its highest speed of 14,400 bps are actually transmitting that many bits per seconds. They do not rely on compression to achieve that high speed. However, with data compression — such as V.42 and V.42 bis — they can achieve higher speeds. The V.32 bis standard also includes "rapid rate renegotiation" feature to allow quick and smooth rate changes when line conditions change. See MODULATION PROTOCOLS, V.42 and V.42 bis.

V.33 CCITT standard for 14,400 and 12,000 bps modem for use on four-wire leased lines.

V.35 CCITT standard for trunk interface between a network access device and a packet network that defines signaling for data rates greater than 19.2 kbps. V.35 was a definition of a GROUP band modem (meaning, one that used the bandwidth of several telephone circuits). V.36 and V.37 are other group band modems. V.35 just happened to describe, in an appendix, electrical characteristics for a high speed interface. IBM decided to use this for other things, but it was never standardized for those purposes. The CCITT, in the 1988 Blue Book, says "It is the opinion of the CCITT that the information contained in Recommendation V.35 is out of date. Therefore it is not recommended to use the techniques described in this Recommendation for new designs. Alternative techniques are described in Recommendations V.36 and V.37. It should be noted that other Recommendations make reference to the electrical characteristics described in Appendix II to this Recommendation [V.35]. As these characteristics are expected to allow interworking with V.11 characteristics, use of V.11 circuits is recommended in those cases." V.35 is no longer published by the CCITT.

V.42 ERROR CORRECTION CCITT error-correction standard specifying both MNP4 and LAP-M. The CCITT title says "Error-correcting procedures for DCEs using Asynchronous-to-Synchronous Conversion". It also notes in the text that it applies only to full-duplex devices. The CCITT modulation schemes with which V.42 may be used are V.22, V.22 bis, V.26 ter, and V.32, and V.32 bis. LAPM, based on HDLC, is the "primary" protocol, on which all future extensions will be based. The Alternative Protocol specified in Annex A of the Recommendation is for backward compatibility with the "installed base" of error-correcting modems. See V.42 bis.

V.42 bis DATA COMPRESSION Recently-approved CCITT data compression standard. It compresses files "on the fly" at an average ratio of 3.5:1 and can yield file transfer speeds of up to 9,600 bps on a 2,400 bps modem, 38,400 bits per second with a 9,600 bps modem, or 57,600 bps with a 14,400 bps V.32 bis modem. Data compression only has value if you use it to transfer and receive material that is not already compressed. Compressing stuff a second time yields no significant improvement in speed (assuming your compression technique the first time around was OK). So the decision to buy a V.42 bis modem depends on the material you're working with and your pocketbook. Obviously V.42 bis modems are more expensive.

V.42 bis was approved by the CCITT because of its technical merits. Existing data compression methods (MNP 5 for example) only provided up to two-to-one compression. Also, V.42 bis provides for built-in "feedback" mechanisms, so that the modem can monitor its own compression performance. If the DTE starts send pre-compressed or otherwise uncompressible data, V.42 bis can automatically suspend its operation to avoid expansion of the data. It continues to monitor performance even when sending data "in the clear," and when a performance improvement can be gained by reactivating compression, it will do so automatically.

V.42 bis was selected because it would work with a wide variety of different implementations — different amounts of memory, different processor speeds, etc. Because of this, there WILL be differences between various manufacturer's products in terms of THROUGHPUT performance (although they will all properly compress and decompress, some will do it faster than others). If maximum throughput is important, you should check published benchmark tests to find the modem that provides the best performance.

V.54 CCITT standard for loop test devices in modems. Defines local and remote loopbacks.

V.FAST An upcoming modem standard in the early stages of development. If approved by the CCITT, it would support speeds to 24,000 bits per second for uncompressed data transmission rates over regular dial-up, voice-grade lines. V-FAST (from Very Fast) modems are not expected to be widely available until 1994.

VAB Value Added Business partner. A term which Hewlett-Packard uses for developers which write software for its computers. HP helps its VABs sell software. Clearly, by doing so, it helps sell more HP computers.

VAC Voice Activity Compression.

VACANT CODE An unassigned area code, central office or station code.

VACANT CODE INTERCEPT Routes all calls made to an unassigned "level" (first digit dialed) to the attendant, a busy signal, a "reorder" signal or to a recorded announcement.

VACANT NUMBER INTERCEPT Routes all calls of unassigned numbers to the attendant, a busy signal or a prerecorded announcement.

VAD Value Added Dealer. Another term for Value Added Reseller (VAR). Essentially, VARs or VADs are companies who buy equipment from computer or telephone manufacturers, add some of their own software and possibly some peripheral hardware to it, then resell the whole computer or telephone system to end users, typically corporations.

VAIL, THEODORE N. Theodore N. Vail began his career with the Bell System as general manager of the Bell Telephone Company in 1878. He later became the first president of the American Telephone & Telegraph Company in 1885. He left AT&T two years later. After pursuing other interests for 20 years, he returned as president of AT&T in 1907, retiring in 1919 as chairman of the board. Vail believed in "One policy, one system, universal service." He regarded telephony as a natural monopoly. He saw the necessity for regulation and welcomed it.

VALIDATION 1. Generally, all long distance carriers, operator service providers and private payphone companies will not put a call through unless they can "validate," the caller's telephone company calling card, home/business phone number or credit card. Until the advent of US West's Billing Validation Service and other similar databases in 1987, the companies who needed to validate their callers' billing requests had to turn back the caller or accept the call on faith. Validating a user's calling card is, simply, a Yes-No. If the card number is validated, it is Yes. Getting the validation involves a data call from the provider to the owner of the database. There are many ways of doing this, including a dedicated trunk and an port through an X.25 network.

2. Tests to determine whether an implemented system fulfills its requirements. The checking of data for correctness or for compliance with applicable standards, rules, and conventions. The portion of the development of specialized security test and evaluation, procedures, tools, and equipment needed to establish acceptance for joint usage of an automated information system by one or more departments or agencies and their contractors.

VALIDITY CHECK Any check designed to insure the quality of transmission.

VALUE ADDED Refers to a voice or data network service that uses available transmission facilities and then adds some other service or services to increase the value of the transmission.

VALUE ADDED CARRIER A voice or data common carrier that adds special service features, usually computer related, to services purchased from other carriers and then sells the package of service and features.

VALUE ADDED NETWORK VAN. A data communications network in which some form of processing of a signal takes place, or information is added by the network. No one knows, however, exactly what a VAN is. The general idea is that a VAN buys "basic" transmission and sometimes switching services from local and long distance phone companies and adds something else — typically an interactive computer with a database, a computer and massive storage. In this way, the VAN adds value to basic communications services. Dial-up stockmarket quoting services are VANs. Electronic mail providers are VANs. But VANs can also simply be basic X.25 packet switching networks which are open to the public. Such a network will use X.25 packet switching to provide error correction, redundancy, and other forms of network reliability. Private organizations (companies, universities, etc.) may set up their own value-added networks, or — as in the case of PDNs (Public Data Networks) — another fancy name for a VAN that offers its services to the public. The classic VAN is a packet-switched operation like Tymnet, GTE Telenet, MCI Mail or AT&T Mail.

VALUE ADDED RESELLER See VAR.

VALUE DRIVEN RE-ENGINEERING A fancy term for Re-Engineering, which is a term probably invented by Michael Hammer in the July-August,

1990 issue of Harvard Business Review. In that issue, he wrote "It is time to stop paving the cowpaths. Instead of embedding outdated processes in silicon and software, we should obliterate them and start over. We should 're-engineer' our business: use the power of modern information technology to radically redesign our business processes to achieve dramatic improvements in their performance." The term re-engineering now seems to me mean taking tasks presently running on mainframes and making them run on file servers running on LANs — Local Area Netwotks. The idea is to save money on hardware and make the information more freely available to more people. More intelligent companies also redesign their organization to use the now, more-freely available information. See RE-ENGINEERING.

VALUE ADDED SERVICE A communications facility using common carrier networks for transmission and providing extra data features with separate equipment. Store and forward message switching, terminal interfacing and host interfacing features are common extras. See also VALUE ADDED NETWORK.

VALUFLEX A New York Telephone service which lets you make and receive regular phone calls and 800-number calls from local areas on your normal business phone lines. There are big advantages here. You don't have to rent additional phone lines. You don't have to expand your existing phone system — or buy a new one (if getting extra lines means you'd grow out). And you can combine your incoming 800 lines with features you can get on business lines — like call forwarding, conferencing, etc. Have your 800 calls come into your office during the day. Have them call forwarded at night to your home. 800 Valuflex is aimed at smaller business.

VALVE The original British word for an electron tube.

VAMPIRE TAP In local area networking technology, a cable tap that penetrates through the outer shield to make connection to the inner conductor of a coax cable.

VAN See VALUE ADDED NETWORK.

VAPORWARE A semi-affectionate slang term for software which has been announced, perhaps even demonstrated, but not delivered to commercial customers. Hyperware is hardware which has been announced but has not yet been delivered. Slideware is hardware or software whose reason for existing (eventually) has been explained in 35-mm slides, foils, charts and/or PC presentation programs. Slideware is usually less real than vaporware or hyperware, though some people would argue with this.

VAR Value Added Reseller. Typically VARs are organizations that package standard products with software solutions for a specific industry. VARs include business partners ranging in size from providers of specialty turn-key solutions to larger system integrators.

VARI-A-BILL A new 900 service of AT&T whereby the call's price varies depending on certain events — the caller punching out some tones on his phone, or a service technician coming on line, etc.

VARIABLE CALL FORWARDING An optional feature of AT&T's 800 IN-WATS service. It allows the subscriber to route calls to certain locations based on time of day or day of week.

VARIABLE FORMAT MESSAGE A message in which the page format of the output is controlled by format characters embedded in the message itself. The alternative is to have the format determined by prior agreement between the origin and the destination.

VARIABLE LENGTH BUFFER A buffer into which data may be entered at one rate and removed at another, without changing the data sequence. Most first-in, first-out (FIFO) storage devices serve this purpose in that the input rate may be variable while the output rate is constant or the output rate may be variable while the input rate is fixed. Various clocking and control systems are used to allow control of underflow or overflow conditions.

VARIABLE LENGTH RECORD A file in a database containing records not of uniform length and in which the distinctions between fields are made with commas, tabs or spaces. Records become uniform in length either because they are uniform to start with or they are "padded" with special characters.

VARIABLE QUANTIZING LEVEL VQL. A speech-encoding technique that quantizes and encodes an analog voice conversation for transmission at 32,000 bits per second.

VARIABLE RESISTOR A resistance element which may be varied to afford various values.

VARIABLE TERM PRICING PLAN VTPP. A rate plan developed by AT&T to replace two-tier pricing. VTPP generally provides for two, four, five or six year contracts, over which period the customer is promised stable prices for some — not all — of the equipment and/or tariffed services he uses. Generally, under VTPP, the customer does not end up owning any of the equipment. VTPP has now been replaced by more normal ways of doing commercial business — outright sale, leasing, etc.

VARIABLE TIMING PARAMETER Timing durations for features such as hold recall, camp-on recall, off-hook duration, and many other programmable telephone system services.

VARIOLOSSER A device with a variable level of attenuation which is controlled by an external signal. Often this signal is the level of the signal being attenuated, that is the higher the level of the signal the more it is attenuated.

VARTI Value Added Reseller Telephone Integrator. A term coined at Telecom Developers '92. It refers to the VARs and interconnects of the 90s that are combining telephony and personal computers to offer products that tie the telephone network to personal computer applications.

VAX A line of minicomputers made by Digital Equipment Corporation (DEC).

VAX MAILGATE FOR MCI MAIL An MCI product that enables users of DEC's ALL-IN-1 Integrated Office and Information System to communicate with others outside their internal network via MCI Mail.

VBI Vertical Blanking Interval. The vertical blanking interval is the portion of the television signal which carries no visual information and appears as a horizontal black bar between the pictures when a TV set needs vertical tuning. The VBI is used for carrying close-captioned signals for the hearing impaired. Digitized data can also be inserted into the VBI for transmission at rates greater than 100,000 bps. Information services such as stock market quotations and news offerings are now available via the VBI of a CATV signal. The data embedded in the VBI signal is retrieved from a standard cable or satellite receiver wall outlet by a receiver set, which connects to a RS-232 port on a microcomputer. Software packages then allow subscribers instant access to the information, which may be displayed in a number of formats.

VBR Variable Bit Rate. Referring to processes such as LANs which generate messages in a random, bursty manner rather than continuously.

VC 1. Virtual Channel or Virtual Circuit — a communications path between two nodes identified by label rather than fixed physical path. 2. Virtual Circuit. In packet switching, network facilities that give the appearance to the user of an actual end-to-end circuit. A dynamically variable network connection where sequential user data packets may be routed differently during the course of a "virtual connection." Virtual circuits allow many users to share transmission facilities simultaneously.

VCA See VOICE CONNECTING ARRANGEMENT.

VCEP Video Comrpession/Expansion Processor chip.

VCI Virtual Channel Identifier. The address or label of a VC (a virtual circuit).

VCN Virtual Corporate Network. Stentor's name for a service it later changed to Advantage VNet. It's similar to MCI's VNet.

VCPI An acronym for the Virtual Control Program Interface, a standard developed by Quarterdeck and Phar Lap Software for running multiple programs and controlling the Virtual-86 mode of 386 microprocessors. A program that's VCPI-compatible and can run in the protected mode under DOS without conflicting with other programs in the system.

VCR VideoCassette Recorder (or Player).

VDISK Virtual DISK. Part of the computer's Random Access Memory assigned to simulate a disk. VDISK is a feature of the MS-DOS operating system.

VDM Voice Data Multiplexer.

VDS Vocabulary Development System

VDT Video Display Terminal. A data terminal with a TV screen. Another name for computer monitor. VDT is the term you hear in Europe.

VDU Visual Display Unit.

VECTOR A quantity in the visual (video) telecommunications industry that describes the magnitude and direction of an object's movement — for example, a head moving to the right. See VECTOR IMAGES.

VECTOR IMAGES Images based on lines drawn between specific coordinates. A vector image is based on the specific mathematics of lines. In contrast, a raster image is a bit-mapped (i.e. bit-drawn) image. A vector engineering image is more useful for engineering, since it can be changed easier than a bit-mapped image. A vector image can easily be converted to a raster image. But it's much more difficult to go from a raster image to a vector image. Some storage systems now store iamges as combination raster/vector.

VECTOR PROCESSOR Array Processor.

VELOCITY OF LIGHT The speed of light in a vacuum is 186,280 miles per second, or 299,792 kilometers per second. The speed of light is very important because today we can measure time more accurately than length. In effect, we define the meter as the time traveled by light in 0.000000003335640952 of a second as measured by the cesium clock.

VELOCITY OF PROPAGATION The speed at which a signal travels from a sender, through a transmission line and finally arrives at the receiver.

VELOCITY OF SOUND The velocity of sound varies with the medium carrying it. In air at 0 degrees centigrade, it's 331 meters per second. In glass at 20 degrees centigrade, its 5485 meters per second.

VENDOR CODE Software written by the same company that manufactured the computer system on which it is running (or not running...).

VENDOR INDEPENDENCE The ability to allow devices manufactured by different vendors, often using different protocols, to talk to (communicate) with each other.

VENDOR INDEPENDENT MESSAGING GROUP A group of software and software companies who are trying to create non-proprietary, standard programming interfaces to help software and corporate developers write messaging and mail-enabled applications. Ultimately, end users should be able to work together more effectively and be able to exchange information from within desktop applications in a work group environment regardless of vendor platform. Members of the group include Apple, Borland, IBM, Lotus, Novell and Wordperfect.

VERIFICATION A service of a phone company operator who dials into a busy or otherwise impossible-to-reach line and checks that line and reports on that check to the caller. Phone companies are beginning to charge for this service. As of writing, AT&T, for example, was charging 40 cents to verify the line was busy and 70 cents additional for the operator to interrupt the conversation and say another call was coming in.

VERIFICATION TRUNK A trunk to which an operator has access and which will switch through to a called line even if the line is busy.

VERIFIED OFF-HOOK In telephone systems, a service provided by a unit that is inserted on each of a transmission circuit for the purpose of verifying supervisory signals on the circuit. Off-hook service is a priority telephone service for key personnel, affording a connection from caller to receiver by the simple expedient of removing the phone from its cradle or hook.

VERIFIER A device that checks the correctness of transcribed data, usually by comparing with a second transcription of the same data or by comparing a retranscription with the original data.

VERTICAL That part of a wiring grid which connects the host computer of Main Distribution Frame (MDF) to equipment located on other fields.

VERTICAL BLANKING INTERVAL The interval between television frames in which the picture is blanked to enable the trace (which "paints" the screen) to return to the upper left hand corner of the screen, from where the trace starts, once again, to paint a new screen. Several companies are eyeing the vertical blanking interval as a place to send digital data, including news and weather information. The vertical blanking interval was the basis of teletext, a 1970s technology that, with the help of a decoder, displays printed information on the TV screen. Teletext has never caught on in the U.S. in part because the amount of data that could be transmitted comfortably was small.

VERTICAL REDUNDANCY CHECK VRC. A check or parity bit added to each character in a message such that the number of bits in each character, including the parity bit, is odd (odd parity), or even (even parity). See PARITY.

VERTICAL SERVICE Options that the customer can add to his basic service such as touchtone, conference calling, speed dialing, etc. No one can explain why it's called "vertical" service.

VERY HIGH FREQUENCY VHF. Frequencies from 30 MHz to 300 MHz.

VERY LARGE SCALE INTEGRATION VLSI. Semiconductor chip with several thousand active elements or logic gates — the equivalent of several thousand transistors on a single chip. VLSI is the technique for making the micro chip, the so-called "computer on a chip."

VERY LOW FREQUENCY VLF. Frequencies from 3 KHz to 300 KHz.

VESA Video Electronics Standards Association. Along with eight leading video board manufacturers, NEC Home Electronics founded VESA in the late 1980s. The association's main goal is to standardize the electrical, timing, and programming issues surrounding 800 x 600 pixel resolution video displays, commonly known as Super VGA. VESA has also issued a standard called "local bus," a new high-speed bus for the PC designed to move video between the CPU and the screen a lot faster than the conventional AT bus.

VESTIGIAL SIDEBAND TRANSMISSION VSB. A modified double-sideband transmission in which one sideband, the carrier, and only a portion of the other sideband are transmitted.

VF Voice Frequency.

VFAST More commonly spelled V.FAST. A future modem standard in the early stages of development, expected to be released in the early part of 1994. If approved by the CCITT, it would raise modem speeds to about 19,200 bps.

VFTG Voice Frequency TeleGraph.

VG Voice Grade.

VGA Variable Graphics Array. A graphics standard developed by IBM for the IBM PC. VGA allows the PC's screen to generate any of four levels of resolution — with one of the sharpest being 640 horizontal picture elements, known as pels or pixels, by 480 pels vertically with 16 colors. VGA is superior to earlier graphics standards, such as CGA and EGA. VGA is barely adequate for CAD-CAE. See MONITOR for all the numbers on pixels in various screens. VGA was the graphics standard introduced for IBM PS/2 line and quickly adopted by PC compatibles; supports analog monitors with a 31.5 Hz horizontal scan rate.

VHF Very High Frequency. The portion of the electromagnetic spectrum with frequencies between 30 and 300 MHz.

VHI Virtual Host Interface.

VIA NET LOSS VNL. A planning factor used in allocating the attenuation losses of trunks in a transmission network. A specified value for this loss is selected to obtain a satisfactory balance between loss and talker echo performance. The lowest loss in dB at which it is desirable to operate a trunk facility considering limitations of echo, crosstalk, noise and signing.

VIBRATORY PLOW A plow that rips open the ground by vibrating a plow share.

VIDEO CAPTURE Video Capture means converting a video signal into a format that can be saved onto a hard disk or optical storage device and manipulated with graphics software. This is accomplished with a device internal in a computer called a "frame grabber" or video capture board. Images thus captured are digitized, and can be dropped into a document or database record and may be transmitted locally on a LAN or long distance over a WAN.

VIDEO COMPRESSION A method of transmitting analog television signals over a narrow digital channel by processing the signal digitally. You can compress an analog TV signal into one T-1 signal of 1.544 megabits per second. More advanced compression techniques will enable video signals to be compressed into fewer bits per second. One increasingly common method allows a full-color reasonably full-motion video to be compressed into two 56 kbps channels.

VIDEO CONFERENCE See VIDEOCONFERENCE.

VIDEO DIAL TONE Video dial tone in telco-speak means the phone company, in competition with the cable TV business, provides video to houses and offices. It does not affect the content of that video signal in any way. Thus the term video dial tone, which is like voice dial tone, whose content the phone company also does not affect or change in any way, shape or form. The definition contributed by Stephen Butera, staff director, technical training, New England Telephone.

This is Northern Telecom's explanation of video dial tone: "Recent advances in communications and computer technology, such as fiber optic cables, digital switching and hyperspeed computing, make it possible to transmit extraordinary volumes of interactive electronic information in digital form through telephone networks. Consumers may soon be able to access an intriguing array of multi-media electronic entertainment and information services from the comfort of their homes via a gateway service called Video Dial Tone, which is part of what multi-media is all about. Multi-media means interactive full-motion video, sound, text and graphics all available on your TV, computer terminal or advanced intelligent telecomputer. There may soon be a proliferation of so-called 'intelligent phones' that will transform the touch-tone telephone into a versatile home computer. By means of simple push-button commands, customers will be able to:

● Select entertainment on demand (movies, music, video).

● Order groceries or other services or products.

● Record customized news and sports programming.

● Enroll and participate in education programs from the convenience of their living rooms.

● Find up-to-minute medical, legal and encyclopedic information.

● Pay bills and manage finances.

● Make airline, rental car and hotel reservations.

● Buy sports and entertainment tickets."

VIDEO ELECTRONICS STANDARDS ASSOCIATION See VESA.

VIDEO SERVER A jukebox like device that would stack several hundred movies and allow someone to download a movie they chose. The device would be used in conjunction with the local telephone companies' service called video dial tone — providing movies over normal phone lines to their subscribers. The Video Server doesn't exist as of writing. But other optical file servers do exist, though they are not used for storing movies.

VIDEO SIGNAL Transmission of moving frames or pictures of information requiring frequencies of 1 to 6 MegaHertz. A commercial quality full-color, full-motion TV signal requires 6 MHz.

VIDEO TELECONFERENCING Also called Videoconferencing. The real-time, and usually two-way, transmission of digitized video images between two or more locations. Transmitted images may be freeze-frame (where television screen is repainted every few seconds to every 20 seconds) or full motion. Bandwidth requirements for two-way videoconferencing range from 6 MHz for analog, full-motion, full-color, commercial grade TV to two 56 kbps lines for digitally-encoded reasonably full motion, full color, to 384 kbps for even better video transmission to 1,544 Mbit/s for very good quality, full-color, full motion TV. See also VIDEOCONFERENCING.

VIDEO WINDOWS A Bellcore invention which is basically a large, high capacity video conferencing device. Bellcore's Video Windows are connected by two optical links, each carrying 45 million bits of information per second. Though impressive, Bellcore's Video Windows is not considered "high definition" TV. For that to happen, you'd probably need 100 to 150 million bits being transmitted in both directions each second.

VIDEOCONFERENCE Videoconference is to communicate with others using video and audio software and hardware to see and hear each other. Audio can be provided through specialized videoconferencing equipment, through the telephone, or through the computer. Videoconferencing has traditionally been done with dedicated video equipment. But, increasingly personal computers communicating over switched digital lines are being used for videoconferencing.

VIDEOPHONE 2500 In January, 1992 AT&T introduced a product called VIDEOPHONE 2500, which transmitted moving (albeit slowly-moving) color pictures over normal analog phone lines. The phone carried a price tag $1,500 a piece. It was not compatible with one MCI later introduced, made for it by GEC-Marconi of England and costing only $750 retail. Videophone 2500 relies on video compression from Compression Labs, Inc. of San Jose, CA. According to the New York Times, the phone took two years, about $10 million and 30 full-time people at AT&T to develop. The January 3, 1993 New York Times carried a quote from John F. Hanley, group VP for AT&T consumer products division, "We could make an AT&T phoe talk to an MCI phone. It would be in both of our interests."

VIDEOTEX Two-way interactive electronic data transmission or home information retrieval system using the telephone network. Videotex has not been successful because of its (erstwhile) need for expensive, proprietary (i.e. dedicated) equipment and lack of variety in information offered. There are various forms of videotex. The "classic" European version of interactive videotext typically works at 75 baud going out from the terminal and 1200 baud coming in from the central office. Some American versions ape the European system. Some have 1200 baud both ways. In interactive videotext, you can do everything from sending serious electronic mail to your business suppliers to holding raunchy conversations with perverts in distant cities. As long as you pay your bills, no European PTT seems to care about what you transmit or receive. In France, videotex is called Minitel. And it's a succcess because the French phone company funds it.

VIEW 1. In satellite communications, the ability of a satellite to "see" a satellite earthstation, aimed sufficiently above the horizon and clear of other obstructions so that it is within a free line of sight. A pair of satellite earthstations has a satellite in "mutual" view when both enjoy unobstructed line-of-sight contact with the satellite simultaneously. 2. An alternative way of looking at the data in one or more database tables. A view is usually created as a subset of columns from one or more tables.

VIEWDATA An information retrieval system that uses a remote database accessible through the public telephone network. Video display of the data is on a monitor or television receiver. Another name for Videotex, the original English (UK) name for it. See VIDEOTEX.

VIM The Vendor-Independent Messaging (VIM) Group. VIM includes Apple, Borland, IBM, Lotus, MCI Mail, Novell and WordPerfect. Together, the Group is intent will collaborate on developing an open, industry-standard interface that will allow e-mail features to be built into a variety of software products.

VINES Virtual networking software which is the core of the LAN from Banyan, Westboro, MA.

VIRTUAL In the telephone industry, "Virtual" is something that pretends to be something it isn't, but can be made to appear to be that thing. A virtual private line is effectively a dial-up phone line with an auto-dialer on it. To the user, it appears to be a private line. (But the phone company can re-sell that capacity when it's not in use.) The concept of "virtual" is to give the telephone company an excuse to lower the price to the end user. See VIRTUAL NETWORK.

VIRTUAL 8086 MODE Virtual 8086 mode allows the Intel 80386 and beyond microprocessors to emulate multiple real mode processors and still switch to and from protected modem. The processor can load and execute real mode applications (in virtual 8086 mode), then switch to protected mode and load and execute another application that requires access to the full extended memory available. The microprocessor, together with a control program like Microsoft Windows 3.x or OS/2 assumes the responsibiity of protecting applications from one another. See REAL MODE and PROTECTED MODE.

VIRTUAL BANDING 1. In WATS services, virtual banding is the ability of trunks to carry traffic to all WATS bands, with billing based on the end points of the call instead of the band over which the traffic went. 2. MCI's definition: Allows customers of MCI's, PRISM, Hotel WATS, and University WATS to call nationwide while only paying for the distance to the actual area. For example, if a customer calls to a Band 1 rea, Band 1 pricing is used. Similarly, if a call is placed to a Band 4 area, Band 4 pricing is used.

VIRTUAL BASIC A version of the programming language BASIC written by Microsoft Corporation for Windows. The new program promises to make it much easier for businesses to develop customized applications of Windows. Some programmers are calling the software a major breakthrough in ease of programming.

VIRTUAL BYPASS Virtual bypass is a way smaller users can fill the unused portion of local T-1 dedicated loops going from a user site to a local office of a long distance company, called a POP (Point of Presence).

VIRTUAL CALL CAPABILITY Provides set-up and clearing on a per call basis. Each call placed appears to have a dedicated connection for the duration of the call.

VIRTUAL CELL A call, established over a network, that uses the capablities of either a real or virtual circuit by sharing all or any part of the resources of the circuit for the duration of the call.

VIRTUAL CALL CAPABILITY A datacommunications packet network service feature in which a call set-up procedure and a call-clearing procedure will determine a period of communication between two DTEs. This service requires end-to-end transfer control of packets within a network. Data may be delivered to the network before the call setup has been completed but it will not be delivered to the destination address if the call setup is not successful. The user's data are delivered from the network in the same order in which they are received by the network. See also VIRTUAL CIRCUIT.

VIRTUAL CIRCUIT A communications link — voice or data — that appears to the user to be a dedicated point-to-point circuit. Virtual circuits are generally set up on a per-call basis and disconnected when the call is ended. The concept of a virtual circuit was first used in data communications with packet switching. A packetized data call may send packets over different physical paths through a network to its destination, but is considered to have a single virtual circuit. Virtual circuits have become more common in ultra-high speed applications, like frame relay or SMDS. There the connection might be permanently connected like a LAN. When the user wants to transmit he simply transmits. There's no dialing in the conventional sense, just the addition of an address field on the information being transmitted. A virtual circuit is referred to as a logical, rather than physical path for a call. A virtual voice circuit is anything from as simple as a phone with an auto dialer in it to a high-speed link in which voice calls are digitized and send on the equivalent of a ultra high-speed, wide-area equivalent of a local area network. There are two basic reasons people buy virtual circuits. They're cheaper and faster. See PERMANENT VIRTUAL CIRCUIT.

VIRTUAL CIRCUIT CAPABILITY A network service feature providing a user with a virtual circuit. This feature is not necessarily limited to packet mode transmission. e.g., an analog signal may be converted at its network node to a digital form, which may then be routed over the network via any available route. See VIRTUAL CIRCUIT.

VIRTUAL COLOCATION Someone other than the local phone company (called in an interconnector) can designate his choice of transmission equipment to be located within a local exchange carrier's central office and dedicated to its use. The interconnector would have the right to remotely monitor and control the equipment, but the local exchange carrier would install, maintain, and repair it.

VIRTUAL CONNECTION A logical connection that is made to a virtual circuit.

VIRTUAL DEVICE A device that software can refer to but that doesn't physically exist.

VIRTUAL DISK A portion of RAM (Random Access Memory) assigned to simulate a disk drive. Also called a ram disk. See RAM DISK.

VIRTUAL HARD DRIVE MEMORY FACTOR The available space on a hard drive partition that Windows can address as phyiscal memory.

VIRTUAL MACHINE FACILITY VM/370. An IBM system control program, essentially an operating system that controls the concurrent execution of multiple virtual machines on a single System/370 mainframe.

VIRTUAL MACHINE VM. Software that mimics the performance of a hardware device. For Intel 80386 and higher processors, a virtual machine is protected memory space that is created through the processor's hardware capabilities.

VIRTUAL MEMORY 1. In computer systems, the memory as it appears to the operating programs running in the CPU. This memory may appear smaller, equal to, or larger than the real memory present in the system. 2. The term used with Apple Macintoshes to connote the ability to use disk swap files as RAM. This requires the Macintosh to be running System 7 and PMMU. 3. The space on your hard disk that Windows NT uses as if it were actually memory. Windows NT does this through the use of swap files. The benefit of using virtual memory is that you can run more applications at one time than your system's physical memory would otherwise allow. The drawbacks are the disk space required for the virtual-memory swap file and the decreased execution speed when swapping is requried.

VIRTUAL MEMORY MANAGER Virtual Memory Manager is a software-only approach to Expanded Memory. These work almost identically to the EMS emulators, except that they use your hard disk rather than extended memory as the storage medium for blocks of memory copied out of your program. As you can imagine, this is painfully s-l-o-w. Use this approach only as a last resort.

VIRTUAL NETWORK A network that is programmed, not hard-wired, to meet a customer's specifications. Created on as-needed basis. Also called Software Defined Network by AT&T. See SOFTWARE DEFINED NETWORK and VIRTUAL PRIVATE NETWORK.

VIRTUAL PRIVATE NETWORK A carrier-provided service in which the public switched network provides capabilities similar to those of private lines, such as conditioning, error testing, and higher speed, full-duplex, four-wire transmission with a line quality adequate for data. A virtual private network eliminates or partly eliminates the need for fixed point-to-point private line because it provides on-demand dial-up circuits or bandwidths that can be dynamically allocated. AT&T, a major provider of virtually private networks, defines them as the equivalent of a private network designed logically within a public network,thus achieving the economy of scale of a public network while offering the user control of the simulated private network. Virtual private network resources are occupied only while information is transiting the network.

VIRTUAL PRIVATE NETWORK SERVICE An MCI software-defined network service with multiple locations that customers can access through the use of customized dialing plans.

VIRTUAL REALITY VR. The publisher of Virtual Reality Report says, "Virtual reality is a way of enabling people to participate directly in real-time, 3-D environments generated by computers." Virtual reality involves the user's immersion in and interaction with a graphic screen/s. Using 3-D goggles and sensor-laden gloves, people "enter" computer-generated environments and interact with the images displayed there. Says Business Week, "Imagine the difference between viewing fish swimming in an aquarium and donning scuba gear to swim around them. That's the sensory leap between regular computer graphics and VR. There are three kinds of VR (Virtual Reality) immersion. First, the toe in the water experience of beginners who stand outside the imaginary world and communicate by computer with characters inside it. next, wading up to the hips, are the "through the window" users, who use a "flying mouse" to project themselves into the virtual, or artificial, world. Then there are the hold-the-nose plungers: "first persona interaction within the computer-generated world via the use of head-mounted sterescopic dislay, gloves, bodysuits and audio systems providing binaural sound. The trick with virtual reality is not only to simulate another world but to interact with it — pouring in data affecting its plots, changing its characters and introducing real-world unpredictability into this "mirror world." Once virtual reality was called artificial reality. But artificial means "fake," while virtual means "almost." The father of virtual reality is Joran Lanier. A term to virtual reality is telepresence. See TELEPRESENCE.

VIRTUAL ROUTE Virtual circuit in IBM's SNA. See SYSTEMS NETWORK ARCHITECTURE.

VIRTUAL ROUTE PACING CONTROL SNA congestion control at the path control level. See SYSTEMS NETWORK ARCHITECTURE.

VIRTUAL STORAGE Storage space that may be viewed as addressable main storage to a computer user, but is actually auxiliary storage (usually peripheral mass storage) mapped into real addresses. The amount of virtual storage is limited by the addressing scheme of the computer.

VIRTUAL TELECOMMUNICATION ACCESS METHOD VTAM (Pronounced "Vee-Tam.") A program component in an IBM computer which handles some of the communications processing tasks for an application program. VTAM also provides resource sharing, a technique for efficiently using a network to reduce transmission costs.

VIRTUAL TERMINAL VT. A universal terminal. The ISO virtual terminal (VT) protocol is designed to describe the operation of a so-called universal terminal so any terminal can talk with any host computer.

VIRTUAL TRIBUTARY VT. 1. A structure designed for transport and switching of sub-DS3 payloads. 2. A unit of sub-Sonet bandwidth that can be combined, or concantenated, for transmission through the network; VT1.5 equals 1.544 Mbps; VT2 equals 2.048 Mbps; VT3 equals 3 Mbps; VT6 equals 6 Mbps.

VIRUS A software program capable of replicating itself and usually capable of wreaking great harm on the system.

VISIBLE LIGHT Electromagnetic radiation visible to the human eye at wavelengths of 400-700 nm.

VISION ONE Vision One "is a strategy for evolution of telecommunications developed by Siemens AG, Siemens companies worldwide and GPT. Vision One comprises all the innovative, homogeneous and compatible network elements required for the high performance universal network of the future." This from an advertisement Siemens ran in conjunction with Telecom '91 in Geneva Switzerland.

VISTA A videotext service offered in Canada.

VISUAL DISPLAY UNIT VDU. Another term for a computer monitor. VDU is preferred in Europe.

VISUAL SOLUTIONS A family of AT&T products which do videoconferencing, first announced on March 23, 1993.

VISUAL VOICE MESSAGING A term created by Microsoft as part of its At Work announcement in June of 1993. There'll be At Work-based visual voice messaging servers sitting on a LAN. Messages for PC users on the LAN will be able to be displayed in a list, much like electronic mail, including the caller's name or number, the time he or she called and the length of the call. This information would let the user browse all messages and select the order for listening to the messages. Administrative options, such as creating a new greeting, will be accessed with a single button. Operations that are difficult today, such as forwarding a voice message to multiple people, will be dramatically simplified, according to Microsoft. One will simply select the recipients from the phone book and broadcast the message. Using visual voice messaging, users will be able to bypass today's inconsistent, time-consuming and confusing audio menus and access their voice messages with the push of a button or the click of a mouse on a Windows type icon. Messages will be able to be retrieved in any order and even delivered to a single mailbox along with other messages such as e-mail and faxes. These visual voice messaging servers will, according to Microsoft, provide applications beyond basic voice messaging, such as supporting voice annotation of PC documents or reading electronic mail over the phone to a traveler.

VISUALIZATION A combination of computerized graphics and imaging technology that provides high-resolution, video-like results on the workstation or personal computer's screen.

VISUALLY IMPAIRED ATTENDANT SERVICE Visually impaired attendant service capability is achieved by augmenting the normal visual signals provided on a standard attendant position with special tactile devices and/or audible signals which enable a visually impaired person to operate the position.

VITREOUS SILICA Glass consisting of almost pure silicon dioxide.

VLF Very Low Frequency. That portion of the electromagnetic spectrum having continuous frequencies ranging from about 3 Hz to 30 kHz.

VLSI Very Large Scale Integration. The art of putting hundreds of thousands of transistors onto a single quarter-inch square integrated circuit. Compare with LSI and ULSI.

VM Voice Mail, Voice Messaging or Virtual memory. See VIRTUAL STORAGE.

VME A bus commonly found on mainframe computers.

VMEC Voice Messaging Educational Committee. An organization formed by voice messaging manufacturers and service providers to promote a better understanding of voice mail and its business benefits, and to help business implement voice mail systems in ways that meet the needs of callers and mailbox owners alike.

VMI Voice Messaging Interface.

VMF Validation Message Fraud

VMR Violation Monitoring and Removal. The process of removing a violations which are detected, so that violations do not propagate beyond the maintance span.

VMS Virtual Memory System

VMUF Voice Messaging User Interface Forum. A standards body formed by voice messaging end users, service providers and manufacturers to define a minimum set of common human interface specifications for voice messaging systems.

VNET Virtual private NETwork. An MCI term for a service it offers to customrs who want to join geographically dispersed switches (typically PBXs). Instead of private lines joining the PBX, Vnet uses fast switched lines.

VO Vertification Office.

VOCABULARY DEVELOPMENT Development of specific word sets to be used for speaker independent ord recognition applications.

VODAS Voice Operated Device Anti-Sing. A device used to prevent the overall voice frequency singing of a two-way telephone circuit by ensuring that transmission can occur in only one direction at any given instant.

VOCODER An early type of voice coder, consisting of a speech analyzer and a speech synthesizer. The analyzer circuitry converts analog speech waveforms into digital signals. The synthesizer converts the digital signals into artificial speech sounds. For COMSEC purposes, a vocoder may be used in conjunction with a key generator and a modulator-demodulator device to transmit digitally encrypted speech signals over normal narrowband voice communication channels. These devices are used to reduce the bandwidth requirements for transmitting digitized speech signals. There are analog vocoders that move incoming signals from one portion of the spectrum to another portion.

VOGAD Voice Operated Gain Adjusting Device. A device used to give a substantially constant output amplitude for a wide range of input amplitudes.

VOICE ACTIVATED DIALING A feature that permits you to dial a number by calling them out to your cellular phone, instead of punching them in yourself.

VOICE ACTIVITY COMPRESSION VAC. A method of conserving transmission capacity by not transmitting pauses in speech.

VOICE APPLICATIONS PROGRAM System software providing the necessary logic to carry out the functions requested by telephone system users. It is responsible for actual call processing, making the various voice connections and providing user features, such as Call Forwarding, Speed Dialing, Conference, etc.

VOICE BOARD Also called a voice card or speech card. A Voice Board is an IBM PC- or AT-compatible expansion card which can perform voice processing functions. A voice board has several important characteristics: It has a computer bus connection. It has a telephone line interface. It typically has a voice bus connection. And it supports one of several operating systems, e.g. MS-DOS, UNIX. At a minimum, a voice board will usually include support for going on and off-hook (answering, initiating and terminating a call); notification of call termination (hang-up detection); sending flash hook; and dialing digits (touchtone and rotary). See VOICE BUS and VRU.

VOICE BULLETIN BOARDS These are voice mailboxes which contain pre-recorded information that can be updated as frequently as the provider of the mailboxes desires and can be accessed by the public 24 hours a day. Voice bulletin boards can be used by city or county departments which receive a large number of calls asking for routine information, e.g., summer programs for kids as listed by a parks and recreation department; jobs currently open in the city as listed by the personnel departments; etc.

VOICE BUS Picture an open PC. Peer down into it. At the bottom of the PC, you'll see a printed circuit board containing chips and empty connectors. That board is called the motherboard. Fatherboards are inserted into the connectors on the motherboard. These fatherboards do things on the PC — like pump out video to your screen or material to your printer or your local area network. The motherboard controls which device does what WHEN by sending signals along the motherboard's data bus — basically a circuit that connects all the various fatherboards through their connectors. That data bus was not designed for voice. For voice you need another bus. Several voice processing manufacturers have addressed that need by creating a voice bus at the top of their PC-based voice processing cards. They have tiny pins sticking out of their cards. You attach a ribbon cable from one set of pins on one voice processing card to the next set on the adjacent card and then the next. There are several voice bus "standards." Two come from Dialogic. One is called AEB, Analog Expansion Bus. And one is called PEB, PC Expansion Bus (a digital version). One comes from a consortium of companies and is called MVIP. There are many advantages to having a voice bus. It gives you enormous flexibility to mix and match voice processing boards, like voice recognition, voice synthesis, switching, voice storage, etc. You can build really powerful voice processing systems inside today's fast '386 and '486 PCs with the great variety of voice processing now available. For more information on this exciting field, read TELECONNECT Magazine. 212-691-8215. See MVIP.

VOICE CALLING One manufacturer describes this as allowing a phone user to have calls automatically answered and connected to his phone's loudspeaker. Not a common definition. A Northern Telecom Norstar definition: This feature allows a voice announcement to be made, or a conversation to begin, through the speaker of another telephone in the system.

VOICE CIRCUIT A circuit able to carry one telephone conversation or its equivalent, i.e. the typical analog telephone channel coming into your house or office. It's the standard subunit in which telecommunication capacity is counted. It has a bandwidth between 300 Hz and 3000 Hz. The U.S. analog equivalent is 3 KHz. The digital equivalent is 56 Kbps in North American and 64 Kbps in Europe. This is not sufficient for high fidelity voice transmission. You'd probably need at least 10,000 Hz. But it's sufficient to recognize and understand the person on the other end.

VOICE COIL The element in a dynamic microphone which vibrates when sound waves strike it. The coil of wire in a loudspeaker through which audio frequency current is sent to produce vibrations of the cone and reproduction of sound.

VOICE COMPRESSION Refers to the process of electronically modifying a 64 Kbps PCM voice channel to obtain a channel of 32 Kbps or less for the purpose of increased efficiency in transmission.

VOICE CONNECTING ARRANGEMENT VCA. A device that, once upon a time, was necessary for connecting your own phone system to the nation's switched telephone network. Most phones now meet FCC (and other) safety standards, so VCAs are no longer necessary. Most phone systems (as opposed to phones) do have internal protection circuitry, as shown by the "F" (for fully protected) in their FCC registration number.

VOICE COUPLER An interface arrangement once provided by the telephone company to permit direct electrical connection of customer-provided voice terminal equipment to the national telephone network. No longer needed because of the FCC's Registration Program.

VOICE DIALING The ability to tell your phone to dial by talking to it. Say, "Call Police" and it will automatically dial the police. This feature has enormous benefits for handicapped people. It will have greater benefits for normal people when the technology of voice recognition improves.

VOICE DIGITIZATION The conversion of an analog voice signal into binary (digital) bits for storage or transmission.

VOICE DTMF FORMS APPLICATIONS This Voice DTMF (DUAL TONE MULTIPLE FREQUENCY) application allows a use of a voice mail system to take specific information from its customers 24 hours a day. By prompting callers to respond by speaking or pressing the keys of their touch-tone phones, a city department, for example, could plan service calls, building inspections or send out appropriate forms.

VOICE FRAME See VOICE FRAME.

VOICE FREQUENCY VF. An audio frequency in the range essential for transmission of speech. Typically from about 300 Hz to 3000 Hz. See VOICE FREQUENCIES.

VOICE FREQUENCIES VF. Those frequencies lying within that part of the audio range that is employed for the transmission of speech. In telephony, the usable voice-frequency band ranges from a nominal 300 Hz to 3400 Hz. In telephony, the bandwidth allocated for a single voice-frequency transmission channel is usually 4 KHz, including guard bands.

VOICE FREQUENCY TELEGRAPH SYSTEM A telegraph system permitting use of up to 20 channels on a single voice circuit by frequency division multiplexing.

VOICE GRADE A communications channel which can transmit and receive voice conversation in the range of 300 Hertz to 3000 Hertz.

VOICE HOGGING See VOICE SWITCHED.

VOICE MAIL You call a number. A machine answers. "Sorry. I'm not in. Leave me a message and I'll call you back." It could be a $50 answering machine. Or it could be a $200,000 voice mail "system." The primary purpose is the same — to leave someone a message. After that, the differences become profound. a voice mail system lets you handle a voice message as you would a paper message. You can copy it, store it, send it to one or many people, with or without your own comments. When voice mail helps business, it has enormous benefits. When it's abused — such as when people "hide" behind it and never return their messages — it's useless. Some people hate voice mail. Some people love it. It's clearly here to stay.

In the fall of 1991, the Wall Street Journal carried a story negative on voice mail. Les Lesniak, Rolm's Senior VP Marketing disagreed. His reply published in the Journal is one of the finest explanations of voice mail's virtues:

● The writer's observations ignore the way today's voice communication technology is making communication between people easier and more convenient, and is elevating the level of service savvy companies provide their customers. Manufacturers use it to take orders after hours and on weekends. Financial services companies use it to provide account information to customers on a 24-hour basis. Colleges use it to register students. A retail executive uses it to broadcast messages to her staff. And a lawyer uses it to respond to calls when traveling.

● Voice messaging keeps calls confidential, simplifies decision making, saves time and money, eliminates inaccurate messages and "telephone tag," allows people to use their time more productively. In short, it keeps communication crisp, clear and constant. The writer's line of thinking would demand that people remain at their desk 24 hours a day. If they don't, the phone goes unanswered, a receptionist answers the phone and takes a message, or an answering machine records the message and cuts off the caller at will. None of these scenarios is ideal.

● To be successful, voice-mail technology must be understood by users and supported by top management, And it must meet the needs of the customer. Training for all employees must be mandatory and the system must be administered and managed properly. 'Must answer' lines and greetings that are changed daily are only two ideas that make voice mail not just helpful, but essential to customer service and an enhanced company image.

● Contrary to the writer's view, voice mail contributes to effective business communication and is far superior to an unanswered phone call, a misplaced message or an answering machine."

here are some statistics which add weight to voice mail's logic:

● 75% of all business calls are not completed on the first attempt.

● This can easily waste $50 to $150 per employee per month in toll charges.

● Half of the calls are for one-way transfers of information.

● Two-thirds of all-phone calls are less important than the work they interrupt.

● The average length of a voice mail message is 43 seconds. The average long distance call is 3.4 minutes. Voice mail is 80% faster.

Here are the standard benefits of voice mail:

1. No more "telephone tag." Voice mail improves communications. It lets people communicate in non-real time.

2. Shorter calls. When you leave messages on voice mail, your calls are invariably shorter. You get right to the point. Live communications encourage "chit chat" - wasting time and money.

3. No more time zone/business hour dilemma. No more waiting till noon (or rising at 6 A.M.) to call bi-coastally or across continents.

4. Reduce labor costs, Instead of answering phones and taking messages, employees are free to do more vital tasks.

5. Fewer callbacks. In some cases, as many as 50%.

6. Improved message content. Voice mail is much more accurate and private than pink slips. Messages are in your own voice, with all the original intonations and inflections.

7. Less paging and shorter holding times.

8. Less peakload traffic.

9. 24-hour availability.

10. Better customer service.

11. Voice mail allows work groups to stay in contact - morning, noon and night.

12. Voice mail reduces unwanted interruptions.

See Also VOICE MAIL SYSTEM.

VOICE MAIL JAIL What happens when you reach a voice mail message and you try and reach a human by punching "0" (zero) and you get transferred to another voice mail box and you try again by punching "0" or some other number you're told to punch...and you never reach a human. You're stuck forever inside the bowels of a voice mail machine, being instructed to go from one box to another, never reaching a real human. You're in voice mail jail.

VOICE MAIL SYSTEM A device to record, store and retrieve voice messages. There are two types of voice mail devices — those which are "stand alone" and those which profess some integration with the user's phone system. A stand alone voice mail is not dissimilar to a collection of single person answering machines, with several added features. You can instruct the machines (voice mail boxes) to forward messages among themselves. You can organize to allocate your friends and business acquaintances their own mail boxes so they can dial, leave messages, pick up messages from you, pass messages to you, etc. You can also edit messages, add comments and deliver messages to a mailbox at a pre-arranged time. Messages can be tagged "urgent" or "non-urgent" or stored for future listening. The range of voice mail options varies among manufacturers.

An integrated voice mail system includes two additional features. First, it will tell you if you have any messages. It does this by lighting a light on your phone and/or putting a message on your phone's alphanumeric display. Second, if your phone rings for a certain number of rings (you set the number), the phone will transfer your caller automatically to your voice mail box, which will answer the phone, deliver a little "I am away" message and then receive and record the caller's message.

There are other levels of integration. You might have a phone which has "soft" buttons and an alphanumeric display. That display might label your phone's soft buttons like those on a cassette recorder — forward, reverse, slow, fast, stop, etc. so you can go through your messages any way you like. Telenova has such a phone. It's very impressive.

There are pros and cons to voice mail systems. Some employees will hide behind them, forwarding calls from their customers into voice mail boxes and never returning them. Some employees will make good use of them. They dial in for their messages, research what the customer wants and return the voice mail calls quickly. Many voice mail systems are being combined with automated attendants. Many are being combined with interactive voice processing systems, including sophisticated tie-ins to mainframe databases. Some people hate voice mail systems. Others love them. It all depends on how the system is used, managed and sold. See also VOICE MAIL, AUDIOTEX, AUTOMATED ATTENDANTS, INFORMATION CENTER MAILBOXES, ENHANCED CALL PROCESSING and VOICE PROCESSING.

VOICE MESSAGE SERVICE A leased service typically over dial up phone lines which provides the ability for a phone user to access a voice mail system and leave a message for a particular phone user. See VOICE MAIL SYSTEM.

VOICE MESSAGING Recording, storing, playing back and distributing phone messages. New York Telephone has an interesting way of looking at voice messaging. NYTel sees it as four distinct areas: 1. Voice Mail, where messages can be retrieved and played back at any time from a user's "voice mailbox"; 2. Call Answering, which routes calls made to a busy/no answer extension into a voice mailbox; 3. Call Processing, which lets callers route themselves among destinations via their touch-tone phones; and 4. Information Mailbox, which stores general recorded information for callers to hear.

VOICE OPERATED RELAY (VOX) CIRCUIT A voice-operated relay circuit that permits the equivalent of push-to-talk operation of a transmitter by the operator.

VOICE OVER TIE/communications name for a totally wonderful feature on a phone system — namely that while you are speaking to someone on the phone, your operator can talk to you "over" the conversation you're having. What happens is that you hear your operator in your telephone's handset receiver, but the person you're speaking with can't. You can reply to the operator (telling him/her you'll be one minute, please call back, etc.) by hitting a DND/MIC (Do Not Disturb/Microphone) button on your phone. Voice Over has major benefits. It saves on long distance calls you don't have to return. It closes deals that can't wait. And it gives customers immediate answers. In short, it improves corporate efficiency and customer satisfaction.

VOICE PAGING ACCESS Gives attendants and phone users the ability to dial loudspeaker paging equipment throughout the building. An unbelievably useful feature, if your people are prone to wander.

VOICE PRINT A voice recognition term. A voice print is a speech template used to "train" systems, in particular voice patterns. When a system is operating, the user's speech is compared to the stored voice prints. If they match, the system recognizes the word and executes the command.

VOICE PROCESSING Think of voice processing as a voice computer. Where a computer has a keyboard for entering information, a voice processing system recognizes touchtones from remote telephones. It may also recognize spoken words. Where a computer has a screen for showing results, a voice processing system uses a digitized synthesized voice to "read" the screen to the distant caller.

Whatever a computer can do, a voice processing system can too, from looking up train timetables to moving calls around a business (auto attendant) to taking messages (voice mail). The only limitation on a voice processing system is that you can't present as many alternatives on a phone as you can on a screen. The caller's brain simply can't remember more than a few. With voice processing, you have to present the menus in smaller chunks.

VOICE RECOGNITION The ability of a machine to understand human speech.

VOICE RESPONSE UNIT VRU. Think of a Voice Response Unit (also called Interactive Voice Response Unit) as a voice computer. Where a computer has a keyboard for entering information, an IVR uses remote touchtone telephones. Where a computer has a screen for showing the results, an IVR uses a digitized synthesized voice to "read" the screen to the distant caller. An IVR can do whatever a computer can, from looking up train timetables to moving calls around an automatic call distributor (ACD). The only limitation on an IVR is that you can't present as many alternatives on a phone as you can on a screen. The caller's brain simply won't remember more than a few. With IVR, you have to present the menus in smaller chunks. See VOICE BOARD.

VOICE RING Multiple Digital Intertie Buses connected in series to all nodes. Provides extra channels for voice data transmission when direct link (DI) channels are busy.

VOICE SERVER A PC sitting on a LAN (Local Area Network) and containing voice files which are accessible by the PCs on the LAN. Such voice files may be transmitted on the LAN or over phone lines under the control of the PCs on the LAN. A voice server might contain voice mail. It might contain voice annotated electronic mail. Its primary function is to store voice in such a way that it's accessible easily. Voice servers are typically faster, have more disk capacity and more backup provisions than normal PCs. According to a letter I received in early May, 1993 from the lawyers for a company called Digital Sound Corporation, that company owns federal trademark registration number 1,324,258 for the mark Voiceserver, spelled as one word, not two.

VOICE STORE AND FORWARD Voice mail. A PBX service that allows voice messages to be stored digitally in secondary storage and retrieved remotely by dialing access and identification codes. See VOICE MAIL SYSTEM.

VOICE SWITCHED A device which responds to voice. When the device hears a voice, it turns on and transmits it, muting the receive side. The most common voice-switched device is the desk speakerphone. With voice switching, it's easy to hog a circuit. Just keep making a noise. Watch out for voice hogging. If you're calling someone and waiting for them by listening in on your speakerphone, mute your speakerphone. This way you'll hear them when they answer.

VOICE TERMINAL A sappy, pretentious AT&T term for TELEPHONE.

VOICE VERIFICATION The process of verifying one's claimed identity through analyzing voice patterns.

VOICEFRAME VoiceFrame is Harris Digital Telephone Systems' name for their open application platform for voice and call processing. According to Harris, VoiceFrame allows businesses to create a comprehensive set of applications that link computers, telephone networks and the telephone. Examples of applications that use the VoiceFrame platform include

● touchtone driven transaction processing such as telebanking * operator services

● advanced paging systems

● intelligent call routing via host computer database inquiries

● other call center applications.

VoiceFrame serves as a communications controller whose primary responsibility is the disposition of inbound and outbound call traffic under computer control. VoiceFrame has these abilities

● It interprets call signaling information and translates it into protocols for host computer use.

● It accepts commands from the host and interprets them to switch, route and complete calls.

● It provides host computer access to private and public network services, such as DNIS, DID, SMSI, ANI, 950, 900 and 800 services.

● It allows the host computer to perform those tasks for which it is best suited — real-time call routing decision making, database lookup, complex calculations and detailed billing.

VOICEMUX 100 Trademark for MICOM's combined TDM and APV products.

VOICEVIEW The family name for the concept and the product line from Radish Communications. It is also used to describe the protocol, the transaction, and the platform.

VOICEVIEW AGENT Also known as Agent software, the software capable of sending PC screens or files as messages to VoiceView callers. This includes the VoiceView Formatting Toolkit. See VOICEVIEW.

VOICEVIEW BRIDGE Also known as a Viewbridge, a device that allows a provider to send information from a VoiceView-equipped PC or other computer to a caller. The Viewbridge may also be used in conjunction with Peer software on the PC to receive as well as send information. The Viewbridge can also emulate a Viewset. See VOICEVIEW.

VOICEVIEW PEER Also known as Peer software, the software that allows a caller equipped with a PC and a Viewbridge to send and receive VoiceView messages. See VOICEVIEW.

VOICEVIEW SET Also known as a Viewset, the unit used by a caller to receive visual information in the course of a VoiceView transaction. See VOICEVIEW.

VOLATILE STORAGE Computer storage that is erased when power is turned off. RAM is volatile storage.

VOLSER An MCI term used to denote a volume of calls. Based on the words "Volume Serial." The term "Volser" can be applied to the manual collection of calls from a switch on a switch tape or through call data transmitted via NEMAS.

VOLT The unit of measurement of electromotive force. Voltage is always expressed as the potential difference in available energy between two points. One volt is the force required to produce a current of one ampere through a resistance or impedance of one ohm.

VOLT METER An instrument for measuring voltages, resistance and current.

VOLTAGE Electricity is a essentially a flow of electrons. They're pushed into a gadget — toaster, computer, phone — on one wire and they sucked out on the other wire. For this movement of electrons to occur there must be "pressure," just as there must be pressure in the flow of water. The pressure under which a flow of electrons moves through a gadget is called the electric voltage. Voltage doesn't indicate anything about quantity, just the pressure.The amount of electricity moving through a wire is called its current and is measured in amps. You figure the power in an electron flow (i.e. in electricity) by multiplying the flow's current by the voltage under which it flows.

VOLTAGE RATING The highest voltage that may be continuously applied to a wire in conformance with standards or specifications.

VOLTAGE STANDING WAVE RATIO VSWR. The ratio of the maximum effective voltage to the minimum effective voltage measured along the length of mis-matched radio frequency transmission line.

VOLTMETER A device for measuring the difference of potential in volts.

VOLUME A volume is a partition or collection of partitions that have been formatted for use by a computer system. A Windows NT volume can be

NEWTON'S TELECOM DICTIONARY

assigned a drive letter and used to organize directories and files. In NetWare a volume is a physical amount of hard disk storage space. Its size is specified during installation. NetWare v2.2 volumes, for example, are limited to 255MB and one hard disk, but one hard disk can contain several volumes. A NetWare volume is the highest level in the NetWare directory structure (on the same level as a DOS root directory). A NetWare file server supports up to 32 volumes. NetWare volumes can be subdivided into directories by network supervisors or by users who have been assigned the appropriate rights.

VOLUME LABEL A name you can assign to a floppy or hard disk in MS-DOS. The name can be up to 11 characters in length. You can assign a label when you format a disk or, at a later time, using the LABEL command.

VOLUME SERIAL NUMBER A number assigned to a disk by MS-DOS. The FORMAT command creates the serial number on a disk.

VOLUME UNIT VU. The unit of measurement for electrical speech power in communications work. VUs are measured in decibels above 1 milliwatt. The measuring device is called a VU meter.

VOM Abbreviation for VOLT-OHM-MILLIAMETER, probably the most common form of electronic test equiment. It measures voltage, resistance and current, and may have either a digital or analog meter readout. Some VOMs have other test functions such as audible continuity signals and special tests for semiconductors.

VOTING RECEIVERS A group of mobile base phone receivers operating on the same frequency as a control unit to pick the best signal from among them.

VOX Voice Operated eXchange. Your voice starts it. When you stop speaking, it stops. Tape recorders use it to figure when to start recording and when to stop. There are pros and cons to VOX. With VOX you often miss the beginning of the conversation. And the tape goes on for 3 or 4 seconds after you've stopped talking. Also if ambient noise is high, VOX might mistake it for speaking and turn the recorder on and keep it running. Cellular phones also use VOX to save battery. A cellular phone without VOX is continuously transmitting a carrier back to the cell cite the entire time your call is in progress. The VOX operation used in smaller phones allows the phone to transmit only when you're actually talking. This reduces battery drain and enables handheld phones to operate longer on a smaller battery.

VOYCALL An early key system manufacturer, which made a combination 1A2 handsfree intercom telephone system. It was wood grained, inlaid into black plastic. An impressive phone system. Sadly, no more.

VP Virtual Parth. A collection of VCs (Virtual Channels) all traveling between common points.

VPI Virtual Path Identifier. The address of a Virtual Path.

1076

VPDN Virtual Private Data Network. A private data communications network built on public switching and transport facilities rather than dedicated leased facilities such as T1s.

VPDS Virtual Private Data Services. MCI's equivalent of Vnet for data.

VPN Virtual Private Network. Virtual Private Network is a software-defined network offering the appearance, functionality and usefulness of a dedicated private network, at a price savings. Here's how it works: Your company buys a bunch of leased lines from your offices to the nearest local offices of your chosen long distance carrier. You're in your New York offices. You want to dial your offices in Chicago. You pick up the phone, dial perhaps seven digits. The phone rings in Chicago. What's happened is that your local PBX has recognized that call as belonging to your VPN. So it shunts the calls over the dedicated local loop to your long distance carrier. Your carrier then checks your dialed number, perhaps changing it with the aid of a database lookup table, and completes the call over the carrier's own switched telephone facilities (fiber optic, microwave, copper, etc.). These are the same facilities which you and I use when we dial 1 and the long distance number (assuming we're equal accessed to that carrier).

There are several differences between a VPN and normal dial service:

1. VPN's price per minute is cheaper, often a lot cheaper.

2. You dial fewer digits with VPN. Sometimes you can get right to the distant desk, without going through the operator at the distant end.

3. You have to pay for the dedicated phone lines at the various ends of the VPN which have those dedicated phone lines. But they're often T-1, and thus not expensive on a per voice circuit basis.

4. You have to commit to use VPN for much longer than you do with normal dial-up service — which is typically month-to-month.

VPN 56 Sprint's Switched 56 kbps service, supports advanced voice, data and image network communication tools including Group IV Fax, high resolution image transfer, file transfer, videoconferencing and switched data service via access to SprintNet, a large public data network.

VPOTS Very Plain Old Telephone Service. No automated switching.

VPU Virtual Physical Unit.

VQL Variable Quantizing Level. Speech-encoding technique that quantizes and encodes an analog voice conversation for transmission, nominally at 32 Kbps.

VR Virtual Reality. See VIRTUAL REALITY.

VRAM Video RAM. Memory used to buffer an image and transfer it onto the display. VRAM has two data paths — a technique known as dual porting — rather than the single path of traditional RAM; thus, it can move data in and out simultaneously. This speeds up screen drawing.

VRC Vertical Redundancy Check.

VREPAIR A Novell NetWare program somewhat analogous to MS-DOS's CHKDSK program. VREPAIR fixes FAT (File Allocation Table) and DIR (Directory) Tables. It's a most useful program. Highly recommended.

VROOMM Virtual Runtime Object-Oriented Memory Manager. VROOMMM is Borland's proprietary technology designed to save memory by reducing commands to compact objects. Because of VROOMM Quattro Pro has had three fully-featured releases without compromising spreadsheet capacity or performance on current machines — even if it's an 8088-based PC with 512K or RAM. How does VROOOMM make more memory available for your spreadsheet data? According to Borland, most spreadsheet programs work with only a small number of large overlays, loading one or another into memory depending on the operations being performed. In contrast, VROOMM moves hundreds of small program modules, which are in effect code objects in and out of memory as necessary. Individual areas of Quattro Pro use different code objects, so it's possible to have very large spreadsheets in memory while significantly increasing functionality. Quattro Pro;s graphics subsystem also take advantage of VROOMM by storing the graphics you, the user, create in available EMS.

VRPRS Virtual Route Pacing Response in SNA.

VRU See VOICE BOARD and VOICE RESPONSE UNIT.

V-SERIES RECOMMENDATIONS Sets of telecommunications protocols and interfaces defined by CCITT Recommendations.

VS See VIRTUAL STORAGE.

VS&F Voice Store and Forward. Voice is digitally encoded, sent to large storage devices and later forwarded to the recipient. See VOICE MAIL.

VSAT Very Small Aperture Terminal. A relatively small satellite antenna, typically 1.5 to 3.0 meters in diameter, used for transmitting and receiving one channel of data communications. You see VSATs on top of retail stores which use them for transmitting the day's receipts and receiving instructions for sales, etc.

VSB Vestigial SideBand. A form of AM modulation that compresses required bandwidth.

VSCBX A Rolm PBX called a Very Small Computerized Branch EXchange.

VSE Virtual Storage Extended.

VSS Voice Server System.

VSWR Voltage Standing Wave Ratio. The ratio of the maximum effective voltage to the minimum effective voltage measured along the length of mismatched radio frequency transmission line.

VT Virtual Tributary. A structure designed for transport and switching of sub-

DS3 payloads. VT1.5 equals 1.544 Mbps; VT2 equals 2.048 Mbps; VT3 equals 3 Mbps; VT6 equals 6 Mbps. These are measures of speed in Sonet. See SONET.

VTAM Virtual Telecommunications Access Method. A program component in an IBM computer which handles some of the communications processing tasks for an application program. In an IBM 370 or compatible, VTAM is a method to give users at remote terminals access to applications in the main computer. VTAM resides in the host. It performs addressing and path control functions in an SNA network that allows a terminal or an application to communicate with and transfer data to another application along some sort of transmission medium. VTAM also provides resource sharing, a technique for efficiently using a network to reduce transmission costs. See SYSTEMS NETWORK ARCHITECTURE.

VTP Virtual Terminal Protocol.

VU METER VU is the unit of measurement for electrical speech power in communications work. VUs are measured in decibels above 1 milliwatt. The measuring device is called a VU meter.

VUI First came the CLI (Command-Line Interface). Then came the GUI (Graphical User Interface). Get ready for the VUI: the Video User Interface. Actually, you don't need to get ready for it any time soon, but you might start wondering how to use it.

VW-1 A test used by Underwriters Laboratories to classify wires and cables by their resistance to burning. (Formerly designated as FR-1.)

W

W 1. Abbreviation for WATT. 2 The Hayes AT Command Set describes a standard language for sending commands to asychronous modems. One of the commands is "W." If you embed a W in your dialing string, i.e. 212-691-8215-W-10045, the modem will dial 212-691-8215 and wait until it hears dial tone. When it hears dial tone, it will dial out 10045. That is the standard Hayes command set interpretation of W. There is another. When using some of the communications software products from Crosstalk (now a subsidiary of DCA) you can place a [W] in your dialing string. If you do, your modem will dial the number until it encounters a [W]. It will then wait until you hit any button on your keyboard. The purpose of W commands is to allow you to dial through private networks (your own), through public networks (MCI, Sprint, etc.), through fax/modem/telephone switches and through any other device or network.

W-DCS Wideband Digital Cross-connect System. W-DCS is an electronic digital cross-connect system capable of cross-connecting signals below the DS3 rate.

WACK Wait before transmitting positive ACKnowledgement. In Bisynch, this DLE sequence is sent by a receiving station to indicate it is temporarily not ready to receive.

WAFER A thin disk of a purified crystalline semiconductor, typically silicon, that is cut into chips after processing. Typically, a wafer is about one fiftieth of an inch thick and four or five inches in diameter.

WAIT ON BUSY An English term for the American term "Camp On" or "Call Waiting." A service allowing the subscriber to make a call to a busy phone line, wait until the call is over, then be connected automatically.

WAIT STATE A period of time when the processor does nothing; it simply waits. A wait state is used to synchronize circuitry or devices operating at different speeds. Wait states are introduced into computers to compensate for the fact that the central microprocessor might be faster than the memory chips next to it. For example, wait states used in memory access slow down the CPU so that all components seem to be running at the same speed. A wait state is a "missed beat" in the cycle of information to and from the CPU that is necessary for a memory transaction to be completed.

WALK TIME The time required to transfer permission to poll from one station to another.

WALKAWAYS People who walk from coin phones though they owe it extra money. You can tell a phone that has just been visited by walkaway: It's typically ringing. And when you answer it, the operator will ask you to deposit some additional coins.

WALKIE-TALKIE Hand-held radio transmitter and receiver. Like the police carry. Probably the best named device in telecom. You walkie, you talkie.

WALL OUTLET A phone outlet positioned at shoulder height to accept a wall telephone set. The typical installation includes a special modular jack containing two mounting bosses that insert into key-hole slots in the base of the telephone set. Electrical connection is made by a short cord or a lug element that is integral to the telephone set base.

WALL PHONE A phone that is mounted on the wall. Where else would a wall phone be mounted? Some new phones — especially some key systems — come so you can use them on the desk or mount them on a wall, without extra hardware. Some desk phones cannot be mounted on a wall. This is a disadvantage when you run out of space on your desk, as you will with all the computers and workstations you'll be putting there.

WALL THICKNESS A term expressing the thickness of a layer of applied insulation or jacket.

WAN Wide Area Network. Uses common carrier-provided lines that cover an extended geographical area. Contrast with LAN. This network uses links provided by local telephone companies and usually connects disperse sites. See WIDE AREA NETWORK.

WANDER Long-term random variations of the significant instants of a digital signal from their ideal position in time. Wander variations are usually considered to be those that occur over a period greater than 1 second. See also WANGNET. As I wrote this, WANG had just filed for Chapter 11 protection under US Bankruptcy laws. For more, see CHAPTER 11.

WANG Wang's name for its telephony link is STEP, which stands for Speech and Telephony Environment for Programmers.

WANGNET Wang Laboratories' proprietary broadband LANs. Used as the brand name for Wang's LAN products.

WARBLE TONE A tone changing in frequency at a slow enough rate to give the effect of warbling. A warble tone is the sound of an electronic ringer, according to many people.

WARC World Administrative Radio Conference. Sets international frequencies. Just before Telecom '87, WARC allocated important new frequencies for satellite-based land mobile (satellite to truck, etc.) and radiodetermination navigation services (electronic maps for your car). WARC is part of the 154-member International Telecommunication Union. CCITT is part of the ITU. See CCITT.

WARM START Restarting or resetting a computer without turning it off (also called "soft boot"); press Ctrl + Alt + Del on an IBM or IBM compatible.

WATCH COMMANDS Watch Commands are found in programming. They allow you to "watch" the value of selected application variables while the application is executing (e.g., see the last-entered touchtone digits from a caller).

NEWTON'S TELECOM DICTIONARY

WATER PIPE GROUND A water pipe to which connection is made for the ground.

WATS Wide Area Telecommunications Service. Basically, a discounted toll service provided by all long distance and local phone companies. AT&T started WATS but forgot to trademark the name, so now every supplier uses it as a generic name. There are two types of WATS services — in and out WATS, i.e. those WATS lines that allow you to dial out and those on which you receive incoming calls (the typical 800 line service). You subscribe to in- and out-WATS services separately. In the old days you needed separate in and out lines to handle the in and out WATS services. But these days you can choose to have in- and out-WATS on the same line. This is not particularly brilliant traffic engineering, since you can't receive an incoming 800 call if you're making an outgoing call. But I do know someone who has an 800 line on his cellular phone!

Many users inside companies think their company's WATS lines (and thus their WATS calls) are free, so they speak longer. This can kill the idea of buying WATS lines to save money. In the old days, interstate WATS was charged at effectively a flat rate and thus, there was some reason to believe that marginal WATS calls were 'free.' These days EVERY WATS call costs money. EVERY one! Without exception. See 800 SERVICE and PLANT TEST NUMBER.

WATT The unit of electrical power and representing the product of amperage and voltage. See OHM's LAW.

WATTS A unit of electrical power. That amount of power required to maintain a current of one amp under the pressure of one volt. In other words if you want to figure out WATTS, multiply the voltage (say 120) by the current — the number of amperes listed on the rear panel of your equipment. See OHM's LAW. Don't confuse WATTS (the measure of electricity) with WATS, which stands for Wide Area Telecommunications Service. See WATS.

WAVE LENGTH The distance between peaks of an electromagnetic (or other) wave. The distance traveled by a wave during one complete cycle. See also WAVELENGTH.

WAVEFORM The characteristic shape of a signal usually shown as a plot of amplitude over a period of time.

WAVEFORM EDITOR A word processor for sound. You record something. Then you "play" it back on your PC's screen. Your PC screen now looks like an oscilloscope. Then you use this wave form editor to edit (i.e. change, replace. amplify, echo, fade in or out, cut out noise, cut/paste from other files, or generally muck with) the sound. A wave form editor is used in voice processing.

WAVEGUIDE A conducting or dielectric structure able to support and propagate one or more modes. More specifically, a waveguide is a hollow,

1082

finely-engineered metallic tube used to transmit microwave radio signals from the microwave antenna to the radio and vice versa. Waveguides comes in various shapes — rectangular, elliptical or circular. They are very sensitive and should be handled very gently. Waveguides may contain a solid or gaseous dielectric material. In optical, a waveguide used as a long transmission line consists of a solid dielectric filament (optical fiber), usually circular. In integrated optical circuits an optical waveguide may consist of a thin dielectric film.

WAVEGUIDE SCATTERING Scattering (other than material scattering) that is attributable to variations of geometry and refractive index profile of an optical fiber.

WAVELENGTH The length of a wave measured from any point on one wave, to the corresponding point on the next wave, such as from crest to crest. In other words, a wavelength is the distance an electromagnetic wave travels in the time it takes to oscillate through a complete cycle. There is a direct proportion between the wavelength of a radio signal and its frequency.

WAVELENGTH DIVISION MULTIPLEXING WDM. A way of increasing the capacity of an optical fiber by simultaneously operating at more than one wavelength. With WDM you can multiplex signals by transmitting them at different wavelengths through the same fiber. Similar to frequency division multiplexing. In optical fiber communications, any technique by which two or more optical signals having different wavelengths may be simultaneously transmitted in the same direction over one fiber, and then be separated by wavelength at the distant end.

WAY OPERATED CIRCUIT A circuit shared by three or more phones on a party line basis. One of the phones usually operates as the control point.

WAY STATION One of the phones, other than the central controller, on a way operated circuit. See WAY OPERATED CIRCUIT.

WCV See Weighted Call Value.

WDM Wavelength Division Multiplexing. A technique in fiber-optic transmission for using different light wavelengths to send data parallel-by-bit (one discrete wavelength per bit), serial-by-character. One multimode fiber can act as an 8-bit parallel bus.

WDMA Wavelength-Division Multiple Access: a technique which is used to provide multiple channels on different wavelengths on the same fibre-optic cable.

WEATHER TRUNK GROUP A trunk group used to provide customers with weather information.

WEATHERMASTER METHOD A distribution method where the unused wall space inside heating and cooling units beneath windows is used for satellite location. Cables are fed from a riser or other serving closet to the location through baseboards, conduit, or underfloor system.

WECO Western Electric COmpany.

WEIGHTED CALL VALUE WCV. The average handling time of a call transaction. ACD vendors count this differently. Typically, a combination of the talk time and the after-call work or wrap-up time.

WESTAR Family of communications satellites owned and operated by Western Union.

WESTERN UNION INTERNATIONAL WUI. Acquired by MCI in 1982 to establish MCI in the International Telex and communications market. WUI is now part of MCI International.

WET CIRCUIT A circuit carrying direct current.

WET LOOP POWERING Defined as local power (non-Span provided) with use of copper pairs (power is looped at the last repeater).

WET T-1 A T-1 line with a Bell Operating Company powered interface.

WETTING AGENT A chemical which reduces surface tension in a liquid, motivating the liquid to spread more evenly on a surface.

WHEATSTONE BRIDGE An instrument for measuring resistances.

WHETSTONES How well does a computer work? Let's test it. The Whetstone benchmark program, developed in 1976, was designed to simulate arithmetic intensive programs used in scientific computing. It is applicable in CAD and other engineering areas where floating-point and trigonometric calculations are heavily used. The Whetstone program is completely CPU-bound and performs no I/O or system calls. The speed at which a system performs floating point operations is measured in units of Whetstones per second or floating point operations per second (flops). Whetstone I tests 32-bit, and Whetstone II tests 64-bit operations. See also DHRYSTONES.

WHISPER TECHNOLOGY A call comes into a call center. The voice response unit prompts the caller to the enter their account number. When the call is transfered to the agent, the VRU "whispers" the account number to the agent, who then manually types it into his computer. This technology is now obsolete, since VRUs can now transfer their account number directly into the agent's database and have the lookup done automatically. And the call is transferred simultaneously.

WHITE FACSIMILE TRANSMISSION In an amplitude-modulated facsimile system, that form of transmission in which the maximum transmitted power corresponds to the minimum density of the subject copy. In a frequency-modulated system, that form of transmission in which the lowest transmitted frequency corresponds to the minimum density of the subject copy.

WHITE LINE SKIP A facsimile transmission technique used to speed up the transmission time by bypassing redundant areas such as white space. (Also known as skip scan.)

WHITE NOISE A signal whose energy is uniformly distributed among all frequencies within a band of interest. Seldom occurring in nature, white noise is a useful tool for theoretical research. White noise is also used less scientifically to simply mean background noise. When the first digital PBXs came out, their intercom circuits were so "clean," they spooked users out who were used to some noise on the line. And some PBX manufacturers added a little "white noise" to their PBXs.

WHITE SIGNAL In facsimile, the signal resulting from the scanning of a minimum-density area of the subject copy.

WHO-ARE-YOU CODE WRU. A control character which operates the answerback unit in a terminal (typically a telex terminal) for identification of sending and receiving stations in a network.

WHOIS An interoperability protocol specified. Whois is an option of the Finger protocol, and requests additional information to the Finger protocol.

WHOLE PERSON PARADIGM This is one of the more fascinating telecom concepts in a while. General Magic created it as some sort of psychological basis for the product/s it is producing. Here's General Magic's definition:

A psychological or behavior model of needs that all people experience. This paradigm is the design center for General Magic's personal intelligent communication products and services. It consists of three elements. 1. Remember - managing your internal agenda, such as things to do and people to see. 2. Communicate - maintaining relationships with your friends, family, and associates. 3. Know - getting information about the world.

WIDE AREA NETWORK WAN. An data network typically extending a LAN (local area network) outside the building, over telephone common carrier lines to link to other LANs in remote buildings in possibly remote cities. A WAN typically uses common-carrier lines. A LAN doesn't. WANs typically run over leased phone lines — from one analog phone line to T1 (1.544 Mbps). The jump between a local area network and a WAN is made through a device called a bridge or a router. Bridges operate independently of the protocol employed. They will work, according to Jeff Weiss, of Cryptall Communications, with all present and expected future communications packages. Routers are specific to the protocol being employed. New routing software is needed for each new protocol or protocol deviation. See BRIDGE, ROUTER, CORPORATE NETWORK and DIGITAL HIERARCHY.

WIDE AREA TELEPHONE SERVICE See WATS and 800 SERVICE.

WIDE FREQUENCY TOLERANT POWER PLANT PBX power facilities are provided that will operate from AC energy sources which are not as closely regulated as commercial AC power. The wide tolerant plant will tolerate average frequency deviations of up to plus or minus 3 Hz or voltage variations of -15% to +10% as long as both of the conditions do not occur simultaneously. This feature permits operation with customer provided emergency power generating equipment.

WIDEBAND Refers to a channel wider in bandwidth than a voice-grade channel.

WIDEBAND CHANNEL Any channel wider in bandwidth that a single voice-grade channel. That's the more modern definition. An older definition is a communication channel of a bandwidth equivalent to twelve or more analog voice-grade channels.

WIDEBAND MODEM A modem whose modulated output signal can have an essential frequency spectrum that is broader than that which can be wholly contained within a voice channel with a nominal 4-kHz bandwidth. A modem whose bandwidth capability is greater than that of a narrowband modem.

WIDEBAND PACKET TRANSPORT Transmission of addressed, digitized message fragments (packets) interleaved among the addressed fragments of other messages at a rate high enough to support general purpose telecommunications services.

WIDEBAND SWITCH Switch capable of handling channels wider in bandwidth than voice-grade lines. Radio and TV switches are examples of wideband switches.

WILDCARDS Special characters you use to represent one or more characters in an MS-DOS filename. An asterisk (*) represents several characters and a question mark (?) represents a single character. For example, the command

ERASE *.BAK

would erase all the files with the suffix "BAK."

The command

ERASE *.?A?

would erase all the files with "A" as the middle letter in a three-letter suffix.

WILL A name Motorola uses for its Wireless Local Loop (WiLL) product, which was developed to serve the basic telephony needs of people in urban and difficult to reach rural areas. Cellular based, WiLL technology is intended to provide fixed telephony services in areas with little or no existing wireline telephone service or as a supplement to the existing wireline service. It uses very few cellular transmitt/receivers — often just one at the end of the landline.

The WiLL system provides three major benefits to the telecom operator looking to expand their service area: more rapid deployment of telephone service; lower cost alternative to copper wire installation, and increased flexibility in system implementation and design. A WiLL system can be operational in weeks, compared to the huge amounts of time it would take to lay and install copper wire from an end office to each of the subscriber points in a typical local loop. Although WiLL is cellular-based, the system does not require a cellular switch. This makes the WiLL system a lower cost alternative to using "typical" cellular systems for fixed telephony applications because the total system outlay costs as well as associated backhaul and maintenance costs are reduced.

WiLL has three elements: the WiLL System Controller (WiSC), a Digital Loop Concentrator (DLC), and a Motorola cellular base station. It interfaces directly to the central office switch via 2-wire analog subscriber loops.

WILLFUL INTERCEPT The act of intercepting messages intended for a station experiencing a line or equipment malfunction.

WIMP INTERFACE Stands for Windows, Icons, Menus and a Pointing device. A derogatory reference to GUI. See GRAPHICAL USER INTERFACE.

WIN Wireless In-building Network. WIN is a technology from Motorola which uses microwaves to replace local area network cabling.

WINCH A machine for pulling cable into conduit (in the street or in the building) or duct liner. A winch has a rotating drum that winds up the pulling line.

WINCHESTER DISK A sealed hard disk. The Winchester magnetic storage device was pioneered by IBM for use in its 3030 disk system. It was called Winchester because "Winchester" was IBM's code name for the secret research project that led to its invention. A Winchester hard disk drive consists of several "platters" of metal stacked on top of each other. Each of the platter surfaces is coated with magnetic material and is "read" and "written" to by "heads" which float across (but don't touch) the surface. The whole system works roughly like the old-style Wurlitzer jukebox. There are several advantages to a Winchester disk system:

1. It can store, read and write enormous quantities of information. Some Winchesters have a capacity of over 100 megabits; 2. You can access information on a Winchester faster than on most computer storage medium (RAM and ROM are obviously faster); and 3. Winchesters are reliable and relatively inexpensive. There are also disadvantages: 1. They are very sensitive to rough handling (they hate being moved); 2. They are very sensitive to the organization of their directory track (lose that and you're in big trouble); and 3. When Winchesters "crash" (i.e. the heads touch the surface of the rotating platters), you can lose an enormous amount of precious data — possibly millions of bytes of data.

WINDING Coils of wire usually found in transformers and used to boost inductance.

WINDOW 1. A band of wavelengths at which an optical fiber is sufficiently transparent for practical use in communications applications. 2. A flow-control mechanism in data communications, the size of which is equal to the number of frames, packets or messages that can be sent from a transmitter to a receiver before any reverse acknowledgment is required. It's called a pacing group in IBM's SNA. 3. A box on the CRT (cathode ray tube) of your personal computer or terminal. A software program is running inside the box. It's possible with new "windows" software to run several programs simultaneously, each accessible and visible through the "window" on your CRT. 4. A technique of displaying information on a screen in which the viewer sees what appears to be several sheets of paper much as they would appear on a desktop. The viewer can shift and shuffle the sheets on the screen. Windowing can show two files simultaneously. For example, in one window you might have a letter you're writing to someone and in another window, you might have a boilerplate letter from which you can take a paragraph or two and drop it in your present letter. Being able to see the two letters on the screen makes writing the new letter easier.

WINDOW CONTROL A credit or token scheme in which a limited number of messages or calls are allowed into the system.

WINDOW SIZE The minimum number of data packets that can be transmitted without additional authorization from the receiver.

WINDOW TREATMENT You take the world's most beautiful window and you screw it up with expensive stuff you affix around it. Paula Friesen invented the term.

WINDOWING A technique of running several programs simultaneously — each in running a separate window. For example, in one window you might run a word processing program. In another, you might be calculating a spreadsheet. In a third, you might be picking up your electronic mail.

WINDOWS A popular Microsoft operating system that hides the cryptic DOS system of typed commands behind a graphical facade (also called a Graphical User Interface, GUI). Windows let you issue commands (i.e. run programs and complete tasks within programs) by pointing (with or without a mouse) at symbols or menu items and clicking, or hitting "Enter." Most Windows programs have the same "look and feel" to them. So issuing commands becomes almost intuitive. The idea is that "use one Windows program, you can use them all." Sort of. The latest version of Windows is 3.1 which contained two big improvements over 3.0 — namely OLE (Object Linking and Embedding) and DLL (Dynamic Link Library). See DLL, OLE, WINDOWS FOR WORKGROUP, WINDOWS NT and WINDOWS TELEPHONY.

WINDOWS APPLICATION A term used in this document as a shorthand term to refer to an application that is designed to run with Windows and does not run without Windows. All Windows applications follow similar conventions for arrangement of menus, style of dialog boxes, and keyboard and mouse use.

WINDOWS CHARACTER SET The character set used in Windows and Windows applications. Most TrueType fonts have a set of about 220 characters.

WINDOWS FOR WORKGROUPS Windows for Workgroup is a local area networked version of Microsoft Windows operating system version 3.1 that offers integrated file sharing, electronic mail (Microsoft Mail) and workgroup scheduling (Schedule+), thus bringing the graphical user interface to the workgroup. Windows For Workgroups also has Network DDE, which allows users to creat compound douments that share data across network.

WINDOWS METAFILE WMF. A method of encoding files. Other methods include EPS, PCX and TIFF.

WINDOWS NT Windows New Technology is a 32-bit operating system from Microsoft, designed to supplement and/or replace Windows and MS-DOS. As an operating system, Windows NT is targeted at the top 10% "power" users who need the power of a big, powerful operating system. Other less demanding souls will continue to run Windows and MS-DOS and possibly access Windows NT through a local area network to a server running Windows NT. Windows NT will require a minimum of 16 megabytes of RAM and 75 megs of free hard disk space. Here are the main advantages of Windows NT, as explained by Microsoft:

● Interoperability. Windows NT delivers support for open computing benefits through its protected subsystem architecture. Windows NT was also designed to be protocol independent. As such it will interoperate with all leading network systems, regardless of the native protocol of the system.

● Portability. Windows NT was designed to be portable across a variety of hardware systems. The Hardware Abstraction Layer (HAL) limits and isolates the amount of code necessary to port Windows NT to a new platform. Windows NT will run on processors other than those made by Intel. MS-DOS, for example, doesn't.

● Scalability. Windows NT scales to work on both single and multiprocessor computer systems. This scalability gives users the flexibility to implement their own solutions, today or over time, on machines that meet the performance needs of sophisticated client-server solutions.

● System Management. Windows NT supports SubNetwork Access Protocol (SNMP) and NetView network management standards.

● Published Interfaces. The interfaces to the Windows NT operating system are fully documented and published. Software developers are free to add functionality to the system based on their interface definitions.

● Support of Industry Standards. These include POSIX.1, OSF DCE, TCP/IP and WOSA, which is Microsoft's Windows Open Services Architecture. WOSA is a standard set of interfaces to connect a variety of applications with a range of back-end devices and services, such as messaging, telephony, databases, etc. Windows Telephony is part of WOSA. See WINDOWS NT ADVANCED SERVER.

WINDOWS NT ADVANCED SERVER Windows NT Advanced Server is the version of Windows NT designed specifically to run on servers in a client/server computing environment. It requires a minimum of 16 megs of RAM and 85 megs of free space on a hard disk. Microsoft's goal for Windows NT was to create "a high-end PC operating system tht supports access to high-performance, scalable hardware and provides the underpinings needed for a secure, distributed computing environment. For network management, the Windows NT Advanced Server also provides customers with centralized security and server management, along with graphical tools to manage multiple systems, and gives users a single log on for the enterprise. A superset of the Windows NT operating system, Windows NT Advanced Server provides additional reliability by supporting advanced fault tolerance including RAID 5. It also delivers Macintosh connectivity and the Remote Access Service — providing network and client-server connections to telecommuters, traveling executives and remote system managers over phone lines, X.25 and ISDN networks. See WINDOWS NT.

WINDOWS OPEN SERVICES ARCHITECTURE See WOSA.

WINDOWS TELEPHONY Introduced in the spring of 1993 jointly by Microsoft and Intel, Windows Telephony is actually a piece of software called a Windows Telephony DLL and two standards. The first standard is the Service Provider Interface (SPI). If a hardware manufacturer's product honors that SPI, that product can happily talk to the Windows Telephony DLL. The second standard is called the Application Programming Interface and it is directed at software developers who write applications programs. If those developers' programs adhere to the API, they can take advantage of the Windows Telephony DLL to drive whatever telephony devices or services adhere to the SPI. DLL stands for Dynamic Link Library. It is a Windows feature that allows executable code modules to be loaded on demand and linked at run time.

Windows Telephony should bring about an explosion of shrink-wrapped Windows-based telephone software applications — from simple personal rolodexes to power dialers, to customized phone systems for banks and for bakers. It should also bring about an explosion of new telephony hardware devices — from telephones that look more like PCs than phones, to PCs that are phones, to blackbox telehpony devices that hook to laptops and transform hotel phones.

Windows Telephony effectively removes earlier overwhelming barriers to creating PC-driven telephony applications, namely the wide enormity of telephony "network" services — from the many telephone company interfaces (POTS to T-1), to the many many more proprietary interfaces behind dozens of proprietary PBXs, key systems and hybrid phone systems. The goal is to bundle the Windows Telephony DLL in the next major release of Windows, sometime in the first half of 1994. It will also be included in Windows NT. Although the Windows NT code may be different, the API and SPI interfaces will be the same, thus causing no re-write of software code or necessitating redesign of telephony hardware.

The original work on the Windows Telephony DLL was done by Herman D'Hooge at the Intel Architecture Development Lab in Hillsboro Oregon. The final effort is a result of joint development effort with Microsoft, where the team was headed by Charles Fitzgerald. It also includes input from 40-odd companies — including virtually all major switch vendors and several major telephony developers. When I wrote this article, the list hadn't passed through the lawyers.

The goal of joint Microsoft/Intel package is to get rid of the bottleneck to bringing the power of the PC to telephony. Intel and Microsoft believe that the bottleneck exists because of two factors:

First, it has been incredibly difcult to interface to the variety of telecom switches in existence today. For example, no manufacturer's switch will talk to another's manufacturer's proprietary phone.

Second, it has been incredibly redundant and time-consuming for software to talk to the various switches. The big analogy is word processing in the old days. In those days, each word processing software company could easily spend 99% of his R&D budget writing drivers to get his program to work with yet another printer. That is no longer necessary under Windows. Windows takes care of interfacing the printers. All you have to do, as a developer is to make sure you conform to Windows specs.

Herman D'Hooge, the primary author of the Windows Telephony API specification, is a senior software architect with Intel's Architecture Development Lab in Hillsboro, Oregon.

On June 9, 1993 Microsoft introduced AT WORK, a new architecture which includes a set of software building blocks that reside in both office machines and PC, including

- Desktop and network-connected printers.
- Digital monochrome and color copiers.
- Telephones and voice messaging systems.
- Fax machines and PC fax products.
- Handheld systems.
- Hybrid combinations of the above.

See AT WORK, FAX AT WORK, WINDOWS TOOLKITS and WOSA.

WINDOWS TOOLKITS Windows toolkits are libraries of code that implement the graphical user interface objects that every software application uses. The toolkits save time by eliminating the need for software developers to re-implement the same code repeatedly for each application. Toolkits also have the benefit of consistent user interface implementation across all applications that use the toolkit. See also WINDOWS.

WINK A signal sent between two telecommunications devices as part of a hand-shaking protocol. It is a momentary interruption in SF (Single Frequency) tone, indicating that the distant central office is ready to receive the digits that have just been dialed. In telephone switching systems, a single supervisory pulse. On a digital connection such as a T-1 circuit, a wink is signaled by a brief change in the A and B signaling bits. On an analog line, a wink is signaled by a change in polarity (electricl + and -) on the line.

WINK OPERATION A timed off-hook signal normally of 140 milliseconds, which indicates the availability of an incoming register for receiving digital information from the calling office. A control system for phone systems using address signaling.

WINK PULSING Recurring pulses of a type where the off-pulse is very short with respect to the on-pulse, e.g., on key telephone instruments, the hold position (condition) of a line is often indicated by wink pulsing the associated lamp at 120 impulses per minute, 94 percent make, 6 percent break (470 ms on, 30 ms off).

WINK RELEASE On most modern central offices when the person or device at the other end hangs up, your local central office will send you a single frequency tone. That tone is called wink release. Such a tone can be used to alert a data device that the device at the other end has hung up. (Remember it can't tell by just listening — like you and me.) When a data device hears a wink release, it usually takes it as a signal to hang up also.

WINK SIGNAL A short interruption of current to a busy lamp causing it to flicker. Indicates there is a line on hold.

WINK START Short duration off hook signal. See WINK OPERATION.

WIRE CENTER The location where the telephone company terminates subscriber outside cable plant (i.e. their local lines) with the necessary testing facilities to maintain them. Usually the same location as a class 5 central office. A wire center might have one or several class 5 central offices, also called public exchanges or simply switches. A customer could get telephone service from one, several or all of these switches without paying extra. They would all be his local switch.

WIRE CENTER SERVING AREA That area of an exchange served by a single wire center.

WIRE PAIR Two separate conductors traveling the same route, serving as a communications channel.

WIRE PRINTER A matrix printer which uses a set of wire hammers to strike the page through a carbon ribbon, generating the matrix characters.

WIRE STRIPPER A tool which takes the insulation off a wire without hurting the metal conductor.

WIRE TELEPHONY The transmission of speech over wires.

WIRED LOGIC A required logic function implemented in hardware, not software.

WIRED-FOR CAPACITY The wired-for capacity represents the upper limit of capacity for a particular configuration. To bring to a phone system to its "wired for capacity," all that's necessary is to fill the empty slots in the system's metal shelving (its cage) with the appropriate printed circuit boards. "Wired-for Capacity" is a marginally useful term, giving little indication of the type of printed circuit boards — trunk, line, special electronic line, special circuit, etc. — that can be installed. And many PBXs allow only their printed circuit boards to go into assigned slots. Your PBX cabinet might, for example, have plenty of empty space for extra printed circuit boards, but it may not have any more space for boards which service electronic phones. Thus, it is effectively maxed out.

WIRELESS Without wires. An English and Australian word for radio and, now in the U.S., a phone system that operates locally without wires. Cellular is wireless in the strictest sense of the term. But "wireless" has come to mean wire-less systems that work within a building. See WIRELESS ACCESS CONTROLLER.

WIRELESS ACCESS CONTROLLER The first component in an in-building wirelss phone systems is the wireless access controller. It does many things. It provides access to the host network, be it a host PBX or the public switched telephone network (including Centrex). The access controller also manages the picocellular infrastructure of the wireless system through connections to the radio base stations. In the case of a Northern Telecom wireless business systems, base stations are connected to the controller via 144-kilobit-per-second (kbit/s) digital links that offer 2B+D interface connectivity. This digital connectivity (two 64-kbit/s channels for voice and data, and one 16-kbit/s channel for signaling information) provides the high-speed signaling capability needed by the controller to offer advanced business services and to manage mobility across several base stations. These digital links also make it possible to enhance radio system capacity by having the controller synchronize all base stations.

The controller software structures are designed so that untethered personal directory numbers and physical ports (specific interface circuits wired to a particular location) are dynamically associated at every call and at every hand-off to another base station. This dynamic assignment makes it possible for the same personal or group directory number to be used for a variety of wireless and wireline terminals, irrespective of location. The controller also handles user registration, roaming, and hand-off.

Roaming which is the capability to redirect incoming calls to the appropriate base station, is accomplished through a combination of radio protocols, system software, and databases. The databases make it possible to locate portable terminals, through various broadcasting or polling schemes, without incurring excessive search delays.

Hand-off, on the other hand, is the capability needed in order to cope with the fact that a user will continuously move from one location, and hence one cell, to another, while communicating. As this happens, the link must be maintained in a manner transparent to the end user, always maintaining communications with the strongest base station signal in the neighborhood of the portable terminal. The controller monitors the radio signal strength of the portable and, when the signal weakens, switches it to a base station with a stronger signal. It then switches the communications link from the former base station to the new one and signals the terminal to begin radio communication on the new channel. Interference could be caused, for example, by other portable terminals in the same cell or an adjacent cell, or by external influences, such as nearby traffic or people moving partitions in an office. In such cases, the base station redirects the call rapidly to a less noisy channel in the same cell or an adjacent cell.

WIRELINE Another name for a telephone company that uses cables, not radio. See WIRELINE CELLULAR CARRIER.

WIRELINE CELLULAR CARRIER Also called the Block B carrier. Under the FCC's initial cellular licensing procedures, the Block B carrier is the local telephone company. The FCC reserved one of the two systems in every market for the local telephone — or wireline company. Wireline or Block B systems operate on the frequencies 869 to 894 Megahertz. See NON-WIRELINE CELLULAR COMPANY.

WIRETAPPING To listen in clandestinely to someone else's conversation. Other than scrambling, there is no known method to protect your telephone call against wiretapping, no matter what equipment you buy from companies advertising their wares nationally. Wiretapping can be accomplished without physical connection to a phone line, though technically this would be called "bugging." For all intents and purposes you should consider your telephone conversations as public and treat your conversations as such.

WIRING CLOSET Termination point for customer premises wiring, offering access to service personnel. Generally serves a specific area, with cross-connected multiple wiring closets.

WIRING CONCENTRATOR A wiring concentrator is an FDDI node that provides additional attachment points for stations that are not attached directly to the dual ring, or for other concentrators in a tree structure. The concentrator is the focal point of Digital's Dual Ring of Trees topology.

WIRING DENSITY Refers to the number of wires that may be terminated on a connecting block in a given area. A high density block may terminate twice as many wires as a low density block, while a low density block may provide better wire management since fewer wires are being dressed into and out of the connecting block.

WIRING GRID The overall architecture of building wiring.

WITS Wireless Interface Telephone System.

WOO WOO TONE A tone on a phone line indicating the number is unavailable. Also the words to a neat Jeffrey Osborne song, as in "Will you woo woo with me?"

WORD A collection of bits the computer recognizes as a basic information unit and uses in its operation. Usually defined by the number of bits contained in it, e.g. 8, 16 or 32 bits. Using DOS, the IBM PC defines a word as eight bytes. Here's another explanation: A group of characters capable of being processed simultaneously in the processor and treated by computer circuits as an entity.

WORD LENGTH The number of characters or bits in a word.

WORDS PER MINUTE WPM. The speed of printing, typing or communications. 100 WPM is 600 characters per minute (six characters per average word) or 10 characters per second. In ASCII, asynchronous transmission at this rate is also 100 or 110 bits per second, depending on the number of stop bits.

WORK LOCATION WIRING SUBSYSTEM The part of a premises distribution system that includes the equipment and extension cords from the information outlet to the terminal device connection.

WORD SPOTTING The process whereby specific words are recognized under specific speaking conditions (i.e. natural, unconstrained speech). Can refer to the ability to ignore extraneous sounds during continuous word recognition.

WORK STATION In this dictionary I spell it as one word WORKSTATION. See WORKSTATION.

WORKFLOW The way work moves around an organization. It follows a path. That path is called workflow. Here's a more technical way of defining workflow: The automation of standard procedures (e.g. records management in personnel operations) by imposing a set of sequential rules on the procedure. Each task, when finished, automatically initiates the next logical step in the process until the entire procedure is completed.

WORKGROUP A fancy new word for a department, except that the members of the workgroup may belong to different departments. The idea is that members of the workgroup work with themselves, so they'd be perfect candidates to buy electronic mail packages that could send stuff between them and other packages that would allow them to share their collective wisdoms.

WORKGROUP MANAGER An assistant network supervisor with rights to create and delete bindery objects (such as users, groups, or print queues) and to manage user accounts. A Workgroup Manager has supervisory privileges over a part of the bindery. When several groups share a file server, Workgroup Managers can provide autonomous control over their own users and data.

WORKSTATION In the telecom indsutry, a workstation is a computer and a telephone on a desk and both attached to a telecom outlet on the wall. The computer industry tends to refer to workstations as high-speed personal computers, such as Sun workstations, which are used for high-powered processing tasks like CAD/CAM, engineering, etc. A common PC — like the one you find on my desk — is not usually considered a workstation. The term workstation is vague.

WORLD NUMBERING ZONE One of eight geographic areas used to assign a unique telephone address to each telephone subscriber.

WORM Write Once, Read Many times. Refers to the new type of optical disks (similar to compact discs) which can be written to only once, but read many times. In other words, once the data is written, it cannot be erased. WORM disks typically hold around 600 megabytes. See also ERASABLE OPTICAL DRIVE.

WORST HOUR OF THE YEAR That hour of the year during which the median noise over any radio path is at a maximum. This hour is considered to coincide with the hour during which the greatest transmission loss occurs.

WOSA Windows Open Services Architecture. According to Microsoft, WOSA provides a single system-level interface for connecting front-end applications with back-end services. Windows Telephony, announced in May 1993, is part of WOSA. According to Microsoft, application developers and users needn't worry about conversing with numerous services, each with its own protocols and interfaces, because making these connections is the business of the operating system, not of individual applications. WOSA provides an extensible framework in which Windows-based applications can seamlessly access information and network resources in a distributed computing environment. WOSA accomplishes this feat by making a common set of APIs available to all applications. WOSA's idea is to act like two diplomats speaking through an interpreter. A front-end application and back-end service needn't speak each other's languages to communicate as long as they both know how to talk to the WOSA interface (e.g. Windows Telephony). As a result, WOSA allows application developers, MIS managers, and vendors of back-end services to mix and match applications and services to build enterprise solutions that shield programmers and users from the underlying complexity of the system.

This is how WOSA works: WOSA defines an abstraction layer to heterogeneous computing resources through the WOSA set of APIs. Initially, this set of APIs will include support for services such as database access, messaging (MAPI), file sharing, and printing. Because this set of APIs is extensible, new services and their corresponding APIs can be added as needed.

WOSA uses a Windows dynamic-link library (DLL) that allows software components to be linked at run time. In this way, applications are able to connect to services dynamically. An application needs to know only the definition of the interface, not its implementation. WOSA defines a system-level DLL to provide common procedures that service providers would otherwise have to implement. In addition, the system DLL can support functions that operate across multiple service implementations. Applications call system APIs to access services that have been standardized in the system. The code that supports the system APIs routes those calls to the appropriate service provider and provides procedures and functions that are used in common by all providers.

The primary benefit of WOSA is its ability to provide users of Windows with relatively seamless connections to enterprise computing environments. Other WOSA benefits, according to Microsoft include:

- Easy upgrade paths.
- Protection of software investment.
- More cost-effective software solutions.
- Flexible integration of multiple-vendor components.
- Short development cycle for solutions.
- Extensibility to include future services and implementations.

WPM See WORDS PER MINUTE.

WRAP 1. In data communications, to place your diagnostic and test equipment around parts of a network so you can monitor their use (i.e. do network diagnostics on them). You are, in essence, wrapping your products around theirs. 2. To make a connection between a flexible wire and a hard tag by tightly wrapping the cable around the tag. There are automatic wire wrapping tools available for this job.

WRAP-UP Between-call work state that an ACD agent enters after releasing a caller. It's the time necessary to complete the transaction that just occurred on the phone.

WRAP-UP DATA Ad hoc data gathered by an agent in the ACD system following a call.

WRITE To record information on a storage device, usually disk or tape.

WRITE HEAD A magnetic head capable of writing only. You find write heads on everything from tape recorders to computers.

WRITE PROTECT Using various hardware and software techniques to prohibit the computer from recording (writing) on storage medium, like a floppy or hard disk. You can write protect a 5 1/4 diskette by simply covering the little notch with a small metal tag. The idea of "Write Protect" is to stop someone (including yourself) from changing your precious data or program. You can't write protect a hard disk easily. The easiest way to stop someone changing a file is to use the program ATTRIB.EXE. See ATTRIBUTES.

WRITE PROTECTION A scheme for protecting a diskette from accidental erasure. 5 1/4" diskettes have a notch which must be uncovered to allow data on the diskette to be modified. 3 1/2" diskettes have small window with a plastic tab which must be slid into place to cover the window to allow data on the diskette to be modified. See WRITE PROTECT and ATTRIBUTES.

WRITE PROTECTION LABEL A removable label, the presence or absence of which on a diskette prevents writing on the diskette.

WTAC World Telecommunications Advisory Council. WTAC is comprised of telecommunications leaders from the private and public sectors and from every region of the world. WTAC gives advice to the ITU — the International Telecommunications Union. The WTAC held its first meeting in Geneva, Switzerland, in April, 1992. In February 1993, it published a small booklet called "Telecommunications Visions of the Future."

WTNG WaiTiNG.

WYPIWYF Acronym for "What You Print Is What You Fax," also "The Way You Print Is the Way You Fax." Coined by Intel to describe its one-step pop-up menu that makes sending faxes from the PC as easy as sending a document to a printer.

WYSIWYG (pron. Whiz-i-wig) What You See Is What You Get. A word processing term meaning what you see on your computer screen is what you will see printed on paper. The exact typeface, the correct size, the right layout, etc. Some word processors do WYSIWYG. Others don't. You usually need a screen with graphics to get the full effect.

WZ1 World Zone One. The part of the earth covered by what used to be called The North American Numbering Plan. It includes the U.S., Canada, Alaska, Hawaii, and the Caribbean islands, but does not include Mexico or Cuba.

X

X An abbreviation for the word "cross," as in crossbar. 5XB would be the abbreviation for a No. 5 Crossbar.

X Windows See X-WINDOWS below.

X-AXIS Horizontal axis on a graph or chart.

X-BASE A term used to describe any database application capable of generating custom programs with dBASE-compatible code.

X-OFF/X-ON A flow control protocol for asynchronous serial transmission. Flow control is a method of adjusting information flow. For example, in transmitting between a computer and a printer, the computer sends the information to be printed at 9600 baud. That's several times faster than the printer can print. The printer, however, has a small memory. The computer dumps to the memory, called a buffer, at 9600 baud. When it fills up, the printer signals the computer that it is full and please stop sending. When the buffer is ready to receive again, the printer (which also has a small computer in it) sends a signal to the desktop computer (the one doing the printing) to please start sending again. X-OFF means turn the transmitter off (xmit in Ham radio terms). It is the ASCII character Control-S. X-ON means turn the transmitter on. It is the ASCII character Control-Q. You can use these characters with many microcomputer functions. For example, if you do DIR in MS-DOS and you want to stop the fast rush of files, then type Control-S.

X-DIMENSION OF RECORDED SPOT In facsimile, the center-to-center distance between two recorded spots measured in the direction of the recorded line. This term applies to facsimile equipment that responds to a constant density in the subject copy by yielding a succession of discrete recorded spots.

X-DIMENSION OF SCANNING SPOT In facsimile, the center-to-center distance between two scanning spots measured in the direction of the scanning line on the subject copy. The numerical value of this term will depend upon the type of system used.

X-OPEN An international consortium of computer vendors working to create an internationally supported vendor-independent Common Applications Environment based on industry standards.

X-SERIES RECOMMENDATIONS Set of data telecommunications protocols and interfaces defined by the CCITT.

X-WINDOWS The UNIX equivalent of Windows. What Windows is to MS-DOS, X-Windows is to Unix. A network-based windowing system that provides a program interface for graphic window displays. X-Windows permits graphics produced on one networked station to be displayed on another. Almost all UNIX graphical interfaces, including Motif and OpenLook, are based on X-Windows. X-Windows is a networked window system developed and specified by the MIT X Consortium. Members of the X Consortium include IBM, DEC, Hewlett-Packard and Sun Microsystems. Sun Microsystems has been contracted by the MIT X Consortium to implement PEX (PHIGS Extensions to X), which will be the standard networking protocol for sending PHIGS (Programmers Hierarchical Graphics System) graphics commands through X-Windows. Some people spell it X-Windows and some spell it X Windows.

X-Y A specific variety of electromechanical switch. Does the same things as a Stronger step-by-step switch but in a horizontal plane. It's so called because it's a two motion switch with horizontal and vertical movements. The first pulse sends the switch horizontally to the right place, then the next pulse sends it vertically up to the right place and so on, until it has switched the call through. One of the most reliable switches ever produced. Unfortunately, it's slow, space-consuming and unable to be programmed with many new customer pleasing features.

X.1 International user classes of service in public data networks and ISDNs.

X.121 International Numbering Plan for public data networks. X.121 defines the numbering system used by data devices operating in the packet mode.

X.150 DTE and DCE test loops in public data networks.

X.2 International user services and facilities in public data networks.

X.20 Interface between data terminal equipment (DTE) and data circuit-terminating equipment (DCE) for start-stop transmission services on public data networks.

X.20 bis Used on public data networks of data terminal equipment (DTE) that is designed for interfacing to asynchronous duplex V-series modems.

X.21 Interface between data terminal equipment (DTE) and data circuit-equipment (DCE) for synchronous operation on public data networks.

X.21 bis Used on public data networks of data terminal equipment (DTE) that is designed for interfacing to synchronous V-series modems.

X.24 List of definitions for interchange circuits between data terminal equipment (DTE) and data circuit-terminating equipment (DCE) on public data networks.

X.25 From its beginning as an international standards recommendation from CCITT, the term X.25 has come to represent a common reference point by which mainframe computers, word processors, mini-computers, VDUs, microcomputers and a wide variety of specialized terminal equipment from many manufacturers can be made to work together over a type of data communications network called a packet switched network. On a packet switched data network (private or public), the data to be transmitted is cut up into blocks. Each block has a header with the network address of the sender and that of the destination. As the block enters the network, the number of bits in the block are put through some mathematical functions (an algorithm) to produce a check sum.

The check sum is attached as a "trailer" to the packet as it enters the network. Packets may travel different routes through the network. But, ultimately, the packets are routed by the network to the node where the destination computer or terminal is located. At the destination, the packet is disassembled. The bits are put through the same algorithm, and if the digits computed are the same as the ones attached as the trailer, there are no detected errors. An ACK, or acknowledgement, is then sent to the transmitting end. If the check sum does not match, a NAK, or Negative Acknowledgement is sent back, and the packet is retransmitted. In this manner, high speed, low error rate information can be transmitted around the country using shared telecommunications circuits on public or private data networks.

X.25 is the protocol providing devices with direct connection to a packet switched network. These devices are typically larger computers, mainframes, minicomputers, etc. Word processors, personal computers, workstations, dumb terminals, etc. do not support the X.25 packet switching protocols unless they are connected to the network via PADs — Packet Assembler/Disassemblers. A PAD converts between the protocol used by the smaller device and the X.25 protocol. This conversion is performed on both outgoing (from the network) and incoming data (to the network), so the transmission looks transparent to the terminal. (See TRANSPARENT.) There's a very good book on X.25 called X.25 Explained, Protocols for packet switching networks by R. J. Deasington of IBM. It is available from Telecom Library on 1-800-LIBRARY, or 1-212-691-8215.

X.25 NETWORK Any network that implements the internationally accepted CCITT standard governing the operation of packet-switching networks. The X.25 standard describes a switched communications service where call setup times are relatively fast. The standard also defines how data streams are to be assembled into packets, controlled, routed, and protected as they cross the network.

X.28 DTE/DCE interface for start-stop-mode data terminal equipment accessing the packet assembly/disassembly facility (PAD) in a public data network situated in the same country.

X.29 Procedures for the exchange of control information and user data between a packet assembly/disassembly facility (PAD) and a packet mode DTE or another PAD.

X.3 CCITT recommendation describing the operation of a Packet Assembly/Disassembly (PAD) device or facility in a public data network. X.3 defines a set of 18 parameters that regulate basic functions performed by a

PAD to control an asynchronous terminal. The setting of these parameters governs such characteristics as terminal speed, terminal display, flow control, break handling and data forwarding conditions, and so on.

X.32 Interface between Data Terminal Equipment (DTE) and Data Circuit Terminating Equipment (DCE) operating in a packet mode and accessing a packet switched public data network via a public switched telephone network or a circuit switched public data network. X.32 describes the functional and procedural aspects of the DTE/DCE interface for DTEs accessing a packet switched public data network via a public switched network.

X.38 CCITT recommendation for the access of Group 3 facsimile equipment to the Facsimile Packet Assembly/Disassembly (FPAD) facility in public data networks situated in the same country.

X.39 CCITT recommendation for the exchange of control information and user data between a Facsimile Packet Assembly/Disassembly (FPAD) facility and a packet mode Data Terminal Equipment (DTE) or another pad, for international networking.

X.400 X.400 is an international standard which enables disparate electronic mail systems to exchange messages. Although each e-mail system may operate internally with its own, proprietary set of protocols, the X.400 protocol acts as a translating software making communication between the electronic mail systems possible. The result is that users can now reach beyond people on their same e-mail system to the universe of users of interconnected systems.

X.500 The CCITT international standard designation for a directory standard to coordinate the dispersed file directories of different electronic mail systems.

X.75 An international standard for linking X.25 packet switched networks. X.75 defines the connection between public networks, i.e. for a gateway between X.25 networks. See X.25.

X/OPEN A consortium of computer-industry vendors, chartered to specify an open system platform based on the Unix operating system.

X3.15 Bit sequencing of ASCII in serial-by-bit data transmission.

X3.16 Character structure and character parity sense for serial-by-data communications in ASCII.

X3.36 Synchronous high speed data signaling rates between data terminal equipment and data circuit-terminating equipment.

X3.41 Code extension techniques for use with 7-bit coded character set of ASCII.

X3.44 Determination of the performance of data communications systems.

X3.79 Determination of performance of data communications systems that use bit-oriented control procedures.

X3.92 Data encryption algorithm.

XA-SMDS Exchange Access SMDS. An access service provided by a local exchange carrier to an interexchange carrier. It enables the delivery of a customer's data over local and long distance SMDS networks.

XBAR Crossbar.

XC Cross connect.

XENIX Microsoft trade name for a 16-bit microcomputer operating system derived from AT&T Bell Labs' UNIX.

XEROGRAPHIC RECORDING Recording by action of a light spot on an electrically charged photoconductive insulating surface where the latent image is developed with a resinous powder.

XEROX NETWORK SERVICES XNS. A multilayer protocol system developed by Xerox and adopted, at least in part, by Novell and other vendors. XNS is one of the many distributed-file-system protocols that allow network stations to use other computers files and peripherals as if they were local. XNS is used by some companies on Ethernet LANs. In local area networking technology, special communications protocol used between networks. XNS/ITP functions at the 3rd and 4th layer of the Open Systems Interconnection (OSI) model. Similar to transmission control protocol/internet protocol (TCP/IP).

XFR TransFeR.

XGA eXtended Graphics Array. A new IBM level of video graphics which has a screen resolution of 1,024 dots horizontally by 768 vertically, yielding 786,432 possible bits of information on one screen, more than two and a half times what is possible with VGA. See also MONITOR.

XIP eXecute-In-Place. Refers to specification for directly executing code from a PCMCIA Card without first having to load it into system memory.

XMA eXtended Memory specificAtion. Interface that lets DOS programs cooperatively use extended memory in 80286 and higher computers. One such driver is Microsoft's HIMEM.SYS, which manages extended memory and HMA (high memory area), a 64k block just above 1Mb.

XMIT Transmit.

XMODEM Also called "Christiansen Protocol". An error-correcting file transfer, data transmission protocol created by Ward Christiansen of Chicago for transmitting files between PCs. A file might be anything — a letter, an article, a sales call report, a Lotus 1-2-3 spreadsheet. The XMODEM protocol sends information in 128 bytes blocks of data. Some sums (check sums) are done on each block and the result is sent along with the block. If it does not check out at the other end, the computer at the other end sends a request (a NAK — Negative AcKnowledgement) to re-transmit that block once again. If the block checks out, the computer sends an ACK — an Acknowledgement. In this way, relatively error-free transmission can be accomplished.

XMODEM protocol used to be common among computer hobbyists but is now popular among business users of microcomputers. If you're buying a telecommunications software program for your microcomputer — IBM, Radio Shack, Compaq, Apple, etc. — it's a good idea to buy a program with XMODEM present. AT&T Mail supports XMODEM protocol. So does TELECONNECT Magazine's own E-mail InfoBoard system (212-989-4675). MCI Mail does not support XMODEM protocol. We don't know why. We wish they did. There are many variations of XMODEM including XMODEM 1K (which uses blocks of 1,025 bytes), MODEM7, YMODEM, Y-MODEM-G and ZMODEM. Most common communications software packages only support (i.e. will handle) the original version of XMODEM (checksum) and the newer CRC variation. A study in Byte Magazine (March, 1989) showed ZMODEM to be a far more efficient file transfer protocol than XMODEM, YMODEM, or W/XMODEM. See also DATA COMPRESSION PROTOCOLS, ERROR CONTROLS PROTOCOLS, FILE TRANSFER PROTOCOL, YMODEM and ZMODEM.

XMODEM-1K Xmodem-1K is an error-correcting file transfer, data transmission protocol for transmitting files between PCs. It it is essentially Xmodem CRC with 1K (1024 byte) packets. On some systems and bulletin boards it may also be referred to as Ymodem.

XMS An acronym for eXtended Memory Specification. To run this standard, your system must have 350K of extended memory. XMS creates the HMA (High Memory Area), then governs access to and the allocation of the remainder of extended memory.

XNMS Trademark for MICOM's IBM PC-based packet data network (PDN) network management system software products.

XNS Xerox Network Services. A multilayer protocol system developed by Xerox and adopted, at least in part, by Novell and other vendors. XNS is one of the many distributed-file-system protocols that allow network stations to use other computers files and peripherals as if they were local. XNS is used by some companies on Ethernet LANs. In local area networking technology, special communications protocol used between networks. XNS/ITP functions at the 3rd and 4th layer of the Open Systems Interconnection (OSI) model. Similar to transmission control protocol/internet protocol (TCP/IP).

XO Crystal Oscillator.

XPAD An eXternal Packet Assembler/Disassembler.

XRB Transmit Reference Burst.

XT Abbeviation for crosstalk.

XTEND EXTEND Telecommunications Integration Platform, a series of network software utilities and calls that allow a PBX to be integrated and directed by workstations on a a local area network. XTEND is an offering of XTEND Communications, Inc. New York City.

XWINDOWS See X-WINDOWS.

Y

Y-DIMENSION OF RECORDED SPOT In facsimile, the center-to-center distance between two recorded spots measured perpendicular to the recorded line.

Y-DIMENSION OF SCANNING SPOT In facsimile, the center-to-center distance between two scanning spots measured perpendicular to the scanning line on the subject copy. The numerical value of this term will depend upon the type of system used.

YAGI ANTENNA A type of directional antenna.

YELLOW ALARM A T-1 alarm signal sent back toward the source of a failed transmit circuit in a DS-1 2-way transmission path. A yellow sends 0's (zeros) in bit two of all time slots. See also T-1.

YELLOW PAGES A directory of telephone numbers classified by type of business. It was printed on yellow paper throughout most of the twentieth century until it was obsoleted in the late 1990s by dial-up yellow page directories operated by voice processing systems and in the early 21st century by electronic directories delivered on disposable laser disks. As a concession to history, the laser disks are now painted bright yellow. Actually, yellow pages remain one of the phone companies' most lucrative sources of revenues. Advertising rates are not cheap. There is now competition. There are many "Yellow Pages" directories, since AT&T never trademarked the term "Yellow Pages." Some "yellow page" directories are better value than others. And some are more legitimate than others. Some actually never get printed or, if they are printed, are not printed in great quantity and are not distributed as widely as their sales literature implies. Many businesses have been suckered into paying money for listings and advertisements in directories that never appeared. This fictitious directory scam also has happened with "telex" and "fax" directories. This "scam" is fraud by mail and is heavily stomped upon by the US Postal Service. As a result, many fake directories (especially the telex ones) are "published" abroad.

YMODEM A faster transfer variation of XMODEM. In YMODEM, XMODEM's 128-byte block grew to YMODEM's 1024 bytes (1 kilobyte). YMODEM combines the 1K block and the 128-byte block modems into the same protocols. YMODEM, or 1K as it is known, became the thrifty way to send files (i.e. it saved on phone time). Enhancements were added, such as auto-fallback to 128-byte blocks if too many errors were encountered (because of bad phone lines, etc.) See XMODEM for a much larger explanation of file transfer using X, Y and ZMODEM protocols.

YMODEM-G Ymodem-g is a variant of Ymodem. It is designed to be used with modems that support error control. This protocol does not provide software error correction or recovery, but expects the modem to provide it. It is a streaming protocol that sends and receives 1K packets in a continuous stream until told to stop. It does not wait for positive acknowledgement after each block is sent, but rather sends blocks in rapid succession. If any block is unsuccessfully transferred, the entire transfer is canceled. See also ZMODEM, which we prefer.

Z Abbreviation for Zulu time.

ZAP To eradicate all or part of a program or database, sometimes by lightning, sometimes intentionally.

ZBTSI Zero Byte Time Slot Interchange. A technique used with the T carrier extended superframe format (ESF) in which an area in the ESF frame carries information about the location of all-zero bytes (eight consecutive "O"s) within the data stream.

ZENER DIODE A particular type of semiconductor which acts as a normal rectifier until the voltage applied to it reaches a certain point. At this point — at the zener voltage or the avalanche voltage — the zener diode becomes conducting.

ZERO BEAT RECEPTION Also called "homodyne" reception. A method of reception using a radio frequency current of the proper magnitude and phase relation so that the voltage impressed on the detector will be of the same nature as that of the wave. An old radio term.

ZERO BIT The high-order bit in a byte or a word.

ZERO CODE SUPPRESSION The insertion of a "one" bit to prevent the transmission of eight or more consecutive "zero" bits. Used primarily with digital T1 and related telephone-company facilities which require a minimum "ones density" keep the individual subchannels of a multiplexed, high-speed facility active. Several different schemes are currently employed to accomplish this. Proposals for a standard are being evaluated by the CCITT. See also ZERO SUPPRESSION.

ZERO FILL See ZEROFILL.

ZERO FREQUENCY The frequency (wavelength) at which the attenuation of the lightguide is at a minimum.

ZERO SLOT LAN A Local Area Network (LAN) that uses a PC's serial port to transmit and receive data. It doesn't require a network interface card to be installed in a slot in the PC, thus the name "zero-slot" LAN. RS-232 LANs usually use standard RS-232 or phone cable to link PCs. Software does the rest of the work. Due to the slow speed of serial communications on a PC, RS-232 LANs are usually restricted to speeds of around 19.2K bits per second. What they lose in speed, however, they make up in low price.

ZERO STUFFING Get a cup of coffee right now. Synchronous data transmission is done by sending what IBM and AT&T call Frames, and what everyone else calls Packets. A frame starts off by sending a bit pattern of 01111110 (notice the six 1's in a row). Synchronous transmission is for sending a bit stream, which means that the bits may (but probably do not) have any relation to the transmission of characters. This is especially true when sending digitized voice. As the bits pass to the receiver, they go through a shift register. When the flag signifying the end of a frame goes by, the last 16 bits in the shift register are the check digits.

The receiver computes the check digits based on the data bits that have gone by. As the sender sent the data, it computed the check digit, sent it after the end of the frame, and then sent the flag. If the receiver computes the same check digit that the sender sent, then one can be reasonably assured the data came through without error. But that's not what I came to talk to you about. I came to talk about Zero Stuffing. The problem is that somewhere in the bit stream, there is the possibility of there being six 1 bits in a row. To the receiving computer, six 1's means a flag. Therefore the sending computer, if it "sees" six 1 bits, will send five 1 bits, and stuff a zero in the bit stream.

In fact, if it sees even five 1 bits, it will stuff a zero anyway, so there will be no ambiguity. The rule is, "If there are five ones in a row and it is NOT the end of a frame, stuff a zero into the bit stream." This way the receiver will know that this is in no way the end of the frame yet. Now if the receiver sees six 1's in a row, it knows without a doubt that it IS at the end of a frame, and should proceed with the error checking.

ZERO SUPPRESSION The elimination of nonsignificant zeros from a numeral. Zero suppression is the replacement of leading zeros in a number with blanks so that when the number appears, the leading zeros are gone. The data becomes more readable. For example, the number 00023 would be displayed on the monitor or printed as 23.

ZERO TEST LEVEL POINT A level point used as a reference in determining loss in circuits. Analogous to using sea level when defining altitude. Written as 0 TLP.

ZERO TRANSMISSION LEVEL POINT ZTLP. In telephony, a reference point for measuring the signal power gain and losses of telecommunications circuit, at which a zero dBm signal level is applied.

ZERO TRANSMISSION LEVEL REFERENCE POINT A point in a circuit to which all relative transmission levels are referenced. The transmission level at the transmitting switchboard is frequently taken as the zero transmission level reference point.

ZERO USAGE CUSTOMER An MCI definition. An MCI customer who has not placed a call over the network, even though he/she is an active customer. Sometimes used interchangeably, but incorrectly, with the term "no usage customer."

ZEROFILL 1. To fill unused storage locations with the character "O." 2. Here's definition from GammaLink, a fax board maker: A traditional fax device is mechanical. It must reset its printer and advance the pages as it prints each scan line it receives. If the receiving machine's printing capability is slower than the transmitting machine's data sending capability, the transmitting machine adds "fill bits" (also called Zero Fill) to pad out the span of send time, giving the slower machine the additional time it needs to reset prior to receiving the next scan line.

ZIF Zero Insertion Force. Intel makes a bunch of math co-processor chips which are used with their 80XXX range of microprocessors. ZIF is a special device which is typically soldered to the motherboard. You place an 80387 chip on this device, move the handle down, it grabs the chip and pulls the chip down, seating it electrically. When you want to remove the chip, you simply lift the handle and up the chip comes. The device was invented by Intel because so many people were apparently breaking the legs on their math co-processor chips each time they removed them. Apparently the problem was most prevalent in the computer rental business.

ZINC SPARK GAP A spark gap having zinc as the electrode.

ZIP CODE The specific five-digit code assigned to each post office to facilitate mail delivery. The Postal Service is beginning to use nine-digit zip codes. The additional four digits will determine the precise letter carrier routing from the post office into the street. Some post offices now optically read zip codes. Allegedly this speeds up delivery.

ZIP TONE Short burst of dial tone to an ACD agent headset indicating a call is being connected to the agent console.

ZMODEM ZMODEM is an error-correcting file transfer, data transmission protocol for transmitting files between PCs. A file might be anything — a letter, an article, a sales call report, a Lotus 1-2-3 spreadsheet. Always use ZMODEM if you can. It's the best and fastest data transmission protocol to use. This is not my sole advice. Virtually every writer in data communications recommends it. Here's an explanation, beginning with XMODEM, an older, more common and less efficient protocol.

Both XMODEM and YMODEM transmit, then receive, then transmit. The handshake (ACK or NAK) happens when the sender isn't sending. ZMODEM adds full duplex-transmission to the transfer protocol. ZMODEM does not depend on any ACK signals from the host computer. It keeps sending unless it receives a NAK, at which time it falls back to the failed block and starts to retransmit at that point. ZMODEM was written by Chuck Forsberg. According to PC Magazine (April 30, 1991) ZMODEM is the first choice of most bulletin boards. ZMODEM, according to PC Magazine, features relatively low overhead and significant reliability and speed. ZMODEM dynamically adjusts it packet size depending on line conditions and uses a very reliable 32-bit CRC error check. It has a unique file recovery feature. Let's say ZMODEM aborts a transfer because of a bad line (or whatever), it can start up again from the point it aborted the transfer. Other file transfer protocols have to start all over again. ZMODEM's ability to continue is a major benefit. ZMODEM in some communications program is a little more automated than other protocols. For example, ZMODEM will start itself when the other end gives a signal — thus saving a keystroke or two and speeding things up. See FILE TRANSER PROTOCOL, XMODEM and YMODEM.

ZONE 1. A telephony definition: One of a series of specified areas, beyond the base rate area of an exchange. Service is furnished in zones at rates in addition to base rates. 2. A LAN definition. Part of a local area network, typically defined by a router. A router will let you get into one part of someone else's network. They define what you are able to get access to. You might get to that router by an external telecommunications circuit — dial-up, ISDN, Switched 56, T-1 etc.

ZONE BITS 1. One or two leftmost bits in a commonly used system of six bits for each character. 2. Any bit in a group of bit positions that are used to indicate a specific class of items, i.e., numbers, letters, commands.

ZONE METHOD A ceiling distribution method in which ceiling space is divided into sections or zones. Cables are then run to the center of each zone to serve the information outlets nearby. See also CEILING DISTRIBUTION SYSTEMS.

ZONE OF SILENCE Skip zone.

ZONE PAGING Ability to page a specific department or area in or out of a building. "Page John in the Accounting Department." Zone paging is useful for finding people who wander, as most of us do.

ZULU TIME Coordinated Universal Time.

ZZF Zentralamt fur Zulassungen im Fernmeldewessen (Approval Authority — Germany).

ZZZYRMIDGEON, A. The last name in the Manhattan Telephone directory. Zzzyrmidgeon beat out Archimedes Zzzyandottie for the honor.